THE FILMS OF GENE KELLY

SONG AND DANCE MAN

THE FILMS OF
GENE KELLY
SONG AND DANCE MAN

by TONY THOMAS

Foreword by FRED ASTAIRE

THE CITADEL PRESS   Secaucus, N. J.

First edition
Copyright © 1974 by Tony Thomas
All rights reserved
Published by Citadel Press
A division of Lyle Stuart, Inc.
120 Enterprise Ave., Secaucus, N.J. 07094
In Canada: George J. McLeod Limited
73 Bathurst St., Toronto 2B, Ont.
Manufactured in the United States of America by
Halliday Lithograph Corp., West Hanover, Mass.
Designed by A. Christopher Simon
Library of Congress catalog card number: 73-90949
ISBN 0-8065-0400-5

To the memory of Jeanne Coyne Kelly

ACKNOWLEDGMENTS

For the help I received in putting this book together I am grateful for the kindness of the following people: to Fred Astaire, Vincente Minnelli, John Green and Rudy Behlmer; to Mildred Simpson and her staff at the library of the Academy of Motion Picture Arts and Sciences in Los Angeles; to Gerald Pratley and his staff at the Ontario Film Institute in Toronto; and to Glen Hunter and the staff of the Theatre Section of the Metropolitan Toronto Central Library. My thanks also to Lois McClelland, secretary to Mr. Kelly, and to Dale Olson of Rogers, Cowan and Brenner, Inc. (Beverly Hills). For aid in collecting the photographs I gratefully thank John Lebold, Paula Klaw of *Movie Star News* (New York), Larry Edmund's Bookshop (Hollywood), Cherokee Bookshop (Hollywood), Diane Goodrich and Eddie Brandt. Many of the photographs are from Mr. Kelly's private collection and for his permission to use them I am most particularly grateful.

Tony Thomas

CONTENTS

THE FILMS OF GENE KELLY

SONG AND DANCE MAN

FOREWORD

BY FRED ASTAIRE

Writing a foreword about Gene Kelly is not all that easy for me. I mean there would naturally be some opinions—"Oh, of course, he had to say that." Many people think of dancers as being too aware or jealous of one another. Such is not the case here. I think I know Gene pretty well. He has his easier, lighter moods and also his very serious moments, which are only natural with an artistic temperament.

I worked with him in one movie—a massive MGM production, *Ziegfeld Follies,* filmed in 1944–45. We got along fine with the many discussions, not particularly arguments, that are bound to occur when you're in rehearsal together on a creative basis. It's "How about this?" or "No—not that" sort of thing that goes on, but I don't recall that we ran into any particular obstacles. I had heard that he was sometimes tough to work with, being a perfectionist and all that. And when you

A recent photo of Fred Astaire and Gene Kelly

have two so-called perfectionists belting away at each other, you might get some kind of fireworks when it applies to a couple of hoofers. That gave me some concern.

However, Gene was not tough with me. He was very respectful—maybe because of my seniority in years. Besides, I was doing my utmost not to be objectionable because I was aware of the fact that he was a very strong and gymnastic young man. I had seen him pick up Ed Sullivan once and carry him off stage like a suitcase. Well—joking aside, as I said there were really no obstacles that deterred us from arriving at what I think proved to be an enjoyable and successful song-and-dance version of a number called "The Babbitt and the Bromide," which was originally written by the Gershwins, George and Ira, for my sister Adele and me in our Broadway stage production musical comedy *Funny Face* in 1927.

Doing that number with Gene in a totally different form was, of course, a challenge for both of us but we always felt that it did work out well, largely due to his creative contributions, and I feel that it became somewhat of a memorable screen musical item.

That was the only thing we did together.

Kelly is a man of multiple talents—dancer —singer—actor—director—producer—completely engulfed when at his work. His many successes speak for themselves.

Gene is also a devoted family man. My respect for him as a person and an artist is unbounded.

While Kelly and Donald O'Connor were making *Singin' in the Rain* they were visited by Fred Astaire, who was working on *The Belle of New York* on the next sound stage.

This strobe photo was taken
by Gjon Mili at the time
Kelly was doing *Cover Girl*.

6

Gene Kelly—his first role

THE LONELINESS OF THE LONG-DISTANCE DANCER

A conspicuous peculiarity in the history of Hollywood is the emergence of only two male dancers as major stars. Through all the decades of high productivity and the popularity of thousands of players of every kind only Fred Astaire and Gene Kelly among the song-and-dance men have scaled the heights of film fame and stayed there. This inevitable tandem reference has lead to perpetual comparison, and an assumption that they have more in common than is actually the case. Both as men and as dancers Astaire and Kelly are more different than they are alike. In their only performance together, a routine in the MGM revue, *Ziegfeld Follies,* they were directed by Vincente Minnelli, who also directed Kelly in *An American in Paris* and Astaire in *The Band Wagon.* In Minnelli's eyes: "Gene bases a lot of his work on ballet, combing modern and tap dancing with ballet movements in great strength and athleticism. Fred, of course, is light as air and has a style completely his own—it hasn't been approached by any other dancer. He's a shy, retiring man who doesn't like to talk about his work whereas Gene is more earthy, very gregarious and eloquent on the subject of dancing. What they have in common is perfectionism, the capacity to work long and hard to get the smallest detail right. They are both originators, both have devised marvelous dance material for movies and each is, in his own way, a great showman."

By the time Gene Kelly arrived in Hollywood at the end of 1941 Fred Astaire had been in films for nine years and occupied an unrivaled position of affection and esteem. Once Kelly had established himself he began hearing references to himself as "another Astaire," not that he was obviously similar to the older dancer, but because the public could find no other simple way to describe him.

8

Age four

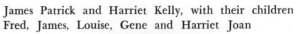
James Patrick and Harriet Kelly, with their children
Fred, James, Louise, Gene and Harriet Joan

Louise, Gene, Harriet Joan, James and Fred

There was never any rivalry because there was never any competition between them. It never bothered Kelly that he was, particularly in his early years in films, continually compared with Astaire: "I was delighted to be compared with Fred because he's a genius in his own right and a man can do worse than being compared with the best. Anyone dancing on the screen today who doesn't admit his debt to Astaire is either a fool or a liar. I used to envy his cool, aristocratic style, so intimate and contained but I was wise enough to know it wasn't for me. Fred wears top hat, white tie and tails to the manner born—I put them on and look like a truckdriver. We've been good friends all these years but even if we weren't I think we would have gotten together now and then just to commiserate with one other. We were like two men on a desert island, the only ones aware of our mutual problem—trying to make dances come alive before the cameras as a bored crew stood and watched. Stage dancers couldn't understand what concerned us. Ours was a kind of splendid isolation."

According to Kelly the shortage of dancer-actors is due to the long and totally absorbing training necessary in order to dance professionally. "A dancer works so hard at training his anatomy that he doesn't give much time to training the rest of himself. Nobody asks, 'Why aren't there any violinists who have become movie stars?' and yet a dancer can spend as much time perfecting his craft as a violinist. And after years of training he discovers he has trouble saying 'hello' on the stage. It's a rare dancer who can hold his own in an acting role. This concentration on perfecting dancing to the exclusion of other areas of being an entertainer is strange to anyone who isn't involved. The point is simply that nature is against you—by the time you've learned your craft your anatomy is starting to run down. The older you get as a dancer the harder it is to grind up the physical forces. A writer can still pound a typewriter at fifty—an actor is usually better at fifty than he was at thirty, but it's the reverse with a dancer. Just when he is experienced and mature he starts running out of steam. The dancer's life is probably the shortest artistic life in the world and you have to face that fact when you get into it."

The ideal performer is the man who combines the discipline of the dancer with the emotional expertise of the actor, but such men are rare—and made all the more rare by an unpredictable public. "There are better dancers than Astaire or myself, and certainly better actors and singers but the public won't have them. The trouble with movies is that no matter how talented a person is, he will flop unless the public takes to his personality. As a director my eyes are peeled all the time for some young man who can act, sing and dance, and who is personable enough to build a show around but even if you found such a person there is no guarantee that the public would accept him."

When Gene Kelly first appeared in Hollywood pictures it was often remarked that he seemed a little like James Cagney. In Kelly's estimation the reason for this comparison is George M. Cohan: "Cohan set the style for the American song-and-dance man—a tough, cheeky, Irish style. Cohan wasn't a great dancer, but he had wonderful timing and a winning personality. He influenced a whole breed of American actors, including Cagney, Spencer Tracy and Pat O'Brien—and when Cagney did Cohan in *Yankee Doodle Dandy* he was an improvement on the original. Cohan *was* the American theatre up until the impact of Eugene O'Neill, and I have a lot of Cohan in me. It's an Irish quality, a jaw-jutting, up-on-the-toes cockiness—which is a good quality for a male dancer to have. And it's a legacy from George M. Cohan."

Eugene Curran Kelly was born in the Highland Park district of Pittsburgh, Pennsylvania, on August 23rd, 1912. He was the third of five children —Harriet, James, Eugene, Louise and Fred—born to James Patrick Kelly and his wife Harriet, née Curran. Kelly senior, born in Peterborough, Ontario, of Irish parents, was employed by the Columbia Gramophone Company as a salesman and held a good position until the economic crash of 1929, when he was dismissed. Recalls Kelly: "Until then it had been a good, comfortable, lower-middle-class home and I look back on it as a very happy childhood. With the Depression we had to pull in our belts but we kids were in our teens by then and we pitched in and got through that period better than many. It was a marvelous family. My father was an easygoing man with the usual Canadian love of ice hockey, and on freezing days he would flood the back yard and have his three boys out there shooting the puck around. By the time I was in high school I had my letter as a peewee halfback and at fifteen I was working out with a semipro ice hockey team, the Pittsburgh Yellow Jackets. I was encouraged to take it up professionally, but I wasn't that interested. However, much of my style as a dancer springs from that early training in ice hockey."

Kelly's emergence as a dancer is due his mother, a lively lady with a strong interest in the theatrical arts and a firm believer in the "American Dream" precept of cultural and social improvement. "She loved dancing and she sent my older brother James and I—I was about eight then—to the Fairgreaves School in the East End of Pittsburgh to take dancing lessons. We didn't like it much and we were continually involved in fistfights with the neighborhood boys who called us sissies. Strong-willed as my mother was, she had to give in, and I didn't dance again until I was fifteen. By that time I'd been on several athletic teams and I wasn't afraid of anyone calling me names. Also, it had come to my attention that girls liked dancing and any guy who could dance had a head start. So I went back to Miss Fairgreaves and asked her if she could teach me some steps. I found I had great adaptability for it, so I got a tap routine together and did it in the high school show. This made me quite a hero with the girls, and I had no trouble with boys because I was a sports nut—hockey, football, baseball, gymnastics, everything."

Gene Kelly spent his first year of high school at the Sacred Heart School, then three years at Peabody High in his final year appearing in several school plays. In 1929 he enrolled at Pennsylvania State College to study journalism but the economic crash also made it necessary for him to get a job to supplement the family finances. He first worked for the YMCA as an instructor in gymnastics. At the same time, he and his brother Fred, three years younger, worked up dance routines in order to appear in amateur talent contests and pick up occasional prize money. The following year Kelly began a course in economics at the University of Pittsburgh, later switching his interest to law. He graduated with a Bachelor of Arts degree in 1933.

At Penn State he had joined the college theatrical club and discovered an increasing taste for entertaining and at the University he devised a dance act with a friend named Jim Barry. In the summer of 1931 Kelly was hired as the dance and stage coach at the YMCA's Camp Porter. In what used to be an American tradition, he worked his way through college, among the evening, weekend and vacation jobs he lists stacking tires in a warehouse, soda-jerking, ditch-digging and concrete-mixing, all in addition to entertainment engage-

James, Gene and Fred Kelly

Counselor Kelly at Camp Porter in the summer of 1931

ments with Fred, then considered the dancer of the family and the one most likely to make dancing his profession.

By his senior year at the University of Pittsburgh Gene Kelly was well known on campus as an entertainer in their *Cap and Gown* shows, and he was put in charge of directing the student company. After graduating in 1933 he went to law school for two months, but quit when he realized his appetite for dancing was now dominant in his thinking. A great factor in making this decision was his mother, who had maintained her interest in dancing and with a group of local parents had put together a kind of school, for which they hired a dancing teacher on the weekends. Mrs. Kelly had inveigled her son to assist the teacher, and she had also taken a job in a dancing school in order to learn the business side of it—and get free lessons for Fred. Mother and son Gene then founded a dancing school in the family basement: "I found I had a penchant for teaching, that I liked it and that I was good with children. This eventually led to choreography—and to be a good choreographer you must first be a good teacher, because you have to show people what to do and convince them they can do it. The man who changed the course of dancing, one of the first great choreographers, Michael Fokine, was before that a star dancer and you must be able to dance in order to teach. So much of it has to do with inspiring confidence. However, with time I became disenchanted with teaching because the ratio of girls to boys was more than ten to one, and once the girls reached sixteen the dropout rate was very high. They would lose interest, or get fat or gauche, or take up other lines. A dancer must be dedicated, yet that dedication can make girls tense and nervous. Many haven't the stamina to stay with it, and others have the dedication without the ability."

The family dance enterprise was quickly successful and soon moved from the basement to a hired hall. It was decided to call it *The Gene Kelly Studio of the Dance,* and the next year the farsighted Mrs. Kelly opened up a branch in Johnstown: "We had relatives there and they said they needed dancing lessons for their children. We organized a class in the Legion Hall, then a bigger hall, and finally it turned into a studio bigger than the one in Pittsburgh. We drew on all the mill communities around Johnstown and as the times improved and the mills opened up, we did very good business. My Fridays and Saturdays were

Louise and Gene in 1932

spent in Johnstown, and so it went for three years, with me all the time dreaming about one day being a great choreographer."

As a teacher Gene Kelly also sought tuition for himself, in order to be at least a step ahead of his pupils. He and Fred each summer attended the sessions of the Chicago National Association of Dancing Masters, where expert instructors gave advice on all manner of dances. Fred had already made the decision to dance for a living but Gene had loftier aims. "I read everything I could get my hands on about ballet and in Chicago I studied with Bernice Holmes, a lady who had the ability to teach men and she had learned her business from Adolph Bolm of the Diaghilev company."

To carry them through the summers in Chicago the Kelly brothers had to find work to pay for their lessons and their lodgings. They danced in an exhibition at the World's Fair but most of their jobs were far less impressive. As a pair of song-and-dance men doing numbers like "It's the Irish in Me," they played for small wages in sleazy nighteries. "I remember one in particular, a grubby joint out in the boondocks. An agent had sent us there to do two shows for five dollars, but the owner demanded four, and with a pair of bruisers at his side we weren't about to argue. It was 4:30 in the morning when we finished, and dawn by the time we got back into town. I went to the agent to complain, but all he did was demand his fifty cents commission. So I hit him—so hard I broke a finger in my hand, and had to spend the money getting it fixed in a hospital. I hadn't learned to control my temper—and I didn't really get to control it until years after I'd been in Hollywood."

In the summer of 1937 Gene Kelly went to New York with the object of finding work as a choreographer. Now twenty-five, his taste for the musical stage had been whetted by contact with many professionals. He had acquired a reputation as an advisor on improving song-and-dance material: "I had routined quite a lot of acts by now, for people coming through Pittsburgh on tour. They needed somewhere to rehearse and my studio came to their attention, and after a while I found myself known as a kind of dance-doctor. They would call on me to spruce up their dancing and occasionally I would get as much as a hundred dollars to devise a new routine. That was big money in those days." However, despite the feeling of affluence and the confidence borne of knowing people in the business, Kelly's rounds of the agents and the producers came to naught and he returned to Pitts-

The proprietor of The Gene Kelly School of the Dance in 1934

13

The director of the *Cap and Gown* show at the University of Pittsburgh, also in 1934

Lt. (j.g.) Gene Kelly, USN

Kelly, to the left of Mary Martin, and his comrades back up her famous debut singing "My Heart Belongs to Daddy" in *Leave It to Me* - Broadway, 1938

In New York in 1938 and the start of a career in show business

14

With Grace McDonald in *One For the Money* - Broadway, 1939

With Vivienne Segal in *Pal Joey*

With Vivienne Segal in *Pal Joey*

With Shirley Paige in *Pal Joey*

burgh at the end of the summer to resume supervision of the dancing schools, now bringing the Kelly family an annual net income of eight thousand dollars.

Kelly's first extended job as a choreographer came in April of 1938, when he was hired by Charles Gaynor to help stage the musical revue *Hold Your Hats* at the Pittsburgh Playhouse, for which Gaynor wrote the sketches, the lyrics and the music. The show ran for a month, with Kelly appearing in six of the sketches and doing one solo, "La Cumparsita," which piece of music would be the basis of his elaborate Spanish number in MGM's *Anchors Aweigh* eight years later.

His applause in this revue encouraged Kelly to take another crack at Broadway. His timing, and his luck, were good. Robert Alton had been hired as the dance director of the Cole Porter musical *Leave It To Me*, which went into rehearsal in the late summer of 1938 and opened on Broadway at the Imperial Theatre on November 21. He invited Kelly to audition as a dancer. Still not having landed himself a position as a choreographer, he accepted and won a part. Alton and his wife had staged a show at the Pittsburgh Playhouse the previous Christmas, and they had been impressed with Kelly's work as a teacher. The Porter show was about an American ambassador, played by Victor Moore, who is sent to Russia against his preference for London and how a shrewd newspaperman, played by William Gaxton, helps him deliberately ruin his assignment in order to be recalled. Kelly played one of the ambassador's secretaries and in the fourth scene of the second act he and the other secretaries, all in fur parkas, backed up the newspaperman's stripper-girlfriend as she sang "My Heart Belongs to Daddy." Mary Martin, fresh from Texas, started her career with this saucy song, admitting years later that she then had little understanding of some of the Porter lines.

By the time *Leave It To Me* made its first appearance Robert Alton was already working on John Murray Anderson's revue *One for the Money*, with music by Morgan Lewis and sketches and lyrics by Nancy Hamilton. Kelly auditioned and won a leading part, requiring him to act, sing and dance in eight routines. The response to his work gave him reason to feel he had found his place in the scheme of things, and he had little trouble finding other jobs. He spent the summer of 1939 as a choreographer with the famed summer stock company of Westport, Connecticut, working on a revue and a musical treatment of O'Neill's *The Emperor Jones,* with Paul Robeson. The director of these shows, John Haggott, was employed by The Theatre Guild as a stage manager for its winter season; he had been responsible for Kelly's getting the job at Westport and he also arranged for him to audition for the Guild's presentation of William Saroyan's new play, *The Time of Your Life.* The actor playing the part of Harry, a hopeful hoofer, had been discharged after the Boston tryout and Kelly was given the role. It called for an actor with some style as a dancer and a dancer with the ability to build a character, this being the part of a rather sad man whose ambitions as a dancer will probably never come to be. Harry is one of a number of assorted, ordinary characters who loiter in a waterfront saloon in San Francisco. Kelly's hoofer gently danced his way through the show, giving the impression of improvisation but actually doing the same routine every night. It was, in fact, dance-acting, and his first chance to perform in material of his own invention. *The Time of Your Life* was the real beginning of Kelly's career; it opened at the Booth Theatre on November 13, 1939, ran for twenty-two weeks and won a Pulitzer Prize.

The summer of 1939 saw Gene Kelly back at Westport, where he directed the dances for Lynn Riggs's play *Green Grow the Lilacs,* this being the vehicle that Rodgers and Hammerstein three years later turned into *Oklahoma!* Returning to New York at the close of the summer season, Kelly applied for the job of dance director for *Billy Rose's Diamond Horseshoe.* Recalls Kelly: "Rose was the hardest, toughest man I've ever met in this business, but I'm grateful to him because he was the man who gave me my first job as a choreographer in New York. When I arrived at the audition he was mean and rude and negative, so I swore at him in return. He said something like, "Don't you talk to me that way," and I replied I wouldn't want to work for him anyway. This amused him, so he invited me to sit and talk and tell him my ideas on the show. He liked this and offered me $115 a week. I said I wouldn't work for that, so he laughed again and added another twenty dollars." Also hired for this show was a seventeen-year-old dancer named Betsy Blair, whom Kelly shortly thereafter began to court. They were married on September 22, 1941 and their only child, a daughter named Kerry, was born on October 16, 1942. She is married and working as a child psychologist in London.

With wife Betsy Blair in 1944

The new movie star - Hollywood, 1942

After setting up the dances for *Billy Rose's Diamond Horseshoe* Kelly was called to audition for a musical comedy Rodgers and Hart had written with John O'Hara, *Pal Joey*. George Abbott was hired as director and Kelly's friend Robert Alton was brought in to direct the dancing. The musical play was a departure from standard Broadway musicals, being considerably more adult in its material and more subtle in the fusion of songs and dances with the characters and the situations. It called for a leading man of unusual ability, someone who could not only sing and dance but who could act well enough to create an ingratiating cad, a nightclub entertainer called Joey Evans, who makes his unscrupulous way through life using people, mainly women, and succeeding, never conscious of the pain he causes. *Pal Joey* opened at the Ethel Barrymore Theatre on December 25, ran for 270 performances, and made a star of Kelly. "It was a case of being the right man in the right place at the right time, and also a case of tremendous luck to have a part like that to play—to have a script by John O'Hara and songs by Rodgers and Hart, and a director like Abbott. I think I did well in it because it gave me a chance to use my own style of dancing to create a character. I wanted to dance to American music and at that time nobody else was doing it. And Joey was a meaty character to play. He was completely amoral. After some scenes I could feel the waves of hate coming from the audience. Then I'd smile at them and dance and it would relax them. It was interesting to be able to use the character to manipulate the audience."

In reviewing *Pal Joey* for *The New York Times*, John Martin wrote: "If Kelly were to be judged exclusively by his actual performance of the dance routines that fall to him, he would still be a good dancer, but when his dancing is seen in this fuller light he becomes an exceptional one. A tap dancer who can characterize his routines and turn them into an integral element of an imaginative theatrical whole would seem to be pretty close, indeed, to unique . . . he is not only glib-footed, but he has a feeling for comment and content that both gives his dancing personal distinction and raises it several notches as a theatre art."

At the time he was appearing in *Pal Joey* Kelly told interviewers, "I don't believe in conformity to any school of dancing. I create what the drama and the music demand. While I am a hundred percent for ballet technique, I use only what I can adapt to my own use. I never let technique get in the way of the mood or the continuity." That viewpoint appears not to have altered—it would seem, in fact, to have been his credo all through the years as a performer-choreographer in Hollywood. Backing up that attitude has been an inordinate capacity for hard work. Van Johnson had a small role in *Pal Joey* and he recalls: "I watched him rehearsing, and it seemed to me that there was no possible room for improvement. Yet he wasn't satisfied. It was midnight and we had been rehearsing since eight in the morning. I was making my way sleepily down the long flight of stairs when I heard staccato steps coming from the stage . . . I could see just a single lamp burning. Under it, a figure was dancing . . . Gene."

Gene Kelly believes that love of work is at least as important as possessing talent in order to succeed as an entertainer: "You have to love being in this business otherwise you couldn't stand it because it's so hard. It's almost masochistic and you couldn't do it if you didn't enjoy it. *The Loneliness of the Long-Distance Runner* could just as well be the story of a dancer, it's the same kind of effort. And you have to be born with a love of movement. As a boy I loved to run and jump—to move through the air and against the ground. You can't dance without that love."

Pal Joey is interesting to anyone studying the nature of the entertainment industry and its people. Says Kelly: "There are a lot of Pal Joeys in this business and perhaps a little of him in every man who has become a successful actor. There's a tendency to believe one's publicity and to forget the people who helped you. It's the kind of business that forces a man to be self-seeking, and it's childlike and narcissistic in many ways. Most male actors realize this after a while and look to do other things. The reason I escaped the problem early is that I didn't want to be an actor—I acted because I couldn't get a job as a choreographer or director, which is what I really wanted to do. I succeeded as an actor because I was a good dancer. The musical theatre needs male dancers all the time, and the fact that here was one who could say "hello" convincingly and carry a tune made it easy for me. I was never out of work in New York."

Hollywood offers began to arrive soon after *Pal Joey* was launched, but Kelly bided his time before accepting any. He finally signed a contract with David O. Selznick, agreeing to go to Hollywood in October of 1941, at the completion of his commitment to *Pal Joey* and after having done the choreography for the stage version of *Best Foot*

Forward. The problem with being signed to Selznick was that he produced very few films and had no interest in making musicals. He was convinced of Kelly's ability as an actor and prepared him to play the young priest in *The Keys of the Kingdom,* the part that was later played by Gregory Peck. Kelly finally talked Selznick out of the assignment but the great producer insisted on having him in the picture and asked him to take the part of the Scottish doctor. Kelly protested that his Scots accent was ridiculous but Selznick hired a dialect coach. "We worked together for a few weeks and then shot a scene. David and I looked at it, and then at each other—and began to laugh. I still sounded like a third-rate vaudevillian, so he wisely called in Thomas Mitchell to play the doctor. Selznick had nothing else on tap, so he sold fifty percent of my contract to MGM and loaned me to them to do *For Me and My Gal.*"

Kelly was not impressed with his debut in Hollywood: "They previewed the picture in Riverside and I was appalled at the sight of myself blown up twenty times. I had an awful feeling that I was a tremendous flop, but when I came outside executives started pumping my hand and Judy Garland came up and kissed me. I went home thinking they were just being nice, and I really didn't believe them until the picture opened in New York and did well. After that I wasn't sure how to handle all the things that quickly happened—the phone calls from newspapers and interviews for the radio. It was a new world and quite different from the theatre. In the theatre you can chug along for years, but being a success in the movies is like suddenly being turned into a rocket. Yet I still feel I'm better on the stage than on film."

MGM purchased the second half of Kelly's contract from Selznick, although there were a number of Metro executives who were not in favor of so doing. He was championed by Judy Garland and producer Arthur Freed, both of whom had seen him in *Pal Joey* and believed he had a future in film musicals. However, for his next assignment the studio used him purely as an actor in an inexpensive programmer, *Pilot No. 5,* followed by a filming of Cole Porter's *Du Barry Was a Lady,* minus most of the Porter songs. Kelly got his first chance at doing a self-choreographed dance in the all-star *Thousands Cheer* in which, as a soldier confined to barracks, he did a mock love-dance with a mop. His major impact as a persuasive, inventive dancer came when MGM loaned him to Columbia for *Cover Girl.* It was then apparent to

the industry that Kelly had a unique quality to bring to films and in his next MGM musical, *Anchors Aweigh,* he was given almost *carte blanche* to devise several extensive routines, including the breakthrough in film choreography, the animated sequence with cartoon figures. It had taken him a couple of years, but Kelly had now hit his stride in Hollywood.

After completing his segment of *Ziegfeld Follies,* the famous dance-duet with Fred Astaire, Kelly left the studio for wartime service. At the end of 1944 he joined the United States Naval Air Service as an enlisted man and applied for a commission. After completing his training he was given the rank of lieutenant, junior grade. "I was in the Photographic Section, and they assumed I knew how to handle a camera, which I didn't. But I learned a lot about cameras the hard way, staying up nights. I was on my way to Japan when The Bomb dropped, and I didn't have to go. I was sweating that one out. You don't know how scared you can get when you ask for active duty and they finally give it to you."

Kelly was discharged from the navy in the spring of 1946; as an officer stationed at the photographic center in Washington, D.C. he had been responsible for writing and directing a number of documentaries, which had increased his interest in being involved in more production work when he returned to Hollywood. But MGM had nothing lined up for him and in looking around for a project they decided to use him in *Living in a Big Way,* a film so feeble that he was asked to devise musical sequences to interpolate afterwards. The film did little business but it drew the attention of the industry to Kelly's ability to create his own material. Believing that they were making a step forward in the maturing of the movie musical as a species, MGM gave Kelly, Judy Garland and Vincente Minnelli a fanciful yarn complete with an original Cole Porter score, *The Pirate.* Now regarded as a major achievement in the art of presenting songs and dances in an imaginative manner, the picture was given a poor reception by the general public. Fearing they had come up with something too sophisticated, MGM lost no time in putting both stars in more conventional and reliable formats.

But Gene Kelly was not content to appear in conventional and reliable movies, and kept hammering away at the management until he was given a film of his own to direct, one that was not at all conventional in its approach to telling a

On the set of *The Pirate* with visitor Irving Berlin

Rehearsing with Leonard Bernstein for *On the Town*

story in song and dance—*On the Town*. He shared the directing credit with Stanley Donen, whom he had brought to Hollywood shortly after his own arrival. Donen met Kelly when he arrived in New York at the age of eighteen and got a job in the chorus of *Pal Joey*. The two became friends, and Kelly gives Donen full credit as his invaluable assistant in most of his major movie musicals. Says Kelly: "To direct and be in front of the cameras at the same time is too hard, as I found out when I did my first picture without Stanley, *The Happy Road*. And when you are involved in doing choreography for film you must have expert assistants. I needed one to watch my performance, and one to work with the cameraman on the timing, which is the most difficult part because cameramen are not musicians and a dancing sequence is all timing and movement. Without such people as Stanley, Carol Haney and Jeanne Coyne I could never have done these things. When we came to do *On the Town*, I knew it was time for Stanley to get screen credit because we weren't boss-and-assistant any more but co-creators, and in time he became a director in his own right."

The success of *On the Town* triggered off two fantastic years for Gene Kelly. By 1952 he was the star of the fabulous *An American in Paris* and the vastly amusing *Singin' in the Rain,* possibly the most popular of all movie musicals. He managed to develop the artistry of film choreography in a manner so apparently non-arty and so vital and appealing that the public was hardly aware of aesthetic pioneering. At all times in his films Kelly gave the appearance of being a likable, easygoing man but as John Green, his friend and head of music at MGM in this heyday period explains: "Gene is easygoing as long as you know exactly what you're doing when you're working with him. He's a hard taskmaster and he loves hard work. If you want to play on his team you'd better love hard work too. He isn't cruel but he is tough, and if Gene believed in something he didn't care who he was talking to, whether it was Louis B. Mayer or the gatekeeper. He wasn't awed by anybody and he had a good record of getting what he wanted. Gene's a survivor, and a good pupil of changing times."

Times changed for Kelly in the early fifties in a way that neither he nor his employers could have predicted. Television had made itself felt by this time and box-office earnings fell drastically. Most of the major studios either let go most of their stars or renegotiated their contracts in terms that

A pair of Von Stroheims. Stanley Donen and Kelly on the set of *On the Town* just prior to the first days' shooting

As a favor to director Stanley Donen, Kelly did a fleeting bit playing himself in *Love Is Better Than Ever* (1952). Here, leaving a Broadway restaurant, he stops to say hello to Larry Parks, playing a theatrical agent, while Elizabeth Taylor, as Parks' stagestruck girlfriend, looks on in awe.

With Maurice Chevalier in Paris in 1956, having hired the great entertainer to sing the title song for Kelly's *The Happy Road*

With assistant Jeanne Coyne and Sugar Ray Robinson, rehearsing the television show *Dancing - A Man's Game*

called for fewer commitments. Further, in releasing their libraries to television, the film producers created their own stiffest competition. Ironically, the film which suffered most was the musical, and by the end of the decade the original movie musical was veritably a thing of the past.

Despite his great popularity due to *Singin' in the Rain*, Kelly signed a contract with MGM in December of 1951 which sent him overseas for a period of nineteen months. It was signed for two major reasons—to allow MGM to take advantage of film funds frozen in Europe, with Kelly to make three pictures using those funds, and to allow him to qualify for income tax exemption under a new ruling stipulating that the earnings of Americans living abroad for a year and a half would be tax-free. While it seemed a feasible decision at the time, it backfired somewhat, in keeping Kelly away from Hollywood at a time when he might have benefited from staying. It also allowed him to produce his dream-project, the all-dancing film, *Invitation to the Dance*, which involved his time and efforts for far too long and resulted in box-office failure—a failure that did nothing to assuage the worries of MGM.

Invitation to the Dance was not released until 1956, four years after it first went into production in England. By that time Gene Kelly was a dissatisfied employee of a studio not at all sure of its future direction. MGM had several times refused

21

to loan Kelly to other studios—the last loan-out had been in 1944—but with their refusal to let Kelly play "Sky Masterson" in Sam Goldwyn's production of *Guys and Dolls,* the relationship between the star and the studio became strained. Goldwyn gave the role to Marlon Brando and, in a bitterly ironic move, turned over the film to MGM to distribute. Looking back on this period, Kelly commented: "I couldn't stand being inactive, it drove me almost berserk. They had cold feet about doing musicals and I was a song-and-dance man wondering what the hell I was going to do. Finally I asked for a settlement on the contract and we came to terms. I was to do two more films for them in addition to MGM coming in with me on a co-production of my own picture *The Happy Road.* This all worked out fairly well except that in severing myself from MGM I also cut myself off from the pension plan. Had I hung on a few years longer I believe I would have qualified for several thousands of dollars a year for life. But I just couldn't take sitting around with nothing to do."

After directing *The Tunnel of Love* and appearing in *Les Girls,* Kelly was clear of his contract with MGM. The sixteen-year association had been a glorious one for much of the time, and Kelly speaks well of his former employers: "It's become fashionable to sneer at the establishment and deride the old movie moguls but I don't go along with that. They were tough men and they mostly knew what they were doing. They made Hollywood the fifth largest industry in America. The mogul was a special breed—part tycoon and part artist, and we could use some of that breed even now. I admired their kind of toughness. They gave in to the talent more than you might think, and in the heyday of the Metro musical they scouted the country for the best dancers, writers, directors and musicians. For anyone connected with musicals it was Mecca. It's sad that it all had to come to an end but you can't blame the moguls for that."

Kellys first film after leaving MGM was *Marjorie Morningstar* for Warners. The picture met with mixed reviews, but some critics felt that it was his best dramatic work and assumed this would be the tone of his future in films. But Kelly was no longer interested in being a movie star; he wanted to devote his time to film production and accept whatever offers came his way for his services as an actor or director in any medium provided they were of sufficient interest.

Kelly's first job in this new phase of his career

was directing Rodgers and Hammerstein's new musical play *Flower Drum Song,* a considerable feather in his cap. Shortly after, still in New York, he devised, produced and performed in a television documentary for the prestigious NBC series, "Omnibus," calling it "Dancing—A Man's Game." Kelly here stated the case for his art in a no-nonsense manner. His appeal to the public has always rested on his image as a muscular, likable workingman, in no way highbrow or effete, and he is well aware of the stigma attached to male dancers: "There's a strong link between sports and dancing, and my own dancing springs from my early days as

an athlete. I played ice hockey as a boy and some of my steps come right out of that game—wide open and close to the ground. I think dancing is a man's game, and if a man does it well he does it better than a woman. Unfortunately, in the western world dancing is treated as a woman's game. This isn't so in the east. In Russia the dancer is a hero, and they can't understand why we make heroes of crooners. I don't want this to sound as if I'm against women dancing—we just have to remember that each sex is capable of doing things the other can't.

"Also, dancing *does* attract effeminate young men. I don't object to this as long as they don't dance effeminately. I know nothing about homosexuality, so I'm not qualified to discuss it. I only say that if a man dances effeminately he is dancing badly—just as if a woman comes out on the stage and starts to sing bass. It's wrong. As for the personal sexual tendencies, and their bearings on being a dancer, I think this has been overemphasized. This stigma on dancing is tragic because a great many boys would benefit from dancing lessons. It's the finest kind of exercise and it teaches poise. Unfortunately, people confuse gracefulness with softness. John Wayne is a graceful man and so are

With Claude Bessy, Helen Rae and Attilio Labis, rehearsing *Pas de Deux* at the Paris Opera House in 1960

many of the great ball players. A quarterback making a forward pass can be as beautiful as a ballet movement, and a double-play in baseball, if it's done well, has a choreographic feeling. Boxers, from James J. Corbett to Sugar Ray Robinson use dancing as part of their art but, of course, they don't run any risk of being called sissies. One of our problems is that so much dancing is taught by women. You can spot many male dancers who have this tuition by their arm movements—they're feminine and soft and limp. The main problem is that we badly need male dancers and so many young men who have talent are put off by the belief that it is an effeminate business. I like to think things have improved in recent years but I have no proof that they have."

Among the highlights in this latter stage of the Gene Kelly career is his staging of the first jazz ballet at the Paris Opera House. A Francophile and fluent in French, Kelly has been a hero to the French ever since *An American in Paris* and a cult-figure among French film makers because of his work in musicals. Early in 1960 he was invited by A. M. Julien, the general administrator of the Paris Opéra and Opéra-Comique to choose material of his own liking and invent a modern ballet for the company. The result was *Pas de Dieux*, combining a telling of Greek mythology with the music of George Gershwin's *Piano Concerto in F*. The story has Zeus coming to earth to win back his wife Aphrodite, who has taken up with the low life on the Left Bank. He manages to do this after the usual quota of problems. Kelly's major problem was in teaching the rigidly, classically trained corps de ballet how to relax their concepts and move in different ways. "It was like an athlete learning to ski after having spent years training to be a boxer. The jazz dancing required the use of different muscles, but they were willing subjects." *Pas de Dieux* was a conspicuous success, and at its opening night received twenty-two curtain calls. Where the French had formally liked Kelly, now they honored him, and his creation for the Paris Opera House was the major consideration in his being elected a Chevalier of the Legion of Honor by the French government.

It was in 1960 that Gene Kelly married for the second time. He and Betsy Blair separated in 1956 and were divorced the following year. The second Mrs. Kelly had known her husband for years prior to the marriage; Jeanne Coyne was a student at Kelly's dancing school in Pittsburgh when she was a teenager. Later she danced in musicals in New

York and went to Hollywood in the late forties. She was a dancer in *The Pirate* and Kelly hired her as an assistant choreographer in 1949, thereafter working with him on all productions and retiring with their marriage. They have two children: Timothy, born March 3, 1962, and Bridget, born June 10, 1964.

Aside from a few appearances in films Kelly in the 1960s was engaged mostly in production work and in directing, occasionally with disappointing results. His directing of Jackie Gleason in *Gigot* in Paris was a particularly unhappy instance of a film's being so drastically cut and reedited by others that the intent of the original was spoiled. Another French endeavor, Jacques Demy's ambitious *hommage* to the MGM musical, *The Young Girls of Rochefort*, with Kelly as one of the stars, was too limp to make any impression.

Kelly was active on television throughout the decade, appearing on most of the major variety shows as a guest doing light dancing, "The heavy dancing is all behind me, but this mini-dancing on variety shows is fun and it helps me stay in shape." Among his major TV efforts were a special called "New York, New York" in 1966, and his direction and production of "Jack and the Beanstalk" in 1967, for which he won an Emmy.

Kelly's only fling at a TV series was a failure. He appeared in late 1962 as Father O'Malley in "Going My Way," in the role originated by Bing Crosby, but the timing was wrong. "I was hemmed in by the strict censorship then in effect, which allowed a Catholic priest to do nothing untoward. Our idea was that he be a two-fisted character and a social crusader, but the censors cut us down. It would have been interesting to have made the series years later when the medium and the public were more mature."

Gene Kelly was honored on November 18, 1969 when a tribute to him delivered by the Hon. Thomas M. Rees, Representative from California, was entered in the *Congressional Record*. The tribute saluted his contributions to the entertainment industry, but also mentioned that he had been cited by the government in 1945 and 1947 for services rendered and that he had traveled as a goodwill ambassador for the State Department in 1964.

But it is as a film dancer and choreographer that Kelly will be remembered, and especially for his development of screen dancing in a way that was acceptable to the mass public. "I belonged to the sweatshirt generation, and I felt uncomfortable

Being invested a Chevalier of the Legion of Honor at the Paris Opera House by director A.M. Julien

With daughter Kerry at the investiture of the Legion of Honor

At a Paris party in 1961 with another ex-M-G-M Kelly - Princess Grace, with Prince Rainier

With Bobby Riha in the television special *Jack and the Beanstalk*

With Nadia Westmore and Leo G. Carroll in the TV series *Going My Way*

26

in a tuxedo. I couldn't be another Fred Astaire and I had very little interest in doing *Swan Lake*. I grew up at a time when the American theatre was coming into its own and by the time I got to New York I knew I wanted to dance to American music, and try and find a style that could be called American. For me it was an extention of being a sports-oriented Pittsburgh kid. I wanted reality and vitality in addition to sophistication. I wasn't alone in this movement—people like Martha Graham and Humphrey Weidman were creating a whole new art form while I was struggling to find a style for myself. And by the time I found my style I got into films, and then found I was into something completely different from the stage and its dancing requirements. Dancing for the camera is comparatively very difficult."

The main difference between stage and screen dancing is one of perspective. Kelly explains: "On the stage you dance in the framework of the proscenium arch, the audience is in front of you and they see a three-dimensional image. They see with two eyes and they can absorb the environment. The one-eyed lens of the camera allows the audience to see only that portion of the scenery behind the dancer, and he becomes a two-dimensional figure. So you lose one of the most vital aspects of the dance—the sense of kinetic force, and the feeling of that third dimension. To compensate for that I put myself and my colleagues to thinking of dances that were purely cinematic—dancing with a cartoon, dancing with yourself in double exposure, dancing across interesting locations and being tracked by the camera. You have to construct a dance so it can be cut and edited, and do it in a way that won't disturb the viewer. You learn to use the camera as part of the choreography. It's possible that a lot of fine dancing has been ineffectual in the movies because it was never photographed imaginatively. Filming dancing will always be a problem because the eye of the camera is coldly realistic, demanding that everything looks natural, and dancing is unrealistic. That's the challenge, and all art is a compromise between your ideas and whatever means you have at your disposal."

There seems little likelihood that the movie musical will ever again become a staple of the cinema. The odds are all against it. The outlet for musical presentations will undoubtedly be television, ever improving in technical and artistic quality. Since 1960 most movie musicals have been filmed treatments of established stage vehicles, but

With wife Jeanne and their children Timothy and Bridget in the Kelly back garden on Bridget's third birthday, June 10, 1967

27

so many of them have been financial disasters that backers have come to regard the film musical as the worst of risks. The problems of costs and risks also apply to the wellspring of such films—the New York theatre, which in the 1960s produced an ever-diminishing number of successful musicals. This shortage is allied to the great changes in taste in popular music since the early fifties, with the accent of the music industry attuned to the younger generation. In the opinion of Gene Kelly: "This is a peculiar problem. Much of the youth-oriented music is admirable in its own right but hardly any of it lends itself to dramatic treatment. Many of the songs are charming, but they are not really for dancing. The authors of *Hair* came to see me about doing it as a film, but they had no script and you can't ad lib a movie musical. And the discotheque kind of dancing, this weird mixture of African tribal rites and the varsity drag, electrifying as it may be in person, means nothing when you put it on film. You need discipline and coordinated team work to make musicals—it's one area of filmmaking where the now popular *auteur* theory just does not make sense."

Gene Kelly, a hale and hearty sixty-one as this book goes to press, has long been considered one of the more solid citizens of Beverly Hills. He has lived in the same house since 1946 and prefers the conservative lifestyle, but is politically liberal and an active supporter of the Democrats. Nothing about Kelly smacks of the bizarre or the flamboyant, and his manner is more that of a successful, dignified business executive than that of a movie star. However, this demeanor is somewhat at variance with his feelings for the business world. "I have little talent for business. Actually the only thing I don't get a kick out of in show business is 'business.' But I still feel it's fun to act, fun to direct, fun to dance, fun to do all the things one does either in front of or behind the camera. And I'll continue to participate whenever and however fortune dictates."

In reviewing his career Kelly expresses no serious regrets: "I think I would like to have made a picture with Cary Grant or a western with John Ford but I've been very fortunate in doing most of the things I wanted to do. I'd like to make a few more movies, mainly as a director, and I have a notion to direct something entirely different from what I've done before, perhaps a Shakespearean tragedy. But even if it never comes to be, I have no cause to complain. A career came my way —I didn't set out in pursuit of one. I took it as it came, and it turned out to be very nice. A man can hardly be luckier than that."

With French director Jacques Demy while making *The Young Girls of Rochefort*

With Adolph Zukor on his 100th birthday - January 7, 1973

THE FILMS

With Judy Garland

FOR ME AND MY GAL

CREDITS:

An MGM Production 1942. Produced by Arthur Freed. Directed by Busby Berkeley. Screenplay by Richard Sherman, Fred Finklehoffe and Sid Silvers. Based on a story by Howard Emmett Rogers. Photographed by William Daniels. Art direction by Cedric Gibbons. Edited by Ben Lewis. Dances directed by Bobby Connolly. Music direction by George Stoll. Running time: 100 minutes.

CAST:

Jo Hayden: Judy Garland; *Harry Palmer:* Gene Kelly; *Red Metcalfe:* George Murphy; *Eve Minard:* Marta Eggerth; *Sid Sims:* Ben Blue; *Lily Duncan:* Lucille Norman; *Danny Duncan:* Richard Quine; *Eddie Miller:* Kennan Wynn; *Bert Waring:* Horace McNally.

The difficulty of playing a leading role in his first film was somewhat eased for Gene Kelly by the nature of the material. *For Me and My Gal* required him to play a charming, but conceited and selfish young song-and-dance man, a part not greatly removed from the characterization of *Pal Joey.* The songs and dances themselves were all familiar ones—at least familiar to anyone with knowledge of the American entertainment business in the years of the First World War, the milieu of the film. In Busby Berkeley Kelly had a director who knew this kind of story from personal experience. Berkeley had served in the U.S. Army in France and had started his career staging shows for the troops. Says Kelly, "I knew nothing about filming when we started and I was scared, but by the time we finished I had picked up quite a lot of know-how, thanks to Berkeley and thanks to Judy, who had a lot to do with persuading MGM to use me in the picture."

For Me and My Gal opens in a little town in Ohio; a troupe of entertainers arrive to play the local theatre, among them Jo Hayden (Judy Garland, Red Metcalfe (George Murphy), Lily Duncan (Lucille Norman) and Sid Sims (Ben Blue), a quartet of singer-dancers who travel the vaudeville circuit. Also in the company is a breezy hoofer, Harry Palmer (Kelly), who makes up to Jo and persuades her they will be a good team, and that they should set their sights on the Palace Theatre in New York, the high spot of the vaudeville circuit. She becomes his partner and gradually falls in love with him, a feeling the ambitious Harry fails either to recognize or reciprocate. He falls under the spell of singing star Eve Minard (Marta Eggerth) and the romance shows every sign of helping his career. Although Jo and Harry have been together for two years they still have not reached the top of the business, and realizing how much he wants to get there, the unselfish Jo goes to Eve and asks her to help him. This she is prepared to do, but when Harry hears about it he has a change of heart; he realizes his own love for Jo and decides to stick with her.

Eventually Jo and Harry receive an offer from the Palace but when they get to the theatre in New York they learn there has been an error—the booking should have made clear it was the Palace Theatre in Newark. They do their act in Newark and do it so well they get an offer of a contract for the big Palace but in the midst of their celebrations Harry receives his draft call to join the army. Determined to let nothing stand in the way of his career, Harry smashes his hand in a trunk and sustains a injury sufficient to get him a deferment. His timing turns out to be bad; Jo learns of his cowardly ruse just as she learns that her young brother has been killed on active duty in France, and she walks out on Harry.

A contrite Harry tries to make amends by enlisting but he is turned down. He then joins a YMCA entertainment unit, along with Sid Sims, and they are shipped to France. He finds that Jo is traveling around the battle areas entertaining the troops, and in order to vindicate himself in her eyes he performs an act of heroism. The lovers are united and with the signing of the armistice they resume their career, which takes them to the Palace in New York.

The plot of *For Me and My Gal* is banal and frequently maudlin, but it is generously laced with musical numbers and the performances are altogether pleasing if not striking. It is really Judy

With George Murphy and Judy Garland

With George Murphy, Lucille Norman and Judy Garland

With Judy Garland

Garland's picture—it was, in fact, her first solo billing—and Kelly is a little bland as the cocky cad, although his performance was sufficient to win him approval as a "likable new find" wherever the picture played. The part of Harry was originally slated for George Murphy but pressure from Arthur Freed and Judy Garland got Kelly the job, with Murphy then taking the next-best role as the faithful friend of the heroine—the nice guy who doesn't get the girl.

The score of the film includes eighteen songs and dances; the title song and "When You Wore a Tulip" are sung by Garland and Kelly as duets, and they also perform the classic jazz-dance "Ballin' the Jack." Kelly does the solo "Tramp Dance," and with Ben Blue he does the vaudeville ditty, "Frenchie, Frenchie." Garland has several extended solos—"Oh, You Beautiful Doll," "Smiles," "Till We Meet Again," and "After You've Gone"—but much of her footage is spoiled by Berkeley's exceedingly sentimental direction. *For Me and My Gal* is very old-fashioned entertainment and now comes within the boundaries of what is vaguely known as "camp."

Gene Kelly looks back on the filming as an exciting but uncomfortable period: "I still feel more at ease on a stage than I do before the cameras but at that time I was constantly thrown by the piecemeal way pictures are made. I knew nothing about playing to the camera, and I didn't know whether I was being shot close, medium or long, or about the intricate business of hitting all the marks laid out on the studio floor for the movements of the actors. It was Judy who pulled me through. She was very kind and helpful, and more helpful than she even realized because I watched her to find out what I had to do. Judy was only twenty, but she had been in pictures for six years. I was amazed at her skill; she knew every mark and every move. All I could do for her then was help with the dancing. She wasn't a dancer, but she could pick up a step instantly, and as a singer she was incredible—she had only to hear a melody once and it was locked in her mind. I learned a great deal about making movies doing this first one, and much of it was due to Judy Garland."

With Martha Eggerth

With George Murphy, Judy Garland, Ben Blue and Keenan Wynn

With Judy Garland

With Ben Blue

With Addison Richards and Ben Blue

With Judy Garland

With Marsha Hunt and Franchot Tone

PILOT NO. 5

CREDITS:

An MGM Production 1943. Produced by B. P. Fineman. Directed by George Sidney. Screenplay by David Hertz. Photographed by Paul C. Vogel. Art direction by Cedric Gibbons and Howard Campbell. Edited by George White. Musical score by Lennie Hayton. Running time: 70 minutes.

CAST:

George Braynor Collins: Franchot Tone; *Freddie:* Marsha Hunt; *Vito S. Alessandro:* Gene Kelly; *Everett Arnold:* Van Johnson; *Winston Davis:* Alan Baxter; *Henry Willoughy Claven:* Dick Simmons; *Major Eichel:* Steve Geray; *Hank Durban:* Howard Freeman; *Nikola:* Frank Puglia; *American Soldier:* William Tannen.

For his second film Gene Kelly opted for a straight dramatic story with no songs and dances, eager to prove his interest in being known as an actor as well as a musical performer. The film was made under the title *Skyway to Glory*, but MGM wisely decided against that pretentious label and chose to release it as *Pilot No. 5*, an uninspired choice that did nothing to draw the public. It was then shown as a "programmer"—something between an A and a B film, to be used as either top or bottom of a double bill depending on location and the studio's investment in the companion feature.

The story begins in March of 1942, at a bomb-blasted air base in Java, where a group of Allied survivors must decide what course to take in the face of the oncoming Japanese forces. The senior officer is a Dutch major, who finds he has five

34

With Marsha Hunt

With Marsha Hunt and Franchot Tone

With Dick Simmons, Steve Geray, Alan Baxter and Van Johnson

With Howard Freeman, Dick French,
Marsha Hunt and Franchot Tone

American pilots at his disposal but only one aircraft fit for service. The decision is made to use the plane, a fighter, to attack the Japanese in what will probably be a suicidal mission. The major calls for a volunteer and when all five men offer to make the flight he decides to choose the

man who has the most logical plan of attack. The winner is George Collins (Franchot Tone), and after he has taken off the major wonders about him, about his character and background. Three of the pilots are acquainted with Collins and their recollections are depicted in flashback sequences which form most of the footage of *Pilot No. 5*.

The divergent opinions about Collins confuse the Dutch officer. Lt. Winston Davis (Alan Baxter) tells how, as an enlistment officer, he was hesitant about accepting Collins's application to join the Air Corps because of an unsavory reputation. Lt. Everett Arnold (Van Johnson) gives a better picture of the man remembered from school days as a law student, eager to succeed because of his love for Freddie (Marsha Hunt). The bulk of the story is learned, somewhat reluctantly, from Lt. Vito Alessandro (Gene Kelly), a former partner of Collins in the employ of a powerful but crooked state governor, Hank Durban (Howard Freeman). Alessandro reveals how the ambitious Collins went along with the venal politician until he himself quit in disgust. Eventually Collins followed suit, with his reputation subsequently blackened by the governor, and his spirit broken by the collapse of his career and the false belief that Alessandro had stolen the affections of Freddie, a lie fostered by Durban. Collins gradually regains respect when he fights back and exposes the governor. As Alessandro ends his story, radio reception from Collins informs them he is about to crash-dive his plane on a Japanese aircraft carrier.

The performance of Kelly as a moody Italian-American surprised those who had little reason to consider him an actor on the basis of his work in *Me and My Gal*. Slight though *Pilot No. 5* was, it proved that Kelly was not merely a visiting Broadway performer and that he obviously had a future in films. As Kelly recalls: "The picture started out to be something bigger and stronger than it finally emerged. The original idea was a statement against fascism, to draw a parallel between the malpractice of political power in America and the kinds of fascism that had drawn America into the war. It was a warning against incipient fascism, somewhat based on Huey Long and the danger of one man's gaining control of a state. But the studio shied away from taking that kind of stand at that time, which isn't hard to understand—we were in the entertainment business and this was wartime. So the script was defanged."

With Marsha Hunt

With Marsha Hunt and Franchot Tone

With Lucille Ball

DU BARRY WAS A LADY

CREDITS:

An MGM Production 1943. Produced by Arthur Freed. Directed by Roy del Ruth. Screenplay by Irving Brecher, adapted by Nancy Hamilton from the musical play by Herbert Fields and B. G. DeSylva. Songs by Cole Porter, Lew Brown, Ralph Freed, Burton Lane, Roger Edens and E. Y. Harburg. Musical direction by George Stoll. Photographed in Technicolor by Karl Freund. Art direction by Cedric Gibbons. Edited by Blanche Sewell. Running time: 96 minutes.

CAST:

Louis Blore, King Louis: Red Skelton; *May Daly, Madame Du Barry:* Lucille Ball; *Alec Howe, Black Arrow:* Gene Kelly; *Ginny:* Virginia O'Brien; *Charlie, Dauphin:* Rags Ragland; *Rami, the Swami, Taliostra:* Zero Mostel; *Mr. Jones, Duc de Choiseul:* Donald Meek; *Willie, Duc de Rigor:* Douglas Dumbrille; *Cheezy, Count de Roquefort:* George Givot; *Niagara:* Louise Beavers; *and Tommy Dorsey and his Orchestra.*

Cole Porter's *Du Barry Was a Lady* suffered the same fate that every stage musical suffered when bought by a Hollywood studio in those years when the studios were all-powerful—the script was thoroughly rewritten, most of the songs were dropped and new ones added. The Porter show, which opened on Broadway in December of 1939, was a smash hit with Ethel Merman and Bert Lahr, but neither was considered strong enough with the moviegoing public to risk using in the film version. In the film their parts were played by Red Skelton and Lucille Ball, with the second

With Red Skelton and Lucille Ball

With Lucille Ball and Red Skelton

With Zero Mostel

leads, those played on Broadway by Ronald Graham and Betty Grable, going to Gene Kelly and Virginia O'Brien. Grable was then under contract to 20th Century-Fox and though they were agreeable to her playing on Broadway, they felt differently about her appearing in a Metro musical. The script of the Porter original was considered quite racy and spicy at the time, and the tone was much softened for the film; whereas the character played by Lahr on stage was a washroom attendant he was played as a cloakroom clerk by Skelton. The twenty songs written by Porter for the original were whittled down to three, and six new ones were written by Lew Brown, Ralph Freed, Burton Lane, E. Y. Harburg and Roger Edens.

Much of the film is set in the period of King Louis XIV with all of that footage in the form of a dream sequence. A hat-check boy, Louis Blore (Red Skelton), in a swank nightclub, is deeply in love with glib showgirl May Daly (Lucille Ball), who disdains to pay him attention—until he wins $75,000 in the Irish Sweepstake. She then becomes his fiancee, to the disappointment of song-and-dance man Alec Howe (Kelly). Due to his good fortune Louis is dubbed "King Louis" by newspapermen, and to further impress his bride-to-be he buys the nightclub. Alec's friend, Swami the Rami (Zero Mostel), a comic seer, predicts May will never marry Louis, and Louis, afraid that Alec may cause trouble at the engagement party, slips a drug into Alec's drink to render him unconscious. But it is Louis who downs the drink, causing him to fall sleep—and dream. The dream transports Louis and his friends back two hundred years, with Louis as the King, May as Du Barry and Alec as a dashing revolutionary leader known as The Black Arrow.

The situations in the dream reveal the same doubts Louis had in his real situation, with Du Barry showing the King little interest. He finds himself the intended victim of a plot, contrived by several of his courtiers and led by The Black Arrow. After a chain of ludicrous circumstances King Louis finds himself among the very crowd marching on the palace to kill him. He manages to gain control of the situation and sentences The Black Arrow to the guillotine, but Du Barry pleads for the life of the handsome rebel—for obvious reasons—promising Louis she will do anything for him in return. The King then tries to stop the execution but his cries are lost in the cries of the mob, and as The Black Arrow kneels under the knife, the dream fades and Louis wakes up in the nightclub, being attended by his friends. Taking the dream as a lesson and a warning, Louis comes to his senses about May and calls off his engagement. He promotes the engagement of May and Alec and realizes he loves Ginny, the club's cigarette girl, who has loved him all along.

Du Barry Was a Lady did good business at the box office, but was far from the blockbuster MGM had hoped for Robbed of the sauciness of the stage original and the brilliant comic performance of Bert Lahr, the film's devices seem limp. Skelton and Lucille Ball are amusing, but only suggestive of the comic experts they would later become. More memorable are the smaller parts—Zero Mostel at the age of twenty-eight and making his film debut; Rags Ragland, whose death in 1946 cut short a thriving comic career, as a nightclub flunky who becomes the Dauphin of France in the dream sequence; and the deadpan chanteuse Virginia O'Brien singing a song about sex, "No Matter How Thin You Slice It, It's Still Salome."

Gene Kelly's role called for no great effort on his part, dance-romancing Lucille Ball and doing a lively group dance with beautiful chorus girls in the nightclub. His swashbuckling as The Black Arrow was a sign of things to come, and he was involved in the only two lasting songs from the film—both from Porter's original score—the ballad "Do I Love You, Do I?" and the catchy "Friendship," sung as the finale by all the main characters.

With Zero Mostel and Red Skelton

With Lucille Ball, Red Skelton, Virginia O'Brien and Tommy Dorsey

The Mop Dance

THOUSANDS CHEER

CREDITS:

An MGM Production 1943. Produced by Joe Pasternak. Directed by George Sidney. Screenplay by Paul Jarrico and Richard Collins. Photographed in Technicolor by George Folsey. Art direction by Cedric Gibbons. Edited by George Boemler. Musical direction by Herbert Stothart. Running time: 125 minutes.

CAST:

Kathryn Jones: Kathryn Grayson; *Eddy Marsh:* Gene Kelly; *Hyllary Jones:* Mary Astor; *Col. William Jones:* John Boles; *Chuck Polansky:* Ben Blue; *Marie Corbino:* Frances Rafferty; *Helen:* Mary Elliott; *Sergeant Kozlack:* Frank Jenks; *Alan:* Frank Sully; *Capt. Fred Avery:* Dick Simmons; *Private Monks:* Ben Lessy.

GUEST STARS: Mickey Rooney, Judy Garland, Red Skelton, Eleanor Powell, Ann Sothern, Lucille Ball, Virginia O'Brien, Frank Morgan, Lena Horne, Marsha Hunt, Marilyn Maxwell, Donna Reed, Margaret O'Brien, June Allyson, Gloria de Haven, John Conte, Sara Haden, Jose Iturbi, Don Loper and Maxine Barrat, and the bands of Kay Kyser, Bob Crosby and Benny Carter.

Thousands Cheer holds especial interest for film students because it is a prime example of a Hollywood product never likely to be produced again. These glittering all-star packages were purportedly made in the national interest as morale boosters in wartime and they were made at a time when the film studios were at the peak of their affluence and creativity. The rich resources of MGM and its talent roster were available to producer Joe Pasternak to make this film, and con-

With Ben Blue

With Ben Blue and Kathryn Grayson

temporary producers might well look with envy at what Pasternak then had at his disposal. The plot was thin, but musical numbers and sketches by twenty guest stars pumped it up to a pleasing two hours. The working title was *Private Miss Jones*, but this was dropped after the completion of the film in favor of *Thousands Cheer*, thereby causing some confusion with Irving Berlin's stage musical *As Thousands Cheer*, to which it bore no resemblance.

Much of the action of the story takes place at an army camp, where Kathryn Jones (Kathryn Grayson) gives up her career as a concert singer in favor of keeping house for her father, Col. William Jones (John Boles), long separated from his wife, Hyllary (Mary Astor). At a railway station, Private Eddie March (Kelly) spots Kathryn and despite his being a stranger, he kisses her because he is alone and feels the urge to kiss somebody goodbye. He is unaware that she is the daughter of the commandant of the camp for which he is bound, and when he later discovers this he is resentful because to him the girl represents military authority, which he hates. Eddie is a trapeze artist, a daring and successful aerialist and he has been drafted much against his wishes. He is conceited in his manner, and rude to Kathryn, until he is advised by his buddies to play up to her if he wants to make his desired transfer to the Air Corps. The idea backfires when Eddie finds himself in love with Kathryn and she with him. The colonel is alarmed at the affair and asks for the advice of his estranged wife. Meanwhile Eddie has taken Kathryn

With Kathryn Grayson and John Boles

41

With Kathryn Grayson and Mary Astor

With Will Kaufmann, Kathryn Grayson, Mary Elliot and Frances Rafferty

42

to meet his circus family, the Corbinos, and she discovers he was, in fact, the star of the act.

Eddie is worried when Kathryn's mother appears on the scene, bound to persuade the girl to return with her to New York. Kathryn begs for more time because she is producing a camp show, to which she has invited various famous entertainers, including Jose Iturbi. Eddie, by now a model soldier, panics when he learns of the arrival of her mother, deserts his guard post and barges into the colonel's office to plead his case, which results in his being confined to barracks. The day of the show arrives and among the talent are The Corbinos, who manage to persuade the colonel to release Eddie in order to perform with them. His family understands Eddie's problems in adjusting to discipline and cooperation, and while performing their high-flying act they graphically impress upon him the need for teamwork and reliance on others. After the show, Hyllary is about to discuss her plans for taking Kathryn away when the camp receives its orders to proceed overseas. At the fadeout, mother and daughter wave goodbye to the colonel and his future son-in-law.

Hollywood was unstinting in its wartime efforts to entertain the armed forces, sending units to every camp on every front, but it's doubtful if any camp received the kind of lavish show staged for the troops in *Thousands Cheer*. One of the plot devices in the film is for the heroine to be a friend of the Spanish concert pianist Jose Iturbi, who here made the first of what would be several appearances in MGM musicals, helping to popularize classical music and occasionally "letting his hair down" with pop pieces. In this picture Iturbi has a fling at boogie-woogie and accompanies Judy Garland in a raucous, and now terribly dated, song called "The Joint is Really Jumping Down at Carnegie Hall," written by Roger Edens. Standing the test of time far better is Lena Horne with "Honeysuckle Rose." The camp show has Mickey Rooney as the master of ceremonies and aside from introducing a raft of sketches he does his impersonation of Clark Gable. Among the better sketches are Red Skelton as a soda-jerk with a weak stomach, made bilious by the appetite of Margaret O'Brien for ice cream, and Frank Morgan as a fake navy doctor delighting over the prospect of examining WAVE inductees Lucille Ball and Ann Sothern. A variety of dance bands play typical songs of the day like "I Dug a Ditch and Struck it Rich in Wichita," and "Let There be Music." Kathryn Grayson is heard to advantage in an aria from *La Traviata,* and a song called "Daybreak," based on a melody by Ferde Grofe, with lyrics by Harold Adamson. The huge finale is "The United Nations Hymn," sung by Grayson and an army orchestra under Iturbi.

Despite the generous amounts of music in *Thousands Cheer,* Gene Kelly appears in only one sequence calling for dancing. As the private confined to barracks and ordered to clean the floor, he makes the job lighter by imagining his mop to be a girl. He glides around the floor waltzing to the tune "Let Me Call You Sweetheart," gradually making the dance more complex. At one point he aims the mop at a picture of Hitler and rat-a-tat-tats with his heel like a machine gun. Kelly's work in the picture was a clear step up in MGM's plan to register him with the public, and he was well received by most of the critics. In his review for The *New York Herald Tribune* Howard Barnes went so far to say Kelly dominated the film and "saves the picture from being merely a parade of personalities."

With Frances Rafferty and Mary Elliot

With Kathryn Grayson

43

THE CROSS OF LORRAINE

CREDITS:

An MGM Production 1943. Produced by Edwin Knopf. Directed by Tay Garnett. Screenplay by Michael Kanin, Ring Lardner, Jr., Alexander Eskay and Robert D. Andrews, based on a story by Lilo Damert and Robert Aisner and *A Thousand Shall Fall* by Hans Habe. Photographed by Sidney Wagner. Art direction by Cedric Gibbons and Daniel Cathcart. Edited by Dan Miller. Musical score by Bronislau Kaper. Running time: 89 minutes.

CAST:

Paul: Jean-Pierre Aumont; *Victor:* Gene Kelly; *Father Sebastian:* Sir Cedric Hardwicke; *Francois:* Richard Whorf; *Rodriguez:* Joseph Calleia; *Sergeant Berger:* Peter Lorre; *Duval:* Hume Cronyn; *Louis:* Billy Roy; *Major Bruhl:* Tonio Stewart; *Jacques:* Jack Lambert; *Pierre:* Wallace Ford; *Marcel:* Donald Curtis; *Rene:* Jack Edwards, Jr.; *Lt. Schmidt:* Richard Ryen.

The majority of Hollywood movies made during the years of the Second World War, dealing with that war, appear ludicrous when viewed a generation later. It can hardly be otherwise. This was entertainment with an intentional propagandistic purpose, and those films which dealt with the German occupation of various European countries suffer most in the time gap. *The Cross of Lorraine* is a case in point; despite its production values and some fine performances the unrelieved depiction of all Germans as vicious brutes and most Frenchmen as noble heroes robs it of any credibility. However, credit must be given the Hollywood studios for following through on requests from Washington for pictures of this nature. MGM was asked to make *The Cross of Lorraine* to inculcate a better regard for France among the Allies.

It is, basically, a prison picture and like others of this genre it quickly sets up the backgrounds of a group of main characters, all of whom join the French army at the outbreak of the war and all of whom are captured when the French government capitulates. Chief among them are a promising Parisian lawyer, Paul (Jean-Pierre Aumont), a taxi driver with a scrappy nature, Victor (Gene Kelly), and Rodriguez (Joseph Calleia), a Spanish Republican intent on carrying on the fight against oppression. The film is little else but an indictment of German ruthlessness. The soldiers find themselves tricked—instead of being returned to their homes they are herded into railway boxcars and shipped off to a camp behind the German lines, there to be indoctrinated into belief in the New Order, a process that hardly seems feasible in view of the brutality meted out to them. A priest, Father Sebastian (Sir Cedric Hardwicke) is one of the captives and he is treated no better than the others —the heathen Huns even deny him the right to hold services. A nasty little German sergeant (Peter Lorre in one of his less memorable roles) steals from the prisoners, and a weasellike Frenchman, Duval (Hume Cronyn) makes use of his knowledge of the German language and decides to work for his captors.

Victor suffers torture and humiliation because of his belligerent attitude. At the initial interrogation he gives a weak Nazi salute and asks, "Heil, er, what's his name?" at which he is knocked unconscious and thrown into solitary confinement, where his spirit is sapped. The French soldiers find their plight little different from the inmates of concentration camps, with near-starvation, sickness, beatings and the idea of escape their sustaining force. Duval meets his due fate when the inmates put him on trial, find him guilty and then push him out into the night to be shot by the guards. Father Sebastian dies when he defies the Germans and holds a burial service—they shoot him as he intones the rites. Meanwhile, Paul assumes Duval's place, feigning loyalty to the Germans in order to facilitate the escapes of his comrades.

Paul arranges the escape of the ailing Victor; he substitutes him for a wounded German soldier, whose head is completely bandaged, and tricks the sergeant into letting him drive the soldier for badly needed attention at a nearby hospital. The sergeant accompanies Paul in the ambulance but he is dumped out and the two Frenchmen makes their way on foot until they are picked up by the French underground forces, who lead them to a village in a less densely occupied part of France. But while Paul and Victor are recuperating, a German army unit arrives in the village to recruit men for labor battalions. They make a show

With Billy Roy, Wallace Ford, Jean Pierre Aumont and Jack Lambert

of requesting volunteers but they clearly mean to arrest the required number of men. As the German officer addresses the crowd, Paul walks to the front to seemingly offer himself as a model volunteer but he then turns and incites the populace into revolt, which act costs him his life. At this, Victor snaps out of the defeatist stupor into which he had fallen and leads the villagers in a pitched battle to wipe out the German soldiers. With this accomplished, they burn the village to prevent its usefulness to other German units and march away to join the Resistance.

The Cross of Lorraine, with the flag of the Free French fluttering in the credit titles and numerous paraphrases of "La Marseillaise" in Bronislau Kaper's score, probably drew the political response it sought, provided it was paired with something more entertaining on a double bill. It also provided Gene Kelly with his most dramatic role in films, one which brought him good notices and one he considers among his best performances.

With Peter Lorre

With Richard Whorf and Jean Pierre Aumont

With Jean Pierre Aumont and Sir Cedric Hardwick

With Jean Pierre Aumont, Jack Lambert, Wallace Ford and Joseph Calleia

With Sir Cedric Hardwick and Joseph Calleia

With Jean Pierre Aumont and Richard Whorf

With Rita Hayworth

COVER GIRL

CREDITS:

A Columbia Production 1944. Produced by Arthur Schwartz. Directed by Charles Vidor. Screenplay by Virginia Van Upp, adapted by Marion Parsonnet and Paul Gangelin from a story by Erwin Gelsey. Photographed in Technicolor by Rudolph Maté and Allen M. Davey. Art direction by Lionel Banks and Cary Odell. Edited by Viola Lawrence. Songs by Jerome Kern and Ira Gershwin. Musical direction by Morris W. Stoloff. Running time: 107 minutes.

CAST:

Rusty Parker: Rita Hayworth; *Danny McGuire:* Gene Kelly; *Noel Wheaton:* Lee Bowman; *Genius:* Phil Silvers; *Jinx:* Jinx Falkenburg; *Maurine* *Martin:* Leslie Brooks; *Cornelia Jackson:* Eve Arden; *John Coudair:* Otto Kruger; *John Coudair (as a young man):* Jess Barker; *Anita:* Anita Colby; *Chef:* Curt Bois; *Joe:* Ed Brophy; *Tony Pastor:* Thurston Hall.

In the history of the Hollywood musical *Cover Girl* marks a major turning point, a transitional point at which the long-familiar concept of the movie musical as a string of songs strung together by a skimpy plot gave way to a broader concept in which the musical sequences would form part of the plot. However, the plot of *Cover Girl* is paper-thin and in direct line with the many corny backstage musicals stretching back over the previous dozen years. Its value lies in the quality of the songs supplied by Jerome Kern and Ira Gershwin and how those songs are sung and danced. The film also marks a turning point in the career of

48

With Phil Silvers

Gene Kelly; until now he had been well received by the public as a pleasant entertainer with an obvious talent for dancing, but with *Cover Girl* it was apparent that he was not merely a dancer. It was here that Kelly made it known to both the public and the industry that he was capable of imaginative choreography of a purely cinematic kind, and equally capable of performing the highly complex and athletic dancing that choreography required.

Much of the story is set in a small Brooklyn nightclub owned by Danny McGuire (Kelly). One of his dancing girls, Rusty Parker (Rita Hayworth), with whom he also happens to be in love, attracts the attention of a magazine editor, John Coudair (Otto Kruger) when that magazine conducts a search for cover girls. His choice of Rusty is influenced by the fact that she is the granddaughter of the young lady he loved and lost when he was a young man. This story twist allows for an elaborate flashback sequence in which Hayworth is seen as the lady in question, a star of Tony Pastor's musical theatre. In this sequence she sings "Sure Thing" against a racetrack backdrop, and the lyrics draw a parallel between betting on horses and being lucky in love.

Danny, Rusty and the club's comic, known as Genius (Phil Silvers), are all show-biz hopefuls, a fact that is clearly stated in one of the film's most memorable segments; after a good night's work they close the club and cavort along a Brooklyn street singing a breezy song of optimism, "Make Way for Tomorrow," leaping over various objects, running up and down stairways, and giving merry

With Phil Silvers and Rita Hayworth

49

With Rita Hayworth

With Eve Arden, Otto Kruger, Rita Hayworth and Lee Bowman

With Rita Hayworth

greetings to whomever comes their way. In total contrast, the film contains another street dance, Kelly's moody "Alter Ego" dance, in which he expresses his fears over the possible loss of his girlfriend. This fear proves groundless; after the ups and downs of the story have allowed for the presentation of several elaborate musical sequences, Rusty makes the decision to stay with Danny and not pursue a career.

The seven Kern-Gershwin songs all perform plot functions. The title song is used in the lavish staging of a cover-girl contest, and for this number Columbia recruited fifteen actual winners of magazine contests. The song "The Show Must Go On" is used in the nightclub in a simple, obvious manner, and Phil Silvers has a solo number, "Who's Complaining?" a topical ditty about rationing and wartime shortages. "Put Me to the Test" is a challenging love song for Kelly to express his feelings for Hayworth; the song begins in a dress shop and Kelly first tries out the lyrics on a dummy before later summoning up the courage to put them directly to his girl. The major song of the picture, the one which Ira Gershwin claims was the easiest to write, is the enduring "Long Ago and Far Away," which was also written for Kelly to sing to Hayworth. The setting is the nightclub after the close of business, with Kelly putting up chairs on tables as Silvers tinkles on the piano. Kelly is sad as he worries about his girl, but then

50

With Rita Hayworth

With Rita Hayworth, Phil Silvers and Ed Brophy

With Rita Hayworth and Phil Silvers

51

she comes onto the scene and he realizes she is his. The beautiful song then becomes the basis of an elegant, sensuous dance, and in this performance Kelly and Hayworth come close to matching Astaire and Rogers at their best. As a dancing partner Kelly is better suited to Hayworth than Astaire.

Cover Girl contains a number of moments which progress the art of presenting dancing on the screen and by far the most significant is Kelly's "Alter Ego" dance, the like of which had never been filmed before—or since. "It was the most difficult thing I've ever done, a technical torture, and I wouldn't want to have to do it again." The setting of the dance is a dim, deserted street late at night, and it springs from the hero's despondency over what he believes to be the loss of his girl. The situation is one of personal conflict, with part of his psyche deeply unhappy and another part trying to tell him it is for the best. To express this Kelly conceived the idea of a double dance, with the two disparate views in visual conflict: Kelly spots his reflection in a shop window and it comes to separate life, jumping into the street to confront him. The two figures pursue each other, leap over each other, run up and down stairs and generally vent their feelings in fancy footwork, all of it of a decidedly tough, masculine nature.

The "Alter Ego" dance came about after the rest of the film had been shot and Harry Cohn, the fabled hard-headed boss of Columbia, told Kelly he would like to see him do a solo. Having outlined his idea, no one at Columbia thought it could be done—but Cohn was convinced and told him to go ahead. Says Kelly: "I wanted to do something that couldn't be done in the theatre. The scene called for a man to show the conflict within himself and on a stage I could have done that easily with a few contortions and a fall to the

52

floor, but I'd found out by now that what worked in a theatre didn't always work on the screen. For example, on the stage I would hoof around for a minute or two and wink at the audience, and they'd love it. But in a film that falls flat—the personality is missing and you have to replace it with something that has meaning for the camera. It's a matter of fitting a three-dimensional art into a two-dimensional medium, and there's nothing easy about it—everything works against you. With this situation I had to invent two dances that could be synchronized, and the main problem was rehearsing the cameraman. We had to use a fixed-head camera in order to get the precision and Stanley Donen—without whom the piece couldn't have been done—would call out the timings for the cameraman, like "one–two–three–stop." We worked for about a month on that dance, then shot it in four days, with a lot more time spent editing all this double-printed footage. Having been told it couldn't be done, I was delighted to bring it off."

Somewhat ironically, Gene Kelly made *Cover Girl* not for MGM, famed for its musicals, but on a loan-out to Columbia. At his own studio he had been unable to persuade his employers to allow him more freedom in devising dances for the screen but with *Cover Girl* in release and bringing him wide acclaim MGM viewed him in a different light. With this picture Kelly's career—and the art of film choreography—took a giant step forward.

The Alter Ego Dance

54

With Rita Hayworth

With Rita Hayworth, director Charles Vidor and Phil Silvers

With Rita Hayworth, Otto Kruger, director Charles Vidor, Eve Arden, Phil Silvers and Leslie Brooks

With Deanna Durbin

CHRISTMAS HOLIDAY

CREDITS:

A Universal Production 1944. Produced by Felix Jackson. Directed by Robert Siodmak. Screenplay by Herman J. Mankiewicz, based on the novel by Somerset Maugham. Photographed by Woody Bredell. Art direction by John B. Goodman and Robert Clatworthy. Edited by Ted Kent. Musical score by Hans J. Salter. Running time: 93 minutes.

CAST:

Jackie Lamont, Abigail Martin: Deanna Durbin; *Robert Manette:* Gene Kelly; *Simon Fenimore:* Richard Whorf; *Charles Mason:* Dean Harens; *Valerie de Merode:* Gladys George; *Mrs. Manette:* Gale Sondergaard; *Gerald Tyler:* David Bruce.

Christmas Holiday is an interesting item. It con-

tains Gene Kelly's most offbeat performance, as a charming killer, and it was designed by Universal to give Deanna Durbin her first opportunity with drama. As a teenager she had been the studio's lifesaver, her early musicals having kept Universal from bankruptcy, but with time it became a problem to find suitable vehicles to maintain her popularity as she changed from a girl into a woman. Durbin was twenty-two when she made this picture, and her studio was greatly relieved when it grossed bigger earnings than her previous productions. However, it is neither the performance of Durbin or Kelly that keeps *Christmas Holiday* alive in the minds of film enthusiasts so much as the fact that it is work of the remarkable German director Robert Siodmak. He left Germany in 1934, having offended the Nazis, and settled in Paris, where he continued his career as a filmmaker. Siodmak arrived in Hollywood in

56

With Richard Whorf and Deanna Durbin

1940, leaving Paris just ahead of the German occupation, and over the course of the next dozen years directed a number of highly regarded films, mostly of the crime-fear-mystery *genre,* the best of them being *The Spiral Staircase* (1945) and *The Killers* (1946).

The screenplay is based, so roughly as to be barely recognizable, on a novel by Somerset Maugham, with the French location of the original switched to Louisiana and the role of the principal character, a girl reduced by dramatic circumstances to prostitution softened to that of a singer-hostess in a second-rate nightclub. The film opens at a military post as a group of officer candidates receive their commissions. One of them, Charles Mason (Dean Harens), is about to leave to visit his fiancee but he receives a telegram from her telling him she has just married someone else. Despondent, he catches a plane to visit his home in San Francisco but because of bad weather the plane is forced down in New Orleans. Mason's depression is increased by his not being able to get a hotel room, and a breezy reporter, Simon Fenimore (Richard Whorf) takes it upon himself to cheer him up. He takes him to the Maison Lafitte and persuades one of the girls, Jackie Lamont (Durbin) to spend some time with him. Jackie herself is quiet and rather glum and the young lieutenant finds himself trying to cheer *her* up. It is Christmas Eve and he offers to take her anywhere she would care to go, and somewhat to his surprise she asks to be taken to church to attend mass.

With Deanna Durbin and the Rev. Neal Dodd, a Hollywood Episcopalian minister frequently used by the studios to perform screen weddings.

With Deanna Durbin

With Deanna Durbin and Gale Sondergaard

With Deanna Durbin

The Christmas mass acts as a catharsis for the unhappy Jackie and with some persuasion she breaks down and tells Mason her story. Her real name is Abigail Martin and she is the wife of a jailed murderer, Robert Manette (Kelly). She had met this charming young man at a symphony concert and after a brief courtship married him and gone to live at the home of his mother (Gale Sondergaard). The Manettes appear to be wealthy and Robert has no occupation, but time proves him to be a psychopath, gambling away the family fortune and getting into trouble. He is always able to charm his wife and smile away their problems, until the day she finds he has unsuccessfully tried to burn a pair of bloodstained trousers. It is soon revealed that Manette has murdered a bookmaker and that his mother has helped him hide the body. Manette is apprehended, convicted and jailed, with the shocked young wife left to fend for herself.

At the end of the film Manette, having escaped prison, appears at the Maison Lafitte in a vengeful

58

mood and threatens his wife with a gun, believing she has betrayed him. Seeing her with the lieutenant increases his resolve to kill her, but before he can do so the police arrive and he is mortally wounded in the subsequent shooting. He dies in her arms, asking to be forgiven, and the audience is left to assume the long-suffering girl will have better luck with the young officer.

Gene Kelly is convincing as the personable cad, as is the remarkable Gale Sondergaard as the fiercely protective mother and her subtle playing suggests a love beyond the norm. The mother-son relationship is one of the best realized aspects of the film, doubtlessly due to Siodmak's direction. In this, as in most of his films, there is a subdued atmosphere of menace, with hints of things unspoken. The style is thoroughly Germanic—slightly cynical and photographed with accent on lighting, on shadows and rays. Unfortunately the film has more style than its substance warrants, but Siodmak was luckier with his next picture, *The Suspect,* starring Charles Laughton, based on the ghastly Crippen murders.

Deanna Durbin was not able to persuade the studio to let her avoid singing in *Christmas Holiday;* in this she sings "Spring Will Be a Little Late This Year," and "Always." Frank Loesser wrote the former especially for the picture and the Irving Berlin song was used as the heroine's pledge to her husband. Miss Durbin, who ended her film career in 1947 and left Hollywood, considers this her best performance, but Gene Kelly recalls her as being nervous and doubtful about it at the time, worrying that the public would not accept this dramatic change in her established image as a lilting, lighthearted singer. For Kelly the film was another loan-out assignment, and one which required no great effort on his part. The commitment was made prior to the release of *Cover Girl,* but with the impact of that picture on the public and the critics, MGM never again loaned Kelly's services to another studio.

With Deanna Durbin

With Frank Sinatra

ANCHORS AWEIGH

CREDITS:

An MGM Production 1945. Produced by Joe Pasternak. Directed by George Sidney. Screenplay by Isobel Lennart, based on a story by Natalie Marcin. Photographed in Technicolor by Robert Planck and Charles Boyle. Art direction by Cedric Gibbons and Randall Duell. Edited by Adrienne Fazan. Musical direction by George Stoll. Songs by Jule Styne (music) and Sammy Cahn (lyrics). Cartoon sequence directed by Fred Quimby. Running time: 143 minutes.

CAST:

Clarence Doolittle: Frank Sinatra; *Susan Abbott:* Kathryn Grayson; *Joseph Brady;* Gene Kelly; *Jose Iturbi:* Himself; *Donald Martin:* Dean Stockwell; *Brooklyn Girl:* Pamela Britton; *Police Sergeant:* Rags Ragland; *Cafe Manager:* Billy Gilbert; *Admiral Hammond:* Henry O'Neill; *Carlos:* Carlos Ramirez; *Police Captain:* Edgar Kennedy; *Bertram Kraler:* Grady Sutton; *Admiral's Aide:* Leon Ames; *Little Beggar Girl:* Sharon McManus.

It was with *Anchors Aweigh* that Gene Kelly came into his own right; the vitality and the joyousness of his performance in this highly entertaining film fairly shouts with the triumph of a man who has hit his own unique stride, and to the approval of every onlooker. This is a kingpin of a musical, filling more than two hours with a variety of music and humor, some of which is now dated due to its wartime slant. But the film retains much of its appeal; its producer, Joe Pasternak, was a man with the Midas touch in popular entertainment and a shrewd judge of talent. He

With Sharon McManus

With Kathryn Grayson, Frank Sinatra and Dean Stockwell

allowed Kelly free rein in devising his dance routines, with the happiest of results. *Anchors Aweigh* contains several memorable dances and with his animated sequence, "The King Who Couldn't Dance," Kelly came up with a classic. Pasternak also had the inspired idea of teaming Kelly with Frank Sinatra, who had appeared in five previous movies but never to advantage, despite his being the crooning rage of the day. But as a gawky, girl-shy sailor, Sinatra greatly widened his following with this picture.

The plotline of *Anchors Aweigh* is no more substantial than that of most other movie musicals but it serves as a good thread: two sailors, Joseph Brady and Clarence Doolittle (Kelly and Sinatra) decide to spend their shore leave in Hollywood and take advantage of the hospitality the movie colony is offering servicemen. Joseph, a nautical Don Juan, imagines he will have a field day with the many attractive girls who work in the studios, and that he will also be able to arrange something for his bashful buddy. They meet Susan Abbott (Kathryn Grayson), who works as an extra in the movies while studying to be a singer. She lives with her small brother Donald (Dean Stockwell) and proves to be too conservative for the tastes of Joseph, so he tries to foist her off on Clarence. She does not take kindly to this since she feels a strong attraction to Joseph, and his scheming backfires as he finds himself falling in love with her.

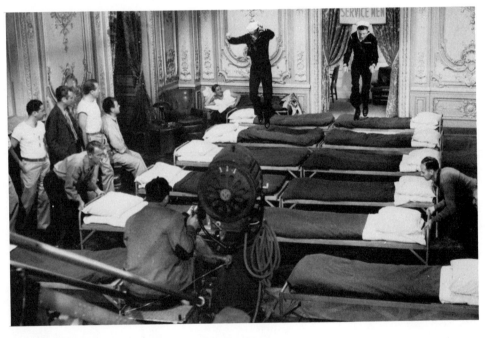

With Frank Sinatra, Kathryn Grayson and Billy Gilbert

Clarence meets a girl from Brooklyn (Pamela Britton) in the Hollywood Canteen and they fall in love. By the end of the picture the two sailors return to their ships having gained the affections of girls likely to be their future wives.

The device of having Kathryn Grayson play a movie extra is the hook on which much of the entertainment hangs. Joseph—and the audience—thereby gain entrance to MGM, and with the girl also a music student auditioning for pianist-conductor Jose Iturbi we get to hear a little popular concert music as well as the songs and dances of Kelly and Sinatra. Iturbi plays a bit of the famous Tchaikowsky concerto and, to prove he's no square, a boogie-woogie version of "The Donkey Serenade." He also accompanies Grayson as she sings "Jalousie." She also sings "All of a Sudden My Heart Sings." Sinatra was well served by the songs written by Jule Styne and Sammy Cahn. He and Kelly sing "We Hate to Leave," a cheeky song of farewell as the holiday-bound gobs leave their comrades, and Sinatra sings a song of fake conquest, "I Begged Her," which is resolved into a sprightly dance for Sinatra and Kelly in a service dormitory. The dance ends with their leaping from bed to bed—actually a series of small trampolines. Sinatra's most charming song is "I Fall in Love Too Easily," and his most maudlin his crooning of Brahms' "Lullaby" to little Dean Stockwell.

Gene Kelly has three major dance routines in *Anchors Aweigh*, in a wide range of style. He does "The Mexican Hat Dance" with a little Mexican girl (Sharon McManus), a very appealing routine somewhat limited by the fact that the partner is a child. But there are no limitations on his elaborate Spanish fandango, using a huge set in the form of a castle and danced like a combination of Rudolph Valentino and Douglas Fairbanks, Sr. The number comes about when Kelly, as the sailor being shown around the film studio by his girlfriend, imagines what it would be like if he were courting her in a costume movie. He dances around a courtyard, scales the walls of the castle, leaps from one parapet to another to reach the balcony of his princess, and leaves by making a huge swing on a hanging drapery from one building to another. And all this to the tune of "La Cumparsita!"

The highlight of *Anchors Aweigh*, and one of the most marvelous pieces of dance-fantasy ever done in films, is the sequence combining a cartoon with live action, "The King Who Couldn't Dance," the basis of which is "The Worry Song," with lyrics by Ralph Freed and music by Sammy

With Jose Iturbi, Frank Sinatra and Pamela Britton

With Henry O'Neill and Frank Sinatra

Fain. The setting is a mythical kingdom, with MGM's familiar Jerry the Mouse as the monarch. William Hanna and Joseph Barbera of the cartoon department and Irving G. Reis of the optical effects department were responsible for the production. The four minutes of screen time involved some ten thousand painted frames to synchronize with Kelly's movements. After devising a meticulous storyboard, Kelly was first photographed doing his part of the sequence, and then the mouse was animated frame by frame. The two figures were later linked optically. The story has Kelly as a French sailor who finds himself in a sad country where dancing is forbidden. He then visits the throne room of the castle and persuades the king to change his mind.

With Jerry, the King Mouse

With Tom and Jerry

The cartoon sequence took two months to complete. It came about through Kelly's desire to do something that had not been done before on film: "Stanley Donen and I sat around for a couple of days trying to think of something and after one long period of silence Stanley suggested, 'How about doing a dance with a cartoon?' This was it. The MGM brass didn't think it could be done, but Pasternak went to bat for us and got a budget of $100,000, to do it as an independent production, warning us that it likely would not appear in the movie. Stanley and I went to Walt Disney, to get his advice and possibly hire some of his men to work for us. But this wasn't possible because the Disney studio was so busy it couldn't accept any extra work. Disney was himself experimenting with live action and animation at that time although he had nothing as difficult in mind as what we hoped to do. But he gave us his blessings, and the fact that Disney considered the idea feasible helped us persuade the MGM cartoon department to do the job. I get all the credit for this, but it would have been impossible for me without Stanley, he worked with the cameraman and called the shots in all these intricate timings and movements. It wasn't easy for the cameraman—he was being asked to photograph something that wasn't there."

Anchors Aweigh was a solid hit wherever it played and it firmly registered Kelly as a star entertainer from whom the public now had the right to expect interesting future performances. It also won him a nomination for the Academy Award.

With Fred Astaire

ZIEGFELD FOLLIES

CREDITS:

An MGM Production 1946. Produced by Arthur Freed. Directed by Vincente Minnelli. Photographed in Technicolor by George Folsey and Charles Rosher. Art direction by Cedric Gibbons, Merrill Pye and Jack Martin Smith. Edited by Albert Akst. Musical direction by Lennie Hayton. Dance direction by Robert Alton. Running time: 118 minutes.

CAST:

Fred Astaire, Lucille Ball, Lucille Bremer, Fanny Brice, Judy Garland, Kathryn Grayson, Lena Horne, Gene Kelly, James Melton, Victor Moore, Red Skelton, Esther Williams, William Powell, Edward Arnold, Marion Bell, Cyd Charisse, Hume Cronyn, William Frawley, Robert Lewis, Virginia O'Brien, and Keenan Wynn.

When *Ziegfeld Follies* was reviewed by the press in New York in March of 1946, several critics made the point that it was a filmed version of the kind of plush, all-star stage revue which was even then a thing of the past. A similar comment can now be made about the film itself. We are never again likely to see such a movie production because the studio system which produced it no longer exists. Gone are the rosters of contracted performers, the stables of producers, directors and writers, and the various departments supplying all the resources the creators could possibly want. *Ziegfeld Follies* is, perhaps, the greatest of all Hollywood musicals although it is difficult to compare it to others because it has no plot at all; it is a collection of twelve unrelated segments of music and

With Fred Astaire

With Fred Astaire

With Fred Astaire

comedy using as its connective tissue the premise that if Florenz Ziegfeld had been able to return from the grave, this is the show he would have produced—assuming that he had MGM at his command.

William Powell appears at the start of the film in the guise of Ziegfeld (Powell had played the fabulous showman in the 1936 picture *The Great Ziegfeld*), occupying a plush apartment in Heaven. He muses about a new show and draws up a list of possible stars. After a puppet sequence—depicting some of Ziegfeld's early stars—Fred Astaire addresses the audience and pays tribute to Ziegfeld, thereby touching off the fantasy revue. The real producer of the show, Arthur Freed, is, of course, never seen—but it might be said that he out-Ziegfelded his subject.

The twelve sections, averaging eight to ten minutes each, are:

1. "Bring on the Beautiful Girls," a girlie merry-go-round with Lucille Ball as the ring mistress, and Virginia O'Brien singing a satirical ditty in praise of men—a counterpoint to the usual Ziegfeldian stand.
2. "A Water Ballet" starring Esther Williams and her aquabatics in an exotic marine setting.
3. "The Drinking Song," from Verdi's *La Traviata*, sung by James Melton and Marion Bell.
4. "Pay the Two Dollars," a classic sketch with Victor Moore as a man fined for spitting in a subway and Edward Arnold as the lawyer who refuses to allow him to pay the fine, making an issue of the case and causing Moore to be jailed.
5. "This Heart of Mine," a dance story with Fred Astaire and Lucille Bremer.
6. "Number Please," a skit with Keenan Wynn ribbing the telephone operator's errors in giving wrong numbers.
7. "Love," a sensuous torch song by Lena Horne.
8. "When Television Comes," with Red Skelton imagining the future problems of commercial announcers on TV, in particular those dispensing liquor.
9. "Limehouse Blues," a dramatic ballet with Fred Astaire and Lucille Bremer.
10. "The Great Lady Has an Interview," with Judy Garland lampooning a celebrated actress about to portray a lady inventor.
11. "The Babbit and the Bromide," a comedy dance by Fred Astaire and Gene Kelly.
12. "There's Beauty Everywhere," with Kathryn Grayson singing in a fantastic setting of multi-

colored bubbles and surrealistic shapes, that looks like a blend of Dali and Busby Berkeley, but isn't.

Ziegfeld Follies has much to recommend it and one of its better numbers is "The Babbitt and the Bromide," marking the only appearance together in a film by Fred Astaire and Gene Kelly. The decision to use this piece of material was made by Arthur Freed, who had seen Fred and his sister Adele do the number in the 1927 Broadway musical *Funny Face*, for which George and Ira Gershwin provided the songs. Freed also considered it a good idea to use the two dancers together, since Kelly by this time had been hailed as a rival to Astaire's position as the premier Hollywood dancer, with some assumption by the public that there might be jealousy between them. Says Freed: "There was no rivalry at all, each is a genuine admirer of the other. My only problem was their deference for each other. Each was willing to do whichever dance the other wanted. I had suggested Babbitt-Bromide to Fred and he liked the idea, but after the first rehearsal Gene privately told me he didn't think too much of the material. I mentioned this to Fred, who then said we should drop it and do whatever Gene wanted, which was an Indian dance and song written for him by Ralph Blane and Hugh Martin. But when Gene heard this he said no, we should do the number that Fred liked. It was a real Alphonse and Gaston routine."

"The Babbitt and the Bromide," is, truth to tell, not a great piece of material and it is a pity that in their only work together they could not have agreed on something more substantial. The routine concerns a pair of gentleman acquaintances, both glib bores, who meet at intervals in their lives and cheerily mouth the same clichéd greetings, "Hello, how are you? Howzafolks? What's new?" and a whole stream of vacuous comments, none of which ever registers in the mind of the other. Part of the lyrics give the narrative of the plot, the fact that they are young men when they first meet and angels in Heaven at the end—but always saying the same things. Their characters are limned in fancy, identical footwork by Astaire and Kelly, all of it bright and bouncing, and giving the viewer an opportunity to compare the two dancers. However, little comparison can be made because the routine is typical of neither one, except to state the obvious facts that Astaire is a lighter man and a shade more graceful, and that Kelly is more muscular and a little more forceful because of it.

Astaire and Kelly rehearsed the dance for a week and shot it in two days during May of 1944, but it was a full two years before *Ziegfeld Follies* was ready for showing, by which time Gene Kelly had been in and out of the United States Navy.

With Fred Astaire

Rehearsing with Astaire

LIVING IN A BIG WAY

CREDITS:

An MGM Production 1947. Produced by Pandro
S. Berman. Directed by Gregory LaCava. Screen-
play by Gregory La Cava and Irving Ravetch. Pho-
tographed by Harold Rosson. Art direction by
Cedric Gibbons and Williams Ferrari. Edited by
Ferris Webster. Musical score by Lennie Hayton.
Running time: 103 minutes.

CAST:

Leo Gogarty: Gene Kelly; *Margaud Morgan:*
Marie McDonald; *D. Rutherford Morgan:* Charles
Winninger; *Peggy Randall:* Phyllis Thaxter; *Mrs.
Morgan:* Spring Byington; *Abigail Morgan:* Jean
Adair; *Everett Hanover Smythe:* Clinton Sund-
berg; *Stuart:* John Warburton; *Schultz:* William
"Bill" Phillips; *Attorney Ambridge:* John Alexan-
der; *Annie Pearl:* Phyllis Kennedy; *Dolly:* Berna-
dine Hayes.

When Gene Kelly concluded his naval service in
early 1946 he advised MGM of his availability and
found they had nothing immediately prepared for
him. The studio at that time had the problem of
finding vehicles for a number of stars returning
to the fold after years away in the services, and
Kelly's experience in this regard proved to be
typical. Not having danced for two years he
moved to get himself back into form by practicing
at a studio in New York, and it was while limber-
ing up that he received a phone call from an
excited Louis B. Mayer, telling him he had just
signed to a contract Marie McDonald, a beautiful
blonde they would publicize as "The Body" and
that he wanted Kelly to co-star with her in a film
to be written and directed by Gregory La Cava.
Since La Cava had a good reputation, as a kind

With Marie McDonald

turned over as living quarters for returning servicemen. Mr. Morgan has grown wealthy during
the war—a hint of profiteering—and his daughter
has become spoiled and pampered in the process.
He therefore looks upon the level-headed Leo as a
sensible addition to the family, a sentiment felt
even more strongly by Margaud's feisty old grandmother Abigail (Jean Adair), who backs Leo in
his plans for building a housing project for veterans. Margaud gradually changes her mind about
Leo—and he about her. They both blow hot and
cold in their feelings and finally agree on a divorce, but at the hearing the judge decides against
a decree to end the marriage, to the relief of both
Leo and Margaud.

Without its interpolated musical moments *Living in a Big Way* would barely qualify as a Grade
B supporting feature, and without Kelly it would
have almost no vitality. The performances of
Charles Winninger and Spring Byington as the
scatterbrained parents are charming and Phyllis
Thaxter is pleasing as a war widow who secretly
loves Kelly because he reminds her of her husband.

All that can be said for Marie McDonald in this
film is that she is pretty of face and figure. Mayer's
faith in her future was completely misfounded;

of minor-league Ernst Lubitsch, Kelly agreed.
Upon meeting La Cava he found there was no
script, only a hazy outline—Irving Ravetch was hired
to work on the screenplay with La Cava—and after
working with Marie McDonald for a few days it
was apparent the girl had very little ability as an
actress. When *Living in a Big Way* (a senseless
title) was completed, MGM then asked Kelly to
invent several musical sequences to add to it, to
make the shallow picture marketable. The effort
proved to be in vain.

The story: Army lieutenant Leo Gogarty (Kelly)
woos and marries the lovely Margaud Morgan
(Marie McDonald) after only a few days of courtship, and gets orders to proceed overseas immediately, barely an hour or so after the wedding. He
returns three years later, eagerly looking forward
to his delayed honeymoon but instead receiving
the cold shoulder from Margaud, who informs him
that all hasty wartime marriages are a mistake and
that she wants a divorce. Gogarty disagrees, so do
her parents (Charles Winninger and Spring Byington) who take a liking to Leo and offer him accommodation in an old house of theirs they have

With Phyllis Thaxter and Jimmy Hunt

With Marie McDonald

72

she never won respect as an actress and seemingly suffered a similar lack of luck in her private life. She died in 1965 at the age of forty-two. *Living in a Big Way* was a sad letdown for Gregory La Cava; it proved to be his last film, and he died two years later. La Cava had been a cartoonist before making films, and in Hollywood he was appreciated for his humor and his direction of several stylish comedies, among them *My Man Godfrey* (1936) and *Stage Door* (1937).

In the original script *Living in a Big Way* called for Kelly to do a dance with Marie McDonald to the tune of "It Had to Be You," but three routines, of Kelly's invention, were added later. One is a dance with an amazingly well-trained dog, "Fido and Me," another is Kelly's comedic dance-serenade to a large female statue, and the most elaborate one takes place on a building project with a group of children. The dance is built around children's games, and later involves Kelly performing all over a half-completed apartment house. He feels, somewhat ruefully, that his dance creations for this film are among his best but he takes some consolation in this largely lost work in that it brought him praise from the esteemed American dancer-choreographer, Martha Graham.

With Judy Garland

THE PIRATE

CREDITS:

An MGM Production 1948. Produced by Arthur Freed. Directed by Vincente Minnelli. Screenplay by Albert Hackett and Frances Goodrich based on the play by S. N. Behrman. Songs by Cole Porter. Musical direction by Lennie Hayton. Photographed in Technicolor by Harry Stradling. Art direction by Cedric Gibbons and Jack Martin Smith. Edited by Blanche Sewell. Running time: 101 minutes.

CAST:

Manuela: Judy Garland; *Serafin:* Gene Kelly; *Don Pedro Vargas:* Walter Slezak; *Aunt Inez:* Gladys Cooper; *The Advocate:* Reginald Owen; *The Viceroy:* George Zucco; *Gandsmith Brothers:* Nicholas Brothers; *Uncle Capucho:* Lester Allen; *Isabella:* Lola Deem; *Mercedes:* Ellen Ross; *Lizarda:* Mary Jo Ellis; *Casilda:* Jean Dean; *Eloise:* Marion Murray; *Gumbo:* Ben Lessy; *Bolo:* Jerry Bergen; *Juggler:* Val Setz; *Trillo:* Cully Richards.

Vincente Minnelli, the son of an Italian violinist and a French actress, grew up in a theatre environment and showed a talent for artistic design while still a boy. At sixteen he was employed by Balaban and Katz as a designer of costumes and scenery and by the time he was twenty-three he was the art director of Radio City Music Hall in New York. This eventually led to Minnelli's becoming a director of stage musicals, and in 1940 he was brought to Hollywood by Arthur Freed. He put in two years as a handyman-designer-advisor-director of musical sequences in Freed productions, and was finally assigned as director

74

of *Cabin in the Sky*. With his directing of the exceptional *Meet Me in St. Louis*, it was clear to all that Minnelli was a director of unusual artistry and sensitivity, and the only man Arthur Freed would consider using as director of *The Pirate*. Freed had purchased the rights to the stage play especially for Judy Garland, who was by now Mrs. Minnelli, and Gene Kelly jumped at the opportunity to play the male lead since it offered not only the chance to sing and dance in a bravura period setting, but also to indulge in some swashbuckling, for which he had a definite taste.

During a break with Judy Garland

The Pirate was made in an atmosphere of loving care and enthusiasm. Freed contracted Cole Porter to write the song-score and after he had written it, with the film well into production Gene Kelly visited Porter and implored him to write an additional song, a knock-about clown number for Judy and himself. And as soon as Freed heard "Be a Clown," it was written into the script. The screenplay is based on the stage comedy S. N. Behrman wrote for Alfred Lunt and Lynn Fontanne, and produced by the Theatre Guild in 1943, which in turn was based on a 1911 German play, *Der Seeräuber* by Ludwig Fulda. In the original the main character was a notorious pirate who retires and, under a new name, becomes the respectable mayor of a little town in the Caribbean. In his version Behrman made this a secondary theme, giving the leading strains to a young, romantic girl who dreams of a legendary pirate and an itinerant actor who impersonates the pirate in order to win her love. The humor rises from the actual pirate, now an older man, not only being the mayor of the town but being engaged to the girl and unable to reveal his identity. This is also the thematic material of the film. Minnelli saw this as the basis for a fantasy-parody of operetta form, and the end result is a sumptuous, highly imaginative and sophisticated movie musical. He and Kelly were completely in accord in this approach, with Kelly deliberately setting out to caricature his part in the style of the elder Fairbanks and John Barrymore in his last, flamboyantly hammy years.

As if to warn the audience of its fairy-tale intent, *The Pirate* opens with a dainty hand turning the pages of a book about Black Macoco, a feared pirate of the Spanish Main, and an enthralled girlish voice reading his exploits. The hand and the voice belong to Manuela (Garland), the daughter of a wealthy house. Her dreams are shattered by her Aunt Inez (Gladys Cooper), who informs

With Judy Garland

Manuela that a good marriage has been arranged for her with Don Pedro Vargas (Walter Slezak), the affluent mayor of their town, San Sebastian. Don Pedro is a rotund, bumbling social climber, and the idea of marriage with him does not please Manuela. On a shopping trip into the town to purchase things for her wedding she notices Serafin (Kelly) and his troupe of entertainers, who have just arrived and who make their presence known to the townspeople. As his troupe prepare for their evening performance, the amorous Serafin wanders around the town eyeing the girls and calling each one of them Niña. A puzzled merchant asks him why and Serafin launches into a song and dance by way of explanation—Niña is his generic name for all beautiful women. He glides from one lovely girl to the next, beaming at each and serenading with lines like: "Niña, you're so sweet, I mean ya, fairly drive me wild!" and "I'll be having neurasthenia, 'til I make you mine." Serafin scales walls and leaps from balcony to balcony, across a roof and down a drainpipe into the street, all the time passing from girl to girl and after dancing in the town square he artfully winds up next to a poster advertising his show.

The only Niña Serafin fails to amuse is Manuela, who finds him annoying and hammy. But that night, unable to sleep, she wanders into town to see his show. Serafin is about to dazzle his audience with an act of mesmerism and needing a subject he chooses Manuela. He hypnotizes her and in a trance she confesses she has a dream lover, a handsome pirate who will one day sweep down and carry her away. So intense is her passion that she breaks into song and extols this paragon, "Mack the Black." The audience applaud her and Serafin brings her back from the trance with a kiss. Indignantly she takes her leave. Later, while trying on her wedding gown in her bedroom, she looks out the window to find that Serafin has followed her. He has also strung a tightrope leading to her window and as he makes his way across the wire to her, she cautions him, "No, it looks so bad," but the ardent lover persists and enters the room to theatrically plead his case. Don Pedro arrives, whip in hand, but before he can flog Serafin, the actor takes him aside and tells the mayor he recognizes him—he is Macoco, whom Serafin once encountered on the high seas. Don Pedro begs him to keep it secret, thinking that his identity as a former pirate would spoil his marriage. He is unaware of Manuela's enchant-

76

With Walter Slezak

wounded performer to defend his art, "I have a review . . . comparing me with David Garrick . . ." But Manuela explodes in fury and pelts him with every object she can lay her hands to, leaving the room covered with broken china and bric-a-brac. As the poor actor lies unconscious on the floor, Manuela realizes her true feelings for him and, with his head cradled on her lap, she sings "You Can Do No Wrong." Their idyll is interupted by Don Pedro, arriving with a company of militia and arresting Serafin as a jewel thief—having already planted the evidence in the actor's trunk.

Sentenced to hang, Serafin asks for a last request, a farewell performance, and over Don Pedro's objections the Viceroy (George Zucco) gives his approval. Serafin has decided to depart the world with a happy song and dance, "Be a Clown," which he does with a pair of equally athletic black dancers (The Nicholas Brothers). Meanwhile, Manuela notices that her engagement ring matches the jewelry planted in Serafin's trunk, and guesses the real culprit. After his dance Serafin tries to mesmerize Don Pedro, but Aunt Inez interrupts. Sensing what he is trying to do, Manuela fakes a trance

ment with the name of Macoco. But Serafin spots his opportunity and rushes into the street to proclaim himself the famed pirate. Soldiers attack him but he easily wards them off as the astounded Manuela looks from her window. The romantic girl fantasizes and imagines herself joining him in his exploits. In this, "The Pirate Ballet," Serafin, in boldly heroic guise, leads his ferocious men, fights off enemies, swings through the rigging of his ship, taunts danger in a fire dance and celebrates his capture of booty with a fearful spear dance. The sequence is an exhaustingly acrobatic, lurid abstract.

Serafin announces he will raze the town unless Manuela is brought to him. He takes possession of the mayor's house, knowing Don Pedro can't object, and the townspeople beg Manuela to sacrifice herself. She feigns terror, as she eagerly prepares herself for the rendezvous. But once in the mayor's house she overhears a servant who accidentally reveals that Serafin is pretending to be the pirate. Before he can confess the ruse Manuela tells him she knew all the time that he was an actor, and not a very good one, which leads the

78

With Judy Garland

and he leads her onto the stage where she denounces Don Pedro as a miserable, miserly coward, a man who is "even afraid to go to sea." She states her undying devotion to the memory of Macoco and sings "Love of My Life," ending the passionate song with a kiss for Serafin. Don Pedro can stand it no longer, he leaps on the stage and yells at Manuela, "If you want to worship Macoco, worship *me!*" He pulls out a pistol to kill Serafin but other members of the troupe attack and disarm him. Serafin then announces the new star of his show, Manuela, and together in clown costumes and makeup they sing a spirited reprise of "Be a Clown."

In the opinion of many film enthusiasts, *The Pirate* is among the most marvelous of all Hollywood musicals. The script is witty and highly literate, although possibly a bit too "inside" in its show-business allusions. The sets and costumes are delightful, the color photography of Harry Stradling is the work of a master, the songs are top-

notch Porter, the direction of Vincente Minnelli is an almost perfect balance of story and music, and the performances of Garland and Kelly reflect their obvious love of working together. Despite all this, *The Pirate* came close to being a flop in the first year of its release. The critics hailed it but the mass movie audience resisted it. Many of the top MGM executives disliked it, feeling it was too different and too artistic for the fans, and Louis B. Mayer ordered "The Pirate Ballet" changed and reshot—in his view the original was far too erotic. One number, "Voodoo," was eliminated. Ludicrous as this managerial stand may seem on the aesthetic level, it certainly was borne out by the reaction of the public, who obviously wanted the simple, appealing Garland and not a sophisticated comedienne. Similarly it proved to Gene Kelly that it was dangerous to step far from his image as the likable, all-American hoofer. Some years later Arthur Freed made the comment that *The Pirate* was twenty years ahead of its time, and

"Be a Clown!" with Judy Garland

the reception the film now receives when shown to film students proves him right.

It was a disappointment for Gene Kelly: "I had decided on this Fairbanks-Barrymore approach to the role at the very start and Minnelli entirely agreed with it. It didn't occur to us until the picture hit the public that what we had done was indulge in a huge inside joke. The sophisticates probably grasped it—all three of them—but the film died in the hinterlands. It was done tongue-in-cheek but it didn't come off, and that's my fault. But I thought Judy was superb—what Minnelli did with color and design in that film is as fine as anything that has ever been done."

The Kelly performance may have puzzled the fans, but his singing and dancing in *The Pirate* are among his best work in films. "Niña" is almost perfect as a saucy Don Juan testament—the number has such fluidity and is so expertly edited that it gives the illusion of being shot in a single take, and musically it is Cole Porter's neat little

With director Vincente Minnelli

With the Nicholas Bros.

satire on Ravel's *Bolero.* "The Pirate Ballet" is an astonishing piece of business in its athletics, although the original concept of it as a love dance —a manifestation of Manuela's romanticism— would have made more sense. "Be a Clown" is a classic statement of its kind and Kelly's dancing with the memorable Nicholas Brothers is thoroughly zesty. Kelly chose the brothers to work with him in this routine, despite the warning of MGM that the sight of a white man dancing with blacks would cost them a few bookings in southern states, which turned out to be the case. As soon as the studio detected lack of success with *The Pirate,* they immediately assigned Garland and Kelly to *Easter Parade,* a more conventional musical vehicle aimed directly at the tastes of the fans and planned to recoup any possible loss of interest in the stars. But Kelly broke his ankle during rehearsals and suggested to Louis B. Mayer that Fred Astaire be contacted as a replacement. Astaire had been retired for two years but he had been showing signs of wanting to get back to work. Says Kelly, "I was pleased to be responsible for getting Fred back but every time I see him and Judy singing 'A Couple of Swells' I do get a twinge of regret."

With Van Heflin, Gig Young
and Robert Coote

THE THREE MUSKETEERS

CREDITS:

An MGM Production 1948. Produced by Pandro
S. Berman. Directed by George Sidney. Screenplay
by Robert Ardrey, based on the novel by Alexandre Dumas. Photographed in Technicolor by
Robert Planck. Art direction by Cedric Gibbons
and Malcolm Brown. Edited by Robert J. Kern
and George Boemler. Musical score by Herbert
Stothart, based on themes by Tchaikowsky. Running time: 126 minutes.

CAST:

Lady de Winter: Lana Turner; *D'Artagnan:* Gene
Kelly; *Constance:* June Allyson; *Athos:* Van Hef-
lin; *Queen Anne:* Angela Lansbury; *King Louis
XIII:* Frank Morgan; *Richelieu:* Vincent Price;
Planchet: Keenan Wynn; *The Duke of Bucking-
ham:* John Sutton; *Porthos:* Gig Young; *Aramis:*
Robert Coote; *Treville:* Reginald Owen; *Roche-
fort:* Ian Keith; *Kitty:* Patricia Medina; *Albert:*
Richard Stapley.

Alexandre Dumas's splendid, swashbuckling ad-
venture story of a young cavalier named D'Artagnan and his friendship with three of King Louis
XIII's musketeers has been a favorite subject of
the movies almost from the beginning of the
medium. Aside from numerous European versions,
there were several American attempts even before
the famous filming by Douglas Fairbanks, Sr. in
1921. Walter Abel was a not very inspiring
D'Artagnan at RKO in 1935 and Don Ameche
and the Ritz Brothers did a musical lampoon at
Fox in 1939. By far the most ambitious attempt
to put *The Three Musketeers* on the screen was

With Ian Keith

With Sol Gorss

MGM's 1948 production, on which they lavished two-and-a-half million dollars—then a considerable budget. Gene Kelly was a natural choice for D'Artagnan; he was in the peak of athletic condition and looking a dozen years younger than his actual age of thirty-six. Says Kelly, "I loved playing this part. As a boy I idolized Fairbanks, Sr. and I raised myself to be a gymnast."

Robert Ardrey's screenplay hews fairly closely to the original, necessarily capsulizing it somewhat but giving it a more comedic slant than Dumas intended. This is a weakness in the film and its general tongue-in-cheek tone diminishes the overall effectiveness of the handsome production values and the visual splendor. Nevertheless, this is a version hard to resist as pure entertainment. Its familiar beginning has the young D'Artagnan leaving his country home and proceeding to Paris with a letter of introduction to the commander of the musketeers, Treville (Reginald Owen) but *en passant* he is humiliated by an arrogant nobleman, Rochefort (Ian Keith), who cannot be bothered to duel with the young man and has one of his henchmen knock him out. In Paris D'Artagnan enrolls in the King's service as a musketeer but from Treville's office he spots Rochefort in the street. In a mad dash to catch him D'Artagnan bumps into veteran musketeer Athos (Van Heflin) then Porthos (Gig Young), and then Aramis (Robert Coote), accepting challenges from each one—at the same time and place, in the gardens behind the Luxembourg. D'Artagnan loses Rochefort but he keeps the appointment with the musketeers, offering to fight all three together if they wish. Athos, as the senior challenger, has priority and soon finds the youngster is a brilliant swordsman. A party of guards in the employ of Cardinal Richelieu (Vincent Price) arrive to arrest the musketeers for breaking the Cardinal's rule outlawing dueling, but D'Artagnan joins with the musketeers and together they thoroughly trounce the guards.

The musketeers have immediate cause to serve King Louis XIII (Frank Morgan). Richelieu is plotting to overthrow the King by promoting war with England. It has come to the attention of Richelieu that Queen Anne (Angela Lansbury) is having an affair with the Duke of Buckingham (John Sutton) and he commands his mistress, the beautiful Lady de Winter (Lana Turner) to conspire in an attempt to discredit the Queen. The Queen's lady-in-waiting, Constance (June Allyson) overhears information concerning the gift of the

Queen's necklace to Buckingham, which information Richelieu will use to his advantage. Constance tells this to D'Artagnan, with whom she has fallen in love, and this pains the young man because he has fallen in love with Lady de Winter. It becomes the mission of the musketeers to ride to Calais, cross the Channel to England, retrieve the necklace from Buckingham and return it to the Queen in time for her to wear at an official function, thereby foiling Richelieu's plan to discredit her in public for not having the necklace in her possession. This retrieval has to take place in short order, and D'Artagnan and the musketeers are hounded all the way by Richelieu's guards. But with their mission accomplished, the Cardinal is forced to drop his plans and deny any complicity, which denial costs Lady de Winter her life. It also enables D'Artagnan to settle his score with Rochefort, dispatching him forever.

This spanking production of *The Three Muske-* teers suffers from some bad casting: the beautiful Lana Turner and June Allyson are less than comfortable in period costumes and situations, Gig Young and Robert Coote make rather limp musketeers and Frank Morgan, his genial comic image against him, is no King. Angela Lansbury is, however, elegant as the Queen and the late Van Heflin powerful as the moody Athos, a tough man capable of crying in his beer at memories of past loves. As the evil Richelieu Vincent Price is urbanity personified. None of the acting, whether good or mediocre, is helped by the musical scoring of Herbert Stothart who made a major error in deciding to use popular themes by Tchaikowsky as his motifs. In the many excellent action sequences of this film the scoring is acceptable but in using the love theme from *Romeo and Juliet* as a surging accompaniment for scenes between D'Artagnan and Constance, the effect is ludicrous. Balanced against this demerit is the gorgeous Technicolor

With Frank Morgan, Reginald Owen, Van Heflin, Gig Young and Robert Coote

With Van Heflin, Gig Young and Robert Coote

With John Sutton and June Allyson

With Lana Turner

photography of Robert Planck and the art direction of Cedric Gibbons and Malcolm Brown. The film is visually magnificent, and George Sidney's direction is excellent in the pacing of the action, although too languid in the dialogue passages.

But *The Three Musketeers* is Gene Kelly's picture, and without his dashing D'Artagnan it would be much the poorer. Some critics found his bouncing, tumbling, vaulting, flipping and leaping performance tending toward burlesque, but it is entirely conceivable that the man Dumas described as the finest swordsman in France would be this kind of zesty athlete. Other critics pointed out that no other actor had ever come this close to matching the performances of Fairbanks, Sr. at his swashbuckling best. In his article "Swordplay on the Screen," for the June–July, 1965, issue of

With Angela Lansbury and June Allyson

With Vincent Price and Ian Keith

Films in Review, Rudy Behlmer dealt at length with Kelly's D'Artagnan:

MGM . . . hired Jean Heremans, a Belgian fencing champion who succeeded Uyttenhove * as fencing instructor at the Los Angeles Athletic Club, to work out fencing routines for Gene Kelly. . . . The resulting action scenes were strikingly set up and executed, and are among the best of their kind. The early encounter of D'Artagnan, Athos, Porthos and Aramis with the Cardinal's Guards—filmed at (the old) Busch Gardens in Pasadena—was particularly effective. As this sequence progresses and the Cardinal's Guards are being disposed of, D'Artagnan singles out Jussac, Captain of the Guard (Saul Gorss), and the two engage in an acrobatic—and comedic—choreographed routine, accompanied by burlesqued Tchaikowsky. It runs five minutes, and was, up to that time, the longest duel on record. It's a delight.

In later, more serious action sequences, Kelly proved he could help set up and perform—straight—far-from-standard acrobatic feats.

Heremans appeared, in various costumes and makeups, as several different fencers throughout this film, and in an extended fight with Kelly on the beach he finally fell backward into the surf following Kelly's death thrust.

Since screen duels are routined in a manner similar to musical numbers, and since Kelly's dancing style emphasizes a strong, vigorous line and athletic movement, he was able to make the transition from musical comedy to swashbuckling heroics with ease.

With Van Heflin

With John Sutton

Of his nonmusical films, *The Three Musketeers* is Gene Kelly's favorite. MGM continues to earn money from this constantly profitable picture, and on his tours for the U.S. State Department Kelly finds himself followed by small boys in distant lands and greeted as D'Artagnan: "I was in Ghana some years ago and arrived in a town where *The Three Musketeers* had only just played. Hundreds of kids with shining black faces happily trooped after me. At the same time the Russians had sent a lady cosmonaut as their goodwill ambassador but when I showed up the kids deserted her *en masse* to cheer D'Artagnan. I'm very happy to have made that picture, although it didn't get me what I was really after, which was to do a musical version of *Cyrano de Bergerac.* I love the part and although I knew I couldn't, because of my American speech, handle the original text I did believe I could manage a musical version. I pestered MGM for years on that one but I could never get them to go for it."

* Henry J. Uyttenhove, Belgian fencing master and the coach of Fairbanks, Sr. on *The Mark of Zorro* (1920), *The Three Musketeers* (1921) and *Robin Hood* (1922).

With Van Heflin

With Sol Gorss

With John Heremans

With June Allyson

90

With Vera-Ellen

WORDS AND MUSIC

CREDITS:

An MGM Production 1948. Produced by Arthur Freed. Directed by Norman Taurog. Screenplay by Fred Finklehoffe, based on a story by Guy Bolton and Jean Halloway, adapted by Ben Feiner, Jr. Photographed in Technicolor by Charles Rosher and Harry Stradling. Art direction by Cedric Gibbons and Jack Martin Smith. Edited by Albert Akst and Ferris Webster. Musical direction by Lennie Hayton. Musical numbers staged and directed by Robert Alton. Running time: 119 minutes.

CAST:

Lorenz Hart: Mickey Rooney; *Richard Rodgers:* Tom Drake; *Herbert Fields:* Marshall Thompson; *Dorothy Feiner:* Janet Leigh; *Peggy Lorgan McNeil:* Betty Garrett; *Joyce Harmon:* Ann Sothern; *Eddie Lorrison Anders:* Perry Como; *Mrs. Hart:* Jeanette Nolan; *Shoe Clerk:* Clinton Sundberg; *Dr. Rodgers:* Harry Antrim; *Ben Feiner, Jr.:* Richard Quine; *Mrs. Rodgers:* Ilka Gruning; *Mr. Feiner:* Emory Parnell; *Mrs. Feiner:* Helen Spring; *James Fernby Kelly:* Edward Earle.

Most of the major American songwriters have been saluted in Hollywood biographies, but seldom with any accuracy. Perhaps this is to be expected; these films exist only as showcases, as convenient marshaling grounds for the creations of the subject being honored. The career struggles of composers and lyricists tend to a sameness, and of interest mainly to students of music or the theatre. Be that as it may, MGM could have done a lot better for Richard Rodgers and Lorenz Hart than *Words*

91

and Music. In this vapid account, Richard Rodgers, a tough-minded and shrewd producer as well as gifted composer is played in bland manner by Tom Drake, and Mickey Rooney frenetically struts around as the brilliant but tragic Lorenz Hart. The selection of music is generous, touching on nearly two dozen songs of the celebrated team and in some instances the performances are excellent. Lena Horne sings "The Lady is a Tramp" in a magnificently sultry manner, and "Blue Room" is smoothly sung by Perry Como and equally smoothly danced by Cyd Charisse.

The most prestigious segment of *Words and Music* is "Slaughter on Tenth Avenue," choreographed and danced by Gene Kelly, with Vera-Ellen as his partner. The piece was originally presented on Broadway in 1937 as the finale of the musical comedy *On Your Toes,* for which Rodgers and Hart wrote the book, along with George Abbott, as well as the music and lyrics. By the time "Slaughter on Tenth Avenue" appeared in *Words and Music,* it was long familiar as a pop concert selection, but in 1937 it was applauded as a milestone in the American theatre —the first presentation of modern ballet in a Broadway musical. It was, in fact, choreographed by the esteemed George Balanchine, and danced by a young Ray Bolger, who appeared in *On Your Toes* as the dancing son of vaudevillian parents. In its original setting the material was more comedic than as choreographed by Kelly for the film; it had Bolger dancing himself into exhaustion to elude capture by a group of gangsters. For the film Kelly shortened the ballet from eleven to seven minutes, truncating some of the lyrical passages, playing up the dramatic substance and inventing a new story. In Kelly's version the dancer is a tough guy in a low-life section of New York, who falls for a pretty street girl but loses her when a former boyfriend, a jealous hood, shoots and kills her.

Kelly's "Slaughter" is set in a sleazy neighborhood, alongside New York's elevated railway and in a large saloon peopled by gangsters and prostitutes, loafers and police. The opening notes of the music suggest the feisty atmosphere and the cheeky character of Kelly's Dancer, who is first seen in his bedroom stretching and yawning, and then proceeding in a cocky, gymnastic style to the street, wearing a sweatshirt, a beret and dark, tight pants. He spots a blonde (Vera-Ellen) in a yellow sweater and a green slit skirt, and when she notices his interest she responds with a seductive dance

With Vera-Ellen

92

around a lamp post. The mood of the music turns romantic and it becomes clear the two are smitten with each other. The music changes again to a cheerful, breezy theme as they enter the saloon together and dance happily; the music takes on a more serious tone as the dancers begin to feel more concerned, then bold and jazzy as they realize their feelings are mutual. The joyful dance is interrupted by the appearance of a rival and he and Kelly engage in a mimed fight-dance. Police arrive and quell the fighting. The hubbub subsides and a wailing oboe sets a mood of uneasy peace. After the police leave the violence flairs up and in the ensuing melee the girl is shot and flung down a flight of stairs. Kelly and the rival then break into a savage fight, which ends with Kelly being shot. He slides along the floor to the body of the girl, picks her up and carries her to the top of the stairs, where he collapses and lies dying and embracing the girl, as the music swells to a bittersweet ending.

As it had on Broadway in 1937, "Slaughter on Tenth Avenue" broke new ground when it was seen in *Words and Music* in 1948. It was the first long, complete piece of modern ballet in a Hollywood film and it proved that a wide audience would accept such artistry if presented in a vital, interesting manner. It was another triumph for Gene Kelly in his efforts to bring worthwhile dancing to the screen, and the piece was also an excellent showcase for his muscular, masculine style. The tightly paced seven-minute production took three days to shoot, following almost four weeks of rehearsal. Kelly regards Vera-Ellen as among the very best women dancers in films, and she herself looks upon "Slaughter" as the best work of her Hollywood career. The dance called for characterization, gymnastics and drama, and it received all this in full measure from Kelly and Vera-Ellen.

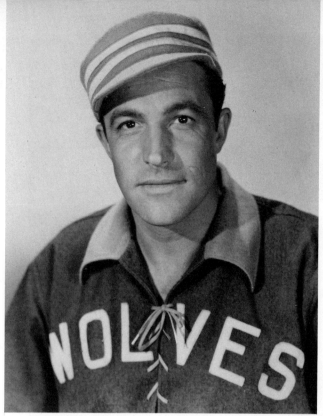

TAKE ME OUT TO THE BALL GAME

CREDITS:

An MGM Production 1949. Produced by Arthur Freed. Directed by Busby Berkeley. Screenplay by Harry Tugend and George Wells. Based on a story by Gene Kelly and Stanley Donen. Photographed in Technicolor by George Folsey. Art direction by Cedric Gibbons and Daniel B. Cathcart. Edited by Blanche Sewell. Songs by Betty Comden, Adolph Green and Roger Edens. Musical direction by Adolph Deutsch. Running time: 94 minutes.

CAST:

Dennis Ryan: Frank Sinatra; *K. C. Higgins:* Esther Williams; *Eddie O'Brien:* Gene Kelly; *Shirley Delwyn:* Betty Garrett; *Joe Lorgan:* Edward Arnold; *Nat Goldberg:* Jules Munshin; *Michael Gilhuly:* Richard Lane; *Slappy Burke:* Tom Dugan; *Za-* *linka:* Murray Alper; *Nick Donford:* William Graff; *Henchmen:* Mack Gray and Charles Regan; *Steve:* Saul Gorss; *Karl:* Douglas Fowley; *Dr. Winston:* Eddie Parkes; *Cop in Park:* James Burke.

The idea behind *Take Me Out to the Ball Game* sprang from the fact that there was once a pair of American vaudevillians, around the turn of the century, who were baseball fanatics and spent their summers playing with professional leagues. Gene Kelly and Stanley Donen developed this into a simple plot outline and took it to Arthur Freed. He liked it and assigned Harry Tugend and George Wells to flesh it out into a comedy-musical, with lyrics by Betty Comden and Adolph Green, and music by Roger Edens.

Kelly and Donen asked Freed if they could direct the picture themselves, but this request coincided with the return to the scene of Busby

95

With Frank Sinatra

Berkeley, and circumstances being what they were, Kelly and Donen agreed with Freed's decision to hire Berkeley. The once-mighty musical director had gone through several years of unemployment due to personal misfortunes and a nervous breakdown, and he came to Freed for help to reestablish himself. Freed was not unmindful of Berkeley's contribution to his own start as a producer, having directed *Babes in Arms* and *Strike Up the Band*, the first two Freed musicals, and four other films. However, despite the directorial credit of *Take Me Out to the Ball Game* going to Berkeley, most of the film's musical sequences were actually directed by Kelly and Donen, and it was this work that persuaded Freed to let them direct *On the Town*.

This is not a great musical, but it does have an easy flow, an amiable atmosphere, and some pleasant but not memorable songs. The plot concerns a popular song-and-dance team—Dennis Ryan (Sinatra) and Eddie O'Brien (Kelly)—who spend each summer as members of a baseball team called The Wolves. The members are anxiously awaiting the arrival of a new owner-manager, K. C. Higgins (Esther Williams), and they are amazed to find this person to be a pretty young woman. Both Dennis and Eddie are romantically attracted to the boss, but she shows them little interest other than in their ability to play baseball, and she turns out to be a tough employer. The ambitious Eddie can't resist an offer to spend his evenings directing a nightclub act, which causes him to be benched for breaking the rules of training, and he allows himself to get involved with a charming, flattering but crooked gambling czar, Joe Lorgan (Edward Arnold), who is scheming to wreck the Wolves in favor of his investment in an opposition club. Eddie unwittingly falls into this trap, until he realizes what is happening. Lorgan tries to keep him from playing in the major game of the season, but Eddie fights his way back to his team and helps them win the pennant. In doing so he also wins the affection of K. C. Higgins, whose friend Shirley (Betty Garrett) has finally managed to get Dennis's mind off the boss and aimed in her own amorous direction.

Aside from the five songs written for the picture, the film employs the famous ditty used as its title, which was written by Albert Von Tilzer and vaudevillian Jack Norworth in 1911—roughly the time period of this picture. For his solo Gene Kelly made his own choice of material, "The Hat My Father Wore on St. Patrick's Day," another vintage

With Esther Williams, Tom Dugan and Richard Lane

With Esther Williams and Tom Dugan

With Richard Lane, Tom Dugan, and Jules Munshin

97

piece, and blatantly Irish in spite of its authors being identified as G. Schwartz and W. Jerome. As performed by Kelly, this is a typical shamrock-and-shillelagh rouser, pleasingly cocky and full of vigorous tap-stepping. Sinatra's solo is a gentle ballad, "The Right Girl for Me," and he and Betty Garrett sing a more vigorous version of the same sentiments in "It's Fate, Baby, It's Fate." Jules Munshin, as a genial, oafish ball player befriended by the two stars, joins them in singing the comic baseball number, "O'Brien to Ryan to Goldberg." Sinatra and Kelly also sing a ragtime ditty, "Yes, Indeedy." The finale, a flag-waver involving the whole cast, "Strictly U.S.A.," was written entirely by Roger Edens. It makes for a spirited wrap-up and steps out of the character of the film by making contemporary allusions in its lyrics, but such is the loose, unimportant nature of this musical that it hardly matters. The picture was obviously aimed by MGM at the summer trade.

Despite the general success of *Take Me Out to the Ball Game,* it proved to be the last film directed by Busby Berkeley. Luck was not with him on his return to the movies. He was next assigned to direct Judy Garland in *Annie Get Your Gun,* but although he and she had worked together in five successful pictures she now took a disliking to him.

With both of them in varying stages of ill health they were taken off the production after several weeks of painful frustrations. In the remainder of his career Berkeley worked as a sequence director in eight musicals, and with the gradual demise of movie musicals he virtually disappeared. It wasn't until the mid-sixties that he was justly heralded for his work as an inventive, highly imaginative devisor of cinematic musical material. Said Gene Kelly: "Buzz was probably the most remarkable talent the Hollywood musical ever had. More than anybody else he showed what could be done with a movie camera—and long before there was such a thing as a zoom lens or a helicopter. He tore away the proscenium arch for the movie musical and anyone interested in making films should study what Berkeley did, particularly in his Warner films of the thirties. Study the shots and the angles and the perpetual movement. Some of it looks a little gimmicky today, but remember that he was the pioneer of the fluid style. In the space of about five years he did everything with a camera that can be done. I was lucky to have him as my first director and I learned a lot from Buzz Berkeley, not the least of which was to keep my eyes open at all times in making films and to look for new ways to do things."

With Jules Munshin, Betty Garrett, Frank Sinatra, and Esther Williams

With Vera-Ellen

ON THE TOWN

CREDITS:

An MGM Production 1950. Produced by Arthur Freed. Directed by Gene Kelly and Stanley Donen. Screenplay by Betty Comden and Adolph Green, based on their musical play. Lyrics by Comden and Green, with music by Leonard Bernstein and additional music for the film by Roger Edens. Musical direction by Lennie Hayton. Photographed in Technicolor by Harold Rosson. Art direction by Cedric Gibbons and Jack Martin Smith. Edited by Ralph E. Winters. Running time: 97 minutes.

CAST:

Gabey: Gene Kelly; *Chip:* Frank Sinatra; *Brunhilde Esterhazy:* Betty Garrett; *Claire Huddesen:* Ann Miller; *Ozzie:* Jules Munshin; *Ivy Smith:* Vera-Ellen; *Mme. Dilyovska:* Florence Bates; *Lucy Shmeeler:* Alice Pearce; *Professor:* George Meader.

The Brooklyn Navy Yard early on a fine summer morning: a beefy dockworker ambles and yawns his way to his job singing "I feel like I'm not out of bed yet . . ." A time whistle blasts the air and the figures "6:00 A.M." appear on the screen. The camera cuts to a naval warship and it fairly explodes with sailors in white uniforms as they eagerly start a twenty-four-hour shore leave. Three of them rush toward the audience to exclaim, "New York, New York, it's a wonderful town . . ." and then proceed to spend a day proving their optimism to be well founded.

Thus the opening of *On the Town*, the most inventive and effervescent movie musical Hollywood had thus far produced and an important

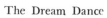

With Frank Sinatra and Jules Munshin

The Dream Dance

With Frank Sinatra

With Frank Sinatra, Betty Garrett, Florence Bates, Jules Munshin and Ann Miller

With Alice Pearce

101

With Betty Garrett, Ann Miller, Jules Munshin, Frank Sinatra and Alice Pearce

one in that it opened up the form and led to more development of modern dancing on the screen and a greater use of locations. More than any other, it took the musical out of the studio and into life. The credit for this belongs to Gene Kelly; he undoubtedly was not the first man to think of it, but he was the first to persuade a studio to let him do it.

By 1949 Kelly was a man to be taken seriously at MGM; for some time he had been given a greater say in the choice and the staging of the dances in his films, and his desire to completely direct musicals was well known. With the powerful Arthur Freed as his champion, Kelly had the studio purchase the rights to the musical comedy, *On the Town*, with music by Leonard Bernstein and book and lyrics by Betty Comden and Adolph Green. This remarkable musical had been a ground-breaker in the theatre and Kelly was determined that it would do the same for the film medium. It began its life as *Fancy Free*, a modernistic ballet by Bernstein and choreographer Jerome Robbins, in which three sailors expressed their shore leave adventures in dances. This inspired Comden and Green, who were at this time

performers in musical revues, to devise a comedic story around the same situation, and they presented it to director George Abbott. He immediately approved the idea and commissioned Comden and Green to write the book and the lyrics, with Bernstein supplying the music and Robbins the choreography.

The project developed very quickly, and *On the Town* made its debut December 28, 1944, barely half a year after *Fancy Free* had made its bow. In its happy fusion of songs, dances and dialogue it was hailed as a milestone in the American musical theatre. And in making it into a film, Gene Kelly fought MGM in order not to have to make it at the studio and to do the whole thing in New York. They compromised and Kelly was allowed one week on location. It is the footage gained in that one frantic week that gives this picture much of its sparkle.

The decision was made to drop most of the score of the original, which MGM believed would not be popular with moviegoers. Also, and this is the reason many stage musicals lost all but their hit numbers when made into films, the studio had its own publishing outlet and more money could

102

be made assigning its staff composers to create new material. Comden and Green were contracted by MGM to write the screenplay and the lyrics for the new songs, with music by Roger Edens. Of the Bernstein original it was deemed necessary to retain the opening recitative and the "New York, New York" exposition song—veritably the theme of the show—and the music for the dances, "Miss Turnstiles" and "A Day in New York," plus one comic song "Come Up to My Place." Six new numbers were written.

The three sailors are Gabey (Kelly), Chip (Frank Sinatra) and Ozzie (Jules Munshin). They begin their day with a whirlwind tour of New York City, and the staging of this sequence is such that the audience sees a dozen locations in the space of a few minutes, with cut-shots matched to the tempo of the music and the flavor of the lyrics. They visit the Statue of Liberty, they prance through Rockefeller Center and scamper around Central Park. A big poster of a beautiful girl catches Gabey's eye—"Miss Turnstiles for June"—Ivy Smith (Vera-Ellen), the choice of the New York Subway System as the monthly symbol of all that is best in the American girl. As Gabey reads the virtues extolled by the poster he fantasizes and sees her in an elaborate ballet of various sports and gymnastics. Then a lady taxi driver comes into view, Brunhilde Esterhazy (Betty Garrett) and they hire her to take them to the Museum of Natural History. Brunhilde takes a fancy to Chip and joins the group. Inside the museum a lovely anthropological student, Claire Huddesen (Ann Miller) tells Ozzie, adoringly, that he has a face like a caveman. After making known her love of studying mankind, Claire launches into a merry song and tap-dance, "Prehistoric Man," which ends with the collapse of the rare bones of a huge dinosaur, causing the group to beat a fast retreat.

Chip and Ozzie have found loving female companionship but Gabey thinks only of Miss Turnstiles and how to locate her. Brunhilde makes her intentions obvious as she sings to Chip, "Come Up to My Place," but when she does get him up there she finds her homely roommate Lucy Schmeeler (Alice Pearce) unexpectedly at home nursing a nasty cold. But poor Lucy is persuaded to leave.

Meanwhile Gabey has wandered into Carnegie Hall. There, in an upper chamber, Ivy Smith is taking ballet lessons from a feisty old teacher,

With Frank Sinatra, Jules Munshin, Ann Miller and Betty Garrett

Madame Dilyovska (Florence Bates). Gabey introduces himself to Ivy and charms her into a date. He succeeds so well that she immediately joins him in a singing and dancing homage to American domesticity, "Main Street."

At about the same time Chip and Brunhilde are at the top of the Empire State Building, where he surrenders to her loving onslaught and croons to her, "You're Awful—Awful Nice to Be With." The other two couples join them and after baffling the policemen who have been warned to look out for the sailors who demolished the dinosaur, the six of them march away singing their intentions, "We're Going on the Town." They visit a string of crowded nightspots and find them all the same.

Suddenly, without explaining herself, Ivy disappears.

Ivy, it turns out, has a secret job as a cooch-dancer in a cheap Coney Island cabaret—to pay for her ballet lessons—and now, short a girl, Brunhilde offers Lucy as a substitute. He accepts, but every time a sailor heaves into view Gabey tries to hide Lucy's face so that it won't be known to the navy that he's had such a dowdy date. To cheer him up Lucy and the others sing, "You Can Count on Me," during which the impulsive Lucy gets carried away by her own passion and, with a tablecloth draped around her, she dances a sultry tango with Gabey. He sees her home and gives her a little kiss goodnight. Touchingly she says, "You bad boy. Now I won't wash that cheek for a year."

But Gabey yearns for his Ivy, and again his

With Frank Sinatra and Jules Munshin

Cavorting on Wall Street

106

mind-wanderings provide an inventive visual for the audience. "A Day in New York" is a surrealistic ballet in which the four other chums are represented by dancers, who join Gabey and Ivy in ensembles. The two principals express their love in a *pas de deux* and in a solo Gabey reacts joyfully to a billboard advertising Miss Turnstiles. This dreamy sequence fades and we are back to reality, with the three sailors and two girlfriends being pursued by the police for their museum damage.

They take refuge at Coney Island, where Gabey discovers Ivy at work. Embarrassed and tearful, she finds she has no cause to worry about the feelings of the adoring sailor. But the arrival of the police sends them all scattering, with the three gobs donning cooch-costumes and joining in the show. They appear in various guises, and as three veiled harem beauties they sing "Pearl of the Persian Sea." They even flirt with the cops but as Ozzie's skirt slips and his navy trousers come into view, the game is up. But the three girls plead with the police—to the tune of "Hearts and Flowers"—and the bewildered officers agree to let the lads get back to their ship, and just in time. The frantic twenty-four-hour leave comes to a close as Ivy, Claire and Brunhilde wave dockside farewells and

With Vera-Ellen

the three tired but happy sailors chant an undeniable "New York, New York, it's a Wonderful Town."

On the Town was budgeted at a reasonable $1,500,000 and a forty-six-day shooting schedule—remarkable in view of the amount of musical sequence and the complicated photography. The New York footage was taken in three shooting days and involved hidden cameras and much shoot-first-and-get-permission-later decisions. Photographer Harold Rosson achieved a difficult 360-degree turn in following the action of the players at the top of the RCA Building, and in the ensemble numbers dozens of camera angles appear in rapid succession—with credit to editor Ralph E. Winters. And as in every production on which he worked the musical direction of the late Lennie Hayton is superlative.

Roger Edens, who served as associate producer as well as composer, often said that the film would never had been made without Arthur Freed's sticking his neck out. The film was not liked by the MGM management when they first saw it, no doubt because it was such a departure from their formula, but they were proved wrong is assuming that it would flop. The result was a victory for Kelly and his co-directing colleague Stanley Donen. Donen worked mainly on the staging of the film, with the choreographic layout entirely left to Kelly. Said Edens: "Freed turned us loose on it. *On the Town* was a very happy wedding of creative spirits. Kelly is a worker—he loves to work. The whole thing was unforgettably exciting for us to put together." And according to Donen: "We had a five-week rehearsal period, and after four weeks we were ready to start shooting . . . we could have shot the picture backwards, we were so excited about the whole production."

New York was in its prime as a tourist attraction at the time of making this film, but the beauty of *On the Town* is not only the buoyant use of locations but the combination of reality with fantasy, the blending of the one with the other. It was also a giant step in the maturing process of the American musical, with songs and dances arising from characterizations and being used to advance plot. And doing it with pleasing exuberance. It is Gene Kelly's point of pride among his films. "I agree it may not be as good as *Singin' in the Rain* or as much of an achievement as *An American in Paris* but I think it meant more to the movies at that time. It's dated now, of course, because the techniques gradually became common

and the theme of sailors on a spree has been done to death, but in 1949 the idea of believable sailors dancing and singing in the streets of New York—using the city as a set—was new, and it paved the way for musicals like *West Side Story*. After *On the Town* musicals opened up."

On the Town has received a great deal of critical study and acclaim over the years but its case was very simply stated by British film historian Roger Manvell in his book, *The Film and the Public* (Penguin, 1955):

I do not know of any musical which pays higher dividends to anyone who sets out to enjoy it in detail. It bears seeing and reseeing for its speed, its subtlety, and its beautiful design, and for that particular kind of captivating American charm which it possesses in almost every sequence.

The dream ballet, with dancers substituting for Sinatra and Munshin

In Rockefeller Plaza

With Sinatra and Munshin on top of the RCA Building

THE BLACK HAND

CREDITS:

An MGM Production 1950. Produced by William H. Wright. Directed by Richard Thorpe. Screenplay by Luther Davis, based on a story by Leo Townsend. Photographed by Paul C. Vogel. Art direction by Cedric Gibbons and Gabriel Scognamillo. Edited by Irving Warburton. Musical score by Alberto Colombo. Running time: 92 minutes.

CAST:

Johnny Columbo: Gene Kelly; *Louis Lorelli:* J. Carrol Naish; *Isabella Gomboli:* Teresa Celli; *Caesar Xavier Serpi:* Marc Lawrence; *Carlo Sabballera:* Frank Puglia; *Captain Thompson:* Barry Kelly; *Benny Danetta:* Mario Siletti; *George Allani:* Carl Milletaire; *Roberto Columbo:* Peter Brocco; *Maria Columbo:* Eleaonora Mendelssohn; *Mrs. Danetta:* Grazia Narciso; *Moriani:* Maurice Samuels; *Judge:* Burk Symon; *Prosecutor:* Bert Freed; *Mrs. Sabballera:* Mimi Aguglia; *Bettini:* Baldo Minuti; *Pietro Riago:* Carlo Tricoli.

Having done nothing but musical and light comedic material for what he considered too long a stretch, Gene Kelly asked MGM for a straight dramatic vehicle. With the edited *On the Town* shaping up as a potential winner, he was in a position to have his wishes taken seriously, although the studio would have preferred to keep him in musicals. However, MGM ran themselves no risk in giving Kelly *The Black Hand*, a modestly budgeted crime melodrama almost certain to recoup its cost on their booking circuit. It did much more than that, being a tough little film with a strong point of view and excellent acting.

The Black Hand was a swipe at the Mafia, long before most people were made aware of that vast, nefarious organization by *The Godfather*. But the attack was cautious, localizing it to New York's Little Italy in the early years of this century and pinpointing a specific group of extortionists and terrorists known as The Black Hand. The film touched on the plight of many immigrants in these times of the great migrations from Europe to America, people who were to discover that the New World was not quite the bright fulfillment they had looked for. They were subject to the exploitation of American industrialists whose agents encouraged them to leave their homelands and thereby supply plentiful labor that helped industry control American wages, after which they were victimized by certain of their own people, of which the Black Handers were the most vivid example.

The film gets its momentum from the defiance of one man not to give in to the system. Johnny Columbo is a New York-born Italian youngster who is taken back to Italy by his mother when his lawyer father is murdered by gangsters for not complying with their demands. After his mother dies Johnny returns to New York, bent on vengeance, but he soon finds it impossible as an individual to gain any evidence or make any impression on other individuals in the Italian community to band together. The Black Handers have the situation firmly under control with their brutal beatings, bombings and kidnappings. Only when Johnny cooperates with police investigator Louis Lorelli (J. Carrol Naish) does he see signs of progress. He also finds his childhood sweetheart Isabella Gomboli (Teresa Celli) and her family are involved in the threats of the secret society, making him more determined to wage his campaign against them.

Columbo and Lorelli finally decide that the best way to gain evidence on the Black Handers is to examine police files in Italy. Lorelli considers it better that Johnny stays in New York while he himself goes to Naples. He there finds the evidence he needs, giving lists of gang members, and he mails this to Johnny, realizing it is too risky to carry it in person. But Lorelli is killed before he can leave Naples and the society seeks to discover the contents of the letter when it arrives in New York. A savage fight for the letter causes Johnny to be badly beaten and Isabella's young brother is held hostage by the society in order to keep Johnny from further action. But he finds out

With J. Carrol Naish

With Teresa Celli

With J. Carroll Naish

With Mario Siletti and J. Carrol Naish

With Teresa Celli and Barry Kelley

where the boy is being held; he manages to blow up the headquarters of the Black Handers and gain possession of the incriminating list. The leaders are exposed and apprehended, and the vicious society—at least this portion of it—is brought to a halt.

The Black Hand is a neat, taut little picture excitingly directed by the veteran Richard Thorpe, and thoroughly convincing as a visualization of life in New York's Italian section several generations ago. MGM wisely sought a good deal of Italian talent in making the film. Gabriel Scognamillo, working under Cedric Gibbons, was responsible for the sets, and an appropriate score was written by Alberto Colombo. Many of the supporting cast were Italians, including leading lady Teresa Celli, whose Hollywood career unfortunately never went beyond this picture. The late J. Carrol Naish, a past master of national types, was superb as the police investigator, and Gene Kelly pleased his public and surprised a few critics with the intensity of his tough, ambitious Columbo. Kelly, a black Celt, thereafter had some problem persuading people he was not really an Italian.

With Judy Garland (center) and Carleton Carpenter, with cigarette in mouth

SUMMER STOCK

CREDITS:

An MGM Production 1950. Produced by Joe Pasternak. Directed by Charles Walters. Screenplay by George Wells and Sy Gomberg. Photographed in Technicolor by Robert Planck. Art direction by Cedric Gibbons and Jack Martin Smith. Edited by Albert Akst. Songs by Harry Warren (music) and Mack Gordon (lyrics). Musical direction by John Green, with Saul Chaplin. Dances staged by Nick Castle. Running time: 108 minutes.

CAST:

Jane Falbury: Judy Garland; *Joe D. Ross:* Gene Kelly; *Orville Wingait:* Eddie Bracken; *Abigail Falbury:* Gloria De Haven; *Esme:* Marjorie Main; *Herb Blake:* Phil Silvers; *Jasper G. Wingait:* Ray Collins; *Sarah Higgins:* Nita Bieber; *Artie:* Carle-

ton Carpenter; *Harrison I. Keith:* Hans Conreid.

Summer Stock was the last of Judy Garland's films for MGM, bringing her spectacular association with that studio to a premature and unhappy end. Until the making of *Easter Parade* in 1948, the public had had no reason to assume that Judy was anything other than secure in her private and professional life. But it now appeared she was bordering on nervous exhaustion and prone to emotional instability. These facts were made known to the management of MGM by her doctors, but the request for leave of absence was denied and she was instructed to proceed with her next assignment, *The Barkleys of Broadway*. Judy collapsed during the period of preproduction and she was replaced by Ginger Rogers. After convalescing she returned to do a short sequence in *Words and Music* and the lead in *In the Good Old*

115

With Judy Garland

With Judy Garland and Phil Silvers

With Phil Silvers

Summertime but it was obvious to those with whom she worked that the strain was too much for her. MGM had purchased the rights to *Annie Get Your Gun* with Judy in mind and insisted she do the picture, but after weeks of fights and problems she was suspended and sent to a clinic in Boston. Three months later she returned to start work in *Summer Stock,* now more plump than she had ever been and possessed with feelings of doubt. The filming stretched out over a period of eight months, more than twice its original schedule.

In his book *Easy the Hard Way* producer Joe Pasternak presents a sympathetic account of this period with Judy, explaining her inability to work and the sympathy given her by her fellow workers. Pasternak singles out Gene Kelly for his patience and his apparent willingness to spend as much time making the film as might be required. Like most of those who knew her well, Kelly is reluctant to discuss Judy Garland, "We loved her and we understood what she was going through, and I had every reason to be grateful for all the help she had given me."

As a movie musical, *Summer Stock* is a decided step back from the progress made by *On the Town,* being the kind of hokey show-biz yarn Judy Garland several times made with Mickey Rooney a few years previously. On the credit side it is pleasant, and it contains nine songs, all good and mostly up-beat. The story is elementary: Jane Falbury (Garland) is a young New England farmer struggling against odds to put her property on a profit-making basis, with the aid of her companion-housekeeper Esme (Marjorie Main) and local merchant Jasper G. Wingait (Ray Collins), whose son Orville (Eddie Bracken) is in love with Jane. Jane's sister Abigail (Gloria De Haven) is a would-be actress who persuades a theatrical company headed by Joe D. Ross (Kelly) to use Jane's barn as a summer theatre and live at the farm during rehearsals—without telling Jane. She at first resents the show people, disliking their conceit and boisterousness, but sensing she needs help around the farm, Joe offers his cast as laborers in return for the use of the premises. As time goes by Jane changes her opinions of the entertainers, she and Joe take a liking to each other that turns to love and, because of her fine singing voice, she accepts his offer to become the star of the show.

Summer Stock is, happily, almost all song and dance. It opens with Garland merrily singing in the shower, "If You Feel Like Singing"—which title was used for the British release of the film. Then, while driving her tractor across the fields she sings the equally optimistic, "Howdy Neighbor, Happy Harvest." As a song to admit their predicament in having to work for their keep, Kelly and Phil Silvers—again the slap-happy sidekick—sing "Dig-Dig-Dig-Dig for Your Supper." Gloria De Haven and Hans Conreid, as a ham actor, satirize old-fashioned musicals in "Memory Island," and a love-smitten Judy gazes at the heavens and sings "Friendly Star."

These five songs are the work of Harry Warren and Mack Gordon, but for the picture's main love song, "You, Wonderful You" the Warren melody has lyrics by Saul Chaplin and Jack Brooks. The melody is first heard as a background as Kelly tells Garland about his love of being an entertainer, leading into his singing the song to her and then doing a soft-shoe dance. This song is later used as a dramatically effective means of expressing his uncertainty, as he dances alone at night on a bare stage. The dance is built around Kelly's using the squeaky boards to motivate his moves and a sheet of spread newspaper as a platform for his footwork. This unique little dance was a Kelly invention whereas Nick Castle was the general dance director for the film.

The show-within-the-show allows for Garland and Kelly to perform a duet, "All for You," and Kelly and Phil Silvers to do a rollicking country-bumpkin routine, "Heavenly Music," in which they caterwaul their love of hillbilly songs, dressed in outlandish costumes with huge feet and end the number when their singing attracts a pack of dogs. Both this and the previous song were written by Saul Chaplin, who shared the musical direction of the film with John Green. For Garland's biggest solo number it was decided to use "Get Happy," the first hit song of Harold Arlen, with lyrics by Ted Koehler, dating from 1930.

Judy Garland's problems are not apparent in her work in *Summer Stock*. During production she was frequently late, sometimes failing to show up at all and at other times so doubting of her talent and the public's affection that she could not bring herself to perform. But once before the cameras, her professionalism gave her strength. Her dancing in this film is very good, particularly in a scene where a stuffy Historical Society dance is jazzed up by the theatrical troupe and Kelly inveigles Garland into a fast and furious "Portland Fancy." "Get Happy" was an afterthought by the studio, who felt the picture needed an extra wallop

With Phil Silvers

With Judy Garland and Gloria De Haven

With Judy Garland

for the Garland fans, and it was filmed two months after the rest of the production had been completed—by which time she was twenty pounds lighter. The byplay between Garland and Kelly in this film is noticeably warm, but despite the excellence of her work and the continued interest of the public her health made her departure from MGM inevitable. Four years would elapse before Judy Garland made another film, and that would be for Warners, the magnificent *A Star is Born*.

With Phil Silvers

With Judy Garland

On the set with Phil Silvers, script clerk Les Martinson and director Charles Walters

With Leslie Caron

AN AMERICAN IN PARIS

CREDITS:

An MGM Production   1951. Produced by Arthur Freed. Directed by Vincente Minnelli. Screenplay by Alan Jay Lerner. Photographed in Technicolor by Alfred Gilks; ballet sequence photographed by John Alton. Art direction by Cedric Gibbons and Preston Ames. Edited by Adrienne Fazan. Music by George Gershwin, lyrics by Ira Gershwin. Musical direction by John Green, with Saul Chaplin. Choreography by Gene Kelly. Running time: 113 minutes.

CAST:

Jerry Mulligan: Gene Kelly; *Lise Bouvier:* Leslie Caron; *Adam Cook:* Oscar Levant; *Henri Baurel:* Georges Guetary; *Milo Roberts:* Nina Foch; *Georges Mattieu:* Eugene Borden; *Mathilde Mat-* *tieu:* Martha Bamattre; *Old Lady Dancer:* Mary Jones; *Therese:* Ann Codee; *Francois:* George Davis; *Tommy Baldwin:* Hayden Rorke; *John McDowd:* Paul Maxey; *Ben Macrow:* Dick Wessel.

Gene Kelly, Vincente Minnelli and others at MGM were concerned over the possible reaction of the French to *An American in Paris,* inasmuch as the French generally despise other people's depictions of their country. In this case they need not have worried; even the French Tourist Bureau could not have devised a sunnier glorification of Paris than this, so full of *joie de vivre.* But to be enjoyed it must be viewed for what it is: a pleasant fantasy barely related to reality. Except for a few establishing shots of Paris, the film was made on the sound stages and on the once-fabulous backlot in Culver City, and it is a purely American idealization of things French. Its great ballet sequence was designed in the style of several master painters, one of whom, Raoul Dufy, saw the film. Says Kelly: "I couldn't resist running it for him—but not without some feelings of trepidation. He was then a sick, very stout old gentleman in a wheelchair. When the lights went up we looked at him, afraid of what he might say, but he was sitting there with a smile on his face, tears in his eyes. He nodded his head at us and asked if we could run the ballet sequence again. With that we knew we would have no trouble in France."

The idea of the film sprang from producer Arthur Freed. He attended a concert with Ira Gershwin at which George Gershwin's tone poem "An American in Paris" was played. Freed mused that the title of the piece would make a good title for a film, and he asked the lyricist for permission to develop the idea. It grew to be an all-Gershwin musical, with Alan Jay Lerner hired to write a

With Oscar Levant

With Georges Guetary, Oscar Levant and Mary Jones

With Leslie Caron

With Leslie Caron

With Georges Guetary

With Mary Jones

simple story to link treatments of various Gershwin songs. For those with a liking for this composer, the film offers a generous sampling of his output, ranging from the early "Tra-La-La," written in 1922 for the Broadway show *For Goodness Sake*, to his last song, "Our Love Is Here to Stay," written for *The Goldwyn Follies* just a few weeks before his death in July of 1937. The choice of material was a group decision, with Vincente Minnelli clearly responsible for the inclusion of "By Strauss." He had been at a party in New York in 1936 and heard the Gershwin brothers kidding around with a parody on Viennese waltzes. Later that year Minnelli directed a stage musical, *The Show is On,* and persuaded the brothers to complete the material as a song for him to include in his musical, which they did.

The American of the title is an ex-G.I., Jerry Mulligan (Kelly), who has stayed on in Paris after the war to study painting. He lives in a tiny room in Montmarte, in the same building with an aspiring American concert pianist, Adam Cook (Oscar Levant), and the two seem to spend much of their time together at a nearby bistro, with the mordantly witty pianist unable to dampen the optimism of the lighthearted painter. Through Adam, Jerry strikes up a friendship with a successful singer, Henri Baurel (Georges Guetary) and offers his congratulations on his forthcoming marriage. His bride-to-be is a little girl he saved from the Germans during the war, Lise Bouvier (Leslie Caron).

Jerry's fortunes pick up when he himself is picked up by a rich, attractive American woman, Milo Roberts (Nina Foch) who promotes his career but fails to ignite any amour in his heart. The honest Jerry prefers not to be a kept man. Meanwhile, he—in a twist of fate familiar in the scripts of musical comedies—spots a lovely young girl in a nightclub and instantly falls in love with her. He pursues her and she rebuffs him, but Jerry is not to be deterred and when she finally agrees to keep a date with him, he learns she is the girl engaged to marry Henri. He attends the Beaux Arts Ball, as do Lise, Henri, Adam and Milo, but the festive atmosphere does nothing to lift Jerry's spirit, especially since he senses Lise now feels the same way about him. His mind drifts and he fantasizes about his predicament, touching off an elaborate imagination sequence. But Henri realizes the situation and releases Lise from the engagement—for a happy ending.

Slight as the story is, it serves as a reasonable

link between the many musical numbers, and the songs themselves occur at well-spaced intervals so as not to bombard the audience. The musical material is well tailored to the characterizations, so that although Kelly is supposed to be a painter, his expert dancing seems a logical expression of his personality and his feelings. The late Oscar Levant here appears in what is really a spinoff from his own career; the part allows for his spouting of barbed jests and much performing of Gershwin. The sequence in which he imagines himself at a concert playing the "Concerto in F," not only at the piano but playing the other instruments, conducting and being seen as members of the audience was his own idea. He had been asked to play a medley of Gershwin tunes but he objected and some time later came up with this suggestion. At other points in the picture he plays snatches of songs and accompanies Kelly in the joyful "Tra-La-La" in which the dancer hoofs around and on the piano. Levant plays and joins in the singing of "By Strauss" in the bistro, and although the piece is designed as a send-up of the Viennese waltz, it has the same lilt and gusto of its target. Another equally happy segment is Kelly's singing "I Got Rhythm" to a crowd of children on the street, leaping around to their amusement.

Georges Guetary, a popular French entertainer, made his only American film appearance in this picture and performed very agreeably with Kelly in a happy street duet, "S'Wonderful," and in a lavish theatre setting he sings "I'll Build a Stairway to Paradise." Leslie Caron, eighteen at the time, was hired for the film by Gene Kelly; he had seen her previously as a dancer with the Ballet des Champs Elysées in Paris and MGM accepted his word that she was right for the film. It was an auspicious debut. With "Embraceable You" as a background, she appears in a montage of different dance styles as the enamored hero images what kind of a girl she might be, and as a tender dance-duet he and she move to the strains of "Our Love is Here to Stay." They are also the principals in the fantasy-ballet.

The ballet sequence of *An American in Paris*, the most impressive thing of its kind ever used in a Hollywood film, was to have been shorter than it actually became. This seventeen-minute production ended up costing $450,000, and not a cent of it needed to be regretted. It was filmed after the rest of the picture had been completed, by which time it was obvious the studio had a highly probable winner in the works. Vincente Minnelli

With Nina Foch

With Leslie Caron

With Leslie Caron

125

worked with Kelly on the libretto and then left to spend five weeks directing *Father's Little Dividend* while Kelly rehearsed his dancers in his own choreography and a team of designers created the sets. Mention must be made of Preston Ames, the art director for this sequence. Ames had been a Beaux Arts student himself from 1927 to 1932, living in a Latin Quarter room similar to the kind depicted in this film, and he designed more than forty sets for *An American in Paris*, assigning skilled painters to recreate huge backdrops in the style of famed French artists. The backdrop for the Dufy-style Place de la Concorde was forty feet high by two hundred and twenty long.

Ames also designed the Beaux Arts Ball sequence and, at Minnelli's suggestion, fashioned it in a black and white motif in order to emotionally pre-

pare the audience for the bright colors of the following ballet. Gershwin's tone poem was re-orchestrated to improve the audio quality—he was not a first-class orchestrator at the time he wrote this (1928)—and a few minor changes were made in the structure of the piece, some deletions and extensions to suit the choreography.

The ballet begins as Kelly sits by himself on a balcony at the Beaux Arts Ball, ignoring the revelry inside, and looks out over the vast scene of Paris at night. His thoughts and his associations with the city and its painters materialize for the audience. Throughout the ballet he continually sees and courts and loses the girl, moving through familiar Parisian locations, all in the style of the painters who have influenced him. The Place de la Concorde swirls with people in a background suggestive of Dufy; he spots the girl and pursues her—through the Renoir-like streets around the

129

Madeleine flower market—through a gaudy fairground as Utrillo might have seen it—through the holiday throngs at the Jardins des Plantes, a favorite subject of Rousseau—and to the Place de L'Opéra, reflecting the art of Van Gogh, and finally to the Montmarte of Toulouse-Lautrec, where Kelly appears as the muscular white-tighted "Chocolat dansant dans le bar d'Achille," complete with Moulin Rouge can-can girls. Having made this whirlwind tour Kelly finds himself back at the Place de la Concorde, standing by the fountain, with all the people suddenly disappearing, leaving him alone looking at a red rose dropped by his elusive love.

This ballet is a summation of Gene Kelly's work as a film dancer and choreographer, allowing him his full range of style—classical ballet, modern ballet, Cohanesque hoofing, tapping, jitterbugging and sheer athletic expressionism. Kelly himself refers to his style as "a synthesis of old forms and new rhythms." He also wrote an article for *Dance Magazine* in which he touched on the problems of filming the *American in Paris* ballet: "We selected each artist's tone and 'felt' for similar tone in the passages of the Gershwin score. For example, that one brassy section could have meant

nothing else to us but Lautrec's "Chocolat" and we all agreed immediately that the "Walking Theme" was most potently related to the lightly sketched style of Raoul Dufy. Our chief trouble was with the Rousseau, which being simply primitive, seemed even more so against the score. But we felt that to omit him would be a kind of misrepresentation, so we made the 'American' tap-dance his way through a Fourth of July celebration in Cohanesque manner, against the theme of the music, while Parisian revelry spins itself out around his figure."

An American in Paris had the distinction of winning an Oscar as the best film of 1951, and six more for various contributions, plus a special Oscar for Gene Kelly by way of saluting his overall work as a dancer-choreographer on the screen. John Green, who shared his Oscar with Saul Chaplin for their work in musical direction, says: "This was the team-job of all time, with Arthur Freed as its captain. Arthur was a real producer, an on-the-floor producer with impeccable musical taste. The whole thing was familial, and the Freed table in the MGM commissary was like the Golden Horseshoe at the Met. Both Gene and I look back on those years with Arthur Freed as among the richest of our lives."

The star, the director and the producer at their party at the close of production

With Janet Leigh

IT'S A BIG COUNTRY

CREDITS:

An MGM Production 1952. Produced by Robert Sisk. Directed by Richard Thorpe, John Sturges, Charles Vidor, Don Weis, Clarence Brown, William A. Wellman and Don Hartman. Written by William Ludwig, Helen Deutsch, George Wells, Allen Rivkin, Dorothy Kingsley, Dore Schary and Isobel Lennart. Photographed by John Alton, Ray June, William Mellor and Joseph Ruttenberg. Edited by Ben Lewis and Frederick Y. Smith. Musical direction by John Green. Running time: 88 minutes.

CAST:

Mrs. Brian P. Riordan: Ethel Barrymore; *Texas:* Gary Cooper; *Adam Burch:* Van Johnson; *Icarus Xenophon:* Gene Kelly; *Rosa Szabo:* Janet Leigh;

Papa Esposito: Fredric March; *Professor:* William Powell; *Stefan Szabo:* S. Z. Sakall; *Mrs. Wrenley:* Marjorie Main; *Mr. Callaghan:* George Murphy; *Sgt. Maxie Klein:* Keefe Brasselle; *Mr. Stacey:* James Whitmore; *Michael Fraser:* Keenan Wynn; *Miss Coleman:* Nancy Davis; *Sexton:* Lewis Stone; *Secret Service Man:* Leon Ames.

Both as entertainment and propaganda *It's a Big Country* fell short of its lofty aims. This compendium of Americana, produced with obvious sincerity by MGM, smacked of sentiment gone somewhat awry; viewed more than twenty years later, in the light of so many changes in attitudes and lifestyle among Americans, it appears ludicrous. Its eight unrelated stories set out to examine America, and MGM lavished eight sets of actors, writers, directors, cameramen and composers to

131

With Janet Leigh

With Janet Leigh and S. Z. Sakall

achieve an understanding and an appreciation of the various social and ethnic strata of life in the United States. It set out to do too much and resulted in too little.

The film begins with William Powell as a college professor lauding America to a dubious citizen played by James Whitmore, and this lecture acts as a springboard to a series of illustrations. Ethel Barrymore is seen as a dignified Bostonian lady angered at being overlooked by the census takers; then comes a tepid tribute to the role played by blacks in America; a young Greek-American (Gene Kelly) wins the love of a Hungarian-American (Janet Leigh) over the protests of her father (S. Z. Sakall); an army sergeant (Keefe Brasselle) delivers from Korea a letter to a stricken mother (Marjorie Main); a Texas cowboy (Gary Cooper) gives a tongue-in-cheek eulogy to his home state; a young Washington minister (Van Johnson) gets to meet the president; and an Italian-American (Fredric March) fumes at having to buy glasses for his son.

In the episode called "Rosita, the Rose" Gene Kelly appears as a breezy young man named Icarus Xenophon, who, because he comes from a Greek family, dislikes an old Hungarian storekeeper, Stefan Szabo (S. Z. Sakall), and the feeling of dislike is mutual. The two men are brought together when Icarus falls in love with Szabo's lovely daughter Rosa (Janet Leigh), to the approval of her impish little sister (Sharon McManus —the same youngster who danced with Kelly in *Anchors Aweigh*). This minor tale is amusing, with no strain on the talents of any of the actors. It was scripted by Isobel Lennart from a story by Claudia Cranston, and directed by Charles Vidor. But in showing how Cupid overcomes national prejudices in America, the episode can hardly be taken seriously.

With Janet Leigh and S. Z. Sakall

With Janet Leigh

SINGIN' IN THE RAIN

CREDITS:

An MGM Production 1952. Produced by Arthur Freed. Directed by Gene Kelly and Stanley Donen. Screenplay by Betty Comden and Adolph Green. Photographed in Technicolor by Harold Rosson. Art direction by Cedric Gibbons and Randall Duell. Edited by Adrienne Fazan. Songs by Nacio Herb Brown (music) and Arthur Freed (lyrics). Musical direction by Lennie Hayton. Running time: 103 minutes.

CAST:

Don Lockwood: Gene Kelly; *Cosmo Brown:* Donald O'Connor; *Kathy Selden:* Debbie Reynolds; *Lina Lamont:* Jean Hagen; *R. F. Simpson:* Millard Mitchell; *Zelda Zanders:* Rita Moreno; *Roscoe Dexter:* Douglas Fowley; *Dancer:* Cyd Cha-

risse; *Dora Bailey:* Madge Blake; *Rod:* King Donovan; *Phoebe Dinsmore:* Kathleen Freeman; *Diction Coach:* Bobby Watson; *Sid Phillips:* Tommy Farrell.

The track record of the late Arthur Freed as a producer is unlike that of any other in the history of films. He produced forty of MGM's celebrated musicals, starting with *Babes in Arms* in 1939, and the most autobiographical of them is *Singin' in the Rain*. The musical score of this picture is made up of songs Freed wrote with Nacio Herb Brown—indeed this is the cream of their catalogue—and the plot, dealing with the coming of sound to Hollywood, is an episode of movie history in which Freed himself was involved. He began as a pianist with a music publishing house and his work as a song plugger led to his be-

133

With Donald O'Connor and Debbie Reynolds

With Donald O'Connor, Douglas Fowley and Bill Lewin

With Jean Hagen

134

coming a performer in vaudeville. By the mid-1920s Freed was collaborating as a lyricist with composer Nacio Herb Brown, supplying songs for musical revues, and in 1929 they were hired by Irving Thalberg to write the songs for MGM's first musical, *Broadway Melody of 1929*, whose score included "You Were Meant for Me." They had written "Singin' in the Rain" in 1926 for a revue but it was also used in MGM's second musical, *Hollywood Revue*, performed by Cliff Edwards, Buster Keaton, Marion Davies, John Crawford, the Brox Sisters and George K. Arthur. Freed and Brown wrote songs for films all through the thirties, and in 1939 Louis B. Mayer contracted Freed as a producer, specifically to develop musical properties.

Plans took shape for *Singin' in the Rain* while Gene Kelly was still working on *An American in Paris*. The studio was anxious to keep the Freed unit at their happy fever pitch of creativity although no project had yet been hit upon as a successor to *American*. The idea of doing something about the early days of the movie musical and the panic caused by the switch from silence to sound germinated, and Betty Comden and Adolph Green were brought from New York to develop it. Says Kelly: "All we began with was a skit about a movie star becoming a sound star, and we all of us dashed around the studio asking the veterans what it was like in the old days and the script was built around the information we picked up. So what happened in the framework of the story was true, this is what it was like around MGM in 1928—with a little comedic exaggeration, of course."

Most Hollywood films about Hollywood have been cruel and strangely frank in exposing the sometimes shallow and vicious characters of its people, and although *Singin' in the Rain* is genial in its tone, its humor is still based on some rather unflattering observations of movie lore. It opens on a scene of tumult at a 1927 film premiere as a gushing Louella Parsons-type commentator greets the celebrated guests. The fans roar as the stars of the film arrive—Don Lockwood (Kelly) and Lina Lamont (Jean Hagen)—and after a few fatuous questions the commentator encourages Don to tell the story of his success.

What Don has to say about his early years is totally at variance with the truth, as we see he and his friend Cosmo Brown (Donald O'Connor) making unappreciated entertainment in tawdry burlesque houses and vaudeville theatre. Don tells

With Donald O'Connor and Bobby Watson

With Donald O'Connor

With Jean Hagen

of his coming to Hollywood and his immediate success, whereas the flashbacks reveal him as an extra who manages to persuade a tough director, Roscoe Dexter (Douglas Fowley) to let him be the butt of comedy stunts, which he does so well he catches the attention of a producer and becomes an actor.

Finally he gets to co-star with Lina Lamont, a none-too-bright beauty with an atrocious speaking voice. He feigns a romance with her to help his career, but Lina imagines he is serious. The egocentric actor doesn't become serious about love until he meets an aspiring entertainer, Kathy Selden (Debbie Reynolds). She rebuffs him, claiming to be a legitimate actress disdainful of the movies but this pose is revealed as false when she turns up as a chorus dancer at a Hollywood party. Needled by Don about this she retaliates by picking up a large iced cake and slinging it at him—but missing and hitting Lina in the face.

It is also at this party that the studio head, R. F. Simpson (Millard Mitchell) shows a new gadget, a short talking movie, but even Simpson doesn't believe it will affect the industry, "The Warner Brothers are making a whole talking picture with this gadget—*The Jazz Singer*. They'll lose their shirts." And Simpson's Monumental Pictures ploughs ahead with silent product. By now Don is more concerned about finding Kathy than pursuing his work and Cosmo does his best to cheer him up. Don proceeds with his new picture, *The Dueling Cavalier*, finding it harder and harder to be civil to the dumb Lina, but as they get into production we see *Variety* headlines telling us about the impact of sound and the revolution in the industry, followed by a montage of excerpts from musicals currently in production.

Kathy comes to the attention of Simpson, who vaguely recalls having seen her before, and he hires her. Don romances her and wins her approval, helped by his singing "You Were Meant for Me," but Lina blocks any plans for her success at the studio. Lina finds it painfully difficult to perform as a talking actress, driving her elocution coach almost mad, and when *The Dueling Cavalier* as a sound picture is sneak-previewed, the audience howls at the hideously bad pickup on the voices and the errors in synchronization.

The studio is about to scrap the picture when Cosmo has the brilliant idea of turning it into a musical and having Kathy dub Lina's voice. The result is a great success, and at the premiere of the picture Don pulls a trick that puts Lina in her place and assures Kathy her future in Hollywood. Asked to reprise one of the songs in the film for the live audience Lina agrees once she knows Kathy is behind the curtain at a microphone. But as Lina mouths the lyrics Don raises the curtain. . . .

This happy movie floats on music from beginning to end, with much of it used for dancing. Freed and Brown wrote one new song, "Make 'Em Laugh," to add to ten old ones and Comden and Green, with Roger Edens, wrote the "Moses" routine in which Kelly and O'Connor make a shambles of a diction teacher's attempts to improve their speech with tongue twisters. "Make 'Em Laugh" is O'Connor's impressive solo, a brilliant and frantic piece of comic dancing full of acrobatics and physical punishment. O'Connor also dances with Kelly and Reynolds in the sprightly "Good Mornin'" and performs several fleeting numbers with Kelly in the vaudevillian montage at the beginning of the film.

O'Connor here proved himself a major dancer. He was also supposed to have been in the film's largest production number, "Broadway Ballet," but a previous television commitment made it impossible for him to stay. This altered the original comedic intent of the number, causing Kelly to develop it into a sequence in which the hero explains to the studio head an idea he has for such a production in a film. The piece is built around two famous Freed-Brown songs, "Broadway Melody" and "Broadway Rhythm" and it was here that Kelly did the little bit of business that becomes almost a trademark—exuberantly chanting in staccato style, "Got-ta sing! Got-ta dance!"

The number tells of an eager young hoofer who comes to the Big Time and carves a career for himself. During one engagement a beautiful moll (Cyd Charisse) flirts with him but drops him when her gangster boyfriend flashes diamonds as a lure. Later, when the dancer is a star he sees her again and imagines himself dancing a love duet with her but when he actually approaches her she spurns him again. He shrugs his shoulders and the elaborate number ends with him seeing another youngster arrive on Broadway bent in the same direction.

This production, admirable though it is, lacks the cohesion of the ballet in *An American in Paris*. The "Broadway Ballet" was filmed after the rest of the picture, requiring a month of rehearsal and two weeks of shooting, and if it doesn't stand out quite as indelibly as Kelly intended it is simply because the uniform excellence of the entire film

With Kathleen Freeman, Jean Hagen and Douglas Fowley

With Carl Milletaire and Jean Hagen

With Donald O'Connor and Debbie Reynolds

doesn't allow for it. Fully sixty of the one hundred and three minutes of running time is taken up by the musical performances. Even the nonmusical performances are impressive, particularly Jean Hagen's horrible-voiced Lina.

The most memorable portion of *Singin' in the Rain* is the title number and Kelly claims it was the easiest of his major dances: "The concept was so simple I shied away from explaining it to the brass at the studio in case I couldn't make it sound worth doing. The real work for this one was done by the technicians who had to pipe two city blocks on the backlot with overhead sprays, and the poor

138

cameraman who had to shoot through all that water. All I had to do was dance and the credit for that delightful little vamp theme which opens and closes the song goes to Roger Edens. My concern with this piece was making the action logical and we arrived at that by setting it up as you would a short story—with a beginning, a middle and an end. The reason for the dance is his happiness in winning the girl—the logic of his antics in the street is the expression of that happiness, and the conclusion is his being spotted by a policeman, snapping him out of his rapture. He then gives the umbrella to a passerby and walks away."

But it is the happiness of Kelly's dance in the rain that gives the piece its lasting life—that plus the lilt of the music and the simple declaration of the lyrics. The sight of a happy man skipping on the sidewalk, climbing a lamppost, letting a drainpipe of rainwater cascade on his face and jump around in puddles is a sight marvelous to behold.

Singin' in the Rain is probably the most popular of all Hollywood musicals, and a favorite subject for film students. Authors Betty Comden and Adolph Green tell of being treated like royalty in Paris by such esteemed filmmakers as François Truffaut and Alain Resnais because of their connection with *Chantons Sous la Pluie*. It rates

second in Gene Kelly's own assessment of his films, although he understands why most people prefer it to *On the Town*. But *Singin' in the Rain* is a testament to the talents of Arthur Freed, and, as Kelly says: "This was the golden age of the musical and it was largely due to Arthur. He knew talent and how to use it, what projects were best to do and which people were best to work on them. He was a nonpareil, and when I think back about all the people I had the good fortune to work with under his gentle command, I'm amazed. They were the finest."

With Debbie Reynolds

With Cyd Charisse

141

With Pier Angeli

THE DEVIL MAKES THREE

CREDITS:

An MGM Production 1952. Produced by Richard Goldstone. Directed by Andrew Marton. Screenplay by Jerry Davis, based on the story by Lawrence Bachmann. Photographed by Vaclav Vich. Art direction by Fritz Maurischat and Paul Markwitz. Edited by Ben Lewis. Musical score by Rudolph G. Kopp. Running time: 89 minutes.

CAST:

Capt. Jeff Eliot: Gene Kelly; *Wilhelmina Lehrt:* Pier Angeli; *Col. James Terry:* Richard Rober; *Lt. Parker:* Richard Egan; *Heisemann:* Claus Clausen; *Hansig:* Wilfred Seyferth; *Cabaret Singer:* Margot Hielscher; *Mrs. Keigler:* Annie Rosar; *Sergeant at Airport:* Harold Benedict; *Mr. Nolder:* Otto Gebuhr; *Mrs. Nolder:* Gertrud Wolle; *Keigler:* Heinrich Gretler; *Girl in Phone Booth:* Charlotte Flemming; *Lt. Farris:* Charles Gordon Howard; *Oberlitz:* Bum Kruger.

Decisions were made by Gene Kelly and MGM in December of 1951 which would affect the future course of his career. The enormous popularity of *Singin' in the Rain* and the high regard in which Kelly was now held in the industry should have resulted in an even greater degree of success but circumstances would prove otherwise. The American film industry was severely shaken by the impact of television, and the 1950s witnessed the deflation of many once-mighty careers. An unexpected casualty was the movie musical, totally unexpected in view of the brilliance that genre had reached, particularly at MGM. But that was not predictable when Kelly and his employers

142

With Richard Egan

In Salzburg, Kelly and Pier Angeli discuss a scene with director Andrew Marton

With Pier Angeli and Austrian slap-dancers

decided that he should leave for Europe early in 1952 and spend the next eighteen months making three films in succession abroad. There were two main reasons for this decision: to use MGM funds frozen in Europe, and to allow Kelly to benefit from a new income-tax ruling whereby the income of Americans who worked overseas for a period of not less than eighteen months would be tax-free. He had persuaded the studio to let him produce his dream-project, *Invitation to the Dance,* and he agreed to star in two nonmusicals, *The Devil Makes Three* and *Crest of the Wave.*

The Devil Makes Three was among the first American films to be made in postwar Germany, utilizing contemporary situations and taking a more compassionate view of the Germans. Films like *The Big Lift* (1950) and *The Desert Fox* (1951) encouraged a more enlightened attitude toward German problems and predicaments and *The Devil Makes Three* delves a little deeper in that spirit. Here, an American army captain, Jeff Eliot (Kelly) decides to spend a Christmas in Munich in order to seek out a German family who had sheltered him during the war. He discovers that the family died in an American air raid and that their daughter Wilhelmina (Pier Angeli) now works as a so-called hostess in a second-rate nightclub. Wilhelmina is bitter about Americans and generally disenchanted with life, but Eliot feels a sympathy for the girl that soon develops into love. Several people involved with the nightclub decide to take advantage of this situation, among them an effete singer-comic named Heisemann (Claus Clausen). Wilhelmina is instructed to use Eliot as a dupe in smuggling black-market items over the border into Austria. Actually it is Wilhelmina who is being duped—her bosses are Nazis smuggling gold in order to restore their party to power.

Army Intelligence is aware of this plot and Eliot is called in to be briefed by Col. James Terry (Richard Rober) and assigned to work on the situation with Lt. Parker (Richard Egan), which involves continuing his affair with Wilhelmina. Her feelings gradually soften toward him and although she still thinks little of the Americans, she makes it clear she loathes the Nazis. Eliot goes along with the smuggling ruse, but he is now primed and ready for trouble. He suddenly realizes the means by which the Nazis are moving their gold—the fenders of the car in which he is riding are solid gold. Before he can get this information back to the army, he and Wilhelmina are captured and

In Salzburg with Pier Angeli

sentenced to death, their demise to take place during a motorcycle race on ice. But Eliot overcomes the situation and takes after the Nazi leader, who turns out to be Heisemann. The chase ends in the ruins of the Adlerhorst, Hitler's former mansion in Berchtesgaden, and the Nazi loses the game.

The film remains of interest because of its location shooting in the Munich, Salzburg and Berchtesgaden of early 1952, and the scenes in the Adlerhorst are of especial interest because the ruins were later obliterated lest they become a tourist attraction. The winter landscapes work in favor of the melodramatics, the suspense and the chase, and the acting by the many German members of the cast is excellent. It is also amusing to note the American influence on the Germans at this time, with nightclub entertainers singing American songs in heavy accents and local youngsters jitterbugging, but there are a few moments of genuine native talent—some singing by the sultry Margot Hielscher and a little slap-dancing in Salzburg. *The Devil Makes Three* is at its best in its action sequences, which is not surprising in view of its director, Andrew Marton, who is famed for his staging of second-unit stunts, such as the chariot race in *Ben-Hur,* and the battles in *The Longest Day* and *Cleopatra.* Gene Kelly played his not very demanding role in a straightforward manner but the sad, beautiful Pier Angeli would have benefited from more sensitive direction than she received here.

With Pier Angeli

With Claus Clausen

With Pier Angeli

145

With Cyd Charisse

BRIGADOON

CREDITS:

An MGM Production 1954. Produced by Arthur Freed. Directed by Vincente Minnelli. Screenplay by Alan Jay Lerner, based on the musical play with book and lyrics by Lerner and music by Frederick Loewe. Photographed in CinemaScope and Ansco Color by Joseph Ruttenberg. Art direction by Cedric Gibbons and Preston Ames. Musical direction by John Green. Edited by Albert Akst. Running time: 108 minutes.

CAST:

Tommy Albright: Gene Kelly; *Jeff Douglas:* Van Johnson; *Fiona Campbell:* Cyd Charisse; *Jane Ashton:* Elaine Stewart; *Mr. Lundie:* Barry Jones; *Harry Beaton:* Hugh Laing; *Andrew Campbell:* Albert Sharpe; *Jean Campbell:* Virginia Bosier;

Charlie Chrisholm Dalrymple: Jimmy Thompson; *Archie Beaton:* Tudor Owen; *Angus:* Owen McGiveney; *Ann:* Dee Turnell; *Meg Brockie:* Dody Heath; *Sandy:* Eddie Quillan.

The pity of MGM's version of *Brigadoon* is that it was made in 1954, at a time when the public interest in musicals had passed its peak. This fall from favor caused the studio to economize, disastrously so in the case of *Brigadoon*. Gene Kelly and Vincente Minnelli had long wanted to make the film version, but legal rights were difficult to finalize. Their original conception called for the picture to be shot on location in Scotland, and to this end they scouted possible settings. After some time in Scotland it became apparent that the project would be defeated by weather, since it could not be relied upon at any time of the year.

146

They settled for shooting their exteriors in the California mountain country but that plan was quashed by the MGM front office, who insisted that the picture would have to be made entirely within the studio. It was also decided that *Brigadoon* would be photographed not in Technicolor but in Ansco Color and in CinemaScope. Few Hollywood directors have ever favored Cinema-Scope and in viewing this picture it is apparent that Minnelli was uncomfortable in his first encounter with the long rectangular frame. It would have been difficult to fill the frame with dancers and singers on location, but even harder in the confines of a studio.

Although *Brigadoon* easily lends itself to criticism, credit is particularly due art directors Cedric Gibbons and Preston Ames, especially the latter. Gibbons was head of MGM's magnificent art department, and his name appeared on every major production. Although he was entirely responsible for the settings of some pictures, he more often than not acted as a supervisor. For *Brigadoon* Ames did the next best thing to the actual location —he created a huge set that filled MGM's largest soundstage, devising it in such a manner that the cameras could shoot a full 360 degrees. This panorama was cleverly designed to give the illusion of great distances, in addition to which Ames built a spacious, attractive Scottish period village.

Brigadoon, the first of Lerner and Loewe's splendid musicals, dealt with fantasy, and for that reason had been a problem whenever it appeared in theatres. It first appeared on Broadway in the spring of 1947, to immediate acclaim, but it was thought from the very outset that it was a musical best suited for the film medium, with natural locations. Ironically, Lerner and Loewe suffered the same disappointment with *Camelot,* which Warner Bros. insisted on making on their backlot rather than in the fabled Arthurian areas of Wales.

No new material was added to the score for the film version, but several selections from the original were dropped. Admirers particularly resented the dropping of the songs "Come to Me, Bend to Me" and "There But for You Go I." Actually, both songs were recorded for the film and both are included in MGM's soundtrack album (E 3135) but they were deleted because they slowed the film. Kelly, ever doubtful about his singing voice, was not pleased with his rendition of the ballad "There But for You Go I" and readily agreed to it being cut. Greater accent was placed on the principal

characters than in the original; the most conspicuous casualty being the part of the soubrette, Meg Brockie, the village flirt, whose two lusty songs, "The Love of My Life" and "My Mother's Wedding Day" do not appear in the film, thereby reducing Meg to a bit part, but nicely played by Dody Heath. A more serious omission is "The Sword Dance," which formed an exciting part of the wedding ceremony in the original.

Brigadoon hangs on a slender thread—the magical possibility of a Scottish village long lost to history and coming to life once every hundred years for a single day. Two Americans hunting in the highlands, Tommy Albright and Jeff Douglas (Kelly and Van Johnson) lose their way in the misty countryside and stumble upon the village of Brigadoon on the very day of its reappearance. They find a happy community, full of people who can sing and dance, but they are puzzled by the costumes and manners, those of centuries ago. The two men assume it to be a carnival and surrender to its hospitality; Jeff enjoys himself at every turn but as the day goes by Tommy finds himself falling in love with Fiona Campbell (Cyd Charisse). She is romantic but cautious and sings about "Waitin' for My Dearie"—in a voice dubbed by Carol Richards—but as she feels more and more drawn to Tommy she joins him in singing and dancing on "The Heather on the Hill." Once he has won her love Tommy wanders through the village singing and dancing "Almost Like Being in Love." With a little rain it might match a previous Kelly routine.

With Van Johnson

147

With Van Johnson
and Cyd Charisse

With Van Johnson

With Cyd Charisse

The village of Brigadoon is in a festive mood over the marriage ceremony of Fiona's sister Jean (Virginia Bosier) to Charlie Chrisholm Dalrymple, who has previously let his intentions be known with the song "I'll Go Home with Bonnie Jean," a song so infectious that Jeff joins in the chorus. The happy occasion is marred by the appearance at the wedding of a jealous, menacing rival, Archie Beaton (Tudor Owen), who threatens to leave the village if the marriage takes place. By now Tommy and Jeff have learned from the schoolmaster, Mr. Lundie (Barry Jones) the story of Brigadoon, a village protected from the evils of the world due to the prayers of one of their former ministers, but with the provision that no villager may ever leave, since should anyone leave, the place will vanish forever. When the drunken Archie Beaton makes haste to escape, the Americans join the gathered clansmen in "The Chase," a spectacular sequence, excitingly scored with Loewe's music, rhythmically dramatic as the villagers run through the heather carrying torchlights. The chase ends with the ac-

With Van Johnson, Barry Jones
and Cyd Charisse

Confronting Hugh Laing

cidental death of Beaton. The village is saved
and the marriage proceeds, but Tommy realizes
he can neither take Fiona with him or stay.

Returning to New York, Tommy is reunited
with his fiancee, Jane Ashton (Elaine Stewart), but
he cannot get Fiona off his mind, or adjust himself to his old way of life. He makes the decision
to return to Scotland one evening in a swank but
noisy nightclub. In this, the most brilliantly directed sequence in the picture, Minnelli cunningly

With Van Johnson and Elaine Stewart

With Cyd Charisse

With Barry Jones

runs the banal chitchat a few frames out of sync, adding to Tommy's irritation and discontent. He resolves to return to Brigadoon, and such is the sincerity of his love for Fiona that the village reappears. She welcomes him and he becomes a part of the legend as they sing and dance "From This Day On."

Brigadoon was greeted as a disappointment by most critics and its impact at the box office was not great. This feeling of disappointment is common with many film treatments of stage musicals, few of which are constructed in a manner which allows for literal filming. The mood created between live performers and an audience in a theatre cannot be duplicated on the screen, and the material almost always needs adaptation, which often drains away some of the original charm and vitality. However, there is much to admire in the filmed *Brigadoon;* the musical arrangements and direction are faultless, as are the costumes of Irene Sharaff and the incredible accomplishment of art director Preston Ames. The performances are pleasing if not outstanding, and Kelly's choreography is sparkling in the Scottish group dances. His dances with the remarkable Cyd Charisse accent the theme of idyllic love in relatively simple balletic style and give the film its best moments.

Rehearsing with Vincente Minnelli and Hugh Laing

Lining up a dance sequence with Jeanne Coyne and Vincente Minnelli

152

CREST OF THE WAVE

CREDITS:

An MGM Production 1954. Produced and Directed by John and Roy Boulting. Screenplay by Frank Harvey and Roy Boulting. Based on the play *Seagulls Over Sorrento* by Hugh Hastings. Photographed by Gilbert Taylor. Art direction by Alfred Junge. Edited by Max Benedict. Musical score by Miklos Rozsa. Running time: 92 minutes.

CAST:

Lieut. Bradville: Gene Kelly; *Lieut. Wharton:* John Justin; *Lofty Turner:* Bernard Lee; *Butch Clelland:* Jeff Richards; *Charlie Badger:* Sidney James; *Petty Officer Herbert:* Patric Doonan; *Sprog Sims:* Ray Jackson; *Shorty Karminsky:* Fredd Wayne; *Lt.-Commander Sinclair:* Patrick Barr; *Haggis Mackintosh:* David Orr.

Crest of the Wave is the American title for MGM's filming of the British stage play *Seagulls Over Sorrento;* the original title was kept for the British release of the picture. It was the first production of the Boulting Brothers, John and Roy, in their contract with MGM, although it is not at all typical of the kind of sophisticated satire with which they built their reputation. Recalls Gene Kelly, "I had seen several of the Boultings' movies and jumped at the chance to do the film when I learned they would be producing and directing it: It was a very deliberate hands-across-the-sea type project, to bolster Anglo-American sentiments and I was all in favor of that."

Seagulls Over Sorrento ran for over three years in the West End of London, but it failed to win similar favor on Broadway. It closed after only twelve performances in New York, the most obvious reason being its humor, much of it alien to

With Patrick Barr

With Sidney James

American ears, especially when spoken by working-class characters. This remained a minor problem in the film, although the story was enlarged and opened up for exterior settings. The main setting is a Royal Navy station on an island off the coast of Scotland, a remote location on which the Admiralty conduct research into new explosive devices for torpedoes.

The story begins with the death of a well-liked naval scientist in an unsuccessful attempt to solve the problems of detonation. Due to the lack of a similarly qualified expert in their own ranks the Admiralty bring in a U.S. Navy scientist to carry on the experimentation. Lt. Bradville (Gene Kelly) arrives with two American assistants, Butch Clelland (Jeff Richards) and Shorty Karminsky (Fredd Wayne), and despite the cordial British greeting there is an underlying resentment at the inclusion of the Americans in the project. This resentment provides both serious and comedic moments, with fairly conventional service characterizations in all ranks, British and American. The film breaks no new ground in this area; the serious differences are reserved for the officers and the comedic for the enlisted men.

Bradville's British counterpart, Lt. Wharton

With John Justin and Patrick Barr

With John Justin, Patrick Barr, Fredd Wayne and Jeff Richards

(John Justin) begins to resent the American when he sees him forging ahead with the work and bringing new ideas to it. Wharton fears Bradville will end up with the credit and rob his predecessor of due respect. The calm, cool Bradville does his best to allay these fears. On the enlisted level the British sailors resent the fact that the Americans don't come under the lash of an obnoxious R. N. petty officer (Patric Doonan), while they themselves suffer his tyranny. The station cook, Charlie Badger (Sidney James) is especially irate when he learns that one of the Americans has stolen the affections of his girlfriend. Through it all the commanding officer, Lt. Commander Sinclair (Patrick Barr) keeps the peace among his company of volunteers in the paternal, civilized manner long familiar in films dealing with the Royal Navy.

Tension increases when two British sailors die in yet another failure to detonate the experimental torpedo. Word is then received from the Admiralty to discontinue the project, but it is at this point that Wharton comes up with what he believes is the solution to the firing device. Rather than risk another man Bradville decides to take the torpedo to the test site himself. But he needs an assistant; lots are drawn to determine who he shall be. The winner is a genial British veteran, Lofty Turner (Bernard Lee), who cheats in the draw in order to save his colleagues. However, the test is a success and both men return safely.

Crest of the Wave is a neatly made film, as are most films made by the craftsmanlike Boulting brothers, and the performances of the British players defy criticism. Gene Kelly surprised a few critics with his restrained and plausible portrait of the naval scientist, carefully avoiding the air of mock heroism that might easily have spoiled the film. Asked by a journalist for a comment on Kelly shortly after the film had been completed, Roy Boulting said, "He's probably the most accomplished player I've worked with. He's absolutely sure of what he's doing."

With John Justin

With John Justin

With John Justin

155

Fred and Gene Kelly

DEEP IN MY HEART

CREDITS:

An MGM Production 1955. Produced by Roger Edens. Directed by Stanley Donen. Screenplay by Leonard Spigelgass, based on the book by Elliott Arnold. Photographed in EastmanColor by George Folsey. Art direction by Cedric Gibbons and Edward Carfagno. Edited by Adrienne Fazan. Musical direction by Adolph Deutsch. Running time: 130 minutes.

CAST:

Sigmund Romberg: Jose Ferrer; *Dorothy Donnelly:* Merle Oberon; *Anna Mueller:* Helen Traubel; *Lillian Romberg:* Doe Avedon; *J. J. Schubert:* Walter Pidgeon; *Florenz Ziegfeld:* Paul Henreid; *Gaby Deslys:* Tamara Toumanova; *Bert Townsend:* Paul Stewart; *Mrs. Harris:* Isobel Elsom; *Harold Butterfield:* Douglas Fowley; *Berrison, Jr.: Berrison:* David Burns; *Ben Judson:* Jim Backus; Russ Tamblyn.

GUEST STARS: Rosemary Clooney, Gene and Fred Kelly, Jane Powell, Vic Damone, Ann Miller, William Olvis, Cyd Charisse, James Mitchell, Howard Keel, Tony Martin, and Joan Weldon.

Sigmund Romberg was a lilting and influential force in the American musical theatre for almost forty years, during which time he composed for some eighty revues, musical comedies and operettas. His total song output is thought to be somewhere in the region of two thousand. A film concept of his life and work was therefore not easy, but MGM acquired the rights to a very respectable book on Romberg by Elliott Arnold and put the project in the hands of two of the studio's major talents—Stanley Donen and Roger Edens. Donen had by now established himself as a director—his *Seven Brides for Seven Brothers* left no doubt about that—but the Romberg picture was Edens's first solo flight as a producer. He was for a long time Arthur Freed's right-hand man, writing lyrics, occasionally composing music, inventing musical sequences, and supervising production. His general role as a mainstay of Metro musicals has yet to be fully credited.

Deep in My Heart did better for Romberg than most other musicals about composers. The two hours of the film touched on sixteen of his songs and the production team astutely included some rare and unfamiliar material as well as obvious selections from *Maytime, The Desert Song,* and *The Student Prince.* To play Romberg MGM settled on Jose Ferrer, an actor with some knowledge of music and capable of musical performance. One of the highlights of the film is Ferrer's doing a frantic audition of the songs and the plotline of the show *Jazzadoo* for the backers in the space of just a few minutes. Another decided asset for the film was the casting of the late Helen Traubel, in her first film role, as Romberg's lifelong friend and booster, Anna Mueller. Miss Traubel at this time had only recently ended her lengthy association with the Metropolitan Opera, having acquired a reputation as America's foremost Wagnerian soprano and it came as a surprise to most people to find this very affable lady had a taste for light music. Her singing of Romberg's "Auf Wiedersehn" is nothing less than gorgeous.

With Donen and Edens making the picture, it was a certainty that Gene Kelly would be among the guest stars, but the selection of material was difficult in view of the limited range of his singing and the almost operatic quality of the Romberg songs. Donen and Edens solved the problem by digging into the composer's earliest work. Romberg arrived in America from Hungary in 1909 and earned his first money playing the piano in restaurants, and later leading small salon orchestras. By 1912 he was conducting his own orchestra at Bustanoby's Restaurant, and writing dance music, some of which was published. A year later he was hired by Broadway producer J. J. Shubert as a staff composer and set to work on a revue called *The Whirl of the World.* His next assignment was *Dancing Around,* starring Al Jolson, which appeared in the latter part of 1914 and told a tale of the British army in France. The song "It's a Long Way to Tipperary," written two years previ-

Jose Ferrer and Helen Traubel

157

On the set with his brother Fred and Ann Miller

ously, was interpolated in the score but among the many Romberg ditties was one called "I Love to Go Swimmin' With Wimmen." According to the film this was performed by a pair known as The O'Brien Brothers.

While "I Love to Go Swimmin' With Wimmen" is far from typical Romberg, it is, however, representative of the kind of music he was required to write in these Shubert shows at this time. It was not until 1917 that he was able to persuade Shubert to let him write the kind of music that interested him most—romantic, sentimental melodies. Hence *Maytime,* the first of his enduring operettas.

To perform the "Wimmen" number with him Gene called in his younger brother Fred, here making his only film appearance but who, before and since, had made a good living as a dance director in television and for stage shows. "Wimmen" called for no great skill from the Kelly brothers but it did require a lot of expended energy and boisterous clowning. The style is near-vaudevillian, the music is rapid ragtime and the lyrics contain couplets like: "I pretend that I'm a crab—and their pretty ankles grab," and "I get those navy notions when I see floating queens, I dive right in the ocean and play submarines." Assuming a taste for Sigmund Romberg, *Deep in My Heart* is a most enjoyable musical, and the love of the Kelly brothers for 'swimmin' with wimmen" is one of its brightest segments.

Rehearsing with Fred

158

With Cyd Charisse

IT'S ALWAYS FAIR WEATHER

CREDITS:

An MGM Production 1955. Produced by Arthur Freed. Directed by Gene Kelly and Stanley Donen. Screenplay and lyrics by Betty Comden and Adolph Green. Music by Andre Previn. Photographed in CinemaScope and Eastman Color by Robert Bronner. Art direction by Cedric Gibbons and Arthur Lonergan. Edited by Adrienne Fazan. Running time: 102 minutes.

CAST:

Ted Riley: Gene Kelly; *Doug Hallerton:* Dan Dailey; *Jackie Leighton:* Cyd Charisse: *Madeline Bradville:* Dolores Gray; *Angie Valentine:* Michael Kidd; *Tim:* David Burns; *Charles Z. Culloran:* Jay C. Flippen; *Rocky:* Hal March.

The third of the celebrated trio of musicals directed by Gene Kelly and Stanley Donen, and written by Betty Comden and Adolph Green, *It's Always Fair Weather,* is admirable as a satire on commercial television and the advertising business, but in its appeal as popular entertainment it falls short of *On the Town* and *Singin' in the Rain.* The musical score of Andre Previn is a factor in point—it functions perfectly at every turn but it lacks the magic that turns a good melody into a touching and memorable melody. In this respect the gifted Previn is less fortunate than some of the songwriters who can barely play the piano. The idea of the film, a good one, was to bring together after an absence of ten years three wartime buddies and see how they feel about each other—a kind of sequel to *On the Town,* with the same trio of actors.

159

With Dan Dailey and Cyd Charisse

With Dan Dailey and Michael Kidd

With Michael Kidd and Dan Dailey

But things had changed, as much in Hollywood as in the lives of the characters in *It's Always Fair Weather*. Frank Sinatra had become more difficult with the years and MGM refused to deal with him. They also refused to accept Jules Munshin in a leading role, despite the efforts of Kelly and Donen. Dan Dailey met with immediate approval and for the third chum, the "little guy" role that would have been played by Sinatra, Kelly and Donen selected Michael Kidd, then held in high regard at MGM for his work as the choreographer of *Band Wagon* and Donen's *Seven Brides for Seven Brothers*. Thus with the selection of Dailey and Kidd, it was decided to build up the dancing in the film.

The film begins with an impressive montage, as we see three soldiers, Ted Riley (Kelly), Doug Hallerton (Dailey) and Angie Valentine (Kidd) making their way through the Second World War, ending with their marching into Tim's (David Burns) Bar on New York's Third Avenue to celebrate V-J Day. The merry warrior-buddies enjoy themselves and vow to meet in the very same bar in ten years' time. Ted is momentarily depressed when he reads a letter from his girl telling him the affair is over, but he puts the letter away and leads his chums in a bar-by-bar binge, dancing under the Third Avenue El, in and out of taxis and then, with garbage can lids attached to their shoes they thump-dance in the street. They depart after vowing eternal friendship with the song, "The Time Has Come for Parting."

Ten years pass and the three ex-comrades keep their rendezvous at Tim's Bar, each hesitant about it and doubting that the others will turn up. They greet each other warmly, but it soon becomes apparent that they are changed men and it is difficult to maintain the joviality. Ted in the intervening years has become a glib, card-sharp fight promoter of dubious ethics, Doug is a well-paid, stuffy, ulcer-ridden advertising executive and Angie runs a hamburger joint in Schenectady, pretentiously calling it "The Cordon Bleu." None of them has become what he hoped to be and their meeting only makes them feel uncomfortable as they realize their lack of self-respect. Their thoughts are revealed to the audience as the camera concentrates on each in turn and their alter egos sing verses of "Once Upon a Time." Too embarrassed to part they agree to have dinner together with Doug, the affluent one, picking an expensive restaurant. As they sit there together, munching celery and barely able to find anything to say, a string quartet

With Michael Kidd and Dan Dailey

in the restaurant plays "The Blue Danube" and their thoughts give voice to the strains of the Strauss waltz—"I shouldn't have come, dum-dum dum-dum . . . can these be the guys I once thought I could never live without?" The loud crunch of celery punctuates each verse in this trenchant little song.

Before the glum trio leave the restaurant a friend and fellow worker of Doug's, an idea girl in advertising, Jackie Leighton (Cyd Charisse) arrives and Ted makes a play for her. His glib technique makes little impression on the cool, intellectual girl but he impresses his work-place on her, Stillman's Gym, and she later turns up there, to the delight of a crowd of pugilists. She amazes them with her encyclopedic knowledge of boxing, and the ugly mugs are moved to sing a song in praise of their alma mater, Stillman's, the landmark of the boxing world, followed by a song in praise of Jackie, "Baby, You Knock Me Out," to which she dances her appreciation. Jackie also has a moralizing force on Ted, who knocks out his own fighter in order to prevent a fixed match. Meanwhile Doug goes through a similar soul-search and at a party of advertising executives he lampoons their absurd jargon in a wild room-wrecking song and dance, "Situation-Wise." Even Angie gets a hold on sanity and changes the name of "The Cordon Bleu" to "Angie's Place."

To speed his necessary departure from Stillman's Gym, in the face of retaliation from his crooked, fight-fixing rival Charles Z. Culloran (Jay C. Flippen), Ted puts on roller skates and makes off through the city. His mood brightens and he becomes his old, happy self again, and as he sails along the sidewalks beaming at people he sings "I Like Myself," following the vocal with nifty

With Michael Kidd and Dan Dailey

tap-dancing and skating figures. The roller skates give him a sense of release.

By now Jackie has learned the story of the three lads and has hit upon the idea of making them the surprise guests on the popular TV show, "Midnight with Madeleine." Madeleine Bradville (Dolores Gray) is a cloyingly sweet, but privately tough, singer-hostess on a nightly New York channel who reveals the lives of the "little people" and showers them with the gifts of her sponsors. Ted makes it known he and the others feel the show is shallow and the charity unwanted, but when he spots Culloran and his thugs entering the studio to get him, Ted realizes an opportunity and goads the unknowing Culloran into revealing his business before an open microphone. Jackie, in the control booth, instantly directs the cameramen to switch to Ted and Culloran, and the brawl which follows is telecast. The three chums whip the Culloran gang and proceed to Tim's Bar to celebrate—with the spirit of ten years ago, their lives

With Dan Dailey, Dolores Gray and Michael Kidd

With Michael Kidd, Dan Dailey and Cyd Charisse

now changed for the better. Also changed is Jackie's opinion of Ted, and when she turns up at the bar Ted knows he's got himself a girl again.

It's Always Fair Weather did only fair business when it was first released, seemingly failing to strike much response with the audiences of the mid-fifties. Its satirical digs at advertising and television seem more pertinent today than then, since the pomposity, bathos and glibness of those media at their worst are even more apparent. The dancing in this film remains its greatest asset, not surprisingly so in view of Kelly's being joined by Dan Dailey and Michael Kidd. The pleasing Dailey is brilliant in his "Situation-Wise" and for a man who had not acted before, Kidd is remarkably good as little Angie, although as soon as he begins to dance it is obvious he is no meek, retiring nonentity. The street dance with the garbage can lids belongs in the select collection of great film choreography, and Kelly's routine on roller skates is amazing in its dexterity, especially in the ease of the tap-dancing. But skating is something Kelly had learned playing ice hockey as a boy, and he claims the tapping was not as difficult as it looks.

The Kelly-Donen direction merits one considerable comment of favor—their clever use of the CinemaScope screen in making it flexible and intimate, something that had escaped previous directors. The giant mail-box-slot shape was always a problem and here the directors hit upon the device of splitting the screen into sections during the passages where the three men soliloquize their thoughts in the restaurant, the photography highlighting the individual and blacking out the other portions of the screen. Kelly and Donen also split the screen into separate independent panels to stage dances showing the three men performing their versions of the same thematic material. And in the television studio brawl the directors employed the wide screen to advantage, showing the several areas of the melee through the windows of the control booth and then picking them up on three different monitors, with each TV screen occupying a third of the movie screen, and showing parallel or contrasting situations. These techniques, while they would never become common in the use of CinemaScope because of the complications and the added expense involved, would however be adopted and further developed by others. But it needs to be remembered that the pioneering was done by Gene Kelly and Stanley Donen in *It's Always Fair Weather*.

INVITATION TO THE DANCE

CREDITS:

An MGM Production 1956. Produced by Arthur Freed. Script, direction and choreography by Gene Kelly. Photographed in Technicolor by F. A. Young and Joseph Ruttenberg. Edited by Raymond Poulton, Robert Watts and Adrienne Fazan. Running time: 93 minutes.

CIRCUS

CREDITS:

Music by Jacques Ibert, conducted by John Hollingsworth.

CAST:

The Lover: Igor Youskevitch; *The Loved:* Claire Sombert; *The Clown:* Gene Kelly.

RING AROUND THE ROSY

CREDITS:

Music composed and conducted by Andre Previn. *The Husband:* David Paltenghi; *The Wife:* Daphne Dale; *The Artist:* Igor Youskevitch; *The Model:* Claude Bessy; *Flashy boyfriend:* Tommy

With Clarie Sombert

period of time. After the success of *On the Town*, which proved to MGM and the general film public that dancing could be used as a story-telling device, Kelly began to hound his employers for the chance to do a film that would consist entirely of dancing. They continually resisted the idea but with *An American in Paris*, and *Singin' in the Rain* to his credit Kelly became impossible to refuse. Recalls John Green, "Gene by now was the Neil Armstrong of MGM. He enjoyed great respect and admiration, and in Arthur Freed he had

Rall; *Debutante:* Belita; *The Crooner:* Irving Davies; *The Hat Check Girl:* Diane Adams; *The Marine:* Gene Kelly; *The Street Walker:* Tamara Toumanova.

SINBAD THE SAILOR

CREDITS:

Music of Rimsky-Korsakov (*Scheherazade*), adapted by Roger Edens and conducted by John Green. Cartoon sequences by Fred Quimby, William Hanna and Joseph Barbera.

CAST:

Scheherazade: Carol Haney; *The Genie:* David Kasday; *Sinbad:* Gene Kelly.

The most ambitious and the most personal of Gene Kelly's film creations is *Invitation to the Dance*, a full-length feature containing three ballets of various style but no dialogue and no singing. For Kelly it was a dream project realized only after much effort and persuasion over a long

164

a powerful ally. It was almost a father-son relationship, with the father having a near-reverence for the son. Also, Gene is not simply a persuasive man—he's a slugging persuader. There's very little velvet glove when he sets his sights on something, and so *Invitation to the Dance* came to be. Freed was nominal producer; it was Gene who determined the road map of the entire film, he sought out the talent, hired it, commissioned the music, devised the choreography, directed it and danced in each of the stories. It is *his* picture."

With Clarie Sombert

165

Having finally won consent, Kelly then embarked on what would turn out to be much longer and more painful then he imagined. MGM stipulated that the film had to be made in England at their Elstree studios in order to utilize frozen British earnings, and production began in October of 1952. Kelly originally conceived the film as having four parts, but the section to be known as "Dance Me a Song" was scrapped before it was completed because the material could not be realized to Kelly's liking. The idea was to have a group of dancers interpret a medley of familiar songs, arranged and conducted by Robert Farnon. The first section, "Circus," was danced to a score commissioned from Jacques Ibert, and it remains the best material in the film. The second section, "Ring Around the Rosy," a modern American ballet, was scored by British composer Malcolm Arnold but the MGM executives disliked his music and told Kelly to get another composer. This was an enormous problem because the same executives were not in favor of spending money to have the ballet refilmed. Andre Previn then performed the incredible feat of writing a score to a ballet already completely filmed to another man's music. Due to the great amount of time *Invitation to the Dance* had required of him, MGM instructed Kelly to proceed with *Crest of the Wave* before continuing with his ballet picture. By the time *Crest* was finished, MGM had decided that the final portion of *Invitation* involving animation, should be made in California, and so complicated were the requirements for that portion, "Sinbad the Sailor," that Kelly made *Brigadoon* while it was being planned.

"Circus" is a relatively simple ballet on a romantic theme, danced in classic style. In this Kelly appears as an eighteenth-century clown with an Italian traveling circus. The libretto is suggestive of *Pagliacci*, as the unhappy Clown reveals in mime his love for the troupe's leading lady (Claire Sombert), who is in love with The High Wire Walker (Igor Youskevitch). The troupe perform in the square of a village; tumblers, jugglers and harlequins create an entertainment that delights the villagers, but after the gaiety has subsided attention focuses on The Clown and it becomes apparent he is sad and lonely, and longing for The Girl. He watches as The Girl dances rapturously with The High Wire Walker. After they have gone The Clown picks up a cloak and dances with it as if he was a daring aerialist. The Girl notices him and in order to keep her

With Tamara Toumanova

166

With David Kasday

With his dance assistant, Carol Haney, who also played the part of Scheherazade in the "Sinbad the Sailor" segment

attention The Clown proceeds with amusing capers, ending with him climbing the aerial apparatus, from which he falls and dies. As he lies on the ground, a crumpled white figure on a red cloak, The Girl and The High Wire Walker realize the tragedy and resolve to love each other the more. The music of Ibert is excellent, fully stating all the joys and sorrows of the plot. "Circus" is Kelly's more serious film dance and he is well matched with Claire Sombert, a student in a ballet school when discovered by Kelly. For the role of The High Wire Walker Kelly says, "There was never any doubt in my mind who I wanted for that part, and I got him—Igor Youskevitch, the finest male classic dancer of the time."

"Ring Around the Rosy" is a takeoff on Arthur Schnitzler's story *Reigen* (*La Ronde*), in which a theme forms a link between a chain of lovers. In Schnitzler's tale the theme was syphilis—in Kelly's ballet it becomes a bracelet. The setting is contemporary American; the bracelet is a pawn passing between people of various kinds. A loving husband gives it to his wife, who gives it to an Artist, who gives it to one of his models. She passes it on to a flashy boyfriend, who uses it as a gift for a Debutante, who gives it to a Singer, and he bedecks the wrist of a Hat-Check Girl with it. A Marine (Kelly) takes it and gives it to a sultry Streetwalker (Tamara Toumanova), who returns it to the husband, who again gives it to his wife. The ballet begins and ends at parties, with other scenes at an artist's studio and on the street. The ten dancers perform a variety of styles, including tap and strong modern movements, as well as classic steps, in trying to set a sophisticated, racy tone to the piece. Previn's score, with him playing the prominent piano part, is suitably saucy and satirically paraphrases the nursery tune, "Ring Around the Rosy." The ballet is of interest to dance students, but lacks appeal for average moviegoers.

The final segment of *Invitation to the Dance* is the one which required the most work. In addition to Kelly and his assistants, the animation requirements of "Sinbad the Sailor" tied up some three dozen artists under the supervision of Fred Quimby, William Hanna and Joe Barbera of the MGM cartoon department for more than a year. A quarter of a million sketches were made to map out the sequence and 57,000 frames of film were painted to synchronize the cartoon characters with the live actors. The story depicts an American sailor (Kelly) on a shopping spree in Baghdad;

he buys an ancient oil lamp and after accidentally rubbing it with his sleeve a genie appears—not the monster usually attached to Aladdin's lamp but a cheerful young boy (David Kasday). The sailor first asks that the boy turn into a sailor like himself, and they then romp together through the pages of the Arabian Nights, with Scheherazade (Carol Haney) as their guide.

The two dance through a world of fantasy, through a valley of diamonds where they outstep serpents and then into the castle of a crooked Sultan, whose guards they elude. The pair foil the Sultan and steal away with his lovely, unwilling, bride-to-be. The lengthy sequence moves in a sprightly manner throughout, but some of the animation is overly cute. Critics were quick to point out that Kelly's results here were not as pleasing or as sharp as his animation sequence in *Anchors Aweigh*. Be that as it may, "Sinbad the Sailor" deserves credit for the sheer weight of effort and the courage it required to do it.

Invitation to the Dance fell far short of the mark Gene Kelly had aimed for. Work on the picture had been spread over three years, and, discouraged by the reactions at sneak previews, MGM held onto the film for another year before releasing it. The delay was costly, it was a case of the wrong picture at the wrong time. By the late fifties movie musicals were no longer the attraction they had been only a few years previously, either in America or Europe. Said Kelly: "When I originally set out to do the film, one of my chief reasons was the lack of filmed dance material available to the public, but in the space of four years that situation changed considerably. By 1956 people were seeing quite a lot of elaborate dancing on television variety shows, and there wasn't as much need for the film. And I must admit there were some things in it that didn't come off as well as I had hoped, although I feel "Circus" is really good. I also didn't want to appear in the film as much as I did, but this was at MGM's insistence. They were investing a million dollars and wanted some protection for their money. My name was about all they could gamble on. As a producer myself, I could see their point of view. And I tend to agree with those who find the whole thing a bit much—each piece is enjoyable by itself, but three in a row is probably more than most people can take."

While *Invitation to the Dance* must be judged an estimable failure it must also be recognized as an admirable piece of filmmaking on the part of a single man. No other entertainer has devoted as much time and effort in trying to interest the public in a movie about the skill and joy of dancing.

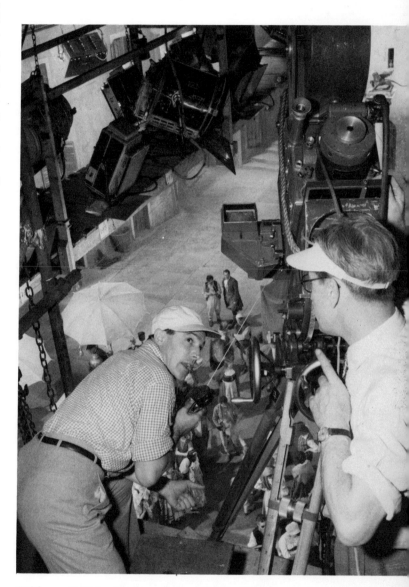

With ace British cinematographer Freddie Young

169

With Barbara Laage

THE HAPPY ROAD

CREDITS:

A Kerry Production, released by MGM 1957. Produced and directed by Gene Kelly. Written by Arthur Julian, Joseph Morhaim and Harry Kurnitz. Photographed by Robert Julliard. Art direction by Alexandre Trauner. Edited by Borys Lewin. Musical score by Georges Van Parys. Running time: 99 minutes.

CAST:

Mike Andrews: Gene Kelly; *Suzanne Duval:* Barbara Laage: *General Medworth:* Michael Redgrave; *Danny Andrews:* Bobby Clark; *Janine Duval:* Brigitte Fossey; *Docteur Solaise:* Roger Treville; *Helene:* Colette Dereal; *Morgan:* Jess Hahn; *Madame Fallere:* Maryse Martin; *Verbier:* Roger Saget; *French Motorcycle Officer:* Van

Doude; *Patronne Hotel:* Claire Gerard; *Armbruster:* Colin Mann; *Bucheron:* Alexandre Rignault.

The Happy Road came about as the result of Gene Kelly wanting to terminate his contract with MGM: "I still had a couple of years to go but they had nothing on tap for me and I'd been sitting around for months waiting for an assignment. I couldn't stand not working so I suggested to them that we come to terms—that I do two more pictures to conclude the deal, provided they enter into a co-production with me on a property of my choice. They agreed to this, with the provision that I also played the lead, which I really didn't want to do because producing and directing plus being the star is too much. But at this point I was very eager to broaden my horizons."

Kelly had bought a script, partly because it was

set in France, where he was held in high regard, and partly because he knew it could be filmed on a modest scale. He set up a company, naming it Kerry after his daughter, and proceeded to Paris to organize his crew and his talent, with further time spent driving around France scouting locations. *The Happy Road* is yet another tale of an American in Paris, but not the cheery, foot-tapping kind Kelly had essayed just a few years previously. Mike Andrews (Kelly) is a brash businessman with little patience for the French manner of conducting business, which to him seems casual and inefficient. He is a widower and he has placed his son Danny (Bobby Clark) in a school in Switzerland. The ten-year-old boy feels his father looks upon him as unable to take care of himself and to prove otherwise he runs away from the school, in company with a female classmate, Janine Duval (Brigitte Fossey), who considers herself unappreciated by her divorced mother, Suzanne Duval (Barbara Laage).

The two youngsters set out for Paris and they are helped everywhere they go by children, who admire the pair for running away. The two parents join forces in the pursuit, with neither one caring much for the other because of their vastly different viewpoints. The failure of the French police to locate the runaways does nothing to increase Mike's feelings for the French, and when he comes across a British army unit on NATO maneuvers he appeals to the commanding officer, General Medworth (Michael Redgrave) for help. But Danny and Janine elude·even the military efforts to trace and trap them. After spending a night with a friendly woodcutter, the two youngsters get caught up with a European bicycle race bound for a Parisian finishing post and they hitch rides. Mike and Suzanne give up the chase and return to his apartment in Paris, where they find their two young escapees safe and soundly asleep. By this time the feelings of the parents have changed from hostility to appreciation, with Mike realizing there is something to be said for the French attitude to life and Suzanne feeling there is a lot to be said for this particular American.

The Happy Road suffers somewhat in overstating national characteristics, it labors the dubious point that children have better ideas on running the world than do adults, but the general feeling of the picture is warm and appealing and in several moments it is genuinely comic. Michael Redgrave gives a knowing send-up of a Blimpish British officer and numerous French character actors pop-

Directing Bobby Clark and Brigitte Fossey

Supervising a French barber cutting Brigitte Fossey's hair as her co-star Bobby Clark looks on

With Barbara Laage

With Van Doude and Barbara Laage

With Colin Mann, Michael Redgrave and Barbara Laage

ulate the picture with amusing bits of business. Barbara Laage is thoroughly believable as the mother, and if Kelly's playing of the father is more restrained than his usual performance it can only be that his mind was mainly on the numerous levels of his job as producer-director. He clearly recognized the slightness of his material and that the best way to treat it was briskly.

The well-photographed chase across France offers some pleasing shots of the countryside. But the point most to Kelly's credit in *The Happy Road* is his handling of his young actors, Bobby Clark and Brigitte Fossey. To find appealing youngsters capable of carrying a film is in itself a talent but to be able to sustain performances from them during the long weeks of filming is the mark of an exceptional director.

Gene Kelly's first film as a producer-director was made for slightly under half a million dollars. He took a small salary and a percentage of the profits, but the profits were few because MGM used it mostly as a companion feature on double bills and the bookkeeping on such arrangements is of a kind best left unchallenged here. But Kelly had proved himself totally responsible for the making of a film and that, as he had planned, altered the course of his career.

With Bobby Clark, Brigitte Fossey and Barbara Laage

172

With Kay Kendall, Taina Elg and Mitzi Gaynor

LES GIRLS

CREDITS:

An MGM Production 1957. Produced by Sol Siegel. Directed by George Cukor. Screenplay by John Patrick, based on a story by Vera Caspary. Photographed in CinemaScope and Metrocolor by Robert Surtees. Art direction by William A. Horning and Gene Allen. Edited by Ferris Webster. Songs by Cole Porter. Musical direction by Adolph Deutsch. Choreography by Jack Cole. Running time: 114 minutes.

CAST:

Barry Nichols: Gene Kelly; *Joy Henderson:* Mitzi Gaynor; *Lady Wren:* Kay Kendall; *Angele Ducros:* Taina Elg; *Pierre Ducros:* Jacques Bergerac; *Sir Gerald Wren:* Leslie Philips; *Judge:* Henry Daniell; *Sir Percy:* Patrick MacNee; *Mr. Outward:* Stephen Vercoe; *Associate Judge:* Philip Tonge.

Gene Kelly's final MGM musical has wit and quality, the script is superior to most others in this genre but the Kelly performance lacks something of the charm of his American painter in Paris, and the vitality of his sailor on a shore leave in New York. He was aware that this was his last performance for Metro, having accepted a directorial assignment as the second of the two items needed to close his contract, and that awareness subtly affects his playing. He declined to direct the choreography, and Jack Cole was given the assignment, although he was ill during part of the production period and Kelly took over in his absence. Cole Porter, whose last Hollywood score

With Mitzi Gaynor, Kay Kendall and Taina Elg

With Mitzi Gaynor

With Mitzi Gaynor, Taina Elg and Kay Kendall

With Mitzi Gaynor

With Mitzi Gaynor

this proved to be, later admitted he felt the script was good enough as a straight comedy and not really in need of songs, other than one for the variety act. But producer Sol Siegel and writer John Patrick, who had just worked with Porter on *High Society,* felt otherwise.

The ladies of the title are three singer-dancers: Joy, a level-headed, uncomplicated American (Mitzi Gaynor); Sybil, a delightfully scatterbrained Briton (Kay Kendall); and Angele, a temperamental French beauty (Taina Elg). They work for, and perform with, an American named Barry Nichols (Kelly) who tours with his nightclub act through Europe. Most of the story is told in flashbacks arising from testimony being given in a court case in London. Sybil, now Lady Wren, the wife of Sir Gerald Wren (Leslie Phillips), has published her memoirs and is being sued by Angele, now married to prominent French industrialist Pierre Ducros (Jacques Bergerac), for defamation of character. According to Sybil, Angele had attempted suicide after being spurned by Nichols but when Angele takes the stand she maintains this is not true and that Sybil was the one who tried to kill herself after being rejected by the boss. The Judge (Henry Daniell) warns the two respectable ladies that one of them is likely to be charged with perjury. Nichols appears on the third day of the trial to give his testimony—and solve the mystery. He declares that he was never in love with either girl and not responsible for their feelings toward him. His real interest among the girls was, and is, Joy and she is his wife. Nichols nonetheless defends the stand taken by both Sybil and Angele, explaining that they have told the truth as they understood it. He recalls arriving at the apartment shared by the two girls and finding them both unconscious as the result of escaping coal gas, an accident in an old, neglected heating apparatus and not the fault of either girl. The judge dismisses the case and the opposing parties embrace one another in an affectionate reunion.

The various pieces of testimony appear in the film à la *Rashomon,* as differing interpretations of the relative truth, and also serve to give the background of Nichols, his girls and their act. The title song is a snappy exposition number in which Nichols, backed by his three stunning employees, states the case for a happy song-and-dance man. The first line of the lyric tells us, "Round the map I've been a dancer, from New Jersey to Japan . . ." and then goes on to give the reason he most likes being a globe-trotting

With Taina Elg

With Kay Kendall

hoofer—working with beautiful girls. The three girls chime in with sentiments suggesting lusty approval.

The most memorable Porter song from this score is the gentle ballad, "Ça, C'Est L'Amour," sung by Taina Elg to Kelly in a little boat on a river, a situation which leads the girl to take seriously the lighthearted advances of her boss. The Finnish-born Miss Elg was a ballet dancer before working in movies and her ability is clear in her dance with Kelly, "The Rope Dance," a sensuous duet in a strange, geometric setting. The three girls appear in French period costume, circa Louis XIV, and sing a saucy ditty about their amorous duties as "Ladies-in-Waiting," and in a comedic dance routine with Mitzi Gaynor, Kelly turns up as a black-leather-jacketed motorcycle punk to sing "Why Am I So Gone About That Girl," an amusing takeoff on Marlon Brando's image in *The Wild One*. And in a typically Cole

With Kay Kendall

With Taina Elg, Kay Kendall, Mitzi Gaynor and Nestor Paiva

Porter joshing of upper-class love sentiments, Kelly and Kay Kendall sing and dance the sprightly "You're Just Too, Too!"

Les Girls was chosen as the Royal Command Film in London in November of 1957 and although it was thought likable most British critics considered it a slightly disappointing vehicle under the prestigious circumstances. But appreciation has grown for the picture over the years, recognizing it not only as the final Kelly-Metro musical but as one of the last films of its kind. By 1957 the Hollywood musical with an original script and score was getting to be a thing of the past, partly due to a curious lack of impressive new talent to take over from the song-and-dance veterans—never a large group at any time—partly due to the public's saturation with musical fare on television, and the definite lack of popularity of original screen musicals in Europe. There was also the factor of cost, rising by the day, causing the studios to reason that the only kind of musical worth risking was one with a built-in reputation— the Broadway hit, but even in making films of famous stage musicals the results were more often than not disappointing. The talented and vivacious Mitzi Gaynor won the lead in the film version of *South Pacific* because of her performance in *Les Girls* but that multimillion-dollar production was a financial disaster and did little to further her career.

There are many enjoyable moments in *Les Girls* and most of them include Kay Kendall, in particular the scene in which she gets drunk on champagne and gives out with a raucous version of an aria from *Carmen*. Unfortunately she would appear in only two more films, *The Reluctant Debutante* and *Once More With Feeling*, dying in 1959 at the age of thirty-two, a victim of leukemia. Gene Kelly: "Kay was a delightful, charming, witty girl and that rarity of rarities—a funny, beautiful woman. Her death was a dumbfounding loss to everybody."

With Leslie Phillips and Jacques Bergerac

With Mitzi Gaynor, Key Kendall and Taina Elg

MARJORIE MORNINGSTAR

CREDITS:

A Beachwold Pictures Production for Warner Bros. 1958. Produced by Milton Sperling. Directed by Irving Rapper. Screenplay by Everett Freeman, based on the novel by Herman Wouk. Photographed in Warner Color by Harry Stradling. Art direction by Malcolm Bert. Edited by Folmar Blangsted. Musical score by Max Steiner. Song "A Very Precious Love" by Sammy Fain (music) and Paul Francis Webster (lyrics). Running time: 123 minutes.

CAST:

Noel Airman: Gene Kelly; *Margorie:* Natalie Wood; *Rose:* Claire Trevor; *Uncle Samson:* Ed Wynn; *Arnold:* Everett Sloane; *Wally:* Marty Milner; *Marsha:* Carolyn Jones; *Greech:* George Tobias; *Dr. David Harris:* Martin Balsam; *Lou Michaelson:* Jesse White; *Sandy Lamm:* Edward Byrnes; *Philip Berman:* Paul Picerni; *Puddles Podell:* Alan Reed; *Imogene:* Ruta Lee; *Carlos:* Edward Foster; *Karen:* Patricia Denise; *Seth:* Howard Best.

Herman Wouk's very popular novel *Marjorie Morningstar* was difficult to make into a film, partly because of its great length but more so because it dealt with a particular segment of American life, the upper-middle-class Jewish society of New York. In turning this into a glossy movie aimed at the widest possible audience Warners had to generalize the philosophy of its protagonists without losing the gist of the heroine's confusion, which is very much a result of her ambivalent attitude towards her background. This uncertainty of approach somewhat undermined the production of the film, with the studio management bothering the producer, the director and the writer all through the filming to popularize the material and avoid too precise a treatment of Jewish customs. By the end of production scenarist Everett Freeman was in favor of his name being removed from the credit titles, but he was persuaded otherwise. The long film, fairly entertaining on the whole, wavers in telling its story and it falls short of the sting and purpose of Wouk's book.

The girl of the title is eighteen-year-old Marjorie Morgenstern—uncertain of everything about her life. Marjorie (Natalie Wood) attends the Bar Mitzvah of her brother Seth, which occasion points to her spiritual doubts about the rigid religious views of her father (Everett Sloane) and her mother (Claire Trevor). Much more understanding is her genial Uncle Samson (Ed Wynn), in whom she confides her troubles. At Hunter College the stage-struck Marjorie receives applause for her perform-

ance in *Romeo and Juliet* and at the end of term she goes to Camp Tamarack in upstate New York as a drama counselor. In company with her saucy friend Marsha (Carolyn Jones), she takes a forbidden ride across the lake to visit South Wind, a resort complex complete with a theatrical company. It is there that she meets the dashing Noel Airman, singer, dancer, songwriter and director of the resort shows. She also meets his assistant, Wally (Marty Milner). He is soon smitten with Marjorie but she has no interest in him because she is dazzled by Noel. She and Marsha become part of the show and Uncle Samson, as a family spy, turns up to work in the kitchen. Noel accepts the love of Marjorie but makes it clear he has no interest in marriage. Her parents visit South Wind but they are unable to dissuade her from the affair with Noel. Uncle Samson, after giving a comic performance as a toreador for the resort customers, has a fatal heart attack and the grief-stricken

With Marty Milner and Natalie Wood

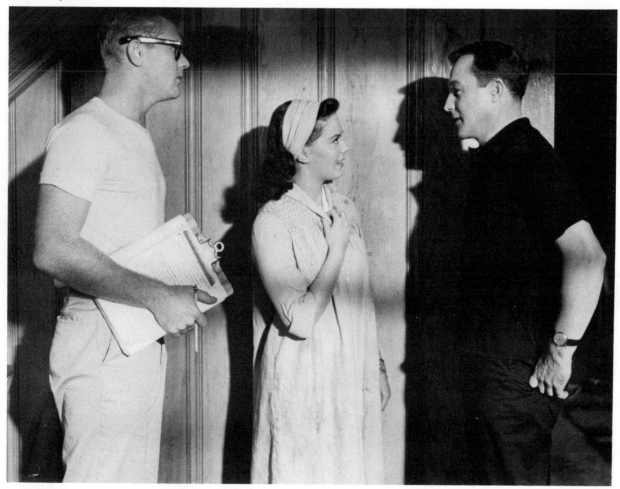

185

With Natalie Wood

186

Marjorie leaves South Wind. She decides to break with Noel and he understands. She takes with her the name he has invented for her, Morningstar instead of Morgenstern, having changed his own name from Ehreman to Airman.

Marjorie graduates from Hunter College the following year and it seems to her happy family that she will marry a respectable doctor, David Harris (Martin Balsam), but Noel reenters her life. Now in New York and employed by a Madison Avenue advertising agency, he tells Marjorie that because of her he has decided to give up the theatre and become a solid citizen, which causes Marjorie to fall even more deeply in love with him.

By this time Wally has become a successful playwright and Noel and Marjorie attend the opening night of his play. Noel, still show-biz at heart, is greatly upset by the triumph of his former assistant and he disappears. Marjorie locates him in Greenwich Village, sharing a room with a blonde, and walks away after slapping his face. Marsha, in the meantime, has become engaged to a theatrical producer, Lou Michaelson (Jesse White) and at their wedding Noel approaches Marjorie and tells her he is sorry and that he is working hard on a musical revue. Marjorie finds it impossible to ignore his need for her, and with her help Michaelson agrees to produce his show. Her parents are reconciled to the match and agree she should marry Noel. But the show is a flop and again Noel disappears. Marjorie trails him to Europe but in London Wally tells her, "Has it ever occurred to you that he doesn't want to be found?" He then tells her that Noel is back at South Wind. She goes there and finds him in his element, surrounded by admiring youngsters, and as she sees Noel escorting a young girl backstage she realizes the hopelessness of the situation. Marjorie returns to the ever-faithful Wally.

Marjorie Morningstar as a film seems to offer more comment on the psyche of those in the entertainment business than people of the Jewish faith. The title role, capably played by Natalie Wood, becomes the story of a girl of almost any background, adolescently rebelling against it, which is less than what Herman Wouk had in mind. His supposition, the anguish of repudiating religious and racial faith, not only affected the heroine but it explained the dilemma of Noel Airman, a Jew who had cut himself off from the stability of his background. It is his uneasy rootlessness, never fully apparent to himself, that sabo-

With Ed Wynn

With Patricia Denise and Natalie Wood

187

With Natalie Wood

188

With Carolyn Jones *(left)* and to the right, Marty Milner and
Natalie Wood

tages his confidence and causes him to drift—and finally retreat.

Danny Kaye was the first choice of Warners for Airman, an excellent choice in view of his own experience as an entertainer on the borscht circuit in the Catskills before his success on Broadway. But Kaye was diffident about the role, perhaps he understood it too well, and it was offered to Gene Kelly. Many consider this his finest dramatic performance and ne says, "I haven't liked all my roles, more often than not I wince when watching myself, but I had some good scenes in this one." A few critics mentioned that in playing a second-rate song-and-dance man Kelly's moments in the picture singing and dancing were too good for such a character, supposedly a summer-camp amateur. Explains Kelly: "Again this is a fault of the film treatment and not the book. Noel Airman is a very talented man, a brilliant fellow, the kind people think will take Broadway by storm. But he lacks either the guts or the drive, the ability or the confidence to push himself beyond the fringes of show business and take his place at the top. There are a lot of people like this. Wouk's concept of Airman was a valid one. Those who succeed in this business are not necessarily those with the most talent, but those with the most stamina and the most luck."

With Natalie Wood

With Doris Day, Gig Young and
Elisabeth Fraser

THE TUNNEL OF LOVE

CREDITS:

An MGM Production 1958. Produced by Joseph Fields and Martin Melcher. Directed by Gene Kelly. Screenplay by Joseph Fields, based on the play by Fields and Peter De Vries, and the novel by De Vries. Photographed in CinemaScope by Robert Bronner. Art direction by William A. Horning and Randall Duell. Edited by John McSweeney, Jr. Music: title song by Patty Fisher and Bob Roberts, and "Runaway, Skidaddle, Skidoo" by Ruth Roberts and Bill Katz, both sung by Doris Day. Running time: 98 minutes.

CAST:

Isolde Poole: Doris Day; *Augie Poole:* Richard Widmark; *Dick Pepper:* Gig Young; *Estelle Novick:* Gia Scala; *Alice Pepper:* Elisabeth Fraser; *Miss MacCracken:* Elizabeth Wilson; *Actress:* Vikki Dougan; *Escort:* Doodles Weaver; *Day Motel Man:* Charles Wagenheim; *Night Motel Man:* Robert Williams; *Themselves:* Esquire Trio.

The Tunnel of Love was Gene Kelly's final movie in his contract with MGM. He was asked to direct the picture as part of the settlement which allowed him to close that contract prior to its original stipulations. Kelly readily accepted, he was looking for projects in order to solidify his reputation as a director and make known to the industry that this was the turn he wanted his career to take. The job was a pleasant one and Kelly claims the picture was shot fairly quickly and without problems, which no doubt accounts for the flowing good-natured mood of this glib sex comedy.

The film is almost a literal treatment of the play *The Tunnel of Love*, which opened on Broadway in February of 1957 and ran for more than a year. Joseph Fields directed the play, which he had written with Peter De Vries, and for the Hollywood version he both produced and wrote the screenplay. None of the leads in the Broadway original were called for the picture—the parts played by Tom Ewell, Nancy Olson and Darren McGavin went to Richard Widmark, Doris Day and Gig Young.

The Tunnel of Love was considered rather naughty in the late fifties, with its many titilating allusions to sex and risqué suggestions. Viewed in the light of later standards of permissiveness it seems almost quaint. It is largely a one-joke vehicle, the joke being the efforts of a childless young couple to acquire a child, either by natural methods or by adoption. The couple are Isolde and Augie Poole (Doris Day and Richard Wid-

mark) who finally apply to an agency for a child after giving up hope of having one of their own, but only after much, apparent effort that has left Augie gaunt and nervous and his wife hale and hearty. He is reduced almost to begging for mercy, and he is constantly needled by his neighbor, Dick Pepper (Gig Young), whose wife Alice (Elisabeth Fraser) is seemingly ever-pregnant. A representative of the adoption agency, Estelle Novick (Gia Scala) calls at their home, a recently converted farmhouse, at a time when the distraught Augie is walking around in his underwear worrying about mice. This does not give Estelle the impression he will make a fit father, and the situation is worsened by the appearance of Dick, who assumes the lady is a solicitor for a charity fund.

The main humor of *The Tunnel of Love* arises from Augie's efforts to win the approval of Estelle. He finds that away from her job she is

Doris Day and Richard Widmark

Richard Widmark, Gia Scala and Gig Young

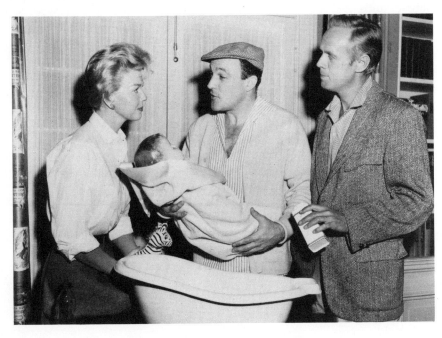

With Doris Day and Richard Widmark

193

With Gia Scala and Gig Young

quite cordial, and he plies her, and himself, with alcohol. But Augie is also on tranquilizers to calm his frazzled nerves, and the mixture of pills and drinks is too much for him. He awakens one morning in a motel room, alone, and not capable of remembering anything about his date with Estelle. Some time later she visits him to borrow a thousand dollars, explaining that she is pregnant. Estelle also tells him she will be able to arrange a child for him. Fearing the worst, Augie grows a moustache so that Isolde won't spot what he assumes will be a resemblance to the forthcoming child, which, to make matters more delicate, arrives nine months after Augie's date with Estelle. When the child arrives, a boy, he does indeed bear a resemblance to Augie, and Isolde threatens divorce. However, Estelle soon arrives to pay back the money she borrowed from Augie, and to show him a photograph of her newly born daughter and of her proud husband. Augie's great relief is then bolstered by Isolde's joyous news—she is pregnant.

The Tunnel of Love hovers on the brink of bad taste but the playing of the principals keeps it from falling. Most critics took a dim view of the film, claiming it to be falsely smutty, although *Variety* viewed it as being "without a snickering leer." Doris Day was here presented at her cheery, wholesome best and Gig Young played his flip, tippling gentleman in the style on which he must hold a patent. The casting of Richard Widmark did not seem to meet general favor with the public. Gene Kelly explains: "This is no criticism of Widmark, who is one of the finest film actors we have and who actually started his stage career playing light comedic parts. It's simply that the public fixes an impression of an actor, they accept him in a certain guise and they don't like him to stray too far from it. Widmark had established himself in serious material and they weren't prepared to accept him in this light, sexy part. The public creates type-casting, not the actors—unfortunately."

194

A dancing lesson for Doris Day as Richard Widmark looks on

Another dancing lesson for Doris Day and Elizabeth Fraser

INHERIT THE WIND

CREDITS:

A Stanley Kramer Production, released by United Artists 1960. Produced and directed by Stanley Kramer. Screenplay by Nathan E. Douglas and Harold Jacob Smith based on the play by Jerome Lawrence and Robert E. Lee. Photographed by Ernest Laszlo. Art direction by Rudolph Sternad. Edited by Frederic Knudtson. Musical score by Ernest Gold. Running time: 126 minutes.

CAST:

Henry Drummond: Spencer Tracy; *Matthew Harrison Brady:* Fredric March; *E. K. Hornbeck:* Gene Kelly; *Mrs. Brady:* Florence Eldridge; *Bertram T. Cates:* Dick York; *Rachel Brown:* Donna Anderson; *Judge:* Harry Morgan; *Davenport:* Elliott Reid; *Mayor:* Philip Coolidge; *Reverend Brown:* Claude Akins; *Meeker:* Paul Hartman; *Howard:* Jimmy Boyd; *Stebbins:* Noah Beery, Jr.; *Sillers:* Gordon Polk; *Dunlap:* Ray Teal; *Radio Announcer:* Norman Fell; *Mrs. Krebs:* Hope Summers; *Mrs. Stebbins:* Renee Godfrey.

Gene Kelly was vacationing in Greece when he received a telegram from Stanley Kramer offering him the role of the newspaperman in *Inherit the Wind*. Kelly was not immediately interested, being more concerned with finding film properties for production, but when he learned that Kramer had engaged Spencer Tracy and Fredric March to play the leads he changed his mind. "An actor need be dumb to turn down the opportunity to watch those two at work. I had known Spence through all the years at MGM and we often talked of doing something together, and I felt the same way

With Donna Anderson and Dick York

With Dick York and Spencer Tracy

about Freddie—veneration. It was a great experience just to be in the picture."

Inherit the Wind, both the stage play of 1955 and this slightly altered screen version, is based on the celebrated "monkey trial" which took place in Dayton, Tennessee in the summer of 1925. The trial was brought on by a biology teacher named John T. Scopes, in discussing Darwin's theory of evolution in a public school, contrary to the statutes of Tennessee. The film makes it appear that he was brought to trial as the result of bigoted public outrage, whereas in fact Scopes volunteered himself for trial in order to make a test case of the Tennessee statutes. The actual trial was conducted in an almost carnival atmosphere and was used for publicity purposes by its principals. The flamboyant Clarence Darrow, *the* lawyer of his day, volunteered, as did others, to defend Scopes, and the even more flamboyant politician William Jennings Bryan declared himself the apostle of

fundamentalist religion—truly a by-the-book man on every issue—and proceeded to speak for Tennessee. In addition, much of the controversy was artfully fanned and reported by journalist H. L. Mencken. For the film Darrow became Henry Drummond (Tracy), Bryan became Matthew Harrison Brady (March) and Mencken became E. K. Hornbeck (Kelly). The issues are idealized and the character of the two main figures somewhat softened, although the newspaperman remains a cynic.

As produced and directed by Stanley Kramer the film generates great sympathy for the teacher on trial, Bertram T. Cates (Dick York), in the face of spiteful prejudice from most of the townspeople, and most of its action takes place in the courtroom in a battle of wits and oratory between Drummond and Brady. The two men have long known each other, respecting their differences, and they seem to enjoy this epic platform. But as the trial drags on the feeling becomes more bitter

198

With Dick York and Spencer Tracy

With Donna Anderson, Dick York and Spencer Tracy

and less ethical, with the stoic Hornbeck quipping on the sidelines. Drummond becomes uncomfortable as he sees Brady bringing in thick-headed fundamentalist witnesses and refusing to accept Drummond's own presentations by scientists. Drummond is forced to make Brady appear ridiculous, laying open his narrow theories and

Fredric March

202

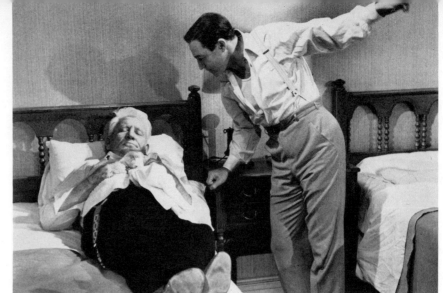

With Spencer Tracy

his apparent belief that his own interpretation of the bible is irrefutable. Cates is ultimately found guilty, but the evidence is such that the fair-minded judge levies only a token fine. Fearing that he has in fact been defeated, Brady launches into a frantic, babbling oration on his views, and as the people turn away his anger brings on a fatal heart attack. Hornbeck makes a flip, derogatory comment and finds himself blasted by Drummond for his cheap humor, his lack of compassion and his failure to grant that Brady had the right to his opinion.

The film is a credit to Stanley Kramer, a filmmaker with a penchant for tackling weighty, social themes. This has brought him adverse comment from the more captious critics but *Inherit the Wind* needs no defending. It is intellectually and emotionally stimulating in its dramatic discourse on the conflict of ancient and new interpretations of religious theory, and in the magnificent performances of Spencer Tracy and Fredric March it is a showcase for the art of acting. Some critics hastened to comment that Gene Kelly was miscast, but without explaining why. His Hornbeck is, in fact, precisely what the script calls for—a superficially amusing, hardhearted and somewhat lost soul.

Kelly's appearance in the film was due entirely to producer-director Stanley Kramer, who cast the picture with precisely the actors he wanted: "I've always thought Gene Kelly was a wonderfully sensitive actor. He had a sharply satirical quality in *Pal Joey* on the stage and he seemed a natural choice for a character based on Mencken in *Inherit the Wind.*"

203

With Marilyn Monroe and Yves Montand

LET'S MAKE LOVE

CREDITS:

A 20th Century-Fox Production 1960. Produced by Jerry Wald. Directed by George Cukor. Screenplay by Norman Krasna, with additional material by Hal Kantor. Photographed in CinemaScope and De Luxe Color by Daniel L. Fapp. Art direction by Lyle R. Wheeler and Gene Allen. Edited by David Bretherton. Musical direction by Lionel Newman. Songs by Sammy Cahn (lyrics) and Jimmy Van Heusen (music). Choreography by Jack Cole. Running time: 118 minutes.

CAST:

Amanda Dell: Marilyn Monroe; *Jean-Marc Clement:* Yves Montand; *Howard Coffman:* Tony Randall; *Tony Danton:* Frankie Vaughan; *John*

Wales: Wilfred Hyde White; *Oliver Burton:* David Burns; *Dave Kerry:* Michael David; *Lily Nyles:* Mara Lynn; *Abe Miller:* Dennis King, Jr.; *Lamont:* Joe Besser; *Miss Manders:* Madge Kennedy.

GUEST STARS: Milton Berle, Bing Crosby and Gene Kelly.

As originally conceived, *Let's Make Love* was to have been a satire on Howard Hughes, with the title *The Billionaire* and Gregory Peck in the leading role. After much deliberation with the legal department at 20th Century-Fox, the producer, the late Jerry Wald, and scenarist Norman Krasna decided to soften the attack by making the subject an international playboy-tycoon and to give the picture a title more in keeping with the charms of its very female star, Marilyn Monroe.

204

With Yves Montand

With Yves Montand

Yves Montand was chosen to play the part of Jean-Marc Clement, a New York-based French businessman of enormous wealth and power.

Let's Make Love assumes that a man like Jean-Marc Clement would take legal action if he learned a theatrical company was in the process of satirizing him—a fair assumption in view of the Fox lawyers' qualms about the original script. First, he decides to take a look at the show in rehearsal. He and his public relations officer, Howard Coffman (Tony Randall), sneak into the theatre to watch the actors. Clement's wrath melts once he sets eyes on the star of the show, Amanda Dell (Marilyn Monroe), a voluptuous, husky-voiced blonde who sings "My Heart Belongs to Daddy" as if she were a cross between Mae West and Shirley Temple. So smitten is Clement with Amanda that he allows himself to be mistaken for an unemployed actor and accepts an offer to be in the show. He orders his attorney, John Wales (Wilfred Hyde White), to purchase fifty-one percent of the show, and he hires the likes of Bing Crosby, Gene Kelly and Milton Berle for a crash course in singing, dancing and comedy. Amanda expresses contempt for the real Clement while growing

With Montand and Wilfred Hyde White

fonder of the man she believes to be an actor. Eventually he confesses his ruse and manages to persuade her he is not the ogre she thought him to be.

The film is uneven and not entirely credible but it does have many amusing moments, particularly those in which Crosby, Kelly and Berle labor to turn Clement into an entertainer. The sexy Marilyn appears to stunning advantage, especially in her Lolita-like opening "Daddy" number, and the talented Montand manages to play down his own ability as a song and dance man in portraying the superwealthy tycoon. Gene Kelly spent exactly one day doing his bit in the picture: "I'd long before promised Jerry Wald I'd do it but by the time they got around to shooting it I was in Paris lining up *Gigot*. He telephoned me, so I got on a plane and flew over the Pole to Los Angeles. Jerry met me in the evening at the airport; we filmed the next day and then he returned me to the airport. Would that all my jobs had been so well arranged!"

During a break with Marilyn Monroe and Yves Montand

206

With Jackie Gleason

GIGOT

CREDITS:

A Seven Arts Production, released by 20th Century-Fox 1962. Produced by Kenneth Hyman. Directed by Gene Kelly. Screenplay by John Patrick, based on a story by Jackie Gleason. Photographed in De Luxe Color by Jean Bourgoin. Art direction by Auguste Capelier. Edited by Roger Dwyre. Musical score by Jackie Gleason, arranged and conducted by Michel Magne. Running time: 104 minutes.

CAST:

Gigot: Jackie Gleason; *Colette:* Katherine Kath; *Madame Brigitte:* Gabrielle Dorziat; *Gaston:* Jean Lefebvre; *Jean:* Jacques Marin; *Alphonse:* Albert Remy; *Lucille Duval:* Yvonne Constant; *Madame Greuze:* Germaine Delbat; *Bistro Proprietor:* Albert Dinan; *Nicole:* Diane Gardner.

Films sometimes fail for reasons other than inferior workmanship and poor material. Often, with the best talent and the best of intentions, the picture doesn't jell—and *Gigot* is a sad case in point. Its star, Jackie Gleason, can be described as gifted rather than merely talented, and the work of director Gene Kelly and scriptwriter John Patrick need no defending. The color filming in Paris is delightful and the acting of a large selection of veteran French character actors is faultless. Despite all this the film was a flop, it drew few customers, and most of those who saw it didn't like it.

Gigot is entirely the creation of Jackie Gleason, his invented character, his performance, his musical scoring. The film grew, in reverse of the usual procedure, from Gleason's musical sketches of the character he had in mind. Gleason, an avid composer and conductor, hit upon the idea while engaged in one of his hobbies—sitting at the elec-

Jackie Gleason

tric organ at his home in Peekskill, New York, and improvising. *Gigot* is also an enlargement on a character often played by Gleason on television, his Poor Soul, a gentle oaf at odds with the world. He roughed out his plot and then hired playwright John Patrick, author of *The Hasty Heart* and *The Teahouse of the August Moon*, to expand it into a screenplay. With this in hand Gleason approached, because of his rapport with the French, Kelly to direct, and the two of them were able to persuade Seven Arts to back the project.

The film is more a character study than a story. Gigot (Gleason) is a mute and a simpleton, but a very warmhearted and genial soul who befriends children and animals, and receives little more than amused tolerance from local adults. He is employed as a janitor in a cheap boarding-house in Montmartre and lives in a dingy little room in the basement. Ever lonely, he ambles around the neighborhood longing to be accepted but the closest he comes to contact with people is when they take advantage of him and make him the butt of jokes. Gigot attends every funeral he can because in being a mourner he feels he can, for a little while, belong to a group of people. One evening he comes across a dejected prostitute, Colette (Katherine Kath), and her small daughter Nicole (Diane Gardner) and befriends them, taking them to his hovel to share his roof. He grows fond of

the child, to the annoyance of the mother, who threatens to leave unless he can give her some money, which he then steals from a local baker.

Colette returns home one morning after a night with a client and finds Gigot and Nicole missing. She assumes he has kidnaped the child and alarms the neighborhood to that belief. Actually he is amusing the child in a cellar of the boarding-house, playing records and dancing for her. But the ceiling collapses on them and Nicole is injured. Gigot, full of anguish, carries the child to a church, where the priest summons a doctor. On the way back to his home to get the phonograph for Nicole, Gigot is spotted by the locals and they give chase. He escapes them but in doing so he falls into the Seine. They see his hat floating in the river and assume that he has drowned. Now filled with sorrow at the passing of the big mute, they hold a funeral service for him—and from a distance an appreciative Gigot watches with tears in his eyes.

The critical consensus was that *Gigot* was admirable in concept and a disaster in construction, and many seemed eager to point out that Gleason had aped Charlie Chaplin's silent little tramp and fallen short of the mark. Gleason, whose gift for mimicry is close to genius, was bitterly disappointed with the attitude of Seven Arts and 20th Century-Fox, who disliked the original finished version of the film and took it upon themselves to edit and change it. Says Gene Kelly: "This was

With Jackie Gleason

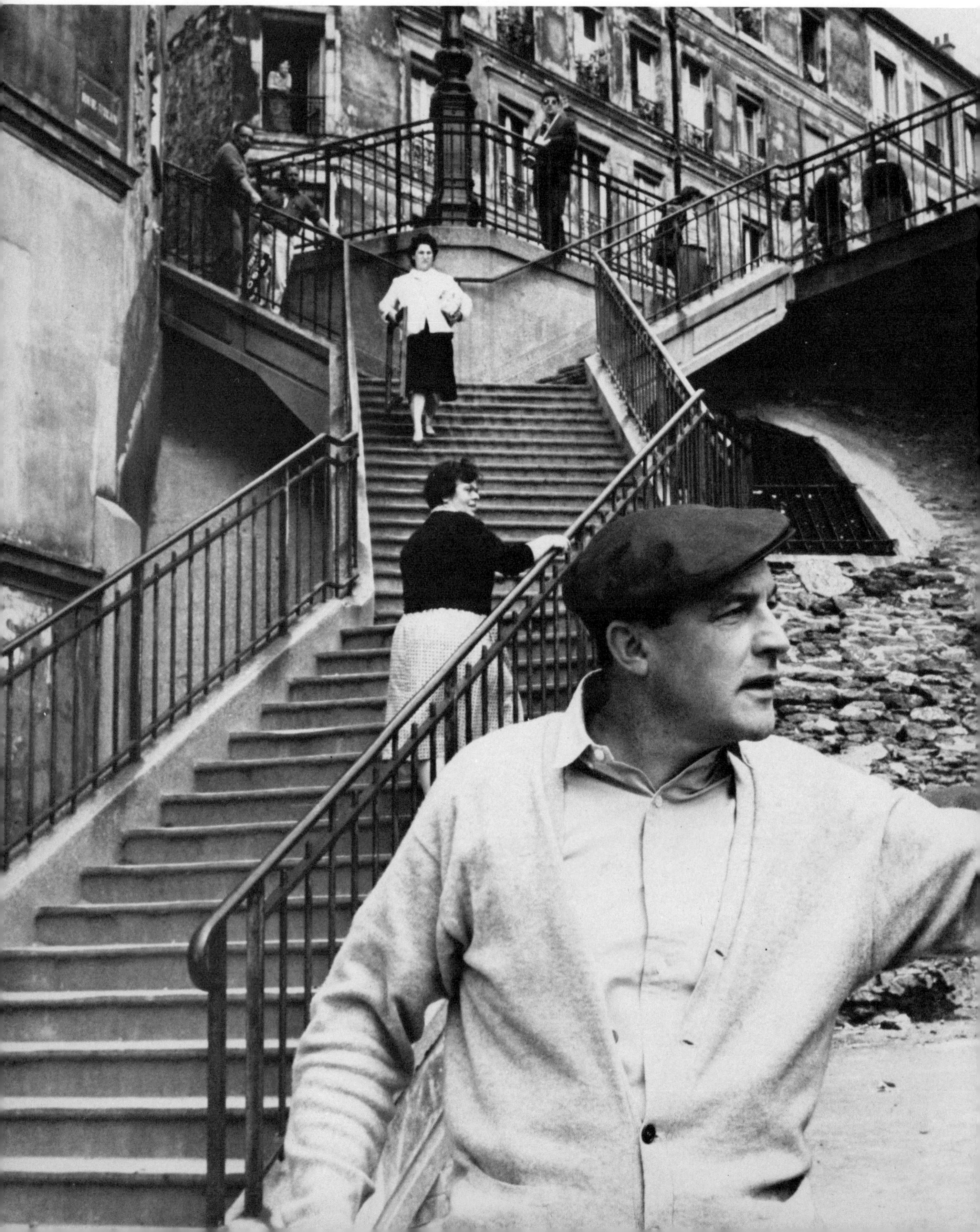

With Diane Gardner

211

During a break with Jackie
Gleason and Diane Gardner

With Jackie Gleason and visitor Brigitte Bardot

my unhappiest experience in the picture business. Our whole idea in making *Gigot* was to accent life in a community, to show its flavor, with the mute as the centrifugal figure. We showed the film to the armed services at camps in Europe and received enthusiastic response. When next I saw the film in New York it had been so drastically cut and reedited that it had little to do with my version. I was never consulted, and I never found out who was responsible for cutting it. Cutting out the material about the other characters caused the picture to look like a continual pantomime, with Gleason following himself in a series of sketches. He was brokenhearted about it. We thought we had a minor classic—but not as it stands."

Showing Jacques Marin how to help the drunken Gigot from the bar

WHAT A WAY TO GO

CREDITS:

A J. Lee Thompson Production, released by 20th Century-Fox 1964. Produced by Arthur P. Jacobs. Directed by J. Lee Thompson. Screenplay by Betty Comden and Adolph Green, based on a story by Gwen Davis. Photographed in CinemaScope and De Luxe Color by Leom Shamroy. Art direction by Jack Martin Smith and Ted Haworth. Edited by Marjorie Fowler. Musical score by Nelson Riddle. Running time: 111 minutes.

CAST:

Louisa: Shirley MacLaine; *Larry Flint:* Paul Newman; *Rod Anderson:* Robert Mitchum; *Leonard Crawley:* Dean Martin; *Jerry Benson:* Gene Kelly; *Dr. Stephenson:* Bob Cummings; *Edgar Hopper:* Dick Van Dyke; *Painter:* Reginald Gardiner: *Mrs.* *Foster:* Margaret Dumont; *Trentino:* Lou Nova; *Baroness:* Fifi D'Orsay; *Rene:* Maurice Marsac; *Agent:* Wally Vernon; *Polly:* Jane Wald; *Hollywood lawyer:* Lenny Kent.

What a Way to Go is a textbook example of all that was wrong with Hollywood in the mid-1960s. Supposedly a satire on the evils of affluence and abundance, the film was sunk by its own excesses, one of them being the assumption that humor can be drawn from death, if a man dies in a funny situation. Some of the studios at this time were misled by the public's apparent appetite for movies, thinking that the great slump of the fifties was over. Such was not quite the case. The public, saturated with mediocre entertainment on television, were eager for films on the particular rather than the general level. 20th Cen-

tury-Fox make the mistake of imagining that *The Sound of Music* heralded the revival of the movie musical, and in a strange moment of antiquated reasoning that same studio assumed that the surest way to make a comedy hilarious would be to spend five million dollars on it. *What a Way to Go* proved anything but.

The film is a group of stories with a single theme —a woman with the Midas touch, who makes a millionaire of every man she marries, but finds that great wealth leads each one to his death. Louisa Benson (Shirley MacLaine) tries to hand over her vast fortune to the Internal Revenue Service, to be free of the curse of money, but the government considers her mad and declines the offer. The distraught woman tells her sad tale to an incredulous psychiatrist, Dr. Stephenson (Robert Cummings).

The daughter of a money-hungry mother, Louisa spurns a rich suitor, Leonard Crawley (Dean Martin) and marries instead a humble storekeeper, Edgar Hopper (Dick Van Dyke). Their simple lifestyle is ridiculed by Crawley, and Hopper is taunted into making something of himself. He becomes a successful merchant and works and works until he drops dead—leaving a fortune. Louisa goes to Paris to forget but meets and marries a struggling American painter, Larry Flint (Paul Newman), who has invented a machine to paint pictures, its arms being driven by soundwaves. Louisa has the idea of feeding classical music into the machine, which results in masterpieces in profusion. This brings wealth—and death to Larry, when he gets caught up in the arms of the machine, leaving an even richer widow.

Louisa next marries a wealthy industrialist, Rod Anderson (Robert Mitchum), thinking that an already rich man will have nothing to fear from her. They both decide to get away from it all by living a simple life running a little farm in the country, but Rod's neglect of his empire ironically causes it to expand and the poor man is killed when, out of sheer ignorance, he tries to milk a bull.

Newly widowed, Louisa happens to visit a dingy nightclub as the entertainer is doing his act. This is Jerry Benson (Gene Kelly), known to friends as Pinky because of his fixation on the color pink, who does a clown act and does it so badly the customers ignore him. But he is a happy, carefree soul with no ambition—until he falls in love with Louisa and marries her. One evening, with not enough time to get into his costume and his grotesque makeup, Pinky goes on the floor and does his act as a straight ballad, to the approval

With Shirley MacLaine

With Shirley MacLaine

215

of the audience. His career blossoms and he goes
from success to success until he becomes a Hollywood star, the kind who does lavish song-and-
dance numbers in splendid settings. He does one
of them with his wife, a nautical musical with
squads of singers and dancers cavorting over the
vast deck of a battleship. Pinky is a smash with the
public and everything in his life is pink—his home,
his wife's clothes and his car—even the coffin he
needs after his adoring fans have trampled him to

With Shirley MacLaine

With Shirley MacLaine

217

death. As Louisa finishes telling her story to Dr. Stephenson he receives a call from the Internal Revenue Service advising him her story is genuine and that they will accept her wealth—news which causes him to faint. The janitor enters the scene, and turns out to be Leonard Crawley, now devoid of funds due to business failures. He and Louisa marry, and live in happy poverty.

The four husband-stories are partly told in the style of various past movie periods—silent, European, Hollywood plush, etc.—but in ribbing old failings the producers of this picture are blind to their own. Allocating, as here, half a million dollars for costumes impresses few other than those who work on the production, and the device of using stars in cameo roles had lost its novelty long before this film was conceived. A movie skit within this movie is labeled a "Lush Budget Production," but the joke hardly comes across under the egregious circumstances.

The best-realized material in *What a Way to Go* is Gene Kelly's knowing lampoon of his own kind of image. The character and the devices are suggestive of *Singin' in the Rain*, which is not surprising, seeing that the scenarists are Comden and Green. The music for the "Musical Extravaganza" was written by Jule Styne, a veteran composer for the American musical, and Kelly devised the choreography. This splendidly dreadful number was an affectionate dig at Busby Berkeley but it is also reminiscent of what another dancer did in *Follow the Fleet*.

With Françoise Dorlèac

THE YOUNG GIRLS OF ROCHEFORT

CREDITS:

A Co-Production of Parc Films, Madeleine Films and Seven Arts, released in the United States by Warner Bros. 1968. Produced by Mag Bodard. Direction, screenplay and lyrics by Jacques Demy. Music composed and conducted by Michel Legrand. Choreography by Norman Maen. Photographed in Franscope and Technicolor by Ghislain Cloquet. Art direction by Bernard Evein. Edited by Jean Hamon. Running time, 126 minutes.

CAST:

Delphine Garnier: Catherine Deneuve; *Solange Garnier:* Françoise Dorléac; *Étienne:* George Chakiris; *Bill:* Grover Dale; *Andy Miller:* Gene Kelly; *Yvonne:* Danielle Darrieux; *Maxence:* Jacques

Perrin; *Simon Dame:* Michel Piccoli; *Judith:* Pamela Hart; *Esther:* Leslie North; *Guillaume Lancien:* Jacques Riberolles; *Dutrouz:* Henri Crémieux; *Boubou:* Patrick Jeantet; *Josette:* Geneviève Thénier.

Although it is obviously Gallic in tone and character, *The Young Girls of Rochefort* is a sincere homage to the Hollywood musical, even to the extent of having Gene Kelly as one of its central figures. Unfortunately the presence of Kelly tends to accentuate the fact that the film fails to emulate the genre it tries to respect. It is pleasing to look at, but it is soft and formless. Writer-director Jacques Demy, a film maker who apparently looks at the world through a rose-colored range-finder, spread his thin story over two hours of screen time and made the mistake of hiring a choreographer, Norman Maen, with very little film experience. The dancing has vitality but it fails to take advantage of the space available in Rochefort, particularly in the huge Colbert Square. The dancers cluster in front of the camera, as they would on a stage, rather than besport themselves through the town. The dancing done in the film by Kelly was devised and staged by himself.

Another deficiency in *The Young Girls of Rochefort* is the music of Michel Legrand, a lengthy score containing more than a dozen songs and five pieces for dancing. Legrand had provided a tuneful score for Demy's charming *The Umbrellas of Cherbourg*, but *Rochefort* failed to fire the prolific composer-arranger. The music, as always with Legrand, has considerable style but in this instance a dulling sameness. The film badly needed a few hit songs, if only to promote it, but there were none. The story called for a flashy, modern piano concerto and Legrand, a gifted pianist, provided a piece that works well within the confines of the picture but not distinctive enough to have a life of its own. Sadly, it is this lack of impressive music that will cause the film to fade into limbo.

As he had in Cherbourg, Demy changed the

With Catherine Deneuve

With Catherine Deneuve

220

With Françoise Dorlèac

face of the town for the better. Once he decided on Rochefort as his location, having considered many other towns, Demy persuaded the town council to let him paint many of the houses and stores in pastel colors. Rochefort, a town of thirty thousand population on the southwest coast of France, is noted mainly as a fishing port and a market for wine and oysters and not as a particular point of interest for tourists. But after Demy's gilding, the town took on a new attractiveness.

The young girls of the title are the Garnier twins, Solange (Françoise Dorléac) and Delphine (Catherine Deneuve). Both are highly romantic in their attitudes toward life and both are musical —Solange teaches various musical instruments and Delphine teaches dancing. Their unmarried mother, Yvonne (Danielle Darrieux) runs a little cafe and dreams of her long-lost lover, Simon Dame (Michel Piccoli), who, unknown to her, operates a music shop in Rochefort. A theatrical company, headed by Étienne (George Chakiris) and Bill (Grover Dale) arrive in the town and set up a fair in Colbert Square. When two of their girl dancers quit, the boys look around for replacements and soon discover Solange and Delphine.

The twins immediately become the stars of the

show, although they decline the friendship of their employers and continue to dream about their ideal men. Such men soon turn up—a handsome young sailor named Maxence (Jacques Perrin), an artist when not in national service and who has painted a portrait of his dream girl, who, by a great coincidence resembles Delphine. The other man is an American concert pianist, Andy Miller (Gene Kelly), who has discovered the score of a piano concerto, which, by another coincidence, happens to be the lost property of composer Solange. The lives of all these people intertwine for a few days, producing a few complications and much singing and dancing. Eventually the entertainers leave the town and the two girls find the romance they wished for in the arms of the sailor and the pianist. Their mother also reunites with Monsieur Dame. Demy pads the flimsy plotline with a few characterizations of townspeople, including a rather unnecessary one of a sadistic killer who carves up women who reject him, but the charm and the wit are strained in this long session in a far-from-fascinating little town.

For Gene Kelly *The Young Girls of Rochefort* is a keenly felt disappointment, particularly so in that Demy clearly meant the enterprise as a tribute to the kind of film Kelly had once made. Demy asked Kelly to be in the film, and in agreeing to take the part Demy was therefore able to raise American financing. Kelly's role in this large soufflé is that of a brash but likable American, an older version of the one in Paris sixteen years previously, and he carried it off with ease. Says Kelly: "It was a good idea, a nice, lyrical concept but it missed. I think Demy made a major mistake in casting Catherine Deneuve and Françoise Dorléac. The parts needed girls of exceptional dancing and singing ability but neither Catherine or Françoise could sing and they had no dancing experience. Almost everyone in the picture had to be dubbed—Daniele Darrieux was about the only one of the leads whose singing voice could be used—and this puts a great strain on a musical. And they all made the mistake of assuming that it's easy to learn to dance for a film, because it looks so easy. It isn't."

With Françoise Dorlèac

222

With Françoise Dorlèac

Directions for Walter Matthau and Inger Stevens

A GUIDE FOR THE MARRIED MAN

CREDITS:

A 20th Century-Fox Production 1967. Produced by Frank McCarthy. Directed by Gene Kelly. Screenplay by Frank Tarloff, based on his book. Photographed in Panavision and De Luxe Color by Joe MacDonald. Art direction by Jack Martin Smith and William Glasgow. Edited by Dorothy Spencer. Musical score by Johnny Williams. Running time: 89 minutes.

CAST:

Paul Manning: Walter Matthau; *Ed Stander:* Robert Morse; *Ruth Manning:* Inger Stevens; *Irma Johnson:* Sue Ane Langdon; *Harriet Stander:* Claire Kelly; *Miss Stardust:* Linda Harrison; *Jocelyn Montgomery:* Elaine Devry.

GUEST STARS: Lucille Ball, Jack Benny, Polly Bergen, Joey Bishop, Ben Blue, Sid Caesar, Art Carney, Wally Cox, Marty Ingels, Ann Morgan Guilbert, Jeffrey Hunter, Sam Jaffe, Jayne Mansfield, Hal March, Louis Nye, Carl Reiner, Phil Silvers and Terry-Thomas.

Sex is not easy to spoof, particularly those areas of it dealing with infidelity, but Gene Kelly came close to perfection with *A Guide for the Married Man*, a film that might have sunk in a mire of tastelessness in less cunning hands. The charm of the film is that it leers without being lewd, it ogles pretty girls in genuine appreciation and while it seemingly sets out as a statement of man's triumph over woman it ends up as anything but. The joke of Kelly's *Guide* is on men, not women.

A Guide for the Married Man is a Hollywood factory product on an expert level. It shines with professional skills, beginning with animated credit titles which touch on the history of the battle of the sexes. Several panels reveal famous quotations, the most apposite being Oscar Wilde's wicked observation: "The one charm of marriage is that it makes a life of deception absolutely necessary for both parties." The color photography of the late Joe MacDonald moves through dozens of attractive locations in Beverly Hills and Los Angeles, catching glimpses of a great variety of young ladies, and the film is paced by Kelly at a brisk clip. The directorial style is suggestive of his musicals, and *Guide* emerges rather like *On the Town* minus the singing and the dancing. The visual aspect of the film is complicated but thanks to the editing of Dorothy Spencer it is also smooth, and backed all the way by the richly comedic score of Johnny Williams.

The film is almost without plot. It deals mainly with the advice of one man to another, and his points are illustrated, both positively and negatively, by a stream of enacted situations featuring famous Hollywood faces. A genial, faithful and happily married man, Paul Manning (Walter Matthau) wonders what it would be like to have an affair with another woman, despite the fact that his wife Ruth (Inger Stevens) is pretty, devoted and perpetually pleasant. No sooner does he start to wonder than his libidinous friend and neighbor, Ed Stander (Robert Morse) begins to proffer advice. Ed considers himself a master of extramarital liaisons, an expert in the art of manipulating women, and he theorizes that a man makes a better husband if he maintains a healthy interest in other women, provided his wife doesn't know about it.

Goaded and encouraged by Ed, Paul decides to take his first fling at adultery. He settles for a handsome, wealthy and willing divorcee named Jocelyn Montgomery (Elaine Devry) and proceeds to rendezvous with her in a remote motel. Once alone with the statuesque Jocelyn, who wastes no time in stripping down to her underwear, Paul loses his nerve and immediately confesses he is a married man. "Congratulations" says the cool lady, intent on the tryst. Paul's predicament is interrupted by a commotion in another part of the hotel. Looking out of a window he sees a room being broken into by Mrs. Ed Stander and her witnesses. Inside the room Ed and his date peer from the bedcovers in horrified embarrassment.

A lesson in seductive walking for Sue Ann Langdon

With photographer Joe MacDonald

225

Instructions for a Go-Go dancer

With Jack Benny

Seeing his tutor so ignominiously defeated Paul, frantically nervous, dashes for his rented car, dragging the half-clad Jocelyn behind him and drives away. He dumps Jocelyn at the car rental lot, climbs into his own convertible and speeds home. As Paul rushes into the arms of his wife, a celestial chorus sings "There's No Place Like Home."

The performance of Walter Matthau is the solid platform on which the humor of the film rests. As a plain, ordinary, decent Everyman Matthau is fully understandable in his anguish. His Paul is a home-loving man only mildly discontented with his lot, and pushed into philandering only after much persuasion. His amiable playing is a good foil for perky Robert Morse as the impish astray-leader, and the late Inger Stevens is so lovely, so kind and so accommodating as the wife that the audience has cause to wonder why the husband would stray. A partial answer to that puzzle is given in one of the picture's many one-line gags. Marty Ingels is seen eating a steak; he holds up a piece and says, "This is the best steak money can buy. But every now and then I feel like fish."

Gene Kelly's direction of *A Guide for the Married Man* is commendable for several reasons, not the least being his decision to pack the proceedings into a brief hour-and-a-half of running time. Within that period a large number of guest stars pop up to illuminate the points given by the *Guide*. Many of them are so brief they are hardly worth the effort of employing a famous name but a few of the stars appear to advantage in vignettes that make good use of their talents. Perhaps the best is Art Carney, as a lusty construction worker who picks on the cooking of wife Lucille Ball in order to provoke her into saying, "If you don't like the food here, go somewhere else." He goes elsewhere, has an enjoyable evening with a girlfriend, and comes home the next day to apologize for his ingratitude.

Jack Benny appears in his familiar guise as a tightwad, pleading financial disaster and suggesting to his mistress that they sell off various pieces of jewelry and clothing to bring in funds. The mistress replies that perhaps they shouldn't see each other for a while, and Jack painfully agrees —while cocking an eye out the window to a new girlfriend sitting in his car. Terry-Thomas illustrates the mistake of entertaining girlfriend Jayne Mansfield in his own home; he is reduced to a nervous wreck by not being able to find her

Directions for Walter Matthau and Inger Stevens

During a break with Walter Matthau

brassiere. Joey Bishop demonstrates how to behave when discovered by the wife in bed with another woman—pretend, with total conviction, that there is no other woman present.

The film's most lavish sketch has Carl Reiner as a hammy Hollywood matinee idol, being so cautious in his amorous plotting that he and a starlet set out for a rendezvous in a snowbound Swiss chalet by going opposite ways around the world to get there—only to have his wife walk in on them, complete with cameramen. *A Guide for the Married Man* is, of course, no guide at all, and therein lies its fun.

The director on location, at a tea room owned by a namesake

HELLO DOLLY

CREDITS:

A Chenault Production, released by 20th Century-Fox 1969. Produced and written for the screen by Ernest Lehman. Directed by Gene Kelly, Associate Producer: Roger Edens. Dances and musical numbers staged by Michael Kidd. Based on the musical play by Michael Stewart and *The Matchmaker* by Thornton Wilder. Music and lyrics by Jerry Herman. Music direction by Lennie Hayton and Lionel Newman. Photographed in TODD-AO and De Luxe Color by Harry Stradling. Art direction by Jack Martin Smith and Herman Blumenthal. Edited by William Reynolds. Running time: 149 minutes.

CAST:

Dolly Levi: Barbra Streisand; *Horace Vandergelder:* Walter Matthau; *Cornelius Hackl:* Michael Crawford; *Orchestra Leader:* Louis Armstrong; *Irene Molloy:* Marianne McAndrew; *Minnie Fay:* E. J. Peaker; *Barnaby Tucker:* Danny Lockin; *Ermenarde:* Joyce Ames; *Ambrose Kemper:* Tommy Tune; *Gussie Granger:* Judy Knaiz; *Rudolph Reisenweber:* David Hurst; *Fritz:* Fritz Feld; *Vandergelder's Barber:* Richard Collier; *Policeman in Park:* J. Pat O'Malley.

Late in 1965, seduced by the flow of millions of dollars profit on *The Sound of Music*, 20th Century-Fox proceeded to set up plans for three expensive musicals. It was the greatest mistake so far made in the history of the film industry. Fox spent twenty million dollars on *Star*, with Julie Andrews playing Gertrude Lawrence, and nearly eighteen million on *Dr. Doolittle*, starring Rex

Harrison. Both were staggering flops and it is doubtful if they will ever realize even half their original costs. Fox compounded this folly by buying the screen rights to *Hello Dolly* for two million dollars and signing a contract with owner David Merrick to the effect that the completed film could not be shown until the original Broadway production closed, or June 20, 1971, whichever came first. The show had already run three years at the time of this agreement and no one at Fox imagined it would run on and on. The film was finished by late summer, 1968, and then sat on the shelf for more than a year with the studio paying interest on the film's financing at the rate of $100,000 per month. Fox threatened to release the film and Merrick countered with a legal suit. Merrick, with money pouring in from every direction, wanted to keep Broadway's *Dolly* running until it broke the record set by *My Fair Lady*. In desperation Fox offered to come to terms with him and in a settlement that allowed them to issue the film in December of 1969 the studio paid David Merrick a further one million dollars.

The final cost of the film is known only to the accountants and management of 20th Century-Fox but it is estimated to be between twenty and twenty-five million dollars. The choice of actress to play the lead was a point of considerable interest after Fox made known its purchase of the property. Choosing Barbra Streisand caused quite a commotion, mostly because at twenty-six she was obviously a different image from the requirements of the role as written—and played on stage by such celebrated middle-aged veterans as Mary Martin, Ginger Rogers and Betty Grable. Much of the point of the story lies in Dolly Gallagher Levi being a warmhearted "older" woman, and in the minds of the public the personification of that role was Carol Channing, who had played it for the better part of four years. However, Miss Channing's charm had never been successfully captured on film, the rather bizarre personality and the raspy voice that work so effectively on stage tends to be grotesque in the intimacy of the camera. Ironically, Barbra Streisand had shown little interest in the vehicle. After being signed for the film she told reporters she considered the musical play, "A piece of fluff. But when everybody was against me as Dolly I took up the challenge."

The story of Dolly Levi, invented by Thorton Wilder for his play *The Matchmaker,* was filmed under that title by Paramount in 1958 with Shirley Booth beautifully cast as the turn-of-the-century

On location in the Hudson Valley, New York. Kelly at left with megaphone

With Barbra Streisand

With Walter Matthau

With Walter Matthau and
Barbra Streisand

230

widow who can't resist playing Cupid. Her matchmaking becomes almost a profession, but in ostensibly trying to find a mate for a wealthy merchant named Horace Vandergelder she moves to nab him for her own. This was also the core of Michael Stewart's musical version, with lyrics and music by Jerry Herman, and in making this into a film, writer-producer Ernest Lehman made little alteration other than making Dolly a younger woman and physically opening up the play to allow for enormous photographic treatment. For the part of Vandergelder Fox selected the popular Walter Matthau, but this move backfired to a minor degree by the inability of Matthau and Streisand to work together amicably. Early in the production they began to quarrel, he calling her Miss Ptomaine and she calling him Old Sewer-Mouth, with director Kelly having to pacify both.

Gene Kelly: "It wasn't until we were well into the picture that I realized Barbra was uncomfortable. I asked her why and she admitted she was scared of the part, feeling, like most everybody else, that she was too young for Dolly. She said she thought Elizabeth Taylor would have been a better choice. I had to reassure her and explain that she had to find ways to make up for this change in concept, to look for other things in the part, and she did. But she was very insecure. I had some trepidation about working with her because she had a reputation for being difficult but I didn't find her so. I asked William Wyler and Vincente Minnelli if they had had any problems with her and they said they hadn't. I'd been told she had had some people fired but I couldn't find any proof of that either. She certainly is direct in her manner and her opinions but I prefer that."

Unfortunately, by the time the film was released the public's fascination with the subject of Dolly Levi and the popularity of the songs had diminished. *Hello Dolly* made no where near the

Rehearsing Barbra Streisand

The street parade, supposedly in New York but actually on the lot at Fox in Beverly Hills

impact the producers hoped for and it has yet to show signs of recouping its hefty costs. It may do this, in time. However, there is much to recommend the picture, certainly from a visual standpoint. Fox spent a further two million dollars turning the main street of its Beverly Hills studio into a New York thoroughfare in the 1890s, and for the mammoth street parade sequence in this setting they hired four thousand extras. According to Kelly it was like having a standing army at his disposal, at a cost of $200,000 per day, a frightening responsibility. The company was on location at Garrison, New York, a little town on the banks of the Hudson River and another half million dollars was spent beautifying the town.

It is a genial, handsome, old-fashioned musical dogged by bad luck in its timing and in the decision to spend so much money making it. Its director admits: "It's not the kind of film I would make as a first choice but what else is there? To make an original musical today you first have to find someone to put up a million dollars just to develop the idea, and that's too much of a risk. What happens now is that studios buy stage shows after they are already dated and then spend a lot of money turning them into dated movies. The musical is the victim of changing times. To make good musicals you need a team of performers, musicians, costume and set designers, choreographers, writers and arrangers, etc., etc. In short, what we used to have at MGM. Well, it's no longer possible. The economics of the business have killed all that. It's all too easy to ridicule Fox for spending all that money making *Dolly* but they took a brave stand—they had spent so much getting hold of the property that they wanted to turn it into a whale of a good show. It takes guts to make that kind of a decision, and as the director I was excited by the challenge of blowing it up into a big and exciting picture. I'm not sorry I did it."

234

With James Stewart

THE CHEYENNE SOCIAL CLUB

CREDITS:

A National General Production 1970. Produced and directed by Gene Kelly. Screenplay by James Lee Barrett. Photographed in Panavision and Technicolor by William Clother. Art direction by Gene Allen. Edited by Adrienne Fazan. Musical score by Walter Scharf. Running time: 103 minutes.

CAST:

John O'Hanlan: James Stewart; *Harley Sullivan:* Henry Fonda; *Jenny:* Shirley Jones; *Opal Ann:* Sue Ane Langdon; *Willouby:* Dabbs Greer; *Pauline:* Elaine Devry; *Barkeep:* Robert Middleton; *Marshall Anderson:* Arch Johnson; *Carrie Virginia:* Jackie Russell; *Annie Jo:* Jackie Joseph; *Sara Jean:* Sharon De Bord; *Nathan Potter:* Rich-ard Collier; *Charlie Bannister:* Charles Tyner; *Alice:* Jean Willes; *Corey Bannister:* Robert J. Wilke; *Pete Dodge:* Carl Reindel; *Dr. Foy:* J. Pat O'Malley; *Dr. Carter:* Jason Wingreen; *Clay Carrol:* John Dehner.

James Stewart brought the script of *The Cheyenne Social Club* to Gene Kelly and asked him if he would be interested in making the picture. Kelly took a liking to the script and said he would do it, provided Henry Fonda could be persuaded to co-star with Stewart. This condition was easily met, and a company was set up with Kelly as producer-director and scriptwriter James Lee Barrett as the executive producer. Barrett had written several of Stewart's previous films and he had acquired a reputation as a man with a particular talent for Western dialogue and characterizations.

With Henry Fonda and James Stewart

James Stewart and Henry Fonda

This is apparent from the very outset in *The Cheyenne Social Club*, as two grizzled old cowpokes, Harley Sullivan (Fonda) and John O'Hanlan (Stewart) slowly make their way across a vast landscape. The voice of Harley is heard droning on and on and on . . . about his family and his dogs and his doings. John, a long-suffering listener, finally gets a chance to speak. "You know where we are now, Harley?" "Not exactly." "We're in the Wyoming territory and you've been talkin' all the way from Texas." Harley looks wounded. "Just been keepin' you company." Replies John, "I ap-preciate it, Harley, but if you say another word the rest of the day I'm gonna kill you."

The two old cowboys are making their way to Cheyenne because John has received an inheritance from a deceased brother, although he doesn't exactly know what it is. It turns out to be a social club, but even with that news he is unaware of the true nature of his fortune—a plush bordello, staffed with half a dozen lovely girls, and the center of life in the town. The madam is Jenny (Shirley Jones), and she and the girls make their new boss welcome, with Harley accepted as a part-

Henry Fonda, James Stewart, Sue Ann Langdon, Elaine Devry, Jackie Russell, Jackie Joseph, Sharon De Bord and Shirley Jones

ner, although he doesn't do anything except enjoy the hospitality of the house. The amiable Harley takes life as it comes, but John is a straitlaced old bachelor and the idea of running the place bothers him. One morning at breakfast John tells the girls he aims to change the house into a respectable saloon and that they will have to leave. The girls are dismayed, but not nearly as dismayed as the local citizens, whose respect for him suddenly turns to scorn.

John is forced to change his mind about selling his social club when he realizes what will happen to Jenny and the girls. He himself is set upon in a barroom and after beating his opponents he is thrown in the local jail. Meanwhile Jenny is beaten by an outlaw, Corey Bannister (Robert J. Wilke) and to avenge her John seeks out Bannister and guns him down. This regains the respect of the citizenry, but it also brings an attack on his establishment by the entire Bannister clan of six brothers and sundry hirelings. Harley, away for a while, arrives back in time to help John and the girls win their battle, but having banished the Bannisters they then learn that more related bandits will descend upon them. Not willing to engage in any more warfare John signs over the social club to Jenny, and he and Harley take their leave, drifting back into the landscape as a kind of Western "Odd Couple," with John presumably doomed to spend his remaining years impatiently listening to the nonstop drawl of Harley.

The Cheyenne Social Club is a good-looking picture, not just because of its girls but through the expertise of veteran cinematographer William Clother, a man with a feeling for the western scene. The budget was set at three million dollars and production designer Gene Allen spent a quarter million of it building a vintage town on the J. W. Eaves Ranch, near Santa Fe, New Mexico. The film has a plausible, genial feel to it, but it did not receive quite the response the producers had hoped. Says Kelly: "Many people considered our bordello too nice and the girls too attractive, thinking that nothing this good could have existed in the real West. Actually, there were houses like this. The wealthy cattlemen and railroad men did indeed set up plush social clubs, calling them that, and they hired only pretty, classy girls. We also ran into another problem with the picture: many people didn't take to the idea of Jimmy Stewart in this setting, it was counter-image. We had one bedroom scene in which Jimmy is approached by a girl wearing a see-through negligee. It seemed funny at the time but looking at it later we both felt it should come out. But the owners, National General, insisted it stay, and I think that was a mistake."

With Shirley Jones and James Stewart

With James Stewart

With James Stewart and Henry Fonda

FORTY CARATS

CREDITS:

A Columbia Picture 1973. Produced by M. J. Frankovich. Directed by Milton Katselas. Written by Leonard Gershe, based on a play by Pierre Barillet and Jean-Pierre Gredy, adapted by Jay Allen. Photographed in Metrocolor by Charles B. Lang. Production designer, Robert Clatworthy. Edited by David Blewitt. Musical score by Michael Legrand. Running time: 108 minutes.

CAST:

Ann Stanley: Liv Ullmann; *Peter Latham:* Edward Albert; *Billy Boylan:* Gene Kelly; *Maud Ericson:* Binnie Barnes; *Trina Stanley:* Deborah Raffin; *J. D. Rogers:* Billy Green Bush; *Mrs. Margolin:* Nancy Walker; *Mr. Latham:* Don Porter; *Mrs. Latham:* Rosemary Murphy; *Mrs. Adams:* Natalie Schaefer; *Arthur Forbes:* Sam Chew, Jr.; *Gabriella:* Claudia Jennings; *Polly:* Brooks Palance.

Difficult, furtive and frustrating though the film business may be, good roles sometimes come to actors in an easy and simple way. Producer Mike Frankovich wanted Gene Kelly for the part of Billy Boylan in *Forty Carats,* but hesitated to offer what was essentially a supporting role to an actor-director of star status. Kelly accepted the role even without seeing the script. "I couldn't see myself declining the opportunity to work with Liv Ullmann, an enchanting actress. Mike said I'd probably want to see the script before I *really* said yes, and I told him to forget it. I think he thought I was putting him on but I wasn't. I wanted to work in a film with that wonderful actress and that was

With Liv Ullman

With Natalie Schafer

enough." The role of Billy Boylan is not a large one but, as Kelly says: "That's not the point. It's good material and it's time we in Hollywood got away from this pretentious business of labeling the appearance of a star in a small part as a *cameo*, as if excusing it. Casting people to type has always been the curse of this business and so has the star syndrome—a lot of talented actors have had their development curtailed by becoming stars. The British and European actors are luckier in that respect, they are not nearly as hidebound or as locked-in as their American brothers."

Liv Ullmann had long been lauded for her work in Swedish films with the prestigious Ingmar Bergman, but it wasn't until her performance in the epic *The Emigrants* that Hollywood began to consider her as an actress of possible wide appeal. Ross Hunter hired her for his lavish but limp musical version of *Lost Horizon,* and after seeing some of the footage of that picture Frankovich decided that Miss Ullmann was the actress for *Forty Carats,* thereby disappointing a number of famed and aging Hollywood actresses. At the age of thirty-seven she was actually too young to play the role, that of a middle-aged woman falling in love with a man young enough to be her son. But, as Kelly explains, "Once Mike had seen Liv, there were suddenly no contenders," and he instructed scenarist Leonard Gershe to alter the part accordingly.

Forty Carats, a French play, was first seen in Paris in late 1967. Among those who saw and liked it was David Merrick, and he purchased the American rights, commissioning Jay Allen to adapt the play into English. It was a hit of the 1968–9 Broadway season and subsequent touring companies. Its romantic plot premise is one common in life, but seldom before touched upon in films. Ann Stanley (Ullmann) is a successful Manhattan real estate agent who meets a personable young American, Peter Latham (Edward Albert), during a vacation in Greece. At first hesitant about his attraction to her, she gradually succumbs to his charm and spends a night with him on a beach. In the morning, before he awakes, she steals away. Some months later, by pure coincidence, Peter turns up at Ann's apartment as a date for her daughter Trina (Deborah Raffin). She discovers that Peter is a brilliant young business executive from a good social background, something which greatly impresses her modish mother Maud (Binnie Barnes), who supports the boy in his campaign to win Ann. Ann tries to deny her own affection for Peter

240

With Binnie Barnes

241

With Binnie Barnes and Liv Ullman

but finds nothing but arguments in favor of the affair—from her mother, her daughter, her sardonic business partner (Nancy Walker), and even from her ex-husband Billy Boylan (Kelly). Eventually Ann surrenders to these arguments, and to her love for Peter, and agrees to marry him.

The title of the play derives from a conversation between Ann and Billy. He is, despite their divorce, still greatly fond of her and concerned about her happiness. She bemoans the age difference between Peter and herself, and laments the fact that she is forty years old. Billy replies, "Don't think of it like that. Think like a diamond. Not years—carats. You're a multi-carated blue-white."

Although Gene Kelly had vowed not to take any more dancing roles in films he did agree to a short sequence in *Forty Carats*, in which Boylan and Maud do a fast-tempo dance to a rock beat in a discotheque. The veteran Binnie Barnes had never before danced in a film, but both she and Kelly appeared in fine form in this amusing moment. The age-defying little dance was in keeping with the character of Billy Boylan, a lighthearted, cheerful but shallow actor pretending to be a decade younger than his years. Boylan is the kind of actor who operates on personality and never quite reaches the level of success that would enable

him to relax his quest for work. In essaying such a character, Kelly clearly drew on many years of close observation.

Forty Carats did not win much favor with the critics. The major magazines dismissed it slick as entertainment, only glibly touching on the problems of age-gap marriages. However, public response was sufficiently strong to assure the producers of profit. The critical reaction to the performance of Liv Ullmann was one of disappointment. In reviewing the picture for the Toronto *Star* Clyde Gilmour sounded a generally felt impression:

Mainly, I think, this is because the talented and delectable Miss Ullmann just doesn't seem to have a talent for comedy. She looks beautiful, and it's not hard to imagine a man of twenty-two falling madly in love with her, but she often seems a bit harried and ill-at-ease in the midst of supposedly hilarious episodes.

Gilmour also commented: "To the film's credit, be it noted that Gene Kelly's work as the irrepressible ex-husband is warm and winning." Kelly won approval from most critics and *Variety* went so far as to claim this one of his finest characterizations:

242

He projects superbly the intricacies of a showbiz character, an aging gypsy so to speak, whose head and heart are together though his career is erratic. It's made to order for his mature abilities in both comedy and drama . . .

Hollywood had probably assumed that because of his success as a producer and director Kelly was no longer interested in acting. His success in *Forty Carats* dispelled that impression and also guaranteed him further roles. During the filming Kelly admitted that it was something of a luxury to be in front of the cameras again, rather than behind them: "When you're a director, you're working every minute, shouldering all that responsibility. On top of that, by the time you prepare a film, shoot it and edit it, that's more than a year out of your life. But as an actor, you rehearse, do your scenes, collect your money and go home. Lovely!" Kelly also admitted that he had let his acting career slide in favor of his family life. "I've turned down some tempting roles the last couple of years because the pictures were being done away off some place. I'm a family man and my kids are in school. I'm not going to uproot them, nor am I going to miss the joy of being with them."

As to what he feels he has yet to accomplish Gene Kelly replies, "A lot. One thing I would like to do is sort of review my career by putting together a clip of everything I've done. Then sit back and appraise it—and from seeing where I've been perhaps I'll decide where I'm going."

With Liv Ullman

Acknowledgments begin on page R79.
ISBN-13: 978-0-618-90552-2   ISBN-10: 0-618-90552-9

Printed in Canada.
1 2 3 4 5 6 7 8 9-TBQC-10 09 08 07

CA2

CLASSZONE

Visit **classzone.com** and get connected.

ClassZone resources provide instruction, practice and learning support for students and parents.

Animated Economics

- Provides interactive maps, charts, and graphs
- Shows how economic concepts apply in changing conditions

Economics Update

- Online statistics and continuous updates keep you at the forefront of news and information

Interactive Review

- Provides a unique way to review key concepts and events
- Includes games, crossword puzzles, and more
- Helps ensure lesson comprehension through graphic organizers, animated flipcards, and review/study notes

Activity Maker

- Create your own review games, graphic organizers, and crossword puzzles

Access the online version of your textbook at classzone.com

Your complete text, along with animated maps, charts and infographics, is available for immediate use!

McDougal Littell
Where Great Lessons Begin

CALIFORNIA EDITION

McDougal Littell

ECONOMICS

Concepts and Choices

McDougal Littell

Senior Consultants

Senior Consultants

Sally Meek has been teaching Economics, AP Microeconomics, and AP Macroeconomics in the Plano Independent School District in Plano, Texas since 1987. She has served as an AP Economics reader since 1998, and is currently a Lead Consultant for AP Economics at Summer Institutes for universities across Texas and a member of the AP Economics Test Development Committee. Additionally, Ms. Meek serves on the National Assessment of Educational Progress Economics Steering Committee and as a test item writer. She served as President of the Global Association of Teachers of Economics and addressed the National Summit on Economic and Financial Literacy in 2005. In 2004, Ms. Meek co-founded the North Texas TINSTAAFL Society and was on the National Council on Economic Education (NCEE) Virtual Economics 3.0 Design Committee. She has received the Southwest College Board Advanced Placement Special Recognition Award and the GATE Distinguished Service Award. Ms. Meek earned her B.A. in political science at the University of Texas at Dallas and her M.Ed. in Secondary Education with a content emphasis on Economics from the University of North Texas.

John Morton is Senior Program Officer for the Arizona Council on Economic Education. He taught economics for 31 years at the high school and university levels. Mr. Morton founded and directed the Center for Economic Education at Governors State University in Illinois for 15 years and founded and served as president of the Arizona Council on Economic Education for 4 years. He served as vice president for program development at the National Council on Economic Education (NCEE) for 5 years. He has authored or co-authored more than 80 publications and chaired the advisory board of *The Wall Street Journal Classroom Edition* from 1991 to 2000. Mr. Morton has won the Leavey Award from the Freedoms Foundation, as well as the Bessie B. Moore Service Award and the John C. Schramm Leadership Award from NCEE and the National Association of Economic Educators. He earned his M.A. from the University of Illinois and pursued postgraduate work at the University of Chicago.

Mark C. Schug is Professor and Director of the University of Wisconsin-Milwaukee Center for Economic Education and served as a Senior Fellow for the National Council for Economic Education from 2002–2005. He has taught for over 35 years at the middle school, high school, and university levels. Dr. Schug has written and edited over 180 publications. Additionally, he edited *The Senior Economist* for the National Council on Economic Education (NCEE) from 1986–1996. Dr. Schug often speaks and writes about economic and financial education, market-based reforms in education, and issues in urban schools, and has addressed local, state, national, and international groups. Similarly, he has done training programs for teachers in several states across the nation. Dr. Schug earned his Ph.D. from the University of Minnesota.

Teacher Consultants

The following educators provided ongoing review during the development of the program.

Sheri Perez
Mesa Community College
Mesa, Arizona

Bill Smiley
Leigh High School (retired)
San Jose, California

Sandra K. Wright
Adlai E. Stevenson High School
Lincolnshire, Illinois

Douglas Young
Croton-Harmon High School
Croton-on-Hudson, New York

Content Reviewers

The content reviewers evaluated the text for depth, accuracy, and clarity in the use of economics concepts.

Joanne Benjamin
Board of Directors, California Council
  on Economic Education
President, California Association of
  School Economics Teachers
San Bernardino, California

Joseph Calhoun
Assistant Director, Stavros Center for
  Economic Education
Florida State Univerisity
Tallahassee, Florida

R. J. Charkins
Executive Director, California Council
  on Economic Education
Sam Bernardino, California

Sarah E. Culver
Director, UAB Center for Economic
  Education
University of Alabama-Birmingham
Birmingham, Alabama

Beth S. Eckstein
Director, Center for Economic Education
  College of Business, East Carolina
  University
Greenville, North Carolina

Gail A. Hawks
Director, Center for Economic Education
Miami-Dade Community College
Miami, Florida

Gary A. Hoover
Associate Professor of Economics
University of Alabama
Tuscaloosa, Alabama

Mary Anne Pettit
Associate Director, Office of
  Economic Education
Southern Illinois
  University-Edwardsville
Edwardsville, Illinois

Dennis Placone
Director, Clemson University Center for
  Economic Education
Clemson University
Clemson, South Carolina

Jennifer Thomas
Senior Director of Operations, Florida
  Council on Economic Education
Largo, Florida

Teacher Reviewers

The following teachers and administrators reviewed the text for its appropriateness for use in high school economics programs.

Julie Barker
Pittsford Mendon High School
Pittsford, New York

Michael D. Bruce
William Fremd High School
Palatine, Illinois

Brett Burkey
Spanish River High School
Boca Raton, Florida

Jan Collins
Franklin High School
Elk Grove, California

Melanie Craven
Nanuet Senior High School
Nanuet, New York

Lisa Herman-Ellison
Kokomo High School
Kokomo, Indiana

Rebecca L. Johnson
Raoul Wallenberg Traditional
  High School
San Francisco, California

Kathleen Ryan Johnston
Rufus King High School
Milwaukee, Wisconsin

Romano Luchini
Encina High School
Sacramento, California

Robert Mira
West Lafayette High School
West Lafayette, Indiana

Michael Noto
Brighton High School
Rochester, New York

Nick Petraccione
K-12 Supervisor
Bethlehem Central School District
Delmar, New York

Elida Petrella-Yocum
Indian Creek High School
Wintersville, Ohio

Heather Price
Eau Gallie High School
Melbourne, Florida

David Sweeney
Dryden High School
Dryden, Michigan

Rick Sydor
C.K. McClatchy High School
Sacramento, California

Gerald Taylor
SEED School
Washington, D.C.

OVERVIEW
California Student Edition

CALIFORNIA CONTENTS

Los Angeles, California © Corbis

Correlations to
California History-Social Science
Content Standards and Analysis Skills

Standards Map—Basic Comprehensive Program
Grade Twelve—History-Social Science
Principles of Economics

In addition to studying government in grade twelve, students will also master fundamental economic concepts, applying the tools (graphs, statistics, equations) from other subject areas to the understanding of operations and institutions of economic systems. Studied in a historic context are the basic economic principles of micro- and macroeconomics, international economics, comparative economic systems, measurement, and methods.

Standard	Instruction	Application
12.1 Students understand common economic terms and concepts and economic reasoning.	PE: 2, 3, 4–5, 6–7, 12, 13, 14, 15–16, 19, 20, 21, 30, 37, 39, 43, 46, 48–49, 54–55, 61, 65, 70–71, 73–74, 92–93, 124–125, 140–141, 174–175, 176–177, 178, 220, 370, 374, 394, 543, 544–545, 549, 554–555, 557	PE: 7, 11, 13, 14, 15, 16, 17, 19, 20, 21, 23, 31, 33, 34–35, 39, 41, 57, 66–67, 178, 179, 188, 394
12.1.1 Examine the causal relationship between scarcity and the need for choices.	PE: 2, 3, 4–5, 6–7, 37, 140–141, 374	PE: 7, 11, 34–35
12.1.2 Explain opportunity cost and marginal benefit and marginal cost.	PE: 12, 14, 15–16, 19, 20, 21	PE: 14, 15, 16, 17, 19, 20, 21, 23, 33, 34–35
12.1.3 Identify the difference between monetary and nonmonetary incentives and how changes in incentives cause changes in behavior.	PE: 12, 13, 30, 124–125, 174–175, 176–177, 178, 220, 557	PE: 13, 17, 178, 179, 188
12.1.4 Evaluate the role of private property as an incentive in conserving and improving scarce resources.	PE: 43, 46, 48–49, 61, 73, 370, 549, 554–555	PE: 57, 66–67
12.1.5 Analyze the role of a market economy in establishing and preserving political and personal liberty (e.g., through the works of Adam Smith).	PE: 30, 39, 54–55, 65, 70–71, 73–74, 92–93, 370, 394, 543, 544–545, 554	PE: 31, 39, 41, 394

Standard	Instruction	Application
12.2 Students analyze the elements of America's market economy in a global setting.	PE: 48, 49, 50, 51, 55–55, 70, 74–75, 78–79, 98–99, 100–101, 102–103, 106–107, 109–114, 117–118, 119–120, 122, 124–125, 130–131, 136, 142–143, 146–147, 148–151, 154–156, 163, 164–166, 167–168, 169–171, 174–175, 176–177, 178, 180–181, 182, 183–184, 186, 187, 191–195, 198–199, 202–204, 206–208, 209–210, 211, 220–221, 226, 301–302, 304–305, 306–307, 318–319, 320–322, 327–328, 330–331, 332–333, 334–335, 336, 338–340, 341, 342, 344–345, 360–361, 370, 373, 384, 399, 511, 512, 513–515, 516–518, 533–535, 549	PE: S14, 51, 57, 75, 77, 101, 105, 107, 111, 113, 114, 115, 120, 123, 124, 126, 127, 131, 137, 143, 147, 150, 153, 157, 160–161, 166, 171, 173, 175, 177, 178, 179, 181, 182, 184, 185, 186, 188–189, 194, 195, 197, 199, 205, 208, 210, 211, 213, 222–223, 303, 305, 308, 311, 314–315, 319, 321, 322, 323, 329, 331, 333, 334, 336, 337, 341, 342, 343, 344–345, 346–347, 361, 514, 515, 517, 519, 533, 540–541
12.2.1 Understand the relationship of the concept of incentives to the law of supply and the relationship of the concept of incentives and substitutes to the law of demand.	PE: 78–79, 98–99, 100–101, 102–103, 106–107, 112–113, 117–118, 119–120, 124–125, 176–177, 178	PE: 101, 105, 107, 113, 115, 120, 123, 126, 177, 178, 179, 188
12.2.2 Discuss the effects of changes in supply and/or demand on the relative scarcity, price, and quantity of particular products.	PE: 109–114, 131, 146–147, 148–151, 154–156, 169–171, 176–177, 183	PE: S14, 111, 124, 131, 147, 153, 157, 160–161, 171, 173, 185, 208
12.2.3 Explain the roles of property rights, competition, and profit in a market economy.	PE: 48, 49, 51, 54–55, 70, 78–79, 130–131, 136, 142–143, 150, 174–177, 191–195, 202–204, 206–208, 209–210, 211, 370	PE: 51, 57, 77, 137, 143, 150, 153, 194, 195, 197, 205, 210, 211, 213
12.2.4 Explain how prices reflect the relative scarcity of goods and services and perform the allocative function in a market economy.	PE: 99, 114, 199, 221, 399	PE: 114, 127, 161, 171, 361, 399
12.2.5 Understand the process by which competition among buyers and sellers determines a market price.	PE: 50, 54–55, 74–75, 100–101, 122, 163, 164–166, 167–168, 174–175, 187, 191–195, 360–361	PE: 75, 166, 173, 175, 179, 188-189, 194, 195, 197
12.2.6 Describe the effect of price controls on buyers and sellers.	PE: 180–181, 182, 183–184, 186, 198–199	PE: 181, 182, 184, 185, 186, 188–189, 199, 222
12.2.7 Analyze how domestic and international competition in a market economy affects goods and services produced and the quality, quantity, and price of those products.	PE: 150–151, 164–166, 178, 206–208, 209–210, 211, 220–221, 360–361, 516–518, 533–535	PE: 150, 179, 189, 208, 210–211, 213, 222–223, 361, 519, 533, 540–541
12.2.8 Explain the role of profit as the incentive to entrepreneurs in a market economy.	PE: 54–55, 70, 78, 122, 136, 142–143, 174, 176–177, 226	PE: 77, 123, 177

Standard	Instruction	Application
12.2.9 Describe the functions of the financial markets.	PE: 301–302, 304–305, 306–307, 318–319, 320–322, 327–328, 330–331, 332–333, 334–335	PE: 303, 305, 308, 311, 314–315, 319, 321, 322, 323, 329, 331, 333, 334, 336, 337, 341, 342, 343, 344–345, 346–347
12.2.10 Discuss the economic principles that guide the location of agricultural production and industry and the spatial distribution of transportation and retail facilities.	PE: 384, 511, 512, 513–515, 516–518, 549	PE: 57, 75, 514, 515, 517, 519

Standard	Instruction	Application
12.3 Students analyze the influence of the federal government on the American economy.	PE: 42, 55, 76, 80–81, 84–88, 89–90, 149–150, 181–182, 183–184, 201, 214–217, 218, 241–242, 262–263, 296–297, 298–299, 300, 307, 312, 336, 338–340, 350–353, 363, 365–366, 392–393, 410–411, 412–414, 415, 416–417, 420, 423, 424–425, 428–430, 431–432, 446–447, 448–450, 451–452, 454–455, 457, 458–460, 462–464, 465–466, 468–469, 474–475, 476–478, 480–481, 482–483, 484–485, 486–487, 488, 490–491, 492–493, 494, 495–496, 498–499, 500–502, 504–505	PE: 55, 81, 86, 87, 90, 91, 94–95, 153, 184, 185, 188–189, 205, 215, 217, 218, 219, 222–223, 295, 297, 299, 300, 303, 307, 311, 312, 314–315, 367, 375, 379, 393, 395, 411, 414, 415, 417, 418, 419, 424, 425, 427, 430, 431, 432, 433, 442–443, 447, 449, 450, 451, 452, 453, 455, 457, 458, 459, 460, 461, 463, 464, 467, 468–469, 470–471, 475, 478, 479, 481, 483, 485, 487, 488, 491, 493, 494, 496, 497, 499, 501, 502, 503, 504–505, 506–507
12.3.1 Understand how the role of government in a market economy often includes providing for national defense, addressing environmental concerns, defining and enforcing property rights, attempting to make markets more competitive, and protecting consumers' rights.	PE: 42, 55, 84–88, 89–90, 181–184, 201, 214–217, 218, 241–242, 262–263, 392–393, 410–411, 463	PE: 55, 86, 87, 90, 91, 94–95, 184, 185, 188–189, 205, 215, 217, 218, 219, 222–223, 375, 393, 395, 411, 418, 419, 442–443
12.3.2 Identify the factors that may cause the costs of government actions to outweigh the benefits.	PE: 181–182, 183–184, 218, 451–452, 457, 466	PE: 184, 185, 189, 219, 375, 452, 453, 467
12.3.3 Describe the aims of government fiscal policies (taxation, borrowing, spending) and their influence on production, employment, and price levels.	PE: 80–81, 149–150, 338–340, 350–353, 365–366, 410–411, 412–414, 415, 416–417, 420, 423, 424–425, 428–430, 431–432, 446–447, 448–450, 451–452, 454–455, 457, 458–460, 462–464, 465–466, 468–469, 498–499, 500–502	PE: 81, 153, 367, 379, 414, 415, 417, 419, 424, 425, 427, 430, 431, 432, 433, 442–443, 447, 449, 450, 451, 452, 453, 455, 457, 458, 459, 460, 461, 463, 464, 467, 468–469, 470–471, 493, 499, 501, 502, 503, 507
12.3.4 Understand the aims and tools of monetary policy and their influence on economic activity (e.g., the Federal Reserve).	PE: 76, 294, 296–297, 298–299, 300, 307, 312, 336, 363, 474–476, 476–478, 480–481, 482–483, 484–485, 486–487, 488, 490–491, 492–493, 494, 495–496, 498–499, 500–502, 504–505	PE: 295, 297, 299, 300, 303, 307, 311, 312, 314–315, 367, 475, 478, 479, 481, 483, 485, 487, 488, 491, 493, 494, 496, 497, 499, 501, 502, 503, 504–505, 506–507

Standard	Instruction	Application
12.4 Students analyze the elements of the U.S. labor market in a global setting.	PE: 158–159, 171, 182, 220–221, 246, 258–260, 261–263, 266–267, 268–269, 270–271, 274–277, 278–279, 280, 336, 350–353, 362–363, 371, 372–373, 385, 390–391, 520, 522, 523, 526–528, 533–535, 538–539	PE: S7, 145, 185, 221, 259, 260, 263, 265, 267, 269, 272, 273, 277, 278, 279, 280, 282–283, 285–285, 363, 366, 375, 385, 387, 391, 403, 406, 447, 522, 525, 528, 533, 537, 538–539, 540
12.4.1 Understand the operations of the labor market, including the circumstances surrounding the establishment of principal American labor unions, procedures that unions use to gain benefits for their members, the effects of unionization, the minimum wage, and unemployment insurance.	PE: 182, 262–263, 274–277, 278–279, 280	PE: 185, 263, 265, 277, 278, 279, 280, 284–285, 387, 403, 447
12.4.2 Describe the current economy and labor market, including the types of goods and services produced, the types of skills workers need, the effects of rapid technological change, and the impact of international competition.	PE: 158–159, 171, 220–221, 246, 266–267, 268–269, 270–271, 352, 362–363, 371, 372–373, 385, 390–391, 520, 522, 523, 538–539	PE: 221, 267, 269, 272, 273, 282–283, 284, 363, 366, 375, 385, 391, 522, 525, 538–539
12.4.3 Discuss wage differences among jobs and professions, using the laws of demand and supply and the concept of productivity.	PE: 258–260, 261–263, 390–391	PE: S7, 259, 260, 261, 263, 265, 284–285, 391
12.4.4 Explain the effects of international mobility of capital and labor on the U.S. economy.	PE: 269, 271, 336, 350–353, 385, 523, 526–528, 533–535, 538–539	PE: 145, 273, 282–283, 385, 406, 528, 533, 537, 538–539, 540

Standard	Instruction	Application
12.5 Students analyze the aggregate economic behavior of the U.S. economy.	PE: 182, 304–305, 350–353, 354–355, 358–359, 360–361, 362–364, 365–366, 368–369, 370–371, 372–373, 382–383, 384–386, 396–398, 399–400, 401–402, 404–405, 495–596, 578–579	PE: A14, 312–313, 352, 353, 355, 356, 357, 359, 363, 364, 366, 369, 371, 373, 375, 378–379, 383, 385, 386, 387, 395, 397, 398, 399, 403, 404–405, 406–407, 497
12.5.1 Distinguish between nominal and real data.	PE: 352–353, 368–369	PE: 352, 353, 357, 378–379
12.5.2 Define, calculate, and explain the significance of an unemployment rate, the number of new jobs created monthly, an inflation or deflation rate, and a rate of economic growth.	PE: 182, 350–353, 354–355, 358–359, 360–361, 362–364, 365–366, 368–369, 370–371, 372–373, 382–383, 384–386, 396–398, 399–400, 401–402, 404–405	PE: 352, 355, 356, 357, 359, 363, 364, 366, 369, 371, 373, 375, 379, 383, 385, 386, 387, 395, 397, 398, 399, 403, 404–405, 406–407
12.5.3 Distinguish between short-term and long-term interest rates and explain their relative significance.	PE: Opportunities to address this objective can be found on the following pages: 304–305, 495–496, 578–579	PE: A14, 312–313, 497

Standard	Instruction	Application
12.6 Students analyze issues of international trade and explain how the U.S. economy affects, and is affected by, economic forces beyond the United States's borders.	PE: 61–62, 200, 292, 352, 512, 513–515, 516–518, 523–524, 526–528, 529, 532–535, 536, 538–539, 562–563, 564–565	PE: 200, 292, 514, 515, 517, 518, 519, 525, 527, 528, 529, 531, 533, 535, 536, 537, 538–539, 540–541, 563, 565
12.6.1 Identify the gains in consumption and production efficiency from trade, with emphasis on the main products and changing geographic patterns of twentieth-century trade among countries in the Western Hemisphere.	PE: 61–62, 200, 352, 512, 513–515, 516–518, 523, 533–534, 536	PE: 200, 514, 515, 517, 518, 519, 533, 536, 537, 540
12.6.2 Compare the reasons for and the effects of trade restrictions during the Great Depression compared with present-day arguments among labor, business, and political leaders over the effects of free trade on the economic and social interests of various groups of Americans.	PE: 523–524, 532–535, 538–539	PE: 525, 533, 535, 537, 538–539, 540–541
12.6.3 Understand the changing role of international political borders and territorial sovereignty in a global economy.	PE: 292, 532–533, 562–563, 564–565	PE: 292, 563, 565
12.6.4 Explain foreign exchange, the manner in which exchange rates are determined, and the effects of the dollar's gaining (or losing) value relative to other currencies.	PE: 526–528, 529	PE: 527, 528, 529, 531, 540

Historical and Social Sciences Analysis Skills

The intellectual skills noted below are to be learned through, and applied to, the content standards for grades nine through twelve. They are to be assessed only in conjunction with the content standards in grades nine through twelve.

In addition to the standards for grades nine through twelve, students demonstrate the following intellectual, reasoning, reflection, and research skills.

Standard	Instruction	Application
CHRONOLOGICAL AND SPATIAL THINKING		
CST(1) Students compare the present with the past, evaluating the consequences of past events and decisions and determining the lessons that were learned.	PE: 22, 44–46, 64–65, 183–184, 270–271, 278–279, 296–297, 298–299, 344–345, 454, 456, 457, 459–460, 465–466, 501, 532–535, 562–565	PE: 65, 67, 184, 185, 273, 279, 281, 284–285, 299, 303, 314, 337, 344–345, 367, 533, 563, 565
CST(2) Students analyze how change happens at different rates at different times; understand that some aspects can change while others remain the same; and understand that change is complicated and affects not only technology and politics but also values and beliefs.	PE: 22, 61–62, 79, 109–113, 169–171, 270–271, 278–279, 298–299, 362–364, 385, 536, 570–571, 572	PE: 22, 34–35, 62, 63, 67, 83, 111, 170, 171, 172, 173, 273, 279, 281, 283, 284, 314, 337, 367, 537, 570–571
CST(3) Students use a variety of maps and documents to interpret human movement, including major patterns of domestic and international migration, changing environmental preferences and settlement patterns, the frictions that develop between population groups, and the diffusion of ideas, technological innovations, and goods.	PE: 64–65, 110–111, 244, 245, 252–253, 268–269, 282–283, 536, 544–545, 548–549, 558	PE: 65, 253, 282–283, 537, 551
CST(4) Students relate current events to the physical and human characteristics of places and regions.	PE: 45–46, 54, 59–60, 61–62, 64–65, 184, 292, 363, 536, 566–567, 568, 570–571	PE: 47, 56, 63, 65, 67, 279, 282–283, 363, 537, 567, 568, 569, 570–571
HISTORICAL RESEARCH, EVIDENCE, AND POINT OF VIEW		
REP(1) Students distinguish valid arguments from fallacious arguments in historical interpretations.	PE: 125, 144, 236, 368, 374, 469	PE: 95, 236, 471, 503, 537
REP(2) Students identify bias and prejudice in historical interpretations.	PE: Opportunities to address this objective can be found on the following pages: 114, 571, R26, R27	PE: R26, R27

Standard	Instruction	Application
REP(3) Students evaluate major debates among historians concerning alternative interpretations of the past, including an analysis of authors' use of evidence and the distinctions between sound generalizations and misleading oversimplifications.	PE: 366, 440–441, 460, 468–469, 496	PE: 440–441, 461, 468–469
REP(4) Students construct and test hypotheses; collect, evaluate, and employ information from multiple primary and secondary sources; and apply it in oral and written presentations.	PE: 32–33, 64–65, 92–93, 124–125, 158–159, 186–187, 220–221, 252–253, 282–283, 312–313, 344–345, 376–377, 404–405, 440–441, 468–469, 504–505, 538–539, 570–571, 573	PE: 32–33, 64–65, 92–93, 95, 124–125, 158–159, 186–187, 220–221, 252–253, 282–283, 312–313, 344–345, 376–377, 404–405, 440–441, 468–469, 471, 504–505, 538–539, 570–571, 573

HISTORICAL INTERPRETATION

Standard	Instruction	Application
HI(1) Students show the connections, causal and otherwise, between particular historical events and larger social, economic, and political trends and developments.	PE: 40, 45–46, 54–55, 64–65, 82, 214–215, 274–279, 292, 297, 298–299, 344–345, 376–377, 501, 532–535, 560, 562–565	PE: 47, 55, 65, 66–67, 80, 279, 281, 285, 292, 299, 337, 344–345, 376–377, 503, 533, 534, 560, 565, 569
HI(2) Students recognize the complexity of historical causes and effects, including the limitations on determining cause and effect.	PE: 22, 64–65, 183–184, 214–215, 270–271, 363	PE: 22, 95, 125, 127, 184, 247, 281, 315, 363, 367, 379
HI(3) Students interpret past events and issues within the context in which an event unfolded rather than solely in terms of present-day norms and values.	PE: 183–184, 214–215, 274–277, 296–297, 298–299, 344–345, 501, R20	PE: 184, 278, 281, 297, 299, 303, 503
HI(4) Students understand the meaning, implication, and impact of historical events and recognize that events could have taken other directions.	PE: 64–65, 183–184, 274–277, 296–297, 298–299, 501	PE: 184, 278, 281, 299, 303, 503
HI(5) Students analyze human modifications of landscapes and examine the resulting environmental policy issues.	PE: 549, 568	PE: 375, 551, 568, 569
HI(6) Students conduct cost-benefit analyses and apply basic economic indicators to analyze the aggregate economic behavior of the U.S. economy.	PE: 32–33, 142–143, 350–353, 355, 358–359, 360–361, 366, 368–369, 372–373, 492–494, 495–496, 498–499, 500–501, 502, 504–505, 533–535, R18	PE: A13, A14, A15, S13, S15, 16, 17, 23, 33, 91, 231, 282, 351, 352, 353, 355, 356, 357, 361, 364, 366, 367, 369, 373, 375, 378–379, 489, 494, 495, 496, 497, 499, 501, 502, 503, 504–505, 506–507, 518, 529, 530, 533, 534, 537, R18

Economics Updates (continued)

Animated Economics   For interactive graphs and lessons, go to **ClassZone.com**

YOUR ECONOMIC CHOICES

Economics Pacesetters

Global Perspectives

Economics Skillbuilders

Math Challenges

Graphs, Charts, Tables, and Maps

Economic Atlas and Statistics

CONTENTS

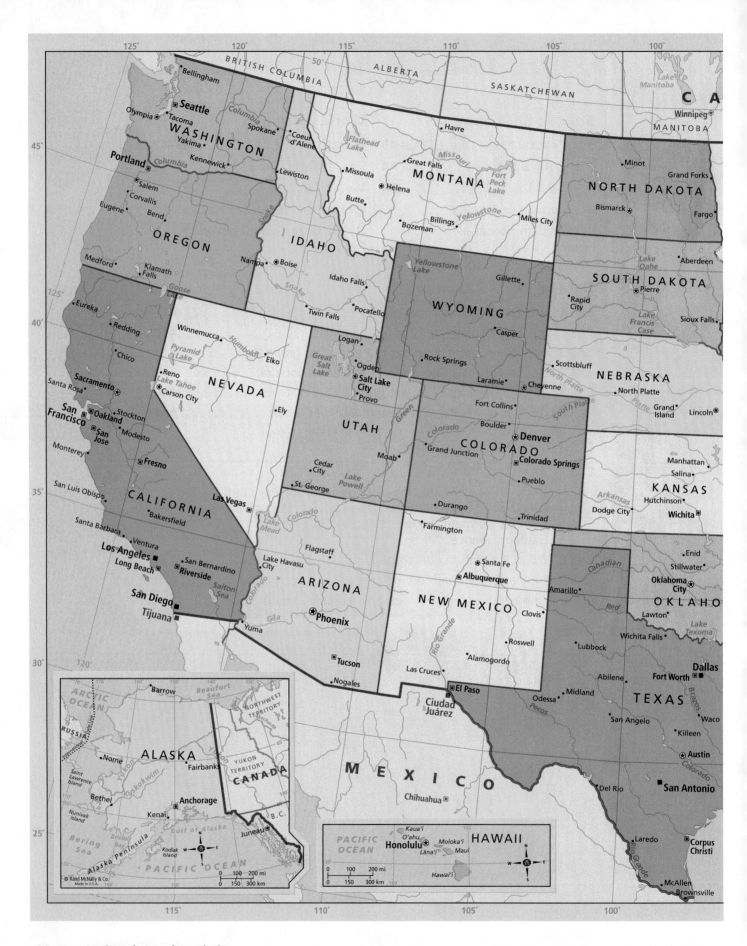

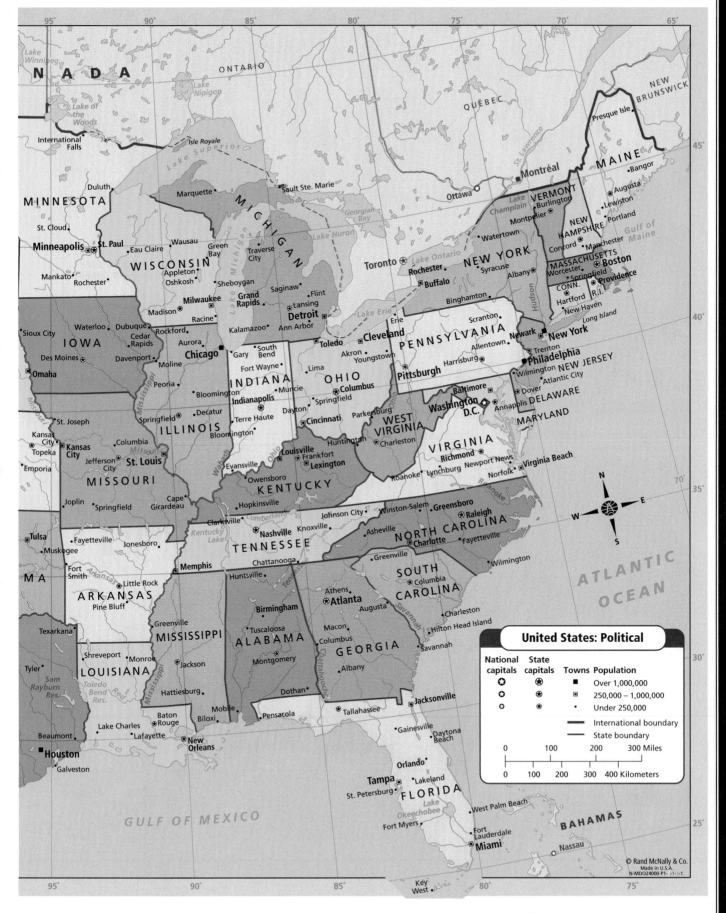

United States: Political

National capitals
⊛ State capitals
Towns Population
■ Over 1,000,000
▣ 250,000 – 1,000,000
• Under 250,000
━ International boundary
── State boundary

| 0 | 100 | 200 | 300 Miles |
| 0 | 100 | 200 | 300 | 400 Kilometers |

© Rand McNally & Co.
Made in U.S.A.
N-MDO24000-P1- -1-1-1

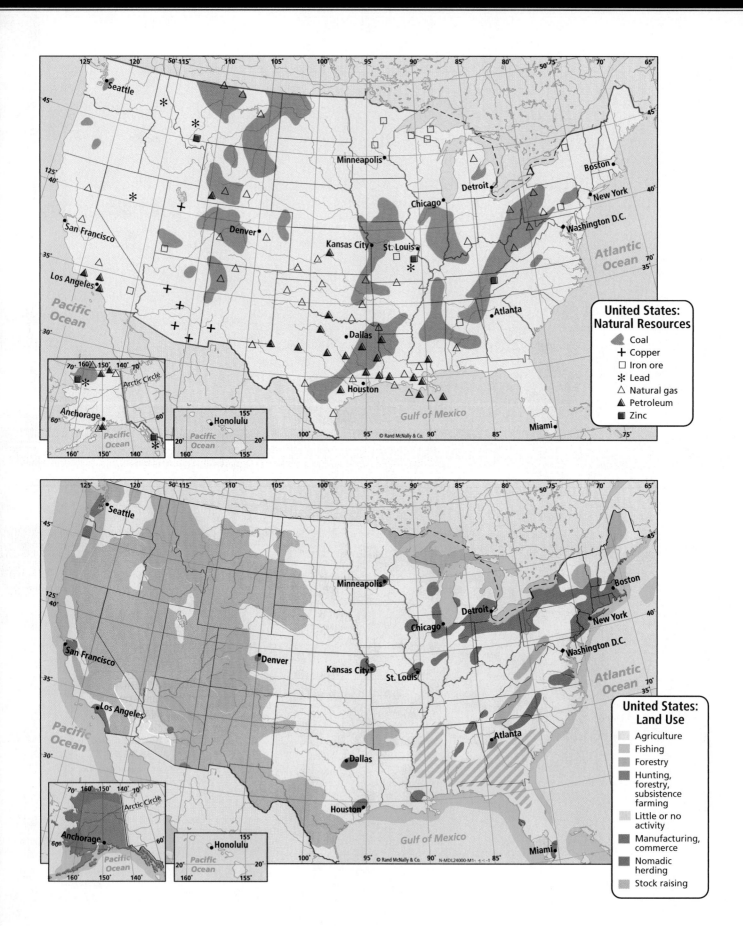

United States: Natural Resources

- Coal
- + Copper
- □ Iron ore
- ✳ Lead
- △ Natural gas
- ▲ Petroleum
- ■ Zinc

© Rand McNally & Co.

United States: Land Use

- Agriculture
- Fishing
- Forestry
- Hunting, forestry, subsistence farming
- Little or no activity
- Manufacturing, commerce
- Nomadic herding
- Stock raising

© Rand McNally & Co.   N-MDL24000-M1:1-1-1

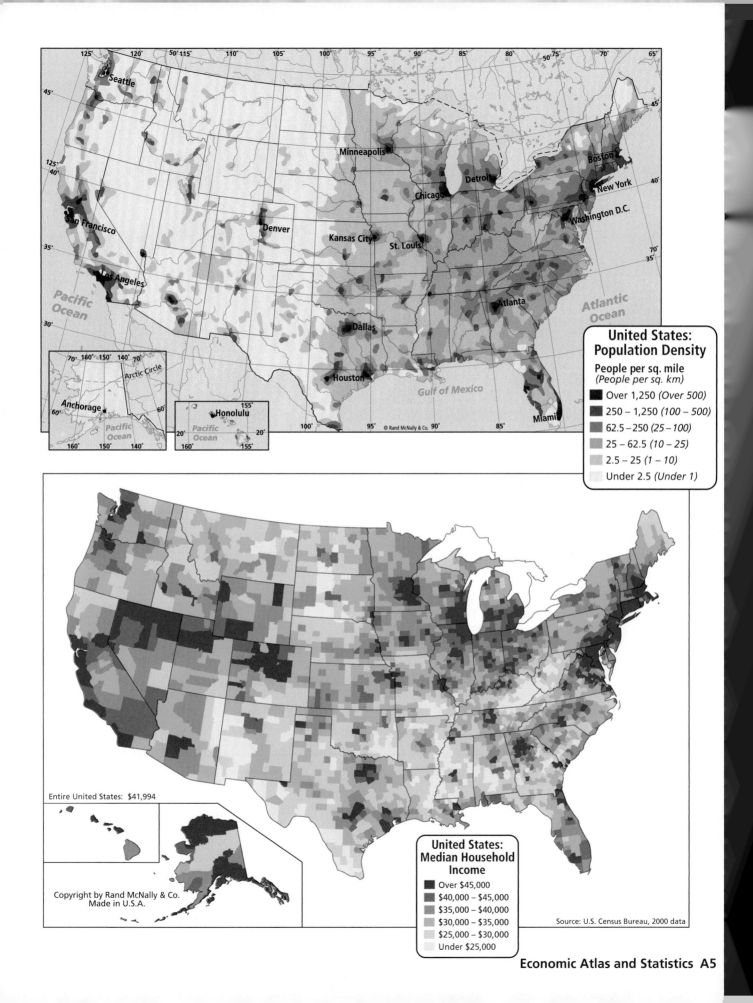

United States: Population Density

People per sq. mile
(People per sq. km)

- Over 1,250 *(Over 500)*
- 250 – 1,250 *(100 – 500)*
- 62.5 – 250 *(25 – 100)*
- 25 – 62.5 *(10 – 25)*
- 2.5 – 25 *(1 – 10)*
- Under 2.5 *(Under 1)*

Seattle
Minneapolis
Boston
Detroit
Chicago
New York
San Francisco
Denver
Washington D.C.
Kansas City
St. Louis
Los Angeles
Atlanta
Pacific Ocean
Dallas
Houston
Atlantic Ocean
Gulf of Mexico
Miami
© Rand McNally & Co.

Arctic Circle
Anchorage
Pacific Ocean
Honolulu
Pacific Ocean

United States: Median Household Income

- Over $45,000
- $40,000 – $45,000
- $35,000 – $40,000
- $30,000 – $35,000
- $25,000 – $30,000
- Under $25,000

Entire United States: $41,994

Copyright by Rand McNally & Co.
Made in U.S.A.

Source: U.S. Census Bureau, 2000 data

Economic Atlas and Statistics A5

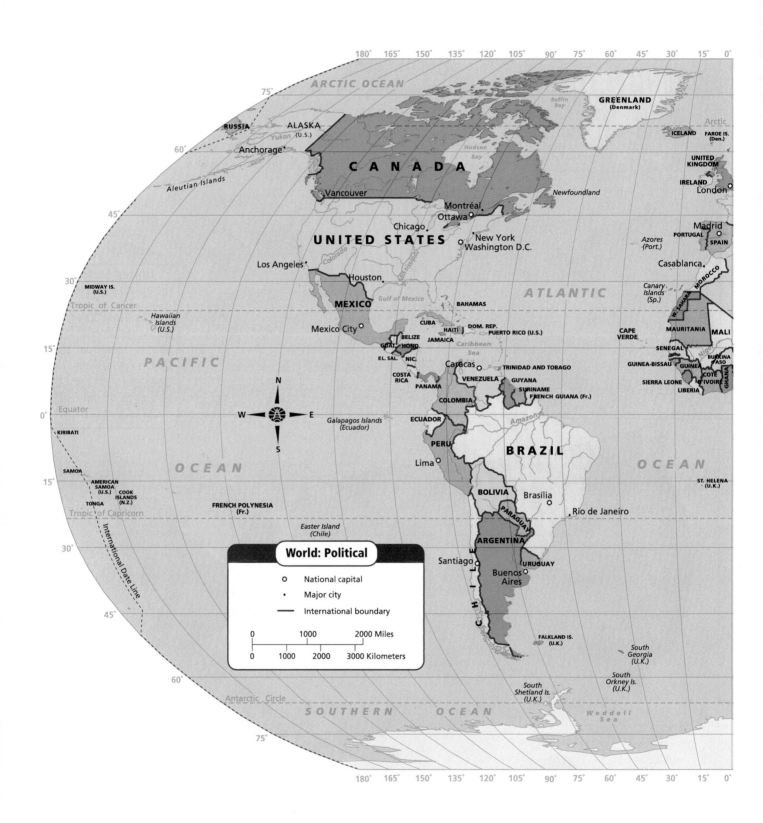

World: Political

- ⊙ National capital
- · Major city
- — International boundary

0   1000   2000 Miles

0   1000   2000   3000 Kilometers

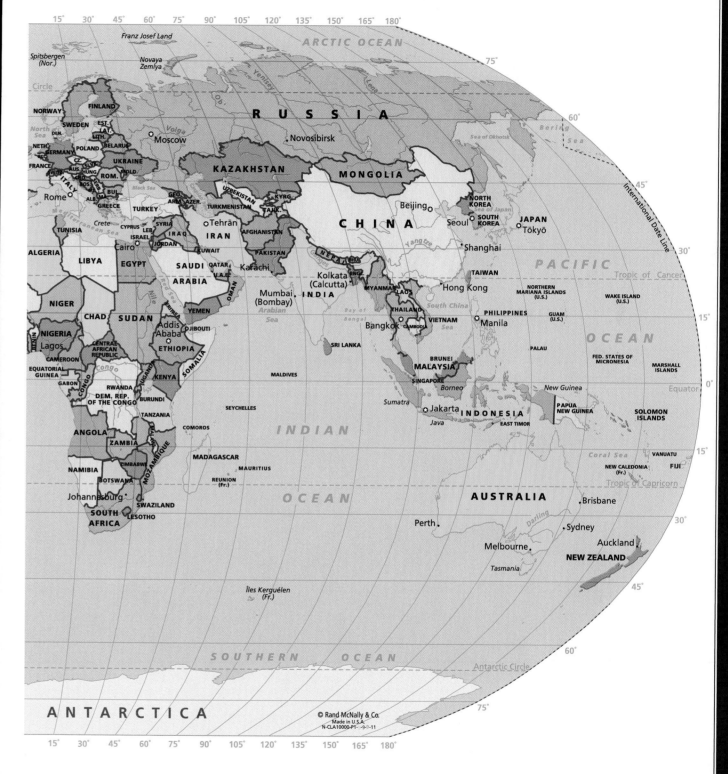

15° 30° 45° 60° 75° 90° 105° 120° 135° 150° 165° 180°

ARCTIC OCEAN

Franz Josef Land

Spitsbergen (Nor.)

Novaya Zemlya

75°

60°

Circle

NORWAY FINLAND

SWEDEN

EST.
LAT.
LITH.

DEN.

NETH.
GERMANY POLAND
BELARUS

FRANCE

ITALY

Rome

ALB.
GREECE

TUNISIA

ALGERIA

LIBYA EGYPT

NIGER

CHAD SUDAN

NIGERIA

Lagos

CENTRAL
AFRICAN
REPUBLIC

CAMEROON

EQUATORIAL
GUINEA

GABON

ANGOLA

ZAMBIA

NAMIBIA

BOTSWANA

Johannesburg

SOUTH
AFRICA LESOTHO

SWAZILAND

Volga

UKRAINE

MOLD.

Black Sea

CYPRUS

Crete

Mediterranean Sea

Cairo

ISRAEL
JORDAN

SAUDI
ARABIA

YEMEN

Addis
Ababa

ETHIOPIA

KENYA

RWANDA

DEM. REP.
OF THE CONGO BURUNDI

TANZANIA

COMOROS

ZIMBABWE

MOZAMBIQUE

MADAGASCAR

MAURITIUS

REUNION
(Fr.)

Moscow

Novosibirsk

R U S S I A

KAZAKHSTAN

UZBEKISTAN

GEO.

ARM. AZER.

TURKMENISTAN

KYRG.

TAJIK.

TURKEY

SYRIA
LEB.

IRAQ

IRAN

AFGHANISTAN

KUWAIT

QATAR

U.A.E.

OMAN

ERITREA

DJIBOUTI

SOMALIA

UGANDA

SEYCHELLES

MALAWI

MONGOLIA

Beijing

CHINA

Yangtze

Tehrān

PAKISTAN

Karachi

Mumbai
(Bombay)

*Arabian
Sea*

INDIA

MALDIVES

SRI LANKA

NEPAL

BHU.

BNG.

Kolkata
(Calcutta)

MYANMAR

Bay of
Bengal

LAOS

THAILAND

Bangkok

CAMBODIA

VIETNAM

*South China
Sea*

NORTH
KOREA

SOUTH
KOREA

Seoul

Shanghai

TAIWAN

Hong Kong

PHILIPPINES

Manila

JAPAN

Tōkyō

Sea of Japan

Sea of Okhotsk

*Bering
Sea*

International Date Line

75°

60°

45°

30°

PACIFIC

Tropic of Cancer

NORTHERN
MARIANA ISLANDS
(U.S.)

GUAM
(U.S.)

WAKE ISLAND
(U.S.)

15°

OCEAN

PALAU

FED. STATES OF
MICRONESIA

MARSHALL
ISLANDS

BRUNEI

MALAYSIA

SINGAPORE

Borneo

Sumatra

Jakarta

Java

INDONESIA

EAST TIMOR

New Guinea

PAPUA
NEW GUINEA

Equator 0°

SOLOMON
ISLANDS

INDIAN

Coral Sea

VANUATU

NEW CALEDONIA
(Fr.)

FIJI

15°

AUSTRALIA

Brisbane

OCEAN

Perth

Darling

Sydney

Melbourne

Auckland

NEW ZEALAND

Tasmania

Tropic of Capricorn

30°

*Îles Kerguélen
(Fr.)*

45°

SOUTHERN OCEAN

60°

Antarctic Circle

A N T A R C T I C A

© Rand McNally & Co.
Made in U.S.A.
N-CLA10000-P1- -9-?-11

75°

15° 30° 45° 60° 75° 90° 105° 120° 135° 150° 165° 180°

Economic Atlas and Statistics A7

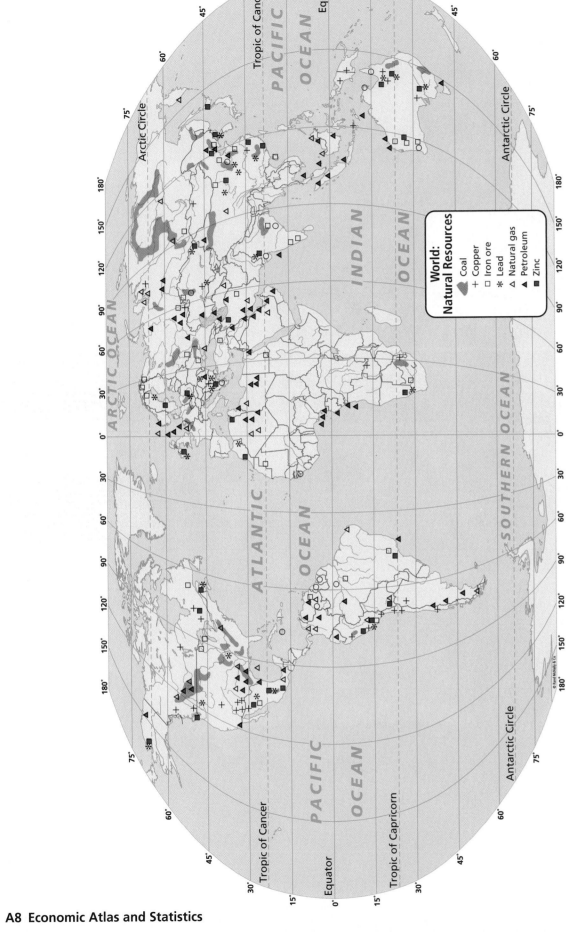

World:
Natural Resources

- Coal
- + Copper
- □ Iron ore
- * Lead
- △ Natural gas
- ▲ Petroleum
- ■ Zinc

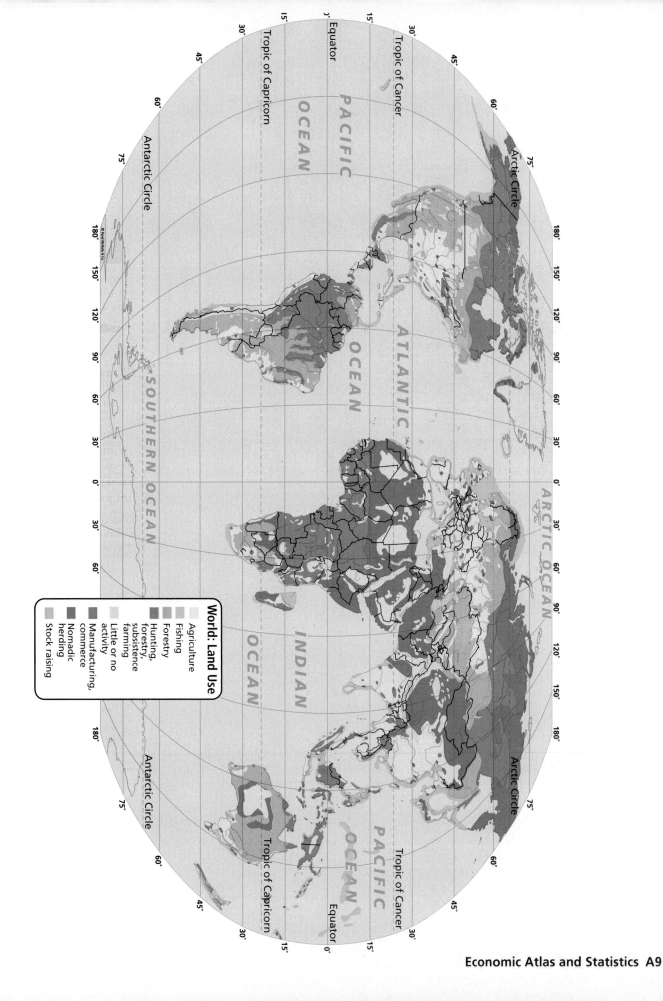

World: Land Use

Agriculture
Fishing
Forestry
Hunting,
forestry,
subsistence
farming
Little or no
activity
Manufacturing,
commerce
Nomadic
herding
Stock raising

PACIFIC OCEAN

ATLANTIC OCEAN

ARCTIC OCEAN

INDIAN OCEAN

SOUTHERN OCEAN

PACIFIC OCEAN

Arctic Circle

Tropic of Cancer

Equator

Tropic of Capricorn

Antarctic Circle

© Rand McNally & Co.

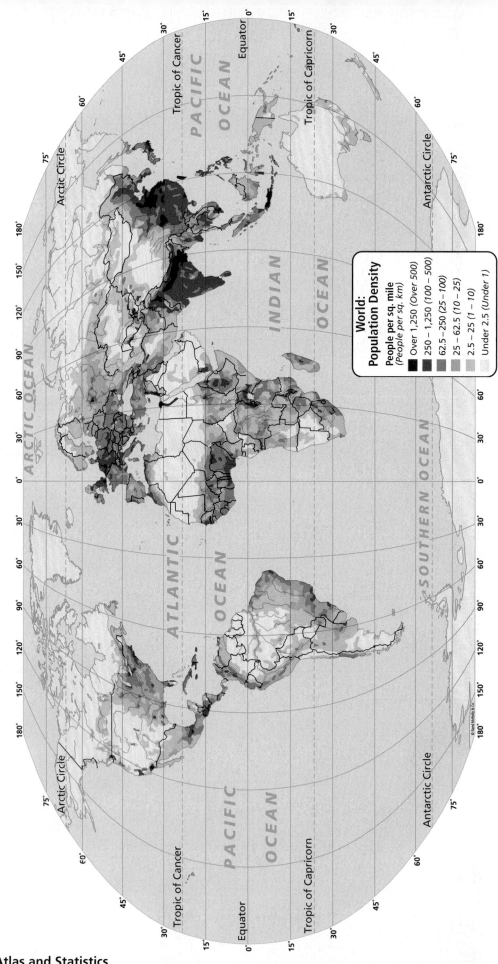

World:
Population Density

People per sq. mile
(People per sq. km)

Over 1,250 (Over 500)
250 – 1,250 (100 – 500)
62.5 – 250 (25 – 100)
25 – 62.5 (10 – 25)
2.5 – 25 (1 – 10)
Under 2.5 (Under 1)

Online Quiz
ClassZone.com

REVIEWING KEY CONCEPTS

1. Explain the relationship between the terms in each of these pairs:

   a. *wants*
   scarcity

   b. *consumer*
   producer

   c. *factors of production*
   entrepreneurship

2. What is the difference between needs and wants? Explain how a need may also be a want.

3. How does scarcity affect consumers? Producers?

4. What services that individuals or businesses provide do you use every day?

5. Describe how the owners of a computer repair store might use the four factors of production to run their business.

6. **Using Your Notes** How does scarcity affect methods of production? Refer to your completed cluster diagram.

   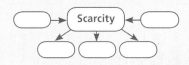

   Use the Graphic Organizer at **Interactive Review @ ClassZone.com**

CRITICAL THINKING

7. **Drawing Conclusions** Many high schools throughout the United States have faced a serious shortage of math and science teachers. Many prospective teachers choose to go into business and industry because of higher salaries. In some communities, businesses are "loaning" employees who want to teach part-time to schools to fill the math and science teacher gap. Does this scenario illustrate scarcity? Why or why not?

8. **Applying Economic Concepts** Consider the following entrepreneurs: Lucy, who runs an organic farm, and Ron, a sports superstar who owns several restaurants. Describe how they may have used entrepreneurship to establish and run their businesses.

9. **Writing About Economics** Select a 10-minute period of time in your day-to-day life—when you are in the cafeteria at lunchtime, for example. Analyze how scarcity affects your activities during this time period. Write your analysis in a paragraph.

10. **Challenge** At one time or another, you have probably made a choice about how to use your scarce resources that you later regretted. For example, you may have purchased a music download instead of going to the movies. What led you to your choice? What did you learn later that might have led you to a different choice?

ECONOMICS IN PRACTICE

Using Scarce Resources
Suppose you are moving into your first apartment like the young woman above. You have saved $1,200 to use for this purpose. When you go shopping, you learn that these are the prices for things you had on your list of furnishings.

Item	Price ($)
Kitchen table and chairs	200
TV set	150
Dishes	45
Silverware	25
Towels	35
Couch	300
Desk & chair	175
Bed	350
Computer	400
Stereo system	300

Make Economic Choices Use these prices to decide how you will spend your budget for furnishings. Make a list of the things you will buy.

Challenge What did you have to give up to get the things you chose? Why did you decide to give those things up?

Economic Choice Today: Opportunity Cost

OBJECTIVES	KEY TERMS	TAKING NOTES
In Section 2, you will • understand why choice is at the heart of economics • explain how incentives and utility influence people's economic choices • consider the role of trade-offs and opportunity costs in making economic choices • demonstrate how to do a cost-benefit analysis	incentives, *p. 12* utility, *p. 12* economize, *p. 12* trade-off, *p. 14* opportunity cost, *p. 14* cost-benefit analysis, *p. 15* marginal cost, *p. 16* marginal benefit, *p. 16*	As you read Section 2, complete a cluster diagram to help you see how the key concepts relate to one another. Use the Graphic Organizer at **Interactive Review @ ClassZone.com** Economic Choice

Making Choices

QUICK REFERENCE

Incentives are methods used to encourage people to take certain actions.

Utility is the benefit or satisfaction received from using a good or service.

To **economize** means to make decisions according to the best combination of costs and benefits.

KEY CONCEPTS

As you recall from Section 1, scarcity forces everyone to choose. But what shapes the economic choices that people make? One factor involves **incentives**, or benefits offered to encourage people to act in certain ways. Grades in school, wages paid to workers, and praise or recognition earned in personal and public life are all incentives. Choice is also influenced by **utility**, or the benefit or satisfaction gained from the use of a good or service. When they economize, people consider both incentives and utility. In common usage, the word *economize* means to "cut costs" or "do something cheaply." In strict economic terms, however, **economize** means to "make decisions according to what you believe is the best combination of costs and benefits."

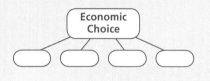

Incentives The chance of winning a championship trophy serves as an incentive for athletes to train and play hard.

ECONOMICS SKILLBUILDER

 For more on cause and effect, see the Skillbuilder Handbook, page R20.

Analyzing Cause and Effect

Causes are the events that explain why something happens and **effects** are what happens. An effect can become the cause of other effects, resulting in a chain of events or conditions. Identifying causes and effects helps economists understand how economic conditions occur. Use the strategies below to help you identify causes and effects using a graphic organizer.

Identify causes by using the word *why* to formulate questions about the topic of the passage. Example: *Why did oil become more scarce in 2003? Why did this situation continue?* The answers you find will be the causes.

Turmoil Reduces Oil Supply

Oil is a scarce resource, but events in the Middle East have made it more so. The invasion of Iraq in 2003 by U.S.- and British-led coalition forces led to an almost immediate shutdown of Iraq's oil exports, thereby reducing the availability of crude oil by some 1.8. million barrels per day. Unrest in Nigeria, Africa's largest oil producer, further added to global scarcity. More than two years later, in part due to continued unrest in the Middle East, oil production was still sluggish. One result of the continued scarcity was a rise in energy prices. Increased energy prices in turn caused shipping costs to rise. The increased costs of shipping led shippers to seek more economical means of transport. Some shippers have decreased their use of planes and trucks. Instead, they have turned to less fuel-dependent modes of transport. One example is the use of double stacked railroad cars that can carry two shipping containers stacked one on top of the other.

Identify effects by looking for results or consequences. These are sometimes indicated by words such as *led to, brought about, thereby,* and *as a result.*

Look for cause-effect chains, where an effect may be the cause of another event and so on.

Diagram the causes and effects in a flowchart like this one.

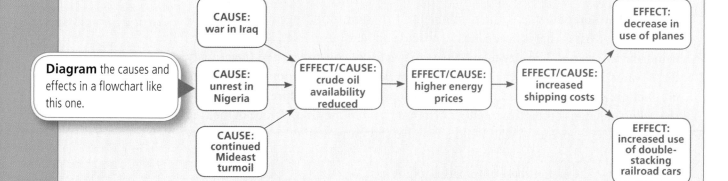

THINKING ECONOMICALLY Analyzing Causes and Effects

Locate and read an economics-related article in a current affairs magazine, such as *Time, Newsweek,* or *U.S. News & World Report.* Make a diagram to summarize the causes and effects discussed in the article.

FIGURE 1.1 Factors of Production

Land All the natural resources found on or under the ground that are used to produce goods and services are considered land.

Labor All the human time, effort, and talent that go into the production of goods and services are considered labor.

What are the Factors of Production?

Entrepreneurship The combination of vision, skill, ingenuity, and willingness to take risks that is needed to create and run new businesses is called entrepreneurship.

Capital All the physical resources made and used by people to produce and distribute goods and services are considered capital. So, too, are the knowledge and skills that make workers more productive.

ANALYZE CHARTS
Two new businesses have opened in your neighborhood—a coffee bar called Lou's Café and a health club called BodyPower. Construct your own Economics Essentials diagram to show how the four factors of production are used in one of these businesses.

FACTOR 4 Entrepreneurship

The fourth factor of production, entrepreneurship, brings the other three factors together. **Entrepreneurship** is the combination of vision, skill, ingenuity, and willingness to take risks that is needed to create and run new businesses. Most entrepreneurs are innovators. They try to anticipate the wants of consumers and then satisfy these wants in new ways. This may involve developing a new product, method of production, or way of marketing or distributing products. Entrepreneurs are also risk takers. They risk their time, energy, creativity, and money in the hope of making a profit. The entrepreneurs who build a massive shopping mall or who open a new health club do so because they think they could profit from these business ventures. The risk they take is that these enterprises might fail.

QUICK REFERENCE

Entrepreneurship involves the vision, skills, and risk-taking needed to create and run businesses.

APPLICATION Applying Economic Concepts

C. Think of a product that you recently purchased. How do you think the four factors of production were used to create this product?

The Factors of Production

To understand how societies answer the first two basic questions—what to produce and how to produce it—economists have identified the **factors of production**, or the economic resources needed to produce goods and services. They divide the factors of production into four broad categories: land, labor, capital, and entrepreneurship. All of these factors have one thing in common—their supply is limited.

FACTOR 1 Land

In everyday terms, the word *land* usually refers to a stretch of ground on the earth's surface. In economic terms, however, **land** includes all the natural resources found on or under the ground that are used to produce goods and services. Water, forests, and all kinds of wildlife belong in the category of land. So, too, do buried deposits of minerals, gas, and oil.

FACTOR 2 Labor

The word *labor* usually brings to mind images of hard physical work. In economic terms, however, its meaning is far broader. **Labor** is all the human time, effort, and talent that go into the making of products. Labor, then, is not only the work done by garbage collectors, factory workers, and construction workers. It also includes the work of architects, teachers, doctors, sales clerks, and government officials.

FACTOR 3 Capital

When you hear the word *capital,* you probably think of money. In economic terms, however, **capital** is all the resources made and used by people to produce and distribute goods and services. Tools, machinery, and factories are all forms of capital. So are offices, warehouses, stores, roads, and airplanes. In other words, capital is all of a producer's physical resources. For this reason capital is sometimes called physical capital, or real capital.

While businesses invest in real capital, workers invest in human capital—the knowledge and skills gained through experience. Human capital includes such things as a college degree or good job training. When workers possess more human capital, they are more productive.

Human Capital Education increases your human capital and makes you more productive in the workplace.

QUICK REFERENCE

Factors of production are the resources needed to produce goods and services.

Land refers to all natural resources used to produce goods and services.

Labor is all of the human effort used to produce goods and services.

Capital is all of the resources made and used by people to produce goods and services.

How to Produce For some societies, using a large amount of human labor is the most efficient way to produce food (left). For other societies, using a lot of machinery is a more efficient method of production (right).

QUESTION 2 How Will It Be Produced?

Once a society has decided what it will produce, it must then decide how these goods and services will be produced. Answering this second question involves using scarce resources in the most efficient way to satisfy society's wants. Again, decisions on methods of production are influenced, in part, by the natural resources a society possesses.

In deciding how to grow crops, for example, societies adopt different approaches. Societies with a large, relatively unskilled labor force might adopt labor-intensive farming methods. For this society, using many workers and few machines is the most efficient way to farm. The United States, however, has a highly skilled work force. So, using labor-intensive methods would be an inefficient use of labor resources. Therefore, the United States takes a capital-intensive approach to farming. In other words, it uses lots of machinery and few workers.

QUESTION 3 For Whom Will It Be Produced?

The third fundamental economic question involves how goods and services are distributed among people in society. This actually involves two questions. Exactly how much should people get and how should their share be delivered to them?

Should everyone get an equal share of the goods and services? Or should a person's share be determined by how much he or she is willing to pay? Once the question of how much has been decided, societies must then decide exactly how they are going to get these goods and services to people. To do this, societies develop distribution systems, which include road and rail systems, seaports, airports, trucks, trains, ships, airplanes, computer networks—anything that helps move goods and services from producers to consumers in an efficient manner.

APPLICATION Analyzing Cause and Effect

B. Why does the basic problem of scarcity lead societies to ask the three fundamental economic questions?

Scarcity Leads to Three Economic Questions

KEY CONCEPTS

If you have ever had to decide whether something you want is worth the money, then you have experienced scarcity firsthand. Scarcity in the lives of individual consumers—the gap between their unlimited wants and limited resources—is all too easy to understand. Scarcity, however, also confronts producers and whole societies. Indeed, scarcity requires every society to address three basic economic questions: What will be produced? How will it be produced? For whom will it be produced?

QUESTION 1 What Will Be Produced?

To answer the first fundamental economic question, a society must decide the mix of goods and services it will produce. Will it produce mainly food, or will it also produce automobiles, televisions, computers, furniture, and shoes? The goods and services a society chooses to produce depend, in part, on the natural resources it possesses. For example, a country that does not possess oil is unlikely to choose to produce petroleum products. Resources, however, do not completely control what a country produces. Japan does not possess large amounts of the iron ore needed to make steel. Yet Japan is a leading producer of automobiles, whose construction requires a great deal of steel.

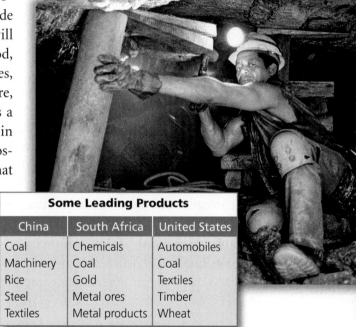

Some Leading Products		
China	South Africa	United States
Coal	Chemicals	Automobiles
Machinery	Coal	Coal
Rice	Gold	Textiles
Steel	Metal ores	Timber
Textiles	Metal products	Wheat

What to Produce? The availability of natural resources, such as gold, influences what the country of South Africa produces.

Some countries, including the United States, resolve the issue of what goods and services to produce by allowing producers and consumers to decide. For example, if consumers want cars with automatic transmissions, automobile companies would be unwise to make only cars that have manual transmissions. In other countries—Cuba and North Korea, for example—the consumer plays little or no part in answering this question. Rather, the government decides what goods and services will be produced.

This first fundamental economic question involves not only what to produce, but also how much to produce. To answer this, societies must review what their wants are at any time. A country at war, for example, will choose to produce more weapons than it would during peacetime.

Shortages and Scarcity Shortages often are temporary. Movie tickets may be in short supply today, but in a few days' time they may be easy to come by. Scarcity, however, never ends because wants always exceed the resources available to satisfy them.

PRINCIPLE 1 People Have Wants

Choice is central to the use of scarce resources. People make choices about all the things they desire—both needs and wants. You might think of food as a need, because it is necessary for your survival. Nevertheless, you make choices about food. What do you want for dinner tonight? Will you cook a gourmet creation or heat up a frozen dinner? Or will you treat yourself to a meal at your favorite restaurant? You make choices about other needs too. For example, consider the choices you make about the clothes you wear.

Wants are not only unlimited, they also are ever changing. Twenty-five years ago, for example, few Americans owned a personal computer. Today, however, few Americans can imagine life without computers and computer-related technology.

PRINCIPLE 2 Scarcity Affects Everyone

Because wants are unlimited and resources are scarce, choices have to be made about how best to use these resources. Scarcity, then, affects which goods are made and which services are provided. **Goods** are physical objects that can be purchased, such as food, clothing, and furniture. **Services** are work that one person performs for another for payment. Services include the work of sales clerks, technical support representatives, teachers, nurses, doctors, and lawyers. Scarcity affects the choices of both the **consumer**, a person who buys goods or services for personal use, and the **producer**, a person who makes goods or provides services.

APPLICATION Applying Economic Concepts

A. Identify five wants that you have right now. Describe how scarcity affects your efforts to meet these wants.

 Economics Update

Find an update about computer ownership in the United States at **ClassZone.com**

QUICK REFERENCE

Goods are objects, such as food, clothing, and furniture, that can be bought.

Services are work that one person does for another.

A **consumer** is a person who buys or uses goods or services.

A **producer** is a maker of goods or a provider of services.

Scarcity: The Basic Economic Problem

OBJECTIVES	KEY TERMS	TAKING NOTES
In Section 1, you will • explain how the economic definition of scarcity differs from the common definition • understand why scarcity affects everyone • learn three economic questions that societies face because of scarcity • describe the four factors of production and their uses	wants, *p. 4* needs, *p. 4* scarcity, *p. 4* economics, *p. 4* goods, *p. 5* services, *p. 5* consumer, *p. 5* producer, *p. 5* factors of production, *p. 8* land, *p. 8* labor, *p. 8* capital, *p. 8* entrepreneurship, *p. 9*	As you read Section 1, complete a cluster diagram showing how scarcity is the central concept of economics. Use the Graphic Organizer at **Interactive Review @ ClassZone.com**

What Is Scarcity?

KEY CONCEPTS

Have you ever felt you wanted a new cell phone, a car, a new pair of running shoes, or the latest MP3 player? You are not alone. Consumers have many economic wants. **Wants** are desires that can be satisfied by consuming a good or service. When making purchases, people often make a distinction between the things they need and the things they want. Some things that people desire, like a house or an apartment, are more important than other things, like a flat-screen television. **Needs** are things, such as food, clothing, and shelter, that are necessary for survival.

People always want more, no matter how much they have already. In fact, wants are unlimited, but the resources available to satisfy them are limited. The result of this difference is **scarcity**, the situation that exists when there are not enough resources to meet human wants. Scarcity is not a temporary shortage of some desired thing. Rather, it is a fundamental and ongoing tension that confronts individuals, businesses, governments, and societies. Indeed, it is so basic to human experience that a social science has developed to understand and explain it. That social science is **economics**, the study of how people choose to use scarce resources to satisfy their wants. Economics involves

1. **examining** how individuals, businesses, governments, and societies choose to use scarce resources to satisfy their wants
2. **organizing, analyzing, and interpreting data** about those economic behaviors
3. **developing theories and economic laws** that explain how the economy works and to predict what might happen in the future.

The Economic Way of Thinking

CONCEPT REVIEW

Economics is the study of how individuals and societies satisfy their unlimited wants with limited resources.

CHAPTER 1 KEY CONCEPT

Scarcity is the situation that exists because wants are unlimited and resources are limited.

WHY THE CONCEPT MATTERS

You confront the issue of scarcity constantly in everyday life. Look again at the caption on page 2. Suppose you have $20 to cover the cost of lunches for the week. How will you use your limited funds to meet your wants (lunch for Monday through Friday)? What if you stayed late at school twice a week and bought a $1 snack each day? How would this affect your lunch choices? Identify one or two other examples of scarcity in your everyday life.

Online Highlights
More at ClassZone.com

 Economics Update

Go to **ECONOMICS UPDATE** for chapter updates and news on the cost of expansion plans at O'Hare Airport in Chicago. (See Case Study, pages 32–33).

 Animated Economics

Go to **ANIMATED ECONOMICS** for interactive lessons on the graphs and tables in this chapter. ▶

Interactive ◀▶ Review

Go to **INTERACTIVE REVIEW** for concept review and activities.

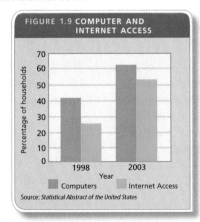

FIGURE 1.9 COMPUTER AND INTERNET ACCESS

Percentage of households / *Year* / Computers / Internet Access

Source: *Statistical Abstract of the United States*

How do economists use graphs? See Section 4 of this chapter.

Scarcity and Choices

Economics is about making choices. Even such an ordinary task as deciding what to have for lunch involves economic choice. Should you spend $5 on a hot meal, $3 on a sandwich, or should you save your money and bring lunch from home?

Directions: Use the graph and your knowledge of economics to answer questions 1 and 2.

Shifts in Aggregate Supply

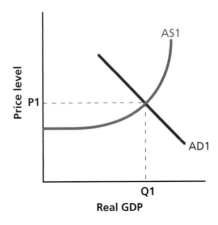

1. The graph above shows an economy at its macroeconomic equilibrium. Copy this graph onto a separate sheet of paper. On the graph, chart how the aggregate supply curve and macroeconomic equilibrium would change if interest rates fell.

2. Write a brief description of these changes and explain why they occurred.

Extended Response

Extended-response questions usually focus on an exhibit of some kind—a chart, graph, or diagram, for example. They are more complex than multiple-choice questions and often require a written response.

Some extended-response questions ask you to complete the exhibit. Others require you to present the information in the exhibit in a different form. Still others ask you to write an essay, a report, or some other extended piece of writing. In most standardized tests, exhibits have only one extended-response question.

① Read the title of the exhibit to get an idea of the subject.

② Carefully read the extended-response questions. (Question 1 asks you to complete the graph by drawing and labeling a new demand curve. Question 2 asks you to write a brief explanation of what is shown in the completed graph.)

③ Study and analyze the exhibit.

④ If the question requires an extended piece of writing, jot down ideas in outline form to get started.

① Shifts in Demand

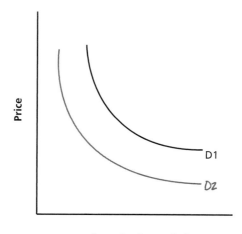

1. The graph above shows the demand for CDs. How would demand for CDs change if the price of CD players rose? Draw a new demand curve to reflect this change. Label the new curve D2.

2. Write a brief explanation of why demand for CDs changed in this way.

④ Sample Response CDs and CD players are used together, so they are complements. If demand for one changes, demand for the other will change in the same way. If the price of CD players rises, then demand for CD players and CDs will decrease and the demand curve shifts to the left.

Directions: Use the graphs and your knowledge of economics to answer questions 1 through 4.

New Jobs Added to the U.S. Economy

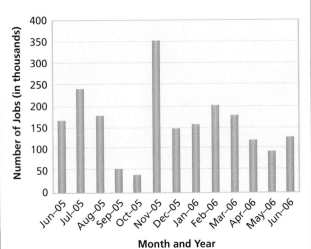

Source: U.S. Department of Labor

Electricity Generation by Energy Source

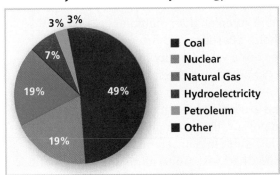

Source: Energy Information Administration,
Electric Power Monthly, June 2006

1. When was the greatest number of jobs added to the economy?

   A. July 2005

   B. November 2005

   C. February 2006

   D. March 2006

2. Which statement is supported by information in the graph?

   A. The graph shows that there were greater fluctuations in job creation in the later months of 2005 than there were in the early months of 2006.

   B. More jobs were added to the economy in all of 2005 than in all of 2006.

   C. The graph shows a steady upward trend in the number of jobs added to the economy.

   D. More jobs were added to the economy between January and June of 2006 than between June and December of 2005.

3. Which source of fuel generated nearly half of all electric power?

   A. coal

   B. natural gas

   C. nuclear

   D. petroleum

4. Which single source generated the least amount of electricity?

   A. coal

   B. natural gas

   C. nuclear

   D. petroleum

Bar and Pie Graphs

A bar graph allows for comparisons among numbers or sets of numbers. A pie, or circle, graph shows relationships among the parts of a whole. These parts look like slices of a pie. The size of each slice is proportional to the percentage of the whole that it represents.

1 Read the title of the graph to learn what it is about.

2 For a bar graph, study the labels on the vertical and horizontal axes to see the kinds of information presented in the graph. Note the intervals between amounts or years.

3 Study the legend, if there is one. The legend on a bar graph provides information on what is being graphed. The legend on a pie graph shows what each slice of the pie represents.

4 Look at the source line and evaluate the reliability of the information in the graph.

5 Study the data on the graph. Make comparisons among the slices of a pie graph. Draw conclusions and make inferences based on the data.

6 Read the questions carefully and use any words to reject incorrect alternatives.

1 **U.S. Imports of Crude Oil and Petroleum Products by Region**

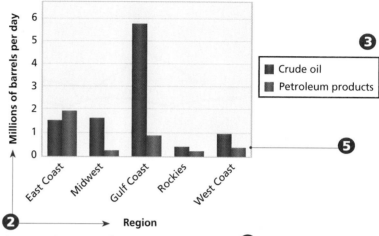

Source: U.S. Energy Information Administration **4**

6 **1.** Which region of the United States imported the most crude oil per day during 2004?

   A. East Coast

   B. West Coast

   C. Gulf Coast

   D. Midwest

1 **Components of M1**

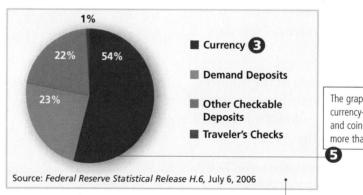

The graph shows that currency—paper money and coins—makes up more than half of M1.

Source: *Federal Reserve Statistical Release H.6,* July 6, 2006

Statistics from government agencies, such as the Federal Reserve, tend to be reliable.

6 **2.** What is the largest component of M1?

   A. currency

   B. demand deposits

   C. other checkable deposits

   D. traveler's checks

answers: 1 (C), 2 (A)

Directions: Use the graph and your knowledge of economics to answer questions 1 through 4.

Retail Prices for Regular Gasoline

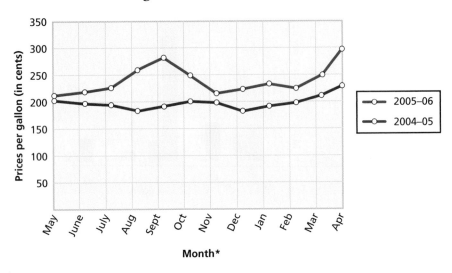

*Survey taken last week of month

Source: U.S. Energy Information Administration

1. During which period did the price of regular gasoline rise toward its peak?

A. May–August 2004

B. November 2004–February 2005

C. August–November 2005

D. February–April 2006

2. Which of the following statements most accurately describes the information shown in the graph?

A. Gas prices were stable during both 12-month periods.

B. There was a severe spike in price during each 12-month period.

C. The price of gas was always higher in 2005–2006.

D. The price of regular gas fluctuated more during 2004–2005.

3. During which period was the price of gasoline lowest?

A. in December 2004

B. in December 2005

C. in May 2004

D. in May 2005

4. In 2005–2006, the price of gasoline per gallon

A. nearly reached $3.00

B. dropped from close to $3.00 to less than $2.20

C. fluctuated more than in 2004–2005

D. all of the above

Line Graphs

Line graphs display information in a visual form. They are particularly useful for showing changes and trends over time.

1 Read the title of the graph to learn what it is about.

2 Study the labels on the vertical and horizontal axes to see the kinds of information presented in the graph. The vertical axis usually shows what is being graphed, while the horizontal axis indicates the time period covered.

3 Review the information in the graph and note any trends or patterns. Look for explanations for these trends or patterns.

4 Carefully read and answer the questions. Note if questions refer to a specific year or time period, or if they focus on trends or explanations for trends.

1 **Nuclear Generation of Electricity in the United States**

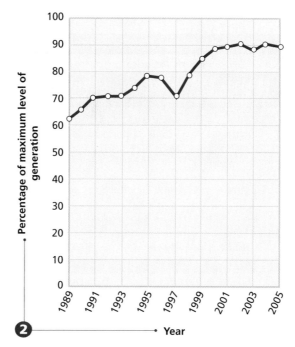

3 One likely explanation for increase in electricity generated is an increase in demand.

Source: U.S. Energy Information Administration

1. Nuclear generation of electricity first exceeded 80 percent of maximum capacity in

A. 1994

B. 1995

C. 1998

D. 1999

2. During which time period did the percentage of maximum capacity increase the most?

A. 1989–1991

B. 1993–1995

C. 1997–1999

D. 1999–2002

answers: 1 (B), 2 (C)

Directions: Use the chart and your knowledge of economics to answer questions 1 through 4.

Refined Copper Production for Selected Countries (in thousands of metric tons)						
	North America			South America		
Year	Canada	Mexico	United States	Brazil	Chile	Peru
1986	493.4	72.3	1,479.9	166.0	783.7	225.6
1987	491.1	128.4	1,541.6	201.7	795.0	224.8
1988	528.7	140.9	1,852.0	185.9	852.9	174.7
1989	515.2	155.8	1,953.8	207.8	1,071.0	224.3
1990	515.8	157.1	2,017.4	201.7	990.8	181.8
1991	538.0	190.1	2,000.0	141.4	1,012.8	244.1
1992	539.3	191.0	2,140.0	158.0	1,242.3	251.1
1993	561.6	197.8	2,250.0	161.1	1,093.2	261.7
1994	527.5	199.5	2,230.0	170.0	1,080.0	253.0
1995	560.0	207.5	2,280.0	165.0	1,288.8	282.0

Source: *2003 Industrial Commodity Statistics Yearbook,* United Nations

1. Which country produced the most refined copper in the years shown?

   A. Canada

   B. Mexico

   C. the United States

   D. Chile

2. From 1986 to 1988, Mexico's copper production

   A. remained fairly constant

   B. nearly doubled

   C. decreased slightly

   D. almost tripled

3. Which North American country showed an increase in copper production each year from 1987 through 1995?

   A. Canada

   B. Mexico

   C. the United States

   D. all of the above

4. Brazil's copper production was greatest in

   A. 1995

   B. 1994

   C. 1990

   D. 1989

STRATEGIES FOR TAKING STANDARDIZED TESTS

Charts

Charts present information in a visual form. Economics textbooks use several types of charts, including tables, flow charts, Venn diagrams, circular flow charts, and infographics. The chart most commonly found in standardized tests, however, is the table. This organizes information in columns and rows for easy viewing.

1 Read the title and identify the broad subject of the chart.

2 Read the column and row headings and any other labels. These will provide more details about the subject of the chart.

3 Note how the information in the chart is organized.

4 Compare and contrast the information from column to column and row to row.

5 Try to draw conclusions from the information in the chart.

6 Read the questions and then study the chart again.

1

Gross Domestic Product (GDP)—Percentage Change Over Previous Year—for Selected Countries		
Country	2002	2003
Canada	3.4	2.0
France	1.1	0.5
Germany	0.1	-0.1
Italy	0.4	0.3
Japan	-0.3	2.5
United Kingdom	1.8	2.2
United States	1.9	3.0

Source: *Historical Statistics of the United States*

3 This chart organizes the countries alphabetically. In some charts, information is organized according to years or the value of the numbers displayed.

4 Notice that the rows contain both positive and negative numbers.

5 Think about what trend or trends the data indicates.

1. The country that had the greatest percentage change in GDP in 2003 was

A. the United States
B. the United Kingdom
C. Japan
D. Canada

2. In 2002, which country experienced a decline in GDP?

A. France
B. Italy
C. Germany
D. Japan

answers: 1 (A), 2 (D)

Directions: Read each question carefully and choose the best answer from the four alternatives.

1. Which of the following is *not* a type of business consolidation?

 A. vertical merger

 B. franchise

 C. conglomerate

 D. multinational corporation

2. Wage rates are influenced by

 A. supply and demand

 B. discrimination

 C. government actions

 D. all of the above

3. As of 2005, the euro had been adopted by

 A. the United Kingdom

 B. all the European countries

 C. some European countries

 D. every member of the European Union

4. The central bank of the United States

 A. has no cash reserves

 B. is the U.S. Treasury

 C. does not lend money

 D. was established by the Federal Reserve Act

STRATEGIES FOR TAKING STANDARDIZED TESTS

Part 2: Test-Taking Strategies and Practice

You can improve your test-taking skills by practicing the strategies discussed in this section. First, read the tips on the left-hand page. Then apply them to the practice items on the right-hand page.

Multiple Choice

① Read the stem carefully and try to answer the question or complete the sentence before looking at the alternatives.

② Look for key words and facts in a question. They may direct you to the correct answer.

③ Read each alternative with the stem. Don't make your final decision on the correct answer until you have read all of the alternatives.

④ Eliminate alternatives that you know are wrong.

⑤ Look for modifiers to help you rule out incorrect alternatives.

⑥ Carefully consider questions that include *all of the above* as an alternative.

⑦ Take great care with questions that are stated negatively.

---

① | stem |

1. The country with the (most) elements of a command economy is

② *Most* is a key word. China has some elements of a command economy but North Korea has more.

③ | alternatives |

A. China

B. North Korea

C. South Korea

D. Japan •

④ You can eliminate **D** if you remember that Japan has a market economy.

2. Economic models

A. (all) present statistical information •

B. represent economic forces

C. must be three-dimensional

D. (always) use graphs to convey information •

⑤ Absolute words, such as *all, always, never, ever,* and *only* often signal an incorrect alternative.

3. Which of these statements about Adam Smith is correct?

A. He is considered to be the founder of modern economics.

B. He was an economic advisor at the Versailles peace conference.

C. He endorsed the trickle-down theory of economics.

D. All of the above. •

⑥ If you select this answer, be sure that all of the alternatives are correct.

4. Which of the following is (not) a factor of production?

A. land

B. labor

C. services

D. capital

⑦ Eliminate incorrect alternatives by identifying those that are factors of production.

---

answers: 1 (B), 2 (B), 3 (D), 4 (C)

Review and Summarize What You Have Read

When you finish reading a section, review and summarize what you've read. If necessary, go back and reread information that was not clear the first time through.

1 Look again at the **blue** heads and **red** heads for a quick summary of the major points covered in the section.

2 Study any tables, charts, graphs, and photographs in the section. These visual materials often convey economic information in condensed form.

3 Complete all the questions in the **Section Assessment.** This will help you think critically about the material you have just read.

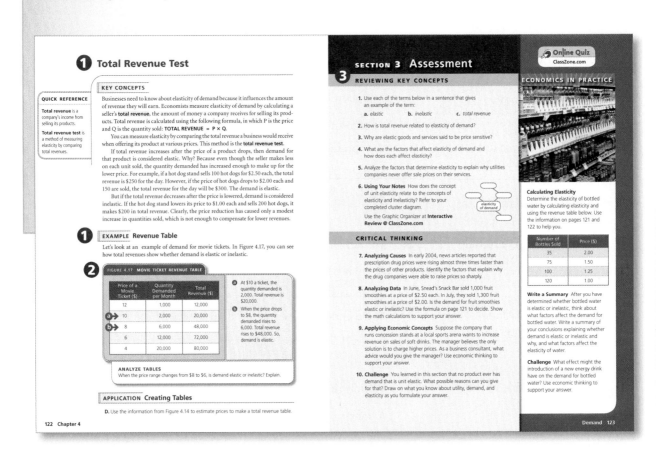

1 Total Revenue Test

QUICK REFERENCE

Total revenue is a company's income from selling its products.

Total revenue test is a method of measuring elasticity by comparing total revenues.

KEY CONCEPTS

Businesses need to know about elasticity of demand because it influences the amount of revenue they will earn. Economists measure elasticity of demand by calculating a seller's **total revenue,** the amount of money a company receives for selling its products. Total revenue is calculated using the following formula, in which P is the price and Q is the quantity sold: TOTAL REVENUE = P × Q.

You can measure elasticity by comparing the total revenue a business would receive when offering its product at various prices. This method is the **total revenue test.**

If total revenue increases after the price of a product drops, then demand for that product is considered elastic. Why? Because even though the seller makes less on each unit sold, the quantity demanded has increased enough to make up for the lower price. For example, if a hot dog stand sells 100 hot dogs for $2.50 each, the total revenue is $250 for the day. However, if the price of hot dogs drops to $2.00 each and 150 are sold, the total revenue for the day will be $300. The demand is elastic.

But if the total revenue decreases after the price is lowered, demand is considered inelastic. If the hot dog stand lowers its price to $1.00 each and sells 200 hot dogs, it makes $200 in total revenue. Clearly, the price reduction has caused only a modest increase in quantities sold, which is not enough to compensate for lower revenues.

1 **EXAMPLE** Revenue Table

Let's look at an example of demand for movie tickets. In Figure 4.17, you can see how total revenues show whether demand is elastic or inelastic.

2 FIGURE 4.17 MOVIE TICKET REVENUE TABLE

Price of a Movie Ticket ($)	Quantity Demanded per Month	Total Revenue ($)
12	1,000	12,000
a → 10	2,000	20,000
b → 8	6,000	48,000
6	12,000	72,000
4	20,000	80,000

a At $10 a ticket, the quantity demanded is 2,000. Total revenue is $20,000.

b When the price drops to $8, the quantity demanded rises to 6,000. Total revenue rises to $48,000. So, demand is elastic.

ANALYZE TABLES
When the price range changes from $8 to $6, is demand elastic or inelastic? Explain.

APPLICATION Creating Tables

D. Use the information from Figure 4.14 to estimate prices to make a total revenue table.

122 Chapter 4

SECTION 3 Assessment

3 REVIEWING KEY CONCEPTS

🔎 **Online Quiz**
ClassZone.com

1. Use each of the terms below in a sentence that gives an example of the term:

   a. elastic   b. inelastic   c. total revenue

2. How is total revenue related to elasticity of demand?

3. Why are elastic goods and services said to be price sensitive?

4. What are the factors that affect elasticity of demand and how does each affect elasticity?

5. Analyze the factors that determine elasticity to explain why utilities companies never offer sale prices on their services.

6. **Using Your Notes** How does the concept of unit elasticity relate to the concepts of elasticity and inelasticity? Refer to your completed cluster diagram.

   Use the Graphic Organizer at **Interactive Review @ ClassZone.com**

CRITICAL THINKING

7. **Analyzing Causes** In early 2004, news articles reported that prescription drug prices were rising almost three times faster than the prices of other products. Identify the factors that explain why the drug companies were able to raise prices so sharply.

8. **Analyzing Data** In June, Snead's Snack Bar sold 1,000 fruit smoothies at a price of $2.50 each. In July, they sold 1,300 fruit smoothies at a price of $2.00. Is the demand for fruit smoothies elastic or inelastic? Use the formula on page 121 to decide. Show the math calculations to support your answer.

9. **Applying Economic Concepts** Suppose the company that runs concession stands at a local sports arena wants to increase revenue on sales of soft drinks. The manager believes the only solution is to charge higher prices. As a business consultant, what advice would you give the manager? Use economic thinking to support your answer.

10. **Challenge** You learned in this section that no product ever has demand that is unit elastic. What possible reasons can you give for that? Draw on what you know about utility, demand, and elasticity as you formulate your answer.

ECONOMICS IN PRACTICE

Calculating Elasticity
Determine the elasticity of bottled water by calculating elasticity and using the revenue table below. Use the information on pages 121 and 122 to help you.

Number of Bottles Sold	Price ($)
35	2.00
75	1.50
100	1.25
120	1.00

Write a Summary After you have determined whether bottled water is elastic or inelastic, think about what factors affect the demand for bottled water. Write a summary of your conclusions explaining whether demand is elastic or inelastic and why, and what factors affect the elasticity of water.

Challenge What effect might the introduction of a new energy drink have on the demand for bottled water? Use economic thinking to support your answer.

Demand 123

STRATEGIES FOR TAKING STANDARDIZED TESTS

S5

Use Active Reading Strategies As You Read

Now you are ready to read the chapter. Read one section at a time, from beginning to end.

1 Read to build your economic vocabulary. Use the marginal **Quick Reference** notes to reinforce your understanding of key economic terms.

2 Use special features and illustrations to reinforce and extend your understanding of content and to apply your knowledge. Study features such as **Your Economic Choices,** which applies economic concepts to a real-world situation. Look closely at the **figures,** which illustrate economic concepts in table, chart, or graph form. Answer the accompanying **Analyze** questions to test your understanding of the visual and the concept it illustrates.

3 At natural breaks in the section, ask yourself questions about what you have just read. Look for **APPLICATION** headings at the bottom of pages and answer the questions or complete the activities. These provide you with opportunities to apply the knowledge you have gained from your reading.

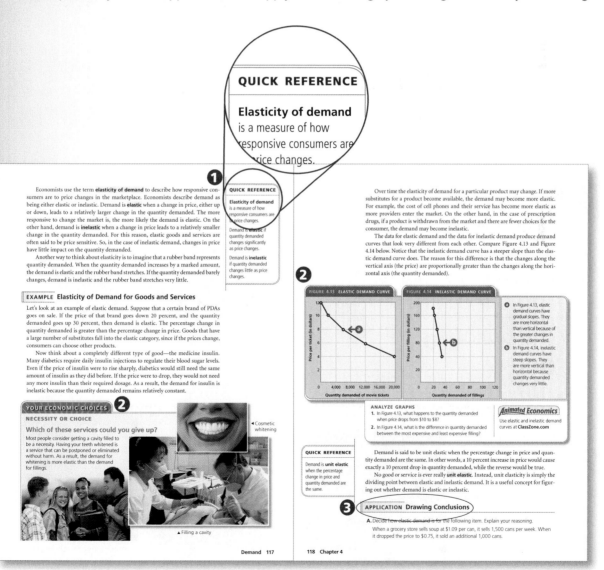

QUICK REFERENCE

Elasticity of demand is a measure of how responsive consumers are to price changes.

1

Economists use the term **elasticity of demand** to describe how responsive consumers are to price changes in the marketplace. Economists describe demand as being either elastic or inelastic. Demand is **elastic** when a change in price, either up or down, leads to a relatively larger change in the quantity demanded. The more responsive to change the market is, the more likely the demand is elastic. On the other hand, demand is **inelastic** when a change in price leads to a relatively smaller change in the quantity demanded. For this reason, elastic goods and services are often said to be price sensitive. So, in the case of inelastic demand, changes in price have little impact on the quantity demanded.

Another way to think about elasticity is to imagine that a rubber band represents quantity demanded. When the quantity demanded increases by a marked amount, the demand is elastic and the rubber band stretches. If the quantity demanded barely changes, demand is inelastic and the rubber band stretches very little.

QUICK REFERENCE

Elasticity of demand is a measure of how responsive consumers are to price changes.

Demand is **elastic** if quantity demanded changes significantly as price changes.

Demand is **inelastic** if quantity demanded changes little as price changes.

EXAMPLE Elasticity of Demand for Goods and Services

Let's look at an example of elastic demand. Suppose that a certain brand of PDAs goes on sale. If the price of that brand goes down 20 percent, and the quantity demanded goes up 30 percent, then demand is elastic. The percentage change in quantity demanded is greater than the percentage change in price. Goods that have a large number of substitutes fall into the elastic category, since if the prices change, consumers can choose other products.

Now think about a completely different type of good—the medicine insulin. Many diabetics require daily insulin injections to regulate their blood sugar levels. Even if the price of insulin were to rise sharply, diabetics would still need the same amount of insulin as they did before. If the price were to drop, they would not need any more insulin than their required dosage. As a result, the demand for insulin is inelastic because the quantity demanded remains relatively constant.

YOUR ECONOMIC CHOICES **2**

NECESSITY OR CHOICE

Which of these services could you give up?

Most people consider getting a cavity filled to be a necessity. Having your teeth whitened is a service that can be postponed or eliminated without harm. As a result, the demand for whitening is more elastic than the demand for fillings.

◄ Cosmetic whitening

▲ Filling a cavity

Demand 117

Over time the elasticity of demand for a particular product may change. If more substitutes for a product become available, the demand may become more elastic. For example, the cost of cell phones and their service has become more elastic as more providers enter the market. On the other hand, in the case of prescription drugs, if a product is withdrawn from the market and there are fewer choices for the consumer, the demand may become inelastic.

The data for elastic demand and the data for inelastic demand produce demand curves that look very different from each other. Compare Figure 4.13 and Figure 4.14 below. Notice that the inelastic demand curve has a steeper slope than the elastic demand curve does. The reason for this difference is that the changes along the vertical axis (the price) are proportionally greater than the changes along the horizontal axis (the quantity demanded).

2

FIGURE 4.13 ELASTIC DEMAND CURVE	FIGURE 4.14 INELASTIC DEMAND CURVE

a In Figure 4.13, elastic demand curves have gradual slopes. They are more horizontal than vertical because of the greater changes in quantity demanded.

b In Figure 4.14, inelastic demand curves have steep slopes. They are more vertical than horizontal because quantity demanded changes very little.

ANALYZE GRAPHS

1. In Figure 4.13, what happens to the quantity demanded when price drops from $10 to $8?
2. In Figure 4.14, what is the difference in quantity demanded between the most expensive and least expensive filling?

Animated **Economics**

Use elastic and inelastic demand curves at ClassZone.com

QUICK REFERENCE

Demand is **unit elastic** when the percentage change in price and quantity demanded are the same.

Demand is said to be unit elastic when the percentage change in price and quantity demanded are the same. In other words, a 10 percent increase in price would cause exactly a 10 percent drop in quantity demanded, while the reverse would be true.

No good or service is ever really **unit elastic.** Instead, unit elasticity is simply the dividing point between elastic and inelastic demand. It is a useful concept for figuring out whether demand is elastic or inelastic.

3 **APPLICATION** Drawing Conclusions

A. Decide how elastic demand is for the following item. Explain your reasoning.
When a grocery store sells soup at $1.09 per can, it sells 1,500 cans per week. When it dropped the price to $0.75, it sold an additional 1,000 cans.

118 Chapter 4

Preview Sections Before You Read

Each chapter consists of three or four sections. These sections explain and build on the **Key Concept.** Use the section openers to help you prepare to read.

❶ Study the information under **Objectives.** This bulleted list tells you the key points discussed in the material you are about to read.

❷ Preview the **Key Terms** list. This list identifies the vocabulary you will need to learn in order to understand the material you are about to read. Use the **Taking Notes** graphic to help you organize information presented in the text.

❸ Notice the structure of the section. **Blue** heads label the major topics; **red** subheads signal smaller topics within a major topic or illustrative examples of the major topic. Together, these heads provide you with a quick outline of the section.

❹ Read the first paragraph under **Key Concepts.** This links the content of the section to previous chapters or sections.

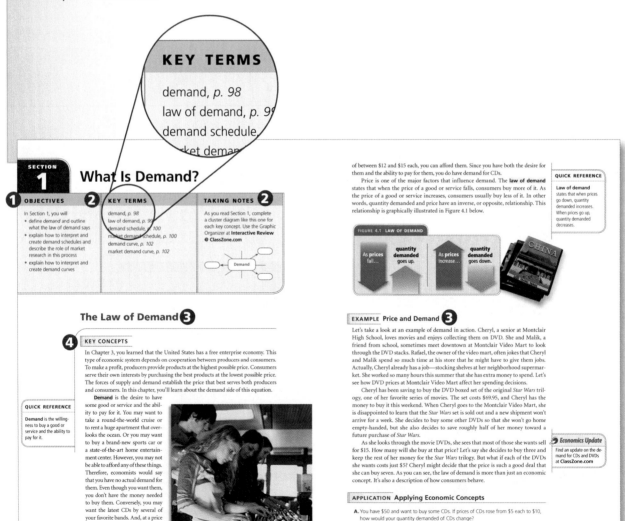

KEY TERMS

demand, *p. 98*

law of demand, *p. 99*

demand schedule,

market deman

SECTION 1

What Is Demand?

❶ OBJECTIVES

In Section 1, you will

• define *demand* and outline what the *law of demand* says

• explain how to interpret and create demand schedules and describe the role of market research in this process

• explain how to interpret and create demand curves

❷ KEY TERMS

demand, *p. 98*
law of demand, *p. 99*
demand schedule, *p. 100*
market demand schedule, *p. 100*
demand curve, *p. 102*
market demand curve, *p. 102*

❷ TAKING NOTES

As you read Section 1, complete a cluster diagram like this one for each key concept. Use the Graphic Organizer at **Interactive Review** @ ClassZone.com

Demand

The Law of Demand **❸**

❹ KEY CONCEPTS

In Chapter 3, you learned that the United States has a free enterprise economy. This type of economic system depends on cooperation between producers and consumers. To make a profit, producers provide products at the highest possible price. Consumers serve their own interests by purchasing the best products at the lowest possible price. The forces of supply and demand establish the price that best serves both producers and consumers. In this chapter, you'll learn about the demand side of this equation.

QUICK REFERENCE

Demand is the willingness to buy a good or service and the ability to pay for it.

Demand is the desire to have some good or service and the ability to pay for it. You may want to take a round-the-world cruise or to rent a huge apartment that overlooks the ocean. Or you may want to buy a brand-new sports car or a state-of-the-art home entertainment center. However, you may not be able to afford any of these things. Therefore, economists would say that you have no actual demand for them. Even though you want them, you don't have the money needed to buy them. Conversely, you may want the latest CDs by several of your favorite bands. And, at a price

98 Chapter 4

of between $12 and $15 each, you can afford them. Since you have both the desire for them and the ability to pay for them, you do have demand for CDs.

Price is one of the major factors that influence demand. The **law of demand** states that when the price of a good or service falls, consumers buy more of it. As the price of a good or service increases, consumers usually buy less of it. In other words, quantity demanded and price have an inverse, or opposite, relationship. This relationship is graphically illustrated in Figure 4.1 below.

QUICK REFERENCE

Law of demand states that when prices go down, quantity demanded increases. When prices go up, quantity demanded decreases.

FIGURE 4.1 LAW OF DEMAND

As prices fall... | quantity demanded goes up. | As prices increase... | quantity demanded goes down.

EXAMPLE Price and Demand ❸

Let's take a look at an example of demand in action. Cheryl, a senior at Montclair High School, loves movies and enjoys collecting them on DVD. She and Malik, a friend from school, sometimes meet downtown at Montclair Video Mart to look through the DVD stacks. Rafael, the owner of the video mart, often jokes that Cheryl and Malik spend so much time at his store that he might have to give them jobs. Actually, Cheryl already has a job—stocking shelves at her neighborhood supermarket. She worked so many hours this summer that she has extra money to spend. Let's see how DVD prices at Montclair Video Mart affect her spending decisions.

Cheryl has been saving to buy the DVD boxed set of the original *Star Wars* trilogy, one of her favorite series of movies. The set costs $69.95, and Cheryl has the money to buy it this weekend. When Cheryl goes to the Montclair Video Mart, she is disappointed to learn that the *Star Wars* set is sold out and a new shipment won't arrive for a week. She decides to buy some other DVDs so that she won't go home empty-handed, but she also decides to save roughly half of her money toward a future purchase of *Star Wars*.

As she looks through the movie DVDs, she sees that most of those she wants sell for $15. How many will she buy at that price? Let's say she decides to buy three and keep the rest of her money for the *Star Wars* trilogy. But what if each of the DVDs she wants costs just $5? Cheryl might decide that the price is such a good deal that she can buy seven. As you can see, the law of demand is more than just an economic concept. It's also a description of how consumers behave.

Economics Update
Find an update on the demand for CDs and DVDs at ClassZone.com

APPLICATION Applying Economic Concepts

A. You have $50 and want to buy some CDs. If prices of CDs rose from $5 each to $10, how would your quantity demanded of CDs change?

Demand 99

Part 1: Strategies for Studying Economics

Reading is the central skill in the effective study of economics or any other subject. You can improve your reading skills by using helpful techniques and by practicing. The better your reading skills, the more you will understand what you read. Below you will find several strategies that involve built-in features of *Economics: Choices and Concepts.* Careful use of these strategies will help you learn and understand economics more effectively.

Preview Chapters Before You Read

Each chapter begins with a two-page chapter opener. Study these pages to help you get ready to read.

1 Read the chapter title and section titles for clues to what will be covered in the chapter.

2 Read the **Concept Review,** which reviews previous learning important to understanding chapter content. Then study the **Key Concept,** which focuses on the main idea explored in the chapter. Finally, read the **Why the Concept Matters** explanation and question. These help place the chapter's main idea in a real-world context.

3 Study the chapter-opening photograph and caption. These provide a visual illustration of the chapter's main idea.

STRATEGIES FOR TAKING STANDARDIZED TESTS

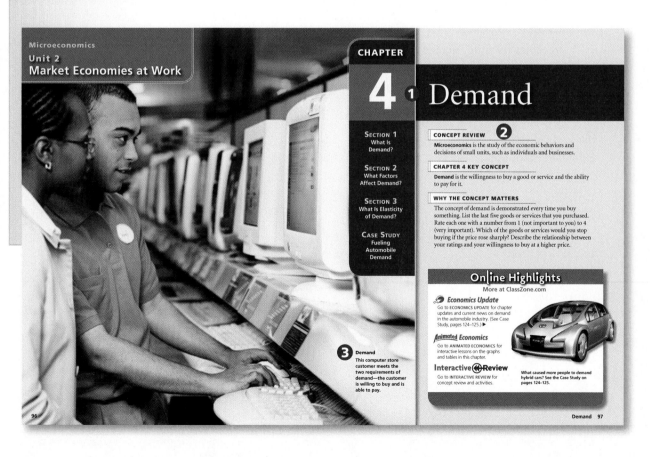

Microeconomics
Unit 2
Market Economies at Work

CHAPTER

4 **1**

Demand

SECTION 1
What Is Demand?

SECTION 2
What Factors Affect Demand?

SECTION 3
What Is Elasticity of Demand?

CASE STUDY
Fueling Automobile Demand

CONCEPT REVIEW **2**

Microeconomics is the study of the economic behaviors and decisions of small units, such as individuals and businesses.

CHAPTER 4 KEY CONCEPT

Demand is the willingness to buy a good or service and the ability to pay for it.

WHY THE CONCEPT MATTERS

The concept of demand is demonstrated every time you buy something. List the last five goods or services that you purchased. Rate each one with a number from 1 (not important to you) to 4 (very important). Which of the goods or services would you stop buying if the price rose sharply? Describe the relationship between your ratings and your willingness to buy at a higher price.

Online Highlights
More at ClassZone.com

Economics Update
Go to ECONOMICS UPDATE for chapter updates and current news on demand in the automobile industry. (See Case Study, pages 124–125.)▶

Animated Economics
Go to ANIMATED ECONOMICS for interactive lessons on the graphs and tables in this chapter.

Interactive Review
Go to INTERACTIVE REVIEW for concept review and activities.

What caused more people to demand hybrid cars? See the Case Study on pages 124–125.

3 Demand
This computer store customer meets the two requirements of demand—the customer is willing to buy and is able to pay.

96

Demand 97

S2

STRATEGIES FOR TAKING STANDARDIZED TESTS

This section of the textbook helps you develop and practice the skills you need to study economics and to take standardized tests. Part 1, **Strategies for Studying Economics,** takes you through the features of the textbook and offers suggestions on how to use these features to improve your reading and study skills.

Part 2, **Test-Taking Strategies and Practice,** offers specific strategies for tackling many of the items you will find on a standardized test. It gives tips for answering multiple-choice and extended-response questions. In addition, it offers guidelines for analyzing charts and line, bar, and pie graphs that often accompany these questions. Each strategy is followed by a set of questions you can use for practice.

CONTENTS for Strategies for Taking Standardized Tests

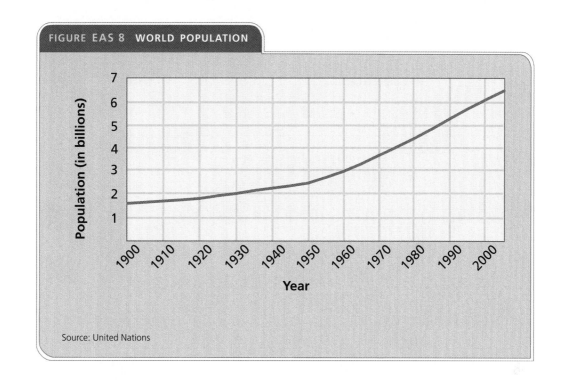

FIGURE EAS 8 WORLD POPULATION

Source: United Nations

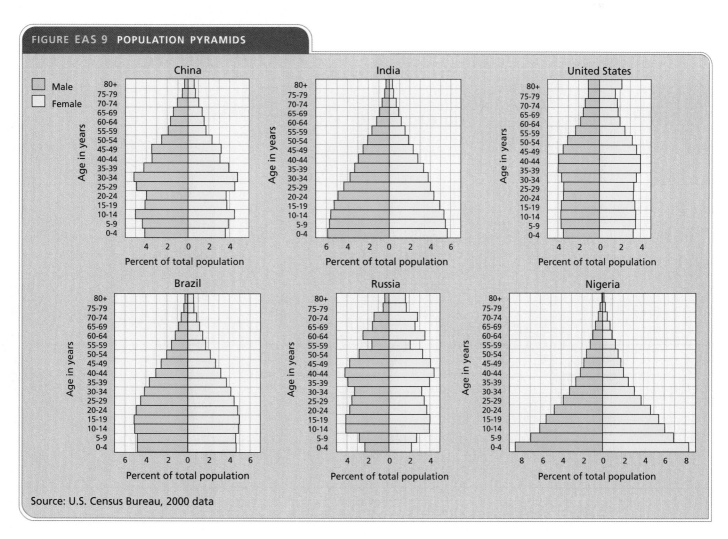

FIGURE EAS 9 POPULATION PYRAMIDS

Source: U.S. Census Bureau, 2000 data

RAND MᶜNALLY

Country	Population	Percent urban / rural	Unemployment rate	GDP (in billions of U.S. dollars)	GDP per capita (in U.S. dollars)	National debt (as percent of GDP)	Inflation rate
China	1,303,701,000	37 / 63	9.0	2,234.1	1,709	24.4	1.8
India	1,103,596,000	28 / 72	8.9	772.0	705	53.8	4.0
United States	296,483,000	79 / 21	5.1	12,455.8	42,000	64.7	3.4
Indonesia	221,932,000	42 / 58	11.8	281.3	1,283	49.9	10.5
Brazil	184,184,000	81 / 19	9.8	795.7	4,320	51.6	6.9
Pakistan	162,420,000	34 / 66	6.6	111.0	728	53.8	9.3
Bangladesh	144,233,000	23 / 77	2.5	60.8	400	44.5	7.0
Russia	143,025,000	73 / 27	7.6	763.3	5,349	12.9	12.6
Nigeria	131,530,000	44 / 56	2.9	99.1	678	11.0	17.9
Japan	127,728,000	79 / 21	4.4	4,567.4	35,757	158.0	–0.6
Mexico	107,029,000	75 / 25	3.6	768.4	7,298	17.4	4.0
Philippines	84,765,000	48 / 52	8.7	98.4	1,168	72.3	7.6
Vietnam	83,305,000	26 / 74	2.4	51.4	618	48.2	8.2
Germany	82,490,000	88 / 12	11.7	2,791.7	33,854	67.3	2.0
Egypt	74,033,000	43 / 57	9.5	89.5	1,265	104.7	11.4
Ethiopia	77,431,000	15 / 85	no data	11.2	153	no data	6.8
Turkey	72,907,000	65 / 35	10.2	362.5	5,062	68.0	8.2
Iran	69,515,000	67 / 33	11.2	192.3	2,767	28.9	12.1
Thailand	65,002,000	31 / 69	1.8	173.1	2,659	47.6	4.5
France	60,742,000	76 / 24	9.9	2,126.7	33,918	66.2	1.9

Sources: International Monetary Fund, Population Reference Bureau, U.S. Central Intelligence Agency; data from 2005 and earlier

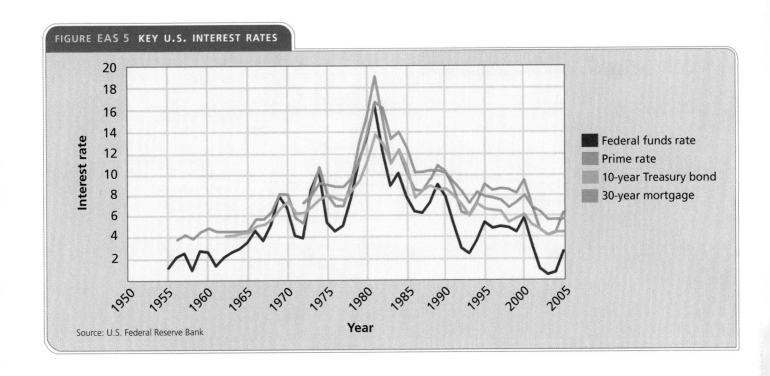

FIGURE EAS 5 KEY U.S. INTEREST RATES

Legend:
- Federal funds rate
- Prime rate
- 10-year Treasury bond
- 30-year mortgage

Y-axis: Interest rate
X-axis: Year

Source: U.S. Federal Reserve Bank

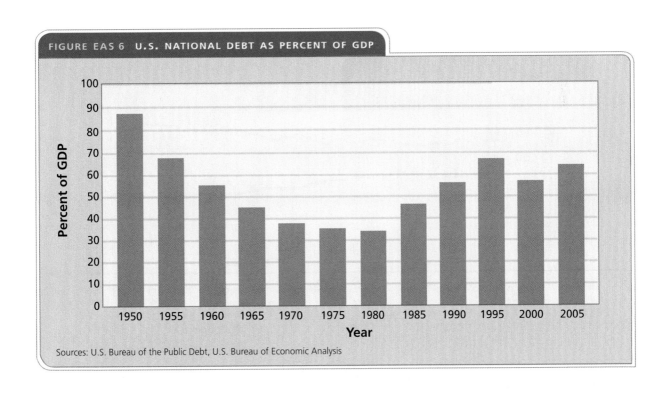

FIGURE EAS 6 U.S. NATIONAL DEBT AS PERCENT OF GDP

Y-axis: Percent of GDP
X-axis: Year

Sources: U.S. Bureau of the Public Debt, U.S. Bureau of Economic Analysis

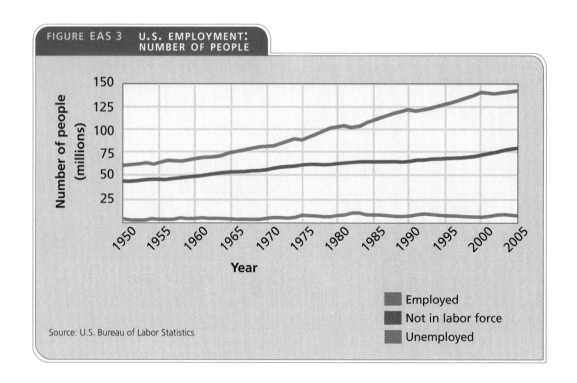

Source: U.S. Bureau of Labor Statistics

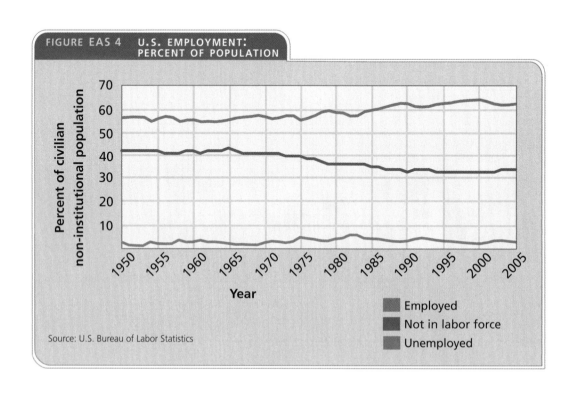

Source: U.S. Bureau of Labor Statistics

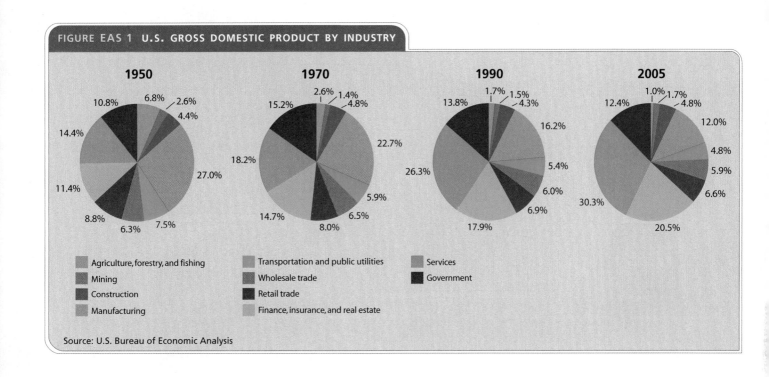

FIGURE EAS 1 U.S. GROSS DOMESTIC PRODUCT BY INDUSTRY

1950

10.8% 6.8% 2.6%
14.4% 4.4%
11.4% 27.0%
8.8%
6.3% 7.5%

1970

2.6% 1.4%
15.2% 4.8%
18.2% 22.7%
5.9%
14.7% 6.5%
8.0%

1990

1.7% 1.5%
13.8% 4.3%
16.2%
26.3% 5.4%
6.0%
6.9%
17.9%

2005

1.0% 1.7%
12.4% 4.8%
12.0%
4.8%
5.9%
30.3% 6.6%
20.5%

- Agriculture, forestry, and fishing
- Mining
- Construction
- Manufacturing
- Transportation and public utilities
- Wholesale trade
- Retail trade
- Finance, insurance, and real estate
- Services
- Government

Source: U.S. Bureau of Economic Analysis

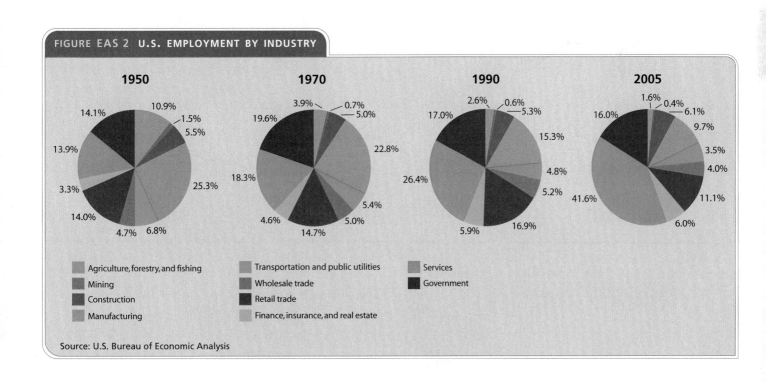

FIGURE EAS 2 U.S. EMPLOYMENT BY INDUSTRY

1950

10.9%
14.1% 1.5%
13.9% 5.5%
3.3% 25.3%
14.0%
4.7% 6.8%

1970

3.9% 0.7%
19.6% 5.0%
18.3% 22.8%
4.6% 5.4%
14.7% 5.0%

1990

2.6% 0.6%
17.0% 5.3%
15.3%
26.4% 4.8%
5.2%
5.9% 16.9%

2005

1.6% 0.4%
16.0% 6.1%
9.7%
3.5%
4.0%
41.6% 11.1%
6.0%

- Agriculture, forestry, and fishing
- Mining
- Construction
- Manufacturing
- Transportation and public utilities
- Wholesale trade
- Retail trade
- Finance, insurance, and real estate
- Services
- Government

Source: U.S. Bureau of Economic Analysis

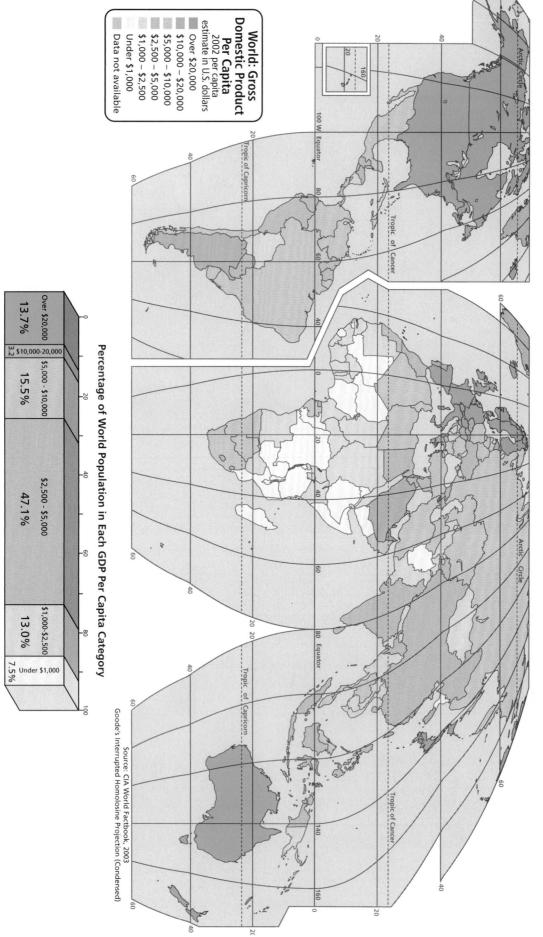

World: Gross Domestic Product Per Capita

2002 per capita estimate in U.S. dollars

- Over $20,000
- $10,000 – $20,000
- $5,000 – $10,000
- $2,500 – $5,000
- $1,000 – $2,500
- Under $1,000
- Data not available

Percentage of World Population in Each GDP Per Capita Category

Over $20,000	$10,000-20,000	$5,000 - $10,000	$2,500 - $5,000	$1,000-$2,500	Under $1,000
13.7%	3.2	15.5%	47.1%	13.0%	7.5%

Source: CIA World Factbook, 2003
Goode's Interrupted Homolosine Projection (Condensed)

160
20

Arctic Circle
Tropic of Cancer
Equator
Tropic of Capricorn
Arctic Circle

RAND McNALLY

MAKING CHOICES

How will you spend time with a friend?

You and a friend have the choice of going to dinner or going to a movie. There is an incentive for choosing the movies, since dinner would surely cost more. On the other hand, your friend has offered to help you with college applications. So dining out, which allows time for conversation, has more utility to you than seeing a movie.

Dinner

Movie

FACTOR 1 **Motivations for Choice**

Choice powers an economy, but what powers choice? The choices people make are shaped by incentives, by expected utility, and by the desire to economize. For example, look at Your Economic Choices above. How will you decide between the two options? Like other economic decision makers, you weigh the costs against the benefits, and you make your choice purposefully. Perhaps you decide to go out to dinner. Even though you'll spend more money, you feel that the tips your friend can give you on writing your college application essay are invaluable. You've economized by choosing what represents the best mix of costs and benefits.

In making this decision, you were guided by self-interest. This does not mean that you behaved selfishly. Rather, it simply means that you looked for ways to maximize the utility you'd get from spending time with your friend.

FACTOR 2 **No Free Lunch**

An old saying can sum up the issue of choice in economics: "There is no such thing as a free lunch." Every choice involves costs. These costs can take the form of money, time, or some other thing you value. Let's revisit your choices. If you chose to go to dinner rather than to a movie, you gained the benefit of a satisfying, informative, and beneficial conversation with a friend. Even so, you also paid a cost—you didn't see the movie. On the other hand, if you chose to go to the movie, you gained the benefit of an entertaining evening and having more money to save or spend on something else. Once again, however, your choice involved a cost. You sacrificed the time you could have spent getting advice and guidance on the college application process from your friend.

APPLICATION **Using a Decision-Making Process**

A. You have enough money to buy either an MP3 player that is on sale or some fitness equipment you want. What incentives and utility would guide your decision?

Trade-Offs and Opportunity Cost

KEY CONCEPTS

QUICK REFERENCE

A **trade-off** is the alternative people give up when they make choices.

Choices, as you have learned, always involve costs. For every choice you make, you give up something. The alternative that you give up when you make an economic choice is called a **trade-off**. Usually, trade-offs do not require all-or-nothing choices. Rather, they involve giving up some of one thing to gain more of another.

EXAMPLE 1 Making Trade-Offs

To understand how trade-offs work, let's take a look at decisions made by Shanti, who has just finished her junior year in high school. Shanti wants to go to summer school to earn some credits she can apply to college. She could take a semester-long course at a local university, or she could take an intensive six-week course at her high school. She decides on the six-week course, even though she'll earn fewer credits. However, she will have several weeks of the summer vacation to have fun and relax.

Trade-Offs All the decisions you make, including selecting school or college courses, involve choosing among alternatives.

EXAMPLE 2 Counting the Opportunity Cost

QUICK REFERENCE

Opportunity cost is the value of something that is given up to get something else that is wanted.

Shanti's friend Dan, who has just graduated, has decided to take off a year before going to college. He's been offered a full-time job for the whole year. However, he decides to take the job for six months and then spend time traveling.

Dan's choice, like all economic choices, involves an opportunity cost. The **opportunity cost** of a decision is the value of the next-best alternative, or what you give up by choosing one alternative over another. Dan decided to travel around the country and visit friends. The opportunity cost of that decision is the income he could have earned at his job. If, however, Dan had decided to work for the whole year, his opportunity cost would have been the trip around the country that he didn't take. Note that Dan's opportunity cost is not the value of all the things he might have done. Rather, it is the value of his next-best alternative, or what he gave up to get what he most wanted.

APPLICATION Applying Economic Concepts

B. Look again at Shanti's decision. What was the opportunity cost of her choice? If she had chosen the semester course, what would her opportunity cost have been?

Analyzing Choices

Shanti and Dan did not make their choices randomly. Rather, they carefully looked at the benefits they would gain and the opportunity costs they would incur from their decisions. This practice of examining the costs and the expected benefits of a choice as an aid to decision making is called **cost-benefit analysis**. Cost-benefit analysis is one of the most useful tools for individuals, businesses, and governments when they need to evaluate the relative worth of economic choices.

QUICK REFERENCE

Cost-benefit analysis is an approach that weighs the benefits of an action against its costs.

EXAMPLE Max's Decision-Making Grid

Perhaps the simplest application of cost-benefit analysis is the decision-making grid, which shows what you get and what you give up when you make choices. Look at Max's decision-making grid in Figure 1.2 below. Max has to decide how to spend his scarce time—studying for his government class or going out with his friends. Max likes nothing better than to spend hours talking with his friends at the local juice bar. However, the F he has in the government class at the moment will not look good on his transcript. So he certainly could benefit from some extra study time.

Max knows that he has six hours available for extra study or socializing each week. He begins to build his decision-making grid by listing all the options he has for using these six hours. He then lists the benefits and opportunity costs of each of these options. After reviewing all of this information, he chooses three extra hours of study a week. He feels that the opportunity cost, three hours of time with his friends, is worth the expected benefit, a B grade.

FIGURE 1.2 Max's Decision-Making Grid

A decision-making grid helps you to see what you gain and what you lose when you make choices. Max's decision-making grid shows the costs and benefits of hours spent studying versus time spent socializing.

Choice	Benefit	Opportunity Cost
One hour of extra study	D in government class	One hour with friends
Two hours of extra study	C in government class	Two hours with friends
Three hours of extra study	B in government class	Three hours with friends
Four hours of extra study	B+ in government class	Four hours with friends
Five hours of extra study	A− in government class	Five hours with friends
Six hours of extra study	A in government class	Six hours with friends

ANALYZE TABLES

1. What is Max's opportunity cost of three extra hours of study?
2. Read the information about marginal costs on the next page. What is Max's marginal cost of moving from a grade of B+ to a grade of A−?

Costs and benefits change over time. So do goals and circumstances. Such changes will influence the decisions people make. For instance, Max learns that Pine Tree State, the college he wants to attend, only considers applicants with a 3.4 or better grade point average. If he needs to get a B+ or better to raise his GPA to 3.4, he might decide to spend less time with his friends and study four or five hours per week rather than three.

EXAMPLE Marginal Costs and Benefits

QUICK REFERENCE

Marginal cost is the additional cost of using one more unit of a product.

Marginal benefit is the additional satisfaction from using one more unit of a product.

How did Max arrive at his decision? To explain it, economists would look at marginal costs and marginal benefits. **Marginal cost** is the cost of using one more unit of a good or service, while **marginal benefit** refers to the benefit or satisfaction received from using one more unit of a good or service. Max's choice was to study three extra hours, which gave him a B grade at the opportunity cost of three hours with his friends. Look again at Max's decision-making grid in Figure 1.2. What would be the marginal cost of one more hour of study? As you can see, it is the loss of one more hour with his friends. The marginal benefit of that extra hour would be an improvement in grade from B to B+. Max decided that the benefit of a slight improvement in his grade was not worth the cost of one less hour with his friends.

The analysis of marginal costs and marginal benefits is central to the study of economics. It helps to explain the decisions consumers, producers, and governments make as they try to meet their unlimited wants with limited resources.

YOUR ECONOMIC CHOICES

MARGINAL BENEFITS AND COSTS

Which will you do—basketball practice or after-school job?

For every hour you practice basketball, you gain in skill and increase your chances of making the team. However, each hour you practice is an hour you could have spent working at an after-school job to save for a car or college or something else you want.

Basketball practice   Part-time job

APPLICATION Using a Decision-Making Process

C. Look at Your Economic Choices above. Construct a decision-making grid that analyzes the potential choices of attending basketball practice and working at an after-school job. Which option would you choose?

REVIEWING KEY CONCEPTS

1. Explain the relationship between the terms in each of these pairs:

   a. *incentive*
   utility

   b. *trade-off*
   opportunity cost

   c. *marginal cost*
   marginal benefit

2. Two action movies are playing at your movie-theater complex. You have a half-price coupon for one. However, you choose to see the other. How might this still be an example of economizing?

3. Think of some of the options you have for spending time after school—sports practice, hobby clubs, work, or extra study, for example. Which option would you choose? What is the opportunity cost of your choice?

4. How is a decision-making grid an example of cost-benefit analysis?

5. Use the concepts of marginal costs and marginal benefits to explain why some people might see the same movie ten times while others will watch it only once or twice.

6. **Using Your Notes** How do marginal costs and benefits relate to trade-offs? Refer to your completed cluster diagram. Use the Graphic Organizer at **Interactive Review @ ClassZone.com**

Economic Choice

CRITICAL THINKING

7. **Applying Economic Concepts** A Web site reviewing new CDs offers you a free subscription. All you have to do is complete a brief online application. What is the opportunity cost of this "free" offer? Why do you think the offer is being made?

8. **Evaluating Economic Decisions** Explain how self-interest is part of each economic choice. Use an example from your own experience that shows how you purposely served your own self-interest in a choice you made.

9. **Conducting Marginal Cost–Marginal Benefit Analysis** You are on a limited budget and planning a four-day camping trip to a national park. Bus fare is $75 each way and the ride takes 12 hours. Plane fare is $150 each way and the ride takes an hour and a half. Conduct a cost-benefit analysis to help you choose your method of travel.

10. **Challenge** Why are all choices economic choices? Illustrate your answer with examples.

ECONOMICS IN PRACTICE

Making Choices
Some of the incentives that spur people to action are money, recognition, self-esteem, good grades, immediate benefit, future benefit, and altruism (doing good for others, such as working for Habitat for Humanity).

Consider Economic Choices Copy and complete the chart by noting the incentives that might motivate people to take the listed actions. (Several incentives might apply in some cases.)

Action	Incentive
Donate to charity.	
Get a promotion.	
Buy a friend a present.	
Attend a good college.	
Buy organic foods.	
Buy inexpensive imported goods.	

Challenge Have you ever had two or more conflicting incentives for a certain behavior? If so, how would you choose among them? If not, which of the incentives above motivates you most often?

Analyzing Production Possibilities

OBJECTIVES	KEY TERMS	TAKING NOTES
In Section 3, you will • describe what a production possibilities curve is and how it is constructed • explain what economists learn from using production possibilities curves • analyze how production possibilities curves show economic growth	economic model, *p. 18* production possibilities curve (PPC), *p. 18* efficiency, *p. 20* underutilization, *p. 20* law of increasing opportunity costs, *p. 21*	As you read Section 4, complete a summary chart to identify the most important points on production possibilities. Use the Graphic Organizer at **Interactive Review @ ClassZone.com** **Analyzing Production Possibilities** | PPC	shows impact of scarcity | |---|---|

Graphing the Possibilities

QUICK REFERENCE

An **economic model** is a simplified representation of economic forces.

The **production possibilities curve (PPC)** is a graph used by economists to show the impact of scarcity on an economy.

KEY CONCEPTS

In Section 2 you learned that all economic choices involve trade-offs. Economists have created **economic models**—simplified representations of complex economic activities, systems, or problems—to clarify trade-offs. One such model is a **production possibilities curve (PPC)**, a graph used to illustrate the impact of scarcity on an economy by showing the maximum number of goods or services that can be produced using limited resources.

Like all other economic models, the PPC is based on assumptions that simplify the economic interactions. For the PPC these assumptions are:

1. **Resources are fixed.** There is no way to increase the availability of land, labor, capital, and entrepreneurship.

2. **All resources are fully employed.** There is no waste of any of the factors of production. In other words, the economy is running at full production.

3. **Only two things can be produced.** This assumption simplifies the situation and suits the graphic format, with one variable on each axis.

4. **Technology is fixed.** There are no technological breakthroughs to improve methods of production.

Since the curve on a PPC represents the border—or frontier—between what it is possible to produce and what it is not possible to produce, this model is sometimes called a production possibilities frontier. It is a useful tool for businesses and even governments, but it works just as well with individual, small-scale economic decisions. For example, suppose you are preparing food for a soup kitchen and have the ingredients to make 12 loaves of whole wheat bread or 100 bran muffins or some combination of the two. A PPC can help you decide what to make.

Production Possibilities Curve

The production possibilities table in Figure 1.3 below shows five production possibilities for loaves of bread and bran muffins. These production possibilities run from the two extremes of all bread or all muffins through several combinations of the two products. The data in the table also can be plotted on a graph, as in Figure 1.4. The line joining the plotted points is the production possibilities curve. Each point on the curve represents the maximum number of loaves of bread that can be produced relative to the number of bran muffins that are produced.

Further, the PPC shows the opportunity cost of each choice in a visual way. Trace the curve from left to right with your finger. Notice that as you move along the curve you make fewer loaves of bread and more muffins. The opportunity cost of making more muffins is the bread that cannot be made.

Production Possibilities A production possibilities curve can show all the possible combinations for producing muffins and bread.

FIGURE 1.3 PRODUCTION POSSIBILITIES TABLE: BREAD vs. MUFFINS

Loaves of Bread	Bran Muffins
a → 12	0
10	35
b → 7	63
4	84
c → 0	100

FIGURE 1.4 PRODUCTION POSSIBILITIES CURVE: BREAD vs. MUFFINS

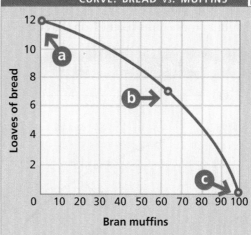

ⓐ Here you are using all the ingredients to make only bread.

ⓑ This point shows a combination of 7 loaves of bread and 63 muffins. The opportunity cost of making the 7 loaves is 37 muffins (100 – 63).

ⓒ At this point, you are making all muffins and no bread.

ANALYZE GRAPHS

1. If you decided to make ten loaves of bread, how many bran muffins could you make?

2. What is the opportunity cost of making the ten loaves of bread?

Animated Economics

Use an interactive production possibilities curve at **ClassZone.com**

APPLICATION Interpreting Graphs

A. Look at the production possibilities curve in Figure 1.4. What is the opportunity cost of increasing bread production from four loaves to seven loaves?

What We Learn from PPCs

QUICK REFERENCE

Efficiency involves producing the maximum amount of goods and services possible.

Underutilization means producing fewer goods and services than possible.

KEY CONCEPTS

No economy actually operates according to the simplified assumptions underlying the PPC. However, economists use the simplified model because it spotlights concepts that work in the real world of scarce resources.

One important concept revealed in a PPC is **efficiency**, the condition in which economic resources are being used to produce the maximum amount of goods and services. Another is **underutilization**, the condition in which economic resources are not being used to their full potential. As a result, fewer goods and services are being produced than the economy is capable of making. Both of these conditions are easy to see in the PPC.

EXAMPLE Efficiency and Underutilization

Figure 1.5 shows the classic production possibilities model of guns vs. butter. In this model, "guns" is shorthand for military spending and "butter" represents consumer products. Every point along this PPC shows a different combination of military and consumer production. Regardless of the combination, each point represents efficiency, the most that can be produced with the available resources.

Any point inside the curve represents underutilization, or the inefficient use of available resources. Look again at Figure 1.5 and notice that point **3** indicates that all resources are not fully employed. The PPC shows that the economy is capable of producing either 47 million more guns (point **1** on the curve) or 30 million more pounds of butter (point

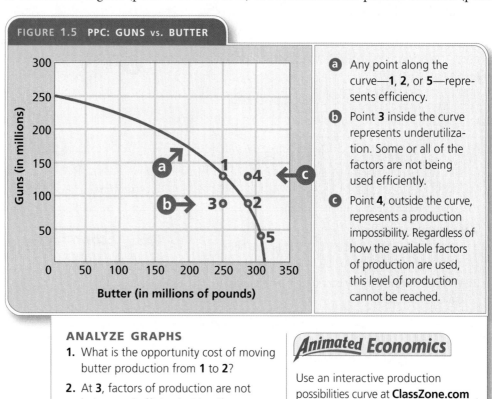

FIGURE 1.5 PPC: GUNS vs. BUTTER

Guns (in millions) / Butter (in millions of pounds)

a Any point along the curve—**1**, **2**, or **5**—represents efficiency.

b Point **3** inside the curve represents underutilization. Some or all of the factors are not being used efficiently.

c Point **4**, outside the curve, represents a production impossibility. Regardless of how the available factors of production are used, this level of production cannot be reached.

ANALYZE GRAPHS

1. What is the opportunity cost of moving butter production from **1** to **2**?

2. At **3**, factors of production are not being used efficiently. Identify a situation where this might occur.

Animated **Economics**

Use an interactive production possibilities curve at **ClassZone.com**

2 on the curve). Any point outside the curve is impossible to meet because resources are fixed. To produce the number of guns indicated at point **4**, fewer pounds of butter would have to be made (point **1** on the curve). Similarly, to produce the amount of butter indicated at point **4**, fewer guns would have to be made (point **2** on the curve).

The shape of the PPC shows a third important economic concept. This is the **law of increasing opportunity costs**, which states that as production switches from one product to another, increasingly more resources are needed to increase the production of the second product, which causes opportunity costs to rise.

EXAMPLE Increasing Opportunity Costs

Return again to Figure 1.5. A nation makes 250 million pounds of butter (point **1** on the curve), but wants to make 280 million pounds (point **2** on the curve). The opportunity cost of making the extra 30 million pounds of butter is 37 million guns. That works out to a cost of about 1.2 guns for every pound of butter. If the nation increases its output of butter to 312 million pounds (point **5** on the curve), the opportunity cost of the change would be 63 millions guns, nearly 2 guns for every pound of butter. This increase in the opportunity cost—each additional unit costs more to make than the last—explains why the curve is bow-shaped.

QUICK REFERENCE

The **law of increasing opportunity costs** states that as production switches from one product to another, increasing amounts of resources are needed to increase the production of the second product.

Opportunity Cost In the guns vs. butter equation, if more resources are used to make military products, such as stealth bombers, there are fewer resources available for other things, such as butter and other consumer goods. The opportunity cost of making more military products is the other products that cannot be made.

The reason for the increasing costs is fairly straightforward. Making butter involves different resources than making guns. Converting from gun production to butter production is not a simple procedure. New machinery must be produced, new factories must be built, and workers must be retrained. The cost of all these actions will be fewer and fewer guns.

APPLICATION Writing about Economics

B. Write a brief paragraph explaining the concepts a PPC shows graphically.

Changing Production Possibilities

The PPC illustrates a country's present production possibilities as if all resources are fixed. However, a country's supply of resources is likely to change over time. When additional resources become available, new production possibilities beyond the original frontier become attainable, and the PPC moves outward.

EXAMPLE A Shift in the PPC

In the late 1700s, the United States occupied a relatively narrow strip of land along the Atlantic Coast. Yet in less than a hundred years, it had expanded to the Pacific Ocean. This additional land provided the United States with an abundance of natural resources. Similarly, successive waves of immigration have added huge numbers of workers to the labor pool. Also, new technology has made the use of land, labor, and capital more efficient.

The addition of new resources or the more efficient use of resources already available meant that the United States could produce more goods and services. This is shown on the PPC as a shift of the curve outward, or to the right, as Figure 1.6 illustrates. Economists refer to this increase in the economy's total output as economic growth. You'll learn more about this concept in Chapter 12.

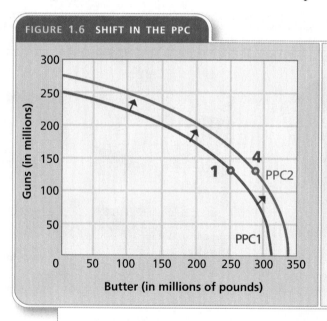

FIGURE 1.6 SHIFT IN THE PPC

Guns (in millions) / Butter (in millions of pounds)

More resources or increased productivity shifts the PPC outward, or to the right, from PPC1 to PPC2. This means that the economy can produce more of both guns and butter and point **4**, which was a production impossibility in Figure 1.5 on page 20, now is located on the curve.

ANALYZE GRAPHS
1. If the curve PPC2 represents current production possibilities, what does point **1** represent?
2. What might cause the PPC to shift inward?

Animated **Economics**

Use an interactive production possibilities curve at **ClassZone.com**

APPLICATION Applying Economic Concepts

C. Identify three developments that would cause the PPC to move outward.

REVIEWING KEY CONCEPTS

1. Explain how each of these terms is illustrated by the production possibilities curve.

   a. *underutilization*   **b.** *efficiency*

2. On what assumptions is the PPC based? Explain how these conditions do not correspond to the real world.

3. What economic data does a PPC bring together?

4. Why do opportunity costs increase as you make more and more butter and fewer guns?

5. Based on what we learn from PPCs, what does an economy need to be able to produce more of both products on the graph?

6. **Using Your Notes** Write a one-paragraph summary of this section. Refer to your completed summary chart for the ideas to use in your summary.

   Use the Graphic Organizer at **Interactive Review @ ClassZone.com**

Analyzing Production Possibilities	
PPC	shows impact of scarcity

CRITICAL THINKING

7. **Applying Economic Concepts** Explain why, in an economy that produces only fish and computers and is working at efficiency, the 500th computer made will cost more in terms of fish than the 450th computer made.

8. **Applying Economic Concepts** Suppose the owners of a car-manufacturing company are thinking of entering the motorcycle production business. How would a PPC model help them make a decision?

9. **Analyzing Cause and Effect** If new technology was introduced but there were not enough skilled workers to use it, where would the nation's production be plotted on the PPC—inside or outside the curve? Explain your answer.

10. **Challenge** During a war, a country suffers massive devastation of its industry. How would the country's PPC change from before the war to after the war? Sketch a PPC to illustrate your answer.

ECONOMICS IN PRACTICE

Creating a PPC
The following information reflects the production possibilities of an economy that makes only corn and television sets. Use the data to create a production possibilities curve.

Bushels of Corn (in thousands)	Television Sets (in thousands)
10	0
9	1
7	2
4	3
0	4

Label Points on a PPC Use the letters to locate the following points on your PPC:

A The point at which the economy makes all TVs and no corn

B A point representing efficiency

C A point representing underutilization

D A point representing an impossible level of production

Challenge Use information from your PPC to explain the law of increasing opportunity costs.

Use ✎ *SMART* *Grapher* @ClassZone.com to complete this activity.

The Economist's Toolbox

OBJECTIVES

In Section 4, you will
- demonstrate how and why economists use economic models
- understand how and why economists use statistics, charts, tables, and graphs
- compare macroeconomics to microeconomics
- contrast positive economics with normative economics

KEY TERMS

statistics, *p. 24*
microeconomics, *p. 27*
macroeconomics, *p. 27*
positive economics, *p. 29*
normative economics, *p. 29*

TAKING NOTES

As you read Section 4, complete a chart to see similarities and differences between key concepts. Use the Graphic Organizer at **Interactive Review @ ClassZone.com**

Concepts	Similarities	Differences
Charts & Tables vs. Graphs		
Micro vs. Macro		
Positive vs. Normative		

Working with Data

KEY CONCEPTS

An old joke notes that economics is everything we already know expressed in a language we don't understand. While many economists might disagree with the second part of this joke, they probably would have little argument with the first part. Economics is something that everybody engages in every day, and in that way everyone has knowledge of it. Individuals, business owners, and government officials make economic decisions all the time. Economists study these decisions and look for logical ways to explain why some nations are rich while others are poor, or why some consumers want one kind of product while others want another.

Since economists can't interview every person in every nation about economic choices, they rely on **statistics**—numerical data or information—to see patterns of behavior. To help organize and interpret the data they collect, they develop economic models. As you recall from Section 3, an economic model is a simplified representation of complex economic forces. The language of economists—these statistics and models—may sometimes be a little hard to understand. However, it is a more efficient way of explaining economic relationships and interactions than everyday language.

QUICK REFERENCE

Statistics are information in numerical form.

Using Economic Models

In science class, you may have seen a model of a lunar eclipse, which shows how, with the sun behind it, the earth casts a shadow on the moon. The model assumes certain laws of planetary orbit and simplifies the relationships among the objects in the solar system. However, these assumptions and simplifications make the process of the eclipse quite clear.

Economic models work in the same way. They are based on assumptions and are simplified because they focus on a limited number of variables. Economists can express their models in words, graphs, or equations. Models help economists explain why things are as they are. In some cases, models can help economists to predict future economic activity. You've already learned how economists construct and use one important economic model—the production possibilities curve—in Section 3. You'll learn about another, the circular flow model, in Chapter 2.

Using Charts and Tables

Economists study statistics in a particular way, looking for trends, connections, and other interesting relationships. They have several tools to help them with this task. Among the most common tools are charts and tables, in which data are arranged and

FIGURE 1.7 DEVELOPMENT ASSISTANCE		
Country	Aid (in millions of U.S. Dollars)	Percentage of Total Economy
Luxembourg	236	0.83
Canada	2,599	0.27

Source: Organization for Economic Co-operation and Development, 2004 Figures

displayed in rows and columns. (See Figure 1.7 above.) By showing numbers in relation to other numbers, charts and tables can reveal patterns in the data.

Suppose, for example, you were curious about how much money various developed countries give to help developing countries. In Figure 1.7, if you looked at one set of numbers, you would see that Luxembourg contributed $236 million, while Canada gave more than ten times that, offering nearly $2.6 billion. Your immediate interpretation of these data might be that Canada gives far more in foreign aid than Luxembourg does. But looking at other sets of numbers might suggest a different interpretation. Luxembourg may have contributed far less than Canada in actual dollar amounts. However, the foreign aid Luxembourg gave represented close to 1 percent of the value of all the goods and services the nation produced. Canada's contribution, in contrast, was about 0.3 percent of its total economy. After studying these numbers, you might conclude that in relative terms Luxembourg gives more than Canada in foreign aid.

Economics Update
Find an update on foreign aid at **ClassZone.com**

Using Graphs

When economists are interested in identifying trends in statistics, they often use graphs, or visual representations of numerical relationships. The most common type is the line graph. Line graphs are particularly useful for showing changes over time.

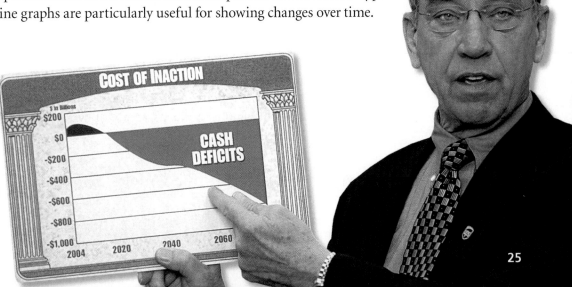

Statistics During a debate in the U.S. Senate on the future of Social Security, Senator Charles Grassley of Iowa illustrates a point using statistics in graph form.

25

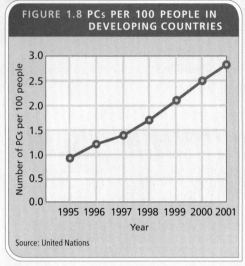

FIGURE 1.8 PCs PER 100 PEOPLE IN DEVELOPING COUNTRIES

Source: United Nations

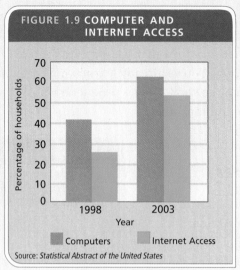

FIGURE 1.9 COMPUTER AND INTERNET ACCESS

Source: *Statistical Abstract of the United States*

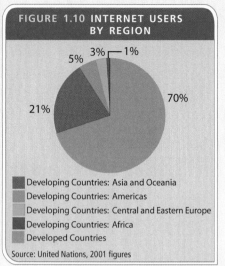

FIGURE 1.10 INTERNET USERS BY REGION

Developing Countries: Asia and Oceania
Developing Countries: Americas
Developing Countries: Central and Eastern Europe
Developing Countries: Africa
Developed Countries

Source: United Nations, 2001 figures

ANALYZE GRAPHS

Graphs show statistics in a visual form. Line graphs (Figure 1.8) are particularly useful for showing changes over time. Bar graphs (Figure 1.9) make it easy to compare numbers or sets of numbers. Pie, or circle, graphs (Figure 1.10) show relationships among the parts of a whole.

Animated Economics

Use a variety of interactive graphs at **ClassZone.com**

NEED HELP?

Throughout this book, you will be asked to interpret and analyze information in graphs. If you need help with these tasks, see "Interpreting Graphs."

Skillbuilder Handbook, page R30

All line graphs use at least two sets of numbers, or variables: one plotted along the horizontal axis, running from left to right, the other plotted along the vertical axis, running from bottom to top. On the line graph in Figure 1.8 above, the range of time between 1995 and 2001 is shown on the horizontal axis. The number of PCs (personal computers) per 100 people in developing countries is shown on the vertical axis.

The number of PCs for each year is plotted on the graph and then these points are joined to form a line. The line may slope upward, showing an upward trend, or downward, showing a downward trend. The line may be straight, keeping the same slope throughout, or it may be curved, having a varied slope. (In later chapters you'll see that where graphs are used to illustrate economic concepts, lines are referred to as curves whether they are straight or curved.) How would you describe the trend shown in Figure 1.8?

A bar graph is especially useful for comparisons. The bar graph in Figure 1.9 above shows information on the percentage of households in the United States that have access to computers and the Internet. The bars vividly illustrate that access to information technology increased dramatically in the United States between 1998 and 2003.

A pie graph, often called a pie chart or circle graph, is especially good for representing numbers in relation to a whole. Take a look at the pie graph in Figure 1.10 above. The whole circle represents all the Internet users in the world. The slices of the pie, which represent regions of the world, are drawn in proportion to the percentage of the whole they constitute.

APPLICATION Interpreting Graphs

A. Look at the bar graph in Figure 1.10 above. Write a generalization based on information in the graph.

Microeconomics and Macroeconomics

For scientists, everything in the earth, air, and water—and beyond—is a source of data to be observed and studied. Yet the data often make little sense until they are seen through the lens of a microscope or telescope. Economic information, as with scientific data, takes on meaning when it is viewed through the most useful lens. Two of the lenses through which economists observe economic behavior are microeconomics and macroeconomics. **Microeconomics** is the study of the behavior of individual players in an economy, such as individuals, families, and businesses. **Macroeconomics** is the study of the behavior of the economy as a whole and involves topics such as inflation, unemployment, aggregate demand, and aggregate supply.

Microeconomics

As the prefix *micro-*, meaning small, would suggest, microeconomics examines specific, individual elements in an economy. The elements include prices, costs, profits, competition, and the behavior of consumers and producers. Microeconomics can help you understand how the sandwich shop owner arrived at the price of the lunch you bought today, why the neighborhood has several sandwich shops offering the same kinds of food, and why some of these shops flourish while others fail. Microeconomics also can offer explanations for why students decide to work only on the weekends and not on school nights, why some families buy a used car rather than a new car, and why the mom-and-pop grocery store in your neighborhood closed after the superstore opened nearby.

Within the field of microeconomics there are areas of specialized concentration. Business organization, labor markets, agricultural economics, and the economics of environmental issues are among the topics that microeconomists might study. You will study the issues of microeconomics in more depth starting in Chapter 4.

Macroeconomics

Macroeconomics, as its prefix *macro-*, meaning large, would suggest, examines the economic "big picture." In other words, macroeconomics is the study of the economy as a whole. While the limited spending power of an unemployed person would be in the realm of microeconomics, the effect of widespread unemployment on the whole nation would be a macroeconomic issue. In a similar way, the rising price of coffee would interest a microeconomist, but a general rise in prices, a sign that the whole economy is experiencing inflation, would be a matter for a macroeconomist.

Microeconomics vs. Macroeconomics Changes in coffee prices might interest a microeconomist. A macroeconomist might study general changes in prices.

Economists
Study

Macroeconomics	Microeconomics
The study of the whole economy	The study of the individual consumer

Units of Study	Units of Study
• Economic growth • Economic stability • International trade	• Consumer markets • Business markets • Labor markets

Topics of Interest	Topics of Interest
• Money, banking, finance • Government taxing and spending policies • Employment and unemployment • Inflation	• Markets, prices, costs, profits, competition, government regulation • Consumer behavior • Business behavior

ANALYZE CHARTS

The division between microeconomics and macroeconomics is not a fixed one. Some topics fall under both areas of study. For example, a microeconomist might be interested in employment levels in the hotel industry, while a macroeconomist looks at employment levels in the economy as a whole. Identify another topic area that might be of interest to both microeconomists and macroeconomists.

While microeconomics considers the *individual* consumer, macroeconomics studies the consumer *sector*, also called the household sector. A sector is a combination of all the individual units into one larger whole. Macroeconomics also examines the business sector, and the public, or government, sector—that part of the economy that provides public goods and services.

Macroeconomists bring a national or global perspective to their work. They study the monetary system, the ups and downs of business cycles, and the impact of national tax policies on the economy. In addition, they look at such global issues as international trade and its effect on rich and poor nations. You will study macroeconomics in depth beginning in Chapter 11.

APPLICATION Categorizing Economic Information

B. Which does each of the news headlines relate to—microeconomics or macroeconomics?

1. National Unemployment Figures Rise
2. World Trade Organization Meets
3. Shipbuilder Wins Navy Contract
4. Cab Drivers on Strike!
5. Gasoline Prices Jump 25 Cents

Positive Economics and Normative Economics

Economics also can be viewed through another pair of lenses. One of those lenses is **positive economics**, a way of describing and explaining economics as it is, not as it should be. Positive economics involves verifiable facts, not value judgments. The other is **normative economics**, a way of describing and explaining what economic behavior ought to be, not what it actually is. Normative economics does involve value judgments because it seeks to make recommendations for actions.

Positive Economics

Positive economics uses the scientific method to observe data, hypothesize, test, refine, and continue testing. Statements made within positive economics can be tested against real-world data and either proved (or at least strongly supported) or disproved (or at least strongly questioned). Suppose, for example, your state is debating the pros and cons of a lottery to raise money for education. In the framework of positive economics, researchers would study data from states with lotteries to see if educational spending increased after the lotteries were begun.

Normative Economics Why is this statement about the North American Free Trade Agreement (NAFTA) an example of normative economics?

Normative Economics

Normative economics, in contrast, is based on value judgments. It goes beyond the facts to ask if actions are good. Since the values of people differ, so do the recommendations based on normative economics.

Consider the issue of using lottery money to fund education. Two economists might agree that the data show that state-run lotteries result in more money for schools, and that many lottery tickets are purchased by people who are poor. Their recommendations, however, might differ because they have different values. One economist might support a lottery because it increases funding for schools. The other might oppose a lottery because it places a burden on the poor.

APPLICATION Applying Economic Concepts

C. Are the following statements examples of positive economics or normative economics?

1. Because of scarcity, everyone must make choices.

2. Americans buy too many cars and do not use mass transit enough.

NAFTA a kinder, gentler way to ruin our economy.

Adam Smith: Founder of Modern Economics

Economics Update

Learn more about Adam Smith at **ClassZone.com**

Some 250 years ago, economics as an academic discipline did not even exist. Any discussion of economic issues usually took place in the fields of politics and philosophy. In 1776, however, Adam Smith completely changed this.

Seeing the Invisible

No other economist has had as much influence as Adam Smith, yet he would not have even considered himself an economist. Smith was born in Kirkcaldy, Scotland, in 1723 and studied, and later taught, literature, logic, and moral philosophy. In 1764 he traveled to France and met many European Enlightenment writers and thinkers. His discussions with them encouraged him to look at the world anew. The result was his groundbreaking work, *An Inquiry into the Nature and Causes of the Wealth of Nations*, which he published in 1776.

In *The Wealth of Nations*, Smith challenged the idea that mercantilism—a system by which the government of the homeland controlled trade with its colonies—was economically sound. Instead, he argued, a nation would be wealthier if it engaged in free trade. It was in this market where goods could be exchanged freely that Adam Smith saw a new economic relationship.

He reasoned that people behave in ways that satisfy their economic self-interest. A tailor will make clothes as long as people will buy them at a price that satisfies him. If he makes more clothes than customers wish to buy, he will cut back and make fewer until he finds the balance again. In this way, according to Smith, an "invisible hand" guides the marketplace. In such a free market, both the buyer and the seller benefit from each transaction. Smith's idea of the "invisible hand," as well as many other principles he explained in *The Wealth of Nations*, became the foundation of modern economic theory.

Founder of Economics
The Wealth of Nations is considered the founding work of the subject of economics—even though Smith never used the word *economics* in the book.

APPLICATION Analyzing Effects

D. What impact do you think individual self-interest has on the economy as a whole? Illustrate your answer with examples.

1. Explain the differences between the terms in each of these pairs:

   a. *statistics*   **b.** *macroeconomics*   **c.** *positive economics*
   economic model   *microeconomics*   *normative economics*

2. Why do economists often choose to present statistics in charts, tables, or graphs?

3. Create a simple model to explain how you decide how much time to study and how much time to unwind each evening. You may use words, charts or graphs, or equations.

4. Think of an example of a macroeconomic issue that affects an individual person, family, or business and explain its effect.

5. Explain the value of statistics and other data to positive economics and to normative economics.

6. **Using Your Notes** In what ways was Adam Smith a microeconomist? In what ways a macroeconomist? Refer to your completed comparison and contrast chart.

Concepts	Similarities	Differences
Charts & Tables vs. Graphs		
Micro vs. Macro		
Positive vs. Normative		

   Use the Graphic Organizer at **Interactive Review @ ClassZone.com**

CRITICAL THINKING

7. **Making Inferences** How do you think politicians might use normative economics statements?

8. **Applying Economic Concepts** In which category does each item below belong—microeconomics or macroeconomics? Why?

   a. Studying statistics to see how well the economy is doing at creating jobs or increasing exports;

   b. Studying statistics on gasoline sales and hotel bookings to explore the impact of higher gas prices on vacation plans.

9. **Distinguishing Fact from Opinion** Consider the example of the state lottery to raise money for education. How might it be possible for two economists to see the same information and arrive at different opinions about what to do?

10. **Challenge** When you go out shopping, do you often worry that there will be a shortage of something you really want? If so, explain why you think there might be a shortage. If not, explain why there seems to be enough of everything you would want to buy.

Ford Motor Company assembly line, 1913

Using Graphs
Graphs are among the most important tools used by economists.

Create Graphs Use the following information about Model T Fords (shown above) to create two line or bar graphs.

Average price per car
1909 — $904
1911 — $811
1913 — $638
1915 — $626

Number of cars sold
1909 —   12,176
1911 —   40,400
1913 —   179,199
1915 —   355,249

Source: Model T Ford Club of America

Challenge As Henry Ford lowered the price of the Model Ts, he potentially reduced his profit—the amount of money he made—on the sale of each car. Why was that a good economic choice?

Use *SMART Grapher* @ **ClassZone.com** to complete this activity.

The Real Cost of Expanding O'Hare Airport

Background Chicago's O'Hare airport is one of the busiest airports in the United States. It is a major hub for both domestic and international airlines, and its smooth running is essential if the many airlines that fly in and out of O'Hare are to remain on schedule. However, delays at O'Hare are commonplace, and this sometimes disrupts air travel throughout the United States and abroad.

Two main factors are responsible for delays at O'Hare: turbulent Midwestern weather and the layout of O'Hare's runways. Because all but one of the runways are interconnected, bad weather results in the shutting down of most of the runway system. A modernization plan to improve efficiency at O'Hare was adopted in 2005. This plan generated considerable, and often heated, discussion and debate.

What's the issue? What are the real costs involved in airport expansion? Study these sources to determine the costs tied to the expansion of O'Hare airport.

A. Online Report

This report describes the anticipated benefits of the O'Hare Modernization Plan to redesign the runway system and expand the airport.

Chicago O'Hare Airport Expansion

The modernization plan is estimated to cost $6.6 billion (in 2001 dollars), which will probably be more like $8 billion by completion. . . .

Supporters of the expansion plan say delays could be cut by 79% and that 195,000 jobs and $18 billion would be put into the local economy. In 2004 the airport played host to 69.5 million arriving, departing and connecting passengers and had total aircraft operations at nearly 929,000, an average of one landing or takeoff every 56 seconds. . . .

The airport has 178 gates on eight connected concourses and one freestanding terminal. The realignment [of the runways] and modernization program could make a great deal of difference to the efficiency of the airport. Overall, delays are expected to drop by 79%. The future airfield will be able to accommodate approximately 1.6 million aircraft operations and 76 million [passengers] per year.

Source: Airport-technology.com/projects/chicago

Thinking Economically What factors led to the development of the plan to expand O'Hare? What are the projected costs and benefits?

B. Political Cartoon

Cartoonist Grizelda drew this cartoon about people protesting noise pollution at an airport.

Source: www.CartoonStock.com

Thinking Economically
Which opportunity cost does this cartoon address? Explain your answer.

C. Organization Website

The Alliance of Residents Concerning O'Hare (AReCo) addresses problems related to the aviation industry. AReCo's website presents the group's findings and views regarding the expansion of O'Hare.

Area Residents Challenge Wisdom of O'Hare Expansion

AReCo cites health hazards, seeks alternatives to enlarging O'Hare.

The [aviation] industry and airport expansionists consistently try to minimize the impacts of airports and aircraft. One example of the harm that has been . . . understated by the federal government . . . [is the] underreporting [of] the amounts of deadly pollution coming from airports/aircraft.

For example, combined aircraft-related amounts of benzene [a known cause of cancer in humans] totaled 20 tons at Logan, Bradley, and Manchester airports in 1999! . . . Mega airports, such as Chicago's O'Hare, operate more aircraft annually than all of the three above-mentioned airports combined, thus emitting even more harmful and even deadly pollution in heavily urban-populated areas. . . .

In the meantime, there are intelligent steps that Chicago (and others) can take that will really modernize the metropolitan air transportation system and retain Chicago's title of "our nation's transportation hub." Such steps include placing a much stronger emphasis on [more than one type of] transportation, such as medium and high-speed rail, that would link O'Hare airport to other airports (becoming a "virtual hub") and building a new airport in a less populated peripheral area.

Source: Areco.org

Thinking Economically What alternatives does AReCo cite to O'Hare's expansion?

THINKING ECONOMICALLY Synthesizing

1. Explain the real cost of expanding O'Hare airport. Use information presented in the documents to support your answer.

2. Who are the most likely winners and losers as a result of the O'Hare expansion? Explain your answer.

3. How might supporters of expansion use a production possibilities model to strengthen their case?

Review this chapter using interactive activities at **ClassZone.com**

- Online Summary
- Quizzes
- Vocabulary Flip Cards
- Graphic Organizers
- Review and Study Notes

◯◯◯ ⬭

 Online Summary

Complete the following activity either on your own paper or online at **ClassZone.com**

Choose the key concept that best completes the sentence. Not all key concepts will be used.

consumer
economic model
economics
efficiency
factors of production
incentive
macroeconomics
microeconomics
opportunity cost

producer
production possibilities curve
scarcity
statistics
trade-off
underutilization
utility
wants

1 is the fundamental economic problem. It arises because human **2** are limitless, while resources are limited. It affects what a **3** buys and what a **4** makes. It affects what is produced, how it is produced, and who gets what is produced. It affects how the four **5** are put to use.

Since people cannot have everything they want, they have to make choices. Every choice, however, involves a **6**, something you have to give up to get what you want. When making an economic decision, you need to consider the **7**, the value of the thing you gave up.

Economists often use an **8**, a simplified representation of reality, to clarify concepts. Economists use such tools in **9**, the study of the economic behavior of individual persons, families, and businesses, and in **10**, the study of the economy as a whole.

One useful model, the **11**, shows the maximum amount of goods that an economy can produce. It also shows **12**, when not all resources are put to full use.

REVIEWING KEY CONCEPTS

Scarcity: The Basic Economic Problem (pp. 4–11)

1. In what ways does scarcity affect both consumers and producers?

2. What are the four factors of production and how do they relate to scarcity?

Economic Choice Today: Opportunity Cost (pp. 12–17)

3. What does the phrase "there's no such thing as a free lunch" mean in economic terms?

4. Why is it important to consider marginal benefits and costs when you do a cost-benefit analysis?

Analyzing Production Possibilities (pp. 18–23)

5. What are three things a PPC shows?

6. What factors could lead to economic growth?

The Economist's Toolbox (pp. 24–33)

7. What are some tools that economists use to draw meaning from large amounts of data?

8. What are the differences between microeconomics and macroeconomics?

APPLYING ECONOMIC CONCEPTS

Look at the bar graph below showing the relationship between educational level and weekly wages.

9. Describe the relationship between education and earnings for males in 1979.

10. Explain why the earnings gap between college and high school graduates might have changed between 1979 and 2004.

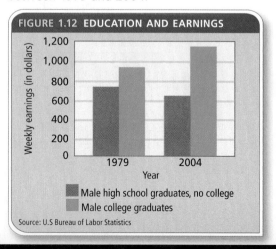

FIGURE 1.12 EDUCATION AND EARNINGS

Weekly earnings (in dollars) — Year

■ Male high school graduates, no college
■ Male college graduates

Source: U.S Bureau of Labor Statistics

11. **Creating Graphs** Use the following information to create a bar graph showing the weekly wages for females with a high school education and those with a college education in 1979 and 2004.

    1979 High school graduates, no college, $424
          College graduates, $605

    2004 High school graduates, no college, $488
          College graduates, $860

    Source: U.S. Bureau of Labor Statistics

    Use ✏ *SMARTGrapher* @ ClassZone.com to complete this activity.

12. **Interpreting Graphs** Compare the graph you created with the one on page 34. Identify three differences between the changes over time for women and for men.

13. **Evaluating Economic Decisions** You plan to open a restaurant that specializes in meals cooked with organic products. You realize that location is very important for this kind of business. You have two options: you can rent an expensive site downtown or you can buy an inexpensive building in a quiet neighborhood. What are the benefits and the opportunity cost for each option?

14. **Conducting Cost-Benefit Analysis** You are considering taking a part-time job after school at a local veterinary surgery. Create a decision-making grid to analyze your potential choices. Include alternative jobs you might take and the costs and benefits of each. Similarly, list activities other than working that you might pursue after school. Indicate which alternative you would choose and explain your choice.

15. **Challenge** You own a small factory that makes widgets and you want to increase production, so you hire new workers. Each new worker increases productivity, but each also must be paid. When will you stop hiring new workers?

Start a Business

Step 1 Team up with a partner or small group of classmates.

Step 2 With your partner or group, decide on a business you want to start. This could be anything that has a realistic chance of succeeding: computer technician, T-shirt printer, caramel-corn producer, dog walker, or anything you think may fulfill a want.

Step 3 On a chart like the one below, list the factors of production you will need to use to start and run your business.

Step 4 Develop a business plan—a way that you can use the factors of production so efficiently that you will be able to make money. Describe your business plan in a paragraph.

Step 5 Present your plan to the rest of the class. When all pairs or groups have made their presentations, hold a class vote to select the best plan.

Factors of Production	
Land	Labor
1.	1.
2.	2.
3.	3.
Capital	Entrepreneurship
1.	1.
2.	2.
3.	3.

Traditional Economy

Some economic activities have changed little over time. This farmer in Guizhou Province, China, employs rice-farming methods that the Chinese have used for centuries.

Economic Systems

CONCEPT REVIEW

Scarcity is the situation that exists when there are not enough resources to meet human wants.

CHAPTER 2 KEY CONCEPT

An **economic system** is the way in which a society uses its scarce resources to satisfy its people's unlimited wants.

WHY THE CONCEPT MATTERS

How does a society decide the ways to use scarce resources to meet unlimited wants? Its economic system determines what to produce, how to produce, and for whom to produce. Although every country today uses a mixture of economic systems, some mixed systems provide more economic and political freedom and create more wealth than others.

Online Highlights
More at ClassZone.com

 Economics Update

Go to **ECONOMICS UPDATE** for chapter updates and current news on the economies of North Korea and South Korea. (See Case Study, pp. 64–65.) ▶

Animated Economics

Go to **ANIMATED ECONOMICS** for interactive lessons on the graphs and tables in this chapter.

Interactive ◀▶ Review

Go to **INTERACTIVE REVIEW** for concept review and activities.

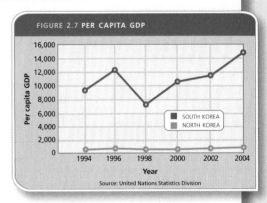

FIGURE 2.7 PER CAPITA GDP

Source: United Nations Statistics Division

How do the economies of North Korea and South Korea compare? See the Case Study on pages 64–65.

Introduction to Economic Systems

OBJECTIVES	KEY TERMS	TAKING NOTES
In Section 1, you will • identify the three main types of economic systems • understand how a traditional economy operates, including its advantages and disadvantages • analyze how modern forces are changing traditional economies	economic system, *p. 38* traditional economy, *p. 38* command economy, *p. 39* market economy, *p. 39*	As you read Section 1, complete a cluster diagram that provides information on the different kinds of economic systems. Use the Graphic Organizer at **Interactive Review @ ClassZone.com** traditional economy Economic System

Types of Economic Systems

KEY CONCEPTS

QUICK REFERENCE

An **economic system** is the way a society uses resources to satisfy its people's wants.

A **traditional economy** is an economic system in which people produce and distribute goods according to customs handed down from generation to generation.

In his book *Utopia,* 16th-century writer Thomas More describes a society without scarcity, where wants are limited and easily fulfilled. It is no accident, however, that the word *utopia* means "no place" in Greek. In the real world, scarcity is a fact of life. To address scarcity, societies must answer three questions:

• What should be produced?

• How should it be produced?

• For whom will it be produced?

The answers to these questions shape the economic system a society has. An **economic system** is the way a society uses its scarce resources to satisfy its people's unlimited wants. There are three basic types of economic systems: traditional economies, command economies, and market economies. In this chapter you will learn about these economic systems, as well as "mixed" economies that have features of more than one type.

TYPE 1 Traditional Economy

A **traditional economy** is an economic system in which families, clans, or tribes make economic decisions based on customs and beliefs that have been handed down from generation to generation. The one goal of these societies is survival. Everyone has a set role in this task. Men often are hunters and herders. Women tend the crops and raise children. The youngest help with everyday chores while learning the skills they will need for their adult roles. There is no chance of deviating from this pattern. The good of the group always takes precedence over individual desires.

Traditional The Kavango people of Namibia use fishing techniques passed down from generation to generation.

Command Food was scarce and expensive in this store in the former Soviet Union, a command economy.

Market Advertisements, like these billboards in New York City, are a common sight in a market economy.

TYPE 2 Command Economy

In the second type of economic system, a **command economy**, the government decides what goods and services will be produced, how they will be produced, and how they will be distributed. In a command economy, government officials consider the resources and needs of the country and allocate those resources according to their judgment. The wants of individual consumers are rarely considered. The government also usually owns the means of production—all the resources and factories. North Korea and Cuba are current examples of command economies. Before the collapse of communism in Europe, countries such as the Soviet Union, Poland, and East Germany also were command economies.

TYPE 3 Market Economy

The third type of economic system, a **market economy**, is based on individual choice, not government directives. In other words, in this system consumers and producers drive the economy. Consumers are free to spend their money as they wish, to enter into business, or to sell their labor to whomever they want. Producers decide what goods or services they will offer. They make choices about how to use their limited resources to earn the most money possible.

In a market economy, then, individuals act in their own self-interest when they make economic choices. However, as they seek to serve their own interests, they benefit others. As a consumer, you choose to buy the products that best meet your wants. However, this benefits the producers who make those products, because they earn money from your purchases. As Adam Smith noted in *The Wealth of Nations* (1776), when you make economic decisions you act in your self-interest, but you are "led by an invisible hand" to promote the interests of others.

QUICK REFERENCE

A **command economy** is an economic system in which the government makes all economic decisions.

A **market economy** is an economic system in which individual choice and voluntary exchange direct economic decisions.

Economics Update

Find an update on issues in a market economy at **ClassZone.com**

APPLICATION Applying Economic Concepts

A. How might economic activities within a family with adults, teenagers, and young children represent aspects of traditional, command, and market economies?

Characteristics of Traditional Economies

KEY CONCEPTS

In the earliest times, all societies had traditional economies. Such systems serve the main purpose of traditional societies—survival—very well. The traditional economic system, however, tends to be inefficient and does not adapt to change.

TRAIT 1 Advantages and Disadvantages

The one great advantage of a traditional economy is that it so clearly answers the three economic questions. A traditional society produces what best ensures its survival. The methods of production are the same as they have always been. Systems of distribution are also determined by custom and tradition. In a traditional economy, then, there is little disagreement over economic goals and roles.

Traditional economies have several major disadvantages, too. Because they are based on ritual and custom, traditional economies resist change. Therefore, they are less productive than they might be if they adopted new approaches. Further, while traditionally defined roles eliminate conflict, they also prevent people from doing the jobs they want to do or are best suited to do. People who are in the "wrong" jobs are less productive. The lower productivity in traditional economies means that people do not acquire the material wealth that people in other societies do. As a result, people in traditional economies have a much lower standard of living.

TRAIT 2 Under Pressure to Change

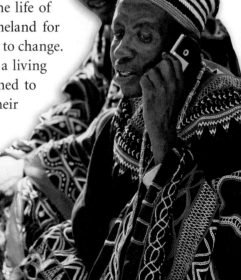

Forces of Change The use of the cell phone has brought changes to many traditional African societies.

Around the world, traditional economies are under pressure from the forces of change. The Kavango people of Namibia in southern Africa, for example, have lived as subsistence farmers for centuries. (Subsistence farmers grow just enough to feed their own families.) Modern telecommunications, however, have bombarded the Kavango with images of the world beyond their homeland. As a result, many young Kavango want something more than the life of subsistence farming. Thousands have left their homeland for the cities. Even the old ways of farming are beginning to change. The vast majority of the Kavango people still make a living from subsistence farming. However, a few have turned to commercial farming, where they grow crops not for their own use, but for sale.

APPLICATION Making Inferences

B. There are no pure traditional economies today. Why do you think this is so?

REVIEWING KEY CONCEPTS

1. Demonstrate your understanding of the following terms by using each one in a sentence.

   a. *traditional economy*

   b. *command economy*

   c. *market economy*

2. Which is more important in a traditional economy, accumulating individual wealth or honoring tradition? Explain your answer.

3. How are economic decisions made in a command economy?

4. What drives the choices of consumers and producers in a market economy?

5. Does Adam Smith's "invisible hand" also function in traditional and command economies? Explain your answer.

6. **Using Your Notes** What do the three kinds of economic systems have in common? Refer to your completed cluster diagram.

   Use the Graphic Organizer at **Interactive Review @ ClassZone.com**

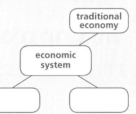

CRITICAL THINKING

7. **Drawing Conclusions** How might strongly defined economic roles and goals be both a strength and a weakness of traditional economies?

8. **Analyzing Cause and Effect** What effect might mass media have on the erosion of traditional economies in today's world?

9. **Generalizing from Economic Information** You have the following information about an economy: 1) People have little choice in the kinds of jobs they do. 2) Producers are not free to use resources as they wish. 3) People have little, if any, say in how the basic economic questions are answered. What kind of economy might this be? Explain your answer.

10. **Challenge** Most modern economies are a mixture of the three economic systems described in Section 1. Identify elements of traditional, command, and market economic systems in the American economy. (You will learn more about mixed economies in Section 4.)

ECONOMICS IN PRACTICE

Market economy in action in Mexico

Identifying Economic Systems
The three economic systems may be identified by the way they answer the basic economic questions: What to produce? How to Produce? For whom to produce?

Complete a Chart Copy the chart below. Complete it by noting how each of the three economic systems answers the basic economic questions.

Economic System	Answers to the Basic Economic Questions
Traditional economy	
Command economy	
Market economy	

Challenge Identify modern countries that have economies that closely resemble each of the three economic systems. Explain each of your choices.

Command Economies

OBJECTIVES	KEY TERMS	TAKING NOTES
In Section 2, you will • describe the main features of a command economy • note how socialism and communism differ • identify modern examples of command economies • explain the advantages and disadvantages of a command economy	centrally planned economy, *p. 42* socialism, *p. 43* communism, *p. 43* authoritarian, *p. 43*	As you read Section 2, complete a hierarchy chart to categorize information about command economic systems. Use the Graphic Organizer at **Interactive Review @ ClassZone.com** Command Economies government controls command economies today

Government Controls

QUICK REFERENCE

A **centrally planned economy** is a system in which central government officials make all economic decisions.

KEY CONCEPTS

In command economies, leaders decide what should be produced and how it should be produced. They also decide for whom it should be produced, in part by setting wages. By determining who earns the highest wages and who the lowest, these leaders decide who has the money to buy available products. A system in which the society's leaders, usually members of the central government, make all economic decisions is called a **centrally planned economy**.

EXAMPLE Government Planning

Think for a moment about how the federal government affects you. If you work, you have to pay taxes. If you're 18 years old and male, you have to register with the Selective Service System. State and local governments exert somewhat more control over your day-to-day life. State laws set both speed limits and the age at which people can drive. Local laws set standards for cleanliness in food stores and restaurants and for honest business practices. And state and local taxes are collected to support such services as police and fire departments and public education.

However, what if the government went further? Suppose that bureaucrats in a government office in Washington, D.C., had the power to decide which businesses could operate in your city. Further, these bureaucrats decided not only what these businesses should produce, but also how much each business should produce each month. Finally, they also decided who could have jobs and set work hours and pay scales for workers. Government controls of this type are a feature of a command, or centrally planned, economy.

EXAMPLE Socialism and Communism

Modern societies that have adopted command economies have done so largely because of the influence of Karl Marx, a 19th-century German philosopher, historian, and economist. According to Marx's analysis, all of history is a struggle between classes. In his own time, the struggle was between the owners of the great industrial factories and the workers who exchanged their labor for wages. While the industrialists grew rich, the workers remained relatively poor. Marx predicted that in time the workers would overthrow this system and transfer ownership of the factories to public hands. With the means of production owned by the government, the class struggle would be resolved and all citizens would share in the wealth.

FIGURE 2.1 Comparing Economic Systems

	Communism	Socialism	Market System
Who owns resources?	Government	Government owns basic resources; the rest are privately owned	All resources privately owned
How are resources allocated?	Government planners decide how resources are used	Government planners allocate basic resources; market forces allocate privately-owned resources	Market forces allocate resources
What role does government play?	Government makes all economic decisions	Government makes decisions in the basic industries	Government's role limited—mostly to ensure market forces are free to work

ANALYZE TABLES
Government involvement varies among economic systems. How do communist systems answer the three basic economic questions?

Socialism, an economic system in which the government owns some or all of the factors of production, developed from the ideas of Marx. **Communism**, a more extreme form of socialism in which there is no private ownership of property and little or no political freedom, also grew out of Marx's thinking. Essentially, it is authoritarian socialism. An **authoritarian** system requires absolute obedience to authority. Figure 2.1 lists the major characteristics of socialism and communism.

Democratic socialism is established through the democratic political process rather than through the violent overthrow of the government. In this form of socialism, the government owns the basic industries, but other industries are privately owned. Central planners make decisions for government-owned industries. Central planners might also control other sectors—health care, for example—to ensure that everyone has access to these important services.

QUICK REFERENCE

Socialism is an economic system in which the government owns some or all of the factors of production.

Communism is an economic system in which the government owns all the factors of production and there is little or no political freedom.

Authoritarian systems require absolute obedience to those in power.

APPLICATION Comparing and Contrasting

A. How are socialism and communism similar yet different?

Karl Marx: Economic Revolutionary

Millions of lives were affected by the work of Karl Marx. Governments were toppled and new political alliances were forged on the strength of his arguments. What was it in the thousands of difficult-to-read pages he wrote that fueled revolutions?

A New View of Economics

Marx was born in what is now Germany in 1818 and grew up in middle-class comfort. In college, however, he became involved in radical politics. In time, his political activism led to his exile from his homeland. He moved from country to country, eventually settling in London. During his travels, he met Friedrich Engels, the son of a factory owner. Through Engels, Marx became aware of the struggles of the working class and he undertook a deep study of economics. He concluded that the Industrial Revolution had created a system of wage slavery.

Factory owners, Marx said, looked upon labor as just another commodity that could be bought. They then used this labor to convert other productive resources into products. The factory owners made a profit by selling products at a higher price than the cost of labor and other resources. By keeping wages low, they could make ever greater profits. The whole industrial system, Marx reasoned, was based on this exploitation of workers.

To Marx, rising tension between worker and owner was an inevitable development in economic history. Over time, more and more wealth would be concentrated in fewer and fewer hands, and dissatisfied workers would revolt and create a new society without economic classes. Marx, assisted by Engels, laid out these ideas in *The Communist Manifesto* (1848). Marx discussed his economic ideas more fully in his enormous study *Das Kapital,* which was published in three volumes between 1867 and 1894.

Because of the way that communist economies worked in practice and the eventual collapse of communism in the early 1990s, Marx's theories have fallen into disfavor. Even so, few people had more impact on 20th-century economic and political thinking than Karl Marx.

Communism Marx's writings influenced revolutionary leaders such as V. I. Lenin in Russia and Mao Zedong in China.

Das Kapital.

Kritik der politischen Oekonomie.

Von

Karl Marx.

Erster B

Buch I. Der Produktion

Das Recht der Ü

Verlag vo

New-York: L. W. &

FAST FACTS

Karl Marx
German philosopher, historian, and economist

Born: May 5, 1818

Died: March 14, 1883

Major Accomplishment:
Detailed analysis of capitalism and foundation for socialist economic theory

Famous Quotation:
Workers of the world unite; you have nothing to lose but your chains.

Influenced:
Russian Revolution, 1917
Chinese Revolution, 1949

Economics Update
Learn more about Karl Marx at **ClassZone.com**

APPLICATION Drawing Conclusions

B. What did Marx think was the logical outcome of the struggle between owners and workers?

Command Economies Today

There are no examples of pure command economies today. The forces that have brought changes to traditional economies are also transforming command economies. However, some countries—North Korea, for example—still have economies with mostly command elements.

North Korea

Once under the control of China and later Japan, Korea was split into North Korea and South Korea following World War II. North Korea came under communist control. The government controlled every economic decision. For example, it diverted many of the country's resources to the military, building up an army of more than 1 million soldiers—out of a population of about 22 million. It also developed a nuclear weapons program. However, this military buildup came at the expense of necessities. During the late 1990s and early 2000s, food was so scarce that millions of North Koreans died from hunger and malnutrition. Many North Koreans survived only because of food aid from other countries, most notably South Korea.

The failure to provide food and other important products was just one result of a flawed economic plan. For much of the 1990s, North Korea produced less and less each year, and its economy actually shrunk. (See Figure 2.2 below.) Since 2003, however, the central planners have relaxed some restrictions on private ownership and market activity. Most North Koreans hope that this tentative experiment with free markets will revive the country's ailing economy. (For more information on North Korea's economy, see the Case Study on pages 64–65.)

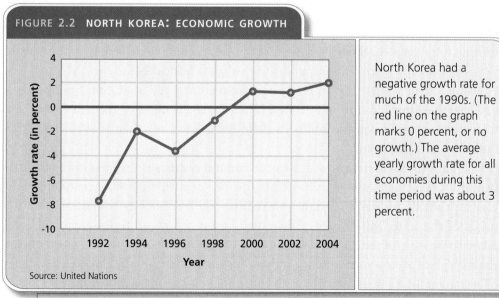

FIGURE 2.2 NORTH KOREA: ECONOMIC GROWTH

Year

Source: United Nations

North Korea had a negative growth rate for much of the 1990s. (The red line on the graph marks 0 percent, or no growth.) The average yearly growth rate for all economies during this time period was about 3 percent.

ANALYZE GRAPHS

1. The North Korean economy began to show positive growth after 1999. To what might this development be attributed?

2. During the 1990s, some newspaper reports noted that the North Korean economy was "shrinking." How is this shown in the graph?

Meeting Demand (Left) In communist East Germany, government planners' decisions left this butcher with just one goose to sell. (Right) In West Germany, a market economy, store shelves were laden with consumer goods.

Impact of Command Economies

In theory, command economies have some advantages. For example, they seek to provide for everyone, even the sick and the old who are no longer productive economically. Also, leaders in a command economy can use the nation's resources to produce items that may not make money in a market economy—certain medicines, for example.

In practice, however, the disadvantages of command economies are abundantly clear. To begin with, central planners often have little understanding of local conditions. Because of this, their economic decisions are frequently misguided or wrong. Also, workers often have little motive to improve their productivity, since they know they will be paid the same wages regardless of their output. And because there is no private property, there is no motivation for workers to use resources wisely.

Centrally planned economies often set prices well below those that would be established in a market system. As a result, command economies face shortages. One scene repeated in many command economies is people standing in long lines waiting to buy goods. Such shortages often lead to creative behavior. In the former Soviet Union, for example, light bulbs were almost impossible to buy for home use. However, burned-out bulbs in factories were regularly replaced. Some people took and sold these burned-out bulbs. Why? Other people would buy them and use them to switch out with working bulbs in their factories. They then took the working bulbs to light their homes.

Perhaps the greatest failing of strict command systems is the great suffering that people living under them endured. Carrying out centrally planned economic policies requires that individual rights—even the right to life—be subordinate to the needs of the state. Millions of people died in the efforts to build huge collective farms in China and the Soviet Union. Millions more were imprisoned for exercising their political or economic rights. Estimates suggest that the deeply flawed policies of command economies are responsible for more deaths than two world wars.

APPLICATION Applying Economic Concepts

C. Why are consumer goods often in short supply in a command economy?

REVIEWING KEY CONCEPTS

1. Write a brief paragraph explaining the links between the following three terms.

   a. *centrally planned economy*   **b.** *socialism*   **c.** *communism*

2. Why do communist countries use authoritarian methods to maintain their economic and political system?

3. List and describe some advantages of centrally planned economies.

4. What are some disadvantages of centrally planned economies?

5. What is the relationship between the individual and the state in a communist nation?

6. **Using Your Notes** Write a sentence that makes a generalization about the nature of command economies. Refer to your completed hierarchy chart to complete this question.

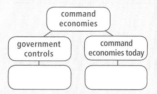

Use the Graphic Organizer at **Interactive Review @ ClassZone.com**

CRITICAL THINKING

7. **Making Inferences** Look again at the sentences about Thomas More's *Utopia* on page 38. Do you think that Karl Marx, like Thomas More, was trying to imagine a utopia in his writings? Give reasons for your answer.

8. **Explaining an Economic Concept** How do command societies address the problem of scarcity? Illustrate your answer with examples.

9. **Analyzing Cause and Effect** Read again the information about the North Korean economy on page 45. What factors caused North Korea's serious economic problems? What steps has the North Korean government taken to improve the dire economic situation?

10. **Challenge** Adam Smith used the "invisible hand" as a metaphor for the forces that balance a free market. What might be a good metaphor for the forces at work in a command economy? Explain your answer.

ECONOMICS IN PRACTICE

Celebration of communism in the Soviet Union

Using Graphs
Presenting information in a graph shows economic changes more clearly.

Create a Graph Use the following data to create a line graph.

Household Expenditures in the Soviet Union ($)	
1979	825.2 million
1981	934.7 million
1983	966.7 million
1985	1,017.1 million
1987	1,064.7 million
1989	1,152.3 million

Source: United Nations

Challenge During the 1980s, Soviet leaders introduced market elements into the economy. How might this explain the increase in household expenditures?

Use *SMART Grapher* @ClassZone.com to complete this activity.

Market Economies

OBJECTIVES	KEY TERMS	TAKING NOTES
In Section 3, you will • describe what a market is and how it works • identify the main features of a market economy • analyze how the circular flow model represents economic activity in a market economy • explain the advantages and disadvantages of a market economy	private property rights, *p. 48* market, *p. 48* laissez faire, *p. 49* capitalism, *p. 49* voluntary exchange, *p. 49* profit, *p. 49* competition, *p. 49* consumer sovereignty, *p. 50* specialization, *p. 50* circular flow model, *p. 52* product market, *p. 52* factor market, *p. 52*	As you read Section 3, complete a chart to identify and describe the features of a market economy. Use the Graphic Organizer at **Interactive Review @ ClassZone.com** 

Fundamentals of a Market Economy

KEY CONCEPTS

QUICK REFERENCE

Private property rights are the rights of individuals and groups to own businesses and resources.

A **market** is any place where people buy and sell goods and services.

Market economies have several distinct characteristics. Earlier in this chapter you read about the fundamental feature of a market economy—the fact that people's economic behavior is motivated by self-interest. Self-interested behavior is behind two other features of a market economy. One is **private property rights**, the rights of individuals and groups to own property. In economic terms, *property* means everything that an individual owns. This includes factories, offices, clothes, furniture, house, car, and other belongings; money; and even intellectual property, such as songs or ideas developed for inventions. It also includes the labor individuals provide to earn money to buy what they own.

The other feature that stems from self-interest is the **market**, any place or situation in which people buy and sell resources and goods and services. It may be the farmers' market on Saturdays in the town square, or it may be an enormous cybermarket on the Internet, such as eBay. Large or small, real or virtual, the market is where people can exchange their private property for someone else's.

Private Property Rights In a market economy, people are free to own and use private property—houses, for example.

FEATURE 1 Private Property and Markets

For markets to operate efficiently, private property rights need to be well defined and actively enforced by law. If you have ever bought a car, you know that an essential part of the transaction is getting possession of the title. You need proof that the person you are buying it from actually owns it and has the right to sell it. Since clear ownership is vital to any sale or exchange, private property rights are necessary to make markets work properly. If buyers could not trust that the sellers actually had the right to offer their products on the market, trade would break down. Further, suppose you are a musician but know that your songs can be downloaded for free, depriving you of your right to exchange what you own for money. In such a situation, it is doubtful that you would be motivated to record music. In protecting private property rights so that producers have motivation and consumers have trust, the government performs an important role in a market economy.

FEATURE 2 Limited Government Involvement

Sometimes the government's economic role is to stay out of the marketplace. The principle that the government should not interfere in the economy is called **laissez faire**, a French phrase meaning "leave things alone." The concept of laissez faire is often paired with **capitalism**, an economic system that is based on private ownership of the factors of production. Capitalism, the foundation of market economies, operates on the belief that, on their own, producers will create the goods and services that consumers demand. Therefore, according to laissez faire capitalism, there is no need for government involvement in the marketplace. Laissez faire capitalism is a market economy in its pure form. However, there are no pure market economies—all real-world market economies have some degree of government involvement.

FEATURE 3 Voluntary Exchange in Markets

When a buyer and seller agree to do business together, they engage in a **voluntary exchange**, a trade in which the parties involved anticipate that the benefits will outweigh the cost. Both sides in a voluntary exchange believe that what they are getting is worth more than what they are giving up. In a market economy, most trade is based on an exchange of a product for money rather than for another product.

Self-interest guides voluntary exchanges. Suppose you buy a new guitar. Even though you spend a good part of your savings, your self-interest is served because you've wanted this particular model of guitar. The seller's self-interest is likely served by **profit**, a financial gain from a business transaction. If you pay more for the guitar than the seller did, the seller earns money. In voluntary exchange, then, both sides must believe that they are gaining by trading.

FEATURE 4 Competition and Consumer Sovereignty

Market economies are also characterized by **competition**, the effort of two or more people, acting independently, to get the business of others by offering the best deal. You are able to choose today between a Macintosh and a Windows PC operating system because of the competition in the computer market. In the case of these competing systems, each has somewhat different features but mainly performs the same

COMPETITION

Where will you buy your computer?

You want to buy a new computer. You could buy a "standard package" from the electronics discount store. The price will be very reasonable, but you won't be able to customize the software package or the service program. Alternately, you could buy from a computer specialty store. You'll pay more, but you can choose the extras that you want and the customer support program is excellent.

Computer specialty store

Electronics discount store

functions as the other. You are free to decide which you prefer based on whatever combination of price and value appeals to you more. When you buy over-the-counter medications, you can also clearly see the competitive aspect of the market. Often next to a well-known brand-name product you will see a product with the same ingredients, similar packaging, but a different name and lower price. The producers of the lower priced item are competing for the business established by the brand-name product. If the producers of the brand-name product want to keep your business, they must lower their prices or find a way to add some other value.

That's because you, the consumer, hold the real power in the market place. **Consumer sovereignty** is the idea that because consumers are free to purchase what they want and to refuse products they do not want, they have the ultimate control over what is produced. Sovereignty means supreme authority, which is what consumers exercise as key economic decision-makers. Let's look at the over-the-counter medications again. If there were no competition, the brand-name producers could charge higher prices. It would be in their self-interest to charge as much as they possibly could. Competition, however, acts as a control on self-interested behavior, guiding the market toward a balance between higher value and lower prices. Rather than lose your business, the brand-name producers will either lower their prices or raise the value of their product. Because producers must compete for the consumer's dollar, they have to work at pleasing you, the consumer, while pleasing themselves.

FEATURE 5 Specialization and Markets

A market economy encourages efficient use of resources by allowing people and businesses to specialize in what they do best. **Specialization** is a situation in which people concentrate their efforts in the areas in which they have an advantage. This allows people to trade what they can most efficiently produce for goods and services

QUICK REFERENCE

Consumer sovereignty is the idea that consumers have the ultimate control over what is produced because they are free to buy what they want and to reject what they don't want.

Specialization is a situation in which people concentrate their efforts in the activities that they do best.

Private Property
Buyers and sellers are free to own and use private property.

Government Involvement
Buyers and sellers must be free to operate with minimal government intervention.

Specialization
Buyers and sellers are able to concentrate their efforts in areas where they have an advantage.

Fundamentals of a Market Economy

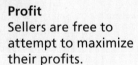

Voluntary Exchange
When a buyer and seller agree to do business together, each believes that the benefits outweigh the costs.

Consumer Sovereignty
Buyers can exercise their dominance over what is produced by freely deciding whether to buy or not to buy.

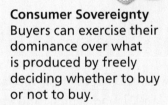

Competition
Sellers are free to attempt to get the business of others by offering the best deal.

Profit
Sellers are free to attempt to maximize their profits.

ANALYZE CHARTS

Identify a business in your community. Consider how the fundamentals of a market economy noted in the diagram are illustrated by the operations of that business. Record your ideas in a two-column table.

produced more efficiently by others. Specialization removes the need for households to be self-sufficient, and markets allow households to trade for what they need.

Suppose one adult in your house is a bank teller and another is a welder. Neither banking nor welding needs to happen within your household, but your household does need groceries. By specializing in what they do best—earning money in their jobs—in a market economy these adults are able to trade the dollars they earn for items and services others specialize in. If, however, they had to grow all the family's food themselves, they'd be less efficient than those who specialized in farming. Also, with each hour spent on growing food they would lose an hour's worth of wages from their jobs. Specialization, then, leads to higher-quality yet lower-priced products.

APPLICATION Applying Economic Concepts

A. Which is more important in determining the format in which recordings are offered by the music industry, new technology or consumer sovereignty? Explain.

Circular Flow in Market Economies

How do all these fundamental characteristics combine to allow a market economy to function? Economists have developed a model to help them answer this question. Called the **circular flow model**, it visualizes how all interactions occur in a market economy. The model represents the two key economic decision makers in a market economy—households, which are made up of individuals like you, and businesses. It also shows the two markets where households and businesses meet—that for goods and services, and that for resources. (See Figure 2.4 on the next page.)

Product Markets

The market for goods and services is called the **product market**. This is the market you probably know best. The product market isn't a place as much as it is a set of activities. Whenever or wherever individuals purchase goods or services—at a local mall, a dentist's office, the phone company, or an online service selling concert tickets—they are doing so in the product market. The suppliers of the product market are businesses, which offer their goods or services for sale and use the money they earn from the sales to keep their businesses going.

Factor Markets

To run a business, firms must, in turn, purchase what they need from the **factor market**, the market for the factors of production—land, labor, capital, and entrepreneurship. Individuals own all the factors of production. They own some factors of production outright, such as their own labor and entrepreneurship. Others they own indirectly as stockholders in businesses. In the factor market, businesses are the customers and individuals are the producers. A restaurant buys your labor as a server, for example, to serve meals prepared by chefs whose labor they have also bought. The chefs make the meals from products bought from farmers who own the fields and farm equipment.

Circular Flow

This set of interactions between businesses and individuals is illustrated in Figure 2.4 on the next page. On the left and right of the model, you can see the two main economic decision makers, businesses and households. At the top and bottom are the two main markets, product and factor. The green arrows represent the flow of money. The blue arrows represent the flow of resources and products.

Circular Flow Individuals, such as restaurant servers, sell their labor to businesses in the factor market.

FIGURE 2.4 The Circular Flow Model

Product
Market

Business
revenue $

Consumer
spending $

Sell
goods and
services

Buy
goods and
services

Businesses

Households
(Individuals)

Buy
productive
resources

Sell
land, labor,
capital,
entrepreneurship

Payments
for resources $

$ Income from
resources

Factor
Market

ANALYZE CHARTS

The circular flow model is a tool for understanding the relationships among economic decision makers and various markets. Why do you think that money always flows in one direction, while resources and products always flow in the opposite direction?

Animated **Economics**

Use an interactive circular flow model at **ClassZone.com**

Find the "Households" box at the right side of the chart. If you follow the green arrow, you see that individuals spend money in the product market to buy goods and services. From the product market, the money goes to businesses as revenue. The businesses spend this in the factor market, paying for the land, labor, capital, and entrepreneurship needed to produce goods and services. The receivers of that money are individuals who own all the factors of production. With the money they receive, individuals can make more purchases in the product market, and so the cycle continues.

If you look at the blue arrows, you can follow the route of the resources and products in the circular flow model. Once again, start with individuals. They sell their land, capital, labor, and entrepreneurship in the factor market. Follow the arrows to see that these factors of production are bought by businesses. The businesses then use these productive resources to make goods and services. The goods and services are then sold in the product market and flow to individuals who purchase them.

APPLICATION Interpreting Economic Models

B. Think of a good or a service you have recently bought. Using the circular flow model as a guide, write an explanation of the impact of your purchase on the economy.

Impact of Market Economies

Economics Update

Find an update about developing market economies in Eastern Europe at **ClassZone.com**

KEY CONCEPTS

Between the late 1940s and the early 1990s, between one-quarter and one-third of the world's population lived under command economic systems. The Soviet Union and its Eastern European neighbors, China and much of Southeast Asia, Cuba, and North Korea all had centrally planned economies. However, with the collapse of communism in the early 1990s, most of these countries have adopted some form of market economy. Also, as you read in Section 2, even those that have clung to communism and central planning have introduced market-economy measures. Why were these countries so ready to embrace the market system?

Advantages

On November 9, 1989, the Berlin Wall, a symbol of the division between the communist and democratic worlds, was finally opened. Over the next few days, hundreds of thousands of East Germans began pouring into West Germany through gates and improvised breaches in the wall. What drew these jubilant East Germans to the west? For most of them, the answer was freedom.

Economic and Political Freedom Freedom is one of the chief advantages of a market economy. A market economy requires that individuals be free to make their own economic choices, since it depends on the consumer's right to buy or refuse products to determine what will be produced. Individuals are also free to develop their interests and talents in work they find satisfying, rather than being assigned to jobs.

Also, since the government does not use a heavy hand to control the economy, the political process can be much freer, with a diversity of viewpoints and open elections. Government bureaucracy is generally less cumbersome and costly in a market economy than in a command economy, since there are fewer areas of

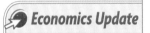

Freedom New shopping malls, like this one in Bucharest, Romania, are a common site in many formerly communist countries.

government involvement. A market economy also can be responsive to changes in conditions and accommodate those changes quickly.

Further, individuals in local communities are free to make their own economic choices without the interference of the government. These individuals' better knowledge of the resources and potential of their area leads to better economic decisions and greater productivity.

Profit The profit motive, a key feature of a market economy, insures that resources will be allocated efficiently, since inefficiencies would result in lower profits. It also serves as a reward for hard work and innovation. Knowing you can earn money

Competition Competition among dairy companies ensures that there is a wide variety of milk and other dairy products.

if you come up with a good idea is an incentive to do so, and the more good ideas people have, the more the economy grows. The incentive to come up with good ideas is related to another advantage of a market economy: it encourages competition, letting consumers have the final say. Competition leads to higher-quality products at lower prices. It also helps to create a diverse product market.

Disadvantages

Market economies, however, have disadvantages as well. In a pure market economy, the economic good of the individual is the primary focus. A pure market economy has no mechanism for providing public goods and services, such as national defense, because it would not be profitable from a strictly economic viewpoint to do so.

Another disadvantage is that a pure market economy cannot provide security to those who, because of sickness or age, cannot be economically productive. Nor can it prevent the unequal distribution of wealth, even though that gap may be the result of unequal opportunities.

The industrial boom in the United States in the late 1800s and early 1900s illustrates the problems that can develop in a market economy with little government regulation. During this time, a few business leaders became very rich. At the same time, most of those who worked for these leaders were paid low—but increasing—wages. Further, most business leaders did little at the time to address the negative consequences of industrialization such as pollution. Issues like these led most industrialized societies to adopt some level of government involvement in the economy. The result was economic systems that mix elements of market and command economies. In Section 4, you'll learn more about such mixed economies.

APPLICATION Analyzing Causes

C. Why did many societies feel it necessary to adopt some level of government involvement in market economies?

For more information on comparing and contrasting information, see the Skillbuilder Handbook, page R19.

Comparing and Contrasting Economic Systems

Comparing means looking at the similarities and differences between two or more things. **Contrasting** means examining only the differences between them. To understand economic systems, economists compare and contrast the ways in which societies use their limited resources to meet unlimited wants.

TIPS FOR COMPARING AND CONTRASTING Look for subjects that can be compared and contrasted.

Comparison This passage compares two economic systems that have both similarities and differences.

Contrast To contrast, look for clue words that show how two things differ. Clue words include *however, in contrast, on the other hand,* and *unlike.*

Similarities To find similarities, look for clue words indicating that two things are alike. Clue words include *both, similarly,* and *likewise.*

Economic Systems

An economic system is the way in which a society uses its resources to satisfy its people's needs and wants. Two common economic systems are the market system and the command system. Both systems provide answers to three basic economic questions: What to produce? How to produce? For whom to produce?

In a command economy, government economic planners decide what goods and services will be produced, how they will be produced, and for whom they will be produced. Individuals, then, have little or no influence on how economic decisions are made. In contrast, in a market economy the individual plays the major role in answering the basic economic questions. Consumers spend their money on the goods and services that satisfy them the most. In response, producers supply the goods and services that consumers want.

Few, if any, "pure" economic systems exist today. Most economic systems are "mixed." For example, market economies generally have some limited form of government control—a characteristic of command economies. Most command economic systems are likewise mixed in that they have some elements of market economies.

THINKING ECONOMICALLY **Comparing and Contrasting**

1. How are market and command economic systems similar?

2. In what ways do these two economic systems differ?

3. Read the paragraphs about North Korea under the heading "Command Economies Today" on page 45. Construct a Venn diagram showing similarities and differences between the economy of North Korea and a typical market economy.

REVIEWING KEY CONCEPTS

1. Explain the relationship between the terms in each of these pairs.

   a. *private property rights*
   market

   b. *laissez-faire*
   capitalism

   c. *specialization*
   profit

   d. *factor market*
   product market

2. What are the essential elements of market economies?

3. What are some advantages of market economies?

4. What are some disadvantages of market economies?

5. How does the profit motive help lead to efficient use of productive resources?

6. **Using Your Notes** Make charts for a traditional economy and a command economy and compare and contrast them with your completed market economy chart.

Use the Graphic Organizer at **Interactive Review @ ClassZone.com**

CRITICAL THINKING

7. **Analyzing Cause and Effect** Review the circular flow model on page 53. Based on the model, how do businesses benefit from the wages they pay?

8. **Creating and Interpreting Economic Models** Return to the answer you gave for Application B on page 53. Create a circular flow model to illustrate your answer.

9. **Solving Economic Problems** How do you think the disadvantages of a market economy can be minimized while its advantages continue to operate?

10. **Challenge** On August 29, 2005, Hurricane Katrina devastated regions of the Gulf Coast states of Louisiana, Mississippi, and Alabama. Most of New Orleans, for example, was flooded after the levees protecting the city broke. How would a pure market economy respond to the devastation and loss?

ECONOMICS IN PRACTICE

Employers and employee discuss salary

Understanding the Market Economy
Market economies can be identified by certain fundamental characteristics. These include self-interested behavior, private property rights, voluntary exchange, profit, competition, consumer sovereignty, specialization, and a limited role for government.

Identify Features Each sentence in the chart illustrates one fundamental feature of a market economy. Complete the chart by identifying these features.

Feature	Description
	An author secures a copyright for her latest novel.
	Declining sales signal the end of production for a model of car.
	A prospective employee and a business reach an agreement on salary and benefits.
	Taking advantage of their beautiful natural environment, local planners approve development of new hotels and resorts.

Challenge Write sentences illustrating two fundamental features of market economies not illustrated in the sentences above.

Modern Economies in a Global Age

OBJECTIVES	KEY TERMS	TAKING NOTES
In Section 4, you will • identify the main characteristics of a mixed economy • understand why most modern economies are mixed economies • explain why modern economies are becoming increasingly global	mixed economy, *p. 58* nationalize, *p. 61* privatize, *p. 61* global economy, *p. 61*	As you read Section 4, complete a cluster diagram to record what you learn about modern economies in a global age. Use the Graphic Organizer at **Interactive Review @ ClassZone.com** Today's Mixed Economies — Trends in Modern Economies — Modern Economies

Today's Mixed Economies

KEY CONCEPTS

QUICK REFERENCE

A **mixed economy** is an economy that has elements of traditional, command, and market systems.

Today, the **mixed economy**—an economic system that has elements of traditional, command, and market economies—is the most common type of economic system. Even the most strongly market-based modern economies have some elements of central planning. Similarly, market influences have penetrated all of today's command economies to some extent. Traditional production methods are still followed in some areas of both market and command systems. And traditional economies everywhere are experiencing greater government involvement and growing pressure from market influences.

Life in a Mixed Economy

Let's look at a farming family in the rural Midwest of the United States to see how elements of all three economic systems may be present in a mixed economy. The family has owned and operated the farm for many generations. While they use the most modern farming methods, family members still cling to some old customs. At harvest time, for example, everybody works to get in the crops. Even the youngest children have their own special tasks to do. The family's crops are sold on the market along with those of their neighbors and of farmers throughout the region. Well-maintained highways connect the farm to the various locations where the crops are sold. Two teenagers in the family attend the public high school. The oldest one works in town at a part-time job during the week, earning the minimum wage. Two grandparents who no longer work full time on the farm each receive a Social Security check every month.

In this scenario, all three types of economic system are blended. The harvest-time customs the family follows represent the influence of a traditional economy. The command aspects of the economy are reflected in the ways that government has become involved. The well-maintained roads, the public high school, the minimum wage, and the Social Security checks are all examples of government benefits and regulations at the local, state, or national level. (You'll learn more about government involvement in the economy, including the minimum wage and Social Security, in later chapters.) The market aspects of the economy are represented in the private property rights and entrepreneurship of the family members. They own their land and have figured out the best ways to use it to make a living. Other aspects of a market economy include the competitive market in which their goods are sold, and the voluntary exchange that takes place when the family sells its crops and when one of the teenagers exchanges labor for wages.

Elements of Command One way the U.S. government intervenes in the economy is to set safety standards for automobiles and other products.

Types of Mixed Economies

Although all modern economies are mixed, they often emphasize one type of system or another. In the scenario you just read, which is based on the economy of the United States, the market economy dominates. Even though there are traditional and command elements, the driving forces of the U.S. economy are such features as private ownership and markets. So, the United States essentially has a market economic system.

Many European countries have a more even mix of market and command economies. France, for example, tried to find a "middle way" between socialism and capitalism. In the years following World War II, its economy emphasized the command system with government ownership of core industries. In the 1980s, however, many people expressed dissatisfaction with the performance of government-owned industry. As a result, the French government pulled back from its ownership role in the economy, privatizing several industries, most notably banking and insurance. Even so, it still has a controlling share of ownership in a number of industries, including energy, automobiles, transportation, communications, and defense. In addition, it provides an array of social services, including health care and education, to the French people.

Sweden, while also a mixed economy, has much greater government involvement. The Swedish government and government-related organizations own about one third of all Swedish companies. In addition, Swedish citizens receive "cradle to grave" social benefits. These include childcare for children ages 1 through 5, schooling for

FIGURE 2.5 Calculating Percentages

Economists often use percentages to express the level of government involvement in a country's economy.

Step 1: Read the table, which contains data on the total economy and government consumption—the value of all the goods and services government buys—for three countries.

Step 2: Using Canada as an example, calculate government consumption as a share of the total economy.

Country	Total Economy (in billions of U.S. dollars)	Government Consumption (in billions of U.S. dollars)
Canada	789.8	152.4
Nigeria	48.8	11.4
Sweden	259.2	72.2

Source: Heritage Foundation

Share of economy consumed by government	=	Government consumption
		Total economy

$$\frac{\$152.4}{\$789.8} = 0.192960243$$

Step 3: Convert the answer to a percentage by multiplying by 100.

$$0.192960243 \times 100 = 19.2960243\%$$

Step 4: Round your answer to a whole number.

$$19.2960243 \text{ rounded to a whole number} \approx 19\%$$

Comparing Economies To compare government consumption in the economies of two different countries, economists can calculate percentages for each country and compare the percents.

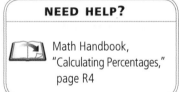

NEED HELP?

Math Handbook, "Calculating Percentages," page R4

children ages 6 through 16, additional years of school and college for those who choose them, health care, dental care, paid time off for raising families, and generous old-age pensions. In return, however, the Swedish pay very high tax rates, in some cases as high as 60 percent of income.

Each country has its own distinct balance of economic types. Namibia, as you read in Section 1, has a large number of people engaged in subsistence farming, following traditional production methods. Since the early 1990s, however, the Namibian government has been encouraging a more market-driven approach, including foreign investment in farming and other businesses. The country's leaders hope that these efforts will help the economy to grow and provide more economic opportunities for all Namibians.

APPLICATION Synthesizing Economic Data

A. Look at the Math Challenge above. What level of government involvement in the economy does each country shown have?

Trends in Modern Economies

KEY CONCEPTS

Economies have changed, and are always changing, in response to changes in natural, social, and political conditions. In the early 1990s, for example, some Eastern European economies experienced abrupt change when their command systems broke down after the collapse of communism in the Soviet Union. Many of these economies have been making reforms to introduce more market elements. (You'll learn more about these economies in Chapter 18.)

TREND 1 Changes in Ownership

Economies in transition often go through predictable processes. Some of the most important relate to changes in ownership. After World War II, some European economies became more centrally planned. For example, the British government, to help the country more effectively recover from the war, nationalized several important industries, including coal, steel, and the railroads. To **nationalize** means to change from private ownership to government or public ownership.

More recently, many economies have moved away from command systems to market systems. In this process, government-owned industries have been privatized. To **privatize** means to change from government or public ownership to private ownership. Poland, for example, is undergoing a transition from a command to a market economy with an extensive privatization program. Since 1990, Poland has privatized a number of manufacturing, construction, trade, and service industries. The Polish government hoped that private ownership of economic resources would provide incentives for greater efficiency, which, in turn, would help the economy to grow.

QUICK REFERENCE

To **nationalize** means to change from private ownership to government or public ownership.

To **privatize** means to change from government or public ownership to private ownership.

The **global economy** refers to all the economic interactions that cross international boundaries.

TREND 2 Increasing Global Ties

One way to help privatize an industry is to open it up to foreign investors. This kind of economic tie between nations is only one example of the global economy. The **global economy** is all the economic interactions that cross international boundaries. Today, American consumers and businesses are actors in a world economy. Businesses now engage in more foreign trade than ever before, and they depend not only on the products they buy from foreign nations, but also on the foreign markets in which they sell their products.

There are several reasons for this surge in economic globalization. One reason is the opening up of the world's markets to trade. Nations have been discussing ways to open trade for many years. The outcome of these talks has been the signing of agreements that ensure that trade among nations flows as

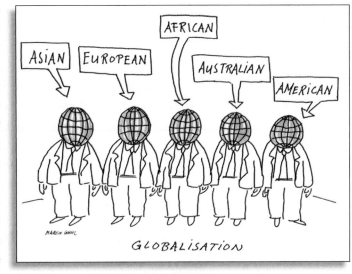

Globalization Some people are opposed to globalization, charging that it results in the loss of national identity.

FIGURE 2.6 The World Student

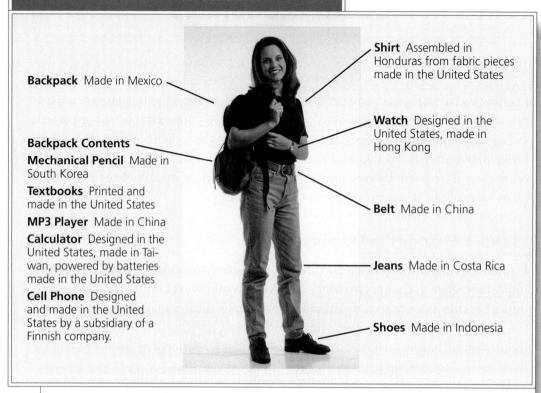

Backpack Made in Mexico

Backpack Contents
Mechanical Pencil Made in South Korea

Textbooks Printed and made in the United States

MP3 Player Made in China

Calculator Designed in the United States, made in Taiwan, powered by batteries made in the United States

Cell Phone Designed and made in the United States by a subsidiary of a Finnish company.

Shirt Assembled in Honduras from fabric pieces made in the United States

Watch Designed in the United States, made in Hong Kong

Belt Made in China

Jeans Made in Costa Rica

Shoes Made in Indonesia

ANALYZE CHARTS

List all the things that you use in a normal day—the clothes you wear, the foods you eat, the appliances you use, and so on. Identify where each item was made—in the United States or in another country.

Economics Update

Find an update on global partnerships at **ClassZone.com**

smoothly and freely as possible. Another reason for the growth of the global economy is the development of faster, safer, and cheaper transportation. Distribution methods have become so efficient that resources and products can be moved around the world relatively inexpensively. In addition, telephone and computer linkages have made global financial transactions quick, inexpensive, and easy.

Globalization also has been enhanced by cross-border business partnerships. For example, Ford Motor Company of the United States and Mazda Motor Corporation of Japan have long worked as partners. They design and engineer cars together, use each other's distribution systems, and share manufacturing plants. Recently, Ford and Mazda have joined with China's Changan Automotive Group to produce engines for Ford and Mazda cars. Such shared efforts lead to greater efficiency, which results in lower production costs and greater profits.

Other global partnerships have grown out of the need to share the enormous costs of researching and developing new technology. For example, Hitachi of Japan has joined with two American companies, Texas Instruments Incorporated and Integrated Device Technology, to develop smaller and more powerful computer memory chips. Such joint efforts are an illustration of today's economic reality—businesses can cooperate and learn from one another even while pursuing their own interests.

APPLICATION Analyzing Effects

B. How do global business alliances benefit the U.S. economy?

REVIEWING KEY CONCEPTS

1. For each of the following key terms, write a sentence that illustrates its meaning.
   a. *mixed economy*
   b. *nationalize*
   c. *privatize*
   d. *global economy*

2. What is a market-driven mixed economy? Illustrate your answer with examples.

3. In the transition from command to market economies, most economic resources are privatized. What is the expected impact of this action?

4. What forces have contributed to the growth of the global economy?

5. How are you, as an individual, affected by the global economy?

6. **Using Your Notes** Write a four-sentence summary of this section, using your completed cluster diagram as a reference.

   Use the Graphic Organizer at **Interactive Review @ ClassZone.com**

Today's Mixed Economies

Trends in Modern Economies

Modern Economies

CRITICAL THINKING

7. **Explaining an Economic Concept** Explain, with examples, how the American economy includes elements of traditional, command, and market economic systems.

8. **Analyzing Cause and Effect** Since the fall of communism in the 1990s, countries in Eastern Europe and the former Soviet Union have abandoned command economies in favor of market economies. How do you think economic life in these countries has changed?

9. **Applying Economic Concepts** Many nations import U.S. capital and technology by purchasing equipment that U.S. businesses manufacture. Explain how this development can benefit the American people.

10. **Challenge** How do market forces operate in the global economy? Illustrate your answer with examples.

ECONOMICS IN PRACTICE

Shopping for shoes

Illustrating the Global Economy
How do you participate in the global economy? Study Figure 2.6 opposite and then complete this exercise.

Conduct a Survey Make a survey of class members to identify the "Made in" labels in their clothes, shoes, and other items they use every day. Use a chart similar to the one below to list the items and the countries in which they were produced.

Product	Where Made
Sweaters	
Shirts	
Pants or dresses	
Shoes	
Jackets	
Backpacks	

Challenge Write a short explanation of how this list illustrates the global economy.

Contrasting Economies: North Korea and South Korea

North Korea
South Korea

Background Korea was an independent kingdom for nearly 1,000 years. After World War II, the country was divided into two nations, North Korea and South Korea. Since then, the two countries have developed in vastly different ways. After the Korean War ended in 1953, North Korea's communist government followed an economic, political, and military policy of isolation. North Korea has a command economy, though elements of a market system are taking root.

South Korea, in contrast, is a democracy with a market economy. South Korea has achieved incredible economic growth, in part because of its *chaebols* (jeh BOLZ), huge technology conglomerates like Samsung and Hyundai that originated from a single family. Strong government support for businesses has aided the country's economic success.

What's the issue? How effective are command and market economies? Use these sources to discover how well the economies of North and South Korea function.

A. Online Article

In this article, the United States Institute of Peace (USIP) summarizes the findings of Andrew P. Natsios about the great famine in North Korea. Natsios is the author of *The Great North Korean Famine: Famine, Politics, and Foreign Policy* (2001).

North Korea Suffers Famine

Workers in "unproductive" industries die from lack of food

According to some estimates, . . . three million people died in the North Korean famine of the mid-1990s. . . .

Faced with a massive food shortage, the North Korean government "made a choice," Natsios said. Making the regime's survival its top priority, the government decided that food would go to the country's elite and its military forces. Most citizens, especially those who lived in regions or worked in industries that the government deemed "unproductive," were considered expendable. As many as three million people may have died.

Before the famine, North Korea relied on food and oil subsidies, mostly from the former Soviet Union. When that aid declined and a series of natural disasters occurred, the North Korean government cut food rations to farmers. Many people started hoarding and stealing. The system collapsed. In Natsios' view, North Koreans lost faith in the state.

Source: "The North Korean Famine." *Peace Watch Online*, June 2002

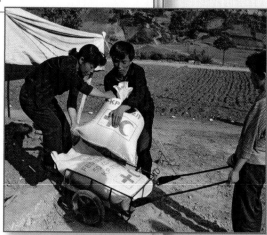

North Koreans receive contributions of rice from an international humanitarian agency.

Thinking Economically What decision described in this document is characteristic of a command economy? Explain your answer.

FIGURE 2.7 PER CAPITA GDP

B. Graph

This graph compares North Korea's and South Korea's per capita GDP—each person's share of everything produced in the economy—from 1994 to 2004.

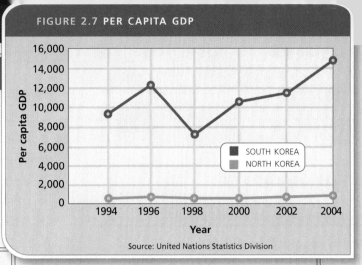

Thinking Economically What does this graph suggest about productivity in the two nations?

C. Magazine Article

This article reflects the contributions of corporations like Samsung to South Korea's growing economy.

Samsung and the "Next Great Tech Revolution"

Heading Towards a Digitized Life

Lee Jong Jin, 51, is no couch potato. But lounging in his apartment overlooking the mountains of Seoul, the international trader has little reason to leave his sofa. As he watches an interactive game show, he uses the remote to send in answers. In a corner of the 50-inch plasma screen, he can link to his online bank or control his air conditioner. Lee is one of thousands of Koreans involved in trials of Samsung Electronics' Home Network, which allows digital products to talk to each other. If Samsung has its way, millions around the world will be running their homes from the comfort of their couch within a few years.

. . . Over the last decade, [Samsung] has . . . become the most diverse and profitable consumer-electronics company on the planet. Samsung leads the global market for color televisions, VCRs, liquid crystal displays for electronic devices and digital memory devices. . . . Since 1999, revenues have doubled, and profits have risen 20 times. . . .

In the digital world all these products will finally be networked to each other . . . creating the sort of "smart" living space imagined only in science fiction. That's the idea, anyway. The change, says analyst Keith Woolcock of Westhall Capital in London, will be "the biggest event in technology for the next 10 years."

Source: "Digital Masters," *Newsweek* (International Edition), October 18, 2004

Thinking Economically What aspects of a market economy are illustrated by Samsung's financial success?

THINKING ECONOMICALLY Synthesizing

1. Based on documents A and C, in which country does the government appear to be more involved in controlling business and the economy?

2. Based on documents A and C, what can you infer about the effects of government activities on productivity in the two nations?

3. In today's global economy, is a command economy or a market economy more likely to succeed? Support your answer with information presented in the three documents.

Interactive Review

Review this chapter using interactive activities at ClassZone.com

- Online Summary
- Graphic Organizers
- Quizzes
- Review and Study Notes
- Vocabulary Flip Cards

 Online Summary

Complete the following activity either on your own paper or online at **ClassZone.com**

Choose the key concept that best completes the sentence. Not all key concepts will be used.

capitalism	global economy	private property rights
centrally planned economy	laissez faire	privatize
circular flow model	market	product market
command economy	market economy	profit
competition	mixed economy	socialism
factor market	nationalize	traditional economy
		voluntary exchange

In a __1__, the three basic economic questions of what to produce, how to produce, and for whom to produce are answered in the same way they have been for generations. In a __2__, in contrast, the government makes most economic decisions. Two systems in which government plays a strong role are communism and __3__. In the transition between types of economic systems, the government may __4__ industries, taking them out of private ownership.

A __5__ economy rests on private ownership, however, so __6__ guaranteed by the government are vitally important. A market economy also depends on __7__ to help produce the highest quality goods at the lowest price. Sellers are motivated by the chance to make a __8__, so they try to use their resources as efficiently as possible. The __9__ shows the flow of money as well as the flow of products and resources in the __10__ that takes place between buyers and sellers in a market economy.

The most common kind of economy today is the __11__ which blends elements from all three systems. Each modern economy is also part of the __12__, which entails all the economic interactions that cross international borders.

REVIEWING KEY CONCEPTS

Introduction to Economic Systems (pp. 38–41)

1. What are the three types of economic systems?

2. What are features of a traditional economy?

Command Economies (pp. 42–47)

3. What role does the government play in a command economy?

4. What are the advantages and disadvantages of a command economy?

Market Economies (pp. 48–57)

5. What are the features of a market economy?

6. What are the advantages and disadvantages of a market economy?

Modern Economies in a Global Age (pp. 58–65)

7. What are the features of a mixed economy?

8. What trends are shaping modern economies?

APPLYING ECONOMIC CONCEPTS

Look at the chart below showing statistics for four nations. Answer the following questions.

9. Which country appears to have the most productive economy?

10. Does a high percentage of GDP from agriculture make a country more or less productive? Support your answer with statistics from the chart.

FIGURE 2.8 GROWTH AND PRODUCTIVITY

Country	GDP* Growth Rate	PPP**	% of GDP from Agriculture
North Korea	1.0	1,800	30.0
Poland	3.3	12,700	2.8
Namibia	4.2	7,800	9.3
China	9.2	6,200	14.4

* Gross Domestic Product (value of everything the country produced)
** Purchasing Power Parity (shows a country's productivity relative to its population)
Source: *The CIA World Factbook, 2006*

11. Creating Charts Create a chart showing a continuum of countries with different types of economic systems. At the left will be the nations with the most command elements in their economic systems. On the right will be the nations with the most market elements in their economies. Use the chart below as a model.

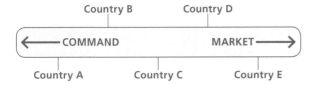

Begin with the countries listed in the chart on the previous page. Then add other countries mentioned in this chapter, such as France, Sweden, and the United States. Conduct extra research if you have difficulty placing these countries on the continuum. One useful source of information is *Economic Freedom of the World Annual Report*.

12. Synthesizing Economic Data Look again at Figure 2.8 on page 66. Why do you think Poland and Namibia had relatively high growth rates? In writing your answer, consider the economic changes that have taken place in these countries in recent years.

13. Evaluating Economic Decisions Using information in Figure 2.8, evaluate Poland's decision to privatize a number of its industries, noting whether you think it was a wise or an unwise action. Explain your evaluation.

14. Explaining an Economic Concept In most of the former command economies in Eastern Europe, one of the first economic changes instituted was establishing the right to own private property. Why do you think the leaders of these countries considered this feature of market economies so important?

15. Challenge Write a brief essay explaining how a country's political system and economic system are intertwined.

Privatize Your Community's Recreation Facilities

Suppose your community felt that its administration of your park district and recreation facilities—pools, gyms, and so on—had become inefficient. As an exercise to understand the issues involved in moving from a government-owned to a privately-owned enterprise, work through the decisions you would face in privatization.

Step 1. With your whole class, divide the recreation facilities into manageable segments. One segment might be park maintenance, another might be fitness classes at the community center, and so on. Then organize pairs or small teams and assign each pair or team one of the segments.

Step 2. In your pairs or teams, discuss how to use the elements of a market economy to make your segment of the project as efficient as possible—to provide the lowest priced services at the highest possible quality.

Step 3. Draw up a plan describing the privately-owned company you think could take over your segment.

Step 4. Share your plans with the teams working on the other segments to see what other ideas came up.

Step 5. With your whole class, discuss whether privatizing services like park district facilities is a beneficial step or not. Discuss possible advantages and possible disadvantages.

Free Enterprise

In the American free enterprise system, everyone is free to start a business like the couple shown here. Businesses will succeed or fail based on how well they respond to market forces.

The American Free Enterprise System

CONCEPT REVIEW

A **market economy** is an economic system based on individual choice, voluntary exchange, and the private ownership of resources.

CHAPTER 3 KEY CONCEPT

Free enterprise system is another name for capitalism, an economic system based on private ownership of productive resources. This name is sometimes used because in a capitalist system anyone is free to start a business or enterprise.

WHY THE CONCEPT MATTERS

Free enterprise is all around you, from huge suburban malls to industrial developments to neighborhood corner stores. Think about ways that the American economic system affects your day-to-day life. Consider where you shop, what you buy, where you work, and what you do there. What do you think allows this huge economic engine to run?

Online Highlights
More at ClassZone.com

 Economics Update
Go to **ECONOMICS UPDATE** for chapter updates and current news on entrepreneurs in the United States. (See Case Study, pages 92–93).

Animated Economics
Go to **ANIMATED ECONOMICS** for interactive versions of diagrams in this chapter. ▶

Interactive Review
Go to **INTERACTIVE REVIEW** for concept review and activities.

How do households, businesses, and government interact in the economy? See Figure 3.4 in Section 2 of this chapter.

Advantages of the Free Enterprise System

In Section 1, you will • explain why the United States is considered to have a capitalist, or free enterprise, system • identify the legal rights that safeguard the free enterprise system • analyze how the profit motive and competition help to make the free enterprise system work	free enterprise system, *p. 70* open opportunity, *p. 73* legal equality, *p. 73* free contract, *p. 73* profit motive, *p. 73*	As you read Section 1, complete a cluster diagram using information on free enterprise. Use the Graphic Organizer at **Interactive Review @ Classzone.com** 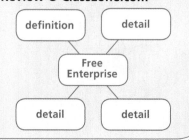

What Is a Free Enterprise System?

KEY CONCEPTS

QUICK REFERENCE

Free enterprise system is another name for capitalism, an economic system based on private ownership of productive resources.

As you recall from Chapter 2, the United States has a capitalist economic system. Capitalism is an economic system based on the private ownership of the factors of production. The central idea of capitalism is that producers are free to produce the goods and services that consumers want. Consumers are influenced by the desire to buy the goods and services that satisfy their economic wants. Producers are influenced by the desire to earn profits, the money left over after the costs have been subtracted from business revenues. A capitalist system is also known as a **free enterprise system** because anyone is free to start a business or enterprise.

EXAMPLE United States

Let's take a look at one American who took advantage of that freedom. Monica Ramirez, a makeup consultant for fashion magazines and television, noticed that very few Hispanic women purchased the cosmetics available in stores. She thought that this might present a business opportunity. So, in 2001, she created Zalia Cosmetics, a line of cosmetics specifically for

Latinas. She put her whole savings account into starting the business. Her creativity and energy attracted attention, and she soon had backers willing to invest their money in the business.

By 2004, Zalia Cosmetics had sales outlets in the major Hispanic markets of New York, Miami, Dallas, Los Angeles, San Antonio, and Houston. Today, the business continues to grow and Ramirez is sharing her success. She donates a percentage of her profits to organizations that help and encourage Latina entrepreneurs.

As you can see in Figure 3.1 below, Zalia Cosmetics was just one of more than 585,000 new businesses started in the United States in 2001. No matter where you go in the United States, you can see similar signs of a free enterprise economy at work. If you walk through a suburban shopping mall you'll see national and regional chain stores next to small boutiques and startup shops. Sometimes you'll even see kiosks in the aisles, competing for business. Similarly, on a stroll through a city neighborhood you'll observe corner grocery stores, dry cleaners, and barber shops. At an industrial park you'll see factories that churn out an immense variety of products. In the countryside beyond the city, you'll notice farms with fields of corn or soybeans, orchards of apples or peaches, or grazing areas for livestock.

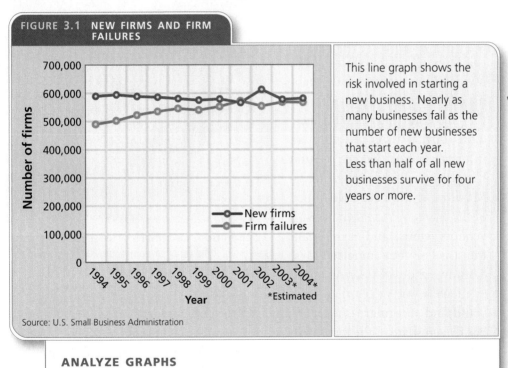

FIGURE 3.1 NEW FIRMS AND FIRM FAILURES

This line graph shows the risk involved in starting a new business. Nearly as many businesses fail as the number of new businesses that start each year. Less than half of all new businesses survive for four years or more.

Source: U.S. Small Business Administration

Economics Update

Find an update on new business firms and business firm failures at **ClassZone.com**

ANALYZE GRAPHS

1. What is notable about 2002 in terms of the relationship between new firms and firm failures?
2. How does this graph illustrate the fact that entrepreneurship involves risk?

What do these examples of free enterprise have in common? They are all illustrations of how individual choices are the basis of a market economy. Business owners freely make the choice to start these enterprises. Also, these owners are free to choose how they will use their scarce productive resources. The managers and workers who operate these businesses voluntarily decide to exchange their labor for the pay the owners offer. Finally, consumers make their own choices on which goods and services they will buy.

As you recall, government plays a relatively limited role in the American free enterprise system. The government sometimes takes actions that limit free enterprise. For the most part, however, these actions are designed to protect or encourage competition or to enforce contracts.

EXAMPLE Emerging Markets

As you read in Chapter 2, most countries today have mixed economic systems with at least some elements of free enterprise. Each economy has its own balance of tradition, free enterprise, and government involvement and its own distinctive ways in which market forces work. To illustrate this, let's look at the countries of Mexico and Singapore

In the Mexican economy, the government plays a much larger role than in the United States. The Mexican government has established many rules and regulations that make starting a new business quite difficult. As a result, an informal market that gets around these barriers has grown up. In Mexico City, for example, much of the city center is taken up with vendors' stalls, and people jam the streets to buy imported toys, clothing, shoes, CDs, and more at much lower prices than they

Competition Popular stalls on the streets of Mexico City, selling everything from candy to clothes, provide considerable competition for established stores.

could find at regular retail stores. Indeed, the stiff competition from street vendors has driven some of the retail stores out of business.

The country of Singapore has a thriving free enterprise system. However, the government is so closely involved in the economy that the country is sometimes called Singapore Inc. The government establishes what benefits employers must provide to workers. It also requires all workers to put a percentage of income in the Central Provident Fund, a government savings scheme. The fund is used to pay pensions and to finance public projects, such as education, housing, and health care. Even so, the government is considered very supportive of free enterprise. Many of its policies keep business rents, taxes, and other costs low so that Singaporean companies remain competitive in the world economy.

APPLICATION Analyzing Cause and Effect

A. What steps can a government take to support free enterprise?

How a Free Enterprise System Works

KEY CONCEPTS

You learned in Chapter 2 that the right to private property is one of the most fundamental freedoms in a capitalist economy. With that freedom comes the right to exchange that property voluntarily. This exchange lies at the heart of a free enterprise economy. Another key freedom of this type of economy is **open opportunity**, the ability of everyone to enter and compete in the marketplace of his or her own free choice. This ensures that the market will reflect a wide range of interests and talents and will provide incentives to everyone to be efficient and productive.

Free enterprise also requires **legal equality**, a situation in which everyone has the same economic rights under the law. In other words, everyone has the same legal right to succeed or fail in the marketplace. Another important element of a market economy is the **free contract**. For voluntary exchange to work, people must be able to decide for themselves which legal agreements they want to enter into, such as business, job, or purchase commitments.

These freedoms assure that people are able to engage in free enterprise. But what motivates people to start a business? For most people, it is the **profit motive**, the incentive that encourages people and organizations to improve their material well-being by seeking to gain from economic activities. Producers, motivated by profit, seek the highest possible price for their products. Competition offsets the drive to earn profits, since it forces prices down. This helps producers find a price that is not so high that it deters buyers and not so low that it inhibits profits.

QUICK REFERENCE

Open opportunity is the ability of everyone to take part in the market by free choice.

Legal equality is a situation in which everyone has the same economic rights under the law.

A **free contract** is a situation in which people decide which legal agreements to enter into.

The **profit motive** is the force that encourages people and organizations to improve their material well being from economic activities.

EXAMPLE Profit in Rocks

One memorable example of how the various economic freedoms and the profit motive come together in the free enterprise system is the pet rock. Talking with friends in April 1975, advertising executive Gary Dahl joked that regular pets were too much trouble. Pet rocks, he suggested, were much easier to care for. Dahl's friends were amused by the idea. In response, he wrote a manual on pet rocks, showing how they could be house trained and taught to do tricks.

In August, Dahl began packaging his pet rocks, complete with a care manual, for sale at gift shows. Intrigued, a buyer from a major department store ordered 500. In a matter of weeks, Dahl's joke had become a national story. Articles appeared in newspapers and magazines and Dahl did several interviews on television. By the end of the year, Dahl had sold more than two tons of pet rocks and had become a millionaire. However, as 1976 began, consumers lost interest, and it quickly became obvious that the pet rock was last year's fad. Dahl decided to get out of the pet rock business, guided by the same market forces that had brought him into the business and made him rich.

Open Opportunity
Because of legal rights built into the free enterprise system, Gary Dahl was free to enter the market for pet rocks.

Open Opportunity
Everyone should have the ability to enter and compete in any marketplace. Open participation serves as an incentive to be efficient and productive.

Legal Equality
Everyone should have the same economic rights under the law. In other words, the law should not give some people a better chance than others to succeed in the marketplace.

What Legal Rights Are Built into the Free Enterprise System?

Marketplace

Free Contract
Everyone should have the right to decide for themselves which legal economic agreements they want to enter into. Voluntary exchange, a cornerstone of free enterprise, cannot function without freedom of contract.

Legal Agreement
x Phil

ANALYZE CHARTS
The American free enterprise system is based on the idea of freedom—producers and consumers are free to pursue their economic self-interest. Certain legal rights have been established to protect and encourage this freedom. Reread the paragraphs on pet rocks on page 73 and those on books on pages 74–75. How do these examples illustrate the legal rights shown in this chart?

EXAMPLE Competition over Books

Gary Dahl did face competition from other producers who jumped into the pet rock market. Competition, however, did not drive him out of business. Rather, consumers simply stopped buying pet rocks. The market for books is somewhat different. Demand for books remains high, but booksellers have been going out of business because of new and fierce competition.

Before 1995, small chain stores and independent neighborhood booksellers dominated the book market. Around 1995, large chain stores such as Barnes & Noble Inc. and Borders Group Inc. began to compete more aggressively. Because of their huge purchasing volume, the large chain stores could buy their books at greatly discounted prices. They passed the savings on to consumers, lowering prices by anywhere from 10 percent to 40 percent. They also created a warm and welcoming atmosphere in their stores, with comfortable reading areas, cafés, and frequent readings and book signings by authors.

The tactics of the large chain stores caused problems for independent booksellers. In 1991, independent booksellers accounted for more than 30 percent of all book sales in the United States. By 2005, their share of sales had fallen to less than 15 percent. And between 1995 and 2005, about 1,200 independent booksellers went out of business.

Soon, however, the large chains faced a challenge themselves: Amazon.com. The online bookseller opened for business in July, 1995 and within a few months had become an important player in the book market. Amazon's easy-to-use Web site, huge database of titles, quick and reliable delivery, and discounted prices attracted many book buyers. By the end of 2004, Amazon's sales stood at $134 million a week. Now Amazon, however, is looking over its shoulder at a new challenger. Online competitors such as Overstock.com and Buy.com have undercut Amazon's prices on hundreds of books by as much as 25 percent while matching Amazon's level of excellence in service.

Consumers have benefited from all of this competition, for they can now easily and conveniently buy books at the lowest prices. Those independent booksellers who have remained in business cannot match the lower prices offered by the large chains and online sellers. However, they can provide some things that their larger competitors cannot: personal service and a focus on local tastes or specialized subject areas. Consumers benefit from this, too. These independent booksellers who stayed in business illustrate an important aspect of free enterprise. Businesses that keep pace with changes in the market and adjust accordingly thrive. Those that do not eventually fail.

YOUR ECONOMIC CHOICES

FREE ENTERPRISE

Where will you open your restaurant?

You've decided to open a restaurant. You can lease one of two buildings. One is in a busy mall next to a highway exit. However, there are already six restaurants in that mall. The other location is in a small strip mall in a quiet neighborhood with no other restaurants nearby. Consider the chance to make profits and the level of competition, and choose.

Mall food court

Neighborhood strip mall

APPLICATION Analyzing Cause and Effect

B. Explain the chain of cause-and-effect reactions since the mid-1990s that led to lower book prices for American consumers.

Milton Friedman: Promoter of Free Markets

At a glittering White House birthday celebration for Milton Friedman in 2002, President George W. Bush declared that the 90-year-old economist "has shown us that . . . in contrast to the free market's invisible hand . . . the government's invisible foot tramples on people's hopes." Economics professors are rarely guests of honor at White House galas. Why did Friedman receive such a tribute?

Free to Choose

Friedman spent most of his career teaching at the University of Chicago, where he helped develop the free-market ideas now linked with what is called the "Chicago School of Economics." Central to his ideas was the belief that the market should be free to operate in all fields, even such professions as the law and medicine. Easing government restrictions in these fields— lowering licensing standards, for example—would bring more doctors and lawyers into the market. This, in turn, would bring down the cost of legal and medical services. Friedman also put forward the theory that the government's most important economic role was to control the amount of money in circulation. Without this control of the money supply, Friedman noted, the economy would experience inflation—a sustained rise in the general level of prices.

Friedman's ideas were very influential. He advised two U.S. presidents and the heads of state of several other countries on economic policy. He gained worldwide recognition in 1976 when he won the Nobel Prize for Economics. Friedman became well known outside the academic world in 1980 when *Free to Choose*, which he wrote with his wife Rose, became the year's best-selling nonfiction book in the United States.

From 1977 until his death in 2006, Friedman served as a scholar at the Hoover Institution, a conservative public-policy research center at Stanford University. In 1996, he and his wife founded the Milton and Rose D. Friedman Foundation, an organization that promotes school choice.

APPLICATION Making Inferences

C. How might Milton Friedman have responded to the problems associated with the informal market in Mexico?

FAST FACTS

Milton Friedman

Born: July 31, 1912

Died: November 16, 2006

Important Publications:
Capitalism and Freedom (1962)
Free to Choose (1980)
Bright Promises, Dismal Performance: An Economist's Protest (1983)

Famous Quotation:
I am in favor of cutting taxes under any circumstances and for any excuse, for any reason, whenever it's possible.

Major Accomplishments:
Economic advisor to Presidents Richard Nixon and Ronald Reagan, and to British prime minister Margaret Thatcher

Economics Update

Find an update on Milton Friedman at **ClassZone.com**

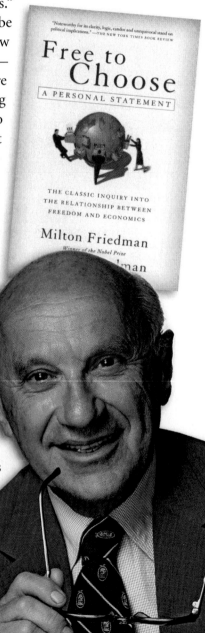

Economic Freedom
Personal freedom is at the center of Friedman's economic theories.

"Noteworthy for its clarity, logic, candor and unequivocal stand on political implications." —THE NEW YORK TIMES BOOK REVIEW

Free to Choose
A PERSONAL STATEMENT

THE CLASSIC INQUIRY INTO THE RELATIONSHIP BETWEEN FREEDOM AND ECONOMICS

Milton Friedman
Winner of the Nobel Prize

SECTION 1 Assessment

REVIEWING KEY CONCEPTS

1. Explain the differences among the following terms.

   a. *open opportunity*   **b.** *legal equality*   **c.** *free contract*

2. What is the role of the profit motive in the American free enterprise system?

3. How is a free enterprise system linked to economic freedom?

4. Give examples of three different economic freedoms in a free enterprise system.

5. What force acts as a balance to the profit motive in the American free enterprise system?

6. **Using Your Notes** Write two or three paragraphs explaining how a free enterprise system works. Refer to your completed cluster diagram.

   Use the Graphic Organizer at **Interactive Review @ ClassZone.com**

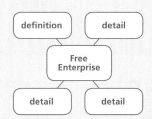

CRITICAL THINKING

7. **Applying Economic Concepts** Explain the role of competition in a free market. Illustrate your answer with examples of businesses in your local economy.

8. **Comparing and Contrasting Economic Information** Monica Ramirez and Gary Dahl both saw business opportunities and started new companies. Compare and contrast Ramirez's response to the market with that of Dahl. Use a Venn diagram to help you organize your ideas.

9. **Predicting Economic Trends** Turn back to page 74 and read again the paragraphs about competitive ideas in the bookselling market. What do you think might be the next new idea to compete with discounted books?

10. **Challenge** In a 1973 magazine interview, Milton Friedman said,

    What kind of society isn't structured on greed? The problem of social organization is how to set up an arrangement under which greed will do the least harm; capitalism is that kind of a system.

    Do you agree with Friedman that societies are structured on greed and that capitalism can reduce the harm caused by greed? Explain your answer.

ECONOMICS IN PRACTICE

A new business in the United States

Analyzing Economic Information
The following chart gives data about the rules and time for setting up new businesses in six countries. The rules are measured according to the number of government procedures a new business has to go through before it can begin operating. The time is the number of days it takes to complete the process of registering a new business.

Draw Conclusions What is the relationship between the rules and the time for setting up a new business?

Country	Rules (Number of Procedures)	Time (Number of Days)
Canada	2	3
Sweden	3	16
United States	5	5
Singapore	6	6
Germany	9	24
Mexico	9	58
China	13	48

Source: World Bank, 2005

Challenge Use the chart and what you know about the economies of the listed countries to write a short paragraph comparing the ease of entry into the marketplace in three countries of your choice.

How Does Free Enterprise Allocate Resources?

OBJECTIVES	KEY TERMS	TAKING NOTES
In Section 2, you will • explain how consumers help determine the way resources are used • explain how producers help determine the way resources are used • analyze a circular flow model of the U.S. economy	profit, *p. 78* modified free enterprise economy, *p. 80*	As you read Section 2, complete a cluster diagram to show how consumers, producers, and the government interact to allocate resources. Use the Graphic Organizer at **Interactive Review @ ClassZone.com**

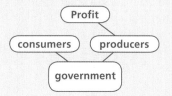

Profit

consumers — producers

government

The Roles of Producers and Consumers

KEY CONCEPTS

QUICK REFERENCE

Profit is the money left over after the costs of producing a good or service have been subtracted from the revenue gained by selling that good or service.

In the marketplace, consumers buy products for their personal use from producers who make or provide goods or services. In these exchanges, consumers look to get the best deal for the money they spend. Producers, on the other hand, are looking to earn the most profit from these transactions. **Profit** is the money left over after the costs of producing a product are subtracted from the revenue gained by selling that product. Seeking opportunities to earn profits is one way producers help allocate scarce resources in the economy.

EXAMPLE Producers Seek Profit

A new neighborhood coffee shop illustrates how producers help to allocate resources. The owners of the coffee shop, motivated by the desire to earn profits, charge the highest price consumers are willing to pay. The possibilities for good profits encourage other people to open coffee shops of their own. As a result, productive resources that might have been used in some other kind of business are directed toward the coffee shops. The profit seeking of producers, then, has helped in the allocation of resources.

EXAMPLE Consumers Vote with Their Wallets

Consumers also play an important role in allocating resources in a free enterprise system. When consumers choose to buy a product, they are "voting" for their choice against competing products. These "votes" help determine what will be produced in the future, since producers, seeking opportunities to profit, try to provide what consumers want. For example, in the early 2000s, when low-carbohydrate diets were popular, consumers "voted" for low-carb and high-protein foods and against high-carb foods. (Figure 3.3 below illustrates this, showing that between 2002 and 2003 sales of typical low-carb/high-protein products increased, while sales of typical high-carb products fell.) How did food producers respond to these "votes"? They moved some of their productive resources into the low-carb market to try to meet consumer demand.

FIGURE 3.3 SALES OF SELECTED FOOD PRODUCTS

High-Carb Foods			Low-Carb/High-Protein Foods		
Product	Unit Sales, 2003 (in millions)	Percentage Change Over 2002	Product	Unit Sales, 2003 (in millions)	Percentage Change Over 2002
Instant Rice	79.1	–8.2	Frozen Meat/ Seafood	483.5	+7.7
Bulk Rice	180.2	–4.9	Meat Snacks	105.4	+7.6
Cookies	1,839.7	–5.5	Nuts	679.3	+8.8
Regular Carbonated Drinks	7,032.5	–5.9	Diet Carbonated Drinks	2,828.6	+1.0
Dry Pasta	1,227.0	–4.6	Cheese	3,424.0	+4.0
White Bread	1,606.1	–4.7	Wheat Bread	873.1	+4.0

Source: ACNielsen

ANALYZE TABLES

1. Which high-carb item showed the greatest percentage drop in sales between 2002 and 2003? Which low-carb/high-protein item showed the greatest percentage gain?

2. Consumer interest in low-carb diets began to decline after 2004. What differences might you expect to see in a similar table for 2004 and 2005?

Interest in low-carb diets peaked early in 2004, but began to fade thereafter. Once again, consumers had cast their votes in the marketplace, buying fewer low-carb and high-protein products. Producers quickly responded. By the beginning of 2005, some companies had gotten out of the low-carb market completely. Others had significantly cut back production of low-carb products. Consumer actions had caused a reallocation of productive resources.

APPLICATION Analyzing Cause and Effect

A. How would the allocation of resources have been affected if the interest in low-carb diets had continued to increase?

Government in the U.S. Economy

KEY CONCEPTS

In Chapter 2 you learned that the United States economy, though based on the market system, is mixed. Government is an important element in the American economic system, but its role is relatively limited. This type of mixed economy, which includes some government protections, provisions, and regulations to adjust the free enterprise system, is sometimes called a **modified free enterprise economy**.

Modified Free Enterprise

In Figure 2.4 on page 53, you saw that the economy could be viewed as a stream of resources and products moving in a circular flow between households and businesses. Money also flows between households and businesses, facilitating this exchange of products and resources. Figure 3.4 shows how the government fits into this circular flow. It also shows how government exacts costs and dispenses benefits. Locate the two main economic decision-makers at the right and left of the chart: households (owners of resources) and businesses (makers of products). The two

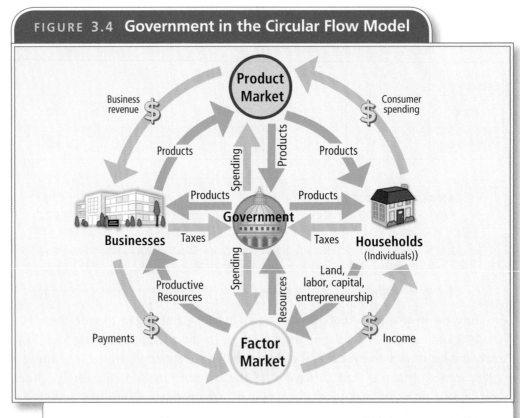

FIGURE 3.4 Government in the Circular Flow Model

ANALYZE CHARTS
This version of the circular flow model shows the flow of resources, products, and money among households, businesses, and the government. Describe the role of government in the economy using information from this chart.

Animated Economics

Use an interactive circular flow model at **ClassZone.com**

markets in the economy, the product market (for goods and services) and the factor market (for economic resources), are located at the top and bottom of the chart. The outer green arrows show the flow of money. The inner blue arrows show the flow of resources and products.

The government is located in the center of the chart. Like the other key actors in the circular flow, the government is both a consumer and a producer. Look at the arrows that run between government and the two markets. The government is a consumer in the resource market, spending money to buy the factors of production. It is also a consumer in the product market, spending money in exchange for products.

Now locate the arrows that run between government and households and government and business firms. Government is a producer here, providing goods and services to both households and businesses. Government collects money from households and businesses, in the form of taxes, as payment for these goods and services. It covers the costs of what it produces with this money. Government also uses this money to make purchases in the resource and product markets, and the cycle continues.

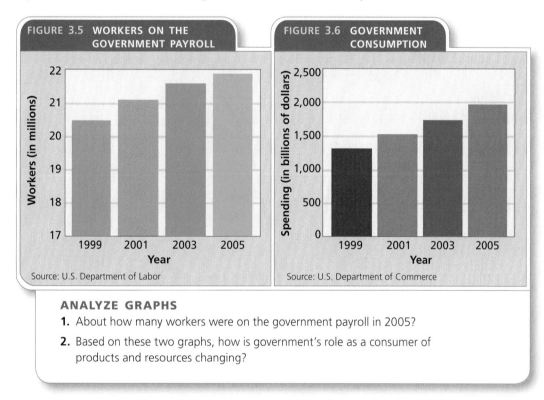

FIGURE 3.5 WORKERS ON THE GOVERNMENT PAYROLL

Workers (in millions) / Year

Source: U.S. Department of Labor

FIGURE 3.6 GOVERNMENT CONSUMPTION

Spending (in billions of dollars) / Year

Source: U.S. Department of Commerce

ANALYZE GRAPHS

1. About how many workers were on the government payroll in 2005?
2. Based on these two graphs, how is government's role as a consumer of products and resources changing?

Figures 3.5 and 3.6 above show that government is a major consumer of both resources and products. As you can see in Figure 3.5, all levels of government, local, state, and federal, employ almost 22 million workers. This is equal to about 16 percent of the labor force—all the labor resources available in the United States. Further, if you look at Figure 3.6 you'll see that government consumption—what all levels of government spend on goods and services—is over two trillion dollars.

Economics Update

Find an update on government workers and government consumption at **ClassZone.com**

APPLICATION Applying Economic Concepts

B. The paycheck that you get for working part-time at the pet store shows what you have earned and how much is withheld for taxes. Explain how the paycheck and the taxes withheld are represented in the circular flow model.

For more on interpreting graphs, see the Skillbuilder Handbook, page R29.

Interpreting Graphs: Public Opinion Polls

Public opinion polls are a useful tool for gathering information. Economists frequently use information obtained from opinion polls to measure public response to economic conditions. Polls conducted at regular intervals show changes in public opinion over a given period of time. The graph below shows the results of a poll that tracks consumer confidence. The poll, which is conducted monthly, is based on a representative sample of 5,000 households in the United States.

Title This indicates the type of data shown. Consumer confidence refers to the way people feel about the economy. Increasing confidence is likely to result in increased purchases of goods.

Subtitle This indicates the months and year of data collection.

Line on Graph This shows the fluctuations in consumer confidence from month to month.

Legend This provides a benchmark for comparison. For example, scores higher than 100 indicate that consumers have more confidence in the economy than they did in 1985.

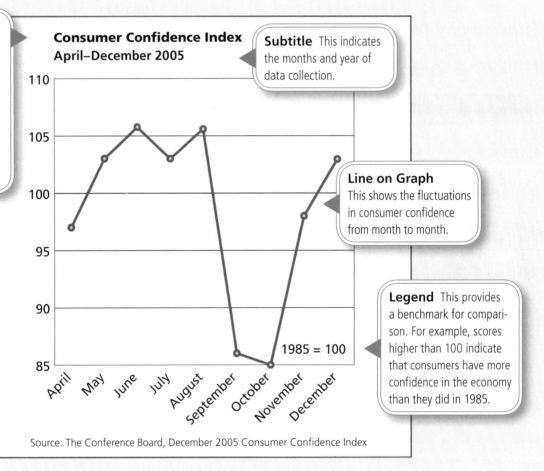

**Consumer Confidence Index
April–December 2005**

1985 = 100

Source: The Conference Board, December 2005 Consumer Confidence Index

According to researchers, consumer confidence in the economy tumbled after Hurricane Katrina hit the Gulf Coast in September 2005. Falling gasoline prices and growth in the job market led to a recovery in confidence in November and December.

THINKING ECONOMICALLY Interpreting

1. During which month was consumer confidence the highest? The lowest?
2. Describe the changes in consumer confidence from August through December.
3. The devastation caused by Hurricane Katrina and resulting increase in gasoline prices led to the abrupt drop in consumer confidence shown in the graph. What other events might cause a decline in consumer confidence?

1. Why is the U.S. economy sometimes referred to as a modified free enterprise system?

2. How does the profit motive work to allocate resources?

3. How do households and business firms interact in the product and resource markets?

4. Describe how the government interacts with the product and resource markets.

5. Study the circular flow models on pages 53 and 80. How are the two models different?

6. **Using Your Notes** Explain how producers, consumers, and the government interact to allocate resources in a free enterprise system.

   Use the Graphic Organizer at **Interactive Review @ ClassZone.com**

Profit

consumers   producers

government

CRITICAL THINKING

7. **Applying Economic Concepts** Think of several examples in which consumers have voted with their dollars and driven a product from the market or into high demand. Record your ideas in a table like the one below.

Consumers Drive Product from the Market	Consumers Drive Product into High Demand

8. **Comparing and Contrasting Economic Information** Compare and contrast the role of consumers and producers in allocating resources. Which do you think has the greater power?

9 **Interpreting Economic Models** Use the circular flow chart on page 80 and what you have learned from this section to explain the ways in which government allocates resources.

10. **Challenge** What industries in today's world do you think would be wise to make changes given consumers' preferences? Give reasons for your selections.

Analyzing Economic Information
Look at the graph below, which shows the sales figures for a company that makes a substance that reduces carbohydrates in baked goods.

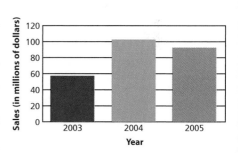

Interpret Information Write a sentence or two explaining the trend that the graph shows.

Challenge If you were the head of the company that made the substance that reduces carbohydrates in baked goods, in what direction would you move your business? How might you reallocate your resources?

Government and Free Enterprise

OBJECTIVES

In Section 3, you will
- understand that one role of government in the U.S. economy is to address market failures
- analyze why governments provide public goods and infrastructure
- explain how governments seek to decrease negative externalities and increase positive externalities

KEY TERMS

market failure, *p. 84*
public goods, *p. 84*
free rider, *p. 85*
infrastructure, *p. 86*
externality, *p. 87*
negative externality, *p. 87*
positive externality, *p. 87*
subsidy, *p. 88*
safety net, *p. 89*
transfer payment, *p. 89*
public transfer payment, *p. 89*

TAKING NOTES

As you read Section 3, complete a cluster diagram to show the role of government in free enterprise. Use the Graphic Organizer at **Interactive Review @ ClassZone.com**

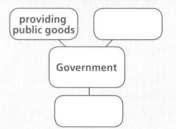

providing public goods

Government

Providing Public Goods

KEY CONCEPTS

In the American economic system, most production decisions are made in the marketplace through the interactions of buyers and sellers. This is the free enterprise sector of our economy. Other decisions are made by different levels of government. This is the public sector of our economy. How do we decide which sector of the economy should produce a good or service? If all the costs are borne by, and all benefits go to, the buyer and seller, the free enterprise sector produces it. If people who are not part of a marketplace interaction benefit from it or pay part of the costs, there is a **market failure.** When market failures occur, the government sometimes provides the good or service. Goods and services that are provided by the government and consumed by the public as a group are **public goods.** Public goods are funded with taxes collected by the government.

QUICK REFERENCE

Market failure occurs when people who are not part of a marketplace interaction benefit from it or pay part of its costs.

Public goods are products provided by federal, state, and local governments and consumed by the public as a group.

Public Goods A city street lighting system is an example of a public good.

EXAMPLE Characteristics of Public Goods

Public goods have two characteristics. First, people cannot be excluded from the benefits of the product even though they do not pay for it. Second, one person's use of the product does not reduce its usefulness to others.

Perhaps the simplest example of a public good is street lighting. When the street lighting is on, it is impossible to exclude people from using it. In addition, the benefit you receive from the safety and security street lighting provides is not diminished because others receive it too. There is simply no way for a private business to establish a realistic price for street lighting and then collect it from all users. Rather, local governments provide street lighting, paying for it with taxes.

Another example of a public good is national defense. Everyone benefits from the country being defended. Further, the security you feel knowing that there is a national defense system in place is not diminished because other people feel secure too. Given these benefits, you would readily pay for this sense of security. However, what if you discovered that your neighbors were not paying for national defense? Would you voluntarily pay then? To avoid this problem, everyone is required to pay taxes to the national government, which provides national defense.

EXAMPLE Free Riders

There is no incentive for businesses to produce public goods, because people will not voluntarily pay for them. After all, people receive the benefits of these products whether they pay for them or not. This situation is called the free-rider problem, and it is one type of market failure. A **free rider** is a person who chooses not to pay for a good or service but who benefits from it when it is provided.

Consider a July 4th fireworks display, which can cost $200,000 or more. If you tried to set up a business to put on such displays, you'd immediately run into problems. There is no way to charge people for watching the display, since it is visible from so many locations. Even if you were able to charge a fee to watch from a particularly good location, many people would still be able to watch it from elsewhere without paying. Those people are free riders—they receive the thrill and enjoyment of the fireworks display, but they do not share in the costs of putting it on. Because of them, there is little interest in providing fireworks displays as a business opportunity.

One way to address the free-rider problem is for government to provide certain goods and services. The city government, for example, could put on the July 4th fireworks display, using taxes to pay for it. In this way, the costs and benefits are shared throughout the community.

Free Riders Free riders will choose not to pay for fireworks displays but will still enjoy the benefits. Because of this, private companies are reluctant to provide such services.

Another example of the free-rider problem is law enforcement. Once a policing system is established, everyone in the community is protected whether they pay for it or not. The best way to ensure that people who benefit from this protection pay a share of the costs is for government to provide the service, paying for it with taxes.

Public and Private Sectors—Shared Responsibilities

Some goods can be provided by either the public sector or the private sector. These often are toll goods—goods consumed by the public as a group, but people can be excluded from using them. For example, toll ways are open for all people to use, but those who do use them have to pay a toll. Similarly, parks are provided for the benefit of everyone, but those who want to enjoy this benefit may have to pay an entrance fee. The initial funding for toll goods is often provided by the public sector. Their day-to-day operation is often the responsibility of the private sector.

The private and public sectors share the responsibility for the nation's **infrastructure**, the goods and services that are necessary for the smooth functioning of society, such as highways; mass transit; power, water, and sewer systems; education and health care systems; and police and fire protection. How important is the infrastructure? Imagine, for example, what the United States would be like without its interstate highways, safe airports and seaports, and passenger and freight train systems. To begin with, the nation's economy would grind to a halt. Further, the nation would lose its ability to move troops in case of attack or to evacuate people in an emergency. A solid infrastructure, then, is essential to economic health.

YOUR ECONOMIC CHOICES

PUBLIC vs. PRIVATE

Will you support tax increases to improve recreational facilities?

The mayor wants to build a water park to attract visitors, who will spend money at your town's restaurants and stores. But what you pay in sales tax will rise by about $100 a year to cover the cost. With that money, you could buy a couple of video games. What will you choose—public wants or private wants?

Water park

Video game

APPLICATION Applying Economic Concepts

A. Identify another example in which the free rider problem makes public goods or services the best solution.

Managing Externalities

Another type of market failure occurs when economic transactions cause externalities. An **externality** is a side effect of a transaction that affects someone other than the producer or the buyer. A **negative externality** is an externality that is a negative effect, or cost, for people who were not involved in the original economic activity. For example, a manufacturing company discharges pollution into a nearby river. The costs of the pollution are borne by everyone who lives by the river, even if they have no connection to the manufacturing company. A **positive externality**, in contrast, is an externality that is a positive effect, or benefit, for people who were not involved in the original economic activity. Another of your neighbors, for example, plants and maintains a beautiful rose garden. All the surrounding homes benefit from the beauty.

EXAMPLE Paying for Negative Externalities

One of the most commonly discussed negative externalities is industrial pollution. The owner of a factory that belches filthy smoke in the air, influenced by such

Paying for Pollution

A 1990 amendment to the Clean Air Act set a limit on the amount of sulfur dioxide that industries could release into the air. The government distributed to those industries only enough "pollution permits" to meet that limit. Instead of using their permits, some companies used cleaner production methods and sold the permits to other companies. As the price of these permits rose, more and more companies developed production methods that did not pollute.

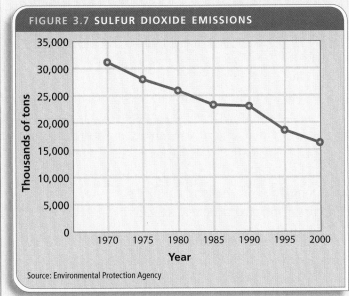

FIGURE 3.7 SULFUR DIOXIDE EMISSIONS

Source: Environmental Protection Agency

ANALYZE GRAPHS
1. How would you describe the trend in sulfur-dioxide pollution, especially since changes in government policy in 1990?
2. How did the government take a market approach to the problem of pollution?

The American Free Enterprise System   87

market forces as the profit motive and competition, has little incentive in the short-term to pay the extra money required to reduce the pollution. Everyone living in the surrounding region suffers from this pollution. Not only do they bear the monetary cost of cleaning up the pollution, they suffer other costs too. They are more likely to suffer pollution-related illnesses and, therefore, face higher medical costs.

Limiting negative externalities, then, is one important role of the government in the American economy. The government taxes or fines the polluter, and in the process accomplishes two economic purposes. The money it raises through taxation and fines can offset the higher medical costs. In addition, the cost of the tax or fine to the factory owner provides an incentive to reduce pollution.

EXAMPLE Spreading Positive Externalities

Positive externalities are benefits that extend to people not involved in the original activity. For example, if a new college is built in your town, local businesses benefit from student purchases of goods and services. Workers benefit too, for as business expands to meet students' wants, more and more jobs become available. The community as a whole benefits from all the taxes collected from students. Local government is able to spend some of these funds to provide more public goods. In addition, the whole community benefits from the potential contribution a more skilled and knowledgeable population can make to the economy.

Just as government attempts to limit negative externalities, it tries to increase positive externalities. One

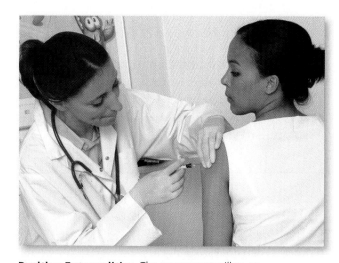

Positive Externalities The government will try to spread the benefit of a flu vaccination program—a healthier population—as widely as possible.

QUICK REFERENCE

A **subsidy** is a government payment that helps cover the cost of an economic activity that has the potential to benefit the public as a whole.

way government does this is through subsidies. A **subsidy** is a government payment that helps cover the cost of an economic activity that is considered to be in the public interest. Since subsidies are paid for with taxes, everyone shares in their cost. Subsidies also spread the benefit of a positive externality as widely as possible. For example, the federal government might provide subsidies to drug companies to develop a new vaccine. This benefits the whole population in the long run because once the vaccine is in use there will be fewer and fewer infected people to spread the disease. Similarly, a local government might subsidize influenza shots for the community. Obviously, those people who take advantage of the free or inexpensive shots benefit because they are protected against infection. Even those people who don't get the shot still receive a benefit because they are less likely to encounter someone with the flu and therefore less likely to catch it themselves.

APPLICATION Explaining an Economic Concept

B. How might a drunk-driving law address negative externalities?

Public Transfer Payments

KEY CONCEPTS

In addition to providing public goods and managing externalities, the government plays another role in the economy. One limitation of free enterprise is that people who are too old or sick to make a full economic contribution do not always have access to all economic opportunities. For these people, and others who are temporarily struggling, there is a public **safety net**, government programs designed to protect people from economic hardships.

Redistributing Income

As many as 37 million people in the United States live below the poverty level, which was defined in 2005 as a yearly income of $9,570 for a single person, with $3,260 added for each additional household member. That is more than 12 percent of the nation's population. However, people move up and down the income ladder in the United States. Many poor families remain poor for a relatively brief time. For example, the median duration of poverty through the 1990s was between four and five months.

How does a modern society address economic issues such as poverty? One way is to encourage economic growth. Another is through **transfer payments**, transfers of income from one person or group to another even though the receiver does not provide any goods or services in return. Some transfer payments are between private individuals. When you receive cash and checks from relatives and friends for your birthday or graduation, you are receiving transfer payments. When someone dies, a transfer payment flows to his or her beneficiaries in the form of inheritance. In both cases, the receiver provides nothing in return for the payment.

A **public transfer payment** is a payment in which the government transfers income from taxpayers to recipients who do not provide anything in return. Public transfer payments, since they do not reflect exchanges within a marketplace, are not a characteristic of pure market economies. They are more characteristic of command economies, and their presence in the United States is one feature that makes the U.S. economy a mixed economy.

Most public transfer payments are in the area of social spending—spending designed to address social issues, such as poverty. Social Security benefits, for example, have significantly reduced poverty among the elderly. This program is funded by the contributions of people currently employed. They pay a social security tax to the federal government, which in turn transfers it to people who are at or past retirement age. The Social Security program also provides income for the disabled.

QUICK REFERENCE

The **safety net** consists of government programs designed to protect people from economic hardship.

Transfer payments are transfers of income from one person or group to another even though the receiver does not provide anything in return.

A **public transfer payment** is a transfer payment in which the government transfers income from taxpayers to recipients who do not provide anything in return.

Public Transfer Payments	
Type	2004 Expenditures (in billions of dollars)
Social Security benefits	517.8
Medicare	303.3
Medicaid	299.7
Supplemental Security Income	37.3
Unemployment compensation	37.1
Veterans' benefits	33.8
Food Stamps	25.8
Temporary Assistance for Needy Families	18.5

Source: U.S. Department of Commerce

Public Transfer Payments Social Security is the largest public transfer program.

Social Spending in Sweden

In market economies, all economic actors—including governments—have to make choices. One economic choice governments must make involves the level of funding for social spending. Sweden's government, for example, has chosen to spend a significant amount in this area. Close to 30 percent of the country's total economy is spent on such programs as free public education through college, national health, and retirement and disability pensions. In comparison, social spending in the United States is about 15 percent of the total economy. U.S. social programs are not as comprehensive as Sweden's.

Such generosity, however, comes at a price. Sweden's workers pay hefty taxes to fund this social spending. Average Swedish workers with two children pay about 22 percent of their income in taxes. In contrast, similar American workers pay only about 9 percent.

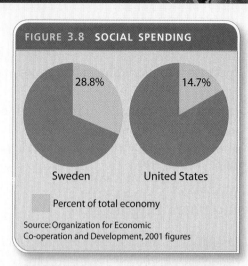

FIGURE 3.8 SOCIAL SPENDING

28.8% Sweden
14.7% United States

Percent of total economy

Source: Organization for Economic Co-operation and Development, 2001 figures

FIGURE 3.9 HOUSEHOLD TAX BURDEN

21.6% Sweden
9.1% United States

Percent of total earnings

Source: Organization for Economic Co-operation and Development, 2003 figures

CONNECTING ACROSS THE GLOBE

1. **Synthesizing Economic Information** How do tax levels relate to the amount of resources devoted to social spending?

2. **Drawing Conclusions** Which country do you think has more of a market economy, Sweden or the United States? Why?

The government makes transfer payments to the very poor as well as to the aged and disabled. For many years, the program known as welfare made payments to the needy to assure their well-being. A debate developed about whether such a program fostered dependence on the government and removed incentives to break out of poverty. In response to this debate, the government introduced sweeping reforms in the mid-1990s. The new program, widely known as workfare, stressed the importance of helping welfare recipients enter or re-enter the workforce as quickly as possible. Since these reforms in 1997, 4.7 million Americans have moved from being dependent on welfare to self-sufficiency.

Public transfer payments also provide a safety net for people who lose their jobs. Unemployment compensation from a mix of federal and state money tides people over until they can find a new job. While people receive it, they must show that they are making an effort to find another job. (You will learn more about unemployment, poverty, and government social spending in later chapters.)

APPLICATION Applying Economic Concepts

C. What are the opportunity costs of public transfer payments?

REVIEWING KEY CONCEPTS

1. Explain the relationship between the terms in each of these pairs:
   a. *market failure*
      free rider
   b. *negative externality*
      positive externality
   c. *subsidy*
      positive externality
   d. *safety net*
      public transfer payment

2. Illustrate the two characteristics of public goods with examples.

3. How is infrastructure linked to the economy?

4. Give an example of a free rider.

5. How can government limit a negative externality? How can it spread a positive one?

6. **Using Your Notes** Explain how the government gets involved in the economy in a modified free enterprise system. Refer to your completed cluster diagram.

   Use the Graphic Organizer at
   Interactive Review @ ClassZone.com

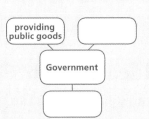

CRITICAL THINKING

7. **Categorizing Economic Information** Unemployment compensation and payment of living expenses for the disabled are examples of what kind of government involvement in the American economy?

8. **Making Inferences** After several incidents of hallway disputes among students, the board of a high school decides to hire hallway guards. In economic terms, what is the school board doing? How might this decision affect other programs at the school?

9. **Evaluating Economic Decisions** As part of the welfare reform of the mid-1990s, the federal government hired 10,000 people who had been dependent on welfare in an initiative called welfare-to-work. How does this approach differ from transfer payments? What are the costs and benefits of this approach?

10. **Challenge** In 2003, Congress passed laws to encourage private charitable organizations to provide social services. They would compete for government funds to carry out community services through their own networks. Do you think this is an effective way to address social issues? Why or why not? Use economic concepts, such as markets, efficiency, and opportunity costs in developing your response.

ECONOMICS IN PRACTICE

Cleaning up a toxic dump

Categorizing Economic Information
Externalities are categorized according to their impact, either positive or negative.

Identify Externalities Decide whether each of the following is a positive or a negative externality and briefly explain its effect.

- A beekeeper establishes a farm next to an apple orchard and the bees move freely into the orchard.

- An airport is constructed near a residential neighborhood.

- A construction company cleans up a toxic dump near a site it is working on.

- Companies pay for programs to help employees get in shape.

Challenge Identify and explain a negative externality and a positive externality that affect you.

The United States: Land of Entrepreneurs

Background The free enterprise system and the belief that everyone has the right to pursue economic success through lawful means is the backbone of American society. Many people achieve that success through working for an employer who provides a place to work, a paycheck, and other benefits. However, an increasing number of people are working for themselves, and for a variety of reasons. These reasons include a desire to market their own products, or to have more freedom.

What's the issue? What are some of the options for opening your own business? Study these sources to learn how others found their way, and the obstacles and opportunities they faced.

A. Magazine Article

This article discusses the development of Fizzy Lizzy, a new soft drink, from initial concept through launch, and introduces the entrepreneur who came up with the idea.

▶ A Business Idea in a Bottle

Getting Fizzy Lizzy Bubbling

[Elizabeth] Marlin . . . got into the beverage business in the summer of 1996, when she set out for a long bicycle ride. . . . Not long into her trip, she realized that her favorite refreshment, which she had packed into a saddlebag—a half-gallon carton of grapefruit juice and a liter bottle of seltzer, which she'd mix together—was not only inconvenient, it was also slowing her down.

"Juice and seltzer is so simple," Marlin said. "I thought, Why can't I buy this is in a bottle?" She . . . was fixated on the idea of creating a carbonated juice, and began researching the beverage industry. She soon discovered she would need to hire a food scientist to help her. . . .

Although Marlin planned to devote her entire checking account to startup costs, that amount was nowhere near what [Abe] Bakal (consultant with 30 years' experience) was asking for R & D alone. . . . [B]ut he was so impressed by her enthusiasm that he offered to consult in return for a 20-percent stake in the business. . . .

Bakal recalled recently, ". . . one of the things I've learned in product development is that sometimes—not always, but sometimes—you can compensate with enthusiasm and commitment for money."

Source: "The Industry: Message in a Bottle," *New York Times*, June 26, 2005

Thinking Economically How did Elizabeth Marlin and Abe Bakal use their productive resources to start this enterprise?

B. Chart

These statistics show the number of self-employed entrepreneurs and their businesses relative to sizes of firms with paid employees.

Number of Employees	Number of Firms	Total Employment
No employees	770,229	0
1–9 employees	3,759,630	12,500,539
10–99 employees	1,135,443	28,516,802
100–499 employees	84,829	16,430,229
500+ employees	16,926	55,950,473
All	5,767,127	113,398,043

Source: *Statistical Abstract of the United States,* 2003 figures

Thinking Economically What is the percentage of entrepreneurial firms with no employees? What percentage of paid employees work in companies with 100 or more workers?

C. Newspaper Article

This article discusses franchises, businesses that offer entrepreneurs an option to start their own business by buying into an established company with an existing business model.

Being The Boss With Backup

The Costs and Benefits of Franchising

In Maryland, there were more than 13,000 franchises employing about 179,000 [people] in 2001, according to [a] study, which was commissioned by the International Franchise Association. More than two dozen of those franchises are headquartered in the state, including Educate Inc., with more than 1,000 Sylvan tutoring center franchises worldwide and MaggieMoos's International with 184 ice cream shops, according to the association.

Opening such a business might be just the right fit for Phil Clark, a mortgage consultant from Elkridge. The mortgage business tends to fluctuate, Clark said. A franchise would give Clark more control over his future, a prospect he finds exciting. "A franchise gives me something more stable," he said. . . .

But it comes at a price. The cost of opening a franchise can vary from $25,000 to millions of dollars.

For some, franchising can mean economic empowerment and a chance at the American dream. But buyer beware: There is no guarantee of success, and a franchise requires the same amount of commitment, sacrifice and sweat equity as any independent business. . . .

Source: "Growing Occupation: Being Your Own Boss," *Baltimore Sun,* April 21, 2006

Thinking Economically If you were to start your own business, would you buy a franchise or build a new enterprise based on your own ideas? What factors would help you in making your decision?

THINKING ECONOMICALLY Synthesizing

1. How do the legal rights built into the free enterprise system affect the businesses in A and C?

2. Which of these two businesses do you feel would provide more stability for its owner? Why?

3. Do you think entrepreneurs make up a large percentage of the work force? Why are entrepreneurs important to the economy?

Review this chapter using interactive activities at **ClassZone.com**

- Online Summary
- Graphic Organizers
- Quizzes
- Review and Study Notes
- Vocabulary Flip Cards

Online Summary

Complete the following activity either on your own paper or online at **ClassZone.com**

Choose the key concept that best completes the sentence. Not all key concepts will be used.

capitalism
externality
free contract
free enterprise system
infrastructure
legal equality

modified free enterprise economy
negative externality
open opportunity
positive externality
profit
profit motive

public goods
public transfer payments
safety net
subsidy
transfer payments

__1__ is another name for capitalism. Three features of this type of economy are open opportunity, legal equality, and __2__, or the right to enter into agreements of one's choice. The __3__ is a driving force in a free enterprise system, urging entrepreneurs to enter the market. The market allocates resources through the activities of both producers and consumers. Producers, seeking __4__, move their resources into the most productive areas. Consumers, through their dollar votes, help determine which products succeed and which fail.

Left on its own, however, a free market cannot address many social issues. The United States has a __5__, mixing government involvement and market forces. One role for the government is to provide __6__, such as national defense. Without a strong __7__ in place, modern economies cannot function. The government also addresses problems created by a __8__, such as the pollution from a factory that affects all those living nearby. It furthers a __9__, such as better health through vaccinations, by offering a __10__ for inoculations. The government also makes direct __11__ in the form of social security, unemployment compensation, and disability coverage.

REVIEWING KEY CONCEPTS

Advantages of the Free Enterprise System (pp. 70–77)

1. What is a free enterprise system?

2. What are some of the rights that must be protected for a free enterprise system to work?

How Does Free Enterprise Allocate Resources? (pp. 78–83)

3. What are the roles of consumers and producers in allocating resources?

4. What role does the government play in the economy's circular flow?

Government and Free Enterprise (pp. 84–93)

5. What problem makes public goods necessary?

6. Besides providing public goods, what two purposes can a government serve in a market economy?

APPLYING ECONOMIC CONCEPTS

Use the information in the table to answer the following questions about changes in the nation since the passage of the Clean Air Act in 1970.

Since the passage of the Clean Air Act:
• Nitrogen oxide emissions have declined by 17%
• Sulfur dioxide emissions have declined by 49%
• Lead emissions have declined by 98%
• Carbon monoxide emissions have declined by 41%
• Particulate emissions caused by combustion have declined by 82%

At the same time:
• U.S. population grew by 42%
• Overall energy consumption grew by 43%
• Total U.S. employment grew by 95%
• The number of registered vehicles grew by 111%
• The economy grew by 175%

Source: Foundation for Clean Air Progress

7. How would you use these statistics to argue that the government has effectively managed a negative externality?

8. Recently, there has been pressure to loosen clean air standards. Use economic arguments to support or oppose this proposed action.

9. **Creating Graphs** Use the statistics below to create a graph titled Businesses in the United States, 1997–2003. Use information from your graph and from Figure 3.1 on page 71 to write a generalization about businesses in the American free enterprise system.

Year	Number of Businesses (in millions)
1997	21.0
1999	21.8
2001	22.6
2003	22.7

Source: U.S. Small Business Administration

Use *SMARTGrapher* @ ClassZone.com to complete this activity.

10. **Distinguishing Fact from Opinion** Look again at the information on changes in the United States after the passage of the Clean Air Act. Which of the following statements represents a fact? Which is an opinion? Explain why.

- Pollution has decreased since 1970.
- Pollution has decreased as a result of the Clean Air Act.
- The government can ease restrictions now that pollution is lower.

11. **Applying Economic Concepts** In the 1990s, efforts were made to reform the healthcare system in the United States so that much of it came under government control. Explain in terms of economic concepts you have learned in this chapter why these efforts failed.

12. **Challenge** Milton Friedman wrote,

Many people want the government to protect the consumer. A much more urgent problem is to protect the consumer from the government.

Explain what you think Friedman meant by this. Illustrate your answer with examples.

Conducting an Economic Impact Study

A manufacturing company has announced plans to open a factory in your town. The plant will consist of a manufacturing area and a warehouse area and will employ about 500 people. Production will be on a 24-hour basis, with workers working one of three 8-hour shifts. At the same time, a national megastore chain wants to open a store on the outskirts of town. The store will employ 60 people, be open 18 hours a day, and have a 200-car parking lot.

Imagine that you have been asked by local government authorities to conduct an economic impact study to identify the positive and negative externalities that the factory or megastore might create.

Step 1 Form a group with three or four classmates. Conduct research on how a factory or a megastore operates—the materials they use, the byproducts they create, and so on. Then do research to discover the impact a new factory or megastore might have on a community.

Step 2 In your group, review your findings and identify the positive and negative externalities of the factory or megastore. Record the information in a chart similar to the one below.

Externalities Created by the Factory/Megastore	
Positive	Negative

Step 3 Use your chart to write your economic impact report. Note the major externalities and suggest steps that the local government might take to limit negative externalities and to encourage positive externalities.

Demand

CONCEPT REVIEW

Microeconomics is the study of the economic behaviors and decisions of small units, such as individuals and businesses.

CHAPTER 4 KEY CONCEPT

Demand is the willingness to buy a good or service and the ability to pay for it.

WHY THE CONCEPT MATTERS

The concept of demand is demonstrated every time you buy something. List the last five goods or services that you purchased. Rate each one with a number from 1 (not important to you) to 4 (very important). Which of the goods or services would you stop buying if the price rose sharply? Describe the relationship between your ratings and your willingness to buy at a higher price.

Demand

This computer store customer meets the two requirements of demand—the customer is willing to buy and is able to pay.

Online Highlights

More at ClassZone.com

 Economics Update

Go to **ECONOMICS UPDATE** for chapter updates and current news on demand in the automobile industry. (See Case Study, pages 124–125.) ▶

Animated Economics

Go to **ANIMATED ECONOMICS** for interactive lessons on the graphs and tables in this chapter.

Interactive ◀◀Review

Go to **INTERACTIVE REVIEW** for concept review and activities.

What caused more people to demand hybrid cars? See the Case Study on pages 124–125.

What Is Demand?

OBJECTIVES	KEY TERMS	TAKING NOTES
In Section 1, you will • define *demand* and outline what the law of demand says • explain how to interpret and create demand schedules and describe the role of market research in this process • explain how to interpret and create demand curves	demand, *p. 98* law of demand, *p. 99* demand schedule, *p. 100* market demand schedule, *p. 100* demand curve, *p. 102* market demand curve, *p. 102*	As you read Section 1, complete a cluster diagram like this one for each key concept. Use the Graphic Organizer at **Interactive Review** @ ClassZone.com 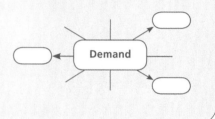

The Law of Demand

KEY CONCEPTS

In Chapter 3, you learned that the United States has a free enterprise economy. This type of economic system depends on cooperation between producers and consumers. To make a profit, producers provide products at the highest possible price. Consumers serve their own interests by purchasing the best products at the lowest possible price. The forces of supply and demand establish the price that best serves both producers and consumers. In this chapter, you'll learn about the demand side of this equation.

Demand is the desire to have some good or service and the ability to pay for it. You may want to take a round-the-world cruise or to rent a huge apartment that overlooks the ocean. Or you may want to buy a brand-new sports car or a state-of-the-art home entertainment center. However, you may not be able to afford any of these things. Therefore, economists would say that you have no actual demand for them. Even though you want them, you don't have the money needed to buy them. Conversely, you may want the latest CDs by several of your favorite bands. And, at a price

of between $12 and $15 each, you can afford them. Since you have both the desire for them and the ability to pay for them, you do have demand for CDs.

Price is one of the major factors that influence demand. The **law of demand** states that when the price of a good or service falls, consumers buy more of it. As the price of a good or service increases, consumers usually buy less of it. In other words, quantity demanded and price have an inverse, or opposite, relationship. This relationship is graphically illustrated in Figure 4.1 below.

QUICK REFERENCE

Law of demand
states that when prices go down, quantity demanded increases. When prices go up, quantity demanded decreases.

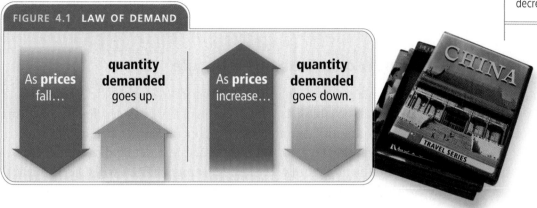

FIGURE 4.1 LAW OF DEMAND

As **prices** fall... quantity demanded goes up.

As **prices** increase... quantity demanded goes down.

EXAMPLE Price and Demand

Let's take a look at an example of demand in action. Cheryl, a senior at Montclair High School, loves movies and enjoys collecting them on DVD. She and Malik, a friend from school, sometimes meet downtown at Montclair Video Mart to look through the DVD stacks. Rafael, the owner of the video mart, often jokes that Cheryl and Malik spend so much time at his store that he might have to give them jobs. Actually, Cheryl already has a job—stocking shelves at her neighborhood supermarket. She worked so many hours this summer that she has extra money to spend. Let's see how DVD prices at Montclair Video Mart affect her spending decisions.

Cheryl has been saving to buy the DVD boxed set of the original *Star Wars* trilogy, one of her favorite series of movies. The set costs $69.95, and Cheryl has the money to buy it this weekend. When Cheryl goes to the Montclair Video Mart, she is disappointed to learn that the *Star Wars* set is sold out and a new shipment won't arrive for a week. She decides to buy some other DVDs so that she won't go home empty-handed, but she also decides to save roughly half of her money toward a future purchase of *Star Wars*.

As she looks through the movie DVDs, she sees that most of those she wants sell for $15. How many will she buy at that price? Let's say she decides to buy three and keep the rest of her money for the *Star Wars* trilogy. But what if each of the DVDs she wants costs just $5? Cheryl might decide that the price is such a good deal that she can buy seven. As you can see, the law of demand is more than just an economic concept. It's also a description of how consumers behave.

Economics Update

Find an update on the demand for CDs and DVDs at **ClassZone.com**

APPLICATION Applying Economic Concepts

A. You have $50 and want to buy some CDs. If prices of CDs rose from $5 each to $10, how would your quantity demanded of CDs change?

Demand Schedules

KEY CONCEPTS

A **demand schedule** is a table that shows how much of a good or service an individual consumer is willing and able to purchase at each price in a market. In other words, a demand schedule shows the law of demand in chart form. A **market demand schedule** shows how much of a good or service all consumers are willing and able to buy at each price in a market.

EXAMPLE Individual Demand Schedule

A demand schedule is a two-column table that follows a predictable format. The left-hand column of the table lists various prices of a good or service. The right-hand column shows the quantity demanded of the good or service at each price.

Cheryl's demand for DVDs can be expressed in a demand schedule. Let's take a look at the price list in Figure 4.2 below. How many DVDs will Cheryl buy if they cost $20 each? How many will she buy when the price stands at $10? Your answers to these questions show one thing very clearly. Cheryl's demand for DVDs depends on their price.

Price and Demand
Storeowners often offer products at sale prices to encourage consumers to make more purchases.

FIGURE 4.2 CHERYL'S DVD DEMAND SCHEDULE

Price per DVD ($)	Quantity Demanded
30	0
25	1
20	2
15	3
10	4
$5	7

a At the top price of $30, Cheryl is not willing to buy any DVDs.

b At $10, she will buy four DVDs.

Notice that when the price falls, the number of DVDs Cheryl will buy rises. When the price rises, the number she will buy falls. So quantity demanded and price have an inverse, or opposite, relationship.

ANALYZE TABLES

1. How many DVDs will Cheryl be likely to buy if the price is $15?

2. What is the relationship between Cheryl's demand for DVDs and various quantities demanded shown on this table?

Animated Economics

Use an interactive demand schedule at **ClassZone.com**

EXAMPLE Market Demand Schedule

The demand schedule in Figure 4.2 shows how many DVDs an individual, Cheryl, is willing and able to buy at each price in the market. The schedule also shows that the quantity of DVDs that Cheryl demands rises and falls in response to changes in price. Sometimes, however, an individual demand schedule does not give business owners enough information. For example, Rafael, who owns Montclair Video Mart, needs information about more than just one consumer before he can price his merchandise to gain the maximum number of sales. He needs a market demand schedule, which shows the quantity demanded by all the people in a particular market who are willing and able to buy DVDs.

Take a look at the DVD market demand schedule below. Notice that it's similar to the individual demand schedule except that the quantities demanded are much larger. It also shows that, like individual demand, market demand depends on price.

FIGURE 4.3 DVD MARKET DEMAND SCHEDULE

Price per DVD ($)	Quantity Demanded
a → 30	50
25	75
20	100
b → 15	125
10	175
c → 5	300

a At the top price of $30, Rafael's customers will buy 50 DVDs.

b At the middle price of $15, the quantity demanded of DVDs is 125.

c At the low price of $5, the quantity demanded rises to 300.

So, markets behave in the same way as individual consumers. As prices fall, the quantity demanded of DVDs rises. As prices rise, the quantity demanded falls.

ANALYZE TABLES

1. How does the quantity demanded of DVDs change when the price drops from $25 to $10?

2. How does this market demand schedule illustrate the law of demand?

How did Rafael create a market demand schedule? First, he surveyed his customers, asking them how many DVDs they would buy at different prices. Next, he reviewed his sales figures to see how many DVDs he sold at each price. Techniques such as these for investigating a specific market are called market research. Market research involves the gathering and evaluating of information about customer preferences. (You'll learn more about market research in Chapter 7.) By tabulating the results of his market research, Rafael created his market demand schedule.

APPLICATION Applying Economic Concepts

B. Imagine that you have discovered a restaurant that makes the best pizza you have ever tasted. Create a demand schedule showing how many pizzas a month you would buy at the prices of $25, $20, $15, $10, and $5.

Demand Curves

QUICK REFERENCE

Demand curve graphically shows the data from a demand schedule.

Market demand curve graphically shows the data from a market demand schedule.

KEY CONCEPTS

A **demand curve** is a graph that shows how much of a good or service an individual will buy at each price. In other words, it displays the data from an individual demand schedule. Creating a demand curve simply involves transferring data from one format, a table, to another format, a graph.

A **market demand curve** shows the data found in the market demand schedule. In other words, it shows the quantity that all consumers, or the market as a whole, are willing and able to buy at each price. A market demand curve shows the sum of the information on the individual demand curves of all consumers in a market.

EXAMPLE Individual Demand Curve

Study the demand curve (Figure 4.4 below) created from Cheryl's demand schedule. How many DVDs will Cheryl buy at the price of $15? How will Cheryl's quantity demanded change if the price rises by $5 or falls by $5? Find the answers to these questions by running your finger along the curve. As you can see, the demand curve is a visual representation of the law of demand. When prices go up, the quantity demanded goes down; when prices go down, the quantity demanded goes up.

You should note that this demand curve and the schedule on which it is based were created using the assumption that all other economic factors except price remain the same. You'll learn more about these factors and how they affect demand in Section 2.

CONNECT TO MATH

One common mistake people make is to look at the downward-sloping graph and think it means that quantity demanded is decreasing. However, if you move your finger downward and to the right on the demand curve, you'll notice that the quantity demanded is increasing.

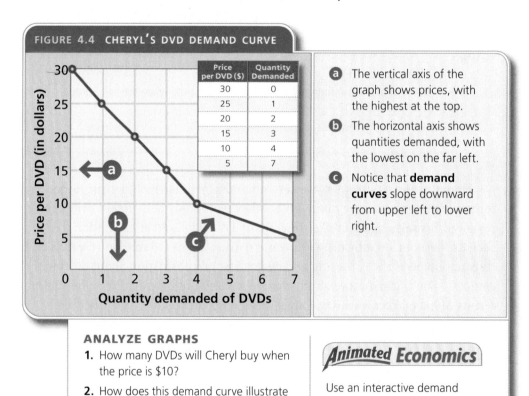

FIGURE 4.4 CHERYL'S DVD DEMAND CURVE

Price per DVD ($)	Quantity Demanded
30	0
25	1
20	2
15	3
10	4
5	7

a The vertical axis of the graph shows prices, with the highest at the top.

b The horizontal axis shows quantities demanded, with the lowest on the far left.

c Notice that **demand curves** slope downward from upper left to lower right.

ANALYZE GRAPHS

1. How many DVDs will Cheryl buy when the price is $10?
2. How does this demand curve illustrate the law of demand?

Animated **Economics**

Use an interactive demand curve at **ClassZone.com**

Market Demand Curve

Like Cheryl's individual demand curve, the market demand curve for Montclair Video Mart shows the quantity demanded at different prices. In other words, the graph shows the quantity of DVDs that all consumers, or the market as a whole, are willing and able to buy at each price. Despite this difference, the market demand curve for Montclair Video Mart (Figure 4.5) is constructed in the same way as Cheryl's individual demand curve. As in Figure 4.4, the vertical axis displays prices and the horizontal axis displays quantities demanded.

FIGURE 4.5 DVD MARKET DEMAND CURVE

Price per DVD ($)	Quantity Demanded
30	50
25	75
20	100
15	125
10	175
5	300

Notice that **market demand curves** slope downward from upper left to lower right, just as individual demand curves do.

The main difference between the two types of demand curves is that the quantities demanded at each price are much larger on a market demand curve. This is because the curve represents a group of consumers (a market), not just one consumer.

ANALYZE GRAPHS

1. At which price will Montclair Video Mart sell 175 DVDs?

2. Cheryl was unwilling to buy any DVDs at $30. Montclair Video Mart can sell 50 DVDs at that price. How do you explain the difference?

NEED HELP?

Throughout this chapter, you will be asked to create and to analyze demand curves. If you need help with those activities, see "Interpreting Graphs."

Skillbuilder Handbook, page R29

Look at Figure 4.5 above one more time. What is the quantity demanded at the price of $15? How will quantity demanded change if the price increases by $5 or drops by $5? Once again, find the answers to these questions by running your finger along the curve. As you can see, the market demand curve—just like the individual demand curve—vividly illustrates the inverse relationship between price and quantity demanded. If price goes down, the quantity demanded goes up. And if price goes up, the quantity demanded goes down. Also, like the individual demand curve, the market demand curve is constructed on the assumption that all other economic factors remain constant—only the price of DVDs changes.

APPLICATION **Applying Economic Concepts**

C. Look back at the demand schedule for pizzas you created for Application B on page 101. Use it to create a demand curve.

SMART Grapher
Create a demand curve at **ClassZone.com**

Vera Wang: Designer in Demand

In this section, you've learned about the law of demand. You've also seen demand in action in some hypothetical situations. The story of fashion designer Vera Wang, however, provides a real-world example of demand at work.

When they married, Mariah Carey, Jennifer Lopez, and several other stars turned to Wang for their wedding dresses. What explains the demand for this one woman's gowns?

Responding to Demand

Vera Wang had worked in the fashion industry for more than 15 years by the time she started planning her own wedding in 1989. So she was frustrated when she couldn't find the type of sophisticated bridal gown she wanted. She knew that many modern brides were savvy career women who preferred designer clothing. Yet, no one was making wedding dresses for those women.

The next year, Wang decided to fill that unmet demand. She created her own line of gowns featuring elegant sleeveless styles rather than the hooped skirts, puffed sleeves, and lace flounces that had dominated wedding-dress designs before.

Soon celebrities such as Uma Thurman were choosing Vera Wang wedding gowns. This generated publicity, and demand for Wang's creations grew. In response, other designers began to create sleeker wedding dresses, and the style spread. Vera Wang is now considered to be one of the country's most influential designers of wedding gowns.

Demand for the sophisticated Wang style has spread beyond weddings. In recent years, Wang has expanded her product line to include ready-to-wear dresses, perfume, accessories, and home fashions.

Changing Styles
Vera Wang wanted to change traditional wedding dress styles that, she thought, made brides look "like the bride on top of a cake, very decorated."

FAST FACTS

Vera Wang

Title: Chairman and CEO of Vera Wang Ltd.

Born: June 27, 1949, New York, New York

Major Accomplishment: Designer of high-fashion wedding gowns

Other Products: Clothing, perfume, eyewear, shoes, jewelry, home fashions

Books: *Vera Wang on Weddings* (2001)

Price Range for Vera Wang Wedding Gowns: about $2,000 to $20,000

Economics Update
Find the latest on Vera Wang's business at **ClassZone.com**

APPLICATION Analyzing Cause and Effect

D. In what ways did Vera Wang respond to consumer demand? In what ways did she generate consumer demand?

REVIEWING KEY CONCEPTS

1. Explain the differences between the terms in each of these pairs:

   a. *demand*
   law of demand

   c. *market demand schedule*
   market demand curve

   b. *demand schedule*
   demand curve

2. Look at Figure 4.1 on page 99. Write a caption for the figure that explains the law of demand.

3. Review the information on Vera Wang on the opposite page. Why is it unlikely that most brides will have demand for an original Vera Wang gown?

4. How might an owner of a bookstore put together a market demand schedule for his or her store?

5. Why does the demand curve slope downward?

6. **Using Your Notes** How are price and quantity demanded related? Refer to your completed cluster diagram.

   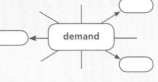

   Use the Graphic Organizer at **Interactive Review @ ClassZone.com**

CRITICAL THINKING

7. **Drawing Conclusions** List three products that you are familiar with and the approximate price of each. Which of the products, if any, do you have a demand for? Consider the two requirements of demand as you answer this question.

8. **Making Inferences** Why might Rafael's market demand schedule and curve not be an accurate reflection of the actual market? To answer this question, consider the assumption that was made when the schedule and curve were created.

9. **Applying Economic Concepts** Return to the demand schedule for pizzas you created for Application B on page 101. Assume that your class is the market for pizzas. Tabulate these individual demand schedules to create a market demand schedule. Then use that schedule to draw a market demand curve.

10. **Challenge** Does quantity demanded always fall if the price rises? List several goods or services that you think would remain in demand even if the price rose sharply. Why does demand for those items change very little? (You will learn more about this topic in Section 3.)

ECONOMICS IN PRACTICE

Making a Market Demand Curve
Suppose that you own a store that sells athletic shoes. You survey your customers and analyze your sales data to see how many pairs of shoes you can expect to sell at various prices. Your research enables you to make the following market demand schedule.

Price per Pair of Shoes ($)	Quantity Demanded
175	0
150	10
125	20
100	40
75	70
50	110

Create a Demand Curve Use this market demand schedule to create a market demand curve.

Challenge Write a caption for your market demand curve explaining what it shows.

Use *SMART Grapher* @ClassZone.com to complete this activity.

What Factors Affect Demand?

OBJECTIVES	KEY TERMS	TAKING NOTES
In Section 2, you will • determine a change in quantity demanded • explain the difference between change in quantity demanded and change in demand • determine a change in demand • analyze what factors can cause change in demand	law of diminishing marginal utility, *p. 106* income effect, *p. 107* substitution effect, *p. 107* change in quantity demanded, *p. 108* change in demand, *p. 109* normal goods, *p. 110* inferior goods, *p. 110* substitutes, *p. 112* complements, *p. 112*	As you read Section 2, complete a chart that shows each factor that causes change in demand. Use the Graphic Organizer at **Interactive Review @ ClassZone.com**

Factor That Changes Demand	Reason Why Demand Changes

More About Demand Curves

KEY CONCEPTS

The demand schedules and demand curves that you studied in Section 1 were created using the assumption that all other economic factors except the price of DVDs would remain the same. If all other factors remain the same, then the only thing that influences how many DVDs consumers will buy is the price of those DVDs. The demand curve graphically displays that pattern.

Now think about the shape of demand curves. Why do they slope downward? The reason is the **law of diminishing marginal utility**, which states that the mar-

QUICK REFERENCE

Law of diminishing marginal utility states that the marginal benefit of using each additional unit of a product during a given period will decline.

ginal benefit from using each additional unit of a good or service during a given time period tends to decline as each is used. Recall that utility is the satisfaction gained from the use of a good or service. Suppose it is a hot day, and you have just gulped down a glass of lemonade. Would you gain the same benefit from drinking a second glass? How about a third? In all likelihood, you'd find the second glass less satisfying than the first, and the third glass less satisfying than the second.

Because consumers receive less satisfaction from each new glass of lemonade they drink, they don't want to pay as much for additional purchases. So, they will buy

two glasses only if the lemonade is offered at a lower price, and they will buy three only if the price is even lower still. This pattern of behavior, which holds true for most consumer goods and services, creates the downward slope of the demand curve. For another example, see Figure 4.6 below, which displays the demand that a young man named Kent has for video games.

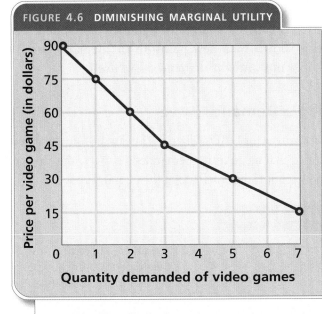

FIGURE 4.6 DIMINISHING MARGINAL UTILITY

Quantity demanded of video games

This graph displays the demand for video games by a high school senior named Kent.

The demand curve slopes downward because of the **law of diminishing marginal utility**, which states that the marginal benefit of using each additional unit of a product during a given period will decline. Because of that declining satisfaction, Kent will buy additional games only at lower prices.

ANALYZE GRAPHS
How many video games is Kent willing to buy at a price of $45? How does the law of diminishing marginal utility explain his refusal to buy more games at that price?

Why do consumers demand more goods and services at lower prices and fewer at higher prices? Economists have identified two patterns of behavior as causes: the income effect and the substitution effect.

The **income effect** is the term used for a change in the amount of a product that a consumer will buy because the purchasing power of his or her income changes—even though the income itself does not change. For example, you can buy more paperback books if they are priced at $7 than if they are priced at $15. If you buy a $7 book, you will feel $8 "richer" than if you buy a $15 book, so you are more likely to buy another book. The income effect also influences behavior when prices rise. You will feel $8 "poorer" if you buy a $15 book instead of a $7 one, so you will buy fewer books overall.

The **substitution effect** is the pattern of behavior that occurs when consumers react to a change in the price of a good or service by buying a substitute product—one whose price has not changed and that offers a better relative value. For example, if the price of paperback books climbs above $10, consumers might decide to buy fewer books and choose instead to buy $4 magazines.

APPLICATION Drawing Conclusions

A. Malik goes to the mall to buy a $40 pair of blue jeans and discovers that they are on sale for $25. If Malik buys two pairs, is this an example of the income effect or the substitution effect? Explain your answer.

Change in Quantity Demanded

QUICK REFERENCE

Change in quantity demanded is an increase or decrease in the amount demanded because of change in price.

KEY CONCEPTS

Remember that each demand curve represents a specific market situation in which price is the only variable. A change in the amount of a product that consumers will buy because of a change in price is called a **change in quantity demanded**. Each change in quantity demanded is shown by a new point on the demand curve. A change in quantity demanded does not shift the demand curve itself.

EXAMPLE Changes Along a Demand Curve

Let's look again at Cheryl's demand curve for DVDs (Figure 4.7 below). Note the quantities demanded at each price. Notice that as quantity demanded changes, the change is shown by the direction of the movement right or left along the demand curve.

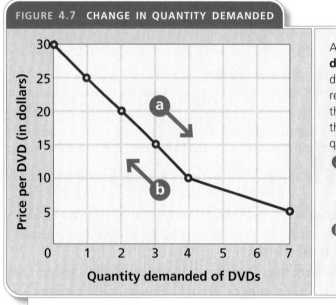

FIGURE 4.7 CHANGE IN QUANTITY DEMANDED

A **change in quantity demanded** doesn't shift the demand curve. The change refers to movement along the curve itself. Each point on the curve represents a new quantity demanded.

a As you move to the right along the curve, the quantity demanded increases.

b As you move to the left, the quantity demanded decreases.

ANALYZE GRAPHS
1. What is the change in quantity demanded when the price drops from $20 to $10?
2. What is the direction of the movement along the demand curve when the quantity decreases?

Animated Economics

Use an interactive demand curve to see changes in quantity demanded at **ClassZone.com**

Figure 4.7 shows change in quantity demanded for one person. A market demand curve provides similar information for an entire market. However, market demand curves have larger quantities demanded and larger changes to quantity demanded because they combine data from all individual demand curves in the market.

APPLICATION Applying Economic Concepts

B. Why do increases or decreases in quantity demanded not shift the position of the demand curve?

Change in Demand

KEY CONCEPTS

Consider what might happen if you lose your job. If you aren't earning money, you aren't likely to buy many CDs or movie tickets or magazines—no matter how low the price. Similarly, when national unemployment rises, people who are out of work are more likely to spend their limited funds on food and housing than on entertainment. Fewer people would be buying DVDs at every price, so market demand would drop.

This is an example of a **change in demand**, which occurs when a change in the marketplace such as high unemployment prompts consumers to buy different amounts of a good or service at every price. Change in demand is also called a shift in demand because it actually shifts the position of the demand curve.

QUICK REFERENCE

Change in demand occurs when something prompts consumers to buy different amounts at every price.

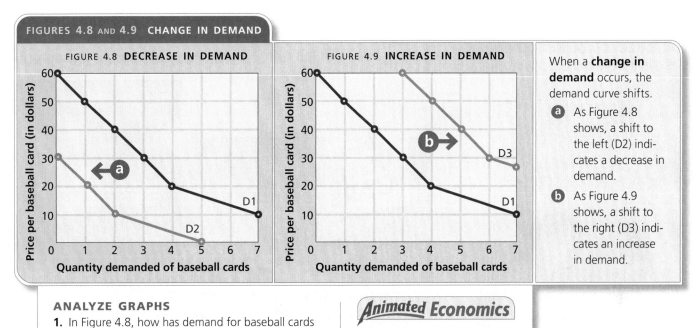

FIGURES 4.8 AND 4.9 CHANGE IN DEMAND

FIGURE 4.8 DECREASE IN DEMAND

FIGURE 4.9 INCREASE IN DEMAND

When a **change in demand** occurs, the demand curve shifts.

a As Figure 4.8 shows, a shift to the left (D2) indicates a decrease in demand.

b As Figure 4.9 shows, a shift to the right (D3) indicates an increase in demand.

ANALYZE GRAPHS

1. In Figure 4.8, how has demand for baseball cards changed at each of these prices: $10, $20, and $30?
2. In Figure 4.9, how has demand for baseball cards changed at each of these prices: $30, $40, and $50?

Animated **Economics**

Use an interactive version of shifting demand curves at **ClassZone.com**

Six factors can cause a change in demand: income, market size, consumer expectations, consumer taste, substitute goods, and complementary goods. An explanation of each one follows.

FACTOR 1 Income

If a consumer's income changes, either higher or lower, that person's ability to buy goods and services also changes. For example, Tyler works at a garden center. He uses his earnings to buy baseball cards for his collection. In the fall, people garden less and buy fewer gardening products, so Tyler works fewer hours. His smaller paycheck means that he has less money to spend, so he demands fewer baseball cards at every price. Figure 4.8 shows this change. The entire demand curve shifts to the left.

Suppose, however, that Tyler is promoted to supervisor and receives a raise of $2 an hour. Now he has more money to spend, so his demand for baseball cards increases and his demand curve shifts to the right—as shown in Figure 4.9 on page 109.

As you might guess, changes in income also affect market demand curves. When the incomes of most consumers in a market rise or fall, the total demand in that market also usually rises or falls. The market demand curve then shifts to the right or to the left.

Increased income usually increases demand, but in some cases, it causes demand to fall. **Normal goods** are goods that consumers demand more of when their incomes rise. **Inferior goods** are goods that consumers demand less of when their incomes rise. Before his raise, Tyler shopped at discount stores for jeans and T-shirts. Now that he earns more, Tyler can afford to spend more on his wardrobe. As a result, he demands less discounted clothing and buys more name-brand jeans and tees. Discounted clothing is considered an inferior good. Other products that might be considered inferior goods are used books and generic food products.

QUICK REFERENCE

Normal goods are goods that consumers demand more of when their incomes rise.

Inferior goods are goods that consumers demand less of when their incomes rise.

YOUR ECONOMIC CHOICES

NORMAL GOODS AND INFERIOR GOODS

If your income rises, which car will you choose?

Most people prefer to buy a new car if they can afford it. Used cars are an example of inferior goods—demand for them drops when incomes rise because people prefer new-car quality to getting a bargain.

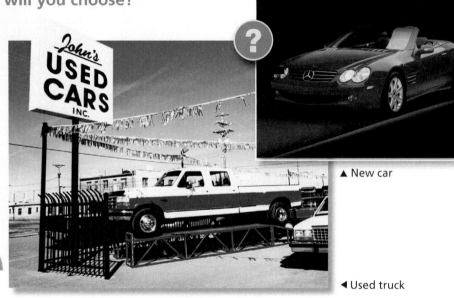

▲ New car

◄ Used truck

FACTOR 2 Market Size

If the number of consumers increases or decreases, the market size also changes. Such a change usually has a corresponding effect on demand. Suppose that the town of Montclair is on the ocean. Each summer, thousands of tourists rent beachfront cottages there. As a result, the size of the population and the market grows. So what do you think happens to the market demand curve for pizza in Montclair in the summer? Check the two graphs at the top of the next page.

Population shifts have often changed the size of markets. For example, in the last 30 years, the Northeast region of the United States lost population as many people moved to the South or the West. The causes of the population shift included the search for a better climate, high-tech jobs, or a less congested area.

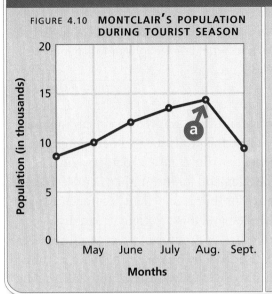

FIGURE 4.10 **MONTCLAIR'S POPULATION DURING TOURIST SEASON**

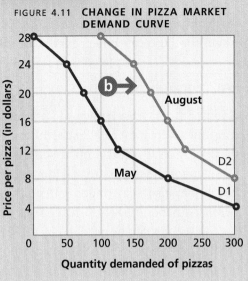

FIGURE 4.11 **CHANGE IN PIZZA MARKET DEMAND CURVE**

When a change in market size occurs, it often causes a change in demand.

a Figure 4.10 shows how the population of Montclair changed during the last tourist season. Notice which month had the highest population.

b Notice that the market demand curve (D2) shifts to the right between May and August.

ANALYZE GRAPHS

1. During what month was the population of Montclair at its highest? What happened to the demand for pizzas during that month? Explain.

2. What would you expect to happen to the market demand curve in September? Explain.

One economic result of the migration is that the overall market size of the Northeast has shrunk, while the market size of the South and the West has grown. This change in market size has altered the demand for many products, from essentials such as homes, clothing, and food to nonessentials such as movie tickets. Demand for most items will grow in booming regions and decrease in regions that are shrinking.

FACTOR 3 Consumer Tastes

Because of changing consumer tastes, today's hot trends often become tomorrow's castoffs. When a good or service enjoys high popularity, consumers demand more of it at every price. When a product loses popularity, consumers demand less of it.

Advertising has a strong influence on consumer tastes. Sellers advertise to create demand for the product. For example, some people stop wearing perfectly good pants that still fit because advertising convinces them that the style is no longer popular and that a new style is better.

Think about your own closet. Doesn't it contain some item of clothing that you just had to have a year ago, but would never pay money for now? You've just identified an instance of consumer taste changing demand. Consumer tastes also affect demand for other products besides clothing. When was the last time you saw someone buying a telephone that had to be attached to the wall by a cord?

Economics Update

Find an update on changing consumer tastes at **ClassZone.com**

FACTOR 4 Consumer Expectations

Your expectations for the future can affect your buying habits today. If you think the price of a good or service will change, that expectation can determine whether you buy it now or wait until later.

Let's look at one example of how consumer expectations shape demand. Automobiles usually go on sale at the end of summer because dealers want to get rid of this year's models before the new models arrive. Would you expect demand for new cars to be higher in May, before the sales, or in August, during the sales? It is higher in August because consumers expect the sales and often choose to wait for them.

FACTOR 5 Substitutes

Goods and services that can be used in place of other goods and services to satisfy consumer wants are called **substitutes**. Because the products are interchangeable, if the price of a substitute drops, people will choose to buy it instead of the original item. Demand for the substitute will increase while demand for the original item decreases. People may also turn to substitutes if the price for the original item becomes too high. Again, demand for the substitute rises while demand for the original item drops.

Substitutes can be used in place of each other. For example, when gasoline prices are high, some people decide to commute to school by bus or train. When gasoline prices are low, a higher number of people choose to drive instead of to take public transportation. As you can see from that example, when the price of one good rises, demand for it will drop while demand for its substitute will rise.

YOUR ECONOMIC CHOICES

SUBSTITUTE SERVICES

How would you decide whether to take a cab or a bus?

Taxis have certain advantages; they will take you to a specific place at a specific time. But if taxi fares rise, you might give up the convenience and go by bus instead.

City bus

FACTOR 6 Complements

When the use of one product increases the use of another product, the two products are called **complements**. An increase in the demand for one will cause an increase in the demand for the other. Likewise, a decrease in demand for one will cause a decrease in demand for the other.

In contrast to substitutes, complements are goods or services that work in tandem with each other. An increase in demand for one will cause an increase in demand for the other. One example is CDs and CD players. Consumers who bought CD players

Income Increased income means consumers can buy more. Decreased income means consumers can buy less.

Complements When the use of one product increases the use of another product, the two are called complements.

Market Size A growing market usually increases demand. A shrinking market usually decreases demand.

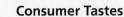

Substitutes Substitutes are goods and services that can be used instead of other goods and services, causing a change in demand.

What Causes a Change in Demand?

Consumer Tastes The popularity of a good or service has a strong effect on the demand for it, and in today's marketplace, popularity can change quickly.

Consumer Expectations What you expect prices to do in the future can influence your buying habits today.

ANALYZE CHARTS
Choose a product used by most consumers, and create a hypothetical demand curve showing demand for that product in a town of 1,000 people. Label it A. On the same graph, add a demand curve showing demand if the population drops to 700. Label it B. Which factor on the chart does the shift in the demand curve represent?

also demanded CDs to play on them. And, as CDs became more popular, demand for CD players grew until they began to appear in places they had never been before, such as in the family minivan.

Therefore, with complements, if the price of one product changes, demand for both products will change in exactly the same way. If the price for one product rises, demand for both will drop. Conversely, if the price for one product drops, demand for both will rise.

APPLICATION Categorizing Information

C. Choose one of the following products: soda, hamburgers, pencils, or tennis rackets. On your own paper, list as many substitutes and complements for the product as you can. Compare your lists with those of a classmate.

For more on analyzing political cartoons, see the Skillbuilder Handbook, page R26.

Analyzing Political Cartoons

Political cartoons often deal with economic themes. Because of this, you will find that the skill of interpreting political cartoons helps you to understand the economic issues on people's minds.

TECHNIQUES USED IN POLITICAL CARTOONS Political cartoonists use many techniques to deliver their message. The techniques used in this cartoon include:

Exaggeration The cartoonist has shown the automobile as towering over humans to make the point that some Americans drive big cars that are gas-guzzlers.

Labels Cartoonists use written words to identify people, groups, or events. Notice the sign on the gas pump referring to OPEC (Organization of Petroleum Exporting Countries) and the license plate on the car.

Stereotyping Here a stereotype image of a man in Arab robes stands for OPEC, even though not all OPEC countries are in the Middle East.

Source: © *The Economist*

Other techniques that political cartoonists use include **caricature**, or creating a portrait that distorts a person's features; **symbolism**, using an object or idea to stand for something else; and **satire**, attacking error or foolishness by ridiculing it.

THINKING ECONOMICALLY Analyzing

1. What does the phrase "Too high!!" mean?

2. What complementary goods are shown in this cartoon? Why are they complementary?

3. How does this cartoon relate to demand? Consider the effect of rising prices, especially rising prices for complementary goods.

1. Explain the differences between the terms in each of the pairs below:

   a. *change in quantity demanded*
      change in demand

   b. *income effect*
      substitution effect

   c. *normal goods*
      inferior goods

   d. *substitutes*
      complements

2. What feature of demand curves is explained by the law of diminishing marginal utility?

3. How does the income effect influence consumer behavior when prices rise?

4. Why might an increase in income result in a decrease in demand?

5. What else besides migration might account for a change in market size?

6. **Using Your Notes** Why does a change in market size affect demand? Refer to your completed chart.

Factor That Changes Demand	Reason Why Demand Changes

   Use the Graphic Organizer at **Interactive Review @ ClassZone.com**

7. **Analyzing Causes** A new version of the computer game Big-Hit Football just came out. Malik buys it now because it has improvements over the current version, which he is bored with. Cheryl decides to wait to see if the price drops. Which of the factors shown in the chart on page 113 affected their decisions?

8. **Applying Economic Concepts** The U.S. government has used many strategies to reduce smoking. It banned television ads for cigarettes, ran public service messages about the health risks of smoking, and imposed taxes on cigarettes. Which factors that affect demand was the government trying to influence?

9. **Analyzing Effects** Take out the market demand curve for athletic shoes that you created on page 105. Add a new curve showing how demand would be changed if the most popular basketball player in the NBA endorses a brand of shoes that your store does not sell. Share your graph with a classmate and explain your reasoning.

10. **Challenge** Do you think changes in consumer taste are most often initiated by the consumers themselves or by manufacturers and advertisers? Explain your answer, using real-life examples.

Explaining Changes in Demand
Think about different types of bicycles: road bikes, mountain bikes, hybrid bikes. What factors affect demand for bicycles?

Identify Factors Affecting Demand The chart below lists examples of a change in demand in the market for bicycles. For each example, identify which factor that affects demand is involved.

Example of Change in Demand	Factor That Affected Demand
Electric scooter sales rise, and bike sales fall.	
The cost of aluminum alloy bike frames is about to rise; consumers buy bikes now.	
Using a folding bicycle becomes a fad among commuters. Sales of this type of bike boom.	
The U.S. birth rate declined for 10 years in a row, eventually causing a drop in sales of children's bikes.	

Challenge Identify which two of the six factors affecting demand that do not appear on this chart. Provide examples of how these factors might affect demand for bicycles.

What Is Elasticity of Demand?

OBJECTIVES	KEY TERMS	TAKING NOTES
In Section 3, you will • define *elasticity of demand* • identify the difference between elastic and inelastic demand • define *unit elastic* • determine how total revenue is used to identify elasticity	elasticity of demand, *p. 117* elastic, *p. 117* inelastic, *p. 117* unit elastic, *p. 118* total revenue, *p. 122* total revenue test, *p. 122*	As you read Section 3, complete a cluster diagram using the key concepts and other terms. Use the Graphic Organizer at **Interactive Review @ ClassZone.com** 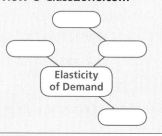

Elasticity of Demand

KEY CONCEPTS

You have learned that there are many factors that influence the demand for a product. However, those factors alone are not the only influences on the sales of goods and services. How does the owner of an electronics store know how to price his or her goods so that the entire inventory of PDAs, or personal digital assistants, are sold?

Store owners know that consumers are responsive to changes in price. Let's examine the relationship between price and demand, and how it affects consumers' buying habits.

Consumer demand is not limitless. It is highly dependent on price. But as you know, demand is seldom fixed. As a result, price is also seldom fixed. Generally, people assume that if prices rise consumers will buy less, and if prices drop consumers will buy more. However, this isn't always the case. The relationship between price and demand is somewhat more complicated than you might think. Change in consumer buying habits is also related to the type of good or service being produced and how important the good or service is to the consumer. The marketplace certainly is very sensitive to changes in price—but not all increases in price will result in a decrease in demand.

Economists use the term **elasticity of demand** to describe how responsive consumers are to price changes in the marketplace. Economists describe demand as being either elastic or inelastic. Demand is **elastic** when a change in price, either up or down, leads to a relatively larger change in the quantity demanded. The more responsive to change the market is, the more likely the demand is elastic. On the other hand, demand is **inelastic** when a change in price leads to a relatively smaller change in the quantity demanded. For this reason, elastic goods and services are often said to be price sensitive. So, in the case of inelastic demand, changes in price have little impact on the quantity demanded.

Another way to think about elasticity is to imagine that a rubber band represents quantity demanded. When the quantity demanded increases by a marked amount, the demand is elastic and the rubber band stretches. If the quantity demanded barely changes, demand is inelastic and the rubber band stretches very little.

QUICK REFERENCE

Elasticity of demand is a measure of how responsive consumers are to price changes.

Demand is **elastic** if quantity demanded changes significantly as price changes.

Demand is **inelastic** if quantity demanded changes little as price changes.

EXAMPLE Elasticity of Demand for Goods and Services

Let's look at an example of elastic demand. Suppose that a certain brand of PDAs goes on sale. If the price of that brand goes down 20 percent, and the quantity demanded goes up 30 percent, then demand is elastic. The percentage change in quantity demanded is greater than the percentage change in price. Goods that have a large number of substitutes fall into the elastic category, since if the prices change, consumers can choose other products.

Now think about a completely different type of good—the medicine insulin. Many diabetics require daily insulin injections to regulate their blood sugar levels. Even if the price of insulin were to rise sharply, diabetics would still need the same amount of insulin as they did before. If the price were to drop, they would not need any more insulin than their required dosage. As a result, the demand for insulin is inelastic because the quantity demanded remains relatively constant.

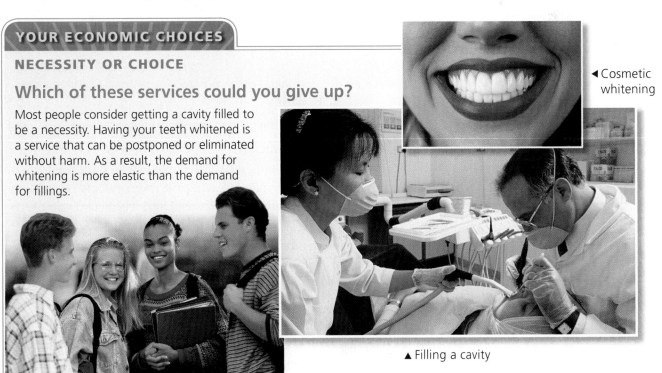

YOUR ECONOMIC CHOICES

NECESSITY OR CHOICE

Which of these services could you give up?

Most people consider getting a cavity filled to be a necessity. Having your teeth whitened is a service that can be postponed or eliminated without harm. As a result, the demand for whitening is more elastic than the demand for fillings.

◀ Cosmetic whitening

▲ Filling a cavity

Over time the elasticity of demand for a particular product may change. If more substitutes for a product become available, the demand may become more elastic. For example, the cost of cell phones and their service has become more elastic as more providers enter the market. On the other hand, in the case of prescription drugs, if a product is withdrawn from the market and there are fewer choices for the consumer, the demand may become inelastic.

The data for elastic demand and the data for inelastic demand produce demand curves that look very different from each other. Compare Figure 4.13 and Figure 4.14 below. Notice that the inelastic demand curve has a steeper slope than the elastic demand curve does. The reason for this difference is that the changes along the vertical axis (the price) are proportionally greater than the changes along the horizontal axis (the quantity demanded).

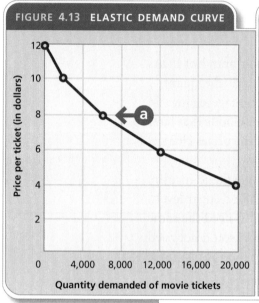

FIGURE 4.13 ELASTIC DEMAND CURVE

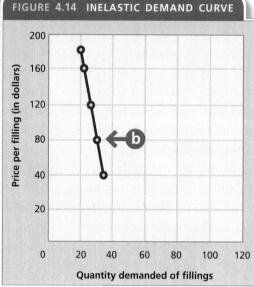

FIGURE 4.14 INELASTIC DEMAND CURVE

ⓐ In Figure 4.13, elastic demand curves have gradual slopes. They are more horizontal than vertical because of the greater changes in quantity demanded.

ⓑ In Figure 4.14, inelastic demand curves have steep slopes. They are more vertical than horizontal because quantity demanded changes very little.

ANALYZE GRAPHS

1. In Figure 4.13, what happens to the quantity demanded when price drops from $10 to $8?

2. In Figure 4.14, what is the difference in quantity demanded between the most expensive and least expensive filling?

Animated Economics

Use elastic and inelastic demand curves at **ClassZone.com**

Demand is said to be unit elastic when the percentage change in price and quantity demanded are the same. In other words, a 10 percent increase in price would cause exactly a 10 percent drop in quantity demanded, while the reverse would be true.

No good or service is ever really **unit elastic**. Instead, unit elasticity is simply the dividing point between elastic and inelastic demand. It is a useful concept for figuring out whether demand is elastic or inelastic.

APPLICATION Drawing Conclusions

A. Decide how elastic demand is for the following item. Explain your reasoning.

When a grocery store sells soup at $1.09 per can, it sells 1,500 cans per week. When it dropped the price to $0.75, it sold an additional 1,000 cans.

What Determines Elasticity?

KEY CONCEPTS

Just as there are factors that cause a change in demand, there are also factors that affect the elasticity of demand. The factors that affect elasticity include the availability of substitute goods or services, the proportion of income that is spent on the good or service, and whether the good or service is a necessity or a luxury.

FACTOR 1 Substitute Goods or Services

Generally speaking, if there is no substitute for a good or service, demand for it tends to be inelastic. Think back to the consumers who need insulin to regulate their blood sugar levels. No substitute exists for insulin, so consumers' demand is inelastic even when the price goes up. If many substitutes are available, however, demand tends to be elastic. For example, if the price shoots up for beef, consumers can eat chicken, pork, or fish. In this case, demand is elastic.

Economics Update

Find an update on factors affecting elasticity at **ClassZone.com**

FACTOR 2 Proportion of Income

The percentage of your income that you spend on a good or service is another factor that affects elasticity. Suppose that photography is your hobby, and you spend about 10 percent of your income on a digital camera, memory cards, software programs, and lenses. If the price for any of these rises even slightly, your demand will likely fall because you just don't have any more money to spend on your hobby. Your demand is elastic. At the same time, demand for products that cost little of your income tends to be inelastic. For example, if the cost of pencils or ballpoint pens rose, would you buy fewer pencils and pens? Probably not. You spend so little on these items that you could easily pay the increase.

YOUR ECONOMIC CHOICES

PROPORTION OF INCOME

How much would you invest in a hobby?

This amateur photographer spends about 10 percent of her income to pay for her digital camera and supplies. If the costs of taking photographs rise sharply, she won't be able to increase her demand by an equal amount because she won't have enough money to pay for the additional expenses.

If the level of your income increases, you are likely to increase your demand for some goods or services. Suppose you ordinarily see one movie per month. If your income increases, you may choose to attend the movies several times a month.

FACTOR 3 Necessities Versus Luxuries

A necessity is something you must have, such as food or water. Demand for necessities tends to be inelastic. Even if the price rises, consumers will pay whatever they can afford for necessary goods and services.

But that doesn't mean that consumers will buy the same quantities no matter what the price. If the price of a necessity such as milk rises too much, consumers may choose to buy a substitute, such as a cheaper brand of milk or powdered milk. The quantity demanded of milk will change as the law of demand predicts; however, the change in quantity demanded is smaller than the change in price, so demand is inelastic.

In contrast, a luxury is something that you desire but that is not essential to your life, such as a plasma television. The demand for luxuries tends to be elastic. Consumers will think twice about paying a higher price for something they don't truly need. The change in quantity demanded is much greater than the change in price.

FIGURE 4.15 Estimating Elasticity

By examining the three factors that affect elasticity, you can often estimate whether demand for a certain good or service will be elastic or inelastic.

Products

Factors that affect elasticity	Table Salt	Ice Cream	Sports Car	Gasoline	Insulin	Braces on Teeth
Are there good substitutes? yes = elastic no = inelastic	no	yes	yes	no	no	no
What proportion of income does it use? large = elastic small = inelastic	small	small	large	small	small	large
Is it a necessity or a luxury? luxury = elastic necessity = inelastic	necessity	luxury	luxury	necessity	necessity	luxury
Conclusion	inelastic	elastic	elastic	inelastic	inelastic	elastic

ANALYZE TABLES
What patterns can you see in the factors that affect elasticity? Write a sentence summarizing your answer.

APPLICATION Evaluating

B. Create a chart like the one above for the following products: mountain bikes, airplane tickets, and home heating oil. Determine if the products are elastic or inelastic.

Calculating Elasticity of Demand

KEY CONCEPTS

Businesses find it useful to figure the elasticity of demand because it helps them to decide whether to make price cuts. If demand for a good or service is elastic, price cuts might help the business earn more. If demand is inelastic, price cuts won't help.

To determine elasticity, economists look at whether the percentage change in quantity demanded is greater than the percentage change in price. To calculate that relationship, economists use mathematical formulas. One such set of formulas is shown below. Another way to determine elasticity is shown on page 122.

MATH CHALLENGE
FIGURE 4.16 Calculating the Elasticity of Demand

Step 1: Calculate percentage change in quantity demanded.
(If the final result is a negative number, treat it as positive.)

Example Calculations

$$\frac{\text{Original quantity} - \text{New quantity}}{\text{Original quantity}} \times 100 = \text{Percentage change in quantity demanded}$$

$$\frac{2{,}000 - 6{,}000}{2000} \times 100 = 200\%$$

Step 2: Calculate percentage change in price.
(If the final result is a negative number, treat it as positive.)

$$\frac{\text{Original price} - \text{New price}}{\text{Original price}} \times 100 = \text{Percentage change in price}$$

$$\frac{10 - 8}{10} \times 100 = 20\%$$

Step 3: Calculate elasticity.

$$\frac{\text{Percentage change in quantity demanded}}{\text{Percentage change in price}} = \text{Elasticity}$$

$$\frac{200\%}{20\%} = 10$$

Step 4: After doing your calculations, if the final number is greater than 1, demand is elastic. If the final number is less than 1, demand is inelastic.

Advanced Calculations Economists use a more complex version of these formulas. In Step 1, instead of dividing the change in quantity demanded by the original quantity demanded, they divide it by the average of the original and new quantities. Similarly in Step 2, they divide change in price by an average of the original price and new price.

NEED HELP?

 Math Handbook, "Calculating Percentages," page R4

APPLICATION Applying Economic Concepts

C. Choose two points on the demand curve shown in Figure 4.13 and determine the price and quantity demanded for each point. Then use that data to calculate elasticity of demand.

Total Revenue Test

QUICK REFERENCE

Total revenue is a company's income from selling its products.

Total revenue test is a method of measuring elasticity by comparing total revenues.

Businesses need to know about elasticity of demand because it influences the amount of revenue they will earn. Economists measure elasticity of demand by calculating a seller's **total revenue**, the amount of money a company receives for selling its products. Total revenue is calculated using the following formula, in which P is the price and Q is the quantity sold: **TOTAL REVENUE = P × Q.**

You can measure elasticity by comparing the total revenue a business would receive when offering its product at various prices. This method is the **total revenue test**.

If total revenue increases after the price of a product drops, then demand for that product is considered elastic. Why? Because even though the seller makes less on each unit sold, the quantity demanded has increased enough to make up for the lower price. For example, if a hot dog stand sells 100 hot dogs for $2.50 each, the total revenue is $250 for the day. However, if the price of hot dogs drops to $2.00 each and 150 are sold, the total revenue for the day will be $300. The demand is elastic.

But if the total revenue decreases after the price is lowered, demand is considered inelastic. If the hot dog stand lowers its price to $1.00 each and sells 200 hot dogs, it makes $200 in total revenue. Clearly, the price reduction has caused only a modest increase in quantities sold, which is not enough to compensate for lower revenues.

EXAMPLE Revenue Table

Let's look at an example of demand for movie tickets. In Figure 4.17, you can see how total revenues show whether demand is elastic or inelastic.

FIGURE 4.17 MOVIE TICKET REVENUE TABLE

Price of a Movie Ticket ($)	Quantity Demanded per Month	Total Revenue ($)
12	1,000	12,000
10	2,000	20,000
8	6,000	48,000
6	12,000	72,000
4	20,000	80,000

ⓐ At $10 a ticket, the quantity demanded is 2,000. Total revenue is $20,000.

ⓑ When the price drops to $8, the quantity demanded rises to 6,000. Total revenue rises to $48,000. So, demand is elastic.

ANALYZE TABLES
When the price range changes from $8 to $6, is demand elastic or inelastic? Explain.

APPLICATION Creating Tables

D. Use the information from Figure 4.14 to estimate prices to make a total revenue table.

REVIEWING KEY CONCEPTS

1. Use each of the terms below in a sentence that gives an example of the term:

   a. *elastic*   **b.** *inelastic*   **c.** *total revenue*

2. How is total revenue related to elasticity of demand?

3. Why are elastic goods and services said to be price sensitive?

4. What are the factors that affect elasticity of demand and how does each affect elasticity?

5. Analyze the factors that determine elasticity to explain why utilities companies never offer sale prices on their services.

6. **Using Your Notes** How does the concept of unit elasticity relate to the concepts of elasticity and inelasticity? Refer to your completed cluster diagram.

   Use the Graphic Organizer at **Interactive Review @ ClassZone.com**

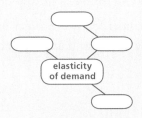

CRITICAL THINKING

7. **Analyzing Causes** In early 2004, news articles reported that prescription drug prices were rising almost three times faster than the prices of other products. Identify the factors that explain why the drug companies were able to raise prices so sharply.

8. **Analyzing Data** In June, Snead's Snack Bar sold 1,000 fruit smoothies at a price of $2.50 each. In July, they sold 1,300 fruit smoothies at a price of $2.00. Is the demand for fruit smoothies elastic or inelastic? Use the formula on page 121 to decide. Show the math calculations to support your answer.

9. **Applying Economic Concepts** Suppose the company that runs concession stands at a local sports arena wants to increase revenue on sales of soft drinks. The manager believes the only solution is to charge higher prices. As a business consultant, what advice would you give the manager? Use economic thinking to support your answer.

10. **Challenge** You learned in this section that no product ever has demand that is unit elastic. What possible reasons can you give for that? Draw on what you know about utility, demand, and elasticity as you formulate your answer.

ECONOMICS IN PRACTICE

Calculating Elasticity
Determine the elasticity of bottled water by calculating elasticity and using the revenue table below. Use the information on pages 121 and 122 to help you.

Number of Bottles Sold	Price ($)
35	2.00
75	1.50
100	1.25
120	1.00

Write a Summary After you have determined whether bottled water is elastic or inelastic, think about what factors affect the demand for bottled water. Write a summary of your conclusions explaining whether demand is elastic or inelastic and why, and what factors affect the elasticity of water.

Challenge What effect might the introduction of a new energy drink have on the demand for bottled water? Use economic thinking to support your answer.

Fueling Automobile Demand

Background Automobiles make up a huge portion of the American economy. In recent years the demand for automobiles and all the services connected with them has accounted for approximately one-fifth of all retail sales. Over the past decade, the total number of automobiles, including light trucks and SUVs (Sport Utility Vehicles), sold has been over 16 million units.

Car dealers are constantly looking for ways to sustain and increase demand for their product. Paul Taylor, chief economist of the National Automobile Dealers Association, observed, "The key to sales of 16.9 million will be the continued strong economy and sustained incentives." Incentives are awards designed to lure potential buyers into an automobile showroom and encourage sales. Manufacturers have tried everything from giving away mountain bikes to zero percent financing.

What's the issue? How does demand affect your selection of a vehicle? Study these sources to discover how the law of demand and the factors that affect demand shape the market.

A. Online Article

Most car dealers offer some sort of incentive. This article discusses Volkswagen's new approach in dealer incentives to car buyers.

Volkswagen Tries 12 Months of Free Car Insurance to Lure Buyers

To fight slumping sales, Volkswagen introduces a new incentive to attract buyers.

The German automaker [Volkswagen]. . . will test the program by offering 12 months of free insurance to people with valid driver's licenses who buy or lease new Golfs, Beetle coupes and Beetle convertibles. . . .

"I think it will be a lure for college graduates and first-time buyers," said Harry Nesbitt, sales manager. . . . "It's a way to get people in the dealership without sounding like everyone else. . . ."

General Motors Corp., the world's largest automaker, has also been varying its ways of luring buyers this year. Its offers have included overnight test drives, 72-hour sales and a program tied to the U.S. federal interest rate increase that allowed buyers to lock in an interest rate this year on a car or truck purchase five years in the future.

The Volkswagen program would be the first insurance giveaway by an automaker.

Source: Bloomberg.com

Thinking Economically Do incentives described in this document change the demand for automobiles or the quantity demanded? Explain your answer.

B. Political Cartoon

Brian Duffy, a cartoonist with the *Des Moines Register,* drew this cartoon about the rising price of gasoline.

Thinking Economically Which of the factors that cause a change in demand does this cartoon address? Explain your answer.

C. Online Report

An auto-buying service linking buyers and sellers examines demand for hybrid automobiles. Hybrid cars get power from a combination of batteries and a gas-powered engine.

The Year of the Hybrid

Stellar Fuel Efficiency, Low Emissions, and More Power

Why do we think 2005 will be The Year of the Hybrid? We can sum it up in two words: Power and SUV. There's something reassuring about how auto manufacturers are helping Americans have their cake and eat it too by offering up more fuel-efficient SUVs. Let's face it, America's love affair with the SUV shows no sign of waning. Yet . . . we can't live in denial that the SUV has a fat appetite for gasoline. And then there's the power argument. Despite the crowd pleasing fuel efficiency standards offered by hybrids, there was still the complaint that they lacked juice, or horsepower. . . . 2005's hybrids will appeal to those of us . . . who absolutely demand a lot of horsepower. As if overcompensating for being picked on when they were little, 2005's hybrids are coming out with more horsepower than their gas-only counterparts.

Though hybrids tend to be more expensive than their gas- or diesel-only powered cousins, the savings in fuel (and sometimes in taxes) can more than offset this difference in the long run.

Source: Invoicedealers.com

Thinking Economically Which of the factors affecting demand is evident in this article? Use evidence from the article to support your answer.

THINKING ECONOMICALLY Synthesizing

1. How would the demand for automobiles be affected by information presented in each of these documents? Support your answer with examples from the documents.

2. Identify and discuss the factors that affect elasticity of demand illustrated in these documents.

3. Explain how Documents B and C illustrate a cause and effect relationship in the demand for SUVs. Use evidence from these documents to support your answer.

Interactive ⟨⟨Review

Review this chapter using interactive activities at ClassZone.com

- Online Summary
- Quizzes
- Vocabulary Flip Cards
- Graphic Organizers
- Review and Study Notes

Online Summary

Complete the following activity either on your own paper or online at **ClassZone.com**

Choose the key concept that best completes the sentence. Not all key concepts will be used.

change in demand	law of demand
change in quantity demanded	market demand curve
demand	market demand schedule
demand curve	normal goods
demand schedule	substitutes
elastic	substitution effect
elasticity of demand	total revenue
income effect	total revenue test
inelastic	unit elastic
inferior goods	

__1__ is the desire for a product and the ability to pay for it. According to the __2__, when price decreases, demand rises, and when price increases, demand falls.

Demand can be displayed in a table called a __3__ or on a graph called a __4__. A __5__ is a table that shows how much demand all consumers in a market have. When that same information is displayed on a graph, it is called a __6__.

The different points on a demand curve show a __7__. A __8__ occurs when consumers are willing to buy different amounts of a product at every price. The six factors that change demand are income, market size, consumer expectations, consumer taste, complement, and __9__.

The term __10__ describes how responsive consumers are to price changes. Demand that changes significantly when prices change is __11__. Demand that doesn't change significantly when prices change is __12__. The dividing line between the two is where demand is __13__.

__14__ is calculated by multiplying price by quantity sold.

CHAPTER 4 Assessment

REVIEWING KEY CONCEPTS

What Is Demand? (pp. 98–105)

1. What two things are necessary for a consumer to have demand for a good or service?

2. What do economists mean when they say that quantity demanded and price have an inverse relationship?

What Factors Affect Demand? (pp. 106–115)

3. What is the difference between change in quantity demanded and change in demand?

4. How do consumer expectations affect demand?

What Is Elasticity of Demand? (pp. 116–125)

5. Explain the difference between elastic and inelastic demand.

6. What are two methods for calculating elasticity of demand?

APPLYING ECONOMIC CONCEPTS

Look at the graph below showing personal spending for two types of products: computers and stationery.

7. What is the general trend of how spending for each of these product types has changed? Are the two trends alike or different?

8. In what way might these products be complements? In what way might they be substitutes?

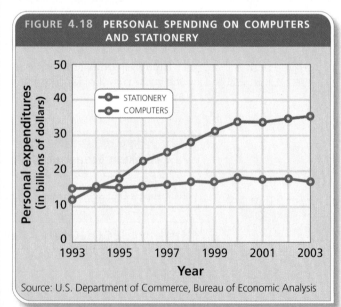

FIGURE 4.18 **PERSONAL SPENDING ON COMPUTERS AND STATIONERY**

Source: U.S. Department of Commerce, Bureau of Economic Analysis

9. **Creating Graphs** A tornado destroys a town. Think of three goods for which demand will rise in the weeks after the storm and three goods for which demand will fall. For each good, create a graph with two demand curves: curve A representing demand before the storm and curve B representing demand after the storm. Under each graph, write a caption explaining the change in demand.

Use *SMARTGrapher* @ ClassZone.com to complete this activity.

10. **Identifying Causes** A certain stuffed toy is popular during the holiday season, but sells for half the listed price after the holidays. Which factor in change in demand is at work here? Explain.

11. **Identifying Causes** In the last few decades, demand for ketchup has dropped in the United States, while demand for salsa has risen. Which factors that affect demand account for this?

12. **Using Economic Concepts** Airlines give discounts to travelers who book in advance and stay over a weekend. Travelers who book at the last minute and do not stay over a weekend usually pay full-price. How does the concept of elasticity explain the difference between the two groups' demand for tickets and the airlines' pricing decisions?

13. **Challenge** Suppose that you read the following article in the newspaper:

Meteorologists announced today that this has been the warmest winter in 57 years. The unusual weather has affected local businesses. According to Pasha Dubrinski, owner of Pasha's Outerwear, sales of winter parkas are 17 percent lower than last year. Dubrinski said, "Instead of buying down-filled parkas, people have been buying substitute items such as leather coats."

Across town, Michael Ellis, owner of Home Hardware, said that his sales of snow blowers are also down. "Next week, I will cut the price. That will increase demand."

Are these two storeowners correct in the way they use economic terms? Explain your answer.

Equip Your Team

Step 1 Choose a partner. Imagine you are the equipment managers for your school's baseball team. You must equip the nine starters with a budget of $5,000. The equipment supplier sends you the list of prices shown in column A of Figure 4.19. Create a list telling how many of each item you will buy.

SPORTING GOODS PRICES

Item	Prices (in dollars)		
	A	B	C
Bat	130	170	200
Baseball	2	3	4
Glove or Mitt	80	130	160
Catcher's Mask	80	90	100
Full Uniform	65	100	135
Jersey Only	30	60	90
Cleats	25	60	90
Sunglasses	20	30	40
Team Jacket	50	75	100

Step 2 When you call in the order, you learn that a big sporting goods factory has burned. Prices have risen to those shown in column B. You must redo your order using the new prices but the same budget.

Step 3 The economy is hit with sudden and severe price hikes. Redo your order using the prices in column C.

Step 4 Share your three purchasing lists with the class. As a class, use the collected data to create a market demand curve for each item.

Step 5 Use the collected data to calculate elasticity for each item. (You may use either method explained in this chapter.) Then as a class discuss your results. What factors influenced elasticity?

Use *SMARTGrapher* @ ClassZone.com to complete this activity.

Supply

The cost of raw materials, the wages paid to workers, and the production decisions made by managers all affect the supply of televisions.

Supply

CONCEPT REVIEW

Demand is the willingness to buy a good or service and the ability to pay for it.

CHAPTER 5 KEY CONCEPT

Supply is the willingness and ability of producers to offer goods and services for sale.

WHY THE CONCEPT MATTERS

You may not think of yourself as a producer, but you are. You offer your labor when you do chores around the house or work at a part-time job. If you have a car, you sometimes provide transportation for your friends. Also, if you belong to a sports or academic team, you supply your skills and knowledge. List five things that you supply. Then list the costs you incur and the rewards you receive for supplying them. How would your willingness and ability to supply these things be affected if these costs and rewards changed?

Online Highlights
More at ClassZone.com

 Economics Update
Go to **ECONOMICS UPDATE** for chapter updates and current news on the use of robots in industry. (See Case Study, pp. 158–159.) ▶

Animated Economics
Go to **ANIMATED ECONOMICS** for interactive lessons on the graphs and tables in this chapter.

Interactive ⟷ Review
Go to **INTERACTIVE REVIEW** for concept review and activities.

How does the use of robots affect the supply of goods and services? See the Case Study on pages 158–159.

What Is Supply?

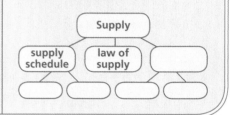

The Law of Supply

KEY CONCEPTS

In Chapter 4, you learned about the demand side of market interactions and how consumers serve their interests by purchasing the best products at the lowest possible price. You also discovered that there are other factors that change demand at every price. Demand, however, is only one side of the market equation. In this chapter, you will learn about the supply side of the equation in order to understand why producers want to provide products at the highest possible price.

Supply refers to the willingness and ability of producers to offer goods and services for sale. Anyone who provides goods or services is a producer. Manufacturers who make anything from nutrition bars to automobiles are producers. So, too, are farmers who grow crops, retailers who sell products, and utility companies, airlines, or pet sitters who provide services.

The two key words in the definition of supply are *willingness* and *ability*. For example, the Smith family grows various fruits and vegetables on their small farm. They sell their produce at a local farmers' market. If the prices at the market are too low, the Smiths may not be willing to take on the expense of growing and

> **QUICK REFERENCE**
>
> **Supply** is the desire and ability to produce and sell a product.

Supplying a Service Service providers, such as utility companies, are producers too.

transporting their produce. Also, if the weather is bad and the Smiths' crops of fruits and vegetables are ruined, they will not be able to supply anything for the market. In other words, they will not offer produce for sale if they do not have both the willingness and the ability to do so.

As is true with demand, price is a major factor that influences supply. The **law of supply** states that producers are willing to sell more of a good or service at a higher price than they are at a lower price. Producers want to earn a profit, so when the price of a good or service rises they are willing to supply more of it. When the price falls, they want to supply less of it. In other words, price and quantity supplied have a direct relationship. This relationship is illustrated in Figure 5.1.

QUICK REFERENCE

The **law of supply** states that when prices decrease, quantity supplied decreases, and when prices increase, quantity supplied increases.

FIGURE 5.1 LAW OF SUPPLY

As **prices** fall... quantity **supplied** falls. As **prices** rise... quantity **supplied** rises.

EXAMPLE Price and Supply

Let's take a closer look at how price and quantity supplied are related by returning to the Smiths and their produce business. The Smiths travel to the Montclair Farmers' Market every Wednesday and Saturday to sell a variety of fruits and vegetables— blueberries, peaches, nectarines, sweet corn, peppers, and cucumbers. However, their specialty crop is the tomato. How should the Smiths decide on the quantity of tomatoes to supply to the farmers' market? The price they can get for their crop is a major consideration.

The Smiths know that the standard price for tomatoes is $1 per pound. What quantity of tomatoes will the Smiths offer for sale at that price? They decide that they are willing to offer 24 pounds. What if the price of tomatoes doubled to $2 per pound? The Smiths might decide that the price is so attractive that they are willing to offer 50 pounds of tomatoes for sale on the market. In contrast, if the price fell to 50 cents, the Smiths might decide to supply only 10 pounds. Furthermore, at prices under 50 cents per pound, they may not be willing to supply any tomatoes. Look again at the definition of the law of supply. As you can see, it provides a concise description of how producers behave.

Economics Update

Find an update on farmers' markets at **ClassZone.com**

APPLICATION Analyzing Effects

A. You sell peppers at the Montclair Farmers' Market. If the price of peppers increased from 40 cents to 60 cents each, how would your quantity supplied of peppers change? How would your quantity supplied change if the price decreased to 25 cents?

Supply Schedules

KEY CONCEPTS

A **supply schedule** is a table that shows how much of a good or service an individual producer is willing and able to offer for sale at each price in a market. In other words, a supply schedule shows the law of supply in table form. A **market supply schedule** is a table that shows how much of a good or service all producers in a market are willing and able to offer for sale at each price.

EXAMPLE Individual Supply Schedule

A supply schedule is a two-column table that is similar in format to a demand schedule. The left-hand column of the table lists various prices of a good or service, and the right-hand column shows the quantity supplied at each price.

The Smiths' supply of tomatoes can be expressed in a supply schedule (Figure 5.2). How many pounds of tomatoes are the Smiths willing to sell when the price is $1.25 per pound? What if the price is $0.50 per pound? Or $2.00 per pound? Your answers to these questions show that the Smiths' quantity supplied of tomatoes depends on the price.

FIGURE 5.2 THE SMITHS' TOMATO SUPPLY SCHEDULE

Price per Pound ($)	Quantity Supplied (in pounds)
a → 2.00	50
1.75	40
1.50	34
1.25	30
1.00	24
0.75	20
b → 0.50	10

a At the top price of $2.00, the Smiths are willing to sell 50 pounds of tomatoes.

b At $0.50, the Smiths are willing to provide only 10 pounds of tomatoes for sale.

Notice that when the price falls, the quantity of tomatoes that the Smiths are willing to sell also falls. When the price rises, the quantity they are willing to sell rises. So quantity supplied and price have a direct relationship.

ANALYZE TABLES

1. How many pounds of tomatoes will the Smiths offer for sale if the price is $1.75?
2. How is this supply schedule different from a demand schedule for tomatoes?

Animated Economics

Use an interactive supply schedule at **ClassZone.com**

EXAMPLE Market Supply Schedule

The supply schedule in Figure 5.2 shows how many pounds of tomatoes an individual producer, the Smith family, is willing and able to offer for sale at each price in the market. The schedule also shows that, in response to changes in price, the Smiths will supply a greater or lesser number of tomatoes. However, sometimes an individual supply schedule does not provide a complete picture of the quantity of a good or service that is being supplied in a given market. For example, several fruit and vegetable stands at the Montclair Farmers' Market sell tomatoes. If you want to know the quantity of tomatoes available for sale at different prices at the entire farmers' market, you need a market supply schedule. This shows the quantity supplied by all of the producers who are willing and able to sell tomatoes.

Take a look at the market supply schedule for tomatoes in Figure 5.3. Notice that it is similar to the Smiths' supply schedule, except that the quantities supplied are much larger. It also shows that, as with individual quantity supplied, market quantity supplied depends on price.

FIGURE 5.3 TOMATO MARKET SUPPLY SCHEDULE

Price per Pound ($)	Quantity Supplied (in pounds)
a → 2.00	350
1.75	300
1.50	250
b → 1.25	200
1.00	150
0.75	100
c → 0.50	50

a At the top price of $2.00, the fruit and vegetable stands will offer 350 pounds of tomatoes for sale.

b At $1.25, the quantity supplied of tomatoes is 200 pounds.

c At the low price of $0.50, the quantity supplied falls to 50 pounds.

So, markets behave in the same way as individual suppliers. As prices decrease, the quantity supplied of tomatoes decreases. As prices increase, the quantity supplied increases.

ANALYZE TABLES

1. How does the quantity supplied of tomatoes change when the price rises from $0.75 a pound to $1.75 a pound?

2. How does this market supply schedule illustrate the law of supply?

In Chapter 4, you learned that Rafael, the owner of Montclair Video Mart, used market research to create a market demand schedule. Market research can also be used to create a market supply schedule. Producers in some markets are able to use research conducted by the government or by trade organizations to learn the prices and quantity supplied by all the producers in a given market.

APPLICATION Applying Economic Concepts

B. Imagine that you own a health food store that sells several brands of nutrition bars. Create a supply schedule showing how many bars you would be willing to sell each month at prices of $5, $4, $3, $2, and $1.

Supply Curves

QUICK REFERENCE

A **supply curve** shows the data from a supply schedule in graph form.

A **market supply curve** shows the data from a market supply schedule in graph form.

KEY CONCEPTS

A **supply curve** is a graph that shows how much of a good or service an individual producer is willing and able to offer for sale at each price. To create a supply curve, transfer the data from a supply schedule to a graph. A **market supply curve** shows the data from the market supply schedule. In other words, it shows how much of a good or service all of the producers in a market are willing and able to offer for sale at each price.

EXAMPLE Individual Supply Curve

Study the supply curve (Figure 5.4) created from the Smiths' supply schedule. How many pounds of tomatoes will the Smiths supply at $1.50 per pound? How will the Smiths' quantity supplied change if the price increases or decreases by 25 cents? Find the answers to these questions by running your finger along the curve. As you can see, the supply curve is a graphic representation of the law of supply. When the price increases, the quantity supplied increases; when the price decreases, the quantity supplied decreases. Note that the supply curve in Figure 5.4, and the schedule on which it is based, were created using the assumption that all other economic factors except price remain the same. You'll learn more about these other factors in Section 3.

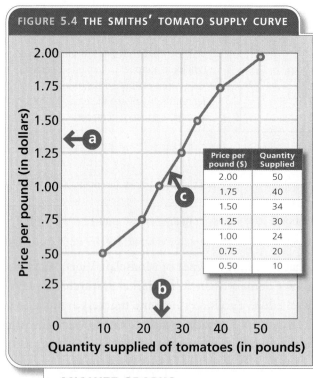

FIGURE 5.4 THE SMITHS' TOMATO SUPPLY CURVE

Price per pound ($)	Quantity Supplied
2.00	50
1.75	40
1.50	34
1.25	30
1.00	24
0.75	20
0.50	10

Notice that **supply curves** always slope upward from lower left to upper right.

a The vertical axis of the graph shows prices, with the highest at the top.

b The horizontal axis shows quantities supplied, with the lowest on the far left.

c The specific quantities supplied at specific prices listed on the supply schedule are plotted as points on the graph and connected to create the supply curve.

ANALYZE GRAPHS

1. How many pounds of tomatoes will the Smiths offer for sale when the price is $1.50?

2. How does this supply curve illustrate the law of supply?

Animated Economics

Use an interactive supply curve at **ClassZone.com**

EXAMPLE Market Supply Curve

Like the Smiths' individual supply curve, the market supply curve for all the stands that sell tomatoes at the Montclair Farmers' Market shows the quantity supplied at different prices. In other words, the graph shows the quantity of tomatoes that all of the producers, or the market as a whole, are willing and able to offer for sale at each price. The market supply curve (Figure 5.5) differs in scope from the Smiths' individual supply curve, but it is constructed in the same way. As in Figure 5.4, the vertical axis displays prices and the horizontal axis displays quantities supplied.

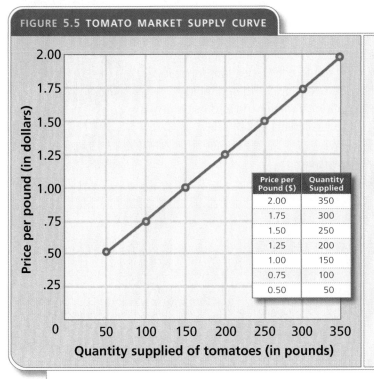

FIGURE 5.5 TOMATO MARKET SUPPLY CURVE

Price per Pound ($)	Quantity Supplied
2.00	350
1.75	300
1.50	250
1.25	200
1.00	150
0.75	100
0.50	50

Notice that **market supply curves** slope upward from lower left to upper right, just as individual supply curves do.

The main difference between the two types of curves is that the quantities supplied at each price are much larger on a market supply curve. This is because the curve represents a group of producers (a market), not just one producer.

ANALYZE GRAPHS

1. At which price will all the fruit and vegetable stands want to sell 200 pounds of tomatoes?
2. How is the slope of this supply curve different from the slope of a market demand curve?

Look at Figure 5.5 one more time. What is the quantity supplied at $1.50? How will quantity supplied change if the price increases by 25 cents or decreases by 25 cents? Once again, find the answers to these questions by running your finger along the curve. As you can see, the market supply curve, just like the individual supply curve, vividly illustrates the direct relationship between price and quantity supplied. If the price of tomatoes increases among all of the suppliers at the farmers' market, then the quantity supplied of tomatoes also increases. And, conversely, if the price decreases, then the quantity supplied decreases as well. As with the individual supply curve, the market supply curve is constructed on the assumption that all other economic factors remain constant—only the price per pound of tomatoes changes.

The NBA Goes International

Until recently, nearly all of the National Basketball Association's (NBA) players were U.S-born. Before 1984, there were only 12 foreign-born players in the league, but that has changed. Opening day rosters in the 2005–06 season listed 82 international players, and they hailed from all over the world—from Spain and Slovenia in Europe to Senegal and the Sudan in Africa. Why has the supply of international players risen so dramatically? The average annual salary of an NBA player, which has risen from about $2 million in 1997 to over $4 million in 2006, is a likely explanation.

The international players are not the only group reaping monetary rewards. With people in China watching Yao Ming (at right), and French fans following Tony Parker, the NBA's overseas merchandise sales have increased rapidly. In 2004, the NBA sold an estimated $600 million in merchandise outside of the United States—about 20 percent of its overall merchandise sales.

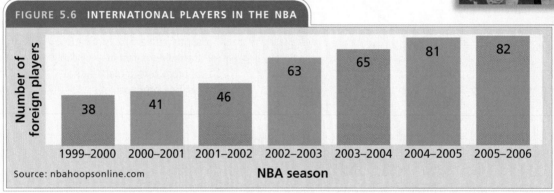

FIGURE 5.6 INTERNATIONAL PLAYERS IN THE NBA

NBA season	Number of foreign players
1999–2000	38
2000–2001	41
2001–2002	46
2002–2003	63
2003–2004	65
2004–2005	81
2005–2006	82

Source: nbahoopsonline.com

CONNECTING ACROSS THE GLOBE

1. **Synthesizing Economic Information** How do price and quantity supplied relate to salaries and labor in the NBA?

2. **Drawing Conclusions** What effect might a large drop in NBA salaries have on international sales of NBA merchandise?

Supply curves for all producers follow the law of supply. Whether the producers are manufacturers, farmers, retailers, or service providers, they are willing to supply more goods and services at higher prices, even though it costs more to produce more. A farmer, for example, spends more on seeds and fertilizer to grow more soybeans. Why are farmers and other producers willing to spend more when prices are higher? The answer is that higher prices signal the potential for higher profits, and the desire to increase profits drives decision making in the market. You will learn more about the costs of production and about maximizing profits in Section 2.

SMART Grapher
Create a supply curve at **ClassZone.com**

APPLICATION Applying Economic Concepts

C. Look back at the supply schedule for nutrition bars you created for Application B on page 133. Use it to create a supply curve.

REVIEWING KEY CONCEPTS

1. Explain the differences between the terms in each of these pairs:

   a. *supply*   **b.** *supply schedule*   **c.** *market supply schedule*
   law of supply   *supply curve*   *market supply curve*

2. Why does a supply curve slope upward?

3. What do the points on a market supply curve represent?

4. If the price of a video game increased, what would the law of supply predict about the quantity supplied of the game?

5. How is the law of supply similar to the law of demand? How is it different?

6. **Using Your Notes** How is a supply schedule different from a market supply schedule? Refer to your completed cluster diagram. Use the Graphic Organizer at **Interactive Review @ ClassZone.com**

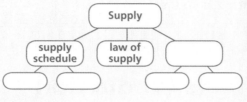

Supply
supply schedule | law of supply

ECONOMICS IN PRACTICE

Making a Market Supply Curve
Suppose that you are the head of the sporting goods dealers' association in your city. You survey all the stores that sell skis and determine how many pairs of skis they are willing to sell at various prices. Your research enables you to make the following market supply schedule.

Price per Pair ($)	Quantity Supplied
500	600
425	450
350	325
275	225
200	150
125	100

Create a Supply Curve Use this market supply schedule to draw a market supply curve. Be sure to label each axis of your graph.

Challenge Write a caption for your supply curve explaining what it shows.

Use *SMART Grapher* @ **ClassZone.com** to complete this activity.

CRITICAL THINKING

7. **Explaining an Economic Concept** Focus on one item you buy regularly for which the price has changed. How did this shift in price influence supply?

8. **Making Inferences** The market supply schedule on page 133 shows that the quantity supplied of tomatoes priced at 50 cents per pound was 50 pounds. However, market research of customers at the farmers' market showed that the market demand at that price was 250 pounds of tomatoes. How do you explain the difference?

9. **Applying Economic Concepts** Return to the supply schedule for nutrition bars you created for Application B on page 133. Assume that the class represents all the sellers of nutrition bars in the market. Tabulate these individual supply schedules to create a market supply schedule. Then use that schedule to draw a market supply curve.

10. **Challenge** Why might producers not always be able to sell their products at the higher prices they prefer? Think about the laws of demand and supply and the different attitudes that consumers and producers have toward price. How might the market resolve this difference? (You will learn more about this in Chapter 6.)

What Are the Costs of Production?

OBJECTIVES	KEY TERMS	TAKING NOTES
In Section 2, you will • analyze how businesses calculate the right number of workers to hire • determine how businesses calculate production costs • explain how businesses use those calculations to determine the most profitable output	marginal product, *p. 138* specialization, *p. 138* increasing returns, *p. 139* diminishing returns, *p. 139* fixed cost, *p. 140* variable cost, *p. 140* total cost, *p. 140* marginal cost, *p. 140* marginal revenue, *p. 142* total revenue, *p. 142* profit-maximizing output, *p. 143*	As you read Section 2, complete a hierarchy diagram like this one to track main ideas and supporting details. Use the Graphic Organizer at **Interactive Review @ ClassZone.com** 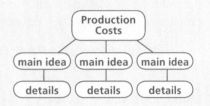

Labor Affects Production

KEY CONCEPTS

Let's look at an individual producer and the costs involved in supplying goods to the market. Janine owns a small factory that produces custom blue jeans. The factory has three sewing machines, and when there are three workers, one day's product is 12 pairs of jeans. She wonders how hiring one more worker will affect production. The change in total product that results from hiring one more worker is called the **marginal product**. With four workers, the factory produces 19 pairs of jeans a day, so the new employee's marginal product is 7 pairs of jeans. With a fifth worker, output jumps from 19 to 29—a marginal product of 10. Why did marginal product increase?

Each of Janine's original three workers had a sewing machine to operate, but they also had to cut cloth, package the finished jeans, and keep the shop clean. So, Janine's employees only spent half of their time sewing. The fourth employee helped with the other tasks, so marginal product increased. But the sewing machines were often still idle. The fifth worker allowed labor to be divided even more efficiently, which caused marginal product to increase markedly. Having each worker focus on a particular facet of production is called **specialization**. But does hiring more workers always cause marginal product to increase?

QUICK REFERENCE

Marginal product is the change in total output brought about by adding one more worker.

Specialization is having a worker focus on a particular aspect of production.

EXAMPLE Marginal Product Schedule

A marginal product schedule shows the relationship between labor and marginal product. As you can see from Janine's marginal product schedule (Figure 5.7), one or two workers produced very little. But marginal product was still slightly larger with each added worker. Then with between three and six workers, the benefits of specialization become increasingly apparent. With up to six employees, Janine's operation experiences **increasing returns**, meaning each new worker adds more to total output than the last, as shown by the marginal product.

FIGURE 5.7 JANINE'S MARGINAL PRODUCT SCHEDULE

Number of Workers	Total Product	Marginal Product
0	0	0
1	3	3
2	7	4
3	12	5
4	19	7
5	29	10
6	42	13
7	53	11
8	61	8
9	66	5
10	67	1
11	65	−2

a Four workers can produce 19 pairs of jeans. **Specialization** causes a healthy increase in **marginal product.**

b With seven workers, total product still increases, but marginal product begins to decrease.

c With eleven workers, total product decreases, and the marginal product is a negative number.

ANALYZE TABLES

1. At what number of workers is total product highest?
2. On the basis of this table, does it make sense for Janine to hire more than six workers? Explain your answer.

Figure 5.7 shows that increasing returns stop with the seventh worker. This is also related to specialization. Workers seven, eight, nine, and ten can still add to productivity, but their work overlaps with that of the first six workers. With between seven and ten employees, Janine's operation experiences **diminishing returns**, as each new worker causes total output to grow but at a decreasing rate. With eleven workers, total output actually decreases, and Janine experiences negative returns. This may happen as employees become crowded and operations become disorganized. It is rare, however, for a business to hire so many workers that it has negative returns.

APPLICATION Drawing Conclusions

A. Why do Janine's increasing returns peak with six employees?

Production Costs

KEY CONCEPTS

The goal of every business is to earn as much profit as possible. Profit is the money that businesses get from selling their products, once the money it costs to make those products has been subtracted. Businesses have different kinds of costs. **Fixed costs** are expenses that the owners of a business must incur whether they produce nothing, a little, or a lot. **Variable costs** are business costs that vary as the level of production output changes. Businesses find the **total cost** of production by adding fixed and variable costs together. Finally, businesses are interested in knowing their **marginal cost**, or the additional cost of producing one more unit of their product.

EXAMPLE Fixed and Variable Costs

Janine's fixed costs include the mortgage on her factory, her insurance, and the utilities that are on even when the factory is closed at night and on weekends. These costs are the same whether she is producing no jeans, 3 pairs, or 42 pairs of jeans per day. She must also pay the salaries of managers who keep the company running but are not involved directly in production.

Wages are one of Janine's chief variable costs. As she hires additional workers to increase the level of production, her costs for wages increase. She also incurs additional costs for more fabric, thread, zippers, and buttons as well as increased electricity costs to run the machines and light the factory. Shipping her jeans to customers is another variable cost. The more pairs of jeans that Janine's factory produces, the more her variable costs increase. Conversely, if she decides to cut back the hours or the number of workers, or if she closes the factory for a week's vacation, her variable costs decrease.

To determine the total cost to produce a certain number of pairs of jeans, Janine can add her fixed and variable costs. And by figuring out her marginal cost, she can determine what it costs to produce each additional pair of jeans.

QUICK REFERENCE

Fixed costs are those that business owners incur no matter how much they produce.

Variable costs depend on the level of production output.

Total cost is the sum of fixed and variable costs.

Marginal cost is the extra cost of producing one more unit.

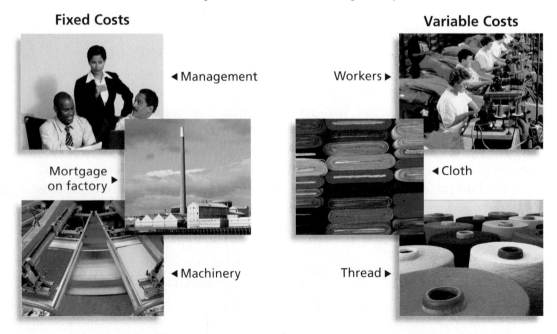

Fixed Costs

◄ Management

Mortgage on factory ►

◄ Machinery

Variable Costs

Workers ►

◄ Cloth

Thread ►

EXAMPLE Production Costs Schedule

By looking at Figure 5.8, we can see Janine's costs and how they change as her quantity of jeans produced changes. Remember that her total product increased through the addition of the tenth worker and declined after the eleventh worker was added. The change in the number of workers is a major factor in the increase in variable costs at each quantity. You'll notice that the fixed costs remain the same no matter what the total product amounts to.

FIGURE 5.8 JANINE'S PRODUCTION COSTS SCHEDULE

Number of Workers	Total Product	(a) Fixed Costs ($)	(a) Variable Cost ($)	Total Cost ($)	Marginal Cost ($)
0	0	40	0	40	—
1	3	40	30 (b)→	70	10
2	7	40	62	102	8
3	12	40	97	137	7
4	19	40	132	172	5
5	29	40	172	212	4
6	42	40	211	251	3
7	53	40	277	317	6
8	61	40	373	413	12
9	66	40	473	513	20
10	67	40	503	543	30
11	65	40	539	579	—

(a) **Fixed costs** remain constant, while **variable costs** change at each quantity.

(b) Calculate **total costs** by adding together fixed costs and variable costs.

CONNECT TO MATH

To determine marginal cost, divide the change in total cost by the change in total product.

1. In Figure 5.8, total cost with four workers is $172; with three workers it is $137. 172−137=35

2. Total product with four workers is 19; with three workers it is 12. 19−12=7

3. Marginal cost in this case is figured by dividing 35 by 7. 35÷7=5

ANALYZE TABLES
1. How do the variable costs change when the total product increases from 7 pairs to 12 pairs?
2. When Janine has no workers, why are her fixed and total costs the same?

Marginal cost is determined by dividing change in total cost by change in total product. Notice in Figure 5.8 that marginal cost declines at first and then increases. The initial decline occurs because of increasing worker efficiency due to specialization. After that the marginal cost increases because of diminishing returns.

Janine now knows when her returns are increasing or diminishing and what it costs her to produce each additional pair of jeans. Her next step is to figure out her revenue, the money she makes from selling jeans, at each level of production.

APPLICATION Analyzing and Interpreting Data

B. Why does it cost Janine more to produce 65 pairs of jeans with 11 workers than to produce 66 pairs of jeans with 9 workers?

Earning the Highest Profit

Marginal revenue is the money made from the sale of each additional unit of output.

Total revenue is a company's income from selling its products.

KEY CONCEPTS

Before a business can decide how much to produce in order to earn as much profit as possible, it must figure its marginal revenue and total revenue. **Marginal revenue** is the added revenue per unit of output, or the money made from each additional unit sold. In other words, marginal revenue is the price. If, for example, baseball hats were priced at $5 each, the money earned from each additional hat sold would be $5. **Total revenue** is the income a business receives from selling a product. It can be expressed by the formula **Total Revenue = P × Q**, where P is the price of the product and Q is the quantity purchased at that price. (Recall that you used this same formula to calculate total revenue on page 101.)

EXAMPLE Production Costs and Revenues Schedule

You have seen how Janine explored the relationship between labor and marginal product. You have also seen what it cost her to produce various quantities of jeans. Next, you will learn how she calculates her revenue and her profits.

Look at Figure 5.9, which shows Janine's costs, revenues, and profit for various levels of total product. Janine calculates her total revenue by multiplying the marginal revenue—$20 per pair of jeans—by the total product. Then she can determine her profit by subtracting her total costs from her total revenue. Remember that Janine is trying to decide how many workers she should hire and how many pairs of jeans she should produce in order to make the most profit. To make these decisions, she needs to perform a marginal analysis, which is a comparison of the added costs and benefits of an economic action. In other words, she needs to look at the costs and benefits of adding each additional worker and producing additional pairs of jeans.

Using Figure 5.9, Janine can see that when she has no employees, and therefore does not produce any jeans, she loses money because she still incurs fixed costs. If she hires one worker who produces three pairs of jeans, her costs are $70, but she only collects $60 in total revenue. Therefore, she still doesn't earn a profit. When she hires a second worker and together the two workers produce seven pairs of jeans, costs are $102 and revenues are $140, so she earns a very small profit of $38. Janine has finally passed the break-even point, the point at which enough revenue is being generated to cover expenses. At the break-even point, total costs and total revenue are exactly equal.

Like all business owners, Janine wants to do a lot better than break even. She wants to earn as much profit as possible. She can see that as she adds additional workers and produces more jeans, her profits increase.

FIGURE 5.9 JANINE'S PRODUCTION COSTS AND REVENUES SCHEDULE

Number of Workers	Total Product	Total Cost ($)	Marginal Cost ($)	Marginal Revenue ($)	(a) Total Revenue ($)	(b) Profit ($)
0	0	40	—	—	0	−40
1	3	70	10	20	60	−10
2	7	102	8	20	140 (c) →	38
3	12	137	7	20	240	103
4	19	172	5	20	380	208
5	29	212	4	20	580	368
6	42	251	3	20	840	589
7	53	317	6	20	1,060	743
8	61	413	12	20	1,220	807
9	66	513	20 (d)	20	1,320	807
10	67	543	30	20	1,340	797
11	65	579	—	20	1,300	721

(a) Total revenue = marginal revenue (price) x total product.

(b) Profit = total revenue – total cost.

(c) When **total revenue** first exceeds total cost, a producer has passed the break-even point.

(d) At profit-maximizing output, marginal cost = marginal revenue.

ANALYZE TABLES

1. How does Janine calculate her total revenue and profits when she produces 42 pairs of jeans?

2. What happens to Janine's profits when she increases production from 66 to 67 pairs of jeans? Why does this happen?

When you look at Figure 5.9 again, you can see that Janine's profits continue to rise as she adds workers—up to and including the ninth worker—and produces more jeans. Why does this happen? Recall that during the stage of diminishing returns (see Figure 5.7 on page 139), total production continues to rise, but it rises more slowly. Although Janine is getting less production from each additional worker, marginal revenue is still greater than marginal cost, so Janine hires more workers, produces more, and increases profits.

When Janine's factory has nine workers producing 66 pairs of jeans, it has reached the level of production where it realizes the greatest amount of profit. This is called **profit-maximizing output**. This level of output is reached when the marginal cost and the marginal revenue are equal (here, both at $20). After that point, profits begin to decline. When Janine adds a tenth worker, the marginal product of one pair of jeans increases total revenue, but the increase in marginal cost is greater than the increase in marginal revenue. Since the goal of every business is to maximize profit, having a tenth employee runs counter to Janine's best interests.

QUICK REFERENCE

Profit-maximizing output is the level of production at which a business realizes the greatest amount of profit.

APPLICATION Analyzing and Interpreting Data

C. If the price of jeans increased to $22 per pair, how would it affect Janine's total revenue and profit?

ECONOMICS SKILLBUILDER

For more on interpreting sources, see the Skillbuilder Handbook, page R28.

Evaluating Sources

There are many sources of economic information, including news articles, reports, books, and electronic media. Knowing how to interpret sources is how we gain economic information.

TECHNIQUES FOR READING SOURCE MATERIAL The following passage appeared on the Web site of the Portland Cement Association. The passage is a source of information about the supply of cement in the United States in 2004. To interpret this source of information, use the following strategies.

> **Identify** the subject of the passage. Then ask yourself what, if any, economic concept is involved. This passage is about cement. The economic concept discussed is supply.

> **Identify** economic factors that are relevant to the discussion. The cement shortage is explained in part by an increase in market demand and by the rising cost and limited availability of ships to carry imported cement.

> **Evaluate** the passage's credibility. Do you think the source of the passage is reliable? Are other cited sources reliable? Information from this association and the U.S. Geological Survey is likely to be reliable.

Cement Supply Falls Short

Several factors have converged to create tight supplies of cement, the key ingredient in concrete, which is used in nearly every type of construction.

First, strong construction markets have increased demand. The flare in demand arrived on the heels of an unusually active winter for construction, traditionally a down period when plants can stockpile cement in anticipation of the spring construction surge. Instead, there was no letup in demand during the 2003/04 winter and little opportunity to prepare a strong inventory for spring when construction activity traditionally increases.

Another factor is freight—limited availability of transport ships and escalating shipping rates. According to figures from the U.S. Geological Survey, 2003 U.S. portland cement consumption was 107.5 million metric tons. Of that total, 23.2 million tons or 21.6 percent was imported cement.

Since the beginning of the spring 2004, shipping rates have skyrocketed and availability of ships is limited. The booming Asian economies are straining worldwide cement capacity and shipping availability.

Source: www.cement.org

THINKING ECONOMICALLY Interpreting

1. According to the passage, what variables affect the supply of concrete in the United States?

2. Do you think cement will continue to be in short supply in the United States? Explain your answer using information from the passage.

3. Who do you think is most likely to benefit from the information provided in the passage? Why?

EXAMPLE Changes Along a Supply Curve

Each new point on the supply curve shows a change in quantity supplied. A change in quantity supplied does not shift the supply curve itself. Let's look again at the Smiths' supply curve for tomatoes (Figure 5.10). Note the quantities supplied at each price. Notice that as quantity supplied changes, the change is shown by the direction of movement, right or left, along the supply curve. A movement to the right indicates an increase in both price and quantity supplied. A movement to the left shows a decrease in both price and quantity supplied.

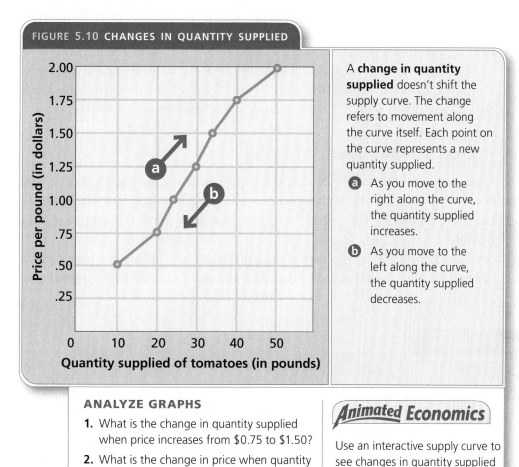

FIGURE 5.10 CHANGES IN QUANTITY SUPPLIED

A **change in quantity supplied** doesn't shift the supply curve. The change refers to movement along the curve itself. Each point on the curve represents a new quantity supplied.

a As you move to the right along the curve, the quantity supplied increases.

b As you move to the left along the curve, the quantity supplied decreases.

ANALYZE GRAPHS

1. What is the change in quantity supplied when price increases from $0.75 to $1.50?

2. What is the change in price when quantity supplied changes from 50 to 24 pounds?

Animated Economics

Use an interactive supply curve to see changes in quantity supplied at **ClassZone.com**

Just as Figure 5.10 shows change in quantity supplied by one individual, a market supply curve shows similar information for an entire market. However, market supply curves have larger quantities supplied, and therefore larger changes to quantity supplied, because they combine the data from all the individual supply curves in the market. For example, when the price increases from $0.75 to $1.75 on the market supply curve (Figure 5.5), the quantity supplied increases from 100 pounds to 300. Compare this with the change in quantity supplied at those prices in Figure 5.10.

APPLICATION Applying Economic Concepts

A. Changes in quantity supplied do not shift the position of the supply curve. Why?

Changes in Supply

QUICK REFERENCE

Change in supply occurs when a change in the marketplace prompts producers to sell different amounts at every price.

KEY CONCEPTS

Consider what might happen if the workers at an automobile factory negotiate a large wage increase so that it's more expensive to produce each automobile. As the firm's costs increase, it is less willing and able to offer as many automobiles for sale. Any action such as this, which changes the costs of production, will change supply. **Change in supply** occurs when something prompts producers to offer different amounts for sale at every price. When production costs increase, supply decreases; when production costs decrease, supply increases.

Just like change in demand, change in supply actually shifts the supply curve. Six factors cause a change in supply: input costs, labor productivity, technology, government actions, producer expectations, and number of producers.

FACTOR 1 Input Costs

QUICK REFERENCE

Input costs are the price of the resources used to make products.

Input costs are a major factor that affects production costs and, therefore, supply. **Input costs** are the price of the resources needed to produce a good or service. For example, Anna makes nutrition bars that contain peanuts. If the price of peanuts increases, Anna's costs increase. She cannot afford to produce as many nutrition bars, and her supply curve shifts to the left (Figure 5.11). When the price of peanuts decreases, her costs decrease. She is willing and able to increase the quantity she can supply at every price, and the curve shifts to the right (Figure 5.12).

FIGURES 5.11 AND 5.12 SHIFTS IN SUPPLY

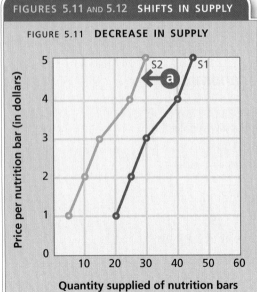

FIGURE 5.11 DECREASE IN SUPPLY

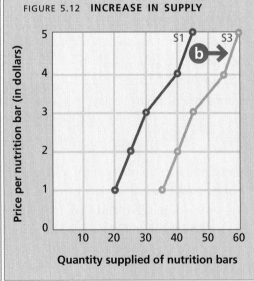

FIGURE 5.12 INCREASE IN SUPPLY

When a **change in supply** occurs, the supply curve shifts.

a As Figure 5.11 shows, a shift to the left (S2) indicates a decrease in supply.

b As Figure 5.12 shows, a shift to the right (S3) indicates an increase in supply.

ANALYZE GRAPHS

1. In Figure 5.11, how has the supply of nutrition bars changed at every price?
2. In Figure 5.12, how has the supply of nutrition bars changed at every price?

Animated Economics

Use an interactive version of shifting supply curves at **ClassZone.com**

FACTOR 2 Labor Productivity

Labor productivity is the amount of goods and services that a person can produce in a given time. Increasing productivity decreases the costs of production and therefore increases supply. For example, a specialized division of labor can allow a producer to make more goods at a lower cost, as was the case at Janine's factory in Section 2. Her marginal costs decreased when there were six workers, each of whom had a separate job to do.

Better-trained and more-skilled workers can usually produce more goods in less time, and therefore at lower costs, than less-educated or less-skilled workers. For example, a business that provides word-processing services can produce more documents if its employees type quickly and have a lot of experience working with word-processing software.

QUICK REFERENCE

Labor productivity is the amount of goods and services that a person can produce in a given time.

Technology entails applying scientific methods and innovations to production.

FACTOR 3 Technology

One way that businesses improve their productivity and increase supply is through the use of technology. **Technology** involves the application of scientific methods and discoveries to the production process, resulting in new products or new manufacturing techniques. Influenced by the profit motive, manufacturers have, throughout history, used technology to make goods more efficiently. Increased automation, including the use of industrial robots, has led to increased supplies of automobiles, computers, and many other products. (See the Case Study on pages 158–159.)

Improved technology helps farmers produce more food per acre. It also allows oil refiners to get more gasoline out of every barrel of crude oil and helps to get that gasoline to gas stations more quickly and more safely. In addition, technological innovations, such as the personal computer, enable workers to be more productive. This, in turn, helps businesses to increase the supply of their services, such as processing insurance claims or selling airline tickets.

The Typewriter's End The move from typewriter to computer shows how technology helps to boost productivity.

FACTOR 4 Government Action

Government actions can also affect the costs of production, both positively and negatively. An **excise tax** is a tax on the production or sale of a specific good or service. Excise taxes are often placed on items such as alcohol and tobacco—things whose consumption the government is interested in discouraging. The taxes increase producers' costs and, therefore, decrease the supply of these items.

Taxes tend to decrease supply; subsidies have the opposite effect. You learned in Chapter 3 that a subsidy is a government payment that partially covers the cost of an economic activity. The subsidy's purpose is to encourage or protect that activity. Most forms of energy production in the United States receive some form of subsidy. For example, subsidies helped to double the supply of ethanol, a gasoline substitute made from corn, between 2000 and 2004.

QUICK REFERENCE

An **excise tax** is a tax on the making or selling of certain goods or services.

QUICK REFERENCE

Regulation is a set of rules or laws designed to control business behavior.

Government **regulation**, the act of controlling business behavior through a set of rules or laws, can also affect supply. Banning a certain pesticide might decrease the supply of the crops that depend on the pesticide. Worker safety regulations might decrease supply by increasing a business's production costs or increase supply by reducing the amount of labor lost to on-the-job injuries.

FACTOR 5 Producer Expectations

If producers expect the price of their product to rise or fall in the future, it may affect how much of that product they are willing and able to supply in the present. Different kinds of producers may react to future price changes differently. For example, if a farmer expects the price of corn to be higher in the future, he or she may store some of the current crop, thereby decreasing supply. A manufacturer who believes the price of his or her product will rise may run the factory for an extra shift or invest in more equipment to increase supply.

FACTOR 6 Number of Producers

When one company develops a successful new idea, whether it's designer wedding gowns, the latest generation of cell phones, or fast-food sushi, other producers soon enter the market and increase the supply of the good or service. When this happens, the supply curve shifts to the right, as you can see in Figure 5.13.

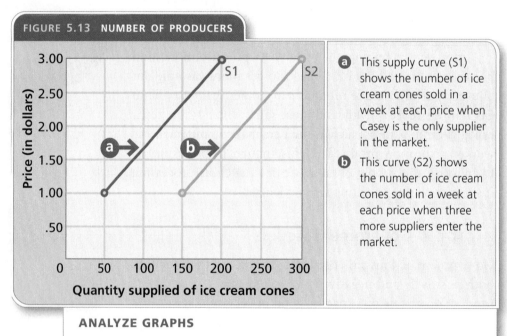

FIGURE 5.13 NUMBER OF PRODUCERS

ⓐ This supply curve (S1) shows the number of ice cream cones sold in a week at each price when Casey is the only supplier in the market.

ⓑ This curve (S2) shows the number of ice cream cones sold in a week at each price when three more suppliers enter the market.

ANALYZE GRAPHS

1. About how many ice cream cones were sold at $1.00 when Casey was the only producer in the market?
2. How do these two curves show the effect of the number of producers on the supply of ice cream cones in the market?

An increase in the number of producers means increased competition, which may eventually drive less-efficient producers out of the market, decreasing supply. (You'll learn more about competition in Chapter 7.) Competition has a major impact on supply, as producers enter and leave the market constantly.

Input Costs Input costs, the collective price of the resources that go into producing a good or service, affect supply directly.

Number of Producers A successful new product or service always brings out competitors who initially raise overall supply.

Labor Productivity Better-trained or more-skilled workers are usually more productive. Increased productivity decreases costs and increases supply.

What Causes a Change in Supply?

Producer Expectations The amount of product producers are willing and able to supply may be influenced by whether they believe prices will go up or down.

Technology By applying scientific advances to the production process, producers have learned to generate their goods and services more efficiently.

Government Action Government actions, such as taxes or subsidies, can have a positive or a negative effect on production costs.

ANALYZE CHARTS

A newspaper article states that the supply of snowboards has risen dramatically over the past six months. Choose four of the six factors that cause a change in supply and explain how each might have resulted in the recent influx of snowboards.

Figure 5.13 shows what happens to the supply of ice cream cones in a neighborhood as more producers enter the market. When Casey opened his ice cream store it was the only one in the area. It was an instant success. Within six months, three competing stores had opened in the neighborhood, and the supply of ice cream cones increased at all price levels. A year later, though, this intense competition forced one of the producers to leave the market.

APPLICATION Applying Economic Concepts

B. Choose an item of food or clothing that you buy regularly. List as many input costs as you can that might affect the supply of that product. Compare your list with a classmate's and see if you can add to each other's lists.

Robert Johnson: Supplying African-American Entertainment

FAST FACTS

Robert Johnson

Title: Chairman of BET Holdings II, Inc., retired

Born: April 8, 1946, Hickory, Mississippi

Major Accomplishment: BET is the leading supplier of cable TV programming aimed at African Americans.

Other Enterprises: Digital music networks, publishing, events production, BET.com Web portal, NBA team Charlotte Bobcats, and WNBA Charlotte Sting

Honors: Broadcasting and Cable Magazine Hall of Fame Award, NAACP Image Award

In this section, you've learned about the factors that influence supply. You've also seen some examples of how these factors work. The story of media entrepreneur Robert Johnson provides a real-world example of how the entrance of a new supplier can affect a market.

EXAMPLE Expanding the Number of Producers

In the late 1970s, Robert Johnson was working as a Washington lobbyist for the National Cable Television Association. He recognized that current suppliers in the cable TV industry were ignoring a substantial market—African Americans. To fill this void, Johnson conceived the idea for Black Entertainment Television (BET), the first cable channel owned by and focused on African Americans.

To launch his dream, Johnson took out a $15,000 bank loan. He also persuaded a major investor to put up $500,000. Next, he secured space on a cable TV satellite for his new channel. BET's first program appeared on January 8, 1980. The company grew from offering two hours of programming a week to round-the-clock programming on five separate channels. Cable operators in the United States, Canada, and the Caribbean saw the value of this kind of targeted programming, and began to buy BET's shows.

At first, BET targeted young viewers with programs similar to those on MTV. As the cable TV industry grew and became more profitable, Johnson invested in more diverse programming. Of this transition he explained, "Now we're a music video channel with a public affairs footprint. . . ." BET could "play music, but also . . . cover issues that are of concern to African Americans." BET.com, the number one Internet portal for African Americans, soon followed.

A Vast Reach BET supplies programming to more than 80 million households in Canada, the United States, and the Caribbean.

In 2001, Johnson sold BET to the giant media company Viacom International Inc. for $3 billion and became the nation's first black billionaire. After the sale, Johnson stayed on at BET and continued to run the company for five more years. His success demonstrated that there was a strong market for African-American entertainment. As a result, many suppliers—some with no traditional ties to the African-American community—now offer the kind of programming Johnson pioneered.

Economics Update

Find an update on Robert Johnson at **ClassZone.com**

APPLICATION Making Inferences

C. What effects might BET's success have on the supply of African-American programming?

1. Explain the differences between the terms in each of these pairs:

   a. *change in quantity supplied*   **b.** *input costs*   **c.** *excise tax*
        change in supply   *technology*   *regulation*

2. What else besides raw materials would be included in input costs?

3. Why might an increase in oil prices lead to a decrease in the supply of fruits and vegetables in your local supermarket?

4. Why do excise taxes and subsidies affect supply differently?

5. Does expectation of a change in price affect supply? Illustrate your answer with examples.

6. **Using Your Notes** How does a change in number of producers affect supply? Refer to your completed chart.

   Use the Graphic Organizer at **Interactive Review @ ClassZone.com**

Factor That Changes Supply	Reason Why Supply Changes

CRITICAL THINKING

7. **Applying Economic Concepts** How do each of these examples of government actions affect the supply of gasoline?

   a. In 2005, the government continued support for ethanol, a gasoline substitute.

   b. The state of California requires a special blend of gasoline that meets stricter environmental standards than other regions in the country.

   c. Many states use gasoline taxes to help fund highway construction and maintenance.

8. **Making Inferences** Why do you think governments want to influence the supply of alcohol and tobacco products by imposing excise taxes?

9. **Analyzing Effects** Take out the market supply curve for skis that you created on page 137. Add new curves showing how supply would be changed in each of the following cases. Share your graph with a classmate and explain your reasoning.

   a. The price of titanium, used in skis, declines dramatically.

   b. A large manufacturer decides to stop producing skis.

10. **Challenge** How does an increased number of producers affect the prices of goods in a market? What is the reason for this effect? Think about what you know about demand and supply and review Figure 5.12 as you formulate your answer.

ECONOMICS IN PRACTICE

Explaining Changes in Supply
Suppose that you are a manufacturer of personal digital music players (PDMPs). What factors affect supply for PDMPs? The chart below lists examples of a change in supply in the market for PDMPs. For each example, identify which factor that affects supply is involved and state whether supply increases or decreases.

Example of Change That Affects Supply	Factor and How It Affected Supply
You give each worker in your factory a specialized job.	
Price of computer chips used in PDMPs rises.	
New machinery speeds up the manufacturing process.	
Your success prompts three new companies to start producing PDMPs.	
A new law requires producers to recycle the wastewater from their factories.	

Challenge Identify which of the six factors that affect supply does not appear on this chart. What would be an example of how that factor might affect the market for PDMPs?

What Is Elasticity of Supply?

OBJECTIVES	KEY TERMS	TAKING NOTES
In Section 4, you will • define the term *elasticity of supply* • explain the difference between elastic and inelastic supply • identify the factors that affect elasticity of supply	elasticity of supply, *p. 154*	As you read Section 4, complete a cluster diagram like the one shown. Use the Graphic Organizer at **Interactive Review @ ClassZone.com** Elasticity of Supply

Elasticity of Supply

KEY CONCEPTS

According to the law of supply, as price increases so will the supply of a good or service. When Toyota Motor Corporation introduced its Prius hybrid in 2000, it was surprised by the automobile's instant popularity. Consumers were willing to pay more than the manufacturer's suggested price. Yet Toyota was not able to increase supply at the same pace that consumer demand and prices rose. Even five years later, Toyota could not meet rising demand. This inability to effectively respond to and meet increased demand suggests that the supply of the Prius was inelastic.

In Chapter 4, you learned that elasticity of demand measures how responsive consumers are to price changes. In a similar way, **elasticity of supply** is also a measure of how responsive producers are to price changes.

If a change in price leads to a relatively larger change in quantity supplied, supply is said to be elastic. In other words, supply is elastic if a 10 percent increase in price causes a greater than 10 percent increase in quantity supplied. If a change in price leads to a relatively smaller change in quantity supplied, supply is said to be inelastic. If the price and the quantity supplied change by exactly the same percentage, supply is unit elastic.

Inelastic Supply The supply of expensive and complicated items, such as this Prius hybrid, is often inelastic.

EXAMPLE Elastic Supply

Let's look at an example of elastic supply. Figure 5.15 illustrates how the quantity supplied of a new style of leather boots was elastic. As the boots gained in popularity, a shortage developed. The boot makers raised the price of the boots from $60 to $150 dollars, and the quantity supplied more than kept up, escalating from 10,000 to 50,000 pairs. The producer was able to rapidly increase the quantity supplied because, unlike car manufacturing for instance, the raw materials needed to make boots are neither particularly expensive nor hard to come by. The actual manufacturing process is also, relatively speaking, fairly uncomplicated and easy to increase.

EXAMPLE Inelastic Supply

In Chapter 4, you learned that demand for gasoline was inelastic. The supply of gasoline is also inelastic. Although gasoline prices rose 20 to 30 percent between 2004 and 2005, producers were not able to increase supply by the same amount because of the limited supply of crude oil and refining capacity.

Figure 5.16 shows how the supply of olive oil is also inelastic. When the price of olive oil rose by a factor of four, supply could not keep pace, as the oil comes from the previous season's olives and is exported from the Mediterranean region.

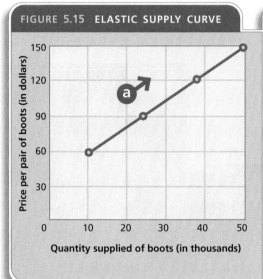

FIGURE 5.15 ELASTIC SUPPLY CURVE

Price per pair of boots (in dollars) / Quantity supplied of boots (in thousands)

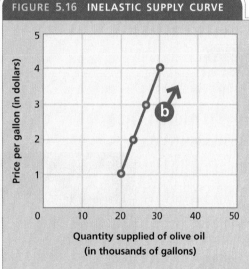

FIGURE 5.16 INELASTIC SUPPLY CURVE

Price per gallon (in dollars) / Quantity supplied of olive oil (in thousands of gallons)

ⓐ The curve in Figure 5.15 slopes gradually. It slopes more horizontally than vertically because of greater changes in quantity supplied.

ⓑ The curve in Figure 5.16 slopes steeply. It slopes more vertically than horizontally because of lesser changes in quantity supplied.

ANALYZE GRAPHS

1. If the price of leather rose dramatically for the boots in Figure 5.15, how might this affect elasticity of supply?

2. In the United States, would the supply of corn oil be more elastic than the supply of olive oil? Why or why not?

Animated **Economics**

Use elastic and inelastic supply curves at **ClassZone.com**

APPLICATION Drawing Conclusions

A. A bakery produces 200 muffins per week that sell for $1.50 each. When the price increases to $2.00, it produces 300 muffins per week. Is supply elastic or inelastic? Explain your answer.

What Affects Elasticity of Supply?

Just as there are factors that cause a change in supply, there are also factors that affect the elasticity of supply. There are far fewer of these factors than for elasticity of demand. The ease of changing production to respond to price change is the main factor in determining elasticity of supply. Given enough time, the elasticity of supply increases for most goods and services. Supply will be more elastic over a year or several years than it will be if the time frame to respond is a day, a week, or a month.

Industries that are able to respond quickly to changes in price by either increasing or decreasing production are those that don't require a lot of capital, skilled labor, or difficult-to-obtain resources. For example, the quantity supplied of dog-walking services can increase rapidly with the addition of more people to walk dogs. A small business that sells crafts made from recycled materials would be able to respond quickly to changes in the price of its various products by applying its resources to increase the supply of its higher priced items.

For other industries, it takes a great deal of time to shift the resources of production to respond to price changes. Automakers and oil refiners are examples of industries that rely on large capital outlays or difficult-to-obtain resources. It might take such suppliers a considerable amount of time to respond to price changes.

YOUR ECONOMIC CHOICES

ELASTICITY OF SUPPLY

Which supply of cupcakes is more elastic?

You're planning to sell cupcakes at your school's football game to raise funds for a charitable cause, but it's hard to say in advance how many fans will attend the game. You can place an order with a bakery (which you need to do a week early) or have volunteers do the baking the night before the game. Which supply of cupcakes is more elastic? Why?

APPLICATION Applying Economic Concepts

B. Is the elasticity of a farmer's crop of sweet corn greater at the beginning of the growing season or in the middle of the growing season? Why?

SECTION 4 Assessment

Online Quiz
ClassZone.com

REVIEWING KEY CONCEPTS

1. Use each of the following three terms in a sentence that gives an example of the term as it relates to supply:

   a. *elastic*   **b.** *inelastic*   **c.** *elasticity of supply*

2. How is elasticity of supply similar to elasticity of demand? How is it different?

3. Is the supply of genuine antique furniture elastic or inelastic? Why?

4. What is the difference between industries that have elastic supply and those that have inelastic supply?

5. What is the main factor that affects elasticity of supply and how does it affect elasticity?

6. **Using Your Notes** How is time related to elasticity of supply? Refer to your completed cluster diagram. Use the Graphic Organizer at **Interactive Review @ ClassZone.com**

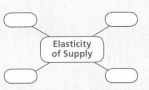

Elasticity of Supply

CRITICAL THINKING

7. **Analyzing Causes** Between 1997 and 2002, many gold producers cut their budgets for exploring for new sources in order to stay profitable when the price of gold was less than $350 per ounce. When the price rose above $400 per ounce in 2004, gold producers were not able to respond quickly to the increase. Use what you know about elasticity of supply to explain this cause-and-effect relationship.

8. **Analyzing Data** In May, Montclair Electronics sold 100 portable DVD players at $150 each. High consumer demand at the start of the summer travel season increased the price to $180. In June, the store sold 115 DVD players at the higher price. Is the supply of DVD players elastic or inelastic? Show your math calculations to support your answer.

9. **Applying Economic Concepts** Analyze the factors that determine elasticity of supply to explain why it is difficult for orange growers to respond quickly to changes in the price of orange juice.

10. **Challenge** Prices are up 8 percent at the local juice shop. Its raw materials are inexpensive and easy to find, and the labor is unskilled. Should the shop be able to raise quantity supplied more than 8 percent? Why?

ECONOMICS IN PRACTICE

Smoothies
bananas $3.75
mangoes
blueberries
raspberries or
strawberries

Calculating Elasticity
The growing market for bottled yogurt smoothies is shown in the supply schedule below. Use the information in the table to determine whether the quantity supplied is growing proportionately more than increases in price. Would you expect supply for yogurt smoothies to be elastic or inelastic over a period of six months?

Price ($)	Quantity Supplied of Smoothies
2.00	600
1.75	450
1.50	300
1.25	200

Create a Supply Curve Use the information in the supply schedule to create a supply curve for yogurt smoothies. What does the slope of this curve indicate about elasticity of supply for yogurt smoothies?

Challenge Adapt the information in the Math Challenge on page 121 to calculate the elasticity of supply using the data in the supply schedule above. Substitute quantity supplied for quantity demanded in the formula.

Use *SMART Grapher* @ ClassZone.com to complete this activity.

Robots—Technology Increases Supply

Background The increasing sophistication of technology continues to have a profound impact on the production and supply of manufactured goods. Robots—machines that can be programmed to perform a variety of tasks—are a prime example of technology's effect on industry.

Today, industrial robots perform a wide variety of functions. Although robots do everything from packaging pharmaceuticals to dispensing genetic material in biotechnical laboratories, half of all industrial robots are used to make automobiles. Robots are ideal for lifting heavy objects and for performing repetitive activities that humans find boring. Lately, though, robots are being used more for tasks that require refined skills.

What's the issue? How does technology increase supply? Study these sources to discover how robots can increase productivity.

A. Online Article

Japan's low birth-rate is likely to result in a shortage of workers. This article discusses how Toyota plans to use robots to solve this problem.

Toyota to Use "Super" Robots

As the Japanese labor pool declines, Toyota turns to robots.

Toyota is deploying at all 12 of its domestic plants robots capable of performing several simultaneous operations. It aims to be the first automaker to introduce robots that, in addition to machine work and engine assembly, perform the finishing touches on the assembly line. . . .

In the automobile industry robots mainly perform relatively dangerous tasks such as welding and coating, while, in order to preserve quality, human workers accomplish such complicated final processes as attaching interior trim.

But Toyota plans to introduce robots to final assembly processes after establishing the necessary control technology and safeguards, and developing parts easily assembled by android [robotic] hands.

Even this super robot will not result in the total replacement of man by machine; rather it will reinforce the strengths of the production line and compensate for manpower shortages in a truly Toyota-style production innovation.

The company plans to use robots to keep production costs at the level of those in China. . . . Toyota presently uses between 3,000 and 4,000 standard robots. It expects a total of 1,000 super robots to join them.

Source: japaninc.net

Thinking Economically Will the use of robots as described in this article affect the supply of Toyota automobiles? Explain your answer.

B. Political
Cartoon

John Morris drew
this cartoon about
the use of robots
in manufacturing.
Parity means
"equality." In the
cartoon, *parity*
refers to equal pay
and benefits.

"The robots have gone on strike - they want parity
with the robots at Ford."

Source: www.CartoonStock.com

Thinking Economically How are the robots in the cartoon
affecting productivity?

**C. Industry
Report**

Epson, a maker of
industrial robots,
presents a case
study involving
the use of robots
in a bakery.

Robots Decorate Cakes

English bakery turns to robots during peak seasons.

Problem: A large English commercial bakery decorates cakes with written messages iced on
the top—a task generally undertaken by skilled staff. . . .

During seasonal holiday periods consumer demand for these decorated cakes increases
fourfold. Training of additional staff to cope with the expanded demand . . . takes a significant period of time and so volume planning is critical.

Solution: System Devices, the EPSON Robots agent for the [United Kingdom], worked with
Integrated Dispensing Systems to design and build a robotic cake decorating cell that . . .
used an EPSON SCARA robot. . . .

Cakes are fed to the EPSON robot via a conveyor. A simple optical positioning system
ensures that the cakes are presented to the robot in a consistent position.

A CAD [computer-aided design] file of the decoration shape is downloaded to the robot.
Because individual cake heights may vary, a laser range finder tells the robot the height of
each cake as it enters the work cell. The robot moves over the top of the cake and writes
the decorative inscription. . . .

Benefits: Ability to boost production during peak seasonal demand periods; consistently
high product quality due to reduced variability on decorations; reduced . . . training costs.

Source: www.robots.epson.com

Thinking Economically In this report, how does the use of robots help the supplier
respond to a seasonal change in demand? Would this robotic solution help a department
store facing a holiday staffing shortage? Why or why not?

THINKING ECONOMICALLY **Synthesizing**

1. Which of the six factors that can cause a change in supply is highlighted in the three
   documents? Does this factor generally increase or decrease supply?

2. Which document, B or C, addresses the issue of elasticity? Explain.

3. In which article, A or C, are the robots an example of variable costs? Why?

Interactive ◄◄ Review

Review this chapter using interactive activities at ClassZone.com

- Online Summary
- Quizzes
- Vocabulary Flip Cards
- Graphic Organizers
- Review and Study Notes

○ ○ ○

🖱 Online Summary

Complete the following activity either on your own paper or online at **ClassZone.com**

Choose the key concept that best completes the sentence. Not all key concepts will be used.

break-even point	marginal product
change in quantity supplied	marginal revenue
change in supply	productivity
diminishing returns	profit-maximizing output
elasticity of supply	supply
fixed cost	supply curve
increasing returns	supply schedule
input costs	total product
law of supply	total revenue
marginal cost	variable cost

__1__ is the quantity of a product that producers are willing and able to offer for sale. According to the __2__, when price increases, quantity supplied increases, and when price decreases, quantity supplied decreases. Quantity supplied can be displayed on a chart called a __3__ or on a graph called a __4__.

__5__ is the change in __6__ caused by hiring one additional worker. When marginal product begins to decrease, production is in the stage of __7__.

Total cost is the sum of __8__ and variable costs. __9__ is the additional cost of producing one more unit. When marginal cost equals __10__, a company has reached __11__.

A __12__ occurs when producers are willing to sell different amounts of a product at every price. The six factors that change supply are input costs, __13__, technology, government action, producer expectations, and number of producers.

The term __14__ describes how responsive producers are to price changes. It is measured by comparing __15__ to change in price.

CHAPTER 5 Assessment

REVIEWING KEY CONCEPTS

What Is Supply? (pp. 130–137)

1. What two requirements of supply must someone meet to be considered a producer?

2. What does it mean to say that quantity supplied and price have a direct relationship?

What Are the Costs of Production? (pp. 138–145)

3. How does marginal product change during the three stages of production?

4. What is the relationship of total costs to profit?

What Factors Affect Supply? (pp. 146–153)

5. What is the difference between change in quantity supplied and change in supply?

6. How do input costs affect supply?

What Is Elasticity of Supply? (pp. 154–159)

7. How are elastic and inelastic supply different?

8. How might you calculate elasticity of supply?

APPLYING ECONOMIC CONCEPTS

Look at the graph below showing price changes for two commodities: crude oil and gasoline.

9. How is the price of gasoline related to the price of crude oil?

10. What factor that affects the supply of gasoline is shown in this graph? How does this factor affect the supply of gasoline?

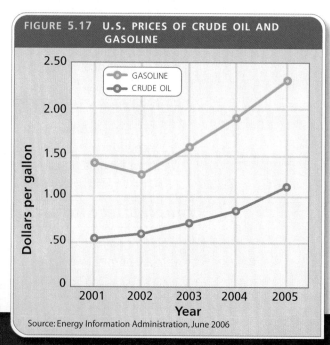

FIGURE 5.17 U.S. PRICES OF CRUDE OIL AND GASOLINE

Source: Energy Information Administration, June 2006

11. Analyzing Data Suppose that you own a factory producing backpacks that sell for $20 each. Use the information in Figure 5.18 to calculate marginal cost, total revenue, and profit at each level of output. Identify the break-even point and profit-maximizing output.

FIGURE 5.18 BACKPACK PRODUCTION COSTS

Production Costs	
Total Product	Total Cost ($)
100	3,500
200	5,300
300	7,000
400	8,000
500	8,800
600	9,800
700	11,800
800	14,300
900	17,000

12. Analyzing Effects A city puts a new rule into effect about the kinds of beverages that may be sold in schools. Sugary sodas must be replaced by bottled water, fruit juices, and sports drinks. How will this decision affect the supply of each category of beverage at the schools? What factor that affects supply is demonstrated in this situation?

13. Drawing Conclusions Both demand and supply for gasoline are inelastic. Would the elasticity of supply and demand be the same for sports cars? Why or why not?

14. Challenge When a string of hurricanes hit Florida, preparation for and cleanup from the storms increased demand for plywood. Yet prices rose only slightly, partly because large chains shipped plywood from stores around the country in anticipation of the increased demand. How does this story illustrate the law of supply and elasticity of supply?

How Much Are You Willing to Supply?

Choose a partner. Imagine that the two of you run a software company. Your best-selling product is a program that helps businesses manage their inventory. Next year you will produce 20,000 units. The following partial supply schedule shows the prices at which you will likely sell your product during that period.

FIGURE 5.19 SOFTWARE SUPPLY SCHEDULE

Price ($)	Quantity Supplied
70	7,500
65	
60	
55	
50	1,000

Step 1 Copy the schedule onto a sheet of paper and fill in the missing amounts in the Quantity Supplied column. Be sure that the amounts you choose adhere to the law of supply.

Step 2 Draw a supply curve to illustrate your schedule. Be sure to label each axis of your curve.

Step 3 Get together with three other groups. These are your competitors. Bring all of your individual supply schedules together to make a market supply schedule. Then convert the market supply schedule into a market supply curve.

Step 4 You and your competitors find out that several other companies are getting ready to introduce similar inventory-control software. On your market supply curve, show how this development causes a shift in supply.

Step 5 Although writing your program was difficult, now that it is written, it is relatively quick and easy to produce copies for sale. Is the supply of your product elastic or inelastic? Why?

Use *SMARTGrapher* @ ClassZone.com to complete this activity.

How are prices set?

Prices greatly influence consumers' buying decisions. A reduced price on this sweater may act as an incentive for these young women to make a purchase.

Demand, Supply, and Prices

CONCEPT REVIEW

Demand is the willingness to buy a good or a service and the ability to pay for it.

Supply is the willingness and ability to produce and sell a product.

CHAPTER 6 KEY CONCEPT

The **equilibrium price** is the price at which quantity demanded and quantity supplied are the same.

WHY THE CONCEPT MATTERS

You've been looking for a vintage concert T-shirt to buy. You see the shirt you want offered on an Internet site, but the price is too high. After exchanging several e-mails, you and the seller set a price. It's higher than you wanted to pay and lower than the seller wanted to receive, but it's acceptable to you both. In a market economy, the forces of demand and supply act in much the same way. They work together to set a price that buyers and sellers find acceptable.

Online Highlights

More at ClassZone.com

 Economics Update

Go to **ECONOMICS UPDATE** for chapter updates and current news on ticketing companies' pricing practices. (See Case Study, pp. 186–187.) ▶

Animated Economics

Go to **ANIMATED ECONOMICS** for interactive lessons on the graphs and tables in this chapter.

Interactive ◀◀Review

Go to **INTERACTIVE REVIEW** for concept review and activities.

Why have some rock bands questioned the pricing practices of certain ticketing companies? See the Case Study on pages 186–187.

Seeking Equilibrium: Demand and Supply

OBJECTIVES	KEY TERMS	TAKING NOTES

OBJECTIVES

In Section 1, you will
- explore market equilibrium and see how it is reached
- explain how demand and supply interact to determine equilibrium price
- analyze what causes surplus, shortage, and disequilibrium
- identify how changes to demand and supply affect the equilibrium price

KEY TERMS

market equilibrium, *p. 164*
equilibrium price, *p. 164*
surplus, *p. 167*
shortage, *p. 167*
disequilibrium, *p. 169*

TAKING NOTES

As you read Section 1, complete a cluster diagram like the one shown using the key concepts and other helpful words and phrases. Use the Graphic Organizer at **Interactive Review @ ClassZone.com**

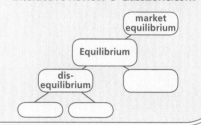

The Interaction of Demand and Supply

KEY CONCEPTS

In Chapters 4 and 5, you learned about how demand and supply work in the market. Recall that a market is any place or situation in which people buy and sell goods and services. Since the market is the place where buyers and sellers come together, it is also the place where demand and supply interact.

As buyers and sellers interact, the market moves toward **market equilibrium**, a situation in which the quantity demanded of a good or service at a particular price is equal to the quantity supplied at that price. **Equilibrium price** is the price at which the quantity of a product demanded by consumers and the quantity supplied by producers are equal.

EXAMPLE Market Demand and Supply Schedule

Let's look at an example of how this concept works in a particular market. Karen runs a sandwich shop near an office park. Recently, she decided to offer a new product at lunchtime—prepared salads. On the first day, she makes up 40 salads and offers them at $10 each. She is disappointed when she sells only 10 and has to throw the rest away. The next day she is more cautious. She lowers

the price to $4 each and makes only 15 salads. She discovers that 35 customers wanted her salads at the lower price. How can Karen find the right price?

Over the course of a week, Karen experiments with different combinations of price and quantity of salads supplied until she discovers market equilibrium at $6 per salad. At that price, she is willing to offer 25 salads for sale, and she sells all of them. When she has either too many or too few salads, she is motivated to change her price. Market equilibrium is the point at which quantity demanded and quantity supplied are in balance.

FIGURE 6.1 KAREN'S MARKET DEMAND AND SUPPLY SCHEDULE

Price per Salad ($)	Quantity Demanded	Quantity Supplied
10	10	40
8	15 →a→	35
6	25 ←b→	25
4	35 ←c←	15
2	40	10

ⓐ At prices above $6, quantity supplied exceeds quantity demanded.

ⓑ At the price of $6, the quantity demanded and the quantity supplied are equal.

ⓒ At prices below $6, the quantity demanded exceeds the quantity supplied.

Only at the **equilibrium price** of $6 are the quantity demanded and the quantity supplied equal.

ANALYZE TABLES

1. What is the difference between quantity supplied and quantity demanded when the price is $10? What is the difference when the price is $2?

2. How does this market demand and supply schedule illustrate the laws of demand and supply?

Animated **Economics**

Use an interactive market demand and supply schedule and curve at **ClassZone.com**

Look at Figure 6.1 to see the information that Karen gathered from her first week selling prepared salads. This table is a combined market demand and supply schedule that shows the quantities of salads supplied and demanded at various prices. Notice that quantity demanded and quantity supplied are different at every line of the schedule except one. That line represents market equilibrium and shows the equilibrium price of $6. When Karen offers salads at prices above $6, she produces more salads than she can sell and has to throw some away. When she offers salads at prices below $6, there is unmet demand because people want more salads than Karen is willing to offer at those prices.

Karen's experience shows how the laws of demand and supply interact in the market. She wants to offer more salads at higher prices than at lower prices because she wants to earn more profit. Her costs would make it impossible to earn much, if any, profit if she were to sell the number of salads that the office workers would like to buy at the lower prices. In a similar way, while the office workers may like the idea of fresh salads for lunch, they are not willing to buy the quantity of salads that Karen wants to sell at higher prices.

Economics Update

Find an update on market equilibrium at **ClassZone.com**

Demand, Supply, and Prices 165

EXAMPLE Market Demand and Supply Curve

Just as it is possible to convert a market demand schedule to a market demand curve or a market supply schedule to a market supply curve, it is possible to graph a combined market demand and supply schedule.

Figure 6.2 portrays Karen's market demand and supply schedule on a combined graph. On the graph, the vertical axis shows the various prices at which salads are offered for sale and bought. The horizontal axis shows the quantity of salads, whether it is the quantity demanded or the quantity supplied. The demand curve (D) is plotted using the prices and the quantities demanded (Figure 6.1, columns 1 and 3). The supply curve (S) is plotted using the prices and the quantities supplied from the combined schedule (Figure 6.1, columns 1 and 2). You can read each individual curve the same way that you did in Chapters 4 and 5, when demand and supply were shown on separate graphs. Each point on the demand curve shows the intersection of price and quantity demanded. Each point on the supply curve shows the intersection of price and quantity supplied.

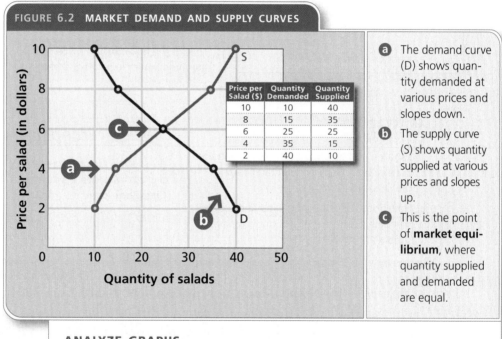

FIGURE 6.2 MARKET DEMAND AND SUPPLY CURVES

Price per Salad ($)	Quantity Demanded	Quantity Supplied
10	10	40
8	15	35
6	25	25
4	35	15
2	40	10

ⓐ The demand curve (D) shows quantity demanded at various prices and slopes down.

ⓑ The supply curve (S) shows quantity supplied at various prices and slopes up.

ⓒ This is the point of **market equilibrium**, where quantity supplied and demanded are equal.

ANALYZE GRAPHS

1. What is the quantity supplied at $8? What is the quantity demanded at $8?

2. How do these market demand and supply curves illustrate the concept of equilibrium price?

Look at Figure 6.2 again and notice that the two curves intersect at only one point; this is the point of market equilibrium. It occurs when quantity demanded and quantity supplied are the same—25 salads at $6. Showing the two curves together allows you to see the interaction of demand and supply graphically.

APPLICATION Applying Economic Concepts

A. Create a combined market demand and supply schedule for pizza at prices of $25, $20, $15, $10, and $5, where $10 is the price at which there is equilibrium.

Reaching the Equilibrium Price

It's clear from the example of Karen's salads that markets don't arrive at equilibrium price instantly; they often require a process of trial and error. The market may experience a **surplus**, which is the result of quantity supplied being greater than quantity demanded, usually because prices are too high. Or a **shortage** may occur, the result of quantity demanded being greater than quantity supplied, usually because prices are too low.

EXAMPLE Surplus, Shortage, and Equilibrium

In Figure 6.3, we can see how Karen's experience demonstrates the concepts of surplus and shortage. It also shows that equilibrium occurs when there is neither a surplus nor a shortage, because quantity demanded and quantity supplied are equal.

> **QUICK REFERENCE**
>
> **Surplus** is the result of quantity supplied being greater than quantity demanded.
>
> **Shortage** is the result of quantity demanded being greater than quantity supplied.

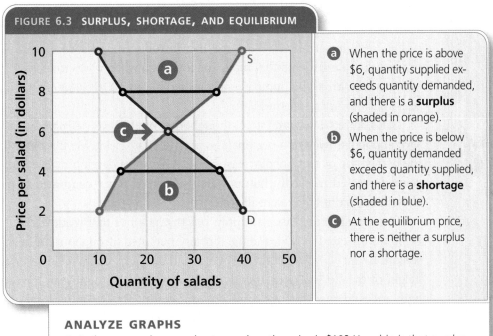

FIGURE 6.3 SURPLUS, SHORTAGE, AND EQUILIBRIUM

a When the price is above $6, quantity supplied exceeds quantity demanded, and there is a **surplus** (shaded in orange).

b When the price is below $6, quantity demanded exceeds quantity supplied, and there is a **shortage** (shaded in blue).

c At the equilibrium price, there is neither a surplus nor a shortage.

ANALYZE GRAPHS

1. Is there a surplus or a shortage when the price is $10? How big is that surplus or shortage? How great is the surplus or shortage when the price is $2?

2. What does this graph illustrate about surplus, shortage, and equilibrium price?

In Figure 6.3, there is a surplus in the area shaded orange. As Karen discovered when she tried to sell salads at prices above $6, she had too many and had to throw some away. The amount of surplus is measured by the horizontal distance between the two curves at each price. For example, at the price of $8, the distance shown by the black line between 15 and 35 shows a surplus of 20 salads.

When there is a surplus, prices tend to fall until the surplus is sold and equilibrium is reached. Producers might also choose to cut back their production to a quantity that is more in line with what consumers demand at the higher prices.

The blue area in Figure 6.3 represents where there is a shortage. When Karen decided to charge less than $6, she had too few salads and lots of unhappy customers who weren't able to get the salads they wanted. As with the surplus, the amount of shortage is measured by the horizontal distance between the two curves at each price. For example, at the price of $4, the distance shown by the black line between 15 and 35 salads shows a shortage of 20 salads.

When there is a shortage, producers raise prices in an attempt to balance quantity supplied and quantity demanded. Producers may also try to increase quantity supplied to meet the quantities demanded at the lower prices.

Holiday Shortages
Consumer tastes often cause spikes in demand for certain items during the holidays.

EXAMPLE Holiday Toys

The concepts of surplus and shortage and the move to equilibrium are active in many markets at different times. Perhaps they are most visible in the market for toys during the holiday shopping season. Toys are often fads, and children's tastes change rapidly. It is difficult for marketers to know how much to supply and at what price to best meet the quantities demanded by consumers. Sometimes they overestimate a toy's popularity and end up with a surplus. If they underestimate popularity, they are faced with a shortage.

In 1996, for example, Tyco Toys Inc. introduced Tickle Me Elmo. The toy included a microchip that made the toy laugh when it was touched. Tyco expected the toy to be popular and ordered about 500,000 for the holiday season. It was priced around $30.

Sales started slowly, and stores thought they might have a surplus. But after several popular television personalities promoted it, Tickle Me Elmo became the hottest toy of that holiday season, and a shortage developed. Even when prices increased markedly, buyers were undeterred. They continued to purchase the toys until they were all gone.

Tyco tried to increase its supply, but the factories that made Tickle Me Elmo were located in Asia, and the shortage persisted throughout the holiday season. By spring, the quantity supplied had doubled. By then, however, the height of the fad was over. Initially, stores tried to sell the toys at the same high prices charged during the holiday season. But consumers were reluctant to buy, and a surplus resulted. Eventually, the market reached equilibrium at a price of about $25.

When you see suppliers reducing prices, it is often because they have a surplus of products to sell. Consider, for example, what happens to the prices of clothing items that are out of season or no longer in fashion. On the other hand, if an item becomes particularly popular or is in short supply for some other reason, suppliers will raise prices. The market does not always reach equilibrium quickly, but it is always moving toward equilibrium.

SMARTGrapher
Create a demand and supply curve at **ClassZone.com**

APPLICATION Applying Economic Concepts

B. Look back at the market demand and supply schedule you created for Application A on p. 166. Use it to create a graph showing the interaction of demand and supply and mark it to show surplus, shortage, and equilibrium.

Equilibrium Price in Real Life

KEY CONCEPTS

In theory, the relationship between demand and supply in the market seems straightforward. The real world, however, is more complex. In earlier chapters, you learned that there are several factors that can cause demand and supply to change. When there is an imbalance between quantity demanded and quantity supplied, a state of **disequilibrium** exists, and the process of finding equilibrium starts over again.

EXAMPLE Change in Demand and Equilibrium Price

Let's take a look at how the market moves from disequilibrium by considering the effect of changes in demand on the equilibrium price for athletic shoes. Recall that a change in demand occurs when one of six factors—income, consumer taste, consumer expectations, market size, substitutes, and complements—prompts consumers to change the quantity demanded at every price.

In Figures 6.4 and 6.5, the intersection of the demand curve (D1) and the supply curves (S) shows an equilibrium price of $75, with quantity demanded and supplied of 3,000 pairs of shoes. When a change in consumer taste causes a decrease in demand for athletic shoes at every price, the demand curve shifts to the left, as shown in Figure 6.4. Notice that this new demand curve (D2) intersects the supply curve at a lower price, around $65. This becomes the new equilibrium price. At this

FIGURES 6.4 AND 6.5 CHANGES IN DEMAND AND EQUILIBRIUM PRICE

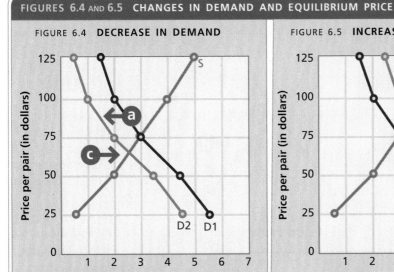

FIGURE 6.4 DECREASE IN DEMAND

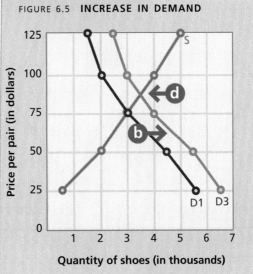

FIGURE 6.5 INCREASE IN DEMAND

a In Figure 6.4, demand decreases; the demand curve shifts left and intersects the supply curve at a lower point.

b In Figure 6.5, demand increases; the demand curve shifts right and intersects the supply curve at a higher point.

c When demand decreases (Fig. 6.4), the equilibrium price falls to about $65.

d When demand increases (Fig. 6.5), the equilibrium price rises to about $90.

ANALYZE GRAPHS

1. What happens to quantity demanded at $100 when demand decreases? What happens to quantity demanded at $100 when demand increases?

2. Does change in demand have a direct or inverse relationship to equilibrium price? Explain your answer.

Animated **Economics**

Use an interactive market demand and supply curve to see changes in demand, supply, and equilibrium price at **ClassZone.com**

new, lower equilibrium price, the quantity demanded decreases to 2,500 pairs of shoes. In other words, when consumers demand fewer goods and services at every price, the equilibrium price will fall and suppliers will sell fewer units—even though the price is lower.

Suppose that an increase in the number of young adults causes demand for athletic shoes to increase. When there is an increase in demand, the demand curve shifts to the right, as shown in Figure 6.5. Notice that the new demand curve (D3) intersects the supply curve at a higher price, around $90. As the equilibrium price increases to this higher level, the quantity demanded also increases to 3,500 pairs of shoes. When consumers demand more goods and services at every price, equilibrium price will rise and suppliers will sell more, even at higher prices.

EXAMPLE Change in Supply and Equilibrium Price

Now let's consider how changes in supply might affect equilibrium price. Recall that a change in supply occurs when something in the market prompts producers to offer different amounts for sale at every price. Remember from Chapter 5 that the six factors that can change supply are input costs, productivity, technology, government action, producer expectations, and number of producers.

In Figures 6.6 and 6.7, the intersection of the supply curve (S1) and the demand curve (D) shows an equilibrium price of $75, with quantity supplied and demanded of 3,000 pairs of shoes. If the price of the raw materials needed to produce athletic shoes increases, the result is a decrease in supply of these shoes at every price.

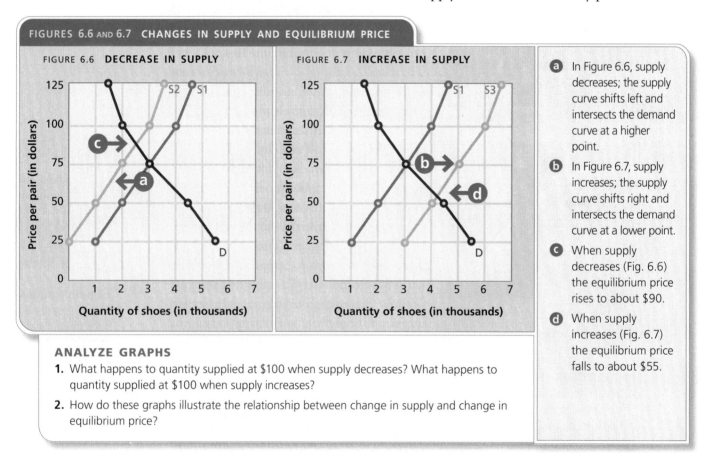

FIGURES 6.6 AND 6.7 CHANGES IN SUPPLY AND EQUILIBRIUM PRICE

FIGURE 6.6 **DECREASE IN SUPPLY**

FIGURE 6.7 **INCREASE IN SUPPLY**

ⓐ In Figure 6.6, supply decreases; the supply curve shifts left and intersects the demand curve at a higher point.

ⓑ In Figure 6.7, supply increases; the supply curve shifts right and intersects the demand curve at a lower point.

ⓒ When supply decreases (Fig. 6.6) the equilibrium price rises to about $90.

ⓓ When supply increases (Fig. 6.7) the equilibrium price falls to about $55.

ANALYZE GRAPHS

1. What happens to quantity supplied at $100 when supply decreases? What happens to quantity supplied at $100 when supply increases?

2. How do these graphs illustrate the relationship between change in supply and change in equilibrium price?

In this situation, the supply curve shifts to the left, as shown in Figure 6.6. Notice that the new supply curve (S2) intersects the demand curve at a higher price, around $90. This is the new equilibrium price. Because of this increase in price, the quantity demanded at equilibrium decreases to 2,500 pairs of shoes. In other words, when there are fewer goods and services available at every price, equilibrium price will rise.

When new technology allows the manufacturer to produce shoes more efficiently, supply increases, and the supply curve shifts to the right, as shown in Figure 6.7. Notice that the new supply curve (S3) intersects the demand curve at a lower price, about

Technology Both supply and equilibrium price are affected when technology improves the manufacturing process.

$55. This is the new equilibrium price. Because of this decrease in price, the quantity demanded at equilibrium increases to about 4,100 pairs of shoes. In other words, when there are more goods and services available at every price, equilibrium price will fall.

Look at Figures 6.4, 6.5, 6.6, and 6.7 once more and notice which situations cause equilibrium price to fall and which cause equilibrium price to rise. The relationships between changes in demand or supply and changes in equilibrium price are illustrated in Figure 6.8. Equilibrium price falls when there is a decrease in demand or an increase in supply. Equilibrium price rises when there is an increase in demand or a decrease in supply. In other words, when consumers want less or producers supply more, prices will fall. When consumers want more or producers supply less, prices will rise.

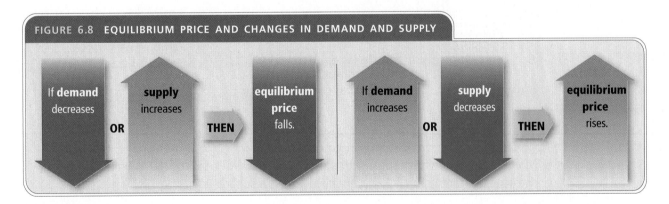

FIGURE 6.8 EQUILIBRIUM PRICE AND CHANGES IN DEMAND AND SUPPLY

If **demand** decreases OR **supply** increases THEN **equilibrium price** falls.

If **demand** increases OR **supply** decreases THEN **equilibrium price** rises.

APPLICATION Analyzing Effects

C. If one of the three pizza parlors in your neighborhood closes, what will happen to the supply of pizza? How will that affect the equilibrium price of pizza?

ECONOMICS SKILLBUILDER

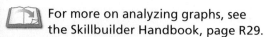 For more on analyzing graphs, see
the Skillbuilder Handbook, page R29.

Interpreting Graphs: Shifting Curves

Graphs show statistical information in a visual manner. A graph that shows a shifting curve should immediately alert the reader to one of the following: a change in quantity demanded at every price, or a change in quantity supplied at every price. In Figure 6.9, a change in the number of producers has caused an increase in supply at every price. The sandwich shop across the street from Forest View High School now has a competitor.

TECHNIQUES FOR ANALYZING SHIFTING CURVES Use the following strategies, along with what you learned throughout Section 1, to analyze the graph.

Use the title to identify the main idea of the graph. If supply has shifted, then we know that quantity supplied at every price has either increased or decreased.

Use the annotations to find key elements of the graph. Annotation **a** shows the equilibrium price where curve S1 meets curve D.

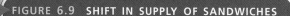

FIGURE 6.9 SHIFT IN SUPPLY OF SANDWICHES

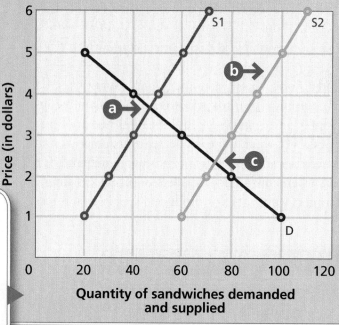

a This is the initial equilibrium price.

b Curve shifts to the right.

c This is the new equilibrium price.

Read the axis labels carefully. When both quantity supplied and demanded are present, look for an intersection to find equilibrium price.

Notice that **b** shows a shift to the right. An increase in supply always shows a rightward shift; a decrease in supply always causes a leftward shift.

Notice the new equilibrium price, **c**. An increase in supply results in a lower equilibrium price.

THINKING ECONOMICALLY Analyzing

1. What are the pre-shift and post-shift equilibrium prices for a sandwich? Will an increase in quantity supplied at every price always result in a lower equilibrium price? Why?

2. Imagine that instead of an increase in supply, there is a decrease in demand. How will the equilibrium price change? Why?

3. On a separate sheet of paper, sketch intersecting quantity supplied and demanded curves with an equilibrium price of $4 at 80 sandwiches. How have the curves shifted from those that appear in Figure 6.9?

REVIEWING KEY CONCEPTS

1. Explain the differences between the terms in each of these pairs:

   a. *market equilibrium*   **b.** *surplus*
      disequilibrium   *shortage*

2. How are surplus and shortage related to equilibrium price?

3. Why is equilibrium price represented by the intersection of the supply and demand curves in a particular market?

4. Why do changes in demand or supply cause disequilibrium?

5. Why is the market always moving toward equilibrium?

6. **Using Your Notes** How is equilibrium price related to market equilibrium? Refer to your completed cluster diagram.

   Use the Graphic Organizer at **Interactive Review @ ClassZone.com**

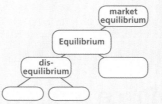

CRITICAL THINKING

7. **Analyzing Data** Look at Figures 6.4, 6.5, 6.6, and 6.7 again. What happens to surplus and shortage as equilibrium price changes in each graph? What general conclusions can you draw from this information?

8. **Analyzing Causes** Suppose that the federal government decides to increase the excise tax on cellular phone services by 0.1 percent. Why will this action cause the equilibrium price of cellular phone services to rise?

9. **Applying Economic Concepts** Between 2003 and 2005, there was huge growth in the market for premium blue jeans priced at $200 or more per pair. The growth was largely fueled by popular magazines showing celebrities wearing certain brands. Then, in the summer of 2005, major department stores started cutting prices on the jeans; they were also found on Web sites that offer jeans at discount prices. Use the economic concepts that you learned in this section to describe what is happening in this market.

10. **Challenge** Study Figures 6.4, 6.5, 6.6, and 6.7 again. What would happen if a change in consumer taste caused an increase in demand for athletic shoes and more suppliers entered the market at the same time? Assume that the increases in demand and in supply are proportionately the same. How would this result be different if each of these changes happened separately?

ECONOMICS IN PRACTICE

Finding Equilibrium Price
Suppose that you are a manufacturer of a new mini refrigerator for college dorm rooms. You expect your product to be popular because of its compact size and high tech design. After a few weeks in the market you are able to develop the following market demand and supply schedule.

Price per Refrigerator ($)	Quantity Demanded	Quantity Supplied
225	500	6,000
200	1,000	4,500
175	1,500	3,500
150	2,500	2,500
125	4,000	1,500

Create a Demand and Supply Curve Use this market demand and supply schedule to create a market demand and supply curve and determine the equilibrium price.

Challenge Calculate surplus or shortage at every price and suggest ways the manufacturer could try to eliminate the surplus and raise the equilibrium price.

Demand, Supply, and Prices **173**

Prices as Signals and Incentives

OBJECTIVES	**KEY TERMS**	**TAKING NOTES**
In Section 2, you will • analyze how the price system works • explain how prices provide information about markets • describe how prices act as incentives to producers	competitive pricing, *p. 174* incentive, *p. 176*	As you read Section 2, complete a chart like the one shown to keep track of how each key concept affects producers and consumers. Use the Graphic Organizer at **Interactive Review @ ClassZone.com**

	Producers	Consumers
Competitive pricing		
Incentive		

How the Price System Works

KEY CONCEPTS

To better understand how price works in the market, let's look at how one kind of change in supply affects the equilibrium price. More producers in a market increases supply, which leads to increased competition and a lower equilibrium price. **Competitive pricing** occurs when producers sell goods and services at prices that best balance the twin desires of making the highest profit and luring customers away from rival producers. By entering a market at a lower price, a new supplier can add to its customer base while it maintains overall profits by selling more units.

EXAMPLE Competitive Pricing

Let's look at an example of competitive pricing. As winter approaches, Elm Street Hardware prices its snow shovels at $20. But Uptown Automotive sees an opportunity to take some customers (mostly for tools, which both stores sell) from Elm Street. Uptown enters the snow shovel market, raising the overall supply. It also prices the shovels at $13. Uptown has a lower profit margin per shovel, but hopes to sell hundreds of them in order to maintain overall profit. Elm Street can choose to lower its prices as well or risk losing customers.

EXAMPLE Characteristics of the Price System

In a market economy, the price system has four characteristics.

1. **It is neutral.** Prices do not favor either the producer or consumer because both make choices that help to determine the equilibrium price. The free interactions of consumers (who favor lower prices) and producers (who favor higher prices) determines the equilibrium price in the market.

2. **It is market driven.** Market forces, not central planning, determine prices, so the system has no oversight or administration costs. In other words, the price system runs itself.

3. **It is flexible.** When market conditions change, prices are able to change quickly in response. Surpluses and shortages motivate producers to change prices to reach equilibrium.

4. **It is efficient.** Prices will adjust until the maximum number of goods and services are sold. Producers choose to use their resources to produce certain goods and services based on the profit they can make by doing so.

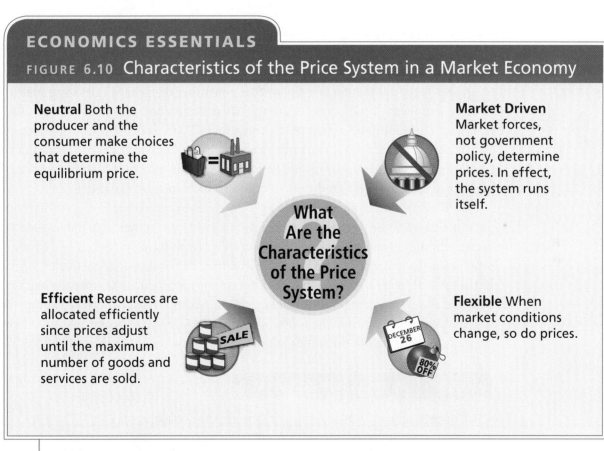

ECONOMICS ESSENTIALS
FIGURE 6.10 Characteristics of the Price System in a Market Economy

Neutral Both the producer and the consumer make choices that determine the equilibrium price.

Market Driven Market forces, not government policy, determine prices. In effect, the system runs itself.

What Are the Characteristics of the Price System?

Efficient Resources are allocated efficiently since prices adjust until the maximum number of goods and services are sold.

Flexible When market conditions change, so do prices.

ANALYZE CHARTS
Choose two of the characteristics of the price system shown in the chart and explain how each is illustrated through the example of competitive pricing.

APPLICATION Analyzing and Interpreting Data

A. If Karen sold 25 salads at $6 each, how many would she need to sell at $5.50 to make at least the same amount of total revenue?

Prices Motivate Producers and Consumers

QUICK REFERENCE

An **incentive** encourages people to act in certain ways.

KEY CONCEPTS

The laws of demand and supply show that consumers and producers have different attitudes toward price. Consumers want to buy at low prices; producers want to sell at high prices. Therefore, prices motivate consumers and producers in different ways. You learned in Chapter 1 that an **incentive** is a way to encourage people to take a certain action. Here, you'll learn that in the price system, incentives encourage producers and consumers to act in certain ways consistent with their best interests.

EXAMPLE Prices and Producers

For producers, the price system has two great advantages: it provides both information and motivation. Prices provide information by acting as signals to producers about whether it is a good time to enter or leave a particular market. Rising prices and the expectation of profits motivate producers to enter a market. Falling prices and the possibility of losses motivate them to leave a market.

A shortage in a market is a signal that consumer demand is not being met by existing suppliers. Recall that a shortage often occurs because prices are too low relative to the quantities demanded by consumers. Producers will view the shortage as a signal that there is an opportunity to raise prices. Higher prices act as an incentive for producers to enter a market. In other words, the prospect of selling goods at higher prices encourages producers to offer products for that market.

As more producers are motivated by high prices to enter a market, quantity supplied increases. When prices are too high relative to consumer demand, a surplus occurs. Producers can respond to a surplus either by reducing prices, or by reducing production to bring it in line with the quantity demanded at a particular price. Either way, falling prices signal that it is a good time for producers to leave the market. Sometimes, less efficient producers leave a market completely, as increased competition and lower prices drive them out of business. More often, producers shift their business to focus on opportunities in markets with higher potential profits.

FIGURE 6.11 CD PRICES AND PRODUCERS

1. Competition from DVDs and video games causes a slump in CD sales–a surplus in CDs.

3. Discount chains begin to sell CDs, often below cost, to attract customers; competitive pricing of CDs.

CD prices decrease

CD prices increase

CD prices decrease

2. Some CD makers switch production to DVDs, video games; fewer CDs are produced–a shortage of CDs.

4. Many small record stores go out of business or devote less shelf space to CDs, more to DVDs and video games.

Competitive pricing in the market often informs the choices made by producers. When a market is growing, and when there is unmet demand, a producer may decide to enter the market with a price that is lower than its competitor's. The new producer can still, however, earn a profit by selling more units at the lower price. So, while prices are the signals that are visible in the market, it is the expectation of profits or the possibility of losses that motivates producers to enter or leave a market.

EXAMPLE Prices and Consumers

Prices also act as signals and incentives for consumers. Surpluses that lead to lower prices tell consumers that it is a good time to buy a particular good or service. Producers often send this signal to consumers through advertising and store displays that draw consumers to certain products. Producers may also suggest that the low prices won't last, encouraging consumers to buy sooner rather than later.

High prices generally discourage consumers from buying a particular product and may signal that it is time for them to switch to a substitute that is available at a lower price. A high price may signal that a particular product is in short supply or has a higher status. Brand marketers rely on the consumer perception that a certain logo is worth a higher price.

Recall what you learned about normal and inferior goods in Chapter 4. Most consumers prefer to buy normal goods at the best possible price. They will buy inferior goods only when they cannot afford something better. While price is a powerful incentive to consumers, the other factors that affect demand also influence consumers' buying habits.

YOUR ECONOMIC CHOICES

PRICES AND CONSUMERS

How Does Price Affect Your Decision?

A new digital video camera with state-of-the-art features costs $500, but you've saved only $250. You can either buy a less expensive substitute with the money you have now, or you can save up to buy the advanced camera later. If other consumers also choose to wait to buy the new camera, a surplus may develop, and the price may decrease.

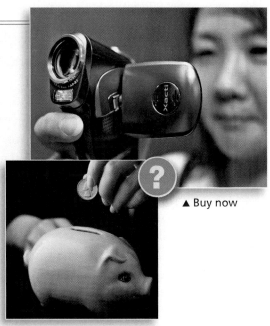
▲ Buy now

▲ Save for later

APPLICATION Making Inferences

> **B.** A cup of gourmet coffee commands a higher price than a regular coffee. How will this fact influence the take-out coffee market?

Michael Dell: Using Price to Beat the Competition

FAST FACTS

Michael S. Dell

Title: Chairman of Dell Inc.

Born: February 23, 1965, Houston, Texas

Major Accomplishment: Pioneered the direct sale of personal computers to consumers

Key Product Lines: Desktop PCs, notebook computers, workstation systems, servers, printers, flat-screen TVs, PDAs

Honors: Youngest CEO of a Fortune 500 company (1992), America's Most Admired Company (2005)

Personal Fortune: $16 billion (2005)

Employees: 65,200 (2006)

High-tech entrepreneur Michael Dell saw an opportunity to use competitive pricing to take business away from much larger companies. By 2005, IBM Corporation, Compaq Computer Corporation, and others had either left the PC market or were facing major problems. How did Dell thrive as its competitors struggled?

Lowering Costs to Reduce Prices

Michael Dell began assembling and selling computers as a freshman in college. He became so successful that he quit college in 1984 to focus on his business. He had sales worth $6 million in his first year.

Dell's success was largely due to his approach to marketing and production. He bypassed computer retailers and sold over the telephone directly to knowledgeable computer users in business and government. Each computer was built to customer requirements and assembled after it was ordered. In this way, Dell lowered his costs significantly and became the low-price leader in the market. The company's sales grew from $69.5 million in 1986 to almost $258 million in 1989.

In Dell's TechKnow program, students learn to assemble and upgrade a computer, which they can then keep.

Dell was also a pioneer in recognizing the potential for sales via the Internet. This strategy allowed the company to maintain close contact with its customers and to adjust its prices frequently, up and down, as market conditions dictated. Competitors who sold only in retail stores found it hard to compete on price because their costs were much higher. By 2005, Dell was the world's leading supplier of PCs, with annual sales of almost $50 billion.

Now Dell is using his experience to make waves in the consumer electronics (flat-panel TVs, MP3 players, and the like) market. He sees the line between these two markets eventually fading. "The whole new ballgame is these worlds [computing and consumer electronics] converging," Dell believes, "and that's a world we're comfortable in."

Economics Update

Find an update on Michael Dell at **ClassZone.com**

APPLICATION Drawing Conclusions

C. What incentive did Michael Dell have to sell computers at lower prices than his competitors?

SECTION 2 Assessment

Online Quiz
ClassZone.com

REVIEWING KEY CONCEPTS

1. Use each of the two terms below in a sentence that illustrates the meaning of the term:

   a. *competitive pricing*   **b.** *incentive*

2. Explain the four characteristics of the price system?

3. Why is the price system an efficient way to allocate resources?

4. How do prices serve as signals and incentives to producers to enter a particular market? to leave a certain market?

5. How does the story of Dell Inc. demonstrate the effects of competitive pricing?

6. **Using Your Notes** How does competitive pricing affect consumers? Refer to your completed chart. Use the Graphic Organizer at **Interactive Review @ ClassZone.com**

	Producers	Consumers
Competitive pricing		
Incentive		

CRITICAL THINKING

7. **Making Inferences** A local supermarket decides to sell a premium brand of meats and cheeses in its deli department. This brand is priced about $2 more per pound than the store brand. About 80 percent of the space in the deli display cases is devoted to the premium brand and 20 percent to the store brand.

   a. How did price serve as an incentive to the supermarket?

   b. What kind of signals is the supermarket sending to its customers with this pricing strategy?

8. **Applying Economic Concepts** A candy company whose products sold in supermarkets for about $3 a bag decided to enter the growing gourmet chocolate market. It purchased two small companies that made premium chocolates that sold for much higher prices. How does this story reveal the way the price system works as an incentive for producers while allocating resources efficiently?

9. **Challenge** A large discount store has built its reputation on offering consumers low prices. However, its customers come from many different income levels. Recently, the store began offering higher priced jewelry and consumer electronics products. What signal might this send to producers of other premium products who have never sold in discount stores before?

ECONOMICS IN PRACTICE

Using Prices as Incentives
As you've learned in Section 2, prices motivate producers to act in certain ways. What actions do producers take in response to rising prices? How about falling prices? Consider each situation that follows. Decide whether the scenario described is associated with rising prices or with falling prices.

- A farmer switches to organic methods when a report says organic foods are healthier.
- To maintain market share, a car wash adjusts its prices to meet a competitor's.
- After a hot, dry spring, a landscaper decides to get out of the business.
- A retailer decides to begin selling this holiday season's must-have toy.

Challenge Which of the above situations descibes a case of competitive pricing? What might happen to the producer if it did not take the action described?

Intervention in the Price System

 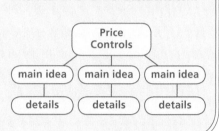
Imposing Price Ceilings

KEY CONCEPTS

You've seen how prices adjust to changes in demand and supply as the market constantly strives for equilibrium. Sometimes, however, people think it is a good idea to interfere with the free market mechanism in order to keep the price of a good or service from going too high. An established maximum price that sellers may charge for a good or service is called a **price ceiling**. The price ceiling is set below the equilibrium price, so a shortage will result.

EXAMPLE Football Tickets and Price Ceilings

Let's look at an example of a price ceiling in ticket prices for college football. The Trenton University Tigers are a winning team with many loyal fans. The university prints 30,000 tickets for every game and sells them for $15 each. At that price, 60,000 fans want to buy the tickets, so there is a shortage of 30,000 tickets for every game.

The university could resolve the shortage by letting the price rise until quantity demanded and quantity supplied are equal. When this solution is proposed, the university president says she would rather keep the tickets affordable for students. Indeed many students get tickets for $15. On game day, however, ticket scalpers stand outside the stadium and sell some tickets for $50 or more.

Rent Control as a Price Ceiling

In the past, many cities passed rent control laws in an effort to keep housing affordable for lower-income families. These laws control when rents can be raised and by how much, no matter what is going on in the market. Of course, the people who live in rent-controlled housing appreciate the lower price in the short term.

But rent control can have unexpected consequences. Without the possibility of raising rents to match the market, there is no incentive to increase the supply of rental housing, and a shortage soon develops. In addition, landlords are reluctant to increase their costs by investing money in property maintenance, so housing conditions often deteriorate. By 2005, rent control was becoming far less common as most cities realized it made housing shortages worse in the long run.

Santa Monica, California, is an example of a city that had strict rent control laws. In the late 1990s, state legislators passed a law that changed the way local communities could regulate rental housing. As a result, property owners in Santa Monica could let the market determine the initial rent when a new tenant moved in, although the city's rent control board still regulated yearly rent increases thereafter. Figure 6.12 illustrates what happened to rents when the new law fully took effect. Rents increased by 40 to 85 percent, showing that the apartments had been priced artificially low. The increases reflect the shortage that rent control had created.

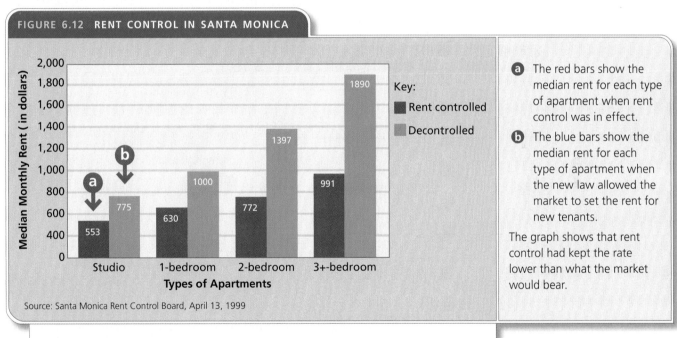

FIGURE 6.12 RENT CONTROL IN SANTA MONICA

Key:
- ■ Rent controlled
- ■ Decontrolled

Median Monthly Rent (in dollars)

Studio: 553 (a), 775
1-bedroom: 630, 1000
2-bedroom: 772, 1397
3+-bedroom: 991, 1890 (b)

Types of Apartments

Source: Santa Monica Rent Control Board, April 13, 1999

a The red bars show the median rent for each type of apartment when rent control was in effect.

b The blue bars show the median rent for each type of apartment when the new law allowed the market to set the rent for new tenants.

The graph shows that rent control had kept the rate lower than what the market would bear.

ANALYZE GRAPHS

1. What happened to the rent for one-bedroom apartments when the new law ended rent control?

2. Who would be more in favor of the changes that happened in the rental market in Santa Monica, landlords or tenants? Why?

APPLICATION **Applying Economic Concepts**

A. Create a demand and supply graph for Trenton University football tickets showing how the price ceiling of $15 is below the equilibrium price.

Demand, Supply, and Prices 181

Setting Price Floors

KEY CONCEPTS

QUICK REFERENCE

A **price floor** is a legal minimum price that buyers must pay for a product.

The **minimum wage** is a legal minimum amount that an employer must pay for one hour of work.

Sometimes the government decides to intervene in the price system to increase income to certain producers. A **price floor** is an established minimum price that buyers must pay for a good or service. For example, the government has used various programs designed to provide price floors under corn, milk, and other agricultural products. The goal of these price floors is to encourage farmers to produce an abundant supply of food.

EXAMPLE Minimum Wage as a Price Floor

Find an update on the minimum wage at **ClassZone.com**

One well-known example of a price floor is a minimum wage. A **minimum wage** is the minimum legal price that an employer may pay a worker for one hour of work. The United States government established its first minimum wage in 1938. The 1930s were a period of low wages, and the government hoped to increase the income of workers. If the minimum wage is set above the equilibrium price for certain jobs in a market, employers may decide that paying the higher wages is not profitable. As a result, they may choose to employ fewer workers, and unemployment will increase. If the minimum wage is set below the equilibrium price, then it will have no effect.

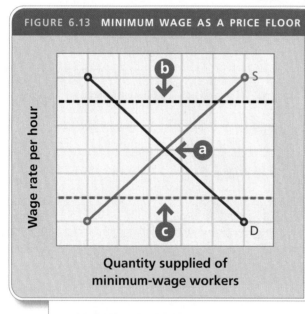

FIGURE 6.13 MINIMUM WAGE AS A PRICE FLOOR

Wage rate per hour

Quantity supplied of minimum-wage workers

a This point shows the equilibrium price for a labor market.

b The black dotted line shows a minimum wage set above the equilibrium price.

c The blue dotted line shows a minimum wage set below the equilibrium price.

The length of black dotted line that falls between the demand curve and the supply curve represents a surplus—in other words, unemployment.

ANALYZE TABLES

1. Assume the minimum wage is set at the dotted black line. What are the costs and benefits of increasing it?

2. Is the minimum wage set at the dotted blue line an effective price floor. Why?

APPLICATION Analyzing Effects

B. Suppose that the Trenton University Tigers were so bad that only 10,000 people want to buy tickets for $15. What effect would keeping $15 as a price floor have?

Rationing Resources and Products

KEY CONCEPTS

The market uses prices to allocate goods and services. Sometimes in periods of national emergency, such as in wartime, the government decides to use another way to distribute scarce products or resources. **Rationing** is a system in which the government allocates goods and services using factors other than price.

The goods might be rationed on a first-come, first-served basis or on the basis of a lottery. Generally, a system is set up that uses coupons allowing each person a certain amount of a particular item. Or the government may decree that certain resources be used to produce certain goods. When such a system is used, some people try to skirt the rules to get the goods and services they want, creating what is known as a black market. In a **black market**, goods and services are illegally bought and sold in violation of price controls or rationing.

QUICK REFERENCE

Rationing is a government system for allocating goods and services using criteria other than price.

The **black market** involves illegal buying or selling in violation of price controls or rationing.

EXAMPLE Rationing Resources

During World War II, the United States government empowered the Office of Price Administration, which was established in 1941, to ration scarce goods. The hope was that these goods would be distributed to everyone, not just those who could afford the higher market prices born of shortages. It also allocated resources in ways that favored the war effort rather than the consumer market. Figure 6.14 shows some of the goods that were rationed. Rationing also led consumers to look for substitutes. Margarine, a butter substitute, was purchased in huge quantities during the war.

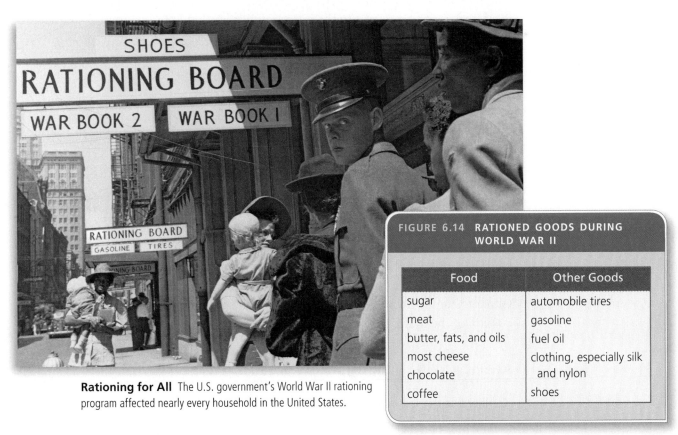

Rationing for All The U.S. government's World War II rationing program affected nearly every household in the United States.

FIGURE 6.14 RATIONED GOODS DURING WORLD WAR II

Food	Other Goods
sugar	automobile tires
meat	gasoline
butter, fats, and oils	fuel oil
most cheese	clothing, especially silk and nylon
chocolate	
coffee	shoes

Rationing in China
Shortages of tofu, a staple of the Chinese diet, led to rationing in 1989.

North Korea maintained a strict rationing system between 1946 and 2002. Most importantly, staple foods—meat, rice, and cabbage—were strictly rationed. However, the system was plagued by inefficiency and corruption. The amount of your ration was generally determined by who you knew, where you lived, and what your occupation was. Government officials in the largest cities often received more than their allotment, while the majority of people got by with less (or received less-nutritious substitutes). Some families had meat or fish only a few times a year.

Between 1996 and 2000, widespread famine in North Korea made the situation desperate. Ration coupons were still distributed, but in most cases, the rations were not. As many as a million people died due to the famine. In response, people established unofficial markets where they traded handicrafts for food. In 2002, the government officially legalized these market activities, and prices rose sharply. Wages also increased. Skeptical of markets, however, the leaders of North Korea were, in 2005, considering a return to the rationing system that failed them in the past.

EXAMPLE Black Markets—An Unplanned Result of Rationing

When rationing is imposed, black markets often come into existence. During World War II, black markets in meat, sugar, and gasoline developed in the United States. Some people found ways, including the use of stolen or counterfeit ration coupons, to secure more of these scarce goods.

During the height of North Korea's rationing system, free trade in grain was expressly forbidden, and most other markets were severely restricted. Prices were very high at the markets that did exist. In 1985, it cost half of the average monthly salary of a typical North Korean to buy a chicken on the black market. Even after the government began allowing some market activities in 2002, the black market flourished because many forms of private property, including homes and cars, were still illegal. Some people started smuggling clothes, televisions, and other goods from China to sell in North Korea. (You'll read more about the black market in the discussion of the underground economy in Chapter 12.)

APPLICATION Making Inferences

C. How does the example of rationing during World War II show that the price system is a more efficient way to allocate resources?

REVIEWING KEY CONCEPTS

1. Explain the relationship between the terms in each of these pairs.

   a. *price floor*
      minimum wage

   b. *rationing*
      black market

2. What is the difference between a price floor and a price ceiling?

3. What kind of surplus might be created by the minimum wage?

4. How does the existence of the black market work against the intended purpose of rationing?

5. Aside from turning to the black market, how do consumers make up for goods that are rationed?

6. **Using Your Notes** What is the usual result of a price ceiling? Refer to your completed diagram. Use the Graphic Organizer at **Interactive Review @ ClassZone.com**

CRITICAL THINKING

7. **Analyzing Causes** Opponents of rent control cite comparisons of cities that regulate rents with cities that do not. Their evidence shows that there is more moderately priced housing available in cities that let the market set the rates for rent. What would account for the differences in availability?

8. **Making Inferences** The percentage of workers who were paid the minimum wage or less decreased from 6.5 percent in 1988 to 3 percent in 2002 to 2.7 percent in 2004. What does this trend tell you about the relationship of the minimum wage to the equilibrium wage for those kinds of work?

9. **Applying Economic Concepts** In the wake of sharply rising gasoline prices in the summer of 2005, several states considered putting a ceiling on the wholesale price of gasoline. What would be the likely result of such a price control? Would it be an effective strategy for lowering gas prices?

10. **Challenge** Many states have laws against so-called price gouging. These laws make it illegal to sell goods and services at levels significantly above established market prices following a natural disaster. What economic argument might be used against such laws?

ECONOMICS IN PRACTICE

Understanding Price Floors

In agriculture, price floors are known as price supports. The government sets a target price for each crop, and if the market price is below that target, it will pay farmers the difference. Suppose that you are a farmer with 400 acres planted in corn. The following graph shows the supply and demand for your crop.

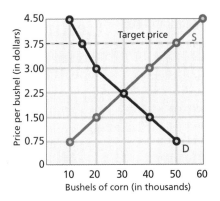

Calculate the Effect of the Price Support How many bushels of corn will you sell at the equilibrium price? How much revenue will you make? How many bushels do you want to sell at the target price? How many bushels are consumers willing to buy at that price? What is the difference? How much will the government have to pay you for that surplus?

Challenge What changes in supply or demand would move the market equilibrium price closer to the target price?

Prices for Concert Tickets

Background Americans spend billions of dollars on concert tickets yearly—an estimated $3 billion in 2005. With ticket prices for the most popular acts averaging more than $50, most younger or less affluent fans can no longer afford to attend many live concerts. And yet, remarkably, forecasters believe that concert ticket prices have yet to peak.

Ticket prices reflect a number of costs. Performers must cover expenses such as travel, costumes, instruments, and equipment before they reap a profit. Venues, or places where concerts are held, also seek to make a profit, as do ticket distributors. However, in the United States, the sale of concert tickets, along with most other goods and services, is driven by three basic elements of a market economy—demand, supply, and pricing.

What's the issue? How do demand, supply, and pricing affect the concert ticket market? Study these sources to discover the factors that affect demand and supply, and their impact on the price of concert tickets.

A. Congressional Transcript

Pearl Jam believed that TicketMaster Corporation, their ticket distributor, was setting too high a price on the band's concert tickets. This statement, submitted to Congress along with oral testimony on June 30, 1994, explains Pearl Jam's stance.

Pearl Jam Tries to Place Ceiling on Ticket Prices

To keep ticket prices affordable, Pearl Jam appeals to Congress.

Many of Pearl Jam's most loyal fans are teenagers who do not have the money to pay the $50 or more that is often charged today for tickets to a popular concert. Although, given our popularity, we could undoubtedly continue to sell out our concerts with ticket prices at that premium level, we have made a conscious decision that we do not want to put the price of our concerts out of the reach of many of our fans. . . .

For these reasons, we have attempted to keep the ticket prices to our concerts to a maximum of $18. . . . Even where a service charge is imposed, our goal is . . . that no one will pay more than $20 to see a Pearl Jam concert.

Our efforts to try to keep prices . . . to this low level and to limit the possibility of excessive service charge mark-ups have put us at odds with TicketMaster . . . a nationwide computerized ticket distribution service that has a virtual monopoly on the distribution of tickets to concerts in this country.

Thinking Economically How would placing a ceiling on the price of Pearl Jam concert tickets have affected demand and supply? Explain your answer based on the information in the document.

FIGURE 6.15 AVERAGE PRICE PER CONCERT TICKET

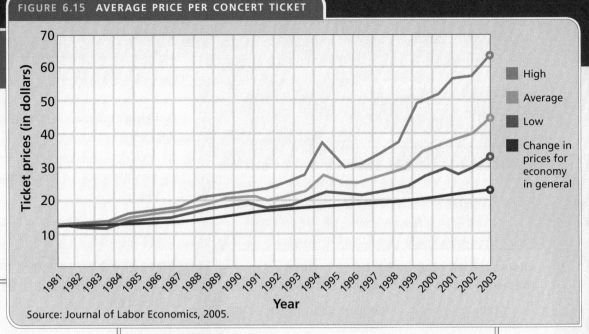

Source: Journal of Labor Economics, 2005.

B. Academic Study

Marie Connolly and Alan Krueger, of Princeton University, compiled these data on concert ticket prices for their study "Rockonomics: The Economics of Popular Music."

Thinking Economically In what three years was the high price per ticket the same as the low price in 2003?

C. Online Newspaper Article

TicketMaster hoped to increase profits by auctioning tickets online. This article discusses the program's potential effect on ticket prices.

TicketMaster Plans to Launch Ticket Auction

The sky's the limit, as bidders compete for the best seats in the house.

Fed up with watching ticket scalpers and brokers rake in the huge bucks for prime seats at their venues, TicketMaster plans to debut an online auction program for choice seats to selected concerts and sports events later this year.

The move may drive up the price of front row seats when they start going to the highest bidder, but some analysts say the impact would likely be minimal. . . .

Princeton University economics professor Alan B. Krueger . . . called the open auction a "positive development."

"For the top artists, tickets are still sold below what the market would bear, even though prices have shot up over the last six years," Krueger told POLLSTAR. "This is especially the case for the best seats in the most expensive cities.

"If the auction is widely used, I suspect price variability will increase; we will see greater dispersion in prices across artists, across cities and seats for the same artist." . . .

Source: **Pollstar.com**

Thinking Economically How might TicketMaster's online auction program lead to market equilibrium for the best tickets?

THINKING ECONOMICALLY   Synthesizing

1. Do you think TicketMaster's plan in document C would help or harm Pearl Jam's wish "that no one will pay more than $20" to see them (document A)? Explain your answer.

2. What do you think happened to quantity supplied of tickets over the span of the graph in document B? Why?

3. In what year in Figure 6.15 did the high price for concert tickets hit $50—the high price that Pearl Jam speaks of in document A? What year was it $20—the desired price they mention?

Demand, Supply, and Prices   187

Online Review

Review this chapter using interactive activities at **ClassZone.com**

- Online Summary
- Quizzes
- Vocabulary Flip Cards
- Graphic Organizers
- Review and Study Notes

○ ○ ○

 Online Summary

Complete the following activity either on your own paper or online at **ClassZone.com**

Choose the key concept that best completes the sentence. Not all key concepts will be used.

black market
competitive pricing
disequilibrium
equilibrium price
incentive
market equilibrium

minimum wage
price ceiling
price floor
rationing
shortage
surplus

__1__ is a situation that occurs when quantity demanded and quantity supplied at a particular price are equal. The price at which that situation occurs is the __2__. If quantity supplied is greater than quantity demanded, a __3__ occurs. If quantity demanded exceeds quantity supplied, then a __4__ occurs.

When a producer enters a market at a lower price (hoping to increase its customer base while maintaining profits by selling more units), it is engaging in __5__. Rising prices are __6__ that draws producers into markets.

Sometimes government intervenes in the price system. A __7__ is the legal maximum that producers may charge for certain goods or services. A __8__ is the legal minimum amount that may be paid for a particular good or service.

When certain goods or resources are scarce, the government may institute a system of __9__, using some criteria besides price to allocate resources. An unplanned consequence of this action by the government is the development of a __10__, where goods are bought and sold illegally.

CHAPTER **6 Assessment**

REVIEWING KEY CONCEPTS

Seeking Equilibrium: Demand and Supply (pp. 164–173)

1. How does the concept of market equilibrium reflect the interaction of producers and consumers in a market?

2. Why are surpluses and shortages examples of disequilibrium?

Prices as Signals and Incentives (pp. 174–179)

3. How are producers and consumers equally involved in the price system?

4. When do prices serve as signals and incentives for producers to enter a market?

Intervention in the Price System (pp. 180–187)

5. What is the usual result of a price floor?

6. What motivates producers and consumers in the black market?

APPLYING ECONOMIC CONCEPTS

Look at the table below showing prices and sales figures for VCRs between 1998 and 2003.

7. Why did dollar sales increase between 1998 and 1999?

8. What is the trend in the average unit price of VCRs between 1998 and 2003? What does this trend signal?

FIGURE 6.16	VCR SALES TO DEALERS		
	Unit Sales (in thousands)	Sales (in millions $)	Average Unit Price ($)
1998	18,113	2,049	133
1999	22,809	2,333	102
2000	23,072	1,869	81
2001	14,910	1,058	71
2002	13,538	826	61
2003*	11,916	727	61

* projected

Source: *Consumer Electronics Association Market Research, January, 2003*

9. **Creating Graphs** Suppose that you are the owner of a toy store. Create demand and supply curves for three products that you expect will sell well during the upcoming holiday shopping season. Then consider the following scenarios: one product becomes much more popular than you expected, one is much less popular than you expected, and the third loses half of its production capacity when a factory is leveled by an earthquake. Draw an additional curve on each of your graphs to show the change in demand or supply represented by these scenarios. Under each graph write a caption explaining the change shown and the effect on the equilibrium price.

Use *SMARTGrapher* @ ClassZone.com to complete this activity.

10. **Analyzing Effects** Consumer concerns about nutrition and obesity contribute to a decrease in white bread sales and an increase in sales of whole wheat bread. This change in consumer taste prompts a major manufacturer known for its white bread to enter the market with a whole wheat bread product. What effect will this action have on the supply and equilibrium price of whole wheat bread?

11. **Using Economic Concepts** In 2004, the price of U.S. butter imports increased by more than 30 percent compared to the previous year. In 2003, Canada and New Zealand together supplied more than 80 percent of the butter imported into the United States. In 2004, their combined market share decreased to about 67 percent. What happened in the market to cause this change? How did price serve as a signal and incentive to producers?

12. **Analyzing Effects** How would U.S. government price supports for U.S.-made tennis rackets affect producers and consumers?

13. **Challenge** How would elasticity of demand help producers decide whether competitive pricing is a good strategy for their businesses?

Find the Best Price

Step 1 Form a group with five other students. Imagine that together you are the market for jeans. Three are buyers and three are sellers, according to Figure 6.17 below. Your goal is to bargain with one another for a pair of jeans. Buyers try to get the lowest price possible, without going above their maximum, and sellers try to get the highest price possible, without going below their minimum.

FIGURE 6.17 SIX-PERSON JEANS MARKET

		Price ($)	
Buyers	A	20	**Maximum** price you are willing to pay for a pair of jeans
	B	30	
	C	40	
Sellers	D	15	**Minimum** price you are willing to sell a pair of jeans for
	E	25	
	F	35	

Step 2 Choose a letter to determine your role. On a piece of paper write your letter and name, identify yourself as a buyer or seller, and show the dollar amount from Figure 6.17.

Step 3 Keep track of each proposed transaction in order on a sheet of paper. Recall what you know about demand, supply, and competitive pricing as you bargain to see who will buy and sell jeans and at what price. Bargaining ends when you reach equilibrium. What is quantity and price at equilibrium?

Step 4 Use the information on the chart to create a demand and supply curve for this market. Does the curve reflect your group's bargaining experience?

Step 5 As a class, discuss what you learned from this exercise about how markets reach equilibrium.

Use *SMARTGrapher* @ ClassZone.com to complete this activity.

Market Structures

In markets where businesses offer similar products, sellers compete by trying to make their products stand out from the competition.

190

Market Structures

CONCEPT REVIEW

Competition involves all the actions that sellers, acting independently, take to get buyers to purchase their products.

CHAPTER 7 KEY CONCEPT

A **market structure** is an economic model that helps economists examine the nature and degree of competition among businesses in the same industry.

WHY THE CONCEPT MATTERS

On trips to the mall, you've probably noticed something about the prices of products you're looking to buy. If there are several different brands of the same kind of product, prices tend to be lower. If there's just one brand, however, prices tend to be higher. The level of competition in a market has a major impact on the prices of products. The more sellers compete for your dollars, the more competitive prices will be.

Online Highlights

More at ClassZone.com

 Economics Update
Go to **ECONOMICS UPDATE** for chapter updates and current news on competition in the cellular telephone industry. (See Case Study, pp. 220–221.) ▶

SMART Grapher
Go to **SMART GRAPHER** to complete graphing activities in this chapter.

Interactive ◀◀ Review
Go to **INTERACTIVE REVIEW** for concept review and activities.

How do cellular phone makers compete for your business? See the Case Study on pages 220–221.

What Is Perfect Competition?

OBJECTIVES	KEY TERMS	TAKING NOTES
In Section 1, you will • learn that perfect competition is the ideal by which economists measure all market structures • explain the characteristics of perfect competition and why it does not exist in the real world • analyze examples of markets that come close to perfect competition	market structure, *p. 192* perfect competition, *p. 192* standardized product, *p. 192* price taker, *p. 193* imperfect competition, *p. 195*	As you read Section 1, complete a cluster diagram to identify the major characteristics of perfect competition. Use the Graphic Organizer at **Interactive Review @ ClassZone.com** 

The Characteristics of Perfect Competition

KEY CONCEPTS

QUICK REFERENCE

A **market structure** is an economic model of competition among businesses in the same industry.

Perfect competition is the ideal model of a market economy.

A **standardized product** is one that consumers see as identical regardless of producer.

When you buy new clothes, you probably shop around for the best deal. But when you buy milk, you know that a gallon will be about the same price no matter where you shop. The market for clothes has a different level of competition than the market for milk. Economists classify markets based on how competitive they are. A **market structure** is an economic model that allows economists to examine competition among businesses in the same industry.

   Perfect competition is the ideal model of a market economy. It is useful as a model, but real markets are never perfect. Economists assess how competitive a market is by determining where it falls short of perfect competition. Perfect competition has five characteristics.

1. **Numerous buyers and sellers.** No one seller or buyer has control over price.

2. **Standardized product.** Sellers offer a **standardized product**—a product that consumers consider identical in all essential features to other products in the same market.

3. **Freedom to enter and exit markets.** Buyers and sellers are free to enter and exit the market. No government regulations or other restrictions prevent a business or customer from participating in the market. Nor is a business or customer required to participate in the market.

4. **Independent buyers and sellers.** Buyers cannot join other buyers and sellers cannot join other sellers to influence prices.

5. **Well-informed buyers and sellers.** Both buyers and sellers are well-informed about market conditions. Buyers can do comparison shopping, and sellers can learn what their competitors are charging.

When these five conditions are met, sellers become price takers. A **price taker** is a business that cannot set the prices for its products but, instead, accepts the market price set by the interaction of supply and demand. Only efficient producers make enough money to serve perfectly competitive markets.

QUICK REFERENCE

A **price taker** is a business that accepts the market price determined by supply and demand.

CHARACTERISTIC 1 Many Buyers and Sellers

A large number of buyers and sellers is necessary for perfect competition so that no one buyer or seller has the power to control the price in the market. When there are many sellers, buyers can choose to buy from a different producer if one tries to raise prices above the market level. But because there are many buyers, sellers are able to sell their products at the market price.

Let's consider the Smith family, whom you met in Chapter 5. The Smiths grow raspberries in the summer to sell at the Montclair Farmers' Market. Because many farmers grow and sell raspberries at the same market, all of the farmers charge about the same price. If one farmer tries to charge more than the market price for raspberries, consumers will buy from the other farmers. Because there are many buyers—in other words, sufficient demand—the Smiths and other producers know that they can sell their product at the market price. Lack of demand will not cause them to lower their prices.

CHARACTERISTIC 2 Standardized Product

In perfect competition, consumers consider one producer's product essentially the same as the product offered by another. The products are perfect substitutes. Agricultural products such as wheat, eggs, and milk, as well as other basic commodities such as notebook paper or gold generally meet this criterion.

Considering the Montclair Farmers' Market, while no two pints of raspberries are exactly alike, they are similar enough that consumers will choose to buy from any producer that offers raspberries at the market price. Price becomes the only basis for a consumer to choose one producer over another.

Perfect Competition
Farmers' markets exhibit many of the characteristics of perfect competition.

CHARACTERISTIC 3 Freedom to Enter and Exit Markets

In a perfectly competitive market, producers are able to enter the market when it is profitable and to exit when it becomes unprofitable. They can do this because the investment that a producer makes to enter a market is relatively low. Market forces alone encourage producers to freely enter or leave a given market.

The Smiths and other farmers consider the market price for raspberries when planning their crops. If they believe they can make a profit at that price, they grow raspberries. If not, they try some other crop.

Economics Update

Find an update about perfect competition at **ClassZone.com**

FIGURE 7.1 Characteristics of Perfect Competition

Many Buyers and Sellers A large number of buyers and sellers ensures that no one controls prices.

Standardized Products All products are essentially the same.

What Are the Characteristics of Perfect Competition?

Well-informed Buyers and Sellers Both buyers and sellers know the market prices and other conditions.

Freedom to Enter and Exit Markets Producers can enter or exit the market with no interference.

Independent Buyers and Sellers Buyers and sellers do not band together to influence prices.

ANALYZE CHARTS
Imagine that you own a farm and that you have decided to sell raspberries at the Montclair Farmers' Market. Construct your own diagram to show how the five characteristics of perfect competition will apply to your enterprise.

CHARACTERISTIC 4 Independent Buyers and Sellers

In a perfectly competitive market, neither buyers nor sellers join together to influence price. When buyers and sellers act independently, the interaction of supply and demand sets the equilibrium price. Independent action ensures that the market will remain competitive. At the Montclair Farmers' Market, the farmers do not band together to raise prices, nor do the consumers organize to negotiate lower prices.

CHARACTERISTIC 5 Well-informed Buyers and Sellers

Buyers and sellers in a perfectly competitive market have enough information to make good deals. Buyers can compare prices among different sellers, and sellers know what their competitors are charging and what price consumers are willing to pay. Buyers and sellers at the Montclair Farmers' Market make informed choices about whether to buy or sell raspberries in that market. With all five characteristics met, the Smiths accept the market price for raspberries. All raspberry producers become price takers.

APPLICATION Making Inferences

A. Can you think of another market that comes close to perfect competition? Which of the characteristics does it lack?

Competition in the Real World

In the real world, there are no perfectly competitive markets because real markets do not have all of the characteristics of perfect competition. Market structures that lack one of the conditions needed for perfect competition are examples of **imperfect competition**. (You'll learn more about imperfect competition in Sections 2 and 3.) However, there are some markets—the wholesale markets for farm products such as corn and beef, for example—that come close to perfect competition.

QUICK REFERENCE

Imperfect competition occurs in markets that have few sellers or products that are not standardized.

EXAMPLE 1 Corn

In the United States, there are thousands of farmers who grow corn, and each one contributes only a small percentage of the total crop. Therefore, no one farmer can control the price of corn, and all farmers accept the market price. Individual farmers decide only how much corn to produce to offer for sale at that price. At the same time, there are a large number of buyers, and the price on the wholesale market is easy to determine. Corn is a fairly standardized product, and buyers usually have no reason to prefer one farmer's corn to another's. Buyers will not pay more than the market price.

In reality, there are several reasons that imperfect competition occurs in the corn market. For one thing, the U.S. government pays subsidies to corn farmers to protect them from low corn prices. In addition, sometimes corn farmers band together to try to influence the price of corn in their favor, and corn buyers sometimes pursue the same strategy. Subsidies, group action, and other deviations from perfect competition interfere with the market forces of supply and demand.

Close to Perfect Competition
Wholesale markets for agricultural products, such as corn, come close to perfect competition.

EXAMPLE 2 Beef

The wholesale market for raw beef is another that comes close to perfect competition. There are many cattle producers, and there is little variation in a particular cut of beef from one producer to the next. Because the beef is so similar, the wholesale buyer's primary concern will be price. Both buyers and sellers can easily determine the market price, and producers sell all their beef at that price. Cattle sellers can adjust only their production to reflect the market price.

As in the corn market, there are several reasons that imperfect competition occurs in the beef market. Cattle ranchers, like corn farmers, may try to join together to influence the price of beef in their favor. In addition, many beef producers try to persuade buyers that there are significant differences in their products that warrant higher prices. For example, cattle that eat corn supposedly produce better tasting beef.

APPLICATION Drawing Conclusions

B. Why is the market for corn closer to perfect competition than the market for corn flakes?

ECONOMICS SKILLBUILDER

For more information on creating and interpreting economic models, see the Skillbuilder Handbook, page R16.

Creating and Interpreting Economic Models

Economic models help solve problems by focusing on a limited set of variables. A production costs and revenue schedule, which you learned about in Chapter 5, is a model that helps businesses decide how much to produce. Creating a graph as part of the model paints a picture of the data that makes it easier to understand.

In this example, imagine you own a business that produces baseballs in a perfectly competitive market. The market price of a baseball is $1, but your costs vary depending on how many you produce. Follow the instructions to create a graph that will help you visualize the way a perfectly competitive market works.

CREATING AN ECONOMIC MODEL OF BASEBALL PRODUCTION

1. Copy the graph below onto your own paper, or use *SMARTGrapher* @ ClassZone.com.

2. Using data from the table below, plot the curve showing the marginal costs of producing different numbers of baseballs. Label the curve "MC."

3. Using data from the table below, plot the curve showing the marginal revenue of producing different numbers of baseballs. Label the curve "MR."

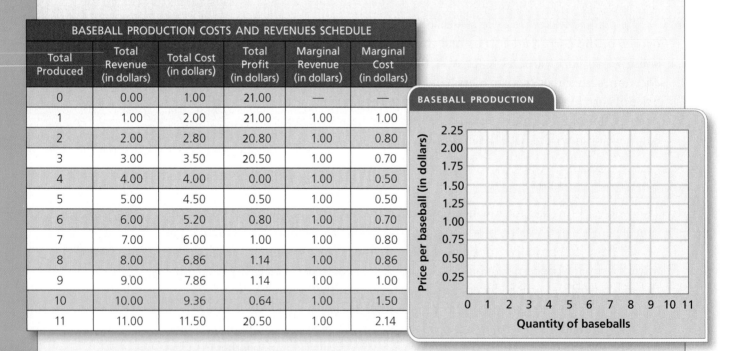

BASEBALL PRODUCTION COSTS AND REVENUES SCHEDULE					
Total Produced	Total Revenue (in dollars)	Total Cost (in dollars)	Total Profit (in dollars)	Marginal Revenue (in dollars)	Marginal Cost (in dollars)
0	0.00	1.00	21.00	—	—
1	1.00	2.00	21.00	1.00	1.00
2	2.00	2.80	20.80	1.00	0.80
3	3.00	3.50	20.50	1.00	0.70
4	4.00	4.00	0.00	1.00	0.50
5	5.00	4.50	0.50	1.00	0.50
6	6.00	5.20	0.80	1.00	0.70
7	7.00	6.00	1.00	1.00	0.80
8	8.00	6.86	1.14	1.00	0.86
9	9.00	7.86	1.14	1.00	1.00
10	10.00	9.36	0.64	1.00	1.50
11	11.00	11.50	20.50	1.00	2.14

BASEBALL PRODUCTION

THINKING ECONOMICALLY Analyzing

1. How many baseballs should you produce each day to maximize profits?

2. Using the same graph, plot the demand curve for this perfectly competitive market. Remember that the market price will not change no matter how many baseballs are demanded.

3. How does the graph help explain the term "price takers"?

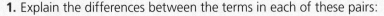

SECTION 1 Assessment

Online Quiz ClassZone.com

REVIEWING KEY CONCEPTS

1. Explain the differences between the terms in each of these pairs:

   a. *market*
   market structure

   b. *perfect competition*
   imperfect competition

2. Why are sellers in a perfectly competitive market known as *price takers*?

3. Why is it necessary to have standardized products in order to have perfect competition?

4. Why is independent action of buyers and sellers important to achieving perfect competition?

5. How is imperfect competition different from perfect competition?

6. **Using Your Notes** What are the five characteristics of perfect competition? Refer to your completed cluster diagram.

   Use the Graphic Organizer at **Interactive Review @ ClassZone.com**

Perfect Competition

CRITICAL THINKING

7. **Drawing Conclusions** Suppose that you went to a farmers' market and found several different farmers selling cucumbers. Would you be likely to find a wide range of prices for cucumbers? Why or why not?

8. **Analyzing Effects** What would happen to a wheat farmer who tried to sell his wheat for $2.50 per bushel if the market price were $2.00 per bushel? Why?

9. **Making Inferences** Why are brand-name products not found in a perfectly competitive market? You will learn more about this topic in Section 3 of this chapter.

10. **Challenge** At an auction, sellers show their goods before an audience of buyers. The goods for sale may be similar to each other, as in an auction of used cars, or they may be one-of-a-kind, as in an art auction. Buyers usually have an opportunity to inspect items prior to the auction. During the auction, buyers bid against one another to see who is willing to pay the highest price. In what ways is an auction similar to a perfectly competitive market? In what ways is it different?

ECONOMICS IN PRACTICE

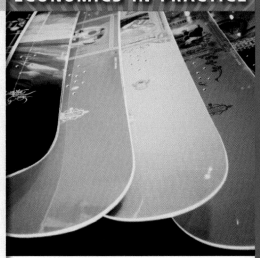

How competitive is the market for snowboards?

Identifying Perfect Competition

Perfectly competitive markets can be identified by specific characteristics. The chart below lists these characteristics.

Characteristics of Perfect Competition	Markets				
	Applesauce	Snowboards	Hairbrushes	Computer games	Paper clips
Many buyers and sellers					
Standardized product					
Freedom to enter and leave the market					
Independent action					
Well-informed buyers and sellers					

Complete a Chart Five different markets are shown in the chart. On your own paper, complete the chart by marking which of the characteristics each market has.

Challenge Choose one market from the chart and explain what would need to be done to make it perfectly competitive.

The Impact of Monopoly

OBJECTIVES	KEY TERMS	TAKING NOTES
In Section 2, you will • describe the characteristics of a monopoly • analyze four different types of monopolies and discuss how they come about • explain how a monopoly sets its prices and production goals	monopoly, *p. 198* cartel, *p. 198* price maker, *p. 198* barrier to entry, *p. 198* natural monopoly, *p. 201* government monopoly, *p. 201* technological monopoly, *p. 201* geographic monopoly, *p. 201* economies of scale, *p. 201* patent, *p. 202*	As you read Section 2, complete a chart to show how different types of monopolies exhibit the characteristics of monopoly. Use the Graphic Organizer at **Interactive Review @ ClassZone.com**

	One Seller	Restricted Market	Control of Prices
Natural Monopoly			
Government Monopoly			
Technical Monopoly			
Geographic Monopoly			

Characteristics of a Monopoly

KEY CONCEPTS

QUICK REFERENCE

Monopoly occurs when there is only one seller of a product that has no close substitutes.

A **cartel** is a group that acts together to set prices and limit output.

A **price maker** is a firm that does not have to consider competitors when setting the prices of its products.

A **barrier to entry** makes it hard for a new business to enter a market.

Perfect competition is the most competitive market structure. The least competitive is **monopoly**, a market structure in which only one seller sells a product for which there are no close substitutes. The term *monopoly* may be used for either the market structure or the monopolistic business. Pure monopolies are as rare as perfect competition, but some businesses come close. For example, a **cartel** is a formal organization of sellers or producers that agree to act together to set prices and limit output. In this way, a cartel may function as a monopoly.

Because a monopoly is the only seller of a product with no close substitutes, it becomes a **price maker**, a business that does not have to consider competitors when setting its prices. Consumers either accept the seller's price or choose not to buy the product. Other firms may want to enter the market, but they often face a **barrier to entry**—something that hinders a business from entering a market. Large size, government regulations, or special resources or technology are all barriers to entry.

Let's take a closer look at the three characteristics of monopoly through the De Beers cartel, which held a virtual monopoly on the diamond market for most of the 20th century. At one time it controlled as much as 80 percent of the market in uncut diamonds. De Beers used its monopoly power to control the price of diamonds and created barriers to entry that kept other firms from competing.

FIGURE 7.2 Characteristics of a Monopoly

What Are the Characteristics of a Monopoly?

Only One Seller
A single business controls the supply of a product that has no close substitutes.

Control of Prices
Monopolies act as price makers because they sell products that have no close substitutes and they face no competition.

Restricted, Regulated Market
Government regulations or other barriers to entry keep other firms out of the market.

ANALYZE CHARTS
Imagine that you are a business person with unlimited funds. Could you gain a monopoly over the market for housing in your neighborhood? Using the chart, explain the steps you would need to take. How might your neighborhood change if one person controlled property prices?

CHARACTERISTIC 1 Only One Seller

In a monopoly, a single business is identified with the industry because it controls the supply of a product that has no close substitutes. For example, De Beers once produced more than half of the world's diamond supply and bought up diamonds from smaller producers to resell. In this way, it controlled the market.

CHARACTERISTIC 2 A Restricted, Regulated Market

In some cases, government regulations allow a single firm to control a market, such as a local electric utility. In the case of De Beers, the company worked with the South African government to ensure that any new diamond mines were required to sell their diamonds through De Beers. The company also restricted access to the market for raw diamonds for producers outside of South Africa. By controlling the supply of diamonds, De Beers made it difficult for other producers to make a profit.

CHARACTERISTIC 3 Control of Prices

Monopolists can control prices because there are no close substitutes for their product and they have no competition. When economic downturns reduced demand for diamonds, De Beers created artificial shortages by withholding diamonds from the market. The reduced supply allowed the cartel to continue charging a higher price.

APPLICATION Analyzing Effects

A. What effect did the De Beers diamond monopoly have on the price of diamonds?

OPEC: Controlling the Oil Pipelines

The Organization of the Petroleum Exporting Countries (OPEC) does not have a monopoly on oil reserves or oil production. However, the 11 member nations of the cartel possess more than two-thirds of the world's oil reserves and produce about two-fifths of the world's oil supply. By regulating the amount of oil that flows through its pipelines, OPEC exerts control over the market price for oil.

   Market forces often counteract OPEC's supply adjustments. For example, in the early 1980s demand for oil fell as consumers and businesses implemented strategies to reduce energy use. Despite OPEC's efforts to reduce supply and stabilize the price, crude oil prices fell through most of the 1980s. Another factor that limits OPEC's control over oil prices is member unity. Members sometimes choose not to follow OPEC moves to reduce oil output—because that would reduce their revenues. Despite these limitations, OPEC continues to play a major role in the world market for petroleum.

FIGURE 7.3 OPEC MEMBERS

Country	Joined OPEC	Location
Algeria	1969	Africa
Indonesia	1962	Asia
Iran	1960	Middle East
Iraq	1960	Middle East
Kuwait	1960	Middle East
Libya	1962	Africa
Nigeria	1971	Africa
Qatar	1961	Middle East
Saudi Arabia	1960	Middle East
United Arab Emirates	1967	Middle East
Venezuela	1960	South America

Source: OPEC

FIGURE 7.4 OPEC Member Nations

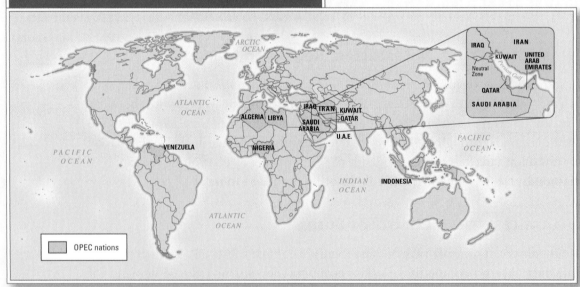

OPEC nations

CONNECTING ACROSS THE GLOBE

1. **Applying Economic Concepts** In what ways does OPEC act like a monopoly?

2. **Making Inferences** What will happen to OPEC's monopolistic power as the world discovers new sources of energy? Explain your answer.

Types of Monopolies

KEY CONCEPTS

There are several reasons why monopolies exist, and not all monopolies are harmful to consumers. A **natural monopoly** is a market situation in which the costs of production are lowest when only one firm provides output. A **government monopoly** is a monopoly that exists because the government either owns and runs the business or authorizes only one producer. A **technological monopoly** is a monopoly that exists because the firm controls a manufacturing method, an invention, or a type of technology. A **geographic monopoly** is a monopoly that exists because there are no other producers or sellers within a certain region.

EXAMPLE 1 Natural Monopoly: A Water Company

In some markets, it would be inefficient to have more than one company competing for consumers' business. Most public utilities fall into this category. Let's look at the water company in your community as an example. It pumps the water from its source through a complex network of pipes to all the homes, businesses, and public facilities in the community. It also monitors water quality for safety and removes and treats wastewater so that it may be recycled.

It would be a waste of community resources to have several companies developing separate, complex systems in order to compete for business. A single supplier is most efficient due to **economies of scale**, a situation in which the average cost of production falls as the producer grows larger. The more customers the water company serves, the more efficient its operation becomes, as its high fixed costs are spread out over a large number of buyers. These economies of scale result in government support for natural monopolies. While supporting natural monopolies, the government also regulates them to ensure that they do not charge excessively high prices for their services.

Natural Monopolies
Most public utilities require complex systems, such as this water treatment facility.

EXAMPLE 2 Government Monopoly: The Postal Service

Government-run businesses provide goods and services that either could not be provided by private firms or that are not attractive to them because of insufficient profit opportunities. One of the oldest government monopolies in the United States is the U.S. Postal Service, which has the exclusive right to deliver first-class mail. Originally, only the government could provide this service in an efficient and cost-effective manner. However, new services and new technologies have been chipping away at this monopoly. Private delivery companies offer services that compete with the U.S. Postal Service. Many people now send information by fax, e-mail, and text messages. In addition, many pay their bills online.

QUICK REFERENCE

A **natural monopoly** occurs when the costs of production are lowest with only one producer.

A **government monopoly** exists when the government either owns and runs the business or authorizes only one producer.

A **technological monopoly** occurs when a firm controls a manufacturing method, invention, or type of technology.

A **geographic monopoly** exists when there are no other producers within a certain region.

Economies of scale occur when the average cost of production falls as the producer grows larger.

▲ E-mail message

▲ Handwritten note

EXAMPLE 3 Technological Monopoly: Polaroid

In 1947, Edwin Land, the founder of the Polaroid Corporation, invented the first instant camera. Land's camera used a special type of film that allowed each picture to develop automatically in about a minute. Through a series of patents, Polaroid created a monopoly in the instant photography market.

A **patent** is a legal registration of an invention or a process that gives the inventor the exclusive property rights to that invention or process for a certain number of years. The government supports technological monopolies through the issuing of patents. Through patents, businesses are able to recover the costs that were involved in developing the invention or technology.

Polaroid's control of instant photography technology through its patents was a barrier to entry for other firms. In 1985, Polaroid won a lawsuit against Eastman Kodak Company for patent infringement. The court ruled that Kodak's instant camera and film had violated Polaroid's property rights, which were protected by several patents. The lawsuit effectively blocked Kodak from the instant photography market.

Technological monopolies last only as long as the patent—generally 20 years—or until a new technology creates close substitutes. The rise of easier-to-use 35mm cameras, one-hour photo processing, and digital cameras all contributed to a steep decline in Polaroid's business. While the company remains the leading seller of instant cameras and film, the technology has become a minor segment of the consumer photography market.

Technological Monopoly Polaroid instant cameras use patented technology.

EXAMPLE 4 Geographic Monopoly: Professional Sports

One type of geographic monopoly in the United States is the professional sports team. The major sports leagues require that teams be associated with a city or region and limit the number of teams in each league. In other words, the leagues create a restricted market for professional sports. Most cities and towns are not directly represented by a team, so many teams draw their fans from a large surrounding geographic region. Because of their geographic monopolies, the owners of these teams are able to charge higher prices for tickets to games than if they faced competition. They also have a ready market for sports apparel and other merchandise featuring the team logo and colors.

Another type of geographic monopoly is created by physical isolation. For example, Joe operates the only gas station at an

Geographic Monopolies The Boston Red Sox is the only baseball team in New England, so it draws fans from across the six-state region.

interstate exit in the middle of a desert. The next station in either direction is more than 50 miles away. Joe has a geographic monopoly because he is the only supplier of a product with no close substitutes. Drivers on the interstate in that area depend on Joe's gas and have no other choice of supplier. They can either buy gas from Joe or risk running out of gas before they reach the next station. Because of his geographic location as the single supplier of a product that has no close substitutes, Joe is able to control the price that he charges—and gas at Joe's is always very expensive.

Isolated locations or small communities may have other examples of geographic monopolies if the market is too small to support two similar businesses. Geographic monopolies have become less common in the United States. Cars allow people to travel greater distances to shop, and catalog marketers and Internet businesses, combined with efficient delivery companies, offer consumers more alternatives to shopping at local stores.

> **Economics Update**
>
> Find an update on monopolies at **ClassZone.com**

APPLICATION Drawing Conclusions

B. Which type of monopoly do you think is least harmful to consumers? Why?

Profit Maximization by Monopolies

Although a monopoly firm is the only supplier in its market, the firm cannot charge any price it wishes. A monopolist still faces a downward-sloping demand curve. In other words, the monopoly will sell more at lower prices than at higher prices. The monopolist controls price by controlling supply. A monopoly produces less of a product than would be supplied in a competitive market, thereby artificially raising the equilibrium price.

It's difficult to study this process in the real world because most countries have laws to prevent monopolies. We have to look at small instances in which a company has a monopoly over one particular specialized product. Such a limited monopoly lasts only for the life of the patent or until a competitor develops a similar product.

EXAMPLE Drug Manufacturer

Pharmaceutical manufacturers offer an example of how companies with limited monopolies try to maximize their profits. On average, drug patents last for about 11 years in the United States. Drug companies try to maximize their profits during that period because when the patent expires they face competition from other manu-

facturers who begin marketing generic versions of the drug. A generic drug contains the same ingredients and acts in the same way as the patented drug, but it is sold at much lower prices.

As an example, consider the Schering-Plough company and its antihistamine Claritin. The drug was originally approved for use as a prescription medication in the United States in 1993, although it had been patented earlier. Unlike many other such

"NOW HERE'S MY IDEA... WE COME UP WITH A REALLY HIGH-PRICED DRUG to TREAT DRUG SIDE EFFECTS..."

drugs, Claritin did not make users drowsy. This advantage, combined with a strong marketing campaign, led Claritin to become a top seller, making as much as $3 billion in annual worldwide sales.

When the patent on Claritin expired in 2002, numerous generic equivalents entered the market. In response, Schering-Plough lowered Claritin's price and gained approval for a nonprescription form of the drug. But sales of Claritin fell to about $1 billion as consumers switched to less costly generic equivalents.

APPLICATION Applying Economic Concepts

C. Using the three characteristics of monopoly, explain what happened to the market for Claritin when its patent expired.

SECTION 2 Assessment

REVIEWING KEY CONCEPTS

1. Explain the differences between the terms in each of these pairs:

   a. *monopoly*   **b.** *natural monopoly*   **c.** *technological monopoly*
      cartel   *geographic monopoly*   *government monopoly*

2. What is the relationship between economies of scale and a natural monopoly?

3. How does a patent awarded to one company act as a barrier to entry to another company wishing to enter the same market?

4. Why is a monopolist a price maker rather than a price taker?

5. Why do technological monopolies exist only for a limited time?

6. **Using Your Notes** Why is a geographic monopoly able to control the price of its product? Refer to your completed chart.

   Use the Graphic Organizer at **Interactive Review @ ClassZone.com**

	One Seller	Restricted Market	Control of Prices
Natural Monopoly			
Government Monopoly			
Technical Monopoly			
Geographic Monopoly			

CRITICAL THINKING

7. **Analyzing Causes and Effects** Companies that produce generic drugs are not required to repeat the clinical tests that the original manufacturer of the drug is required to run before the drug receives its patent. How does this fact affect the prices of generic drugs and why?

8. **Analyzing Effects** A powerful monopoly is broken up into several smaller, competing companies. What are the costs and benefits for the general public?

9. **Drawing Conclusions** In 2003, 95 percent of the households in America had access to only one cable TV company in their area. What kind of monopoly did cable TV companies have? Explain your answer.

10. **Challenge** Among the drugs to fight high cholesterol, the most effective are known as statins. The drugs are similar, but each is different enough to have its own patent. In 2005, there were seven such drugs on the market. In 2006, the patents ended for two of the drugs. What effect did this have on the entire category of statin drugs, including those whose patents were still in effect through 2006? Explain why this might be the case.

ECONOMICS IN PRACTICE

Identifying Types of Monopolies You learned in this section that there are four types of monopolies: natural, government, technological, and geographical.

What Type? The chart below lists examples of several monopolies. For each example, identify the type of monopoly. Some types have more than one example.

Example of Monopoly	Type of Monopoly
U.S. interstate highway system	
Electric utility company	
The only bank in a small town	
The company that received a patent for the Frisbee	
A city's public transportation system	
Natural gas company	

Challenge In which type of monopoly is the government least likely to be involved? Give reasons for your answer.

Other Market Structures

OBJECTIVES

In Section 3, you will
- learn that monopolistic competition and oligopoly are market structures that fall between perfect competition and monopoly
- identify the characteristics of monopolistic competition
- describe the characteristics of oligopoly

KEY TERMS

monopolistic competition, *p. 206*
product differentiation, *p. 206*
nonprice competition, *p. 207*
focus group, *p. 208*
oligopoly, *p. 209*
market share, *p. 209*
start-up costs, *p. 209*

TAKING NOTES

As you read Section 3, complete a chart to compare and contrast monopolistic competition and oligopoly. Use the Graphic Organizer at **Interactive Review @ ClassZone.com**

Monopolistic Competition	Oligopoly

Characteristics of Monopolistic Competition

KEY CONCEPTS

Most markets in the real world fall somewhere between the models of perfect competition and monopoly. One of the most common market structures is **monopolistic competition,** in which many sellers offer similar, but not standardized, products. The market for T-shirts printed with images or slogans is one example. The market is competitive because there are many buyers (you, your friends, and many other buyers) and many sellers (stores at the mall, online merchants, sports teams, and many other sellers). The market is monopolistic because each seller has influence over a small segment of the market with products that are not exactly like those of their competitors. Someone looking for a pink T-shirt with fuzzy kittens would not accept a black monster-truck rally T-shirt as a close substitute.

Product differentiation and nonprice competition are the distinguishing features of monopolistic competition. **Product differentiation** is the attempt to distinguish a product from similar products. Sometimes, the effort focuses on substantial differences between products, such as vehicle gas mileage ratings.

But companies also try to differentiate their products when there are few real differences between products. For example, a battery company might spend millions of dollars on advertising to convince consumers that their batteries last longer than other batteries—even though the real difference in longevity may be minimal.

Another way companies in monopolistic competitive markets try to gain business is through nonprice competition. **Nonprice competition** means using factors other than low price—such as style, service, advertising, or giveaways—to try to convince customers to buy one product rather than another. If you've ever decided to eat at a particular fast food restaurant just to get the cool gizmo it's giving away, you have participated in nonprice competition.

Monopolistic competition has four major characteristics: many buyers for many sellers, similar but differentiated products, limited lasting control over prices, and freedom to enter or exit the market. Let's take a closer look at each of these characteristics by focusing on the market for hamburgers.

QUICK REFERENCE

Nonprice competition occurs when producers use factors other than low price to try to convince customers to buy their products.

CHARACTERISTIC 1 Many Sellers and Many Buyers

In monopolistic competition there are many sellers and many buyers. The number of sellers is usually smaller than in a perfectly competitive market but sufficient to allow meaningful competition. Sellers act independently in choosing what kind of product to produce, how much to produce, and what price to charge.

When you want a hamburger, you have many different restaurants from which to choose. The number of restaurants assures that you have a variety of kinds of hamburgers to choose from and that prices will be competitive. No single seller has a large enough share of the market to significantly control supply or price.

However, there are probably a few restaurants that make burgers you really like and others with burgers you really don't like. The restaurants that make your favorite burgers have a sort of monopoly on your business.

Economics Update

Find an update about monopolistic competition at **ClassZone.com**

CHARACTERISTIC 2 Similar but Differentiated Products

Sellers in monopolistic competition gain their limited monopoly-like power by making a distinctive product or by convincing consumers that their product is different from the competition. Hamburger restaurants might advertise the quality of their ingredients or the way they cook the burger. They might also use distinctive packaging or some special service—a money-back guarantee if the customer is not satisfied with the meal, for example. One key method of product differentiation is the use of brand names, which

Hamburger Valhalla Chili-Cheese Burger

White bread bun

Cheese and chili

All-beef patty

Standard pickles, onions, tomatoes, lettuce

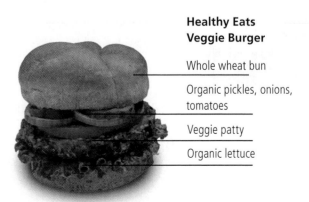

Healthy Eats Veggie Burger

Whole wheat bun

Organic pickles, onions, tomatoes

Veggie patty

Organic lettuce

encourage consumer loyalty by associating certain desirable qualities with a particular brand of hamburger. Producers use advertising to inform consumers about product differences and to persuade them to choose their offering.

How do hamburger restaurants decide how to differentiate their products? They conduct market research, the gathering and evaluation of information about consumer preferences for goods and services. For local restaurants, market research may be limited to listening to their customers' praise or complaints and paying attention to what competing restaurants offer.

The large chain restaurants can afford to use more sophisticated research techniques to gain information about consumers' lifestyles and product preferences. One technique is the **focus group**—a moderated discussion with small groups of consumers. Another market research technique is the survey, in which a large number of consumers are polled, one by one, on their opinions. The results of market research help the restaurants differentiate their hamburgers and attract more customers.

QUICK REFERENCE

A **focus group** is a moderated discussion with small groups of consumers.

CHARACTERISTIC 3 Limited Control of Prices

Product differentiation gives producers limited control of price. Hamburger restaurants charge different prices for their product depending on how they want to appeal to customers. The price of some hamburgers is set as low as possible to appeal to parents of younger eaters or to those on tight budgets. Prices for name-brand hamburgers or burgers with better quality ingredients may be set slightly higher. If consumers perceive that the differences are important enough, they will pay the extra price to get the hamburger they want.

Yet producers in monopolistic competition also know that there are many close substitutes for their product. They understand the factors that affect demand and recognize that consumers will switch to a substitute if the price goes too high.

CHARACTERISTIC 4 Freedom to Enter or Exit Market

There are generally no huge barriers to entry in monopolistically competitive markets. It does not require a large amount of capital for someone to open a hamburger stand, for example. When firms earn a profit in the hamburger market, other firms will enter and increase competition. Increased competition forces firms to continue to find ways to differentiate their products. The competition can be especially intense for small businesses facing much larger competitors.

Some firms will not be able to compete and will start to take losses. This is the signal that it is time for those firms to exit the market. Leaving the restaurant market is relatively easy. The owners sell off the cooking equipment, tables, and other supplies at a discount. If their finances are solid, they may then look for another market where profits might be made.

Ease of Entry and Exit
In monopolistic competition, sellers may enter and exit the market freely.

APPLICATION Applying Economic Concepts

A. Think about an item of clothing that you purchased recently. How did the seller differentiate the product? List several ways, then compare lists with a classmate.

Characteristics of an Oligopoly

KEY CONCEPTS

Oligopoly (OL-ih-GOP-ah-lee), a market structure in which only a few sellers offer a similar product, is less competitive than monopolistic competition. In an oligopoly, a few large firms have a large **market share**—percent of total sales in a market—and dominate the market. For example, if you want to see a movie in a theater, chances are the movie will have been made by one of just a few major studios. What's more, the theater you go to is probably part of one of just a few major theater chains. Both the market for film production and the market for movie theaters are oligopolies.

There are few firms in an oligopoly because of high **start-up costs**—the expenses that a new business must pay to enter a market and begin selling to consumers. Making a movie can be expensive, especially if you want to make one that can compete with what the major studios produce. And getting it into theaters across the country requires a huge network of promoters and distributors—and even more money.

An oligopoly has four major characteristics. There are few sellers but many buyers. In industrial markets, sellers offer standardized products, but in consumer markets, they offer differentiated products. The few sellers have more power to control prices than in monopolistic competition, but to enter or exit the market is difficult.

QUICK REFERENCE

Oligopoly is a market structure in which only a few sellers offer a similar product.

Market share is a company's percent of total sales in a market.

Start-up costs are the expenses that a new business faces when it enters a market.

CHARACTERISTIC 1 Few Sellers and Many Buyers

In an oligopoly, a few firms dominate an entire market. There is not a single supplier as in a monopoly, but there are fewer firms than in monopolistic competition. These few firms produce a large part of the total product in the market. Economists consider an industry to be an oligopoly if the four largest firms control at least 40 percent of the market. About half of the manufacturing industries in the United States are oligopolistic.

The breakfast cereal industry in the United States is dominated by four large firms that control about 80 percent of the market. Your favorite cereal is probably made by one of the big four manufacturers. Although they offer many varieties of cereals, there is less competition than there would be if each variety were produced by a different, smaller manufacturer.

The Breakfast Cereal Industry
Just a few large companies produce the majority of breakfast cereals available.

CHARACTERISTIC 2 Standardized or Differentiated Products

Depending on the market, an oligopolist may sell either standardized or differentiated products. Many industrial products are standardized, and a few large firms control these markets. Examples include the markets for steel, aluminum, and flat glass. When products are standardized, firms may try to differentiate themselves based on brand name, service, or location.

Breakfast cereals, soft drinks, and many other consumer goods are examples of differentiated products sold by oligopolies. Oligopolists market differentiated products using marketing strategies similar to those used in monopolistic competition. They use surveys, focus groups, and other market research techniques to find out what you like. The companies then create brand-name products that can be marketed across the country or around the world.

CHARACTERISTIC 3 More Control of Prices

Economics Update

Find an update about oligopolies at **ClassZone.com**

Because there are few sellers in an oligopoly, each one has more control over product price than in a monopolistically competitive market. For example, each breakfast cereal manufacturer has a large enough share of the market that decisions it makes about supply and price affect the market as a whole. Because of this, a seller in an oligopoly is not as independent as a seller in monopolistic competition. A decision made by one seller may cause the other sellers to respond in some way.

For example, if one of the leading breakfast cereal manufacturers lowers its prices, the other manufacturers will probably also lower prices rather than lose customers to the competition. Therefore, no firm is likely to gain market share based on price, and all risk losing profits. But if one manufacturer decides to raise prices, the others may not follow suit, in order to take customers and gain market share. Consequently, firms in an oligopoly try to anticipate how their competitors will respond to their actions before they make decisions on price, output, or marketing.

CHARACTERISTIC 4 Little Freedom to Enter or Exit Market

Start-up costs for a new company in an oligopolistic market can be extremely high. Entering the breakfast cereal industry on a small scale is not very expensive—but the profits are low too. The factories, warehouses, and other infrastructure needed to compete against the major manufacturers require large amounts of funds. In addition, existing manufacturers may hold patents that act as further barriers to entry.

Firms in an oligopoly have established brands and plentiful resources that make it difficult for new firms to enter the market successfully. For example, breakfast cereal

High Start-up Costs
New firms may not have the funds to construct large factories.

manufacturers have agreements with grocery stores that guarantee them the best shelf space. Existing manufacturers also have economies of scale that help them to keep their expenses low. Smaller firms, with smaller operations, lack the economies of scale.

However, all of the investments by firms in an oligopoly make it difficult for them to exit the market. When a major breakfast cereal manufacturer begins losing money, its operations are too vast and complex to sell and reinvest easily, as a small business might. It must trim its operations and work to stimulate demand for its product.

APPLICATION Categorizing Information

B. Which of these products produced by oligopolies are standardized and which are differentiated: automobiles, cement, copper, sporting goods, tires?

Comparing Market Structures

Each of the four market structures has different benefits and problems. And each type creates a different balance of power—namely, the power to influence prices—between producers and consumers.

Consumers get the most value in markets that approach perfect competition. No actual markets are perfectly competitive, but in those that come close, prices are set primarily by supply and demand. However, such markets usually deal in a standardized product, so consumers have little choice other than the best price.

In monopolistic competition, consumers continue to benefit from companies competing for their business. But businesses gain some control over prices, so they are more likely to earn a profit. Opening a business in such a market is usually relatively affordable, which is another benefit for businesses.

In markets dominated by oligopolies, consumer choices may be more limited than in more competitive markets. Businesses in such markets gain more control of price, making it easier for them to make a profit. However, the cost of doing business in such a market is high.

A market ruled by a monopoly is very favorable for the business that holds the monopoly. It faces little or no competition from other companies. And monopoly gives consumers the least influence over prices. They decide only whether they are willing to buy the product at the price set by the monopolist.

FIGURE 7.5 Comparing Market Structures

	Number of Sellers	Type of Product	Sellers' Control over Prices	Barriers to Enter or Exit Market
Perfect Competition	Many	Standardized	None	Few
Monopolistic Competition	Many	Similar but differentiated	Limited	Few
Oligopoly	Few	Standardized for industry; differentiated for consumers	Some	Many
Monopoly	One	Standardized, but no close substitutes	Significant	Very many—market restricted or regulated

ANALYZE CHARTS
1. If you were starting a business, which market structures would make it easiest for you to enter the market?
2. Which market structures offer the highest potential profits? Why?

APPLICATION Drawing Conclusions

C. What difference does it make to consumers whether a market is ruled by monopolistic competition or by an oligopoly?

Joan Robinson: Challenging Established Ideas

FAST FACTS

Joan Robinson

Career: Economics professor, Cambridge University

Born: October 31, 1903

Died: August 5, 1983

Major Accomplishment: Developed theory of imperfect competition

Books: *The Economics of Imperfect Competition* (1933), *The Accumulation of Capital* (1956), *Economic Philosophy* (1963), *Introduction to Modern Economics* (1973)

Famous Quotation: "*It is the business of economists, not to tell us what to do, but show why what we are doing anyway is in accord with proper principles.*"

Economics Update

Learn more about Joan Robinson at **ClassZone.com**

In this section, you learned about monopolistic competition and oligopoly. British economist Joan Robinson was one of the first to write about these market structures. As strange as it may seem to us now, most economists before 1930 described market competition only in terms of the extremes of perfect competition and monopoly.

Explaining Real-World Competition

In 1933, Joan Robinson challenged the prevailing ideas about competition. Her first major book, *The Economics of Imperfect Competition*, described market structures that existed between monopoly and perfect competition. Robinson's work appeared shortly after Harvard economist Edward Chamberlin published his book *Theory of Monopolistic Competition.* The two economists had developed their ideas independently.

Robinson and Chamberlin described the type of competition that exists among firms with differentiated products. Such firms gain more control over the price of their product, but their control is limited by the amount of competition. They also described the nature of oligopoly and of monopsony, a market structure in which there are many sellers but only one large buyer.

Robinson continued to contribute important ideas throughout her long career in economics. Her theory of imperfect competition remains a key element of the field of microeconomics today. Economists recognized that Robinson's theory more accurately reflected modern market economies in which firms compete through product differentiation and advertising and in which many industries are controlled by oligopolies.

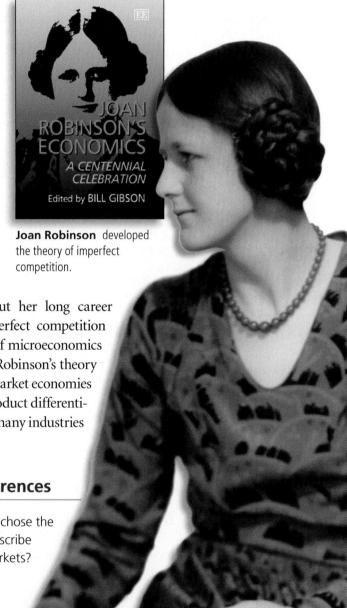

Joan Robinson developed the theory of imperfect competition.

APPLICATION Making Inferences

D. Why do you think Joan Robinson chose the term *imperfect competition* to describe the nature of most real-world markets?

REVIEWING KEY CONCEPTS

1. Explain the relationship between the terms in each of these pairs:

   a. *product differentiation*
      nonprice competition

   b. *focus group*
      market share

   c. *oligopoly*
      start-up costs

2. How is monopolistic competition similar to perfect competition and how is it similar to monopoly?

3. Describe some of the techniques sellers use to differentiate their products.

4. Why are standardized products sometimes found in oligopoly but not in monopolistic competition?

5. Is it easier for a new firm to enter the market under monopolistic competition or oligopoly? Why?

6. **Using Your Notes** How does the number of sellers compare in monopolistic competition and oligopoly? Refer to your completed chart.

Monopolistic Competition	Oligopoly

   Use the Graphic Organizer at **Interactive Review @ ClassZone.com**

CRITICAL THINKING

7. **Contrasting Economic Information** What makes the market for wheat different from the markets for products made from wheat, such as bread, cereal, and pasta?

8. **Applying Economic Concepts** In 2005, a major U.S. automaker announced a new discount plan for its cars for the month of June. It offered consumers the same price that its employees paid for new cars. When the automaker announced in early July that it was extending the plan for another month, the other two major U.S. automakers announced similar plans. What market structure is exhibited in this story and what specific characteristics of that market structure does it demonstrate?

9. **Analyzing Effects** Blue jeans are produced under monopolistic competition, so their prices are higher than if they were produced under perfect competition. Do the positive effects for consumers of blue jeans justify the higher prices? Why or why not?

10. **Challenge** Why do manufacturers of athletic shoes spend money to sign up professional athletes to wear and promote their shoes rather than differentiating their products strictly on the basis of physical characteristics such as design and comfort?

ECONOMICS IN PRACTICE

Perfect competition or monopoly?

The Impact of Market Structure
Each of the four market structures carries different consequences for businesses and consumers. Imagine what would happen if there were only one type of market structure. Use Figure 7.5 on page 211 as a guide as you do this exercise.

a. What would your town look like if every market was perfectly competitive? What would happen to your consumer choices?

b. What would happen if every market was ruled by monopolistic competition?

c. What would the town look like if oligopolies controlled every market?

d. What if every market in your town was ruled by a monopoly? How could you tell the difference between situation A and D?

Challenge Now think about what your town actually looks like. What types of market structures are most prevalent? Are you satisfied with the mix of market structures, or do you think some markets would be better served by different structures?

OBJECTIVES	KEY TERMS	TAKING NOTES
In Section 4, you will • explain how government acts to prevent monopolies • analyze the effects of anti-competitive business practices • describe how government acts to protect consumers • discuss why some industries have been deregulated and the results of that deregulation	regulation, *p. 214* antitrust legislation, *p. 214* trust, *p. 214* merger, *p. 214* price fixing, *p. 216* market allocation, *p. 216* predatory pricing, *p. 216* cease and desist order, *p. 217* public disclosure, *p. 217* deregulation, *p. 218*	As you read Section 4, complete a hierarchy diagram to track main ideas and supporting details. Use the Graphic Organizer at **Interactive Review@ ClassZone.com** Regulation and Deregulation Promoting Competition details

Promoting Competition

KEY CONCEPTS

QUICK REFERENCE

Regulation is a set of rules or laws designed to control business behavior.

Antitrust legislation defines monopolies and gives government the power to control them.

A **trust** is a group of firms combined in order to reduce competition in an industry.

A **merger** is the joining of two firms to form a single firm.

The forces of the marketplace generally keep businesses competitive with one another and attentive to consumer welfare. But sometimes the government uses **regulation**—controlling business behavior through a set of rules or laws—to promote competition and protect consumers. The most important laws that promote competition are collectively called **antitrust legislation,** laws that define monopolies and give government the power to control them and break them up. A **trust** is a group of firms combined for the purpose of reducing competition in an industry. (A trust is similar to a cartel, which you learned about in Section 2.) To keep trusts from forming, the government regulates business mergers. A **merger** is when one company combines with or purchases another to form a single firm.

Origins of Antitrust Legislation

During the late 1800s, a few large trusts, such as Standard Oil, dominated the oil, steel, and railroad industries in the United States. The U.S. government became concerned that these combinations would use their power to control prices and output. As a result, in 1890, the government passed the Sherman

Standard Oil Company This cartoon dramatizes how Standard Oil controlled the oil industry.

Antitrust Act. This gave government the power to control monopolies and to regulate business practices that might reduce competition. Over time, other laws strengthened the government's ability to regulate business and to encourage competition.

To understand why government officials pushed for antitrust laws, consider one of the trusts that developed in the late 1800s—the Standard Oil Company. By merging with other companies and eliminating competitors, Standard Oil gained control of about 90 percent of the U.S. oil industry. Such a huge holding, government officials contended, gave Standard Oil the ability to set production levels and prices. In 1911, the U.S. government won a court case under the Sherman Antitrust Act that required the breakup of the trust. In order to increase competition, Standard Oil was forced to relinquish control of 33 companies that had once been part of the trust.

Antitrust Legislation Today

At various times, the U.S. government has used antitrust legislation to break up large companies that attempt to maintain their market power through restraint of competition. The government might allow a large dominant firm to remain intact because it is the most efficient producer. Or it might order that the company change its business practices to allow other firms to compete more easily.

The responsibility for enforcing antitrust legislation is shared by the Federal Trade Commission (FTC) and the Department of Justice. A major focus of their work is the assessment of mergers. The government tends to support mergers that might benefit consumers. For example, larger firms are often able to operate more efficiently, and lower operating costs may lead to lower prices for consumers. On the other hand, the government tends to block mergers that lead to greater market concentration in the hands of a few firms. A merger that makes it more difficult for new firms to enter a market will also be looked upon with concern.

To evaluate a potential merger, the government looks at how a particular market is defined. A company that is proposing a merger would try to define its market as broadly as possible, in order to make its control of the market seem smaller. For example, a soft drink producer might claim that its market competition includes all beverages, such as water, tea, coffee, and juice.

To determine whether the merger will increase the concentration in the market and decrease competition, the government considers the market share of the firms before and after the proposed merger. Government regulators also look at whether the merger allows a firm to eliminate possible competitors. If this analysis shows that a merger will reduce competition and more than likely lead to higher prices for consumers, the regulators will deny the companies' effort to merge.

The Federal Trade Commission (FTC)
In 2004, Deborah Platt Majoras became head of the FTC, an agency that enforces antitrust laws.

APPLICATION Drawing Conclusions

A. Which of these mergers would the government be more likely to approve and why: two airlines that serve different cities or two banks in a small town?

Ensuring a Level Playing Field

In addition to evaluating mergers, the government also tries to make sure that businesses do not engage in practices that would reduce competition. As you have learned, competition enables the market economy to work effectively. When businesses take steps that counteract the effects of competition, prices go up and supplies go down. In the United States, laws prohibit most of these practices. The FTC and the Department of Justice enforce these laws.

Prohibiting Unfair Business Practices

Businesses that seek to counteract market forces can use a variety of methods. One is **price fixing**, which occurs when businesses work together to set the prices of competing products. A related technique is when competing businesses agree to restrict their output, thereby driving up prices.

For example, in the mid-1990s the five major recorded music distributors began enforcing a "minimum advertised price" for compact discs sold in the United States. As a result, CD prices remained artificially high. The FTC estimated that consumers paid about $480 million more for CDs than they would have if prices had been established by market forces. In 2000 the FTC reached an agreement with the distributors to end this anticompetitive practice.

Another way businesses seek to avoid competition is by **market allocation**, which occurs when competing businesses negotiate to divide up a market. By staying out of each other's territory, the businesses develop limited monopoly power in their own territory, allowing them to charge higher prices.

For example, in the early 1990s agribusiness conglomerate Archer Daniels Midland (ADM) conspired with companies in Japan and Korea to divide the worldwide market for lysine, an additive used in livestock feeds. Around the same time, ADM also conspired with European companies to divide the worldwide market for citric acid, an additive used in soft drinks, canned foods, and other consumer products. Both of these illicit agreements also included price fixing. In 1996, the Department of Justice charged ADM with antitrust violations in both the lysine and citric acid markets. ADM pleaded guilty and paid a $100 million fine.

Occasionally, businesses use anticompetitive methods to drive other firms out of a market. One technique used by cartels or large producers is **predatory pricing**, setting prices below cost so that smaller producers cannot afford to participate in a market. Predatory pricing can be difficult to distinguish from competitive pricing. Larger businesses are usually able to offer lower prices because they have economies of scale unavailable to smaller firms.

APPLICATION Applying Economic Concepts

B. If you owned an ice cream store, could you negotiate with other ice cream store owners to set a standard price for a scoop of ice cream? Why or why not?

Protecting Consumers

KEY CONCEPTS

When the government becomes aware that a firm is engaged in behavior that is unfair to competitors or consumers, it may issue a **cease and desist order**, a ruling that requires a firm to stop an unfair business practice. The government also enforces a policy of **public disclosure**, which requires businesses to reveal product information to consumers. This protects consumers and promotes competition by giving consumers the information they need to make informed buying decisions.

QUICK REFERENCE

A **cease and desist order** requires a firm to stop an unfair business practice.

Public disclosure is a policy that requires businesses to reveal product information.

Consumer Protection Agencies

Besides enforcing laws that ensure competitive markets, the government protects consumers by regulating other aspects of business. Figure 7.6 shows some of the most important federal agencies that protect consumers. The Federal Trade Commission has primary responsibility for promoting competition and preventing unfair business practices. The Federal Communications Commission and Securities and Exchange Commission regulate specific industries. The Food and Drug Administration, Environmental Protection Agency, and Consumer Product Safety Commission protect consumers by regulating multiple industries to ensure the safety and quality of specific products and to protect consumer health.

FIGURE 7.6 Federal Consumer Protection Agencies

Agency	Created	Purpose
Food and Drug Administration (FDA)	1906	Protects consumers from unsafe foods, drugs, or cosmetics; requires truth in labeling of these products
Federal Trade Commission (FTC)	1914	Enforces antitrust laws and monitors unfair business practices, including deceptive advertising
Federal Communications Commission (FCC)	1934	Regulates the communications industry, including radio, television, cable, and telephone services
Securities and Exchange Commission (SEC)	1934	Regulates the market for stocks and bonds to protect investors
Environmental Protection Agency (EPA)	1970	Protects human health by enforcing environmental laws regarding pollution and hazardous materials
Consumer Product Safety Commission (CPSC)	1972	Sets safety standards for thousands of types of consumer products; issues recalls for unsafe products

ANALYZE TABLES

1. What's the difference between the FTC and the SEC?

2. Pick one agency, note the year it was created, and explain what might have led to its creation.

APPLICATION Making Inferences

C. Why do you think the government has decided to set up agencies to protect consumers from unsafe products?

Deregulating Industries

KEY CONCEPTS

QUICK REFERENCE

Deregulation reduces or removes government control of business.

Much government regulation in the 20th century focused on controlling industries that provided important public services. For example, in the 1930s, in response to bank closings and other problems during the Great Depression, the U.S. Congress passed many laws for oversight of the financial services industry. In the 1970s, a trend toward deregulation began. **Deregulation** involves actions taken to reduce or to remove government oversight and control of business.

Deregulation has benefits and drawbacks. Deregulation generally results in lower prices for consumers because the markets become more competitive. Firms in industries with regulated prices have little or no incentive to reduce costs. But deregulation may lead to fewer protections for consumers.

Deregulating the Airlines

The Airline Deregulation Act of 1978 removed all government control of airline routes and rates. Only safety regulations remained in place. Prior to 1978, there was limited competition, and airlines differentiated based on service rather than price.

As a result of deregulation, the industry expanded as many new carriers entered the market. Increased competition led to greater efficiency. Economists estimate that prices fell by 10 to 18 percent, falling most sharply on heavily traveled routes where there was the greatest amount of competition. More people than ever before, lured by lower prices, chose to travel by plane.

However, the quality of service declined as airlines cut back on food and other in-flight amenities to reduce costs. In addition, many travelers encountered crowded airports as a result of the increase in air travel. It took time for local governments to expand facilities to accommodate the increase in traffic.

The financial pressures led to a large number of bankruptcies among the airline companies. Airline employees faced increased layoffs, lower wages, and loss of pensions.

APPLICATION Analyzing Causes

C. Why did deregulation of the airline industry lead to lower prices for many consumers?

REVIEWING KEY CONCEPTS

1. Explain the differences between the terms in each of these pairs:

   a. *trust*
   merger

   b. *price fixing*
   predatory pricing

   c. *regulation*
   deregulation

2. What is the main purpose of antitrust legislation?

3. How does market allocation lead to reduced competition?

4. When would the government issue a cease and desist order?

5. How do public disclosure requirements protect consumers?

6. **Using Your Notes** Why is it important for the government to evaluate and approve mergers? Refer to your completed hierarchy diagram.

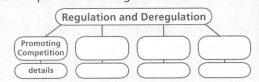

Regulation and Deregulation

Promoting Competition

details

Use the Graphic Organizer at **Interactive Review @ ClassZone.com**

CRITICAL THINKING

7. **Analyzing Causes and Effects** In 2005, the FTC approved the merger of The Gillette Company with Procter & Gamble. Experts who reviewed the merger said it made sense that it was approved because the two companies had few products in the same market categories. In order to satisfy the government, the companies had to sell only two of their brands to other companies. What factors that affect mergers are illustrated in this story?

8. **Applying Economic Concepts** In the early 2000s, a new form of marketing emerged called word-of-mouth marketing or buzz marketing. Companies hired ordinary people to talk about the benefits of their products to others. Marketing industry lawyers warned their clients that it was important that the hired spokespeople reveal that they were paid for their endorsements. What are the lawyers concerned about? Use the concepts from this section to formulate your answer.

9. **Challenge** The Telecommunications Act of 1996 included provisions to deregulate the cable television industry. In 2003, consumer organizations complained that cable rates had increased by 45 percent since the law was passed. Only 5 percent of American homes had a choice of more than one cable provider in 2003. Those homes paid about 17 percent less than those with no choice of cable provider. How effective had deregulation been in the cable industry by 2003? Cite evidence to support your answer.

ECONOMICS IN PRACTICE

Identifying Regulatory Agencies
Several federal agencies provide protection for consumers. Many of them are listed in Figure 7.6 on page 217. Decide which agency or agencies from Figure 7.6 would best protect consumers in each of the situations below.

a. Children's necklaces sold over the Internet are found to contain high levels of lead. Consumers are concerned about the chance of lead poisoning.

b. Advertising for a skin cream claims that it will eliminate acne problems. Consumers find that the product does not live up to its claim and in fact seems to irritate people's faces and cause rashes.

c. Some apple farmers use a pesticide on their trees that causes illness. More and more of the pesticide has been found in groundwater supplies.

Challenge Find out about a government regulatory agency not listed in Figure 7.6. Discuss the agency's purpose with your class.

Case Study

Economics Update
Find an update on this Case
Study at **ClassZone.com**

Competition in Gadgets and Gizmos

Background Cellular phones are a highly successful telecommunications product. Since they first appeared on the market in the 1980s, cell phone sales have grown steadily. Now, billions of people around the world own cell phones.

As the global market becomes saturated with cell phones, sales growth will slow. To counteract this, cell phone producers rely on product differentiation to increase sales. New gadgets and gizmos aim to make the cell phone both irresistible and indispensable. A director of business development at one cell phone maker summed up his strategy this way: "We are trying to drive the cell phone in[to] every aspect of your life."

What's the issue? What affects your selection of a cell phone? Study these sources to discover how producers use product differentiation to compete for your business.

A. Magazine Article

Nokia Corporation, a maker of phone handsets, developed several add-ons to boost sales. This article describes one of Nokia's plans.

Nokia Hopes to Attract Consumers with Mobile-TV

Web-browsing, picture-messaging, videos, and now TV

Nokia, the world's largest handset-maker, has just released the results of a mobile-TV trial in Helsinki which found that 41% of participants were willing to pay for the service, and thought a monthly fee of €10 [€ is the European Union currency, the euro] ($12.50) was reasonable.

As revenue from voice calls has stopped growing in developed markets, the industry has been searching for new avenues for growth. In recent years, it has championed mobile web-browsing, picture-messaging and video-telephony. . . . But . . . consumers have not taken to these things in large numbers. . . .

Ah, but mobile TV is different from all those other services . . . because there is no need to educate the consumer. "Everyone gets it if you say 'mobile TV'," says Richard Sharp of Nokia.

Source: **"Anyone for Telly?"** *The Economist*, September 10, 2005

Thinking Economically What caused Nokia to develop mobile-TV? Explain, using evidence from the article.

B. Cartoon

This cartoon makes light of the dozens of features packed into most cellular phones.

Swiss Army Phone

Source: www.CartoonStock.com

Thinking Economically Why do cellular phone makers include so many features in their phones?

C. Online Press Release

Gartner, Inc. provides research and analysis on the information technology industry. This press release presents its projections on mobile phone sales.

Gartner Says Mobile Phone Sales Will Exceed One Billion in 2009

Sales will increase, but so will competition.

Gartner estimates there will be 2.6 billion mobile phones in use by the end of 2009. . . . "The sales volume cannot be attributed to one region in particular. It's a truly global phenomenon," said Carolina Milanesi, principal analyst at Gartner for mobile terminals. "In mature markets like Europe and North America, subscribers are still buying replacement phones. In emerging markets like Brazil and India, new customers are signing up for mobile services at an even faster rate." . . .

Despite spectacular growth on all fronts, not everything is rosy. [Ben] Wood, research vice president for mobile terminals at Gartner, cautioned that "Sales numbers are impressive, but the big names in this industry will have to deliver value as well as volume. We expect the average wholesale price of a mobile phone will decline from US\$174 in 2004 to US\$161 in 2009. At the same time, phones will keep getting more complex and become ever-more packed with features. Only the sharpest players will survive."

Source: www.gartner.com

Thinking Economically Are manufacturers more likely to offer differentiated products in new markets or in those already established? Explain your answer.

THINKING ECONOMICALLY Synthesizing

1. Compare the product described in document A and the one illustrated in B. Are cell phones likely to become more or less complex? Explain why or why not.

2. Which of the four market structures best fits the market for cellular phones? Use evidence from documents A and C to explain your answer.

3. In documents A and C, compare the role that market research plays in the development of new products. Use evidence from the documents.

Interactive Review

Review this chapter using interactive activities at **ClassZone.com**

- Online Summary
- Graphic Organizers
- Quizzes
- Review and Study Notes
- Vocabulary Flip Cards

○○○

 Online Summary

Complete the following activity either on your own paper or online at **ClassZone.com**

Choose the key concept that best completes the sentence. Not all key concepts will be used.

antitrust legislation	monopoly
barrier to entry	natural monopoly
cartel	nonprice competition
cease and desist order	oligopoly
deregulation	patent
economies of scale	perfect competition
geographic monopoly	price fixing
market structure	price taker
merger	standardized product
monopolistic competition	start-up costs

__1__ is an economic model of the nature and degree of competition among businesses in the same industry. In __2__ there are many buyers and sellers of standardized products.

In a __3__ there is a single seller of a product with no close substitutes. The local water company is an example of a __4__ because __5__ make it most efficient for a single company to provide the service.

A __6__ is a group of sellers that acts together to set prices and limit output. A __7__ is anything that makes it difficult for a business to enter a market.

In __8__ there are many buyers and sellers of similar but differentiated products. In such a market the sellers engage in __9__.

In __10__ there are only a few sellers for many buyers. It is hard for new firms to enter such a market due to high __11__. Sellers in such a market engage in __12__ when they all agree to charge the same price for their products.

__13__ gives the government the power to control monopolies and to promote competition.

REVIEWING KEY CONCEPTS

What Is Perfect Competition? (pp. 192–197)

1. What determines the difference between one market structure and another?

2. Why is perfect competition not found in real markets?

The Impact of Monopoly (pp. 198–205)

3. How does a monopoly control the price of its product?

4. Name three ways in which a monopoly differs from perfect competition.

Other Market Structures (pp. 206–213)

5. Why is product differentiation necessary for monopolistic competition?

6. Why are firms in an oligopoly less independent in setting prices than firms in monopolistic competition?

Regulation and Deregulation Today (pp. 214–221)

7. What factors does the government consider in deciding whether to approve a merger?

8. Why do economists generally favor deregulation of most industries?

APPLYING ECONOMIC CONCEPTS

Look at the table below showing retail sales.

9. Which retail market is the least concentrated? Which market is most concentrated?

10. Which markets are closer to monopolistic competition and which are closer to oligopoly?

FIGURE 7.7 SALES CONCENTRATION IN RETAIL TRADE

Retail Market	Percent of Total Sales by the Four Largest Firms
Furniture	8
Clothing	29
Supermarkets	33
Music	58
Athletic footwear	71
Books	77
Discount department stores	95

Source: U.S. Census Bureau, 2002 data

11. Applying Economic Concepts In 2004, a new trend started in the marketing of music CDs. A variety of retailers, from coffee shop and restaurant chains to large discount stores, began negotiating marketing deals that allowed them to sell a particular recording artist's CDs exclusively for a period of time.

   a. What part of monopolistic competition does this trend reinforce: the monopolistic aspect or the competition aspect?

   b. How is this trend likely to affect prices for these CDs? Give reasons why.

12. Analyzing Causes and Effects After deregulation of the airline industry, many of the largest U.S. airlines struggled financially. These airlines then increased their business in the international market in order to boost their profits. What effect of deregulation caused the airlines to make this move?

13. Making Inferences The company that invented the first xerographic photocopier initially enjoyed 70 percent profit margins and a 95 percent market share. Several years later a Japanese camera company invented another way to make photocopiers. Over time, the original company's market share fell to 13 percent. What specific kind of market structure is illustrated by this example? When a company invents a new product or process, what concerns might they have, if they studied this example?

14. Drawing Conclusions An herbal supplement company claimed that its product would cure serious diseases and promote weight loss. In 2005, the Federal Trade Commission (FTC) required the company to stop making those claims. Why did the FTC rather than the Food and Drug Administration (FDA) handle this case?

15. Challenge Why might a local electric company be in favor of regulations that would allow it to remain a natural monopoly? Why might it oppose regulations that would require monitoring the pollution from its generating plants?

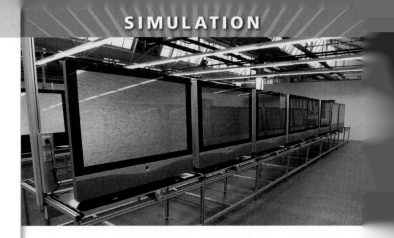

Compete for Buyers

Step 1. Choose a partner. Imagine that together you run a company that produces flat-screen televisions under monopolistic competition. Use the criteria in this table to decide how to differentiate your product.

Product and Marketing Considerations
• Physical characteristics
• Where it will be sold
• Packaging or labeling
• Service
• Advertising and promotion
• Price (from $500 to $1,500)

Step 2. Create a poster that outlines your product and marketing decisions. Include a sketch of one of your televisions along with the price.

Step 3. Display all the posters in the classroom. Allow all students to buy a television from the company of their choice. Tally the results and see how many buyers each company attracted.

Step 4. Merge with two or three other companies to form a larger company. There should now be only three or four producers. Discuss how this new situation might affect your marketing decisions.

Step 5. As a class, discuss what would happen if the three or four firms became a cartel and acted like a monopoly.

Challenge Which of these scenarios would you prefer as a producer? Which would you prefer as a consumer?

Types of Businesses

Businesses are organized in different ways. The organization that suits a small business, such as this florist, may not be appropriate for a large manufacturer.

Types of Business Organizations

CONCEPT REVIEW

A **producer** is a maker of goods or provider of services.

CHAPTER 8 KEY CONCEPT

Most of the producers in a market economy are **business organizations**, commercial or industrial enterprises and the people who work in them. The purpose of most business organizations is to earn a profit.

WHY THE CONCEPT MATTERS

Do you have a part-time job after school or on weekends? Perhaps you work behind the counter at the local flower shop or as a server at the juice bar downtown. Or perhaps you work as a stocker at one of the large clothing stores at the shopping mall. These businesses are of varying sizes and are organized differently. The American free enterprise system allows producers to choose the kind of business organization that best suits their purpose.

Online Highlights
More at ClassZone.com

 Economics Update

Go to **ECONOMICS UPDATE** for chapter updates and current news on Apple Computer, Inc. (See Case Study, pp. 252–253.) ▶

Animated Economics

Go to **ANIMATED ECONOMICS** for interactive lessons on the graphs and tables in this chapter.

Interactive ◀◀Review

Go to **INTERACTIVE REVIEW** for concept review and activities.

How did Apple Computer, Inc., which began in a garage, grow into a major multinational corporation? See the Case Study on pages 252–253.

Sole Proprietorships

Sole Proprietorships

Advantages	Disadvantages

The Characteristics of Sole Proprietorships

KEY CONCEPTS

Every business begins with a person who has an idea about how to earn money and the drive to follow through on the idea and to create a business organization. A **business organization** is an enterprise that produces goods or provides services. Most of the goods and services available in a market economy come from business organizations.

The purpose of most business organizations is to earn a profit. They achieve this purpose by producing the goods and services that best meet consumers' wants and needs. In the course of meeting consumer demand, business organizations provide jobs and income that can be used for spending and saving. Business organizations also pay taxes that help finance government services.

The most common type of business organization in the United States is the **sole proprietorship**, a business owned and managed by a single person. Sole proprietorships include everything from mom-and-pop grocery stores to barbershops to computer repair businesses. They account for more than 70 percent of all businesses in the United States. However, they generate less than 5 percent of all sales by American businesses.

Sole Proprietorships Beauty salons are frequently operated by one owner.

EXAMPLE Bart's Cosmic Comics

To understand how sole proprietorships are set up and run, let's look at the example of Bart's Cosmic Comics. Bart started collecting comic books in grade school. Over the years, he amassed a huge collection of comics as well as other related items—lunch boxes, action figures, and so on. At the same time, he learned a lot about the comic book business. So, few of his friends expressed surprise when Bart announced that he wanted to open a business selling comic books and related merchandise.

Raising Funds Bart needed money to rent and renovate the space he found downtown and to buy new and used comics to stock the store. A hefty withdrawal from his savings account got him started, but he needed to borrow to get the job finished. He tried to get a loan from a local bank. However, because he was not yet an established business owner, bank officers were reluctant to approve the loan. Finally, he turned to his family and friends, who together lent him $15,000.

Preparing to Open After raising the necessary funds, Bart completed the few legal steps required to open his business. These included obtaining a business license and a site permit, a document stating that the local government allowed him to use the space he was renting for business. He also registered the name he had chosen for his business—Bart's Cosmic Comics.

Initial Difficulties At first, business was slow. Bart worried that the store would fail and he would be stuck with no income and no way to repay the loans. He thought the safest course of action might be to hang on to what cash he had so he could keep the store open for as long as possible. After much consideration, however, he decided to take another risk, spending $1,000 on advertisements in local newspapers. He also ran several in-store promotions. His business began to take off.

Economics Update

Find an update on sole proprietorships at **ClassZone.com**

Success Within 18 months, Bart had paid back his loans and was earning a profit. Shortly after, he decided to expand his inventory to include T-shirts and posters and to hire an assistant to help run the store. This time when he asked the bank for a loan to pay for the expansion, bank officers were ready to approve the financing. Bart's success indicated that giving him a loan would be a good business decision.

APPLICATION Applying Economic Concepts

A. Identify two or three examples of businesses you might want to establish as sole proprietorships.

Sole Proprietorships: Advantages and Disadvantages

KEY CONCEPTS

The sole proprietorship has certain advantages and disadvantages that set it apart from other kinds of business structures. For example, sole proprietorships are not governed by as many regulations as other types of businesses. Also, sole proprietorships have **limited life**, a situation in which a business ceases to exist if the owner dies, retires, or leaves the business for some other reason. Finally, sole proprietors have **unlimited liability**, a situation in which a business owner is responsible for all the losses, debts, and other claims against the business.

ADVANTAGES Sole Proprietorships

There is a reason that sole proprietorships are by far the most common type of business structure: they have several significant advantages.

Easy to Open or Close Bart's start-up requirements were typical: funding, a license, a site permit, and a legally registered name. If Bart wanted to get out of the business, he would find that process easy as well. As long as he has settled all his bills, Bart may close the business when he sees fit.

Few Regulations Compared with other business organizations, sole proprietorships are lightly regulated. Bart, for example, must locate his store in an area zoned, or officially set aside, for businesses. He also must treat his employees according to various labor laws.

Freedom and Control Bart makes all the decisions and does so quickly without having to check with partners or boards of directors. Having complete control and seeing his ideas come to life gives Bart, like many other sole proprietors, a strong sense of personal satisfaction. In other words, he enjoys being his own boss.

Owner Keeps Profits Bart also enjoys the chief economic advantage of the sole proprietorship. Since he is the sole owner of the business, he gets to keep all the profits the business earns.

Sole Proprietors Are Fully Responsible The owner bears full responsibility for running the business but also keeps all of the profits.

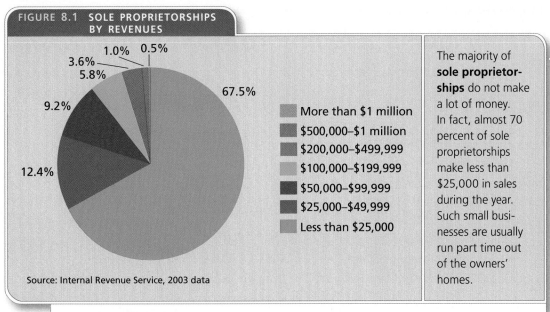

FIGURE 8.1 SOLE PROPRIETORSHIPS BY REVENUES

1.0% 0.5%
3.6%
5.8%
9.2%
67.5%
12.4%

- More than $1 million
- $500,000–$1 million
- $200,000–$499,999
- $100,000–$199,999
- $50,000–$99,999
- $25,000–$49,999
- Less than $25,000

Source: Internal Revenue Service, 2003 data

The majority of **sole proprietorships** do not make a lot of money. In fact, almost 70 percent of sole proprietorships make less than $25,000 in sales during the year. Such small businesses are usually run part time out of the owners' homes.

ANALYZE GRAPHS

1. About what percentage of sole proprietorships make less than $50,000 in annual sales?
2. Make a generalization about sole proprietorships based on information in the graph.

DISADVANTAGES Sole Proprietorships

Bart's story hints at some of the disadvantages of sole proprietorships as well.

Limited Funds Especially at start-up, Bart had very limited funds. This disadvantage is one of the key reasons that sole proprietorships are far more likely to fail than other types of business organizations. Until he had established his business, Bart had trouble securing a bank loan. Without monetary reserves to fall back on, he found it a struggle to stay in business. Even when the business became successful, Bart felt that the lack of funds hurt him. He worried that he would not be able to attract and keep good workers because his limited funds meant he could not pay competitive wages or offer benefits such as health insurance.

Limited Life Bart found that some of the advantages of the sole proprietorship may also prove to be disadvantages. He appreciated the ease with which you can set up or close a sole proprietorship. However, this means that sole proprietorships have limited life. If he leaves the business, Bart's Cosmic Comics ceases to exist.

Unlimited Liability Bart enjoys having total responsibility for running the business, even though that means that he works long hours. Having total responsibility for the business produces perhaps the greatest disadvantage of a sole proprietorship—unlimited liability. Bart is legally responsible for all the financial aspects of the business. If Bart's Cosmic Comics fails, he must still pay all its debts, even without income from the business. If necessary, he may have to sell property and use his personal savings to pay off debts. Sole proprietors, then, may lose their homes, cars, or personal savings if their businesses fail.

APPLICATION Analyzing Cause and Effect

B. Why do you think that sole proprietorships are the most common form of business organization in the United States?

Mary Kay Ash: Going It Alone

Economics Update

Find an update on Mary Kay Inc. at **ClassZone.com**

Do you have what it takes to "go it alone" as an entrepreneur? See how many of these questions you can answer with a "yes."

• Are you willing to take risks?

• Can you live with uncertainty?

• Are you self-confident?

• Are you self-directed, able to set and reach goals for yourself?

• Are you optimistic, energetic, and action-oriented?

Like other entrepreneurs, Mary Kay Ash had all of these qualities. She used them to turn $5,000 in personal savings into Mary Kay Inc., a business that now sells billions of dollars of cosmetics and other merchandise every year.

Building a Business

While raising three children on her own, Ash built a very successful career in direct sales. In 1963, however, Ash suffered a blow when she lost out on a promotion that was given instead to a man she had trained. Feeling she had been treated unfairly, Ash resolved to create an enterprise that would reward women for their hard work. Later that year, she started a cosmetics company with her son Richard and nine sales people—whom Ash referred to as "beauty consultants." In 1964, sales exceeded $198,000. By the end of 1965, sales had skyrocketed to more than $800,000.

Since its founding, Mary Kay® products have been sold at in-home parties rather than in stores. Mary Kay has always had distinctive programs for recognizing women who reached certain goals. Pink Cadillacs, diamond-studded jewelry, luxury vacations, and other incentives spur the sales representatives to greater and greater efforts.

Mary Kay Ash
Mary Kay Ash grew her business into a major corporation.

In 1987, Ash assumed the title of chairman emeritus, though she remained active in the company until her death in 2001. Her company and its culture continued to flourish. In 2005, over 1.6 million Mary Kay beauty consultants operated in more than 30 countries worldwide. As the company expanded globally, China became Mary Kay's largest market outside the United States.

APPLICATION Making Inferences

C. Why do you think Mary Kay Ash proved so successful in her cosmetics venture?

REVIEWING KEY CONCEPTS

1. Explain the relationship between the terms in each of these pairs:

   a. *business organization*
   sole proprietorship

   b. *limited life*
   unlimited liability

2. What are the main advantages of a sole proprietorship?

3. What are the main disadvantages of a sole proprietorship?

4. Who gets the profits from a sole proprietorship? Who has to pay all the debts?

5. What steps do new sole proprietorships usually need to take before they can open?

6. **Using Your Notes** Select one of the businesses you identified in Application A on page 227. If you were starting that business, do you think the advantages of a sole proprietorship would outweigh the disadvantages or vice versa? Why? Refer to your completed chart as you formulate your answer. Use the Graphic Organizer at **Interactive Review @ ClassZone.com**

Sole Proprietorships	
Advantages	Disadvantages

CRITICAL THINKING

7. **Evaluating Economic Decisions** Suppose Cosmic Comics becomes very successful, and Bart decides to try opening a second store. What issues should Bart consider? What challenges will he face?

8. **Making Inferences and Drawing Conclusions** In what ways might limited life be considered an advantage for sole proprietors?

9. **Applying Economic Concepts** Explain how a sole proprietorship rests on the principles of free enterprise.

10. **Writing About Economics** Write a brief paragraph explaining what Bart might learn from Mary Kay Ash.

11. **Challenge** How many "yes" answers did you provide to the questions at the top of page 230? If you had one or more "no" answers, explain how you would change a sole proprietorship in order to suit your skills and abilities. If you answered "yes" to all of the questions, explain what you would like about running your own business.

ECONOMICS IN PRACTICE

Business fairs promote new opportunities.

Starting Your Own Business
Each year, thousands of Americans start businesses as sole proprietorships.

Write a Business Plan Choose a business that you might like to start as a sole proprietorship. Use the following questions to develop a plan that shows how the business will make a profit.

- How much money will it take to start the business? Detail each expense.

- How much money will it take to run the business each month? Detail each expense.

- Who will the customers be and how will you attract them?

- Once the business is established, how much will it earn each month? Detail each source of income.

- How much profit will you earn?

Challenge What challenges do you think you would face in making this business a success? Write a paragraph explaining how you would address these challenges.

Forms of Partnerships

OBJECTIVES	KEY TERMS	TAKING NOTES
In Section 2, you will • identify the characteristics and types of partnerships • compare the economic advantages and disadvantages of partnerships	partnership, *p. 232* general partnership, *p. 233* limited partnership, *p. 233* limited liability partnership, *p. 233*	As you read Section 2, complete a comparison and contrast chart to show similarities and differences between partnerships and sole proprietorships. Use the Graphic Organizer at **Interactive Review @ ClassZone.com**

Sole Proprietorships	Partnerships
One owner	Two or more owners

The Characteristics of Partnerships

KEY CONCEPTS

QUICK REFERENCE

A **partnership** is a business co-owned by two or more partners who agree on how responsibilities, profits, and losses of that business are divided.

In Section 1, you read how Bart set up his business as a sole proprietorship. His sister, Mary, who is a whiz at bookkeeping, began helping him with the accounting tasks. As her role in the business expanded, Bart proposed that they join forces in a partnership. A **partnership** is a business co-owned by two or more people, or "partners," who agree on how responsibilities, profits, and losses will be divided. Bart lacks the bookkeeping skills his sister has, and the extra funds she brings could help Cosmic Comics to grow. Forming a partnership might be a good business decision.

Partnerships are found in all kinds of businesses, from construction companies to real estate groups. However, they are especially widespread in the areas of professional and financial services—law firms, accounting firms, doctors' offices, and investment companies. There are several different types of partnerships—general partnerships, limited partnerships, and limited liability partnerships—but they are all run in the same general way.

TYPE 1 General Partnerships

The most common type of partnership is the **general partnership**, a partnership in which partners share responsibility for managing the business and each one is liable for all business debts and losses. As in a sole proprietorship, that liability could put personal savings at risk. The trade-off for sharing the risky side of the business enterprise is sharing the rewards as well. Partners share responsibility, liability, and profits equally, unless there is a partnership agreement that specifies otherwise. This type of partnership is found in almost all areas of business.

TYPE 2 Limited Partnerships

In a general partnership, each partner is personally liable for the debts of the business, even if another partner caused the debt. There is a way, however, to limit one's liability in this kind of business organization. This is through a **limited partnership**, a partnership in which at least one partner is not involved in the day-to-day running of business and is liable only for the funds he or she has invested.

All limited partnerships must have at least one general partner who runs the business and is liable for all debts, but there can be any number of limited partners. Limited partners act as part owners of the business, and they share in the profits. This form of partnership allows the general partner or partners to raise funds to run the business through the limited partners.

QUICK REFERENCE

In a **general partnership** partners share management of the business and each one is liable for all business debts and losses.

A **limited partnership** is one in which at least one partner is not involved in the day-to-day running of business and is liable only for the funds he or she has invested.

In a **limited liability partnership** (LLP), all partners are limited partners and not responsible for the debts and other liabilities of other partners.

TYPE 3 Limited Liability Partnerships

Another kind of partnership is the **limited liability partnership** (LLP), a partnership in which all partners are limited partners and not responsible for the debts and other liabilities of other partners. If one partner makes a mistake that ends up costing the business a lot of money, the other partners cannot be held liable. In LLPs, partners' personal savings are not at risk unless the debts arise from their own mistakes.

Not all businesses can register as LLPs. Those that can include medical partnerships, law firms, and accounting firms. These are businesses in which malpractice—improper, negligent, or unprincipled behavior—can be an issue. LLPs are a fairly new form of business organization, and the laws governing them vary from state to state.

Partnerships Doctors' offices are often run as limited liability partnerships.

APPLICATION Comparing and Contrasting Economic Information

A. What are the differences in liability that distinguish general partnerships, limited partnerships, and limited liability partnerships?

Partnerships: Advantages and Disadvantages

KEY CONCEPTS

Some of the economic advantages of partnerships are similar to those of sole proprietorships. Like sole proprietorships, partnerships are easy to set up and dissolve and have few government regulations. Compared with sole proprietorships, however, partners have greater access to funds. Also, possibilities exist for specialization among partners, which can promote efficiency.

The disadvantages of partnerships are similar to the disadvantages of sole proprietorships. Like the sole proprietor, at least one of the partners, except in LLPs, faces unlimited liability. Partnerships, too, have limited life. However, partnerships have at least one disadvantage that sole proprietorships avoid. Disagreements among partners can lead to serious problems in running the business.

ADVANTAGES Partnerships

Bart and Mary realized that if they formed a partnership they would benefit from some of the same advantages that sole proprietorships have, plus some important additional advantages.

Easy to Open and Close Partnerships, like sole proprietorships, are easy to start up and dissolve. Ending the partnership would be equally straightforward for Bart and

Economics Update

Find an update on partnerships at **ClassZone.com**

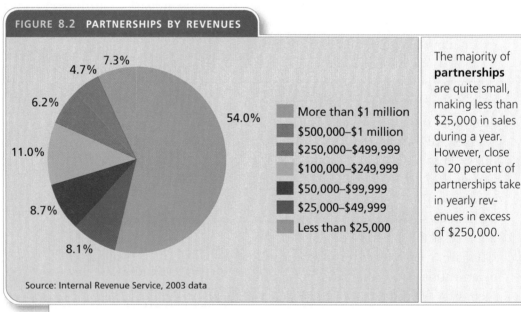

FIGURE 8.2 PARTNERSHIPS BY REVENUES

7.3%
4.7%
6.2%
54.0%
11.0%
8.7%
8.1%

- More than $1 million
- $500,000–$1 million
- $250,000–$499,999
- $100,000–$249,999
- $50,000–$99,999
- $25,000–$49,999
- Less than $25,000

The majority of **partnerships** are quite small, making less than $25,000 in sales during a year. However, close to 20 percent of partnerships take in yearly revenues in excess of $250,000.

Source: Internal Revenue Service, 2003 data

ANALYZE GRAPHS

1. What percentage of partnerships made more than $100,000 in sales?
2. Some 7 percent of partnerships took in more than $1 million in revenues, compared to just 0.5 percent of sole proprietorships. Why do you think partnerships generate more revenues than sole proprietorships?

his sister. As long as they have settled all their bills, Bart and Mary may dissolve the partnership when they see fit.

Few Regulations Bart and Mary would not be burdened with a host of government regulations. They would enter into a legal agreement spelling out their rights and responsibilities as partners. Partners are covered under the Uniform Partnership Act (UPA), a law, adopted by most states, that lays out basic partnership rules.

Access to Resources Mary would bring additional funds to Cosmic Comics. In addition, partnerships generally make it easier to get bank loans for business purposes. A greater pool of funds also makes it easier for partnerships to attract and keep workers.

Joint Decision Making In most partnerships, partners share in the making of business decisions. This may result in better decisions, for each partner brings his or her own particular perspective to the process. The exception is limited partnerships, in which the limited partner does not participate in running the business.

Specialization Also, each partner may bring specific skills to the business. For example, Bart brings knowledge of comic books, while Mary, who studied business accounting in college, brings skills in bookkeeping and finance. Having partners focus on their special skills promotes efficiency.

DISADVANTAGES Partnerships

Bart and Mary also considered the disadvantages of partnerships.

Unlimited Liability The biggest disadvantage of most partnerships is the same as that of sole proprietorships: unlimited liability. Both Bart and Mary are personally responsible for the full extent of the partnership's debts and other liabilities. So they risk having to use their personal savings, and even having to sell their property, to cover their business debts.

Joint Decision Making Partners benefit by making decisions together. But sometimes disagreements can interfere with running the business.

Potential for Conflict As partners, they may encounter a new disadvantage as well. Having more than one decision maker can often lead to better decisions. However, it can also detract from efficiency if there are many partners and each decision requires the approval of all. Further, disagreements among partners can become so severe that they lead to the closing of the business.

Limited Life Like sole proprietorships, partnerships have limited life. When a partner dies, retires, or leaves for some other reason, or if new partners are added, the business as it was originally formed ceases to exist legally. A new partnership arrangement must be established if the enterprise is to continue.

APPLICATION Applying Economic Concepts

B. Consider the businesses you identified in Application A on page 227 of Section 1. Would these businesses work as partnerships? Why or why not?

For more information on interpreting graphs, see the Skillbuilder Handbook, page R27.

Distinguishing Fact from Opinion

Facts are events, dates, statistics, and statements that can be proved to be true. Facts can be checked for accuracy. Economists use facts to develop **opinions**, which may be expressed as judgments, beliefs, or theories. By learning to distinguish between facts and opinions, you will be able to think critically about the economic theories, interpretations, and conclusions of others.

TIPS FOR ANALYZING TEXT Use the following guidelines to analyze economic information in written works:

FIGURE 8.3 STARTS AND CLOSURES OF SMALL EMPLOYER FIRMS

	2000	2001	2002	2003	2004
New Firms	574,300	585,140	569,750	553,500	580,990
Firm Closures	542,831	553,291	586,890	572,300	576,200
Bankruptcies	35,472	40,099	38,540	35,037	34,317

Sources: U.S. Bureau of the Census; Administrative Office of the U.S. Courts; U.S. Department of Labor, Employment and Training Administration.

> **Facts** used by economists are often in the form of statistics, like the ones in this table.

Many Americans have faith that their ideas will bring them wealth or at least a comfortable living. According to the U.S. government, Americans created more than half a million small firms, or businesses, in the United States each year from 2000 to 2005. While prospective entrepreneurs may interpret these figures as a small business bonanza, overall closures of small businesses also exceeded the half-million mark each year during the same period. And in 2002 and 2003, more small firms closed their doors than opened them, suggesting that market conditions for those two years were particularly unfavorable for the prolonged success of small businesses. Yet bankruptcies among small firms declined in 2002 and 2003. Although such data are likely to be of interest to prospective entrepreneurs, it is limited in nature. Anyone planning to start a business venture would be wise to conduct more extensive research.

> **Opinions.** Look for words, such as *suggest, suggesting, belief,* and *believe,* which often express assertions, claims, and hypotheses.

> **Facts** include economic data that can be proved. The writer bases this statement on verifiable facts from the table.

> **Judgments,** another form of opinion, often use descriptive words such as *wise, foolish, sensible,* and *fortunate,* which have an emotional quality.

THINKING ECONOMICALLY Distinguishing Fact from Opinion

1. What facts, if any, does the author use to support the first sentence in the paragraph?

2. Using information from the table and article, write one statement of fact and one statement of opinion. As a class, share your statements and discuss.

Online Quiz
ClassZone.com

REVIEWING KEY CONCEPTS

1. Explain the relationship between the terms in each of these pairs:

   a. *partnership*
   general partnership

   b. *limited partnership*
   limited liability partnership

2. What are the main advantages of a partnership?

3. What are the main disadvantages of a partnership?

4. In what ways do the increased resources of a partnership help a business?

5. What determines how partners will divide responsibilities, profits, and debts?

6. **Using Your Notes** Which type of partnership is most like a sole proprietorship? Explain your answer with specific characteristics. Refer to your completed chart.

Sole Proprietorships	Partnerships
One owner	Two or more owners

   Use the Graphic Organizer at
   Interactive Review @ ClassZone.com

CRITICAL THINKING

7. **Applying Economic Concepts** If you were looking to start a business as a partnership, what traits would you look for in potential partners? Draw up a list of five traits and give a brief explanation for each. Be sure to take the advantages and disadvantages of partnerships into consideration.

8. **Comparing and Contrasting Economic Information** Briefly explore the differences in potential for job satisfaction between sole proprietorships and partnerships. One size does not fit all—try to determine which of these two business organizations would suit you best.

9. **Writing About Economics** American business leader John D. Rockefeller said, "A friendship founded on business is a good deal better than a business founded on friendship." What do you think he had in mind? Write a brief paragraph agreeing or disagreeing, with reference to partnerships.

10. **Challenge** Do you think that major retail or manufacturing businesses would work as partnerships? Why or why not?

ECONOMICS IN PRACTICE

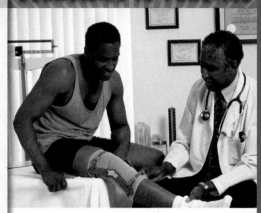

Types of Partnerships
The different types of partnerships suit different types of businesses.

Identify Partnerships Identify the type of partnership represented in each description.

1. Doctors choose this type of partnership because it protects them from malpractice suits brought against other partners.

2. The only role that George plays in the partnership is to collect profits or bear losses based on the amount of funds he contributed.

3. Stephen and Mike start a consulting service to help businesses manage their trademarks and patents. They are the only partners, sharing equally in the work, profits, and losses.

4. Rosa and Serena carefully review expansion plans after new partners provide extra funds. However, they know that they remain fully liable if their decisions are not sound.

Challenge Write a description of three different business partnerships without naming them. Exchange your descriptions with a classmate and identify each other's partnerships.

Corporations, Mergers, and Multinationals

OBJECTIVES	KEY TERMS	TAKING NOTES
In Section 3, you will • identify the characteristics of corporations • compare the advantages and disadvantages of corporations • describe how corporations consolidate to form larger business combinations • explain the role of multinational corporations in the world economy	corporation, *p. 238* stock, *p. 238* dividend, *p. 238* public company, *p. 238* private company, *p. 238* bond, *p. 240* limited liability, *p. 240* unlimited life, *p. 240* horizontal merger, *p. 243* vertical merger, *p. 243* conglomerate, *p. 243* multinational corporation, *p. 243*	As you read Section 3, complete a cluster diagram that categorizes information about corporations. Use the Graphic Organizer at **Interactive Review @ ClassZone.com** 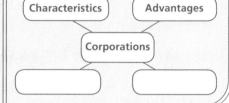

Characteristics of Corporations

KEY CONCEPTS

Corporations are the third main kind of business organization. A **corporation** is a business owned by individuals, called shareholders or stockholders. The shareholders own the rights to the company's profits, but they face limited liability for the company's debts and losses. These individuals acquire ownership rights through the purchase of **stock**, or shares of ownership in the corporation.

For example, suppose a large company sells a million shares in the form of stock. If you bought 10,000 shares, you would own 1 percent of the company. If the company runs into trouble, you would not be responsible for any of its debt. Your only risk is that the value of your stock might decline. If the company does well and earns a profit, you might receive a payment called a **dividend**, part of the profit that the company pays out to stockholders.

A corporation that issues stock that can be freely bought and sold is called a **public company.** One that retains control over who can buy or sell the stock is called a **private company.** Corporations make up about 20 percent of the number of businesses in the United States, but they produce most of the country's goods and services and employ the majority of American workers.

EXAMPLE F & S Publishing, Inc.

To better understand how corporations operate, let's look at F & S Publishing, Inc., a successful publishing business. Frank and Shirley, the founders, decided to turn their business into a corporation because they wished to avoid unlimited liability. A corporation, unlike a partnership or sole proprietorship, is a formal, legal entity separate from the individuals who own and run it. The financial liabilities of F & S

QUICK REFERENCE

A **corporation** is a business owned by stockholders, who own the rights to the company's profits but face limited liability for the company's debts and losses.

Stock is a share of ownership in a corporation.

A **dividend** is part of a corporation's profit that is paid out to stockholders.

A **public company** issues stock that can be publicly traded.

A **private company** controls who can buy or sell its stock.

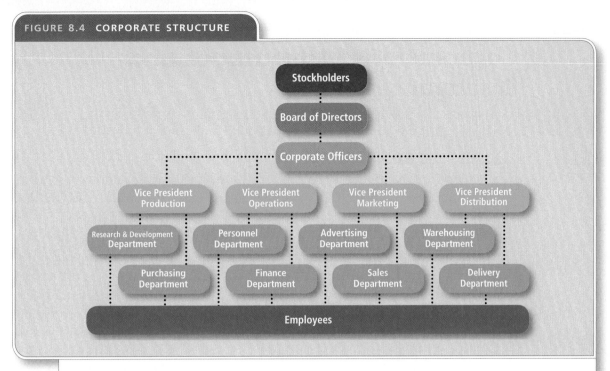

FIGURE 8.4 CORPORATE STRUCTURE

Stockholders

Board of Directors

Corporate Officers

Vice President Production

Vice President Operations

Vice President Marketing

Vice President Distribution

Research & Development Department

Personnel Department

Advertising Department

Warehousing Department

Purchasing Department

Finance Department

Sales Department

Delivery Department

Employees

ANALYZE CHARTS
This chart shows the organization of a typical corporation. Smaller corporations may only have stockholders, corporate officers, and employees. Larger corporations may be much more complex. Imagine you own a company that makes a product you like. Draw an organization chart for your corporation.

Publishing, Inc., are separate from the personal financial liabilities of Frank, Shirley, and other F & S stockholders. If the business fails, only the assets of F & S itself—the office building, equipment, and company bank accounts—are at risk.

Setting up a corporation involves more work and expense than establishing a sole proprietorship or partnership. Frank and Shirley hired a law firm to draw up and file papers requesting permission from the state government to incorporate. The state government agreed to the request and issued a corporate charter. This document named F & S Publishing, Inc., as the business and stated its address and purpose. The charter also specified the maximum amount of stock Frank and Shirley could sell to stockholders.

F & S Publishing, Inc., is organized like the majority of corporations. Stockholders—the owners of the corporation—elect a board of directors. The board hires corporate officers, such as the president and the vice-presidents in charge of sales, production, finance, and so on. These officers are responsible for the smooth running of the corporation. In most corporations, the stockholders and the board of directors are not involved in the day-to-day running of the business. F & S Publishing, Inc., however, is a small company, and Frank and Shirley became members of the board of directors as well as managers.

Frank and Shirley decided to make their business a public company. They bought enough of the stock themselves so that they would each have a seat on the board of directors. They sold the rest of the stock to raise money to expand the business.

APPLICATION Applying Economic Concepts

A. Frank and Shirley were worried about unlimited liability. How did incorporating protect them from this problem?

Corporations: Advantages and Disadvantages

QUICK REFERENCE

A **bond** is a contract issued by a corporation that promises to repay borrowed money, plus interest, on a fixed schedule.

Limited liability means that a business owner's liability for debts and losses of the business is limited.

Unlimited life means that a corporation continues to exist even after an owner dies, leaves the business, or transfers his or her ownership.

KEY CONCEPTS

The advantages of corporations often address the major disadvantages of sole proprietorships and partnerships. For example, corporations are more effective than either of the other business structures at raising large amounts of money. The key methods of raising money are the sale of stock and the issuing of bonds. A **bond** is a contract the corporation issues that promises to repay borrowed money, plus interest, on a fixed schedule. Also, unlike sole proprietorships and most partnerships, corporations provide their owners with **limited liability**, which means that the business owner's liability for business debts and losses is limited. Further, corporations have **unlimited life**—they continue to exist even after a change in ownership. Sole proprietorships and partnerships do not.

Most of the disadvantages of corporations are related to their size and organizational complexity. Corporations are costly and time-consuming to start up; they are governed by many more rules and regulations; and, because of the organizational structure, the owners may have little control over business decisions. Despite these drawbacks, corporations can be efficient and productive business organizations.

Economics Update

Find an update on corporations at **ClassZone.com**

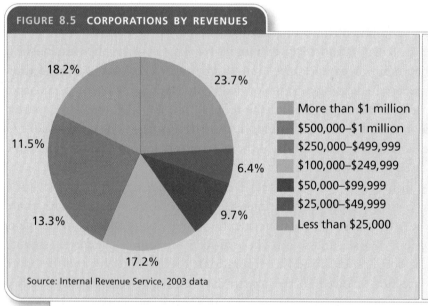

FIGURE 8.5 CORPORATIONS BY REVENUES

- More than $1 million
- $500,000–$1 million
- $250,000–$499,999
- $100,000–$249,999
- $50,000–$99,999
- $25,000–$49,999
- Less than $25,000

23.7%
18.2%
11.5%
13.3%
17.2%
9.7%
6.4%

Source: Internal Revenue Service, 2003 data

Most people think of **corporations** as very large companies with factories and offices that occupy great expanses of land. Actually, more than a third of all corporations in the United States take in less than $100,000 in revenues each year.

ANALYZE GRAPHS

1. What percentage of corporations made more than $250,000 in sales?

2. Compare Figure 8.5 with Figure 8.1 on p. 229 and Figure 8.2 on p. 234. According to the graphs, which type of business has the highest percentage of firms that earn over $1 million in revenues each year?

ADVANTAGES Corporations

Frank and Shirley had operated F & S as a partnership for several years. They decided to incorporate to gain the advantages of the corporate business structure.

Access to Resources Frank and Shirley have ideas to expand their business, but implementing the ideas may require more money than profits from the business will provide. As a corporation, they have better opportunities for obtaining additional money. Besides borrowing from banks, F & S can raise money by selling more stock or by issuing bonds. This greater access to funds leads to greater potential for growth.

Professional Managers Frank and Shirley are involved in the running of F & S Publishing, Inc. Frank serves as chief executive officer (CEO), while Shirley is chief operations officer (COO). However, they decided to hire managers with strong backgrounds in finance and sales as company treasurer and vice-president for sales. Having professionals in charge of financial and sales matters will probably lead to higher profits.

Limited Liability Because of limited liability, F & S Publishing, Inc., alone is liable for any debts or losses it incurs. Frank, Shirley, and F & S stockholders are liable only for the money they paid for their stock. The board of directors and officers of the corporation, too, are protected from liability.

"Our investors' enthusiasm was gratifying... first time I've ever seen a mosh pit at a stockholders' meeting!"

Source: www.CartoonStock.com

Unlimited Life If any of the owners—the stockholders—of F & S dies or decides to end his or her relationship with the company, the business would continue to operate as before. This even applies to Frank and Shirley. If either or both of them move on to another business, F & S Publishing, Inc., can continue without them for as long as it is a viable business.

DISADVANTAGES Corporations

Frank and Shirley discovered some of the disadvantages to incorporating when they first began the process. They learned about other disadvantages of corporations as they ran their business.

Start-Up Cost and Effort When they first started, Frank and Shirley set up their business as a partnership. Compared to setting up the partnership, Frank and Shirley found the process of setting up a corporation more time-consuming, difficult, and expensive. The paperwork they had to prepare and file with the state government was extensive, and they had to hire a law firm to help with this task.

Heavy Regulation As a public company, F & S Publishing, Inc., must prepare annual reports for the Securities and Exchange Commission (SEC), the government agency

FIGURE 8.6 Business Organizations: Advantages and Disadvantages

Type of Organization	Advantages	Disadvantages
Sole Proprietorship	• Easy to start up, close down • Sole proprietor has satisfaction of running business his or her own way • Few regulations • Sole proprietor keeps all the profits	• Limited funds • Limited life • Unlimited liability
Partnership	• Easy to start up, close down • Few regulations • Greater access to funds • Partners share in decision making • Partners may bring complementary skills to the business	• Unlimited liability • Shared decision making may create conflict among partners • Limited life
Corporation	• Greatest access to funds • Business run by professionals • Limited liability • Unlimited life	• Difficult to start up • More regulations • Double taxation • Owners may have less control of running the business

ANALYZE TABLES

All three forms of business organizations have distinct advantages and disadvantages.
If you were starting a business, which form of business organization would you choose? Why?

that oversees the sale of stocks. It also has to prepare and issue quarterly financial reports for stockholders. Further, the company must hold yearly meetings for its stockholders. All of these regulations help ensure that corporations are run for the benefit of the shareholders. Private companies are subject to fewer regulations related to their ownership.

Double Taxation Frank and Shirley experience an effect known as double taxation. As officers of the company, they are well aware of the taxes on profits that the corporation must pay. As stockholders, they know that their dividend income, paid out of the company profits, is also taxed. Some small corporations qualify for S corporation status, a tax status which avoids double taxation.

Loss of Control Frank and Shirley, as founders, owners, and directors, expect to have a major voice in deciding the direction that F & S Publishing, Inc., will take. However, they experienced some loss of control when the rest of the board of directors voted against them and brought in a new sales manager.

APPLICATION Evaluating Economic Decisions

B. F & S was successful as a partnership. What will Frank and Shirley gain by making their company a corporation?

Business Consolidation

You've probably seen news stories about them—business consolidations that merge, or combine, several large companies into one mega-company. These consolidations take place for several possible reasons. These include increasing efficiency, gaining a new identity as a business or losing an old one, keeping rivals out of the marketplace, and diversifying the product line.

There are two main kinds of mergers (see Figure 8.7). A **horizontal merger** describes the joining of companies that offer the same or similar products or services. A **vertical merger** describes the combining of companies involved in different steps of production or marketing of a product or service. An alternative to the two main types is a **conglomerate**, which results from a merger of companies that produce unrelated goods or services. Through growth, consolidations, and other means, an enterprise can grow so big that it becomes a **multinational corporation**, a large corporation with branches in several countries.

QUICK REFERENCE

A **horizontal merger** is the combining of two or more companies that produce the same product or similar products.

A **vertical merger** is the combining of companies involved in different steps of producing or marketing a product.

A **conglomerate** is a business composed of several companies, each one producing unrelated goods or services.

A **multinational corporation** is a large corporation with branches in several countries.

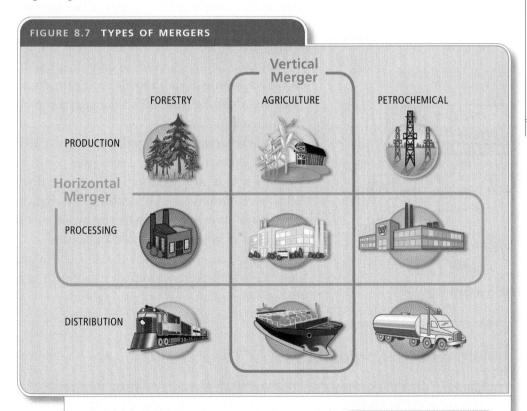

FIGURE 8.7 TYPES OF MERGERS

ANALYZE CHARTS

What kind of mergers took place in each of the following situations?

1. In 1999, Ford Motor Co. purchased Swedish-based car manufacturer Volvo.
2. In 1989, Japanese electronics giant Sony purchased Columbia Pictures Entertainment.

Animated Economics

Use an interactive merger chart at **ClassZone.com**

Mergers

An example of a horizontal merger is the one between Reebok and Adidas in 2005. At the time, they were the second- and third-biggest makers of sports shoes. The subtitle of an article about the merger summed up the potential benefits of all mergers: "Adidas-Reebok merger could trim costs for companies and maybe even some dollars for consumers." The two companies planned to cut production and distribution costs by combining their operations. This, they hoped, would improve their ability to compete against the largest sport-shoe maker, Nike. More efficient production usually leads to lower prices, which would draw consumers away from Nike.

An example of a vertical merger took place in the late 1990s during a period when the oil and gas industry was undergoing major consolidations. Shell Oil, which owned more refineries, joined with Texaco, which owned more gas stations. This type of merger is vertical, since companies involved in different steps of production (refining) or distribution (getting gasoline to customers) combined.

Conglomerates

Another kind of business consolidation, the conglomerate, is formed when two or more companies in different industries come together. In theory, the advantage of this form of consolidation is that, with diversified businesses, the parent company is protected from isolated economic pressures, such as changing demand for a specific product. In practice, it can be difficult to manage companies in unrelated industries.

Conglomerates were popular during the 1960s. One conglomerate of the 1960s was Gulf and Western, which included companies in such diverse fields as communications, clothing, mining, and agricultural products. As with many other conglomerates formed in the 1960s, however, Gulf and Western did not produce the desired financial gains. Gulf and Western sold all its companies but the entertainment and publishing endeavors and became known as Viacom.

"I've come up with our new logo, JB."

Source: www.CartoonStock.com

Multinational Corporations

When you use Google to do an Internet search, you are using the services of a multinational corporation, a large corporation with branches in several countries. Google's headquarters are in Mountain View, California, but it has branch offices in many other countries. Coca-Cola, McDonald's, Nike, and Sony are all examples of multinational, or transnational, corporations.

Multinational corporations like Google are a major force in globalization, commerce conducted without regard to national boundaries. Multinational corporations have many beneficial effects. They provide new jobs, goods, and services around the world and spread technological advances. When such companies open businesses in poorer countries, the jobs and the tax revenues help raise the standard of living.

General Electric: Multinational Corporation

The operations of General Electric (GE), one of the world's largest multinational corporations, span the globe. While its headquarters is located in the United States, GE has manufacturing and production centers located in countries far and near. To supply these centers, GE purchases raw materials from all over the world. Further, the corporation has sales centers on six of the seven continents.

GE is both a multinational and a conglomerate, offering a wide range of services and products. The diagram below offers a view of GE's six major businesses and the units that make up these businesses. GE owns many companies that you know. For example, GE owns 80 percent of NBC Universal, which is made up of the NBC television network, Universal Pictures, and many related businesses. GE's Consumer and Industrial unit manufactures such common products as refrigerators, ovens, and light bulbs. But many of GE's businesses are less well-known because they provide services and products for businesses and governments.

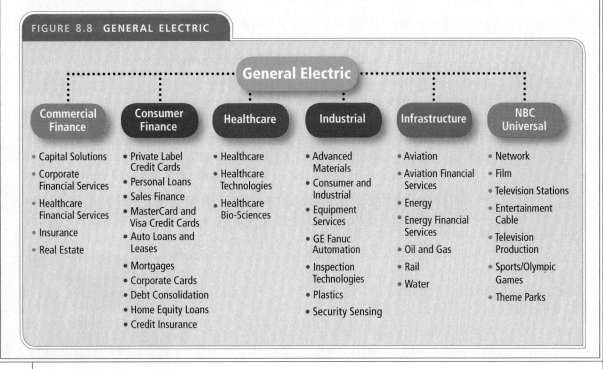

FIGURE 8.8 GENERAL ELECTRIC

General Electric

Commercial Finance	Consumer Finance	Healthcare	Industrial	Infrastructure	NBC Universal
• Capital Solutions • Corporate Financial Services • Healthcare Financial Services • Insurance • Real Estate	• Private Label Credit Cards • Personal Loans • Sales Finance • MasterCard and Visa Credit Cards • Auto Loans and Leases • Mortgages • Corporate Cards • Debt Consolidation • Home Equity Loans • Credit Insurance	• Healthcare • Healthcare Technologies • Healthcare Bio-Sciences	• Advanced Materials • Consumer and Industrial • Equipment Services • GE Fanuc Automation • Inspection Technologies • Plastics • Security Sensing	• Aviation • Aviation Financial Services • Energy • Energy Financial Services • Oil and Gas • Rail • Water	• Network • Film • Television Stations • Entertainment Cable • Television Production • Sports/Olympic Games • Theme Parks

CONNECTING ACROSS THE GLOBE

1. **Applying Economic Information** What characteristics of General Electric define it as "multinational"?

2. **Analyzing Charts** General Electric operates in a wide range of industries. Name some industries in which it does not participate. Make sure to check your answer against the chart.

However, multinational corporations can also create problems. Some build factories that emit harmful waste products in countries with lax government regulation. Others operate factories where workers toil for long hours in unsafe working conditions. You will learn more about the impact of multinationals on the world economy in Chapter 17.

APPLICATION Applying Economic Concepts

C. Make up an imaginary conglomerate based on three real companies.

Bill Gates:
Entrepreneur and Corporate Leader

A reporter once asked multibillionaire Bill Gates, founder of Microsoft Corporation, if he thought there was a larger meaning in the universe. Gates joked, "It's possible … that the universe exists only for me. If so, it's sure going well for me, I must admit." From a small beginning, Bill Gates created the world's largest software company. Microsoft employs more than 60,000 people in more than 100 countries.

Microsoft Corporation

Gates was always fascinated with computers and software. He developed software for his high school to schedule classes and for his hometown of Seattle to monitor traffic. At Harvard, he and his friend Paul Allen developed the BASIC language for personal computers. In 1975, during his third year, Gates left college to form a business with Allen to supply BASIC programming for an early brand of personal computers. Gates and Allen called their company Micro-soft (later changed to Microsoft). "I think my most important work was the early work," Gates said in 2005, "conceiving of the idea of the PC and how important that would be, and the role software would play. . . . "

Microsoft incorporated in 1981. When it struck a deal to provide the operating system for IBM personal computers, it secured its dominance. Microsoft became an international corporation in 1985, when it opened a production facility in Dublin, Ireland. That same year, it released what would become the world's most popular operating system, Microsoft Windows. Initially, Microsoft focused on corporate computing. With the release of Windows 95, however, it turned to the consumer market.

Bill Gates Bill Gates cofounded Microsoft in 1975. It became one of the world's most successful corporations.

Gates led Microsoft as it continued to dominate the computer industry. In 1994, Gates established a foundation for charitable giving that quickly became the largest charitable foundation in the world. The foundation focuses on global health and education. In 2006, Gates began shifting away from the day-to-day responsibilities of running Microsoft and toward running the foundation.

 **Economics Update**

Find an update on Bill Gates and Microsoft at **ClassZone.com**

APPLICATION Categorizing Economic Information

D. Create a timeline showing the development of Microsoft from its founding to its status as a major multinational corporation.

SECTION 3 Assessment

Online Quiz
ClassZone.com

REVIEWING KEY CONCEPTS

1. Explain the relationship between the terms in each of these groups.

   a. *stock*   **b.** *public company*   **c.** *merger*
         bond   *private company*   *conglomerate*

2. What are the main advantages of a corporation?

3. What are the main disadvantages of a corporation?

4. How do corporations raise money?

5. What is a multinational corporation?

6. **Using Your Notes** What is the difference between a vertical merger and a horizontal merger? Refer to your completed cluster diagram.

   Use the Graphic Organizer at **Interactive Review @ ClassZone.com**

   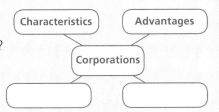

CRITICAL THINKING

7. **Analyzing Cause and Effect** Review the table below. If the two largest bottled water manufacturers consolidated in a horizontal merger, what might the effect be on competition?

Company	Annual Sales (in millions of dollars)	Percent of Market
Nature's Springs	1,000	25
Well Water, Inc.	600	15
Best Taste	400	10
Empyrean Isles	400	10
No-Tap Water	200	5

8. **Writing About Economics** In what ways might a vertical merger in the oil industry influence gas prices?

9. **Explaining an Economic Concept** What are the benefits of combining several companies to form a conglomerate? Name an example of a conglomerate.

10. **Challenge** So far in this chapter, you have learned about business enterprises that seek profits. In Section 4, you will learn about nonprofit organizations. How do you think the structure of such organizations might differ from the structure of profit-seeking organizations?

ECONOMICS IN PRACTICE

Analyzing Data
When companies decide to merge, they must carefully evaluate how to combine their operations.

Will This Merger Work? Leviathan Motion Pictures wants to purchase Pipsqueak Computer Games.

	Leviathan	Pipsqueak
Head of Company	Ivana Getrich, age 60	Bob L. Head, age 30
Board of Directors	15 business executives	Bob and a couple of his buddies
Publicly Owned Shares	200,000,000	250,000
Market Capitalization	$5,000,000,000	$250,000,000
2008 Sales	$1,000,000,000	$10,000,000
Production Studios	4 in California, 1 in New York	1 in Austin
Employees	15,000 worldwide	150 in Austin

Review the table and imagine what would happen if the companies merge. Write a paragraph describing the challenges and the benefits.

Challenge If you were Bob, would you retire after selling Pipsqueak, or would you want to continue running the company? Explain your answer.

Franchises, Co-ops, and Nonprofits

OBJECTIVES	KEY TERMS	TAKING NOTES
In Section 4, you will • explain how franchises function • identify the characteristics and purpose of cooperatives • describe the types and purposes of nonprofit organizations	franchise, *p. 248* franchisee, *p. 248* cooperative, *p. 250* nonprofit organization, *p. 250*	As you read Section 4, complete a summary chart with information on specialized organizations. Use the Graphic Organizer at **Interactive Review @ ClassZone.com**

Franchises	Co-ops	Nonprofits

Franchises

KEY CONCEPTS

QUICK REFERENCE

A **franchise** is a business that licenses the right to sell its products in a particular area.

A **franchisee** is a semi-independent business that buys the right to run a franchise.

A **franchise** is a business made up of semi-independent businesses that all offer the same products or services. Each **franchisee**, as the individual businesses are known, pays a fee to the parent company in return for the right to sell the company's products or services in a particular area. Fast-food restaurants are the most common franchised business. However, this kind of business organization is also found in many other industries, including hotels, rental cars, and car service.

EXAMPLE An Almost Independent Business

The Mango Grove Juice and Nut Bar in the city center provides an illustration of how a franchise works. Tim, who runs the Mango Grove, had worked as assistant manager at a local restaurant for several years. He really wanted to run his own business, but he didn't think he had the experience or the funds to go it alone. On trips to other cities, he had been impressed by the popularity of the Mango Grove Juice and Nut Bar, an organic juice and sandwich restaurant. So he looked into becoming a franchisee of that business in his home city.

FIGURE 8.9 World's Leading Franchises

Corporation	Franchisees
1. McDonald's	30,300
2. Yum! Brands (KFC, Taco Bell, etc.)	29,300
3. 7-Eleven	28,200
4. Cendent (Howard Johnson, Avis Rent-A-Car, etc.)	24,600
5. Subway	21,000

Source: International Franchise Association, 2004 data

Which franchise would you like to run?

Hundreds of different businesses operate as franchises. Fast-food restaurants and coffee bars are among the most common. Which type of franchise would you like to run? Why?

ADVANTAGES Franchises

Becoming a franchisee of Mango Grove Juice and Nut Bar appealed to Tim for several reasons. First, he would have a level of independence he did not have in his job at the restaurant. Second, the franchiser, Mango Grove Fruit and Nut Bar, would provide good training in running the business, since his success affected their own. They would also provide proven products—their famous mango smoothie mixes and nut bread for sandwiches—as well as other materials, such as the décor common to all the Mango Grove juice bars, at a relatively low cost. Further, the franchiser would pay for national or regional advertising that would bring in customers.

DISADVANTAGES Franchises

Tim also thought through the disadvantages. He would have to invest most of the money he had saved, with no assurance of success in the business. He would also have to share some of the profits with the franchiser. Further, he would not have control over some aspects of the business. For example, he would have to meet the franchiser's operating rules, such as buying materials only from the franchiser and limiting the products he offered to those from the franchiser.

After considerable thought, Tim decided to apply to become a franchisee. He was accepted, and before long his business became a success. In time, a number of other Mango Grove bars opened in other parts of the city. Since both the franchiser and franchisees had the same incentive—financial reward if the business was successful—they worked well together to make the juice bars succeed.

APPLICATION Evaluating Economic Decisions

A. What advantage does the franchiser have over a business that owns and operates all of its own shops?

Cooperatives and Nonprofits

KEY CONCEPTS

The primary purpose of most businesses is to earn money for the owners—in other words, to make a profit. But not all businesses exist solely to make a profit. A **cooperative** is a type of business operated for the shared benefit of the owners, who are also its customers. A **nonprofit organization** is an institution that acts like a business organization, but its purpose is usually to benefit society, not to make a profit.

A Business Organization for Its Members

When people who need the same goods or services band together and act as a business, they can offer low prices by reducing or eliminating profit. Such organizations are called cooperatives, or co-ops. There are three basic types of cooperatives: consumer, service, and producer.

Consumer Consumer, or purchasing, co-ops can be small organizations, like an organic food cooperative, or they can be giant warehouse clubs. Consumer co-ops require some kind of membership payment, either in the form of labor (keeping the books or packaging orders) or monetary fees. They keep prices low by purchasing goods in large volumes at a discount price.

Service Service co-ops are business organizations, such as credit unions, that offer their members a service. Employers often form service cooperatives to reduce the cost of buying health insurance for their employees.

Producer Producer cooperatives are mainly owned and operated by the producers of agricultural products. They join together to ensure cheaper, more efficient processing or better marketing of their products.

A Purpose Other Than Profit

There are several different types of nonprofits. Some, like the American Red Cross, have the purpose of benefiting society. They provide their goods or services for free or for a minimal fee. Other nonprofits, like the American Bar Association, are professional organizations. Such organizations exist to promote the common interests of their members. Business associations, trade associations, labor unions, and museums are all examples of organizations pursuing goals other than profits.

The structure of a nonprofit resembles that of a corporation. A nonprofit must receive a government charter, for example, and has unlimited life. Unlike a corporation, however, many nonprofit organizations are not required to pay taxes because they do not generate profits and they serve society. Nonprofits raise most of their money from donations, grants, or membership fees. Some nonprofits sell products or services, but only as a way of raising funds to support their mission.

APPLICATION Making Inferences

B. The National Association of Home Builders promotes the interests of construction companies. Habitat for Humanity builds homes for the disadvantaged. Which of these nonprofits is the government more likely to excuse from paying taxes? Why?

SECTION 4 Assessment

REVIEWING KEY CONCEPTS

1. Give an example of each of the following terms.

   a. *franchise*   b. *cooperative*   c. *nonprofit organization*

2. What are the main advantages of a franchise?

3. What are the main disadvantages of a franchise?

4. How do consumer and service cooperatives save their members money?

5. What are some purposes of nonprofit organizations?

6. **Using Your Notes** What are the chief distinctions among franchises, cooperatives, and nonprofits? Refer to your completed summary chart.

   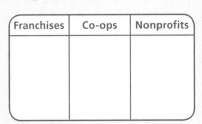

Franchises	Co-ops	Nonprofits

   Use the Graphic Organizer at **Interactive Review @ ClassZone.com**

CRITICAL THINKING

7. **Explaining an Economic Concept** Explain how franchisees share the risk of the business venture with the franchiser.

8. **Making Inferences and Drawing Conclusions** How do nonprofits get the money needed to pay the people who work for them and to provide services?

9. **Evaluating Economic Decisions** You're shopping for a new camera. You could buy it from a specialty camera store that offers expert advice or from a discount retail store that carries hundreds of other products. Or you could join a camera club that offers a buying cooperative. What are the advantages and disadvantages of each option?

10. **Challenge** Helping society can be big business. The largest nonprofits generate annual revenues in the billions of dollars. Even small nonprofit organizations can make as much money as many for-profit businesses. Nonprofits employ professional managers, accountants, and marketers, just as any other business would. Should the chief executive officer (CEO) of a nonprofit with $500 million in annual revenue be paid the same salary as the CEO of a for-profit company with the same amount of revenue? Explain your answer.

ECONOMICS IN PRACTICE

Identifying Business Organizations
Franchises, co-ops, and nonprofits have distinctive features.

What Kind of Organization?
Review the following descriptions of business organizations. Decide what kind of business organization fits each description. Remember that there are three different types of cooperatives.

- Several companies in your city join together to get a better deal on the health insurance they offer to their workers.

- Dan pays a fee for the right to sell Soft Freeze ice cream. Soft Freeze provides all the equipment Dan needs.

- Rachel and Serafina join an association that offers relatively cheap organic products. In return, they pay a small monthly membership fee.

- The Portswood Road Church Club provides a free food service for the poor of the neighborhood.

Challenge Imagine a cooperative you and your friends might form. Describe how it would operate and how it would save you money.

Apple: The Evolution of One Company

Background Steve Jobs and Steve Wozniak joined forces when they were students. Together, they created a personal computer, named it Apple, and in 1976 started a company with the same name. In the years that followed, Apple Computer, Inc., attained worldwide prominence. While the success story of Jobs and Wozniak often sounds like a fairy tale, the evolution of the company was not without its ups and downs. But by 2005, Apple had revenues of nearly $14 billion.

What's the issue? How does a company evolve from an idea into a billion-dollar enterprise? Study these sources to discover the factors behind the success of Apple Computer, Inc.

Steve Wozniak (left) and Steve Jobs (right) founded Apple Computer in 1976.

A. Online Biography

This article describes how two young men with an interest in computers created the basis for Apple Computer, Inc.

▶ Two American Entrepreneurs Start Out in a Garage

Young inventors build their first of many computers.

When the two first met, Wozniak (born 1950) was 18, Jobs (born 1955) only 13. The pair put their electronics and inventing talents to work making unusual devices, and a few years later purchased a $25 microprocessor with the intention of building a computer. Although this first computer was crude and came without memory, a power supply or even a keyboard, it was very reliable. Jobs and Wozniak decided on a name that would convey the simplicity of the product's design and use: the Apple.

Jobs had a passionate belief in bringing computer technology to everyone. So in 1976, Jobs and Wozniak started a company to build and distribute their invention. In true American-dream fashion, their company began in a garage.

To finance their venture, Jobs sold his Volkswagen van and Wozniak sold his programmable calculator to raise $1,300. Weeks later, Jobs secured the company's first sale: 50 Apple I computers at [the retail price of] $666 each.

Source: **Inventor of the Week Archive, MIT**

Thinking Economically According to the document, why were Jobs and Wozniak able to succeed in starting their own company?

1984–Apple Launches Macintosh

Marketing Plays Key Role in Product's Success

They [Apple] were really more attuned to magazines much more than other tech companies, because magazines can reach a mass market. . . . Steve Jobs got on the cover of *Time* right around then.

The press kit was all really well-packaged. There was the press release for the non-techie people that just talked about how wonderful Macintosh was and how it was going to change the world. Then there were techier press releases, where they talked about the RAM, or the keyboard, or other things. . . .

It was really easily digestible, and easy to use by the press. Lots of great photos, professionally done. Now all that is standard.

Source: **Stanford Library; Interview with Evelyn Richards, 22 June 2000**

Thinking Economically How did Apple's marketing of Macintosh contribute to its success?

Highlights in Apple Company History

1976–Jobs and Wozniak incorporate Apple Computer
1977–Apple II computer, the first PC with color graphics, introduced
1980–Apple becomes public company, offering 4.6 million shares for sale
1984–Commercial during Super Bowl XVIII introduces the first Macintosh
1985–Both Jobs and Wozniak leave Apple
1988–Apple sues Microsoft when Windows begins using features similar to those developed by Apple
1989–First portable Macintosh introduced
1993–Debut of Newton, an early personal digital assistant
1995–Apple loses its case against Microsoft
1997–Jobs returns to Apple as chief executive officer
1998–Newton discontinued
2001–Portable digital music player iPod introduced
2003–Safari browser introduced; iTunes Music Store debuts
2006–Apple computers begin using Intel Core Duo processors

Sources: **Macworld March 30, 2006; Apple Computer, Inc.**

Thinking Economically How might Apple's history have been different if it had become a partnership instead of a corporation? Explain your answer.

THINKING ECONOMICALLY **Synthesizing**

1. Based on information in the documents, how would you describe the evolution of Apple Computer, Inc.?

2. How did Apple's advertising and marketing affect its success or failure? Use examples from the documents in your answer.

3. What single overriding concern has defined the evolution of Apple and determined its success? Use information from the documents to support your answer.

Interactive Review

Review this chapter using interactive activities at **ClassZone.com**
- Online Summary
- Graphic Organizers
- Quizzes
- Review and Study Notes
- Vocabulary Flip Cards

○ ○ ○

Online Summary

Complete the following activity either on your own paper or online at **ClassZone.com**

Choose the key concept that best completes the sentence. Not all key concepts will be used.

bond	limited partnership
conglomerate	merger
cooperative	multinational corporation
corporation	nonprofit organization
dividend	partnership
franchise	regulation
general partnership	sole proprietorship
horizontal merger	stock
limited liability	unlimited liability
limited liability partnership	unlimited life
limited life	vertical merger

In a __1__ , the business is owned and managed by a single person. One key drawback of this is that the owner has __2__ , putting even personal savings at risk. A __3__ is a business structure in which two or more owners share the management of the business, profits, and full liability. The __4__ and __5__ provide ways for some partners to risk only the amount of their investment.

A __6__ is a business that can raise money by selling __7__ and allows for limited liability of its owners and __8__ of the enterprise. Two or more businesses can consolidate through a __9__ . If they provide the same kinds of goods or services, their consolidation is known as a __10__ . When a business has branches in other countries, it is known as a __11__ .

If someone pays for the right to sell a company's goods or services in a certain area, that person is operating a __12__ . A business whose owners are also its customers is known as a __13__ . A __14__ is structured like a business but pursues goals other than profits.

CHAPTER 8 Assessment

REVIEWING KEY CONCEPTS

Sole Proprietorships (pp. 226–231)

1. What are the advantages of a sole proprietorship?

2. What are the disadvantages?

Forms of Partnership (pp. 232–237)

3. What are three different kinds of partnerships, and how do they differ?

4. What are the advantages and disadvantages of a partnership?

Corporations, Mergers, and Multinationals (pp. 238–247)

5. What are the advantages and disadvantages of a corporation

6. In what three ways can companies consolidate?

Franchises, Co-ops, and Nonprofits (pp. 248–253)

7. How is a franchise "an almost independent" business?

8. What is the difference between a cooperative and a nonprofit organization?

APPLYING ECONOMIC CONCEPTS

9. What might be the outcome of raising the fees and requiring more paperwork in order to start a corporation? What would happen if fees were lowered and the application process was simplified?

10. Do you think the number of multinationals will continue to increase? Give reasons for your answer.

11. As you have read, sometimes merged companies are not more efficient than they were separately. In some cases, the chief executive officers (CEOs) who arranged the deal make an enormous amount of money from the merger even though the deal itself does not improve profits. What incentives might a board of directors offer to CEOs to make sure they make deals that pay off in profits?

Use the following graph showing the number of mergers in the years from 1970 to 2000 to answer questions 12–14.

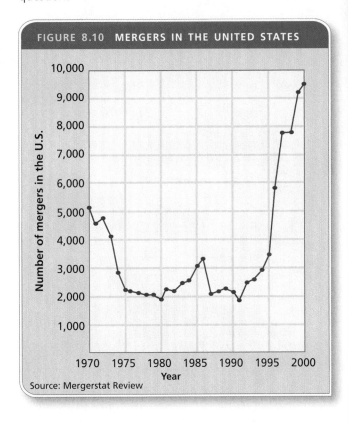

FIGURE 8.10 **MERGERS IN THE UNITED STATES**

Number of mergers in the U.S.

Year

Source: Mergerstat Review

12. **Analyzing Graphs** Which of the following can you determine from the information about mergers in the graph?

    a. how many companies merged in any given year from 1970 to 2000

    b. how many more mergers took place in 2000 than in 1990

    c. how long each of the new companies lasted after the merger

13. **Predicting Economic Trends** Which decade saw the greatest increase in the number of mergers? What probably happened after that decade?

14. **Challenge** The number of mergers can reflect the economic times, which in turn are often affected by national and world events. What events may have contributed to tighter economic times—and therefore a decrease in mergers—in the 1970s?

Design a New Business Structure

Each business structure you have read about in this chapter has both advantages and disadvantages. Follow the steps below to design a new business structure that attempts to avoid the worst disadvantages and to capitalize on the most important advantages of the other structures. You can imagine changing laws to accommodate your new structure, but try to make sure your creation makes economic sense.

Step 1. Break into small groups. In your group, draw up a list of advantages and disadvantages of all the business structures. The table on page 242 will help you begin the list.

Step 2. Discuss how the advantages and disadvantages would affect the ability of a business to earn a profit. Choose the three advantages and three disadvantages that your group feels have the most impact.

Step 3. Brainstorm possible ways to avoid the disadvantages and make the most of the advantages. Remember that in brainstorming any idea is allowed, no matter how crazy or simple it might sound.

Step 4. Sort through your brainstorming ideas. Use them to develop a new "ideal" business structure.

Step 5. Share your business structure with the rest of the class, and compare your efforts to those of your classmates.

The Role of Labor
The service sector makes up the largest part of the U.S. economy. More people work in offices than ever before.

The Role of Labor

CONCEPT REVIEW

Labor productivity is the value of the goods or services a worker can produce in a set amount of time.

CHAPTER 9 KEY CONCEPT

Labor, the human effort used to produce goods and services, is subject to the same forces of demand and supply that govern the rest of the economy.

WHY THE CONCEPT MATTERS

The value of your labor depends on the demand for what you do and the supply of other people able to do the same thing. It's up to you to figure out what you do best and to distinguish yourself from other workers. Maybe what you really want to do will require special training or years of experience. Think of your dream job, and write a plan for how you will get that job. Evaluate the demand for the job and the supply of people capable of performing it.

Online Highlights

More at ClassZone.com

 Economics Update

Go to **ECONOMICS UPDATE** for chapter updates and current news on managing change in your worklife. (See Case Study, pp. 282–283.) ▶

Animated Economics

Go to **ANIMATED ECONOMICS** for interactive lessons on the graphs and tables in this chapter.

Interactive ◀◀Review

Go to **INTERACTIVE REVIEW** for concept review and activities.

The world of work is changing. Will you be able to keep pace? See the Case Study on pages 282–283.

How Are Wages Determined?

<table>
<tr>
<th>OBJECTIVES</th>
<th>KEY TERMS</th>
<th>TAKING NOTES</th>
</tr>
<tr>
<td>

In Section 1, you will
- identify what wages are
- describe how the interaction of supply and demand determines wages
- explain why wage rates differ

</td>
<td>

wages, *p. 258*
equilibrium wage, *p. 258*
derived demand, *p. 259*
wage rate, *p. 261*
human capital, *p. 261*
glass ceiling, *p. 262*
minimum wage, *p. 262*

</td>
<td>

As you read Section 1, complete a cluster diagram like the one below to record what you learn about wages. Use the Graphic Organizer at **Interactive Review @ ClassZone.com**

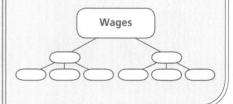

</td>
</tr>
</table>

Labor: Demand and Supply

KEY CONCEPTS

QUICK REFERENCE

Wages are payments received in return for work.

Equilibrium wage is the wage at which the quantity of workers demanded equals the quantity of workers supplied; the market price for labor.

Have you ever wondered why working at a fast food restaurant pays so little? This section will help answer that question. In Chapter 1 you learned about the four factors of production: land, labor, capital, and entrepreneurship. Each of those has a price that must be figured into production costs. The price of labor is **wages**, the payments workers receive in return for work.

Wages, just like the other factors of production, are governed by the forces of supply and demand. The interaction of these two economic forces produces an equilibrium, or balance. An **equilibrium wage** is the wage at which the number of workers needed equals the number of workers available. In other words, an equilibrium wage produces neither a surplus nor a shortage of workers. Let's look at demand and supply separately and see how they affect wages at fast food restaurants.

Demand for Labor

In a competitive labor market, wages reflect a worker's labor productivity—the value of the goods or services a worker produces in a set amount of time. A business hires workers to help it produce goods or provide

services. A producer's demand for labor is therefore a **derived demand**, a demand for a product or resource because of its contribution to the final product.

Workers with higher productivity tend to earn higher wages. In one hour, a fast food chef might be able to produce $50 worth of food that customers want. An attorney, by contrast, might be able to provide services worth $300 in the same hour's time. Employers, then, are willing to pay attorneys higher wages than fast food chefs.

The demand for labor depends in part on its price. As with anything else, when the price goes down, the quantity demanded goes up; and when the price goes up, the quantity demanded goes down. For example, suppose that fast food chefs are paid $12 per hour. If the wage should fall to $10 per hour, many restaurants would hire additional chefs. On the other hand, if the wage rose to $14 per hour, some restaurants would stop hiring and others would have to lay off some chefs. This is illustrated in Figure 9.1. The demand curve for labor, then, is a downward slope—the lower the price of labor, the greater the quantity of labor employers would demand.

QUICK REFERENCE

Derived demand is a demand for a product or resource based on its contribution to the final product.

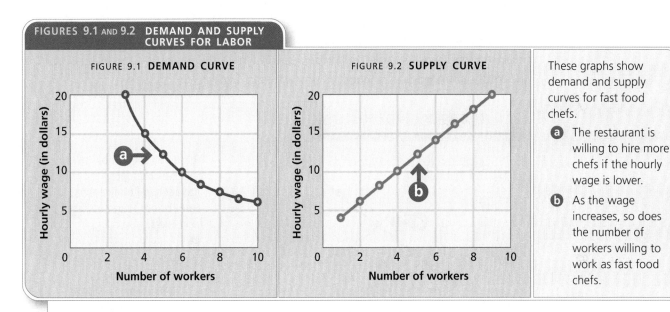

FIGURES 9.1 AND 9.2 DEMAND AND SUPPLY CURVES FOR LABOR

FIGURE 9.1 DEMAND CURVE

FIGURE 9.2 SUPPLY CURVE

These graphs show demand and supply curves for fast food chefs.

ⓐ The restaurant is willing to hire more chefs if the hourly wage is lower.

ⓑ As the wage increases, so does the number of workers willing to work as fast food chefs.

ANALYZE GRAPHS
1. How many fast food chefs would the restaurant hire at the wage $10 per hour?
2. How many workers would be willing to be fast food chefs at the wage of $10 per hour?
3. What would happen if the restaurant tried to hire chefs at $10 per hour?

Animated Economics

Use interactive demand and supply curves for labor at **ClassZone.com**

Supply of Labor

Now let's consider the situation from the worker's point of view, to see how the supply of labor works. Suppose a new fast food restaurant opens and wants to hire chefs. If it puts an ad in the newspaper for chefs who would be paid $10 per hour, fewer people will respond—and probably none of the chefs currently employed at $12 per hour. Workers who are earning less than $10 per hour in some other kind of job might leave their jobs and become fast food chefs because the wages are higher than their current wages.

Economics Update

Find an update on demand and supply of labor at **ClassZone.com**

But suppose the new restaurant offers fast food chefs $15 per hour. Any worker earning less than that will be interested—including experienced chefs currently employed at $12 per hour. More workers will be willing to work at higher wages than at lower wages. For this reason, the supply curve for labor is upward sloping, as illustrated in Figure 9.2 on page 259.

Equilibrium Wage

You learned in Chapter 6 that the equilibrium price for goods or services is the price at which there is neither a surplus nor a shortage—in other words, the point at which the supply curve and the demand curve intersect. Since wages are the price of labor, they too gravitate toward equilibrium.

For example, fast food restaurants might offer higher wages to attract chefs. Given the upward-sloping supply curve, before long there would be more people wanting to be chefs than there are jobs, resulting in a labor surplus. With so many chefs to choose from, restaurants could lower the wage and still attract workers. If they offered a wage that was too low, however, people would have less incentive to work as fast food chefs. A shortage would eventually result, so restaurants would need to raise the wages to attract more. The downward and upward forces push until an equilibrium wage is reached, as illustrated in Figure 9.3.

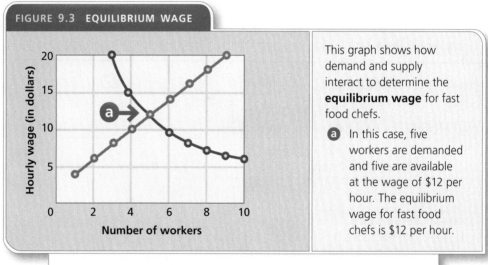

FIGURE 9.3 EQUILIBRIUM WAGE

This graph shows how demand and supply interact to determine the **equilibrium wage** for fast food chefs.

a In this case, five workers are demanded and five are available at the wage of $12 per hour. The equilibrium wage for fast food chefs is $12 per hour.

ANALYZE GRAPHS

1. How many fast food chefs would the restaurant hire at the wage of $15 per hour?

2. How many workers would be willing to be fast food chefs if the wage rose to $15 per hour?

3. What would result if the wage rose to $15 per hour?

APPLICATION Applying Economic Concepts

A. Suppose that a new high school opens next to a popular fast food restaurant. Explain what will happen to the derived demand for chefs at the restaurant.

Why Do Wage Rates Differ?

KEY CONCEPTS

Different jobs have different **wage rates**, the rates of pay for specific jobs or work performed. Wage rates are determined by supply and demand, which in turn are influenced by four key factors: (1) **human capital**, which is the knowledge and skills that enable workers to be productive, (2) working conditions, (3) discrimination in the workplace, and (4) government actions.

FACTOR 1 Human Capital

Economists group workers according to the amount of human capital they have. *Unskilled workers*, such as house cleaners and sanitation workers, have a low level of human capital. *Semiskilled workers*—construction and clerical workers, for example—have received some training, so their human capital is higher. *Skilled workers*, such as plumbers and electricians, have made a significant investment in human capital in the form of specialized training. *Professional workers*—doctors, lawyers, and others with intensive specialized training—have the highest human capital.

The demand for skilled and professional workers is high, but the supply of these workers is relatively low. For this reason and because training increases their productivity, highly skilled workers tend to receive higher wages. The prospect of higher wages leads many people to invest in their human capital and enroll in vocational school, specialist training programs, and higher education.

QUICK REFERENCE

Wage rate is the established rate of pay for a specific job or work performed.

Human capital is the knowledge and skills that enable workers to be productive.

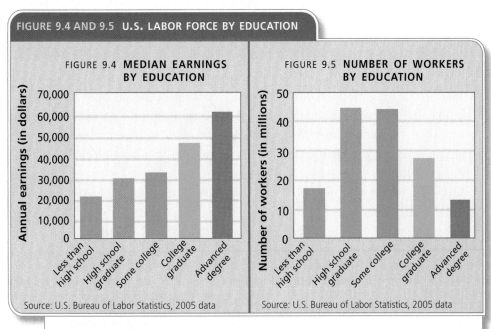

FIGURE 9.4 AND 9.5 **U.S. LABOR FORCE BY EDUCATION**

FIGURE 9.4 **MEDIAN EARNINGS BY EDUCATION**

Source: U.S. Bureau of Labor Statistics, 2005 data

FIGURE 9.5 **NUMBER OF WORKERS BY EDUCATION**

Source: U.S. Bureau of Labor Statistics, 2005 data

ANALYZE GRAPHS

1. In terms of average annual salary, about how much is graduating from high school worth?

2. There are almost as few people without a high school diploma as with an advanced degree. Why doesn't the reduced supply make their salaries as high as the salaries for people with an advanced degree?

Working Conditions
Painters who work at high altitudes receive higher wages.

FACTOR 2 Working Conditions

"It's a tough job, but someone has to do it." That statement is often used humorously by people who have dream jobs, such as vacation planners who get to go on fabulous trips as "research" or taste testers who sample chocolate or other goodies. However, some jobs really are tougher than others. Some jobs, such as washing windows on a skyscraper, are very dangerous. Other jobs can be very unpleasant, such as collecting garbage. Higher wages are often paid to workers in dangerous and unpleasant occupations in order to attract qualified people to those jobs.

While the disadvantages of some jobs may be offset by higher wages, the advantages of other jobs may make up for low wages. These advantages vary widely, depending on the worker. For example, a student who loves movies might take a job as a clerk at a video store. Although the pay is low, the student might get to borrow movies free of charge. Someone tired of a long commute in rush hour traffic might welcome a lower-paying job that is only minutes away from home.

FACTOR 3 Discrimination

Another factor affecting differences in wage rates is discrimination. Wage discrimination may be based on race, ethnicity, gender, or other factors. For example, the average pay of women tends to be lower than that of men doing the same job. Racial prejudices sometimes lead to discrimination in wages. A prejudiced employer might be unwilling to hire a minority candidate except at a lower wage.

However, employers who discriminate may actually lose money. By eliminating qualified candidates because of their gender, ethnic group, or other trait irrelevant to performance, employers may miss out on the best worker for the job.

Wage differences may also result from occupational segregation. Some low-paying jobs have been viewed as the "realm" of women or certain racial or ethnic groups. Occupational segregation becomes a vicious cycle: groups can become trapped in these jobs, unable to earn enough to invest in human capital that could move them upward. In the United States, the federal government has tried to break this cycle by passing such antidiscrimination laws as the Equal Pay Act (1963) and the Civil Rights Act (1964).

Artificial barriers to advancement may also limit the wages of women and minorities. They may have the skills and experience necessary to advance, but find that they are never promoted. The term **glass ceiling** describes these unseen barriers to advancement.

FACTOR 4 Government Actions

In a pure market economy, wages would be set strictly by economic forces. However, in many countries, including the United States, the government steps in when market forces produce results that people disagree with. The **minimum wage**, the lowest wage legally allowed for one hour of work, is one example. As you read in Chapter 6, the minimum wage acts as a price floor designed to boost wages for low-income workers. The forces of supply and demand might set the equilibrium wage

QUICK REFERENCE

Glass ceiling is an artificial barrier to advancement faced by women and minorities.

The **minimum wage** is the legal minimum amount that an employer must pay for one hour of work.

Suppose you are offered two jobs, one that pays $12.50 per hour or another that pays $30,000 per year. In both jobs, you will work 40 hours per week and get two weeks off per year. Assuming both offer the same benefits, which job pays better?

You could either figure out how much you would make in a year at the hourly job or you could convert the annual salary into an hourly wage. In this exercise, we will calculate how much a wage of $12.50 per hour pays for a year's worth of work.

Step 1: Multiply to determine the number of hours worked per year. Assume the job includes two weeks of unpaid vacation.

Example Calculations

Hours per week	×	Weeks per year	=	Total hours per year	40	×	50	=	2,000

Step 2: Then, multiply to find the amount of pay annually.

Total hours per year	×	Hourly wage	=	Annual wages	2,000	×	$12.50	=	$25,000

The job that pays a salary of $30,000 per year pays better than the one that pays a wage of $12.50 per hour.

Comparing Earnings Use the calculations to determine the annual wages of a job that pays $15 per hour for 40 hours per week. What about one that pays $20 per hour but only offers 20 hours of work each week? What other factors do you need to consider when comparing pay between jobs?

for certain jobs so low that no one could reasonably make a living at these jobs. The minimum wage attempts to help the people who hold these jobs to make ends meet. However, businesses point out that they might hire more workers if they were allowed to pay a lower wage.

The first national minimum wage law in the United States was passed in 1933 during the Great Depression. In part, it was intended to raise wages so that workers could consume products and help the economy recover. In 1938, the minimum wage became part of the Fair Labor Standards Act, which included other protections for workers. The U.S. Congress has increased the minimum wage several times, but the increases have not kept up with the general rise in prices. In response, some state and local governments have passed their own laws requiring minimum wages higher than the federal standard.

APPLICATION Applying Economic Concepts

B. Explain how each of the four factors influences wages at fast food restaurants.

Gary Becker:
The Importance of Human Capital

FAST FACTS

Gary Becker

Born: December 2, 1930 Pottsville, Pennsylvania

Major Accomplishment: Extending an economic way of thinking into other areas of life and using economics to explain social behavior

Inspiration for Ideas About Economics and Crime: When he arrived late one day at Columbia University in New York, Becker decided to save time by parking illegally, even though he knew he might get caught and fined. This led him to wonder if people committing other crimes considered the consequences of their decisions rationally.

Famous Quotation: *"No discussion of human capital can omit the influence of families on the knowledge, skills, values, and habits of their children."*

Economics Update

Find an update on Gary Becker at **ClassZone.com**

"I believe an economist should . . . express concepts in simple language and show how to deal with important problems in a fairly simple way." With those words, Nobel laureate economist Gary Becker aptly described his own approach. He proposed that the general economic principle of rational choice could be applied to the decisions people make in all spheres of life. Becker extended an economic way of thinking into new areas, including crime and punishment, households and family relations, and human competence.

Investing in Yourself

When Gary Becker graduated from high school, he was torn between following a career in mathematics and doing something to help solve social problems. He studied economics at Princeton University and the University of Chicago, and he went on to teach at Chicago and at Columbia University. In 1957, Becker published *The Economics of Discrimination*, which examined the "effects of prejudice on the earnings, employment, and occupations of minorities." However, most economists did not pay much attention, feeling that such a study belonged in the fields of sociology or psychology. Today, though, Becker's approach is widely appreciated and has led economists to explore new areas.

Becker is best known for his contributions to the idea of human capital and for formulating the economic theory that explains differences in wages in terms of investments in human capital. To Becker, human capital is more than education and training: it is all the investments people make in themselves to improve their output, including the development of good work habits and receiving good medical treatment. The more abundant the capital, the more productive the labor. Becker helped to quantify the importance of education and on-the-job training and, by doing so, broadened the reach of economics.

Gary Becker won the Nobel Prize for Economics in 1992 and the National Medal of Science in 2000.

APPLICATION Conducting Cost-Benefit Analysis

C. Becker debated with himself about whether to park illegally, weighing the possible costs against the advantages. Explain a decision you made using cost-benefit analysis. Is that always the best way to make a decision? Why or why not?

Online Quiz
ClassZone.com

REVIEWING KEY CONCEPTS

1. Explain the relationship between the terms in each of these pairs.

   a. *wages*
   derived demand

   b. *equilibrium wage*
   minimum wage

   c. *wage rate*
   human capital

2. What market forces influence wages?

3. What nonmarket forces influence wages?

4. Why are education and training considered a kind of capital?

5. Why would a star athlete receive wages so much higher than an insurance sales representative?

6. **Using Your Notes** Suppose you are the owner of a video store. Explain how you would decide what to pay your workers, making reference to the terms in your completed cluster diagram.

   Use the Graphic Organizer at **Interactive Review @ ClassZone.com**

CRITICAL THINKING

7. **Analyzing Cause and Effect** If the equilibrium wage for bowling alley managers is $16 per hour, why would a wage of $20 per hour result in a labor surplus? Why would a wage of $12 per hour lead to a labor shortage?

8. **Solving Economic Problems** What economic problem does the minimum wage try to address?

9. **Applying Economic Concepts** Explain why working conditions can either justify higher wages or make up for lower wages.

10. **Making Inferences and Drawing Conclusions** Despite efforts to close the wage gap between men and women, the gap has actually been widening. Using what you have learned in this section, write a paragraph discussing what could be done to close the gap.

11. **Challenge** Gary Becker said that economics "is easy in the sense that there are only a few principles that really guide most economic analysis." Identify the basic principles behind how wages operate.

ECONOMICS IN PRACTICE

Graphing Equilibrium Wages
Read each job description below. Then make a graph showing a hypothetical equilibrium wage for each job using the same values for both axes in each graph.

Job Description #1	Job Description #2
Structural metal worker for high-rise construction project. Must have at least 2 years of experience.	Filing clerk, small accounting office. No experience necessary, but must have a high school diploma or GED.

Apply Economic Concepts
Using the economic knowledge you gained in this section, briefly explain why each graph appears as it does.

Challenge In many dangerous industries, including mining, safety laws establish standards that protect workers. Explain what effect these laws might have on wages.

Use *SMARTGrapher* @ ClassZone.com to complete this activity.

Trends in Today's Labor Market

OBJECTIVES

In Section 2, you will
- identify the changes that have taken place in the labor force
- explain how occupations have changed
- explain how the way people work has changed

KEY TERMS

civilian labor force, *p. 266*

outsourcing, *p. 269*

insourcing, *p. 269*

telecommuting, *p. 270*

contingent employment, *p. 270*

independent contractor, *p. 270*

TAKING NOTES

As you read Section 2, complete a hierarchy chart like the one below. In each box write the main ideas. Use the Graphic Organizer at **Interactive Review @ ClassZone.com**

Trends in Labor Market

changing labor force

A Changing Labor Force

KEY CONCEPTS

The labor market in the United States has changed dramatically since the 1950s, and it continues to change. For example, in the 1950s, many companies hired workers with the expectation that they would stay with the company for most of their working lives. After a lifetime of service, workers could count on company pension plans to help fund their retirement. Today, few workers stay with the same company their entire career, and workers take more responsibility for funding their retirement.

Those are only some of the profound changes that affect the **civilian labor force**, people who are 16 or older who are employed or actively looking for and available to do work. The civilian labor force excludes people in the military, in prison, or in other institutions. In 2005, about 150 million Americans made up the civilian labor force. That figure was up from 126 million workers in 1990 and is expected to rise almost 165 million workers by 2020.

QUICK REFERENCE

The **civilian labor force** is made up of people age 16 or older who are employed or actively looking for and available to do work.

Labor Force
The civilian labor force is composed of people age 16 or older who are working or looking for work.

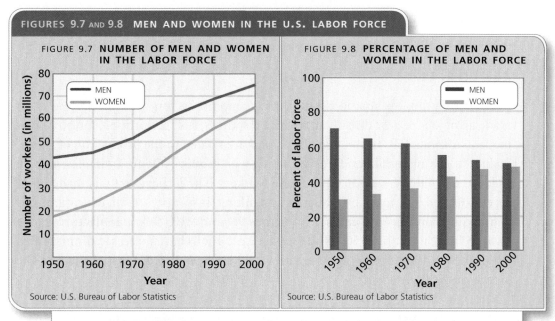

FIGURES 9.7 AND 9.8 MEN AND WOMEN IN THE U.S. LABOR FORCE

FIGURE 9.7 **NUMBER OF MEN AND WOMEN IN THE LABOR FORCE**

Source: U.S. Bureau of Labor Statistics

FIGURE 9.8 **PERCENTAGE OF MEN AND WOMEN IN THE LABOR FORCE**

Source: U.S. Bureau of Labor Statistics

ANALYZE GRAPHS

1. About how many more men were in the labor force than women in 1950? in 2000?
2. What percentage of the labor force did women account for in 1950? in 2000?

Changes in the U.S. Labor Force

To understand some of the changes in the U.S. labor force, consider these two scenes. In the first scene, the year is 1955. A young woman pulls into a gas station, and the attendant fills up her car with gas. Then she picks up her children at school and heads home to get dinner ready in time for her husband's arrival from work. The second scene is set in today's world. A young mother pulls into a gas station, swipes her credit card, and fills up her tank. Her business meeting ran long, and she is late getting to the daycare center. Her husband will pick up dinner for the family on his way home from work.

One obvious change these scenes demonstrate is the addition of many more women to the work force. As shown in Figures 9.7 and 9.8, women have been a significant factor in the growth of the labor market in the United States. Since the 1950s, the kinds of jobs open to women have expanded. As job opportunities have improved, wages for women have risen, and many more women have been drawn into the work force.

The U.S. work force has also become better educated. About 30 percent of people in the labor force have a college degree, and an additional 30 percent of workers have some college credits. In a work force with such a high degree of human capital, productivity and wages are also high compared with many other nations.

Economics Update

Find an update on the U.S. work force at **ClassZone.com**

APPLICATION Evaluating Economic Decisions

A. Explain how rising opportunity costs have led more women into the workplace.

Changing Occupations

KEY CONCEPTS

Economists group occupations into three economic sectors. The *primary sector* is made up of jobs related directly to natural resources, such as farming, forestry, fishing, and mining. Jobs in the *secondary sector* are related to the production of goods, including the materials and energy needed to produce them. Examples include welders, truck drivers, and construction workers. The *tertiary sector* is made up of service-related jobs in such industries as banking, insurance, retail, education, and communications. As you can see in Figures 9.9 and 9.10, U.S. manufacturing jobs have declined since the 1950s, while service-sector jobs have increased dramatically. All of the ten fastest-growing occupations are service related, most of them in the area of medical services.

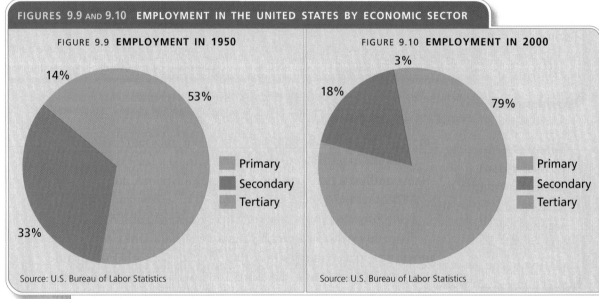

FIGURES 9.9 AND 9.10 EMPLOYMENT IN THE UNITED STATES BY ECONOMIC SECTOR

FIGURE 9.9 **EMPLOYMENT IN 1950**

14%
53%
33%

Primary
Secondary
Tertiary

Source: U.S. Bureau of Labor Statistics

FIGURE 9.10 **EMPLOYMENT IN 2000**

3%
18%
79%

Primary
Secondary
Tertiary

Source: U.S. Bureau of Labor Statistics

ANALYZE GRAPHS
1. Which sector grew the most from 1950 to 2000? By how much did it grow?
2. How much of the civilian labor force was employed in the combined primary and secondary sectors in 1950? How much in 2000?

Technology and Change

Think back for a moment to the young mother at the gas station. In the years between 1955 and today, the job of gas station attendant has been mainly replaced by the computerized, credit-card operated gasoline pump. In the same way, ATMs have greatly affected the occupation of bank teller. Technological changes have eliminated or redefined many other jobs in all three sectors.

The personal computer and the Internet have drastically changed the way on-the-job information is stored, transferred, and used. About half of all American workers use a computer on the job. As a result, those occupations that support the

1950s gas station　　　　**2000s gas station**

use of computers—software engineers and network and data communications analysts, for example—have been among the fastest growing in the United States.

More than 80 percent of managers and professionals use a computer at work. However, even in less skilled jobs, more and more workers are using computers. About 20 percent of machine operators, laborers, and farmers use a computer on the job. Basic computer skills have become necessary for many different types of jobs.

Globalization and Jobs

Today's labor market is global. Technology allows companies to employ people not just all over the country, but all over the world. Many companies have sought to cut their costs by **outsourcing**, the practice of contracting with an outside company to provide goods or services.

Most outsourcing by U.S. companies goes to other U.S. companies. For example, many American businesses hire other American firms to handle their accounting. However, the term outsourcing has become connected with the practice of moving jobs from the United States to foreign countries where wages are lower. As this happens more frequently, it would seem that their American operations would lose jobs. But many companies actually add more jobs in the United States than they outsource abroad, just in different parts of their businesses. In 2004, IBM decided to send about 3,000 jobs overseas. But at the same time, it created about 4,500 jobs in the United States.

The American economy has also benefited from **insourcing**, the practice of foreign companies establishing operations in, and therefore bringing jobs to, the United States. Both outsourcing and insourcing are tied to the trends toward more service-related jobs and more technology-related work.

QUICK REFERENCE

Outsourcing is the practice of contracting with an outside company, often in a foreign country, to provide goods or services.

Insourcing is the practice of foreign companies establishing operations in, and therefore bringing jobs to, the United States.

APPLICATION Predicting Economic Trends

B. Think of an example of an occupation that is likely to be eliminated or substantially redefined as a result of technology.

Changes in the Way People Work

KEY CONCEPTS

QUICK REFERENCE

Telecommuting means working part or all of the time in a location other than the traditional office.

Contingent employment refers to temporary or part-time work.

An **independent contractor** is someone who sells their services on a contract basis.

The way people work has been transformed by technology. In the past, many workers needed to physically commute to and from an office in order to accomplish their work. The Internet and laptop computers have allowed some of these workers to engage in **telecommuting**, the practice of working part or all of the time in a location other than the traditional office.

But the job market has also changed. In the past, companies offered most workers permanent positions. Today, companies offer fewer permanent positions and more **contingent employment**, work that is temporary or part-time. Similarly, more people work as **independent contractors**, selling their services to businesses on a contract basis. People used to enter a field and stay in more or less the same line of work for most of their work life. Now, most people will change careers several times as the world of work continues to evolve.

Working at the Office from Home

Many telecommuters enjoy the reduced stress, flexibility in work time, and increased free time they have by avoiding a commute to work. Employers benefit from an expanded labor pool, increased productivity, and lower real estate costs. Society benefits, too, from fewer drivers on crowded freeways and lower pollution.

However, there are also costs. People who work at home may feel that their work too often spills over into their personal time. Some miss the social life of the office and the chance to network. Some at-home workers also fear that on-site workers might be more likely to get promoted. Still, experts estimate that the number of telecommuting workers grew by about 20 percent each year from 2000 to 2005.

YOUR ECONOMIC CHOICES

TELECOMMUTING

Where would you want to work?

Technology allows people to work in many different places. Alternative work places have different benefits—and drawbacks—than the traditional office.

▲ Work at the office

▲ Work at the coffee shop

Alternatives to Permanent Employment

Through much of the 1900s, U.S. companies would hire workers for permanent, full-time jobs. Employees would work 40 hours per week in exchange for both wages and benefits. In the 1990s, companies began to hire fewer full-time employees and more contingent employees and contract workers. Contingent workers, sometimes called temps, make up over 5 percent of the total work force. Independent contractors make up over 7 percent of the work force.

Hiring contingent employees and contract workers makes it easier for businesses to adjust their work force to suit production demands. Discharging temporary workers is easier and less costly than discharging permanent employees. Since most temporary workers do not receive benefits, labor costs are also lower.

Most contingent workers would prefer to have the steady income and benefits that come with permanent, full-time employment. But many independent contractors prefer the flexibility of being their own boss to working in a permanent position. They are willing to take the risk of not having enough work to support themselves, and they find alternative ways to pay for health insurance and retirement. Businesses sometimes offer permanent positions to contingent and contract workers who have done a good job.

Changing Careers More Often

As technology has advanced, jobs have changed, too. Much of the work done today in the United States and other advanced countries did not exist 100 years ago. Some of the work did not exist even ten years ago. With every new technology, new types of jobs are created. But as technology advances, many older professions become less in demand or even obsolete. To fill the new jobs, workers must learn and adapt to the new technologies. Someone who started out as a radio repair technician might need to learn how to work with cellular phone technology.

In a similar way, the economy changes more quickly than it did in the past. Companies have become more flexible, changing their business plans constantly to maximize profits. Globalization allows companies to move jobs across national boundaries. As the economy changes, workers must change and adapt. The technician who adapted to cellular phone technology might need to change yet again in a few years.

Changing Careers
As the demand for healthcare workers increases, some people will change careers to fill these jobs.

APPLICATION Analyzing Cause and Effect

C. A 2003 report concluded that telecommuters can save their employers $5,000 a year. Explain how that savings may come about.

For more on interpreting graphs, see the Skillbuilder Handbook, page R29.

Drawing Conclusions from Graphs

Drawing conclusions means analyzing a source of information and forming an opinion. You have already had some practice analyzing line and pie graphs in Chapters 6 and 8. These graphs are bar graphs.

PRACTICING THE SKILL Begin by using the following strategies to analyze the graphs. They are similar to the strategies you used in Chapter 6 to analyze a line graph. Your analysis will enable you to draw conclusions about the information shown on the graphs.

Read the title to identify the main idea of the graphs.

Check the vertical axes. Note that the axes use different scales.

Check the horizontal axes. Both axes list a variety of occupations.

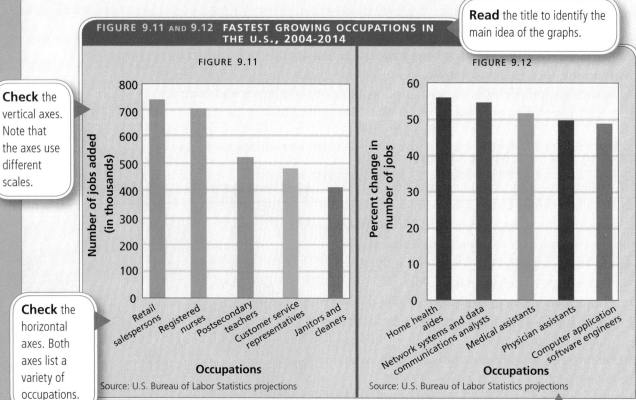

FIGURE 9.11 AND 9.12 FASTEST GROWING OCCUPATIONS IN THE U.S., 2004-2014

FIGURE 9.11

FIGURE 9.12

Source: U.S. Bureau of Labor Statistics projections

Source: U.S. Bureau of Labor Statistics projections

Read the source lines to confirm that the data come from a reliable source.

NOW PUT IT ALL TOGETHER Both graphs claim to present the same information. Compare the two graphs, and consider their differences.

THINKING ECONOMICALLY Drawing Conclusions

1. What is the main difference between the two graphs?

2. Which graph really shows the fastest growing occupations? Explain your answer.

3. What would be a better title for each graph?

4. Which of these jobs are most likely to have higher than average wages? Why?

1. Explain the differences between the terms in each of these pairs.

   a. *outsourcing*
   insourcing

   b. *contingent employment*
   independent contractor

2. Name three of the fastest growing occupations. What do they have in common?

3. What are the economic reasons that explain why so many women joined the labor force in the late 1900s?

4. Name two ways technology has altered the U.S. labor market.

5. For an employee, what are the advantages and disadvantages of telecommuting?

6. **Using Your Notes** Write a paragraph explaining how you can use the information in this section to prepare for your future career. Refer to your completed hierarchy chart to help you anticipate the employment trends you will be facing.

Trends in Labor Market — changing labor force

   Use the Graphic Organizer at **Interactive Review @ ClassZone.com**

CRITICAL THINKING

7. **Making Inferences and Drawing Conclusions** Given the trends in the labor market, do you think today's employees will need to be more independent than the last generation's or less independent? Why?

8. **Analyzing Cause and Effect** Explain how changing technologies have led to workers changing careers more often.

9. **Evaluating Economic Decisions** The United States has shifted to an economy driven by service industries. The primary sector, which deals in natural resources, and the secondary sector, which produces goods, are both shrinking. Do you think the shift toward a service economy is helping American workers or hurting them? Give reasons for your answer.

10. **Challenge** Adam Smith explained that countries maximize their wealth when they concentrate on producing the goods that they produce most efficiently and rely on international trade for goods they don't produce efficiently. Explain how outsourcing is an example of this concept.

Examining Labor Market Trends
Make a copy of the table below. On your copy, list the reasons for the trend toward contingent labor in the left column. In the right column, describe its impact on the labor force.

Move to Contingent Labor	
Why?	Impact on Labor Force

Analyze Cause and Effect
In what ways have women in the work force influenced the growth of contingent labor? In what ways has the growth of contingent labor influenced women?

Challenge What personal issues might lead a worker to seek part-time employment?

Organized Labor in the United States

OBJECTIVES	KEY TERMS	TAKING NOTES
In Section 3, you will • describe how the labor movement developed in the United States • discuss why organized labor has declined in the United States • explain how labor unions affect wage rates and employment	labor union, *p. 274* strike, *p. 274* closed shop, *p. 279* union shop, *p. 279* right-to-work law, *p. 279* collective bargaining, *p. 280* binding arbitration, *p. 280*	As you read Section 3, complete a summary chart like the one below. In each box, write the main ideas for each topic. Use the Graphic Organizer at **Interactive Review @ ClassZone.com**

Topic	Main Ideas	Related Facts
Labor movement's rise to power		

The Labor Movement's Rise to Power

KEY CONCEPTS

Organized labor helped to shape the modern workplace. Most of the benefits that workers in the United States take for granted today did not exist 200 years ago. The eight-hour workday, the five-day work week, vacations, even sick leave—none of these basic amenities would have existed without the efforts of organized labor.

In the industries of the 1800s, workers put in long hours—often 60 hours per week or more—for low pay. Factory laborers often worked in dangerous conditions. Individual workers had little power to demand improvements from a business owner. If a worker complained too much, they would be fired. Workers in industrialized nations around the world faced similar problems, but this section will focus on the labor movement in the United States.

To improve their bargaining power, factory workers in the 1800s began to join together and act as a group. A **labor union** is an organization of workers who collectively seek to improve wages, working conditions, benefits, job security, and other work-related matters. Unions attempted to negotiate with businesses to achieve their goals, but businesses often resisted. As unions sought ways to gain negotiating power, they turned to the **strike**, or work stoppage. The threat of shutting down production demonstrated the power of organized labor.

Different types of unions addressed different needs. Some workers joined a craft union, a union of workers with similar skills who work in different industries for different employers. Examples include typesetters or, more recently, electricians. Others joined an industrial union, a union for workers with different skills who work in the same industry. For example, workers in the textile industry formed some of the earliest industrial unions.

QUICK REFERENCE

A **labor union** is an organization of workers that seeks to improve wages, working conditions, fringe benefits, job security, and other work-related matters for its members.

A **strike** is a work stoppage used to convince an employer to meet union demands.

Early Developments

Local craft unions were the main kind of worker association during the early years of the United States. By the 1830s, local unions began joining together into federations to advance their common cause. The first national federation was the National Trades Union (NTU), founded in 1834. A financial crisis that gripped the country in 1837 brought an end to the NTU and temporarily subdued union activity.

In 1869, organized labor took a huge step forward when Uriah Stephens founded the Knights of Labor. Unlike other unions, it organized workers by industry, not by trade or skill level. The Knights of Labor became a nationwide union and adopted political goals including an eight-hour workday for all workers and the end of child labor. Its membership grew quickly, especially after the union helped workers win concessions from the big railroad companies in the 1880s.

During the explosion of industrialism in the late 1800s, employers strongly resisted the efforts of workers to organize, and many labor protests turned violent.

- In 1886, one person was killed and several others were seriously wounded when police attacked workers protesting for an eight-hour workday outside the McCormick Harvester Company in Chicago. The next day, people gathered at Haymarket Square to protest the deaths, and police troops arrived to disperse the crowd. Someone threw a bomb into the police, killing seven officers, and the riot that followed left dozens of other people dead and hundreds injured.

- In 1892, ten workers were killed in a strike against Carnegie Steel in Homestead, Pennsylvania, and the union was broken up.

- In 1894, a strike in Illinois against the Pullman Palace Car Company won the support of railway workers across the country, who collectively brought the nation's railroads to a halt. The dispute turned violent when National Guard troops were brought in to keep the nation's railroads running. A federal court ruled that the American Railway Union could not interfere with the trains, and the strike was broken.

Union Organizing
A union rally takes place at a shipyard in 1943.

A New Model for Unions

The violence associated with organized labor, as well as its often controversial political agenda, led to a decline in union membership. But Samuel Gompers offered a different model for union organization. In 1886, he founded the American Federation of Labor (AFL), an organization of craft unions that focused on the interests of skilled labor. The AFL continued to seek improvements in wages, benefits, and working conditions, but it focused on achieving these goals through the economic power of workers, instead of through legislation. By the early 1900s, the AFL had a membership of about 1.7 million workers. Legal action against organized labor forced Gompers to modify his stance against political activity, and the AFL began supporting pro-union candidates.

The International Ladies' Garment Workers Union was founded in 1900. The union gained strength following successful strikes in 1909 and 1910. Perhaps the most famous

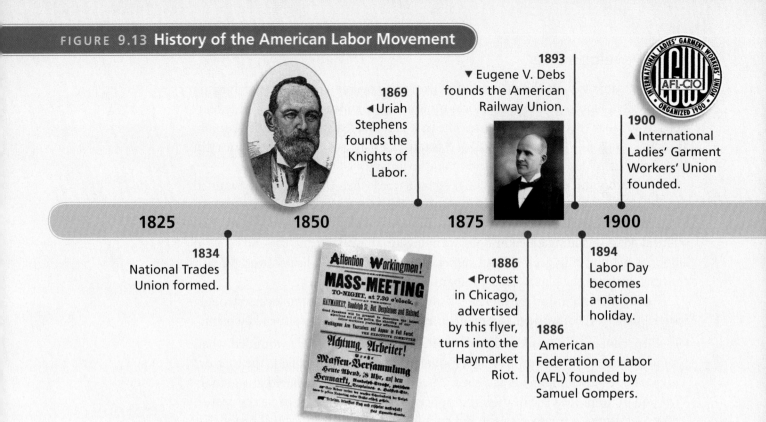

FIGURE 9.13 **History of the American Labor Movement**

1869
◀ Uriah Stephens founds the Knights of Labor.

1893
▼ Eugene V. Debs founds the American Railway Union.

1900
▲ International Ladies' Garment Workers' Union founded.

1825   **1850**   **1875**   **1900**

1834
National Trades Union formed.

Attention Workingmen!
MASS-MEETING
TO-NIGHT, at 7.30 o'clock,
HAYMARKET, Randolph St. Bet. Desplaines and Halsted.

1886
◀ Protest in Chicago, advertised by this flyer, turns into the Haymarket Riot.

1894
Labor Day becomes a national holiday.

1886
American Federation of Labor (AFL) founded by Samuel Gompers.

woman to participate in the U.S. labor movement was Mary Harris Jones, known as Mother Jones. In 1903, she led 80 children, many of whom had been injured while working, on a march to the home of President Theodore Roosevelt. The march helped to emphasize the need for child labor laws.

Unions Gain Power

During the Great Depression of the 1930s, union membership in the United States declined as millions of people lost their jobs. Yet unions gained power through laws passed as part of the New Deal, a series of reforms that attempted to revive the country's economy.

- The Norris-LaGuardia Act (1932) outlawed the practice of hiring only workers who agreed not to join a union. It also required employers to allow workers to organize without interference from their employer.

- The National Labor Relations Act (1935), also known as the Wagner Act, gave most workers in the private sector the right to form unions and to use strikes and other job actions.

- The Fair Labor Standards Act (1938) set a minimum wage, required extra pay for overtime work, and made most child labor illegal.

During this period, the Congress of Industrial Organizations (CIO) organized unions for industrial workers. Originally part of the AFL, which favored skilled workers in craft unions, the CIO broke away in 1938. The two organizations came together again in 1955 as the AFL-CIO.

The AFL succeeded in organizing the United Auto Workers (UAW) union in 1935. After a tense sit-down strike in Flint, Michigan, in 1937, General Motors

1962
◄ Cesar Chavez founds National Farm Workers Association (NFWA), which later becomes United Farm Workers.

2005
Service Employees International Union breaks away from AFL-CIO.

1925

1950

1975

2000

1935
Congress passes the National Labor Relations Act, also called the Wagner Act.

1959
Congress passes Landrum-Griffin Act.

1981
► Air traffic controllers' strike is unsuccessful.

1935
United Auto Workers organized.

became the first automaker to recognize the union. Chrysler and Ford soon followed. In the 1940s, Walter Philip Reuther, as president of the UAW, helped auto workers become some of the nation's highest paid industrial workers. Also in the 1940s, John L. Lewis, the tough-talking, cigar-smoking leader of the CIO, brought his own United Mine Workers back from near failure and waged a fierce and successful fight to organize the nation's steelworkers.

Backlash Against Unions Following World War II

The end of World War II ushered in a period of anti-union legislation. In 1947, over the veto of President Harry S. Truman, the Taft-Hartley Act was passed. It amended the Wagner Act and limited union activities, increasing the government's power to intervene if a strike might threaten national security.

America's fear of Communism, the political and economic system of the Soviet Union, led to further restrictions on unions. The Landrum-Griffin Act (1959) forbade communists from holding union offices and required tighter financial and electoral accounting. George Meany, president of the AFL-CIO from 1955 to 1979, was a strong anti-communist and worked to get rid of unions that he considered sympathetic to communist ideas.

APPLICATION Comparing and Contrasting Economic Information

A. What motivated workers in the 1800s to form unions? Why did they continue to form unions in the early- to mid-1900s?

The Labor Movement's Steady Decline

KEY CONCEPTS

For 30 years following World War II, labor unions represented about 30 percent of the U.S. work force. Since the mid-1970s, membership in unions has declined steadily, falling to about 12.5 percent in 2005. The decline in unions can be traced to three causes: unions' tarnished reputations, changes in the labor force, and laws restricting union influence.

Loss of Reputation and Labor Force Changes

In the late 1900s, labor unions began to lose their luster in the eyes of many Americans. Prolonged strikes both disrupted the public and placed a burden on the striking families. Some unions began requiring companies to employ more workers than necessary, a tactic known as featherbedding. Featherbedding, especially in the railroad industry, raised criticisms of wastefulness. Investigators discovered that a few labor unions had ties to organized crime, which reflected badly on all unions.

The changing nature of the U.S. work force also led to reduced union membership. Union membership was traditionally rooted in manufacturing industries. But the number of manufacturing jobs in the United States fell sharply in the second half of the 20th century as the economy shifted toward service industries. The increase in the number of contingent and contract workers also led to lower union membership because such workers are less likely to pursue union representation.

As manufacturing declined, unions shifted their organizing efforts toward service workers. The American Federation of State, County, and Municipal Employees

Economics Update

Find an update on labor unions at **ClassZone.com**

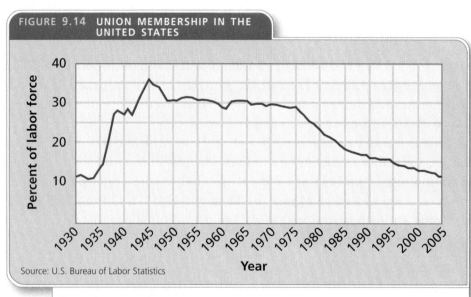

FIGURE 9.14 **UNION MEMBERSHIP IN THE UNITED STATES**

Source: U.S. Bureau of Labor Statistics

ANALYZE GRAPHS

1. During this time period, when was union membership highest? What percent of the labor force belonged to a union that year?

2. Which year was union membership lowest, and what percent of the labor force belonged to a union then?

had about 1.4 million members in 2005. The Service Employees International Union (SEIU), which organizes such service workers as caregivers and janitors, had a membership of 1.8 million in 2005. The SEIU was the largest union in the AFL-CIO, but in 2005 it left the group. Several other smaller unions also left the AFL-CIO and joined SEIU to form a new coalition with different priorities.

Right-to-Work Laws

Another factor in the steady decline of union membership in the United States is legislation that tries to limit union influence. Unions had developed the **closed shop**, a business required to hire only union members. The closed shop was intended to maintain union standards for workers who only work at a business briefly, such as musicians or restaurant employees. Unions also developed the **union shop**, a business where workers are required to join a union within a set time period after being hired. Union shops allowed businesses to hire nonunion workers without diluting the strength of the union.

The Taft-Hartley Act outlawed the closed shop and weakened possibilities for a union shop. It also gave states the power to make it illegal to require workers to join unions. Such laws became known as **right-to-work laws**, a name meant to emphasize that workers are free not to join a union. However, the effect of right-to-work laws and similar legislation is to weaken unions and to help businesses operate without unions. Most right-to-work states are in the Southeast and the central West, and union membership in these areas is low.

QUICK REFERENCE

A **closed shop** is a business where an employer can hire only union members.

A **union shop** is a business where workers are required to join a union within a set time period after being hired.

Right-to-work laws make it illegal to require workers to join unions.

FIGURE 9.15 RIGHT-TO-WORK STATES MAP

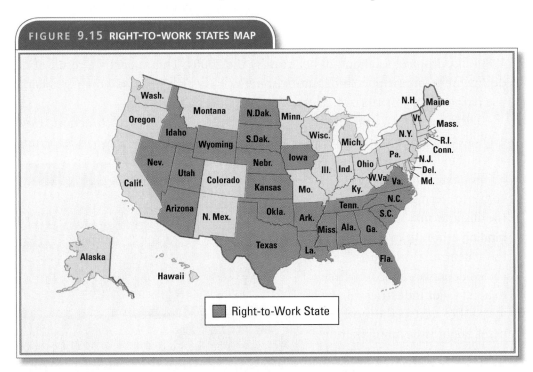

Right-to-Work State

APPLICATION Predicting Economic Trends

B. Consider the trends in today's labor force that you learned about in Section 2. As more service industries unionize, is union membership, as a percent of the labor force, likely to return to the levels of the mid-1900s? Why or why not?

Union Negotiating Methods

QUICK REFERENCE

Collective bargaining is the way businesses and unions negotiate wages and working conditions.

KEY CONCEPTS

Despite the decline in membership, organized labor still wields power in the American economy. Unions continue to use **collective bargaining**, the process of negotiation between businesses and their organized employees to establish wages and to improve working conditions. Since it represents many employees together, a union can arrive at a better deal for workers than if each employee bargained with the employer separately. As a result, unionized companies tend to pay higher wages than companies without unions.

Collective Bargaining

In the 1930s and 1940s, unions negotiated for higher wages, better working conditions, and fair grievance procedures for workers who felt that they had been treated unjustly. As these demands were increasingly met, unions negotiated for job security and such fringe benefits as health insurance. Benefits and job security are important issues in today's negotiations as well, but in many cases today's workers are not pressing for higher wages. Instead they are trying to hold the line against pay cuts and reductions in benefits, including pensions.

Unions have the threat of a strike to provide a motivation for management to come to terms, but strikes occur much less frequently than in the past. Large-scale work stoppages in the United States occurred hundreds of times a year before the 1980s but dropped to about 20 per year by the 2000s. This is partly a result of the decline in union membership, but it also reflects the willingness of management to use replacement workers or to close a plant permanently.

The vast majority of union contracts are settled without such action. However, some negotiations require additional interventions if the two sides cannot agree. First, a mediator may be brought in to help the sides come to terms. If that fails, the dispute may be settled by **binding arbitration**—a decision by a neutral third party that each side agrees ahead of time to accept. For industries related to public safety, the government might issue an injunction to force workers back to work after a stoppage, or to stop protest activities that may interfere with public safety.

QUICK REFERENCE

Binding arbitration is a process in which an impartial third party resolves disputes between management and unions.

Collective Bargaining
Union leaders meet with business management to negotiate the details of union contracts.

APPLICATION Analyzing Cause and Effect

C. Explain why high wages and high employment do not necessarily go hand in hand.

REVIEWING KEY CONCEPTS

1. Explain the differences between the terms in each of these pairs.

   a. *closed shop* **b.** *strike*
   union shop *collective bargaining*

2. Why was the formation of the Knights of Labor a key event for organized labor in the United States?

3. Name two laws that supported labor's rights and two laws that restricted them.

4. Opponents of right-to-work laws sometimes call them "work-for-less" laws. Why do you think they use that name?

5. Why would a business care if its workers went on strike?

6. **Using Your Notes** Write a paragraph explaining why unions grew in the 1800s and the first half of the 1900s. Refer to your completed summary chart to help you develop your argument with strong supporting detail.

Topic	Main Ideas	Related Facts
Labor movement's rise to power		

   Use the Graphic Organizer at **Interactive Review @ ClassZone.com**

CRITICAL THINKING

7. **Analyzing Cause and Effect** What effect might outsourcing have on union membership?

8. **Evaluating Economic Decisions** In 1981, a group of air traffic controllers, employees of the Federal Aviation Administration, went on strike. They wanted to reduce their workweek to 32 hours instead of the usual 40 because of the high stress of their jobs. President Ronald Reagan broke the strike and disbanded the union of air traffic controllers, claiming that they were striking illegally. About 100 strikers were arrested, and all of them were banned for life from jobs in air traffic control. Did Reagan do the right thing by firing the striking workers? Explain your answer.

9. **Challenge** The firing of the air traffic controllers and the breaking of their union was one of the key events for labor in the United States. What trends in organized labor are evident in that event?

ECONOMICS IN PRACTICE

Automated factories reduced the need for assembly line workers.

Analyzing Economic Data
Look at Figure 9.14 on page 278, which shows changes in union membership in the United States.

Analyze Union Membership
Compare the upward and downward movements of the graph to the events going on in the United States and world.

1930s—The Great Depression

1940s—World War II; postwar recovery

1950s—Korean War; economy thrives

1960s—Civil Rights movement; Vietnam War; steady economy

1970s—End of Vietnam War; oil embargo; inflation

1980s—Recession and recovery

1990s—Fall of Communism in Europe and Russia; Internet boom

2000s—September 11; Iraq War; recession and recovery

Challenge Does there seem to be a relationship between how well the economy is doing and union membership? Explain.

Managing Change in Your Work Life

Background The United States economy has shifted from manufacturing to service and knowledge-based industries. New technologies offer increasingly sophisticated tools. Telecommuting provides businesses the option of having employees work effectively from outside the office.

Globalization has revolutionized the way companies do business. Companies are no longer tied to a specific location. Instead, they establish offices around the globe. The outsourcing and insourcing of jobs result both in benefits and challenges. The dynamics of the workplace are defined by a single factor—change.

What's the issue? How will you respond to the changing dynamics of the work environment? Study these sources to discover how change affects the type of work we do, as well as where and how we do it.

A. Online Magazine Article

Call centers in India help businesses reduce costs because local wages are low. But some Westerners accept the low wages for a chance to live in India.

Subcontinental Drift

More Westerners are beefing up their resumés with a stint in India

After a year answering phones for Swiss International Air Lines Ltd. in a Geneva call center, Myriam Vock was eager to see something of the world. So she packed her bags and hopped a plane to India. Two and a half years later she's still there, sharing a five-bedroom apartment in an upscale New Delhi suburb with four other foreigners.

And how does she pay the bills? She works in a call center, getting paid a fraction of what she did back home. "I'm not earning much, but there is enough to live well and travel," says Vock, 21. . . . "I don't pay taxes here, and life is so much cheaper," she says.

Worried about your job fleeing to India? One strategy is to chase it—an option a growing number of twentysomething Westerners are choosing. Sure, the trend will never make up for the thousands of positions lost back home, but for adventurous young people, a spell in a call center in Bangalore or Bombay can help defray the costs of a grand tour of the subcontinent and beyond.

Source: BusinessWeek.com, January 16, 2006

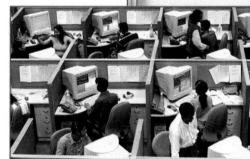

Call centers in India serve customers of companies all over the world.

Thinking Economically Explain Myriam's decision to work in a call center in India using cost-benefit analysis.

B. Business Cartoon

Canadian cartoonist Andrew Toos drew this cartoon about working in an increasingly technological society.

MR. CRENSHAW, TIME FOR OUR TELECONFERENCE.

IS THERE NO ESCAPE?

Source: www.CartoonStock.com

Thinking Economically
What does the cartoon suggest about new technological developments in the world of work? Explain your answer.

C. Online Newspaper Article

Many worry that outsourcing may reduce the number of jobs in the United States. This article presents a different perspective.

Outsourcing Benefits Permac Employees

Permac creates a win-win situation.

Permac Industries in Burnsville [Minnesota] fashions parts ranging from rings that tie parachutes to small planes to parts for soda fountain machines and construction trucks. President and CEO Darlene Miller plans to send some work to China, but she said it's to the benefit of her 27 Minnesota employees.

"No one here will lose a job. We're not planning to let anybody go—in fact, we're hiring," she said.

Miller is investing in a $700,000 piece of equipment to give workers in Burnsville better tools for specialized work that demands higher skills than the work she plans to send to China. A side benefit for the company's Burnsville workers is that the work going to China will reduce the need for what at times has seemed relentless overtime.

"The simple parts eat up a lot of machine time," said John Keith, a Permac team leader. "If we farm that out we have time to look at getting new business, more complicated business."

Source: www.startribune.com, September 5, 2004

Thinking Economically How will Permac employees benefit from outsourcing? Identify others who also will benefit and explain why.

THINKING ECONOMICALLY Synthesizing

1. What skills are you likely to need in order to manage change successfully in your work life? Support your answer with examples from the documents.

2. In documents A and B, are the types of change similar or different? Are their effects on workers positive or negative? Explain your answer.

3. Compare the opportunities afforded by change in documents A and C. How are they similar? How are they different?

The Role of Labor   283

Interactive  Review

Review this chapter using interactive
activities at **ClassZone.com**
- **Online Summary**
- **Quizzes**
- **Vocabulary Flip Cards**
- **Graphic Organizers**
- **Review and Study Notes**

 Online Summary

Complete the following activity either on your
own paper or online at **ClassZone.com**

**Choose the key concept that best completes
the sentence. Not all key concepts will be used.**

civilian labor force	insourcing
closed shop	labor union
collective bargaining	minimum wage
contingent employment	outsourcing
craft union	productivity
derived demand	right-to-work law
equilibrium wage	strike
glass ceiling	telecommuting
human capital	union shop
industrial union	wages

__1__ are the cost of labor. The demand for labor is
a __2__, growing out of the demand for the goods or
services workers can produce. The forces of supply
and demand determine the __3__, at which there is
neither a surplus nor a shortage of workers. Wages
are directly correlated to a worker's __4__. Workers
with the lowest level often earn only the __5__.

Since the 1950s, many women have entered
the __6__. They are sometimes limited by the __7__,
which keeps them from reaching the highest levels
of management. Other trends in the labor market
include __8__, working away from a central office,
and __9__, working part-time or temporary jobs.
U.S. firms sometimes use __10__ to hire workers in
other countries. When foreign companies open
plants in the United States, it is called __11__.

Changes in the work force have reduced the
number of workers who belong to a __12__. Such
organizations press for higher pay and better
working conditions through __13__. If talks fail,
union workers might __14__, putting pressure on
employers to meet their demands.

CHAPTER 9 Assessment

REVIEWING KEY CONCEPTS

How Are Wages Determined? (pp. 258–265)

1. What forces determine the equilibrium wage?

2. What four factors contribute to differences in
wages?

Trends in Today's Labor Market (pp. 266–273)

3. How has the labor market in the United States
changed since the 1950s?

4. Name two new developments in the way
Americans work.

Organized Labor in the United States
(pp. 274–283)

5. Name an important U.S. labor leader and describe
what he or she contributed to the labor movement.

6. What are some of the reasons membership in unions
has declined since the 1950s?

APPLYING ECONOMIC CONCEPTS

The table below shows the median weekly earnings of
full-time wage and salary workers by union affiliation
and selected characteristics.

FIGURE 9.16 UNION AND NONUNION WAGES

Median Weekly Earnings of Full-Time Workers in the United States (in dollars)				
Race or Ethnicity	Union Men	Union Women	Nonunion Men	Nonunion Women
African-American	689	632	523	478
Asian	819	789	827	643
Hispanic	713	609	473	414
White	884	749	714	576

Source: U.S. Bureau of Labor Statistics, 2005 data

7. What is the only group for which union affiliation
does not yield higher pay?

8. Calculate the percentage difference between each
group's union and nonunion wages. Which group
gains the most in wages from union membership?

9. **Creating Graphs** Create a bar graph using the following information about alternative work arrangements in the United States. Include an appropriate title and a source line showing that the data, which are for 2005, come from the Bureau of Labor Statistics.

   Independent contractors (Self-employed workers, such as independent sales consultants or freelance writers): 10.3 million

   On-call workers (Workers called as needed, sometimes working several days or weeks in a row, such as substitute teachers): 2.5 million

   Temporary workers (Workers paid by the hour, such as file clerks, hired through a temporary employment agency): 1.2 million

   Contract workers (Workers paid a salary, such as training specialists, provided by contract firms and hired for a limited contract): 0.8 million

   Use *SMART Grapher* @ ClassZone.com to complete this activity.

10. **Synthesizing Economic Data** Explain the differences in median weekly earnings in Figure 9.16 in terms of this chapter's key concepts.

11. **Explaining an Economic Concept** Have you ever been paid to work? If so, explain how the rate you were paid was determined. If not, think of someone you know who has earned money and explain how that person's wages were determined.

12. **Applying Economic Concepts** Think back to a time when you negotiated with someone in a position of authority for something you strongly wanted. Briefly describe the tactics you used and look for similarities or differences between those and the tactics unions use with employers.

13. **Challenge** In 2003, the Fair Labor Standards Act was amended to clarify who was entitled to overtime pay. At the center of the issue were computer programmers, who lost entitlement to overtime if their regular pay is $65,000 per year or more. What impact might this have had on the workers and the economy?

Collective Bargaining

It's time to renegotiate the union contract at the Acme auto parts factory in Springfield. Read these descriptions of the two sides, then follow the instructions to experience what union negotiations are like.

Union workers currently earn $25 per hour, plus overtime pay if they have to work more than 35 hours per week. Benefits include health-care insurance paid for by the company, plus vision and dental coverage, also funded by the company. The workers' pension fund is handled through the union.

The Acme company is a conglomerate based in the United States. Its auto parts business has been struggling to make a profit, so it is considering outsourcing the work to a factory in China. It would then like to turn the Springfield factory into a computer manufacturing facility.

Step 1 Divide the class evenly into union members and the Acme management team.

Step 2 Separately and privately, each group discusses its objectives and negotiating strategies. Try to keep the conversation quiet so that the other side does not gain an advantage by learning your bargaining points.

Step 3 Each group chooses three representatives to conduct the negotiations.

Step 4 The representatives from both sides meet and negotiate the new contract. The rest of the two groups may listen to the negotiations, but they may not participate. If the two sides still disagree on an issue after several minutes of negotiations, put that issue aside for the moment. Keep a list showing the status of each issue.

Step 5 If time permits, repeat steps 2–4 to address the unresolved issues.

Discuss what happened. Did one side have more bargaining power? How did the two sides resolve their differences? Why were some issues more difficult to resolve than others?

U.S. TREASURY

What constitutes money?

Money isn't born, it's made. Each society decides what it will accept as money, but effective moneys all share certain attributes and perform certain functions.

Money and Banking

CONCEPT REVIEW

Macroeconomics is the study of the behavior of the economy as a whole and how major economic sectors, such as industry and government, interact.

CHAPTER 10 KEY CONCEPT

Money provides a low-cost method of trading one good or service for another. It makes the system of voluntary exchange efficient.

WHY THE CONCEPT MATTERS

What were the last three economic transactions you completed using money? Perhaps you put four quarters in the fare machine on the bus to school or bought a slice of pizza and a drink in the cafeteria at lunch. Or maybe you caught an early movie after school yesterday. To gauge the importance of money to the economy, imagine trying to make such transactions without the familiar paper bills and coins.

Online Highlights
More at ClassZone.com

 Economics Update

Go to **ECONOMICS UPDATE** for chapter updates and current news on student loans. (See Case Study, pp. 312–313.) ▶

Animated Economics

Go to **ANIMATED ECONOMICS** for interactive lessons on the graphs and tables in this chapter.

Interactive ◀▶Review

Go to **INTERACTIVE REVIEW** for concept review and activities.

OH HE'S MY LOANS OFFICER.
Source: www.CartoonStock.com

How important are student loans in the U.S. higher education system? See the Case Study on pages 312–313.

Money: Its Functions and Properties

OBJECTIVES	KEY TERMS	TAKING NOTES
In Section 1, you will • outline the functions that money performs and the characteristics that money possesses • explain why the different types of money have value • describe how the money supply in the United States is measured	money, *p. 288* medium of exchange, *p. 288* barter, *p. 288* standard of value, *p. 289* store of value, *p. 289* commodity money, *p. 291* representative money, *p. 291* fiat money, *p. 291* currency, *p. 293* demand deposits, *p. 293* near money, *p. 293*	As you read Section 1, complete a cluster diagram summarizing key information about money. Use the Graphic Organizer at **Interactive Review @ ClassZone.com**

(cluster diagram with central node labeled "Money")

Functions of Money

KEY CONCEPTS

What do the following things have in common: cattle, corn, rice, salt, copper, gold, silver, seashells, stones, and whale teeth? At different times and in different places, they have all been used as money. In fact, **money** is anything that people will accept as payment for goods and services. Whatever it is that people choose to use as money, it should perform three important functions.

FUNCTION 1 Medium of Exchange

Money must serve as a **medium of exchange**, or the means through which goods and services can be exchanged. Without money, economic transactions must be made through **barter**—exchanging goods and services for other goods and services. Barter is cumbersome and inefficient because two people who want to barter must at the same time want what the other has to offer. For example, suppose you want to trade two T-shirts for a pair of jeans. One classmate might have the jeans but not want your shirts; another might want your shirts but not have jeans to trade. It is much easier for you to buy a pair of jeans by giving money to the seller who, in turn, can use it to buy something else. Money allows for the precise and flexible pricing of goods and services, making any economic transaction convenient.

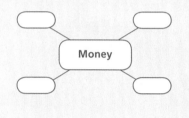

A World of Money Currencies come in a wide variety of colors and sizes. This is a collage of the currencies of South America.

FUNCTION 2 Standard of Value

Money also serves as a **standard of value**, the yardstick of economic worth in the exchange process. It allows people to measure the relative costs of goods and services. A $20 T-shirt is worth two $10 phone cards, four $5 burritos, or twenty $1 bus rides. The basic monetary unit in the United States is the dollar, which serves as the standard by which the economic worth of all goods and services can be expressed and measured.

QUICK REFERENCE

A **standard of value** determines the economic worth in the exchange process.

A **store of value** is something that holds its value over time.

FUNCTION 3 Store of Value

Finally, money acts as a **store of value**, that is, something that holds its value over time. People, therefore, do not need to spend all their money at once or in one place; they can put it aside for later use. They know that it will be accepted wherever and whenever it is presented to purchase goods and services.

One situation where money does not function well as a store of value is when the economy experiences significant inflation—a sustained rise in the general level of prices. For example, in Argentina in the first half of 2002, prices rose by about 70 percent. Basic goods that cost 150 pesos in January cost 255 pesos in June. In other words, in that time period, Argentina's money lost over two-thirds of its purchasing power. You'll learn more about inflation in Chapter 13.

Economics Update

Find an update on the functions of money at **ClassZone.com**

ECONOMICS ESSENTIALS
FIGURE 10.1 **Functions of Money**

What Functions Does Money Perform?

Standard of Value Money provides both a way to express and measure the relative costs of goods and services and a way to compare the worths of different goods and services.

Medium of Exchange Money provides a flexible, precise, and convenient way to exchange goods and services.

Store of Value Money holds its value over time. It can be saved for later use because it can be exchanged at any time for goods and services.

ANALYZE CHARTS
You've read that salt was used as money in the past. How effectively do you think salt would function as money? Use the three functions of money in the chart to frame your answer.

APPLICATION Applying Economic Concepts

A. How does money help to make clear the opportunity cost of an economic decision?

Properties of Money

To perform the three functions of money, an item must possess certain physical and economic properties. Physical properties of money are the characteristics of the item itself. Economic properties are linked to the role that money plays in the market.

PROPERTY 1 Physical

The following are physical properties of useful money:

Durability Money should be durable, or sturdy, enough to last throughout many transactions. Something that falls apart when several people handle it or that spoils easily would not be a good item to use as money.

Portability Money needs to be small, light, and easy to carry. It's easy to see why paper bills are preferable to cattle as money.

Divisibility Money should also be divisible so that change can be made. For example, the dollar can be divided an endless number of ways using different combinations of pennies, nickels, dimes, or quarters. Divisibility also allows flexible pricing.

Uniformity Lastly, money must be uniform, having features and markings that make it recognizable. Coins that are used as money look different from other flat metal disks. Paper money is a consistent size and uses special symbols and printing techniques. All money that represents a certain amount in a given country has distinctive characteristics that help identify its value. These distinctive markings also make it more difficult to counterfeit.

Chinese Coins
Bronze, spade-shaped coins, 8th–7th century B.C.

PROPERTY 2 Economic

Useful money must also have the following economic properties:

Stability of Value Money's purchasing power, or value, should be relatively stable. In other words, the amount of goods and services that you can buy with a certain amount of money should not change quickly. Rapid changes in purchasing power would mean that money would not successfully serve as a store of value.

Scarcity Money must be scarce to have any value. As you recall from Chapter 7, when the supply of a product outstrips demand, there is a surplus and prices for that product fall. Similarly, when the supply of money outstrips demand, money loses value, or purchasing power.

Acceptability People who use the money must agree that it is acceptable—that it is a valid medium of exchange. In other words, they will accept money in payment for goods and services because others will also accept it as payment.

APPLICATION Applying Economic Concepts

B. Describe how U.S. dollars serve each of the three functions of money.

Types of Money

In the discussion of the functions and properties of money, one theme recurs—value. Money draws its value from three possible sources. **Commodity money** derives its value from the type of material from which it is composed. **Representative money** is paper money backed by something tangible—such as silver or gold—that gives it value. **Fiat money** has no tangible backing, but it is declared by the government that issues it, and accepted by citizens who use it, to have worth.

Commodity money has intrinsic value based on the material from which it is made.

Representative money is backed by something tangible.

Fiat money is declared by the government and accepted by citizens to have worth.

TYPE 1 Commodity Money

Commodity money is something that has value for what it is. Items used as commodity money have value in and of themselves, apart from their value as money. Over the course of history, for example, gold, silver, precious stones, salt, olive oil, and rice have all been valued enough for their scarcity or for their usefulness to be used as money.

However, the most common form of commodity money throughout history has been coins made from precious metals. Such coins contain enough of the precious metal that if each was melted down it would be worth at least its face value. One problem with commodity money is that if the item becomes too valuable, people will hoard it rather than circulate it, hoping it will become more valuable in the future. Commodity money is rarely used today.

Commodity Money Until recently, cattle was an important medium of exchange for the Masai people of East Africa.

TYPE 2 Representative Money

Representative money is paper money that can be exchanged for something else of value. The earliest forms of representative money were seen in the Middle Ages, when merchants, goldsmiths, and moneylenders began issuing receipts that promised to pay a certain amount of gold or silver. This came about because it was not always convenient or safe to transport large quantities of those precious metals from place to place for the purpose of trading. These practices signal the beginning of the widespread modern use of paper money.

Eventually, governments got involved with representative money by regulating how much metal needed to be stored to back up the paper money. One problem with representative money is that its value fluctuates with the supply and price of gold or silver, which can cause problems of inflation or deflation—a sustained rise or fall, respectively, in the general level of prices.

The Euro as a Common Currency

On January 1, 2002, a new currency—the euro—was put into full use in 12 European countries, each a member of the European Union (EU). The symbol for the euro is €. This adoption of a common currency marked the first time that such a large area willingly entered into a monetary union. The step was one more milestone in the economic consolidation of Europe. Ten Eastern European countries that were admitted to the EU in 2004 also plan to adopt the European currency in time.

The European Union introduced the euro to make trade among member nations easier and cheaper. Adoption of the euro also was an important step in the economic and political integration of Europe.

Like all modern currencies, the euro is categorized as fiat money. Its value is derived from public confidence in the European Union. Control of the supply of the euro is maintained by the European Central Bank located in Frankfurt, Germany. Each member nation of the EU has a seat on the Central Bank's decision-making board.

EU Members Using the Euro, 2006

	Austria
	Belgium
	Finland
	France
	Germany
	Greece
	Ireland
	Italy
	Luxembourg
	Netherlands
	Portugal
	Spain

CONNECTING ACROSS THE GLOBE

1. **Making Inferences** How do you think having a common currency might benefit the EU?

2. **Recognizing Effects** Why does the euro have value as currency?

TYPE 3 Fiat Money

Unlike representative money, fiat money has value only because the government has issued a fiat, or order, saying that this is the case. The value of the U.S. dollar was linked to the value of gold until 1971. Since then, a $10 bill can no longer be exchanged for gold; it can only be converted into other combinations of U.S. currency that also equal $10.

In fiat money, coins contain only a token amount of precious metal that is worth far less than the face value of those coins. Paper money has no intrinsic value, and people cannot exchange it for a certain amount of gold or silver. Fiat money has value because the government says it can be used as money and because people accept that it will fulfill all the functions of money.

Dollar bills in the United States carry the statement "This note is legal tender for all debts, public and private." This statement assures people that sellers will accept such money from buyers as payment for goods or services and lenders will accept it as payment for debts. A crucial role of the government in maintaining the value of fiat money is controlling its supply—in other words, maintaining its scarcity.

APPLICATION Analyzing Cause and Effect

C. Which type of money's value would be most affected by political instability? Why?

Money in the United States

KEY CONCEPTS

In this section so far, you have learned what has been used as money, what functions money performs, what properties it possesses, and why money has value. But what serves as money in the United States today? In its narrowest sense, money consists of what can be used immediately for transactions—currency, demand deposits, and other checkable deposits. **Currency** is paper money and coins. Checking accounts are called **demand deposits** because funds in checking accounts can be converted into currency "on demand."

There are other monetary instruments that are almost, but not exactly, like money. Known as **near money**, it includes savings accounts and other similar time deposits that cannot be used as a medium of exchange but can be converted into cash relatively easily.

QUICK REFERENCE

Currency is paper money and coins.

Demand deposits are checking accounts.

Near money is savings accounts and time deposits that can be converted into cash relatively easily.

Money in the Narrowest Sense

In the narrowest sense, money is what can be immediately used for transactions. This definition of money sometimes uses the term *transactions money*. Most of the money that you and your friends and family spend is transactions money. About half of such money is currency, both paper money and coins, that is used by individuals and businesses.

Most demand deposits are noninterest-bearing checking accounts that can be converted into currency simply by writing a check. Traveler's checks, which are drafts that can be purchased in a number of money amounts and redeemed in many parts of the world, represent a small share of overall demand deposits. Other checkable deposits include negotiable order of withdrawal (NOW) accounts, which are interest-bearing savings accounts against which drafts may be written.

Are Savings Accounts Money?

Near money, such as savings accounts and other interest-bearing accounts, cannot be used directly to make transactions. Your local sporting goods store will not accept a savings passbook as payment for a new basketball or for your tennis racket to be restrung. But money in a savings account can be easily transferred into a checking account or removed directly from an automatic teller machine and put toward a desired good or service.

Near money takes many forms in addition to traditional savings accounts. Time deposits are funds that people place in a financial institution for a specific period of time in return for a higher interest rate. These deposits are often placed in certificates of deposit (CDs). Money market accounts place restrictions on the number of transactions you can make in a month and require you to maintain a certain balance in the account (as low as $500 but often substantially more) in order to receive a higher rate of interest.

Near Money A savings account contains money but is not, strictly, money.

How Much Money?

How much money is in supply in the United States? Economists use various instruments to measure the money supply, but the most often cited are M1 and M2. M1 is the narrowest measure of the money supply, consisting of currency, demand deposits, and other checkable deposits. It is synonymous with transactions money. The elements of M1 are referred to as liquid assets, which means that they are or can easily become currency.

M2 is a broader measure of the money supply, consisting of M1 plus various kinds of near money. M2 includes savings accounts, other small-denomination time deposits (CDs of less than $100,000), and money market mutual funds. You will learn about these financial instruments in Chapter 11.

Figure 10.2 shows the amounts of the different forms of money that make up M1 and M2. You can see that M1 is almost evenly split between currency and checkable deposits. Notice that more of M2 comes from savings than from M1. You will learn the importance of the money supply in the economy and how the government manages it in Chapter 16.

Economics Update

Find an update on measures of the money supply at **ClassZone.com**

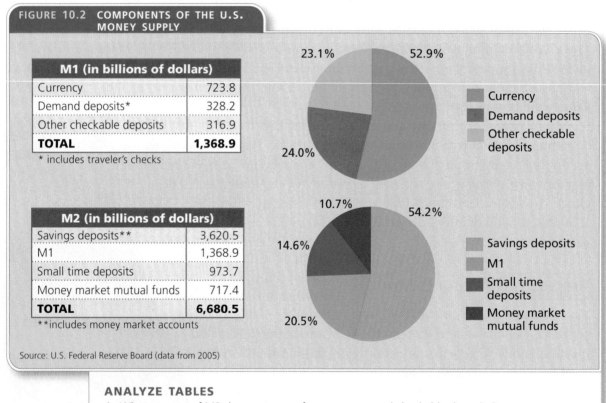

FIGURE 10.2 COMPONENTS OF THE U.S. MONEY SUPPLY

M1 (in billions of dollars)	
Currency	723.8
Demand deposits*	328.2
Other checkable deposits	316.9
TOTAL	**1,368.9**

* includes traveler's checks

Currency — 52.9%
Demand deposits — 24.0%
Other checkable deposits — 23.1%

M2 (in billions of dollars)	
Savings deposits**	3,620.5
M1	1,368.9
Small time deposits	973.7
Money market mutual funds	717.4
TOTAL	**6,680.5**

**includes money market accounts

Savings deposits — 54.2%
M1 — 20.5%
Small time deposits — 14.6%
Money market mutual funds — 10.7%

Source: U.S. Federal Reserve Board (data from 2005)

ANALYZE TABLES
1. What amount of M2 does not come from currency and checkable deposits?
2. If currency is 52.9 percent of M1, and M1 is 20.5 percent of M2, what percentage of M2 is currency?

APPLICATION Applying Economic Concepts

D. Classify each of the following as M1 and M2: **a.** dollar bill; **b.** savings account; **c.** money market account; **d.** traveler's check; **e.** $50,000 CD.

REVIEWING KEY CONCEPTS

1. Explain the difference between the terms in each of these pairs.

   a. *standard of value* **b.** *commodity money* **c.** *demand deposits*
   store of value   *representative money*   *near money*

2. Why are economic transactions easier with money than with barter?

3. Why is it important that money be divisible?

4. Why are checking accounts called demand deposits?

5. What aspect of fiat money allows it to have more stability than representative money?

6. **Using Your Notes** How are the economic properties of money related to its functions? Refer to your completed cluster diagram.

   Use the Graphic Organizer at **Interactive Review @ ClassZone.com**

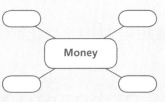

Money

CRITICAL THINKING

7. **Categorizing Economic Information** Which of these forms of money are included in M1:
   - checking accounts
   - coins
   - money market accounts
   - paper money
   - savings accounts
   - time deposits
   - traveler's checks
   - NOW accounts

8. **Making Inferences** The U.S. government has tried to get people to use dollar coins rather than dollar bills. Most consumers prefer to use dollar bills. Which physical properties of money are involved in these different preferences?

9. **Applying Economic Concepts** Maria's parents told her that for the ten years prior to her high school graduation, they saved $200 per month for her college education—$24,000 (plus interest). Which function of money does this example best illustrate? Why?

10. **Challenge** Why is there more near money than transactions money in the U.S. money supply?

ECONOMICS IN PRACTICE

Evaluating Economic Decisions
In the past, indigenous people of Central and South America used cacao beans (the source of chocolate) as currency.

Evaluate Money In Section 1, you learned that money should function as a medium of exchange, a standard of value, and a store of value. Use what you've learned about these functions to evaluate how useful cacao beans might be as money today. Show your answer by filling in the table below.

Function	Possible Problems
Medium of exchange	
Standard of value	
Store of value	

Challenge How well do cacao beans exhibit each of the physical and economic properties of money?

The Development of U.S. Banking

OBJECTIVES	KEY TERMS	TAKING NOTES
In Section 2, you will • describe how banking developed in the United States • identify the banking institutions that operate in the United States	state bank, *p. 296* national bank, *p. 299* gold standard, *p. 299*	As you read Section 2, complete a chart using the key concepts and other helpful words and phrases. Use the Graphic Organizer at **Interactive Review @ ClassZone.com**

Development of U.S. Banking		
Origins	19th Century	20th Century

The Origins of Banking

KEY CONCEPTS

Modern banking arose in Italy in the late Middle Ages. Italian merchants stored money or valuables for wealthy people and issued receipts that promised to return the property on demand. They realized that they did not have to hold all the deposits, since all depositors did not reclaim their property at the same time, but could lend some of the deposits and earn interest on those loans. This was the beginning of fractional reserve banking (see Section 3), the practice of holding only a fraction of the money deposited in a bank and lending the rest.

Early "Bankers" The Italian word *banco,* means "bench." From benches in the street, Italian merchants used some practices that are part of banking today.

In colonial America, many merchants followed the same practice. However, these banks were far from secure. If a merchant's business failed, depositors lost all of their savings. After the Revolutionary War, many **state banks**—banks chartered, or licensed, by state governments—were established. Some of these banks, however, followed practices that tended to create instability and disorder. Many issued their own currency that was not linked to reserves of gold or silver held by the bank.

Alexander Hamilton: Shaping a Banking System

Imagine what it would be like if every bank issued its own currency. How would buyers know if sellers would accept their money? How would sellers know if the money they received was worth anything? That was the confusing situation that Alexander Hamilton faced when he became Secretary of the Treasury in 1789. He immediately set to work to bring stability to U. S. banking.

The First Bank of the United States

Hamilton was a leading Federalist who believed in a strong central government. He proposed chartering a privately owned national bank to put the government on a sound financial footing. This bank would issue a national currency and help control the money supply by refusing to accept currency from state banks that was not backed by gold or silver. It also would lend money to the federal government, state banks, and businesses.

The Constitution did not specifically authorize Congress to charter a national bank. The Anti-federalists, led by Thomas Jefferson and James Madison, interpreted the Constitution strictly and feared putting too much power in the hands of the central government. Hamilton argued that the Constitution implied that the federal government had the authority to create a national bank to carry out its duty to regulate the currency.

Hamilton won the fight, and the First Bank of the United States was chartered in 1791. Over time, it achieved the financial goals that Hamilton had set. However, opponents argued that the bank's policies restrained economic growth, and Congress refused to renew the charter in 1811.

The fact that Hamilton was the architect of the bank was always a strike against it, as he had made many enemies during his career. (One, Aaron Burr, killed him in a duel.) Maybe Hamilton was right when he said, "Men often oppose a thing merely because they have had no agency in planning it, or because it may have been planned by those whom they dislike."

Alexander Hamilton (above) and the First Bank of the United States (right)

FAST FACTS

Alexander Hamilton

Position: First Secretary of the Treasury (1789–1795)

Born: January 11, 1755 in Nevis, British West Indies

Died: July 12, 1804

Writings: *The Federalist Papers* (1787), with James Madison and John Jay; *Report on a National Bank* (1790)

Major Accomplishment: Strengthened the national government and established the First Bank of the United States

Hamilton's Visible Legacy: Portrait on the $10 bill

Economics Update

Learn more about Alexander Hamilton at **ClassZone.com**

APPLICATION Making Inferences

A. How did the First National Bank force state banks to become more stable?

FIGURE 10.3 **Major Developments in American Banking**

1816
◄ Congress charters Second Bank of the United States.

1863
◄ Congress creates national banks and currency.

1775   1800   1825   1850   1875

1791
Congress charters First Bank of the United States.

1837–1865
Wildcat banking leads to unstable currency. ►

19th-Century Developments

KEY CONCEPTS

Without a central bank, the government had difficulty financing the War of 1812 against Britain. Furthermore, state banks soon returned to the unrestrained issuing of currency that was not linked to reserves of gold or silver held by the banks. The resulting increase in the money supply led to inflation during the war.

The Second Bank of the United States

Congress finally agreed to charter the Second Bank of the United States in 1816. The new bank had greater financial resources than the First Bank and succeeded in making the money supply more stable. Opponents continued to see the central bank as too powerful and too closely aligned with the wealthy. President Andrew Jackson was an outspoken critic who mistrusted banks and paper money He vetoed the renewal of its charter in 1832.

Wildcat Banking

After the Second Bank's charter lapsed in 1836, there was no federal oversight of the banking industry. During this period, all banks were state banks, each of which issued its own paper currency, called bank notes. States passed free banking laws that allowed individuals or groups that met its requirements to open banks.

Jackson and the Second Bank This 1828 cartoon lampoons Jackson's battle against the bank.

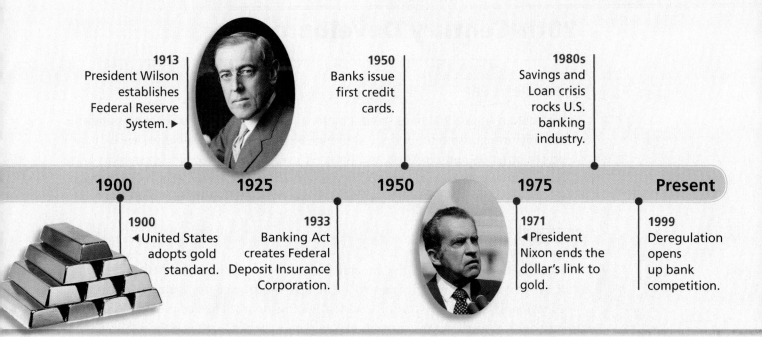

1913 President Wilson establishes Federal Reserve System. ▶

1950 Banks issue first credit cards.

1980s Savings and Loan crisis rocks U.S. banking industry.

1900 | **1925** | **1950** | **1975** | **Present**

1900 ◀ United States adopts gold standard.

1933 Banking Act creates Federal Deposit Insurance Corporation.

1971 ◀ President Nixon ends the dollar's link to gold.

1999 Deregulation opens up bank competition.

Some of these banks were located in remote areas to discourage people from redeeming their bank notes, which were often worth less outside the region where they had been issued. It was this practice, along with the questionable quality of many bank notes that resulted in the term *wildcat bank*. In addition, such banks were susceptible to bank runs when depositors demanded gold or silver for their currency. Since the banks often did not have sufficient reserves of these precious metals, financial panics and economic instability were common results.

The Struggle for Stability

During the Civil War, it was particularly difficult for the government to finance its operations without a national currency and a federal bank. The government's first solution to this problem was to issue a new currency backed by government bonds. These U.S. bank notes, called greenbacks, were printed with green ink.

In 1863, Congress passed the National Banking Act, which led to the creation of a system of **national banks**, banks chartered by the national government. The act provided for a national currency backed by U.S. Treasury bonds and regulated the minimum amount of capital required for national banks as well as the amount of reserves necessary to back the currency. Congress taxed state bank notes issued after 1865, effectively eliminating these notes from circulation.

In 1900, the government officially adopted the **gold standard**, a system in which the basic monetary unit—for example, one dollar—is equal to a set amount of gold. The national currency and gold standard helped to bring some stability to the banking system. Money was now uniform throughout the country, backed by something of intrinsic value, and limited by the supply of gold.

QUICK REFERENCE

National banks are banks chartered by the national government.

The **gold standard** is a system that backs the basic monetary unit with a set amount of gold.

APPLICATION Analyzing Effects

B. How did the National Banking Act of 1863 attempt to eliminate the problems caused by wildcat banking?

20th-Century Developments

KEY CONCEPTS

The system of national banks and a national currency linked to the gold standard initially brought stability to U.S. banking. Yet the economy still experienced periods of inflation and recession and financial panics. This economic instability was largely due to the lack of a central decision-making institution that could manage the money supply in a flexible way to meet the economy's changing needs.

A New Central Bank

In 1913, Congress passed the Federal Reserve Act, which established the Federal Reserve System (commonly known as the Fed)—a true central bank. It consists of 12 regional banks with a central decision-making board. The Fed provides financial services to the federal government, makes loans to banks that serve the public, issues Federal Reserve notes as the national currency, and regulates the money supply to ensure that money retains its purchasing power. You'll learn more about the structure and functions of the Federal Reserve in Chapter 16.

The Great Depression and the New Deal

At the start of the Great Depression in 1929, many banks failed due to bank runs, as consumers panicked and withdrew all of their money. When the banks failed, many more depositors lost their money. Part of President Franklin Roosevelt's New Deal program was the Banking Act of 1933, which instituted reforms such as regulating interest rates that banks could pay and prohibiting banks from selling stocks. The Federal Deposit Insurance Corporation (FDIC) provided federal insurance so that if a bank failed, people would no longer lose their money. This legislation set the tone for almost 50 years by increasing the regulation of banking in the United States.

Deregulation and the S&L Crisis

In 1980 and 1982, Congress passed laws that lifted government limits on savings interest rates. This allowed savings and loans associations (S&Ls) to operate much like commercial banks. Deregulation encouraged the S&Ls to take more risks in the types of loans they made. As a result, many S&Ls failed and lost their depositors' money. Congress agreed to fund the S&L industry's restructuring in order to protect consumers, which cost taxpayers hundreds of billions of dollars.

The S&L Crisis Depositors camp out to withdraw their money in May 1985.

APPLICATION **Comparing and Contrasting**

C. How are the First Bank of the United States and the Federal Reserve different?

Financial Institutions in the United States

The term *bank* is used to refer to almost any kind of financial institution that takes in deposits and makes loans, helping individuals, businesses, and governments to manage their money. In the end, though, the goal of a bank is to earn a profit.

All financial institutions receive a charter from the government, either state or federal. Government regulations set the amount of money the owners of a bank must invest in it, the size of the reserves a bank must hold, and the ways that loans may be made. The term may refer to commercial banks, savings and loan associations, or credit unions.

In the past, these institutions provided very different and distinct services. Today, however, because of the deregulation of banking, these distinctions are much less apparent. The distinctive characteristics of each type of financial institution are described in more detail below. Figure 10.4 on page 302 compares the three types of banks based on numbers of institutions and total assets.

> **Economics Update**
>
> Find an update on U.S. financial institutions at **ClassZone.com**

TYPE 1 Commercial Banks

Privately owned commercial banks are the oldest form of banking and are the financial institutions most commonly thought of as banks. As their name implies, commercial banks were initially established to provide loans to businesses. Now they provide a wide range of services, including checking and savings accounts, loans, investment assistance, and credit cards to both businesses and individual consumers. You will learn more about these services in Section 3.

In 2003, there were about 2,000 national commercial banks and about 5,800 state-chartered banks insured by the FDIC. All national commercial banks belong to the Federal Reserve System, but only about 16 percent of state-chartered banks choose to join the Fed. About 1,500 of these commercial banks are large ones with assets of $300 million dollars or more. In 2005, the seven largest banks in the United States held 50 percent of the total assets controlled by all these large banks.

TYPE 2 Savings Institutions

Savings and loan associations (S&Ls) began in the United States in the 1830s. They were originally chartered by individual states as mutual societies for two purposes— to take savings deposits and provide home mortgage loans. In other words, groups of people pooled their savings in a safe place to earn interest and have a source of financing for families who wanted to buy homes.

The S&Ls continue to fulfill these purposes, but they now also offer many of the services provided by commercial banks. Since 1933, the federal government may also charter S&Ls, and since 1982, many federally chartered S&Ls have chosen to call themselves savings banks. Many savings institutions are now financed through the sale of stock, just as commercial banks are.

In 2003, there were about 800 federally chartered savings institutions and 600 state-chartered institutions. These institutions are now insured under a specific fund of the FDIC as part of the reforms that followed the S&L crisis of the 1980s.

TYPE 3 Credit Unions

Credit unions are cooperative savings and lending institutions, rather like the early S&Ls. They offer services similar to commercial banks and S&Ls, including savings and checking accounts, but specialize in mortgages and auto loans.

The first credit union in the United States was chartered in 1909. The Federal Credit Union Act of 1934 created a system of federally chartered credit unions. In 2003, there were about 5,800 federally chartered credit unions and about 3,600 chartered by the states. Most credit unions have deposit insurance through the National Credit Union Association (NCUA), similar to the FDIC.

The major difference between credit unions and other financial institutions is that credit unions have membership requirements. To become a member, a person must work for a particular company, belong to a particular organization, or be part of a particular community affiliated with the credit union. Credit unions are cooperatives—nonprofit organizations owned by and operated for members, who numbered more than 80 million nationwide in 2003.

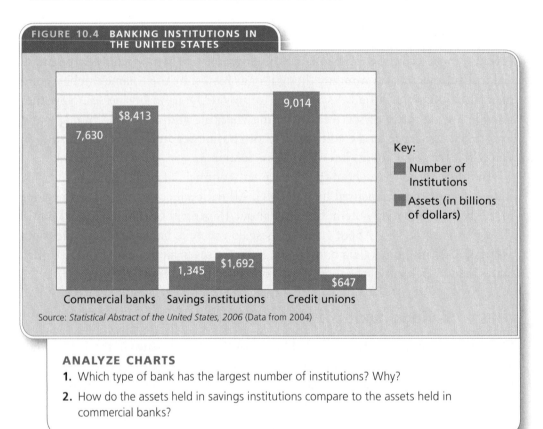

FIGURE 10.4 BANKING INSTITUTIONS IN THE UNITED STATES

Key:
■ Number of Institutions
■ Assets (in billions of dollars)

Commercial banks: 7,630 / $8,413
Savings institutions: 1,345 / $1,692
Credit unions: 9,014 / $647

Source: *Statistical Abstract of the United States, 2006* (Data from 2004)

ANALYZE CHARTS
1. Which type of bank has the largest number of institutions? Why?
2. How do the assets held in savings institutions compare to the assets held in commercial banks?

APPLICATION Analyzing and Interpreting Data

D. Which type of bank described above has the largest percentage of its institutions chartered by the federal government? Why might this situation have developed?

1. Use each of the three terms below in a sentence that illustrates the meaning of the term.

   a. *state bank*   **b.** *national bank*   **c.** *gold standard*

2. Explain the relationship between the gold standard and the concept of representative money.

3. How does the Federal Reserve System serve as a central bank?

4. What is the difference between a national bank and a state bank?

5. How did the FDIC make fractional reserve banking less risky for consumers?

6. **Using Your Notes** What role did state banks play in the era of wildcat banking? Refer to your completed chart.

   Use the Graphic Organizer at **Interactive Review @ ClassZone.com**

Development of U.S. Banking		
Origins	19th Century	20th Century

CRITICAL THINKING

7. **Creating Graphs** Use the information in Figure 10.4 to create two pie graphs, one showing the percentage that each type of bank contributes to the total number of financial institutions and another showing the percentage that each type of bank contributes to total bank assets. State one conclusion that you can draw from the two graphs.

   Use *SMARTGrapher* @ ClassZone.com to complete this activity.

8. **Synthesizing Economic Information** On the basis of what you learned about the history of U.S. banking in the 19th and 20th centuries, were Alexander Hamilton's ideas about the need for a central bank and a national currency shown to be mostly accurate? Cite specific examples to support your answer.

9. **Applying Economic Concepts** Suppose that Mariel deposits $100 in her local bank. If the Fed's reserve requirement is 15 percent, how much can the bank loan out on the basis of Mariel's deposit? What concept does this scenario illustrate?

10. **Challenge** How do banks facilitate saving and borrowing in the same way that money facilitates buying and selling?

Constructing Graphs
Consider what you have learned about different types of financial institutions. The table below shows how the numbers of commercial banks and savings institutions have changed over time.

Year	Commercial Banks	Savings Institutions
1985	14,417	3,626
1990	12,347	2,815
1995	9,942	2,030
2000	8,315	1,589
2004	7,630	1,345

Create Line Graphs Use the information in the table to create two line graphs that show the changes in the numbers of each type of bank.

Use *SMARTGrapher* @ ClassZone.com to complete this activity.

Challenge On the basis of this information, what trends can you identify? Which type of financial institution experienced a greater percentage loss from 1985 to 2004?

Innovations in Modern Banking

OBJECTIVES	KEY TERMS	TAKING NOTES
In Section 3, you will • describe the services that banks provide • discuss the changes that deregulation has brought to banking • explain how technology has changed banking in the United States	automated teller machine, *p. 308* debit card, *p. 308* stored-value card, *p. 308*	As you read Section 3, complete a hierarchy diagram to track main ideas and supporting details. Use the Graphic Organizer at **Interactive Review @ ClassZone.com** 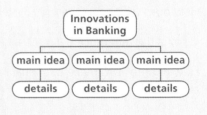

What Services Do Banks Provide?

KEY CONCEPTS

Banks offer a number of services that allow them to act like "money stores." In other words, just as stores are places where goods are bought and sold, banks are places where money can be bought (borrowed) and sold (lent). By using these services, customers are able to do three things—store money, earn money, and borrow money. Banks are businesses that earn money by charging interest or fees on these services.

SERVICE 1 Customers Can Store Money

As you read in Section 2, banks began as safe places to store money and other valuables. They still serve the same purpose today. Customers deposit money in the bank, and the bank stores currency in vaults and is also insured against theft and other loss. Customers' bank accounts are also insured in case the bank fails. Banks are also a safe place to store important papers and valuables—through the use of safe deposit boxes.

SERVICE 2 Customers Can Earn Money

When customers deposit their money in bank accounts, they can earn money on their deposits. Savings accounts and some checking accounts pay some level of interest. Banks offer other accounts, such as money market accounts and certificates of deposits (CDs), that pay a higher rate of interest. You will learn more about saving and investing in Chapter 11 and in Consumer and Personal Finance, which begins on page 576.

SERVICE 3 Customers Can Borrow Money

Banks also allow customers to borrow money through the practice of fractional reserve banking. (See Figure 10.5.) The percent of deposits that banks must keep in reserve is set by the Fed.

Banks provide customers, each of whom must be approved by the bank, with different loans for different circumstances. One common loan is a mortgage. A mortgage loan allows a buyer to purchase a real estate property, such as a house, without paying the entire value of the property up front. The lender and the borrower agree on a time period for the loan (often up to 30 years) and an interest rate to be paid to the lender. From this, a monthly mortgage payment amount is settled. In this arrangement, the real estate property acts as collateral. So if the borrower defaults on the loan (stops making the payments), the lender takes control of the property. It can then be sold by the bank to cover the balance of the mortgage.

It may not seem so, but a purchase made on a credit card is a loan too. Credit cards are issued by banks to users who are, in effect, borrowers. When you use a credit card to buy a new skateboard or a tank of gasoline, the issuing bank pays the seller and lends you the money. When you pay the bank back, you're repaying a loan. And if you don't pay it back within a month, you'll owe the bank extra in interest.

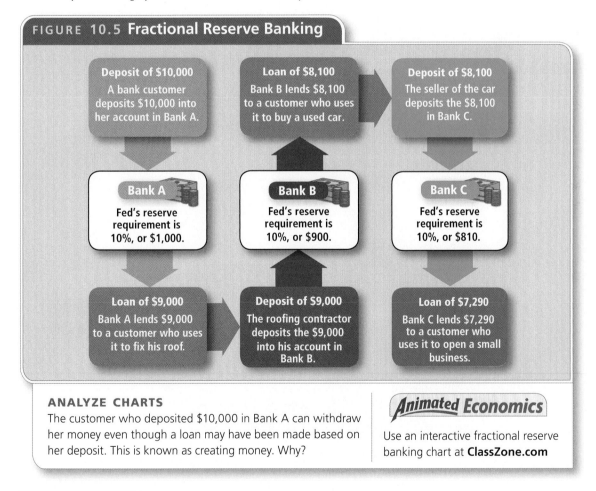

FIGURE 10.5 Fractional Reserve Banking

Deposit of $10,000
A bank customer deposits $10,000 into her account in Bank A.

Loan of $8,100
Bank B lends $8,100 to a customer who uses it to buy a used car.

Deposit of $8,100
The seller of the car deposits the $8,100 in Bank C.

Bank A
Fed's reserve requirement is 10%, or $1,000.

Bank B
Fed's reserve requirement is 10%, or $900.

Bank C
Fed's reserve requirement is 10%, or $810.

Loan of $9,000
Bank A lends $9,000 to a customer who uses it to fix his roof.

Deposit of $9,000
The roofing contractor deposits the $9,000 into his account in Bank B.

Loan of $7,290
Bank C lends $7,290 to a customer who uses it to open a small business.

ANALYZE CHARTS
The customer who deposited $10,000 in Bank A can withdraw her money even though a loan may have been made based on her deposit. This is known as creating money. Why?

Animated Economics

Use an interactive fractional reserve banking chart at **ClassZone.com**

APPLICATION Applying Economic Concepts

A. Explain the ways in which bank transactions are beneficial to customers and banks.

Banking Deregulation

Prior to the 1980s, government tightly regulated the amount of interest that banks could pay on deposits and could charge on loans. Regulations also prevented banks from operating in more than one state. Several states also had limitations on the number of branches that a bank could have within a state. Deregulation in the 1980s and 1990s ended these restrictions and brought major changes to what we think of as banks and how they operate.

Bank Mergers

The end of restrictions on interstate banking led to a large number of mergers, as larger banks acquired smaller ones and smaller ones joined together to be able to enter different geographic markets. The number of mergers has steadily declined since 1998, when there were almost 500, to less than 200 in 2003. Yet as Figure 10.6 shows, mergers that created very large banking organizations continued. In 2004,

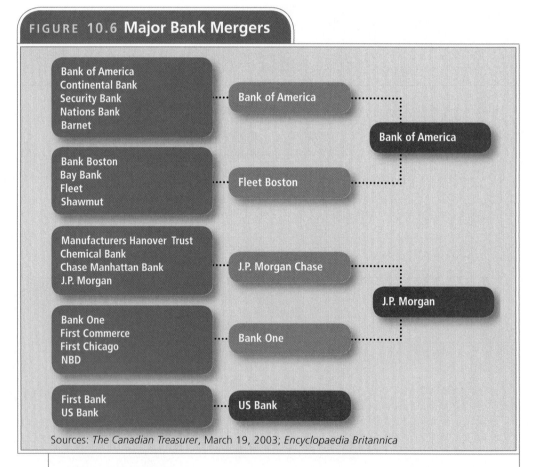

FIGURE 10.6 Major Bank Mergers

Bank of America / Continental Bank / Security Bank / Nations Bank / Barnet	Bank of America	
		Bank of America
Bank Boston / Bay Bank / Fleet / Shawmut	Fleet Boston	
Manufacturers Hanover Trust / Chemical Bank / Chase Manhattan Bank / J.P. Morgan	J.P. Morgan Chase	
		J.P. Morgan
Bank One / First Commerce / First Chicago / NBD	Bank One	
First Bank / US Bank	US Bank	

Sources: *The Canadian Treasurer*, March 19, 2003; *Encyclopaedia Britannica*

ANALYZE CHARTS

In most of the mergers shown here, the acquiring banks hoped to increase their customer base by gaining offices in regions where they had no presence. What reasons might target banks (the banks acquired) have for entering into a merger?

Bank of America Investment Services Inc. and J. P. Morgan Chase & Co. became two of the largest banks in the United States, with assets of around $1 trillion each. In contrast, some 95 percent of commercial banks have assets of $1 billion or less.

One benefit from the mergers has been increased competition that has kept interest rates low and resulted in more consumer services. There has also been an increase in the number of bank branches, even while the number of banks has declined. Larger banks and more branches offer customers greater availability of services. Many banks also cite economies of scale made possible by the mergers, as banks are able to spread their costs, especially for new technology, over more customers. However, some see potential problems associated with mergers. Although competition between these merged banks has heated up, there are increasingly fewer banks to choose from. Further, it is feared that larger banks may show less interest in small customers and local community issues. If this is the case, consumers will choose a bank that provides them with what they want, and the large banks will either respond or lose customers.

Banking Services

The Financial Services Act of 1999 lifted the last restrictions from the Banking Act of 1933 that had prevented banks, insurance companies, and investment companies from selling the same products and competing with one another. This change allowed banks to sell stocks, bonds, and insurance. At the same time, some investment companies and insurance companies began offering traditional banking services.

The change in banking services was based on the idea that consumers would prefer to have a single source for all their financial services needs—something that might function as a kind of "financial supermarket." However, banks have not always been able to effectively realize the benefits they had envisioned from offering this array of services. While banks establish relationships with customers through deposit accounts and loans for homes and autos, they have not been as successful in selling insurance or in helping customers to buy and sell stocks and bonds. Most bank customers continue to look to traditional insurance companies for their insurance needs and investment brokers and mutual fund companies to meet investment desires.

Financial Freedom
President Clinton signs the bill that eliminated restrictions in place since 1933.

▲ Roosevelt and the Banking Act of 1933

▲ Clinton and the Financial Services Act of 1999

APPLICATION Analyzing Effects

B. How did deregulation change the ways that banks competed?

Technology and Banking

KEY CONCEPTS

Deregulation is not the only thing that has changed the nature of banking. Technology—particularly computer technology—has changed the way customers use banks, producing a system generally referred to as electronic banking. For example, banks have begun using **automated teller machines** (ATMs), electronic devices that allow bank customers to make deposits, withdrawals, and transfers and check their account balances at any time without seeing a bank officer. Other innovations include **debit cards**, cards that can be used like an ATM card to withdraw cash or like a check to make purchases, and **stored-value cards**—cards that represent money that the holder has on deposit with the issuer, such as a department store. These cards give customers the ability to use the money in their accounts in more convenient ways. (You'll learn more about ATM and debit cards in Consumer and Personal Finance.)

QUICK REFERENCE

An **automated teller machine** (ATM) is an electronic device that allows bank customers to make transactions without seeing a bank officer.

A **debit card** can be used like an ATM card or like a check.

A **stored-value card** represents money that the holder has on deposit with the issuer.

Automated Teller Machines

Between school, sports practice, and a part-time job, you might find it difficult to get to the bank while it is open to deposit your paycheck and to withdraw spending money. The ATM solves that problem. ATMs are the oldest and most familiar of the developments in electronic banking. They began to be used widely in the 1970s and are now located not just at banks but also at retail stores, workplaces, airports, and entertainment venues, such as movie theaters and sports stadiums.

ATM Boom Between 1998 and 2003, the number of ATMs in the United States nearly doubled, from 187,00 to 371,000. By 2007, there were over 1.5 million ATMs worldwide.

ATMs are basically data terminals that are linked to a central computer that is in turn linked to individual banks' computers. The bank provides you with a plastic ATM card with a magnetic strip on the back that contains your account information. You insert your card into the ATM, enter your personal identification number (PIN), and follow the instructions on the screen. You may check your account balance, make deposits, withdraw cash, transfer money between accounts, and make loan payments through the ATM.

All ATM networks are connected so that consumers can use their ATM cards at any machine, no matter what bank owns it. Some banks charge fees for ATM use, especially to consumers who do not have an account at the bank that owns the particular ATM. ATMs allow people to bank even when the bank is closed and to avoid waiting in line for simple transactions. Many drive-through ATMs allow customers to bank from their cars. ATMs save banks money because it is much less expensive to process ATM transactions than transactions that involve a teller. They also allow banks to provide services at more locations without constructing complete bank branch offices.

Debit Cards

Debit cards are similar to ATM cards but offer additional benefits. Like ATM cards, debit cards can be used to withdraw cash and make other transactions at ATM machines. Debit cards are sometimes called check cards because they are linked to bank accounts and can be used like checks to make purchases at many retail outlets. Retailers often prefer debit cards because they avoid the problem of people writing checks with insufficient funds in their accounts.

Debit cards often look like credit cards, and they are similar in that they can be used to make purchases at stores. An important difference is that credit card purchases involve getting a loan. Your money stays in your account until you pay your credit card bill. With a debit card you make an immediate payment, since the price of your purchase is deducted from the account that is linked to your card. Therefore, it is important to keep track of debit card purchases along with checks so that you know how much money is available in your account at any given time.

Because of the way debit cards work, they are often seen as safer ways to manage your money than with credit cards. With credit cards, if you do not pay your balance in full each month, you pay interest on the outstanding balance and can build up considerable debt. With debit cards, you can only spend money that you actually have in a bank account.

YOUR ECONOMIC CHOICES

CREDIT CARD VS. DEBIT CARD

Which one should you use?

You have $250 in your checking account, and you don't get your next paycheck for a week. You want to buy a $75 birthday gift for a friend, and you have to pay $225 for a car repair. With your classmates, talk through each of the ways to handle the situation to find out what works best.

Entering a PIN for a debit card

Signing for a credit card

Stored-Value Cards

Stored-value cards, which represent money that the holder has on deposit with the card issuer, give consumers another convenient way to use electronic banking. These cards are sometimes called prepaid cards because customers have paid a certain amount of money for the card and can then use it to make payments for various goods and services. Some examples of stored-value cards include transit fare cards, gift cards from retail stores, and telephone cards. Consumers benefit from using transit fare cards and telephone cards because they do not have to worry about having the exact change needed each time they ride the bus or use a pay phone.

Money and Banking 309

In 2004, there were more than 2,000 different stored-value card programs in the United States with about 20 million users. The number of users was expected to be 49 million by 2008. The $42 billion in transactions in 2003 was expected to grow to more than $72 billion by 2006.

Multipurpose stored-value cards—cards that can be used like debit cards—are becoming more popular. This type of card may take the place of a checking account, especially for people who have not traditionally used banks. While stored-value cards are a convenient way for people to make purchases and pay bills, consumers need to evaluate the fees involved in using such cards to determine whether they are less expensive than having a checking account or using a check-cashing service. In addition, the money paid into such cards is not always covered by FDIC insurance to protect customer deposits in case of a bank's failure.

Electronic Banking

Electronic banking allows customers who have set up accounts with a bank to perform practically every transaction without setting foot in a bank. Indeed, some banks are virtual banks with no physical buildings at all. Through the use of the Internet, customers can arrange for direct deposit of their paychecks, transfer funds from account to account, and pay their bills.

Most bank Web sites allow customers to review the most recent transactions on their accounts, view images of canceled checks, and download or print their periodic statements. Through electronic fund transfers, consumers can pay a credit card bill at one bank with funds from a checking account at another bank. Recurring bills, such as mortgage payments, may be paid automatically from a customer's checking account each month or through their bank's bill paying service.

However, electronic banking presents several challenges. Information security and identity theft are related, high-profile issues for the industry. Electronic banking allows banks to amass large amounts of information about their customers. Banks contend that this allows them to provide customers with better service. New laws require that banks make customers aware of privacy policies and offer them the opportunity to decide what information may be shared with others. Consumer concerns have led banks to developing increasingly sophisticated information security systems. (For information on identity theft, see Consumer and Personal Finance, which begins on p. 576.)

Online Convenience Online bill paying cuts time and expense by eliminating the need to mail checks.

APPLICATION Contrasting Economic Information

C. How are debit cards different from most stored-value cards?

REVIEWING KEY CONCEPTS

1. How are these three terms related? How are they different?

   a. *automated teller machine*   b. *debit card*   c. *stored-value card*

2. What are two reasons that people deposit money in banks?

3. It is said that fractional reserve banking allows banks to create money? What is meant by this?

4. How did deregulation lead to a decrease in the number of banks between 1980 and the present?

5. How are debit cards related to automated teller machines?

6. **Using Your Notes** How does computer technology support home banking? Refer to your completed hierarchy diagram.

   Use the Graphic Organizer at **Interactive Review @ ClassZone.com**

CRITICAL THINKING

7. **Analyzing Data** Over the course of one year, Hometown Bank paid Mary Lee 3 percent interest on a $1,000 deposit and charged Owen's Bakery 8 percent interest on a $900 loan. How much net income did Hometown bank make? Show your calculations.

8. **Applying Economic Concepts** Suppose that Liz inherits $2,000 from her grandmother and deposits it into her college savings account at Hamilton Savings Bank. Assume that the reserve requirement is 20 percent. Create a chart showing five successive loans that could be made from this initial deposit.

9. **Making Inferences** Some parents think that allowing teenagers to use a debit card prepares them for using a credit card. What are the possible reasons behind this thinking? Do you think this reasoning is sound? Why or why not?

10. **Challenge** Look again at Figure 10.5, Fractional Reserve Banking, on page 305. Suppose that when Bank A made the $9,000 loan to the man with the leaky roof, it turned out the job cost only $7,000. The contractor deposited that money into Bank B. How much could Bank B then lend to the used-car buyer? If she bought a car for that amount, and the seller of the car deposited the money in Bank C, what size small-business loan could Bank C then turn around and make?

ECONOMICS IN PRACTICE

Starting a Bank
Think about what you have learned about the services that banks provide and how banks make money. Imagine that you are starting a bank for the other members of the class. Consider the following questions:

- What services would you provide? Why?

- How would your bank make a profit?

- What challenges might you face in making your bank profitable?

Write a Proposal Answer the above questions in a one-page proposal outlining what your bank would be like. Share your proposal with a classmate.

Challenge Include a section in your proposal about what you would do to make your bank more attractive to customers than the other banks run by your classmates.

Student Loans

Background In the United States, the cost of higher education may still be affordable to some, but it certainly is not cheap. Because of rising costs, more and more students (and their parents) borrow money to finance at least part of their college education. According to the U.S. Department of Education, about 10 million students take out Stafford loans each year, while about 800,000 parents take out PLUS loans.

Although banks, S&Ls, and credit unions are the primary lenders of money in the United States, this is not the case for student loans. Students and parents have the option of borrowing wherever they choose, but federally guaranteed loans are their main source of funding.

What's the issue? What is the current situation with student loans? What are the future ramifications of the increasing cost of paying for college? Study these sources to learn about student loans.

A. Online News Story

This story explains a change in the way the government figures the interest rate on student loans.

Congres Cuts Funding for Student Loans

Graduates Face Higher Interest Payments, Fewer Options

Congress yesterday cut funding for federal student-loan programs, a move that is expected to increase the debt burden for many future college graduates and their families. . . .

To help limit spending, Congress raised interest rates on the popular Stafford loans to a fixed 6.8%, even if commercial rates are lower. . . .

The changes come at a time when families have been struggling with skyrocketing tuition bills. After adjusting for inflation, private-college tuition and fees have increased 37% over the past decade, while public tuition has risen 54%. Today, most college students borrow money to pay for college. . . .

The interest rate on a Stafford loan is variable and reset annually, depending on a formula that looks at prevailing market interest rates. Today, that rate is as low as 4.7%. . . .

Under the new legislation, the interest rate changes to a fixed rate of 6.8% starting July 1, 2006. . . .

Source: WSJClassroom.com, Anne Marie Chaker, December 22, 2005

FIGURE 10.7 AVERAGE TUITION COST, FOUR-YEAR INSTITUTION

Year	Cost
1999–2000	$12,352
2000–2001	$12,922
2001–2002	$13,639
2002–2003	$14,439
2003–2004	$15,539

Source: National Center for Education Statistics

Thinking Economically If interest rates hit 10 percent, would the new fixed rate established by Congress still harm student borrowers? Why or why not?

Ralph Hagen drew this cartoon about student loans as a factor in higher education.

Thinking Economically What does the cartoon suggest about student reliance on college loans? Explain your answer.

C. Newspaper Article

This article discusses the problems associated with debt and loan repayment after college graduation.

It's Payback Time

More Student Loans Increase Debt Pressure on Graduates

Student loans are two-edged: the more money a student can borrow, the more schooling falls within reach. But of course, the more debt a student has, the more painful repayment becomes. . . .

"More students will be required to take out more money from the federal government and from private" lenders, says Jasmine L. Harris, legislative director at the United States Student Association, a student advocacy group in Washington. Over time, she continues, "It's a great formula for unmanageable levels of debt and hence higher default rates.". . .

The consequences of defaulting, too, are worse than they have been in years past.

A provision of a law that took effect last year, for example, makes it next to impossible to discharge private student loans in personal bankruptcy proceedings (federal loans were already barred). . . .

[Theresa] Shaw of the Education Department advises that a struggling borrower should try to make a payment of any kind, however small, to avoid default.

Source: The *New York Times*, April 23, 2006

Thinking Economically Explain in your own words why you think the article calls student loans "two-edged."

THINKING ECONOMICALLY Synthesizing

1. Compare the financial news presented in documents A and C. What bearing do you think the information in document A might have on what you learned from document C?

2. Document B humorously points to the prominence of student loans in U.S. higher education. Specifically, what parts of documents A and C support this view?

3. In document A, what does the federal government seem to be saying about who should pay for a college education? With this in mind, what does Figure 10.7 mean for students and parents?

Interactive Review

Review this chapter using interactive activities at **ClassZone.com**
- Online Summary
- Quizzes
- Vocabulary Flip Cards
- Graphic Organizers
- Review and Study Notes

○○○

 Online Summary

Complete the following activity either on your own paper or online at **ClassZone.com**

Choose the key concept that best completes the sentence. Not all key concepts will be used.

automated teller machine	M2
barter	medium of exchange
commodity money	money
currency	national bank
debit card	near money
demand deposits	representative money
fiat money	standard of value
fractional reserve banking	state bank
gold standard	store of value
M1	stored-value card

__1__ is anything that people will accept as payment for goods and services. Money makes trade easier by serving as a __2__. As a __3__, money allows people to compare the prices of goods and services. Money must be a __4__, or something that holds its value over time.

Gold coins and salt are both examples of __5__. Most money in the world today is __6__, which has no tangible value but is declared by the government to have worth.

__7__ consists of __8__, which includes paper money and coins and __9__, which is another name for checking accounts. Savings accounts and time deposits are called __10__ because they can be converted into cash easily.

__11__ allows banks to hold only part of their deposits and make loans based on the rest. The Federal Reserve Bank is the central __12__ in the nation.

The __13__ is the oldest form of electronic banking. A __14__ can be used like an ATM card or like a check.

REVIEWING KEY CONCEPTS

Money: Its Functions and Properties (pp. 288–295)

1. What three functions does money serve in the economy?

2. Why do economists make a distinction between M1 and M2?

The Development of U.S. Banking (pp. 296–303)

3. Why does fractional reserve banking leave banks vulnerable to failure if too many consumers demand their money at the same time?

4. How is the Federal Reserve System different from the system of national banks created in the 1860s?

Innovations in Modern Banking (pp. 304–313)

5. How did the automated teller machine change the nature of banking?

6. Which type of stored-value card is most like a debit card?

APPLYING ECONOMIC CONCEPTS

Look at the table below showing changes in use of electronic payments between 1995 and 2001.

7. Which type of electronic banking increased the most among all households between 1995 and 2001?

8. How did education generally affect the use of electronic payments?

FIGURE 10.8 PERCENTAGE OF HOUSEHOLDS USING ELECTRONIC BANKING

Education of head of household	ATM		Debit card		Automatic bill paying	
	1995	2001	1995	2001	1995	2001
All households	61.2	69.8	17.6	47.0	21.8	40.3
No college degree	52.8	63.7	14.3	42.3	18.2	33.7
College degree	80.1	81.6	25.2	56.2	30.1	53.2

Source: *Statistical Abstract of the United States, 2006*

9. **Analyzing Effects** Suppose that the government changes the tax policy so that people pay lower taxes if they save more money. The benefits are significant enough that people shift about 10 percent of their money from their checking accounts into certificates of deposit. How would this change affect the amount of money in M1 and M2?

10. **Drawing Conclusions** Today, there are about three times as many state chartered commercial banks as there are nationally chartered commercial banks. How does the current U.S. economy avoid the kinds of problems caused by state banks in the 19th century?

11. **Applying Economic Concepts** One Saturday, four friends go shopping at the local mall. Catherine uses her ATM card to withdraw some cash. Tara has a gift card that she received for her birthday. It is worth $50 at her favorite clothing store. Charlotte uses a credit card, and Alyssa pays with a debit card.

    a. Which of the shoppers has a stored-value card? Why does she have less flexibility in her shopping than the other shoppers?

    b. If Catherine, Charlotte, and Alyssa each spend $50, which one has not reduced the amount of money in her checking account at the end of the day? Why?

    c. Which shopper may end up paying more than face value for her purchases?

12. **Analyzing Causes** What are the different motives behind these two mergers: a stock brokerage firm buys a bank; a California bank buys a Florida bank?

13. **Challenge** Why are credit cards and debit cards not considered to be money?

Promote Electronic Banking

Step 1 Choose a partner. Imagine that you work for a bank in the late 1990s. Your bank intends to be a pioneer in Internet banking and asks you to design its first Web page. Your boss gives you the following criteria for the Web page:

- Allow existing customers to access account balances and transfer funds between accounts.
- Promote traditional bank products, including checking, savings, CDs, credit cards, mortgages, and auto loans.
- Allow customers to find the most convenient branch or ATM location.

Step 2 Sketch out a design for the Web page to meet your boss's criteria, showing appropriate links.

Step 3 Two years later, deregulation has led to significant changes in the banking industry. In addition, more consumers are interested in Internet banking. Your boss asks you to redesign the Web page with these additional criteria:

- Allow customers to pay bills, apply for loans, buy stocks, and shop for insurance through the bank's Web site.
- Allow customers to view transactions on all their accounts, including credit and debit card transactions, and receive statements and other bank communications electronically.
- Reassure customers that online banking is secure and that their privacy will be protected.

Step 4 Sketch out a new Web page that shows the complete range of services the bank now offers and that meets all six criteria.

Step 5 Share your Web page designs with another pair of students and discuss what aspects would be most important and effective for you as a customer.

Stock Market
The stock market, which consists of institutions such as the NASDAQ, is where stocks and bonds are traded.

Financial Markets

CONCEPT REVIEW

Voluntary exchange is a trade in which both parties involved believe that what they are getting is worth more than what they are giving up.

CHAPTER 11 KEY CONCEPT

The **financial system** consists of institutions, such as banks, insurance markets, bond markets, and stock markets, that help transfer funds between savers and investors.

WHY THE CONCEPT MATTERS

Do you have a savings account? If so, you play a very important role in our economy. Your savings—what you gave up to get those assets—will be borrowed and invested by businesses and the government to build factories, offices, roads, and so on. The jobs and new products and services created by these investments, in turn, further help to fuel the nation's economy.

Online Highlights

More at ClassZone.com

 Economics Update
Go to **ECONOMICS UPDATE** for chapter updates and current news on investing in Internet companies. (See Case Study, pp. 344–345.) ▶

 SMART Grapher
Go to **SMART GRAPHER** to complete graphing activities in this chapter.

Interactive ◀▶ Review
Go to **INTERACTIVE REVIEW** for concept review and activities.

"The good news is we've financed another dot.com for no fathomable reason."

Source: www.CartoonStock.com

Why did the dot-com companies experience such a rapid rise and fall? See the Case Study on pages 344–345.

Savings and Investment

OBJECTIVES	KEY TERMS	TAKING NOTES
In Section 1, you will • identify what constitutes the financial system • describe the various financial intermediaries • explain how economists categorize the various markets where financial assets are sold	savings, *p. 318* investment, *p. 318* financial system, *p. 318* financial asset, *p. 319* financial market, *p. 319* financial intermediary, *p. 319* mutual fund, *p. 320* capital market, *p. 322* money market, *p. 322* primary market, *p. 322* secondary market, *p. 322*	As you read Section 1, complete a hierarchy diagram to track main ideas and supporting details. Use the Graphic Organizer at **Interactive Review @ ClassZone.com** 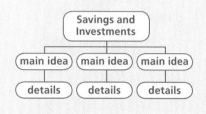

The Financial System

KEY CONCEPTS

There are two things you can do with your money—spend it or save it. **Savings** is income not used for consumption, in other words not spent on immediate wants. Savings that are put to use are investments. In general, **investment** is the use of income today in a way that allows for a future benefit. More specifically, *economic investment* refers to money lent to businesses—to finance the construction of a new factory, for example. *Personal investment* refers to the act of individuals putting their savings into financial assets, such as CDs, stocks, bonds, or mutual funds.

Consider what happens when you put money in a savings account. Through this act, you benefit—your savings account earns interest—but others do too. By saving, you make funds available for the bank to lend. Borrowers use these funds for many purposes, such as investing in new businesses or in new equipment for established businesses. The **financial system**, which consists of institutions such as banks, insurance markets, bond markets, and stock markets, allows for this transfer of funds between savers and investors.

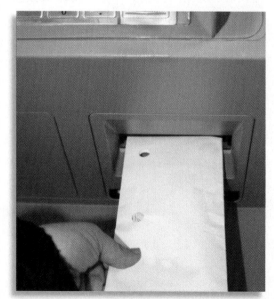

ATM Deposits Using an ATM to make deposits makes saving easy and convenient.

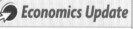
Economics Update
Find an update on saving at **ClassZone.com**

FIGURE 11.1 **The Financial System**

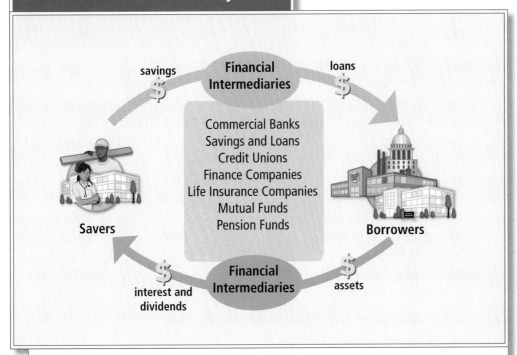

savings   **Financial Intermediaries**   loans

Commercial Banks
Savings and Loans
Credit Unions
Finance Companies
Life Insurance Companies
Mutual Funds
Pension Funds

Savers   Borrowers

interest and dividends   **Financial Intermediaries**   assets

ANALYZE CHARTS

1. What do savers get in exchange for the funds they deposit with financial intermediaries?

2. Why do you think that financial intermediaries perform their vital function? Think back to Chapter 10 if you need help.

Bringing Savings and Investment Together

Individuals and businesses can save surplus funds in many ways, including savings accounts at commercial banks or S&Ls, certificates of deposit (CDs), corporate or government bonds, and stocks. The agent receiving these funds is a borrower, who issues savers written confirmation of the transaction. This written confirmation is called a **financial asset**, or a claim on the property of the borrower.

Sometimes savers and borrowers come together directly in a **financial market**, a situation in which buyers and sellers exchange particular types of financial assets. For example, an individual or business might buy corporate bonds or shares of stock. More often, however, financial intermediaries bring savers, borrowers, and financial assets together. A **financial intermediary** is a financial institution that collects funds from savers and then invests these funds in loans and other financial assets. Figure 11.1 shows how funds flow from savers to investors through the financial markets and financial intermediaries that make up the financial system.

APPLICATION Applying Economic Concepts

A. Look again at the example opposite of a person depositing money into a savings account. How is this an example of Adam Smith's "invisible hand"?

Financial Intermediaries

Financial intermediaries bring savers and investors together. In Chapter 10, you learned about one group of financial intermediaries—commercial banks, S&Ls, and credit unions. These financial institutions take in deposits from savers and provide loans to individuals and businesses. Many offer other financial assets as well.

Other common financial intermediaries include finance companies, which make small loans; pension funds, which invest money for groups of workers; and life insurance companies, which invest funds collected from policyholders. A **mutual fund** is a pool of money managed by an investment company that gathers money from individual investors and purchases a range of financial assets. Investors own shares of the entire fund based on the amount of their investment. These institutions gather their money in different ways and provide many different financial assets to a variety of investors.

EXAMPLE Banking Financial Intermediaries

This group of financial intermediaries includes commercial banks, S&Ls, and credit unions. All of these institutions provide checking and savings accounts. Depositors earn interest on their savings deposits and some checking deposits. Most also offer CDs and money market deposit accounts that pay slightly higher rates of interest. (Figure 11.2 explains how savers earn money from interest.) The federal government insures deposits, including CDs and money market accounts, up to $100,000 per depositor in any given bank.

These institutions lend a portion of their deposits to borrowers. Banks charge borrowers a higher rate of interest than they pay to savers and hope to earn a profit. The loans are financial assets to the bank. If a borrower does not pay back the loan on time, the bank may repossess the property, such as a home or a car.

Deregulation has allowed banks to offer other financial assets, such as money market mutual funds, stocks, bonds, and insurance. The federal government does not insure funds invested in these financial assets.

EXAMPLE Nonbank Financial Intermediaries

This group of financial intermediaries includes finance companies, mutual funds, pension funds, and life insurance companies. Finance companies make loans to households and small businesses. Generally, the loans are under $2,000 and are paid back in monthly installments, including interest, over a few years.

A mutual fund pools money from many personal investors. In return, each investor receives shares in a fund that is made up of a large number and variety of stocks, bonds, or other financial assets. Mutual funds make it easier and more affordable for individual investors to own a wide variety of financial assets. Once investors purchase shares of a fund, they allow its managers to make investment decisions.

The New York Stock Exchange Stocks are an important element of the assets that make up a mutual fund.

Pension funds allow employees to save money for retirement and sometimes include contributions from employers. The pension fund then invests these pooled contributions in various financial assets that will increase in value and provide workers with more money when they retire.

Life insurance companies allow individuals to accumulate savings by building cash values and protect against losses from death or disability. Just as banks lend some of their deposits, insurance companies lend or invest some of the income earned from policyholders in a variety of financial assets.

MATH CHALLENGE

FIGURE 11.2 Calculating Interest

Banks pay savers interest in order to use their money. A saver's initial deposit is called the principal. Simple interest is the interest paid on the principal alone. Compound interest is paid on the principal plus any earned interest. The following steps show how an annual rate of 5 percent interest is paid on the principal ($1,000) over three years.

Year 1 Simple interest is calculated using the following formula:

| Principal | × | Interest rate | = | Interest earned | $1,000 | × | .05 | = | $50.00 |

Year 2 The amount in this account is now $1,050.00. Compound interest, which is paid on the principal plus the earned interest, is calculated as follows:

| (Principal + Year 1 interest) | × | Interest rate | = | Interest earned | ($1,000.00 + $50.00) | × | .05 | = | $52.50 |

Year 3 There is now $1,102.50 in the account. Interest continues to compound.

| (Principal + Year 1 interest + Year 2 interest) | × | Interest rate | = | Interest earned | ($1,000.00 + $50.00 + 52.50) | × | .05 | = | $55.13 |

After three years, the total in the account is $1,157.63.

Using a Formula Instead of using the multiple steps shown above, you can calculate the total value of an account using the following formula (wherein P=principal, r=interest rate, and t=number of years):

| $P(1+r)^t$ | = | total value | $1,000.00(1+.05)^3$ | = | $1,157.63 |

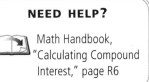

NEED HELP?

Math Handbook, "Calculating Compound Interest," page R6

APPLICATION Comparing and Contrasting

B. How is a pension fund like a savings account? How is it different?

Financial Asset Markets

QUICK REFERENCE

The **capital market** is where long-term financial assets are bought and sold.

The **money market** is where short-term financial assets are bought and sold.

The **primary market** is for buying and selling financial assets that the original buyer must redeem.

The **secondary market** is where financial assets are resold.

KEY CONCEPTS

The different financial assets discussed in this section are bought and sold on various financial markets. Economists tend to categorize these markets based on two factors—time (how long the loan is for) and whether the financial assets can be resold. Based on time, economists distinguish between the **capital market**, the market for buying and selling long-term financial assets, and the **money market**, the market for buying and selling short-term financial assets. In regard to resalability, economists distinguish between the **primary market**, which is the market for buying and selling newly created financial assets directly from the issuing entity, and the **secondary market**, which is the market where financial assets are resold.

FACTOR 1 Time

There are two time-sensitive markets. Capital markets are markets where assets are held for longer than a year. Some examples of assets sold on the capital market include certain kinds of securities, namely stocks and bonds, mortgages, and long-term CDs. Because these loans are for longer periods of time, the money may be invested in projects that require large amounts of capital, such as buying homes, building new factories, retooling established factories, or financing government projects.

Money markets are markets where loans are made for less than a year. Examples of assets traded in these markets include short-term CDs that depositors can redeem in a few months and Treasury bills, which allow the U.S. government to borrow money for short periods of time.

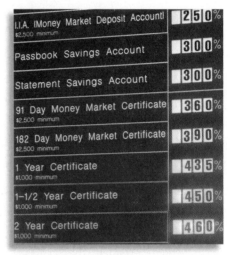

Return on Investment Time is an important factor in the level of return for many investments.

FACTOR 2 Resalability

There also are two kinds of markets based on whether the financial assets can be resold. Primary markets are markets for financial assets that can be redeemed only by the original buyer. Examples include savings bonds and small denomination CDs. The term *primary market* also refers to the market where the first issue of a stock is sold to the public through investment bankers.

Secondary markets are resale markets for financial assets. These markets offer liquidity to personal investors. So, investors are able to turn their assets into cash relatively quickly. Stocks and bonds, which you'll learn more about later in this chapter, are two of the most prominent financial assets sold on the secondary market.

APPLICATION Analyzing Effects

C. Why are stocks and bonds part of the capital market and the secondary market?

REVIEWING KEY CONCEPTS

1. Explain the difference between the terms in each of these pairs.

   a. *savings*   **b.** *capital market*   **c.** *primary market*
   investment   *money market*   *secondary market*

2. What is the purpose of the financial system?

3. Why do banks receive financial assets when they make loans?

4. How does a mutual fund serve as a financial intermediary?

5. What determines whether a loan is part of the capital market or the money market?

6. **Using Your Notes** What is the relationship between financial intermediaries and the financial system? Refer to your completed hierarchy diagram.

   Use the Graphic Organizer at **Interactive Review @ ClassZone.com**

CRITICAL THINKING

7. **Categorizing Information** Which of the following are banking financial intermediaries and which are nonbanking financial intermediaries?
   - Consumer Finance Company
   - Investors' Mutual Fund
   - Family Life Insurance Company
   - Employee Credit Union
   - First National Bank
   - Employee Pension Fund
   - Home Savings and Loan

8. **Making Inferences** A local bank offers savings accounts that have no minimum balance requirement and pay 3 percent interest per year. Account holders can withdraw any amount of money from their accounts at any time. The bank also offers money market accounts that require a $500 minimum balance and pay 4 percent interest each year. Account holders are allowed two withdrawals per month, but each must be for at least $100. Why does the money market account pay a higher interest rate?

9. **Applying Economic Concepts** Suppose that you deposit $100 into your savings account, which earns 3 percent interest per year. Use what you've learned about calculating interest to determine how much money you'll have in your account at the end of one year and at the end of six years.

10. **Challenge** Why might a decrease in household savings have an adverse effect on small businesses in a local community?

ECONOMICS IN PRACTICE

Stock certificates

Identifying Markets
Consider how economists categorize financial markets. Copy the table shown below. Review the bulleted list of financial assets and place each one in the correct location(s) in the table. Assets may be placed in more than one category.

- 15-year mortgage
- 6-month CD for $1,000
- 2-year CD for $25,000
- 5-year corporate bond
- 10-year savings bond
- Shares of stock
- 26-week Treasury bill
- 30-year Treasury bond

Capital Market	Money Market

Primary Market	Secondary Market

Challenge Why do savings bonds and small certificates of deposit have less liquidity than shares of stock?

OBJECTIVES	KEY TERMS	TAKING NOTES
In Section 2, you will • discuss the issues that should be considered when making investment decisions • explain how risk and return are related	investment objective, *p. 324* risk, *p. 327* return, *p. 327* diversification, *p. 327*	As you read Section 2, complete a chart like the one shown using the key concepts and other helpful words and phrases. Use the Graphic Organizer at **Interactive Review @ ClassZone.com**

Investing in a Market Economy	
objectives	risk vs. return

Why Are You Investing?

KEY CONCEPTS

In Section 1, you saw that there are two types of investing: personal and economic. Note that for the remainder of the chapter, we'll be using all forms of the word *invest* as a quick way to refer to personal investing—which is, in effect, saving.

You've now learned that there are a number of assets you can own. But how do you determine which is, or are, right for you? The first thing that you might do is to decide why you are investing. This reason is your **investment objective**, a financial goal that an investor uses to determine if an investment is appropriate. Some possible financial goals are saving money for retirement, for a down payment on a house or an automobile, for college tuition, or for a vacation. Your goal helps you to determine the right investments.

Investment Objectives

Two issues play a major role in determining which investments work best to achieve different investment objectives. The first issue is time. For example, is this a short-term financial goal, such as saving for a vacation, or a long-term financial goal, such as saving for

Savings Goals Saving for a car down payment suggests certain kinds of longer-term investments.

What reasons do you have for investing?

Do you have any investment objectives? Maybe you have a short-term objective, such as saving money to go on spring break. Or your objective is more long term, such as saving for college. What kinds of investments might be appropriate for your objective?

Saving for vacation

Saving for college

retirement? The amount of time you have to build your savings influences the kinds of investments that would be most appropriate.

The second issue is income. How much money do you have available to save after meeting current expenses? The answer to this question is influenced by a series of other questions: Will your income change in the future? Is there money available for emergencies? To respond to all these questions, having a savings plan that is realistic and that is flexible enough to adjust to changing circumstances can be a big help.

Other important questions are: Do you have any outstanding debts? Are you paying taxes on time? Paying off debts is an important first step to investing. Generally, the interest you pay on debts, such as credit card balances, is higher than what you can earn through most investments. Tax considerations are most important for investors with higher incomes who are subject to higher tax rates.

Different types of investments are suitable to various investment objectives. For example, savings for emergencies should be in highly liquid investments, such as savings accounts or money market accounts. With these investments, the risk of loss is low and money can be withdrawn at any time. Saving for a vacation would also require investments that are short-term and liquid. Investors who are saving for longer-term goals may be less concerned with immediate liquidity and may want to invest in stocks that increase in value over a longer period of time. CDs that commit funds for a certain length of time may be chosen to coincide with the timing of certain savings goals, such as making a major purchase or starting college. Many bonds offered by state and local governments offer tax-free earnings.

> **Economics Update**
>
> Find an update on investing at **ClassZone.com**

APPLICATION Drawing Conclusions

A. Would a CD be a more appropriate way to save for a down payment on a car or for emergencies? Why?

Mellody Hobson: Investing in the Future

What do the Chicago Bulls, hip-hop stars, and inner-city elementary school students have in common? All are part of Mellody Hobson's efforts to get investment "discussed around every dinner table." Hobson believes that many people lack the necessary knowledge to determine their investment objectives and manage their money to create wealth. How is she trying to change this situation?

Creating Educated Investors

Mellody Hobson discovered her career in investing as a college intern. When she got her degree in 1991, Hobson landed a position in the marketing department at Ariel Capital Management LLC. In 2000, she became the president of the company, making her the most powerful African-American woman in the mutual-fund industry. As president of Ariel, Hobson runs an operation with over $21 billion in assets.

Ariel was the first minority-owned mutual fund company in the country and pioneered programs to teach inner-city school-children about investing. Hobson's passion for investment education led her to give presentations in locations from PTA meetings to union halls. She developed the first ongoing study of investing by African Americans and looked for ways to increase their participation in the stock market. "The stock market represents a major source of wealth creation in this country," Hobson has stated, "but . . . African Americans have been largely left out." Ariel's marketing efforts to the black community included cosponsoring events with the Chicago Bulls and creating a stock-picking contest involving well-known hip hop stars.

Mellody Hobson

When Hobson became the financial contributor to the *Good Morning America* television program in 2000, she was able to reach millions of people with easy-to-understand information about economic matters. Hobson believes that more knowledge about the benefits of investing in stocks and greater diversity in the investment industry will help bring the benefits of investing to people of all racial and economic backgrounds.

Economics Update

Find an update on Mellody Hobson at **ClassZone.com**

APPLICATION Making Inferences

B. Why might Mellody Hobson think it is important for families to talk about investing at the dinner table?

Risk and Return

KEY CONCEPTS

Once investors have decided their financial objectives, there are two other related issues they might consider—risk and return. **Risk** is the possibility for loss on an investment, and **return** is the profit or loss made on an investment.

While savings deposits in banks are insured against loss, most investments carry some possibility of losing part of the money invested. Return may refer to the interest paid on a savings account or CD or the increase in value of a stock over time. Most investors try to balance risk and return through **diversification**, the practice of distributing investments among different financial assets to maximize return and limit risk.

What Kind of Risk Are You Willing to Take?

When most investors think about risk, they think about the possibility of losing some of their initial investment, often referred to as their principal. Even if they don't earn a lot of money on the investment, they want to get back at least what they put in. Investments that guarantee no loss of principal include insured savings deposits and CDs. Bonds that are backed by the U.S. government are also considered to be almost risk-free because it is highly unlikely that the government would not pay back its loans. Almost all other investments carry some risk.

One of the biggest risks investors face, even with safe investments like those described above, is loss of the purchasing power of the money invested due to inflation. (Remember that inflation is a general rise in the level of prices.) That is why many financial advisers warn against investing everything in safe investments that pay a guaranteed rate of interest that may not keep up with inflation.

Other investments, such as stocks and corporate bonds, carry a higher degree of risk because the return depends on how profitable the company is. Investors who purchase stock with the expectation that it will appreciate in value over time may lose some of their money if the company runs into problems or other economic factors affect the value of the stock. In that case, investors may find that they cannot sell the stock for as much as they paid for it, and they suffer a loss. Investors in corporate bonds face similar risks, although bonds are considered less risky than stocks because creditors such as bondholders are paid off before stockholders if a company has financial problems.

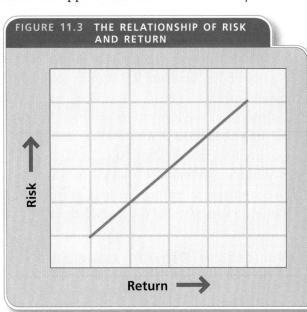

FIGURE 11.3 THE RELATIONSHIP OF RISK AND RETURN

Risk

Return

QUICK REFERENCE

Risk is the possibility for loss on an investment.

Return is profit or loss made on an investment.

Diversification is the practice of distributing investments among different financial assets.

Risk and Return
Risk and return have a direct relationship—the higher the risk of the investment, the greater the possible return.

RISK AND RETURN

How can you balance risk and return?

When you consider what financial assets further your investment objective, you must address both risk and return. A high-risk investment may bring large returns, but can you absorb the potential losses? A low-risk investment may provide a steady return, but because of inflation you may be losing money. How would you decide which type of investment to make?

▲ Return

▲ Risk

What Kind of Return Do You Want?

When making investment decisions, investors decide what kind of return they expect to earn. The safest investments, such as Treasury bills, interest-bearing savings accounts, and shorter-term CDs, generally offer the lowest return in the form of fixed rates of interest. The returns on stocks and bonds are not guaranteed and may vary considerably at different times, depending on how well the economy as a whole and how well the company you choose to invest in is performing. On the whole, stocks provide a higher return over time than do other investments.

As Figure 11.3 on page 327 shows, risk and return are directly related—the higher the risk, the greater the possible return. Investors always want the highest return possible, but they must balance that desire with a realistic understanding about the level of risk they can tolerate. The factors of time and income come into play here. People who are investing for retirement over a period of 20 to 30 years may be willing to take more risk by investing in stocks because their investments are likely to increase over that period, even though they might have losses in some years. People with less time and less income to invest might not be willing to face risking possible losses.

Diversification is the most common way for investors to maximize their return and limit their risks. For example, you might put 70 percent of your investments for retirement in a variety of stocks, 20 percent in bonds, and 10 percent in CDs. By spreading out your money in a variety of assets, you have a better chance of offsetting losses from one investment with gains from another. Mutual funds, which invest in a large number of stocks or bonds, help small investors diversify their investments.

APPLICATION Drawing Conclusions

C. Is it possible to have a low-risk, high-return investment? Why or why not?

REVIEWING KEY CONCEPTS

1. Use each of the three terms below in a sentence that illustrates the meaning of the term:

   a. *investment objective*   **b.** *return*   **c.** *diversification*

2. What is the relationship between risk and return?

3. How would the risk of investing in a single stock compare with the risk of investing in a mutual fund? Why?

4. How is diversification related to risk and return?

5. How are risk and return related to investment objectives?

6. **Using Your Notes** How do time and income influence investment objectives? Refer to your completed chart.

   Use the Graphic Organizer at **Interactive Review @ ClassZone.com**

Investing in a Market Economy	
objectives	risk vs. return

CRITICAL THINKING

7. **Comparing and Contrasting** Matthew's parents started saving for his college education when he was born. When Matthew turned 16, he got a part-time job and saved part of his earnings for his college expenses. Compare and contrast the investment objectives of Matthew and his parents and describe the factors that influenced their investment decisions.

8. **Drawing Conclusions** Ryan owns shares in a single mutual fund that includes stocks and bonds. Maggie invests her money in Treasury bonds, state bonds, and corporate bonds. Joshua invests in shares of stock in five different high-tech companies. Which of these investors best understands the concept of diversification? Give reasons for your answer.

9. **Applying Economic Concepts** Inez bought 100 shares of a mutual fund for $10 each and sold them five years later for $15 each. Ethan put $1,000 in a 5-year CD and received a total of $235 in interest. Which investment provided the better return? How does this illustrate the relationship between risk and return?

10. **Challenge** Stocks that are sold on the secondary market and savings accounts both provide liquidity. For each of these investments, what kinds of risks does this liquidity entail?

ECONOMICS IN PRACTICE

Evaluating Investments
Consider what you have learned about risk and return as they relate to various investments, then study the table below and evaluate each investment.

Identify Risk and Return Place a check mark in the appropriate columns for each investment.

Investment	Risk		Return	
	Low	High	Low	High
$1,000 CD				
100 shares of a mutual fund				
100 shares of stock				
Corporate bond				
Government bond				
Regular savings account				

Challenge Rank the investments in order from the lowest risk to the highest risk and from the lowest return to the highest return. Make a generalization about risk and return based on your rankings.

Buying and Selling Stocks

OBJECTIVES	KEY TERMS	TAKING NOTES
In Section 3, you will • discuss why people buy stocks • describe how stocks are traded • explain how the performance of stocks is measured	stock exchange, *p. 330* capital gain, *p. 330* common stock, *p. 331* preferred stock, *p. 331* stockbroker, *p. 332* future, *p. 333* option, *p. 333* stock index, *p. 334* bull market, *p. 335* bear market, *p. 335*	As you read Section 3, complete a cluster diagram using the key concepts and other helpful words and phrases. Use the Graphic Organizer at **Interactive Review @ ClassZone.com** 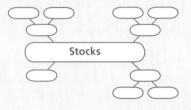

The Stock Market

KEY CONCEPTS

Recall that in Chapter 8 you learned that corporations raise money through stock and bond issues. You will learn more about the sale—and resale—of stocks in this section. When a company first issues stock, it is sold to investment bankers in the primary market. Known as an initial public offering, or IPO, this is the stock sale that raises money for the corporation.

However, most stock is then resold to investors through a **stock exchange**, a secondary market where securities (stocks and bonds) are bought and sold. Most people buy stocks as a financial investment, with the expectation that the stock price will rise and that they can resell the stock for a profit. Gains made from the sale of securities are called **capital gains**.

Why Buy Stock?

Investors buy stock for two reasons. The first is to earn dividend payments, which are a share of the corporation's profits that are paid back to the corporation's stockholders. The second reason is to earn capital gains by selling the stock at a price greater than the purchase price. If stock is sold below the buying price, the seller makes a capital loss. Investors who want to earn income

from their investment will be most interested in dividends. Those who want to see their investment grow over time will be most interested in potential for capital gain.

As you learned in the previous section, investing in stocks carries a higher risk than most other investments but provides the opportunity for higher returns over time. Corporations are not required to pay dividends, so an investor has no guarantee that they will earn income from stocks. Similarly, there is no guarantee that the stock price will be higher when the investor wants to sell the stock.

"IN LIEU OF A DIVIDEND, YOU'LL BE E-MAILED A 'STOCK TIP DU JOUR'."

Source: www.CartoonStock.com

No Guarantees Dividend payments are a possibility, not a certainty; stocks come with risk.

Types of Stock

There are essentially two types of stock—common stock and preferred stock. **Common stock** is share of ownership in a corporation, giving holders voting rights and a share of profits. **Preferred stock** is share of ownership in a corporation giving holders a share of profits (paid before common stockholders) but no voting rights. Most people who buy stock choose to buy common stock.

Figure 11.4 shows the similarities and differences between the two types of stock. Notice that both types of stock give a share of ownership in the corporation that entitles a shareholder to receive dividends. The difference is that holders of preferred stock receive guaranteed dividends and will be paid before common stockholders if the company is liquidated. As a tradeoff for this preference, holders of preferred stock generally have no voting rights in the corporation, and their dividends do not increase if the company's stock increases in value. Each holder of common stock generally gets one vote per share owned to elect the board of directors, which makes important decisions about how the company conducts business.

FIGURE 11.4 Common Stock and Preferred Stock

Characteristic	Preferred Stock	Common Stock
Share of ownership	Yes	Yes
Eligible for dividends	Yes	Yes
Guaranteed dividends	Yes	No
Voting rights	No	Yes

ANALYZE CHARTS
1. What preference do holders of preferred stock have?
2. What do holders of common stock have that holders of preferred stock do not have?

APPLICATION Drawing Conclusions

A. What kind of stock do you think investors who wanted a steady income from their investment would buy? Why?

Trading Stock

Most people who invest in stock do so with the hope of earning capital gains when they sell it. Like anything else sold in a free market, stock prices are determined by demand and supply. Some factors that affect stock prices include company profits or losses, technological advances that may affect a company's business or a whole industry, and the overall state of the economy. When investors perceive that a company's value is likely to increase, the demand for the stock will increase and its price will rise. As the price rises, more people will want to sell the stock for a profit.

Few companies sell stock directly to investors. When investors want to buy or sell stock, they use a **stockbroker**, an agent who, for a commission, buys and sells securities for customers. Stockbrokers, sometimes just called brokers, generally work for brokerage firms. Investors may interact with brokers in person, by phone, or online. The broker's primary job is to carry out the investor's instructions to make trades. Some brokers also provide investment advice. Brokers buy and sell stocks for their customers on a variety of stock exchanges.

Controlled Chaos Don't be fooled by the seeming disorder of the exchange floor. It is a secure and organized trading system.

Organized Stock Exchanges

The New York Stock Exchange (NYSE) is the oldest and largest of the organized stock exchanges in the United States. It is located on Wall Street in New York City, and the street name has become synonymous with the U.S. stock market. Almost 1.5 billion shares of about 2,800 of the largest and most successful U.S. companies are traded on the NYSE each day. Brokerage firms pay for the privilege of being one of the 1,336 members of the exchange.

Traditionally, trading on the NYSE was in an organized auction format. Each stock had a specified location or trading post on the floor of the exchange. A specialist representing that stock ran the auction that matched buyers and sellers through open bidding to determine the price of shares. Prices for a stock often varied from minute to minute as the auction process continued throughout the day.

Changes in technology have brought changes to the NYSE. Since 1996, floor traders have used small hand-held computers to execute many trades, and more than half of the orders to buy and sell are now sent electronically. In 2006, the NYSE merged with Archipelago Exchange, an electronic trading company. This allowed the NYSE not only to speed up its transactions, but also to trade stocks normally traded in electronic markets.

The smaller American Stock Exchange (AMEX) is also located in New York City. Trading at the AMEX is structured in a similar way to the NYSE, although AMEX-traded companies are generally smaller than those listed on the NYSE. In 2006, AMEX introduced new practices that combined the benefits of floor trading and electronic trading.

Electronic Markets

The term *over-the-counter* (OTC) is used to describe the market for stocks that are not traded on the NYSE or AMEX. In 1970, the National Association of Securities Dealers (NASD) introduced a centralized computer system that allows OTC traders around the country to make trades at the best prices possible.

This automated quotation system is known as NASDAQ. In 2005, NASDAQ was the second-largest stock exchange in the world in number of companies listed (about 3,200) and number of shares traded daily. The companies listed on NASDAQ cover many sectors of the U.S. economy, although the majority are involved in technology. The NASD also regulates the OTC Bulletin Board as an electronic market for trading shares in companies that are too small to be traded on NASDAQ.

FIGURE 11.5 SOME NASDAQ STOCKS

Apple Computer	Peets Coffee & Tea
Dell	Priceline.com
Fuji Photo Film Company	Sirius Satellite Radio
Google	Sun Microsystems
Intel Corporation	United Stationers

Futures and Options Markets

Most investors do not trade futures and options because they are complicated and high-risk investments that involve trying to predict the future. A **future** is a contract to buy or sell a stock on a specified future date at a preset price. An investor who wants to buy in the future wants to lock in a low price. An investor who wants to sell in the future wants to lock in a high price.

An **option** is a contract giving the investor the right, but not the obligation, to buy or sell stock at a future date at a preset price. As you can see, the difference between a future and an option is that a futures contract requires the investor to buy or sell, while an option contract offers the possibility of buying or selling but does not require it. In options trading, an investor pays a small fraction of a stock's current price for an option to buy or sell the stock at a better price in the future.

Recent Developments

In the late 1990s, new stock market regulations and advances in computer technology changed the way that stocks were traded. Stocks listed on any exchange are now available to any trading firm. The growth of electronic communications networks (ECNs) increased electronic stock trading, especially on the NASDAQ market. Trades now take place 24 hours a day, not just when the stock exchanges are open.

Many individual investors have access to the Internet and have become more knowledgeable about investing. They wanted ways to trade stocks without relying on traditional stockbrokers. The result has been huge growth in online brokerage companies. Investors now have the ability to make trades at any time and generally pay lower commissions than those charged by traditional brokers. Computer technology matches buyers and sellers automatically, providing rapid trades at the best possible prices.

> **QUICK REFERENCE**
>
> A **future** is a contract to buy or sell a stock on a specific future date at a preset price.
>
> An **option** gives an investor the right to buy or sell stock at a future date at a preset price.

APPLICATION Drawing Conclusions

B. How is NASDAQ similar to the NYSE? How are they different?

Measuring How Stocks Perform

QUICK REFERENCE

A **stock index** measures and reports the change in prices of a set of stocks.

KEY CONCEPTS

About half of all U.S. households now own stocks, and the stock market's performance is followed closely on the nightly news, not just in specialized business media. Perhaps you have heard a statement like this one: "Wall Street responded positively to the latest employment figures, with the Dow making robust gains for the first time in several weeks." The Dow is a **stock index**, an instrument used to measure and report the change in prices of a set of stocks. Stock indexes measure the performance—whether gaining or declining in value—of many individual stocks and the stock market as a whole.

Stock Indexes

Economics Update

Find an update on stocks in the Dow Jones Industrial Average at **ClassZone.com**

Stock indexes provide a snapshot of how the stock market is performing. The Dow—short for the Dow Jones Industrial Average (DJIA)—is the most well known. (For help reading Figure 11.6, turn to the Skillbuilder on page 342.) Other U.S. indexes often cited include the Standard & Poor's 500 (S&P 500) and the NASDAQ Composite. Global stock indexes include the Hang Seng Index (Hong Kong), the DAX (Germany), the Nikkei 225 (Japan), the TSE 300 (Canada), and the FTSE 100 (Britain). Each index measures the performance of a different group of stocks.

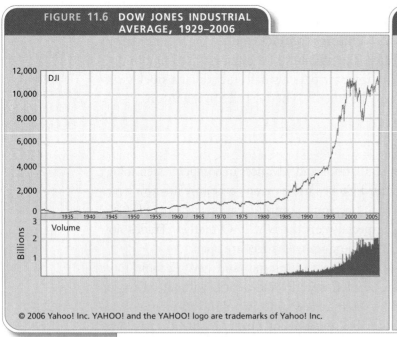

FIGURE 11.6 DOW JONES INDUSTRIAL AVERAGE, 1929–2006

© 2006 Yahoo! Inc. YAHOO! and the YAHOO! logo are trademarks of Yahoo! Inc.

FIGURE 11.7 THE DOW'S BEST AND WORST YEARS

The Dow's Best Years		
Rank	Year	% Change
1	1915	81.66
2	1933	66.69
3	1928	48.22
4	1908	46.64
5	1954	43.96

The Dow's Worst Years		
Rank	Year	% Change
1	1931	-52.67
2	1907	-37.73
3	1930	-33.77
4	1920	-32.90
5	1937	-32.82

ANALYZE CHARTS

1. Does Figure 11.6 suggest a relationship between the level of the DJIA (above) and the volume of shares traded (below)? Explain.
2. What were the most recent best and worst years for the Dow?

FIGURE 11.8 THE 30 STOCKS IN THE DJIA

Alcoa Inc.	Exxon Mobil Corp.	McDonald's Corp.
Altria Group, Inc.	General Electric Co.	Merck & Co.
American Express Co.	General Motors Corp.	Microsoft Corp.
American International Group Inc.	Hewlett-Packard Co.	3M
AT&T Inc.	Home Depot Inc.	Pfizer Inc.
Boeing Co.	Honeywell International Inc.	Procter & Gamble Co.
Caterpillar Inc.	Intel Corp.	United Technologies Corp.
Citigroup Inc.	International Business Machines Corp.	Verizon Communications Inc.
Coca-Cola Co.	J.P. Morgan & Co.	Wal-Mart Stores Inc.
Dupont Co.	Johnson & Johnson	Walt Disney Co

The Dow Jones Company, publisher of the *Wall Street Journal* newspaper, first published the DJIA in 1896. The index included the stocks of 12 companies that reflected the economy of the time, which was focused heavily on agriculture and mining. Since 1928, the Dow has included 30 companies. General Electric is the only one of the original companies that is on the current index. As the U.S. economy has changed from agriculture to industry to services, the companies in the index have changed to reflect the most successful companies in the most important sectors of the economy. These stocks are often referred to as blue chip stocks.

The DJIA is a price index, in other words it measures changes in the prices at which the stocks on the index are traded. The original DJIA was the actual average of the prices of the 12 stocks. Now the average is weighted so that higher-priced stocks have more influence on the average than lower-priced stocks. The number that is quoted is not a price but an average measured in points not dollars.

Tracking the Dow

Changes in the Dow reflect trends in stock market prices. The terms *bull market* and *bear market* are commonly used to describe these trends. A **bull market** is a situation where stock market prices rise steadily over a relatively long period of time. A **bear market** is a situation where stock market prices decline steadily over a relatively long period of time. Those who follow the stock market track the Dow and other indexes to determine if the market is trending toward bull or bear.

The first DJIA measure was 40.94. In 1972, it reached 1,000 for the first time, and in May 1999, it topped 11,000. When the Dow hit its all-time high of 11,722.98 on January 14, 2000, it marked the end of the longest bull market in history. During the 1990s the Dow had climbed from 2,800 to its peak. Most bull markets last two to three years.

A well-known bear market followed the Stock Market Crash of 1929. During the 1920s, the Dow had risen from 60 to a high of 381.17 in early September of 1929. In the month after October 29, 1929, it fell to a low of just under 199. The next time it achieved a closing price of 400 was December 29, 1954.

QUICK REFERENCE

A **bull market** occurs when stock market prices rise steadily over time.

A **bear market** occurs when stock market prices decline steadily over time.

'Better order in more porridge'

Source: www.CartoonStock.com

Investing Money Overseas

In an increasingly international economy, the NYSE is no longer the "only game in town" for U.S. investors. Currently, there are about 21 major stock markets overseas, each listing more than 1,000 large companies. With U.S. stocks representing only about half of the total value of global markets, international investing has become an important option for Americans.

Investing money overseas offers both advantages and risks. For example, an investment in an emerging country—one with an economy that is rapidly growing—offers the prospect of a greater and more rapid return. Such an investment also may involve greater risk, for political instability in an emerging country can drive stock prices down in a hurry. However, many investors view increased diversification as the primary advantage of investing overseas.

FIGURE 11.9 World Markets

Market	Index	Closing Number, May, 2001	Closing Number, May, 2006
Hong Kong Stock Exchange (SEHK)	Hang Seng (HSI)	13,174.41	15,857.89
Buenos Aires Stock Exchange (BCBA)	MERVAL (MERV)	439.22	1,638.01
Bombay Stock Exchange (BSE)	BSE 30 (BSESN)	3,631.91	10,786.63
Tel Aviv Stock Exchange (TASE)	TASE 100 (TA100)	414.21	875.99
Brussels Stock Exchange (BSE)	BEL 20 (BFX)	2786.16	3,987.34

Source: Yahoo Finance

CONNECTING ACROSS THE GLOBE

1. **Synthesizing Economic Information** Do you think it likely that U.S. investment in overseas stock markets will become increasingly common? Explain your answer.

2. **Drawing Conclusions** What does the listing of world markets in Figure 11.9 show about the nature of overseas investment? Explain your answer using information from both the chart and the article.

Many factors affect the Dow's performance. Among these are the market's previous close, actions by the Federal Reserve that affect interest rates or the money supply, the performance of foreign indexes, and the trade balance between imports and exports.

APPLICATION Drawing Conclusions

C. Why have the stocks on DJIA changed over time?

Online Quiz
ClassZone.com

REVIEWING KEY CONCEPTS

1. Explain the relationship between the terms in each of these pairs:

   a. *stock exchange*   **b.** *future*   **c.** *bear market*
   stockbroker   *option*   *bull market*

2. Are owners of common stock generally more interested in dividends or capital gains? Why?

3. Why do most people who buy stock choose common stock over preferred stock?

4. What is the difference between a bear market and a bull market?

5. How has the growth of individual online trading affected stockbrokers?

6. **Using Your Notes** What are the four different ways that stocks are traded? Refer to your completed cluster diagram.

   Use the Graphic Organizer at **Interactive Review @ ClassZone.com**

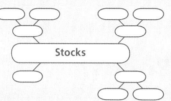

Stocks

CRITICAL THINKING

7. **Applying Economic Concepts** Rachel paid $10 per share for 100 shares of common stock in her favorite clothing store.

   a. If she receives 10 cents per share in dividends each year, about how many years would it take her to earn $100 on her investment?

   b. If the share price increases to $11 in two years and she chooses to sell the stock, how much capital gain would she make?

8. **Analyzing and Interpreting Data** Rearrange the data in Figure 11.7 into one table in chronological order. Use a plus sign to indicate a best year and a minus sign to indicate a worst year.

   a. What relationship, if any, do you see between best years and worst years?

   b. What does the data reveal about the stock market in the 1930s?

9. **Challenge** The Standard and Poor's 500 (S&P 500) is an index composed of 500 stocks, while the Dow Jones Industrial Average is composed of 30 stocks. Many analysts feel the S&P 500 is a better representation of the U.S. stock market. Do you agree? Why?

ECONOMICS IN PRACTICE

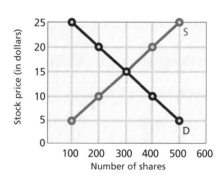

Analyzing Demand for Stock
The graph below shows the combined market demand and supply curve for the stock of a company that makes mp3 players.

Draw New Demand Curves Copy the graph above on your own paper and draw new demand curves to reflect each of the following scenarios:

a. A competitor announces a technological breakthrough that will dramatically cut its production costs.

b. The company announces a new product that offers features that consumers have been asking for.

Challenge How does the change in demand in each scenario affect the price of the stock?

Financial Markets 337

Bonds and Other Financial Instruments

OBJECTIVES	KEY TERMS	TAKING NOTES
In Section 4, you will • discuss why people buy bonds • describe the different kinds of bonds • explain the factors that affect bond trading • outline investment options other than stocks and bonds	par value, *p. 338* maturity, *p. 338* coupon rate, *p. 338* yield, *p. 338* junk bond, *p. 339*	As you read Section 4, summarize what you learn by completing a chart using the key concepts and other helpful words and phrases. Use the Graphic Organizer at **Interactive Review @ ClassZone.com**

Bonds	Other Financial Instruments

Why Buy Bonds?

KEY CONCEPTS

You learned in Chapter 8 that a bond is a contract issued by a corporation promising to repay borrowed money, plus interest, on a fixed schedule. Governments also issue bonds. The amount that the bond issuer promises to pay the buyer at maturity is its **par value. Maturity** is the date when the bond is due to be repaid. The **coupon rate** is the interest rate a bondholder receives every year until a bond matures.

There are two reasons to invest in bonds—the interest paid on bonds and the gains made by selling bonds. Most people buy bonds for the interest. Generally, bonds are considered less risky than stocks because bondholders are paid before stockholders. It is important to determine the **yield**—the annual rate of return—for a bond when deciding to buy and sell bonds. If a bond is sold at par value, the yield is the same as the coupon rate. If a bond is sold for less than par value, the yield will be higher than the coupon rate. On the other hand, if demand is strong and the price of a bond is higher than the par value, the yield will be lower than the coupon rate.

Generally speaking, bonds with longer maturity dates have higher yields than those with shorter dates. This is because there is more uncertainty and risk involved with repayment dates that are farther in the future.

Types of Bonds

Investors may choose to invest in many different kinds of bonds. The yields and risks associated with these bonds vary considerably. As is the case with stocks, the higher the risk the greater the potential yield of a bond. Figure 11.10 shows the yields for different types of bonds. Bonds are classified based on who issues the bonds.

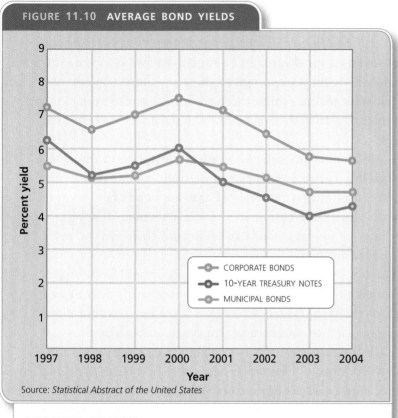

FIGURE 11.10 AVERAGE BOND YIELDS

Percent yield / Year

Legend:
- CORPORATE BONDS
- 10-YEAR TREASURY NOTES
- MUNICIPAL BONDS

Source: *Statistical Abstract of the United States*

ANALYZE GRAPHS
1. Which type of bond had the lowest average yield in most years?
2. Which type of bond carries the highest risk? How do you know?

Corporate bonds
help businesses expand.

Treasury bonds
help keep the federal
government operating.

Municipal bonds
make state and local
projects possible.

The U.S. government issues securities called Treasury bonds, notes, or bills. The different terms denote loans with different maturity dates, with Treasury bonds having the longest maturity (more than ten years) and Treasury bills having the shortest (one year or less). The money borrowed through the sale of these securities helps keep the government running. Because they are backed by the "full faith and credit" of the federal government, these securities are considered to be virtually risk free. Governments all over the world issue bonds for the same reasons as the U.S. government. The risk level of international bonds depends on the financial strength of the particular government.

Bonds issued by state and local governments are called municipal bonds. Funds raised by these bonds finance government projects such as construction of roads, bridges, schools, and other public facilities. The interest earned on many municipal bonds is not subject to federal income tax. Generally, municipal bonds are considered low-risk investments. A major reason for this is that state and local governments collect taxes, so it is assumed that they'll be able to make interest payments and repay the buyer upon maturity. However, there have been instances of governments being unable to repay bondholders the full amount of their loans.

One way that companies finance expansion is by issuing corporate bonds. These bonds generally pay a higher coupon rate than government bonds because the risk is higher. One kind of corporate bond, a **junk bond**, is considered high risk but has the potential for high yields. The risk involved with investing in junk bonds is similar to that of investing in stocks.

QUICK REFERENCE

Junk bonds are high-risk, high-yield corporate bonds.

Buying Bonds

Investors need to determine their reason for buying bonds in order to purchase the right type of bond. Most investors purchase bonds because they want the guaranteed interest income. Yield will be most important to those investors. Coupon rate and price relative to the par value will determine the yield. Investors who want to sell bonds before they reach maturity study the bond market to see if they can sell their investment at a profit.

Market interest rates are another important consideration for bond investors. There is an inverse relationship between the price of existing bonds and interest rates. For example, as interest rates rise, the price of existing bonds falls because bonds that were issued with a lower interest rate will be less in demand. Conversely, if interest rates fall, the price of existing bonds rises because there will be more demand for those bonds issued at a higher interest rate.

The main risk that bond buyers face is that the issuer will default, or be unable to repay the borrowed money at maturity. Therefore, the level of risk is directly tied to the financial strength of the bond issuer. When governments or corporations want to issue bonds, they pay a credit-rating company to evaluate how likely it is that they will repay the loans. In this way, investors have a standard by which to judge the risk of the bonds. The two most well-known systems of bond ratings are those established by Standard & Poor's and Moody's. These companies use a system of letters to designate the relative credit risk of bonds. Bonds are rated from the lowest risk of U.S. Treasury securities (Aaa or AAA) to the higher risks associated with junk bonds. (See Figure 11.11.)

FIGURE 11.11 Bond Ratings

Bond Rating		Grade	Risk
Moody's	Standard & Poor's		
Aaa	AAA	Investment	Lowest risk
Aa	AA	Investment	Low risk
A	A	Investment	Low risk
Baa	BBB	Investment	Medium risk
Ba, B	BB, B	Junk	High risk
Caa/Ca	CCC/CC/C	Junk	Highest risk
C	D	Junk	In default

ANALYZE TABLES

1. What are the lowest-rated investment grade bonds in each system?

2. Why do junk bonds have lower ratings than investment grade bonds?

APPLICATION Drawing Conclusions

A. Why is bond yield not always the same as the coupon rate?

Other Financial Instruments

KEY CONCEPTS

Investors have investment options other than bonds and stocks. The most common of these are certificates of deposit (CDs) and money market mutual funds. Both of these investments have very low risk and provide income in the form of interest. Individual investors do not generally sell these financial instruments for profit.

Certificates of Deposit

As you learned earlier, CDs are a form of time deposit offered primarily by banks, savings and loans, and credit unions. Like bonds, CDs have a maturity date (usually 6 months to 5 years), when the investor receives the principal back with interest.

The issuer of the CD pays the investor a rate of either fixed or variable interest during the period that the CD is held. Usually the interest is reinvested in the CD so that the investor enjoys the benefits of compound interest. In general, CDs with longer maturity dates pay higher rates of interest. For example, a 6-month CD might pay 3.4 percent interest while a 5-year CD might pay 4.4 percent.

The federal government insures funds deposited in CDs at most banks and credit unions up to $100,000 per depositor in any given institution. The main risk that investors in CDs face is the loss of interest or possibly some principal if funds are withdrawn before the maturity date. In addition, investors might face interest-rate risk if rates rise and funds are locked in for a length of time at a lower rate.

Money Market Mutual Funds

Recall from Section 1 that the money market involves financial assets with maturities of one year or less. Also, remember that mutual funds allow investors to buy shares that represent an investment in all the financial assets held by the fund. Money market mutual funds (MMMF) allow investors to own a variety of short-term financial assets, such as Treasury bills, municipal bonds, large-denomination CDs, and corporate bonds.

These mutual funds give investors a higher yield than bank savings accounts, but provide a similar level of liquidity. Investors can redeem their shares by check, by phone, or by electronic transfer to a separate checking account.

Although the federal government does not insure MMMFs, the funds are tightly regulated, and these investments are considered to be quite safe with regard to loss of principal. There is less interest-rate risk than with CDs because the money is not committed for a specified length of time. The yield of the MMMF varies based on the yield of the assets in the fund.

"'Oh, no,' said Goldilocks, 'don't tell me that the return on invested capital is only *three* percent—less than you can earn on a money-market account!'"

Source: www.CartoonStock.com

APPLICATION Making Inferences

B. Why do longer-term CDs pay higher interest rates than shorter-term CDs?

For more information on evaluating online sources, see the Skillbuilder Handbook, page R29.

Interpreting Graphs: Online Financial Information

Evaluating means to make a judgment about information. Investors make judgments about stocks based on their analysis of financial information. Many use the Internet as a resource for acquiring minute-to-minute information about stock market trading. The graphs on this page provide information about Apple Computer Inc., a stock traded on the NASDAQ. These graphs, which are updated online throughout trading, offer an example of the type of online information investors use to evaluate stocks.

TIPS FOR EVALUATING ONLINE INFORMATION Use the following guidelines to evaluate economic information online:

Read the title to identify the company for which stock information is shown. Here it is Apple Computer (AAPL), traded on the NASDAQ (Q).

Read the vertical axis. This graph has two parts. The upper part shows the stock's price; the lower part shows the volume of shares traded.

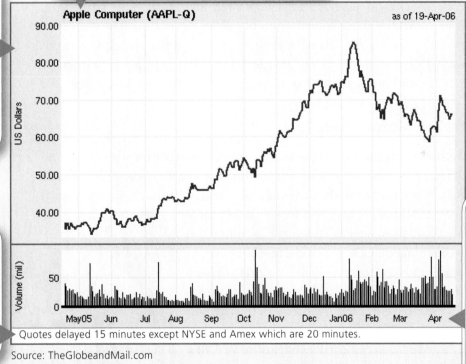

Read the horizontal axis. This graph shows stock prices and volume traded from May 2005 through April 2006.

Look for other information This statement shows the lag time for information—15 minutes in this case.

Source: TheGlobeandMail.com

THINKING ECONOMICALLY Evaluating

1. As an investor, which month would have been best for you to acquire Apple stock? Why?

2. How does the price per share at the beginning of June 2005 compare with the price in mid-January 2006? Use information from the graph in your answer.

3. From January through April of 2006, the price of Apple shares fluctuated greatly. Volume of trading was also very heavy. Are these two facts related? Why?

Online Quiz
ClassZone.com

REVIEWING KEY CONCEPTS

1. Use each of the three terms below in a sentence that illustrates the meaning of the term:

   a. *coupon rate*   **b.** *maturity*   **c.** *yield*

2. What does par value represent to the issuer of a bond?

3. What is the relationship between par value and maturity?

4. When does yield equal the coupon rate?

5. Why do junk bonds offer a higher yield than other types of bonds?

6. **Using Your Notes** Compare the risk of investing in a CD with the risk of investing in a money market mutual fund. Refer to your completed chart.

Bonds	Other Financial Instruments

   Use the Graphic Organizer at **Interactive Review @ ClassZone.com**

CRITICAL THINKING

7. **Comparing and Contrasting** Dmitri bought a $1,000 bond at par value with a coupon rate of 5 percent. He determines the yield by dividing the amount of interest he earns by the price.

   a. How much interest would he earn in the first year and what would be the yield?

   b. How much interest would he earn in the first year and what would be the yield if he had paid $950 for the bond? What would be the interest and yield if he paid $1,050?

8. **Making Inferences** In 2003, Molly bought a 10-year Treasury note for $1,000. The market interest rate was 3.5 percent. In 2005, Molly wanted to sell the note to pay for college expenses. Interest rates had risen to 4.5 percent. How would the change in interest rates affect the price that Molly was likely to receive for her note? Give reasons for your answer.

9. **Applying Economic Concepts** Julie has accumulated $1,000 in a bank savings account, which pays 2.7 percent interest. She investigates several options and finds that she can invest her money in a 1-year Treasury note paying 4.4 percent interest, a 1-year CD paying 3.9 percent interest, or a money market mutual fund with an average yield of 3.7 percent. What are the pros and cons of each of these investment options?

10. **Challenge** How would a lower bond rating by Moody's or Standard & Poor's affect the coupon rate that a corporation has to offer when it issues its bonds? Give reasons for your answer.

ECONOMICS IN PRACTICE

Making Investment Decisions
Suppose that you have been advised to invest in bonds. Recall what you have learned about the factors to consider when buying and selling bonds and then complete the following activities.

Ask Investment Questions Fill in the chart by developing a series of questions you might ask to help you decide which type of bond to buy.

Categories of Questions to Ask About Bonds	My Questions
Investment objectives	
Tolerance for risk	
Desired return	
Resalability of bonds	

Challenge How might you apply the concept of diversification to a portfolio of bond investments?

Economics Update
Find an update on this Case Study at **ClassZone.com**

The Rise and Fall of Dot-Coms

Background The availability of products and services on the Internet is old news. But when the Internet first emerged, it provided a unique and exciting tool for almost instant access to potential buyers worldwide. Young people in particular were quick to grasp the possibilities of the electronic marketplace. As a result, many new companies, known as dot-coms, quickly appeared on the Internet.

Like the stock of many companies based on new technologies, the value of dot-com stocks rose quickly. Investors, attracted by the initial success of dot-coms and spurred on by low interest rates in the late 1990s, were quick to join the dot-com boom. The boom, however, proved to be a financial bubble. In 2000 and 2001, the bubble burst as dot-com stocks fell dramatically. Many dot-coms went out of business, and their investors sustained heavy financial losses.

What's the issue? Why did so many dot-com companies fail? Study these sources to discover what investors learned when the dot-com bubble burst.

A. Online Encyclopedia Article

Many young entrepreneurs jumped into the dot-com market, often with disastrous results. This article describes one such venture.

Kozmo.com Offered New Yorkers Free, One-Hour Delivery

Despite millions in capital investment, Kozmo.com's choices led to failure.

Kozmo.com was a venture-capital-driven online company that promised free one-hour delivery of anything from DVDs to Starbucks coffee. It was founded by young investment bankers Joseph Park and Yong Kang in March 1998 in New York City. The company is often referred to as an example of the dot-com excess.

Kozmo promoted an incredible business model; it promised to deliver small goods free of charge. The company raised about $280 million, including $60 million from Amazon.com. The business model was heavily criticized by business analysts, who pointed out that one-hour point-to-point delivery of small objects is extremely expensive and there was no way Kozmo could make a profit as long as it refused to charge delivery fees. Not surprisingly, the company failed soon after the collapse of the dot-com bubble, laying off its staff of 1,100 employees and shutting down in April 2001.

Source: **Wikipedia.org**

Thinking Economically Why do you think Park and Kang were so successful in raising capital to fund their business venture?

B. Cartoon

Cartoonist Andrew Toos drew this commentary about the dot-com bubble.

"The good news is we've financed another dot.com for no fathomable reason."

Source: www.CartoonStock.com

Thinking Economically What comment does the cartoon make about investing in the dot-com financial market?

C. Online News Story

Early dot-coms typically spent huge amounts of money on advertising. This article compares purchases of advertising during the 2000 Super Bowl telecast to Napoleon's 1815 defeat at Waterloo.

The Bubble Bowl

Expensive advertising failed to market dot-com products.

It was just five years ago, although it seems like a different age entirely. It was a time of singing-sock-puppets, 21-year-old chief executives, gravity-defiant stock prices, revolutionary technologies and half-baked business plans.

And in this atmosphere, during the final, halcyon days of the Internet boom, the St. Louis Rams played the Tennessee Titans in Super Bowl XXXIV, a moment that will be forever remembered as the dot-com bubble's Waterloo.

Football fans got a heavy dose of the fever that day: More than a dozen internet companies spent an average of $2.2 million for 30-second spots, amounting to more than $40 million of stockholder cash and not-so-hard-won venture capital.

These startups hoped that Super Bowl exposure would sear their web address into the minds of consumers. But most viewers were left with only vague memories of chimpanzees dancing to "La Cucaracha" to promote whatchamacalit.com... while the businesses themselves were left with empty wallets.

Today, most of these Internet pioneers are dead and gone, forgotten as the score of the game (St. Louis 23, Tennessee 16).

Source: **"The Bubble Bowl," by David M. Ewalt. Forbes.com, January 27, 2005**

Thinking Economically Why do you think the author compares the dot-com Super Bowl advertising to Waterloo, a major military defeat?

THINKING ECONOMICALLY Synthesizing

1. During the dot-com bubble, do you think it was relatively easy or difficult for Internet start-up companies to raise capital? Explain your answer, using information from the documents.

2. Why do you think so many dot-coms failed? Use evidence from the documents in your answer.

3. What lessons might investors learn from the information presented in documents A and C?

Interactive ◄◄Review

Review this chapter using interactive activities at ClassZone.com
- **Online Summary**
- **Quizzes**
- **Vocabulary Flip Cards**
- **Graphic Organizers**
- **Review and Study Notes**

○○○

🔖 Online Summary

Complete the following activity either on your own paper or online at **ClassZone.com**

Choose the key concept that best completes the sentence. Not all key concepts will be used.

capital gain	money market
capital market	par value
common stock	preferred stock
coupon rate	primary market
diversification	return
financial asset	risk
financial intermediary	savings
investment	secondary market
investment objective	stock index
maturity	yield

__1__ is income not used for consumption. __2__ is the use of income today that allows for greater production in the future.

A __3__ is a claim on the property of a borrower. A __4__ collects funds from savers and invests the funds in loans and other financial assets. Examples include banks and mutual funds. The __5__ is the market for buying and selling short-term financial assets. The __6__ is the market where financial assets are resold.

The two issues that play a major role in setting an __7__ are time and income. Investors try to maximize __8__ and limit __9__ through __10__, the practice of distributing investments among different financial assets.

__11__ is profit made from the sale of securities. __12__ is share of ownership in a corporation that gives holders voting rights and a share of the profit. The Dow Jones Industrial Average is a __13__ that measures the performance of a group of 30 stocks. __14__ is the interest rate paid on a bond. The __15__ is the amount that a bond issuer promises to pay the buyer at maturity.

CHAPTER **11 Assessment**

REVIEWING KEY CONCEPTS

Savings and Investment (pp. 318–323)

1. How are savings and investment related?

2. What is the role of financial intermediaries in the circular flow of the financial system?

Investing in a Market Economy (pp. 324–329)

3. Why do investors need to determine their investment objective before they invest?

4. Explain the relationship between risk and return.

Buying and Selling Stocks (pp. 330–337)

5. How do people earn money by investing in stocks?

6. How does the Dow Jones Industrial Average reveal trends in the stock market?

Bonds and Other Financial Instruments (pp. 338–345)

7. What are the two reasons people buy bonds?

8. How are interest rates and bond prices related?

APPLYING ECONOMIC CONCEPTS

Look at the graph below showing savings as a percentage of after-tax income in various countries.

9. Which country has the lowest rate of savings?

10. What is the overall trend from 1980 to 2000?

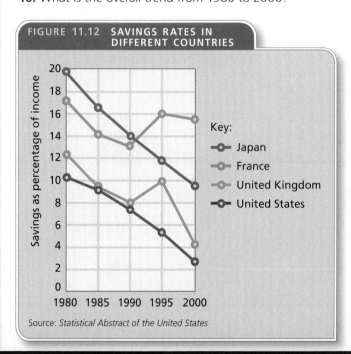

FIGURE 11.12 **SAVINGS RATES IN DIFFERENT COUNTRIES**

Key:
- Japan
- France
- United Kingdom
- United States

Source: *Statistical Abstract of the United States*

11. **Analyzing Causes and Effects** In 2005, many leading advertisers announced plans to increase use of online advertising and to decrease the amount of advertising dollars spent in traditional print media, such as newspapers. In addition, newspaper circulation figures declined steadily as more people read news on the Internet.

   a. How was this situation likely to affect the stock prices of online search-engine companies that featured banner ads and sponsored links on their Web pages?

   b. How would it affect the stock prices of newspapers? Explain your answers.

12. **Comparing and Contrasting** What are the similarities and differences between stock dividends, a bond coupon rate, and interest on a CD?

13. **Drawing Conclusions** Alex, Kate, and Rashid all invested money in a software company. Alex bought a corporate bond, Kate bought shares of common stock, and Rashid bought shares of preferred stock. Which of these investors would be least at risk of losing money if the company became unprofitable?

14. **Making Inferences** Suppose that you heard the following statement on the financial news: "Bonds fell as the yield on 10-year Treasury notes rose to 4.56 percent, the highest in two years." What does "bonds fell" mean and how is it related to the increase in yield?

15. **Challenge** Steve purchases an option contract to buy 100 shares of stock in a big high-tech company for $50 per share in six months. The stock is currently selling for $40 per share. Steve pays $5 per share for the option contract. If the share price rises to $60, Steve exercises his option to buy the shares at $50 and then resells the stock on the market for $60 per share. How much profit does Steve make per share? If the price never rises to $50 before the option expires, how much money does Steve lose?

Advise Your Clients

Choose a partner. Imagine that you are financial planners whose job is to help clients meet their investment objectives and use diversification to maximize return and limit risk.

Step 1 Make a list of several possible financial instruments that you might recommend and rate them for risk and return.

Step 2 Review each client's objectives and risk tolerance to consider what investments to recommend.

   a. Carlos and Juanita Diaz want to invest for their two young children's college education. They would like a return of 7 to 10 percent a year and have a moderate tolerance for risk.

   b. Patrick Hurd is 30 years old and wants to begin saving for his retirement. He wants the highest return possible and is willing to take risks.

   c. Alison Leveridge has recently retired. She wants to invest the money from her pension fund so that she can have a guaranteed amount of income and little risk of losing her capital.

Step 3 Decide what percentage of each client's money to invest in different types of financial instruments. Create pie graphs to show your recommendations for each client.

Step 4 Present your recommendations to another pair of students. Discuss the choices that each of you made.

Step 5 As a class, discuss how changes in your clients' financial circumstances or changes in the stock market might affect your recommendations.

Use *SMART Grapher* @ ClassZone.com to complete this activity.

Measuring the Economy
Millions of workers and
businesses participate in the
U.S. economy. Measuring the
country's economy requires
special economic tools.

WORLD STOCK MARKETS

Bourses up but volatility remains
WORLD OVERVIEW

There was a bounce in
European shares following
Monday's rout, while US
markets opened firmer after
consumer confidence figures
turned out less gloomy than
feared.

The meeting of the Federal
Open Market Committee,
which concludes today, is
not expected to alter the 1.75
per cent interest rate.
Markets will be looking for
any change in the Fed's
opinion on whether the
dangers of inflation are
lessening or increasing.

Biggest gainers in Europe
were the stocks that led the
previous session, while
telecoms and IT compa-

FTSE Eurotop 300
Indices rebased

BMW
Share price (€)

SAP

Eurotop 300
Automobile

Sep 2001 02 Apr

Source: Thomson Datastream

Techs and telecoms lead gains
EUROPE

European indices

Economic Indicators and Measurements

CONCEPT REVIEW

Macroeconomics is the study of the economy as a whole and how major sectors of the economy interact.

CHAPTER 12 KEY CONCEPT

National income accounting uses statistical measures of income, spending, and output to help people understand what is happening to a country's economy.

WHY THE CONCEPT MATTERS

Your economic decisions—combined with those of millions of other people—determine the fate of the nation's economy. Can you afford to buy a new car? Is now a good time to change jobs? Should you take a risk in the stock market or keep your money safe in the bank? Understanding what is happening to the country's economy will help you make better economic decisions.

Online Highlights

More at ClassZone.com

 Economics Update

Go to **ECONOMICS UPDATE** for chapter updates and current news on the economy of Poland. (See Case Study, pp. 376–377.) ▶

Animated Economics

Go to **ANIMATED ECONOMICS** for interactive lessons on the graphs and tables in this chapter.

Interactive ◀◀ Review

Go to **INTERACTIVE REVIEW** for concept review and activities.

How has manufacturing transformed Poland's economy? See the Case Study on pages 376–377.

Gross Domestic Product and Other Indicators

OBJECTIVES	KEY TERMS	TAKING NOTES
In Section 1, you will • define GDP and describe how it is measured • explain how GDP has certain limitations • identify other national income accounting measures	national income accounting, *p. 350* gross domestic product (GDP), *p. 350* nominal GDP, *p. 352* real GDP, *p. 352* nonmarket activities, *p. 354* underground economy, *p. 354* gross national product (GNP), *p. 355* net national product (NNP), *p. 355* national income (NI), *p. 355* personal income (PI), *p. 355* disposable personal income (DPI), *p. 355*	As you read Section 1, complete a hierarchy chart like the one below to record what you learn about national income accounting. Use the Graphic Organizer at **Interactive Review @ ClassZone.com**

What Is GDP?

QUICK REFERENCE

National income accounting is a way of evaluating a country's economy using statistical measures of its income, spending, and output.

Gross domestic product (GDP) is the market value of all final goods and services produced within a nation in a given time period.

KEY CONCEPTS

As you have read, microeconomics and macroeconomics look at the economy through different lenses. While microeconomics examines the actions of individuals and single markets, macroeconomics examines the economy as a whole. Macroeconomists analyze the economy using **national income accounting**, statistical measures that track the income, spending, and output of a nation. The most important of those measures is **gross domestic product (GDP)**, the market value of all final goods and services produced within a nation in a given time period.

The Components of GDP

To be included in GDP, a good or service has to fulfill three requirements. First, it has to be final rather than intermediate. For example, the fabric used to make a shirt is an intermediate good; the shirt itself is a final good. Second, the good or service must be produced during the time period, regardless of when it is sold. For example, cars made this year but sold next year would be counted in this year's GDP. Finally, the good or service must be produced within the nation's borders. Products made in foreign countries by U.S. companies are not included in the U.S. GDP.

Products Included in GDP
Cars made in the United States are an example of goods counted toward U.S. gross domestic product (GDP).

Calculating GDP

Although there are several different ways to calculate GDP, economists often use the expenditures approach. With this method, they group national spending on final goods and services according to the four sectors of the economy: spending by households, or consumption; spending by businesses, or investment; government spending; and total exports minus total imports, or net exports. Economists identify consumption with the letter C; investment with the letter I; government spending with the letter G; and net exports with the letter X. To calculate GDP, economists add the expenditures from all sectors together: C+I+G+X=GDP.

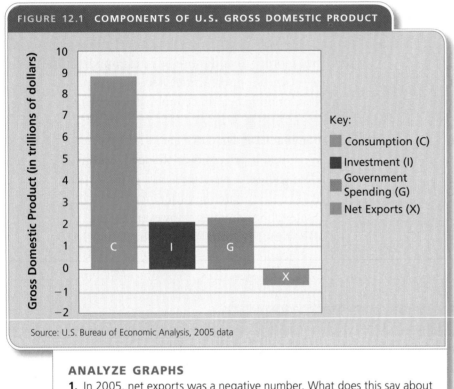

FIGURE 12.1 COMPONENTS OF U.S. GROSS DOMESTIC PRODUCT

Key:
- Consumption (C)
- Investment (I)
- Government Spending (G)
- Net Exports (X)

Source: U.S. Bureau of Economic Analysis, 2005 data

ANALYZE GRAPHS

1. In 2005, net exports was a negative number. What does this say about the relative amounts of exports and imports?

2. Did households, businesses, or the government contribute the most to U.S. GDP in 2005?

Economics Update

Find an update on the U.S. GDP at **ClassZone.com**

Consumption includes all spending by households on durable goods, nondurable goods, and services. You drive to the movies in a durable good (an item that does not wear out quickly). You purchase a service when you pay for the movie (since you are not buying to own something). And you obtain a nondurable good (a good that is used up relatively soon after purchase) when you buy popcorn.

Investment, which measures what businesses spend, has two categories. One is fixed investment, which includes new construction and purchases of such capital goods as equipment, machinery, and tools. The other is inventory investment. This category, also called unconsumed output, is made up of the unsold goods that businesses keep on hand.

Government spending includes all the expenditures of federal, state, and local governments on goods and services. Examples include spending for defense, highways,

and public education. However, government spending on transfer payments, such as social security and unemployment benefits, is not included. These payments allow the recipients to buy goods and services, and these are counted as consumption.

Net exports, the final component of GDP, represents foreign trade. This component takes into account the goods and services produced in the United States but sold in foreign countries—in other words, exports. However, U.S. consumers and businesses also buy, or import, goods made in foreign countries. Cars, car parts, and crude oil are the largest imports in dollar value. The GDP counts only net exports—the value of U.S. exports minus the value of U.S. imports.

Two Types of GDP

Economists use GDP to gauge how well a country's economy is doing. When GDP is growing, an economy creates more jobs and more business opportunities. When GDP declines, jobs and more business opportunities become less plentiful. To get a clearer picture of a country's economic health, economists calculate two forms of GDP—nominal and real.

The most basic form is **nominal GDP**, which is stated in the price levels for the year in which the GDP was measured. If prices never changed, nominal GDP would be sufficient. But prices tend to increase over time. In Figure 12.2, find the line that represents nominal GDP. If you estimate the difference from 1990 to 2005, the nominal GDP of the United States about doubled. However, during this time prices went up, adding dollars to GDP without adding value to the nation's output.

To factor out rising prices, economists use **real GDP**, which is nominal GDP adjusted for changes in prices. Real GDP is an estimate of the GDP if prices were to

QUICK REFERENCE

Nominal GDP states GDP in terms of the current value of goods and services.

Real GDP states GDP corrected for changes in prices from year to year.

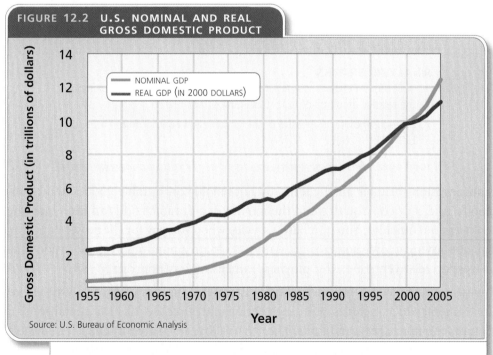

FIGURE 12.2 U.S. NOMINAL AND REAL GROSS DOMESTIC PRODUCT

NOMINAL GDP
REAL GDP (IN 2000 DOLLARS)

Gross Domestic Product (in trillions of dollars)

Year

Source: U.S. Bureau of Economic Analysis

ANALYZE GRAPHS
1. About how much did nominal GDP increase from 1990 to 2000?
2. About how much did real GDP increase over the same period?
3. Why do the two lines cross at the year 2000?

352 Chapter 12

FIGURE 12.3 Understanding Nominal and Real GDP

To better understand nominal and real GDP, imagine a country that produces only one good: TVs. If you know the price of TVs and the number produced, you can calculate that country's nominal and real GDP. Use the table to find the data for these calculations.

	2004	2005	2006
TVs Produced	500	600	600
TV Price	$100	$100	$120
Nominal GDP	$50,000	$60,000	$72,000
Real GDP, base: 2004	$50,000	$60,000	$60,000

Step 1: Calculate nominal GDP for 2004. Nominal GDP is the product of the number of TVs produced and the price of TVs that year.

Number produced	3	Price in that year	5	Nominal GDP	500 3 $100 5 $50,000

The table shows that nominal GDP grew each year. If you judged only by nominal GDP, the economy of this country would seem to be growing.

Step 2: Analyze the nominal GDP figures. Why did nominal GDP increase from 2004 to 2005? The number of TVs produced increased. Why did nominal GDP increase from 2005 to 2006? The price of TVs increased.

The output of the country's economy grew from 2004 to 2005, but it stayed the same from 2005 to 2006, despite the increase in prices. Calculating real GDP produces a better estimate of how much a country's economy is growing.

Step 3: Calculate real GDP for 2006. Real GDP is the product of the number of TVs produced in the current year and the price of TVs in the base year. In this case, use 2004 as the base year.

Number produced	3	Price in the base year	5	Real GDP	600 3 $100 5 $60,000

Since 2004 is the base year, nominal and real GDP are the same for 2004. Real GDP allows you to compare the output of the country's economy in different years.

remain constant from year to year. To find real GDP, economists compare nominal GDP to a base year. Look again at Figure 12.2, which uses 2000 as a base year. Since real GDP eliminates price differences, the line for real GDP rises more gradually than the line for nominal GDP. Real GDP provides a more accurate measure of economic performance.

APPLICATION Applying Economic Concepts

A. If output remained the same, how would a year of falling prices affect nominal GDP? How would it affect real GDP?

What GDP Does Not Measure

KEY CONCEPTS

Although GDP provides an important estimate of how well the economy is performing, it does not measure all output. It does not measure **nonmarket activities**, such as home childcare or performing one's own home repairs. GDP also does not measure output from the **underground economy**, market activities that go unreported because they are illegal or because those involved want to avoid taxation. Further, GDP does not measure "quality of life" issues related to economic output.

QUICK REFERENCE

Nonmarket activities are services that have potential economic value but are performed without charge.

Underground economy describes market activities that go unreported because they are illegal or because those involved want to avoid taxation.

Nonmarket Activities

Some productive activities do not take place in economic markets. For example, there is no effective way to measure the output of plumbers who install or repair plumbing systems in their own homes or people who do volunteer work for schools or hospitals. By far the biggest nonmarket activity, also left out of GDP, consists of the many services—cooking, cleaning, childcare—provided by homemakers.

Nonmarket Activities Housework is an example of a productive activity not measured by GDP.

Underground Economy

Also missing from GDP is the underground sector of the economy. Some activities are kept underground because they are illegal—drug dealing, smuggling, gambling, and selling stolen goods, for example. When goods are rationed or otherwise restricted, illegal trading occurs on what is called the black market. Other underground activities are themselves legal, but the way the payment is handled is not. For example, a plumber who does repairs for a neighbor might receive payment in cash and not declare it as taxable income. Estimates suggest that the underground economy would make up 8 to 10 percent of the U.S. GDP.

Quality of Life

Countries with high GDPs have high living standards. But GDP does not show how the goods and services are distributed. The United States has the largest GDP of any country, but more than 10 percent of its people still live in poverty. GDP also does not express what products are being built and services offered: for example, are there more jails being built than schools?

APPLICATION Explaining an Economic Concept

B. If you get paid in cash to baby-sit, mow lawns, or do other chores for neighbors, are you part of the underground economy? Why or why not?

Other Economic Performance Measures

KEY CONCEPTS

GDP is not the only measure that economists use to gauge economic performance. Several other measures are derived by making adjustments to GDP.

- **Gross national product (GNP)** is the market value of all final goods and services a country produces in a given time period. GNP equals GDP plus the income from goods and services produced by U.S. companies and citizens in foreign countries but minus the income foreign companies and citizens earn here.

- **Net national product (NNP)** is GNP minus depreciation of capital stock—in other words, the value of final goods and services less the value of capital goods that became worn out during the time period.

- **National income (NI)** is the total income earned in a nation from the production of goods and services in a given time period. It is calculated by subtracting indirect business taxes, such as property and sales taxes, from NNP.

- **Personal income (PI)** is the income received by a country's people from all sources in a given time period. It can be calculated from NI by subtracting social security taxes, corporate profit taxes, and corporate profits not paid to stockholders and by adding social security, unemployment, and welfare payments.

- **Disposable personal income (DPI)** is personal income minus personal income taxes. It shows how much money is actually available for consumer spending.

QUICK REFERENCE

Gross national product (GNP) is the market value of all final goods and services produced by a country.

Net national product (NNP) is the value of final goods and services less the value of capital goods that have become worn out.

National income (NI) is the total income earned in a nation from the production of goods and services.

Personal income (PI) is the income received by a country's people from all sources.

Disposable personal income (DPI) is personal income minus taxes.

FIGURE 12.4 National Income Accounting

GDP + income earned abroad by U.S. businesses and citizens
− income earned in U.S. by foreign businesses and citizens

= GNP − depreciation of capital stock

    = NNP − indirect business taxes

        = NI − income earned but not received
             + income received but not earned

           = PI − personal taxes

              = DPI

ANALYZE CHARTS
What three figures do you need in order to calculate personal income (PI)?

APPLICATION Making Inferences

C. Under what circumstances might a country's GNP be greater than its GDP?

ECONOMICS
SKILLBUILDER

For more on synthesizing economic data,
see the Skillbuilder Handbook, page R23.

Synthesizing Economic Data

Synthesizing is a skill used by economists to interpret economic trends. Synthesizing involves interpreting various data to form an overview of economic performance. A synthesis is often stated as a broad summary statement.

PRACTICING THE SKILL National income accounting involves the collection and analysis of data on key economic variables. Economists synthesize the data to arrive at an overview of national economic performance. The table below presents data for variables used to determine gross domestic product (GDP), a key factor in national income accounting.

> **Read** the title to learn the main idea of the table. This table shows the components of U.S. GDP for selected years.

> **Read** the column heads carefully. The four types of expenditures are used to determine GDP.

> **Determine** how the types of data relate to one another. For 1990, calculating the sum of the four expenditures yields $5,803 billion, the nominal GDP for 1990.

> **Check** the source of the data to evaluate its reliability.

> **Look** for patterns in the data. For example, notice that net exports have been negative.

FIGURE 12.5 COMPONENTS OF U.S. GDP (IN BILLIONS OF DOLLARS)

Year	Consumption Expenditure	Investment Expenditure	Government Expenditure	Net Export Expenditure	Nominal GDP
1980	1,757	479	566	−13	2,789
1985	2,720	736	879	−115	4,220
1990	3,840	861	1,180	−78	5,803
1995	4,976	1,144	1,369	−91	7,398
2000	6,739	1,736	1,722	−380	9,817
2005	8,746	2,105	2,363	−727	12,487

Source: U.S. Bureau of Economic Analysis

THINKING ECONOMICALLY Synthesizing

1. What trend can be seen in U.S. nominal GDP? What can you tell from this about the growth of the U.S. economy? Do you need more information?

2. Which expenditure accounts for most of GDP?

3. Does the proportion of this expenditure to the other two positive expenditures remain about the same in the six years shown here? Briefly explain how you estimated this.

REVIEWING KEY CONCEPTS

1. Explain the relationship between the terms in each of these pairs.

   a. *nominal GDP*
   real GDP

   b. *gross national product*
   net national product

   c. *personal income*
   disposable personal income

2. What are the four components of GDP?

3. What is an example of a durable good? a nondurable good?

4. Name two economic activities that GDP does not measure.

5. Why are transfer payments not included as a government expenditure when calculating GDP?

6. **Using Your Notes** Write a brief summary of the methods used to calculate national income and the purposes of each accounting method. Refer to your completed hierarchy chart.

Use the Graphic Organizer at **Interactive Review @ ClassZone.com**

CRITICAL THINKING

7. **Drawing Conclusions** List some things that have become more expensive during your lifetime. Explain how a rise in price level affects nominal GDP and real GDP.

8. **Making Inferences** If consumption is especially high compared with other years, what might you generalize about the health of the economy?

9. **Explaining an Economic Concept** What is the underground economy? What impact does it have on a nation's GDP?

10. **Drawing Conclusions** Imagine that a new country is discovered on an island in the middle of the Pacific Ocean. The country's people have never left the island, and no foreigners have ever been there. What would the relationship be between the country's GDP and its GNP? Why?

11. **Challenge** How would the following affect GDP?
    a. Government transfer payments increase.
    b. Student sells used CD to record store.
    c. Car owner pays auto repair shop $500 to fix his car.

ECONOMICS IN PRACTICE

Identifying Intermediate and Final Goods

Look at the following list of goods and who purchased them.

Goods	Purchaser
copier paper	accounting firm
refrigerator	home consumer
stainless steel	manufacturer
eggs	home consumer
eggs	factory that makes frozen baked goods
battery	car owner
paint	furniture maker

Categorize Economic Information Decide whether each good is an intermediate good or a final good.

Challenge Why is it important to make a distinction in national income accounting between intermediate and final goods?

357

Business Cycles

OBJECTIVES	KEY TERMS	TAKING NOTES
In Section 2, you will • describe the phases of the business cycle • discuss aggregate demand and aggregate supply • identify the causes of the changes in the business cycle • explain how economists predict business cycle changes • outline major business cycles in U.S. history	business cycle, *p. 358* economic growth, *p. 358* recession, *p. 359* depression, *p. 359* stagflation, *p. 359* aggregate demand, *p. 360* aggregate supply, *p. 360* macroeconomic equilibrium, *p. 361* leading indicators, *p. 364* coincident indicators, *p. 364* lagging indicators, *p. 364*	As you read Section 2, complete a cluster diagram like the one below to record what you learn about business cycles. Use the Graphic Organizer at **Interactive Review @ ClassZone.com** 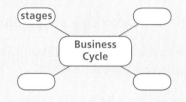

What Is the Business Cycle?

KEY CONCEPTS

Economic changes often follow a broad pattern. During the 1990s, the U.S. economy expanded. In 2001, the economy slowed down. It then returned to a period of growth. Such changes are an example of the **business cycle**, a series of periods of expanding and contracting economic activity. The business cycle is measured by increases or decreases in real GDP. The cycle has four distinct stages: expansion, peak, contraction, and trough.

STAGE 1 Expansion

In the expansion phase, real GDP grows from a low point, or trough, as you can see in the graph in Figure 12.6. The expansion is a period of **economic growth**, an increase in a nation's real gross domestic product (GDP). During an expansion, jobs are relatively easy to find, so unemployment goes down. More and more resources are needed to keep up with spending demand. As resources become more scarce, their prices rise. The length of each phase may vary both within a cycle and from cycle to cycle. The longest expansion in U.S. history took place over the course of ten years from 1991 to 2001.

Business Cycles Workers and businesses ride the ups and downs of the economy.

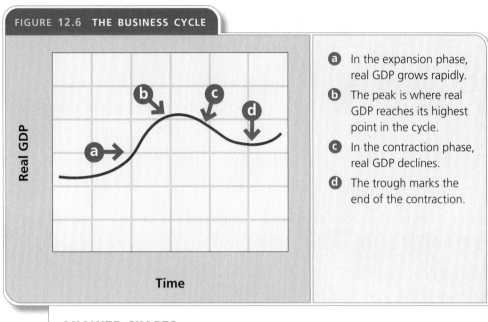

FIGURE 12.6 THE BUSINESS CYCLE

Real GDP

Time

a In the expansion phase, real GDP grows rapidly.

b The peak is where real GDP reaches its highest point in the cycle.

c In the contraction phase, real GDP declines.

d The trough marks the end of the contraction.

ANALYZE CHARTS
1. What stage occurred before point A?
2. What stage will occur after point D?
3. How might the business cycle curve change if nominal GDP was used instead of real GDP?

STAGE 2 Peak

The point at which real GDP is the highest represents the peak of the business cycle. As prices rise and resources tighten, businesses become less profitable. From that point on, real GDP declines as businesses curtail production.

STAGE 3 Contraction

The contraction phase begins after the peak. As producers cut back, resources become less scarce and prices tend to stabilize or fall. Unemployment rises because employers produce less. Sometimes the contraction phase becomes a **recession**, a contraction lasting two or more quarters (six months or more). On rare occasions, as in the 1930s, a contraction turns into a **depression**, an extended period of high unemployment and limited business activity. While prices usually remain about the same or go down during the contraction phase, sometimes they go up. These are periods of **stagflation**—stagnation in business activity and inflation of prices.

STAGE 4 Trough

The final phase of the business cycle is the trough, the point at which real GDP and employment stop declining. A business cycle is complete when it has gone through all four phases, from trough to trough or from peak to peak.

APPLICATION Explaining an Economic Concept

A. In terms of the business cycle, what is unusual about stagflation?

QUICK REFERENCE

Recession is a prolonged economic contraction lasting two or more quarters (six months or more).

Depression is an extended period of high unemployment and reduced business activity.

Stagflation describes periods during which prices rise at the same time that there is a slowdown in business activity.

Aggregate Demand and Supply

One way to understand business cycles is through the concepts of demand and supply. In this case the concepts apply not to a single product or business but to the economy as a whole.

Aggregate Demand

Aggregate demand is the total amount of goods and services that households, businesses, government, and foreign purchasers will buy at each and every price level. In Figure 12.7, the vertical axis, labeled "Price level," shows the average price of all goods and services. The horizontal axis, labeled "Real GDP," shows the economy's total output. The aggregate demand curve (AD) is downward sloping. As the price level decreases the purchasing power of money increases.

Aggregate Supply

Aggregate supply is the total amount of goods and services that producers will provide at each and every price level. Note that in Figure 12.8 the aggregate supply curve (AS) does not look like the supply curves in Chapter 5. The aggregate supply curve is almost horizontal when real GDP is low—during times of recession or depression—because businesses try not to raise their prices when the economy is weak. The middle part of the aggregate supply curve slopes upward, with prices increasing as real GDP increases. But during times of high inflation, prices rise without contributing to real GDP, and the aggregate supply curve becomes almost vertical.

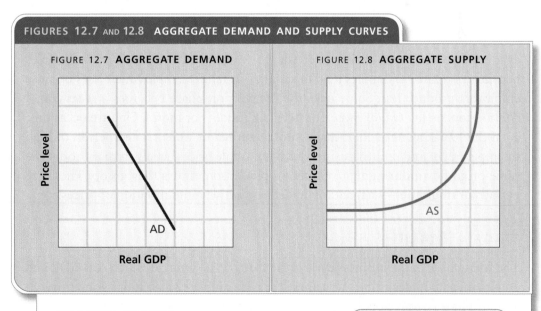

FIGURES 12.7 AND 12.8 AGGREGATE DEMAND AND SUPPLY CURVES

FIGURE 12.7 **AGGREGATE DEMAND**

Price level / Real GDP / AD

FIGURE 12.8 **AGGREGATE SUPPLY**

Price level / Real GDP / AS

ANALYZE GRAPHS

1. What does a normal demand or supply graph use as an x-axis? What does it use as a y-axis?

2. Why are the x and y axes different for the aggregate demand and supply graphs?

Animated **Economics**

Use an interactive aggregate demand and aggregate supply graph at **ClassZone.com**

Macroeconomic Equilibrium

When the quantity of aggregate demand equals the quantity of aggregate supply, the economy reaches **macroeconomic equilibrium**. Figures 12.9 and 12.10 illustrate a variety of different possibilities, but let's consider one particular example shown in Figure 12.9. Macroeconomic equilibrium occurs where the aggregate demand curve (AD1) intersects the aggregate supply curve (AS). P1 indicates the equilibrium price level, and Q1 shows the equilibrium level of real GDP.

Think about business cycles. An increase in aggregate demand shifts the aggregate demand curve to the right (AD2). Aggregate demand becomes greater at all price levels, and equilibrium real GDP rises (Q2), marking an expansion phase. If aggregate demand were to decrease, the aggregate demand curve would shift to the left (AD3). This would result in a lower equilibrium real GDP (Q3)—in other words, an economic contraction.

Shifts in aggregate supply affect real GDP in a similar way, as you can see in Figure 12.10. An increase in aggregate supply shifts the aggregate supply curve to the right (AS2). As aggregate supply increases, the price level goes down (P2) and equilibrium real GDP rises (Q2), marking an expansion phase. If aggregate supply were to decrease, the aggregate supply curve would shift to the left (AS3). The result would be a higher price level (P3) and lower equilibrium real GDP (Q3)—in other words, stagflation.

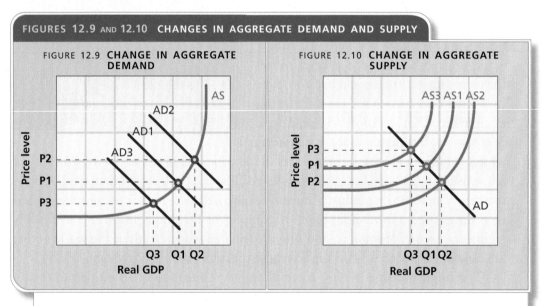

FIGURES **12.9** AND **12.10** CHANGES IN AGGREGATE DEMAND AND SUPPLY

FIGURE 12.9 **CHANGE IN AGGREGATE DEMAND**

FIGURE 12.10 **CHANGE IN AGGREGATE SUPPLY**

ANALYZE GRAPHS

1. As aggregate demand decreases, what happens to price level and real GDP?

2. As aggregate supply decreases, what happens to price level and real GDP?

APPLICATION Analyzing Cause and Effect

B. Assuming aggregate demand remains the same, why does the price level go up when aggregate supply decreases?

Why Do Business Cycles Occur?

KEY CONCEPTS

You have seen that shifts in aggregate demand and aggregate supply indicate changes in the business cycle. But what causes these shifts? Four factors are especially important: (1) decisions made by businesses, (2) changes in interest rates, (3) the expectations of consumers, and (4) external shocks to the economy. These factors involve the "ripple effect," the cause-and-effect interactions that ripple through the economy.

FACTOR 1 Business Decisions

When businesses decide to decrease or increase production, their decisions can have far-reaching effects. If enough businesses make similar decisions, it can lead to a change in the business cycle.

Demand slump Consider the ripple effect of a decision by businesses in the recording industry. In response to a slump in demand, the producers decide to reduce production of compact discs. First, they reduce the number of hours worked at their compact disc manufacturing facilities. Some workers get laid off, others work shorter hours. In a related move, the recording businesses cut back on their investment in new CD manufacturing equipment. That decision will lead to a decrease in the demand for machinery, which puts producers of the machinery in the same situation that the recording businesses were in. The machinery businesses will also cut back on production and lay off workers. The recording industry businesses also decide to reduce the number of new recordings they commission, thereby reducing the income of musicians, recording engineers, record promoters, and other associated workers. All of the workers that are now unemployed or working less must cut back on their purchases.

The single decision by the recording industry businesses had numerous consequences. By itself, it might not be enough to change the business cycle for the entire country. But if enough businesses make similar decisions, a contraction in the business cycle might result.

New technology Alternatively, business decisions can also increase aggregate supply and fuel an expansion. For example, suppose computer chip manufacturers adopt a new technology that greatly reduces production costs. Those manufacturers become more productive—the supply of their products increases and the cost of their products goes down. Businesses that make products that use computer chips can make their products more cheaply. Other businesses may now be able to make new products with the more readily available computer chips. All of these businesses hire more workers to handle the increased production. The aggregate supply increases, and the economy experiences an expansion.

Economics Update

Find an update on factors affecting the business cycle at **ClassZone.com**

FACTOR 2 Changes in Interest Rates

Another event that has a ripple effect in the economy and causes shifts in aggregate demand and supply is a change in interest rates. Rising interest rates, for example, make it more costly for consumers to borrow money to make purchases—from televisions to cars to houses. This decreased purchasing power lowers the level of aggregate demand and promotes a contraction in the economy. When interest rates fall, the opposite happens. Aggregate demand rises, promoting an expansion.

Consider what may happen to businesses when interest rates rise. With the higher cost of borrowing money, businesses may cut back on their investment in capital goods. As you saw earlier, such a cutback would lead to less business activity for the producers of capital goods. As the aggregate supply decreases, a contraction in the economy is likely. But falling interest rates would lead to an increase in aggregate supply and an economic expansion.

Higher or lower interest rates also affect the housing market. When interest rates are low, people are inclined to purchase housing rather than rent, so housing sales and all related economic activities increase, contributing to an economic expansion. When interest rates rise, the high cost of loans limits mortgage eligibility, so more people rent. Housing sales slow down, contributing to an economic contraction.

FACTOR 3 Consumer Expectations

Every month, 5,000 households are surveyed to find out how people are feeling about the economy, and the results are published in the Consumer Confidence Survey report. Why? The way consumers are feeling about prices, business activity, and job prospects influences their economic choices, and their choices can bring about changes in aggregate demand. For example, when consumers are confident about the future and believe that they are economically secure, they tend to consume more, driving up aggregate demand and encouraging an economic expansion.

FACTOR 4 External Issues

A nation's economy can also be strongly influenced by issues and events beyond its control or outside of its borders. Examples include such natural disasters as Hurricanes Katrina and Rita, which struck the Gulf Coast in the summer of 2005. The hurricanes damaged oil refineries, oil wells, and offshore oil platforms. The effects of Katrina and Rita, combined with conflicts in other oil-producing countries, led to higher oil prices and slowed down the growth of the U.S. economy.

The oil embargo of 1973 is another example. The Organization of the Petroleum Exporting Countries (OPEC) reduced the amount of oil supplied to Western nations that had supported Israel in the Yom Kippur and October wars. The price of oil rose by 400 percent. The higher prices raised production costs and resulted in an economic contraction in the United States.

External Issues
Natural disasters can affect the economy. Hurricane Katrina washed this oil-drilling platform into this bridge.

APPLICATION Analyzing Cause and Effect

C. Describe the ripple effect of a natural disaster like Hurricane Katrina on the economy.

Predicting Business Cycles

KEY CONCEPTS

Economists try to predict changes in the business cycle to help businesses and the government make informed economic choices. They base their predictions on sets of economic indicators.

- **Leading indicators** are measures of economic performance that usually change six to nine months *before* real GDP changes. Examples include new building permits, orders for capital goods and consumer goods, consumer expectations, average manufacturing workweek, stock prices, and the money supply. Economists look for trends in these indicators that last several months before they predict a change.

- **Coincident indicators** are measures of economic performance that usually change *at the same time as* real GDP changes. These indicators include such items as employment, sales volume, and personal income.

- **Lagging indicators** are measures of economic performance that usually change *after* real GDP changes. Such indicators are useful for confirming the end of an expansion or contraction in the business cycle. They include length of unemployment and the ratio of consumer credit to personal income.

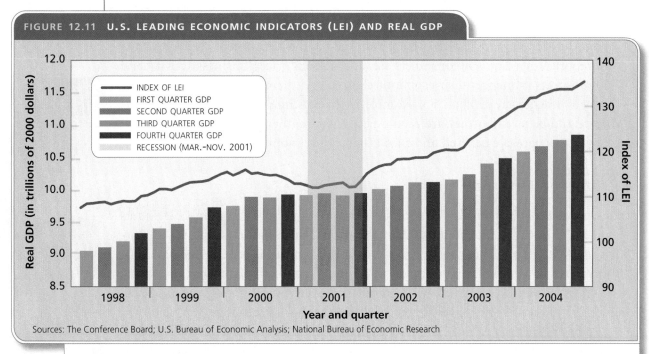

FIGURE 12.11   U.S. LEADING ECONOMIC INDICATORS (LEI) AND REAL GDP

Sources: The Conference Board; U.S. Bureau of Economic Analysis; National Bureau of Economic Research

ANALYZE GRAPHS

1. Find a period of at least four quarters in which the index of leading economic indicators accurately predicted a change in real gross domestic product.

2. Do changes in the real gross domestic product always echo changes in the index of leading economic indicators? What does this say about predicting changes in the nation's economy?

APPLICATION   Using a Decision-Making Process

D. If you were the manager of an electronics store, how might you use the news that leading indicators suggest a contraction in the economy in six months?

Business Cycles in U.S. History

KEY CONCEPTS

The agency that tracks economic indicators and business cycles in the United States is the National Bureau of Economic Research (NBER). It measures contractions from peak to trough and expansions from trough to peak. NBER identified about 20 extended contractions, or recessions, in the American economy in the 20th century. The worst of these by far was the Great Depression.

The Great Depression

"Back in those dark depression days," President Ronald Reagan once recalled, "I saw my father on a Christmas Eve open what he thought was a Christmas greeting from his boss. Instead, it was the blue slip telling him he no longer had a job. The memory of him sitting there holding that slip of paper and then saying in a half whisper, 'That's quite a Christmas present' –it will stay with me as long as I live." Millions of people who lived through the Great Depression were haunted by such memories. For more than a decade, beginning with the stock market crash in 1929, the United States and much of the world suffered a terrible economic contraction. Not until the United States entered World War II in 1941 did the American economy begin a full recovery.

Between the years 1929 and 1933, when the depression was at its worst, U.S. real GDP declined by about a third. Sales in some big businesses, including General Motors Corporation, declined by as much as 50 percent. In the resulting cutbacks, millions of workers lost their jobs. The unemployment rate skyrocketed from 1929 to 1933, leaving one in four American workers jobless. Businesses failed at a higher than usual rate, and banks failed at a tremendously high rate. The number of bank closings, either temporary or permanent, soared from 659 in 1929 to 4,000 in 1933.

The New Deal

President Herbert Hoover, who had been elected in 1928, was not able to bring about a recovery. Franklin D. Roosevelt, accepting the nomination to run for president against Hoover in 1932, promised Americans "a new deal," and the programs he enacted after winning the election came to be known by that name. Roosevelt's New Deal programs focused on federal spending to help the economy revive. Through a number of government agencies created just for this purpose, the American economy came under closer government regulation and many Americans were put back to work—employed by the federal government itself. Spending by the federal government rose from about 3 percent of GDP in the 1920s to about 10 percent in the mid-1930s.

The Great Depression
Millions of Americans were thrown into poverty during the 1930s. These people received soup from a charity kitchen.

In this cartoon, Franklin D. Roosevelt is surrounded by children representing programs created as part of the New Deal.

Economists debate whether the New Deal programs led to sustained economic growth. But when the United States entered World War II in 1941, spending on the war effort also helped the economy to recover. Unemployment plunged to 1.2 percent by 1944.

Business Cycles Since the Great Depression

According to NBER, there have been about a dozen economic contractions and expansions in the U.S. economy since the Great Depression. The recessions have been less severe and have occurred less often than those before the 1930s. However, the contraction of the mid-1970s was an especially difficult time, triggered in part by the Oil Embargo of 1973. The unemployment rate rose from an average of 5.4 percent in the first half of the decade to an average of 7.4 percent from 1975 to 1979. At the same time, prices also rose, creating stagflation.

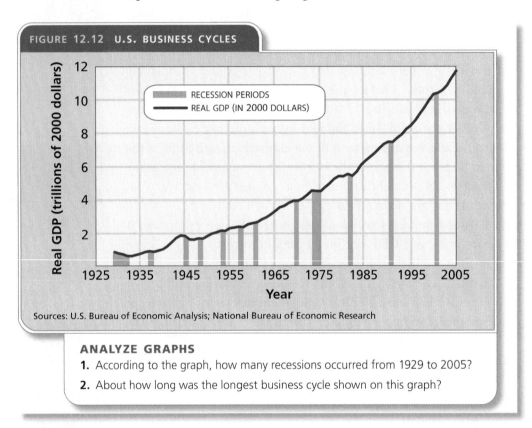

FIGURE 12.12 U.S. BUSINESS CYCLES

Sources: U.S. Bureau of Economic Analysis; National Bureau of Economic Research

ANALYZE GRAPHS
1. According to the graph, how many recessions occurred from 1929 to 2005?
2. About how long was the longest business cycle shown on this graph?

The 1990s, in contrast, saw strong economic expansion, fueled in part by the explosive growth of information technology. The economy experienced a brief recession in the early 2000s, which was extended slightly by the terrorist attacks on September 11, 2001. Through 2005, the U.S. economy continued to expand, although not at the heated pace of the 1990s.

APPLICATION Making Inferences and Drawing Conclusions

E. One industry that flourished during the Great Depression was the movie industry. Comedies were especially popular, and stories often portrayed the lives of the wealthy. Why do you think the movie industry fared so well?

REVIEWING KEY CONCEPTS

1. Explain the relationship between the terms in each of these pairs.

   a. *contraction*   **b.** *aggregate demand*   **c.** *leading indicators*
   expansion   *aggregate supply*   *lagging indicators*

2. Between which two points of the business cycle is a contraction measured?

3. What is the difference between *demand* and *aggregate demand*?

4. Name four factors that can trigger changes in the business cycle.

5. Name three coincident indicators of the Great Depression.

6. **Using Your Notes** Write a brief statement of your expectations for the economy from the point of view of the consumer. Use your completed cluster diagram and make references to what you have learned about the business cycle.

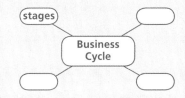

   Use the Graphic Organizer at **Interactive Review @ ClassZone.com**

CRITICAL THINKING

7. **Comparing and Contrasting Economic Information** What were the similarities and differences between the Great Depression and the recession in the 1970s?

8. **Solving Economic Problems** Did President Roosevelt's New Deal focus on generating aggregate demand, or was its main focus on increasing aggregate supply? Explain.

9. **Analyzing Cause and Effect** Are the components that are considered leading economic indicators causes or effects of changes in the business cycle?

10. **Challenge** In the 1990s many people speculated that the economy had been transformed by new technologies. Paul A. Volcker, former chairman of the U.S. Federal Reserve Bank, described it this way: "The speed of communication, the speed of information transfer, the cheapness of communication, the ease of moving things around the world are a difference in kind as well as degree." Do you think that business cycles are inevitable? Can they ever be eliminated entirely? Explain your answer.

ECONOMICS IN PRACTICE

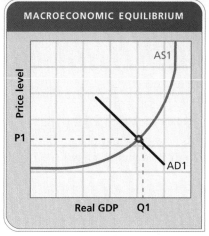

MACROECONOMIC EQUILIBRIUM

Interpreting Graphs

The graph shows an economy at its macroeconomic equilibrium, where the aggregate demand curve (AD1) intersects the aggregate supply curve (AS1). P1 indicates the equilibrium price level, and Q1 shows the equilibrium level of real GDP.

Draw Aggregate Demand and Aggregate Supply Curves

Read the following scenarios. Copy the graph onto your own paper, then graph the changes that would occur in the Scenario 1 in blue. Graph the changes that would occur in the Scenario 2 in red.

Scenario 1: In a booming economy, interest rates begin to rise. Manufacturers and other producers, wary of borrowing money at higher rates, begin to cut back on production.

Scenario 2: Consumer confidence is high. Most people are optimistic about their job prospects and security, and they are willing to spend money on luxuries.

Challenge As a consumer, how might your confidence be affected in Scenario 1?

Use *SMARTGrapher* @ ClassZone.com to complete this activity.

Stimulating Economic Growth

OBJECTIVES	KEY TERMS	TAKING NOTES
In Section 3, you will • explain how economists measure growth • analyze the causes of economic growth • discuss how productivity and economic growth are related	real GDP per capita, *p. 369* labor input, *p. 371* capital deepening, *p. 371* productivity, *p. 372* multifactor productivity, *p. 372*	As you read Section 3, complete a summary chart like the one below to record what you learn about economic growth. Use the Graphic Organizer at **Interactive Review @ ClassZone.com** What Is Economic Growth?

What Is Economic Growth?

KEY CONCEPTS

In Section 2 you learned about the business cycle, the pattern of expansion and contraction in a nation's economy. In this section you will learn more about economic growth, as measured by changes in real gross domestic product (GDP).

Gauging Economic Growth

Before Adam Smith (whom you learned about in Chapter 1, Section 4), many people believed that population growth and higher taxation were the secrets to economic growth. The theory held that more people paying more taxes was the best way to fill a nation's treasury. Another view, called mercantilism, argued that increased national wealth came through exporting more goods than a country imports. In this way, the country would gain gold or silver currency from other countries.

Adam Smith, however, saw that the real "wealth of nations" lay in their productive capacities. Taxes could be so high that they limit the amount of funds available for business investment and consumer spending, thereby reducing economic growth. In Smith's view, foreign trade allows a country to focus its resources on what it does best. The more efficiently a nation uses its resources, the more productive it will be and the larger its economy will grow. Smith's views proved to be accurate, and they serve as the basis for modern economics.

The best measure of economic growth is not simply the amount of money a nation has or how much its population increases, but rather the increase in its real GDP. The rate at which real GDP changes is a good indicator of how well a country's resources are being utilized.

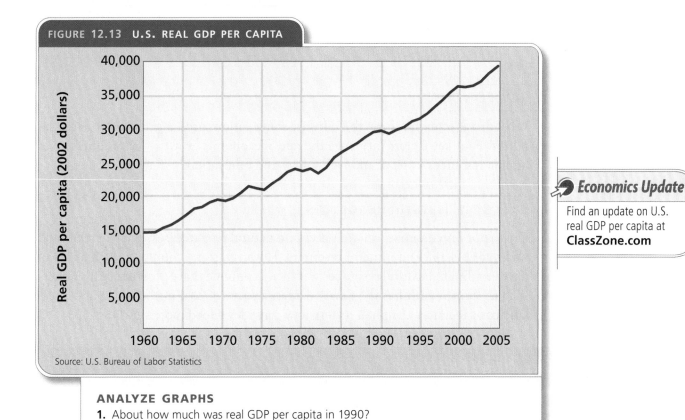

FIGURE 12.13 U.S. REAL GDP PER CAPITA

Real GDP per capita (2002 dollars)

Source: U.S. Bureau of Labor Statistics

ANALYZE GRAPHS

1. About how much was real GDP per capita in 1990?
2. About how many years did it take for real GDP per capita to double from its level in 1960?

Population and Economic Growth

Population growth influences economic growth. A country's real GDP might be growing, but if its population is growing at an even faster rate, the increase in real GDP might simply reflect more workers contributing to the economy. Think of a potluck dinner. If each person brings one dish, the amount of food per person will be the same whether you invite 10 people or 100.

To get a clearer picture of economic growth, economists use a measure called **real GDP per capita**, which is real GDP divided by total population. Real GDP per capita reflects each person's share of real GDP. In terms of the potluck dinner, if each person brings more than one dish to the next potluck, the amount of food per person will have increased.

Real GDP per capita is the usual measure of a nation's standard of living. Nations with higher real GDP per capita tend to have populations that are better educated and healthier. However, real GDP per capita does not mean that each person gets that amount of money. Some people will get more, others less. It also does not measure quality of life. For example, people might have to work longer hours to achieve higher rates of economic growth, leaving them with less leisure time.

QUICK REFERENCE

Real GDP per capita is real GDP divided by total population.

APPLICATION Explaining an Economic Concept

A. Why does a nation's real GDP have to increase at a faster rate than its population for significant economic growth to take place?

Economic Indicators and Measurements 369

What Determines Economic Growth?

KEY CONCEPTS

What drives economic growth? Why are some nations growing at a faster pace than others? Four key factors influence the rate of economic growth—natural resources, human resources, capital, and technology and innovation.

FACTOR 1 Natural Resources

One factor in economic growth is access to natural resources, especially arable land, water, forests, oil, and mineral resources. However, some countries, such as Japan, have very limited natural resources, yet their economies have grown rapidly. Others, such as India, which has the fourth-largest reserve of coal in the world and arable land covering more than half its territory, have developed more slowly.

A GLOBAL PERSPECTIVE

Do Natural Resources Guarantee Wealth?

Not necessarily. In fact, countries with abundant natural resources generally do not perform as well economically as countries with fewer natural resources—a phenomenon economists refer to as "the resource curse." In Nigeria, for example, although oil is plentiful, personal income is low. GDP per capita is about $1,400 (in U.S. dollars). Poverty is widespread, with an estimated 60 percent of Nigeria's population below the poverty line—and Nigeria has the largest population of any African country.

At the other end of the spectrum is Japan. Although the country has few natural resources, the strength of Japan's economy is second only to that of the United States. GDP per capita is about $30,000 (in U.S. dollars). What Nigeria lacks, but Japan has, are the basic structures of a free market economy—private ownership, the profit motive, an effective government, and economic competition. These economic institutions are more important than natural resources for generating economic growth. Japan, with few natural resources, achieved economic success by developing alternative sources of wealth—industry and foreign trade.

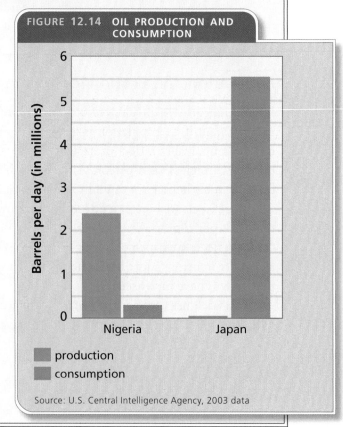

FIGURE 12.14 OIL PRODUCTION AND CONSUMPTION

Barrels per day (in millions)

Nigeria   Japan

■ production
■ consumption

Source: U.S. Central Intelligence Agency, 2003 data

CONNECTING ACROSS THE GLOBE

1. **Synthesizing Economic Information** What role do natural resources play in a country's economic strength? Explain your answer.

2. **Drawing Conclusions** Figure 12.14 illustrates oil production and consumption in Nigeria and Japan. What would happen to each country's economy if it produced less oil? What if each produced more?

FACTOR 2 Human Resources

Another key factor in economic growth is the labor force. Economists measure this partly through **labor input**—the size of the labor force multiplied by the length of the workweek. The steady declines in the length of the workweek in most countries since the early 1900s have been more than made up for by the growth in the population, so labor input has grown. Perhaps even more important than the raw numbers, however, is the level of human capital—the skills and knowledge—that the labor force brings to its tasks. Some economists believe that human capital is the single most important component in economic growth.

QUICK REFERENCE

Labor input is the size of the labor force multiplied by the length of the workweek.

FACTOR 3 Capital

You learned in Chapter 1 that natural resources, labor, and capital come together through the creativity of an entrepreneur to produce goods and services. Capital is critical to this process and to economic growth. More and better capital goods increase output: the more machines a factory has and the better designed they are, the more goods the factory can churn out. Multiply this by the number of factories across a nation and the increased output equals higher GDP.

The economy also grows when more capital is available per worker. An increase in the capital to labor ratio is called **capital deepening**. In other words, workers are provided with more and better equipment to work with. The Industrial Revolution is a prime example of capital deepening. Sewing machines, for example, allowed clothing manufacturers to make more clothing per worker than if the workers had been sewing by hand.

QUICK REFERENCE

Capital deepening is an increase in the ratio of capital to labor.

FACTOR 4 Technology and Innovation

Technology and innovation are also important factors in economic growth. These factors promote the efficient use of other resources, which in turn leads to increased output. Some of the key technological developments that have contributed to economic growth include steam power, electricity, and the automobile.

Innovations can also increase economic growth. Something as simple as adjusting an order form can contribute to economic growth by reducing the amount of time needed to complete a task. Other innovations might improve customer service or reduce the amount of material needed to create a product.

Information technology has had a strong impact on economic growth. Technological advances in producing the information technology itself have led to a dramatic decline in prices. With lower prices for technology, firms are engaging in capital deepening without having to spend more money.

Technology and Innovation
Technological advancements have increased economic growth.

APPLICATION Writing About Economics

B. Using the four factors, explain how developing countries like Nigeria might improve their economic growth.

Productivity and Economic Growth

Productivity refers to the amount of output produced from a set amount of inputs. When the same amount of inputs produces more output, productivity has increased. In Chapter 9, you learned about labor productivity—the amount of goods or services produced by a worker in an hour. But the broader sense of productivity includes the productivity of both labor and capital.

For example, imagine that you begin building bookshelves. The inputs would include your labor plus capital, in the form of the workshop, hammers, glue, and other supplies. At first, it may take you a week to complete one bookshelf. In the process, you may waste materials as you make mistakes, and you may find that some of your tools are not ideal for the task. But after you have built several bookshelves and acquired the right tools for the job, your productivity increases. Using the same amount of input, you might now be able to produce two bookshelves per week.

This section concerns the productivity of a country's entire economy. As a country becomes more productive, its economy is likely to grow.

How Is Productivity Measured?

To measure the productivity of a single business, you would compare the inputs to the outputs. Using the bookshelf example, you would compare the amount of capital and number of hours worked to the number of bookshelves produced. But how can we measure the productivity of a nation's economy, which is made up of millions of different people and businesses? Economists use a measurement called **multifactor productivity**, the ratio between an industry's economic output and its labor and capital inputs. By collecting multifactor productivity data on a country's major industries and business sectors, economists can estimate the productivity of the entire economy.

What Contributes to Productivity?

Several factors contribute to changes in productivity.

Quality of Labor A better educated, healthier workforce tends to be more productive. Using the bookshelf example, if you were to take classes in woodworking, your enhanced knowledge would enable you to produce more and better shelves. In general, the more educated the workforce, the more productive it is. As for health, people are usually more productive when they feel well than when they feel sluggish or ill.

Technological Innovation Historically, as during the Industrial Revolution, new machines and technologies helped countries produce more output from the same amount of inputs. In recent times, the desktop computer and computer technology generally have generated productivity gains.

Energy Costs Gas, electricity, and other fuels power the technologies that increase productivity. When energy costs rise, those tools become more expensive to use and productivity declines. By the same token, when energy costs fall, using advanced tools becomes less expensive and productivity rises.

Financial Markets The easier it is for funds to flow to where they are needed, the more productive the economy becomes. Banks, stock markets, and similar institutions allow a country's funds to be put to their best use. When such institutions do not exist or when they do not function efficiently, productivity is reduced.

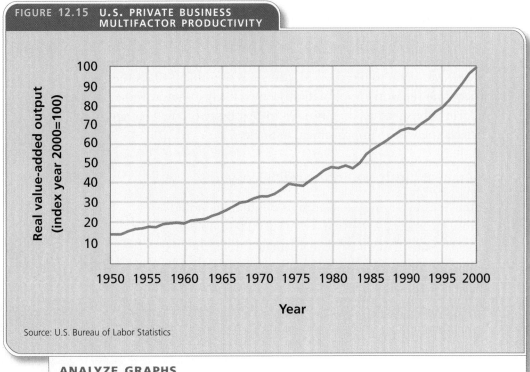

FIGURE 12.15 U.S. PRIVATE BUSINESS MULTIFACTOR PRODUCTIVITY

Source: U.S. Bureau of Labor Statistics

ANALYZE GRAPHS

1. What happened to productivity in the three years after the 1973 oil embargo? Why?

2. Compare this graph with Figure 12.13 on page 369, which shows real per capita GDP. How closely is economic growth related to productivity?

How Are Productivity and Growth Related?

Economic growth is a measure of change in production. It does not consider how much effort or how many resources it took to produce that quantity of production. Productivity, on the other hand, is a measure of efficiency. It reflects the amount of effort and resources it took to produce a certain quantity.

A country could experience economic growth—as measured by real GDP—without increasing its productivity. Such growth would be tied to an increase in the quantity of natural resources, labor, capital, or technology. If the productivity of a country increases, its real GDP can grow without increasing the quantity of inputs.

As shown in Figure 12.15, productivity in the United States grew at a steady pace from 1950 to 2000. Among other things, a better educated labor force and advances in information technology contributed to the increase. The dips in the graph represent productivity setbacks, such as tighter financial markets during recessions.

APPLICATION Drawing Conclusions

C. Some countries have limited natural resources but high economic growth. Does this prove that worldwide economic growth is unlimited by natural resources? Why or why not?

Thomas Robert Malthus: The Population Problem

Economics Update

Find an update on Thomas Robert Malthus at **ClassZone.com**

In the late 1700s, many European thinkers and writers predicted a future of peace and harmony in which poverty and hunger would be eliminated. Discussing humanity's future with his father led Thomas Robert Malthus to question whether the prevailing view was perhaps too rosy. Malthus saw a problem that others had overlooked, namely, that the world's population seemed likely to outgrow the available supply of food. He published his ideas in 1798 in "An Essay on the Principle of Population as It Affects the Future Improvement of Society."

A Natural Limit to Economic Growth?

Malthus's essay argued that human population would increase geometrically—that is, it would double—every 25 years. Malthus also estimated that food production would only increase arithmetically—that is, by the same amount each time—over that time period. Figure 12.16 uses hypothetical numbers to illustrate the problem. As time went on, agriculture would produce less food per person, and millions would be thrown into poverty and starvation.

"An Essay on the Principle of Population" caused a tremendous backlash. People could not accept that the rosy future they had imagined might not come to pass. Malthus and his essay were widely attacked and criticized—but no one could ignore his argument.

Malthus's estimates turned out to be flawed. Human population increased at a slower pace than he predicted. World population was about 1 billion in 1800, but it took until 1930 to reach 2 billion. Agricultural productivity rose dramatically with the introduction of mechanized farming and advances in fertilization and pest control. Although world population accelerated around 1950, reaching about 6.5 billion by 2005, agricultural production kept pace with the growing population.

Thomas Robert Malthus
Malthus predicted a population explosion that would result in poverty and famine.

FIGURE 12.16 MALTHUS'S POPULATION PROBLEM			
Elapsed Years	Bushels of Wheat (in millions)	Population (in millions)	Bushels per Person
0	10	10	1.00
25	20	20	1.00
50	30	40	0.75
75	40	80	0.50
100	50	160	0.31

APPLICATION Applying Economic Concepts

D. How is Malthus's population problem an example of the problem of scarcity?

REVIEWING KEY CONCEPTS

1. Explain the differences between the terms in each of these pairs.

   a. *economic growth*
   real GDP per capita

   b. *capital deepening*
   labor input

2. Name the key measurement of economic growth.

3. What four factors drive economic growth?

4. How are productivity and growth related?

5. Briefly explain the problem Malthus identified.

6. **Using Your Notes** Write a persuasive paragraph arguing one side or the other of economic growth possibilities. Refer to your completed summary chart.

What Is Economic Growth?		

   Use the Graphic Organizer at **Interactive Review @ ClassZone.com**

CRITICAL THINKING

7. **Solving Economic Problems** In 2000, the world's population was about 6 billion, and about 800 million of those people did not have enough to eat. By 2050, the world's population is expected to grow to about 9 billion. What steps should we take now to avoid having more than 1 billion people without enough to eat by 2050? Employ the ideas you learned about in this section in formulating your solution.

8. **Explaining an Economic Concept** Why is real GDP per capita a useful measure? Why couldn't real GDP or GDP per capita be used for the same purpose?

9. **Analyzing Cause and Effect** Globalization opens international boundaries to companies, creating markets that stretch around the world. What role might global competition play in the development of innovations?

10. **Challenge** Going to school is your job. Your product is increasing your knowledge, and your grades are the main measure of this. Increasing your productivity would result in better grades—and more free time. Adapt the factors that contribute to economic productivity to explain how you might increase your productivity as a student.

ECONOMICS IN PRACTICE

A busy factory is one route to economic growth.

Stimulating Economic Growth
Government policies affect economic growth. Some policies have immediate effects that last for a short time. Other policies take longer to show results but have lasting impact.

Create a Healthy Economy
Reflecting on what you learned in this section, consider the following possible government actions.

- open a protected wilderness area for coal mining

- increase funding for scholarships for low-income students

- provide tax breaks for companies purchasing new equipment

- strengthen laws protecting the rights of inventors

Explain how each potential action might lead to economic growth.

Challenge Estimate the costs and the benefits of each action. Which actions would have the most lasting positive effect on the economy?

Poland: Economic Freedom and Economic Growth

Background Communists ruled Poland and controlled its economy from 1948 to 1989. After holding its first free elections in 1990, Poland made rapid progress toward full democracy and a free market economy. Economic reforms included ending government price controls, privatizing industries formerly controlled by the government, and entering the international marketplace. As Poland moved away from government control of the economy, it experienced a surge in economic growth—outdistancing many other former Communist countries in eastern and central Europe. In 2004, Poland became a member of the European Union, further increasing its economic potential.

What's the issue? How successful is Poland's economy? Read these documents to learn about the challenges and rewards of the country's economic transition.

A. Online News Article

Wroclaw, a city in southwest Poland, offers one example of the country's success through embracing global capitalism. This article describes that phenomenon.

Wroclaw, Poland: Europe's Next Appliance Capital?

Appliance Manufacturers Pour into Southwest Poland

Money and companies are pouring in—not just the prestige nameplates like Bombardier, Siemens, Whirlpool, Toyota, and Volvo, but also the network of suppliers that inevitably follows them. At first, most of the new jobs were of the semi-skilled variety. Now they have been followed by design and engineering work that aims to tap into the largest concentration of university students in Eastern Europe.

"Everyone is coming, and they are coming very fast," reports Josu Ugarte . . . who heads the appliance manufacturing operations here of Mondragon, the giant Spanish industrial cooperative. He predicts, confidently, that the region around Wroclaw will soon surpass Northern Italy as Europe's appliance capital. . . .

The secret isn't just lower wages. It's also the attitude of workers who take pride and are willing to do what is necessary to succeed, even if it means outsourcing parts production or working on weekends or altering vacation schedules. . . .

Source: "Europe's Capitalism Curtain" WashingtonPost.com July 23, 2004

Many manufacturers have opened factories in Wroclaw, Poland. This Volvo factory produces buses.

Thinking Economically How has Poland's human capital contributed to the country's economic growth?

Poland's farmers were sceptical about the benefits of European Union membership. This cartoon reflects their change of heart as agricultural exports increased and they received new subsidies from the European Union.

Source: The Economist

Thinking Economically Does the cartoon emphasize the free market benefits of the European Union or other benefits?

C. Magazine Article

Joining the European Union brought tremendous growth to Poland's economy. This article explains some of the elements that led to the success.

Reaping the European Union Harvest

How the new central European members learnt to stop worrying and love the European Union

After grumbling furiously about dangers to their sovereignty and their social values when they joined the European Union in May, Poles are discovering themselves now to be among the Union's most loyal citizens. Some three-quarters say they are happy with EU membership—and no wonder. In its first eight months of membership Poland got some €2.5 billion [€ is the euro, the currency of the European Union] ($3.4 billion) from the EU budget, or roughly twice what it paid in, according to the newspaper Rzeczpospolita. Rural incomes have risen by one-third for small farmers and two-thirds for big ones, reversing eight years of stagnation and decline, thanks to munificent EU subsidies and an influx of foreign buyers offering high prices for Polish meat and fruit.

Poland's total exports rose by more than 30% in the first nine months of 2004, helped by the abolition of customs formalities. EU rules have opened the skies to budget airlines, boosting tourist numbers by 20% last year. Higher-than-expected tax revenues have meant lower-than-expected budget deficits. . . .

Source: *The Economist*, January 8, 2005

Thinking Economically According to the document, how has membership in the EU helped Poland's economic growth?

THINKING ECONOMICALLY **Synthesizing**

1. Which economic measurements and indicators are evident in documents A and C? Explain what they convey about the strengths and weaknesses of Poland's economy.

2. What factors have driven Poland's economic growth?

3. Compare documents A and C, written about six months apart. What continued economic trends and new economic strengths do they describe?

Interactive ←→ Review

Review this chapter using interactive
activities at **ClassZone.com**
- Online Summary
- Quizzes
- Vocabulary Flip Cards
- Graphic Organizers
- Review and Study Notes

 Online Summary

Complete the following activity either on your
own paper or online at **ClassZone.com**

Choose the key concept that best completes
the sentence. Not all key concepts will be used.

aggregate demand
aggregate supply
business cycle
capital deepening
coincident indicators
depression
disposable personal income (DPI)
economic growth
gross domestic product (GDP)
gross national product (GNP)
lagging indicators
leading indicators

macroeconomic equilibrium
national income (NI)
national income accounting
net national product (NNP)
nominal GDP
nonmarket activities
per capita real GDP
personal income (PI)
real GDP
recession
stagflation
underground economy

__1__, the market value of all goods and services
produced in a nation, is one of the key measurements used in __2__. __3__ is especially useful because
it gives the market value of all goods and services
corrected for price level changes. Another very
useful measurement is __4__, which shows the
actual amount of money people have to spend.

The economy goes through regular changes
called the __5__. Economists watch __6__, such as
building permits issued and stock prices, to
predict changes in the economy. Low points in the
economy are usually self-correcting, but in times
of a __7__, such as the one that happened in the
1930s, government intervention may be needed.

Several factors influence __8__, including an
increase in capital. __9__, an increase in the ratio
between capital and labor, increases productivity,
helping the economy grow. Economists use
__10__, real GDP divided by whole population,
to distinguish an increase in population from a
higher level of economic output.

CHAPTER **12 Assessment**

REVIEWING KEY CONCEPTS

**Gross Domestic Product and Other Indicators
(pp. 350–357)**

1. What is the purpose of national income
accounting?

2. In what way is GDP a baseline for other economic
indicators?

Business Cycles (pp. 358–367)

3. What do leading indicators say about the economy?

4. Explain how a business decision might have a ripple
effect that would tilt the economy on a new phase
of the business cycle.

Stimulating Economic Growth (pp. 368–377)

5. Explain how a country with few natural resources
can still have economic growth.

6. What are the four key factors that influence economic
growth?

APPLYING ECONOMIC CONCEPTS

The table below shows the size of the underground
economies of selected countries.

FIGURE 12.17	UNDERGROUND ECONOMIES IN SELECTED COUNTRIES	
Country	GDP Per Capita (in U.S. dollars)	Underground Economy as Percent of GDP
Egypt	3,900	69
Thailand	8,300	70
Russia	11,100	44
Chile	11,300	19
Singapore	28,100	14
Italy	29,200	27
Switzerland	32,300	9
United States	41,800	10

Sources: International Monetary Fund, U.S. Central
Intelligence Agency, 1998-2005 data

7. Is there a relationship between GDP per capita and
the size of a country's underground economy?

8. If a country incorporated its underground economy
into the main economy, what would happen to its
GDP per capita? Why?

9. **Creating Graphs** Copy the blank graph onto your own paper. Then use the data in the table to create a line graph showing the percent change in U.S. real gross domestic product from 1999 through 2003.

Use 🖉**SMART**Grapher @ ClassZone.com to complete this activity.

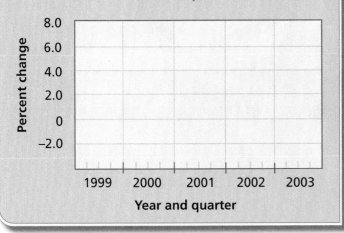

FIGURE 12.18 **PERCENT CHANGE IN REAL GDP FROM PRECEDING PERIOD**

Year	Quarter 1	Quarter 2	Quarter 3	Quarter 4
1999	3.4	3.4	4.8	7.3
2000	1.0	6.4	0.5	2.1
2001	0.5	1.2	1.4	1.6
2002	2.7	2.2	2.4	0.2
2003	1.7	3.7	7.2	3.6

Source: U.S. Bureau of Economic Analysis

10. **Analyzing and Interpreting Data** Which year had the highest growth? The lowest?

11. **Analyzing Cause and Effect** The government enacted tax cuts and issued child tax credit refunds in 2003. What component of GDP would likely have increased because of these?

12. **Distinguishing Fact from Opinion** Does the graph support or counter the idea that the September 11, 2001 terrorist attacks caused a recession?

13. **Challenge** How could GDP grow by 5 percent a year but leave the economy no better off—or even worse off? Give two different explanations.

Surveying Consumer Confidence

The Consumer Confidence Survey is one poll used to determine consumer expectations. Another is the ABC/Washington Post Consumer Comfort Index, which makes 1,000 phone calls to adults each month and asks the following questions:

• National Economy: "Would you describe the state of the nation's economy these days as excellent, good, not so good, or poor?"

• Personal Finances: "Would you describe the state of your own personal finances these days as excellent, good, not so good, or poor?"

• Buying Climate: "Considering the cost of things today and your own personal finances, would you say now is an excellent time, a good time, a not so good time, or a poor time to buy the things you want and need?"

To understand the consumer comfort index better, take a survey of your class.

Step 1. Break into five small groups and discuss each of the questions. The point is to share your thoughts, not to debate who is right or wrong.

Step 2. Return to your desk and write down your answers to each of the questions anonymously.

Step 3. Collect the anonymous answers from the whole class. Have one person tabulate the answers to each question on the board.

Step 4. Now calculate the consumer confidence of your class. For each question, add up the number of positive responses (either "excellent" or "good"). Then subtract the number of negative responses (either "not so good" or "poor"). Divide by the total number of students and multiply by 100.

Add the result from all three questions together, and then divide by three. That will yield an overall comfort level. A level of 100 would mean everyone is satisfied with everything. A level of −100 would mean that everyone felt negatively about everything.

Step 5. Discuss the result. Does it seem to accurately reflect the mood of the class? What would happen to the nation's GDP if all consumers felt as you do?

Economic Challenges
The national economy faces many challenges. Economics can help us understand and cope with these challenges.

Facing Economic Challenges

CONCEPT REVIEW

Business cycle is the series of growing and shrinking periods of economic activity, measured by increases or decreases in real gross domestic product.

CHAPTER 13 KEY CONCEPT

Unemployment has a variety of causes. Some level of unemployment is expected, even when an economy is healthy.

WHY THE CONCEPT MATTERS

As the nation's economy goes through business cycles, it will face the twin problems of unemployment and inflation. You may find yourself unemployed at some point during your working years, if only for a short period. For some people, persistent unemployment leads to poverty. During periods of inflation, you may have a job but your wages may buy less.

Online Highlights

More at ClassZone.com

 Economics Update
Go to **ECONOMICS UPDATE** for chapter updates and further information on inflation in the 1970s. (See Case Study, pp. 404–405.) ▶

SMART Grapher
Go to **SMART GRAPHER** to complete graphing activities in this chapter.

Interactive ◀◀Review
Go to **INTERACTIVE REVIEW** for concept review and activities.

How did inflation in the 1970s affect people and businesses? See the Case Study on pages 404–405.

Unemployment in Today's Economy

OBJECTIVES	KEY TERMS	TAKING NOTES
In Section 1, you will • explain how economists measure unemployment • identify the different types of unemployment • discuss the impact that unemployment has on the economy and on individuals	unemployment rate, *p. 382* underemployed, *p. 383* full employment, *p. 383* frictional unemployment, *p. 384* seasonal unemployment, *p. 384* structural unemployment, *p. 384* cyclical unemployment, *p. 384*	As you read Section 1, complete a cluster diagram like the one below to record and organize what you learn about unemployment. Use the Graphic Organizer at **Interactive Review @ ClassZone.com** 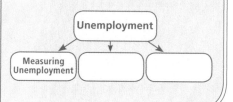

Measuring Unemployment

KEY CONCEPTS

In November 2005, General Motors Corporation announced that it would close or scale back about a dozen plants and lay off about 30,000 workers. The impact of a decision like that on the towns where the factories are located can be extensive. Because the unemployed cannot buy as many goods and services as they did when they had a paycheck, other area businesses might decrease output, and they might even lay off some of their own workers. If businesses across the country decide to stop hiring or to cut back, the decreased production might reduce gross domestic product (GDP), the leading measure of a country's economic health. Economists use unemployment figures to judge the performance of the economy. The measure they use most is the **unemployment rate**, the percentage of the labor force that is jobless and actively looking for work.

Unemployment Job fairs allow people looking for work to meet with many potential employers.

The Unemployment Rate

The civilian labor force, as you learned in Chapter 9, is made up of people over the age of 16 who are employed or actively looking and available for work. It does not include people in the military or those in schools, prisons, or other institutions. To determine the unemployment rate, the U.S. Bureau of Labor Statistics (BLS) surveys the labor

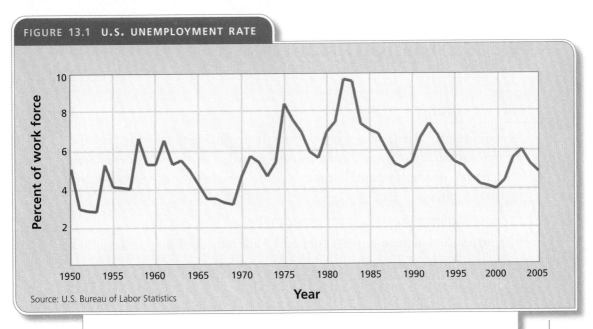

FIGURE 13.1 U.S. UNEMPLOYMENT RATE

Source: U.S. Bureau of Labor Statistics

ANALYZE GRAPHS

1. From 1950 to 2005, when was the unemployment rate the highest?
2. From 1950 to 2005, when was the unemployment rate the lowest?

Economics Update

Find an update on the U.S. unemployment rate at **ClassZone.com**

force in 60,000 households each month. Workers over the age of 16 who are not working but are able to work and who have looked for work sometime during the previous four weeks are considered unemployed. The BLS then divides the number of unemployed persons by the total number of workers in the civilian labor force to arrive at the unemployment rate. While very useful, the unemployment rate does not account for discouraged workers who have stopped looking for work. Nor does it count the **underemployed**, those who work part-time when they want full-time employment or those who work at a job below their skill level. These include recently laid-off workers who may be in a temporary, lower-paying job.

Full Employment

Despite its name, **full employment** does not mean a zero unemployment rate. Instead, it means a level of unemployment in which none of the unemployment is caused by decreased economic activity. Even in a healthy economy there is always some level of unemployment. Sometimes people become unemployed when they relocate or when they leave one job to try to find another job that suits them better. Sometimes the available jobs do not match up with the skills of the available workers. In other words, some amount of unemployment is inevitable.

Economists generally agree that an unemployment rate of four to six percent indicates full employment in the United States. In other countries, with different labor markets and economic policies, full employment may occur at higher or lower rates of unemployment.

QUICK REFERENCE

The **underemployed** are part-time workers who want to work full-time or people working below their skill level.

Full employment means no unemployment caused by decreased economic activity.

APPLICATION Explaining an Economic Concept

A. Explain why the unemployment rate is based on a country's civilian labor force, not its entire population.

Types of Unemployment

KEY CONCEPTS

KEY CONCEPTS

Economists pay attention not only to the unemployment statistics, but also to the reasons for unemployment. Economists recognize four types of unemployment:

- **Frictional unemployment**, temporary unemployment experienced by people changing jobs
- **Seasonal unemployment**, unemployment linked to seasonal work
- **Structural unemployment**, a situation where jobs exist but workers looking for work do not have the necessary skills for these jobs
- **Cyclical unemployment**, unemployment caused by a part of the business cycle with decreased economic activity

QUICK REFERENCE

Frictional unemployment is temporary unemployment of people changing jobs.

Structural unemployment is when jobs exist but do not match the skills of available workers.

Seasonal unemployment is unemployment linked to seasonal work.

Cyclical unemployment is unemployment caused by a part of the business cycle with decreased economic activity.

TYPE 1 Frictional Unemployment

Frictional unemployment refers to the temporary unemployment of workers moving from one job to another. The frictionally unemployed might include a parent who has spent time at home raising children and decides to move back into the work force; a magazine designer who leaves his job to seek work as a designer at a book publisher; or a recent college graduate who is looking for her first full-time job. Frictional unemployment is a reflection of workers' freedom to find the work best suited for them at the highest possible wage. Economists consider frictional unemployment normal and not a threat to economic stability.

TYPE 2 Seasonal Unemployment

Demand for some jobs changes dramatically from season to season, resulting in seasonal unemployment. Demand for construction workers, for example, typically falls in the winter months when construction activities are more difficult. Tourism peaks at certain times of the year, and different regions have different tourist seasons. Migrant farm workers, who move from one area to another following the growing schedules of the crops, are hard hit by seasonal unemployment. The winter months are especially slow, resulting in economic hardship for many migrant families.

TYPE 3 Structural Unemployment

Structural unemployment results when the available jobs do not match up well with the skills and experience of the available workers. A dynamic economy will often create structural unemployment as businesses become more efficient and require fewer workers to create the same amount of output. There are a number of possible triggers for structural unemployment. New technology can replace human workers or require workers to retrain. New industries requiring specialized education can leave less well-educated workers

Seasonal Unemployment
Demand for lifeguards is high during the warmer months.

Offshore Outsourcing: Scourge or Boon?

Many American workers fear losing their jobs to offshore outsourcing—the contracting of work to suppliers in other countries. But the likelihood of offshore outsourcing varies widely from one occupation to the next. According to a report issued by the McKinsey Global Institute in 2005, about 11 percent of all service jobs in the United States have the potential to be outsourced to another country. Jobs in information technology, engineering, and accounting are much more likely to be outsourced than jobs in health care, retail sales, and other fields that require direct personal interaction.

Office worker in India

The offshore outsourcing trend has created some structural unemployment, as laid-off workers seek new jobs. But ultimately, it should make the U.S. economy more efficient. The firms that save money by outsourcing will be more competitive. As these businesses grow, they will hire more U.S. workers.

For some U.S. workers, outsourcing may offer unique opportunities. India has been so successful in securing business outsourced by other countries that it has a shortage of qualified labor. Because many jobs outsourced to India require workers to be fluent in English or European languages, one study predicts that 120,000 Europeans, Americans, and Australians will be working in India by 2010.

CONNECTING ACROSS THE GLOBE

1. **Synthesizing Economic Information** Explain how outsourcing might change the American economy.

2. **Evaluating** What career do you want to pursue? Explain whether it has the potential to be outsourced.

out of work. A change in consumer demand—from compact discs to computer music files, for example—can shift the type of workers needed. Offshore outsourcing, when jobs once held by Americans are staffed overseas, is another cause of structural unemployment.

TYPE 4 Cyclical Unemployment

Cyclical unemployment results when the economy hits a low point in the business cycle and employers decide to lay off workers. Workers who lose their jobs during a recession can have trouble finding new jobs because the economy as a whole is scaling back, and the demand for labor declines. When the economy picks up again, many workers are again able to find jobs.

The duration of unemployment in these four types ranges widely, but the average duration of unemployment is relatively short. More than a third of the unemployed are out of work for five weeks or less.

APPLICATION Making Inferences

B. If you owned a clothing factory, how would a high rate of unemployment affect your business?

The Impact of Unemployment

KEY CONCEPTS

Although some unemployment is unavoidable, excessive or persistent unemployment hurts the economy in several ways. It reduces efficiency; it hurts the least economically secure; and it damages workers' self-confidence.

Efficiency Unemployment is inefficient. It wastes human resources, one of the key factors of economic growth.

Inequality Unemployment does not follow equal opportunity rules. In an economic slowdown, those with the least experience lose their jobs first—usually minorities and the young (see the graphs below). Also, with fewer jobs available, people on the lower rungs of the employment ladder have less opportunity to advance.

Discouraged Workers People who are unemployed—or underemployed—for long periods of time may begin to lose faith in their abilities to get a job that suits their skills. Potentially productive workers may give up their search for work. If they are underemployed, they may not be motivated to do their best work.

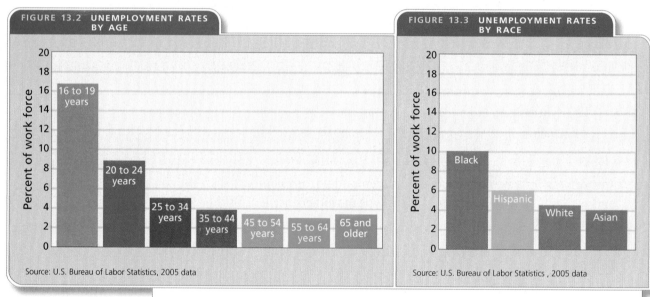

FIGURE 13.2 UNEMPLOYMENT RATES BY AGE

Percent of work force

16 to 19 years
20 to 24 years
25 to 34 years
35 to 44 years
45 to 54 years
55 to 64 years
65 and older

Source: U.S. Bureau of Labor Statistics, 2005 data

FIGURE 13.3 UNEMPLOYMENT RATES BY RACE

Percent of work force

Black
Hispanic
White
Asian

Source: U.S. Bureau of Labor Statistics , 2005 data

ANALYZE GRAPHS

1. Which group, either age or race, has the highest rate of unemployment?
2. What happens to the unemployment rate as people get older?
3. If the majority of people aged 65 and older are retired, why is the unemployment rate for that group so low?

APPLICATION Writing About Economics

C. In 1889, Jane Addams founded the Hull House Association in Chicago to help newly arrived immigrants adjust to the challenges of city life. In 1910, she wrote that "of all the aspects of social misery nothing is so heartbreaking as unemployment." Write a paragraph explaining the impact of unemployment on immigrants.

REVIEWING KEY CONCEPTS

1. Explain the relationship between the terms in each of these pairs.

   a. *frictional unemployment*
   structural unemployment

   b. *seasonal unemployment*
   cyclical unemployment

2. Explain how the unemployment rate is calculated.

3. Why are economists interested in the unemployment rate?

4. Name a job that might be affected by structural unemployment. Explain why it might be affected.

5. What is full employment?

6. **Using Your Notes** Write a brief summary of this section, covering measuring unemployment, types of unemployment, and the impact of unemployment. Refer to your completed cluster diagram.

   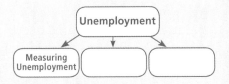

   Use the Graphic Organizer at **Interactive Review @ ClassZone.com**

CRITICAL THINKING

7. **Solving Economic Problems** Unemployment insurance provides money to workers who have lost their jobs through no fault of their own. In most states, the insurance is funded entirely by employers. What else might business and government do to help unemployed workers?

8. **Analyzing Cause and Effect** In June 2005, claims for unemployment insurance in Illinois from construction workers made up about 14 percent of all claims. In December 2005, they made up about 21 percent. Why might more construction workers file for unemployment benefits in December than in June? What type of unemployment best explains the difference?

9. **Applying Economic Concepts** Give specific examples from the Great Depression of the 1930s of ways in which the widespread unemployment (1) affected efficiency, (2) was distributed unequally, and (3) eroded self-esteem.

10. **Challenge** Think about the type of career you hope to have when you are finished with your education. Do you think it is more likely or less likely than others to be affected by each of the various types of unemployment? Explain each of your answers.

ECONOMICS IN PRACTICE

Identifying Types of Unemployment
Read the following descriptions of unemployment scenarios.

Categorize Economic Information Decide which of the four types of unemployment each scenario describes.

- Because of reduced demand, an appliance company temporarily closes one of its factories and lays off workers.

- In September, a part-time student at the University of Central Florida in Orlando loses his job at a theme park.

- A newspaper journalist leaves her job to make a switch into television journalism. She has been looking for a new job for several months.

- A local travel agency has to close down because of the widespread availability of direct online booking options.

Challenge Young people are two to three times more likely than older people to be unemployed. Why is this?

Poverty and Income Distribution

OBJECTIVES	KEY TERMS	TAKING NOTES
In Section 2, you will • explain how economists measure poverty • discuss the causes of poverty • describe how economists measure income inequality • identify what antipoverty programs are available	poverty, *p. 388* poverty threshold, *p. 388* poverty rate, *p. 389* income distribution, *p. 390* income inequality, *p. 390* Lorenz curve, *p. 391* welfare, *p. 392* workfare, *p. 393*	As you read Section 2, complete a summary chart like the one below to pull together the most important ideas about poverty and income distribution. Use the Graphic Organizer at **Interactive Review @ ClassZone.com**

What Is Poverty?			

What Is Poverty?

KEY CONCEPTS

QUICK REFERENCE

Poverty is the condition where a person's income and resources do not allow them to achieve a minimum standard of living.

Poverty threshold is the minimum income needed to pay for the basic expenses of living.

Persistent unemployment sometimes leads to **poverty**, a situation in which a person lacks the income and resources to achieve a minimum standard of living. This minimum standard varies from country to country because different countries have different ways of life. Someone who herds sheep and lives in a hut would probably be considered poor in the United States. But such a person might be thought to have a comfortable life in some other countries. Because of such disparities, there is no universal standard for what constitutes poverty.

The U.S. government has established its own standard for poverty based on income levels. This **poverty threshold** is the official minimum income needed for the basic necessities of life in the United States.

The Poverty Threshold

The poverty threshold, also called the poverty line, is the amount of income the government has determined to be necessary for meeting basic expenses. People with incomes below that threshold are considered to live in poverty. The threshold, first formulated in the early 1960s, was calculated by finding the cost of nutritionally sound food and then multiplying by three, on the assumption that food costs are about a third of a person's expenses.

The threshold differs according to the size of the household and is adjusted annually to reflect changing prices. In 2005, the poverty threshold for a family of four in the United States was about $20,000. That same year, the median income for a family of four was over $65,000.

The Poverty Rate

The **poverty rate** is the percentage of people living in households that have incomes below the poverty threshold. Unlike the unemployment rate, the poverty rate is based on the population as a whole. Through census information, the poverty rate can be estimated for individuals, households, or specific segments of the population, such as African-American children or single-parent households.

The overall poverty rate in the United States declined between 1993 and 2000 to a low of 11.3 percent. It began to rise in 2000 and by 2004 had climbed to 12.7 percent, with 37 million people living below the poverty line. (See Figure 13.4.)

Poverty, like unemployment, does not hit all sectors of society equally. Children are especially at risk. Children made up more than half of the 1.3 million increase in the number of people living in poverty between 2002 and 2003. The number of families below the poverty line that are headed by a single mother also rose. Minorities and families that live in either an inner city or a rural area tend to have higher than average poverty rates. While the numbers tell the statistical story of poverty, only personal voices can convey the toll of being poor. James Baldwin, an African-American writer born in poverty, wrote that "anyone who has ever struggled with poverty knows how extremely expensive it is to be poor."

QUICK REFERENCE

The **poverty rate** is the percentage of people living in households that have incomes below the poverty threshold.

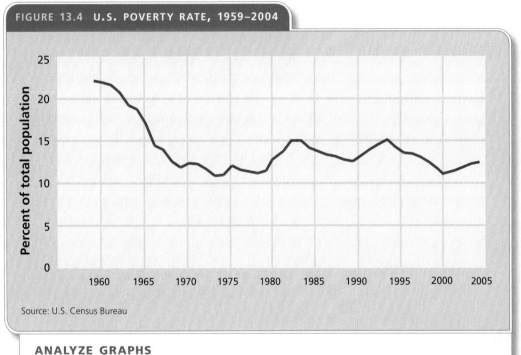

FIGURE 13.4 U.S. POVERTY RATE, 1959–2004

Source: U.S. Census Bureau

Economics Update

Find an update on the U.S. poverty rate at **ClassZone.com**

ANALYZE GRAPHS

1. From 1959 to 2004, when was the poverty rate the highest? When was it lowest?

2. What decade saw the largest drop in the rate of poverty?

APPLICATION Drawing Conclusions

A. Why is the poverty rate based on the entire population, while the unemployment rate is based on the civilian work force?

The Problem of Poverty

KEY CONCEPTS

Across the globe, about half of the world's 6 billion people live in poverty. In the United States, one of the world's wealthiest countries, almost 40 million people live below the poverty level. Even good economic times, such as the boom that the United States experienced in the 1990s, do little to move large numbers of people out of poverty. Why is an adequate income out of reach for so many people?

Factors Affecting Poverty

Four major factors have the strongest influence on who lives in poverty in the United States: education, discrimination, demography, and changes in the labor force.

Education As you learned in Chapter 9, usually there is a direct relationship between level of education and income: the higher the level of education, the higher the income. In the United States, the poverty rate of people who did not complete high school is 12 times higher than that of people with a college education.

Discrimination White males tend to have higher incomes than racial minorities and women, even when there are no differences in education or experience. Certain groups sometimes face wage discrimination or occupational segregation and may find it difficult to move beyond low-paying jobs. Government initiatives, as well as the pressures of the competitive marketplace, have helped to reduce job discrimination.

Demographic Trends In the 1950s, about one-fourth of all marriages ended in divorce. Now, almost half of all marriages end in divorce. Over the same period, births to unmarried mothers jumped from about 5 percent of all births to over 30 percent. Such demographic trends lead to higher poverty rates because single-parent families are more likely to have economic problems than two-parent families.

Changes in the Labor Force The shift in the labor force from mainly manufacturing to mainly service industries is one of the changes that affects the distribution of poverty. When manufacturing jobs were plentiful, even relatively low-skilled workers were able to earn a good wage. As the jobs shifted from manufacturing to service, the wages did not always follow. Workers in many service jobs, such as fast-food clerks, tend to earn lower wages than similarly skilled workers in manufacturing.

Income Distribution

QUICK REFERENCE

Income distribution is the way income is divided among people.

Income inequality is the unequal distribution of income.

The United States has one of the highest median family incomes in the world, yet millions of Americans live below the poverty line. This disparity is reflected in the country's **income distribution**, the way income is divided among people in a nation.

All countries have some degree of **income inequality**, an unequal distribution of income. Unless everyone earns the same amount, there will always be a difference between the incomes of the wealthiest citizens and those of the poorest. Compared to other advanced nations, the United States has relatively high income inequality. However, less advanced countries tend to have the most extreme differences between what the rich earn and what the poor earn.

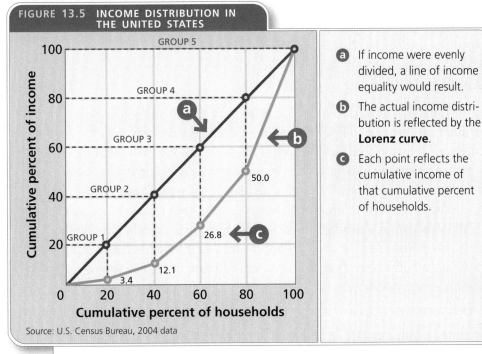

FIGURE 13.5 INCOME DISTRIBUTION IN THE UNITED STATES

GROUP 5

GROUP 4

GROUP 3

GROUP 2

GROUP 1

50.0

26.8

12.1

3.4

Cumulative percent of income

Cumulative percent of households

a If income were evenly divided, a line of income equality would result.

b The actual income distribution is reflected by the **Lorenz curve**.

c Each point reflects the cumulative income of that cumulative percent of households.

Source: U.S. Census Bureau, 2004 data

ANALYZE GRAPHS

1. According to the graph, about how much of the total income in the United States is earned by the lowest 60 percent of households?

2. How would the graph change if the lower groups earned a greater percent of the nation's total income?

A **Lorenz curve** graphically illustrates the degree of income inequality in a nation. The Lorenz curve in Figure 13.5, for example, plots income distribution in the United States. If income were distributed equally, then 20 percent of the population would receive 20 percent of the income, 40 percent would receive 40 percent, and so on. That distribution would be represented with a diagonal line.

However, income is not equally divided. The Lorenz curve in Figure 13.5 shows that the lowest 20 percent of the population (Group 1) receives only about 3.4 percent of the nation's total income. The lowest 40 percent (Group 2)—which includes the lowest 20 percent plus the next 20 percent—receive about 12.1 percent of the nation's total income. The more the Lorenz curve dips away from the diagonal line of equality, the greater the level of income inequality.

In the United States, the income gap between the lower 80 percent of the population and the top 20 percent grew steadily throughout the late 1900s. In 1970, the richest 20 percent of Americans earned on average 9 times more than the poorest. By 1997, they were earning 15 times more.

Households are not stuck in one group. When people gain experience and education, their incomes tend to increase. When they retire or make poor economic decisions, their incomes decrease.

APPLICATION **Applying Economic Concepts**

B. In 2004, the richest 20 percent of households in the United States received about 50 percent of the nation's income. Based on that proportion, if $100 was shared among five people, how much would the richest one receive? How much would each of the other four get if they shared the rest equally?

Antipoverty Programs

KEY CONCEPTS

In 1964, in his first State of the Union Address, President Lyndon Johnson pledged: "This administration today, here and now, declares unconditional war on poverty in America." Johnson's antipoverty programs were among many that the U.S. government has tried in an effort to close the income gap. These programs are often referred to as **welfare**, government economic and social programs that provide assistance to the needy. Some of these programs, however, have been criticized for wasting government funds and for harming rather than helping the recipients. During the 1980s and 1990s, the government changed its approach, and it now uses tax breaks, grants, job training, and other "self-help" initiatives in addition to cash benefits.

QUICK REFERENCE

Welfare is government economic and social programs that provide assistance to the needy.

Programs for Low-Income Households

The national food stamp program, which was established by the Food Stamp Act of 1964, helps ensure that no one will go hungry. Qualifying individuals and families receive electronic benefit transfers, which have replaced the paper food stamps that had been used originally. Recipients are given a card tied to an account into which the government makes monthly deposits of food benefits. The card can be used only to purchase food at grocery stores. Since 1975, the number of food stamp recipients has fluctuated from year to year from about 16 million to about 27 million. In 2005, almost 26 million people participated in the program.

Food Stamps The food stamp program helps those with low incomes to buy groceries.

The Medicaid program is another antipoverty measure for low-income households. Medicaid offers health care for the poor and is funded by both the federal and state governments. The expense to each state is often as much as 25 percent of the state budget. Medicaid is the only health care coverage for about 40 million Americans, nearly half of them children.

Another antipoverty program is the earned-income tax credit. This program provides the working poor a refund of payroll taxes and other taxes deducted from their paychecks. About 21 million people received these credits in 2004. One benefit of the program is that the money refunded to the recipients generally gets spent in their own communities. This spending helps to boost the economies of poor neighborhoods.

General Programs

The U.S. government's Social Security program—which pays benefits to retirees, survivors, and the disabled—is the largest government program in the world. In the year 2004 alone, it paid out $500 billion, and that amount is expected to increase as people born during the baby boom after World War II reach retirement age. It was established in 1935 by the Social Security Act.

The Social Security program is funded through a special payroll tax. At retirement, all workers—rich and poor alike—are entitled to monthly checks to help with living expenses. Another payroll tax helps to fund Medicare, a government health insurance program for seniors. Medicare became part of the Social Security program in 1965. These benefits have been key in reducing the number of older Americans in poverty. From 1960 to 1995, the poverty rate of those aged 65 and over fell from about 35 percent to about 10 percent.

The Social Security Act also established a system of unemployment insurance administered through state governments. People who lose their jobs through no fault of their own are eligible to receive income while they look for work. Each state administers its own unemployment insurance program. Most of the programs are funded by taxes paid by employers, but in a few states employees contribute too. These benefits, which usually last no more than 26 weeks, help people avoid financial problems while they seek new employment.

Other Programs

Other antipoverty programs supplement the largest programs. One is the Community Services Block Grant program, which provides blocks of federal money to local communities to address such issues as employment, education, and housing. Job training is another. One such program provides grants to community colleges to develop training for high-tech, high-growth jobs. Another way to provide jobs for the unemployed and at the same time boost the economy of a struggling neighborhood is through Empowerment Zones. The government tries to attract businesses to these specially designated neighborhoods by not charging them certain taxes. Businesses that operate in Empowerment Zones provide needed services and offer employment opportunities to area residents.

Job Training Job training helps unemployed people to learn new skills.

In 1996, the federal welfare program underwent substantial revision in a series of changes often referred to as welfare-to-work. These changes included new incentives for working, which older welfare programs often did not provide. **Workfare**, for example, is a program that requires welfare recipients to do some kind of work in return for their benefits. Their work provides a useful service and also helps prepare the workers for future jobs. Direct financial aid, now called Temporary Assistance for Needy Families (TANF), now has a limit of five years.

APPLICATION Explaining an Economic Concept

C. In terms of government spending, what is a fundamental difference between the food stamp program and the Empowerment Zone initiative?

Hernando de Soto: Another Path out of Poverty

FAST FACTS

Hernando de Soto

Title: President and Chief Executive Officer of the Institute for Liberty and Democracy

Born: 1941 in Arequipa, Peru

Major Accomplishments: Founded Institute for Liberty and Democracy

Major Publications: *The Other Path* (1986); *The Mystery of Capital: Why Capitalism Triumphs in the West and Fails Everywhere Else* (2000)

Reputation: "The poor man's capitalist"—*New York Times Magazine*

One of the "100 most influential people in the world"—*Time Magazine*

Economics Update

Find an update on Hernando de Soto at **ClassZone.com**

Peruvian economist Hernando de Soto has attacked the problem of poverty by redefining it: "The poor . . . are essentially the biggest source of wealth within [a] country." According to de Soto, the poor have numerous assets—but in most countries they lack the basic property rights they need to grow economically. "They have houses but not titles; crops, but not deeds; businesses, but not statutes of incorporation." In short, their wealth is not protected by the rule of law.

Prosperity Through Property Rights

As a young man, de Soto was struck by the sharp contrast between the poverty in Peru's shantytowns and the energetic industry of the people. These thoughts led him, in time, to establish the Institute for Liberty and Democracy (ILD), which addresses this contrast in Peru and throughout the world.

De Soto estimates that 4 billion of the world's 6 billion people are shut out of the formal economy. Antiquated and needlessly complex laws make it difficult for these people to gain legal ownership of their homes and businesses, assets that are recognized as theirs in the informal economy.

De Soto estimates that the assets of the world's poor add up to about $10 *trillion*. He argues that until legal systems change to accommodate the poor, they will continue to prefer to operate in the informal economy—at the cost of lost economic opportunity for everyone. If the resources of the poor could be brought into the formal economy and developed, the wealth they would create could lift struggling nations out of poverty into prosperity.

Hernando de Soto
De Soto developed innovative ideas about the origins of poverty.

De Soto's critics point to his non-scholarly approach, but he says that he purposely "closed the books and opened his ears" as he traveled throughout the world listening to the voices of the poor. Former U.S. President Bill Clinton echoed the sentiments of many world leaders when he described de Soto's ILD as "the most promising antipoverty initiative in the world."

APPLICATION Writing About Economics

D. De Soto said: "Capitalism . . . allowed the people that came from humble origins of the world to have economic rights the way only nobility . . . had it before. So capitalism is essentially a tool for poor people to prosper." Do you agree with that explanation? Write a paragraph to explain your answer.

SECTION 2 Assessment

Online Quiz
ClassZone.com

REVIEWING KEY CONCEPTS

1. Explain the relationship between the terms in each of these pairs.

  a. *poverty threshold*   **b.** *income distribution*   **c.** *welfare*
     poverty rate   *income inequality*   *workfare*

2. Why is it difficult to determine a universal poverty threshold?

3. What groups are especially hard hit by poverty?

4. What four factors help explain the distribution of poverty?

5. What does the Lorenz curve show?

6. Using Your Notes Describe five different antipoverty programs and the problems each combats. Refer to your completed summary chart.

What Is Poverty?			

Use the Graphic Organizer at **Interactive Review @ ClassZone.com**

CRITICAL THINKING

7. Making Inferences and Drawing Conclusions A number of antipoverty programs are targeted specifically at children:

- State Children's Health Insurance Program (SCHIP) provides health insurance to low income children who do not qualify for Medicaid and have no health insurance

- National School Lunch Program provides free or reduced price lunches to eligible children

- School Breakfast Program provides cash to schools for offering breakfasts to more than 8 million children nationally

What are the economic benefits of antipoverty programs aimed at children?

8. Solving Economic Problems Antipoverty programs in the United States are least effective for immigrant families and for non-elderly people without children. Why might this be so?

9. Analyzing Cause and Effect How does the earned income tax credit aid both the working poor and their communities?

10. Challenge In 2005, the poverty threshold for a family of four was an annual income of just over $19,800. Based on this income, devise a monthly budget for a family of four. Assume that no taxes or payroll deductions will reduce the family's income. Also assume that the family lives in an apartment that costs $700 per month. Provide a detailed account of your estimated allowances for food, clothing, and other expenses.

ECONOMICS IN PRACTICE

Food aid from the United States and other nations assists those in extreme poverty.

Understanding World Poverty
Different parts of the world have different levels of poverty.

FIGURE 13.6 PERCENT OF POPULATION IN POVERTY	
Region	**Percent**
Sub-Saharan Africa	75
South-Central Asia	75
World	53
China	47
North Africa	29
Latin America / Caribbean	26
Eastern Europe	14

Source: World Bank, 2004 data

Analyze and Interpret Data Use the information in the table to answer these questions.

1. The table uses a poverty threshold of living on less than $2 a day. Why doesn't North America appear?

2. China has a population of about 1.3 billion people. About how many of them, in millions, live in poverty?

Challenge Do the same factors that affect poverty in the United States apply to the rest of the world?

Causes and Consequences of Inflation

OBJECTIVES	KEY TERMS	TAKING NOTES
In Section 3, you will • explain how economists measure inflation • identify what causes inflation • describe how inflation affects the economy	inflation, *p. 396* consumer price index (CPI), *p. 396* producer price index (PPI), *p. 397* inflation rate, *p. 397* hyperinflation, *p. 398* deflation, *p. 398* demand-pull inflation, *p. 399* cost-push inflation, *p. 399* wage-price spiral, *p. 400*	As you read Section 3, complete a cluster diagram like the one below to record what you learn about inflation. Use the Graphic Organizer at **Interactive Review @ ClassZone.com** Inflation How Is Inflation Measured?

What Is Inflation and How Is It Measured?

KEY CONCEPTS

In 2006, militants attacked many of Nigeria's oil installations, demanding that more of the country's oil wealth be shared with the Nigerian people. Before the attacks, Nigeria produced about 2.5 million barrels of oil a day, and the country was the fifth largest source of oil imported by the United States. On news of the attacks, the price of oil rose by almost 20 percent. Some economists predicted that if oil stayed at those price levels, manufacturers might raise the prices of their products to compensate for higher fuel costs. They suggested that the high oil prices might ultimately lead to **inflation**, a sustained rise in the level of prices generally or a sustained fall in the purchasing power of money. Economists have several instruments for measuring inflation.

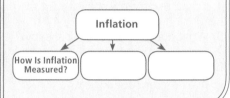

Consumer Price Index

One tool for gauging inflation is the **consumer price index (CPI)**, a measure of changes in the prices of goods and services commonly purchased by consumers. Creating the index requires many different steps, but the following describes the basic process. The U.S. government surveys thousands of people across the country to find out what goods and services they buy on a regular basis. The government then creates a "market basket" of about 400 different

QUICK REFERENCE

Inflation is a sustained rise in the general price level or a fall in the purchasing power of money.

Consumer price index (CPI) is a measure of changes in the prices of goods and services commonly purchased by consumers.

goods and services purchased by a typical household. The basket is adjusted to account for how much of a household's budget goes to purchase each type of item. For example, families tend to spend more on food than on lawn care, so the market basket is balanced to reflect this.

Each month, government workers research the current prices of the items in the market basket. What consumers spend to fill the basket can then be compared to prices in the reference base, which reflects the level of prices in the three years 1982 to 1984. Those numbers are given the value of 100. See the Connect to Math sidebar for more information.

Economics Update

Find an update about the U.S. consumer price index at **ClassZone.com**

FIGURE 13.7 U.S CONSUMER PRICE INDEX

Source: U.S. Bureau of Labor Statistics

ANALYZE CHARTS

1. If you paid $500 to fill the market basket in 1984, about how much would you pay to fill the basket in 2005?

2. Prices doubled from 1971 to 1980. How long did it take them to double again after 1980?

CONNECT TO MATH

Suppose the original value of the market basket was $500 and the current year's value is $550. To determine CPI, you divide the new value by the original value and multiply by 100. The current CPI, then, is 110.

$550 / $500 x 100 = 110

Producer Price Index

The CPI shows the level of inflation experienced by consumers, but producers also experience inflation. The tool that gauges that kind of inflation is the **producer price index (PPI)**, a measure of changes in wholesale prices. The PPI is constructed in roughly the same way as the CPI, but it reflects the prices producers receive for their goods rather than the prices consumers pay. The difference between consumer prices and producer prices lies in all the additional fees consumers pay, such as sales taxes or shipping charges. Like the CPI, the PPI is tied to a reference base of producer prices. More than 10,000 PPIs for individual products and groups of products are available. The indices are grouped either by stage of production (finished goods, intermediate goods, and raw materials, for example) or by industry. Index changes from period to period are calculated in the same general way as the CPI.

Because producers tend to encounter inflation before consumers, PPI tends to lead CPI as an indicator of inflation. Economists use CPI and PPI to calculate the **inflation rate**, the rate of change in prices over a set period of time.

QUICK REFERENCE

Producer price index (PPI) is a measure of changes in wholesale prices.

Inflation rate is the rate of change in prices over a set period of time.

FIGURE 13.8 Calculating the Rate of Inflation

To calculate the rate of inflation, economists evaluate the prices of many different goods. This hypothetical example uses a simplified market basket consisting of prices for milk, bread, and juice. The table shows that the prices of milk and bread increased from Year B to Year C, but the price of juice decreased. To see the general trend in prices, you must look at the total price of the market basket of milk, bread, and juice. The steps below show how to use this simplified market basket to calculate the rate of inflation for Year C. The base year is Year A.

Price of a Market Basket			
	Year A	Year B	Year C
1 gallon milk	$2.50	$2.40	$2.60
1 loaf bread	$1.00	$1.35	$1.53
1 gallon juice	$2.00	$2.30	$2.20
Price of basket	$5.50	$6.05	$6.33
CPI, base: Year A	100	110	115

Step 1: Calculate each year's consumer price index (CPI).

Calculations for Year C

$$\frac{\text{Price of market basket}}{\text{Price of basket in base year}} \times 100 = \text{CPI}$$

$$\frac{\$6.33}{\$5.50} \times 100 = 115$$

Step 2: Use the CPI to calculate the rate of inflation.

$$\frac{\text{CPI} - \text{CPI for preceding year}}{\text{CPI for preceding year}} \times 100 = \text{Rate of Inflation}$$

$$\frac{115 - 110}{110} \times 100 = 4.5$$

The rate of inflation in Year C was about 4.5 percent.

Choosing a market basket To calculate the rate of inflation, economists use a complicated market basket of hundreds of goods. The market basket is intended to represent the goods that are purchased by a typical urban consumer.

Types of Inflation

QUICK REFERENCE

Hyperinflation is a rapid, uncontrolled rate of inflation in excess of 50 percent per month.

Deflation is a decrease in the general price level.

The different types of inflation are defined according to the degree or level of the inflation rate. Rates below 1 percent are negligible, and those between 1 and 3 percent are moderate. If a moderate rate continues over a period of time, the result is *creeping inflation*. A rapid increase in price level is known as *galloping inflation*. If galloping inflation gets out of hand, the result is **hyperinflation**—a rapid, uncontrolled rate of inflation in excess of 50 percent per month. One of the most dramatic episodes of hyperinflation happened in Germany in 1922 and 1923. At the height of the crisis, prices rose at a rate of about 322 percent per month. **Deflation**, a decrease in the general price level, happens more rarely. The Great Depression of the 1930s in the United States was marked by deflation.

APPLICATION Applying Economic Concepts

A. If the price of milk goes up, is that inflation? Why or why not?

What Causes Inflation?

Economists generally distinguish between two kinds of inflation, each with a different cause. When the inflationary forces are on the demand side of the economy, the result is **demand-pull inflation**, a situation where total demand is rising faster than the production of goods and services. When the forces that lead to inflation originate on the supply side of the economy, the result is **cost-push inflation**, a situation where increases in production costs push up prices.

Demand-Pull Inflation

In demand-pull inflation, total demand rises faster than the production of goods and services, creating a scarcity that then drives up prices. Suppose, for example, that consumers gain confidence in the economy and decide they want to buy more durable goods—new refrigerators, stoves, second cars, and so on. It takes producers some time to recognize this rise in demand and to gear up for higher production. During this lag period, consumer demand pushes up prices on the currently available goods. Figure 13.9 illustrates how demand-pull inflation happens.

As you will learn in Chapter 16, the U.S. government creates and controls money through the Federal Reserve Bank. If the government creates too much money during the lag period before an increase in production makes more goods available, there will be too much money chasing too few goods, and prices will rise. The creation of excess money is the main reason for demand-pull inflation.

QUICK REFERENCE

Demand-pull inflation results when total demand rises faster than the production of goods and services.

Cost-push inflation results when increases in the costs of production push up prices.

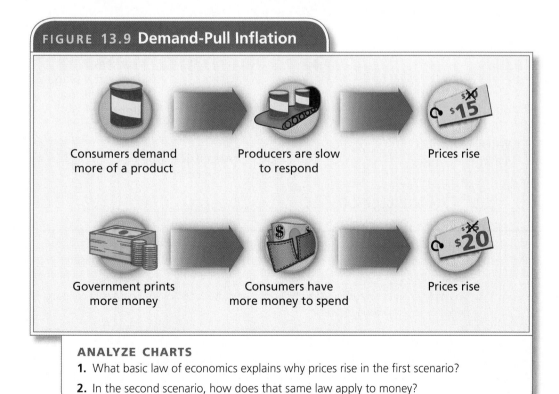

FIGURE 13.9 **Demand-Pull Inflation**

Consumers demand more of a product → Producers are slow to respond → Prices rise $15

Government prints more money → Consumers have more money to spend → Prices rise $20

ANALYZE CHARTS
1. What basic law of economics explains why prices rise in the first scenario?
2. In the second scenario, how does that same law apply to money?

Cost-Push Inflation

In cost-push inflation, prices are pushed upward by rising production costs. When production costs increase, producers make less of a profit. If consumer demand is strong, producers may raise their prices in order to maintain their profits. A general trend of rising prices leads to inflation.

Cost-push inflation is often the result of supply shocks—sharp increases in prices of raw materials or energy. For example, in 1973 and 1974, many members of the Organization of Petroleum Exporting Countries (OPEC) limited the amount of oil they sold to the United States and other Western countries. The resulting rapid rise in the price of oil led to cost-push inflation.

Cost-Push Inflation Shortages of raw materials or energy can lead to cost-push inflation.

Wages are a large part of the production costs for many goods, so rising wages can lead to cost-push inflation. A **wage-price spiral** is a cycle in which increased wages lead to higher production costs, which in turn result in higher prices, which then lead to demands for higher wages. You can see the wage-price spiral in motion in Figure 13.10.

QUICK REFERENCE

A **wage-price spiral** is a cycle that begins with increased wages, which lead to higher production costs, which in turn result in higher prices, which result in demands for even higher wages.

FIGURE 13.10 Wage-Price Spiral

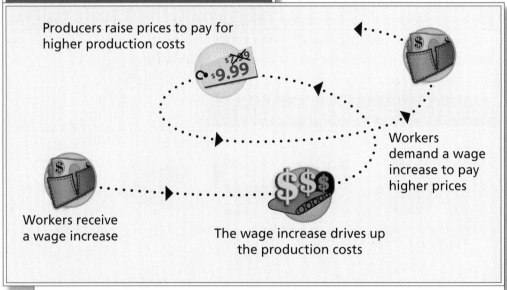

Producers raise prices to pay for higher production costs

$9.99

Workers demand a wage increase to pay higher prices

Workers receive a wage increase

The wage increase drives up the production costs

ANALYZE CHARTS

1. Using the cotton industry as an example, explain how the cycle might proceed. Use the cotton workers, cotton growers, textile mills, and other intermediate industries in your explanation.

2. Do employers grant wage increases whenever employees ask for a raise? What economic principles determine wage levels?

APPLICATION Categorizing Economic Information

B. What type of inflation would result if bad weather hit farmers hard over a long stretch of time?

What Is the Impact of Inflation?

KEY CONCEPTS

Since the 1960s, the impact of inflation on the United States economy has been significant. Inflation has raised interest rates, limited the growth of the stock market, forced agricultural bankruptcies, and slowed production. It has also had a huge impact on politics. More than half of those who voted for Ronald Reagan in 1980 said that his promise to stop the long-running inflation of the 1970s was the decisive factor. Inflation is a major challenge to economic stability. For the economy as a whole and for individual consumers, inflation has an especially strong impact on the purchasing power of the dollar and on interest rates.

EFFECT 1 Decreasing Value of the Dollar

With inflation, today's dollar buys less than last year's. The consumer price index, illustrated in Figure 13.7, shows that the real value of a dollar has declined steadily. The rising index represents the declining value of the dollar.

Consider how this declining value affects people who are on a fixed income. Suppose, for example, that your cousin started college with a savings of $10,000 to see him through. He planned to spend $2,500 a year on carefully budgeted expenses. However, because of inflation, each of those dollars bought less each year. To pay for exactly the same things he bought in his freshman year for $2,500, by the time he was a senior he needed $2,750. Inflation had pushed prices up by 10 percent over the four-year period. Senior citizens living on a fixed retirement income—as well as anyone else with a fixed income—are especially vulnerable to the decreasing value of the dollar through inflation.

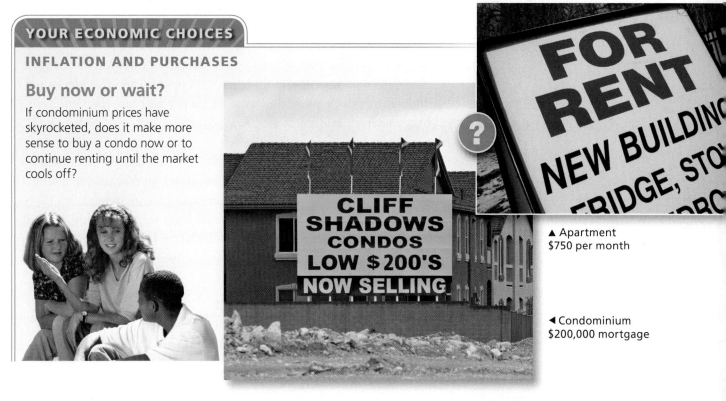

YOUR ECONOMIC CHOICES

INFLATION AND PURCHASES

Buy now or wait?

If condominium prices have skyrocketed, does it make more sense to buy a condo now or to continue renting until the market cools off?

CLIFF SHADOWS CONDOS LOW $200'S NOW SELLING

▲ Apartment
$750 per month

◄ Condominium
$200,000 mortgage

Conversely, inflation can help borrowers. With inflation, those who borrow at a fixed rate of interest can repay their debts with dollars that are worth less, making their repayments smaller than they would have been without inflation. Suppose someone borrows $100 at 5 percent interest, promising to pay the lender $105 after a year. If inflation rises at 5 percent, the $105 the borrower pays the lender will have the same purchasing power as the $100 of the original loan. The borrower essentially paid no real interest on the money he borrowed.

Increasing Interest Rates Higher interest rates make borrowing more expensive.

EFFECT 2 Increasing Interest Rates

As prices increase, interest rates also tend to increase. Lenders raise their interest rates to ensure they earn money on their loans despite inflation. Higher interest rates mean that borrowing money becomes more expensive. For example, a $10,000 loan at 10 percent interest to be repaid over the course of five years would have a monthly payment of $212.47. At 5 percent interest, the monthly payment would be only $188.71. At the end of five years, you would have paid over $1,425 more for the loan at the higher rate. When interest rates are high, businesses are less likely to borrow to expand or to make capital improvements. Consumers are less likely to make purchases of high-priced items that they would need to finance. People carrying debt on credit cards have to make higher monthly payments as their rates rise.

EFFECT 3 Decreasing Real Returns on Savings

Inflation also has a significant effect on savings. People who save at a fixed interest rate get a lower rate of return on their savings. While the interest paid on savings tends to increase during inflationary times, the difference between the rate of return and the rate of inflation still leaves them at a disadvantage.

For example, if someone puts $100 in a savings account that pays 5 percent interest per year, they will have $105 at the end of a year. But if the rate of inflation for the year was 10 percent, that $105 will buy only about what $95 bought when they deposited their money. Although they have more dollars, that money will buy less. Inflation, then, can discourage savings, leading more people to make purchases today rather than saving for tomorrow.

Inflation is the most commonly used economic term in the popular media, far outpacing the distant second, *unemployment*. Inflation worries many people, especially those who remember the volatile 1970s. Much of the worry centers on a person's individual standard of living: Will my wages keep up with rising prices? Will my savings see me through retirement? Fear of inflation has contributed to the shift away from the traditional American belief in saving over consumption.

APPLICATION Writing About Economics

C. According to opinion polls, most Americans feel inflation is a more serious problem than unemployment. Write a paragraph stating your view on which is more serious. Use convincing reasons and examples.

1. Explain the relationship between the terms in each of these pairs.

   a. *consumer price index*   **b.** *hyperinflation*   **c.** *demand-pull inflation*
   producer price index   *deflation*   *cost-push inflation*

2. What are the stages in a wage-price spiral?

3. Use a specific example to explain cost-push inflation.

4. Use a specific example to explain demand-pull inflation.

5. What are three effects of inflation?

6. **Using Your Notes** If you were a business owner, what decisions might you make on news of a steady rise in inflation? Refer to your completed cluster diagram and provide specific examples.

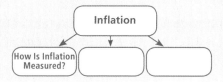

   Use the Graphic Organizer at **Interactive Review @ ClassZone.com**

7. **Analyzing Cause and Effect** Why would producers tend to experience inflation before consumers? What type of inflation would the producers experience?

8. **Explaining an Economic Concept** How does the creation of excess money cause a demand-pull inflation? Refer to Figure 13.9 to help you answer this question.

9. **Applying an Economic Concept** Imagine that union leaders are meeting with the owners of a steel manufacturer to negotiate a new five-year contract for union employees. Explain how both sides of the union-management negotiation team must take the unpredictability of future inflation into account.

10. **Challenge** The cost of attending college has been rising faster than the inflation rate, at times twice as fast. For proof, ask your school guidance counselor for a catalog from a private college that shows prices from several years ago. Compare the old prices to the current prices shown on the college website. Calculate the percentage increase for this school.

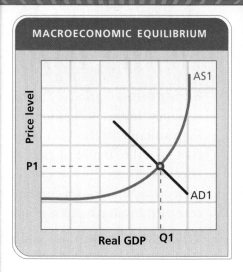

Estimating the Effects of Inflation
Suppose that a natural disaster disrupts the production of oil so dramatically that prices for oil and related products double in a short period of time. In this graph of macroeconomic equilibrium, P1 shows the price level before the natural disaster.

Draw Aggregate Supply and Demand Curves On your own paper, recreate the graph of macroeconomic equilibrium. Then draw the new aggregate supply curve that would result from the natural disaster scenario, and indicate where P2 would fall.

Challenge Explain what will happen to total economic output because of the change in prices. How does the new graph show this?

Use **SMART Grapher @ ClassZone.com** to complete this activity.

The Effects of Inflation in the 1970s

Background Periods of high inflation can wreak havoc with a country's economy. In the 1970s, for example, the United States experienced the biggest and most sustained period of inflation in the country's history. By 1979, inflation had risen into the "double digits," that is, to 10 percent per year or higher. The prices of consumer goods—everything from food and gas to cars and houses—rose dramatically. Those on fixed incomes were particularly hard-hit, because as prices rose their limited budgets bought less.

What's the issue? How did inflation affect people and businesses in the 1970s? Study these sources to discover what it was like to live with a high rate of inflation.

A. Economic Analysis

In the late 1960s, the rate of inflation began rising in many countries. This article explains inflation's effects on the U.S. economy.

The Industrialized World and Inflation

How inflation affected the U.S. economy

For the years 1967 through 1978, the U.S. inflation rate averaged 6.1 per cent a year, compared with an average of 2 per cent for the years 1952 through 1967. Even during the 1973–74 recession, unlike most previous recessions, the inflation rate continued at a relatively high rate. In the late 1970s inflation speeded up again, reaching unprecedented levels.

Inflation would not be so bad, in the opinion of some economists, if it were accompanied by substantial increases in output and employment. But economic growth in the United States slowed during the high-inflation 1970s, bringing on a condition that economists describe as "stagflation." Another measure of economic health—productivity, or output per worker—also slowed dramatically in [those] years throughout the industrialized world, and in the United States and Great Britain for a time failed to increase at all. For the United States, a country long accustomed to ever-increasing material wealth, the fall-off in economic growth and the constantly eroding value of the dollar were traumatic developments. If the trends continued, the average American could no longer anticipate a constantly rising standard of living.

Source: *The Search for a New Economic Order*, The Ford Foundation, 1982

Thinking Economically Explain how the effects of inflation might be offset by increases in output and employment.

In this cartoon by Larry Katzman, a father offers an early lesson in economics.

Source: www.CartoonStock.com

"... but if daddy raised your allowance he'd be hurting the economy by stimulating inflation. You wouldn't want him to do that, would you?"

Thinking Economically Which type of inflation does the cartoon reflect? Explain your answer.

C. Newspaper Editorial

Prices rose dramatically during the 1970s. This editorial reflects the anger many consumers felt about the situation.

Protesting Inflation

Consumers grew impatient with the government's inability to control inflation.

Here we are, spending more and getting less, but the [government] economists are optimistic. What makes them so happy? The rate of inflation may have dropped 1 per cent. Just suppose the rate of inflation had gone down from 5 per cent to 4 per cent. . . . To me this is another increase of four cents, and a further shrinkage of my dollar.

Obviously this type of economics is good for someone. It certainly isn't good for me, or my friends, or my relatives. Everyone is complaining, but the experts are satisfied.

I have a family of meat eaters. . . . Long ago I discovered a marvelous cut of meat called skirt steak. It used to cost 89 cents a pound. It has inched its way up and has recently taken a leap to $1.59 and overtaken sirloin steak. Chopped meat is now where my skirt steak used to be. . . . Even the lowly onion is no longer cheap. A weekly trip to the supermarket, which in 1969 cost $50, now costs $70.

Source: *The New York Times*, September 29, 1972

Thinking Economically Why might a small decrease in a large rate of inflation satisfy government economists but frustrate consumers?

THINKING ECONOMICALLY Synthesizing

1. Name one example from each document that shows how inflation has a negative impact on the economy.

2. Inflation is a general rise in price levels. Are the examples of price increases in documents B and C symptoms of inflation or isolated price increases?

3. Compare the tone of documents A and C. Do economists care as much about inflation as consumers? Explain your answer.

Interactive Review

Review this chapter using interactive activities at **ClassZone.com**

- Online Summary
- Quizzes
- Vocabulary Flip Cards
- Graphic Organizers
- Review and Study Notes

 Online Summary

Complete the following activity either on your own paper or online at **ClassZone.com**

Choose the key concept that best completes the sentence. Not all key concepts will be used.

consumer price index (CPI)
cost-push inflation
cyclical unemployment
deflation
demand-pull inflation
frictional unemployment
full employment
hyperinflation
income distribution
income inequality
inflation
inflation rate

Lorenz curve
poverty
poverty rate
poverty threshold
producer price index (PPI)
seasonal unemployment
structural unemployment
underemployed
unemployment rate
wage-price spiral
welfare
workfare

There are different types of unemployment. __1__ represents workers changing jobs to increase their working satisfaction or to accommodate a move to another region. __2__ results from significant changes in the economy and in the way work is done. Even during periods of __3__ about 4 to 6 percent of the work force is still unemployed.

Nearly 40 million people in the United States have incomes below the __4__, even though the nation has one of the highest median incomes in the world. The poorest receive assistance through __5__. In recent years __6__, which requires an exchange of labor for government benefits, has replaced some direct cash payments.

__7__, a rise in the general level of prices, is another economic challenge. To monitor it, government economists developed the __8__, which tracks what consumers pay for a market basket of items, and the __9__, which tracks prices from the producers' point of view. They monitor the __10__ using these indices.

CHAPTER 13 Assessment

REVIEWING KEY CONCEPTS

Unemployment in Today's Economy (pp. 382–387)

1. What are the four main kinds of unemployment and how do they differ from one another?

2. What are three negative impacts of unemployment?

Poverty and Income Distribution (pp. 388–395)

3. Which of the following persons is most likely to live in poverty: a senior citizen, a disabled adult, a college graduate, or a child? Explain your answer with specific facts and reasons.

4. Describe three antipoverty programs you feel are most useful and give reasons for your position.

Causes and Consequences of Inflation (pp. 396–405)

5. Describe two causes of inflation.

6. Which consequence of inflation would be the most troublesome to you personally? Explain your answer.

APPLYING ECONOMIC CONCEPTS

The table below shows employees laid off from selected industries in 2004. It also shows how many of these jobs were replaced by outsourcing.

7. What type of unemployment is it when an industry lays off workers but outsources their jobs? Name an example from the table.

8. Which industries' job cuts are probably due to changes in the business cycle?

FIGURE 13.11 LAYOFFS AND OUTSOURCING

Industry	Employees Laid Off	Replaced by Outsourcing
Mining	6,123	0
Apparel Manufacturing	11,583	4,102
Computer and Electronic Products	14,979	6,481
Transportation Equipment	40,634	6,223
Retail Trade	143,660	5,298
Transportation and Warehousing	59,098	2,090
Educational Services	1,429	0
Health Care and Social Assistance	44,212	621

Source: U.S. Census Bureau, 2004 data

9. **Creating Graphs** The population can be divided into five equal groups—or quintiles—according to income. Income mobility means moving from one quintile to another. A study done by the U.S. Treasury Department between 1979 and 1988 showed the following about taxpayers who started out in the lowest quintile:

   • 14.2 percent of the taxpayers in the bottom quintile in 1979 were still there in 1988

   • 20.7 percent had moved to the next higher quintile

   • 25 percent had moved to the middle quintile

   • 25.3 percent had moved to the second highest quintile

   • 14.4 percent of those who started in the lowest quintile had moved into the highest quintile

   Create a bar graph that illustrates these facts about income mobility in the United States. Use **SMART Grapher @ ClassZone.com** to complete this activity.

10. **Analyzing and Interpreting Data** What conclusions can you draw about income mobility based on the above data?

11. **Analyzing Cause and Effect** Think of three possible reasons a person might be able to move from one level of income to another.

12. **Explaining an Economic Concept** Which antipoverty programs use market forces to achieve their goals? Explain your answer.

13. **Analyzing and Interpreting Data** Consider the following data:

Consumer Price Index:	up by 6 percent
Unemployment Rate:	up to 7 percent
Gross Domestic Product:	up by 1 percent

    What's the economic problem? To correct the problem, which of these measures would you address first and why?

14. **Challenge** Which economic challenge—unemployment, poverty, or inflation—represents the greatest threat to social stability, in your opinion? Explain your answer with reasons and examples.

The Pursuit of Happiness

Do you need money to be happy? Since income alone does not tell the whole story of someone's quality of life, some people think other measures besides income should be used to determine a household's well-being. Many elements beyond material possessions also affect a person's quality of life.

To better understand the relationship between wealth and happiness, create a quality-of-life threshold by following the steps below.

Step 1. As a whole class, discuss the differences between income and quality of life.

Step 2. Break into five small groups and devise a quality-of-life threshold, a standard below which a person would be considered seriously impoverished.

Step 3. Try to find a measure for each of your criteria. For example, if one standard is "lives in warm climate," define the temperature range that qualifies as warm.

Step 4. Report your criteria to the rest of the class and explain how you would measure each.

Step 5. With the whole class, debate the relative merits of each quality-of-life threshold and its measurement.

Challenge Write a paragraph explaining how the quality-of-life threshold you developed relates to Hernando de Soto's ideas about property and prosperity (see page 394).

Macroeconomics

Unit 6
The Role of Government in the Economy

Government Spending

Government funds pay for national parks such as the Grand Canyon National Park. Government raises the money for such services through taxation.

Government Revenue and Spending

CONCEPT REVIEW

A **modified free enterprise economy** is an economic system, like that of the United States, that includes some government involvement that influences the free enterprise system.

CHAPTER 14 KEY CONCEPT

A **tax** is a mandatory payment to a local, state, or national government, while **revenue** is government income from taxes and other nontax sources.

WHY THE CONCEPT MATTERS

Taxes are a part of your everyday life—from the income tax withheld from your paycheck to the sales tax you pay on the snack you bought at the sandwich shop. The revenues raised from these taxes fund programs that are familiar to you. For example, the highways you drive on, the police that protect you, and the parks that you use are all paid for by government revenues.

Online Highlights

More at ClassZone.com

Economics Update
Go to **ECONOMICS UPDATE** for chapter updates and current news on sales taxes on Internet purchases. (See Case Study, pages 440–441.)

Animated Economics
Go to **ANIMATED ECONOMICS** for interactive lessons on the graphs and tables in this chapter. ▶

Interactive Review
Go to **INTERACTIVE REVIEW** for concept review and activities.

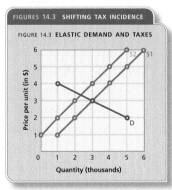

FIGURES 14.3 SHIFTING TAX INCIDENCE

FIGURE 14.3 ELASTIC DEMAND AND TAXES

Who pays more of a tax—the consumer or the producer? See Figures 14.3 and 14.4 on page 415.

How Taxes Work

OBJECTIVES

In Section 1, you will
- explain why the government establishes taxes
- identify the principles and structure of taxes
- examine the incidence of taxes
- describe how taxes affect the economy

KEY TERMS

tax, *p. 410*
revenue, *p. 410*
tax base, *p. 412*
individual income
   tax, *p. 412*
corporate income
   tax, *p. 412*
sales tax, *p. 412*
property tax,
   p. 412
proportional tax,
   p. 412

progressive tax,
   p. 412
regressive tax,
   p. 412
incidence of a
   tax, *p. 415*
tax incentive,
   p. 417

TAKING NOTES

As you read Section 1, complete a cluster diagram, using the key concepts and other helpful words and phrases. Use the Graphic Organizer at **Interactive Review @ ClassZone.com**

Taxes

Government Revenue

KEY CONCEPTS

Governments provide certain public goods that generally are not provided by the market, such as street lighting, highways, law enforcement, and the court system. Government also provides aid for people in need. Where does the money come from to pay for such goods and services? The most important source is taxes. A **tax** is a mandatory payment to a local, state, or national government. **Revenue** is government income from taxes and nontax sources. Nontax sources include borrowing and lotteries. The rights of government to tax are set down in the U.S. Constitution and in state constitutions.

Principles of Taxation

When Chelsea started her 20-hour-per-week job at the local library, she expected to receive $120 in her weekly paycheck. However, she was surprised to see that some money was deducted from her pay for various taxes. She wondered why she had to pay these taxes.

Economists use certain principles and criteria to evaluate whether or not taxes should be paid and who should pay them. These principles most often are based on the benefits taxpayers receive from taxes and their ability to pay.

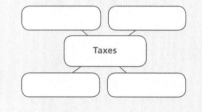

Benefits-Received Principle The benefits-received principle of taxation holds that people who benefit directly from public goods should pay for them in proportion to the amount of benefits received. One example of this principle is the financing of road construction and maintenance through taxes on gasoline. However, it is difficult for governments to assess exactly how much different taxpayers benefit from services like national defense, national parks, local police and fire protection, and public education.

Ability-to-Pay Principle The ability-to-pay principle of taxation holds that people should be taxed on their ability to pay, no matter the level of benefits they receive. According to this principle, people with higher incomes will pay more than people with lower incomes. The level of benefits received is not a consideration. Yet, income alone might not completely determine someone's ability to pay taxes. Other questions also arise. For example, should everyone pay the same percentage of income, which still results in wealthier people paying more in taxes, or should those with higher incomes pay a higher percentage of their income in taxes?

Criteria for Taxation

Tax systems attempt to meet three criteria: equity, simplicity, and efficiency. However, the criteria are sometimes in conflict, and a given tax may not meet all of the criteria equally well.

Simplicity One criticism of the U. S. tax code is that it is too complicated.

Frank and Ernest

U. S. DEPT. OF TAX SIMPLIFICATION

USE OTHER DOOR →

NOT AN ENTRANCE

©1987 Thaves. Reprinted with permission. Newspaper dist. by NEA, Inc.

Equity The equity, or fairness, of a tax is established by how uniformly the tax is applied. Equity requires that people in similar situations pay a similar amount of taxes. For example, everyone who buys gasoline pays the same tax, or all people with the same level of income pay the same amount in taxes. In addition, some believe that equity requires that people with higher incomes pay more than people with lower incomes.

Simplicity The simplicity of a tax is determined by how easy it is for the taxpayer to understand and how easy it is for the government to collect. In addition, there should be no confusion about the time the tax is due and the amount to be paid. The sales tax, which you'll read about on the next page, meets the criterion of simplicity. A set percentage of the price of a taxed item is collected every time that item is purchased.

Efficiency The efficiency of a tax can be judged by how well the tax achieves the goal of raising revenue for the government with the least cost in terms of administration. From the taxpayers' viewpoint, tax efficiency can be judged by the amount of effort and expense it takes to pay the tax. Of all the types of taxes levied, the individual income tax—which you'll learn more about on the next page—best meets the criterion of efficiency.

Economics Update

Find an update on taxation at **ClassZone.com**

APPLICATION Drawing Conclusions

A. Businesses and homeowners both benefit from police protection. How does this statement show the limitations of the benefits-received principle of taxation?

Tax Bases and Structures

KEY CONCEPTS

Government imposes taxes on various forms of income and wealth in order to raise the revenue to provide public goods and various other services. Each type of wealth subject to taxes is called a **tax base.** The four most common tax bases are individual income, corporate income, sales, and property.

Tax Bases

Individual income tax is a tax based on an individual's income from all sources: wages, interest, dividends, and tips. All taxes are ultimately paid from income, but using income as a tax base means that the amount of tax is directly linked to a person's earnings. For most individuals, income is earned mainly from work in the form of wages or tips. It may also come from savings and investment in the form of interest and dividends. Corporations pay income tax too. **Corporate income tax** is a tax based on a corporation's profits.

Sales tax is a tax based on the value of designated goods or services at the time of sale. Generally, sales taxes are imposed on a wide range of goods and services. The tax usually is a percentage of the posted price of the good or service and is included in the final price that the buyer pays. The seller then passes the tax revenue collected from customers on to the government that has imposed the tax.

Property tax is a tax based on the value of an individual's or business's assets, generally real estate. Homeowners and business owners pay property taxes based on the value of their buildings and the land on which the buildings stand. Property tax is generally included in the rents charged by property owners to individuals or businesses that rent the property, whether it is an apartment, an office, a factory, or a retail store. Property tax may also be imposed on other assets such as automobiles.

You may have heard references to a particular government's tax base growing or shrinking. Such statements refer to the amount of wealth that is available to be taxed. If overall personal income rises, the individual income tax base grows. If there are fewer homes or businesses in a certain locality or if their value declines, the property tax base shrinks because there is less wealth for the government to tax.

Tax Structures

The way in which taxes are imposed on the different tax bases gives rise to three different tax structures. These tax structures are distinguished from one another based on the percentage of income that a particular tax takes. A **proportional tax** takes the same percentage of income from all taxpayers regardless of income level. A **progressive tax** places a higher percentage rate of taxation on high-income earners than on low-income earners. A **regressive tax** takes a larger percentage of income from people with low incomes than from people with high incomes.

Proportional Tax A proportional tax is sometimes called a flat tax, because the rate of tax is the same for all taxpayers. For example, all taxpayers in a given country or state might be charged a flat 15 percent tax on their income, no matter how much

Step 1: Study the table to the right, which shows income tax brackets for a progressive tax. Each marginal tax rate is applied only to the income in that tax bracket. For example, for a taxable income of $12,000, $10,000 is taxed at 10 percent and the remaining $2,000 is taxed at 15 percent.

Income Bracket	Marginal Tax Rate
$0–$10,000	10%
$10,000–$30,000	15%
$30,000–$50,000	25%

Step 2: Assume you have a taxable income of $40,000. The table to the right shows how much of that income is in each tax bracket.

Income in Each Bracket	Tax Bracket
$10,000	10%
$20,000	15%
$10,000	25%

Step 3: Calculate the marginal tax for the income in each bracket. Add these figures to get the total tax for a taxable of income of $40,000. The total tax on $40,000 of taxable income is $6,500.

Income in bracket	×	Marginal tax rate	=	Marginal tax
$10,000	×	10%	=	$1,000
$20,000	×	15%	=	$3,000
$10,000	×	25%	=	$2,500

Total tax: $6,500

More Calculations Repeat calculations for taxable incomes of $25,000 and $45,000.

NEED HELP?

Math Handbook, "Understanding Progressive Taxes," page R7

their income is. An individual who earns $20,000 would pay $3,000 in taxes, and an individual who earns $50,000 would pay $7,500 in taxes. In the United States, some state and local governments have proportional taxes on individual income. For example, the state of Michigan has a flat income tax rate of 3.9 percent, while the state of Massachusetts has a 5.3 percent rate. Similarly, the city of Bowling Green, Ohio, collects a flat rate of 1.92 percent on its residents' incomes.

Progressive Tax As you saw above, even with a proportional tax, the amount of tax increases as income increases. A progressive tax is one in which the tax rate also increases as a person's income increases. In other words, under a progressive tax structure, a high-income person not only pays more in the amount of taxes but also pays a higher percentage of income in taxes. Figure 14.1 shows how a progressive income tax works. You can see that a progressive tax is most closely linked to the ability-to-pay principle.

In the United States, the federal income tax is a progressive tax, because the tax rate increases as income increases. (You'll learn more about the federal income tax in Section 2.) Many states, including California, Kansas, New York, and South Carolina, also have progressive income taxes.

What is the impact of each of the tax structures?

Proportional Tax
A proportional tax takes the same percentage of income from all taxpayers, regardless of income level.

Progressive Tax A progressive tax is based on income level. It takes a larger percentage of income from high-income earners and a smaller percentage of income from low-income earners.

Regressive Tax
A regressive tax hits low-income earners harder than it hits high-income earners. This is because the proportion of income that goes to taxes falls as income rises.

ANALYZE CHARTS
Look again at the description of the various tax bases on page 412. Consider which kind of tax structure applies to each of these tax bases. Write a brief paragraph explaining your choices.

Regressive Tax With a regressive tax, the percentage of income paid in taxes decreases as income increases. Some taxes are regressive because they are applied to sales, not income. For example, although a sales-tax rate is applied equally to all items subject to the tax, the tax as a percentage of income is regressive. This is because low-income earners tend to spend a higher proportion of income than do high-income earners. Suppose that a state charges 5 percent sales tax on certain goods sold in the state. If the Jones family earns $20,000 and spends $15,000 on taxable goods, they pay $750 in sales taxes (5 percent of $15,000), or 3.75 percent of their income. If the Smith family earns $50,000 and spends $25,000 on taxable goods, they pay $1,250 in sales tax (5 percent of $25,000), or 2.5 percent of their income.

For similar reasons, property taxes on homes are also considered regressive. Low-income homeowners usually spend a higher percentage of their income on housing than do high-income homeowners. Therefore, property taxes take a higher percentage of their income. In addition, poorer communities often charge a higher tax rate, because the property has a lower value and therefore the property tax base is smaller. Even those who do not own homes are subject to the regressive property tax, because property taxes are generally passed on to renters. Figure 14.2 above shows the impact of each type of tax structure on low-income earners and high-income earners.

APPLICATION Comparing and Contrasting

B. How do proportional, progressive, and regressive taxes meet the criteria of simplicity and equity?

Who Pays the Tax?

KEY CONCEPTS

The impact of a tax can also be measured by who actually pays it. The **incidence of a tax** is the final burden of that tax. In other words, it is the impact of the tax on a taxpayer. For example, taxes imposed on businesses may get passed on to the consumer in the form of higher prices or rents. To understand this, you need to apply the concepts of supply and demand.

QUICK REFERENCE

The **incidence of a tax** is the final burden of the tax.

Effect of Elasticity on Taxes

Suppose that the government imposes a $1 tax on a product. Demand elasticity influences the incidence of this tax. If a product has elastic demand, the seller pays more of the tax, because the seller faces decreased quantity demanded if prices rise. If the product has inelastic demand, the consumer pays more of the tax in the form of higher prices. The seller recognizes that quantity demanded will go down only slightly for goods or services that have inelastic demand, because they are less price-sensitive. Figures 14.3 and 14.4 illustrate the difference in tax incidence between products with elastic and inelastic demand.

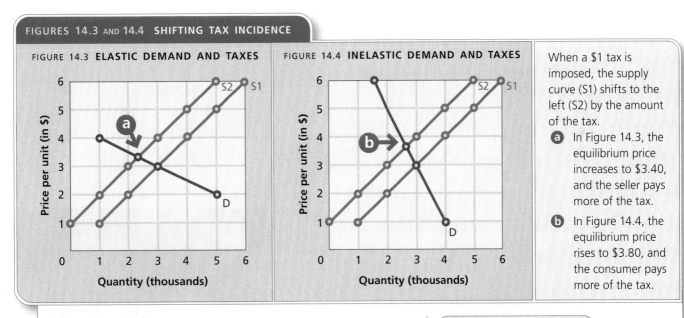

FIGURES 14.3 AND 14.4 SHIFTING TAX INCIDENCE

FIGURE 14.3 ELASTIC DEMAND AND TAXES

FIGURE 14.4 INELASTIC DEMAND AND TAXES

When a $1 tax is imposed, the supply curve (S1) shifts to the left (S2) by the amount of the tax.

ⓐ In Figure 14.3, the equilibrium price increases to $3.40, and the seller pays more of the tax.

ⓑ In Figure 14.4, the equilibrium price rises to $3.80, and the consumer pays more of the tax.

ANALYZE GRAPHS
1. In Figure 14.3, how does quantity demanded at equilibrium change?
2. Which producer's revenues would be least affected by the $1 tax?

Animated **Economics**

Use interactive demand elasticity curves at **ClassZone.com**

APPLICATION Applying Economic Concepts

C. Who would bear the greater incidence of these taxes: a. $1 tax on movie tickets? b. $1 tax on gasoline? Give reasons for your answers.

Impact of Taxes on the Economy

KEY CONCEPTS

Taxes do more than provide government with the revenue that allows it to provide public goods and other programs. Taxes have an economic impact on resource allocation, productivity and growth, and the economic behavior of individuals and businesses. Government chooses what to tax and how to tax based on the amount of income it wants to raise and the other economic effects it wants to achieve.

IMPACT 1 Resource Allocation

A tax placed on a good or service will increase the costs of production and therefore shift the supply curve to the left. If the demand remains the same, the price of the good or service will go up. This shift will likely result in a shift in resources. Recall what you learned about tax incidence earlier. If a supplier is not able to pass increased costs along to the consumer in the form of higher prices, the supplier may choose to shift production to another good that will be more profitable.

For example, if the government imposed a 10 percent tax on luxury yachts, which have elastic demand, the producer of the yachts would not be able to raise prices enough to cover the full cost of the tax. If it were no longer profitable to sell the yachts because of the extra cost of the tax, the producer might decide to shift resources to producing small fishing boats or go into a different business.

IMPACT 2 Productivity and Growth

When taxes on interest and dividends are high, people tend to save less than when taxes on this source of income are low. Therefore, taxes also have an impact on the amount of money available to producers to invest in their businesses. Some economists also believe that high taxes reduce incentives to work. They suggest that people may spend more time on activities other than work if a large percentage of their income goes to taxes.

Other economists suggest that the underground economy is a result of high taxes. The underground economy refers to jobs, services, and business transactions conducted by word of mouth and, for the most part, paid for in cash to avoid paying taxes. For example, Bob has a part-time landscaping business. He works on the weekends, charges lower prices than larger landscaping companies, and insists that his customers pay him in cash. Since there are no records of Bob's business transactions, it is difficult for the government to tax his income.

Underground Economy Bob avoids paying taxes on his landscaping business by working on a cash-only basis.

IMPACT 3 Economic Behavior

A **tax incentive** is the use of taxes to encourage or discourage certain economic behaviors. By providing tax credits or rebates, the government may encourage behavior that it believes is good for the economy and for society. For example, it may give tax rebates to businesses for opening new factories, offices, and stores in economically depressed areas. Or government may give tax credits to consumers for activities such as recycling or using energy more efficiently. The positive tax incentive with the widest impact is perhaps the home mortgage interest deduction, which is designed to encourage home ownership. (You'll learn more about tax deductions later in this chapter.)

So-called sin taxes are often imposed on products or activities considered to be unhealthful or damaging to society, such as gambling, alcohol, and cigarettes. These taxes are generally levied on products or activities for which there is relatively inelastic demand, so that the incidence of the tax will fall on the consumer. Yet because demand for such products is relatively inelastic, the government knows that decline in quantity demanded will not cause tax revenues to decrease dramatically. (Figure 14.5 shows how the quantity demanded of cigarettes changes when states enact higher cigarette taxes.) Demand for sin-tax products becomes somewhat more elastic as tax increases get steeper. For example, cigarette sales in Washington fell by nearly 19 percent in the year after the state imposed a 60-cents-per-pack tax increase in 2002. Even so, since the tax increase was so large, cigarette tax revenues went up by more than 40 percent.

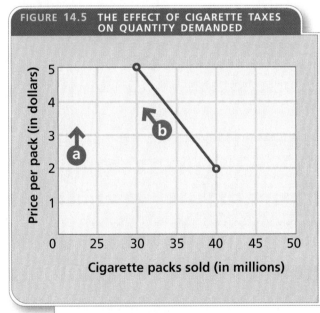

FIGURE 14.5 THE EFFECT OF CIGARETTE TAXES ON QUANTITY DEMANDED

Price per pack (in dollars) / Cigarette packs sold (in millions)

a Price increases reflect increases in state taxes on cigarettes.

b Read the curve from right to left to see that as increased taxes lead to higher cigarette prices, the quantity demanded falls somewhat. The steep slope of the demand curve indicates that demand for cigarettes is relatively inelastic.

ANALYZE GRAPHS

1. How does the quantity demanded of cigarettes change when the price rises from $4 to $5 per pack?
2. How does this graph illustrate the concept of tax incentives?

APPLICATION Analyzing Effects

D. What effect does the underground economy have on government revenue?

ECONOMICS SKILLBUILDER

For more information on evaluating sources, see the Skillbuilder Handbook, page R28.

Using the Internet for Research

The Internet is a powerful tool for researching information. The Web site of the U.S. Treasury Department, for example, provides information on government revenue and spending.

RESEARCHING ON THE INTERNET Below is an example of FAQs, or "frequently asked questions." Use the following tips to help you navigate this and similar Internet Web sites that you might use for research.

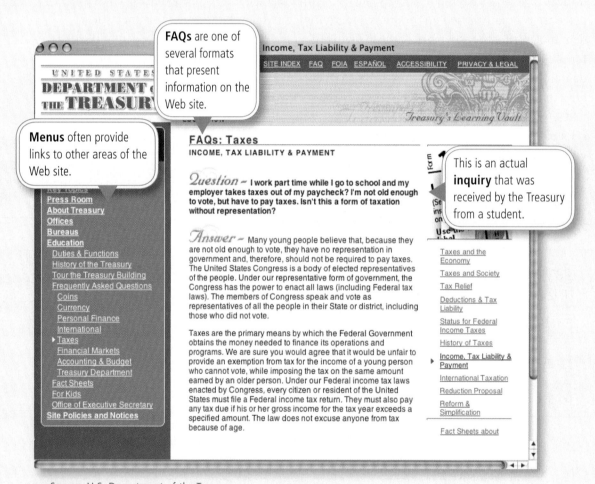

FAQs are one of several formats that present information on the Web site.

Menus often provide links to other areas of the Web site.

This is an actual **inquiry** that was received by the Treasury from a student.

FAQs: Taxes
INCOME, TAX LIABILITY & PAYMENT

Question – I work part time while I go to school and my employer takes taxes out of my paycheck? I'm not old enough to vote, but have to pay taxes. Isn't this a form of taxation without representation?

Answer – Many young people believe that, because they are not old enough to vote, they have no representation in government and, therefore, should not be required to pay taxes. The United States Congress is a body of elected representatives of the people. Under our representative form of government, the Congress has the power to enact all laws (including Federal tax laws). The members of Congress speak and vote as representatives of all the people in their State or district, including those who did not vote.

Taxes are the primary means by which the Federal Government obtains the money needed to finance its operations and programs. We are sure you would agree that it would be unfair to provide an exemption from tax for the income of a young person who cannot vote, while imposing the tax on the same amount earned by an older person. Under our Federal income tax laws enacted by Congress, every citizen or resident of the United States must file a Federal income tax return. They must also pay any tax due if his or her gross income for the tax year exceeds a specified amount. The law does not excuse anyone from tax because of age.

Source: U.S. Department of the Treasury

THINKING ECONOMICALLY Using the Internet

1. Why do you think the student used the phrase "taxation without representation"? (If you are unfamiliar with the phrase, use a search engine to research its origin.)

2. How might you navigate this page of the U. S. Department of the Treasury Web site to locate a press release on new tax legislation?

3. Access this Web site and use the FAQs to discover how the Treasury Department answers the question: Why do I have to pay taxes?

REVIEWING KEY CONCEPTS

1. Explain the difference between the terms in each of these pairs.

   a. *tax*
   revenue

   b. *sales tax*
   property tax

   c. *progressive tax*
   regressive tax

2. Why do governments collect taxes?

3. What are the four most used tax bases?

4. How does demand elasticity influence the incidence of a tax?

5. What is the purpose of a tax incentive?

6. **Using Your Notes** What are the major criteria for a good tax system? Refer to your completed cluster diagram.

   Use the Graphic Organizer at **Interactive Review @ ClassZone.com**

CRITICAL THINKING

7. **Categorizing Economic Information** Colorado has a state income tax of 4.63 percent on all income and a sales tax of 2.9 percent. Are these taxes proportional, progressive, or regressive? Give reasons for your answers.

8. **Drawing Conclusions** In 2005, Hurricane Katrina destroyed many homes and businesses along the Gulf Coast of the United States. How did this natural disaster affect the tax bases in communities in that region?

9. **Analyzing Effects** Where does the burden of an increase in a sin tax usually fall? Illustrate your answer with supply and demand curves.

   Use 🏈 **SMART Grapher @ ClassZone.com** to complete this activity.

10. **Applying Economic Concepts** Demand for insulin is highly inelastic. Would the government be likely to use a tax on insulin as a tax incentive? Why or why not?

11. **Challenge** Pennsylvania and Illinois each have state income taxes of about 3 percent of income. In Illinois, the first $2,000 of individual income is exempt from taxation. Pennsylvania has no similar individual tax exemptions. Is one state's tax more progressive than the other? Why or why not? (You'll learn more about tax exemptions in Section 2.)

ECONOMICS IN PRACTICE

Driver's license

Evaluating Taxes

Review what you have learned about the principles and criteria used to evaluate the effectiveness of a tax, and then complete the following activities.

Draw Conclusions Evaluate the effectiveness of each tax listed in the chart below by indicating with a checkmark whether it meets each principle and criterion.

Tax	Principles		Criteria		
	Benefits received	Ability to pay	Equity	Simplicity	Efficiency
Fee for driver's license					
Sales tax					
Flat rate income tax					
Progressive income tax					
Highway tolls					
Property tax					
Corporate income tax					

Challenge How would you evaluate a tax to support public education that was imposed only on families with children?

Federal Taxes

OBJECTIVES	KEY TERMS	TAKING NOTES
In Section 2, you will • describe the process of paying individual income taxes • explain taxes for Social Security, Medicare, and unemployment • identify other taxes that are collected by the federal government	withholding, *p. 421* taxable income, *p. 421* tax return, *p. 421* FICA, *p. 423* Social Security, *p. 423* Medicare, *p. 423* estate tax, *p. 425* gift tax, *p. 425* excise tax, *p. 425* customs duty, *p. 425* user fee, *p. 425*	As you read Section 2, complete a cluster diagram using the key concepts and other helpful words and phrases. Use the Graphic Organizer at **Interactive Review @ ClassZone.com** Federal Taxes

Individual Income Tax

KEY CONCEPTS

The federal government takes in around $2.5 trillion in revenue each year. This money comes from several sources, including individual income tax, social insurance taxes, corporate income taxes, estate taxes, gift taxes, excise taxes, and customs taxes. The largest source of taxes for the federal government is the individual income tax. (You can see the contribution of the various taxes to total revenue in Figure 14.8 on page 425.) The government began using the income tax after the Sixteenth Amendment to the U.S. Constitution, which recognized this type of direct taxation on individuals, was ratified in 1913. Prior to that time, excise taxes and customs duties were the main sources of federal revenue. (Figure 14.8 shows that today only a very small portion of federal tax revenue comes from excise taxes and customs duties.) Social insurance taxes are the second largest source of federal tax revenue. Workers and employers share the burden of these taxes.

EXAMPLE Paying Your Taxes

If taxpayers had to pay their income taxes in one lump sum at the end of each year, some people would have difficulty coming up with all the money at once. Also, receiving revenue just once a year would create problems for the government. Drawing up a budget for the year would be very difficult, and developing sound economic plans for the future would be almost

impossible. Therefore, to make it easier for taxpayers and the government, a payroll tax—a tax that is taken from a worker's paycheck—is collected. The payroll tax is deducted from a paycheck as **withholding**, or money taken from a worker's pay before the worker receives it.

To see how this works, let's look at the example of Scott, who works part-time during the school year and full-time during the summer at the Main Street Grocery Store. For every hour Scott works, he earns $6. Because of withholding for taxes, the amount he receives in his paycheck is less than the total amount he earns. In this way, he pays his taxes as he earns income, and the government receives a steady stream of revenue. The Main Street Grocery Store forwards the money withheld from Scott's paycheck to the Internal Revenue Service (IRS). The IRS is the government agency that collects the money for the federal government and administers the federal tax system.

The federal income tax is a progressive tax based on the ability-to-pay principle of taxation. This means that people with higher incomes not only pay more in total taxes but also pay a higher percentage of their income in taxes. The amount owed is based on **taxable income**, the portion of income subject to taxation. Under federal income tax laws, taxpayers may take certain exemptions and deductions from their total earned income to reduce the amount of their taxable income. Exemptions are allowed for each individual adult and child, so larger families reduce their taxable income by a greater amount than do smaller families. In addition, taxpayers may take a standard deduction or itemize deductions, such as interest paid on a home mortgage, state and local taxes, charitable contributions, and a certain portion of medical expenses. Figure 14.6 below provides information on some of the itemized deductions taken by taxpayers in 2004.

Each year, taxpayers must complete a **tax return**, a form used to report income and taxes owed to various levels of government. The federal tax return shows how much income has been earned, the exemptions being claimed, and how much tax has been paid through withholding. State and local tax returns show similar, but less detailed, information. Taxpayers who have too much tax withheld receive a refund for overpayment. Taxpayers who have not had enough withheld must then pay any additional taxes owed directly to the IRS or to state or local revenue departments.

FIGURE 14.6 SELECTED ITEMIZED DEDUCTIONS ON INDIVIDUAL INCOME TAX RETURNS

Deduction	Number of Returns	Amount Claimed (in $)
Interest Paid	37,961,584	346.0 billion
State and Local Sales and Income Taxes	44,685,865	217.2 billion
Charitable Contributions	40,594,576	156.2 billion
Medical and Dental Expenses	9,458,443	61.3 billion

Source: Internal Revenue Service, 2004 figures

About 132.4 million individual income tax returns were filed in 2004. Some 46.2 million—or 35 percent—of these returns claimed itemized deductions to taxable income. Total itemized deductions equaled close to $972 billion, or just over $21,000 for each return.

ANALYZE GRAPHS

1. Which was the largest deduction taken in terms of the dollar amount claimed?

2. What percentage of total deductions taken in 2004 did state and local sales and income taxes represent?

EXAMPLE Indexing

Because the federal income tax is a progressive tax, the tax rate increases as taxable income increases. The level of income that causes someone to pay a higher rate of tax is the dividing point between tax brackets. The tax bracket is identified by the tax rate for that income span. For example, the tax schedule at the bottom of this page shows that in 2006 a single taxpayer with $7,550 or less in taxable income is in the 10 percent tax bracket. Someone with taxable income between $7,550 and $30,650 is in the 15 percent tax bracket, someone with taxable income between $30,650 and $74,200 would be in the 25 percent bracket, and so on.

Tax Return Checking your taxable income against the various tax brackets is an important step in completing your tax return.

Look again at the tax schedule below. Suppose that Scott has $7,000 in taxable income. He is in the 10 percent bracket and pays 10 percent, or $700, in taxes. If, however, he had $8,000 in taxable income, he would be in the 15 percent tax bracket. He would pay 10 percent on the first $7,550 of his earnings and 15 percent on the remaining $450. His total taxes would be $822.50 ($755 + $67.50) or about 10.3 percent of his income.

Indexing is a revision of tax brackets to prevent workers from paying more taxes due to inflation. For example, suppose Scott's taxable income rises from $8,000 to $8,320—a 4 percent increase—due to inflation. Without indexing, $770 of his income is taxed at the 15 percent rate and he pays $870.50 in taxes, or about 10.5 percent of his income. With indexing, the beginning level of the 15 percent bracket is adjusted by 4 percent to $7, 852. So Scott continues to pay 10.3 percent of his income in taxes. Indexing, therefore, combats the effect of inflation and keeps the rate of taxation relatively constant.

Economics Update

Find an update on tax schedules at **ClassZone.com**

2006 Tax Rates: Schedule X—Single

If your taxable income is:		The tax is:
Over—	But not over—	
$0	$7,550	**10% of the amount over $0**
7,550	30,650	**$755 plus 15% of the amount over $7,550**
30,650	74,200	**$4,220 plus 25% of the amount over $30,650**
74,200	154,800	**$15,108 plus 28% of the amount over $74,200**
154,800	336,550	**$37,676 plus 33% of the amount over $154,800**
336,550	No limit	**$97,653 plus 35% of the amount over $336,550**

APPLICATION Analyzing Effects

A. How much of Scott's income of $8,320 would be taxed at 15 percent if the 10 percent tax bracket were indexed and increased to $7,780? What effect would this have on his overall tax rate?

FICA: Taxes to Ease Hardships

KEY CONCEPTS

FICA is the Federal Insurance Contributions Act, a payroll tax that provides coverage for the elderly, the unemployed due to disability, and surviving family members of wage earners who have died. Also known as social insurance, FICA encompasses Social Security and Medicare. Both employees and employers make payments into FICA accounts.

Social Security Social Security is a federal program to aid older citizens who have retired, children who have lost a parent or both parents, and people with disabilities. The program began during the Great Depression of the 1930s as a way to help people who were in desperate need of economic assistance. The employer and employee each pay 6.2 percent of the employee's income up to an annual maximum. In 2006, Social Security tax was applied to $94,200 of earned income. The limit generally rises each year.

Medicare Introduced in 1966, **Medicare** is a national health insurance program for citizens over 65 and certain other groups of people. Employers and employees each pay 1.45 percent of employee income. There is no limit on the amount of income subject to the tax for Medicare.

Unemployment Taxes Unemployment compensation is a program funded by federal and state taxes and administered by the states. It provides benefits for a certain period of time to employees who lose their jobs through no fault of their own. Unemployment tax applies to the first $7,000 earned by an employee and, for the most part, is paid only by employers.

"SURELY YOU CAN EARN MORE THAN THIS! SOMEONE HAS to SUPPORT MEDICARE AND SOCIAL SECURITY."

Source: www.CartoonStock.com

FICA Accounts As the American population ages, fears are growing that there will not be enough workers to fund FICA.

APPLICATION Applying Economic Concepts

B. How would the employee portion of total FICA taxes for an individual earning $100,000 be split between Social Security and Medicare? Show your calculations.

Corporate Income and Other Taxes

KEY CONCEPTS

The federal government collects more than individual income and FICA taxes. It also uses corporate income, estate, gift, and excise taxes, as well as customs duties and user fees, to finance its operations.

Corporate Income Taxes

As you recall from earlier in this chapter, corporate income tax is tax on corporate profits. This tax is the third largest source of tax revenue for the federal government. Between 1941 and 1968, corporate income tax was the second largest source of revenue. Since that time, however, it has been surpassed by social insurance taxes. As Figure 14.7 shows, corporate income tax receipts have increased in total dollars since the mid-1900s, but have decreased relative both to total federal tax revenues and to the overall size of the economy.

Only certain types of corporations are subject to corporate income tax. These corporations are about 8 percent of all businesses that file tax returns. While the tax rate for most corporations is 35 percent of profits, most pay only about 26 percent of their profits in taxes. Like individuals, corporations can deduct certain expenses from their profits to reduce their taxable income. Some of the most important tax breaks for corporations include deductions for investment in buildings, equipment, and research, and rules that benefit multinational corporations.

A common criticism of the corporate income tax is that corporate profits are subject to double taxation. Profits are taxed at the corporate level and again at the individual level, since shareholders pay taxes on the income they receive in the form of dividends or capital gains. In recent years, the tax rate on capital gains has decreased in answer to this criticism.

FIGURE 14.7 CORPORATE INCOME TAX RECEIPTS, 1950–2009

	Receipts (in millions of $)	As Percentage of Total Federal Tax Revenue	As Percentage of GDP
1950–59	185,406	27.5	4.8
1960–69	262,891	21.3	3.8
1970–79	437,564	15.0	2.7
1980–89	675,358	9.3	1.7
1990–99	1,434,246	10.5	1.9
2000–09*	2,189,162	10.0	1.8

Source: The Budget of the United States, FY 2007

*Reflects government budget estimates for 2006–2009

ANALYZE GRAPHS
1. What overall trend is shown in the chart?
2. Which decade diverges from this overall trend? How does it differ from the overall trend?

Other Taxes

Several miscellaneous taxes provide a small part of total federal revenue, as you can see in Figure 14.8 below. The **estate tax** is a tax on property that is transferred to others on the death of the owner. Most estates are not subject to this tax, because the government only taxes large estates. In 2006, estates valued at less than $2 million were not subject to this tax. The **gift tax** is a tax on money or property given by one living person to another. As with the estate tax, there are exemptions to the gifts that are subject to the tax. For the most part, these exemptions allow family members to give money to other family members tax-free.

The **excise tax** is a tax on the production or sale of a specific product, such as gasoline or telephone service. The sin taxes discussed earlier in this chapter are other examples of excise taxes. In general, the government places excise taxes on goods or services for which there is relatively inelastic demand in order to maintain a steady stream of revenue. The **customs duty** is a tax on goods imported into the United States from another country. Customs duties are basically excise taxes on imports and are also known as tariffs. (You'll read more about tariffs in Chapter 17.)

The **user fee** is money charged for the use of a good or service. These fees are based on the benefits-received principle of taxation. For example, the federal government charges entrance, parking, and camping fees to visitors to national parks. So the people enjoying the parks the most pay for the benefits provided by the parks.

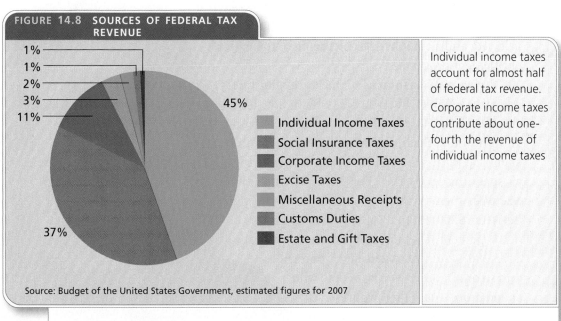

FIGURE 14.8 SOURCES OF FEDERAL TAX REVENUE

- 1%
- 1%
- 2%
- 3%
- 11%
- 45%
- 37%

Legend:
- Individual Income Taxes
- Social Insurance Taxes
- Corporate Income Taxes
- Excise Taxes
- Miscellaneous Receipts
- Customs Duties
- Estate and Gift Taxes

Individual income taxes account for almost half of federal tax revenue.

Corporate income taxes contribute about one-fourth the revenue of individual income taxes

Source: Budget of the United States Government, estimated figures for 2007

ANALYZE GRAPHS

1. What percentage of federal tax revenue comes from individual income taxes and social insurance taxes combined?

2. If total tax revenue for 2007 is estimated to be about $2.35 trillion, about how much revenue will come from individual income taxes?

APPLICATION Drawing Conclusions

C. There are plans to eliminate the estate tax. Who will benefit most from this?

Maya MacGuineas: Reforming the Tax System

Economics Update

Find an update on Maya MacGuineas at **ClassZone.com**

For the most part, tax reform measures of the last few years have involved tinkering with tax rates, exemptions, and deductions. Maya MacGuineas, a tax policy analyst, thinks that it's time for far more dramatic change—a complete overhaul of the U.S. tax system, in fact.

A Tax Revolution?

Why does MacGuineas think that such drastic action is needed? The present tax system, she says, is complicated, inefficient, and unfair, and doesn't raise the revenue to fund all of the government's programs. The new tax system, she argues, ought to be based on simplicity, efficiency, equity, and responsible budgeting.

To this end, MacGuineas suggests that the income tax should be simplified by ending most tax deductions and exemptions. This, she says, would also make the system more equitable, since taxpayers in higher marginal tax brackets gain the greatest benefit from these measures. In part for reasons of efficiency, MacGuineas believes that the corporate income tax should be phased out. She also supports new environmental taxes, a different approach to how the estate tax is levied, and a complete restructuring of the nation's entitlement programs.

Perhaps MacGuineas's most revolutionary measure involves FICA taxes, which she thinks should be replaced with a progressive consumption tax. Such a tax would be tied to total spending rather than income, with rates rising as spending levels rise. For example, the first $20,000 spent would be tax-free, spending between $20,000 and $50,000 would be taxed at 10 percent, spending between $50,000 and $175,000 would be taxed at 15 percent, and so on. In other words, people who spend more would face progressively higher marginal tax rates. A progressive consumption tax would not only be simpler and fairer, MacGuineas argues, it would also provide tremendous incentives to save.

Tax Reform Maya MacGuineas wants to make the tax system more equitable and less complex.

APPLICATION Making Inferences

D. Should spending on education and housing be exempt from MacGuineas's consumption tax? Why or why not?

REVIEWING KEY CONCEPTS

1. Explain the relationship between the terms in each of these pairs.

   a. *taxable income*   **b.** *FICA*   **c.** *estate tax*
      tax return   *Social Security*   *gift tax*

2. Why is indexing important to taxpayers?

3. What is the role of the IRS in relationship to federal taxes?

4. How are excise taxes and customs duties similar? How are they different?

5. How are payroll taxes and user fees different?

6. **Using Your Notes** What two programs are financed by FICA? Refer to your completed cluster diagram. Use the Graphic Organizer at **Interactive Review @ ClassZone.com**

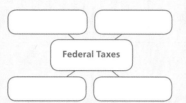

Federal Taxes

CRITICAL THINKING

7. **Analyzing and Interpreting Data** In 2005, the 10 percent tax bracket limit was $7,300. In 2006, it increased to $7,550. By what percentage did the tax bracket limit increase? How does this example illustrate the concept of indexing?

8. **Applying Economic Concepts** The Social Security tax rate for employees is 6.2 percent, and the Medicare tax rate is 1.45 percent. Are both parts of the FICA tax proportional? Give reasons for your answer.

9. **Drawing Conclusions** Study these two statements about tax payments for the 2005 tax year:

   • On average, an individual with $100,000 in taxable income paid about 29.5 percent in combined income and FICA taxes.

   • On average, an individual with $150,000 in taxable income also paid about 29.5 percent in combined taxes.

   Why were the combined tax rates the same for these two taxpayers?

10. **Challenge** Review the data in Figure 14.7. As a share of federal tax revenue and as a share of GDP, by what percentage have corporate income taxes declined between the 1950s and the first decade of the 21st century?

ECONOMICS IN PRACTICE

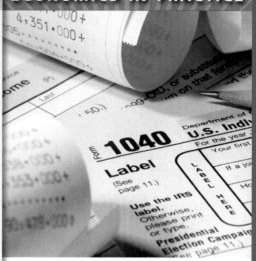

Analyzing Tax Schedules
The IRS provides tax schedules, or tables, to help taxpayers calculate their taxes.

Calculate Taxes Suppose that you work for a tax preparation company. Use the tax schedule on page 422 to answer the questions about the taxpayers described below.

a. Chris has $8,500 in taxable income. What is her tax bracket, how much tax does she pay, and what is her actual tax rate?

b. Miguel earned $35,000 in taxable income this year. How much more does he pay in taxes than if he had earned $30,000?

c. Meredith had $125,000 in taxable income and had $30,000 in taxes withheld. Will she receive a refund or owe money? How much?

Challenge Calculate the FICA taxes and tax rates for each of the above taxpayers.

Federal Government Spending

OBJECTIVES	KEY TERMS	TAKING NOTES
In Section 3, you will • compare the two types of government expenditures • explain how the federal budget is developed • describe how government payments are made • identify the impact that federal spending has on the economy	mandatory spending, *p. 428* discretionary spending, *p. 428* entitlements, *p. 428* Medicaid, *p. 429* federal budget, *p. 431* fiscal year, *p. 431* appropriations, *p. 431* transfer payments, *p. 432* grant-in-aid, *p. 432* private sector, *p. 432*	As you read Section 3, complete a hierarchy diagram to track main ideas and details. Use the Graphic Organizer at **Interactive Review** **@ ClassZone.com**

Federal Expenditures

KEY CONCEPTS

QUICK REFERENCE

Mandatory spending is required by law.

Discretionary spending has to be authorized each year.

Entitlements are social welfare programs with specific requirements.

As you have seen, the federal government takes in a huge amount of money in taxes. The programs and services the federal government funds with this revenue are divided into two categories. These are **mandatory spending**, or spending that is required by current law, and **discretionary spending**, or spending that the government must authorize each year. For example, the law requires that the government spend money to fund the Social Security and Medicare programs. However, the federal government can decide to fund or not fund highway construction or maintenance of national parks. The federal government, then, has certain expenses that must be paid under current law, while other expenses are covered with what is left after those required expenses have been met.

TYPE 1 Mandatory Spending

Mandatory spending makes up well over half of all federal spending. Most of this spending is in the form of **entitlements**, which are social welfare programs with specific requirements. Social Security and Medicare are entitlement programs that provide payments to anyone who is eligible based on age or disability. Many

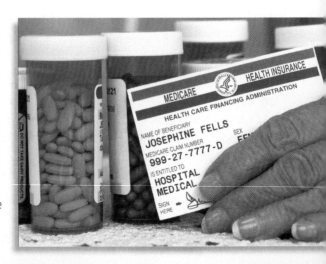

Medicare About 42 million Americans are enrolled in the Medicare program.

of these programs are not "means tested." In other words, anyone who meets the eligibility requirements receives the benefits, regardless of income level. For some other programs, however, income level is part of the requirement.

Social Security The Social Security program takes the largest amount of federal spending. It provides benefits to older retired workers, disabled workers with limited incomes, and survivors of workers who have died. Social Security is financed through a payroll tax. Therefore, workers must have worked for a certain period of time before they are eligible to receive full benefits under the program.

As the population of the United States has gotten older and more people have retired, costs for Social Security have increased. To help control costs, the government has gradually raised the age of full retirement—the point at which a worker is eligible to receive maximum benefits. Full retirement age ranges from 65 to 67, depending on the person's year of birth. Retirement benefits are not means tested. However, if retirees have additional income, benefits may be subject to withholding. For example, in 2006 retirees could earn $1,040 a month and still receive full Social Security benefits. However, retirees who earned more than this amount had their benefits reduced by $1 for every $3 over the income limit.

Economics Update

Find an update on Social Security at **ClassZone.com**

Medicare The Medicare program was introduced in 1966 as an additional old-age benefit under Social Security. Originally, Medicare provided hospital insurance, funded by a payroll tax, for people over 65, as well as optional medical coverage for items such as doctor bills. This part of Medicare is funded by premiums paid by those choosing the coverage and by general tax revenues.

Because of increasing numbers of retirees and increasing health care costs, Medicare costs have risen dramatically since the program began. Beginning in 2006, reforms to the program required Medicare to compete with private health insurance providers. Means testing was added for all but the lowest-income group of senior citizens. In addition, some coverage was added for prescription drugs.

QUICK REFERENCE

Medicaid is a government medical insurance program for low-income people.

Medicaid Established at the same time as Medicare, **Medicaid** is a joint federal-state medical insurance program for low-income people. The federal government funds about 63 percent of the costs of the program, and the states pay about 37 percent. In recent years, states have tightened their eligibility requirements for Medicaid in an effort to control costs.

Other Mandatory Spending Programs There are a variety of other mandatory spending programs that define eligibility requirements and are then funded based on an estimate of how many people meet those requirements. The Food Stamp program provides funds for about 26 million low-income people to purchase food. Veterans' benefits include health care coverage and disability payments for service-related illness or injury. People who have served in the military are also eligible for education assistance. The federal government spends about $50 billion a year on veterans' benefits.

Payments for the federal portion of unemployment insurance are also part of mandatory spending. In addition, the federal government pays its workers some retirement benefits. Federal employees hired after 1983 are also eligible for some Social Security retirement benefits.

Services for Veterans The Veterans Administration serves the needs and represents the interests of some 26 million veterans and their dependents.

429

TYPE 2 Discretionary Spending

More than one-third of federal revenue is devoted to discretionary spending. The programs covered by discretionary spending fall into several different categories. These categories include

• interstate highway system and transportation programs, such as Amtrak;

• natural resources and the environment, including conservation programs, pollution clean-up, and national parks;

• education, most notably college tuition assistance;

• science, space, technology, and other research programs;

• justice administration, including enforcement agencies, such as the Federal Bureau of Investigation (FBI), and the federal court system.

The largest discretionary expenditure category, however, is national defense, which takes up about 50 percent of the total discretionary budget. National defense includes a large amount of the nation's military spending, including the salaries of military personnel, weapons, and the construction and maintenance of military bases. Not all national defense spending is discretionary. Some spending on homeland security—border protection and the enforcement of some immigration laws, for example—falls in the mandatory expenditures category. In addition, certain military spending, such as additional funding requests for the wars in Iraq and Afghanistan, is outside the basic federal budget.

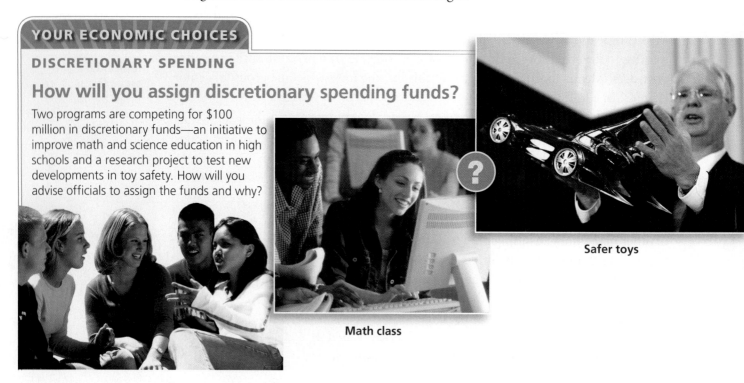

YOUR ECONOMIC CHOICES

DISCRETIONARY SPENDING

How will you assign discretionary spending funds?

Two programs are competing for $100 million in discretionary funds—an initiative to improve math and science education in high schools and a research project to test new developments in toy safety. How will you advise officials to assign the funds and why?

Math class

Safer toys

APPLICATION Categorizing Economic Information

A. Categorize the following items as either mandatory spending or discretionary spending: AIDS prevention programs, air traffic regulation, medical coverage for low-income people, pollution control, retirement benefits for older workers.

The Federal Budget and Spending

KEY CONCEPTS

Each year the President and Congress work together to establish the **federal budget**, a plan for spending federal tax money. The budget is prepared for a **fiscal year**, a 12-month period for which an organization plans its expenditures. The federal government's fiscal year runs from October 1 through September 30. The President's budget is prepared by the Office of Management and Budget (OMB) and takes into account estimated tax receipts and requests by all federal departments and agencies. Figure 14.9 shows the OMB budget estimate for fiscal year 2007.

QUICK REFERENCE

The **federal budget** is a plan for spending federal tax money.

A **fiscal year** is a 12-month period for which an organization plans its expenditures.

Appropriations are specific amounts of money set aside for specific purposes.

Congress Acts on the Budget

The Congressional Budget Office helps the House and Senate develop guidelines for different **appropriations**, which are set amounts of money set aside for specific purposes. Members of Congress often make deals to gain votes for appropriations that they support. Congress votes on the final budget and sends it to the president for approval. If the budget is not approved by the beginning of the new fiscal year, Congress passes resolutions to keep the government running on a day-to-day basis.

Methods of Federal Spending

After budget approval, the funds are spent in several ways. One way is direct spending, by which the government buys goods and services that it needs to operate, such as military equipment and office supplies. Paying the salaries of government

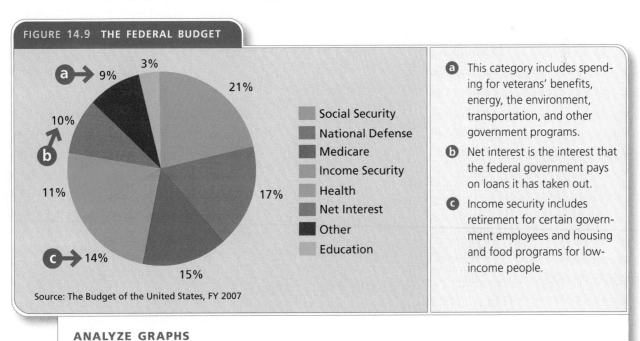

FIGURE 14.9 THE FEDERAL BUDGET

Social Security
National Defense
Medicare
Income Security
Health
Net Interest
Other
Education

ⓐ This category includes spending for veterans' benefits, energy, the environment, transportation, and other government programs.

ⓑ Net interest is the interest that the federal government pays on loans it has taken out.

ⓒ Income security includes retirement for certain government employees and housing and food programs for low-income people.

Source: The Budget of the United States, FY 2007

ANALYZE GRAPHS
1. What is the largest category of spending in the federal budget?
2. Approximately how much of the federal budget goes to health and education?

QUICK REFERENCE

Transfer payments are money distributed to taxpayers who do not provide anything in return.

A **grant-in-aid** is a transfer payment from the federal government to state or local governments.

The **private sector** is the part of the economy owned by individuals or businesses.

employees is another type of direct spending. A second way the government spends the money is through **transfer payments**—money distributed to taxpayers who do not provide goods or services in return. A **grant-in-aid** is a transfer payment from the federal government to state or local governments.

Transfer Payments These payments are generally part of the mandatory spending you learned about earlier. For example, Social Security retirement or disability benefits and health care benefits from Medicare or veterans' programs are transfer payments from the government to individual taxpayers. The taxpayers do not provide specific goods or services in exchange for these government funds.

Grants-in-aid These grants are transfer payments between levels of government. The federal government makes grants to states, local governments, and regions. The grants are designated for specific categories of activities such as highway construction, certain school services, or Medicaid funding.

The Impact of Federal Spending

Because the federal government spends trillions of dollars, it is a big factor in the economy. The federal government influences the economy in three ways: resource allocation, income redistribution, and competition with the **private sector**, which is that part of the economy owned by individuals or businesses.

Resource Allocation The federal government makes choices concerning where to spend money and on what to spend it, and that influences how resources are allocated. For example, if money goes to urban transit, it cannot go to fix rural roads. Similarly, money spent on weapons systems for the military cannot be spent on some other program, such as environmental protection.

Income Redistribution Government spending affects the incomes of families, individuals, and businesses. Transfer payments for health care, retirement, and Food Stamp benefits, for example, provide income support for many low-income earners. How the government awards work contracts can also influence the distribution of income. For example, if the government awards a contract to build several submarines to a shipyard in the Northeast, workers there will be assured work and an income. However, workers at a California shipyard that failed to get the contract may lose their jobs. In turn, they will not have income to spend at local businesses.

Competition with the Private Sector The government may produce goods or services that are also produced in the private sector. Examples include veterans' hospitals that compete with privately owned hospitals, or federal housing that competes with homes and apartments provided by private developers and landlords.

Government Contracts
A government contract, such as one to build submarines, has a huge impact on local, state, and regional economies.

APPLICATION Drawing Conclusions

B. How are transfer payments related to income redistribution?

1. Explain the relationship between the terms in each of these pairs.

a. *mandatory spending* **b.** *federal budget* **c.** *transfer payment*
   entitlement   *fiscal year*   *grant-in-aid*

2. What is the difference between mandatory spending and discretionary spending?

3. Why is Medicaid an example of an entitlement program?

4. What does Congress do when it decides on appropriations?

5. How does the government compete with the private sector?

6. Using Your Notes How is the
federal budget established?
Refer to your completed hierarchy
diagram. Use the Graphic
Organizer at **Interactive
Review @ ClassZone.com**

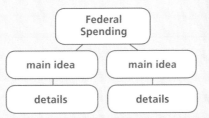

7. Making Inferences Between 2007 and 2009, spending on Social Security is projected to remain at 21.5 percent of the federal budget, while spending on education is projected to decline from 3.4 percent to 3.1 percent of the budget. How does this show the difference between mandatory and discretionary spending?

8. Categorizing Economic Information Categorize each of these examples of federal spending as direct spending, transfer payment, or grant-in-aid:

- computers for IRS
- disability benefits
- flood control in Gulf Coast region
- highway funds for states
- medical care for elderly
- money for urban housing
- price supports for farmers
- repair of space shuttle
- salaries for national park rangers

9. Challenge Molly's grandmother was born in 1943. If she retires in 2005, she'll receive $750 per month in Social Security benefits. If she waits until 2009, she will receive $1,000, and if she waits until 2010, her monthly benefit increases to $1,080. Why do you think Congress structured the Social Security benefit payments program in this way?

Military base entrance

Studying Economic Impact
Consider what you have learned about the impact of federal spending on the economy. The chart below shows information on the impact of a hypothetical military base on an area's economy.

Direct military base employment	27,400 jobs, $1 billion payroll
Additional related jobs	19,500 jobs, $800 million payroll
Payments to private health care providers	$19 million
Contracts for goods and services	$115 million
State and local taxes	$102.8 million

Analyze Data Study the chart to answer these questions:

- What is the total number of jobs attributable to the military base?

- How much does the base spend on health care?

Challenge Write a summary of the economic impact of the military base.

State and Local Taxes and Spending

OBJECTIVES

In Section 4, you will
- identify the major sources of revenue for both state and local governments
- examine the concept of a balanced budget
- describe the major categories of state and local expenditures

KEY TERMS

balanced budget, *p. 436*
operating budget, *p. 436*
capital budget, *p. 436*
tax assessor, *p. 437*

TAKING NOTES

As you read Section 4, complete a chart using the key concepts and other helpful words and phrases. Use the Graphic Organizer at **Interactive Review @ ClassZone.com**

State Government		Local Government	
Revenue	Spending	Revenue	Spending

State Revenues

KEY CONCEPTS

As you recall from earlier in this chapter, all levels of government may impose taxes to raise revenue to support their activities. The federal government has the broadest tax base, while the smallest tax base is at the local level. There are thousands of local governmental units, from towns, cities, and counties to districts set up to handle a specific problem such as mosquito control or sewage treatment.

State revenues come from a variety of sources, the largest of which is intergovernmental revenue, mostly grants-in-aid from the federal government. States also raise funds from state sales taxes and from state income tax, both on individuals and on corporations. (See Figure 14.11 on page 437.)

TYPE 1 Sales and Excise Taxes

All states except Alaska, Delaware, New Hampshire, Montana, and Oregon levy a state sales tax. Rates range from 2.9 percent in Colorado to 7.25 percent in California. These taxes generally are applied to most goods and services sold within the state. However, many states exempt food and prescription drugs from sales tax. Some other states tax these goods, over-the-counter drugs, and certain other medical supplies at a lower rate. In addition, charitable, religious, and educational organizations are often exempt from paying sales taxes.

All states also have excise taxes on cigarettes, alcohol, gasoline, and diesel fuel. Certain government organizations, volunteer fire-fighting companies, and farmers may be exempt from fuel taxes. Many states also have special sales taxes that mostly affect tourists, such as taxes on car rentals and hotel and motel room rates.

Economics Update

Find an update on state sales taxes at **ClassZone.com**

TYPE 2 Income Tax and Other Revenue Sources

Income taxes account for some 16 percent of states' total revenue. Most states levy taxes on both individual and corporate income. However, Alaska, Florida, and Texas have no individual income tax. And Nevada, South Dakota, Washington, and Wyoming levy neither individual nor corporate income taxes. Most states have progressive tax rates on individual income and flat tax rates on corporate income. Individual income tax rates range from a low of 0.36 percent for the lowest tax bracket in Iowa to 9.5 percent for the highest tax bracket in Vermont. Figure 14.10 below compares average individual income tax rates and sales tax rates for several states.

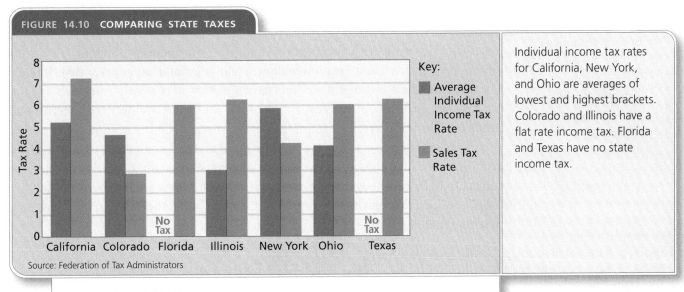

FIGURE 14.10 COMPARING STATE TAXES

Key:
- Average Individual Income Tax Rate
- Sales Tax Rate

Individual income tax rates for California, New York, and Ohio are averages of lowest and highest brackets. Colorado and Illinois have a flat rate income tax. Florida and Texas have no state income tax.

Source: Federation of Tax Administrators

ANALYZE GRAPHS
1. Which state has the highest income tax rate? Which has the highest sales tax rate?
2. Which state has the heaviest tax burden?

The average state corporate tax rate is about 6.8 percent, ranging from a low of 1 percent for the lowest brackets in Alaska and Arkansas to Pennsylvania's flat rate of 9.99 percent. Many state governments structure their corporate tax rates to attract businesses to the state. These governments have used billions of dollars in tax cuts and incentives for businesses to promote economic development. However, states receive benefits from these tax practices in the increased economic activity that development brings.

States also raise revenue from several other sources. Many of these sources, including estate taxes and user fees, are the same as those used by the federal government. (See Figure 14.8 on page 426.) Most states also levy property taxes. In addition, most states charge several fees related to business operations. These include registration fees for certain types of businesses and license fees for doctors, dentists, lawyers, and accountants.

APPLICATION Comparing Economic Information

A. How do state income tax rates compare to federal income tax rates?

State Budgets and Spending

All states except Vermont are required to have a **balanced budget**, in which total government revenue from all sources is equal to total government spending. However, balanced-budget requirements usually apply only to certain kinds of spending. Further, nearly every state has a reserve fund or may run a surplus, both of which can be used to balance the budget in subsequent years.

State Budgets

States actually work with two types of budgets—an **operating budget,** a plan for day-to-day expenses, and a **capital budget**, a plan for major expenses or investments. The operating budget generally covers expenses that occur each year, such as salaries for state government employees, payments for health and welfare benefits, and funds for education systems. Capital budgets provide funds for large construction and maintenance projects on state buildings, roads, and bridges, as well as for land acquisition for state construction needs or state parks. Usually, operating budgets are subject to balanced-budget requirements. Capital budgets are not, because they are usually funded through borrowing. In fact, capital budgets often are run at a deficit, meaning that more is spent than is collected in revenues.

Deficit Spending Both federal and state governments practice deficit spending—spending more than they collect in revenues—to cover their expenses.

State Expenses

Education is a major expense for the states, which not only support community colleges and state university systems but also provide assistance to local school districts. For example, state assistance accounted for about 49 percent of public school funding in 2002. Public safety, too, is a significant state expense. Spending on public safety includes state police, crime labs, and prisons and other correctional facilities. States also support a court system.

Public welfare expenses involve funds for state-run hospitals as well as cash assistance and medical care payments to the needy. States also fund programs that help citizens with problems related to housing, disability, unemployment, and job training. Other expenses include state government administration, retirement funds for state employees, natural resources, and economic development.

APPLICATION Categorizing

B. Would a grant to a city to build a new sewage treatment plant be part of the city's operating budget or capital budget?

Local Revenue and Spending

Local government units include counties, cities, towns, villages, townships, school districts, and other special districts. They have fewer options for raising revenue than do other levels of government. Their major revenue sources are intergovernmental revenue—or transfers—from state and federal governments and property taxes. Local governments also tap other sources, many of which are similar to the state tax base. Figure 14.11 shows revenue sources for state and local governments.

Property Tax

Recall that you read about property tax in the first section of the chapter. This tax can be levied on real estate and on personal property such as motor vehicles, boats, expensive jewelry, or computers. Local governments rely on a **tax assessor**, a government official who determines the value of the property. They then enact a tax based on a percentage of the property's value.

Other Taxes

Local governments also use sales taxes, sin taxes on activities such as gambling, hospitality taxes on hotels and restaurants, entertainment taxes on tickets or entrance fees, and payroll taxes. The local payroll tax is a tax on people who work in a city but live outside the city. Such a tax is often used in large metropolitan areas where workers from the suburbs benefit from city services such as police and fire protection.

QUICK REFERENCE

A **tax assessor** determines the value of property.

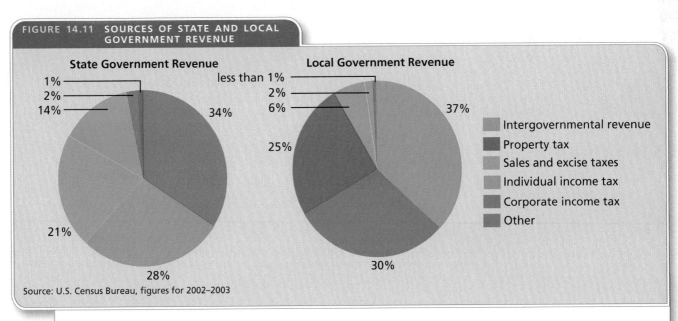

FIGURE 14.11 SOURCES OF STATE AND LOCAL GOVERNMENT REVENUE

State Government Revenue

Local Government Revenue

- Intergovernmental revenue
- Property tax
- Sales and excise taxes
- Individual income tax
- Corporate income tax
- Other

Source: U.S. Census Bureau, figures for 2002–2003

ANALYZE GRAPHS
1. What are the two largest sources of revenue for both state and local governments?
2. Which type of government gets a larger percentage of its revenue from sales and excise taxes?

Local Spending

Local governments provide most of the direct services that citizens receive. To deliver these services, local governments employ almost three times the number of workers as state governments do. Some of the most important areas of local spending are described below.

Public Schools Local governments have the main responsibility for elementary and secondary schools. About 46 percent of local government spending goes to education. Government funds pay for construction and maintenance of school buildings, salaries for teachers, administrators, and other personnel, as well as for items such as textbooks and computers. Reliance on the property tax has led to difficulties for many local governments, since communities with lower property values have smaller tax bases to finance education.

Public Safety Local governments provide police and fire protection to secure lives and property in their communities. They are also responsible for emergency medical equipment and personnel to provide on-site treatment and transportation to medical facilities. Local governments maintain the 911 emergency telephone number system. Other expenditures in this category include animal control, consumer protection, and preparation for and response to natural disasters.

Public Welfare Local governments spend less than state governments on direct payments for medical care and assistance to the needy. However, many local governments maintain public health departments, and some own and operate their own hospitals. Local health departments are concerned with immunization programs, environmental health, and maintaining birth and death records. They also are responsible for making sure that restaurants meet health standards.

Public Safety Ensuring the safety of life and property in the community—by providing fire protection, for example—is the responsibility of local government.

Other Responsibilities Local governments also have primary responsibility for providing most public utilities such as water, public transit, sewage systems, and trash removal. They maintain local highways, roads, and streets, including traffic control lights and signs, snow removal, and pothole repair. Finally, local governments provide many kinds of recreational and cultural facilities including parks, recreation centers, swimming pools, and libraries.

APPLICATION Drawing Conclusions

B. Why do local governments rely more on property taxes as a source of revenue than do state governments?

SECTION 4 Assessment

Online Quiz
ClassZone.com

REVIEWING KEY CONCEPTS

1. Use each of the three terms below in a sentence that illustrates the meaning of the term.

   a. *balanced budget*   **b.** *capital budget*   **c.** *tax assessor*

2. What is the difference between an operating budget and a capital budget?

3. How is an operating budget related to a balanced budget?

4. What is the largest revenue source for state governments? What is the largest source for local governments?

5. Why do local governments need tax assessors?

6. **Using Your Notes** What kinds of education do state and local governments spend money on? Refer to your completed chart. Use the Graphic Organizer at **Interactive Review @ ClassZone.com**

State Government		Local Government	
Revenue	Spending	Revenue	Spending

CRITICAL THINKING

7. **Comparing and Contrasting** What are the similarities and differences in the sources of revenue for state and local governments?

8. **Analyzing Effects** Which level of government would be most affected if the federal government decided to limit the amount of money that it spent on the Medicaid program? Give reasons for your answer.

9. **Making Inferences** Voters in your city must decide whether to raise revenue by increasing the rate of property tax for owners of homes and businesses or by placing a new tax on motel and hotel room rates and car rentals. Which tax are voters more likely to choose? Give reasons for your answer.

10. **Challenge** Between 1992 and 2002, average state funding for public schools increased from 46 percent of all state expenditures to 49 percent of all state expenditures. At the same time, local government funding of public schools decreased from 47 percent to 43 percent. Why do you think the source of school funding has changed in this way?

ECONOMICS IN PRACTICE

School board meeting

Using a Decision Making Process
Suppose that you are on a local school board. Total budget for the school district is $25,000,000. The chart below lists the items to be funded out of this budget.

Spending Category	Priority
Administrative salaries	
Classroom computers	
School lunch program	
Special education programs	
Teacher salaries	
Textbooks and other instructional materials	
Utilities	

Decide on Funding Priorities Use a decision-making process to decide how to allocate the budget. Complete the chart by ranking the items from 1 to 7, from most important to least important.

Challenge Based on your priorities, allocate a percentage of the budget to each category.

439

Should Online Sales Be Taxed?

Background In 1992 the Supreme Court upheld a law making Internet retailers exempt from collecting most sales taxes. The ruling was based on the fact that, at the time, the various state and local rules for tax collection varied widely. The differing rules would have placed a heavy burden on Internet retailers charged with having to collect taxes on what they sold.

Today, however, tax collection is becoming simpler and more streamlined. In addition, Internet purchases have become commonplace, with shoppers buying everything from computers to airplane tickets. Many online shoppers fail to realize that they are required to pay sales tax for Internet purchases at their home state's rate. To date, most states have tried to collect Internet sales tax on a voluntary basis. Needless to say, results have been poor. Given this and other considerations, Internet sales tax once again is a subject for debate.

What's the issue? Should there be sales tax on Internet purchases? Study these sources to discover arguments for and against taxing purchases online.

A. Online News Story

This news story on whether to impose the "iPod tax"—a tax on digital products—illustrates the differences of opinion on online sales tax.

Entertainment Lovers May Soon Pay Tax on Downloads

Wisconsin governor and legislators disagree over "iPod" tax.

Wisconsin Gov. Jim Doyle now wants his state to start collecting taxes on digital music, videos and software. Key Republicans in the GOP-dominated legislature say they will block the proposal, but administration officials say they're just trying to make things fair.

"It's an issue of tax equity," said Jessica Iverson, a spokeswoman for the Wisconsin Department of Revenue. "If you go into a Main Street business and purchase a CD, you are paying tax. . . ."

Economists are split . . . as to whether adding these kinds of taxes is a good idea. Some say that taxes on digital goods will hamper the growth of a potentially vibrant new marketplace, while others say that having taxes only on offline versions of the same goods distorts the operation of free markets.

Source: **News.com, March 10, 2005**

Thinking Economically What do you think economists mean when they say that taxing only offline versions of the same goods "distorts the operation of free markets"?

This graph shows the growth of online purchases during the 2000s.

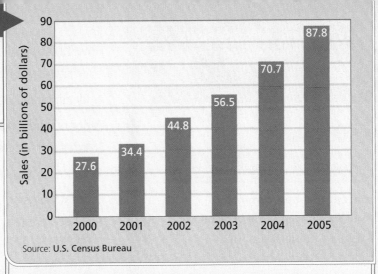

Sales (in billions of dollars)

Year	Sales
2000	27.6
2001	34.4
2002	44.8
2003	56.5
2004	70.7
2005	87.8

Source: U.S. Census Bureau

Thinking Economically How might state and local governments use the information in the graph to support their demand to levy sales taxes on online purchases?

C. Newspaper Editorial

Some states are becoming pro-active in their efforts to promote Internet sales tax. This newspaper editorial describes one multistate project to facilitate the collection of the tax.

Internet Sales Tax

Eighteen states agree to establish uniform sales tax rules.

Last week, 18 state tax collectors met in Chicago to announce an interstate agreement establishing uniform sales tax rules. Starting in October, the group will offer free software that will allow any business to easily collect the required taxes online.

The states' demonstration project will drive home the point that online sales-tax collection can be done nationwide. Many retailers already collect the taxes. Now Congress should step up and pass a law overturning the court's exemption in states that have streamlined their tax systems. That would allow hard-pressed states to take in roughly $20 billion a year in annual sales tax revenue that is rightfully theirs, and perhaps much more, depending on the growth in online shopping. It would also help level the playing field between local and online retailers.

Source: "Internet Sales Tax," *New York Times*, July 5, 2005

Thinking Economically What impact has Internet shopping had on state and local revenues? Explain your answer.

THINKING ECONOMICALLY Synthesizing

1. Summarize the arguments for and against an Internet sales tax as presented in the documents.

2. Who is most likely to benefit from Internet sales tax revenue? Explain your answer, using information from the documents.

3. How has government responded to e-commerce—the selling of goods and services online? Use information from the documents in your answer.

Interactive Review

Review this chapter using interactive activities at **ClassZone.com**

- Online Summary
- Quizzes
- Vocabulary Flip Cards
- Graphic Organizers
- Review and Study Notes

Online Summary

Complete the following activity either on your own paper or online at **ClassZone.com**

Choose the key concept that best completes the sentence. Not all key concepts will be used.

ability-to-pay principle of taxation	proportional tax
balanced budget	regressive tax
benefit principle of taxation	revenue
capital budget	tax
discretionary spending	tax base
entitlement	tax incentive
incidence of tax	tax return
indexing	taxable income
mandatory spending	transfer payment
progressive tax	withholding

__1__ is a mandatory payment to a government. __2__ is government income. The __3__ holds that people should be taxed on their ability to pay, no matter the level of benefits they receive.

A __4__ is the income, property, goods or services subject to taxes. A __5__ takes the same percentage of income from all taxpayers. A __6__ places a higher rate of taxation on high-income people, and a __7__ takes a larger percentage of income from low-income people. The __8__ is the final burden of tax.

__9__ is money taken from a worker's pay before the worker receives it. __10__ is a revision of tax brackets to prevent workers from paying more taxes due to inflation. Social Security is an example of an __11__, a social welfare program with specific requirements. Such programs make up most of federal __12__, which is spending that is required by law.

States are required to have a __13__, in which government revenue and spending are equal.

REVIEWING KEY CONCEPTS

How Taxes Work (pp. 410–419)

1. What is the relationship between tax and revenue?

2. Identify three ways that taxes affect the economy.

Federal Taxes (pp. 420–427)

3. What is the largest source of federal revenue?

4. Which tax pays for Social Security and Medicare?

Federal Government Spending (pp. 428–433)

5. What are three programs that make up most mandatory spending?

6. How does federal spending affect the economy?

State and Local Taxes and Spending (pp. 434–441)

7. What are the two types of state budgets?

8. What tax base are tax assessors concerned with?

APPLYING ECONOMIC CONCEPTS

Look at the chart below showing average combined city and state tax rates for families with different incomes in several cities.

FIGURE 14.13 STATE AND LOCAL TAXES FOR A FAMILY OF FOUR					
City	Total taxes paid as a percent of income				
	$25,000	$50,000	$75,000	$100,000	$150,000
Atlanta	8.1	10.3	11.4	11.5	11.7
Chicago	9.3	9.5	10.0	9.7	9.3
Houston	6.2	6.0	6.3	5.9	5.5
Jacksonville	4.3	4.6	5.0	4.8	4.6
Los Angeles	8.6	8.7	10.3	11.2	12.3
New York	5.6	10.8	12.7	13.4	14.1
Philadelphia	11.0	13.2	13.0	12.6	12.2

Source: *Statistical Abstract of the United States, 2002 figures*

9. Which city has the lowest tax rate for the lowest-income families? Which has the lowest tax rate for the highest-income families?

10. Which combined city and state tax structures are progressive and which are regressive?

11. Creating Graphs The state legislature proposes new 10 percent excise taxes on the following goods and services: gasoline, ice cream, local telephone service, and sports cars. For each good or service create supply and demand curves showing the supply curve before the tax and how the supply curve shifts after the tax. Under each graph, write a caption explaining who will pay more of the tax—the consumer or the producer—and why.

Use *SMARTGrapher* @ ClassZone.com to complete this activity.

12. Analyzing Data Shandra earns $30,000 per year from her job as a radiology technician. She takes a personal exemption of $3,200 and the standard deduction of $5,000 to reduce her taxable income.

a. If she pays 10 percent tax on the first $7,300 of taxable income and 15 percent on the rest, how much does she pay in income tax?

b. Shandra's FICA tax rate is 7.65 percent. What are her FICA taxes?

c. How much total tax does Shandra pay? What is her effective tax rate as a percentage of her taxable income and of her total income?

13. Making Inferences When Rajiv goes shopping for a new MP3 player, he notices that he pays 7.35 percent sales tax on the purchase. He knows that the state sales tax rate is 4.22 percent. What accounts for the difference?

14. Comparing and Contrasting All states have excise taxes on cigarettes and gasoline. What are the similarities and differences in the reasons why states tax these two items?

15. Challenge In 2003, Congress reduced the tax rate paid by individual investors on dividends and capital gains to 15 percent. Previously the rate for dividends had been as high as 38.6 percent, and capital gains had been taxed at 20 percent. Which of these changes addressed the charge that corporate income is subject to double taxation? Give reasons for your answer.

Develop a Federal Budget

Step 1 Choose a partner. Imagine that you are members of Congress who must determine the discretionary spending portion of the federal budget. The table below shows the categories of spending. You have a total of $960 billion to spend. Determine your spending priorities by deciding what percent of the budget to allocate to each category.

FEDERAL DISCRETIONARY SPENDING CATEGORIES	
Administration of justice	Health (non-Medicaid)
Agriculture	International affairs
Community & regional development	National defense
Education	Natural resources & environment
Energy	Science, space & technology
General government	Transportation

Step 2 Form a group with two or three other pairs of students so that there are now a total of four groups in the class. Compare your budgets, noting areas of agreement and disagreement. Negotiate to develop a single budget proposal for your group.

Step 3 Present your group's budget proposal to the class. Include a list of reasons to support your budget choices.

Step 4 As a class, decide on a final recommendation that resolves any differences among the four budget proposals.

Step 5 Present your final budget to your teacher, who is acting as the President. Make necessary changes to the budget to resolve any differences between the Congress and the President.

Government

Federal government actions in the areas of taxing and spending are designed to enhance the nation's economic stability.

CHAPTER

15

Using Fiscal Policy

CONCEPT REVIEW

The **business cycle** is the series of growing and shrinking periods of economic activity.

CHAPTER 15 KEY CONCEPT

Fiscal policy uses taxes and government spending in an effort to smooth out the peaks and troughs of the business cycle.

WHY THE CONCEPT MATTERS

In history classes, you've probably read about instances of rampant inflation when people needed bags and bags of cash to pay for their groceries. Or you might have read about periods of economic depression when millions of workers lost their jobs. By using a combination of spending and taxation, the federal government tries to reduce the impact of such economic extremes.

Online Highlights
More at ClassZone.com

 Economics Update
Go to **ECONOMICS UPDATE** for chapter updates and current news on the federal deficit. (See Case Study, pp. 468–469.) ▶

Animated Economics
Go to **ANIMATED ECONOMICS** for interactive lessons on the graphs and tables in this chapter.

Interactive ◀▶ Review
Go to **INTERACTIVE REVIEW** for concept review and activities.

BUREAU OF SPENDING INCREASES AND DEFICIT REDUCTION

SCHWADRON
"WAIT A MINUTE! HOW CAN THAT BE?"

Source: www.CartoonStock.com

How big a problem is the federal deficit? See the Case Study on pages 468–469.

What Is Fiscal Policy?

OBJECTIVES	KEY TERMS	TAKING NOTES
In Section 1, you will • examine the tools used in fiscal policy • determine how fiscal policy affects the economy • identify the problems and limitations of fiscal policy	fiscal, *p. 446* fiscal policy, *p. 446* expansionary fiscal policy, *p. 446* contractionary fiscal policy, *p. 446* discretionary fiscal policy, *p. 446* automatic stabilizers, *p. 447* rational expectations theory, *p. 452* Council of Economic Advisers, *p. 452*	As you read Section 1, complete a cluster diagram that organizes the main ideas about fiscal policy. Use the Graphic Organizer at **Interactive Review @ ClassZone.com** 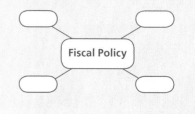

Fiscal Policy Tools

KEY CONCEPTS

In Chapter 14, you learned that the government puts the tax dollars it collects to a variety of uses. The term **fiscal** refers to anything related to government revenue, spending, and debt. **Fiscal policy** is the federal government's use of taxes and government spending to affect the economy. Fiscal policy has one of two goals: to increase aggregate demand or to fight inflation.

To stabilize or strengthen the economy, the government may use one of two basic policies. When the economy slows, the government may use **expansionary fiscal policy**, a plan to increase aggregate demand and stimulate a weak economy. When the economy is in an inflationary period, the government may use a **contractionary fiscal policy**, a plan to reduce aggregate demand and slow the economy in a period of too-rapid expansion. The federal government has two basic fiscal tools to influence the economy: taxation and government spending.

Discretionary Fiscal Policy

As you learned in Chapter 14, discretionary spending is spending that the government must authorize each year. In other words, the government must make a choice about this type of spending. Similarly, **discretionary fiscal policy** involves actions taken by the government by choice to correct economic instability. This type of policy involves an active government response, through choices about taxes or government spending, to help stabilize the economy. Congress must enact legislation for these policies to be implemented. This type of fiscal policy is discussed in more depth later in this section and in Section 2.

Automatic Stabilizers

Unlike discretionary fiscal policy, **automatic stabilizers** are features of fiscal policy that work automatically to steady the economy. Both of these approaches use taxes and government spending to influence the economy. Discretionary fiscal policy involves government choices about whether an expansionary or contractionary policy is needed and how the chosen policy should be put into action. Automatic stabilizers, such as public transfer payments and progressive income taxes, may work in an expansionary or contractionary manner, but they work automatically rather than through active policy choices.

Public Transfer Payments As you recall from Chapter 14, public transfer payments include programs such as unemployment compensation, food stamps, and other entitlements. These payments automatically set up a flow of money into the economy. Therefore, this form of government spending helps stabilize the economy automatically.

For example, during a recession more people are unemployed and qualify to receive unemployment compensation and other government benefits, such as food stamps or welfare payments. When people receive these benefits, they gain a certain amount of income to spend, and the effects of the recession are less severe than they would be without the transfer payments.

Automatic Stabilizers Unemployed workers wait to register for unemployment compensation, a program designed to stabilize the economy by providing temporary replacement wages.

When the economy improves, fewer people qualify for food stamps, unemployment compensation, and other entitlements, and government spending automatically decreases. This automatic decrease keeps the economy from growing too fast. By helping to control aggregate demand, this automatic stabilizer keeps prices from rising too quickly and leading to inflation.

Progressive Income Taxes The individual income tax is progressive. As income increases, so do the tax rate and the amount of taxes paid. The progressive nature of the income tax allows it to act as an automatic stabilizer to the economy without additional government action.

For example, during prosperous times, individual incomes rise, and some individuals move into higher tax brackets. These taxpayers pay more in taxes and do not have all of their increased income to spend or save. By preventing some of the increased income from entering the economy, this automatically higher taxation keeps the economy from growing too quickly and helps keep inflation in check. On the other hand, during a recession, individuals earn less income and may move into lower tax brackets. Therefore, lower incomes result in lower taxes, which automatically reduce the impact of the recession.

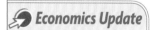
APPLICATION Applying Economic Concepts

A. Programs such as unemployment insurance ensure that people experiencing economic hardship have a basic level of income. How does this help to stabilize the economy?

The Purpose of Fiscal Policy

KEY CONCEPTS

Fiscal policy can be used for expansionary or contractionary purposes. The choice of policy depends on whether the economy is weak or strong. Expansionary fiscal policy is designed to stimulate a weak economy to grow. Contractionary fiscal policy is used to slow the economy down in order to control inflation.

POLICY 1 Expansionary Fiscal Policy

Government may use expansionary policy to increase the level of aggregate demand so that growth occurs in the economy. As you recall from Chapter 13, increased aggregate demand causes prices to rise, providing incentives for businesses to expand and causing GDP to increase. Expansionary fiscal policy also reduces the rate of unemployment, as there are more jobs available when businesses are expanding. Expansionary fiscal policy may involve increased government spending, decreased taxes, or both.

For example, suppose the economy is in recession and, in response, the government decides to increase spending for highways. The government spends the money by contracting with private firms in many cities to build new roads. This spending creates additional jobs as the contractors hire more and more construction workers to complete the projects. If employment increases, more people will have income to spend, and aggregate demand increases for all goods and services in the economy.

The government may also choose to cut taxes to stimulate the economy. By lowering individual and corporate income tax rates, the government allows individuals and businesses to have more income left after taxes. Individuals may spend their increased income and thereby increase demand for numerous goods and services. Increased income may allow them to increase their savings, which makes more money available to businesses to invest. Lower taxes also leave businesses with more money to invest in new equipment or plants, or in additional workers to produce more goods and services to meet increased demand.

Whether the government increases spending, decreases taxes, or uses some combination of the two, the result is somewhat similar. As Figure 15.1 on the opposite page shows, expansionary fiscal policy leads to an increase in aggregate demand (the curve shifts to the right) and, therefore, economic growth.

Expansion Increased construction of new housing is an indication that the economy is expanding.

POLICY 2 Contractionary Fiscal Policy

The federal government may use contractionary policy to decrease the level of aggregate demand so that inflation is reduced. When the economy is growing too rapidly, aggregate demand may increase faster than aggregate supply, leading to demand-pull inflation. This type of inflation, which you read about in Chapter 13, is characterized by a steadily rising price level and a decrease in the purchasing power of people's incomes.

When the government faces such an economy, it may employ contractionary fiscal policy and use spending and taxes in ways opposite to expansionary fiscal policy. In other words, it may choose to decrease government spending or increase taxes in order to control inflation.

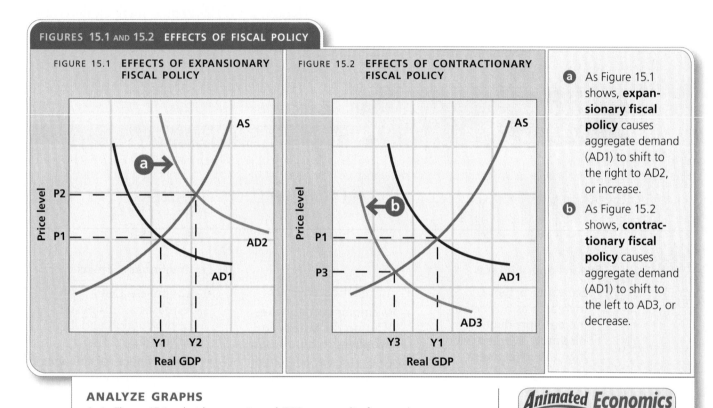

FIGURES 15.1 AND 15.2 EFFECTS OF FISCAL POLICY

FIGURE 15.1 EFFECTS OF EXPANSIONARY FISCAL POLICY

FIGURE 15.2 EFFECTS OF CONTRACTIONARY FISCAL POLICY

a As Figure 15.1 shows, **expansionary fiscal policy** causes aggregate demand (AD1) to shift to the right to AD2, or increase.

b As Figure 15.2 shows, **contractionary fiscal policy** causes aggregate demand (AD1) to shift to the left to AD3, or decrease.

ANALYZE GRAPHS
1. In Figure 15.1, what happens to real GDP as a result of expansionary fiscal policy?
2. In Figure 15.2, what happens to the price level as a result of contractionary fiscal policy?

Animated Economics

Use interactive aggregate demand and aggregate supply curves at **ClassZone.com**

For example, if the economy is growing too rapidly, the government may cut its spending on a variety of programs such as highway construction, education, and health care. By cutting spending, the government takes money out of the economy. This decreased government spending results in less income for individuals or businesses that are directly affected by the cuts in government programs. So these individuals have less money to spend on goods and services, and aggregate demand decreases. Businesses may cut production in response to decreased aggregate demand. As aggregate demand decreases, the rise in the price level is stopped, and inflation is brought under control.

Rather than cut spending, the government may choose to increase taxes. This leads to a decrease in consumer spending and, therefore, a slowdown in the rate of inflation. In other words, when individuals and businesses have to pay higher taxes, they have less income left over to spend or invest. As a result, aggregate demand will decrease. As aggregate demand decreases, businesses may cut back production and lay off workers. This will cause a further decrease in aggregate demand, because workers will have less to spend on goods and services. And as aggregate demand falls, so will the price level.

Whether the government decreases spending or increases taxes or uses some combination of the two, the impact of contractionary fiscal policy on aggregate demand and inflation is somewhat similar. Turn back to Figure 15.2 on page 449. Notice that contractionary fiscal policy results in the aggregate demand curve shifting to the left. This indicates that aggregate demand is decreasing. This decline in aggregate demand, in turn, helps control inflation. (The major fiscal policy tools, and their impact on the economy, are reviewed in Figure 15.3.)

ECONOMICS ESSENTIALS
FIGURE 15.3 Effects of Fiscal Policy on the Economy

Fiscal Policy Tools

Expansionary Effects

- Economic activity increases as businesses increase production, hire more workers, and increase investment
- More workers have more income to spend on goods and services
- Aggregate demand increases, resulting in economic growth

- Automatic stabilizers
- Raising or cutting taxes; offering tax breaks and incentives to businesses
- Increasing or decreasing government spending

Contractionary Effects

- Economic activity decreases as businesses cut production and lay off workers
- Workers have less income to spend on goods and services
- Aggregate demand decreases, bring inflation under control

ANALYZE CHARTS

The government can use a combination of taxing and spending policies to stimulate a sluggish economy or to slow down an overheated economy. At what point in the business cycle do you think the economy is today? What type of fiscal policy do you think the government should apply at this time?

APPLICATION Analyzing Cause and Effect

B. What effect does expansionary fiscal policy have on consumer spending? Explain your answer.

Limitations of Fiscal Policy

The purpose of fiscal policy is to reduce economic slowdowns, which result in unemployment, and to curb inflation. The success of fiscal policy, however, is limited by a number of issues, including policy lags and timing.

LIMITATION 1 Policy Lags

Fiscal policy lags behind the economic conditions it is designed to address. This situation is often related to identifying the problem and getting Congress to move on the issue. Months of debate may precede policy change. The lag also may be related to how quickly the change in policy takes effect. For example, the time for tax changes to take effect is shorter than that for government spending. In particular, it may take a long time for public spending programs to get started and money to begin flowing into the economy. Therefore, tax changes may be more effective than policy changes in dealing with short-term recessions.

LIMITATION 2 Timing Issues

The goal of fiscal policy is to provide a stable economic environment. This means that it should coordinate with the business cycle. Fiscal policy is described as countercyclical because the goal is to smooth out the peaks and troughs of the business cycle. If the timing of the policy is good, fluctuations in the business cycle will be less severe, as Figure 15.4 illustrates. If the timing is bad, however, it could make matters worse. For example, if the economy is already moving out of a recession when an expansionary fiscal policy takes effect, the result could be inflation.

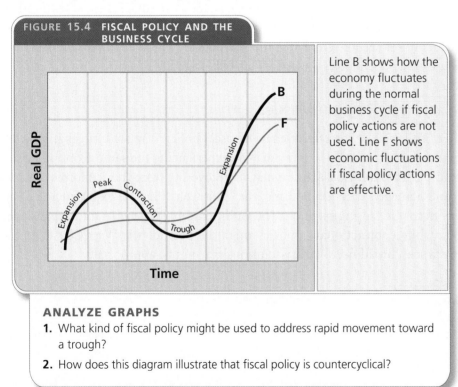

FIGURE 15.4 FISCAL POLICY AND THE BUSINESS CYCLE

Line B shows how the economy fluctuates during the normal business cycle if fiscal policy actions are not used. Line F shows economic fluctuations if fiscal policy actions are effective.

ANALYZE GRAPHS

1. What kind of fiscal policy might be used to address rapid movement toward a trough?

2. How does this diagram illustrate that fiscal policy is countercyclical?

LIMITATION 3 Rational Expectations Theory

QUICK REFERENCE

The **rational expecta-tions theory** states that people anticipate that changes in fiscal policy will affect the economy in a particular way and that, as a result, people will take steps to protect their interests.

A second phenomenon affecting timing is explained by the **rational expectations theory**, which states that individuals and business firms expect that changes in fiscal policy will have particular outcomes, and they take actions to protect their interests against those outcomes. These actions may limit the effectiveness of fiscal policy. For example, expansionary fiscal policy attempts to stimulate aggregate demand to increase employment. An increase in aggregate demand might also pull up the price level, causing inflation. In anticipation of rising inflation, people spend more to keep their buying power from decreasing. However, this increased spending causes more inflation and defeats the aims of the expansionary policy.

LIMITATION 4 Political Issues

Fiscal policy decisions are not always based on economic considerations. Sometimes, political considerations, most notably enhancing the chances of reelection, may influence the kind of fiscal policy that a government follows. The **Council of Economic Advisers** is a three-member group that advises the President on fiscal policy and other economic issues. Because of political pres-

QUICK REFERENCE

The **Council of Economic Advisers** is a group of economic advisors to the president.

Fiscal Policy and Politics Decisions on economic policy often are influenced by politics.

sures, however, the President may not always follow their advice. Even if the President does accept the council's guidance, members of Congress—again because of political considerations—may not agree with proposed policies. This is an important issue, since the House of Representatives is where all tax bills originate.

LIMITATION 5 Regional Issues

Another limitation of the effectiveness of fiscal policy is related to geography. Not every state or region of the country may be experiencing the same economic issues. For example, the Gulf Coast region may be recovering from the economic effects of hurricane damage. At the same time, the West Coast may be experiencing a high tech boom that is causing inflation. The Gulf Coast might benefit from expansionary policies, while contractionary policies might be best for the West Coast. In such circumstances, broad fiscal-policy solutions may not be appropriate.

APPLICATION Making Inferences

C. How do policy lags and timing issues work together to limit the effectiveness of fiscal policy?

SECTION 1 Assessment

Online Quiz
ClassZone.com

REVIEWING KEY CONCEPTS

1. Use each of the three terms below in a sentence that illustrates the meaning of the term.

   a. *expansionary fiscal policy*   **b.** *discretionary fiscal policy*   **c.** *rational expectations theory*

2. What are the two basic goals of fiscal policy?

3. How do expansionary fiscal policy and contractionary fiscal policy use the same fiscal policy tools in different ways?

4. What is the difference between discretionary fiscal policy and automatic stabilizers?

5. What is the role of the Council of Economic Advisers?

6. **Using Your Notes** What are the limitations of fiscal policy? Refer to your completed cluster diagram.

   Use the Graphic Organizer at **Interactive Review @ ClassZone.com**

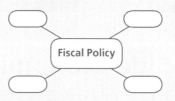

CRITICAL THINKING

7. **Making Inferences** Between 2001 and 2004, Congress passed a series of tax cuts and increased government spending. Do these actions reflect expansionary or contractionary fiscal policy? Explain your answer.

8. **Applying Economic Concepts** Agricultural price supports provide farmers with government subsidies when market prices of certain crops are low. What kind of fiscal policy is at work in this situation and how does it work?

9. **Drawing Conclusions** Federal government officials want to prevent a slowing economy from going into recession. They debate whether to increase spending on new public transit systems or decrease individual and corporate income tax rates.

   a. How would an understanding of policy lags help them decide which government action would be most effective?

   b. What other issues might affect their decision?

10. **Challenge** Make a copy of Figure 15.4 on page 451 and label the part of line F that might represent expansionary fiscal policy and the part that might represent contractionary fiscal policy.

ECONOMICS IN PRACTICE

Analyzing Economic Conditions Consider what you've learned about economic instability and fiscal policy. Then complete the following activities.

Propose Fiscal Policies For each situation listed in the chart, identify the problem and decide whether the fiscal policy should be expansionary or contractionary.

Economic Situation	Problem/Fiscal Policy Needed
Business investment spending declines for six straight months	
Consumer Price Index rises for four straight months	
Unemployment rate increases from 4% to 6.5% over six months	
Consumer confidence falls for five straight months	

Challenge Choose one situation and give examples of how fiscal policy might be applied to it.

Demand-Side and Supply-Side Policies

OBJECTIVES	KEY TERMS	TAKING NOTES
In Section 2, you will • describe how demand-side fiscal policy can be used to stimulate the economy • describe how supply-side fiscal policy can be used to stimulate the economy • identify the role that fiscal policy has in changing the economy	Keynesian economics, *p. 454* demand-side fiscal policy, *p. 454* spending multiplier effect, *p. 455* supply-side fiscal policy, *p. 458* Laffer Curve, *p. 459*	As you read Section 2, complete a chart to show the major features of demand-side and supply-side policies. Use the Graphic Organizer at **Interactive Review @ ClassZone.com**

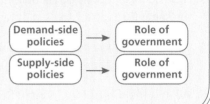

Demand-Side Economics

KEY CONCEPTS

Economists have not always supported the idea of discretionary fiscal policy. Historically, most think that the national government should have a limited role in the economy. When the country experienced financial panics and depressions, the government did little to help the economy get back on track.

The Great Depression of the 1930s changed many people's minds about the role of the government. High unemployment and low production persisted for several years. Many economists concluded that the old ways were ineffective in this situation. One economist, John Maynard Keynes, proposed a new way to address the problem.

The theories that Keynes put forward are called **Keynesian economics**, the idea that in times of recession aggregate demand needs to be stimulated by government action. Keynes believed that such an approach would lower unemployment. Keynesian economics forms the basis of **demand-side fiscal policy**, fiscal policy to stimulate aggregate demand.

QUICK REFERENCE

Keynesian economics states that aggregate demand needs to be stimulated by government action.

Demand-side fiscal policy is a plan to stimulate aggregate demand.

Demand-Side Policies The Civilian Conservation Corps (CCC), an employment program for young men, was one government action aimed at stimulating the economy during the Great Depression.

Keynesian Theory

Keynes argued that changes in aggregate demand influence the business cycle, and he expressed this idea in an equation. His equation states that the GDP equals the total market value of all consumer goods (C), investment goods (I), government goods (G), and net exports (F). The equation looks like this: GDP = C + I + G + F.

Keynes believed that net exports played only a small role in the economy and that government and consumer expenditures were fairly stable. He reasoned that it was investment that caused the economy to fluctuate and that investment creates a greater than one-for-one change in national income. That is, one dollar spent in investment has a **spending multiplier effect**, meaning that a change in spending is multiplied into a larger change in GDP. (See Figure 15.5.)

QUICK REFERENCE

The **spending multiplier effect** states that a small change in spending causes a much larger change in GDP.

MATH CHALLENGE
FIGURE 15.5 Spending Multiplier Effect

If Zain receives a $100 raise and spends $60 of it to buy products from Joan, Joan's income increases too. Similarly, if Joan uses $36 of her increased income to buy products from Ravi, Ravi's income increases. Ravi then buys from Sarah, and so on. Each increase in income contributes to the GDP, so the total effect of Zain's spending is multiplied. To quantify how spending increases GDP, economists use the spending multiplier.

Step 1: Determine the percentage of the money that is spent on domestic goods and services each time the money is reused. In the example, this is 60 percent.

NEED HELP?

Math Handbook, "Calculating Percentages," page R24

Step 2: Use this equation, where A is the percentage, to calculate the spending multiplier.

Sample Calculations

$$\frac{1}{1-A} = \text{Spending multiplier} \qquad \frac{1}{1-60\%} = \frac{1}{1-0.60} = 2.5$$

Step 3: Use the spending multiplier to calculate the total increase in GDP.

$$\text{Initial investment} \times \text{Spending multiplier} = \text{Total increase in GDP} \qquad \$100 \times 2.5 = \$250$$

If businesses invest less, the spending multiplier effect means that the decrease in overall spending is greater than the initial decrease in business investment. Because this effect touches the entire economy, the government may need to step in to offset changes in investment. This idea became the basis of demand-side fiscal economics, which favors the use of fiscal policy to stimulate aggregate demand.

APPLICATION Making Inferences

A. How did Keynes's equation help him conclude that if investment declined, government needed to increase spending or cut taxes to stimulate aggregate demand?

John Maynard Keynes: Architect of Demand-Side Policy

Many Americans are accustomed to the idea that the government plays an active role in the market economy. However, when John Maynard Keynes proposed his ideas in the 1930s, they were considered revolutionary. He questioned the principles of economics that had been accepted since the time of Adam Smith. How did Keynes's work change the way that people viewed the role of government in the economy?

Using Government Action to Stimulate Demand

The economic situation of the 1920s led John Maynard Keynes to question the classical economic theories of supply and demand. Classical economists believed that a free market would eventually correct any imbalances. However, as aggregate demand fell, businesses invested and produced less, which led to layoffs. As a result, consumers had even less money to spend, and businesses cut back production even further.

As early as 1929, Keynes proposed that the British government spend money on public works projects to help ease unemployment. However, he had no theoretical backing for his proposal until he read an article in 1931 about the spending multiplier. This concept proved to be the key to his new economic theory, which he published in *The General Theory of Employment, Interest, and Money* (1936). This ground-breaking book marked the beginning of the field of macroeconomics.

Keynes's first revolutionary idea was to define aggregate demand as the sum of investment, consumer spending, and government spending. He further stated that only active government intervention could break the patterns in the business cycle that caused so much economic suffering. Even more revolutionary, however, was his argument that it was better for the government to spend money to help stabilize the economy than to have a balanced budget.

A Continuing Influence
Keynes's ideas continue to influence the way some governments deal with economic depressions.

FAST FACTS

John Maynard Keynes

Career: British academic and government economist

Born: June 5, 1883, in Cambridge, England

Died: April 21, 1946

Major Accomplishment: Introduced the idea of using government action to stimulate aggregate demand

Books: *A Treatise on Money* (1930); *The General Theory of Employment, Interest, and Money* (1936)

Famous Quotation: *The difficulty lies, not in the new ideas, but in escaping from the old ones.*

Jobs: Lecturer in economics, Cambridge University; editor of the *Economics Journal*; positions with the British Treasury office during World Wars I and II

 **Economics Update**
Learn more about John Maynard Keynes at **ClassZone.com**

APPLICATION Contrasting Economic Information

B. What made Keynes's ideas different from those of classical economists?

Government and Demand-Side Policies

KEY CONCEPTS

Discretionary fiscal policy involves choices about how to use government spending and taxation to increase aggregate demand or control inflation. Demand-side policies advocate use of these fiscal policy tools to control aggregate demand and stabilize the economy.

The Role of Government

Keynes proposed an active role for government in the economy. He argued that the federal government ought to step into the economy using expansionary fiscal policy to promote full employment. The Great Depression had shown that the economy could reach equilibrium with less than full employment and that business was unable to break out of this cycle because of insufficient aggregate demand. Therefore, Keynes advocated increased government spending and decreased taxation to end recessions. Increased government spending helps create jobs and increases income, and decreased taxation encourages consumers to spend more, which prompts businesses to invest more. Such actions help increase aggregate demand.

On the other hand, Keynes thought that when inflation was high the government should use contractionary fiscal policy to keep prices from rising. The government would take an active role through decreasing government spending or increasing taxes. Both of these actions help decrease aggregate demand and control inflation.

Wartime Spending
Massive government spending on wartime industries brought the United States out of economic depression.

Demand-Side Policies—Analysis

In some circumstances, an increase in government spending may lead to economic recovery. For example, government spending on public works programs and on production related to World War II brought the United States out of the Great Depression. However, it is not easy to limit such spending to times of recession, because federal programs seem to take on a life of their own and are difficult to terminate. Politicians are often reluctant to discontinue programs that are popular.

Excessive aggregate demand due to government or consumer spending can lead to inflation. Contractionary fiscal policy requires decreases in government spending or increases in taxation. Just as it is difficult to decrease government spending, it is difficult to enact the tax increases. Politicians must often choose between doing what is best for the economy and doing what is most likely to ensure their reelection. Furthermore, when the economy experiences stagflation—slow economic growth with high unemployment and inflation—as it did in the 1970s, demand-side policies seem to be ineffective.

APPLICATION Drawing Conclusions

C. Why are demand-side policies more effective against recession than against inflation?

Supply-Side Economics

KEY CONCEPTS

Some economists believe that the best way to influence the economy is through the supply side rather than through the demand side. **Supply-side fiscal policy** is designed to provide incentives to producers to increase aggregate supply. In other words, demand-side economics uses fiscal policy to encourage consumers to spend more, while supply-side economics focuses on cutting the cost of production to encourage producers to supply more. Figure 15.6 compares supply-side economics to demand-side economics.

The Role of Government

As you have learned, the role of the government in the economy falls into three categories: taxation, spending, and regulation. For the most part, supply-side economists favor less government involvement in these three areas.

Supply-side economists favor cutting the tax rates on individual and corporate income because they believe that high tax rates slow economic growth by discouraging working, saving, and investing. Lower tax rates, on the other hand, encourage individuals and businesses to work, save, and invest more. Specifically, reducing the highest tax brackets provides more available income to the people most likely to invest in new business activities. Spending cuts are another way that supply-side economics seeks to stimulate aggregate supply. Cuts in spending are related to tax cuts. If the government spends less, it needs to take in less in revenue and, therefore, is able to lower taxes. Finally, decreased government regulation can also stimulate business production. Government regulations add to the costs of production and make it harder for businesses to grow. Deregulation, however, cuts costs and leads to increases in aggregate supply.

FIGURE 15.6 Supply-Side and Demand-Side Economics

Supply-Side Economics	Demand-Side Economics
• Focuses on stimulating production (supply) to increase business output	• Focuses on stimulating consumption (demand) to increase business output
• Lower taxes + decreased government spending + deregulation = greater incentives for business investment	• Increased government spending results in more money in people's hands
• Businesses expand and create jobs; people work, save, and invest more	• People spend more
• Greater investment and productivity cause businesses to increase output	• Increased demand causes business to increase output

ANALYZE CHARTS

1. What is similar about supply-side and demand-side tax policies?

2. Which system favors less government involvement in the economy?

The Laffer Curve

Supply-side economists refer to the **Laffer Curve**, a graph developed by economist Arthur Laffer, to illustrate how tax cuts affect tax revenues and economic growth. As Figure 15.7 shows, Laffer theorized that tax revenues increase as tax rates increase up to a certain point. After that point, higher tax rates actually lead to decreased tax revenues. The reasoning behind the curve is that higher taxes discourage people from working, saving, and investing. So, at a tax rate of 100 percent, the government would theoretically collect no tax revenues, because people would have no incentive to earn income if it all went to the government for taxes.

In other words, the higher the tax rate, the likelier it is that people will take some type of action to avoid paying more taxes. When people find alternatives to income-producing activity, total taxable income declines, tax revenues decrease, aggregate supply falls, and economic growth slows. Conversely, as tax rates fall, people are more inclined to undertake income-producing activity because less of their income will go to taxes. Further, they are more likely to save and invest this extra income, which will lead to increasing aggregate supply and greater economic growth.

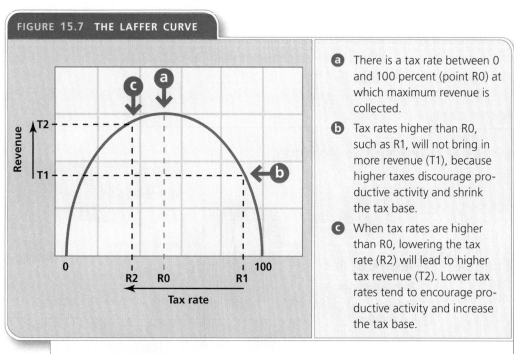

FIGURE 15.7 THE LAFFER CURVE

ⓐ There is a tax rate between 0 and 100 percent (point R0) at which maximum revenue is collected.

ⓑ Tax rates higher than R0, such as R1, will not bring in more revenue (T1), because higher taxes discourage productive activity and shrink the tax base.

ⓒ When tax rates are higher than R0, lowering the tax rate (R2) will lead to higher tax revenue (T2). Lower tax rates tend to encourage productive activity and increase the tax base.

ANALYZE GRAPHS

1. There is no tax revenue at two points on the graph—when the tax rate is 0 percent and when it is 100 percent. Why is this so?

2. How does this graph support the ideas of supply-side economists?

Supply-Side Policies—Analysis

When the principles of the Laffer Curve were applied in the United States in the 1980s, the results were much as Laffer had predicted. Legislation passed in that decade reduced federal income tax rates substantially. For example, the top bracket went from 70 percent to around 30 percent. At the same time, federal government receipts from income taxes over the whole decade were about 13 percent higher than

they had been in the 1970s. Inflation and unemployment rates both fell during the decade. Further, the economy grew steadily in the 1980s, with real GDP increasing by about 3 percent each year.

Even so, some of Laffer's predictions did not hold true. The supply-side approach suggests that with lower tax rates, people will work more. However, while some people did choose to work more, others chose to work less, since they could earn the same amount of after-tax income by working fewer hours. In addition, supply-side theory states that lower tax rates encourage people to save and invest. In fact, the savings rate declined during the 1980s.

Some economists have suggested that the success of supply-side policies depends on where the economy is located on the Laffer Curve. Look again at Figure 15.7 on page 459. Find the tax rate R0 on the horizontal axis and trace the broken line from that point to where the line intersects the curve. Tax revenue is maximized at this point. If the economy is not at this point on the curve, then tax rate cuts will decrease tax revenue rather than increase it. Supply-side theory offers no measures for establishing where on the curve an economy might be. Other economists have argued that it is difficult to isolate the effects of supply-side incentives from demand-side results to determine what caused unemployment and inflation rates to fall and the economy to grow during the 1980s. They suggest that tax cuts and increased government spending on defense drove up aggregate demand, resulting in economic growth. This increased spending was fueled by deficits, which you'll learn more about in Section 3.

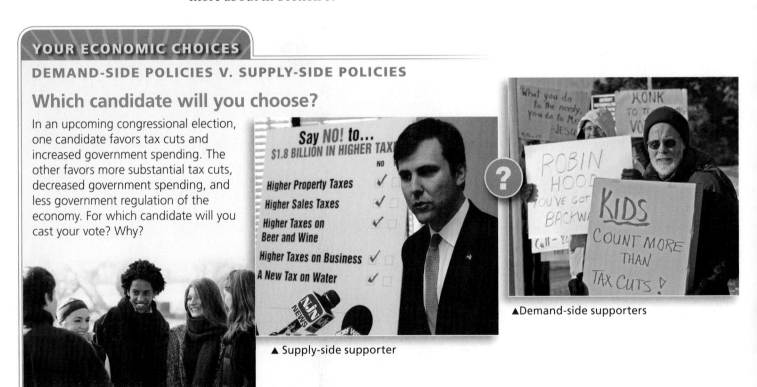

YOUR ECONOMIC CHOICES

DEMAND-SIDE POLICIES V. SUPPLY-SIDE POLICIES

Which candidate will you choose?

In an upcoming congressional election, one candidate favors tax cuts and increased government spending. The other favors more substantial tax cuts, decreased government spending, and less government regulation of the economy. For which candidate will you cast your vote? Why?

Say NO! to...
$1.8 BILLION IN HIGHER TAX
NO
Higher Property Taxes ✓
Higher Sales Taxes ✓
Higher Taxes on ✓
Beer and Wine
Higher Taxes on Business ✓
A New Tax on Water ✓

▲ Supply-side supporter

▲Demand-side supporters

APPLICATION Analyzing Causes

D. What fiscal policy techniques do supply-side economists advocate to reduce unemployment and fight inflation at the same time?

REVIEWING KEY CONCEPTS

1. Explain the relationship between the terms in each of these pairs.

   a. *Keynesian economics*
      demand-side fiscal policy

   b. *supply-side fiscal policy*
      Laffer Curve

2. How did the Great Depression influence Keynesian economics?

3. How is the spending multiplier effect related to demand-side economics?

4. How are supply-side and demand-side economics different?

5. Which fiscal policy tool does the Laffer Curve address?

6. Using Your Notes How does the role of government differ in demand-side and supply-side economics? Refer to your completed flow chart.

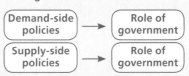

Use the Graphic Organizer at
Interactive Review @ ClassZone.com

CRITICAL THINKING

7. Creating Graphs Create a graph showing aggregate demand and aggregate supply in the economy. Then add new curves to show the expected shifts based on expansionary demand-side policies and supply-side policies. What happens to price level and GDP as a result of each type of policy?

Use *SMARTGrapher* @ ClassZone.com to complete this activity.

8. Applying Economic Concepts Suppose that the federal government decides to increase its spending on highway construction by $5 billion to keep the economy from falling into a recession. Explain the real impact on GDP of this spending.

9. Analyzing Effects Tom, Cia, and Julie were all in the 50 percent tax bracket. When a tax cut program reduced their tax bracket to 28 percent, they all made changes in their lives. Tom decided to work fewer hours so he could begin training to run in a marathon. Cia bought the new sports car she'd been wanting. Julie chose to work more hours so she could save extra money for her daughter's college education. Explain the effects of the tax cut for each individual. Use supply-side or demand-side economics reasoning in your answer.

10. Challenge Why is it difficult for demand-side economics to solve the problems of high unemployment and high inflation when they occur at the same time?

ECONOMICS IN PRACTICE

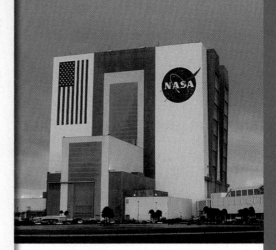

Space research center

Categorizing Economic Information Consider what you've learned about demand-side or supply-side fiscal policy. Then complete the following activities.

Identify Policies Complete the chart by indicating whether each action reflects a demand-side or a supply-side policy.

Government Action	Demand-Side or Supply-Side
Cut capital gains tax rates to encourage investment	
Expand government spending on space exploration	
Increase federal grants for education	
Reduce safety rules that businesses must follow	

Challenge Why is it difficult to tell if a cut in individual income tax rates is the result of a demand-side or a supply-side policy?

Deficits and the National Debt

OBJECTIVES	KEY TERMS	TAKING NOTES
In Section 3, you will • examine the difference between the deficit and the debt • explain why national deficits occur • describe how deficits are financed • identify the impact of the national debt on the economy	budget surplus, *p. 462* budget deficit, *p. 462* deficit spending, *p. 462* national debt, *p. 462* Treasury bills, *p. 464* Treasury notes, *p. 464* Treasury bonds, *p. 464* trust funds, *p. 465* crowding-out effect, *p. 466*	As you read Section 3, complete a comparison chart to show the similarities and differences between federal deficits and the national debt. Use the Graphic Organizer at **Interactive Review @ ClassZone.com** | Federal Deficits	National Debt | |---|---| | | |

The Federal Deficit and Debt

KEY CONCEPTS

Governments have frequently made efforts to balance their budgets so that spending equals the revenues collected. In reality, however, all levels of government often struggle to achieve a balanced budget. As you recall, Congress and state legislatures make budget decisions with both economic and political considerations in mind.

Federal government spending falls into one of three categories: a balanced budget; a **budget surplus**, when the government takes in more than it spends; or a **budget deficit**, when government spends more than it takes in. In recent years, the federal government has rarely achieved a budget surplus. Since 1970, a surplus was recorded only between 1998 and 2001. Figure 15.8 on the opposite page shows the pattern of budget deficits and surpluses since 1940.

It is important to note that a budget surplus or budget deficit refers to only one year. **Deficit spending** occurs when a government spends more than it collects in revenue for a specific budget year. Annual deficits contribute to the **national debt**, which is the total amount of money that the government owes. In effect, the national debt is equal to the sum of annual budget deficits minus any budget surpluses or other payments against the debt.

Source: www.CartoonStock.com

Controlling the Deficit This cartoon suggests one way to deal with a budget deficit.

Causes of the Deficit

There are four main causes of deficit spending: national emergencies, a desire for more public goods, stabilization of the economy, and the role of government in society. Many times a budget deficit may be the result of more than one of these causes.

National Emergencies Generally speaking, national emergencies are wars in which the United States is involved. Deficit spending has been used in wartime from the Revolutionary War to the war in Iraq that began in 2003. The terrorist attacks of September 11, 2001, and catastrophic weather events are other examples of national emergencies. All may require massive spending beyond the normal outlay of funds.

Need for Public Goods and Services Public goods and services benefit many different people and groups. The interstate highway system, dams, flood-control projects, and airports are examples of public goods. Building such infrastructure is expensive and lasts many years. The public expects the government to provide these goods to facilitate commerce, agriculture, and transportation.

Stabilization of the Economy As you learned earlier in this chapter, fiscal policy can include government spending to stimulate the economy. The classic example of this occurred during the Great Depression. The government spent money on a variety of public works projects to build roads, bridges, schools, and parks, putting millions of unemployed people to work. This government spending led to budget deficits.

Role of Government in Society As you have seen, people have also come to depend on government programs such as Social Security, Medicare, Medicaid, and unemployment insurance to provide help for those in need. These programs are expensive, and because they are entitlement programs, they require funding each year.

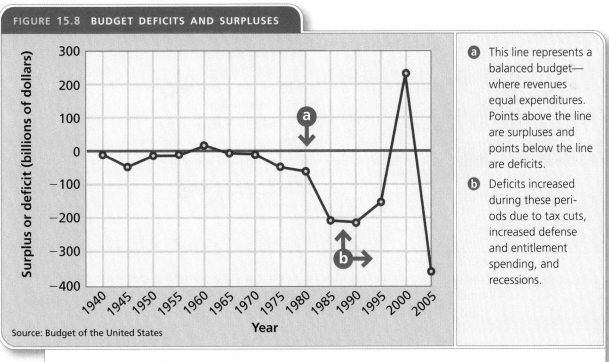

FIGURE 15.8 BUDGET DEFICITS AND SURPLUSES

Source: Budget of the United States

ⓐ This line represents a balanced budget—where revenues equal expenditures. Points above the line are surpluses and points below the line are deficits.

ⓑ Deficits increased during these periods due to tax cuts, increased defense and entitlement spending, and recessions.

ANALYZE GRAPHS

1. When did the largest deficit occur and about how much was it? The largest surplus?
2. How would the trends shown on this graph affect the national debt?

Raising Money for Deficit Spending

When the federal government does not receive enough revenue from taxes to finance its spending, it can borrow money to expand the economy. In effect, the government pays for its present needs by borrowing money that it will have to repay at some future date. It does this by issuing government bonds, through the Department of the Treasury.

Perhaps the best known type of bond issued by the government is the savings bond. Savings bonds mature in 20 years and are available in both small and large denominations—from $25 up to $10,000. The Department of the Treasury issues three other types of bonds. **Treasury bills** (T bills) are short-term bonds that mature in less than one year. **Treasury notes** are bonds that mature between two and ten years. And finally, **Treasury bonds** are issued for 30 years. Interest is paid on all these bonds, with higher interest rates sometimes being paid on instruments with longer maturity dates.

Individuals, state and local governments, insurance companies, pension funds, financial institutions, the Federal Reserve banks, and foreign investors hold these bonds. Figure 15.9 shows the percentage of federal debt held by different types of investors. A trend in recent years has been an increase in the percentage of the federal debt owned by foreign investors. Most foreign investors in U.S. Treasury bonds are the central banks of other countries. Japan and China hold the largest amount of foreign investors' share of the debt.

> **QUICK REFERENCE**
>
> **Treasury bills** mature in less than one year.
>
> **Treasury notes** mature between two and ten years.
>
> **Treasury bonds** mature in 30 years.

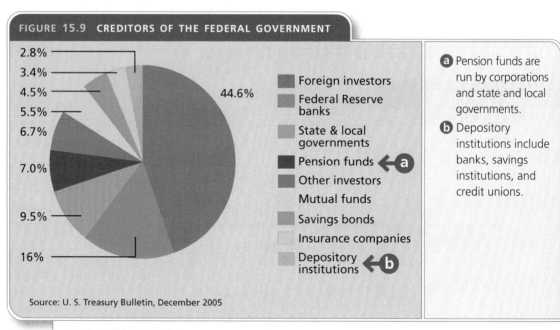

FIGURE 15.9 CREDITORS OF THE FEDERAL GOVERNMENT

- 2.8%
- 3.4%
- 4.5%
- 5.5%
- 6.7%
- 7.0%
- 9.5%
- 16%
- 44.6%

- Foreign investors
- Federal Reserve banks
- State & local governments
- Pension funds ← a
- Other investors
- Mutual funds
- Savings bonds
- Insurance companies
- Depository institutions ← b

a Pension funds are run by corporations and state and local governments.

b Depository institutions include banks, savings institutions, and credit unions.

Source: U. S. Treasury Bulletin, December 2005

ANALYZE GRAPHS

1. What percentage of the federal debt is owed to U.S. investors? What percentage is owed to foreign investors?

2. How do savings bonds compare to other government bonds as a form of government borrowing?

APPLICATION Drawing Conclusions

A. Why do all levels of government often struggle to achieve balanced budgets or budget surpluses?

The National Debt

KEY CONCEPTS

As you have seen, the national debt consists of the total accumulation of government deficits and surpluses over time. The money is owed to savers for the bonds they purchase and the interest paid on them. However, the actual debt situation is somewhat more complicated. The government also borrows from **trust funds**, which are funds being held for specific purposes to be expended at a future date. Examples of government trust funds include Social Security, Medicare, Medicaid, and government pension funds. When the trust funds accumulate surpluses by taking in more tax revenue than is needed for annual benefit payments, the surplus is invested in government bonds until the specific programs need the funds. In essence, therefore, the government borrows from itself to cover some deficit spending.

Some economists do not consider this to truly be debt. The money is transferred from one part of the government to another. This borrowing does not place a burden on the current economy because the current budget is not used to pay for it.

QUICK REFERENCE

Trust funds are held for specific purposes to be expended at a future date.

The Current Debt

Economics Update
Find an update about the national debt at **ClassZone.com**

In August 2006, the total national debt was about $8.4 trillion. About $4.8 trillion was privately owned by the creditors shown in Figure 15.9, and about $3.6 trillion was in government trust funds.

In Figure 15.8 on page 463, you saw that federal deficits increased during the 1980s and most of the 1990s. As deficits grew, the federal debt increased by more than five times between 1980 and 1997. Before that time the debt roughly kept pace with inflation, but since the 1980s it has grown faster than inflation. In other words, the debt has been growing in real terms and not just because of inflation.

Economists often look at the country's debt as a percentage of GDP. That perspective allows them to see how the burden of borrowing compares to the strength of the overall economy. The national debt was 33 percent of GDP in 1981. By 2006, it had doubled to nearly 68 percent of GDP. However, in 1981 about 80 percent of the debt was privately owned. In 2006, less than 60 percent was privately owned.

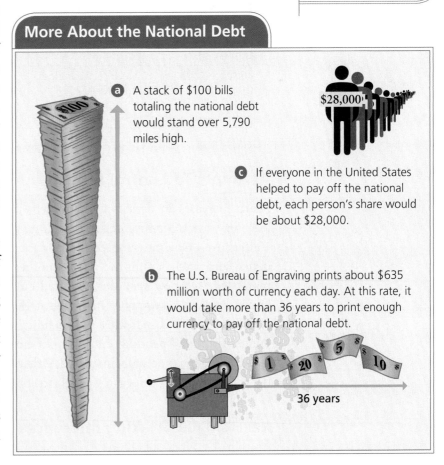

More About the National Debt

a A stack of $100 bills totaling the national debt would stand over 5,790 miles high.

c If everyone in the United States helped to pay off the national debt, each person's share would be about $28,000.

$28,000

b The U.S. Bureau of Engraving prints about $635 million worth of currency each day. At this rate, it would take more than 36 years to print enough currency to pay off the national debt.

36 years

The Effect of the Debt on the Economy

The national debt can have positive or negative effects on the economy. When government spending stimulates the economy, jobs are created and public goods such as the infrastructure may be improved. These improvements benefit everyone. However, when the government competes with the private sector to raise money by paying higher interest rates to get the savers' dollars, the results often are negative. The **crowding-out effect** is what happens when the government outbids private bond interest rates to gain loanable funds. Money leaves the private sector, and interest rates increase.

Repaying the interest on government bonds, or servicing the debt, also can have a negative impact on the economy. The 2007 federal budget estimate showed interest payments to be nearly 10 percent of all federal spending. Constant borrowing raises the amount of interest to be paid. This, in turn, increases the need for taxes to service the debt. Higher taxes mean less spending by consumers and less investment by businesses, both of which may hurt the economy.

FIGURE 15.10 Actions to Control Deficits and Debt

Budget Action	Goal	Key Points	Analysis
Gramm-Rudman Hollings (1985)	Eliminate the deficit by 1991	Set annual deficit targets; automatic spending cuts	Unrealistic goals; deficits increased
Budget Enforcement Act (1990)	Ensure new laws do not increase deficits	Caps on discretionary spending; "pay-as-you-go" financing	Deficits declined after 1992
Omnibus Budget Reconciliation Act (1993)	Cut deficit by $500 billion over 5 years	Make income tax more progressive; some spending cuts	Deficits declined significantly; strong economy
Balanced Budget Agreement (1997)	Balance the budget by 2002	Cut some entitlement spending; increase education spending; targeted tax cuts	Budget surpluses 1998–2001

Attempts To Control Deficits and Debt

Sharp increases in deficits and the debt in the 1980s led government officials to look for ways to control deficit spending. (These efforts are summarized in Figure 15.10 above.) One measure set annual deficit targets with the goal of eliminating the deficit completely within five years. Another set limits on discretionary spending and mandated that new spending required cuts elsewhere in the budget, an approach known as "pay-as-you-go" financing. A third attempted to trim the deficit with a combination of tax increases and spending cuts. Still another sought to balance the budget through spending cuts in entitlement programs. Some of these measures failed, and deficits actually increased. Others enjoyed only limited success. As a result, the government continues to struggle to control the national debt.

APPLICATION Making Inferences

B. Why is paying interest on the national debt considered mandatory spending?

SECTION 3 Assessment

CRITICAL T

9. **Analyzing C**
   federal budg
   three fiscal ye
   do so. The Pr
   thing to do w
   taxpayers thr
   economics de
   tax cuts?

10. **Applying Ec**
    got a better j
    pay each wee
    you spent 80
    examples to s
    a multiplier e

11. **Drawing Co**
    and in 2001 l
    and were rela
    overall econo
    effectiveness
    the country o

12. **Making Infe**
    the annual fe
    the amount c
    decreased by
    federal debt g
    same time pe
    this differenc

13. **Challenge** Ir
    proposed a cc
    require the fe
    Opponents ar
    make recessic
    to use contrac
    Why would a
    fiscal policy?

REVIEWING KEY CONCEPTS

1. Explain the difference between the terms in each of these pairs.
   a. *budget surplus*   b. *national debt*   c. *Treasury bills*
      budget deficit   *deficit spending*   *Treasury bonds*

2. How do budget deficits affect the national debt? Why?

3. What do Treasury bills, Treasury notes, and Treasury bonds have in common?

4. Why is government borrowing from trust funds different from privately-owned debt?

5. How is the crowding-out effect related to the national debt?

6. **Using Your Notes** What are the four causes of budget deficits? Refer to your completed chart.

Federal Deficits	National Debt

   Use the Graphic Organizer at **Interactive Review @ ClassZone.com**

CRITICAL THINKING

7. **Applying Economic Concepts** In 2007, the federal government was expected to have tax revenue of $2,350.8 billion. Total federal spending was estimated at $2,592.1 billion. Would the government have a budget deficit or a budget surplus that year? How much would it be?

8. **Analyzing Causes** Each of the following headlines reflects an example of deficit spending. Which of the causes of budget deficits is suggested by each headline?
   a. President Proposes Tax Cut Extensions to Keep Economy on Track
   b. Baby Boomers' Retirement Will Strain Social Security and Medicare
   c. Hurricane Recovery Effort to Require Massive Federal Aid

9. **Analyzing Data** Assume that the privately-owned part of the debt is $4,900 billion and the amount held by government trust funds is $3,500 billion. Use the percentages shown in Figure 15.9 to calculate the dollar amounts held by different creditors.

10. **Challenge** The Social Security Administration estimates that annual revenue from payroll taxes will be insufficient to meet annual benefit payments beginning in 2018. The Social Security trust fund will be used to make up the difference. How will this change affect the nature of the national debt?

ECONOMICS IN PRACTICE

Government bonds

Applying Economic Concepts
Recall what you learned about the crowding-out effect and then complete the following activities.

Analyze the Crowding-Out Effect The graph below shows the crowding-out effect in terms of supply and demand. Why would some private bond issuers be crowded out as a result of government borrowing?

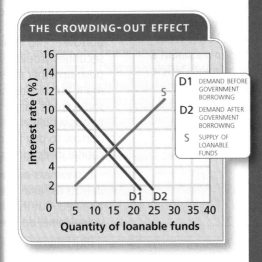

THE CROWDING-OUT EFFECT

D1 DEMAND BEFORE GOVERNMENT BORROWING
D2 DEMAND AFTER GOVERNMENT BORROWING
S SUPPLY OF LOANABLE FUNDS

Interest rate (%) — Quantity of loanable funds

Challenge What part of the national debt might cause the crowding-out effect, the public-owned portion, the portion in government trust funds, or both? Explain your answer.

Intera...

Review this
activities at

- Online Su
- Quizzes
- Vocabula

Onlin

Complet
own pap

**Choose the key
the sentence. M

automatic stabilizer
budget deficit
budget surplus
contractionary fisca
Council of Economic
crowding-out effect
deficit spending
demand-side fiscal p
discretionary fiscal p
expansionary fiscal

1 is the gove
government sp
is a plan to sti
plan to slow th
too rapidly. **4**
government to
transfer payme
are examples o

6 is the i
to be stimulate
the basis of **7**
in income caus

9 is fisca
producers to i
illustrates how
economic grow

A **11** occ
more than it sp
takes in **12** o
of money owed
results when th
interest rates.

The Money Supply
Paper currency—an
important part of the
money supply—is
distributed by the
Federal Reserve.

The Federal Reserve and Monetary Policy

CONCEPT REVIEW

Fiscal policy is the federal government's use of taxes and government spending to affect the economy. It has one of two goals: to decrease unemployment or to fight inflation.

CHAPTER 16 KEY CONCEPT

Monetary policy includes all the Federal Reserve actions that change the money supply in order to influence the economy. Its purpose is to curb inflation or to reduce economic stagnation or recession.

WHY THE CONCEPT MATTERS

All economies experience the business cycle, a series of periods of growing and shrinking economic activity. Sometimes, these ups and downs become extreme, and the government takes action to even out the business cycle. The government has many tools available to do this—monetary policy is one of the most important.

Online Highlights
More at ClassZone.com

 Economics Update
Go to **ECONOMICS UPDATE** for chapter updates and current news on monetary policy. (See Case Study, pp. 504–505).

Animated Economics
Go to **ANIMATED ECONOMICS** for interactive lessons on the graphs and tables in this chapter. ▶

Interactive ◀◀Review
Go to **INTERACTIVE REVIEW** for concept review and activities.

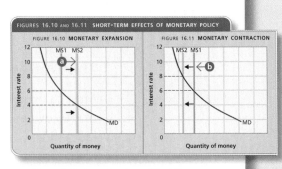

How do interest rates affect the demand for money? See Figures 16.10 and 16.11 on page 495.

The Federal Reserve System

OBJECTIVES	KEY TERMS	TAKING NOTES
In Section 1, you will • examine the purpose and duties of a central bank • identify the distinctive features of the Federal Reserve System • explain the structure of the Federal Reserve System	central bank, *p. 474* monetary, *p. 474* Federal Reserve System, *p. 474* currency, *p. 475* Board of Governors, *p. 476* Federal Open Market Committee, *p. 477* thrift institution, *p. 478*	As you read Section 1, complete a cluster diagram to identify the major characteristics of the Federal Reserve System. Use the Graphic Organizer at **Interactive Review @ ClassZone.com**

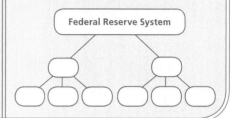

Creating the Fed

KEY CONCEPTS

QUICK REFERENCE

A **central bank** is a nation's main monetary authority.

Monetary is a term that means "relating to money."

The **Federal Reserve System** is the central bank of the United States.

As you recall from Chapter 10, there were times when the U.S. economy suffered from panics and banking was very unstable. The government made many efforts to address this problem, but had only limited success. Perhaps the most far-reaching of these efforts to stabilize the American financial system was the passage of the Federal Reserve Act in 1913. This act created a central bank for the United States. A **central bank** is a nation's main monetary authority, which is able to conduct certain monetary practices. (**Monetary** means "relating to money.") The **Federal Reserve System** is the central bank of the United States and is commonly called the Fed. The Fed is an independent organization within the government, which has both public and private characteristics.

The Duties of a Central Bank

Most countries have a central bank to oversee their banking system. The central bank may be owned and controlled by the government or it may have considerable political independence. There are three common duties that all central banks perform: holding reserves, assuring stability of the banking and monetary systems, and lending money to banks and the government.

Holding Reserves Central banks are sometimes called reserve banks. You learned in Chapter 10 that banks lend only a part of their funds to individuals and businesses and keep the rest in reserve. The central bank holds these reserves to influence the amount of loanable funds banks have available. This allows the central bank to control the money supply.

Assuring Stability The central bank also acts to assure stability in the national banking and monetary systems. For example, it is one of the banking regulatory agencies that regulate and supervise banks to make sure that they act in ways that serve the interests of depositors and of the economy. Also, by controlling the way money is issued and circulated, the central bank attempts to avoid the confusion that might result when individual banks issue their own bank notes.

Lending Money The final duty of the central bank involves one of the primary functions of all banks—it lends money. Its lending practices are unlike those other banks, however. It does not seek to make a profit through lending, and it serves private banks and the government rather than individual customers and businesses.

Creating the Fed
President Woodrow Wilson proposed the Federal Reserve Act, in part, to break the power of the nation's biggest banks.

The Duties of the Fed

With the passage of the Federal Reserve Act of 1913, Congress created the first national bank in the United States that could truly fulfill the duties of a central bank. The Fed supervises banking in the United States by providing regulation and oversight to make sure that banks follow sound practices in their operations. The Fed also takes steps to ensure that banks do not defraud customers and works to protect consumers' rights as they relate to borrowing money.

Like all central banks, the Fed provides banking services for both private banks and the national government. It accepts and holds deposits in the form of cash reserves, transfers funds between banks or between banks and the government, and makes loans to these institutions. Because it performs such functions, the Fed is sometimes referred to as the bankers' bank.

This responsibility of the Fed is especially important in times of emergency. Shortly after the Fed was created, it played a major role in financing U.S. involvement in World War I by purchasing government war bonds. The Fed also took emergency action after the terrorist attacks on New York City and Washington, D.C. in 2001. It issued $45 billion in loans to banks throughout the United States in order to ensure that there would be as little disruption to the banking system as possible in light of the destruction in these cities.

The Fed also distributes currency, which is coins and paper money, and regulates the supply of money. The supply of money does not mean actual cash but all available sources of money. Specifically, the amount of money that banks have available to lend has important effects on the whole economy. You will learn more about these functions of the Fed in Section 2.

Economics Update

Find an update on the duties of the Fed at **ClassZone.com**

QUICK REFERENCE

Currency is coins and paper money.

APPLICATION Comparing and Contrasting

A. Recall what you learned about the structure and functions of commercial banks in Chapter 10. What are the similarities and differences between the Federal Reserve and a commercial bank?

The Structure of the Fed

The Fed is different from most countries' central banks because it is not a single national bank but has both a national and a regional structure. This structure represents a compromise between power resting at the regional level and at the national level. As you may recall from Chapter 10, many U.S. citizens were hesitant to give too much power to a national bank. In addition, the United States is a large and economically diverse country with a complex banking system.

Elements of the Fed

The elements that make up the Fed reflect this balance between national and regional authority. An appointed board sets national Fed policy, and a regional system of district banks carries out this policy and performs the duties of the central bank. This approach gives the Fed some independence from political influence. Even so, the Fed is ultimately accountable to Congress. Figure 16.1 shows how the Fed is organized.

Board of Governors The **Board of Governors** is a board of seven appointed members who supervise the operations of the Fed and set policy. The president appoints members for a single 14-year term, with the approval of the Senate. One board member's term expires every two years, and the president may also appoint replacements to fill vacancies created by members who leave before the end of their terms. The president chooses the chairman and vice-chairman, who serve four-year terms, from among

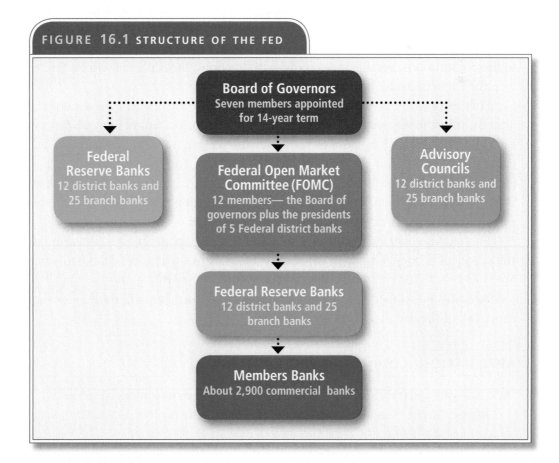

FIGURE **16.1** STRUCTURE OF THE FED

Board of Governors
Seven members appointed for 14-year term

Federal Reserve Banks
12 district banks and 25 branch banks

Federal Open Market Committee (FOMC)
12 members— the Board of governors plus the presidents of 5 Federal district banks

Advisory Councils
12 district banks and 25 branch banks

Federal Reserve Banks
12 district banks and 25 branch banks

Members Banks
About 2,900 commercial banks

the seven members. The chairman is considered the most influential member and is the spokesperson for the board. Alan Greenspan, who held the position for nearly 20 years, was so influential as Fed chairman that he almost came to personify the institution. (You can read more about Alan Greenspan on page 494.)

Twelve District Banks The Federal Reserve System is organized into 12 districts. Figure 16.2 shows these districts and the cities where the Federal Reserve district banks and the offices of the Board of Governors are located. While the district banks are responsible for carrying out the national policy set forth by the Board of Governors, each one also serves the needs of its particular region.

FIGURE 16.2 FEDERAL RESERVE DISTRICTS

★ Board of Governors
● Federal Reserve Bank City

Member Banks All nationally chartered banks automatically are members of the Federal Reserve System. State-chartered banks, if they wish, may apply to join the Fed. In 2004, there were about 2,000 national bank members and 900 state bank members, about 37 percent of all commercial banks.

Each member bank must purchase stock in its Federal Reserve district bank. However, this stock ownership is not the same as ownership of stock in a private corporation or a commercial bank. It may not be bought or sold on the open market. Member banks earn a set dividend rate on the stock they hold. This helps to make up for the interest they do not earn on the reserves that the Fed requires them to hold. (See the information on reserve requirements on page 484.)

Federal Open Market Committee The **Federal Open Market Committee (FOMC)** is a board of the Fed that supervises the sale and purchase of federal government securities. The term *open market* refers to the way that government securities are bought and sold. The FOMC consists of 12 voting members, including the Board of Governors, the president of the Federal Reserve Bank of New York, and four other Fed district bank presidents who take turns serving one-year terms. All Fed bank presidents attend the meetings and provide input even when they have no vote.

QUICK REFERENCE

The **Federal Open Market Committee (FOMC)** supervises the sales and purchase of government securities.

Comparing Central Banks

Today, more than 160 nations have central banks. These banks function as the main monetary authority for their respective nations. They also serve the same purpose—maintaining economic stability. Further, they use similar tools to fulfill this purpose. Even so, these central banks do have several differences. One difference is historical. The Federal Reserve, for example, was established by an act of Congress in 1913. The Bank of England, Great Britain's central bank, claims a royal pedigree, having been established in 1694 during the reign of William and Mary. In China, the People's Bank of China (PBC) began as a commercial bank in 1948. It functioned as a central bank and a commercial bank until 1983, when it was reorganized solely as a central bank.

Chinese bank note

British bank note

Another difference lies in the production of money. The central banks of Great Britain and China both produce and distribute currency. In the United States, the Treasury produces currency and the Federal Reserve distributes it.

CONNECTING ACROSS THE GLOBE

1. Why do you think central banks are common to countries that have very different forms of government, such as the United States and China?

2. In terms of money production, how does the Bank of England differ from the Federal Reserve?

The sale and purchases of federal government bonds on the open market are the principal tools used by the Fed to promote a stable, growing economy. At the end of each of its meetings, the FOMC issues a public statement to explain its assessment of the economy and its latest actions. You will learn more about the functions of the FOMC in Section 3.

Advisory Councils Three committees provide advice directly to the Board of Governors. The 12 members of the Federal Advisory Council, one from each Fed district, represent the commercial banking industry. The Consumer Advisory Council advises the board on matters concerning the Fed's responsibilities in enforcing consumer protection laws related to borrowing. Its 30 members, for the most part, are drawn from consumer groups and the financial services industry.

The Federal Reserve Board created the Thrift Institutions Advisory Council in 1980 to provide advice about the needs of this important segment of the financial services industry. **Thrift institutions** are savings and loan institutions, savings banks, or other institutions that serve savers. While the Fed does not regulate thrift institutions, the thrifts must conform to the Fed's reserve requirements and may borrow from the Fed.

> **QUICK REFERENCE**
>
> A **thrift institution** is a financial institution that serves savers.

APPLICATION Making Inferences

B. How does the 14-year term of members of the Board of Governors help make the Fed an independent government agency?

REVIEWING KEY CONCEPTS

1. Explain the relationship between the terms in each of these pairs.

   a. *central bank*
   Federal Reserve System

   c. *Board of Governors*
   Federal Open Market Committee

   b. *monetary*
   currency

2. What are the three duties of a central bank?

3. How is the Fed different from other central banks?

4. How does the composition of the Federal Open Market Committee reflect the blend of national and regional power in the Fed?

5. What do all thrift institutions have in common?

6. **Using Your Notes** What are the five elements of the Fed? Refer to your completed cluster diagram.

   Use the Graphic Organizer at
   Interactive Review @ ClassZone.com

   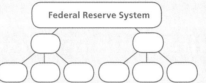

CRITICAL THINKING

7. **Analyzing Causes and Effects** If all members of the Board of Governors served 14-year terms, no president would appoint more than four members during two terms in office. However, many board members do not serve full terms, and vacancies occur on average more than once every two years. How does this situation affect a president's influence on the Board?

8. **Drawing Conclusions** The four rotating members on the Federal Open Market Committee are chosen from these groups:
   • Boston, Philadelphia, and Richmond
   • Cleveland and Chicago
   • Atlanta, St. Louis, and Dallas
   • Minneapolis, Kansas City, and San Francisco
   Why does the Fed mandate that one of the rotating members must come from each of these four groups?

9. **Challenge** The Federal Reserve Act of 1913 created the Federal Advisory Council. The Consumer Advisory Council was not created until 1976. How does this difference reflect changes in the duties of the Fed?

ECONOMICS IN PRACTICE

Analyzing Information

Refer to Figure 16.2 on page 477 to answer the following questions about the creation and present alignment of the Fed.

Analyze Maps Complete the chart below by indicating your answer to each question in the space provided.

Question	Response
Which region of the country has the most Fed district banks?	
How does the size of Fed districts 1–5 compare with districts 9–12?	
Where is the Board of Governors located?	
In which Fed district is your community located?	
How do the Federal Reserve Districts reflect U.S. geographic and economic diversity?	

Challenge How might the Federal Reserve districts be different if they were created today?

Functions of the Federal Reserve

OBJECTIVES	KEY TERMS	TAKING NOTES
In Section 2, you will • identify the services the Fed provides for the banking system • explain how the Fed acts as a banker for the federal government • describe the creation of money • discuss what factors influence the money supply	check clearing, *p. 480* bank holding company, *p. 481* bank exams, *p. 481* required reserve ratio, *p. 484* deposit multiplier formula, *p. 485*	As you read Section 2, complete a chart to identify the major functions of the Federal Reserve. Use the Graphic Organizer at **Interactive Review @ ClassZone.com** **Functions of the Federal Reserve** <table><tr><td>Serving the banking system</td><td>Serving the federal government</td><td>Creating money</td></tr><tr><td></td><td></td><td></td></tr></table>

Serving the Banking System

KEY CONCEPTS

As the banker's bank, the Fed has the responsibility of helping banks do their jobs. The Fed serves the banking system in a variety of ways, including providing check clearing and other services that facilitate the transfer of funds, lending money, and regulating and supervising banking activity.

SERVICE 1 Check Clearing

One of the services that the Fed offers to banks is **check clearing**, a process in which banks record the receipts and expenditures of their clients. Each Fed district processes millions of checks every day, but most checks clear in two days or less. Figure 16.3 on the next page shows how a check is cleared by following its path from the time it is written until the money is taken from the check writer's account. Electronic-payment methods, such as credit and debit cards, have begun to replace checks. Further, more private companies are involved in the check-clearing process. As a result, check clearing has become a less important function of the Fed.

SERVICE 2 Lending Money

Banks often loan each other money on a short-term basis. Sometimes all the banks in a region are faced with short-term cash flow issues, usually during natural disasters. At such times, the Fed will provide

FIGURE 16.3 **The Federal Reserve and Check Clearing**

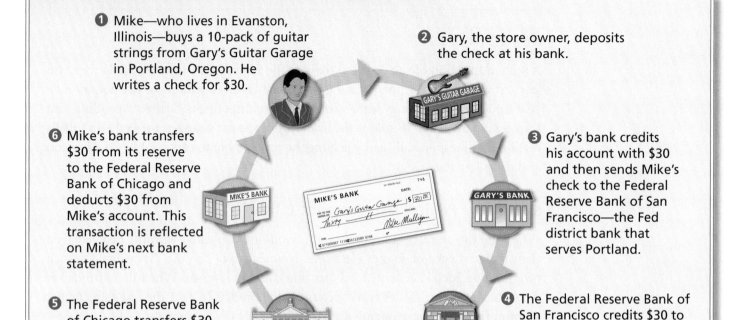

① Mike—who lives in Evanston, Illinois—buys a 10-pack of guitar strings from Gary's Guitar Garage in Portland, Oregon. He writes a check for $30.

② Gary, the store owner, deposits the check at his bank.

③ Gary's bank credits his account with $30 and then sends Mike's check to the Federal Reserve Bank of San Francisco—the Fed district bank that serves Portland.

④ The Federal Reserve Bank of San Francisco credits $30 to Gary's bank's reserve account and then sends Mike's check to the Federal Reserve Bank of Chicago—the Fed district bank that serves Evanston.

⑤ The Federal Reserve Bank of Chicago transfers $30 from its reserves to the San Francisco Fed district bank and then sends Mike's check to his bank in Evanston.

⑥ Mike's bank transfers $30 from its reserve to the Federal Reserve Bank of Chicago and deducts $30 from Mike's account. This transaction is reflected on Mike's next bank statement.

ANALYZE CHARTS

This diagram illustrates the steps in the check-clearing process for a typical check transaction. Note how many banks handle Mike's check during the process. What is the importance of the Fed's role in clearing Mike's check?

loans to banks and may charge reduced interest rates. Banks must have sufficient assets and capital to qualify for Fed loans. In addition, smaller banks that have seasonal cash flow needs due to the nature of their local economy may borrow from the Fed. The Fed also acts as the lender of last resort to prevent a banking crisis.

SERVICE 3 Regulating and Supervising Banks

Each Federal Reserve Bank supervises the practices of state-chartered member banks and bank holding companies in its district. A **bank holding company** is a company that owns, or has a controlling interest in, more than one bank. This supervision includes **bank exams**, which are audits of the bank's financial practices. These exams make sure that banks are not engaged in risky or fraudulent practices, especially in lending. The Fed monitors bank mergers to ensure that competition is maintained and enforces truth-in-lending laws to protect consumers in such areas as home mortgages, auto loans, and retail credit.

APPLICATION Making Inferences

A. Why might the Fed help a small bank in an agricultural region stabilize its cash flow?

> **QUICK REFERENCE**
>
> A **bank holding company** owns, or has a controlling interest in, more than one bank.
>
> A **bank exam** is an audit of the bank's financial practices.

Serving the Federal Government

A second function of the Fed is to serve as the federal government's banker. As you learned in Chapter 14, the federal government receives billions of tax dollars each year and uses this money on a variety of programs through direct spending and transfer payments. In its role as the federal government's banker, the Fed also fulfills certain fiscal responsibilities by helping the government to carry out its taxation and spending activities.

SERVICE 1 Paying Government Bills

When the IRS collects tax revenues, the funds are deposited with the Fed. The Fed then issues checks or makes electronic payments, via the U.S. Treasury, for such programs as Social Security, Medicare, and IRS tax refunds. When these funds are deposited in the recipient's bank account or the check is cashed, the Fed deducts that amount from the government's account.

Including military personnel, the federal government employs about 4.6 million people, and their wages and benefits are processed through the Fed. Direct government spending also comes from accounts at the Fed. Whether the government is buying office supplies or military equipment or paying contractors to maintain federal highways, the money is funneled through the Fed. The Fed also processes food stamps, which are issued by the Department of Agriculture, and postal money orders, which are issued by the U.S. Postal Service. The Fed, therefore, facilitates government payments in a way that is similar to the way it clears checks and processes electronic payments in the private sector.

Economics Update

Find an update on the Fed's role in the sale of government securities at **ClassZone.com**

SERVICE 2 Selling Government Securities

As you learned in Chapter 15, the federal government has different kinds of securities that it sells when it wants to borrow money. (Remember that securities are another name for bonds and stocks.) The Fed processes U.S. savings bonds and auctions other kinds of securities for the U.S. Treasury to provide funds for various government activities.

The Fed has many roles in this process. It provides information about the securities to potential buyers, receives orders from customers, collects payments from buyers, credits the funds to the Treasury's account, and delivers the bonds to their owners. It also pays the interest on these bonds on a regular basis or at maturity. Many of these transactions are now handled electronically. Even when individuals purchase government securities on the Treasury Department's Web site, the Fed transfers funds between the purchaser and the Treasury and pays the interest when it is due. The Fed does not charge fees for these services.

In addition to selling government securities to raise money to fund government activities, the Federal Open Market Committee supervises the sales and purchases of government securities as a way to stabilize the economy. You'll learn more about this aspect of the Fed's work in Section 3.

One of the important functions of a central bank is to issue a standard currency that is used throughout the economy. In the United States, Federal Reserve notes are the official paper currency. These notes are fiat money backed by the confidence of the federal government and managed by the Federal Reserve. The government's backing is made plain by the statement on each note: "This note is legal tender for all debts, public and private." Figure 16.4 highlights several important features of Federal Reserve notes.

The Department of the Treasury's Bureau of Engraving and Printing prints Federal Reserve notes, which are distributed by the Fed to its district banks. The notes are then moved on to depository institutions and finally into the hands of individuals and businesses. The Fed makes sure that bills are distributed to banks in the amounts that they need. Paper money has a life span of between two and five years. Smaller denomination bills tend to have a shorter life span. Larger denomination bills stay in circulation longer. When bills get worn out, they are taken out of circulation, destroyed, and replaced with new ones. In a similar way, the Fed distributes coins that are produced by the U.S. Mint.

FIGURE 16.4 A FEDERAL RESERVE NOTE

ⓐ Federal Reserve Notes are the official U.S. paper **currency**.

ⓑ Code indicates to which Federal Reserve Bank the Treasury issued the note. For example, B2 is New York, E5 is Richmond, and K11 is Dallas.

ⓒ Each note has a unique serial number. The second letter identifies the Fed district to which the note was issued.

ⓓ The Federal Reserve seal is on the left, the Treasury Department seal on the right.

ⓔ The signature of the Treasurer is on the left, the signature of the Secretary of the Treasury on the right.

ⓕ In 1955, Congress required that the phrase "In God We Trust" be used on all currency and coins.

ANALYZE

1. To which Federal Reserve Bank was this bill issued?
2. How might serial numbers help the authorities detect counterfeit bills?

APPLICATION **Comparing Economic Information**

B. How are the banking services the Fed provides to the government similar to the services it provides to banks?

Creating Money

QUICK REFERENCE

Required reserve ratio (RRR) is the fraction of a bank's deposits that it must keep in reserve.

KEY CONCEPTS

Creating money does not mean printing paper currency and minting coins. It refers to the way money gets into circulation through deposits and loans at banks. (You learned briefly about this process in Chapter 10.) Because the United States has a fractional reserve banking system, banks are not allowed to loan out all the money they have in deposits. The Fed establishes a **required reserve ratio (RRR)**, which is the fraction of the bank's deposits that must be kept in reserve by the bank, to control the amount a bank can loan. Money on deposit in excess of the required reserve amount can be loaned out. The money in reserve may be stored as cash in the bank's vault or deposited with the Fed.

EXAMPLE Money Creation

The banking system creates money whenever banks receive deposits and make loans. The level of the RRR determines how much money may be loaned and, therefore, how much money gets created. Let's see how this works by studying Figure 16.5. At the top of the chart, the RRR is set at 20 percent. If Bank A has $10,000 in deposits, it must keep 20 percent, or $2,000, on reserve. It lends the remaining $8,000 to Kecia's Fitness Studio, which Kecia deposits in Bank B. Bank B keeps 20 percent of the $8,000, or $1,600, on reserve as required. Bank B lends the remaining $6,400 to Juan's Computer Repair, and Juan deposits it in Bank C. At this point, the money supply has increased by $14,400, the total of the loans made. The process could continue until there was nothing left to lend.

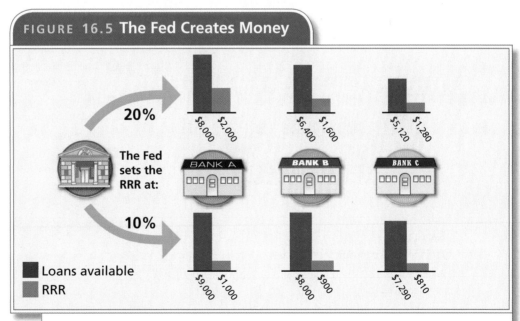

FIGURE 16.5 The Fed Creates Money

ANALYZE CHARTS
Remember that the amount of money that each bank can loan is limited by the RRR. Suppose that Bank C loaned its available funds to Miles and Miles deposited the money in Bank D. How much money would Bank D have to hold in reserve and how much would it have available for loans if the RRR is set at 20 percent? What would these figures be if the RRR were set at 10 percent?

Now look at what happens if the Fed reduces the RRR to 10 percent. The change is shown at the bottom of Figure 16.5. Bank A can now lend $9,000 to Kecia and Bank B can lend $8,100 to Juan. In this scenario, the money supply would increase by $17,100. The decrease in the RRR allowed the money supply to increase by an additional $2,700.

How do you figure out how much the money supply will increase after all possible loans have been made? The **deposit multiplier formula** is a mathematical formula that tells how much the money supply will increase after an initial cash deposit in a bank. The formula is 1/RRR. For example, if the RRR is 10 percent the deposit multiplier equals 10. Figure 16.6 illustrates how the deposit multiplier formula is used to determine the amount of increase in the money supply from an initial deposit of $100 and a reserve requirement of 10 percent.

MATH CHALLENGE

FIGURE 16.6 Deposit Expansion Multiplier

Step 1: Study the table below, which shows how an initial deposit of $100 can increase the money supply. To quantify the total amount of money that can be created from this initial deposit, economists use the deposit expansion multiplier.

	Money deposited	=	10% held as reserves	+	90% loaned out
Bank A	$100.00	=	$10.00	+	$90.00
Bank B	$90.00	=	$ 9.00	+	$81.00
Bank C	$81.00	=	$ 8.10	+	$72.90
Bank D	$72.90	=	$ 7.29	+	$65.61
---	---		---		---
Total			$100.00		$900.00

Step 2: Calculate the deposit expansion multiplier.

Sample Calculations

$$\frac{1}{\text{Required reserve ratio}} = \text{Deposit expansion multiplier}$$

$$\frac{1}{10\%} = \frac{1}{0.10} = 10$$

Step 3: Use the deposit expansion multiplier to calculate the total money that can be loaned.

$$\text{Initial deposit} \times \left[\text{Deposit expansion multiplier} - 1 \right] = \text{Total available for loans}$$

$100 \times [10-1] = \$100 \times 9 = \$900$

APPLICATION Analyzing Effects

C. If the Fed raised the RRR from 10 percent to 12 percent, how would it affect the money supply and by approximately how much, if the initial deposit was $5,000? Show your calculations.

Factors Affecting Demand for Money

KEY CONCEPTS

The Fed monitors two major indicators of the money supply, namely M1 and M2. Recall that you learned in Chapter 10 that M1 includes cash and checkable deposits, while M2 includes M1 plus savings deposits and certain time deposits. The Fed needs to know how large each type of money is in order to act appropriately to manage the supply of money. Four factors influence how much money individuals and businesses need—cash on hand, interest rates, the cost of consumer goods and services, and the level of income.

FACTOR 1 Cash on Hand

Individuals and businesses need cash to complete certain financial transactions. Recall that M1, which includes cash and checkable deposits, is also called transactions money. Consumers use this money to pay for things such as food, clothing, transportation costs such as gasoline and bus or train fares, and entertainment. Businesses also use cash and checks for many day-to-day expenses. The fastest growing form of payment is the debit card, which was used for more than 23 billion transactions in 2005. While a debit card is not money, it is linked to a checking account, and the funds in the account are considered money.

The Fed understands that there are certain times when people need more cash. It routinely increases the amount of cash at banks during the holiday season because people want more money to buy gifts. Similarly, during the summer months the Fed ensures that banks in areas popular with tourists have more cash. Natural disasters also influence the amount of cash the Fed puts into circulation. In response to Hurricane Katrina's devastation of the Gulf Coast in 2005, the Fed shipped large amounts of currency to banks in several nearby districts because of the immediate demand for more cash by residents. Since many parts of the Gulf Coast were without electricity, people were not able to use debit cards and credit cards as they ordinarily would.

Cash on Hand Portable ATMs dispensed much-needed cash to evacuees from the Gulf Coast after Hurricane Katrina.

FACTOR 2 Interest Rates

When interest rates are high, individuals and businesses may place excess cash in savings instruments, such as bonds, stocks, or savings accounts. This of course pulls cash out of circulation. The money then exists as a part of M2. Figure 16.7 shows how the demand for money is affected by interest rates. When interest rates are high, the demand for money is lower because there is less incentive for individuals and businesses to spend and more incentive to save and earn interest. When interest rates are lower, however, more money is demanded because people have less incentive to save and more incentive to spend.

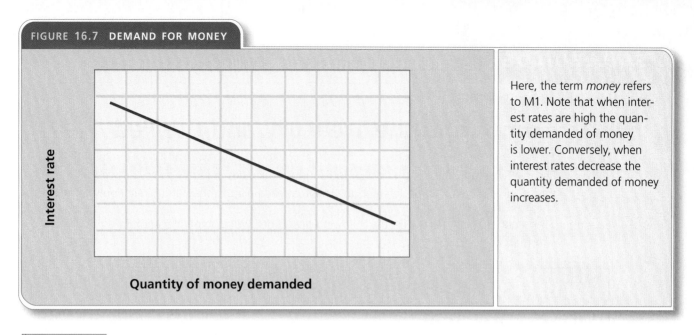

FIGURE 16.7 DEMAND FOR MONEY

Interest rate

Quantity of money demanded

Here, the term *money* refers to M1. Note that when interest rates are high the quantity demanded of money is lower. Conversely, when interest rates decrease the quantity demanded of money increases.

FACTOR 3 Cost of Consumer Goods and Services

As the cost of consumer goods or services increases, buyers may wish to have more money available. Suppose that adverse weather conditions and higher energy prices have driven up the prices of fresh fruits and vegetables. People may need to have more cash when they buy groceries at the supermarket than they did before the prices increased. They might also find that it takes more cash to buy gasoline than it used to.

Businesses face the same challenges. They would also wish to have more cash to purchase the goods and services they need for their operations. Of course, when businesses pay more for goods and services, production costs increase and the higher costs are often passed on to consumers. This, in turn, may lead consumers to want to have more money available.

FACTOR 4 Level of Income

As income increases, individuals and companies have a tendency to hold more cash. Recall that level of income is one of the factors that affect demand. Suppose that Bob has a part-time job cooking at a restaurant. When he gets a raise, he notices that he keeps more money in his wallet because he feels he can afford to spend more on clothes and DVDs. The same holds true for businesses. When their income increases, they will keep more cash because they are able to spend more on the goods and services that they need to pay for operations. In general, when income levels rise, so will the demand for money.

The Fed can take several actions to change the money supply in response to changes in demand for money. More important, the Fed can use these methods of increasing or decreasing the money supply to stabilize the economy. In the next section, you'll learn about the nature of these methods and how they are used to establish economy stability.

APPLICATION Analyzing Effects

D. Which factor is likely to increase the size of M2? Why?

For more information on comparing economic
information, see Skillbuilder Handbook, page R19

Comparing the Treasury and the Fed

The following passage provides information about the U.S. Treasury and the Federal
Reserve System. Compare the two by looking for similarities and differences between
them. This will help you understand the role that each plays in the nation's economy.

TIPS FOR COMPARING Use the following tips to help you compare economic
information.

The U.S. Treasury and the Federal Reserve System

Although the U.S. Treasury and the Federal Reserve are both essential to
the functioning of the nation's economy, they differ in many ways. The
U.S. Treasury Department was established by an act of Congress in 1789.
It is the primary federal agency responsible for the economic prosperity
of the United States. As such, it is responsible for managing federal
finances, including the collection of taxes, duties, and other monies due
to the United States; the paying of the nation's bills; and the management
of government accounts and the public debt. In addition, the Treasury
Department produces stamps, currency, and coinage.

> **Look** for words that
> signal similarities, such
> as *both, similarly,* and
> *also.*

The Federal Reserve System similarly was established by an act of
Congress but much later, in 1913. Unlike the U.S. Treasury, which is a
department of the federal government, the Fed is the nation's central
bank. According to its mission statement, the purpose of the Federal
Reserve is "to provide the nation with a safer, more flexible, and more
stable monetary and financial system."

> **Look** for words that
> signal differences,
> or contrasts, such
> as *unlike, differ,* and
> *varies.*

The duties of the Federal Reserve fall into four general areas:
conducting the nation's monetary policy in pursuit of maximum
employment and economic stability; supervising and regulating the
nation's banking institutions; maintaining the stability of the financial
system; and providing financial services such as check clearing and short-
term loans to member banks. The Fed consists of a board of governors
and 12 regional banks, a structure that varies considerably from that of
the Treasury.

THINKING ECONOMICALLY **Analyzing**

1. In what ways are the Treasury and the Fed similar?

2. What are some important differences between the Fed and the Treasury?

3. Which do you think is more policy oriented, the Fed or the Treasury? Explain why
you think so.

SECTION 2 Assessment

Online Quiz
ClassZone.com

REVIEWING KEY CONCEPTS

1. Use each of the three terms below in a sentence that illustrates the meaning of the term.
   a. *check clearing*
   b. *bank holding company*
   c. *required reserve ratio*

2. Why are bank exams an important way for the Fed to help create a sound banking system?

3. What is the relationship between the required reserve ratio and the deposit multiplier formula?

4. How does the Fed's check-clearing service help the banking system?

5. How does the deposit multiplier formula allow the Fed to create money through the banking system?

6. **Using Your Notes** What are the three services that the Fed provides to the federal government. Refer to your completed chart.

   Use the Graphic Organizer at **Interactive Review @ ClassZone.com**

Functions of the Federal Reserve		
Serving the banking system	Serving the federal government	Creating money

CRITICAL THINKING

7. **Applying Economic Concepts** Daniel is a high school senior living in California. He receives a check from his grandmother in Florida as a graduation gift. How is the Federal Reserve involved in transferring the money from Daniel's grandmother's bank account to his account? Illustrate your answer with a flow chart.

8. **Applying Economic Concepts** You've been planning your college finances and you know that you'll have to take a bank loan to cover tuition costs. You read that the Fed intends to raise the RRR from 10 percent to 20 percent. How will this change affect the money supply and your ability to borrow money for college tuition?

9. **Analyzing Data** The Fed sets the required reserve ratio at 10 percent. What is the initial deposit if the money supply increases by $40,000? Use the deposit multiplier formula to determine your answer and show your calculations.

10. **Challenge** Banks do not earn interest on the funds they hold as reserves. How does this provide an incentive to banks to create money by making loans rather than to deposit excess funds in a Fed bank?

ECONOMICS IN PRACTICE

Buying school supplies

Evaluating Demand for Money
Consider the factors that affect the demand for money and then complete the following activities.

Identify Changes in Demand The chart below shows some scenarios that would cause demand for money to change. For each example, note if demand is increasing or decreasing.

Factor Affecting Demand for Money	Increasing or Decreasing?
Back-to-school shopping begins	
Banks lower the interest rate on CDs from 6% to 3%	
Energy costs for home heating are up by 20%	
Interest rates on savings deposits increase from 1% to 4.5%	

Challenge What type of potential economic instability is suggested by rising prices? How might the Fed adjust the money supply in such a situation? You will learn more about this topic in Section 3.

Monetary Policy

OBJECTIVES	KEY TERMS	TAKING NOTES
In Section 3, you will • examine the Fed's tools for monetary policy • explain how the Fed's monetary policy promotes growth and stability • analyze the challenges the Fed faces in implementing its policy	monetary policy, *p. 490* open market operations, *p. 490* federal funds rate, *p. 490* discount rate, *p. 491* prime rate, *p. 491* expansionary monetary policy, *p. 492* contractionary monetary policy, *p. 492* easy-money policy, *p. 492* tight-money policy, *p. 493* monetarism, *p. 496*	As you read Section 3, complete a hierarchy diagram to track main ideas and supporting details about monetary policy. Use the Graphic Organizer at **Interactive Review @ ClassZone.com** 

The Fed's Monetary Tools

QUICK REFERENCE

Monetary policy includes the Fed's actions that change the money supply in order to influence the economy.

Open market operations are the sales and purchase of federal government securities.

The **federal funds rate (FFR)** is the interest rate that banks charge one another to borrow money.

KEY CONCEPTS

Monetary policy involves Federal Reserve actions that change the money supply in order to influence the economy. There are three actions the Fed can take to manage the supply of money: open market operations, adjusting the reserve requirement, and adjusting the discount rate. They may be taken individually or in combination with one another. The impact of these actions is shown in Figure 16.8.

ACTION 1 Open Market Operations

Open market operations are the sales and purchase of marketable federal government securities. This is the monetary policy tool most used by the Fed to adjust the money supply. When the Fed wants to expand the money supply, it buys government securities. The Fed pays for the bonds it buys from commercial banks or the public by writing checks on itself. When sellers receive the funds from the Fed, they deposit them in banks. The banks can then lend their new excess reserves. When the Fed wants to contract the money supply, it sells government bonds on the open market. The purchasers of the bonds transfer funds to the Fed to pay for the bonds. These funds are taken out of circulation, and the reserves available for loans decrease.

The Fed communicates its intention to buy or sell bonds by announcing a target for the federal funds rate. The **federal funds rate (FFR)** is the interest rate at which a depository institution lends immediately available funds (balances at the Federal Reserve) to another depository institution overnight. When the Fed lowers the target for the FFR, it buys bonds. When it raises the target, it sells bonds. The Fed does not set the rate directly but influences it through its actions.

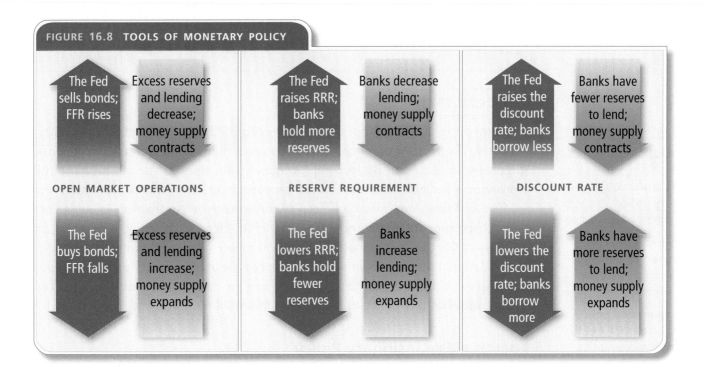

FIGURE 16.8 TOOLS OF MONETARY POLICY

OPEN MARKET OPERATIONS

The Fed sells bonds; FFR rises → Excess reserves and lending decrease; money supply contracts

The Fed buys bonds; FFR falls → Excess reserves and lending increase; money supply expands

RESERVE REQUIREMENT

The Fed raises RRR; banks hold more reserves → Banks decrease lending; money supply contracts

The Fed lowers RRR; banks hold fewer reserves → Banks increase lending; money supply expands

DISCOUNT RATE

The Fed raises the discount rate; banks borrow less → Banks have fewer reserves to lend; money supply contracts

The Fed lowers the discount rate; banks borrow more → Banks have more reserves to lend; money supply expands

ACTION 2 Adjusting the Reserve Requirement

As you recall from Section 2, the Fed sets the required reserve ratio (RRR) for all depository institutions. The RRR affects the money supply through the deposit multiplier formula. Increasing the RRR can reduce the money supply; decreasing the RRR can expand the money supply. Since the early 1990s, the RRR has been between 10 and 12 percent for transaction deposits and between 0 and 3 percent for time deposits.

ACTION 3 Adjusting the Discount Rate

The **discount rate** is the interest rate that the Fed charges when it lends money to other banks. The discount rate affects the money supply because it sets the reserves that banks have available to lend. When the Fed increases the discount rate, banks tend to borrow less money from the Fed. They must then use their existing funds to meet reserve requirements and have less excess reserves to lend. Therefore, the money supply decreases. The opposite happens when the discount rate is lowered. Banks borrow more money from the Fed and increase their reserves. When this happens, they have more money to lend, and the money supply increases.

The Fed's actions also impact businesses and individuals who borrow. The **prime rate** is the interest rate that banks charge their best customers. Interest rates for other borrowers tend to be two or three percentage points above prime. To make a profit on the loans they make, banks need to charge higher rates than they pay to borrow. So when the discount rate increases, so does the prime rate and, therefore, the cost of business and consumer credit.

APPLICATION Analyzing Causes

A. Which open market operation causes the money supply to expand? Why?

Approaches to Monetary Policy

QUICK REFERENCE

Expansionary monetary policy is a plan to increase the money supply.

Contractionary monetary policy is a plan to reduce the money supply.

Easy-money policy is another name for expansionary monetary policy.

KEY CONCEPTS

The most important job of the Fed is to promote growth and stability in the American economy. The purpose of monetary policy is to curb inflation and reduce economic stagnation or recession. By focusing on these goals, the Fed tries to promote full employment and growth without rapid increases in prices or high interest rates.

The Fed uses two basic policies—expansionary or contractionary monetary policy. **Expansionary monetary policy** is a plan to increase the amount of money in circulation. **Contractionary monetary policy** is a plan to reduce the amount of money in circulation. When the economy slows, the Fed uses expansionary monetary policy to pump more money into the economy. When the economy is overheated, the Fed uses a contractionary policy to reduce the amount of money in the economy.

POLICY 1 Expansionary Policy

In Chapter 15 you studied expansionary policy as it related to the federal government's fiscal-policy actions. This type of fiscal policy is used during a slowdown in economic activity. The Fed's expansionary monetary policy is used at the same point in the business cycle. It is sometimes called the **easy-money policy** because it puts more money into circulation by making it easier for borrowers to secure a loan.

During a recession, when unemployment is high, the Fed wants to have more money circulating in the economy to stimulate aggregate demand. When it is easier to borrow money, consumers will take out more loans to buy homes, automobiles, and other goods and services. In response, businesses then produce more, which creates jobs and decreases unemployment. An easy-money policy allows businesses to borrow funds to help them expand. When more loans are made, more money is created in the banking system.

The Fed enacts an easy-money policy by buying bonds on the open market, by decreasing reserve requirements, by decreasing the discount rate, or by some combination of these tools. The Fed's most common action in this situation is to buy bonds on the open market. When the Fed decides to buy more bonds, it increases the demand for them, which raises their price. Recall that bond prices have an inverse, or opposite, relationship to interest rates. When bond prices rise, interest rates fall. Lower interest rates will encourage more lending. More lending increases consumer spending and investment. This, in turn, increases aggregate demand, resulting in the growth of GDP and lower unemployment. If the Fed expands the money supply too much, however, aggregate demand may increase to a level that causes inflation.

Monetary Policy The Fed's monetary policy must be well-timed and well-balanced to have the required effect.

Frank and Ernest

NEWS AND MAGAZINES

DEFLATION TREND

IT SAYS NOT ONLY HAS THE THREAT OF INFLATION PASSED, IT'S REVERSED DIRECTION!

YOU MEAN IT'S COMING BACK TO GET US?!

THAVES

©1998 Thaves. Reprinted with permission. Newspaper dist. by NEA, Inc.

POLICY 2 Contractionary Policy

In Chapter 15, you also studied the federal government's contractionary fiscal policy, used during an expansionary period. The Fed's contractionary monetary policy also is used when economic activity is rapidly increasing. It is sometimes called a **tight-money policy** because it is designed to reduce inflation by making it more difficult for businesses and individuals to get loans.

Suppose that aggregate demand is increasing faster than aggregate supply, leading to higher prices and concerns about inflation. The Fed would want to have less money circulating because more money fuels demand and may lead to inflation in wages and prices. In other words, the Fed would want to make it harder for businesses and individuals to borrow money. Therefore, it would decrease the money supply by decreasing reserves available for loans.

The Fed enacts a tight-money policy by selling bonds on the open market, increasing reserve requirements, or increasing the discount rate. As with easy-money policy, the Fed's most likely action involves open market operations. Selling bonds causes bond prices to fall and interest rates to increase. Higher interest rates discourage lending. Less lending decreases aggregate demand, which decreases growth in GDP, and lowers the general price level. If the Fed contracts the money supply too much, however, aggregate demand may decrease to a level where unemployment increases. Figure 16.9 summarizes how the Fed uses expansionary and contractionary monetary policies.

QUICK REFERENCE

Tight-money policy is another name for contractionary monetary policy.

ECONOMICS ESSENTIALS
FIGURE 16.9 Approaches to Monetary Policy

How does the Fed use its monetary policy tools?

Expansionary Policy
- Buy bonds on the open market
- Lower the reserve requirement
- Reduce the discount rate

Contractionary Policy
- Sell bonds on the open market
- Raise the reserve requirement
- Increase the discount rate

ANALYZE CHARTS
Monetary policy is designed to even out the extremes of the business cycle by expanding or contracting the money supply. Explain how the actions listed under Expansionary Policy increase the supply of money and those under Contractionary Policy decrease the supply of money.

APPLICATION Comparing and Contrasting

B. What are the similarities and differences between expansionary fiscal policy and expansionary monetary policy?

Alan Greenspan: Fighting Inflation

FAST FACTS

Alan Greenspan

Title: Chairman of the Federal Reserve Board (1987–2006)

Born: March 6, 1926, New York City

Major Accomplishment: Controlled inflation while supporting unprecedented economic growth

Presidents Served Under: Ronald Reagan, George H. W. Bush, Bill Clinton, George W. Bush

Time as Fed Chairman: 18 years, 5 months (second longest tenure)

Notable Quotation: *I guess I should warn you, if I turn out to be particularly clear, you've probably misunderstood what I've said.*

🔁 *Economics Update*

Find an update about Alan Greenspan at **ClassZone.com**

During his 18-plus years as chairman of the Fed, Alan Greenspan came to personify the institution. The worldwide financial community and the media waited eagerly to hear what he would say after each meeting of the FOMC. Why did so many people come to believe that one man's decisions could have such a profound impact on everything from the performance of the stock market to mortgage rates?

Managing Monetary Policy

President Ronald Reagan appointed Alan Greenspan chairman of the Federal Reserve Board of Governors in 1987. He had a reputation as a committed inflation fighter and fulfilled that role with great success. The core inflation rate was 3.9 percent when he became chairman and was 2 percent in 2005.

Although the chairman has only one vote on the FOMC, Greenspan's economic insight and persuasiveness gave him much greater power. He led the Fed in using open market operations to help raise interest rates to cool down the economy when it experienced inflationary periods. At other times, for example, when the stock market crash of October 1987 threatened to lead the economy into a severe recession, Greenspan responded by expanding the money supply as needed to cushion the shock. Then, in the late 1990s, he pushed the Fed to edge up interest rates, and the economy experienced a period of unprecedented growth without inflation.

Greenspan's success was due to his clear understanding of the tools of monetary policy and how to apply them, as well as in-depth knowledge of a wide range of economic indicators. Also, throughout his years as chairman, he developed a sense of timing, knowing just when to direct the Fed to expand the money supply and when to contract it.

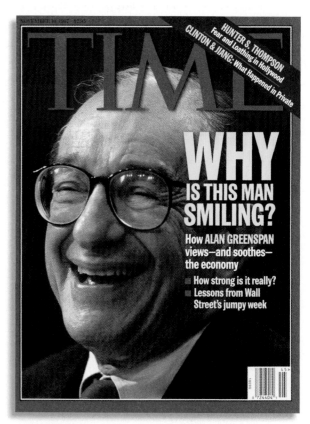

A Celebrity During his tenure as Fed chairman, Alan Greenspan practically achieved celebrity status.

APPLICATION Making Inferences

C. Did Greenspan advocate a tight-money policy or an easy-money policy in the late 1990s? How do you know?

Impacts and Limitation of Monetary Policy

As you recall, the purpose of monetary policy is to curb inflation and to halt recessions, which result in unemployment. But what impact does monetary policy have on the economy, and how successful is it in fulfilling its purpose?

IMPACT 1 Short-Term Effects

Adjustments to monetary policy have both short-term and long-term effects. The short-term effect is change in the price of credit—in other words, the interest rates on loans. The Fed's open market operations influence the FFR fairly quickly by increasing or decreasing the level of reserves that banks have available to lend. Figure 16.10 shows that when the Fed uses an easy-money policy to expand the money supply, interest rates decline. When the Fed uses a tight-money policy, as shown in Figure 16.11, interest rates rise.

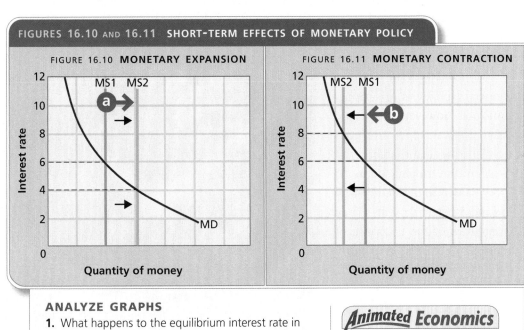

FIGURES 16.10 AND 16.11 SHORT-TERM EFFECTS OF MONETARY POLICY

FIGURE 16.10 **MONETARY EXPANSION**

FIGURE 16.11 **MONETARY CONTRACTION**

The money supply (MS1, MS2) is a vertical line because it represents the fixed amount of money available as determined by the Fed.

Demand for money (MD) is the same as demand for any product. As prices (interest rates) fall, demand increases. As prices rise, demand falls.

a The supply curve shifts to the right when the money supply expands.

b The supply curve shifts to the left when the money supply contracts.

ANALYZE GRAPHS

1. What happens to the equilibrium interest rate in Figure 16.10? What happens to it in Figure 16.11?

2. How do these graphs show the effects of easy-money and tight-money policy?

Animated **Economics**

Use an interactive money supply curve at **ClassZone.com**

IMPACT 2 Policy Lags

Some lags, or delays, that affect monetary policy are related to identifying the problem. The Fed needs specific information and statistics in order to identify the problem and take action. Other lags have to do with how quickly the change in policy takes effect. Many economists suggest that it may take as long as two years for adjustments in monetary policy to take full effect. This may have long-term effects on the economy. For example, businesses often delay plans for expansion if interest rates are too high. Because policies designed to lower rates may take some time to take effect, actual investment in expansion may lag months or years behind the plans.

IMPACT 3 Timing Issues

As with fiscal policy, monetary policy must be coordinated with the business cycle in order to provide a stable economic environment. If the policy is correct and the timing is good, extremes in the business cycle will be evened out. If the timing is bad, a business cycle phase may be exaggerated. For example, high interest rates in 1990 that were intended to help fight inflation actually took effect as the economy was going into a recession, worsening the effects of that recession.

Supporters of monetarism cite such situations to show that using monetary policy to influence short-term changes in the business cycle can create major problems. **Monetarism** is a theory that suggests that rapid changes in the money supply are the main cause of economic instability. Milton Friedman is the most prominent monetarist. (You can read more about Friedman on page 76.) He studied how changes in the growth rate of the money supply affected prices and concluded that inflation is always accompanied by rapid monetary growth. Conversely, he noted that there has been little or no inflation when the money supply has grown slowly and steadily.

Monetarists do believe that monetary policy is an important tool. However, they argue that best way to ensure economic growth and stability is to allow the money supply to grow slowly and steadily—by around 3 percent a year. They disapprove of the Fed's use of monetary policy to constantly tinker with the money supply.

Monetarism According to monetarists, a slow, steady growth in the amount of money in circulation is the best monetary policy.

Other Issues

The use of the monetary policy tools is just one way the economy can be corrected. It is more effective if it is coordinated with fiscal policy. In addition, the goals of the Fed may clash with those of Congress or the president. Since members of the Fed's Board of Governors serve for 14-year terms, they are not as susceptible to political pressure as are politicians, who are elected every two to six years.

APPLICATION Analyzing Causes

D. What will happen to interest rates when the Fed sells bonds in open market operations? Why?

REVIEWING KEY CONCEPTS

1. Explain the difference between the terms in each of these pairs.

   a. *monetary policy*
   monetarism

   b. *easy-money policy*
   tight-money policy

   c. *discount rate*
   prime rate

2. How should a contractionary monetary policy affect interest rates and the rate of inflation? Why?

3. How should an expansionary monetary policy affect interest rates and the unemployment rate? Why?

4. How does the Fed use open market operations as a monetary policy tool?

5. What is the main short-term effect of monetary policy?

6. **Using Your Notes** Which monetary policy tool does the Fed use least often? Refer to your completed hierarchy diagram.

   Use the Graphic Organizer at **Interactive Review @ ClassZone.com**

   Monetary Policy
   → main ideas → main ideas → main ideas
   → details → details → details

CRITICAL THINKING

7. **Analyzing Causes** To curb inflation, why is it easier for the Fed to use monetary policy to raise interest rates than it is for Congress to implement contractionary fiscal policy?

8. **Making Inferences** What are the Fed's underlying assumptions about the state of the economy, based on these Fed actions?

   a. The Fed's open market operations caused the FFR to drop from 6.25 percent to 1 percent.

   b. The FFR rose from 1 percent to 4.25 percent.

9. **Applying Economic Concepts** In 2005, the Fed set the discount rate for banks in good financial condition at 1 percent above the targeted FFR.

   a. Would these banks be more likely to borrow short-term funds from another bank or from the Fed? Why?

   b. How does this policy help keep the federal funds rate close to the target set by the Fed?

10. **Challenge** Explain how the Fed buying bonds affects interest rates, aggregate demand, price level, and GDP. Illustrate your answer using two graphs, one showing the money market and one showing aggregate supply and aggregate demand.

ECONOMICS IN PRACTICE

Durable goods—washing machines

Applying Economic Concepts
Think about the ways monetary policy is used to address economic problems. Then complete the following activities.

Determine Monetary Policy The chart below lists several economic situations. For each one, decide whether an easy-money or tight-money policy is needed.

Economic Situation	Monetary Policy Needed
Consumer spending on durable goods rises faster than production	
Rising energy prices are pushing prices of many products higher	
Unemployment rate increases from 5.4% to 6.8% over six months	

Challenge Choose one example that requires an easy-money policy and one that requires a tight-money policy and explain how open market operations would be used in each case.

Applying Monetary and Fiscal Policy

In Section 4, you will
- describe how monetary and fiscal policy can coordinate to improve the economy
- understand how monetary and fiscal policy can work against each other
- identify other measures that can be used to manage the economy

wage and price controls, *p. 501*

As you read Section 4, complete a cause-and-effect chart using the key concepts and other helpful words and phrases. Use the Graphic Organizer at **Interactive Review @ ClassZone.com**

Expansionary Policies → results

Contractionary Policies → results

Conflicting Policies → results

Policies to Expand the Economy

KEY CONCEPTS

The goals of both fiscal and monetary policy are to stabilize the economy by easing the effects of recession and controlling inflation. Fiscal policy relies on government spending and taxation to achieve its goals. Monetary policy uses open market operations, the discount rate, and reserve requirements as its tools.

These policies, as well as affecting the economy, also have an impact on each other. As you recall, both monetary and fiscal policy have limitations. These include policy lags, political constraints, and timing issues. Policy lags relate to the time it takes to identify the problem and for policy actions to take effect. Political considerations may limit government's ability to do what is best for the economy. Timing, too, is important because to be effective government actions must counteract the negative effects of the business cycle. Intervention at the wrong time may skew the cycle and make the problem worse.

A second phenomenon affecting timing is explained by the rational expectations theory. As you recall from Chapter 15, this states that individuals and business firms learn, through experience, to anticipate changes in monetary and fiscal policy and take steps to protect their interests. For example, if there is debate in Congress about tax cuts, individuals and businesses may take actions before the legislation is even passed, based on their expectations that tax cuts will increase their income. Individuals may decide to purchase durable goods, such as automobiles, refrigerators, and washing machines. Similarly, businesses may decide to expand their operations by building new factories and hiring more workers. On the other hand, if individuals and businesses think the tax cuts will be temporary, they may choose not to spend as the policy intended.

Rational Expectations

Expectations that tax cuts will increase their incomes may cause people to buy "big-ticket" items such as refrigerators.

People who disagree with the use of most discretionary policy often support their argument with the rational expectations theory. They suggest that rather than fiddling with fiscal and monetary policy, the government should aim for a stable monetary policy so that business decisions are made for economic reasons and not in anticipation of new policies.

EXAMPLE Expansionary Monetary and Fiscal Policy

The goal of expansionary policy is to stimulate the economy by reducing unemployment and increasing investment. As you recall, expansionary fiscal policy involves increased government spending or tax cuts. Also, to enact expansionary monetary policy, the Fed buys government bonds or reduces the discount rate or the reserve requirement.

For example, suppose that the unemployment rate is 9.5 percent and the Consumer Price Index (CPI) is at 2 percent. The economy is in recession and inflation is a minimal concern. In order to increase the money supply, the Fed buys bonds on the open market and lowers the discount rate. The federal government also cuts personal income taxes and increases government spending. These expansionary policies are designed to increase aggregate demand and decrease unemployment. Real GDP will expand and prices will rise as aggregate demand increases. Figure 16.12 shows how expansionary policies affect these key economic indicators.

Expansionary fiscal policy is likely to raise interest rates, while expansionary monetary policy should decrease interest rates. Therefore, the actual change in interest rates will depend on the relative strength of the two policies. The amount of investment spending will depend on what happens with interest rates.

FIGURE 16.12 Effects of Expansionary Policies

Policies

a

Monetary Policy
The Fed buys bonds and lowers the discount rate to increase money supply

Fiscal Policy
Increased spending/ tax cuts to increase aggregate demand

Effects

b

Real GDP increases and **prices** rise

Unemploy-ment falls

a Here, fiscal and monetary policies work together to expand the economy.

b These policies tend to increase aggregate demand, increase real GDP, and lower unemployment.

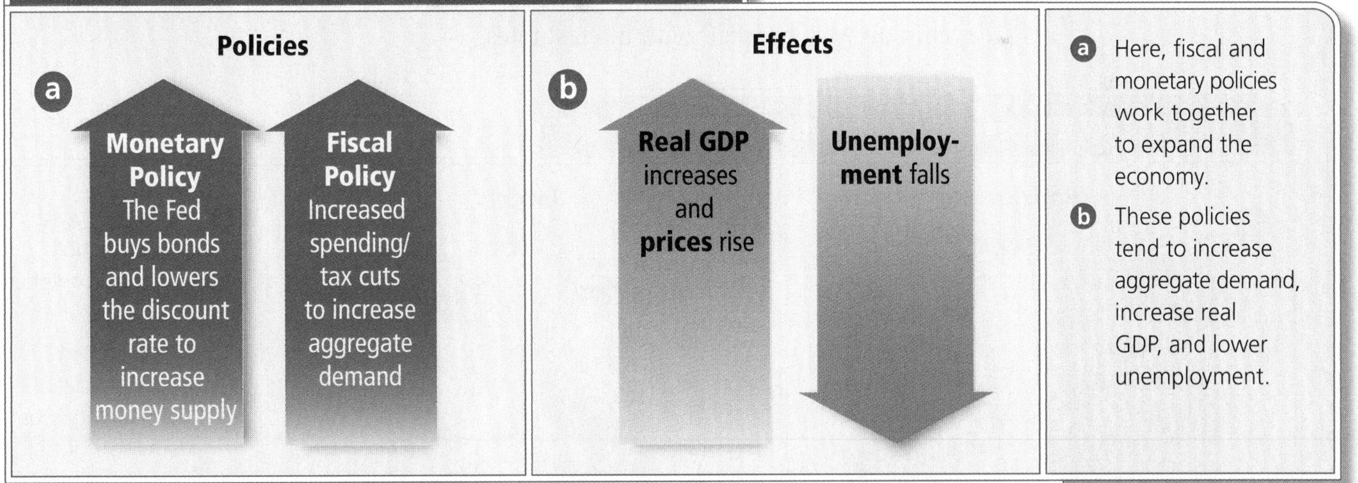

ANALYZE CHARTS
1. According to the chart, what are the goals of expansionary policies?
2. Which indicator in the chart suggests that expansionary policy might lead toward inflation?

APPLICATION Analyzing Effects

A. What effect would government borrowing to finance increased spending have on interest rates and why?

Policies to Control Inflation

KEY CONCEPTS

The goal of contractionary monetary policy is to tighten up the economy by decreasing inflation and increasing interest rates. Contractionary fiscal policy tools include decreased government spending or tax increases. The Fed will sell bonds on the open market or raise the discount rate or the reserve requirement as contractionary monetary policy tools.

EXAMPLE Contractionary Monetary and Fiscal Policy

Suppose that the unemployment rate is 4.5 percent and the CPI is running in excess of 10 percent. The economy is operating at or above a sustainable level of output, and inflation is very high. In order to decrease the money supply, the Fed sells bonds on the open market and raises the discount rate. The federal government cuts spending on government programs. It also may raise taxes. These contractionary policies are designed to decrease aggregate demand and bring inflation under control. Real GDP will decrease, and prices will fall as aggregate demand decreases. Further, unemployment tends to rise as real GDP decreases. Figure 16.13 shows how contractionary monetary and fiscal policies affect the key economic indicators of unemployment and real GDP.

Contractionary fiscal policy is likely to lower interest rates because decreased government spending will decrease demand for loans. Contractionary monetary policy should raise interest rates. Therefore, the actual change in interest rates will depend on the relative strength of the two policies. The amount of investment spending depends on what happens with interest rates.

FIGURE 16.13 Effects of Contractionary Policies

Policies

a

Monetary Policy
The Fed sells bonds and raises the discount rate to cut money supply

Fiscal Policy
Decreased spending/ tax increases to decrease aggregate demand

Effects

b

Real GDP and **prices** fall

Unemployment increases

a Here, fiscal and monetary policies work together to contract the economy.

b These policies decrease aggregate demand, control inflation, and raise unemployment.

ANALYZE CHARTS

1. According to the chart, what are the goals of contractionary policies?

2. In what way might the fiscal policy shown here not help to control inflation?

CHAPTER

17

SECTION 1
Benefits and Issues of International Trade

SECTION 2
Trade Barriers

SECTION 3
Measuring the Value of Trade

SECTION 4
Modern International Institutions

CASE STUDY
Analyzing Tariffs: Who Wins and Who Loses?

International Trade

CONCEPT REVIEW

The **global economy** is the sum of all economic interactions that cross international boundaries.

CHAPTER 17 KEY CONCEPT

Economic interdependence involves producers in one nation that depend on producers in other nations to supply them with certain goods and services.

WHY THE CONCEPT MATTERS

Japan is a world-class producer of automobiles, in spite of the fact that it has few mineral resources. How can this be? The answer lies in the realm of international trade, where nations choose to produce some things and trade for others. In the case of Japan, it must trade for the raw materials it uses in order to produce automobiles. It then turns around and trades the automobiles for other goods.

Online Highlights
More at ClassZone.com

🏃 Economics Update
Go to **ECONOMICS UPDATE** for chapter updates and current news on how tariffs and subsidies affect the sugar market. (See Case Study, pp. 538–539). ▶

Animated Economics
Go to **ANIMATED ECONOMICS** for interactive lessons on the graphs and tables in this chapter.

Interactive ◀▶ Review
Go to **INTERACTIVE REVIEW** for concept review and activities.

Why do many people believe that U.S. government susidies to sugar producers are a problem? See the Case Study on pages 538–539.

Benefits and Issues of International Trade

OBJECTIVES	KEY TERMS	TAKING NOTES
In Section 1, you will • determine why nations choose to specialize their economies • examine the difference between absolute and comparative advantage • explain how international trade impacts prices and quantity	specialization, *p. 510* economic interdependence, *p. 510* absolute advantage, *p. 513* comparative advantage, *p. 513* law of comparative advantage, *p. 514* exports, *p. 516* imports, *p. 516*	As you read Section 1, complete a diagram that shows how the concepts in the section relate to international trade. Use the Graphic Organizer at **Interactive Review @ ClassZone.com** 

Resource Distribution and Specialization

KEY CONCEPTS

A nation's economic patterns are based on its unique combination of factors of production: natural resources, human capital, physical capital, and entrepreneurship. For example, a nation rich in arable land but lacking well-educated workers is less likely to develop a strong technology sector than a country with better-educated citizens and diverse natural resources. Economic patterns may also change over time. The United States, for example, once relied heavily on its agricultural sector, but the U.S. economy is now also extremely high-tech and highly skilled.

Because each nation has certain resources and cannot produce everything it wants, individuals and businesses must decide what goods and services to focus on. The result is **specialization**, a situation that occurs when individuals or businesses produce a narrow range of products. Through specialization, businesses can increase productivity and profit—the driving force of world trade. Specialization also leads to **economic interdependence**, a situation in which producers in one nation depend on others to provide goods and services they do not produce.

Specialization A coal-rich nation that lacks advanced technology can trade its coal for manufactured goods, such as automobiles, from nations with higher levels of technology.

SPECIALIZATION

Will you specialize in lawn mowing or babysitting?

Do you have a lawn mower? Do you know children that need to be watched? What other questions might you ask yourself before deciding what you will specialize in?

Mow lawns

Babysit

EXAMPLE Specialization

The concept of specialization can be illustrated by looking at the agricultural production of two nations: Costa Rica and New Zealand. The climate, the labor conditions, and the level of technology of each nation have made some agricultural products more important than others. In other words, each nation has decided to specialize in certain agricultural areas because they have an advantage in doing so.

For Costa Rica, the product of choice is bananas. It is the world's seventh-largest producer and second-largest exporter of bananas. For New Zealand, the product of choice is sheep. It is the world's third-largest producer and second-largest exporter of wool and is responsible for about 50 percent of the world's lamb and mutton exports. What explains each nation's specialization?

Costa Rica has the necessary climate for bananas—warm and wet. In addition, agricultural wages are relatively low, an important point as banana production is quite labor intensive.

On the other hand, New Zealand has the temperate climate, water resources, and vast expanses of open grasslands to support the grazing of millions of sheep. (Today, there are about 10 sheep for every person in New Zealand.) Raising sheep is not nearly as labor intensive as banana production, and this suits the fairly low population density of this remote island nation. Also, scientific breeding practices and mechanized wool- and meat-processing operations are available to a developed nation such as New Zealand.

It makes sense for each nation to specialize as it does and to trade for the things it cannot produce as efficiently.

> **Economics Update**
>
> Find an update on Costa Rica's economy at **ClassZone.com**

APPLICATION Drawing Conclusions

A. Why should nations specialize in what they produce most efficiently and trade for the rest?

David Ricardo: The Theory of Comparative Advantage

FAST FACTS

David Ricardo

Title: Economist, stockbroker

Born: 1772

Died: 1823

Major Accomplishment: Brilliantly thinking through economic principles and laying the foundation for free trade

Major Work: *On the Principles of Political Economy and Taxation* (1817)

Famous Quotation:

"*The labor of 100 Englishmen cannot be given for that of 80 Englishmen, but the produce of the labor of 100 Englishmen may be given for the produce of the labour of 80 Portuguese, 60 Russians, or 120 East Indians.*"

Economics Update

Learn more about David Ricardo at **ClassZone.com**

Many things about London-born economist David Ricardo make him a memorable figure. He was one of 17 children in a Jewish family. At age 14, he went to work in his father's stockbrokerage. He married a Quaker at age 21 and broke from the Jewish faith, at which time his father disinherited him. And finally, when he died at age 51, he left a $126 million fortune.

Ricardo is most remembered, however, for the idea that has become the backbone for free trade—comparative advantage. It states, in short, that a trading nation should produce a certain product if it can do so at a lower opportunity cost than that of another trading nation.

EXAMPLE Trading in Opportunity

The prevailing view about international trade in Ricardo's time was based on the idea of absolute advantage, the ability of one trading nation to make a product more efficiently than another trading nation. Most people believed that if Portugal, for example, could make grape juice more efficiently than England, and if England could make cloth more efficiently than Portugal, then trade would be beneficial to both.

Ricardo, however, set up a different problem, one that challenged this outlook. What if, he thought, Portugal makes both products more efficiently than England? Would trade, at least for Portugal, no longer be beneficial? His surprising answer was that trade would indeed still be beneficial. He based his conclusion on the opportunity costs each nation spends to make its products.

Suppose that in Portugal, it takes two hours of labor to produce a jug of grape juice, while in England, it takes four hours. Suppose also that in Portugal, a yard of cloth takes six hours to make; in England it takes eight hours. Ricardo reasoned that in Portugal, every yard of cloth costs three jugs of grape juice in lost opportunity. In England, however, every yard of cloth costs only two jugs of grape juice. Portugal, then, would be wise to buy cloth from England and to specialize in grape juice. This understanding has become known as the law of comparative advantage: countries gain when they produce items they are most efficient at producing and that have the lowest opportunity cost.

David Ricardo

APPLICATION Applying Economic Concepts

B. Does the law of comparative advantage apply only to nations, or does it apply to individuals as well? Explain your answer.

Absolute and Comparative Advantage

KEY CONCEPTS

Absolute advantage is the ability of one trading nation to make a product more efficiently than another trading nation. Some regions or nations have absolute advantage in producing certain products or services because of the uneven distribution of production factors.

Comparative advantage, in contrast, is the idea that a nation will specialize in what it can produce at a lower opportunity cost than any other nation. When determining comparative advantage, you look not for the absolute cost of a product, but for its opportunity cost.

QUICK REFERENCE

Absolute advantage is the ability of one trading nation to make a product more efficiently than another trading nation.

Comparative advantage is a trading nation's ability to produce something at a lower opportunity cost than that of another trading nation.

EXAMPLE Absolute Advantage

Consider the trade relations between two countries on the Pacific Rim today, China and Australia. Both countries produce iron ore; both also produce steel. Suppose that every week, Australia produces 5,000 tons of iron ore and 1,000 tons of steel. In the same period of time, and with the same amount of labor, China produces 2,700 tons of iron ore and 900 tons of steel. In this case, Australia has an absolute advantage over China in both areas.

Before Ricardo, the standard logic held that, in this situation, the nation that held the absolute advantage for both commodities would trade for neither. But, as you've read, when the important factor of opportunity cost is considered, this logic doesn't stand up. Why would it benefit Australia to import steel from China, in spite of its absolute advantage? The answer is comparative advantage.

What Does Opportunity Cost? Should Australia specialize in mining iron ore (left) and leave the steel production (right) to China? Where does the comparative advantage lie?

EXAMPLE Comparative Advantage

Let's start with a simple example of comparative advantage. After years as an office manager at a law firm by day and a law student by night, Ellen becomes a lawyer and starts her own practice. She charges $150 per hour for her legal services. She hires Miguel to run her office, and she pays him $25 per hour. Although Miguel works hard and is good at his job, Ellen soon realizes that, due to her years of experience, she could run her own office better than Miguel. Should she take over these duties? The answer lies in opportunity cost. Every hour that Ellen spends engaged in the duties that are worth $25 per hour costs her an hour that could be spent doing work that is worth $150 per hour. Clearly it makes sense for her to employ an office manager and concentrate on the legal end of her practice.

Back to our previous example of Australia and China, we see that Australia's production ratio of steel to iron ore is 1:5. In other words, Australia's opportunity cost for one ton of steel is five tons of iron ore. Applying the same logic to China, we find that its production ratio of steel to iron ore is 1:3. Its opportunity cost for one ton of steel is three tons of iron ore. So, in the procrution of steel, China has a comparative advantage. Australia would benefit by trading for Chinese steel. This is the **law of comparative advantage**: countries gain when they produce items that they are most efficient at producing and that are at the lowest opportunity cost.

FIGURE 17.1 Specialization and Trade

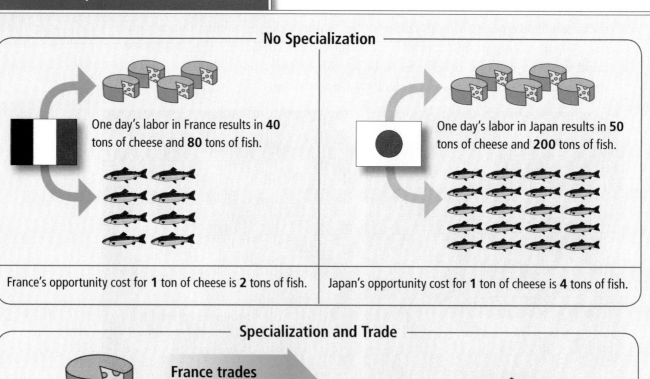

No Specialization

One day's labor in France results in **40** tons of cheese and **80** tons of fish.

One day's labor in Japan results in **50** tons of cheese and **200** tons of fish.

France's opportunity cost for **1** ton of cheese is **2** tons of fish.

Japan's opportunity cost for **1** ton of cheese is **4** tons of fish.

Specialization and Trade

France trades 1 ton of cheese.

Japan trades 3 tons of fish.

It used to cost France **1** ton of cheese to get **2** tons of fish; now it trades **1** ton of cheese for **3** tons of fish.

It used to cost Japan **4** tons of fish for **1** ton of cheese; now it trades only **3** tons of fish for **1** ton of cheese.

Economic Success with Few Natural Resources

Some economies thrive as a direct result of natural resources—Saudi Arabia and its oil, for instance. But, many nations, such as the Republic of Ireland, thrive economically in spite of a relative lack of natural resources.

It is not rich in mineral resources and relies on imports for the majority of its energy supply. However, it has formulated and carried out certain policies that have helped to produce today's dynamic economy.

In the mid-1950s, Ireland began a continuing process of reversing protectionist tariff and quota policies. The Programmes for Economic Expansion (1958 and 1963) attracted large amounts of foreign direct investment through financial grants and tax concessions. Levels of human capital were increased through educational reforms in the 1960s. It was also an original member of the EU and took advantage of EU funds to shore up its infrastructure. These and other policies set the stage for Ireland's economic boom of the 1990s. During this decade, it became a major manufacturer of high-tech electronics, computer products, chemicals, and pharmaceuticals. It has also become an important center for banking and finance.

The headquarters of the Industrial Development Agency of Ireland, in Dublin

CONNECTING ACROSS THE GLOBE

1. **Drawing Conclusions** What specialization has, for the most part, driven Ireland's economic boom?
2. **Applying Economic Concepts** Why might an economy like Ireland's be more desirable than one that relies solely on natural resources?

EXAMPLE Advantages of Free Trade

If China and Australia decide to specialize and trade, they can improve their ratio of return. Previously, China's ratio of steel production to iron ore production was 1:3 and Australia's was 1:5. If the two nations establish a trade ratio of 1:4 (China trades one ton of its steel for four tons of Australian iron ore), both countries win. China now gets four tons of iron ore for a ton of steel; it got three before. Also, one ton of steel now costs Australia only four tons of iron ore; it previously cost five.

When countries specialize and trade, they not only improve their production ratios but they also increase world output. If China specializes in steel and Australia in iron ore, each can make more of their products than the two nations could have made together if they had not specialized. Increased output is a mark of economic growth, which is a factor in raising standards of living.

APPLICATION Interpreting Tables

C. Use the example in Figure 17.1 to explain how output for both nations increases through specialization and trade.

International Trade Affects the National Economy

Because of the law of comparative advantage, nations gain through trading goods and services. Goods and services produced in one country and sold to other countries are called **exports**. Goods and services produced in one country and purchased by another are called **imports**.

The costs and benefits of international trade vary by nation. To understand how trade affects a nation's economy, economists use supply and demand analysis. They look at the impact of exports and imports on prices and quantity.

IMPACT 1 Exports on Prices and Quantity

Suppose that a county called Plecona existed and that it did not trade with other countries. Figure 17.2 shows the equilibrium price for Plecona's motorbikes.

What would happen to prices and demand if Plecona decided to become a trading nation and export its motorbikes? In some countries, such as Nepocal, people would give up their bicycles and begin to buy Pleconese motorbikes. This results in an increase in demand for Pleconese motorbikes, shifting the demand curve to the right and establishing a new equilibrium price. Motorbikes will now cost more in Plecona too. However, the greater demand resulting from exporting offsets this by creating more jobs and more income in Plecona, as the motorbike producer invests its profits to expand production and hire more workers.

IMPACT 2 Imports on Prices and Quantity

Now suppose that Nepocal and Plecona agree that Nepocal may sell its major product, microwave ovens, in Plecona. Instead of having only Pleconese-made microwaves, consumers in Plecona may now purchase ovens imported from Nepocal. This change adds to the number of microwave oven producers in the Pleconese market. Adding producers shifts the supply curve of microwave ovens to the right and thereby establishes a new, lower equilibrium price. (See Figure 17.3.)

In other words, there are now more microwave ovens in Plecona, and the consumers are paying a lower price for them. However, because of the lower price, Pleconese producers of microwave ovens will choose to offer fewer microwaves for sale. So imports have the effect of initially increasing supply and of providing consumers with greater selection and lower prices. The competition also establishes incentives for domestic producers to become more efficient in production, improve worker productivity, and enhance customer service.

Both consumers and producers, then, benefit from international trade. Consumers benefit from imports because the selection of goods increases and prices decrease. Producers benefit from exports by gaining a new market for their products, and thereby giving them the opportunity to increase revenues and earn a profit.

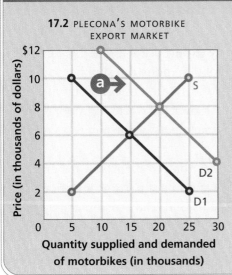

17.2 PLECONA'S MOTORBIKE EXPORT MARKET

Price (in thousands of dollars)

Quantity supplied and demanded of motorbikes (in thousands)

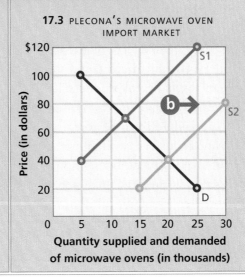

17.3 PLECONA'S MICROWAVE OVEN IMPORT MARKET

Price (in dollars)

Quantity supplied and demanded of microwave ovens (in thousands)

a Increased demand causes the demand curve to shift to the right.

b Increased supply causes the supply curve to shift to the right.

ANALYZE GRAPHS

What are the initial and then post-shift equilibrium prices for motorbikes in Figure 17.2? for microwaves in Figure 17.3?

Animated Economics

Use an interactive supply and demand graph at **ClassZone.com**

IMPACT 3 Trade Affects Employment

As nations specialize in their changing areas of strength, the availability of certain jobs can undergo dramatic changes. For example, if Australia specializes in producing iron ore or providing educational services (another area of strength for that nation) at the expense of making steel, then some Australian steelworkers may lose their jobs. At the same time, however, the overall number of Australian jobs may increase significantly. The Australian Trade Commission estimates that a ten percent increase in exports results in 70,000 new jobs for workers in Australia.

In the United States, manufacturing output increased 600 percent between 1950 and 2000. During the same period, however, employment in manufacturing, as a share of total employment, declined by nearly two-thirds. The United States was shifting its specialization from manufacturing to technology. In the process, it became a world leader in technology exports. So, while many manufacturing jobs in some sectors were lost, the shift in specialization and the result-ing trade had positive effects on U.S. employment in general. During the 1990s, for example, U.S. exports were responsible for about 25 percent of the nation's economic growth, supporting about 12 million jobs. About 20 percent of all U.S. factory jobs depend on trade. Also, jobs in plants that export their products pay an average of 18 percent higher wages than jobs in non-exporting plants.

Biotech Jobs The U.S. economy's move to the technology sector has meant a sharp rise in biotechnology employment.

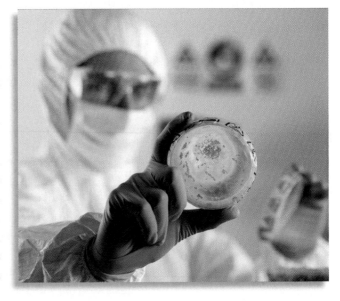

The United States in the World Economy

The United States is a leading nation in a number of aspects of the world economy. It is the largest exporter in the world, selling more than $900 billion in goods and services in 2005. The United States mostly exports capital goods (computers, machinery, civilian aircraft, and so on), automobiles, industrial supplies, consumer goods, and agricultural products. It is also the world's largest importer, buying nearly $1.7 trillion worth of goods and services from all over the world. It imports mainly crude oil and refined petroleum products, machinery, automobiles, consumer goods, and industrial raw materials.

Economics Update

Find an update on U.S. imports at **ClassZone.com**

While the United States imports more goods than it exports, it exports more services than it imports. Such services as travel and tourism, transportation, architecture and construction, and information systems find ready customers in Europe, Japan, Canada, and Mexico. The four most important trading partners for the United States in goods and services are Canada, accounting for 20 percent of trade, China (12 percent), Mexico (11 percent), and Japan (7 percent). Trade with these four partners accounts for half of U.S. foreign trade.

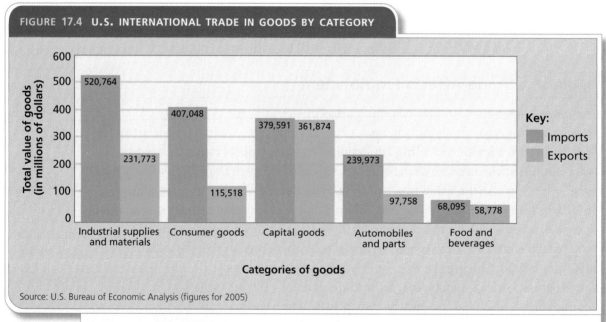

FIGURE 17.4 U.S. INTERNATIONAL TRADE IN GOODS BY CATEGORY

Source: U.S. Bureau of Economic Analysis (figures for 2005)

ANALYZE GRAPHS

1. In what two areas do U.S. export totals approach import totals?
2. What do these graphs show about the United States and specialization?

In recent years, as shown in Figure 17.4, the United States has imported an increasingly larger amount than it has exported. You will learn more about this in Section 4 of this chapter.

APPLICATION Interpreting Graphs

D. In what category of goods is the difference between imports and exports the greatest? Why do you think this is so?

REVIEWING KEY CONCEPTS

1. Explain the difference between the terms in the following pairs:

   a. *specialization* and *economic interdependence*

   b. *absolute advantage* and *comparative advantage*

   c. *export* and *import*

2. What principle explains why nations specialize and trade?

3. Explain why trade is good for nations that produce exports as well as buy imports.

4. What effect do imports have on price and supply? Why?

5. What effect do exports have on price and demand? Why?

6. **Using Your Notes** Write a speech for the president of Australia, explaining why your nation should specialize in the production of iron ore and trade for steel. Use the Graphic Organizer at **Interactive Review @ ClassZone.com**

International Trade

CRITICAL THINKING

7. **Analyzing Cause and Effect** You have just learned that high-quality electric guitars made in South Korea will soon be exported to the United States. Should you buy a new guitar now or wait until after the imports begin arriving? Explain your answer.

8. **Making Inferences and Drawing Conclusions** Why does the law of comparative advantage explain that all people and nations can trade?

9. **Explaining an Economic Concept** How does international trade help create jobs? How does it shift jobs?

10. **Challenge** Shelley started her own comedy improvisation club right after college, and at first she did everything: developed new material, starred in the show, handled publicity, and sold tickets. As the enterprise grew, however, she hired an assistant to handle publicity and sell tickets, even though she was better at doing those things than he was. Explain why that was a good idea, using terms from this lesson.

ECONOMICS IN PRACTICE

Figuring Absolute and Comparative Advantage

Review the following scenario that describes cordless drill and drill bit production in the fictional nations of Freedonia and Sylvania.

Freedonia and Sylvania both produce cordless drills and drill bits. Over the span of a month, Freedonia can produce 3,000 cordless drills and 21,000 drill bits. During this same period, Sylvania can produce 2,000 cordless drills and 10,000 drill bits.

Drawing Conclusions Use what you've learned in this section to answer the following questions:

1. For each product, which nation has the absolute advantage?

2. What are the production ratios for each nation? What is each nation's opportunity cost for each cordless drill produced?

3. Which country has the comparative advantage in cordless drill production?

Challenge Draw up and explain a scenario whereby Freedonia and Sylvania agree to trade, and each gets a better deal by adjusting its trade ratio.

Trade Barriers

OBJECTIVES	KEY TERMS	TAKING NOTES
In Section 2, you will • identify barriers to trade • examine the economic consequences of trade barriers • describe protectionism and the arguments for it	trade barrier, *p. 520* quota, *p. 520* dumping, *p. 521* tariff, *p. 521* revenue tariff, *p. 521* protective tariff, *p. 521* voluntary export restraint, *p. 521* embargo, *p. 521* trade war, *p. 522* protectionism, *p. 523* infant industries, *p. 523*	As you read Section 2, complete a chart that shows the causes and effects of trade barriers. Use the Graphic Organizer at **Interactive Review @ ClassZone.com** | Cause	Effect
---	---
quota	higher prices

Barriers to Trade

KEY CONCEPTS

In order to offer some short-term protection to jobs and industries located within their borders, almost all nations pass some sort of laws that limit trade. These laws lead to higher prices on the restricted items or to economic retaliation by other nations. In the end, these industries and the jobs they provide can only be saved by becoming more competitive. The issue of trade restrictions is basically political in nature, and governments struggle to find the best policies to enact.

Types of Trade Barriers

A **trade barrier** is any law passed to limit free trade among nations. There are five basic types of trade barriers. Most are mandatory, but some are voluntary.

Quotas Nations often impose **quotas**, limits on the amount of a product that can be imported. For example, the United States had quotas on the amount of textiles allowed to be imported. These quotas limited supply and kept textile prices relatively high.

Quota Lifted Chinese textiles cross the Great Wall on their way to markets in the United States and the EU.

These quotas expired on January 1, 2005. Chinese producers then flooded the United States (and the European Union) with low-priced textiles. Prices for Chinese textiles increased, however, in other nations. This practice of **dumping**, the sale of a product in another country at a price lower than that charged in the home market, hurts domestic producers but provides consumers a lower price.

Tariffs Another trade barrier is the **tariff**, a fee charged for goods brought into a country from another country. There are two types of tariffs: revenue and protective. **Revenue tariffs**, taxes on imports specifically to raise money, are rarely used today. In the past, however, nations regularly used them as a source of income. Today nations use **protective tariffs**, taxes on imported goods, to protect domestic goods. Protective tariffs raise prices on goods produced more cheaply elsewhere, thereby minimizing the price advantage the imports have over domestic goods. Tariff rates have fallen worldwide since the late 1980s. (See Figure 17.5.)

Voluntary Export Restraint Sometimes, to avoid a quota or a tariff, a country may choose to limit an export. This is called a **voluntary export restraint (VER)**. It usually comes about when a trade ambassador from one nation makes appeals to a counterpart, warning of possible consequences without the VER.

Embargoes An **embargo** is a law that cuts off most or all trade with a specific country. It is often used for political purposes. Since the early 1960s, for example, the United States has had an embargo on trade with Communist Cuba.

Informal Trade Barriers Other trade restrictions are indirect. Licenses, environmental regulations, and health and safety measures (such as a ban on the use of certain herbicides) are, in effect, trade barriers.

QUICK REFERENCE

Dumping is the sale of a product in another country at a price lower than in the home market.

A **tariff** is a fee charged for goods brought into one country from another.

A **revenue tariff** is a tax levied on imports specifically to raise money.

A **protective tariff** is a tax on imported goods to protect domestic goods.

A **voluntary export restraint (VER)** is a country's self-imposed restriction on exports.

An **embargo** is a law that cuts off trade with a specific country.

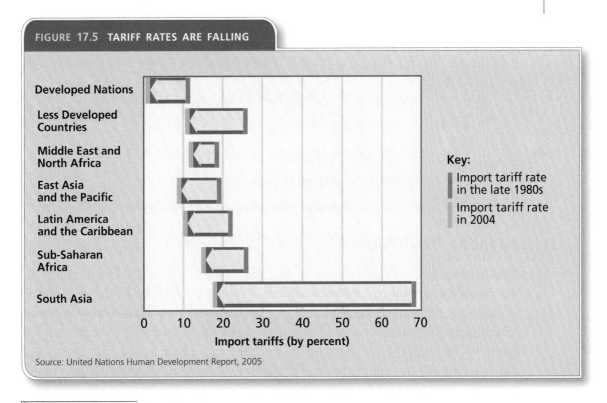

FIGURE 17.5 TARIFF RATES ARE FALLING

Key:
Import tariff rate in the late 1980s
Import tariff rate in 2004

Import tariffs (by percent)

Source: United Nations Human Development Report, 2005

APPLICATION Categorizing Economic Information

A. Aside from imposing an embargo, how might one nation limit the import of a product from another nation?

The Impact of Trade Barriers

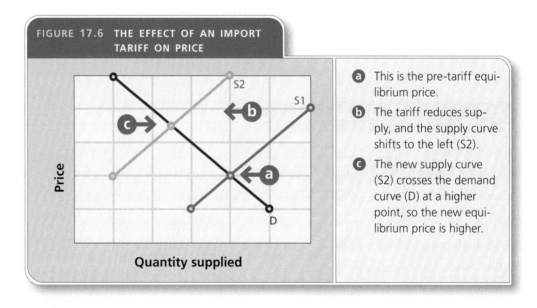

KEY CONCEPTS

Trade barriers have numerous effects. They may temporarily save domestic jobs in certain industries, but without competition, those industries might continue to operate inefficiently. In the end, consumers pay higher prices. Further, limits on trade sometimes lead to a **trade war**, a succession of trade barriers between nations.

IMPACT 1 Higher Prices

Trade barriers raise prices or keep them high. For example, in the early 2000s, the United States and Japan, who both produce semiconductor chips, imposed tariffs on chips from South Korea. The reason for the tariff was that the Korean government had subsidized the chip maker, allowing the chips to be sold at a very low price. The result was a higher price in U.S. and Japanese markets for both the Korean chips (up 27 to 44 percent) as well as for those produced domestically. (See Figure 17.6.)

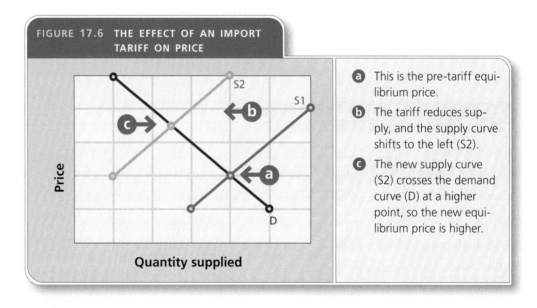

FIGURE 17.6 THE EFFECT OF AN IMPORT TARIFF ON PRICE

Price / Quantity supplied

S2 S1 D

ⓐ This is the pre-tariff equilibrium price.

ⓑ The tariff reduces supply, and the supply curve shifts to the left (S2).

ⓒ The new supply curve (S2) crosses the demand curve (D) at a higher point, so the new equilibrium price is higher.

IMPACT 2 Trade Wars

Trade wars often occur when nations disagree on quotas or tariffs. One recent trade war, however, came about in 1999 when the European Union banned the importation of hormone-treated U.S. beef. Many U.S. ranchers treat their cattle with hormones, which cause the animals to develop muscle faster than untreated animals. But EU scientists, citing health concerns, helped push through a ban. In response, the United States levied 100 percent tariffs on a range of EU products, including ham, onions, mustard, chocolate, and Roquefort cheese.

APPLICATION Applying an Economic Concept

B. Boeing, a U.S. airplane producer, and Airbus, its European competitor, each claim the other receives unfair governmental support. Why does each object to the alleged unfair support?

Arguments for Protectionism

KEY CONCEPTS

Considering all the disadvantages of trade barriers, why would a country enact such laws? The answer lies in the concept of **protectionism**, the use of trade barriers between nations to protect domestic industries. Protectionists argue that trade barriers protect domestic jobs, promote **infant industries** (new industries that are often unable to compete against larger, more established competitors), and protect national security.

QUICK REFERENCE

Protectionism is the use of trade barriers between nations to protect domestic industries.

Infant industries are new industries that are often unable to compete against larger, more established competitors.

ARGUMENT 1 Protects Domestic Jobs?

Between 2000 and 2003, Stark County, Ohio, lost ten percent of its manufacturing jobs, including hundreds at a plant that makes Hoover vacuum cleaners. Imports from Asia and Mexico forced a ten percent drop in the price of vacuum cleaners. The U.S. workers, many of whom earned high wages to do their skilled work, were understandably upset by the shift of their jobs to overseas facilities.

In Ohio and elsewhere, people argue that trade barriers are needed to protect domestic jobs, even though, in reality, these actions generally protect inefficient production and result in higher prices for everyone. Voters in industrial areas bring their voices to the national debate about foreign trade. By doing so, they have helped bring about federal job training programs for workers who find themselves unemployed as a result of the movement of jobs to places where the per unit cost of labor is lower.

Irish Success Bono suggested that Ireland's ability to protect its industries helped the Irish economy become stronger.

ARGUMENT 2 Protects Infant Industries?

What was an Irish rock star, Bono, doing at the 2006 World Economic Conference in Davos, Switzerland? For one thing, this performer, known for his commitment to Africa, was arguing that African infant industries should be protected. Referring to the history of his own country, he said that Irish infant industries were protected in their day but that such protection is "denied . . . to the poorest countries in the world."

The idea behind protecting infant industries is to assist newly developing industries in their growth process until they are able to compete with better-developed foreign rivals. This argument is often used by newly developing nations to keep out goods from economically well developed nations. In Africa, for example, Uganda has received protection for its infant industries in the form of tariffs on exports from neighboring Kenya. However, even with these protective tariffs, Ugandan industry has not yet found a way to become competitive on its own and continues to request extensions of the tariff.

This example points to a potential problem. Critics say that, provided with a sheltered existence that is free from the need to compete on equal terms, these industries settle into perpetual infancy. And a perpetual infant needs perpetual support.

Non-Economic Trade Barriers

Some nations impose trade barriers for religious reasons. Iran, for instance, has banned any Western movies that portray secularism, feminism, and other activities deemed unethical. Western popular music has also been deemed indecent and "un-Islamic" and, therefore, banned. These barriers have driven demand for Western movies and music underground, where they can be found on the black market.

Some nations enact trade barriers based on more general notions of culture. During the 1994 round of negotiations related to the Global Agreement on Tariffs and Trade (GATT), the French movie industry won a victory on a principal close to its heart.

It's known as the cultural exception, and it basically states that cultural goods are different from other goods and should not be covered by trade agreements. The cultural exception has been used, notably by France and Canada, to boost domestic television and film industries (through subsidies and quotas) and limit foreign competition, mostly from the United States.

Without these protections, the exception's proponents say, a handful of U.S. media multinationals would be able to dominate the area of audiovisual entertainment, thereby overwhelming the traditional cultures of other nations.

French movie poster

CONNECTING ACROSS THE GLOBE

1. **Explaining an Economic Concept** Some would argue that all trade barriers lack sound, economic reasoning. Do you agree? Why?

2. **Making Inferences and Drawing Conclusions** Which one of the three arguments for protectionism most resembles the actions taken by France and Canada? Explain.

ARGUMENT 3 Protects National Security?

National security affects the trade of industries that nations consider to be vital to their safety. The energy industry is considered vital by most. In 2005, a government-run Chinese company bid on U.S. oil company UNOCAL. Many in Congress and elsewhere in the United States warned against allowing a foreign government to take over an important U.S. energy supplier. After the House of Representatives voted 398 to 15 to ask President Bush to step in, the Chinese company withdrew its bid.

But sharp political differences exist over what industries are truly vital to national security. In 2006, a company from Dubai, which had purchased the rights to operate port facilities in New York, Miami, New Orleans, and elsewhere, was forced to abandon the deal in light of political pressure over port security. Many analysts were skeptical of the security concerns, however, and worried more about the implications of interference in free international trade for purely political reasons.

APPLICATION Making Inferences and Drawing Conclusions

C. Do you think that political pressure for protectionist trade barriers rises or falls during a recession? Explain your answer.

SECTION 2 Assessment

Online Quiz
ClassZone.com

REVIEWING KEY CONCEPTS

1. Explain the relationship between the terms in the following pairs:

   a. *trade barrier* **b.** *tariff*   **c.** *trade war*   **d.** *infant*
      quota   *voluntary export* *protective tariff*   *industries*
              restraint   *protectionism*

2. Why would a country engage in dumping?

3. How does a trade war get started? What effects does it have?

4. Why do some people feel that barriers to free trade are essential for national security?

5. Who benefits from trade barriers, inefficient or efficient producers?

6. **Using Your Notes** Take a position on free trade vs. protectionism and explain your position in a brief essay. Refer to your completed cause-and-effect chart. Use the Graphic Organizer at **Interactive Review @ ClassZone.com**

Cause	Effect
quota	higher prices

CRITICAL THINKING

7. **Analyzing Cause and Effect** In 1996, the United States expanded the embargo against Cuba, declaring that any foreign corporation that engaged in trade with Cuba would lose its privilege of trading with the United States. Give two possible effects of this embargo expansion.

8. **Solving Economic Problems** If you were the CEO of a manufacturing company facing stiff foreign competition, what are some ways you could adjust your business to stay competitive? What are the advantages and disadvantages of these changes?

9. **Applying Economic Concepts** Give three examples of U.S. citizens earning an income by selling products domestically that were made in other countries. Give three examples of U.S. citizens earning an income by selling products or services that are ultimately purchased by people in other countries.

10. **Challenge** A trade agreement between Kenya and some nations in Europe requires Kenyan farmers, most of whom have small peasant farms, to comply with 400 conditions before they can export their produce to European countries. They must be able to document the fertilizers, pesticides, and other additives used in the growing of their crops. How would you categorize this trade restriction? What impact do you think it will have on Kenyan exports and prices in the European nations?

ECONOMICS IN PRACTICE

Analyzing Tariff Rates
Look at the graph below showing selected U.S. tariff rates for nations with which it has "Normal Trade Relations" (NTR), also known as the "most-favored nation" (MFN) status.

Item	NTR/MFN Tariff (%)
Ceramic tableware	4.5
Cars	2.5
Trucks	25.0
Most bicycles	11.0
Sports footwear	10.5

Analyzing and Interpreting Data How much does the cost of a $32,000 truck increase because of the tariffs? If you pay $245.31 for a bicycle, what amount is the tariff?

Challenge Suppose a pair of imported running shoes costs $10. With the tariff added, the importer has to pay $11.50. The importer, however, has to raise the price of the shoes to cover the expense of selling and shipping them to retailers, and retailers have to raise the price to cover their expenses in selling the shoes. Assuming the price increases by 50 percent at each stage of the process, what amount does the initial $1.50 tariff grow into?

Measuring the Value of Trade

TAKING NOTES

As you read Section 3, complete a cluster diagram summarizing key information about measuring trade. Use the Graphic Organizer at **Interactive Review @ ClassZone.com**

Measuring Trade

Foreign Exchange

KEY CONCEPTS

If a certain good costs $100, how many euros does it cost? How many Mexican pesos? Or Russian rubles? International trade requires some way to establish the relative value of the different currencies of the nations doing the trading. So nations have worked out systems that facilitate the exchange of currencies between buyers and sellers. One key element is the **foreign exchange market**, a market in which currencies of different countries are bought and sold. This market is a network of major commercial and investment banks that link the economies of the world. Another key element in facilitating international trade is the **foreign exchange rate**, the price of one currency in the currencies of other nations.

Rates of Exchange

During the 1800s and early 1900s, gold was the standard against which the value of a nation's currency was determined. Nations traded on the basis of a **fixed rate of exchange**, a system in which the currency of one nation

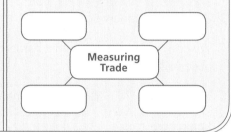

Currency Exchange The Mexican peso, the Australian dollar, and the Chinese yuan are all bought and sold on the foreign exchange market.

is fixed, or constant, in relation to other currencies—in this case to gold. After the profound economic disruption of World War II, other currencies were "pegged" to the stable U.S. dollar. That is, their currency was valued according to its relation to the U.S. dollar. The price of an ounce of gold was fixed at $35.

The volatile 1970s brought another change. As the United States ran up a trade deficit and the dollar declined in value, the standard of $35 per ounce of gold was no longer sustainable, and the **flexible exchange rate**, also called the floating rate, became predominant. This is a system in which the exchange rates for currencies change as the supply of and demand for the currencies change. For example, suppose that one British pound (GBP) is worth two U.S. dollars (USD). If an American importer wants to buy 100 British-made watches valued at 100 GBP each, then the importer would sell 20,000 USD in the foreign exchange market to obtain the necessary 10,000 GBPs. As the supply of dollars increases, their relative value drops. So the next time the importer wants to buy watches, the exchange rate might be 1 GPB:2.5 USD, and the watches would cost 25,000 U.S. dollars, making them less attractive as imports. Over time, the flexible exchange rate acts as a regulator on foreign exchange, balancing imports and exports.

QUICK REFERENCE

The **flexible exchange rate** is a system in which the exchange rate for currency changes as supply and demand for the currency changes.

MATH CHALLENGE
FIGURE 17.7 Calculating Exchange Rates

Suppose you want to buy a book in Germany, where the currency is the euro (€). The book costs €25, and the seller wants you to pay in euros, but you have U.S. dollars. To buy the book you must first buy euros.

To find out how much €25 costs in U.S. dollars, you must know the exchange rate. In this case, let's say the exchange rate is 1.25, which means that one euro costs $1.25. Now use the following formula.

Example Calculation

Amount of currency you want to buy	×	Exchange rate	=	Cost in currency you have		€25 × 1.25 $/€ = $31.25

To buy €25, you must pay $31.25.

Reciprocal exchange rate The exchange rate 1.25 can be written as a fraction: $1.25/€1. You can use this fraction to find the exchange rate a German must use to buy U.S. dollars with euros. First take the reciprocal of the fraction by swapping the numerator and the denominator; then use a calculator to write the fraction as a decimal.

The reciprocal of	$\dfrac{\$1.25}{€1}$	is	$\dfrac{€1}{\$1.25}$,	which is 0.80 €/$

So to convert from U.S. dollars to euros, multiply by the exchange rate 0.80.

Strong and Weak Currencies

QUICK REFERENCE

The **trade-weighted value of the dollar** is a measure of the international value of the dollar.

The Federal Reserve keeps a measure of the international value of the dollar called the **trade-weighted value of the dollar**. It determines if the dollar is strong or weak as measured against another currency. Because of the flexible exchange rate, as currencies are traded, some increase or decrease in value when measured against another currency.

For example, if the U.S. dollar becomes stronger in comparison to the Mexican peso, then the U.S. dollar buys more Mexican pesos than it could previously. What this means is that imports from Mexico now cost less. As you can see in Figure 17.8, importers in the United States benefit because they are able to buy foreign goods and services relatively cheaply.

At the same time, however, goods made in the United States may have a hard time competing with these inexpensive imports in the U.S. domestic market. Also, the strong dollar has a negative effect on U.S. exporters, since goods made here would be more costly to purchase abroad at the strong dollar rate. The weak dollar has the same effects but in reverse, as imported goods become more expensive and exporters are able to sell relatively cheaply.

FIGURE 17.8   THE STRONG DOLLAR AND U.S. TRADE

As the **value of the dollar** increases → **imports** to the U.S. become less expensive and increase → but **exports** from the U.S. become more expensive and decrease

YOUR ECONOMIC CHOICES

STRONG DOLLAR AND WEAK DOLLAR

Which sweater will you buy?

The U.S. dollar is very weak versus the Hong Kong dollar (HKD). How might this influence your decision to buy a new sweater made in the United States, or one imported from Hong Kong?

Domestically produced

100% MERINO EXTRA FINE WOOL MADE IN HONG KONG RN 77219 SEE REVERSE FOR CARE

Imported from overseas

APPLICATION Applying Economic Concepts

A. If you are an American exporter, does a strong dollar help your business? Explain.

REVIEWING KEY CONCEPTS

1. Explain the differences between the terms in each of these pairs:

   a. *foreign exchange market* **b.** *fixed rate of exchange* **c.** *trade surplus*
   foreign exchange rate   *flexible rate of*   *trade deficit*
                                 exchange

2. What is an advantage of a trade surplus? A disadvantage?

3. What is an advantage of a trade deficit? A disadvantage?

4. How does the value of the U.S. dollar affect the U.S. trade surplus or deficit?

5. How does a flexible exchange rate help to stabilize trade balances?

6. **Using Your Notes** Write a brief essay arguing for or against a single world currency. Refer to your completed cluster and use the section's key words.

   Use the Graphic Organizer at **Interactive Review @ ClassZone.com**

Measuring Trade

CRITICAL THINKING

7. **Analyzing Cause and Effect** In July 2005, the Chinese RMB became fixed to a "market-basket" of currencies, including the U.S. dollar and the Japanese yen, removing a decade-long peg to the U.S. dollar alone. The new formula slightly raised the value of the RMB. If China's trade surpluses continue, what will happen to the value of the RMB?

8. **Applying an Economic Concept** While you are in France on a business trip, you find out that the euro has gained strength against the U.S. dollar. Will your hotel room and food now be more or less expensive? Why? What about the goods you're trying to sell on your trip; will they be more or less expensive to your customers in France? Why?

9. **Making Inferences and Drawing Conclusions** Japan has the world's largest foreign currency reserves, followed by China. State two conclusions you can draw about the economies of these two nations based on their foreign currency reserves.

10. **Challenge** What are the advantages of a large supply of foreign investment in a domestic economy? What are the disadvantages?

ECONOMICS IN PRACTICE

Analyzing Exchange Rates
Look at the rate table for five major currencies below and answer the questions that follow.

U.S. Dollar	Euro	Canadian Dollar	British Pound	Swiss Franc
1	0.7917	1.1434	0.5401	1.2459
1.2631	1	1.4441	0.6822	1.5736
0.8746	0.6925	1	0.4724	1.0897
1.8514	1.4658	2.1168	1	2.3067
0.8026	0.6355	0.9177	0.4335	1

10:33 A.M. eastern standard time, 7/24/06

Analyzing Data How much of each of the other four currencies will $5 U.S. purchase? If the exchange rate for a British pound changed from $1.85 to $1.90, which currency has gotten weaker? How would this affect exporters in Great Britain?

Challenge Why do foreign exchange rates vary from hour to hour?

Modern International Institutions

OBJECTIVES	KEY TERMS	TAKING NOTES
In Section 4, you will • describe what agreements were made to start the free-trade movement • identify international and regional trade groups • explain what role multinationals play in world trade	free-trade zone, *p. 532* customs union, *p. 532* European Union, *p. 532* euro, *p. 533* NAFTA, *p. 533* OPEC, *p. 535* cartel, *p. 535* WTO, *p. 535*	As you read Section 4, complete a summary chart like the one shown, using the key concepts and other helpful words and phrases. Use the Graphic Organizer at **Interactive Review @ ClassZone.com** | Regional	International
---	---

Regional and World Trade Organizations

KEY CONCEPTS

QUICK REFERENCE

A **free-trade zone** is a specific region in which trade between nations takes place without protective tariffs.

A **customs union** is an agreement that abolishes trade barriers among its members and establishes uniform tariffs for non-members.

The **European Union**, the EU, is an economic and political union of European nations established in 1993.

Following the failed protectionist policies of the 1930s, nations have sought to expand trade and reduce or eliminate trade barriers. They have organized regional trading groups to create **free-trade zones**, specific regions in which trade between nations takes place without protective tariffs. Some have created **customs unions**, agreements that abolish trade barriers among the members and establish uniform tariffs for non-members. Some of these organizations are called common markets. As a result of these efforts, global tariffs have dropped by about one-third.

GROUP 1 The European Union

In 1957, six European nations recognized the benefits of abolishing trade barriers and formed a customs union called the European Economic Community. It was widely known as the Common Market. In 1993 the Common Market evolved into the **European Union**, or EU , which tightly bound its member nations to one another both economically and politically. The political nature of the EU, the fact that its members surrender some sovereignty in specified areas, makes it unique among

EU Expansion Lithuanians celebrate their nation's admission to the EU in 2004.

regional trading groups. Specifically, the Treaty on European Union had monetary union and a common European foreign policy as key goals. Monetary union was effectively established in 2002, as 12 member states adopted the **euro**.

In 2004, the EU's membership swelled to 25 nations, as several Eastern European nations (Poland, the Czech Republic, Hungary, and Slovakia), the former Baltic republics of the Soviet Union (Estonia, Latvia, and Lithuania), Slovenia (formerly of Yugoslavia), and the Mediterranean island nations Cyprus and Malta joined.

The EU accounts for about 20 percent of global exports and imports, making it the world's biggest trader. It has removed barriers to free trade among member nations, with the ultimate goal that Europe's national borders will be no more a barrier to free trade than are the borders of U.S. states. It is also committed to the reduction and removal of barriers to international free trade. Its average tariff rate, 4 percent, is among the world's lowest.

QUICK REFERENCE

The **euro** is the currency of the European Union.

GROUP 2 NAFTA

In 1990, negotiations began on a free-trade agreement among the United States, Canada, and Mexico. The result of these negotiations, the North American Free Trade Agreement, or **NAFTA**, created the largest free-trade zone in the world. When it went into effect on January 1, 1994, it immediately eliminated tariffs on half of the goods exported to Mexico from the United States. The agreement calls for an eventual phase-out of all trade barriers on goods and services within 15 years. It also calls for improved protection under Mexican law of intellectual property rights, environmental and worker protections, and investment policies that treat investors from the three participating nations equally.

The advantages of NAFTA include specialization and increased efficiency, a competitive advantage over the EU and Japan, expanded markets, and new jobs. And while some object to NAFTA on a number of political, social, and even environmental grounds, the economic results appear robust. (See Figure 17.11.) Between 1993 and 2003, Mexico and Canada experienced economic gains as well. Two-way agricultural

QUICK REFERENCE

NAFTA, the North America Free Trade Agreement, is designed to ensure trade without barriers between Canada, Mexico, and the United States.

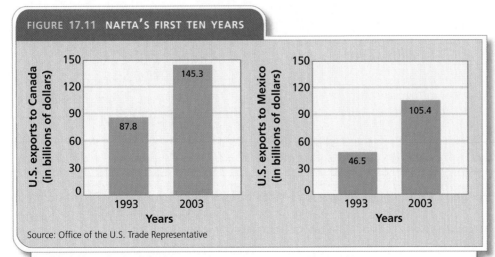

FIGURE 17.11 NAFTA'S FIRST TEN YEARS

U.S. exports to Canada (in billions of dollars): 1993 = 87.8, 2003 = 145.3

U.S. exports to Mexico (in billions of dollars): 1993 = 46.5, 2003 = 105.4

Source: Office of the U.S. Trade Representative

ANALYZE GRAPHS

1. Which nation, Canada or Mexico, increased its trade with the United States by a larger percentage?

2. Is an increase in trade typically beneficial for nations? Explain..

trade between Mexico and the United States increased 125 percent—from $6.2 billion in 1993 to $14.2 billion in 2003. Productivity in Mexico increased a remarkable 55 percent. Canada's exports to its NAFTA partners increased by 104 percent, and its overall economy grew by over 30 percent. Overall trade between the three partners more than doubled during this period, from $289.3 billion in 1993 to $623.1 billion in 2003.

GROUP 3 Other Regional Trade Groups

Throughout the world, nations are forming trade organizations to specialize, promote free trade, and stay competitive with other trade groups. Descriptions of a number of these agreements from all parts of the world follow:

Mercosur (*Mercado Comun del Cono Sur*) This group promotes the movement of goods and people in South America. Formed in 1995, Mercosur eliminated tariffs on 90 percent of goods traded between the group's full members (Argentina, Brazil, Paraguay, and Uruguay). Venezuela became a full member in July of 2006. Counting associate members Mexico, Chile, Bolivia, and Peru, Mercosur has become the world's fourth-largest trade association.

ASEAN The Association of Southest Asian Nations was formed in 1967 to accelerate economic growth, social progress, and cultural development in the region, and to promote regional peace and stability. Its members include Indonesia, the Philippines, Singapore, Thailand, Vietnam, Laos, Cambodia, and others.

FIGURE 17.12 Some Regional Trade Groups

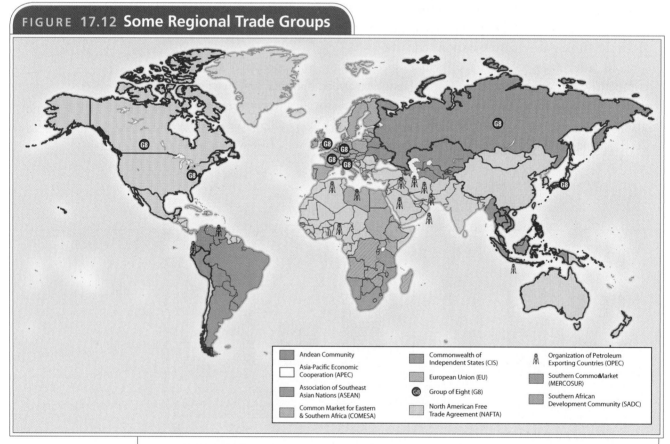

Andean Community	Commonwealth of Independent States (CIS)	Organization of Petroleum Exporting Countries (OPEC)
Asia-Pacific Economic Cooperation (APEC)	European Union (EU)	Southern Common Market (MERCOSUR)
Association of Southeast Asian Nations (ASEAN)	Group of Eight (G8)	Southern African Development Community (SADC)
Common Market for Eastern & Southern Africa (COMESA)	North American Free Trade Agreement (NAFTA)	

ANALYZE MAPS

How many trading groups do the United States and Canada belong to? Why does it make sense for such developed nations to be part of multiple trading groups?

APEC The Asia-Pacific Economic Cooperation group is a trade organization of nations on the Pacific Rim—those that are adjacent to or within the Pacific Ocean. It includes developed nations such as Australia, Japan, and the United States, transitional economies such as Russia and China, as well as less developed countries such as Thailand, Papua New Guinea, and Chile. The group has set ambitious goals for trade liberalization throughout the region by 2020. However, since all APEC decisions require a unanimous vote, progress toward its goals has been slow.

OPEC The Organization of Petroleum Exporting Countries is a **cartel**—a group of producers who regulate the production, pricing, and marketing of a particular product. In OPEC's case, that product is petroleum, or oil. It has had mixed results in controlling the oil market since its formation in 1960. However, surging demand, from nations such as China and the United States, and periods of regional political instability have strengthened OPEC's position in recent years.

SADC Founded in 1979, the South African Development Community's original goal was to act as a counterbalance to the region's main economic power—South Africa. (After South Africa finally abandoned minority white rule—the apartheid system—it also became a member in 1994.) A regional free-trade zone was established in 2000.

Dedication to free trade is a key element in boosting the region's economies. However, corruption, political instability, various health issues (most importantly, AIDS), substandard education, and poor infrastructure consistently hamper development. (You'll learn about these and other development issues in Chapter 18.)

QUICK REFERENCE

OPEC is the Organization of Petroleum Exporting Countries.

A cartel is a group of producers that regulates the production, pricing, and marketing of a product.

GROUP 4 World Trade Organization

In 1944, the Allied nations met to plan for recovery after World War II. Among other important outcomes, they produced the General Agreement on Tariffs and Trade (GATT), which laid out rules and policies for international trade. In 1995, the GATT principles were incorporated into a new organization, the **World Trade Organization**, or WTO. At the end of 2005, the WTO had 149 member nations.

The purposes of the WTO include negotiating and administering trade agreements, resolving trade disputes, monitoring the trading policies of member nations, and providing support for developing countries. The principles underlying these purposes are that trade rules should apply equally to domestic and imported products. To that end all member nations should extend one another Normal Trade Relation (NTR) status, formerly known as Most Favored Nation (MFN) status. This means that no nation should extend more favorable trade terms to one WTO member than it does to another. Members should also work toward lowering trade barriers of all kinds and support fair trade as well as free trade.

To varying degrees, the WTO has been successful. It has helped reduce tariffs on manufactured goods, lower trade barriers in agriculture, and promote intellectual property rights. It has also resolved disputes among members while maintaining each nation's sovereignty, and promoted stability among member nations.

QUICK REFERENCE

The World Trade Organization, or **WTO**, is a group of nations that adhere to the policies of the General Agreement on Tariffs and Trade.

APPLICATION Making Inferences and Drawing Conclusions

A. Why do you think the term *most favored nation* has been replaced by *normal trade relations*?

Multinationals Bring Changes to International Trade

KEY CONCEPTS

Multinational corporations (see Chapter 8) cross many borders and must deal with tariffs, labor restrictions, and taxes in different nations. They often bring jobs and technology to developing nations, while boosting overall levels of international trade—something that benefits everyone involved.

International Trade Within Multinationals

As multinationals have become more prevalent, trade between the various divisions of multinationals has become an area of increasing interest. Intrafirm trade, as it is known, can simply be the exchange of goods between two parts of a multinational. But international intrafirm trade also covers the coordination of production between parts of a multinational. This means, for instance, that when a U.S. parent company sends parts to an overseas affiliate to assemble, that is counted in the export column for U.S. statistics on trade. Likewise, when the assembled goods are shipped back to the U.S. parent from its overseas affiliate, that is counted in the import column. In general, intrafirm imports account for about 40 percent of total U.S. imports. Intrafirm exports account for about one-third of total U.S. exports.

EXAMPLE A Multinational Telecom Corporation

Consider the case of Worldwide Cellular, a U.S.-based multinational that makes, markets, and services cellular phones. It imports an essential raw material from its mining arm in Australia, manufactures the phones at its facility in South Korea, markets the phones in Europe, and then directs customers who have questions or complaints to technical support and customer service representatives in India. Throughout the process, the people and the economies of each nation benefit.

▲ Australian mining

▼ South Korean manufacturing

▲ European marketing and sales

▼ Indian call center

APPLICATION to come

B. In 1969, there were about 7,200 known multinationals. By 2000, that number had grown to more than 63,000. Give three possible contributing reasons for that growth.

REVIEWING KEY CONCEPTS

1. Explain the relationship between the terms in each of these pairs:

   a. *free-trade zone*
   customs union

   b. *EU*
   NAFTA

   c. *OPEC*
   cartel

2. What circumstances led to a liberalization in global trading?

3. How do customs unions help member nations?

4. How is the EU different from other regional trading groups?

5. What are some advantages of NAFTA?

6. **Using Your Notes** Write a brief summary of the major regional and international trade organizations. Refer to your completed summary chart and use the section's key words. Use the Graphic Organizer at **Interactive Review @ ClassZone.com**

Regional	International

CRITICAL THINKING

7. **Making Inferences and Drawing Conclusions** Some regional trade associations are viewed as an attempt by less developed countries to protect themselves and their regions from globalization's aggressive momentum. Explain how regional groups might have that effect.

8. **Analyzing Cause and Effect** Many multinationals grew out of exporting businesses. How might the exporting business prepare a company to become a multinational?

9. **Predicting Economic Trends** Before NAFTA was passed, some experts predicted a reduction in illegal immigration from Mexico to the United States. In fact, in the first few years after NAFTA went into effect, illegal immigration increased. What reasoning might have explained the prediction that illegal immigration would decline? What reasons might explain the increase?

10. **Challenge** At the Hong Kong gathering of the World Trade Organization in 2005, Supachai Panitchpakdi, secretary general of the United Nations Conference on Trade and Development (UNCTAD) said: "Rich countries will have to reject not just protectionism, but populism, too. They will have to speak honestly to their people about the changing economies of the 21st century, and about global interdependence and the fact that prosperity elsewhere means prosperity and jobs at home." Write a brief essay that "speaks honestly" to the rich countries about the changing economies of the 21st century.

ECONOMICS IN PRACTICE

The Effects of NAFTA
Between 1993 and 2002, the total trade among Canada, the United States, and Mexico more than doubled. The table below shows export figures for NAFTA members Canada and Mexico in each of those years.

Nation	Exports (in billions of dollars)	
	1993	2002
Canada		
to United States	113.6	213.9
to Mexico	.9	1.6
Mexico		
to United States	31.8	136.1
to Canada	2.9	8.8

Analyzing and Interpreting Data Canada has a higher export amount than Mexico, but did its level of trade increase more than Mexico's in the interval? Explain.

Challenge Can Canadian companies produce, package, and market products for both of its NAFTA partners in the same way? Explain why or why not.

Analyzing Tariffs—Who Wins and Who Loses?

Background Tariffs on foreign sugar have been around almost as long as the United States itself. Although early tariffs were a form of revenue, their purpose expanded in the 19th century to provide protection for the domestic sugar industry. That protection continues to this day.

Globalization, however, is having a direct impact on the way nations trade. Agricultural subsidies and tariffs have become a point of contention in recent WTO talks, with less-developed countries unhappy about the lack of market access for their goods and about their price disadvantage.

What's the issue? How do the trade barriers set up by the U.S. government affect producers (both foreign and domestic) and consumers?

A. Online Article

This article describes how the U.S. government supports sugar prices. Note that sugar subsidies are paid to the processor, rather than the farmer. The farmer receives a share once the sugar is processed.

Sugar Interests Harm the National Interest

USDA loan rates set floor on price of sugar.

The [government] program allows sugar processors to take out loans from the USDA [U.S. Department of Agriculture] by pledging sugar as collateral. The loan rates—18 cents per pound for cane sugar, 22.9 cents per pound for beet sugar—are significantly higher than average world sugar prices. These loans must be repaid within nine months, but processors also have the option of forfeiting their sugar to the government in lieu of repaying their debt.

This arrangement effectively guarantees that the processors receive a price for their sugar that is no lower than the loan value: If prices fell below that level, they would simply forfeit their sugar and keep the government's money.

In order to avoid that scenario, the USDA must prop up the domestic price of sugar. It does this by controlling supply through two mechanisms. First, it sets quotas on how much foreign sugar can be imported without facing prohibitive tariffs; second, it regulates the amount of sugar that domestic processors can sell.

Source: Jason Lee Steorts, *National Review*, July 18, 2005

CANE LOADING AREA AHEAD

Thinking Economically In your own words, describe the mechanisms by which the U.S. government props up domestic sugar prices.

FIGURE 17.13 U.S. AND WORLD RAW SUGAR PRICES

B. Government Report

This information from the U.S. Department of Agriculture charts U.S. raw sugar prices versus raw sugar prices for the rest of the world.

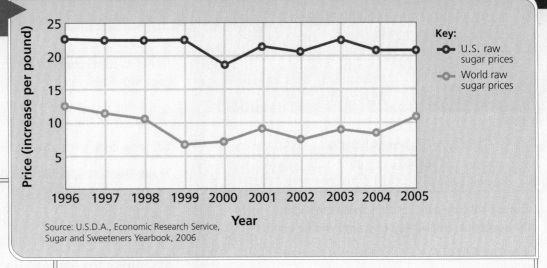

Source: U.S.D.A., Economic Research Service, Sugar and Sweeteners Yearbook, 2006

Thinking Economically On average, how much greater are U.S. raw sugar prices than those for the rest of the world?

C. Trade Association Web Page

The American Sugar Alliance's Web site makes the case that the U.S. sugar industry is an important part of the overall U.S. economy.

Sweetener Impact on the U.S. Economy

Do the industry's jobs come at too high a cost?

- Economic impact: $21.1 billion of economic activity in 42 states are generated in the U.S. each year by the sugar and corn sweetener industries.
- Beet sugar industry: Over 1,400,000 acres of sugarbeets are grown in 12 states and are processed in 25 sugarbeet factories. The industry creates 88,200 full time direct and indirect jobs for people across the nation.
- Jobs: 372,000 jobs in the U.S. rely on a strong U.S. sweetener industry.
- Cane sugar industry: Seven cane refineries and 22 mills process sugar cane raised in four states: Florida, Hawaii, Lousiana and Texas. The production and processing of sugarcane creates 71,900 full time direct and indirect jobs.

Source: www.sugaralliance.org

Thinking Economically How many jobs in the U.S. sweetener industry are not directly or indirectly created by the beet sugar or cane sugar industries?

THINKING ECONOMICALLY Synthesizing

1. Which argument for protection does document C seem to make? Use the document and pages 523 and 524 to formulate your answer. Is this argument economically valid? Explain.

2. Is the difference in price shown in document B an unavoidable outcome of the program outlined in document A? Explain your answer.

3. How does U.S. government intervention in the sugar industry limit the functioning of the economy as a free market? Use examples from the documents in your answer.

Interactive Review

Review this chapter using interactive
activities at **ClassZone.com**
- Online Summary
- Quizzes
- Vocabulary Flip Cards
- Graphic Organizers
- Review and Study Notes

Online Summary

Complete the following activity either on your
own paper or online at **ClassZone.com**

**Choose the key concept that best completes
the sentence. Not all key concepts will be used.**

absolute advantage	NAFTA
balance of trade	protectionism
comparative advantage	quota
economic interdependence	revenue tariffs
embargo	tariff
exports	trade barrier
foreign exchange market	trade deficit
foreign exchange rate	trade surplus
free trade zone	trade war
imports	WTO

When nations can produce something at a lower
cost than other nations, they are said to have a(n)
__1__. This is different from a(n) __2__, which means
that goods or services are produced at a lower
opportunity cost. Through trade, nations develop
__3__, relying on one another.

Policies of __4__ have created __5__ between
nations, including __6__—limits on imports—and
__7__—fees charged on goods brought into a country.

International trade would not be possible
without the __8__, where currencies of different
countries are bought and sold. Nations keep track
of their __9__, the difference between their exports
and their imports. With a __10__, large reserves
of foreign currency accumulate. With a __11__,
domestic consumers enjoy lower prices.

The trend since the end of World War II has
been toward free trade. Nations have formed
regional __12__ that abolish trade barriers among
members. In 1994 the United States became part
of a trading organization with Mexico and Canada
known as __13__.

REVIEWING KEY CONCEPTS

Benefits and Issues of International Trade
(pp. 510–519)

1. How do nations gain by specializing in products
for which they have a comparative advantage?

2. How does trade affect a national economy?

Trade Barriers (pp. 520–525)

3. Name and describe four trade barriers.

4. What three reasons are protectionists likely to
offer to support their position?

Measuring the Value of Trade (pp. 526–531)

5. Explain how an importer purchases a foreign
product and what effect those actions would have
on the value of each currency.

6. What does the term *strong dollar* mean?

Modern International Institutions (pp. 532–539)

7. What agreements helped launch the free trade
movement?

8. Create a fictional multinational and explain how
it might operate from raw materials all the way
through marketing the finished product.

APPLYING ECONOMIC CONCEPTS

Look at the graph below showing U.S. imports and
exports to and from various trading regions.

9. To which group does the United States export the
lowest dollar value of goods and services?

10. With which group does the United States have the
largest trade deficit? the smallest trade deficit?

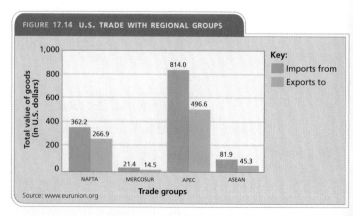

FIGURE 17.14 U.S. TRADE WITH REGIONAL GROUPS

Source: www.eurunion.org

11. **Creating Graphs** Create a graph of your choice to show the following trade data from the year 2003. Figures that are not in percentages are in billions of U.S. dollars. *EU25* is the 25 European Union members and soon to be members in 2003.

Measure	United States	EU25	Japan
Total imports	1,517	1,047	477
Total exports	1,021	1,250	597
World import share	22.9%	14%	6.8%
World export share	13.8%	13.1%	8.5%

Use *SMART Grapher* @ ClassZone.com to complete this activity.

12. **Analyzing and Interpreting Data** Which two of the three trading entities in the table above are likely to have good reserves of foreign currency?

13. **Synthesizing Economic Data** In which trading entity in the table above are imports the highest percent of total trade value? The lowest?

14. **Comparing and Contrasting Economic Information** What are developed nations hoping to gain through reduced global trade barriers? What are developing nations hoping to gain?

15. **Challenge** The World Trade Organization, unlike GATT, has an organizational structure to implement its principles. However, it has no authority to force a nation to do something against its own laws. How is it able, then, to resolve disputes among members?

The Advantages of International Trade

The concept of comparative advantage explains why specialization and international trade are so important to economic success. Complete this exercise with a partner to help further your understanding.

Each of you will represent a trading nation. One of you will be El Estado, and the other will be Lichtenbourg. Both countries produce lemons and televisions. The following table shows monthly production by each nation.

	El Estado	Lichtenbourg
Lemons (in pounds)	20,000	9,000
Televisions	4,000	3,000

Step 1 Decide whether El Estado or Lichtenbourg has the absolute advantage for each product. Explain why this is so.

Step 2 Each student should calculate what his or her nation's production ratio is. Express your ratio in terms of opportunity cost. How many pounds of lemons does it cost to make one TV?

Step 3 With your ratios calculated, decide which nation has the comparative advantage in the production of TVs. On this basis, decide which nation should specialize in the production of each product.

Step 4 Now that you've decided to specialize and trade, calculate a trade ratio that makes trade between your two nations even more advantageous. Explain how the new ratio achieves this goal.

Economic Development
Issues of economic development are as much about the basic building blocks of societies as they are about money. When governments are stable and help to provide their people with resources and opportunities, economic development can become a reality.

18

Issues of Economic Development

CONCEPT REVIEW

Free enterprise system is another name for capitalism, an economic system based on private ownership of productive resources.

CHAPTER 18 KEY CONCEPT

A **transitional economy** is a country that has moved (or is moving) from a command economy, such as communism, to a market economy.

WHY THE CONCEPT MATTERS

The development of the world's less developed countries has grown increasingly important as globalization has taken hold. Promoting development also promotes good government and economic opportunity in less developed countries. When a nation's government is democratic and stable and its citizens are prosperous, the benefits reach beyond that emerging economy to the world community, which gains a new economic and political partner.

Online Highlights
More at ClassZone.com

 Economics Update
Go to **ECONOMICS UPDATE** for chapter updates and current news on trade and China's transition to a market economy. (See Case Study, pp. 570–571.) ▶

 SMART Grapher
Go to **SMART GRAPHER** to complete graphing activities in this chapter.

Interactive ⊛ Review
Go to **INTERACTIVE REVIEW** for concept review and activities.

China's development depends on international trade. Is everyone satisfied with China's trade dominance? See the Case Study on pages 570–571.

Definitions of Development

OBJECTIVES

In Section 1 you will
- determine how economic development is defined
- explain how certain indicators can illustrate the level of economic development of a nation

KEY TERMS

developed nations, *p. 544*

transitional economies, *p. 545*

less developed countries (LDC), *p. 545*

infrastructure, *p. 545*

per capita GDP, *p. 546*

infant mortality rate, *p. 547*

life expectancy, *p. 547*

literacy rate, *p. 547*

human development index (HDI), *p. 547*

TAKING NOTES

As you read Section 1, complete a summary table like the one shown. Use the Graphic Organizer at **Interactive Review @ ClassZone.com**

Definitions of Development	
Levels of Development	Standards of Economic Development

Levels of Development

KEY CONCEPTS

Do you have at least $1 in your pocket at the moment? If so, you have more money than over a billion of the world's people have for food, shelter, and clothing for today. Economists gather this type of data to compare the economies of nations and the impact of those economies on people's standard of living. They use the data to measure the nations' level of economic development.

Developed Nations

Economists have defined three major levels of economic development. The nations with the highest standards of living are known as **developed nations**. In addition to a relatively high standard of living, these nations have a market economy, a high GDP, industrialization, widespread private ownership of property, and stable and effective governments. The nations of Western Europe, the United States, Canada, Australia, New Zealand, Japan, and South Korea are all developed nations.

You can identify some of the features of a developed nation by looking around you. Most people live fairly comfortable lives and enjoy such consumer goods as television sets, washing machines, and cars. You will also see that most people live in urban areas, where they have jobs in service and industrial enterprises: banks, insurance companies, auto parts manufacturing, and so on. Even though few people work in agriculture, the nation produces a surplus of agricultural products using advanced science and technology and highly efficient farming methods. You will also see that, on the whole, people are generally healthy and well-educated. They have political and economic freedom, and they exercise those freedoms in pursuit of well-being. You will see exceptions to all of these features—poverty, unemployment, poor living conditions—but they are not the prevailing features of the society.

Transitional Economies

Economists have also defined the development that occurs in **transitional economies**. These are countries that have moved (or are moving) from a command economy to a market economy. China, Russia, and a number of Eastern European countries are considered to be transitional economies.

Poland, in Eastern Europe, is in transition and categorized as a less developed country. Like other transitional economies, however, it is on a clear path toward improving standards of living. As democracy and economic freedom begin to take hold, Poland's economy and its citizens' quality of life have steadily improved.

QUICK REFERENCE

A **transitional economy** is a country that has moved (or is moving) from a command economy to a market economy.

In Transition A developed economy, such as the United States (left), generally has greater access to technology than a transitional economy, such as China (right).

Less Developed Countries

Less developed countries (LDCs), such as many African, South American, and Eastern European countries, have a lower GDP, less well developed industry, and a lower standard of living. Often, these nations have ineffective or even outright corrupt governments that fail to protect private property rights. LDCs are sometimes called emerging economies, but some have emerged, so to speak, more than others. As a result, they can be divided into middle-income nations, such as Brazil and Thailand, and low-income nations, such as Mozambique and Cambodia.

The picture in the low-income nations is starkly different from what you see when you look around the United States. A high percentage of people live in substandard housing. Few families own televisions or washing machines. Even if they owned cars, there are few good roads to drive them on, since developing nations often lack infrastructure. **Infrastructure** is the basic set of support systems needed to keep an economy going. It includes such things as power, communications, transportation, water, sanitation, and education systems.

In these economies, a relatively high percentage of the people work at subsistence farming and have little savings. Often, even children toil with the rest of the family. Some go to school for only three or four years; some children receive no schooling. Health conditions are substandard, as medical care is hard to come by in rural areas. In many developing nations, political freedom is still a dream.

QUICK REFERENCE

A **less developed country** (LDC) has a lower GDP, less well developed industry, and a lower standard of living.

Infrastructure is the basic support systems needed to keep an economy going, including power, communications, transportation, water, sanitation, and education systems.

🖱 *Economics Update*

Find an update on health statistics in LDCs at **ClassZone.com**

APPLICATION Economies

A. What role does technology play in economic development?

Standards of Economic Development

How is it possible to compare economies when each country may have its own ideas of what is valuable? For example, the number of television sets per thousand households yields valid information about the economic conditions in most nations. However, not every culture values television ownership to the same extent. Such statistics need to be used in conjunction with others, so that a more nuanced image of a nation's overall level of development can be obtained. Economists use the following standards of development to bring this detailed image into focus.

Per Capita Gross Domestic Product

The most popular measure of economic development is **per capita gross domestic product**, a nation's overall GDP divided by its total population. This statistic is informative because it estimates the amount of goods and services produced per person in a given year. These figures can be used to compare one country to another. (See Figure 18.1.) For example, the per capita GDP of the United States is among the world's highest—over $40,000. In Tanzania, in east Africa, it is $700—among the lowest. Often these figures are adjusted to take into account the idea that a dollar may go further in some less developed countries where goods and services are less costly.

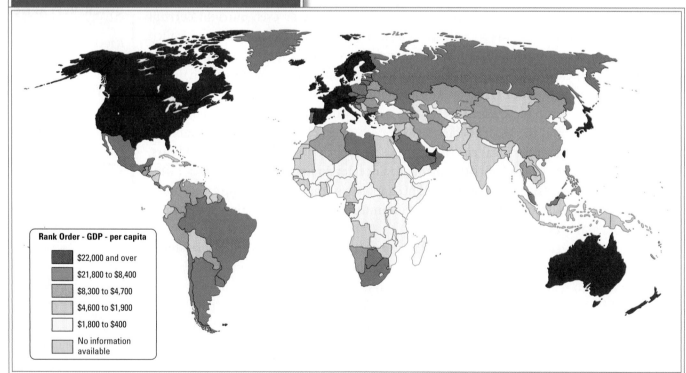

FIGURE 18.1 World Per Capita GDPs

Rank Order - GDP - per capita

- $22,000 and over
- $21,800 to $8,400
- $8,300 to $4,700
- $4,600 to $1,900
- $1,800 to $400
- No information available

ANALYZE MAPS

1. Which continent is the least developed?

2. Which continent has no countries in the top GDP bracket?

Health

Statistics showing various aspects of health and health care are also useful in determining economic development. Especially indicative are statistics on the survival rate of babies. This measure is called the **infant mortality rate**, the number of children who die within the first year of life per 1,000 live births.

The infant mortality rate in Japan is 3. In China it is 23. In Angola it is 185. What can economists learn from these figures? The answer lies in understanding the conditions in which infants thrive. These conditions include a safe and sanitary birth environment with access to needed emergency care, adequate nutrition, an adequately fed mother who has access to clean drinking water and acceptable shelter, and protection from disease in the form of early-childhood vaccinations. A subsistence society, or one in extreme poverty, is unlikely to be able to provide these conditions. Less developed economies may be able to provide them to some degree, but in developed economies, these conditions are the norm.

Dangerous Water More than a billion people worldwide use unsafe drinking water sources. Disease and death can be real consequences of this fact.

Another useful standard is **life expectancy**, the average number of years a person could expect to live if current mortality trends were to continue for the rest of that person's life. For example, people born today in Japan can expect to live to age 82, in China, to age 72, while in Angola, only to age 39.

Education

The World Education Forum declares in its Framework for Action that "education is . . . the key to sustainable development and peace and stability within and among countries, and thus an indispensable means for effective participation in the societies and economies of the twenty-first century. . . ." Since education is so clearly tied into the economy, education statistics are tracked as useful indicators of the development level of a nation. One key education figure is the **literacy rate**, the percentage of people older than 15 who can read and write. Japan's literacy rate is 99 percent; Somalia's is 38 percent. Another useful statistic is student enrollment at all levels. This figure tells the percentage of school-age individuals who are actually going to school. In Belgium and Japan, for example, primary-school enrollment is 100 percent. In Niger, it is about 40 percent.

In 1990, another standard was introduced that combines some of these other statistics. It is the **human development index** (HDI)—the brainchild of Pakistani economist Mahbub ul Haq. A nation's HDI is a combination of its real GDP per capita, life expectancy, adult literacy rate, and student enrollment figures. Its measures are an important indicator of what life is like in a specific country.

QUICK REFERENCE

Infant mortality rate is the number of children who die within the first year of life per 1,000 live births.

Life expectancy is the average number of years a person can expect to live if current mortality trends were to continue for the rest of that person's life.

Literacy rate is the percentage of people older than 15 who can read and write.

The **human development index** (HDI) uses targeted economic, education, and health statistics to assess a nation's level of development.

Consumption of Goods and Services

In the mid-1990s, home appliances were still relatively rare in less developed countries like China. By the year 2000, however, the refrigerator had become a familiar part of Chinese city life; three out of four dwellings in major urban areas had one. Refrigerators have even begun to reach the secondary cities and rural areas, though they are still so rare there that they are sometimes displayed proudly in the living room rather than hidden away in the kitchen. Washing machines are also becoming increasingly commonplace. China's consumption of cell phones has risen rapidly in recent years too. At the beginning of 2001, there were approximately 65 million cell phones in use in China; by 2004, there were about 335 million—more than in any other country. The number of personal computers owned in China is doubling every 28 months.

What do these statistics say about China's economic development? These data show how people choose to spend their income after they have food and shelter. When consumption of such big-ticket items as refrigerators, automobiles, and washing machines increases, an economy is growing and developing. This indicates that people's living standards are rising. Goods that once were available only to the rich are now purchased by middle- and even low-income families.

In the less developed nations of China and India, 16 percent of the population is following this consumption pattern, compared with 89 percent of the population in Europe. The less developed nations therefore have the greatest room for growth in the consumption of consumer goods and services. For now, however, consumers in North America and Western Europe, whose population is about 12 percent of the global total, are responsible for 60 percent of the global total of consumption of goods and services. The 30 percent of the world population that lives in South Asia and sub-Saharan Africa, on the other hand, spends only 3.2 percent. Comparisons like the one below in Figure 18.2 offer another way to measure relative growth.

FIGURE 18.2 Ownership of Typical Consumer Goods

(per thousand residents)

Country	Television Sets	Telephone Mainlines
United States	835	659
Ukraine	456	212
India	83	40

Source: The State of the World, 2004

Energy Use

Of the roughly 6.5 billion people in the world, as many as 2 billion are without electricity. Since electricity and other forms of energy contribute to economic development, statistics on energy use can reveal an aspect of a nation's economic development. Energy use is not spread evenly throughout the population. Asia, with 50 percent of the world's people, accounts for just over 21 percent of annual energy consumption. For another example, the average global consumption of electricity is 2,744 kilowatt hours (KWh) per capita. Japan's annual per capita consumption of electricity, like that of other industrialized nations, is well over 7,000 KWhs. Colombia's annual rate of about 820 KWh per capita is typical of LDCs, which average about 750 KWh per capita each year.

Wind Power Wind farms, such as this one in northwest China, contribute a small but growing part of the world's electricity.

How the energy is put to use is another revealing statistic, especially the amount used for commercial purposes. The United States, for example, uses the equivalent energy of 8,148 kilograms of oil per person in commercial enterprises. India uses the equivalent of about 494 kilograms of oil per person for commercial activities. The amount of energy used for commercial purposes correlates to a nation's level of technological achievement and other economic measures.

Projected energy use to the year 2025 follows the same pattern as the projected consumption of consumer goods and services, with LDCs outpacing developed nations. The LDCs are expected to increase their energy use by about 3.2 percent a year. In Asia, including China and India, the demand for energy is expected to double between 2002 and 2025. The relatively rapid increase in energy use coincides with the move toward industrialization and technological advances. In fact, transportation and industry account for nearly all of the projected increase in the use of fossil fuels.

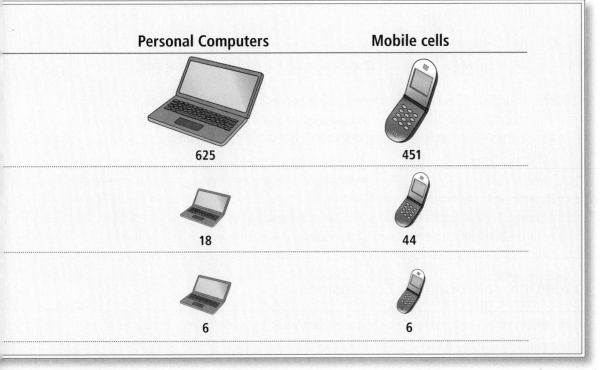

Personal Computers	Mobile cells
625	451
18	44
6	6

In contrast, the developed nations are projected to increase their energy use by only 1.1 percent a year. Developed economies use fuel more efficiently, which accounts in part for their slower rate of increase in energy use. Transitional economies are expected to increase their energy use by 1.6 percent each year as they face the challenges of moving to a market economy.

Labor Force

In what kind of job do most of a nation's workers find themselves employed? The answer to this question reveals one aspect of a nation's level of development. According to the World Bank, this measure includes all the economically active people between the ages of 15 and 65 in a country—including the employed, the unemployed, and soldiers, but excluding students and unpaid caregivers. The fewer workers there are engaged in agriculture, and the greater the number of workers in manufacturing and service industries, the more developed the nation.

A GLOBAL PERSPECTIVE

Botswana's Growing Economy

Since it became independent in 1966, Botswana's per capita income growth has been among the fastest of any nation in the world. This small African country transformed itself from one of the world's poorest countries to a middle-income nation in under 50 years. In 2004, Botswana received an A credit rating from Moody's and from Standard and Poor's.

Botswana has succeeded largely by maintaining a stable and responsible governmental system. The government has managed the income from large-scale mining operations wisely, reinvesting it in the nation's physical and human infrastructure. In recent years, the development of the financial services and tourism industries has been stressed. Together, they now represent about one-quarter of the nation's GDP.

Botswana still faces a number of social and economic challenges, including high unemployment, low manufacturing output, and one of the world's highest rates of HIV/AIDS infection. But through its moves to diversify the economy, the government has put the nation on a solid development track.

CONNECTING ACROSS THE GLOBE

1. How has the government of Botswana helped keep the nation's economy growing?

2. In the article, what tells investors that Botswana is a relatively safe place to invest?

APPLICATION Drawing Conclusions

B. Would you expect a positive or negative correlation between literacy rates and infant mortality rates? Explain.

REVIEWING KEY CONCEPTS

1. Explain the relationship between the terms in each of these pairs:

   a. *developed nations*
   less developed countries

   b. *human development index*
   infant mortality rate

2. What does the state of a nation's infrastructure say about the country's level of economic development?

3. Why is per capita GDP a more useful statistic than overall GDP when comparing nations?

4. What does an analysis of the labor force and energy usage tell economists about a nation?

5. Why are health and longevity statistics useful in determining a nation's level of development?

6. **Using Your Notes** Pick one example of a developed nation, one of a transitional economy, and one of a less developed nation. Use your notes to explain why you chose each.

   Use the Graphic Organizer at **Interactive Review @ ClassZone.com**

Definitions of Development	
Levels of Development	Standards of Economic Development

CRITICAL THINKING

7. **Comparing and Contrasting** Compare and contrast three characteristics of a developed nation and a less developed nation.

8. **Making Inferences and Drawing Conclusions** One measure of economic development is the extent to which a nation buys big-ticket consumer goods. Does the production of those goods also indicate a level of economic development? Explain your answer.

9. **Writing About Economics** Some economists argue that GDP does not give an accurate picture of a nation's well-being. They point out that GDP reflects economic activity that pollutes the environment and depletes resources as well as economic activity that counteracts the pollution. In other words, it shows both the polluting enterprises and the cost of cleaning up the pollution on the plus side of the balance sheet. Write a paragraph speculating on how to revise GDP figures to reflect this concern.

10. **Challenge** In poorer countries, where does the money for development initiatives come from?

ECONOMICS IN PRACTICE

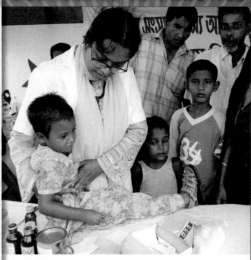

Health care in Bangladesh

Understanding Levels of Development

The chart below shows life expectancy, infant mortality rates, and literacy rates for five countries.

Country	Life Expectancy (years)	Infant Mortality (per 1,000 live births)	Literacy Rate (%)
Bolivia	65.8	51.8	87.2
Germany	78.8	4.1	99.0
Moldova	65.7	38.4	99.1
Philippines	70.2	22.8	92.6
Bangladesh	62.5	60.8	43.1

Source: *CIA World Factbook, 2006*

Drawing Conclusions Which nation is probably the most developed? Which nation is probably the least developed? Which nation is more developed, Bolivia or the Philippines? Explain your answers.

Challenge If you were "weighting" the various measures used to show economic development, which would you consider most meaningful: life expectancy, infant mortality, or literacy rate? Explain your answer.

A Framework for Economic Development Objectives

OBJECTIVES	KEY TERMS	TAKING NOTES
In Section 2 you will • evaluate the importance of developing human and physical capital • examine the importance of stability and opportunity in economic development • describe how developing nations raise money for development programs	capital flight, *p. 558* default, *p. 559* World Bank, *p. 559* International Monetary Fund (IMF), *p. 559* debt restructuring, *p. 559* stabilization program, *p. 559*	As you read Section 2, complete a cluster diagram like the one shown for each major concept. Include key concepts and other helpful words and phrases. Use the Graphic Organizer at **Interactive Review @ ClassZone.com** Development Framework stability stable prices

Resources

KEY CONCEPTS

What does a nation need to develop economically? Natural resources such as minerals and fossil fuels play a role in economic development. A nation's climate and the amount of land suited for agriculture are also factors. Each nation uses the resources it has. However, natural resources are not enough. Investing in human capital and physical capital, for example, are ways that many nations promote economic expansion.

High Levels of Human Capital

People are the most valuable resources in a market economy. One element of a healthy and growing market economy is a commitment to make the most of its human resources through education and training. Education and training help people develop the skills to enter into and function productively in the economy.

Human Capital Societies benefit in many ways when their citizens are well educated.

Investing in education also affects other aspects of a society. Educated citizens are able to make informed decisions about health matters. Educated parents are likely to vaccinate their children and invest in their children's education. Furthermore, educated citizens are likely to vote, participate in civic affairs, rise above poverty, and avoid criminal activity.

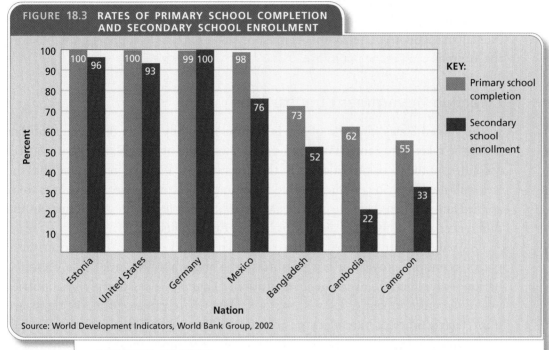

FIGURE 18.3 RATES OF PRIMARY SCHOOL COMPLETION AND SECONDARY SCHOOL ENROLLMENT

KEY:
Primary school completion
Secondary school enrollment

Nation

Source: World Development Indicators, World Bank Group, 2002

ANALYZE GRAPHS

1. What nation shows the largest drop-off between the percentage of students that complete primary school and the percentage who go on to secondary school?

2. Do you think the amount of drop-off between education levels is a clue to a nation's level of development? Explain your answer.

High Levels of Physical Capital

Physical capital is also an important factor contributing to economic growth. As you read in Chapter 1, physical capital consists of the human-made goods—machines— that are used in the production of other goods and services. Investments in physical capital make people more productive.

Fortunately, LDCs do not have to reinvent the wheel. Technology and other innovative capital resources are always being refined in developed nations. LDCs need only copy or import the technology. The desire to copy or import technologies points to the link between human and physical capital. Copying technology requires educated and well-trained people. Importing technology requires money, which is generally in short supply in LDCs, so these nations look to foreign investment. However, a country that lacks human capital is less attractive to investors that might supply this money.

APPLICATION Explaining an Economic Concept

A. Think of your own examples to explain the ripple effect that education has on a society and economy.

Stability

While such inputs as human capital and physical capital are necessary for increased output, they are only part of the framework for economic growth. The overall governmental and economic environments must be stable enough to support growth before those inputs can best be put to use.

Effective Government Institutions

In the United States, the rule of law is so fundamentally a part of the culture that it may be taken for granted. We are used to laws made by a legislature that we elect according to the principles laid out in the Constitution. We take for granted that the laws will then be made public for all to know and follow. We expect those laws to be applied fairly. When there are disputes, we trust that our legal system will sort out the differences according to the law, not by bribery or intimidation.

In many countries, however, the rule of law is still out of reach, and in those places, economic growth suffers. Business investment always carries risk, even in a nation with effective government institutions. That risk rises sharply in countries where the enforcement of laws is unpredictable, where private property rights are unprotected, where a bureaucracy is corrupt or bloated or both, and where judges can be bought and sold. The rule of law provides a foundation of predictability and certainty that reduces economic risk.

Democracy itself is a key factor of economic growth. Democratic nations have a higher rate of economic growth than nations with a different form of government. In nations where people can choose their representatives in free and open elections, they can promote their economic self-interest with the same degree of power as other citizens. When the press is uncensored, views that oppose government policy can be aired and debated. In a famous study, one Nobel Prize–winning economist, Amartya Sen, concluded that crop failures are not the chief cause of famines: political systems are. He points out that no widespread famine has ever occurred in a democratic nation. India has had famines, but none since it became a democracy in 1947. The democratic process reduces the likelihood that the government will interfere with the self-correcting market forces that could prevent widespread famine.

Law Enforcement A fair and transparent court system is key to the kind of governmental stability that promotes development.

Stable Prices

In areas where prices are stable and where the governments' fiscal and monetary policies are sound, economic growth can take root. Investors in such an environment know what to expect. They do not see volatile changes in interest rates, prices, or the level of the government debt.

With price stability, businesses can make long-term plans with some assurance that conditions will not change too dramatically and that the government will not go bankrupt. In contrast, in nations with a high inflation rate or with unstable interest rates, investors run a high risk. Many will choose to avoid investing in such an environment in the first place. And even if they do take a chance, they are likely to withdraw their investment at the first sign of trouble. That leaves the unstable country further behind, since the funds it could use for economic expansion are placed in more stable nations.

Monetary Stability Runaway prices in post–World War I Germany made money into children's toys (left). A stable currency and stable prices create real purchasing power (right).

Protected Property Rights

Guaranteed protection of private property provides an incentive for economies to grow. If businesses have no way to assert ownership of their enterprises, they will have little incentive to take economic risks, since they will have no guarantee of reaping the rewards if they succeed. Assured property rights give investors confidence and stimulate entrepreneurship.

Business owners also need private property rights to prevent the government from interfering with or restricting their operations. In such unstable nations as Haiti, Kazakhstan, and Indonesia, where corruption and favoritism are widespread, private property rights are insecure. This lack of stability is more than enough to cause investors to look elsewhere to locate their enterprises.

In some LDCs, especially former colonies of Western nations, land ownership is in the hands of a very small percentage of the population—usually the descendants of the colonists. In some cases, this land is seized by the government for redistribution to the majority population. Foreign investors are wary of locating businesses in countries that threaten private property.

APPLICATION Drawing Conclusions

B. Why is the rule of law a stabilizing force that promotes development?

Issues of Economic Development 555

Opportunity

KEY CONCEPTS

Economic opportunity depends on a number of functions that fall to the government. These include opening international trade, helping people move up the income ladder, controlling corruption, and limiting regulations.

Open International Trade

The government can also create opportunities for economic growth by lowering restrictions on international trade. As you read in Chapter 17, trade benefits the trading nations by allowing them to produce what they are most efficient at producing and trading for the rest. Partners in a trading relationship produce more than they would without trade, leading to economic growth.

However, in less developed countries, governments have imposed high tariffs on imports and instituted other protectionist measures in an effort to give local producers an advantage. Governments often justify these protections as a short-term effort to help local industries until they grow strong enough to compete with foreign competitors. Protectionist measures come with costs, though. Consumers have to pay more for goods than they would in a market open to imports. Also, government protections may reduce incentives for producers to become more efficient. Industries may become dependent on tariffs and other trade barriers.

Increase Social and Economic Mobility

Economic opportunity leads to the most vigorous economic growth when that opportunity is open to the entire population. If all citizens have an equal opportunity under the law to engage in economic enterprise, many will be motivated to lift themselves into a higher income bracket. A number of studies have found that in the United States, for example, about 25 to 33 percent of the population moves into a new income quintile each year. Over a ten-year period, that number rises to 60 percent. In the process of seeking personal economic reward, these people are also helping the economy to grow.

In some traditional cultures, however, social conditions do not promote equal opportunity. For example, in some LDCs with a traditional culture, the lower status of women keeps half the labor force from developing its full potential. Further, an entrenched class structure in some nations hampers growth, since the rich do not want changes that could deprive them of their wealth. Governmental changes that promote equal opportunity will help create a successful framework for economic growth.

Economic Potential In many traditional societies, women are an untapped resource that could give development a boost.

Economics Update

Find an update on women in the workplace in LDCs at **ClassZone.com**

Control Corruption

Corruption, the abuse of public office for private gain, is an especially urgent problem that helps explain why some nations are able to develop and others are not. When government officials are at liberty to enrich themselves and others—by taking bribes and kickbacks, funneling lucrative government jobs and contracts to relatives and allies, skimming aid and loan money, and so on—the rest of the nation, especially the poor, pays the price. (See Figure 18.4.) Although there is not an exact correlation between corruption and per capita GDP, much more often than not, countries with less corruption have higher per capita GDPs.

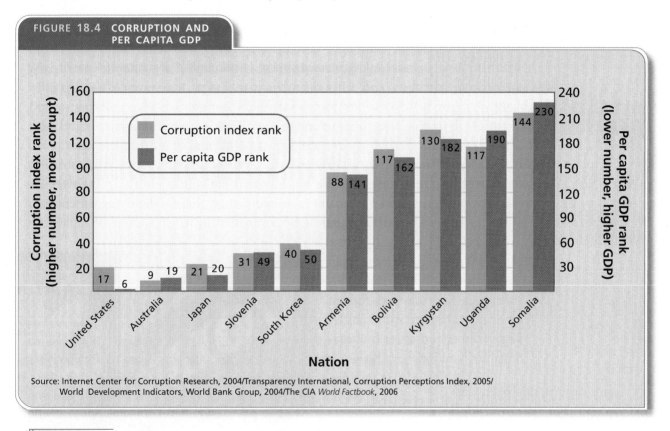

FIGURE 18.4 CORRUPTION AND PER CAPITA GDP

Source: Internet Center for Corruption Research, 2004/Transparency International, Corruption Perceptions Index, 2005/ World Development Indicators, World Bank Group, 2004/The CIA *World Factbook*, 2006

Limit Regulation

Governments with reasonable tax levels and business regulations help to create economic opportunity. Businesses and other investors are more likely to be attracted to nations with relatively little "red tape."

Even in the United States, which has relatively few regulations on business, it is estimated that companies with 20 or fewer employees have to pay over $7,500 per employee each year to comply with government regulations. In many LDCs, the number of regulations is significantly higher. In a climate of instability, the high number of regulations can lead to corruption. Rather than comply with all the regulations, businesses are tempted to bypass them through payoffs. As you have read, a corrupt environment removes economic incentive and slows economic growth.

APPLICATION Applying Economic Concepts

C. Nations with the highest corruption index tend to have their wealth distributed less evenly, with a large percentage of people living in poverty. Why might this be so?

Issues of Economic Development   557

Financing Development

KEY CONCEPTS

Nations seeking to finance economic development can look to four main sources: internal investment, foreign investment, aid from foreign governments, or investments from international agencies. A developing nation must consider both the positive and negative aspects of each source.

Internal Investment

Investment funds for economic development can come from both public and private internal investment. Banks within the nation invest in economic enterprises, such as roads, bridges, and other infrastructure. Egypt, for example, has a goal to make domestic savings the key force in development and has been working toward increasing the savings rate to 25 percent of GDP. To do so, it has an initiative to bolster the insurance industry, which is successful at pooling and channeling savings.

In poorer nations, personal savings are very low, so banks have little to invest. The wealthy citizens sometimes do not invest in the country but take their wealth where they think it will be safer and more productive, thereby depriving the country of the funds. This is called **capital flight**, a situation in which sources of capital are sent outside the country. If private banks are not able to invest, then the government itself may provide funds, or it may seek foreign investment through such vehicles as government bonds or multinational corporations.

QUICK REFERENCE

Capital flight occurs when sources of capital are sent outside a country.

Foreign Direct Investment Multinational corporations, such as those pictured, contribute to development in LDCs by providing employment and training and by introducing technology.

Foreign Investment

There are several ways in which foreign interests can invest in an economy. One is foreign direct investment (FDI), the establishment of a business enterprise in a foreign country. A second is foreign portfolio investment, through which foreign investors take part in a nation's stock and other financial markets. Foreign investment in less developed countries has increased dramatically, from $44 billion in 1990 to $226 billion in 2000. One reason for the increase is that the less developed nations have been working to create a more attractive business climate for investors. Multinationals that open manufacturing plants in foreign nations provide jobs and training to the local population and reap the benefits of cheaper labor.

Loans and Aid

Developing nations have also turned to loans to help finance their economic development. External debt, money borrowed from foreign banks or governments, has become an issue of great concern in some LDCs. Some countries, especially in South America and Africa, have more debt than they can pay back. When a nation cannot pay interest or principle on a loan, it is said to be in **default**.

Nations may also seek foreign aid—money from other nations. (See Figure 18.5 for aid figures from the U.S. Agency for International Development [USAID]).

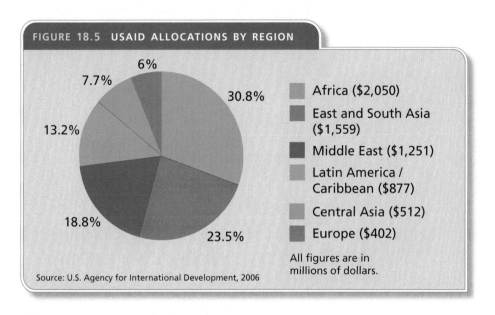

FIGURE 18.5 USAID ALLOCATIONS BY REGION

6%
7.7%
30.8%
13.2%
18.8%
23.5%

- Africa ($2,050)
- East and South Asia ($1,559)
- Middle East ($1,251)
- Latin America / Caribbean ($877)
- Central Asia ($512)
- Europe ($402)

All figures are in millions of dollars.

Source: U.S. Agency for International Development, 2006

International Help Agencies

LDCs also receive aid from several important international organizations. The World Bank, the International Monetary Fund, and the United Nations Development Program are the main international organizations devoted to economic development.

- **World Bank** is a financial institution that provides loans, policy advice, and technical assistance to low- and middle-income countries to reduce poverty.

- **International Monetary Fund (IMF)** is an international organization established to promote international monetary cooperation, foster economic growth, and provide temporary financial assistance to countries to help ease balance of payments adjustment. The IMF helps nations overloaded with debt to develop **debt restructuring**, a method used by countries with outstanding debt obligations to alter the terms of the debt agreements in order to achieve some advantage. It often oversees **stabilization programs**, in which it requires these troubled nations to carry out reforms—reducing foreign trade deficits and external debt, eliminating price controls, closing inefficient public enterprises, and slashing budget deficits.

- **United Nations Development Program** (UNDP) is a United Nations agency working to fight poverty. In 2006 it had active programs in 174 nations.

APPLICATION Making Inferences and Drawing Conclusions

D. Why would Kuwait, a developing nation, offer aid to countries in its region?

Anne Krueger: Reforming IMF Development Policy

FAST FACTS

Anne O. Krueger

Title: First Deputy Managing Director of the IMF, September 2001 to August 2006

Born: February 12, 1934, New York City

Major Publications Edited:

Reforming India's Economic, Financial, and Fiscal Policies. Edited with Sajjid Z. Chinoy, 2003

Latin American Macroeconomic Reform: The Second Stage. Edited with Jose Antonion Gonzales, Vittorio Corbo, and Aaron Tornell, 2003

Selected Awards:

- Distinguished Fellow and past President of the American Economic Association

- Frank E. Seidman Distinguished Award in political economy (1993)

- Bernard Harms Prize awarded by the Kiel Institute of World Economics (1990)

Economics Update

Find an update on Anne Krueger at **ClassZone.com**

On September 1, 2001, Anne Krueger became First Deputy Director of the International Monetary Fund. Ten days later, the terrorist attacks on the United States sent shockwaves through the global economy. Three months later, Argentina suspended payments on its $132 billion foreign debt. At the time, this was the biggest default in history. All the while, there were significant economic upheavals as well as international protests over the burden of debt in developing nations. Clearly, she didn't have the luxury of easing into her new position.

A New Role for IMF

Luckily, Krueger came very well prepared for her new job. In addition to her professorships at Stanford University, Duke University, and the University of Minnesota, Krueger had also been Director of the Center for Research on Economic Development and Policy Reform, at Stanford, and the Vice President of Economics and Research at the World Bank.

In November 2001, anticipating Argentina's default, Krueger put forward a proposal for the role of the IMF in debt restructuring and dispute resolution. In her proposal, the IMF would oversee the restructuring of the debt rather than simply providing bailout funds. The reform effort also called for collective action clauses, measures that let a supermajority of creditors overrule a creditor who is holding out for more repayment than may be possible. In fact, after several years of negotiations, most of Argentina's creditors accepted 35 cents on the dollar in early 2005, and Argentina's credit rating climbed once again.

Even 35 cents on the dollar, however, seems too high to many critics, who believe that debt in most developing nations should be forgiven 100 percent so the money used to service the debt can be put to use providing such needed human services as health care and education. Krueger has disagreed: ". . . Unless there is radical change from past behavior on the part of the debtors, their priorities for the use of released resources are not likely to be on education, health, or other expenditures that will enable the poor to improve their lot." Nonetheless, the IMF is part of a plan to forgive debt completely in 18 of the most heavily indebted poor nations in exchange for economic policies that favor trade liberalization and other development goals.

Anne Krueger

APPLICATION Solving Economic Problems

C. Krueger believes that direct aid to nongovernmental organizations working in health or education are more effective than debt cancellation. Critics argue that grants with conditions show the IMFs desire to control nations' economies. Who do you agree with? Give reasons for your answers.

REVIEWING KEY CONCEPTS

1. Explain the relationship between this pair of terms:

   a. *International Monetary Fund* **b.** *stabilization program*

2. What are four key sources of funding for development?

3. How can a nation develop its human capital?

4. How can a nation improve its business climate?

5. What roles do foreign nations play in a country's development?

6. **Using Your Notes** Use your completed cluster diagram to help you explain how the economic development of one nation might be an opportunity for growth for another nation. Use the Graphic Organizer at **Interactive Review @ ClassZone.com**

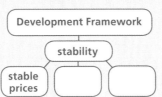

Development Framework

stability

stable prices

CRITICAL THINKING

7. **Analyzing Cause and Effect** How might the bailout by an international agency of a nation that has defaulted on foreign debt lead to more corruption in the future?

8. **Writing About Economics** Many economists believe that a country that is rich in a particular natural resource may actually be at a developmental disadvantage. They point out that nations such as these tend to put all of their resources into this one industry. Write a paragraph about how you, as leader of a nation, would use the large income from your nation's natural resource to take other avenues to developing your economy.

9. **Applying Economic Concepts** Look again at Figure 18.5. The United States grants aid money each year to nations in the developing world. Do you think Anne Krueger would think this aid money should come with certain terms or conditions? Explain.

10. **Challenge** If you were in charge of development efforts for a poor nation, which source of development funds would you focus on? Why?

ECONOMICS IN PRACTICE

Understanding the Path to Development

Read the following scenarios of fictional less developed countries:

- In nation A, there is a democratically elected government, but a corrupt law enforcement system has made property rights shaky. There is little foreign trade, and few foreign firms have set up manufacturing facilities. However, a foreign nation gives nation A hundreds of millions of dollars in aid each year.

- In nation B, the move toward democracy has begun. A system of fair and transparent law enforcement is in place, and international trade and foreign direct investment are on the rise. High levels of foreign debt, however, could pose a problem in the future.

Categorizing Economic Information Is nation A or nation B more likely on a path to successful development? Explain why you think so.

Challenge What's more beneficial to development— a connection to a large amount of foreign aid money or a plan to increase social, political, and economic stability? Why?

Transition to a Market Economy

OBJECTIVES	KEY TERMS	TAKING NOTES
In Section 3 you will • identify problems that emerge when an economy goes from command to market • describe the transitions to a market economy in the former Soviet Union and nations it dominated • discuss the transitions to a market economy in China	privatization, *p. 563* shock therapy, *p. 563* perestroika, *p. 564* special economic zone (SEZ), *p. 567*	As you read Section 3, complete a cluster diagram like the one shown, using the key concepts and other helpful words and phrases. Use the Graphic Organizer at **Interactive Review @ ClassZone.com** 

New Challenges

KEY CONCEPTS

In Chapter 2, you read about different economic systems, including a command, or centrally planned, economy in which all economic decisions are made by the society's leaders, usually government officials acting in a central location. For a while, much of the world's population lived in a command economy. However, China, the nations that formerly made up the Soviet Union, and many Eastern European countries have taken steps toward a market economy. The transition requires new answers to the basic economic questions that central planners used to answer. Both the government and private individuals and companies face a number of challenges.

CHALLENGE 1 Poor Infrastructure

A market economy needs a solid infrastructure to facilitate the production and distribution of goods and services. In a command economy, transportation, communications, banking, and education—the infrastructure of an industrialized nation—are as inefficient as other industries tend to be. With no competition there is little incentive to create a more robust physical and institutional infrastructure. Modernized airports, phone systems, roads, harbors, bridges, and computer connections help a transitional economy support and spread the goods and services it produces.

Bridging the Gap Transportation infrastructure is a vital part of the overall infrastructure needed to develop a successful market economy.

CHALLENGE 2 Privatization

Under communism, the government owns all property. As transitional nations move toward a market economy, they have all undertaken the challenges of **privatization**, the process of transferring state owned-property and businesses to individuals. A major problem with privatization is how to sell the property. It can, for example, be auctioned off, but command economies have little private savings, and few people have the needed finances. Also, as you'll read later, these auctions can sometimes be rigged to benefit those close to the ruling elites. A second method is to sell shares of businesses through a vehicle like the stock market. A third way is to give vouchers to people to purchase shares of a business, making cash unnecessary.

QUICK REFERENCE

Privatization is the process of transferring state owned property and businesses to individuals.

CHALLENGE 3 Rise in Prices

In a command economy, some goods may have artificially low prices. Part of the switch to a market economy is the removal of price controls, allowing the market to operate. On January 1, 1990, Poland's government gave the go-ahead for an economic program referred to as **shock therapy,** involving the abrupt shift from a command to a free-market economy. The initial result indeed shocked consumers; the inflation rate that first month was 78 percent. However, this inflationary "correction" eased as the free-market policies were allowed to take hold. (See Figure 18.6.)

QUICK REFERENCE

Shock therapy is an economic program involving the abrupt shift from a command economy to a free-market economy.

FIGURE 18.6 POLAND'S INFLATION RATE AFTER SHOCK THERAPY

Source: "The Polish Zloty 1990–1999: Success and Under-Performance," Dominico Nuti

ANALYZE GRAPHS
1. After 1991, how many years did it take Poland to cut its inflation rate in half?
2. Why did the inflation rate consistently decrease after the initial "shock" of 1991?

APPLICATION Making Inferences and Drawing Conclusions

A. Which of the challenges above do you think is the most serious? Give reasons for your answer.

Economic Change in the Former Soviet Bloc

QUICK REFERENCE

Perestroika was a gradual plan to incorporate markets into the Soviet Union's command economy.

KEY CONCEPTS

In the 1980s, Soviet leader Mikhail Gorbachev introduced **perestroika**, a plan to gradually incorporate markets into the Soviet Union's command economy. People began to push for political freedom as well, and in 1991 the Soviet Union dissolved. The collapse of the Soviet Union caused a period of dramatic transition throughout Eastern Europe and Central Asia.

EXAMPLE 1 Russia

The transition has been a turbulent time for Russia. Like Poland and several other Eastern European nations, it pursued a program of economic "shock therapy." The resulting inflation was devastating. Supplies of goods were very low, and many industries were forced into bankruptcy when faced with the need to become "self-financing." Further, the state was poorly equipped to carry out even the most basic functions of government, such as tax collection. As a result, with little revenue to work with, it could not offer welfare services to cover the disruptions of the economic shift, and the burden of government debt began to rise.

Amid the upheaval, some market forces began to exert themselves. Without directives from central planners, regional business initiatives could address the real demands of consumers. In 1992, a program of privatization began to put the means of production into private ownership, introducing incentives for success.

The privatization process, however, was fixed in favor of certain individuals. As a result, a small group of politically well-connected business people snapped up many of Russia's former public assets through a series of rigged auctions. These oligarchs, as they're known, went on to build massive corporations and became the most powerful economic force in modern Russia.

The best-known oligarch, Mikhail Khodorkovsky, has recently been sentenced to nine years in prison on fraud and tax evasion charges. In addition, his giant oil company, Yukos, was taken over by the government. It is widely believed that the charges against him were motivated by his support for political parties that were opposed to Russia's president, Vladimir Putin. Many saw this case and others as symptoms of Putin's reluctance to truly adopt democratic reforms and a market economy. Taken together, Putin's actions, the power of Russian organized crime, and the persistence of widespread corruption threatened to undermine Russia's successful development.

At Will Oligarchs? The prosecution of Khodorkovsky was seen by many as a warning to Russia's oligarchs: the price of opposition to Putin's government may be your freedom.

EXAMPLE 2 Former Soviet Republics

The transition of the former Soviet Republics has been varied. The Baltic Republics—Latvia, Lithuania, and Estonia—have fared better than others, experiencing a 45 percent inflation rate while Ukraine had a 400 percent rate and Kazakhstan in Central Asia had a rate higher than 1,000 percent. Of all the former republics, only the Baltic Republics, Armenia, Belarus, and Kazakhstan have a higher output now than they did before the collapse of the Soviet Union. Nevertheless, many economists believe the quality of goods and services produced is higher. In the other republics, poor infrastructure, complicated bureaucracies, undeveloped property laws, and corruption have interfered with economic growth.

Vilnius Since independence, the capital of Lithuania has thrived. It accounts for one-third of the nation's GDP and attracted 2.815 billion euros in FDI in 2005.

EXAMPLE 3 Eastern Europe

The formerly Communist nations of Eastern European have faced some of the same challenges as their neighbors and had similarly varying degrees of success. The largest nations, the Czech Republic, Hungary, and Poland, are now much like Western countries. They are members of the European Union, but some experts believe they will need until 2035 to catch up economically with other member nations. Nonetheless, progress is apparent. Since the transition, Poland's economy has been growing at an average rate of 6 percent annually, industrial productivity has increased by more than 20 percent, and the private sector is responsible for more than 70 percent of the national income. There are more than 2.5 million small- or medium-sized businesses operating today, and Western franchises, such as the McDonald Corporation and the IKEA Group, have become entrenched.

However, Poland also has problems that are common across the nations of Eastern Europe. Its infrastructure is out of date, and telephone and internet services are very costly. The laws for registering to do business in the Polish market are confusing, and the patent process that protects property rights is slow. The health care and pension systems have weakened, and unemployment is high. Averaged throughout the country, the unemployment rate is about 18 percent, but in some regions it is as high as 40 percent, and workers are discouraged. In Hungary, the illegal "hidden economy" may account for up to 30 percent of GDP.

APPLICATION Comparing and Contrasting Economic Information

B. Which of the three regions—Russia, the former Soviet Republics, or Eastern European nations—has had the hardest transition? Explain your answer.

China Moves Toward a Market Economy

China became a Communist country in 1949, but it began a transition to a free market economy in 1978. At that time, its leader, Deng Xiaoping, introduced free market economic principles to stimulate China's economy. The result was a vastly changed and rapidly growing economy.

EXAMPLE Rapid but Uneven Growth

In the early years of China's Communist economy, central planners focused on redistributing land, developing heavy industry, and improving China's transportation system. In 1958, the government introduced the Great Leap Forward. This plan focused on the building of huge collective farms and the development of the steel industry. For a while, both agricultural and steel output increased. However, the gains were short-lived. Poor economic planning and a series of natural disasters led to stark times. Millions of people died in famines.

When Deng Xiaoping came to power in the late 1970s, hundreds of millions of Chinese villagers lived in poverty, sometimes sharing one pair of trousers among a whole family. Deng brought hope and practical programs to the people. "It is time to prosper. . . . To get rich is glorious," he said. Deng began a far-reaching but gradual program to relax government control over the economy and let market forces drive economic growth.

In agriculture, farmland that had been confiscated was returned to the farmers in household units. Under this "household responsibility system," farms still had to supply a quota of staple goods to the government at set prices, but beyond that the farmers could grow what they wanted and sell any surplus on the open market. China reported a ten percent annual growth in agricultural output between 1979 and 1984. Brick homes began to replace thatched huts as farmers' income soared.

A Growing Divide
Modernization has come at breakneck speed in many of China's urban centers, while life in rural China can seem to be in a different century.

In the mid-1980s, Deng focused his reform effort on industry, where two-thirds of the manufacturing plants were still state-owned. Deng moved slowly and cautiously. Instead of privatizing suddenly or making drastic, uniform changes, he scattered the reforms among different industries. In one industry, local managers might have more decision-making power. In another, workers might get raises based on the profits of the factory. Deng's reforms also called for localities to invest in the industries they thought would thrive. In this process, resources were re-allocated from heavy to light industry, a key factor in China's rapid growth.

Deng also created **special economic zones (SEZs)**, geographical regions that have economic laws that are different from a country's usual economic laws, with the goal of increasing foreign investment. The first four were begun in 1979 as an experiment. In 1984, fourteen more were created in cities along the coast, including Shanghai; now there are hundreds. The SEZs have tax incentives for foreign investment, and the economic activities are driven entirely by market forces. Further, when capitalist Hong Kong was returned to China in 1997 after a 99-year lease by Great Britain, it was reunified under the "one country, two systems" framework. The government would not interfere with its economy; in fact, it would be a model for the nation.

Areas with high foreign investment have raced ahead of other parts of the country economically, contributing to China's annual growth in GDP of between 5 and 15 percent since the reforms began. Some people, encouraged by Deng's proclamation, have become very rich. However, in 2003, the number of people living in extreme poverty (on less that $77 a year) rose for the first time in 25 years, to about 3 percent of the population. In some villages of western China, 90 percent of the people live on government welfare and do not have indoor plumbing or telephones.

QUICK REFERENCE

A **special economic zone (SEZ)** is a geographical region that has economic laws that are different from a country's usual economic laws, with the goal of increasing foreign investment.

Economics Update

Find an update on China's special economic zones at **ClassZone.com**

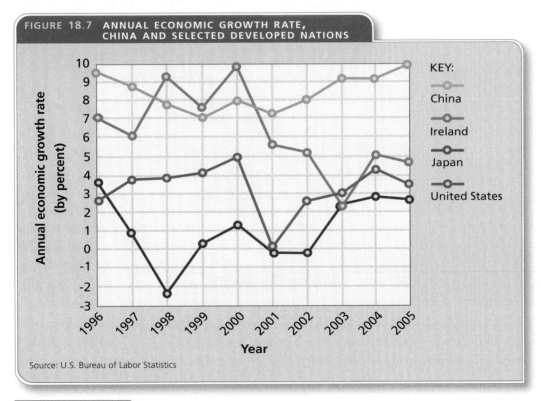

FIGURE 18.7 ANNUAL ECONOMIC GROWTH RATE, CHINA AND SELECTED DEVELOPED NATIONS

Source: U.S. Bureau of Labor Statistics

APPLICATION Explaining an Economic Concept

C. What role do the SEZs play in China's transition to a market economy?

For more on using a decision-making process, see the Skillbuilder Handbook, page R17.

Using a Decision-Making Process

Making decisions in complicated situations can be extremely difficult. Having a plan, or process, in place can be quite helpful.

TECHNIQUES USED IN MAKING DECISIONS Making decisions involves (1) gathering information to identify the situation in question, (2) identifying options, (3) predicting consequences, and (4) implementing a decision. The following passage describes the problem of flooding on China's Chang River. It illustrates the decision-making process.

Look for information that points to a situation that requires a decision. Figures on the deadly toll of flooding show that a decision on damming was needed.

Predict possible consequences. The positive and negative results of the dam are listed.

Controlling the Chang River

In the past 100 years, more than 1 million people have died as a result of flooding along China's Chang (Yangtze) River. After devastating floods in the 1950s, Chinese leader Mao Zedong ordered studies to see whether damming the river was feasible. Finally, in the 1990s, construction began on the Three Gorges Dam, which—when completed—will be the largest dam in the world. In addition to providing flood control, the dam will be a source of hydropower. Its turbines are expected to produce up to one-ninth of China's electricity. The dam's series of locks will allow ocean-going ships to sail 1,500 miles inland.

Nevertheless, the project has serious drawbacks. For one thing, it will require the resettlement of an estimated 1.2 million people. Environmentalists warn of water pollution, as well as the eradication of migratory fish and rare plants. The dam is scheduled for completion in 2009. In the meantime, the Chinese government has already begun to address the problem of pollution with the building of at least one comprehensive sewage treatment plant.

Look for any options that are offered. Here, only the option of damming the river is considered.

Decide what the result was. The dam is scheduled to be completed in 2009.

THINKING ECONOMICALLY Making Decisions

1. What choice did the government have regarding the flooding of the Chang River?

2. What economic incentives do you think may have added to the government's decision?

3. What consequences of the decision might be contrary to economic growth? Explain your answer.

REVIEWING KEY CONCEPTS

1. 1. Explain the difference between these terms:
   a. *shock therapy*   **b.** *perestroika*

2. What makes privatization a challenge in transitional economies?

3. What role does infrastructure play in transitional economies?

4. Why are special economic zones important to the growth of the Chinese economy?

5. In what way(s) is privatization an element of China's shift to a market economy?

6. **Using Your Notes** Write a summary of the challenges of economic transitions and explain how they have been addressed in the former Soviet bloc and in China. Refer to your completed cluster diagram.

   Use the Graphic Organizer at **Online Review @ ClassZone.com**

CRITICAL THINKING

7. **Comparing and Contrasting Economic Information** What are three key differences between the economic transitions of the former Soviet bloc and China?

8. **Making Inferences and Drawing Conclusions** While China has welcomed western economic principles, it has continued to come down hard on political freedoms. For example, Deng crushed protesters in Tiananmen Square in 1989. Why do you think capitalism can grow in China under a restrictive government when in the former Soviet bloc it went hand in hand with political freedom?

9. **Applying Economic Concepts** Explain how life in the former Soviet bloc changed for each of the following during a transition to a market economy.
   a. factory worker **b.** farmer **c.** consumer **d.** factory manager

10. **Challenge** Do businesses from foreign nations with strong anti-pollution laws have a responsibility to voluntarily limit pollution when located in a less developed country with less developed pollution laws? Give reasons for your answer.

ECONOMICS IN PRACTICE

Budapest, Hungary

Assessing Transition and Development

The chart below shows statistics from 2004 for Kyrgyzstan and Tajikistan, in Central Asia, and Hungary and Romania, in Eastern European.

	Kyrgyzstan	Tajikistan	Hungary	Romania
Gross national income ($ per capita)	$268	154	4,913	1,729
Real GDP growth rate (%)	6.0	10.5	3.9	8.1
Industrial production growth rate (%)	6.0	8.2	9.6	4.0
Human development index (HDI)*	0.702	0.652	0.862	0.792

* Highest HDI is 1.0; lowest is 0.0.

Comparing and Contrasting Economic Information Write a paragraph comparing and contrasting the transition to a market economy in the selected Central Asian and Eastern European countries. Use the figures from the chart to explain the similarities and differences.

Challenge Why might the nation with the highest HDI, Hungary, also have the lowest real GDP growth?

China's Campaign for Economic Power

Background Since 1978, when China's former leader, Deng Xiaoping, made the decision to adopt free-market reforms, China's economy has been steadily gaining momentum. Deng's "four modernizations" (agriculture, industry, science and technology, and defense) have helped China become a player in the global economy in less than a generation.

Its success is based in part on its encouragement of foreign investment, the establishment of a number of special economic zones, and the opening of 14 coastal cities to foreign investment in 1984. Also, in 2001, China joined the World Trade Organization. Today, China's economic impact is too big to ignore.

What's the issue? What accounts for China's successful transition to a market economy? Study these sources to discover what fuels China's economic growth and how it affects the rest of the world.

A. Magazine Article

This article discusses some of the underlying reasons for China's growing impact on the global economy.

▶ The Dragon Awakes

China is changing the dynamics of the global economy.

[China's] contribution to global GDP growth since 2000 has been almost twice as large as that of the next three biggest emerging economies, India, Brazil and Russia, combined. Moreover, there is [a] crucial reason why China's integration into the world economy is today having a bigger global impact than other emerging economies, or than Japan did during its period of rapid growth from the mid-1950s onwards. Uniquely, China combines a vast supply of cheap labor with an economy that is (for its size) unusually open to the rest of the world, in terms of trade and foreign direct investment. The sum of its total exports and imports of goods and services amounts to around 75% of China's GDP; in Japan, India and Brazil the figure is 25–30%. . . . As a result, the dragon's awakening is more traumatic for the rest of the world.

Source: *The Economist*, July 28, 2005

Thinking Economically Identify the aspect of China's economy that, according to the article, has had the most significant impact on the global economy, and explain why its impact has been so great.

The volume of China's exports has gotten a lot of attention in recent years.

Why is it worth pointing out that China's exporting power seems to outstrip that of other nations?

C. Online News Story

China's economic growth frequently is referred to as an "economic miracle." The miracle, however, is not without problems.

China's Economic Miracle: the High Price of Progress

China's progress is uneven and sometimes problematic.

[China's] GDP is growing by 10 percent a year. Industrial production is galloping ahead at an annual rate of 17 percent. Its economy is now the second-biggest in the world, behind only the U.S., and there are predictions it will assume the top spot as early as 2020. . . .

China's explosive growth has come at a price. The economic gains have not been shared equally. Millions have become richer. But hundreds of millions have not. More than 60 percent of the population still toils in agriculture; the country's "economic miracle" has yet to make an appearance in much of the country. Corruption also remains well entrenched . . . [and] millions of workers have lost their jobs in the restructuring, prompting frequent protests. . . .

Source: **CBC News Online, April 20, 2005**

Thinking Economically Will China's economic growth alone increase the incomes of its poorest people? Why or why not?

THINKING ECONOMICALLY Synthesizing

1. All three documents point to China's success in international trade. What key element of financing development does document A cite as a component of China's success?

2. Documents A and B hint that the rest of the world is uneasy with China's economic growth, while document C discusses some of China's problems at home. Discuss these fears and problems in the context of what you've learned throughout Chapter 18.

3. Which factors do you think are most significant relative to China's economic growth? Explain why you think so. Use evidence from the documents in your answer.

Interactive ◀▶ Review

Review this chapter using interactive activities at **ClassZone.com**

- Online Summary
- Quizzes
- Vocabulary Flip Cards
- Graphic Organizers
- Review and Study Notes

○○○

 Online Summary

Complete the following activity either on your own paper or online at **ClassZone.com**

Choose the key concept that best completes the sentence. Not all key concepts will be used.

debt restructuring
default
developed nations
infant mortality rate
International Monetary Fund (IMF)
less developed countries (LDC)

per capita GDP
"shock therapy"
stabilization program
privatization
World Bank

Nations with little industry and relatively low GDP are said to be **1**, while nations with a market economy and higher standard of living are known as **2**. Economists measure the level of a nation's development through such statistics as **3**, which allows for easy comparison with other countries because it shows the nation's output in relation to its population.

When nations set a course for development, they often seek loans from other nations. Some heavily indebted nations have gone into **4** on their loans, being unable to pay them back. In those cases, nations can negotiate a **5** plan to extend the payback and/or lower the payback rate.

Some economies are moving from central planning to an open market. These nations face a number of challenges. For example, there are questions about how to carry out **6**, the transfer of public property into individually owned property. There are also questions about the pace of change. **7** involved suddenly removing governmental restrictions on the economy.

CHAPTER 18 Assessment

REVIEWING KEY CONCEPTS

Definitions of Development (pp. 542–551)

1. What are some features of a developed nation?

2. Name five measures economists use to gauge a nation's level of development.

A Framework for Economic Development Objectives (pp. 552–561)

3. Describe the internal and external goals a developing nation may set for itself.

4. In what ways can developing nations receive aid from other countries?

Transition to a Market Economy (pp. 562–571)

5. Name five challenges nations face when moving from a command economy to a market economy.

6. Briefly summarize the transition to a market economy in the former Soviet bloc and in China.

APPLYING ECONOMIC CONCEPTS

Look at the graph below showing life expectancy in various entities from 1980 to 2003.

7. What explanation can you offer for the regions in which life expectancy declined?

8. In 2003, how much longer can someone living in a country that belongs to OECD expect to live than someone living in sub-Saharan Africa?

FIGURE 18.8 LIFE EXPECTANCY IN WORLD REGIONS

Life expectancy (in years) vs Year (1980, 1985, 1990, 1995, 2000 2003)

- HIGH-INCOME OECD (ORGANIZATION FOR ECONOMIC COOPERATION AND DEVELOPMENT) NATIONS
- LATIN AMERICA & THE CARIBBEAN
- EAST ASIA & THE PACIFIC
- ARAB STATES
- CENTRAL & EASTERN EUROPE & THE COMMONWEALTH OF INDEPENDENT STATES
- SOUTH ASIA
- SUB-SAHARAN AFRICA

Source: U.N. Human Development Report, 2005

9. **Creating Graphs** Create a graphic of your choice to show the figures below on the percentage of people living on $1 a day or less between 1981 and 2001.

Region	1981	1990	2001
East Asia & Pacific	56.7	29.5	14.3
Europe & Central Asia	0.8	0.5	3.5
Latin America & Caribbean	10.1	11.6	9.9
Middle East & North Africa	5.1	2.3	2.4
South Asia	51.5	41.3	31.9
Sub-Saharan Africa	41.6	44.5	46.4
World	40.4	26.3	20.7

Source: U.N. Human Development Report, 2005

Use ✏️ *SMARTGrapher* @ ClassZone.com to complete this activity.

10. **Analyzing and Interpreting Data** Refer to the graph you created. In which region was the improvement in poverty most dramatic? In which regions did the situation worsen?

11. **Analyzing Cause and Effect** What might explain why this measure of poverty increased in Europe and Central Asia during this time period?

12. **Making Inferences and Drawing Conclusions** For each dollar spent on foreign aid by members of OECD, $10 is spent on the military. What can you conclude about the OECD member nations' concerns for the future?

13. **Challenge** A recent study found that an increase of ten mobile phones per 100 people raised GDP growth in a developing nation by ten percent. What might explain this? What does it suggest as a way to speed development?

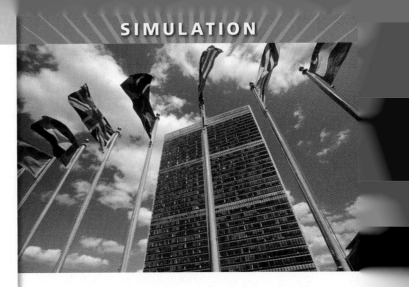

Work Toward Development Goals

In 2005, all the 191 members of the United Nations voted to adopt the Millennium Development Goals, with a target date of 2015 to have the goals realized.

Step 1 As a whole class, discuss the following eight goals that are part of this program:

1. Eradicate extreme poverty and hunger
2. Achieve universal primary education
3. Promote gender equality and empower women
4. Reduce child mortality
5. Improve maternal health
6. Combat HIV/AIDS, malaria, and other diseases
7. Ensure environmental sustainability
8. Develop a global partnership for development

Step 2 Break into eight small groups, one for each of the goals.

Step 3 Meet with your group and discuss concrete ways that the international community (either through such organizations as the IMF or World Bank or United Nations Development Program or through the efforts of individual nations or trading entities) can meet your goal and why it is important that it be met.

Step 4 Present your recommendations to the rest of the class.

Step 5 Follow up on the presentations with a discussion of how many different ways of approaching the problem surfaced and which seem most likely to lead to success.

1 Budgeting and Money Management

1.1 Budgeting

As an independent adult you have the freedom to make your own financial decisions. But with freedom comes responsibility. It takes planning and practice to learn how to use your income wisely, to pay your bills on time, and to have money left to save for the future.

What Would a Budget Do for Me?

QUICK REFERENCE

A **budget** is a plan for allocating income for saving and spending.

Everyone has a limited amount of money. A **budget**—a plan for how to save and spend your income—can help you focus your limited financial resources on what's most important to you. It will help you pay for basics like food, clothing, and shelter. After those expenses are met, it can include optional items such as travel or entertainment. And with savings as part of your budget, you will be on the path to achieve your long-term financial goals.

How Do I Set Up a Budget?

Determine Your Income Make a list of all the steady income you receive, including your pay from after-school and summer jobs and occasional work such as mowing lawns. List only the money you take home after taxes have been withheld from your paycheck.

Track Your Expenses To learn where your money goes, keep a record of all your expenses for a month. Save your receipts, and carry a small notebook to jot down purchases when you make them. The list should cover a full month, because not all expenses occur every week.

Categorize Expenses When you have a record of your expenses, put them into categories, such as transportation, food, clothing, savings, and entertainment. Figure CPF 1 shows how monthly expenses might be categorized to help set up a budget.

EXPENSES for month
Week 1
parking $6.00
movie $9.00
pizza $13.00

Figure CPF 1 Creating a Budget

(a) Fixed Expenses Your car payment and auto insurance are examples of fixed expenses.

(b) Spending Wisely Food is a necessity. But packing a lunch, cutting back on snacks, or eating out less often can help your budget.

(c) Savings Pay yourself each month. Limiting fixed expenses and reducing flexible expenses will help you meet your savings goals.

(d) Flexible Expenses Make room in the budget for entertainment, travel, and other fun stuff.

Monthly Expenses		
Category	**Current Expenses**	**Budget**
Transportation		
Car payment	#200	#200
Insurance	70	70
Gas	60	40
Parking	6	0
Maintenance	50	25
Food		
School lunches	#85	#80
Snacks	35	30
Eating out	30	15
Savings	20	50
Clothing	100	50
Entertainment		
Movie tickets	#27	#18
Movie rentals	12	12
Recorded music	20	20
TOTALS	#715	#610

Determine Fixed and Flexible Expenses Identify which expenses must be paid every month and determine what portion of your income they take. Savings should be a fixed amount, not a flexible amount. Money from savings pays for emergencies, large insurance bills that only come due once or twice a year, and major investments such as cars or real estate. What's left is available for flexible expenses like entertainment.

Set Up a Spending Plan Now look at your income and expenses. Set out a plan for fixed expenses. Look at the amount left over and allocate it to cover the flexible expenses. If your flexible expenses are cutting into your savings or leading to debt, look for ways to cut your spending. For example, you might eat more meals at home instead of at restaurants, or rent DVDs to watch with friends instead of going out to the movies.

Check It Out!

☑ Create an emergency fund for unexpected expenses.

☑ Save in advance for holiday or birthday gifts.

☑ Resist the temptation of impulse buying.

APPLICATION Budgeting

1. Which of the expenses in Step 3 will be monthly bills?

2. **Planning a Budget** Suppose you have a job that brings in $1,150 a month after taxes. You contribute $350 toward rent and utilities each month for an apartment you share with two other people. You put $100 each month into a savings account, and you spend about $50 per month for a cell phone. Of course, you also eat, wear clothes, and go out with friends. You want to buy a car that will cost $300 per month for payments and insurance. Can you afford it? Plan a budget to see if you can take on this new fixed expense.

1.2 Checking Accounts

Banks offer two basic types of accounts: checking and savings. Checking accounts are for immediate expenses. They can help you manage your expenses and pay your bills. The bank records deposits and withdrawals on your checking account, whether they are in the form of paper checks, automated teller machine (ATM) transactions, debit card purchases, or electronic transactions.

What Are the Benefits of Checking Accounts?

When you earn money on a regular basis, you should have a place to put it. Most people use checking accounts. Not only is your money safe in the bank, but a checking account makes it easy to pay your bills. In order to use electronic banking and ATMs, you need a checking account.

If you keep all your money as cash, your cash may be lost or stolen. It's also difficult to pay bills with cash. A checking account is safe and convenient.

Opening an Account By shopping around, you can find an account that suits your situation. Ask questions about fees, interest rates paid on the checking account, charges for printing checks, and any restrictions on the number or size of checks you write. Find out the bank's **minimum balance requirement**, which is the amount of money you must keep in the account in order to avoid fees. Most banks charge a high fee for an **overdraft**, a check or other withdrawal for more than the existing account balance.

You'll need several documents to open an account. Most banks require two forms of identification, one of which should have your photo on it. You must provide your Social Security number, address, and phone number. The bank may also ask for a personal or work reference. The money for an initial deposit may be in the form of cash or a check.

Figure CPF 2 Writing a Check

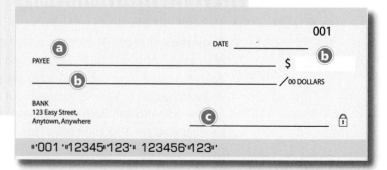

a Write the full name of the person or business receiving the check.

b Enter the amount in numbers and then in words on the next line.

c Sign the check to make it valid. Never sign a blank check.

What's the Difference Between an ATM Card and a Debit Card?

Once you have a checking account, you have several options for making deposits and withdrawals. You could go to the bank, but that can be time-consuming, and some banks charge a fee for using a human teller. Instead, automated teller machines (ATMs) give you access to your checking account.

At ATMs Both ATM cards and debit cards allow you to use an ATM to access your checking account. You can withdraw cash, deposit cash or checks, or transfer money between linked accounts. Both cards require that you enter your personal identification number (PIN) when you use the ATM.

Using an ATM can cost you money. Most ATMs charge a service fee unless you have an account with that bank. Fees range from $1 to $3 or more. To avoid this expense, learn where your bank has ATMs near your home, school, and workplace.

At Stores You can also use ATM and debit cards at businesses to purchase goods and services. However, debit cards can be used like a credit card—the business swipes your card and you sign for the purchase. With an ATM card, the business must have a keypad for you to enter your PIN. In either case, the money comes directly out of your account. Some stores let you get cash back—with no additional charge—when you make a purchase. For example, if you buy $20 worth of groceries, you can charge your ATM or debit card $50 and receive the $30 difference in cash.

Register all the transactions you make with your ATM or debit card in your checkbook. These transactions will be recorded on the monthly account statement that the bank will send to you, but keep track of them as you go along to avoid overdrawing your account.

Check It Out!

☑ Research banking services at several banks.

☑ Immediately record your deposits and withdrawals—including checks, cash withdrawals, and purchases—in your checkbook register.

☑ Review your bank statement every month.

APPLICATION Checking Accounts

1. How is a debit card different from an ATM card?

2. **Finding a bank** Using the Internet, research checking accounts at three banks in your neighborhood. Create a table comparing the services offered and fees charged by the banks. Then write a paragraph identifying the bank you would choose if you wanted to open an account and why you would choose it.

1.3 Saving and Investing

What are your dreams? Do you want to go to college, to travel, to own a car and a home, or perhaps to retire early? Saving some of your income each month can help you achieve your dreams. Accidents and unforeseen problems happen to everyone, so it is good to have an emergency fund, too. When you save your money at a bank or invest in a company, they pay you for the privilege of using your funds. If you save and invest wisely, your money will grow, and you won't have to work as hard to achieve your dreams.

What Are the Benefits of Savings Accounts?

Savings accounts allow you to save money for future expenses. Your money grows in a savings account because banks pay **interest**, a fee for the use of your money. To open a savings account, you'll need the same kinds of identification and other information that you needed to open a checking account.

Types of Accounts Banks and credit unions offer a variety of savings accounts including standard accounts, money market deposit accounts, and certificates of deposit (CDs). The minimum balance, interest rates, and other features vary by type of account. Some banks offer better rates than others, so it's important to shop around for the best deal.

Deposits in these accounts are insured by the government. If the bank should fail, the Federal Deposit Insurance Corporation (FDIC) would make sure you got your money back. The FDIC insures each depositor up to $100,000 at each bank. Retirement accounts are insured up to $250,000.

Unlike stocks, bonds, and many other investments, you are guaranteed to get a positive return on your money in a government-insured account. Figure CPF 3 summarizes the features of the most common types of accounts used for savings.

QUICK REFERENCE

Interest is the price paid for the use of money.

Figure CPF 3 Government-Insured Accounts

Standard Savings Account	Money Market Account	Certificate of Deposit
A standard savings account requires a small initial deposit and allows you the most access to your money. However, it pays the lowest rate of interest.	A money market account pays higher interest and allows you to write a limited number of checks. But it also requires a higher minimum balance.	Certificates of Deposit (CDs) usually offer the highest interest rates. But you pay a penalty if you withdraw any money before the CD matures.

When Should I Start Investing?

The purpose of saving is to accumulate readily available cash. Most financial advisors recommend saving an emergency fund that would cover three to six months of expenses. After you have created your emergency fund, you can begin saving for short-term goals such as buying a car or paying for college tuition.

The purpose of investing is to build wealth—that is, to acquire assets that will grow in value over time and give you a pool of assets beyond the income you earn from a job. Building wealth comes from making your money work for you over a long period of time. It is never too early to start this process, even if you can only allocate a small portion of your income to investment. Investing even small amounts on a regular basis over a long period of time can lead to significant growth.

Before saving or investing, pay off any credit card debt. It is almost impossible to earn more from your investments than you are paying in interest on your debt. For example, if you are paying 15 percent interest on a loan, it doesn't make sense to put some of your money in a savings account that only pays 3 percent interest. Pay off the expensive loan first, then start saving.

Determining Risk As you learned in Chapter 11, there is an inverse relationship between risk and return—the riskier the investment, the greater the potential return. Figure CPF 4 shows this relationship, with the least risky investments at the bottom of the graph and the riskiest ones at the top.

Savings accounts and CDs carry little or no risk because the government insures the principal, and they pay a guaranteed rate of interest. Treasury bonds carry little risk because the U.S. government backs them. Corporate bonds carry greater risk because a company may go bankrupt and be unable to repay its creditors. Stocks offer higher possible returns but are subject to market risks and may decrease rather than increase in value.

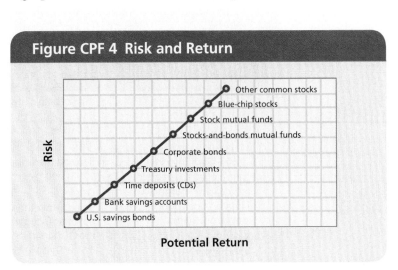

Figure CPF 4 Risk and Return

Risk (vertical axis), Potential Return (horizontal axis)

- Other common stocks
- Blue-chip stocks
- Stock mutual funds
- Stocks-and-bonds mutual funds
- Corporate bonds
- Treasury investments
- Time deposits (CDs)
- Bank savings accounts
- U.S. savings bonds

How Should I Invest?

Consider your investment objective when choosing the type of investment. If you want to use the money to buy a house in five years, you would choose a different type of investment than if you are investing for your retirement. Generally, the sooner you plan to use the money, the more conservatively you should invest. Conversely, the longer you have before you need the money, the easier it will be to recover from any downturns. Figure CPF 5 shows different ways of investing to reach long-term goals.

There are three basic rules for building wealth: start early, buy and hold, and diversify.

Start Early By starting to invest early you have a longer time for wealth to build. A longer investment time frame also allows you to take more risks, because you can ride out the fluctuations in the market.

Buy and Hold The phrase "buy and hold" describes a disciplined approach to investing. Do research and talk to a financial adviser to make wise decisions, and then hold the investments you make for a long enough period of time to allow your wealth to build. Jumping in and out of the market can lead to significant losses of potential return.

Diversify Diversifying helps you maximize your returns and limit risks. You've probably heard the saying "Don't put all your eggs in one basket." Putting your money in different types of investments allows you to choose different levels of risk.

Figure CPF 5 Investment Options

Stocks, Bonds, and Mutual Funds	Employer-Sponsored Retirement Plans	Individual Retirement Accounts (IRAs)
• Stocks let you share in corporate profits. • Government and corporate bonds pay a fixed rate of interest. • Mutual funds are an easy way to invest in a large number of different stocks or bonds. • See Chapter 11 for more information.	• 401(k) plans let workers invest money for retirement and defer taxes. Employers may also contribute. • Pension plans are controlled by employers. • Employers may fund employee retirement benefits through profit sharing or stock ownership plans.	• Workers may invest money each year for retirement, tax deferred. • Traditional IRA contributions may be tax deductible. • Roth IRA contributions are not tax deductible but earn tax-free income. • Funds must be held until age 59½—with some exceptions.

FIGURE CPF 6 THE POWER OF COMPOUNDING

Year	Annual Investment (in dollars)	5 Percent Return (in dollars)	Year-end Balance (in dollars)
1	2,000.00	100.00	2,100.00
2	2,000.00	205.00	4,305.00
3	2,000.00	315.25	6,620.25
4	2,000.00	431.01	9,051.26
5	2,000.00	552.56	11,603.82
6	2,000.00	680.19	14,284.01
7	2,000.00	814.20	17,098.21
8	2,000.00	954.91	20,053.12
9	2,000.00	1,102.66	23,155.78
10	2,000.00	1,257.79	26,413.57

FIGURE CPF 7 BUILDING WEALTH OVER TIME

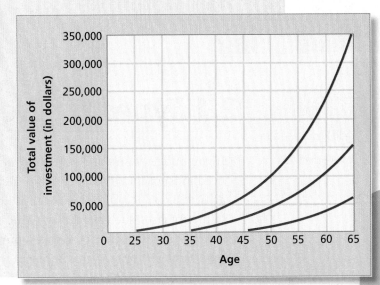

CONSUMER & PERSONAL FINANCE

What Are the Benefits of Starting Early?

Figures CPF 6 and CPF 7 graphically illustrate the benefits of starting your investment program when you are young. The table, Figure CPF 6, shows how a savings account that pays 5 percent interest would grow. Investing $2,000 each year for 10 years—a total of $20,000—yields a balance of more than $26,000 through the benefits of compounding and reinvesting the earnings. If the investments continued at the same pace for 45 years, the total balance would reach almost $1 million.

The graph, Figure CPF 7, shows the benefits of starting to save for retirement early. The graph shows what happens to three people who invest $100 per month in a retirement account. It assumes they receive a return on their investments of 8 percent, which approximates the historical average return for the stock market. Someone who begins investing $100 per month at age 25 has over twice as much at retirement as someone who waits until age 35 and almost six times as much as someone who waits until age 45.

Check It Out!
✔ Make regular contributions to your savings account.
✔ Commit to investing for the long term.
✔ Diversify your investments.

Interactive ⏪Review

Review Budgeting and Money Management using interactive activities at **ClassZone.com**

APPLICATION Saving and Investing

1. Suppose you have saved $1,000 toward the purchase of a car. Which type of savings plan would be best for this money until you are ready to use it? Why?

2. **Listing Financial Goals** Make a list of financial goals you might want to reach by the time you are 30 years old, then 50 years old, then at retirement age. Think about a plan that might help you achieve these goals. What sort of investments will you make? Write a summary paragraph describing your goals and plans.

Budgeting and Money Management 581

2 | Credit

2.1 Types of Credit

If you budget wisely and save your money, you will be able to buy what you need most of the time. But sometimes, waiting to accumulate the money to achieve a goal is not the best economic choice. Using credit to make important purchases, such as a college education or a home, often has economic benefits. If you decide to finance a purchase by using credit, you first need to decide what type of credit to use.

What Is Credit?

Credit is the practice of buying goods or services now and paying for them in the future. One form of credit is a **loan**, which is borrowed money that must be repaid with interest. Just as banks pay you interest for the use of your money in a savings account, you have to pay them interest if you want to use their money to buy something.

Loans are usually used for large purchases such as a home, automobile, or school tuition.

Credit cards are like short-term loans, because they allow you to buy things without having the cash at the time of purchase. But you will be charged interest if the credit card balance is not paid in full each month, and credit cards usually charge higher interest rates than other loans.

REMEMBER THAT NEAT CREDIT CARD YOU FOUND WHEN THE INTEREST WAS SO LOW?

GOLLY!

RATE HIKES

WWW.CAGLECARTOONS.COM

How Much Does Credit Cost?

The cost of credit is called the **finance charge**. It includes the total amount of interest you will pay plus any service charges. The amount of interest you pay depends on the **annual percentage rate (APR)**, the length of the loan, and how often you make payments. With all of these variables, it can be challenging to figure out how much a loan actually costs. But all lenders are

Figure CPF 8 Costs of Borrowing $10,000

Loan	APR (in percent)	Length of Loan (in months)	Monthly Payment (in dollars)	Total Payments (in dollars)	Finance Charge (in dollars)
A	4	36	295.24	10,628.63	628.63
B	8	36	313.36	11,281.11	1,281.11
C	8	60	202.76	12,165.89	2,165.89

required to tell you the total finance charges and the APR. This information should allow you to understand how much a loan will cost and to compare offers from different lenders.

For example, suppose you want to borrow $10,000 to purchase a car. The finance charge will vary depending on the length of the loan and the interest rate. As you can see in Figure CPF 8, a longer loan might have a lower monthly payment, but it will also have the highest total cost.

How Do Lenders Decide If I Can Get Credit?

Lenders use three basic criteria to determine if you are creditworthy and can be trusted to repay a loan. The criteria—character, capacity, and capital—are often referred to as the three Cs. These three criteria are based on your past, present, and future financial situation.

Character refers to your past record of paying your bills on time. Lenders want to know if you can live within your means, which makes it more likely that you will be able to repay the loan. When you make car payments on time or pay off a department store charge card each month, you build a positive credit history. These actions show that you are financially responsible.

Capacity refers to your level of income relative to the size of the loan. A lender will check to see if you have a steady income and if the amount of your income is enough to make the loan payments. The lender may look at your past employment history to see if you are likely to keep your current job or may check with your employer to see if your income will remain steady over the projected term of the loan.

Capital—specifically, financial capital—includes your income, savings, and other investments. Lenders will consider how much money you have in the bank as well as assets such as a car or house. If you fail to repay the loan, the lender may be able to take these assets to recover the cost of the loan.

If you are weak on any of these criteria a lender might ask for a cosigner for the loan. A **cosigner** is a person who will assume responsibility for the debt if you fail to repay the loan. Taking out a loan with a cosigner but repaying it yourself is one way you can build up a positive credit history.

QUICK REFERENCE

A **cosigner** assumes responsibility for debt if a borrower doesn't repay.

What Should I Consider When Choosing a Credit Card?

Credit card companies are eager to get young adults to use their cards. But these companies offer a variety of terms, and some of them can be costly. Before you apply for a credit card, carefully examine the terms.

Annual Fee Many cards have no annual fee, but some charge $60 per year or more for membership.

Interest Rate The Truth in Lending Act requires that credit card companies state the interest rate in the form of an annual percentage rate (APR). Rates may be fixed, meaning that they will stay the same, or variable, meaning that they are tied to an index and likely to change frequently.

Grace Period The grace period is the time between your billing date and the date your payment is due. Late payments may result in stiff fees.

Minimum Payment The minimum payment may be a flat amount or a certain percentage of your balance. Paying this amount allows you to avoid paying penalties, but not interest.

Credit Limit The credit limit is the maximum amount you can charge. Your available credit is your credit limit minus any outstanding balance.

Other Fees There are usually fees for paying late or for spending over your credit limit. There may be a minimum finance charge or amount of interest due, or transaction fees for cash advances.

Bonuses Many credit cards offer to give you a bonus based on how much you charge as an incentive to use the card. Some cards offer "cash back"—a refund of a small percentage of your total purchases. Others offer discounts on merchandise or air travel.

What Should I Know About My Credit Card Statement?

When you pay by credit card, you will receive a record of what you have spent each month called a statement. It will also show any payments or credits to your account. Check your credit card statement right away to make sure all the purchases shown are ones that you made. Also check to be sure the credit card company received your last payment.

Figure CPF 9 points out some of the important information to notice on your credit card statement. Your new balance is the amount you must pay by the due date to avoid paying interest. The finance charge is the interest due on any unpaid balance from your last statement. Notice that the minimum payment is only a small percentage of your new balance. Credit card companies make money if you pay less than the full balance, because they charge you interest on the rest of your balance.

Figure CPF 9 Understanding Your Credit Card Statement

(a) The new balance includes all of your purchases for the month, plus any unpaid balance from the last month and interest, plus any fees. To avoid finance charges, pay the entire balance by the due date.

(b) If you cannot pay the entire balance, pay at least the minimum balance by the due date to avoid late fees. The minimum balance may be only a small percentage of your total balance but is usually at least $10.

(c) The periodic rate is the daily interest rate, that is, the APR divided by the number of days in the year.

CREDITCard PLATINUM _____ BILLING STATEMENT

CARD NUMBER	CREDIT LIMIT	AVAILABLE CREDIT	STATEMENT DATE	NEW BALANCE	PAYMENT DUE	MINIMUM PAYMENT DUE
1234 5678 9012 3456	2,000.00	1,954.83	04/25/10	45.17	05/20/10	15.00

TRANSACTION REFERENCE NUMBER	TRANSACTION DESCRIPTION	TRANSACTION CHARGE DATE	ACTUAL POST	CHARGES (+)	CREDITS (−)
0123	MANGO GROVE JUICE & NUT BAR	03/26	03/28	13.76	
6543	BART'S COSMIC COMICS	03/30	04/01	25.41	
8901	MONTCLAIR VIDEO MART	03/31	04/03	6.00	

FINANCE CHARGE CALCULATIONS

ANNUAL PERCENTAGE RATE	DAILY PERIODIC RATE
13.65%	0.037397%

FINANCE CHARGE SCHEDULE

CATEGORY	DAILY PERIODIC RATE	CORRESPONDING APR
CASH ADVANCES		
A. BALANCE TRANSFERS, CHECKS	0.037397%	13.65 %
B. ATM, BANK	0.065041%	23.74 %
PURCHASES	0.037397%	13.65 %

DAYS IN BILLING CYCLE: 30

PREVIOUS BALANCE	−	PAYMENTS	−	CREDITS	+	PURCHASES	+	CASH ADVANCES	+	PERIODIC RATE FINANCE CHARGE	+	CASH ADVANCE FINANCE CHARGE	=	NEW BALANCE
53.26		53.26		0.00		45.17		0.00		0.00		0.00		45.17 (a)

TO REPORT LOST OR STOLEN CARD(S) CALL: (800) 555 5555

NOTICE: SEE REVERSE FOR IMPORTANT INFORMATION

Pay at least the minimum balance by the due date. Most credit card companies charge high fees for late payments. Allow time for your payment to arrive and be processed before the due date.

How Is a Credit Card Different from a Debit Card?

Both cards can be used to make purchases. But when you use a credit card you create a loan to repay, while a debit card takes money directly from your checking account. You can use your debit card to get cash from your checking account at an ATM. But if you use your credit card to get cash, you are essentially taking out a loan. Interest begins accruing right away on the amount of the cash advance, and most cards charge an additional transaction fee. It is a very expensive way to get cash.

Check It Out!
✔ Determine all costs and fees for a credit card or loan.
✔ Check your statement every month for unauthorized expenses.
✔ Pay on time.

APPLICATION Types of Credit

1. What are the three Cs, and who uses them?

2. Determining the Best Offer Suppose you have offers from three credit card companies. Company A offers a fixed APR of 12 percent and has an annual fee of $60.00. Company B has no annual fee and offers an introductory rate of 9 percent—but it rises to 18 percent after the first 3 months. Company C offers a fixed APR of 15 percent with an annual fee of $30. If you pay off your balance each month, which offer is best for you?

2.2 Credit Reports

How you handle your finances can determine your ability to qualify for a loan or credit card, to be hired for a job, or to rent an apartment. Your credit report contains much of the information on the three Cs discussed earlier.

What's a Credit Report?

A **credit report** is a statement by a credit bureau that details a consumer's credit record. Equifax, Experian, and Trans Union are the three companies that handle most credit reporting. The report includes information on your employment, bank accounts, and credit history. It will also indicate if you've had any legal problems regarding your finances, such as bankruptcy. The report shows how well you have handled your financial obligations over the previous 7 to 10 years so lenders can determine if you are a good credit risk.

Credit agencies use the information in your credit report to assign you a **credit score**, a number that rates your credit worthiness. Different agencies use different scoring systems, but higher scores indicate a better credit history. Lenders may charge a lower interest rate to someone with a high credit score.

QUICK REFERENCE

A **credit report** describes a consumer's credit record.

A **credit score** is a number that summarizes your credit worthiness.

Where Do I Get My Credit Reports?	
online:	www.annualcreditreport.com
phone:	1-877-322-8228
mail:	Annual Credit Report Request Service P.O. Box 105281 Atlanta, GA 30348-5281 (print form at www.annualcreditreport.com)

Do not contact the three nationwide consumer credit reporting companies directly for free reports.

Credit Report Users Lenders evaluate your credit report when you apply for a loan or a credit card. Buying the report from one of the three major companies saves them the time of contacting all your creditors to see how well you've paid your bills. Landlords may also check your credit report before agreeing to rent you an apartment. Some employers check credit scores before hiring people. Because so many people rely on these reports, you should verify the accuracy of the information in the report. Checking your credit reports also helps guard against identity theft. (See 2.3 Identity Theft for more information on this topic.)

How Do I Get a Copy of My Credit Report?

The Fair Credit Reporting Act makes it easy to access your credit reports (see "Where Do I Get My Credit Reports?" sidebar). By law, you may use this service to order one free copy from each company every 12 months. You provide your name, address, Social Security number, and date of birth. You may be asked other questions to verify your identity.

The government is the only legitimate source for free credit reports.

Good Rating
- You pay bills in full
- You pay bills on time
- You can cover payments in case of emergency
- You can make payments if you lose your job

Danger
- More than 25 percent of your take-home pay goes to pay off debt
- You only make minimum payments
- You make payments after the due date
- You open new accounts because the old ones are maxed out
- Creditors harass you

Overextended
- Creditors repossess (take back) what you bought on credit
- Creditors garnish your wages (take money from your paycheck before you get it)
- You must declare bankruptcy

Avoid other sources that claim to offer free credit reports. Some of them want to sell you unnecessary services, and others want to steal your identity. Also avoid firms that promise to fix your credit rating. Only you can do that.

How Do I Solve Credit Problems?

The best cure is prevention. You can avoid credit problems by following your budget and paying off your bills on time. But if you recognize any of the signs of danger or overextension shown in Figure CPF 10, you can take action to avoid financial problems.

Self-Help These are the first steps for restoring your credit rating.
- Talk to your creditors and explain your situation and your desire to correct it.
- Cut up your credit cards and pay off your debts as soon as possible.
- Create a strict budget and follow it.

Professional Help If you are unable to resolve the problems yourself, see a professional counselor. Try nonprofit agencies first. The National Foundation for Credit Counseling can provide referrals. These agencies will provide services and help you to straighten out your debt problems.

Check It Out!
✔ Check your credit report yearly.
✔ Pay your bills on time.
✔ Watch for the danger signs, and act promptly to correct the problem.

APPLICATION Credit Reports

1. What groups might use your credit score?

2. **Paying Off Your Bills** Suppose you have a student loan, a car payment, and a credit card with debt. The student loan debt is $4,000 with interest at APR 8 percent. The car loan is $8,000 with APR of 4 percent. The credit card debt is $1,500 with APR of 18 percent. Your grandmother sends you a check for $1,000 for graduation. Which bill would you put the money towards?

2.3 Identity Theft

Your bank accounts, credit cards, and other financial tools are all tied to your name. You've seen what can happen if your credit report shows a poor credit history. What if a poor credit rating is not your fault?

What Is Identity Theft?

Identity theft is the use of personal information—such as Social Security numbers, credit card or bank account numbers—to commit fraud and other crimes. Identity thieves steal personal information to run up charges on existing accounts or to open new ones. They may withdraw money from your bank accounts, apply for loans, or use your telephone calling card. It takes victims weeks, months, and sometimes years to correct the damage done after their identity has been stolen.

How Can I Protect Myself?

If you know how these thieves operate, you can take measures to protect yourself. While some victims lose their identity through loss or theft of their wallet or purse, almost half of the victims don't know how the thief obtained their information. Here are some of the most common techniques.

Shoulder Surfing Identity thieves may watch you as you punch in a calling card or credit card number or your PIN. They might overhear you giving out an account number over the phone. Be conscious of those around you when you use an ATM or give out personal financial information.

Dumpster Diving Thieves look through the trash to find discarded credit card statements or other documents with financial information. Put such documents through a shredder before throwing them away.

Economics Update

Find an update on identity theft at **ClassZone.com**

Spamming or Phishing Identity thieves may send unsolicited e-mail (spam) that appears to be from a legitimate source. Or they may telephone and say there is a problem with your account or offer you some benefit if you confirm information.

Hacking Sometimes identity thieves will use programs that invade your computer and find your personal data. Or they might direct you to a fake Web site set up to look like that of a bank or other business. Security software can help prevent hacking, but you must pay attention when you give out credit card and other personal information over the Internet. Confirm that the site you visit is legitimate.

Where Do I Get More Information?

Department of Justice	www.usdoj.gov
Federal Trade Commission	www.consumer.gov or 1-877-ID-THEFT 1-877-(438-4338)
Consumer Action Web Site	www.consumeraction.gov

What If I Become a Victim?

If you learn that your personal information has been stolen, act immediately to limit the damage. Keep good records of all the steps you take. First, contact one of the three credit reporting companies to place a fraud alert on your credit report. The fraud alert will make it necessary for creditors to contact you before opening new accounts in your name. The Federal Trade Commission and Department of Justice Web sites (see "Where Do I Get More Information?" sidebar) provide toll-free phone numbers and Web site addresses for the credit reporting companies. When you notify one company it will notify the others to place a similar alert on their reports. Once you have placed such an alert, you may order free copies of your report to check for fraudulent activity.

Contact your creditors or banks to close out accounts that have been accessed by thieves or that have been opened without your permission. The FTC Web site also provides a form to dispute new accounts that you did not authorize. You may want to stop payment on any checks that have not cleared and change your ATM account and PIN number.

File a report with the police and get a copy of the report or the report number. Provide as much information as you can. The report will provide proof to your creditors or financial institutions that a crime has been committed. Also file a report with the FTC, which maintains a database of reported cases of identity theft.

Check It Out!

Remember the word SCAM.

☑ Be **S**tingy. Only give personal information to people you trust.

☑ **C**heck your bank and credit card statements regularly.

☑ **A**sk for your credit report every 12 months.

☑ **M**aintain careful records of all your financial accounts.

Interactive ← Review

Review Credit using interactive activities at **ClassZone.com**

APPLICATION Identity Theft

1. What are some ways that identity theft can occur?

2. Planning a Response Take a look in your wallet or purse. What items there could be the source of identity theft? How do you protect yourself from having these items stolen? Review how you would respond if these items were stolen.

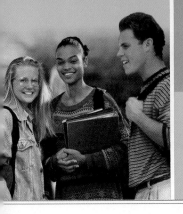

3 Wise Choices for Consumers

3.1 Buying a Car

A car is a symbol of freedom and independence. It is convenient to be able to travel where and when you want. Yet owning a car includes financial obligations. Since it's expensive to own a car, first consider whether you really need one. Is good public transportation, such as a bus or a train, available to get you to work or school? Do you live close enough to ride a bike or to walk? If you don't need a car most of the time, would it make sense to rent a car occasionally or to join a car sharing plan?

What Should I Consider When Buying a Car?

If a vehicle is definitely in your future, take your time before you make a purchase. A car is a major investment, so it makes sense to do some research. Use the information in Figure CPF 11 as a starting point.

One decision is whether to buy a new car or a used car. New cars cost a lot and **depreciate**, or decrease in value, quickly. On average a new car loses 10 percent of its value as soon as you drive it off the lot. The biggest advantage new cars have is that they are covered by warranties. If something goes wrong, you probably won't have to dip into your savings to pay repair bills.

A used car will cost less but may be less reliable. Many experts suggest that cars that are two to three years old offer the best value. Certified used cars come with limited warranties to cover certain major repairs.

How Can I Finance the Purchase of a Car?

If you have not saved enough for the total purchase price of a car, you might consider applying for a car loan. Investigate loans before you shop for the car, so that you will know how much you can afford to spend. Call banks and credit unions and check out online banks to find the best interest rate. Find out the length of available loans, total finance charges, and the amount of your monthly payment. Most lenders will require that you have a down payment on the loan. You may also need a cosigner for your loan.

Beware of financing packages offered by car dealers. Combining price negotiations with financing terms generally results in a good deal for the dealer, not for you.

Research

- Decide what kind of vehicle best suits your needs and budget.
- Use Internet or library resources to find out such information as gas mileage, repair costs, safety record, and prices.
- If it's a new car, find out what the dealer paid for the car so you can negotiate a good price.
- If it's a used car, look up the average resale value in a "blue book" (used car price guide).

Looking for cars

- Visit dealer lots when they are closed to get an idea of what's available without sales pressure.
- Ask family and friends about their car-buying experiences. See if they know a reliable dealer or anyone selling a car.
- Check out "for sale" ads in newspapers, on local bulletin boards, or on Web sites.
- Look for dealer ads in newspapers or on the Internet.

Used cars

- Check the odometer. Avoid cars with an average of 15,000 miles per year or more.
- Look for rust, dents, and signs of the car having been in an accident.
- Review the vehicle's repair record. Check for regular maintenance such as oil changes.
- Find the vehicle identification number (VIN), and use it to research the car's history through an Internet service.
- Take a test drive. Test the air conditioner, heater, radio, and other equipment.
- Pay a mechanic you trust to examine the car and to list what needs to be repaired.

The buying experience

- Always go prepared with the information you have gathered.
- Know which options you want and which ones you can live without.
- Get any offer in writing. That way you are very clear on the exact costs.

Check It Out!

- ✔ Consider whether you really need a car.
- ✔ Research the car and its price before you talk to a salesperson.
- ✔ Be sure you have all the necessary legal documents.

What Should I Do After I Buy a Car?

Each state has laws about vehicle titles, taxes, registration, and insurance. You can learn what is required from a car dealership or your state's motor vehicle department. Call several insurance agencies to find out how much insurance for your vehicle will cost (also see 3.3 Getting Insurance). Keep the title, sales receipts, and other important documents in a safe place—not in the glove compartment. Only the registration and proof of insurance should be carried in the vehicle.

APPLICATION Buying a Car

1. Why should you do research on vehicles before you talk to a dealer?

2. **Planning a Purchase** Choose a particular model of car, new or used. Go to the library or look on the Internet and find information about the car from at least three different sources. Try to learn as much as you can about the car's features, reliability, and pricing, and write down what you learn.

3.2 Financing Your Education

Choosing to go on to college or vocational or technical school after graduation from high school is one of the biggest economic decisions you will make. Getting more schooling will cost you money, but it will pay off in higher salaries and a greater lifetime income. As you learned in Chapter 9, each additional amount of education you receive increases your chances of earning a higher income. More highly educated workers are also less likely to be unemployed. Although the costs of higher education can be daunting, there are many alternatives to help finance your education.

How Do I Decide About Higher Education?

What type of higher education do you want? Choices include college, vocational school, and technical school. Costs at different types of schools vary widely and may influence the type of education you choose. Generally, public colleges are less expensive than private ones, and community colleges are less expensive than four-year schools. Consider your career goals, interests, and aptitudes, and think about what type of school offers the best value that meets your needs.

Do you want to start right after high school? If you want to take a year off, think about what you will do and who will provide your financial support. Consider your income and expenses during that time and what kind of help your parents might give you. Postponing education postpones your future higher earnings and may lead to increased education costs.

Where do you want to go for schooling? Are there schools in your state that would meet your needs? Out-of-state tuition is significantly higher than tuition at a public college in your own state. Going away to school generally means higher costs for housing, food, and travel, but it may be important for other reasons.

What Will Be the Total Cost of Going to School?

Paying for tuition to cover the costs of your coursework is just the beginning of school expenses. A variety of fees to cover student activities, connection to the school's computer network, and other costs are added to tuition. In the 2005–2006 school year, average tuition and fees ranged from about $2,200 at a public two-year college to about $5,500 at a public four-year college and more than $21,200 at a private four-year college. Room and board costs cover housing and food and average more than $6,600 per year at a public four-year college. You must also buy your textbooks, which may cost as much as $1,000 per year. Transportation for visits home as well as other personal expenses are also part of the costs of going to school.

Economics Update

Find an update on the cost of higher education at **ClassZone.com**

Where Can I Get the Money for Higher Education?

Once you have determined the costs of going to school, you can begin to make decisions about how to pay for your education. Here are some things to think about: Do I have the money to pay for it myself? Will my parents or family help me out? Can I work and study at the same time? Answers to these questions will help you decide if you need financial aid to go on to school.

All the costs of going to school can be daunting. Over 60 percent of students find that they need some financial help. In fact, most students pay much less than the published costs because of financial aid. There are three basic types of financial aid: grants and scholarships, loans, and work-study programs. Figure CPF 12 outlines the characteristics of each type of aid.

Figure CPF 12 Financial Aid Options

Grants	Scholarships	Loans	Work-Study Programs
• do not need to be repaid • usually based on need • sometimes based on academic merit • given by federal and state governments and colleges	• do not need to be repaid • usually based on academic merit or athletic or artistic ability • awarded by colleges, private groups, and the U.S. military	• must be repaid • federal loans for students • federal and private loans for parents • subsidized—based on need, some interest paid by government • unsubsidized—student pays all interest	• college helps student find a job • federal government helps pay the salary • earnings do not need to be repaid • students who work part-time often do better in school

CONSUMER & PERSONAL FINANCE

3 Wise Choices for Consumers

How Much Aid Can I Get?

In general, the amount of aid you receive is determined by the difference between the cost of attending school and the amount you and your family can contribute. Schools consider the following when awarding financial aid:

• Income—yours and your parents. This is the single most important factor in determining financial aid based on need. Students and families with higher incomes are expected to contribute more.

• Number of higher education students in your family. A family with more than one student in college would be expected to contribute less for each one.

• Family assets and expenses. Students are expected to contribute a higher percentage of their savings than parents are, so it's better to have more savings in parents' accounts. In general, schools do not consider the value of retirement funds, a home, or personal assets such as automobiles in figuring out a family's contribution. Some schools do consider these assets, so it's important to know how the schools you are interested in figure their aid awards. Unusual medical expenses and other large expenses may be considered in determining a family's contribution.

• Pool of aid dollars at the school you want to attend. Schools award aid based on a combination of federal, state, and school funds. A wealthy private school may have more funds available than a state school.

• Number of students applying for aid at the school you want to attend. Since each school has a limited amount of funds available for aid, if more students apply for aid there may be less available for each student. The level of need of the students applying might also affect how much individual students receive.

How Do I Apply?

Start Early Meet with your guidance counselor and request financial aid information from schools at least a year before you plan to start school. Begin to research scholarships. Make note of all application deadlines.

Get a PIN A personal identification number (PIN) allows you to submit your Free Application for Federal Student Aid (FAFSA) online for faster results. Go to www.pin.ed.gov.

Gather All the Documents You Need You'll need income tax returns and W-2 forms for you and your parents, as well as information on nontaxable income. You'll also need your Social Security number and driver's license number, along with bank statements and information on mortgage payments and investments.

Complete the FAFSA Fill out a paper form or go to www.fafsa.ed.gov to apply online. Follow the instructions carefully. You only need to complete one form, which will be used by all the schools to which you are applying.

Fill Out Any Additional Aid Forms These forms may be required for some nonfederal aid such as state and school aid or private scholarships. Ask for recommendations from your teachers and other adults who know you well at least a month before scholarship application deadlines. Provide them any necessary forms and a stamped envelope for the recommender to send to the school.

Review Your Student Aid Report (SAR) This report is the result of your FAFSA application. Make sure all the information is accurate. Your SAR shows your Expected Family Contribution (EFC), which determines your eligibility for federal student aid based on need.

Contact Schools' Financial Aid Offices Make sure all schools you've applied to received all the information they need.

Compare Your Aid Awards After you receive responses, decide which school's aid package offers the best combination of grants, scholarships, loans, and work-study.

Where Do I Get More Information?	
Federal Student Aid Information Center	studentaid.ed.gov 1-800-4-FED-AID (1-800-433-3243)
FAFSA on the Web	www.fafsa.ed.gov
The College Board	www.collegeboard.com
SallieMae® loans	www.salliemae.com
Your school guidance counselor and the financial aid offices of the schools you are considering also have information.	

Check It Out!

☑ Get forms in on time.

☑ Photocopy all information or print copies of online applications.

☑ Make sure information is consistent on all forms.

APPLICATION Financing Your Education

1. What criteria are used to determine who gets financial aid?

2. **Using a Decision-Making Grid** Using the questions on page 592 and a decision-making grid, determine which type of schooling makes the most economic sense for you.

3.3 Getting Insurance

Insurance protects people from the financial effects of unexpected losses. When you buy insurance coverage, your money joins a pool of money from many different people who face similar risks. The system works because the risk is spread over a large group of people. The chances of any one individual suffering a loss are small.

What Are the Benefits of Insurance?

Most people take out insurance for problems that may be unlikely but would be expensive if they happened: medical treatment for a serious illness or accident, repairing a car damaged in an accident, or replacing valuables stolen from your residence. Such losses are potentially so large that it would be difficult to save enough in an emergency fund to pay for them. Insurance protects you financially against those kinds of losses.

What Kinds of Insurance Should I Get?

When you buy an insurance policy you purchase a certain amount of protection or coverage. Your payment for this protection is called an insurance **premium**. Many types of insurance require you to pay a **deductible**, which is the amount you pay before the insurance company pays on a loss. Some health insurance requires a **co-pay**, an amount you must pay each time you receive health care under your policy. When you have a loss you submit a **claim**, which is a request for payment, to the insurance company.

Most people start out with car insurance, health insurance, and renter's or personal property insurance. There are other options as well. See Figure CPF 13 for an overview of the basic types of insurance.

Most states require that you carry at least a minimum amount of car insurance in case of injury or property damage caused by your car. Premiums are based on the type of vehicle, your age, your driving record, and other related information. The more coverage you have the more the insurance will cost. If you carry a high deductible, it will reduce the premium.

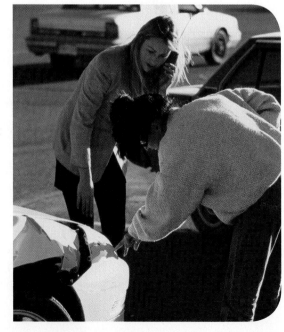

QUICK REFERENCE

A **premium** is amount paid for insurance.

A **deductible** is an amount paid by the insured before the insurance company pays.

A **co-pay** is an amount due when an insured receives health care.

A **claim** is a request for payment on an insured loss.

Figure CPF 13 Types of Insurance

Type of Insurance	Protects	Pays
Car	vehicle in case of accident or theft; occupants in case of accident	for property damage and bodily injury, legal costs, and related expenses
Health	policyholder in the event of illness or injury	for doctor and hospital visits, prescription drugs
Homeowner's	structures, land, and personal property	for damage due to fire, theft, or natural disaster
Renter's	personal property	for loss of or damage to personal items
Disability	income when a person cannot work	a percentage of income when a person is out of work due to injury or illness
Life	family when a wage-earner dies	money to the family to meet expenses after death

Health insurance is very costly. Your employer or school may offer insurance plans to cover some or all of your needs. In some states, you may be covered by your parents' health insurance until you graduate from college or reach age 25.

If you live in rented housing, you may want to protect your belongings with renter's insurance or with personal property insurance. Some policies cover the full replacement cost of insured items; others cover only the current value of the items. For example, actual cash value coverage will not cover the full cost of replacing a three-year-old bike that gets stolen.

Check It Out!

✔ Find out if you have insurance coverage at work or through your educational institution.

✔ See if your insurance covers the current value or the full replacement cost.

✔ Determine how much you can afford in deductibles.

What Questions Should I Ask an Insurance Agent?

• How much does the policy cover? Are there limits each year or for each accident or illness? Are there maximums for certain kinds of losses?

• What levels of deductibles are available? Higher deductibles lower the premiums.

• Are claims paid on actual cash value or on replacement value? The former may cost less, but you will receive less in the event of a loss.

• How often are premiums due—monthly or once or twice per year?

APPLICATION Getting Insurance

1. What reasons do people cite for getting insurance?

2. **Selecting Insurance** Explain how having insurance could help in each of the following situations. Case A: Your CD player and 10 CDs are stolen from your car. Case B: You have to have emergency surgery for a fractured leg. Case C: Your car is smashed up by a hit-and-run driver. The damage is well over $2,000.

3.4 Contracts: Reading the Fine Print

Buying insurance, taking out a loan, signing up for a credit card—all of these involve a formal, legally binding agreement known as a **contract**. The contract may be in the form of a signed document or may be executed on a Web site when you download something from the Internet. These terms and conditions are called the "fine print" because they are often set in small type.

Why Should I Read the Fine Print?

There's an old saying: "Education is when you read the fine print. Experience is what you get when you don't." By reading the fine print, you will understand exactly what you are agreeing to when you sign a contract. The fine print often contains information about extra charges and fees that may not be displayed in marketing brochures or advertisements.

Consider Michele, a student who signed a cell phone service contract without reading it. When the first bill arrived, it was over $1,000. She checked the contract and found fine print stating that all text messaging both sent and received was subject to a charge. Even though Michele hadn't read these terms, she had signed the contract, and she had to pay the bill.

What Should I Do Before Signing a Contract?

- First, actually read the contract. If it is long or complicated, ask for a copy and take it home to read.
- Clarify all terms or provisions you don't understand. In a cell phone contract, for example, be clear on peak and off-peak hours, roaming charges, and the cancellation policy. Ask questions until you understand everything clearly. If there are parts you can't figure out, get advice from a friend before signing.
- Check all figures in the contract. Bring a calculator and figure the costs yourself—don't depend on the salesperson's math.
- Make sure any mistakes or omissions are corrected on the contract and initialed by the salesperson.

Source: www.CartoonStock.com

"Sign here to indicate you have no idea what you've signed."

Figure CPF 14 A Cell Phone Contract

(a) Note how many minutes are included in the basic monthly price.

(b) Asterisks or footnotes often lead to small print that provides important information.

(c) If you exceed the allotted number of text messages, you pay a fee for each one.

(d) If you want to end your contract before it expires, you pay the cancellation fee.

(e) Your signature here shows that you have read and agree to the fine print.

CellPhone ——————— Service Agreement

Monthly calling plan	$24.95
Total minutes/month (peak)	**400** (a)
Unlimited off-peak	$5.95
Voice mail	Included* (b)
Additional minutes	$0.40/minute
Roaming charges (See coverage map and terms for details)	$1.00/minute
Text messaging	$3.95
Total outgoing messages/month	**100**
Additional outgoing messages	$0.10/each (c)
Incoming messages	Unlimited Free
Plus federal, state, and local taxes and fees	
Contract length	**24 months**
Cancellation fee	$150.00 (d)

(b) *Accessing voice mail through cellular phone accrues minutes like any other call.

I acknowledge that I have read and agree to the company's Terms and Conditions

(e) _____ (your signature)

What Should I Beware of?

• Don't let the salesperson rush you. Take your time and make sure you are certain of the terms of the contract. Even if the salesperson says certain desirable terms are about to expire, you should not sign anything you do not thoroughly understand and agree to.

• Never sign a contract with blank spaces. Make sure every blank on the contract is either filled in or marked through as being not applicable. If you leave blanks, someone might enter something after you sign that you did not want to agree to.

• Don't agree to verbal contracts. Make sure everything is in writing. If you agree to a verbal contract and run into a problem, you have no evidence of what the agreement was. Business agreements are generally too complex for either side to remember all the details.

• Don't leave without getting a copy of the contract. Keep the contract in a safe place. Check your first bill carefully to make sure everything matches the contract. If you have questions, call the company to resolve your concerns.

Check It Out!

✔ If it seems too good to be true, it probably is.

✔ Check all figures on the contract.

✔ Never sign a contract with blanks not filled in or crossed out.

Interactive ⟨◄⟩Review

Review Wise Choices for Consumers using interactive activities at **ClassZone.com**

APPLICATION Contracts

1. Why shouldn't you agree to a verbal contract?

2. **Evaluating an Offer** Study the ads or commercials for cell phone service. Suppose you are ready to sign a contract for cell phone service. Make a list of the questions you will ask before you sign the contract.

4 Getting Out on Your Own

4.1 Getting a Job

An important step to becoming an independent adult is getting a job. A job allows you to earn money, gain experience, and learn new skills. A career is more than a job. It is a work path that provides satisfaction, challenge, and opportunities for self-expression. Your first jobs help you learn about the world of work and what kind of career you might enjoy.

Where Can I Look for a Job?

Finding a job that suits your skills and helps advance you along your career path can be challenging. There are many sources of information about jobs, and the more you use, the better your chances of finding a good fit.

Friends and Family Talk to them to find out if they know of any job openings. They are the beginning of your network—people who will support you in what you attempt, and whom you support in turn.

School Guidance Counselor, or Career Planning or Placement Office These offices have listings of jobs and intern positions. You can also learn about different careers.

Internet Many Web sites offer job listings, places to post your resumé, and other services. America's Job Bank, managed through a partnership between federal and state governments, allows you to tap into career resources, look at job listings all over the country, and post a resumé.

Newspaper Want Ads Your local newspaper is a good source for jobs in your area.

Employment Agencies Your state and local governments may offer employment services. These public agencies often offer job counseling and training as well as job listings. Private agencies also offer job listings and placement, but they sometimes charge a fee for their services.

Job Fairs Job fairs offer the opportunity to talk to many employers in an area or a specific job category in a very short period of time.

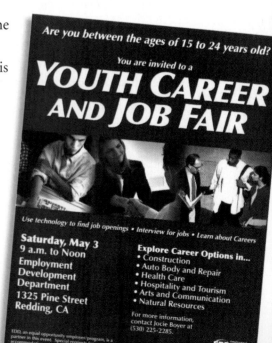

Are you between the ages of 15 to 24 years old?

You are invited to a

YOUTH CAREER AND JOB FAIR

Use technology to find job openings • Interview for jobs • Learn about Careers

Saturday, May 3
9 a.m. to Noon
Employment
Development
Department
1325 Pine Street
Redding, CA

Explore Career Options in...
• Construction
• Auto Body and Repair
• Health Care
• Hospitality and Tourism
• Arts and Communication
• Natural Resources

For more information, contact Jocie Boyer at (530) 225-2285.

EDD, an equal opportunity employer/program, is a partner in this event. Special requests for accommodation need to be made...

EDD

What Do I Need to Apply for a Job?

Before you apply for a job, you will need to prepare materials that introduce you to potential employers and tell them about your qualifications. You will need a resumé, a cover letter, and a list of references. References are people who know you and your work habits and are willing to talk to potential employers. Many jobs will also require that you fill out an application form.

Resumé A resumé is a record of your job history and education. It should be truthful and succinct—no more than one page long. Since employers judge you by your resumé, be sure it is visually appealing and free of errors. Figure CPF 15 shows a sample resumé for a recent high school graduate. If you apply for different kinds of jobs, you may want to develop more than one resumé.

Cover Letter A cover letter briefly explains why you want the job and how you are qualified for it. Address your letter to the specific individual who is

---

Cheryl A. Miller **(a)**
1909 E. Walnut St.
Long Beach, CA 90811
310-555-5678
camiller89@isp.net

(b) Objective To obtain an entry-level customer service position

Education Jefferson High School, 2003-2007

(c) Experience
September 2006–Present
Sales Associate, Electronics Super Center
· Advised customers on product features and helped them choose the ones that best met their needs
· Met or exceeded weekly sales quotas
· Developed promotional materials for in-store use
Summer 2006
Administrative Assistant, Oceanside Computer Center
· Tracked customer sales and repair orders to improve response time
· Responded to customer questions by phone and email
· Provided office support for staff of six
September 2005–June 2006
User support, Jefferson High computer lab
· Developed an orientation program for incoming students
· Helped students use a variety of software applications
· Led a workshop on Web page design

(d) Other Skills
· Proficient in a wide range of application software, including word processing, spreadsheet, database, and presentations
· Internet research

(e) Activities and Honors
· Member of varsity girls' track team
· Captain of debate team

References available upon request

Figure CPF 15
Writing a Resumé

(a) Include all the information an employer might need to contact you.

(b) Make your objective specific and succinct. Tailor it to the job you are applying for.

(c) List your work experience in reverse chronological order. Include volunteer work if you have little paid work experience. Focus on skills and accomplishments.

(d) List other skills you have that might be useful on the job, even if you have not been able to use them in previous jobs.

(e) Include a section that lists activities, honors, and community service.

designated to receive applications. Open your letter with a strong statement of your interest in this particular job. In the body of the letter, use information from your resume to explain why you are the best candidate. Close by restating your interest and indicate your intention to follow up to request an interview. Internet and library resources can give you samples of strong cover letters.

References Before you list someone as a reference, talk with him or her about your job hunt and ask their permission. The list of references should include the person's name, address (either business or home), telephone number, and an e-mail address, if they have one. It's also a good idea to indicate the person's position or relationship to you.

The people you choose as references should know you well enough to be able to describe your skills, experiences, and work habits. Choose people who will be enthusiastic about your abilities based on their experience with you. Typical references include former or current employers, teachers or coaches, or family friends who can vouch for your personal character. Stay in touch with your references during your job hunt. Let them know when they might expect to hear from an employer, and discuss what you would like them to emphasize when they are contacted.

Figure CPF 16 References

Cheryl A. Miller
1909 E. Walnut St.
Long Beach, CA 90811
310-555-5678
camiller89@isp.net

References

Barry Woods
Assistant Manager
Electronics Super Center
1234 Main St.
Long Beach, CA 90811
310-555-1357
bwoods@esc.com

Cynthia North
Director
Jefferson High Computer Lab
461 Grand Oak Boulevard
Long Beach, CA 90811
310-555-1234
c_north@jefferson.lb.ca.edu

Danielle Curran
Office Manager
Oceanside Computer Center
4916 Oceanside Road
Long Beach, CA 90812
310-555-2468
dmcurran@occ.com

Julie Barnes
Moderator
Jefferson High Debate Team
461 Grand Oak Boulevard
Long Beach, CA 90811
310-555-1345
j_barnes@jefferson.lb.ca.edu

How Can I Ace the Interview?

If an employer gets a good impression of you from your resume and cover letter, they may invite you to come in for an interview. The interview is a chance for the employer to learn more about you and for you to learn more about the job and the company.

The Company and the Job Do some research on the company to which you are applying. A company's Web site will tell you more about the organization, but you might also find newspaper articles with information about the company. This research will help you to confirm that you are interested in working for the company. It will also show the company that you cared enough about the job to do some investigating before the interview.

Use your research to prepare a set of questions about the organization and the job. Find out as much as you can about the job requirements and responsibilities before discussing such things as pay, hours, or benefits. In some cases, those topics may not come up until a later interview. Remember that both you and the employer want to confirm that you are a good fit for the job and the organization.

Presenting Yourself Be ready to answer questions about your qualifications and about how you will fit into the company. You may want to practice answering questions in front of a mirror or with a friend or family member. Make sure your answers are clear and succinct. Take time to think about your responses to unexpected questions. Books and online resources can provide examples of many common interview questions.

Dress appropriately for the job you are seeking. Don't show up to the interview in business attire if you are applying to work where you will get very dirty. By the same token, don't go to an interview for an office job dressed in jeans and a T-shirt. Always appear neat, clean, and well groomed.

Determine how long it will take to get to the interview. Plan to arrive about ten minutes early. Take weather conditions and traffic into consideration. If you are delayed, be sure to call and explain that you will be late.

Bring extra copies of your resumé and list of references. You may want to bring a pad of paper to take notes during the interview. Be sure to get the name and title of each person who interviews you.

Check It Out!

☑ Learn about the company where you are applying.

☑ Prepare a list of questions about the job and the company.

☑ Bring extra copies of your resumé and your list of references.

☑ Be on time for your interview.

Follow-Up Write a short thank-you note immediately after the interview to each interviewer. Thank the interviewer for spending time with you. If you still want the job, restate your interest in it. Refer to something you learned in the interview. Express your desire to learn more about the position.

APPLICATION Getting a Job

1. What is the purpose of a resumé?

2. **Writing Your Resumé** Study the resumé in this section. Prepare a personal resumé based on the model. Also assemble a list of people whom you might want to use as references.

4.2 Paying Taxes

Benjamin Franklin once said, "In this world nothing is certain but death and taxes." As you learned in Chapter 14, taxes provide the government with revenue to provide needed services. Recall that the Internal Revenue Service (IRS) is the government agency that collects the federal taxes owed by Americans. Most states also collect taxes. Taxes for the previous year must be paid by April 15 of the current year. For example, taxes for income earned in 2010 would need to be paid by April 15, 2011.

How Are My Taxes Determined?

The amount you pay in taxes is determined by your filing status and your taxable income. **Filing status** is based on your marital status or whether you have any dependents. A dependent is a child or relative in your household whom you support. People with more dependents have less tax withheld. Employers use the W-4 form, shown in Figure CPF 17, to determine your filing status for withholding taxes from your paycheck. You fill out a W-4 form when you begin a job. As long as you are still dependent on your parents, you claim only one withholding allowance.

The second determinant is your **taxable income**, which is the amount of income subject to taxation after all exemptions and deductions. The higher your income, the higher your taxes will be. Certain income may not be taxed. For example, money can be deducted from your paycheck before taxes to pay for health insurance. Income above a certain level is not subject to Federal Insurance Contributions Act (FICA) taxes for Social Security.

QUICK REFERENCE

Filing status is based on your marital status or support of dependents.

Taxable income is the income subject to taxation after exemptions and deductions.

Figure CPF 17 The W-4 Form

(a) Instructions help you determine how many allowances to claim. A single person with one job who is claimed as a dependent gets one allowance.

(b) Your Social Security number is required on all IRS forms.

G Child Tax Credit (including additional child tax credit):
- If your total income will be less than $55,000 ($82,000 if married), enter "2" for each eligible child.
- If your total income will be between $55,000 and $84,000 ($82,000 and $119,000 if married), enter "1" for each eligible child plus "1" **additional** if you have four or more eligible children.   **G** _____

H Add lines A through G and enter total here. (**Note.** This may be different from the number of exemptions you claim on your tax return.) ▶ **H** _____

For accuracy, complete all worksheets that apply.
- If you plan to **itemize or claim adjustments to income** and want to reduce your withholding, see the **Deductions and Adjustments Worksheet** on page 2.
- If you have **more than one job** or are **married and you and your spouse both work** and the combined earnings from all jobs exceed $35,000 ($25,000 if married) see the **Two-Earner/Two-Job Worksheet** on page 2 to avoid having too little tax withheld.
- If **neither** of the above situations applies, **stop** here and enter the number from line H on line 5 of Form W-4 below.

Cut here and give Form W-4 to your employer. Keep the top part for your records.

Form **W-4** — Department of the Treasury, Internal Revenue Service

Employee's Withholding Allowance Certificate

▶ Whether you are entitled to claim a certain number of allowances or exemption from withholding is subject to review by the IRS. Your employer may be required to send a copy of this form to the IRS.

OMB No. 1545-0074

20**06**

1 Type or print your first name and middle initial.   Last name   2 Your social security number

3 Home address (number and street or rural route)   ☐ Single ☐ Married ☐ Married, but withhold at higher Single rate.
Note. If married, but legally separated, or spouse is a nonresident alien, check the "Single" box.

City or town, state, and ZIP code   4 If your last name differs from that shown on your social security card, check here. You must call 1-800-772-1213 for a new card. ▶ ☐

5 Total number of allowances you are claiming (from line **H** above **or** from the applicable worksheet on page 2)   **5** ____

6 Additional amount, if any, you want withheld from each paycheck   **6** $ ____

7 I claim exemption from withholding for 2006, and I certify that I meet **both** of the following conditions for exemption.
- Last year I had a right to a refund of **all** federal income tax withheld because I had **no** tax liability **and**
- This year I expect a refund of **all** federal income tax withheld because I expect to have **no** tax liability.
If you meet both conditions, write "Exempt" here . . . . ▶ **7**

Under penalties of perjury, I declare that I have examined this certificate and to the best of my knowledge and belief, it is true, correct, and complete.
Employee's signature
(Form is not valid ...) ▶   Date ▶

Where Do I Get Tax Forms?

Federal and state tax forms are available starting in January each year at post offices (federal forms only), libraries, banks, and IRS or state tax offices. They are also available through official Web sites, or you can order forms through the mail or by phone. The first year you file taxes, you will need to find the forms yourself. After that, you should receive forms in the mail from the state and federal governments at the end of each year. If your tax situation changes significantly from the previous year, you may need to pick up additional forms.

Form 1040 Most young adults do not have to file complicated tax forms. Generally, the 1040EZ form should be sufficient for your federal taxes. This is a one-page form that has only 12 lines to fill out. The back of the form explains who is eligible to use it. See Figure CPF 18 for a sample of a 1040EZ form.

If you receive more than $1,500 in interest, you cannot use the 1040EZ form. Likewise, if you receive any dividends or other income from stocks, bonds, or similar investments, you cannot use 1040EZ. Instead, you will need to use form 1040A or 1040. These forms have related forms, known as schedules, for reporting investment income.

Most state tax forms are simple because they are based on the results you obtain from filling out your federal forms.

The W-2 Form The W-2 form shows how much you earned during the year and how much you paid in taxes through withholding. The form shows your total gross earnings and the amount of earnings subject to taxation. The amount withheld for each type of tax is also shown, including federal income tax, Social Security and Medicare taxes, and state and local taxes.

At the end of each year, any employer that you have worked for that year must send you a W-2 form. Employers must send the forms in time to arrive at your home by January 31. The W-2 will include copies to file with your federal, state, and local tax returns, as well as one copy for your files.

Other Forms When you have savings or investments, your bank or financial institution will send you other forms. Form 1099-INT for savings interest and form 1099-DIV for investment gains should arrive about the same time as your W-2.

How Do I Fill Out a Tax Form?

Instruction booklets are available in most locations where you find tax forms. You may also download them for free from the IRS or state tax Web sites or request them by mail or phone. The instructions will take you through the steps to fill out the form line by line. They will also provide additional background information that may be helpful, as well as telling you where to go if you need help. Perhaps most important, the instructions contain the tax tables that will tell you how much tax you have to pay once you have determined your taxable income.

Follow the step-by-step instructions to complete each form. Always use correct and verifiable numbers. Making up numbers is considered tax fraud, which can be punishable with severe penalties. Figure CPF 18 shows a sample of a 1040EZ form.

Figure CPF 18 Filling Out the 1040EZ

ⓐ Use your W-2 form(s) to find the amount to enter here.

ⓑ The 1099-INT form shows how much interest you earned.

ⓒ The amount you enter here depends on your filing status. If you are a dependent, you get the standard deduction but not the personal exemption.

ⓓ The amount of tax withheld is found on your W-2 form along with earnings.

ⓔ If you had more withheld than you owe in taxes, you will get money back in the form of a refund. If you didn't have enough withheld, you will have to pay the amount you still owe to the IRS.

How Do I File My Taxes?

Everyone who receives more than a certain amount of income during the year must file a tax return. Check the tax form instructions or the IRS Web site to determine if you are required to file. Even if you don't owe money, you must file a form if you meet the requirements. And, of course, you will not receive a refund for excess taxes withheld unless you file a tax return. See the "What if I get stuck?" sidebar to find out how to receive help with your taxes.

Before you send in your forms, double check your work. Confirm that you have entered the correct Social Security number; that your income, withholding, and tax figures are correct; and that you have signed your forms. Then make a photocopy of the forms for your own records.

When everything is ready, you can mail all the paperwork to the IRS service center listed on your form. You can also file your tax forms electronically. Electronically filed returns are generally more accurate, and refunds are processed more quickly. The IRS has formed a partnership with several tax software companies to offer the Free File service that allows most taxpayers to prepare and file their taxes electronically for free. You can find more information and instructions on e-filing options on the IRS Web site.

After you file your return, be sure to keep all your forms and copies in a safe place. Keep your tax returns and all related documents for at least three years—the limit if the IRS wants to contest your return.

Mistakes The IRS and state tax auditors usually catch simple math mistakes and inform you of them. They then recalculate your taxes and adjust the amount of your refund or taxes owed. If you discover a major error or omission on your form after you submit it, file an amended return as soon as possible. You must file an amended return within three years of the time when the original return was filed. You may have to pay a penalty depending on the type of error involved.

WHAT IF I GET STUCK?

- Ask a parent or other trusted adult. Most have many years of experience filling out tax forms.

- For federal tax help, go to the IRS Web site. For state tax help use the name of your state and the key words *tax help* to find the Web site.

- For additional help, call the local IRS office (1-800-829-1040) or your state tax office.

CONSUMER & PERSONAL FINANCE

Check It Out!

☑ The filing deadline is April 15, every year.

☑ Check everything on your form carefully before submitting it.

☑ Save your forms and copies for at least three years.

APPLICATION Paying Taxes

1. Where can you go to get tax forms?

2. Preparing to Do Your Taxes Make a list of the documents and information you will need to file federal and state income tax forms. Decide on a location where you will keep the list and the information until it is time to file your taxes.

4.3 Finding an Apartment

Most young adults will rent an apartment when they start out on their own because apartments are an affordable type of housing. Moving out of your parents' home or out of a college dormitory into an apartment will give you more freedom. But it also means more responsibilities. You will have to pay monthly bills, shop for groceries, fix meals, clean your apartment, and do laundry. With a little effort, you can find an apartment that suits you.

What Should I Consider About Renting an Apartment?

How much should I spend? Your housing expenses should amount to no more than about one-fourth to one-third of your take-home pay. These expenses include not only your rent, but also utilities, cable, and any other housing costs. Spending a higher proportion of your income on housing may not leave you enough to meet your other expenses or to have the money you want to enjoy life.

Should I live by myself or with roommates? If one-third of your take-home pay only pays rent for a storage locker, you may want to consider sharing a larger apartment with one or more roommates. Roommates can make living in an apartment cheaper and more fun, but they can become a problem if they are irresponsible or have a lifestyle that clashes with your own. Think about how to balance the desire for privacy and your own space with the desire for companionship and help with household expenses and chores. If you decide to live with roommates, consider looking for an apartment together. That way, everyone can commit to the same place, and people will be less likely to grow dissatisfied and leave.

How do I choose roommates? Look for individuals you are compatible with, whose personalities and lifestyles are similar to your own. Roommates should be people you can count on, whether it's to pay their share of the rent or to do their share of household chores. Living with other people can bring up conflicts about how to share expenses, use the living space, and keep it clean. You and your roommates will need to communicate to resolve such issues. Consider drawing up an agreement together that spells out the rules that everyone must obey and the responsibilities that each roommate accepts.

Location
- Is it convenient to where you work?
- Is there nearby public transportation or parking?
- Are there grocery stores, self-service laundries, or other stores you need nearby?
- Is the neighborhood safe?

The Building
- Is it clean and well taken care of?
- Do the other tenants seem friendly?
- Are the lobby and stairwells safe?
- Are there sufficient parking spaces, laundry facilities, or bike rooms?

Space
- Is there enough room for the number of people living in the apartment?
- Is it suitable for your way of life?
- Are all the roommates happy with the living space and available storage?

Furnished or Unfurnished
- Do you want it furnished with furniture or do you want to use your own furniture?
- Can you get used furniture from family or friends or purchase inexpensive furniture?
- Does the apartment include appliances, such as a stove and refrigerator?

What Do I Need to Know About Signing a Lease?

- A **lease** is a contract for renting an apartment for a specific period of time. The contract is between you and your **landlord**, who is the owner of the rental property. A lease is a legal document that obligates you to pay rent and to follow certain rules for a specific period of time. The landlord has responsibilities as well. If you have roommates, whoever signs the lease is responsible even if other roommates fail to pay their part of the rent.

- You may be asked for the first and last months' rent, a security deposit, and possibly cleaning and key fees. When you move out, the landlord will inspect the property and return some or all of the security deposit and fees, depending on what repairs need to be done.

- You may need to provide character references—name, address, and phone number. Generally you should use three people who are not relatives, such as teachers, employers, or supervisors of volunteer work, who can vouch for you.

- You must provide your Social Security number and bank information. If you are employed you will provide employment information.

- If this is your first apartment or you are not employed, you may be asked to have a responsible adult act as a cosigner. This ensures that the landlord will be paid the rent due if you fail to pay.

QUICK REFERENCE

A **lease** is a contract for renting an apartment.

A **landlord** is the owner of rental property.

Check It Out!

- ✔ Provide a list of references.
- ✔ Be prepared for up-front costs such as a security deposit.
- ✔ Look at several places before committing to an apartment.

Interactive ⟨⟩Review

Review Getting Out on Your Own using interactive activities at **ClassZone.com**

APPLICATION Finding an Apartment

1. What is a lease?

2. Analyzing Your Needs Decide if you would prefer to live alone or with others. If you prefer to live alone, write a paragraph explaining your decision. If you would like to live with others, create a list of roommate rules and responsibilities.

Reference Section

McDougal Littell
ECONOMICS
Concepts and Choices

Math Handbook

Table of Contents

Refer to the Math Handbook when you need help with the mathematical concepts that you might encounter in your study of economics.

1.1 Working with Decimals and Percents

Understanding the Skill

A decimal is a number that uses the base-ten value system where a decimal point separates the ones' and tenths' digits. Each place value is ten times the place value to its right. For example, 5.2 is five and two tenths and 12.45 is twelve and forty-five hundredths.

The word *percent* means "per hundred." For example, 5 percent means "5 per 100," or 5/100. If 5 percent of the population is unemployed, then, on average, 5 out of 100 people are unemployed.

To write a decimal as a percent, multiply by 100 percent. To write a percent as a decimal, divide by 100 percent.

Example 1: A company's February sales were 0.125 of its total annual sales. Express this as a percentage.

$$0.125 = 0.125 \times 100\% \qquad \text{Multiply by 100 percent.}$$

$$= 12.5\% \qquad \text{Move the decimal point two places to the right.}$$

Check your answer: 12.5 should be larger than 0.125 because you multiplied by 100.

Example 2: A company's workforce was 105 percent of what it was a year earlier. Express this as a decimal.

$$105\% = \frac{105\%}{100\%} \qquad \text{Divide by 100 percent.}$$

$$= \frac{105}{100} \qquad \text{Cancel the \% signs.}$$

$$= 1.05 \qquad \text{To divide by 100, move the decimal point 2 places to the left.}$$

Check your answer: 1.05 should be smaller than 105 because you divided by 100.

Applying the Skill

1. In 2002, the total personal income in the United States was $8.922 trillion and the total personal taxes were $1.112 trillion. What percent of income were taxes? Round your answer to the nearest hundredth.

2. The GDP of the United States is $11.750 trillion and the GDP of the world is $55.500 trillion. What percent of the world's GDP is from the United States? Round your answer to the nearest tenth.

1.2 Calculating Averages

Understanding the Skill

There are three ways to express the average of a group of numbers. The most common way is to divide the total by the number of values. This kind of average is called the *mean.*

Mean, Median, and Mode Notice that, in Example 1, most workers earn much less than the mean of $27,000; the mean doesn't describe typical earnings well. Typical earnings are often described better by the two other kinds of average: the mode and the median. To determine the mode and the median of a group of numbers, write the numbers in order from smallest to largest. The *mode* is the most common value. The *median* is the middle value. If the number of values is even, the median is the mean of the two middle values.

Example 1: The annual earnings of five workers are shown below. Calculate the mean earnings.

   $14,000 $18,000 $14,000 $75,000 $14,000

Solution

Divide the total by the number of values. There are five numbers to average, so the number of values is 5.

$$\text{Mean} = \frac{\text{Total}}{\text{Number of values}}$$

$$= \frac{135,000}{5} \qquad \text{\textit{Simplify the numerator.}}$$

$$= \$27,000 \qquad \text{\textit{Divide.}}$$

The workers have mean   *Answer the question.*
earnings of $27,000

Example 2: Find the mode and the median of the earnings in Example 1.

Solution

Write the values in order from smallest to largest.

   $14,000 $14,000 $14,000 $18,000 $75,000

The most common value is $14,000, so the mode is $14,000.

   $14,000 $14,000   **$14,000** $18,000 $75,000

The middle value is also $14,000, so the **median** is $14,000.

Applying the Skill

Calculate the mean, the median, and the mode of each group of numbers.

1. $40,000 $32,000 $38,000 $40,000 $40,000

2. $80,000 $50,000 $35,000 $35,000 $40,000 $60,000

1.3 Calculating and Using Percents

Understanding the Skill

As you recall, the term *percent* means "per hundred." For example, 25% is 25/100. To change a decimal to a percent, move the decimal point two places to the right and add the % symbol.

$$0.253 = 25.3\% \qquad 1.63 = 163\%$$

To calculate and use percents, first write a question. Then rewrite your question as an equation. Replace "percent" with /100, "of" with ×, and "is" with =. Replace the unknown value with a variable, like x.

Example 1: Sweden's gross domestic product (GDP) is $255,400,000,000. Agriculture accounts for about $5,108,000,000 of the GDP. What percent of the GDP is from agriculture?

Solution

What **percent of** the GDP **is** from agriculture?	*Write a question.*
What percent of $255,400,000,000 **is** $5,108,000,000?	*Substitute numbers.*
x**/100** × $255,400,000,000 = $5,108,000,000	*Rewrite as an equation.*
$x = \dfrac{\$5,108,000,000}{\$255,400,000,000} \times 100$	*Solve the equation.*
$x = 2$	*Use a calculator.*
Two percent of Sweden's GDP is from agriculture.	*Answer the question.*

Example 2: Sweden's unemployment rate is 5.6% and its labor force is 4.46 million. About how many people are unemployed?

Solution

5.6 **percent of** the labor force **is** how many people?	*Write a question.*
5.6 **percent of** 4.46 million **is how many**?	*Substitute numbers.*
5.6**/100** × 4,460,000 = x	*Rewrite as an equation.*
249,760 = x	*Use a calculator.*
About 250,000 people are unemployed.	*Round your answer.*

Applying the Skill

1. What is 10% of $65?

2. What is 150% of 256,000?

3. $3.75 is 15% of how much?

1.4 Using Ratios

Understanding the Skill

A ratio compares two numbers that have the same units of measure. For example, if Tina runs 8 miles per hour and Maria runs 7 miles per hour, the ratio of their speeds is 8 to 7, or 8:7. A ratio can also be written as a fraction: $\frac{8}{7}$.

You can simplify ratios in the same way that you simplify fractions.

Example 1: Raul runs 8 miles per hour and his little brother Ben runs 4 miles per hour. What is the ratio of Raul's speed to Ben's speed?

Solution

$$\frac{\text{Raul's speed}}{\text{Ben's speed}} = \frac{8}{4} \qquad \textit{Write a fraction.}$$

$$= \frac{8 \div 4}{4 \div 4} \qquad \textit{To simplify the fraction, divide both the top and the bottom by 4.}$$

$$= \frac{2}{1} \qquad \frac{2}{1} \textit{ means the same as 2:1 and "2 to 1."}$$

The ratio of Raul's speed to Ben's speed is 2 to 1.

Ratios are sometimes written as decimals. For example, a company's price-earnings ratio is the ratio of the price of a share of the company's stock to the earnings per share.

Example 2 Suppose a share of a company's stock costs $54.75 and the earnings per share are $2.73. What is the company's price-earnings ratio?

Solution

$$\text{Price-earnings ratio} = \frac{\text{Price of a share of stock}}{\text{Earnings per share}} \qquad \textit{Write a fraction.}$$

$$= \frac{\$55.75}{\$2.73} \qquad \textit{Substitute numbers.}$$

$$= 20.421245 \qquad \textit{Use a calculator.}$$

$$\approx 20.4 \qquad \textit{Round your answer.}$$

The company's price-earnings ratio is about 20.4. \qquad *Answer the question.*

Applying the Skill

1. The GDP of the world is about $55 trillion and the GDP of the United States is about $11 trillion. What is the ratio of the GDP of the world to the GDP of the United States?

2. Suppose a share of a company's stock costs $26.24 and the earnings per share are $3.19. What is the company's price-earnings ratio?

1.5 Calculating Compound Interest

Understanding the Skill

For some savings instruments, interest is calculated and paid multiple times each year. To calculate the amount of each interest payment, you can use the following formula.

$$\text{Interest} = \frac{\text{Balance} \times \text{Interest rate}}{\text{Number of times calculated each year}}$$

If interest on your savings is *compounded,* that means the interest you earn is added to your total savings, and is included in future calculations of interest.

Notice that the interest for the second half of the year is greater than the interest for the first half of the year. In the second half of the year, you earn interest not only on your original balance, but also on the interest you earned in the first half of the year.

Compound interest on loans works the same as compound interest on savings. But for loans, if interest is compounded, you must *pay* interest on interest you haven't yet paid.

> **Example:** If interest on $1,000 is compounded biannually with an interest rate of 5 percent, how much interest do you earn for each compounding period in the first year?
>
> **Solution**
>
> If interest is compounded *biannually,* that means it is calculated **two** times a year and each compounding period is a half of a year. Calculate the interest for each half.
>
> **First half of year** $\text{Interest} = \dfrac{\text{Balance} \times \text{Interest rate}}{\text{Number of times calculated each year}}$
>
> $= \dfrac{\$1,000 \times 5\%}{2}$ Substitute numbers.
>
> $= \dfrac{\$1,000 \times 0.05}{2}$ Convert the percent to a decimal.
>
> $= \$25.00$ Use a calculator.
>
> **Second half of year**
>
> First, calculate the new balance by adding the interest to the old balance.
>
> New balance $=$ Old balance $+$ Interest on old balance
>
> $= \$1,000 + \textbf{\$25.00}$
>
> $= \textbf{\$1,025.00}$
>
> $\text{Interest} = \dfrac{\textbf{New balance} \times \text{Interest rate}}{\text{Number of times calculated each year}} = \dfrac{\$1,025.00 + 5\%}{2} \approx \$25.63$
>
> The interest for the first half of the year is $25.00 and for the second half is $25.63.

Applying the Skill

1. If interest on $2,000 is compounded biannually with a rate of 6 percent, what is the interest for each compounding period in the first year? What is the total interest for one year?

2. If interest on $2,000 is compounded four times a year with a rate of 6 percent, what is the interest for each compounding period in the first year? What is the total interest?

3. Look at your answers to Questions 1 and 2. Do you earn more if the interest is compounded twice a year or if it is compounded four times a year?

1.6 Understanding Progressive Taxes

Understanding the Skill

The federal income tax is progressive: a person with a low income is taxed at a lower rate than a person with a higher income. The table at the bottom of the page shows the 2006 income tax brackets for a single person. If you file as single and your taxable income is **$7,125,** you are in the **10 percent** tax bracket because $7,125 is between **$0** and **$7,550.** If your taxable income is **$7,750,** then you are in the 15 percent tax bracket, but your tax is not 15 percent of $7,750. Instead, you pay 10 percent on the first $7,550 of your income. You pay 15 percent on the rest.

Example 1: Calculate tax in the 10 percent tax bracket on $7,125.

Tax = Tax rate x Income in bracket

= **10%** × **$7,125**	*Substitute numbers.*
= 0.10 × $7,125	*Write 10 percent as a decimal.*
= $712.50	*Multiply.*

The tax on $7,125 is $713. *Answer the question. Round to the nearest dollar.*

Example 2: Calculate tax in the 15 percent tax bracket on $7,550.

Pay **10 percent** on the first **$7,550.**

Tax = Tax rate x Income in bracket = **10%** × **$7,550** = **$755.00**

Pay 15 percent on the rest of the income.

Income in 15% bracket = Total income – **Income in 10% bracket**

= **$7,750** – **$7,550**

= **$200**

Tax = Tax rate x Income in bracket = **15%** × **$200** = **$30.00**

Add the tax from the two brackets together to find the total tax.

$755.00 + **$30.00** = **$785.00**

Applying the Skill

Using the tax bracket table on the right, calculate the taxes on the following taxable incomes:

A. $7,175 **B.** $17,225
C. $74,100 **D.** $98,975

2006 Federal Income Tax Brackets (Single)	
Income Bracket	Tax Rate
$0–$7,550	10%
$7,550–$30,650	15%
$30,650–$74,200	25%
$74,200–$154,800	28%

1.7 Creating Line Graphs

Understanding the Skill

A line graph is useful for showing how a value changes over time. You can use a spreadsheet or graphing software to make a line graph. In the example, type the years and inflation rates into the software. The software will do most of the above steps for you. See the software's tutorials or help feature for guidance.

United States Inflation Rate (in percent)									
1970	1971	1972	1973	1974	1975	1976	1977	1978	1979
5.7	4.4	3.2	6.2	11.0	9.1	5.8	6.5	7.6	11.3
1980	1981	1982	1983	1984	1985	1986	1987	1988	1989
13.5	10.3	6.2	3.2	4.3	3.6	1.9	3.6	4.1	4.8
1990	1991	1992	1993	1994	1995	1996	1997	1998	1999
5.4	4.2	3.0	3.0	2.6	2.8	3.0	2.3	1.6	2.2

Source: U.S. Bureau of Labor Statistics

❶ Write the title of the graph and make a grid under it.

❷ Write numbers along the left side, or verticle axis, of the grid with 0 at the bottom. The top number should be larger than the largest rate in the table. Label the axis.

❸ Write years from the table evenly along the bottom line, or horizontal axis, of the grid. Label the axis.

❹ Graph each point where the horizontal line from the **inflation rate** meets the vertical line from the **year.**

❺ Draw a straight line to connect each point to the point for the next year.

Example: Make a line graph showing the rate of inflation between 1970 and 1999. Find the largest rate in the table. It is **13.5.**

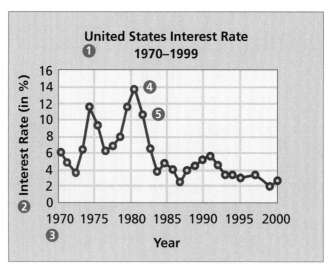

Applying the Skill

Make a line graph to show the unemployment rate from 1993 to 2002.

Unemployment Rate (in percent)									
1993	1994	1995	1996	1997	1998	1999	2000	2001	2002
6.9	6.1	5.6	5.4	4.9	4.5	4.2	4.0	4.8	5.8

Source: U.S. Bureau of Labor Statistics

1.8 Creating Bar Graphs

Understanding the Skill

A bar graph is useful for comparing different values. You can use a spreadsheet or graphing software to make a bar graph. In the example, type the oil consumption information into the software. The software will do most of the above steps for you. See the software's tutorials or help feature for guidance.

Leading Oil Consumers (in millions of barrels per day)							
United States	European Union	China	Japan	India	Brazil	Russia	Canada
20.0	14.6	6.4	5.6	2.3	2.1	2.8	2.2

Source: CIA World Factbook

1. Write the title of the graph. Draw a box under it.

2. Write numbers evenly along the vertical axis. The largest number should be larger than 20.0 and the smallest number should be 0. Label the axis.

3. Write the names evenly along the horizontal axis. Label the axis.

4. Draw each bar. Find the **oil consumption** on the vertical axis. Imagine a horizontal line from the oil consumption to directly above the **name.** Draw the bar as shown. Each bar should be the same width.

Example: Make a bar graph of the oil consumption of the four greatest oil consumers: the United States, the European Union, China, and Japan.

Solution

Begin by finding the highest level of oil consumption—the United States with 20 million barrels a day. Then complete the following steps.

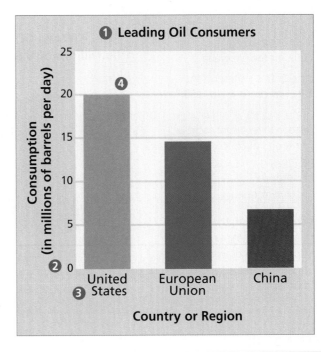

Applying the Skill

Use the information in the table at the top of the page to make a bar graph of the oil consumption of the three leading oil consumers in Asia: China, Japan, and India.

1.9 Creating Pie Graphs

Understanding the Skill

A pie graph is useful for showing the relationship of parts to the whole. The table at the right and the pie graph below show the GDP for various countries and the European Union. The graph makes it easy to see how each GDP contributes to the world's total GDP. The example shows how to make the pie graph.

Country	GDP	Population	Country	GDP	Population
United States	11.8	296	Russia	1.4	143
European Union	11.7	457	Canada	1.0	33
China	7.3	1,306	Mexico	1.0	106
Japan	3.7	127	South Korea	0.9	49
India	3.3	1,080	Indonesia	0.8	242
Brazil	1.5	186	Other	11.1	2,421

GDP (trillions of U. S. dollars) and Population (millions of people) of Various Countries and the European Union

Source: CIA World Factbook

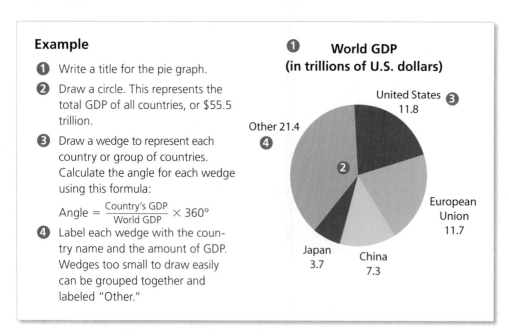

Example

❶ Write a title for the pie graph.

❷ Draw a circle. This represents the total GDP of all countries, or $55.5 trillion.

❸ Draw a wedge to represent each country or group of countries. Calculate the angle for each wedge using this formula:

$$\text{Angle} = \frac{\text{Country's GDP}}{\text{World GDP}} \times 360°$$

❹ Label each wedge with the country name and the amount of GDP. Wedges too small to draw easily can be grouped together and labeled "Other."

Applying the Skill

Use the information in the table at the top of the page to make a pie graph of the populations of the world. Include wedges for the four largest countries, and one for all others.

1.10 Creating a Database

Understanding the Skill

A database is a large collection of information that can be organized and searched. You can use a spreadsheet to make a database. First enter information into the spreadsheet. Label each row and column, including units of measure. You can use the spreadsheet software to manipulate the information and answer questions.

Example Which country has the largest per capita oil consumption?

	A	B	C	D	E	F	G
1		United States	European Union	Japan	Russia	Canada	Mexico
2	Oil Consumption (**millions** of barrels per day)	20.0	14.6	5.6	2.8	2.2	1.8
3	Population (**millions** of people)	296	457	127	143	33	106

Solution

Per capita oil consumption is **oil consumption** divided by **population.** For the U.S. it is

$$\frac{20.0 \ \text{million barrels per day}}{296 \ \text{million people}} = \frac{20.0 \ \text{barrels per day}}{296 \ \text{people}} \approx 0.07 \ \text{barrels per person per day.}$$

❶ Divide row 2 by row 3. Put the answer in row 4.

❷ Sort the whole database by row 4, from largest to smallest.

	A	B	C	D	E	F	G
1		United States	Canada	Japan	European Union	Russia	Mexico
2	Oil Consumption (**millions** of barrels per day)	20.0	2.2	5.6	14.6	2.8	1.8
3	Population (**millions** of people)	296	33	127	457	143	106
4	Per capita oil consumption (barrels/person/day)	0.07	0.07	0.04	0.03	0.02	0.02

Once the database is sorted, the United States and Canada are the first in the new order. So the United States and Canada are the countries in the database that have the greatest per capita oil consumption, with consumptions of 0.07 barrels per person per day.

Applying the Skill

Make a database of the information in the table on page R10, by entering the information into spreadsheet software. Multiply each GDP by 1 trillion so the units are "dollars" instead of "trillions of dollars." Multiply each population by 1 million so the units are "people" instead of "millions of people".

Contents

Refer to the Economics Skillbuilder Handbook when you need help in answering Application questions or questions in Section Assessments and Chapter Assessments. In addition, the handbook will help you answer questions about charts, graphs, databases, and economic models.

Skills for Understanding Economics

Using Print, Visual, and Technology Sources

1.1 Explaining an Economic Concept

EXPLAINING ECONOMIC CONCEPTS involves clarifying and communicating the basic ideas of economics. Some of these concepts are simple, while others are complex. Three basic steps will help you develop an explanation of a concept, regardless of its complexity.

Understanding the Skill

STRATEGY: Use the steps in the concept-explanation process. The following passage provides information on economic recessions. The table below that provides an analysis of the concept of economic recession based on the concept-explanation process.

1 Identify and define the economic concept.

2 Describe the impact of the concept on the economy.

3 Give an example of the concept. Providing an illustrative example will help underscore your explanation of the concept.

1 An economic recession may be defined as a downturn in the business cycle. During a recession, both production and employment decline. **2** As a result, the economy experiences little, if any, growth. **3** In 1990 and 1991, the United States experienced the greatest recession since the Great Depression. According to some economic analysts, the 1990–1991 recession caused the loss of 1.9 million jobs in 1992.

Make a Table

Use a table like the one shown here to help you explain an economic concept with the three-step process.

Explaining an Economic Concept	
Concept	Economic recession
Definition	A downturn in the business cycle, characterized by a decline in production and employment
Impact	Slows economic growth
Example	U.S. recession of 1990–1991

Applying the Skill

Turn to Chapter 7, Section 4, and read about deregulation on page 218. Use a table to explain the economic concept of deregulation with the three-step process.

1.2 Analyzing and Interpreting Data

DATA, or factual information, is the most basic tool of the economist. Economic data is most often in the form of statistics. Economists **ANALYZE** data to learn about economic conditions and trends. They **INTERPRET** data to draw conclusions or make predictions based on their analysis.

Understanding the Skill

STRATEGY: Analyze and interpret the data. Data usually is presented in visual form as a graph or a table like the one below.

1 Read the title. The title provides a good indication of the kind of data shown. Here, the data concerns average food expenditures for several large cities in the Midwest of the United States.

2 Determine how the data is organized. Here, data in each horizontal row provides information on a category of food expenditure. Each vertical column shows expenditures by food category for one of five metropolitan areas.

3 Ask what kinds of questions may be answered from the data. Answering such questions helps in the analysis and interpretation of the data.

① Average Annual Household Food Expenditures in Selected Midwestern Metropolitan Areas, 2003–2004 (in dollars)

	Chicago	Detroit	Milwaukee	Minneapolis-St. Paul	Cleveland
Cereals and Bakery	472	470	460	509	388
Meats, Fish, and Eggs	855	863	837	779	854
Dairy	366	339	309	431	310
Fruits and Vegetables	606	542	506	610	449
Other Foods at Home	1,128	1,073	950	1,236	822
Food Away from Home	2,597	2,439	2,126	2,983	1,765

Source: Consumer Expenditure Survey, 2003–2004, U.S. Bureau of Labor Statistics

Write a Summary

Summarize your analysis and interpretation of the data in the table

> Data in the above table reflects average annual household food expenditures for one year (2003-2004) for 5 Midwestern metropolitan areas. Food expenditures are shown according to type of food purchased: a food at home versus food away from home. The data may be analyzed and interpreted in a number of ways, including the following: comparing expenditures in different cities for foods in a single category or comparing expenditures for two or more food categories within a city; computation of percentages of total expenditure spent on specific food categories.

Applying the Skill

Turn to Chapter 14, Section 2, page 421, and study the table showing data on itemized tax deductions. Write a summary of your analysis and interpretation of data in the table.

1.3 Applying Economic Concepts

When attempting to understand complex economic behavior, economists make constant use of fundamental economic concepts, such as supply, demand, and price. By **APPLYING ECONOMIC CONCEPTS** to everyday situations, economists develop a better understanding of how the economy works.

Understanding the Skill

STRATEGY: Examine the information carefully. The news story below describes a fall in the price of crude oil. The supply and demand curves beneath it graphically illustrate this shift.

1 **Look for economic concepts as you read.** Such words as *prices, supplies, inventories,* and *capacity* indicate that the topic of this story is the relationship between supply and price.

2 **Look for relationships among concepts.** The story states that OPEC, the oil-producing cartel, has decided not to curtail production. It also notes that BP could restore lost oil production. So, even if demand remains constant, an increase in supply will cause the equilibrium price to fall.

3 **Express the relationship in graphic form.** Supply and demand curves provide a vivid picture of the impact of increased supply on price.

Crude Oil Prices Sink Below $66 a Barrel

1 Oil prices fell below $66 a barrel Monday as concerns over **1** supplies eased in expectation that **2** OPEC ministers would not change their production targets. . . .

1 Supplies remain ample. . . . OPEC maintains about 2 million barrels a day of spare **1** capacity, and stocks are high elsewhere; the U.S. Department of Energy said last week that **1** inventories have hit their highest levels since 1998. . . .

2 The possibility that [British Petroleum] could restore 180,000 barrels per day of lost Alaskan production at Prudhoe Bay by the end of October also calmed the market.

Source: Associated Press, September 11, 2006

Draw Demand and Supply Curves

Draw demand and supply curves to illustrate the situation described in the news story. Assume that demand stays constant. The increased supply shifts the supply curve to the right (from S1 to S2), causing prices to fall (from P1 to P2).

Applying the Skill

In the business section of a newspaper, find a story about a change in price. Analyze the information in the story to determine why the price changed. Then draw supply and demand curves that illustrate the shifts that caused such a change.

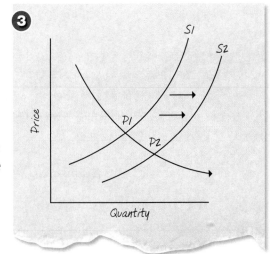

1.4 Creating and Interpreting Economic Models

CREATING an economic model involves using information and ideas to show an economic concept or situation in a visual way. An **ECONOMIC MODEL** might be a graph, a diagram, a three-dimensional representation, or a computer program. **INTERPRETING AN ECONOMIC MODEL** involves carefully studying the model in order to draw conclusions or make predictions based on the information it provides.

Understanding the Skill

STRATEGY: Create an economic model. The model below is a circular flow diagram. Economists use the circular flow model to help understand and describe how a market-based economy operates. Use the following steps to create an economic model.

1 Gather the information you need to create an economic model. In this case, you need to show the rules that govern the relationships between economic actors and economic markets in a market economy.

2 Visualize and sketch an idea of your model. The creator of this economic model used a circular diagram to convey the relationships between economic markets and economic actors.

3 Think of symbols you may want to use. Here, different colored arrows indicate the flow of money and the flow of resources and products.

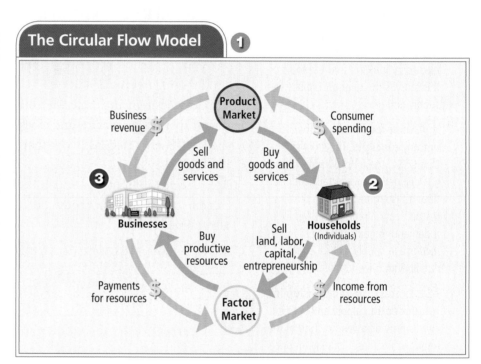

Interpret the Model

Write a summary of your interpretation of the information in the model.

This model illustrates the interactions between businesses and individuals in the economy. The two main economic decision makers, businesses and households, are shown on the left and right of the model. The two main economic markets, product and factor, are shown at the top and bottom. The green arrows represent the flow of money between actors and through the markets. The blue arrows represent the flow of resources and products through the economy.

Applying the Skill

Turn to Chapter 7, Section 1, and read the information on perfect competition on pages 192–194. Create an economic model that shows the relationship between two actors—buyers and sellers—in a perfectly competitive market.

1.5 Using a Decision-Making Process

USING A DECISION-MAKING PROCESS involves choosing between two or more options or courses of action. Organized decision-making involves four steps: 1) identify the problem or situation that requires a decision; 2) identify options; 3) predict possible consequences of the decision; 4) put the decision into effect.

Understanding the Skill

STRATEGY: Use the steps in the decision-making process. The following passage describes how a Polish food producer used a decision-making process to introduce a new product into Poland's convenience food market. The flow chart organizes the elements of the process that was used.

1 **Identify the decision that needs to be made.** In this passage, the title offers a clue to the problem, which is stated more fully in the text.

2 **Identify options.** The company might have chosen to stay out of the convenience food market because most Poles did not own microwave ovens.

3 **Identify possible consequences of the decision.** Remember that there can be more than one possibility. Also look for factors that could affect the consequences.

4 **Note what decision was made and the impact it had.**

---

1 **Polish Meals in the Microwave?**

At the beginning of the current millennium, Pudliszki, a Polish firm owned by Heinz, was faced with a decision. **1** Should the company introduce full-course microwaveable meals into Poland's market for convenience foods? Poland's accession into the European Union promised to have a positive effect on both employment and disposable income. And with Polish workers averaging 40 hours on the job, projected demand for convenience foods appeared promising—a strong indication for the product's success. **2** However, households owning microwaves were very much in the minority, which could result in the product's failure. **3** Perhaps banking on an increase in household microwaves, Pudliszki introduced Meals from the Four Corners of the World. According to Euromonitor, an international market research firm, **4** Pudliszki's four full-course meals were "reasonably priced and accepted rather well by the market."

Source: Adapted from "Poland's EU Membership Presents Packaging Opportunities" by Chris Mercer. *Food Industry News*, February 2, 2005.

Make a Flow Chart

In a flow chart, state the decision to be made, its possible consequences, the actual decision, and the actual consequences of the decision.

Applying the Skill

Read the Chapter 1 Case Study, "The Real Cost of Expanding O'Hare Airport," on pages 32–33. From this information, identify the four steps of the decision-making process. Present your findings in a flow chart like the one shown at the right.

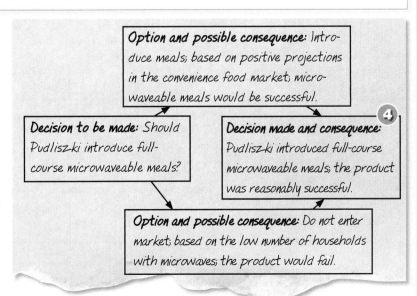

Option and possible consequence: Introduce meals; based on positive projections in the convenience food market; microwaveable meals would be successful.

Decision to be made: Should Pudliszki introduce full-course microwaveable meals?

Decision made and consequence: Pudliszki introduced full-course microwaveable meals; the product was reasonably successful. **4**

Option and possible consequence: Do not enter market; based on the low number of households with microwaves; the product would fail.

1.6 Conducting Cost-Benefit Analyses

A **COST-BENEFIT ANALYSIS** involves determining the economic costs and benefits of an action and then balancing the costs against the benefits.

Understanding the Skill

STRATEGY: Look for the trade-offs that are a part of every economic decision.
The passage below describes the costs and benefits of a government-subsidized business development in Hong Kong. The decision-making grid beneath it summarizes the trade-offs in the project.

1 **Identify the decision that is being made.** The article notes that the Hong Kong government signed an agreement with a large private company to construct a new business.

2 **Note the potential benefits of the decision.** Here, government officials provide estimates of the economic benefits—jobs and money pumped into the economy.

3 **Note the potential costs of the decision.** The article focuses on the huge cost of the project to the government.

4 **Determine if the decision is beneficial.**

---

1 Hoping to jump-start their economy, government officials in Hong Kong inked an agreement with Walt Disney to build the U.S. company's third overseas theme park. . . . Government officials estimate that **2** construction of Hong Kong Disneyland will create 16,000 jobs. Another 18,400 jobs will be created once the park opens in 2005. Further, they hope that the park will draw millions of tourists to this city every year, raising more than US $1 billion a year.

Few doubt that the project will provide the city with a shot of confidence. Yet John Whaley, a Virginia-based economist, says the construction jobs provided by the project will be short-term positions, with little long-term economic impact. Also, since many tourists to Hong Kong are people of modest means from China, there is no guarantee that they will spend the money to go to the park.

3 Nevertheless, much of the costs for the new park will be paid by the Hong Kong government, which is spending more than US $2.83 billion to build the park. Estimates suggest the government is spending about US $100,000 for every new job it will create when the park is running.

Source: Adapted from "Disney-Park Deal May Not Wave A Magic Wand Over Hong Kong" by Jon E. Hilsenrath and Zach Coleman. *The Wall Street Journal*, November 4, 1999.

Make a Diagram

Summarize the costs and benefits of the Hong Kong government's decision in a diagram. Consider the wisdom of the decision by analyzing these costs and benefits.

Applying the Skill

Turn to page 125 and read the article titled "2005–Year of the Hybrid." Based on the information you find there, conduct a cost-benefit analysis of buying a hybrid automobile.

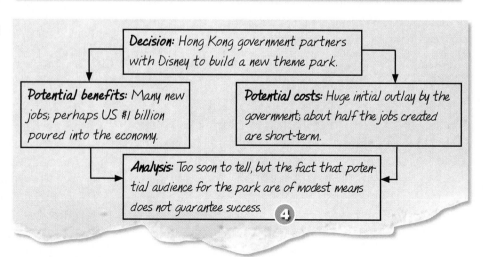

Decision: Hong Kong government partners with Disney to build a new theme park.

Potential benefits: Many new jobs; perhaps US #1 billion poured into the economy.

Potential costs: Huge initial outlay by the government; about half the jobs created are short-term.

Analysis: Too soon to tell, but the fact that potential audience for the park are of modest means does not guarantee success. **4**

1.7 Comparing and Contrasting Economic Information

Economists compare and contrast economic programs, concepts, and trends in order to understand them better. **COMPARING** involves finding both similarities and differences between two or more things. **CONTRASTING** means examining only the differences between them.

Understanding the Skill

STRATEGY: Look for similarities and differences. The following passage describes pension reform in Chile and in Britain. The Venn diagram that follows the passage shows some of the similarities and differences between the two economic programs.

---

1 **Compare: Look for features that two subjects or ideas have in common.** Here, you learn that both Chile and Britain needed to reform their pension systems.

2 **Compare: Look for clue words indicating that two things are alike.** Clue words include *all*, *both*, *as*, *likewise*, and *similarly*.

3 **Contrast: Look for clue words that show how two things differ.** Clue words include *different*, *however*, *unlike*, and *except*.

4 **Contrast: Look for ways in which two things are different.** Here you learn that the structure and the administration of the two programs were different.

Pension Reform in Chile and Britain

In the late 20th century, Chile and Britain faced **1** the same problem: how to reform their overburdened pension systems. **2** Both countries had social welfare budgets that were stretched to the limit. And both had pension systems that were nearly bankrupt. To provide for their aging population, Chile and Britain chose privatization as the means to reform their pension programs.

3 However, **4** the structure and administration of the two programs were very different. For example, in Chile a monthly payroll deduction became mandatory for all employees. The payments are administered by one of six private pension funds. In Britain, however, the plan was voluntary. Six million people chose the plan when it was first offered. They received a government rebate, along with responsibility for managing their own retirement money.

Source: Adapted from "In Britain and in Chile, Lessons for Social Security" by Mark Rice-Oxley and Jennifer Ross. *The Christian Science Monitor*, March 14, 2005

Make a Venn Diagram

Summarize similarities and differences in a Venn diagram like the one shown here. In the overlapping area, list characteristics shared by both subjects. Then, in one oval, list the characteristics of one subject not shared by the other. In the other oval, list characteristics unique to the second subject.

Applying the Skill

Turn to Chapter 8 and read Sections 1 and 2, pages 226–235. Construct a Venn diagram comparing and contrasting sole proprietorships and partnerships.

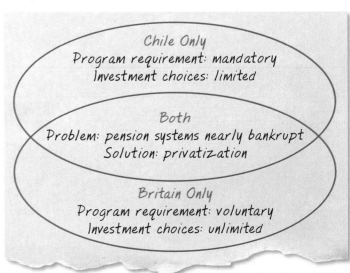

Chile Only
Program requirement: mandatory
Investment choices: limited

Both
Problem: pension systems nearly bankrupt
Solution: privatization

Britain Only
Program requirement: voluntary
Investment choices: unlimited

1.8 Analyzing Cause and Effect

CAUSES are the events, factors, and other reasons that lead to an event or condition. Causes happen before the event in time; they explain why it happened. **EFFECTS** are the results or consequences of the event. One effect often becomes the cause of other effects, resulting in a chain of events. Causes and effects can be both short-term and long-term.

Understanding the Skill

STRATEGY: Keep track of causes and effects as you read. The passage below describes factors leading to a shortfall of qualified staff in India's call centers. The diagram that follows the passage summarizes the economic chain of causes and effects.

1 Causes: Look for clue words that show cause. These include *due to, cause,* and *therefore.*

2 Look for multiple causes and multiple effects. Increased outsourcing to India caused the series of effects discussed in the rest of the article.

3 Effects: Look for results or consequences. Sometimes these are indicated by clue words such as *as a result* and *consequence.*

4 Notice that an effect may be the cause of another event. This begins a chain of causes and effects.

Each year, three thousand English speakers graduate from India's universities. **1** Largely due to this pool of job seekers fluent in English, India has been able to establish a highly successful business process outsourcing industry. **2** As businesses in more and more countries outsourced to India, call centers there have become increasingly successful. As a result, salaries for entry-level positions have continued to rise. An unintended **3** consequence of the **4** higher salaries has been a greater tendency of workers to job hop. Increasing success also has created increasing stress, as employees often are required to work long hours. Therefore, employment in call centers, once considered glamorous, has begun to lose its appeal. Analysts claim that such conditions will cause a shortfall of as many as 260,000 qualified workers by 2009.

Source: Adapted from "Busy Signals," *The Economist,* September 10, 2005

Make a Cause-and-Effect Diagram

Summarize cause-and-effect relationships in a diagram. Starting with the first cause in a series, fill in the boxes until you reach the end result.

Cause ⟶	Effect / Cause ⟶	Effect / Cause ⟶	Effect / Cause ⟶	Effect
Many of India's college graduates speak English.	Outsourcing industry enjoys success.	• Pay improves for entry-level jobs. • On-the-job stress increases.	• Workers change jobs often. • Fewer people apply.	There will soon be a shortage of qualified workers.

Applying the Skill

Turn to Chapter 2 and read "Under Pressure to Change" on page 40. Construct a Cause-and-Effect diagram summarizing the information you find.

1.9 Making Inferences and Drawing Conclusions

MAKING INFERENCES involves reading between the lines to extend the information provided.
DRAWING CONCLUSIONS involves analyzing what has been read and forming an opinion about its meaning.

Understanding the Skill

STRATEGY: Develop inferences from the facts. Use the facts to draw conclusions. The passage below describes the U.S. trade deficit in 2005. The diagram that follows shows how to organize the facts and inferences to draw conclusions.

1 **Read carefully to understand all the facts.** Fact: The U.S. trade deficit rose almost 18 percent in 2005.

2 **Use the facts to make an inference.** Inference: It's unlikely that the United States will see a trade surplus in the foreseeable future.

3 **Read between the lines to make inferences.** Inference: Continued dependence on foreign oil will continue to increase the deficit.

4 **Ask questions of the material.** How can the United States reduce its trade deficit?

5 **Use all this information to draw a conclusion.** Conclusion: In order to reduce the deficit, the United States will need to reduce its dependence on foreign oil.

1 The U.S. trade deficit jumped nearly 18 percent in 2005, the government reported Friday, hitting its fourth consecutive record as consumer demand for imports increased, energy prices soared and the dollar strengthened against other currencies.

The $725.8 billion gap, **1** which is almost exactly twice the deficit in 2001, was driven by a 12 percent jump in imports and a more muted 10 percent increase in exports, the Commerce Department reported in Washington. **2** The nation last had a trade surplus, of $12.4 billion, in 1975.

3 The nation's deficit in trade for petroleum products accounted for 29 percent of the total gap, up from 25 percent in 2004. **4** Imports of petroleum goods climbed 39 percent, to $251.6 billion, after rising by 39 percent in 2004. Excluding oil and other petroleum products, the trade deficit would have grown 10 percent, to $537 billion.

Source: "The U.S. Trade Deficit Hit Record High in 2005" by Vikas Bajaj. *The New York Times*, February 10, 2006

Applying the Skill

Read the online news story "China's Economic Miracle; the High Price of Progress" on page 571. Use the chart at the right as a model for organizing facts, inferences, and conclusions about the passage.

Facts	Inferences	Conclusion about Passage
The U.S. trade deficit rose almost 18 percent in 2005. The deficit nearly doubled between 2001 and 2005.	The deficit is growing at a marked rate.	**5** In order to reduce the deficit, the United States will need to reduce its dependence on foreign oil.
Last trade surplus was in 1975.	Trade surplus is unlikely in foreseeable future.	
Trade in petroleum products accounted for 29 percent of deficit.	Continued dependence on foreign oil will continue to increase the deficit.	

1.10 Evaluating Economic Decisions

EVALUATING ECONOMIC DECISIONS means making judgments about decisions that individuals, businesses, and governments make on economic matters. Economists evaluate a decision based on its outcome and the choices available when that decision was made.

Understanding the Skill

STRATEGY: Look for choices and reasons. The following passage describes the marketing decisions Joe Sillett made to promote a cricket bat he had begun to manufacture. As you read the passage, look for alternative decisions he could have made.

1 **Look at decisions made by individuals or by groups.** Identify the decision Sillett made to market his company's product.

2 **Look at the outcome of the decisions.**

3 **Analyze a decision in terms of the choices that were possible.** Sillett could have chosen a marketing strategy that was less expensive and therefore less risky. Make a simple chart of your analysis.

Applying the Skill

Pages 234–235 of Chapter 8 describe Bart's decision to open his comic store as a partnership rather than a sole proprietorship. Make a chart like the one shown to summarize the pros and cons of his decision and your evaluation of that decision.

Marketing Woodworm

When Joe Sillett formed his company, Woodworm, to make cricket bats, he was up against stiff competition. . . Sillett had to decide how to break into the market. Should he utilize traditional marketing techniques, such as the development and purchase of print and media ads, to introduce his product? Or should he try something bolder? **1** Sillett decided to risk most of his marketing budget on a single idea: the sponsorship of two English heavy hitters—Andrew Flintoff and Kevin Pietersen. Sillett's idea proved to be a winner. **2** In just three years, Woodworm bats succeeded in capturing ten percent of the cricket bat market. **3** Sillett knew that a less expensive approach would have allowed him to grow his company over a more extended period of time. But because he believed that linking Woodworm bats with high profile players would quickly create brand recognition, Sillett risked the future of his company on a single marketing idea and won.

Source: Adapted from "The Benefits of Woodworm." *The Economist*, September 8th, 2005

3 Sillett's Choices	Pros	Cons	Evaluation
Sponsor popular players	Possible to gain market share quickly	Risky and expensive	In your opinion, which was the better choice? Why?
Pursue a less expensive marketing strategy	Less risky	Market share likely to grow slowly	

1.11 Synthesizing Economic Data

SYNTHESIZING ECONOMIC DATA is the skill economists use to develop interpretations of past economic events. Like detective work, synthesizing involves putting together clues from data to form an overall picture of an economic event.

Understanding the Skill

STRATEGY: Build an interpretation as you read. The passage below describes the collapse of Enron, a giant American energy company. Note how combining different data leads to a synthesis—an overall picture of Enron's fall and its significance.

1 Read carefully to understand the data. These statements explain why Enron borrowed money and how it succeeded in hiding $600 million in debt.

2 Look for variables in the data that need an explanation. Here, the data in the two statements present a puzzling picture. They lead one to question how a large company that tripled its profits could experience a loss of $638 million less than a year later.

3 Form a synthesis based on the data. This interpretation brings together the different pieces of data to arrive at a new understanding of the subject. Summarize your synthesis in a graphic organizer, such as a table or a cluster diagram.

Enron's Downfall

1 Enron began to borrow money to invest in new projects. Enron then created partnerships to keep the debt off its books. One partnership . . . allowed Enron to keep $600 million in debt off the books it showed to the government and to people who own Enron stock. **2** In December 2000, Enron claimed to have tripled its profits in two years. **2** The collapse began in October [2001], when Enron announced a loss of $638 million. In November, Enron said that it had overstated earnings for the past four years and it now owed over $6 billion. With these announcements, Enron's stock price took a dive. **3** Since Enron had made deals based on the assumption that the stock would go up, it suddenly had to repay lots of money. When Enron could not come up with the cash, it declared bankruptcy. **3** [One] consequence of [Enron's] failure may be new laws that change how much money big businesses can give politicians. Enron gave over $5 million to [political] campaigns since 1998. Lawmakers [also] are considering whether to make new laws to better regulate accounting practices.

Source: "Not Business as Usual," by Elisabeth Bauman. Online NewsHour Extra, January 30, 2002 (www.pbs.org)

Applying the Skill

Read the information on income distribution and income inequality on pages 390–391. Look for data to support a synthesis about the effectiveness and limitations of measuring income inequality. Organize your findings in a table or cluster diagram.

1.12 Generalizing from Economic Information

GENERALIZING involves making broad judgments based on information from more than one source. When you form generalizations, you need to be sure they are based on sufficient evidence and that they are consistent with the information given.

Understanding the Skill

STRATEGY: Look for common themes. The following three excerpts reflect concern regarding the economic deprivation of the elderly during the Great Depression.

1 **Determine what information the sources have in common.** All the sources suggest the need for a government program to provide pensions to the elderly.

2 **Form a generalization about the common information.**

3 **State your generalization in sentence form.** A generalization often needs a qualifying word, such as *most, many,* or *some,* to make it valid.

Plight of the Elderly

1 We also propose to give the old-age pensions to the old people . . . so that the people who reach the age of sixty can be retired from the active labor of life and given an opportunity to have surcease [rest] and ease for the balance of the life that they have on earth.
—*Governor Huey Long of Louisiana*

1 "Old age dependent pensions . . . are not gifts from charity. They are for compensation well earned."
—*Flyer attached to a letter written to President Franklin D. Roosevelt by a woman asking for help for her 81-year-old mother*

1 "It is estimated that the population of the age of 60 and above in the United States is somewhere between nine and twelve millions. I suggest that the national government retire all who reach that age on a monthly pension of $200 a month or more."
—*Francis E. Townsend*

Make a Web Diagram

Using a diagram can help you make generalizations. The diagram below records relevant information from the three statements that leads to a valid generalization.

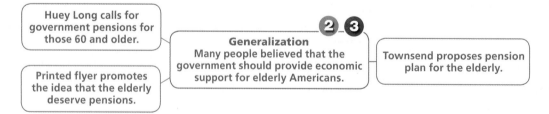

Huey Long calls for government pensions for those 60 and older.

Printed flyer promotes the idea that the elderly deserve pensions.

Generalization
Many people believed that the government should provide economic support for elderly Americans.

2 **3**

Townsend proposes pension plan for the elderly.

Applying the Skill

Read the information under the headings "Changing Occupations" and "Changes in the Way People Work" on pages 268–271. Use a diagram like the one above to make a generalization about technology and work in the United States today.

1.13 Predicting Economic Trends

PREDICTING ECONOMIC TRENDS involves projecting the outcome or the continuation of an economic condition or trend. Economists use their knowledge of past economic events and conditions and related decisions to predict the outcome of current economic events and conditions.

Understanding the Skill

STRATEGY: Identify decisions. The following passage describes how the United States government, under the leadership of President Franklin D. Roosevelt, dealt with a nationwide banking crisis during the Great Depression.

1 **To help you identify decisions, look for clue words.** These words include *decide, decision,* and *chose.*

2 **Notice how one economic decision often leads to others.**

3 **Notice that decisions may have positive or negative impacts.**

4 **Consider alternatives to the decisions that were made.**

5 **Make a chart to record decisions, suggest alternative decisions, and predict a possible outcome for each alternative decision.**

During the Great Depression, many banks in the United States failed. In 1933 Americans, fearing the loss of their money, created "runs" on banks throughout the country. A bank run occurs when large numbers of people attempt to withdraw money within a short period of time. Banks did not have enough money to meet the demand.

In response, President Roosevelt **1** decided to temporarily shut down the nation's banks by proclaiming a bank holiday. **2** Congress **1** chose to pass a law in support of Roosevelt's decision. The law also provided for the rehabilitation of the nation's banking facilities. To avoid an epidemic of bank failures, **3** it was decided not to reopen all the banks at the same time. Instead, banks would open once they had been examined and judged to be sound. In addition, the government made the **1** decision to issue new currency—based on sound assets—so that banks, once reopened, would have enough currency to meet increased demand. Finally, it was decided to include state banks that were not members of the Federal Reserve in the rehabilitation process. The government response to the banking crisis served to stabilize the U.S. banking system.

Source: Franklin D. Roosevelt's First Fireside Chat, March 12, 1933

Applying the Skill **5**

Read the document titled "Two American Entrepreneurs Start Out in a Garage" on page 252 and identify three business decisions that "the two Steves" made. Record them in a chart similar to the one shown for the passage above, along with an alternative decision for each. Then predict a possible outcome for each alternative decision.

Decisions	Alternative Decisions **4**	Prediction of Outcome
FDR proclaimed a nation-wide bank holiday.	FDR did not proclaim a bank holiday.	The run on banks continued.
Congress passed a law to rehabilitate banking facilities.	Congress passed no law to rehabilitate banking facilities.	Banks were not rehabilitated.
New currency was issued.	New currency was not issued.	There was not enough money to meet depositors' demands.
State banks would receive assistance.	Fed did not assist non-member state banks.	State banks failed to reopen.

2.1 Analyzing Political Cartoons

POLITICAL CARTOONS are drawings that express the artist's point of view about a local, national, or international situation or event. They may criticize, show approval, or draw attention to a particular issue, and may be either serious or humorous. Political cartoonists often use symbols as well as other visual clues to communicate their message.

Understanding the Skill

STRATEGY: Examine the cartoon carefully. The cartoon below was drawn as a comment on the process of globalization.

1 **Look at the cartoon as a whole to determine the subject.**

2 **Look for symbols, which are especially effective in communicating ideas visually.** Here, the cartoonist uses symbols that stand for a global economy. The arm in a suit stands for big business. The globe stands for Earth and its resources. The people represent consumers.

3 **Analyze the visual details, which help express the artist's point of view.** The Western-style house and clothing suggest that the people are Americans or Europeans. The people are smiling, indicating that they are happy about what is being offered to them.

Make a Chart

Summarize your interpretation in a chart. Look for details and interpret their significance. Then decide on the message of the cartoon.

Symbols and Visual Details	Significance	Message
Oversized arm in business suit	Corporations	Big business is the driving force behind globalization.
Disproportionately small Earth	Earth as the property of big business	
Happy people reaching out	Consumers	

Applying the Skill

Turn to page 283 and study the political cartoon. Note the clothing and apparent attitudes of the figures in the cartoon, as well as how they relate to one another. Then analyze the cartoon by making a chart like the one to the right.

2.2 Distinguishing Fact from Opinion

FACTS are events, dates, statistics, or statements that can be proved to be true. Facts can be checked for accuracy. **OPINIONS** are judgments, beliefs, and feelings of the writer or speaker.

Understanding the Skill

STRATEGY: Find clues in the text. The following excerpt describes economist Sir William Beveridge's 1942 recommendations for creating a welfare state in Great Britain.

1 Facts: Look for specific names, dates, statistics, and statements that can be proved. The first paragraph gives a factual account of the government's plan.

2 Opinion: Look for assertions, claims, hypotheses, and judgments. Beveridge expresses his opinion regarding provision for old age and for medical care.

3 Opinion: Look for judgment words that the writer uses to describe policies and events. Judgment words are often adjectives that are used to arouse a reader's emotions.

1 The coalition British Government has unveiled plans for a welfare state offering care to all from the cradle to the grave. The Beveridge report proposes a far-reaching series of changes designed to provide a financial safety net to ensure a "freedom from want" after the war is over. Everyone of working age would be expected to pay a weekly national insurance contribution. In return benefits would be paid to the sick, widowed, retired, unemployed and there would also be an allowance for families.

The architect of the report, economist Sir William Beveridge, drew on advice from various government departments. **2** He found provision for old age represented one of the most pressing problems. But there were other failings too. Medical provision was not universally available to all and Britain's achievement, in his words, "fell seriously short" compared with other countries of the world.

At a time when the war was destroying landmarks of every kind, [Beveridge] said, it was a **3** "revolutionary moment in the world's history, a time for revolutions, not for patching."

Source: BBC News

Make a Chart

Divide facts and opinions in a chart. Summarize and separate the facts from the opinions expressed in the passage.

Facts	Opinions
In 1942 the British government unveiled plans for a welfare state. The plan was based on a report by Sir William Beveridge and was designed to provide British citizens with a financial safety net.	• The British government's provision for old age represented one of the most pressing problems. • Britain's medical provision fell seriously short as compared to that of other countries. • It was a revolutionary moment in history.

Applying the Skill

Read "Government and Demand-Side Policies" on page 457. Using a chart like the one to the left, summarize the facts, opinions, and judgments stated. Look carefully at the language used in order to separate one from the other.

2.3 Evaluating Online Sources

EVALUATING ONLINE SOURCES involves making judgments about sites that are available on the Internet—a network of computers associated with universities, libraries, news organizations, government agencies, and other information providers. Each location on the Internet has a home page with its own address, or URL. The international collection of home pages, known as the **WORLD WIDE WEB,** is a good source of up-to-the-minute information as well as in-depth research on economic subjects.

Understanding the Skill

STRATEGY: Explore and evaluate the elements on the screen. The computer screen below shows "Treasury's Learning Vault," the education page of the United States Department of the Treasury.

1 **Go directly to a Web page.** Access the Internet using your Internet Service Provider (ISP). If you know the address of the Web site you want, type it in the address box at the top of your computer screen, then press ENTER or RETURN. (To access the page shown here, type in www.treas.gov/education.)

2 **Explore the features and links.** Click on any one of the images or topics to find out more about a specific subject. These links take you to other pages at this Web site. Some links take you to related information that can be found at other places on the Internet.

3 **Evaluate the Web site.** Use the information you gathered in Step 2 to evaluate the Web site. Ask yourself the following questions: Is the information provided by the site useful to an economist or a student of economics? How reliable is this information?

Applying the Skill

Access the Bureau of Labor Statistics (www.bls.gov) and the Census Bureau (www.census.gov) Websites through ClassZone.com. How useful do you think these sites might be to economists? How might economists use the information on these sites?

2.4 Interpreting Graphs

GRAPHS show statistical information in a visual manner. Economists use graphs to show comparative amounts, ratios, trends, and changes over time. Interpreting graphs will increase your understanding of economic trends and data. **LINE GRAPHS** can show changes over time, or trends. Usually, the horizontal axis shows a unit of time, such as years, and the vertical axis shows quantities. **PIE GRAPHS** are useful for showing relative proportions. The circle represents the whole, such as the entire population, and the slices represent the different groups that make up the whole. **BAR GRAPHS** compare numbers or sets of numbers. The length of each bar indicates a quantity. With bar graphs, it is easy to see at a glance how different categories compare.

Understanding the Skill

STRATEGY: Study all the elements of the graph. The double line graph to the right shows the number of new firms started and the number of firm failures from 1994 to 2004.

1 **Read the title to identify the content of the graph.** Here, the title explicitly states the content of the graph—new firms and firm failures.

2 **Read the vertical and horizontal axes.** The vertical axis shows the number of firms, and the horizontal axis shows years.

3 **Look at the legend to understand what colors and symbols represent.** In this graph, different colored lines are used to represent new firms and firm failures.

4 **Summarize the information shown in each part of the graph.** What trend does each line show?

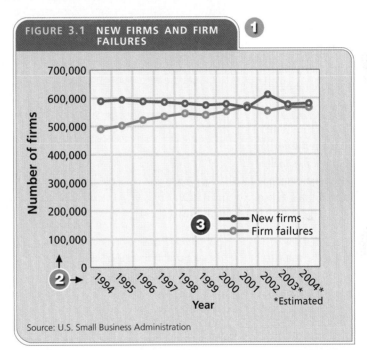

FIGURE 3.1 NEW FIRMS AND FIRM FAILURES

Number of firms / Year

New firms
Firm failures

*Estimated

Source: U.S. Small Business Administration

Write a Summary

Write a summary paragraph to show what you have learned from the graph.

4 Each year between 1994 and 2004, about 600,000 new firms opened in the United States. During the same time period, anywhere from 500,000 to about 575,000 firms failed. In 2001, there actually were more firm failures than new firms opened. The overall trend shows that nearly as many firms fail as open each year.

Applying the Skill

Turn to page 267 and study Figure 9.7, a graph that provides information on the U.S. labor force. Write a paragraph summarizing what you learn from the graph.

2.5 Interpreting Tables

TABLES present information in a visual form. Tables are created by simplifying, summarizing, and organizing information into a format that is easy to understand. Tables are the most commonly used charts in Economics books.

Understanding the Skill

STRATEGY: Study all the elements of the table. The table shown here provides statistical information about employment in the United States.

① Read the title to identify the main idea of the table. This table provides information on selected aspects of the United States labor force during 2006.

② Read the headings to determine how the table is organized. In this table, data is organized by category and by month.

③ Study the data in the table to understand what the table was designed to show. This table shows economic data regarding employment in the United States during a six-month period in 2006.

④ Be sure to read any footnotes provided with the table. Footnotes clarify information. For example, (P) indicates that a statistic is preliminary rather than final.

⑤ Summarize the information shown in each part of the table. Use the title and side headings to help you focus on what information the table is presenting.

Selected Labor Force Statistics, February to July, 2006 ①			
② Month	Unemployment Rate (percent)	New Jobs Added (thousands)	Average Hourly Earnings[1] (in dollars)
February	4.8	200	16.47
March	4.7	175	16.51 **③**
April	4.7	112	16.61
May	4.6	100	16.62
June	4.6	124^p	16.69^p
July	4.8	113^p	16.76^p

Footnotes: **④**
(P) Preliminary
(1) For production and nonsupervisory workers, in dollars and cents
Source: Bureau of Labor Statistics

⑤ *The table provides statistical information about employment in the United States. Statistics are given for each of six months, from February through July 2006. The unemployment rate fluctuated between 4.6 and 4.8 percent. There was an increase in the number of jobs each month, with the greatest increase occurring in June and the smallest in May. Average hourly earnings rose fairly steadily from $16.47 in February to $16.76 July.*

Applying the Skill

Turn to page 79 and study Figure 3.3. Then write a paragraph summarizing the information presented in the table.

2.6 Analyzing Databases

A **DATABASE** is a collection of data, or information, that is organized so that you can find and retrieve information on a specific topic quickly and easily. You can search for specific information without going through the entire database. A database provides a list of all information related to a specific topic.

Understanding the Skill

STRATEGY: Study the elements of the database. First identify the topic. The title "World's Top Oil Consumers" indicates the criterion for listing the six nations in the database. Look at the categories shown and pose questions about what you can learn from them. For example, in this database you could search for "countries consuming more than 10 million bbls (barrels) per day" and discover that the United States and the European Union fall into that category.

1 **Determine the order of presentation of information.** The six countries in this database are listed according to the amount of oil they consume, from most to least.

2 **Identify the entries included under each heading.** Here, the data in each row relates to one of the six countries listed.

3 **Determine how the categories in the database relate to one another.** This database includes the categories "oil production" and "proved oil reserves." Both relate to oil consumption. These related categories enable you, for example, to determine which countries, if any, produce less oil than they consume.

4 **Read any labels or footnotes that clarify the nature of the data.** In this database, the figures represent barrels (bbl) of oil. Also note that for purposes of providing statistical information, the EU is considered to be one country.

5 **Note the source of the data.** Is the source reliable? The source of data here is *The CIA World Factbook*, a respected and reliable source of data on the countries of the world.

World's Top Oil Consumers			
Country	Oil Consumption (Millions of bbl[1] / day)	Oil Production (Millions of bbl[1] / day)	Proved Oil Reserves (Billions of bbl[1])
United States	20.0	7.6	22.5
European Union[2]	14.6	3.4	7.3
China	6.4	3.5	18.3
Russia	2.8	9.1	69.0
Saudi Arabia	1.8	9.5	262.7
Iran	1.4	4.0	133.3

Footnotes: **4**
(1) Barrels
(2) For data presentation, treated as a single country
Source: *The CIA World Factbook* **5**

Analyze the Database

Consider the kinds of information that you could quickly find from the database. For example, you can search for countries that produce or consume more or less oil than a specific number of barrels per day. Make a list of the kinds of information you could search for in this database.

Applying the Skill

Turn to page A12 in the Economic Atlas and Statistics and review the information in the two graphs. Create a database for United States industry using statistics for the most recent year shown. Consider the steps listed above when creating your database.

Glossary

A

absolute advantage *n.* the ability of one trading nation to make a product more efficiently than another trading nation (p. 513)

aggregate demand *n.* the sum of all the demand in the economy (p. 360)

aggregate supply *n.* the sum of all the supply in the economy (p. 360)

antitrust legislation *n.* laws that define monopolies and give government the power to control or dissolve them (p. 214)

appropriations *n.* set amounts of money put aside for specific purposes (p. 431)

authoritarian *adj.* requiring absolute loyalty and obedience to authority (p. 43)

automated teller machine (ATM) *n.* an electronic device that allows bank customers to make transactions without seeing a bank officer (p. 308)

automatic stabilizer *n.* a feature of fiscal policy that works automatically to steady the economy (p. 447)

B

balanced budget *n.* a budget in which total government revenue is equal to total government spending (p. 436)

balance of payments *n.* a record of all the transactions that occurred between the individuals, businesses, and government units of one nation and those of the rest of the world (p. 529)

balance of trade *n.* the difference between the value of a country's imports and exports (p. 529)

bank exam *n.* an audit, conducted by the Federal Reserve, of a bank's financial practices (p. 481)

bank holding company *n.* a company that owns more than one bank (p. 481)

barrier to entry *n.* anything that hinders a business from entering a market (p. 198)

barter *n.* the exchange of goods and services without using money (p. 288)

bear market *n.* a situation in which stock market prices decline steadily over time (p. 335)

binding arbitration *n.* a process by which an impartial third party resolves disputes between management and unions (p. 280)

black market *n.* the illegal business of buying or selling goods or services in violation of price controls or rationing (p. 183)

Board of Governors *n.* the board of seven appointed members that supervises the operations of the Federal Reserve System and sets monetary policy (p. 476)

bond *n.* a contract a corporation issues that promises to repay borrowed money, plus interest, on a fixed schedule (p. 240)

bounced check *see* overdraft

break-even point *n.* a situation in which total costs and total revenues are the same (p. 142)

budget *n.* a monthly plan for saving and spending (p. 574)

budget deficit *n.* a situation in which the government spends more than it takes in (p. 462)

budget surplus *n.* a situation in which the government takes in more than it spends (p. 462)

bull market *n.* a situation in which stock market prices rise steadily over time (p. 335)

business cycle *n.* the series of growing and shrinking periods of economic activity, measured by increases or decreases in real gross domestic product (p. 358)

business organization *n.* an enterprise that produces goods or provides services, usually to make a profit (p. 226)

business structure *see* business organization

C

capital *n.* all the resources people make and use to produce and distribute goods and services (p. 8)

capital budget *n.* a plan for major expenses or investments (p. 436)

capital deepening *n.* an increase in the ratio of capital to labor (p. 371)

capital flight *n.* a situation in which sources of capital are sent outside the country (p. 558)

capital gain *n.* the profit made from the sale of securities (p. 330)

capitalism *n.* an economic system based on private ownership of the factors of production (p. 49)

capital market *n.* a market in which long-term financial assets are bought and sold (p. 322)

cartel *n.* a formal organization of sellers or producers who regulate the production, pricing, and marketing of a product (pp. 198, 535)

cease and desist order *n.* a ruling requiring a firm to stop an unfair business practice (p. 217)

central bank *n.* a nation's main monetary authority (p. 474)

centrally planned economy *n.* a system in which the society's leaders make all economic decisions (p. 42)

change in demand *n.* a situation in which a change in the marketplace prompts consumers to buy different amounts of a good or service at every price (p. 109)

change in quantity demanded *n.* a change in the amount of a product that consumers will buy because of a change in price (p. 108)

change in quantity supplied *n.* an increase or decrease in the amount of a good or service that producers are willing to sell because of a change in price (p. 146)

change in supply *n.* a situation in which a change in the marketplace prompts producers to offer different amounts for sale at every price (p. 148)

check clearing *n.* a service provided by the Federal Reserve to record receipts and expenditures of bank clients (p. 480)

circular flow model *n.* a visualization of all interactions in a market economy (p. 52)

civilian labor force *n.* people age 16 or older who are employed or actively looking for and available to do work (p. 266)

claim *n.* a request to an insurance company for payment on an insured loss (p. 596)

closed shop *n.* a business in which an employer can hire only union members (p. 279)

coincident indicators *n.* measures of economic performance that usually change at the same time as real gross domestic product changes (p. 364)

collective bargaining *n.* the process of negotiation between a business and its organized employees to establish wages and improve working conditions (p. 280)

command economy *n.* an economic system in which the government makes all economic decisions (p. 39)

commodity money *n.* money that has intrinsic value based on the material from which it is made (p. 291)

common stock *n.* a share of ownership in a corporation that gives the holder voting rights and a share of profits (p. 331)

communism *n.* an economic system in which there is no private ownership of property and little or no political freedom (p. 43)

comparative advantage *n.* the ability of one trading nation to produce something at a lower opportunity cost than that of another trading nation (p. 513)

competition *n.* the effort of two or more people acting independently to get business by offering the best deal (p. 49)

competitive pricing *n.* a situation in which producers sell goods and services at prices that best balance the twin desires of making the highest profit and luring customers away from rival producers (p. 174)

complements *n.* products that are used together, so the increase or decrease in demand for one will result in an increase or decrease in demand for the other (p. 112)

conglomerate *n.* a business composed of companies that produce unrelated goods or services (p. 243)

consumer *n.* a person who buys goods or services for personal use (p. 5)

consumer price index (CPI) *n.* a measure of changes in the prices of goods and services that consumers commonly purchase (p. 396)

consumer sovereignty *n.* the idea that consumers have the ultimate control over what is produced because they are free to buy what they want and refuse products they do not want (p. 50)

contingent employment *n.* temporary or part-time work (p. 270)

contract *n.* a formal, legally binding agreement (p. 602)

contraction *n.* a decrease in economic activity (p. 359); *see* business cycle

contractionary fiscal policy *n.* a plan to reduce aggregate demand and slow down the economy during a period of too-rapid economic expansion (p. 446)

contractionary monetary policy *n.* a plan to reduce the amount of money in circulation; also called tight-money policy (p. 492)

cooperative *n.* a type of business operated for the shared benefit of the owners, who are also its customers (p. 250)

co-pay *n.* an amount the insured owes when an insured receives health care (p. 596)

corporate income tax *n.* a tax based on a corporation's profits (p. 412)

corporation *n.* a business owned by shareholders, also called stockholders, who own the rights to the company's profits but face only limited liability for the company's debts and losses (p. 238)

cosigner *n.* a person who assumes responsibility for the debt if the borrower fails to repay the loan (p. 583)

cost-benefit analysis *n.* the practice of examining the costs and the expected benefits of a choice as an aid to decision making (p. 15)

cost-push inflation *n.* a situation in which increases in production costs push up prices (p. 399)

Council of Economic Advisers *n.* the three-member group that advises the President on fiscal policy and other economic issues (p. 452)

coupon rate *n.* the interest rate a bond-holder receives every year until the bond matures (p. 338)

craft union *n.* an organization of workers with similar skills who work in different industries for different employers (p. 274)

credit *n.* the practice of buying goods or services now and paying for them in the future (p. 582)

credit report *n.* a statement by a credit bureau that details a consumer's credit record (p. 586)

credit score *n.* a number that summarizes a consumer's creditworthiness (p. 590)

crowding-out effect *n.* a situation in which the government outbids private bond interest rates to gain loanable funds (p. 466)

currency *n.* paper money and coins (pp. 293, 475)

customs duty *n.* a tax on goods imported into the United States (p. 425)

customs unions *n.* agreements that abolish trade barriers among the members and establish uniform tariffs for non-members (p. 532)

cyclical unemployment *n.* unemployment caused by the part of the business cycle with decreased economic activity (p. 384)

D

debit card *n.* a card one can use like an ATM card to withdraw cash or like a check to make purchases (p. 304)

debt restructuring *n.* a method countries with outstanding debt obligations use to alter the terms of debt agreements to achieve some advantage (p. 559)

deductible *n.* the amount the insured pays before the insurance company pays (p. 596)

default *n.* the condition that occurs when a nation cannot pay interest or principle on a loan (p. 559)

deficit spending *n.* the government practice of spending more than it collects in revenue for a specific fiscal year (p. 462)

deflation *n.* a decrease in the general price level (p. 398)

demand *n.* the desire to have some good or service and the ability to pay for it (p. 98)

demand curve *n.* a graph that shows a demand schedule, or how much of a good or service an individual is willing and able to purchase at each price (p. 102)

demand deposits *n.* checking accounts, so called because checking accounts can be converted into currency "on demand" (p. 293)

demand-pull inflation *n.* a condition that occurs when total demand rises faster than the production of goods and services (p. 399)

demand schedule *n.* a table that shows how much of a good or service an individual is willing and able to purchase at each price (p. 100)

demand-side fiscal policy *n.* a plan to stimulate aggregate demand (p. 454)

deposit multiplier formula *n.* a mathematical formula that tells how much the money supply will increase after an initial cash deposit in a bank (p. 485)

depreciate *v.* to decrease in value (p. 590)

depression *n.* an extended period of high unemployment and reduced business activity (p. 359)

deregulation *n.* the reduction or elimination of government oversight and control of business (p. 218)

derived demand *n.* a demand for a product or resource based on its contribution to the final product (p. 259)

developed nations *n.* nations that have a market economy, a relatively high standard of living, a high GDP, industrialization, widespread private ownership of private property, and stable and effective governments (p. 544)

differentiated product *see* product differentiation

diminishing returns *n.* a situation in which new workers cause marginal product to grow but at a decreasing rate (p. 139)

discount rate *n.* the interest rate that the Federal Reserve charges when it lends money to other banks (p. 491)

discretionary fiscal policy *n.* actions taken by the federal government by choice to correct economic instability (p. 446)

discretionary spending *n.* spending that the government must authorize each year (p. 428)

disequilibrium *n.* a situation in which quantity supplied and quantity demanded are not in balance (p. 169)

disposable personal income (DPI) *n.* personal income minus taxes (p. 355)

diversification *n.* the practice of distributing investments among different financial assets to maximize return and limit risk (p. 327)

dividend *n.* the part of a corporation's profit that the company pays the stockholders (p. 238)

dumping *n.* the sale of a product in another country at a price lower than that charged in the home market (p. 521)

Dumpster diving *n.* technique used by identity thieves to gather personal information in the garbage (p. 588)

E

easy-money policy *see* expansionary monetary policy

economic cycle *see* business cycle

economic growth *n.* an increase in a nation's real gross domestic product (p. 358)

economic interdependence *n.* a situation in which producers in one nation depend on others to provide goods and services they do not produce (p. 510)

economic model *n.* a simplified representation of economic activities, systems, or problems (p. 18)

economics *n.* the study of how individuals and societies satisfy their unlimited wants with limited resources (p. 4)

economic system *n.* the way in which a society uses its scarce resources to satisfy its people's unlimited wants (p. 38)

economies of scale *n.* a situation in which the average cost of production falls as the producer grows larger (p. 201)

economize *v.* to make decisions according what is believed to be the best combination of costs and benefits (p. 12)

efficiency *n.* the condition in which economic resources are used to produce the maximum amount of goods and services (p. 20)

elastic *adj.* referring to a situation in which a change in price, either up or down, leads to a relatively larger change in the quantity demanded or the quantity supplied (pp. 117, 154)

elasticity of demand *n.* a measure of how responsive consumers are to price changes in the marketplace (p. 117)

elasticity of supply *n.* a measure of how responsive producers are to price changes in the marketplace (p. 154)

embargo *n.* a law that cuts off most or all trade with a specific country (p. 521)

entitlement *n.* a social welfare program with specific eligibility requirements (p. 428)

entrepreneurship *n.* the combination of vision, skill, ingenuity, and willingness to take risks that is needed to create and run new businesses (p. 9)

equilibrium price *n.* the price at which the quantity demanded equals the quantity supplied (p. 164)

equilibrium wage *n.* the wage at which the quantity of workers demanded equals the quantity of workers supplied; the market price for labor (p. 258)

estate tax *n.* a tax on the assets of a person who has died (p. 425)

European Union (EU) *n.* the economic and political union of European nations that was established in 1993 (p. 532)

euro *n.* the single currency of the European Union (p. 533)

excise tax *n.* a tax on the production or sale of a specific good or service (pp. 149, 425)

expansion *n.* an increase in economic activity (p. 358); *see* business cycle

expansionary fiscal policy *n.* a plan to increase aggregate demand and stimulate a weak economy (p. 446)

expansionary monetary policy *n.* a plan to increase the amount of money in circulation; also called easy-money policy (p. 492)

exports *n.* goods or services produced in one country and sold to other countries (p. 516)

externality *n.* a side effect of a transaction that affects someone other than the producer or buyer (p. 87)

F

factor market *n.* the market for the factors of production—land, labor, capital, and entrepreneurship (p. 52)

factors of production *n.* the economic resources needed to produce goods and services (p. 8)

federal budget *n.* a plan for spending federal tax money (p. 431)

federal funds rate (FFR) *n.* the interest at which a depository institution lends available funds to another depository institution overnight (p. 490)

Federal Insurance Contributions Act (FICA) *n.* a payroll tax that provides coverage for the elderly, the unemployed due to disability, and surviving family members of wage earners who have died (p. 423)

Federal Open Market Committee (FOMC) *n.* the Federal Reserve System board that supervises the sale and purchase of federal government securities (p. 477)

Federal Reserve System *n.* the central bank of the United States; commonly called the Fed (p. 474)

fiat money *n.* money that has no tangible backing but is declared by the government and accepted by citizens to have worth (p. 291)

filing status *n.* for filing taxes, based on marital status or support of dependents (p. 604)

financial asset *n.* a claim on a borrower's property (p. 319)

financial intermediary *n.* an institution that collects funds from savers and invests these funds in financial assets (p. 319)

financial market *n.* a situation in which buyers and sellers exchange financial assets (p. 319)

financial system *n.* all the institutions that help transfer funds between savers and investors (p. 318)

fiscal *adj.* of or relating to government revenue and spending (p. 446)

fiscal policy *n.* the federal government's use of taxing and spending to affect the economy (p. 446)

fiscal year *n.* a 12-month period for which an organization plans its expenditures (p. 431)

fixed costs *n.* expenses that business owners incur no matter how much they produce (p. 140)

fixed rate of exchange *n.* a system in which the currency of one nation is fixed or constant in relation to other currencies (p. 526)

flexible exchange rate *n.* a system in which the exchange rate for currency changes as supply and demand for the currency changes; also called the floating rate (p. 527)

focus group *n.* a moderated discussion with small groups of consumers (p. 208)

foreign exchange market *n.* a market in which currencies of different countries are bought and sold (p. 526)

foreign exchange rate *n.* the price of one currency in the currencies of other nations (p. 526)

franchise *n.* a business made up of semi-independent businesses that all offer the same products or services (p. 248)

franchisee *n.* a semi-independent business that pays a fee for the right to sell the parent company's products or services in a particular area (p. 248)

free contract *n.* a situation in which people decide for themselves which legal agreements to enter into (p. 73)

free enterprise system *n.* another name for capitalism, an economic system based on private ownership of productive resources (p. 70)

free rider *n.* a person who does not pay for a good or service but who benefits from it when it is provided (p. 85)

free-trade zone *n.* a specific region in which trade between nations takes place without protective tariffs (p. 532)

frictional unemployment *n.* the temporary unemployment of workers moving from one job to another (p. 384)

full employment *n.* a level of unemployment in which none of the unemployment is caused by decreased economic activity; generally marked by an unemployment rate of 4 to 6 percent (p. 383)

future *n.* a contract to buy or sell a stock on a specified future date at a preset price (p. 333)

G

general partnership *n.* a partnership in which each partner shares the management of the business and is liable for all business debts and losses (p. 233)

geographic monopoly *n.* a monopoly that exists because there are no other producers or sellers within a certain region (p. 201)

gift tax *n.* a tax on money or property given by one living person to another (p. 425)

glass ceiling *n.* an unseen, artificial barrier to advancement that women and minorities sometimes face (p. 262)

global economy *n.* all the economic interactions that cross international boundaries (p. 61)

gold standard *n.* a system in which the basic monetary unit is equal to a set amount of gold (p. 299)

goods *n.* physical objects, such as food, clothing, and furniture, that can be purchased (p. 5)

government monopoly *n.* a monopoly that exists because the government either owns and runs the business or authorizes only one producer (p. 201)

grant-in-aid *n.* a transfer payment from the federal government to state or local governments (p. 432)

gross domestic product (GDP) *n.* the market value of all final goods and services produced within a nation in a given time period (p. 350)

gross national product (GNP) *n.* the market value of all final goods and services produced by a country in a given time period (p. 355)

H

hacking *n.* technique used by identity thieves to gather personal information using computers and related technology (p. 588)

horizontal merger *n.* the joining of two or more companies that offer the same or similar products or services (p. 243)

human capital *n.* the knowledge and skills that enable workers to be productive (p. 261)

human development index (HDI) *n.* a combination of a nation's real GDP per capita, life expectancy, adult literacy rate, and student enrollment figures that indicates what life is like in a specific country (p. 547)

hyperinflation *n.* a rapid, uncontrolled rate of inflation in excess of 50 percent (p. 398)

I

identity theft *n.* the use of someone else's personal information for criminal purposes (p. 588)

imperfect competition *n.* a market structure that lacks one or more of the conditions needed for perfect competition (p. 195)

imports *n.* goods or services produced in one country and purchased by another (p. 516)

incentive *n.* a benefit offered to encourage people to act in a certain way (pp. 12, 176)

incidence of a tax *n.* the final burden of a tax (p. 415)

income distribution *n.* the way income is divided among people in a nation (p. 390)

income effect *n.* a change in the amount of a good or service a consumer will buy because his or her income (and therefore purchasing power) changes (p. 107)

income inequality *n.* the unequal distribution of income (p. 390)

increasing returns *n.* a situation in which hiring new workers cause marginal product to increase (p. 139)

independent contractor *n.* someone who sells his or her services on a contract basis (p. 270)

individual income tax *n.* a tax based on an individual's income from all sources (p. 412)

industrial union *n.* an organization of workers with many different skills who work in the same industry (p. 274)

inelastic *n.* a situation in which quantity demanded or quantity supplied changes little as price changes (pp. 117, 155)

infant industries *n.* new industries that are often unable to compete against larger, more established competitors (p. 523)

infant mortality rate *n.* the number of children who die within the first year of life per 1,000 births (p. 547)

inferior goods *n.* goods that consumers demand less of when their incomes rise (p. 110)

inflation *n.* a sustained rise in the general price level, or a sustained fall in the purchasing power of money (p. 396)

inflation rate *n.* the rate of change in prices over a set period of time (p. 397)

infrastructure *n.* the basic set of support systems—such as power, communications, transportation, water, sanitation, and education systems—needed to keep an economy and society going (pp. 86, 545)

input costs *n.* the price of the resources needed to produce a good or service (p. 148)

insourcing *n.* the practice of foreign companies establishing operations in, and therefore bringing jobs to, the United States (p. 269)

interest *n.* a fee a bank pays for the use of money (p. 578)

International Monetary Fund (IMF) *n.* the international organization established to promote international monetary cooperation, foster economic growth, and provide temporary financial assistance to countries to help ease balance-of-payments adjustment (p. 559)

investment *n.* the use of income today in a way that allows for a future benefit (p. 318)

investment objective *n.* a financial goal that is used to determine if an investment is appropriate (p. 324)

J

junk bond *n.* a high-risk, high-yield corporate bond (p. 339)

K

Keynesian economics *n.* the idea, first advanced by John Maynard Keynes, that the government needs to stimulate aggregate demand in times of recession (p. 454)

L

labor *n.* all the human time, effort, and talent used to produce goods and services (p. 8)

labor input *n.* the size of the labor force multiplied by the length of the workweek (p. 371)

labor productivity *n.* the amount of goods and services a person can produce in a given time (p. 149)

labor union *n.* an organization of workers that seeks to improve wages, working conditions, fringe benefits, job security, and other work-related matters for its members (p. 274)

Laffer Curve *n.* a graph that illustrates how tax cuts affect tax revenues and economic growth (p. 459)

lagging indicators *n.* measures of economic performance that usually change after real gross domestic product changes (p. 364)

laissez faire *n.* the principle that the government should not interfere in the economy (p. 49)

land *n.* all the natural resources on or under the ground that are used to produce goods and services (p. 8)

landlord *n.* the owner of rental property (p. 609)

law of comparative advantage *n.* the law stating that countries gain when they produce items that they are most efficient at producing and that are at the lowest opportunity cost (p. 514)

law of demand *n.* states that when the price of a good or service goes down, quantity demanded increases, and when the prices go up, quantity demanded falls (p. 99)

law of diminishing marginal utility *n.* states that the marginal benefit from using each additional unit of a good or service during a given time period tends to decline as each is used (p. 106)

law of increasing opportunity costs *n.* states that as production switches from one product to another, increasingly more resources are needed to increase the production of the second product, which causes opportunity costs to rise (p. 21)

law of supply *n.* states that producers are willing to sell more of a good or service at a higher price than they are at a lower price (p. 131)

leading indicators *n.* measures of economic performance that usually change before real gross domestic product changes (p. 364)

lease *n.* a contract for renting an apartment, vehicle, or other item for a specific period of time (p. 609)

legal equality *n.* a situation in which everyone has the same economic rights under the law (p. 73)

less developed countries (LDCs) *n.* countries with lower GDPs, less well-developed industry, and lower standards of living; sometimes called emerging economies (p. 545)

life expectancy *n.* the average number of years a person could expect to live if current mortality trends were to continue for the rest of that person's life (p. 547)

limited liability *n.* a situation in which a business owner's liability for business debts and losses is limited (p. 240)

limited liability partnership (LLP) *n.* a partnership in which all partners are not responsible for the debts and other liabilities of the other partners (p. 233)

limited life *n.* a situation in which a business ceases to exist if the owner dies, retires, or leaves (p. 228)

limited partnership *n.* a partnership in which at least one partner is not involved in running the business and is liable only for the funds he or she invested (p. 233)

literacy rate *n.* the percentage of people older than 15 who can read and write (p. 547)

loan *n.* borrowed money that is usually repaid with interest (p. 582)

Lorenz curve *n.* a curve that shows the degree of income inequality in a nation (p. 391)

M

macroeconomic equilibrium *n.* the point where aggregate demand equals aggregate supply (p. 361)

macroeconomics *n.* the study of the behavior of the economy as a whole; concerned with large-scale economic activity (p. 27)

mandatory spending *n.* government spending that is required by current law (p. 428)

marginal benefit *n.* the benefit or satisfaction gained from using one more unit of a good or service (p. 16)

marginal cost *n.* the additional cost of producing or using one more unit of a good or service (pp. 16, 140)

marginal product *n.* the change in total output that results from adding one more worker (p. 138)

marginal revenue *n.* the money made from each additional unit sold (p. 142)

market *n.* any place or situation in which people buy and sell goods and services (p. 48)

market allocation *n.* an agreement among or between competing businesses to divide up a market (p. 216)

market demand curve *n.* a graph that shows data from a market demand schedule, or how much of a good or service all consumers are willing and able to purchase at each price (p. 102)

market demand schedule *n.* a table that shows how much of a good or service all consumers are willing and able to purchase at each price in a market (p. 100)

market division *see* market allocation

market economy *n.* an economic system based on individual choice and voluntary exchange (p. 39)

market equilibrium *n.* a situation in which the quantity supplied and the quantity demanded at a particular price are equal (p. 164)

market failure *n.* a situation in which people who are not part of a marketplace interaction benefit from it or pay part of its costs (p. 84)

market research *n.* the gathering and evaluation of information about consumer preferences for goods and services (p. 208)

market share *n.* a company's percent of total sales in a particular market (p. 209)

market structure *n.* an economic model of competition among businesses in the same industry (p. 192)

market supply curve *n.* a graph that shows data from a market supply schedule (p. 134)

market supply schedule *n.* how much of a good or service all producers in a market are willing and able to offer for sale at each price (p. 132)

maturity *n.* the date when a bond is due to be repaid (p. 338)

Medicaid *n.* a government-run medical insurance program for low-income people (p. 429)

Medicare *n.* a government-run, national health insurance program mainly for citizens over age 65 (p. 423)

medium of exchange *n.* a means through which goods and services can be exchanged (p. 288)

merger *n.* the combining of two or more companies to form a single company (p. 214)

microeconomics *n.* the study of the behavior of individual players—such as individuals, families, and businesses—in an economy (p. 27)

minimum balance requirement *n.* the amount of money needed in an account to avoid fees (p. 576)

minimum wage *n.* the lowest amount, established by law, that an employer may pay a worker for one hour of work (pp. 182, 262)

mixed economy *n.* an economic system that has elements of traditional, command, and market economies; the most common economic system (p. 58)

modified free enterprise economy *n.* a mixed economic system that includes some government protections, provisions, and regulations to adjust the free enterprise system (p. 80)

monetarism *n.* an economic theory that suggests that rapid changes in the money supply are the main cause of economic instability (p. 496)

monetary *adj.* of or relating to money (p. 474)

monetary policy *n.* the Federal Reserve's actions that change the money supply to influence the economy (p. 490)

money *n.* anything that people will accept as payment for goods and services (p. 288)

money market *n.* a market in which short-term financial assets are bought and sold (p. 322)

monopolistic competition *n.* a market structure in which many sellers offer similar, but not standardized, products to consumers (p. 206)

monopoly *n.* a market structure in which only one seller sells a product for which there are no close substitutes (p. 198)

monopsony *n.* market structure in which there are many sellers but only one large buyer (p. 212)

multifactor productivity *n.* the ratio between an industry's economic output and its labor and capital inputs (p. 373)

multinational corporation *n.* a corporation with branches in several countries (p. 243)

mutual fund *n.* an investment company that gathers money from individual investors and uses the money to purchase a range of financial assets (p. 320)

N

NAFTA *n.* the North America Free Trade Agreement, which ensures free trade throughout the continent and constitutes the largest free-trade zone in the world (p. 533)

national accounts *see* national income accounting

national bank *n.* a bank chartered by the national government (p. 299)

national debt *n.* the total amount of money that the federal government owes (p. 462)

national income (NI) *n.* the total income earned in a nation from the production of goods and services in a given time period (p. 355)

national income accounting *n.* a way of analyzing a country's economy using statistical measures of its income, spending, and output (p. 350)

nationalize *v.* to change from private ownership to government or public ownership (p. 61)

natural monopoly *n.* a market situation in which the costs of production are lowest when only one firm supplies a product or service (p. 201)

near money *n.* savings accounts and other similar time deposits that can be converted into cash relatively easily (p. 293)

needs *n.* things such as food, clothing, and shelter that are necessary for survival (p. 4)

negative externality *n.* an externality that costs people who were not involved in the original economic activity (p. 87)

net national product (NNP) *n.* the gross national product minus depreciation of capital stock—in other words, the value of final goods and services less the value of capital goods that became worn out during the year (p. 355)

nominal GDP *n.* the gross domestic product stated in terms of the current value of goods and services (p. 352)

nonmarket activities *n.* services that have potential economic value but are performed without charge (p. 354)

nonprice competition *n.* the use of factors other than price—such as style, service, advertising, or giveaways—to try to convince customers to buy from one producer rather than another (p. 207)

nonprofit organization *n.* an institution that acts like a business but exists to benefit society rather than to make a profit (p. 250)

normal goods *n.* goods that consumers demand more of when their incomes rise (p. 110)

normative economics *n.* a way of describing and explaining what economic behavior ought to be, not what it actually is (p. 29)

not-for-profit *see* nonprofit organization

O

oligopoly *n.* a market structure in which only a few sellers offer a similar product (p. 209)

OPEC *n.* the Organization of Petroleum Exporting Countries, a regional trade group (p. 535)

open market operations *n.* the Federal Reserve's sale and purchase of federal government securities; the monetary policy tool most used by the Federal Reserve to adjust the money supply (p. 490)

open opportunity *n.* the ability of everyone to enter and compete in the market of his or her own free choice (p. 73)

operating budget *n.* a plan for day-to-day expenses (p. 436)

opportunity cost *n.* the value of something that is given up by choosing one alternative over another (p. 14)

option *n.* a contract giving an investor the right to buy or sell stock at a future date at a preset price (p. 333)

outsourcing *n.* the practice of contracting with an outside company, often in a foreign country, to provide goods or services (p. 269)

overdraft *n.* a check or other withdrawal that exceeds the existing account balance (p. 576)

P

par value *n.* the amount that a bond issuer promises to pay the buyer at maturity (p. 338)

partnership *n.* a business co-owned by two or more people, or "partners," who agree on how responsibilities, profits, and losses should be divided (p. 232)

patent *n.* a legal registration of an invention or a process that gives the inventor the exclusive property rights to that invention or process for a certain number of years (p. 202)

peak *n.* the end of an expansion in the economy (p. 359); *see* business cycle

per capita gross domestic product *n.* a nation's GDP divided by its total population (p. 546)

perestroika *n.* Russian leader Mikhail Gorbachev's plan to gradually incorporate markets into the Soviet Union's command economy (p. 564)

perfect competition *n.* the ideal model of a market economy; the market structure in which none of the many well-informed and independent sellers or buyers has control over the price of a standardized good or service (p. 192)

personal income (PI) *n.* the annual income received by a country's people from all sources (p. 355)

phishing *n.* technique used by identity thieves to gather personal information through deceptive telephone calls (p. 588)

PIN *n.* personal identification number (p. 577)

positive economics *n.* a way of describing and explaining economics as it is (p. 29)

positive externality *n.* an externality that benefits people who were not involved in the original economic activity (p. 87)

poverty *n.* the situation in which a person's income and resources do not allow him or her to achieve a minimum standard of living (p. 388)

poverty line *see* poverty threshold

poverty rate *n.* the percentage of people living in households that have incomes below the poverty threshold (p. 389)

poverty threshold *n.* the official minimum income needed to pay for the basic expenses of living (p. 388)

predatory pricing *n.* the setting of prices below cost for a time to drive smaller competitors out of a market (p. 216)

preferred stock *n.* a share of ownership in a corporation giving the holder a share of profits but, in general, no voting rights (p. 331)

premium *n.* an amount paid for insurance (p. 596)

price ceiling *n.* an established maximum price that sellers may charge for a product (p. 180)

price fixing *n.* conspiring among or between businesses to set the prices of competing products (p. 216)

price floor *n.* an established minimum price that buyers must pay for a product (p. 182)

price maker *n.* a business that does not have to consider competitors when setting its prices (p. 198)

price taker *n.* a firm that must accept the market price set by the interaction of supply and demand (p. 193)

primary market *n.* a market for buying and selling newly created financial assets directly from the issuing entity (p. 322)

prime rate *n.* the interest rate that banks charge their best customers (p. 491)

private company *n.* a corporation that controls who can buy or sell its stock (p. 238)

private property rights *n.* the rights of individuals and groups to own resources and businesses (p. 48)

private sector *n.* the part of the economy that is owned by individuals or businesses (p. 432)

privatization *n.* the process of transferring state-owned property and businesses to individuals (p. 563)

privatize *v.* to change from government or public ownership to private ownership (p. 61)

producer *n.* a person who makes goods or provides services (p. 5)

producer price index (PPI) *n.* a measure of changes in wholesale prices (p. 397)

product differentiation *n.* the attempt to distinguish a product from similar products (p. 206)

product market *n.* the market in which goods and services are bought and sold (p. 52)

production possibilities curve (PPC) *n.* a graph used to illustrate the impact of scarcity on an economy (p. 18)

productivity *n.* the amount of output produced from a set amount of inputs (p. 372)

productivity, labor *see* labor productivity

profit *n.* the financial gain a seller makes from a business transaction (p. 49); the money left over after the costs of producing a product are subtracted from the income gained by selling that product (p. 78)

profit-maximizing output *n.* the point in production at which a business has reached its highest level of profit (p. 143)

profit motive *n.* the incentive that encourages people and organizations to improve their material well-being by seeking to gain from economic activities (p. 73)

progressive tax *n.* a tax that places a higher percentage rate of taxation on high-income earners than on low-income earners (p. 412)

property tax *n.* a tax based on the value of an individual's or a business's assets (p. 412)

proportional tax *n.* a tax that takes the same percentage of income from all taxpayers regardless of income level (p. 412)

protectionism *n.* the use of trade barriers between nations to protect domestic industries (p. 523)

protective tariff *n.* a tax on imported goods to protect domestic goods (p. 521)

public company *n.* a corporation that issues stock that can be freely traded (p. 238)

public disclosure *n.* a policy requiring businesses to reveal product information to consumers (p. 217)

public goods *n.* goods and services provided by the government and consumed by the public as a group (p. 84)

public transfer payment *n.* a transfer payment in which the government transfers income from taxpayers to recipients who do not provide anything in return (p. 89)

pure competition *see* perfect competition

Q

quota *n.* a limit on the amount of a product that can be imported (p. 520)

R

rational expectations theory *n.* the theory that states that individuals and business firms expect changes in fiscal policy will have particular effects and take action to protect their interests against those effects (p. 452)

rationing *n.* a system in which the government allocates goods and services using factors other than price (p. 183)

real GDP *n.* the gross domestic product corrected for changes in prices from year to year (p. 352)

real GDP per capita *n.* the real gross domestic product divided by total population (p. 369)

recession *n.* a prolonged economic contraction lasting two or more quarters (six months or more) (p. 359)

regressive tax *n.* a tax that takes a larger percentage of income from low-income earners than from high-income earners (p. 412)

regulation *n.* a set of rules or laws designed to control business behavior (pp. 150, 214)

representative money *n.* paper money that is backed by something tangible (p. 291)

required reserve ratio (RRR) *n.* the fraction of a bank's deposits, determined by the Federal Reserve, that it must keep in reserve so that it can loan out money (p. 484)

return *n.* the profit or loss made on an investment (p. 327)

revenue *n.* government income from taxes and nontax sources (p. 410)

revenue tariff *n.* a tax on imports specifically to raise money; are rarely used today (p. 521)

right-to-work laws *n.* legislation that makes it illegal to require workers to join unions (p. 279)

risk *n.* the possibility for loss on an investment (p. 327)

S

safety net *n.* government programs designed to protect people from economic hardships (p. 89)

sales tax *n.* a tax based on the value of goods or services at the time of sale (p. 412)

savings *n.* income not used for consumption (p. 318)

scarcity *n.* a situation that exists when there are not enough resources to meet human wants (p. 4)

seasonal unemployment *n.* unemployment linked to seasonal work (p. 384)

secondary market *n.* a market in which financial assets are resold (p. 322)

service *n.* work that one person does for another for payment (p. 5)

shadow economy *see* underground economy

share *n.* part of the stock of a corporation (p. 238); *see* stock

shock therapy *n.* an economic program involving the abrupt shift from a command economy to a free-market economy (p. 563)

shortage *n.* a situation in which demand is greater than supply, usually the result of prices being set too low (p. 167)

shoulder surfing *n.* technique used by identity thieves to gather personal information as you disclose private information in public (p. 588)

socialism *n.* an economic system in which the government owns some or all of the factors of production (p. 43)

Social Security *n.* a federal program to aid older citizens, orphaned children, and the disabled (p. 423)

sole proprietorship *n.* a business owned and controlled by one person (p. 226)

spamming *n.* technique used by identity thieves to gather personal information through deceptive e-mails (p. 588)

special economic zone (SEZ) *n.* a geographic region that has economic laws that are different from a country's usual economic laws, with the goal of increasing foreign investment (p. 567)

specialization *n.* a situation that occurs when individuals or businesses concentrate their efforts in the areas in which they have an advantage for increased productivity and profit (pp. 50, 138, 510)

spending multiplier effect *n.* a situation in which a small change in spending eventually results in a much larger change in GDP (p. 455)

stabilization programs *n.* programs that require troubled nations to carry out reforms such as reducing foreign trade deficits and external debt, eliminating price controls, closing inefficient public enterprises, and slashing budget deficits (p. 559)

stagflation *n.* a period during which prices rise at the same time that there is a slowdown in business activity (p. 359)

standardized product *n.* a product that consumers consider identical in all essential features to other products in the same market (p. 192)

standard of value *n.* the yardstick of economic worth in the exchange process (p. 289)

start-up costs *n.* the expenses that a new business must pay to enter a market and begin selling to consumers (p. 209)

state bank *n.* a bank chartered by a state government (p. 296)

statistics *n.* numerical data (p. 24)

stock *n.* shares of ownership in a corporation (p. 238)

stockbroker *n.* an agent who buys and sells securities for customers (p. 332)

stock exchange *n.* a secondary market where securities are bought and sold (p. 330)

stock index *n.* an instrument used to measure and report the change in prices of a set of stocks (p. 334)

stored-value card *n.* a card that represents money that the card holder has on deposit with the card issuer (p. 308)

store of value *n.* something that holds its value over time (p. 289)

strike *n.* a work stoppage used to gain negotiating power while attempting to convince an employer to improve wages, working conditions, or other work-related matters (p. 274)

structural unemployment *n.* unemployment that exists when the available jobs do not match the skills of available workers (p. 384)

subsidy *n.* a government payment that helps cover the cost of an economic activity that can benefit the public as a whole (p. 88)

substitutes *n.* products that can be used in place of other products to satisfy consumer wants (p. 112)

substitution effect *n.* the pattern of behavior that occurs when consumers react to a change in price of a product by buying a substitute product that offers a better relative value (p. 107)

supply *n.* the willingness and ability of a producer to produce and sell a product (p. 130)

supply curve *n.* a graph that shows data from a supply schedule (p. 134)

supply schedule *n.* a table that shows how much of a good or service an individual producer is willing and able to offer for sale at each price (p. 132)

supply-side fiscal policy *n.* a plan designed to provide incentives to producers to increase aggregate supply (p. 458)

surplus *n.* a situation in which supply is greater than demand, usually the result of prices being set too high (p. 167)

T

tariff *n.* a fee charged for goods brought into a country from another country (p. 521)

tax *n.* a mandatory payment to a government (p. 410)

taxable income *n.* the portion of income subject to taxation after all deductions and exemptions (pp. 421, 604)

tax assessor *n.* a government official who determines the value of property to be taxed (p. 437)

tax base *n.* a form of wealth—such as income, property, goods, or services—that is subject to taxes (p. 412)

tax incentive *n.* the use of taxes to encourage or discourage certain economic behaviors (p. 417)

tax return *n.* a form used to report income and taxes owed to the government (p. 421)

technological monopoly *n.* a monopoly that exists because a firm controls a manufacturing method, invention, or type of technology (p. 201)

technology *n.* the application of scientific methods and innovations to production (p. 149)

telecommuting *n.* the practice of doing office work in a location other than the office (p. 270)

telework *see* telecommuting

temp, temps, temping *see* contingent employment

thrift institution *n.* a financial institution that serves savers (p. 478)

tight-money policy *see* contractionary monetary policy

total cost *n.* the sum of fixed and variable costs (p. 140)

total revenue *n.* the income a business receives from selling its products (pp. 122, 142)

total revenue test *n.* a method of measuring elasticity by comparing the total revenue a business would receive when offering its product at various prices (p. 122)

trade barrier *n.* any law passed to limit free trade between nations (p. 520)

trade deficit *n.* an unfavorable balance of trade that occurs when a nation imports more than it exports (p. 529)

trade-off *n.* the alternative someone gives up when making an economic choice (p. 14)

trade surplus *n.* a favorable balance of trade that occurs when a nation exports more than it imports (p. 529)

trade union *see* labor union

trade war *n.* a succession of trade barriers between nations (p. 522)

trade-weighted value of the dollar *n.* a measure of the international value of the dollar that determines if the dollar is strong or weak as measured against another currency (p. 528)

traditional economy *n.* an economic system in which people make economic decisions based on customs and beliefs that have been handed down from one generation to the next (p. 38)

transfer payment *n.* money distributed to taxpayers who do not provide goods or services in return (pp. 89, 432)

transitional economy *n.* a country that has moved (or is moving) from a command economy to a market economy (p. 545)

Treasury bill (T bill) *n.* a short-term bond that matures in less than one year (p. 464)

Treasury bond *n.* a long-term bond that matures in 30 years (p. 464)

Treasury note *n.* an intermediate-term bond that matures in between two and ten years (p. 464)

trough *n.* the end of a contraction in the economy (p. 359); *see* business cycle

trust *n.* a group of firms combined in order to reduce competition in an industry (p. 214)

trust fund *n.* a fund held for a specific purpose to be expended at a future date (p. 465)

U

underemployed *n.* people employed part-time who want to work full-time, or those who work at a job below their skill level (p. 383)

underground economy *n.* market activities that go unreported because they are illegal or because those involved want to avoid taxation (p. 354)

underutilization *n.* the condition in which economic resources are not being used to their full potential, resulting in fewer goods and services (p. 20)

unemployment rate *n.* the percentage of the labor force that is jobless and actively looking for work (p. 382)

union *see* labor union

union shop *n.* a business in which workers are required to join a union within a set time period after being hired (p. 279)

unit elastic *adj.* relating to a situation in which the percentage change in price and quantity demanded are the same (p. 118)

unlimited liability *n.* a situation in which a business owner is responsible for all the losses and debts of a business (p. 228)

unlimited life *n.* a situation in which a corporation continues to exist even after a change in ownership (p. 240)

user fee *n.* a tax charged for the use of a good or service (p. 425)

utility *n.* the benefit or satisfaction gained from using a good or service (p. 12)

V

variable costs *n.* business costs that vary with the level of production output (p. 140)

vertical merger *n.* the combining of two or more businesses involved in different steps of producing or marketing a product or service (p. 243)

voluntary exchange *n.* a trade in which the parties involved anticipate that the benefits will outweigh the cost (p. 49)

voluntary export restraint (VER) *n.* a self-imposed limit on exports to certain countries to avoid quotas or tariffs (p. 521)

W

wage and price controls *n.* government limits on increases in wages and prices (p. 501)

wage-price spiral *n.* a cycle that begins with increased wages, which lead to higher production costs, which in turn result in higher prices, which result in demands for even higher wages (p. 400)

wage rate *n.* the established rate of pay for a specific job or work performed (p. 261)

A

absolute advantage [ventaja absoluta] *n.* capacidad de un país para hacer un producto más eficientemente que otro país (pág. 513)

aggregate demand [demanda agregada] *n.* suma de las demandas totales existentes en la economía (pág. 360)

aggregate supply [oferta agregada] *n.* suma de las ofertas totales existentes en la economía (pág. 360)

antitrust legislation [legislación antimonopolio] *n.* leyes que definen los monopolios y dan al gobierno el poder de controlarlos o disolverlos (pág. 214)

appropriations [asignaciones] *n.* cantidades fijas de dinero destinadas a fines determinados (pág. 431)

authoritarian [autoritario] *adj.* lo que exige una lealtad y una obediencia absolutas ante la autoridad (pág. 43)

automated teller machine (ATM) [cajero automático (ATM)] *n.* dispositivo electrónico que permite a los clientes de un banco hacer transacciones sin ver al personal del banco (pág. 308)

automatic stabilizer [estabilizador automático] *n.* característica de la política fiscal que actúa automáticamente para mantener estable la economía (pág. 447)

B

balanced budget [presupuesto balanceado] *n.* presupuesto en el que el total de ingresos del gobierno es igual al total de gastos del gobierno (pág. 436)

balance of payments [balanza de pagos] *n.* registro de todas las transacciones ocurridas entre las personas, las empresas y las unidades gubernamentales de un país y las del resto del mundo (pág. 529)

balance of trade [balanza de comercio] *n.* diferencia entre el valor de las exportaciones y el de las importaciones de un país (pág. 529)

bank exam [inspección bancaria] *n.* auditoría, realizada por la Reserva Federal, de las prácticas financieras de un banco (pág. 481)

bank holding company [compañía tenedora de acciones bancarias] *n.* compañía que posee más de un banco (pág. 481)

barrier to entry [barrera de entrada] *n.* todo factor que impide que una empresa entre en un mercado (pág. 198)

barter [trueque] *n.* intercambio de bienes y servicios sin utilizar dinero (pág. 288)

bear market [mercado a la baja (mercado "oso")] *n.* situación en la que los precios del mercado de valores bajan constantemente con el tiempo (pág. 335)

binding arbitration [arbitraje vinculante] *n.* proceso por el que un tercero imparcial resuelve los conflictos entre la dirección de una empresa y los sindicatos (pág. 280)

black market [mercado negro] *n.* compra o venta ilegal de bienes o servicios, violando los controles de precios o el racionamiento (pág. 183)

Board of Governors [Junta de Gobernadores] *n.* junta de siete miembros nombrados que supervisa las operaciones del Sistema de la Reserva Federal y establece la política monetaria (pág. 476)

bond [bono] *n.* contrato emitido por una sociedad anónima que promete reembolsar el dinero prestado, más intereses, según las fechas establecidas (pág. 240)

bounced check [cheque rebotado] véase overdraft [sobregiro]

break-even point [punto de equilibrio] *n.* situación en la que el total de costos y el total de ingresos son iguales (pág. 142)

budget [presupuesto] *n.* plan mensual referente a los ahorros y a los gastos (pág. 574)

budget deficit [déficit presupuestario] *n.* situación en la que los gastos del gobierno son mayores que los ingresos (pág. 462)

budget surplus [superávit presupuestario] *n.* situación en la que los ingresos del gobierno son mayores que los gastos (pág. 462)

bull market [mercado alcista (mercado "toro")] *n.* situación en la que los precios del mercado de valores suben constantemente con el tiempo (pág. 335)

business cycle [ciclo económico] *n.* serie de períodos de ascenso y descenso de la actividad económica, medida por los aumentos o las disminuciones del producto interior bruto real (pág. 358)

business organization [organización comercial] *n.* empresa que produce bienes o presta servicios, generalmente para obtener ganancias (pág. 226)

business structure [estructura comercial] véase business organization [organización comercial]

C

capital [capital] *n.* todos los recursos que se crean y utilizan para producir y distribuir bienes y servicios (pág. 8)

capital budget [presupuesto de capital] *n.* plan referente a los principales gastos o inversiones (pág. 436)

capital deepening [intensificación del uso del capital] *n.* aumento de la razón entre el capital y el trabajo (pág. 371)

capital flight [fuga de capitales] *n.* situación en la que las fuentes de capital se envían fuera del país (pág. 558)

capital gain [ganancias de capital] *n.* ganancias obtenidas de la venta de valores (pág. 330)

capitalism [capitalismo] *n.* sistema económico basado en la propiedad privada de los factores de producción (pág. 49)

capital market [mercado de capitales] *n.* mercado en el que se venden y compran activos financieros a largo plazo (pág. 322)

cartel [cártel] *n.* organización formal de vendedores o productores que regulan la producción, la fijación de precios y la comercialización de un producto (págs. 198, 535)

cease and desist order [orden de cese de actividades comerciales] *n.* decisión judicial que obliga a una compañía a dejar de realizar una práctica comercial injusta (pág. 217)

central bank [banco central] *n.* principal autoridad monetaria de un país (pág. 474)

centrally planned economy [economía de planificación centralizada] *n.* sistema en el que los dirigentes del país toman todas las decisiones económicas (pág. 42)

change in demand [cambio en la demanda] *n.* situación en la que un cambio en el mercado incita a los consumidores a comprar una cantidad diferente de un bien o de un servicio a cada precio (pág. 109)

change in quantity demanded [cambio en la cantidad demandada] *n.* cambio en la cantidad de un producto que los consumidores comprarán debido a un cambio en el precio (pág. 108)

change in quantity supplied [cambio en la cantidad ofertada] *n.* aumento o disminución de la cantidad de un bien o de un servicio que los productores están dispuestos a vender debido a un cambio en el precio (pág. 146)

change in supply [cambio en la oferta] *n.* situación en la que un cambio en el mercado incita a los productores a ofrecer para su venta una cantidad diferente a cada precio (pág. 148)

check clearing [compensación de cheques] *n.* servicio proporcionado por la Reserva Federal para registrar las entradas y las salidas de los clientes de los bancos (pág. 480)

circular flow model [modelo de flujo circular] *n.* visualización de todas las interacciones de una economía de mercado (pág. 52)

civilian labor force [fuerza laboral civil] *n.* personas de 16 años o mayores que trabajan o que buscan activamente un trabajo y están en condiciones para trabajar (pág. 266)

claim [reclamación] *n.* petición presentada ante una compañía de seguros para recibir un pago sobre una pérdida asegurada (pág. 596)

closed shop [compañía de sindicación obligatoria] *n.* compañía en la que el empleador sólo puede contratar miembros del sindicato (pág. 279)

coincident indicators [indicadores coincidentes] *n.* medidas del rendimiento económico que generalmente cambian al mismo tiempo que cambia el producto interior bruto real (pág. 364)

collective bargaining [negociación colectiva] *n.* proceso de negociación entre una empresa y sus empleados sindicalizados para establecer los salarios y mejorar las condiciones de trabajo (pág. 280)

command economy [economía autoritaria] *n.* sistema económico en el que el gobierno toma todas las decisiones económicas (pág. 39)

commodity money [dinero-mercancía] *n.* dinero que tiene un valor intrínseco basado en el material del que se compone (pág. 291)

common stock [acciones ordinarias] *n.* participación en la propiedad de una sociedad anónima que da al titular derecho a voto y parte de las ganancias (pág. 331)

communism [comunismo] *n.* sistema económico en el que no existe la propiedad privada y hay poca o ninguna libertad política (pág. 43)

comparative advantage [ventaja comparativa] *n.* capacidad de un país para producir algo a un costo de oportunidad más bajo que el de otro país (pág. 513)

competition [competencia] *n.* esfuerzo de dos o más personas que actúan independientemente por obtener clientes ofreciéndoles la mejor opción (pág. 49)

competitive pricing [fijación de precios competitivos] *n.* situación en la que los productores venden bienes y servicios a precios que intentan el mejor equilibrio entre dos deseos: obtener las mayores ganancias y atraer a los clientes de los productores rivales (pág. 174)

complements [complementarios] *n.* productos que se usan conjuntamente, de manera que el aumento y la disminución de la demanda de uno produzca el aumento o la disminución de la demanda del otro (pág. 112)

conglomerate [conglomerado] *n.* empresa compuesta de compañías que producen bienes o servicios no relacionados (pág. 243)

consumer [consumidor] *n.* persona que compra bienes o servicios para su uso personal (pág. 5)

consumer price index (CPI) [índice de precios al consumo (IPC)] *v* medida porcentual de los cambios en los precios de una cesta de los bienes y los servicios que los consumidores compran frecuentemente (pág. 396)

consumer sovereignty [soberanía del consumidor] *n.* idea de que los consumidores tienen el control definitivo sobre lo que se produce ya que son libres para comprar lo que quieren y para rechazar productos que no quieren (pág. 50)

contingent employment [empleo contingente] *n.* trabajo temporal o a tiempo parcial (pág. 270)

contract [contrato] *n.* acuerdo formal con fuerza jurídica (pág. 602)

contraction [contracción] *n.* reducción de la actividad económica (pág. 359); *véase* business cycle [ciclo económico]

contractionary fiscal policy [política fiscal restrictiva] *n.* plan para reducir la demanda agregada y desacelerar la economía durante un período de expansión económica demasiado rápido (pág. 446)

contractionary monetary policy [política monetaria restrictiva] *n.* plan para reducir la cantidad de dinero en circulación; también llamada política de dinero escaso (pág. 492)

cooperative [cooperativa] *n.* tipo de negocio dirigido a favor del beneficio compartido de los propietarios, que son también los clientes (pág. 250)

co-pay [copago] *n.* cantidad que el asegurado debe pagar cuando una persona asegurada recibe atención médica (pág. 596)

corporate income tax [impuesto de sociedades anónimas] *n.* impuesto basado en las ganancias de una sociedad anónima (pág. 412)

corporation [sociedad anónima] *n.* empresa que pertenece a los titulares de acciones, o accionistas, que poseen los derechos a las ganancias de la compañía pero cuya responsabilidad es limitada respecto a las deudas y pérdidas de la compañía (pág. 238)

cosigner [cofirmante, aval, avalista] *n.* persona que asume la responsabilidad de la deuda si el prestatario no reembolsa el préstamo (pág. 583)

cost-benefit analysis [análisis costo-beneficio] *n.* práctica de examinar los costos y los beneficios previstos de una opción, como ayuda en la toma de decisiones (pág. 15)

cost-push inflation [inflación de costos] *n.* situación en la que el aumento de los costos de producción hace subir los precios (pág. 399)

Council of Economic Advisers [Consejo de Consejeros Económicos] *n.* grupo de tres miembros que aconseja al Presidente sobre la política fiscal y otros asuntos económicos (pág. 452)

coupon rate [tasa de cupón] *n.* tasa de interés que el titular de un bono obtiene cada año hasta que vence el bono (pág. 338)

craft union [sindicato gremial] *n.* organización de trabajadores con aptitudes similares que trabajan en diferentes industrias para diferentes empleadores (pág. 274)

credit [crédito] *n.* práctica de comprar bienes o servicios en el presente y pagarlos en el futuro (pág. 582)

credit report [informe crediticio] *n.* documento emitido por una agencia de informes crediticios que explica detalladamente el historial de crédito de un consumidor (pág. 586)

credit score [calificación del riesgo crediticio] *n.* número que resume la reputación crediticia de un consumidor (pág. 590)

crowding-out effect [efecto de exclusión] *n.* situación en la que el gobierno supera la oferta de las tasas de interés de bonos privados para obtener fondos prestables (pág. 466)

currency [moneda] *n.* papel moneda y monedas metálicas (págs. 293, 475)

customs duty [derecho arancelario] *n.* impuesto aplicado en Estados Unidos a los bienes importados (pág. 425)

customs unions [uniones aduaneras] *n.* acuerdos que eliminan las barreras al comercio entre los miembros y establecen aranceles uniformes para los no miembros (pág. 532)

cyclical unemployment [desempleo cíclico] *n.* desempleo causado por la parte del ciclo económico que presenta una actividad económica reducida (pág. 384)

D

debit card [tarjeta de débito] *n.* tarjeta que se puede usar como tarjeta de cajero automático (ATM) para retirar dinero o como cheque para hacer compras (pág. 304)

debt restructuring [reestructuración de la deuda] *n.* método que utilizan los países con obligaciones de deuda pendientes para alterar los términos de los acuerdos de la deuda, a fin de conseguir alguna ventaja (pág. 559)

deduction [deducible] *n.* cantidad que el asegurado paga antes de que pague la compañía aseguradora (pág. 596)

default [incumplimiento] *n.* condición que se presenta cuando un país no puede pagar los intereses o el capital sobre un préstamo (pág. 559)

deficit spending [gastos deficitarios] *n.* práctica del gobierno de gastar más de lo que obtiene en ingresos en un determinado año fiscal (pág. 462)

deflation [deflación] *n.* disminución del nivel general de precios (pág. 398)

demand [demanda] *n.* deseo de obtener algún bien o servicio y la capacidad para pagarlo (pág. 98)

demand curve [curva de la demanda] *n.* gráfica que muestra una tabla de demanda, o la cantidad de un bien o de un servicio que una persona puede y está dispuesta a comprar a cada precio (pág. 102)

demand deposits [depósitos a la vista] *n.* cuentas corrientes, llamadas así porque las cuentas corrientes pueden convertirse en dinero "a la vista" (pág. 293)

demand-pull inflation [inflación de demanda] *n.* condición que se presenta cuando la demanda total sube más rápido que la producción de bienes y servicios (pág. 399)

demand schedule [tabla de demanda] *n.* tabla que muestra la cantidad de un bien o de un servicio que una persona puede y está dispuesta a comprar a cada precio (pág. 100)

demand-side fiscal policy [política fiscal sobre la demanda] *n.* plan para estimular la demanda agregada (pág. 454)

deposit multiplier formula [fórmula del multiplicador de depósitos] *n.* fórmula matemática que indica cuánto aumentará la oferta monetaria tras realizar un depósito inicial de dinero en un banco (pág. 485)

depreciate [depreciar] *v.* disminuir de valor (pág. 590)

depression [depresión] *n.* período prolongado con un alto nivel de desempleo y una reducción de la actividad económica (pág. 359)

deregulation [desregulación] *n.* reducción o eliminación de la vigilancia y el control de las empresas por parte del gobierno (pág. 218)

derived demand [demanda derivada] *n.* demanda de un producto o un recurso que se basa en su aportación al producto final (pág. 259)

developed nations [países desarrollados] *n.* países que tienen una economía de mercado, un nivel de vida relativamente alto, un PIB alto, industrialización, propiedad privada generalizada y un gobierno estable y efectivo (pág. 544)

differentiated product [producto diferenciado] véase product differentiation [diferenciación de productos]

diminishing returns [rentabilidad decreciente] *n.* situación en la que nuevos trabajadores hacen que el producto marginal aumente pero a un ritmo decreciente (pág. 139)

discount rate [tasa de descuento] *n.* tasa de interés que aplica la Reserva Federal cuando presta dinero a otros bancos (pág. 491)

discretionary fiscal policy [política fiscal discrecional] *n.* medidas que toma el gobierno federal a voluntad para corregir la inestabilidad económica (pág. 446)

discretionary spending [gastos discrecionales] *n.* gastos que el gobierno debe autorizar cada año (pág. 428)

disequilibrium [desequilibrio] *n.* situación en la que la cantidad ofertada y la cantidad demandada no se encuentran en equilibrio (pág. 169)

disposable personal income (DPI) [renta personal disponible (RPD)] *n.* renta personal menos los impuestos (pág. 355)

diversification [diversificación] *n.* práctica de distribuir las inversiones entre diferentes activos financieros para maximizar la rentabilidad y limitar el riesgo (pág. 327)

dividend [dividendo] *n.* aquella parte de las ganancias de una sociedad anónima que la compañía paga a los accionistas (pág. 238)

dumping [dumping] *n.* venta de un producto en otro país a un precio más bajo del que tiene en el mercado de origen (pág. 521)

Dumpster diving [buceo en la basura] *n.* técnica utilizada por los ladrones de identidad para recoger información personal en la basura (pág. 584)

E

easy-money policy [política de dinero barato] véase expansionary monetary policy [política monetaria expansiva]

economic cycle [ciclo económico] véase business cycle [ciclo económico]

economic growth [crecimiento económico] *n.* aumento del producto interior bruto real de un país (pág. 358)

economic interdependence [interdependencia económica] *n.* situación en la que los productores de un país dependen de otros para conseguir bienes y servicios que ellos no producen (pág. 510)

economic model [modelo económico] *n.* representación simplificada de las actividades, sistemas o problemas económicos (pág. 18)

economics [economía] *n.* estudio de cómo las personas y la sociedad satisfacen sus deseos ilimitados con recursos limitados (pág. 4)

economic system [sistema económico] *n.* forma en que la sociedad utiliza sus recursos escasos para satisfacer los deseos ilimitados de su población (pág. 38)

economies of scale [economías de escala] *n.* situación en la que el costo promedio de producción disminuye al crecer el productor (pág. 201)

economize [economizar] *v.* tomar decisiones según lo que se cree la mejor combinación de costos y beneficios (pág. 12)

efficiency [eficiencia] *n.* condición en la que los recursos económicos se utilizan para producir la cantidad máxima de bienes y servicios (pág. 20)

elastic [elástica] *adj.* situación en la que un cambio en el precio, ya sea para más o para menos, produce un cambio relativamente más grande en la cantidad demandada o en la cantidad ofertada (págs. 117, 154)

elasticity of demand [elasticidad de la demanda] *n.* medida de la reacción de los consumidores ante los cambios de los precios en el mercado (pág. 117)

elasticity of supply [elasticidad de la oferta] *n.* medida de la reacción de los productores ante los cambios de los precios en el mercado (pág. 154)

embargo [embargo] *n.* ley que prohíbe la mayor parte o todo el comercio con un país determinado (pág. 521)

entitlement [derechos sociales adquiridos] *n.* programa de asistencia social que tiene determinados requisitos de admisión (pág. 428)

entrepreneurship [capacidad empresarial] *n.* combinación de visión, aptitud, ingenio y disposición de asumir riesgos, necesaria para crear y dirigir nuevas empresas (pág. 9)

equilibrium price [precio de equilibrio] *n.* precio al que la cantidad demandada equivale a la cantidad ofertada (pág. 164)

equilibrium wage [salario de equilibrio] *n.* salario en el que la cantidad de trabajadores demandados equivale a la cantidad de trabajadores ofertados; precio de mercado de la mano de obra (pág. 258)

estate tax [impuesto de sucesiones] *n.* impuesto aplicado a los activos de una persona que ha muerto (pág. 425)

European Union (EU) [Unión Europea (UE)] *n.* unión económica y política de los países europeos, establecida en 1993 (pág. 532)

euro [euro] *n.* moneda única de la Unión Europea (pág. 533)

excise tax [impuesto sobre consumos] *n.* impuesto aplicado a la producción o a la venta de un bien o un servicio determinado (págs. 149, 425)

expansion [expansión] *n.* aumento de la actividad económica (pág. 358); *véase* business cycle [ciclo económico]

expansionary fiscal policy [política fiscal expansiva] *n.* plan para aumentar la demanda agregada y estimular una economía débil (pág. 446)

expansionary monetary policy [política monetaria expansiva] *n.* plan para aumentar la cantidad de dinero en circulación; también llamada política de dinero barato (pág. 492)

exports [exportaciones] *n.* bienes o servicios producidos en un país y vendidos a otros países (pág. 516)

externality [externalidad] *n.* efecto secundario de una transacción que afecta a alguien que no sea el productor o el comprador (pág. 87)

F

factor market [mercado de factores] *n.* mercado para los factores de producción: tierra, trabajo, capital y capacidad empresarial (pág. 52)

factors of production [factores de producción] *n.* recursos económicos necesarios para producir bienes y servicios (pág. 8)

federal budget [presupuesto federal] *n.* plan para gastar los ingresos obtenidos mediante los impuestos federales (pág. 431)

federal funds rate (FFR) [tasa de interés para fondos federales (TFF)] *n.* interés al que una institución de depósitos presta por un día fondos disponibles a otra institución de depósitos (pág. 490)

Federal Insurance Contributions Act (FICA) [Ley de Contribuciones al Seguro Federal] *n.* impuesto sobre nóminas que proporciona cobertura a las personas mayores, a los desempleados por incapacidad y a los familiares supervivientes de asalariados que han muerto (pág. 423)

Federal Open Market Committee (FOMC) [Comité Federal del Mercado Abierto] *n.* junta del Sistema de la Reserva Federal que supervisa la venta y la compra de valores del gobierno federal (pág. 477)

Federal Reserve System [Sistema de la Reserva Federal] *n.* banco central de Estados Unidos, llamado comúnmente la Fed (pág. 474)

fiat money [dinero fiduciario] *n.* dinero que no tiene respaldo tangible pero cuyo valor es declarado por el gobierno y aceptado por los ciudadanos (pág. 291)

filing status [estado personal] *n.* para la declaración de impuestos, se basa en el estado civil o en las cargas familiares (pág. 604)

financial asset [activo financiero] *n.* derecho de la propiedad del prestatario (pág. 319)

financial intermediary [intermediario financiero] *n.* institución que reúne fondos de los ahorradores e invierte estos fondos en activos financieros (pág. 319)

financial market [mercado financiero] *n.* situación en la que los compradores y los vendedores intercambian activos financieros (pág. 319)

financial system [sistema financiero] *n.* todas las instituciones que ayudan a transferir fondos entre los ahorradores y los inversionistas (pág. 318)

fiscal [fiscal] *adj.* lo relacionado a los ingresos y a los gastos del gobierno (pág. 446)

fiscal policy [política fiscal] *n.* uso que hace el gobierno federal de los impuestos y los gastos para afectar a la economía (pág. 446)

fiscal year [año fiscal] *n.* período de 12 meses en el que una organización planifica sus gastos (pág. 431)

fixed costs [costos fijos] *n.* gastos en los que incurren los propietarios de empresas, independientemente de cuánto produzcan (pág. 140)

fixed rate of exchange [tasa de cambio fija] *n.* sistema en el que la divisa de un país es fija o constante respecto a las otras divisas (pág. 526)

flexible exchange rate [tasa de cambio flexible] *n.* sistema en el que la tasa de cambio para una divisa fluctúa al fluctuar la oferta y la demanda de la divisa; también llamada tasa flotante (pág. 527)

focus group [grupo focal] *n.* discusión dirigida por un moderador y realizada con pequeños grupos de consumidores (pág. 208)

foreign exchange market [mercado de divisas] *n.* mercado en el que se compran y venden divisas de diferentes países (pág. 526)

foreign exchange rate [tasa de cambio de divisas] *n.* precio de una divisa expresado en las divisas de otros países (pág. 526)

franchise [franquicia] *n.* negocio formado por negocios parcialmente independientes que ofrecen todos los mismos productos o servicios (pág. 248)

franchisee [franquiciado] *n.* negocio parcialmente independiente que paga un cargo por el derecho a vender en una determinada zona los productos o servicios de la compañía matriz (pág. 248)

free contract [contrato libre] *n.* situación en la que las personas deciden por sí solas qué contratos legales aceptar (pág. 73)

free-enterprise system [sistema de libre mercado] *n.* otro nombre del capitalismo, sistema económico basado en la propiedad privada de los recursos productivos (pág. 70)

free rider [beneficiario gratuito] *n.* persona que no paga un bien o un servicio pero que se beneficia de él cuando se le da (pág. 85)

free-trade zone [zona de libre comercio] *n.* determinada región en la que el comercio entre los países se realiza sin aranceles proteccionistas (pág. 532)

frictional unemployment [desempleo friccional] *n.* desempleo temporal de los trabajadores que pasan de un puesto de trabajo a otro (pág. 384)

full employment [pleno empleo] *n.* nivel de desempleo en el que ninguna parte del desempleo se debe a la reducción de la actividad económica; por lo general, está marcado por una tasa de desempleo del 4 al 6 por ciento (pág. 383)

future [futuro] *n.* contrato para comprar o vender acciones en una fecha futura determinada y a un precio establecido (pág. 333)

G

general partnership [sociedad colectiva] *n.* sociedad en la que cada socio participa en la dirección de la empresa y es responsable de todas las deudas y pérdidas de la empresa (pág. 233)

geographic monopoly [monopolio geográfico] *n.* monopolio que existe debido a la ausencia de otros productores o vendedores en cierta región (pág. 201)

gift tax [impuesto sobre donaciones] *n.* impuesto aplicado al dinero o a las propiedades que una persona viva le da a otra (pág. 425)

glass ceiling [techo de cristal] *n.* barrera artificial e invisible que a veces afrontan las mujeres y las minorías y que les impide avanzar profesionalmente (pág. 262)

global economy [economía global] *n.* todas las interacciones económicas que cruzan las fronteras internacionales (pág. 61)

gold standard [patrón oro] *n.* sistema en el que la unidad monetaria básica es igual a una cantidad de oro establecida (pág. 299)

goods [bienes] *n.* objetos físicos, como los alimentos, la ropa y los muebles, que pueden comprarse (pág. 5)

government monopoly [monopolio gubernamental] *n.* monopolio que existe debido a que el gobierno posee y dirige esa empresa o autoriza un solo productor (pág. 201)

grant-in-aid [donativo del gobierno federal] *n.* pago de transferencia del gobierno federal a gobiernos estatales o locales (pág. 432)

gross domestic product (GDP) [producto interior bruto (PIB)] *n.* valor de mercado de todos los bienes y servicios finales producidos en un país durante un determinado período de tiempo (pág. 350)

gross national product (GNP) [producto nacional bruto (PNB)] *n.* valor de mercado de todos los bienes y servicios finales producidos por un país durante un determinado período de tiempo (pág. 355)

H

hacking [hacking] *n.* técnica empleada por los ladrones de identidad para recoger información personal mediante computadoras y tecnología relacionada (pág. 588)

horizontal merger [fusión horizontal] *n.* unión de dos o más compañías que ofrecen productos o servicios iguales o similares (pág. 243)

human capital [capital humano] *n.* conocimientos y aptitudes que permiten a los trabajadores ser productivos (pág. 261)

human development index (HDI) [índice de desarrollo humano (IDH)] *n.* combinación del PIB real per cápita, la esperanza de vida al nacer, la tasa de alfabetización de adultos y la tasa de matriculación de los estudiantes de un país y todo esto indica cómo es la vida en un país determinado (pág. 547)

hyperinflation [hiperinflación] *n.* tasa de inflación acelerada y no controlada superior al 50 por ciento (pág. 398)

I

identity theft [robo de identidad] *n.* uso de la información personal de otra persona con fines criminales (pág. 588)

imperfect competition [competencia imperfecta] *n.* estructura de mercado que carece de una o más de las condiciones necesarias para la competencia perfecta (pág. 195)

imports [importaciones] *n.* bienes o servicios producidos en un país y comprados por otro (pág. 516)

incentive [incentivo] *n.* beneficio ofrecido para estimular a las personas a que actúen de cierta manera (págs. 12, 176)

incidence of a tax [incidencia fiscal] *n.* carga final de un impuesto (pág. 415)

income distribution [distribución de la renta] *n.* forma en que la renta se divide entre las personas de un país (pág. 390)

income effect [efecto renta] *n.* cambio en la cantidad de un bien o de un servicio que un consumidor comprará debido a la variación de su renta (y por ello su poder adquisitivo) (pág. 107)

income inequality [desigualdad de la renta] *n.* distribución desigual de la renta (pág. 390)

increasing returns [rentabilidad creciente] *n.* situación en la que la contratación de nuevos trabajadores hace aumentar el producto marginal (pág. 139)

independent contractor [contratista independiente] *n.* alguien que vende sus servicios mediante un contrato (pág. 270)

individual income tax [impuesto sobre la renta personal] *n.* impuesto basado en las rentas que una persona recibe de todas las fuentes (pág. 412)

industrial union [sindicato industrial] *n.* organización de trabajadores con muchas y diversas aptitudes y que trabajan en la misma industria (pág. 274)

inelastic [inelástica] *n.* situación en la que la cantidad demandada o la cantidad ofertada cambia poco al cambiar el precio (págs. 117, 155)

infant industries [industrias nacientes] *n.* nuevas industrias que frecuentemente son incapaces de competir contra los competidores más grandes y establecidos (pág. 523)

infant mortality rate [tasa de mortalidad infantil] *n.* número de niños que mueren durante el primer año de vida por 1,000 nacimientos (pág. 547)

inferior goods [bienes inferiores] *n.* bienes que tienen menos demanda por parte de los consumidores cuando aumentan sus ingresos (pág. 110)

inflation [inflación] *n.* aumento persistente del nivel general de precios, o disminución persistente del poder adquisitivo del dinero (pág. 396)

inflation rate [tasa de inflación] *n.* tasa de variación de los precios durante un período de tiempo establecido (pág. 397)

infrastructure [infraestructuras] *n.* conjunto básico de los sistemas de soporte, como los sistemas energéticos, de comunicaciones, de transporte, de agua, sanitarios y de educación, que se necesitan para el funcionamiento de la economía y la sociedad (págs. 86, 545)

input costs [costos de los insumos] *n.* precio de los recursos necesarios para producir un bien o un servicio (pág. 148)

insourcing [uso de recursos internos] *n.* práctica de las compañías extranjeras que establecen operaciones en Estados Unidos y por lo tanto crean puestos de trabajo en este país (pág. 269)

interest [interés] *n.* cargo que paga un banco por el uso del dinero (pág. 578)

International Monetary Fund (IMF) [Fondo Monetario Internacional (FMI)] *n.* organización internacional establecida para promocionar la cooperación monetaria internacional, fomentar el crecimiento económico y proporcionar apoyo financiero temporal a los países para ayudar a mitigar el ajuste de la balanza-de-pagos (pág. 559)

investment [inversión] *n.* uso actual de la renta de manera tal que permita obtener un beneficio futuro (pág. 318)

investment objective [objetivo de inversión] *n.* meta financiera utilizada para determinar si una inversión es apropiada (pág. 324)

J

junk bond [bono basura] *n.* bono de empresa que es de alto riesgo y de alto rendimiento (pág. 339)

K

Keynesian economics [economía keynesiana] *n.* idea, propuesta inicialmente por John Maynard Keynes, de que el gobierno necesita estimular la demanda agregada en períodos de recesión (pág. 454)

L

labor [trabajo] *n.* todo el tiempo, esfuerzo y talento humano usado para producir bienes y servicios (pág. 8)

labor input [factor trabajo] *n.* magnitud de la fuerza laboral multiplicada por la duración de la semana laborable (pág. 371)

labor productivity [productividad del trabajo] *n.* cantidad de bienes y servicios que una persona puede producir en un tiempo determinado (pág. 149)

labor union [sindicato laboral] *n.* organización de trabajadores que trata de mejorar para sus miembros los salarios, las condiciones laborales, los beneficios suplementarios, la seguridad en el empleo y otros asuntos relacionados con el trabajo (pág. 274)

Laffer Curve [curva de Laffer] *n.* gráfica que ilustra cómo afecta la reducción de los impuestos a los ingresos fiscales y al crecimiento económico (pág. 459)

lagging indicators [indicadores retrasados] *n.* medidas del rendimiento económico que suelen cambiar después de cambiar el producto interior bruto real (pág. 364)

laissez faire [laissez faire] *n.* principio según el cual el gobierno no debe interferir en la economía (pág. 49)

land [tierra] *n.* todos los recursos naturales sobre o bajo el suelo que se utilizan para producir bienes y servicios (pág. 8)

landlord [propietario de una propiedad] *n.* dueño de una propiedad de alquiler (pág. 609)

law of comparative advantage [ley de la ventaja comparativa] *n.* ley según la cual los países se benefician cuando producen artículos cuya fabricación realizan con la mayor eficiencia y con el menor costo de oportunidad (pág. 514)

law of demand [ley de la demanda] *n.* establece que cuando el precio de un bien o de un servicio baja la cantidad demandada aumenta, y cuando los precios suben la cantidad demandada disminuye (pág. 99)

law of diminishing marginal utility [ley de la utilidad marginal decreciente] *n.* establece que el beneficio marginal obtenido al consumir cada unidad adicional de un bien o de un servicio durante un determinado período de tiempo tiende a disminuir tras el consumo de cada una (pág. 106)

law of increasing opportunity costs [ley de costos de oportunidad crecientes] *n.* establece que al pasar de fabricar un producto a fabricar otro, se necesitan cada vez más recursos para aumentar la fabricación del segundo producto, lo cual hace aumentar los costos de oportunidad (pág. 21)

law of supply [ley de la oferta] *n.* establece que los productores están dispuestos a vender más de un bien o de un servicio a un precio más alto que a un precio más bajo (pág. 131)

leading indicators [indicadores principales] *n.* medidas del rendimiento económico que generalmente cambian antes de que cambie el producto interior bruto real (pág. 364)

lease [contrato de arrendamiento financiero] *n.* contrato para alquilar un apartamento, vehículo u otro objeto durante un determinado período de tiempo (pág. 609)

legal equality [igualdad legal] *n.* situación en la que todo el mundo tiene los mismos derechos económicos bajo la ley (pág. 73)

less developed countries (LDCs) [países menos desarrollados (PMD)] *n.* países con un PIB más bajo, menos industrias bien desarrolladas y un nivel de vida menor; a veces, se llaman economías emergentes (pág. 545)

life expectancy [esperanza de vida al nacer] *n.* promedio de años que se prevé que una persona vivirá si las tendencias de mortalidad actuales continúan durante el resto de la vida de esa persona (pág. 547)

limited liability [responsabilidad limitada] *n.* situación en la que la responsabilidad del propietario de una empresa respecto a las deudas y a las pérdidas de la empresa es limitada (pág. 240)

limited liability partnership (LLP) [sociedad de responsabilidad limitada (SRL)] *n.* sociedad en la que no todos los socios son responsables de las deudas y de otras obligaciones de los otros socios (pág. 233)

limited life [vida limitada] *n.* situación en la que una empresa deja de existir si el propietario muere, se jubila o abandona la empresa (pág. 228)

limited partnership [sociedad limitada] *n.* sociedad en la que hay al menos un socio que no participa en la gestión de la empresa y es responsable sólo de los fondos que invirtió (pág. 233)

literacy rate [tasa de alfabetización] *n.* porcentaje de personas mayores de 15 años que saben leer y escribir (pág. 547)

loan [préstamo] *n.* dinero prestado que se reembolsa generalmente con intereses (pág. 582)

Lorenz curve [curva de Lorenz] *n.* curva que muestra el grado de desigualdad de la renta de un país (pág. 391)

M

macroeconomic equilibrium [equilibrio macroeconómico] *n.* punto donde la demanda agregada equivale a la oferta agregada (pág. 361)

macroeconomics [macroeconomía] *n.* estudio del comportamiento de la economía en su conjunto; lo relacionado a la actividad económica a gran escala (pág. 27)

mandatory spending [gastos obligatorios] *n.* gastos que debe realizar el gobierno según las leyes actuales (pág. 428)

marginal benefit [beneficio marginal] *n.* beneficio o satisfacción obtenido al consumir una unidad adicional de un bien o de un servicio (pág. 16)

marginal cost [costo marginal] *n.* costo adicional de producir o consumir una unidad adicional de un bien o de un servicio (págs. 16, 140)

marginal product [producto marginal] *n.* cambio en el producto total que es resultado de añadir un trabajador más (pág. 138)

marginal revenue [ingreso marginal] *n.* dinero obtenido al vender cada unidad adicional (pág. 142)

market [mercado] *n.* cualquier lugar o situación en que las personas compran y venden bienes y servicios (pág. 48)

market allocation [reparto de mercado] *n.* acuerdo entre dos o más empresas competidoras por el que se divide un mercado (pág. 216)

market demand curve [curva de demanda de mercado] *n.* gráfica que muestra datos de una tabla de demanda de mercado, o la cantidad de un bien o de un servicio que todos los consumidores pueden y están dispuestos a comprar a cada precio (pág. 102)

market demand schedule [tabla de demanda de mercado] *n.* tabla que muestra la cantidad de un bien o de un servicio que todos los consumidores pueden y están dispuestos a comprar a cada precio de un mercado (pág. 100)

market division [repartición de mercado] *véase* market allocation [reparto de mercado]

market economy [economía de mercado] *n.* sistema económico basado en la elección individual y el intercambio voluntario (pág. 39)

market equilibrium [equilibrio del mercado] *n.* situación en la que la cantidad ofertada y la cantidad demandada a un precio determinado son iguales (pág. 164)

market failure [fallo del mercado] *n.* situación en la que personas no participantes de una interacción del mercado se benefician de ella o pagan parte de sus costos (pág. 84)

market research [investigación de mercados] *n.* recogida y evaluación de información sobre las preferencias de los consumidores respecto a bienes y servicios (pág. 208)

market share [cuota de mercado] *n.* porcentaje del total de ventas de una empresa en un mercado determinado (pág. 209)

market structure [estructura de mercado] *n.* modelo económico de competencia entre las empresas de la misma industria (pág. 192)

market supply curve [curva de oferta de mercado] *n.* gráfica que muestra datos de una tabla de oferta de mercado (pág. 134)

market supply schedule [tabla de oferta de mercado] *n.* tabla que muestra la cantidad de un bien o de un servicio que todos los productores de un mercado pueden y están dispuestos a ofrecer para su venta a cada precio (pág. 132)

maturity [vencimiento] *n.* fecha en la que un bono debe reembolsarse (pág. 338)

Medicaid [Medicaid] *n.* programa de seguro médico gubernamental destinado a las personas de baja renta (pág. 429)

Medicare [Medicare] *n.* programa de seguro de salud nacional y gubernamental destinado principalmente a los ciudadanos mayores de 65 años (pág. 423)

medium of exchange [medio de intercambio] *n.* medio por el que se pueden intercambiar bienes y servicios (pág. 288)

merger [fusión] *n.* unión de dos o más compañías para formar una sola compañía (pág. 214)

microeconomics [microeconomía] *n.* estudio del comportamiento de los participantes individuales de una economía, como las personas, las familias y las empresas (pág. 27)

minimum balance requirement [requisito de saldo mínimo] *n.* cantidad de dinero que se debe mantener en una cuenta para evitar los cargos (pág. 576)

minimum wage [salario mínimo] *n.* la menor cantidad, según establece la ley, que un empleador puede pagar a un trabajador por una hora de trabajo (págs. 182, 262)

mixed economy [economía mixta] *n.* sistema económico que presenta elementos de las economías tradicional, autoritaria y de mercado; sistema económico más común (pág. 58)

modified free enterprise economy [economía de libre mercado modificada] *n.* sistema económico mixto que incluye algunas medidas protectoras, disposiciones y reglamentos del gobierno, para ajustar el sistema de libre mercado (pág. 80)

monetarism [monetarismo] *n.* teoría económica que sugiere que los cambios rápidos en la oferta monetaria son la causa principal de la inestabilidad económica (pág. 496)

monetary [monetario] *adj.* lo relacionado al dinero (pág. 474)

monetary policy [política monetaria] *n.* medidas de la Reserva Federal que cambian la oferta monetaria para influir en la economía (pág. 490)

money [dinero] *n.* todo lo que las personas aceptan como pago de bienes y servicios (pág. 288)

money market [mercado monetario] *n.* mercado en el que se compran y venden activos financieros a corto plazo (pág. 322)

monopolistic competition [competencia monopolista] *n.* estructura de mercado en la que un gran número de vendedores ofrecen a los consumidores productos similares pero no estandarizados (pág. 206)

monopoly [monopolio] *n.* estructura de mercado en la que un único vendedor vende un producto para el que no existen sustitutos adecuados (pág. 198)

monopsony [monopsonio] *n.* estructura de mercado en la que existe gran número de vendedores pero sólo un comprador grande (pág. 212)

multifactor productivity [productividad multifactorial] *n.* razón entre la producción económica de una industria y los factores trabajo y capital (pág. 373)

multinational corporation [empresa multinacional] *n.* sociedad anónima que tiene establecimientos en varios países (pág. 243)

mutual fund [fondo de mercado monetario, fondo mutual] *n.* compañía de inversión que reúne dinero de inversionistas individuales y lo utiliza para comprar una variedad de activos financieros (pág. 320)

N

NAFTA [NAFTA] *n.* Tratado de Libre Comercio con América del Norte, convenio que asegura el libre comercio por todo el continente y constituye la zona de libre comercio más grande del mundo (pág. 533)

national accounts [cuentas nacionales] *véase* national income accounting [contabilidad nacional]

national bank [banco nacional] *n.* banco autorizado por el gobierno nacional (pág. 299)

national debt [deuda pública] *n.* cantidad total de dinero que debe el gobierno federal (pág. 462)

national income (NI) [renta nacional (RN)] *n.* renta total percibida en un país por la producción de bienes y servicios durante un determinado período de tiempo (pág. 355)

national income accounting [contabilidad nacional] *n.* método de analizar la economía de un país usando medidas estadísticas de los ingresos, los gastos y la producción (pág. 350)

nationalize [nacionalizar] *v.* pasar de la propiedad privada a la propiedad gubernamental o pública (pág. 61)

natural monopoly [monopolio natural] *n.* situación del mercado en la que los costos de producción son más bajos cuando una única empresa proporciona un producto o un servicio (pág. 201)

near money [cuasidinero] *n.* cuentas de ahorro y otros depósitos a plazo similares que pueden convertirse en dinero de manera relativamente fácil (pág. 293)

needs [necesidades] *n.* objetos como los alimentos, la ropa y los lugares de vivienda, que son necesarios para la vida (pág. 4)

negative externality [externalidad negativa] *n.* externalidad que supone un costo para personas no participantes en la actividad económica original (pág. 87)

net national product (NNP) [producto nacional neto (PNN)] *n.* producto nacional bruto menos la depreciación del capital social. Es decir, es el valor de los bienes y los servicios finales menos el valor de los bienes capitales que quedaron desgastados durante el año (pág. 355)

nominal GDP [PIB nominal] *n.* producto interior bruto expresado en función del valor actual de los bienes y los servicios (pág. 352)

nonmarket activities [actividades no comerciales] *n.* servicios que tienen un valor económico en potencia pero que se prestan sin cobrar (pág. 354)

nonprice competition [competencia no basada en el precio] *n.* uso de factores distintos al precio, como el estilo, el servicio, la publicidad o los regalos, para tratar de convencer a los clientes para que compren algo de un productor y no de otro (pág. 207)

nonprofit organization [organización sin fines de lucro] *n.* institución que actúa como empresa pero que existe para beneficiar a la comunidad en lugar de obtener ganancias (pág. 250)

normal goods [bienes normales] *n.* bienes que tienen más demanda por parte de los consumidores cuando aumentan sus ingresos (pág. 110)

normative economics [economía normativa] *n.* forma de describir y explicar cómo debería ser el comportamiento económico y no cómo es en realidad (pág. 29)

not-for-profit [sin fines de lucro] *véase* nonprofit organization [organización sin fines de lucro]

O

oligopoly [oligopolio] *n.* estructura de mercado en la que un número reducido de vendedores ofrecen un producto similar (pág. 209)

OPEC [OPEP] *n.* Organización de Países Exportadores de Petróleo, grupo comercial regional (pág. 535)

open market operations [operaciones de mercado abierto] *n.* compraventa por parte de la Reserva Federal de valores del gobierno federal; instrumento de política monetaria de mayor uso por la Reserva Federal para ajustar la oferta monetaria (pág. 490)

open opportunity [oportunidad abierta] *n.* capacidad para que todo el mundo pueda entrar y competir en el mercado según su libre elección (pág. 73)

operating budget [presupuesto de operación] *n.* plan para los gastos diarios (pág. 436)

opportunity cost [costo de oportunidad] *n.* costo de elegir una alternativa económica en lugar de otra (pág. 14)

option [opción] *n.* contrato por el que se da al inversionista el derecho a comprar o vender acciones en una fecha futura y a un precio establecido (pág. 333)

outsourcing [subcontratación] *n.* práctica de contratar una empresa externa, a menudo en un país extranjero, para que proporcione bienes y servicios (pág. 269)

overdraft [sobregiro] *n.* cheque u otra forma de retirar fondos que excede del saldo existente en la cuenta (pág. 576)

P

par value [valor a la par] *n.* cantidad que el emisor de un bono promete pagar al comprador en la fecha de vencimiento (pág. 338)

partnership [sociedad] *n.* empresa que pertenece a dos o más personas, o "socios", que acuerdan la forma de repartir las responsabilidades, las ganancias y las pérdidas (pág. 232)

patent [patente] *n.* inscripción legal de un invento o de un proceso que da al inventor los derechos exclusivos de la propiedad sobre ese invento o proceso durante cierto número de años (pág. 202)

peak [punto máximo, pico] *n.* fin de una expansión de la economía (pág. 359); *véase* business cycle [ciclo económico]

per capita gross domestic product [producto interior bruto per cápita] *n.* PIB de un país, dividido por la población total (pág. 546)

perestroika [perestroika] *n.* plan del dirigente ruso Mijaíl Gorbachov de incorporar de forma gradual mercados en la economía autoritaria de la Unión Soviética (pág. 564)

perfect competition [competencia perfecta] *n.* modelo ideal de una economía de mercado; estructura de mercado en la que ninguno de los numerosos vendedores y compradores independientes y bien informados tiene control sobre el precio de un bien o un servicio estandarizado (pág. 192)

personal income (PI) [renta personal (RP)] *n.* renta anual recibida por el conjunto de personas de un país y procedente de todas las fuentes (pág. 355)

phishing [phishing] *n.* técnica empleada por los ladrones de identidad para recoger información personal mediante llamadas telefónicas engañosas (pág. 588)

PIN [PIN] *n.* número de identificación personal (pág. 577)

positive economics [economía positiva] *n.* forma de describir y explicar la economía tal como es (pág. 29)

positive externality [externalidad positiva] *n.* externalidad que beneficia a personas no participantes en la actividad económica original (pág. 87)

poverty [pobreza] *n.* situación en la que la renta y los recursos de una persona no le permiten obtener un nivel de vida mínimo (pág. 388)

poverty line [línea de pobreza] *véase* poverty threshold [umbral de pobreza]

poverty rate [tasa de pobreza] *n.* porcentaje de personas que viven en hogares cuya renta es inferior a la del umbral de pobreza (pág. 389)

poverty threshold [umbral de pobreza] *n.* renta mínima oficial necesaria para pagar los gastos básicos de la vida (pág. 388)

predatory pricing [establecer precios predatorios] *n.* fijar los precios por debajo del costo durante un tiempo para excluir de un mercado a los competidores de menor tamaño (pág. 216)

preferred stock [acciones preferentes] *n.* participación en la propiedad de una sociedad anónima que da al titular parte de las ganancias pero generalmente no da derecho a voto (pág. 331)

premium [prima] *n.* cantidad que se paga por un seguro (pág. 596)

price ceiling [precio máximo] *n.* precio máximo establecido que los vendedores pueden cobrar por un producto (pág. 180)

price fixing [imposición de precios] *n.* pactos entre dos o más empresas por los que fijan los precios de productos competidores (pág. 216)

price floor [precio mínimo] *n.* precio mínimo establecido al que los compradores deben pagar un producto (pág. 182)

price maker [fijador de precio] *n.* empresa que no tiene que tomar en cuenta a los competidores cuando fija sus precios (pág. 198)

price taker [tomador de precio] *n.* compañía que debe aceptar el precio de mercado fijado por la interacción de la oferta y la demanda (pág. 193)

primary market [mercado primario] *n.* mercado en el que se compran y venden activos financieros de reciente creación directamente de la entidad emisora (pág. 322)

prime rate [tasa preferencial] *n.* tasa de interés que los bancos aplican a sus mejores clientes (pág. 491)

private company [compañía privada] *n.* sociedad anónima que controla quién puede comprar o vender sus acciones (pág. 238)

private property rights [derechos a propiedad privada] *n.* derechos de las personas y de los grupos a poseer recursos y empresas (pág. 48)

private sector [sector privado] *n.* parte de la economía que pertenece a las personas o a las empresas (pág. 432)

privatization [privatización] *n.* proceso de transferir a las personas propiedades y empresas públicas (pág. 563)

privatize [privatizar] *v.* pasar de la propiedad gubernamental o pública a la propiedad privada (pág. 61)

producer [productor] *n.* persona que produce bienes o presta servicios (pág. 5)

producer price index (PPI) [índice de precios al por mayor (IPM)] *n.* medida de los cambios en los precios al por mayor (pág. 397)

product differentiation [diferenciación de productos] *n.* intento de distinguir un producto de otros productos similares (pág. 206)

product market [mercado de productos] *n.* mercado en el que se compran y venden bienes y servicios (pág. 52)

production possibilities curve (PPC) [curva de posibilidades de producción (CPP)] *n.* gráfica utilizada para ilustrar el efecto de la carencia sobre una economía (pág. 18)

productivity [productividad] *n.* cantidad de producto obtenido a partir de una cantidad establecida de insumos (pág. 372)

productivity, labor [productividad, trabajo] *véase* labor productivity [productividad del trabajo]

profit [ganancias] *n.* ganancias financieras que obtiene un vendedor al realizar una transacción comercial (pág. 49); dinero que queda tras restar los costos de fabricar un producto a los ingresos obtenidos al vender ese producto (pág. 78)

profit-maximizing output [nivel de producción de máxima ganancia] *n.* punto de la producción en el que una empresa ha alcanzado su mayor nivel de ganancias (pág. 143)

profit motive [afán de lucro] *n.* incentivo que estimula a las personas y a las organizaciones para que mejoren su bienestar material buscando obtener ganancias de actividades económicas (pág. 73)

progressive tax [impuesto progresivo] *n.* impuesto que aplica una tasa impositiva más alta a las personas de alta renta que a las personas de baja renta (pág. 412)

property tax [impuesto sobre la propiedad] *n.* impuesto basado en el valor de los activos de una persona o de una empresa (pág. 412)

proportional tax [impuesto proporcional] *n.* impuesto que extrae el mismo porcentaje de renta a todos los contribuyentes, independientemente de su nivel de renta (pág. 412)

protectionism [proteccionismo] *n.* uso de barreras al comercio entre los países para proteger las industrias nacionales (pág. 523)

protective tariff [arancel proteccionista] *n.* impuesto aplicado a los bienes importados para proteger los bienes nacionales (pág. 521)

public company [empresa que cotiza en Bolsa] *n.* sociedad anónima que emite acciones que pueden negociarse libremente (pág. 238)

public disclosure [divulgación pública] *n.* política que exige que las empresas revelen a los consumidores información sobre sus productos (pág. 217)

public goods [bienes públicos] *n.* bienes y servicios proporcionados por el gobierno y consumidos por el público como grupo (pág. 84)

public transfer payment [pago de transferencia público] *n.* pago de transferencia por el que el gobierno transfiere ingresos de los contribuyentes a los beneficiarios sin que éstos den nada a cambio (pág. 89)

pure competition [competencia pura] *véase* perfect competition [competencia perfecta]

Q

quota [cuota] *n.* límite sobre la cantidad de un producto que puede importarse (pág. 520)

R

rational expectations theory [teoría de las expectativas racionales] *n.* teoría según la cual las personas y las empresas prevén que los cambios en la política fiscal tendrán efectos determinados y actúan para proteger sus intereses contra esos efectos (pág. 452)

rationing [racionamiento] *n.* sistema en el que el gobierno asigna bienes y servicios aplicando factores distintos al precio (pág. 183)

real GDP [PIB real] *n.* producto interior bruto corregido respecto a los cambios en los precios de un año a otro (pág. 352)

real GDP per capita [PIB real per cápita] *n.* producto interior bruto real dividido por la población total (pág. 369)

recession [recesión] *n.* contracción económica prolongada que dura dos o más trimestres (seis meses o más) (pág. 359)

regressive tax [impuesto regresivo] *n.* impuesto que extrae un mayor porcentaje de renta a las personas de baja renta que a las personas de alta renta (pág. 412)

regulation [regulación] *n.* serie de reglas o leyes diseñadas para controlar el comportamiento comercial (págs. 150, 214)

representative money [dinero representativo] *n.* papel moneda respaldado por algo tangible (pág. 291)

required reserve ratio (RRR) [coeficiente de reservas exigidas (CRE)] *n.* fracción de los depósitos de un banco, tal como lo determina la Reserva Federal, que debe tener en forma de reservas para poder dar préstamos de dinero (pág. 484)

return [rentabilidad] *n.* ganancias o pérdidas derivadas de una inversión (pág. 327)

revenue [ingresos] *n.* renta gubernamental procedente de los impuestos y de fuentes no impositivas (pág. 410)

revenue tariff [arancel financiero] *n.* impuesto aplicado a las importaciones específicamente para recaudar fondos; actualmente se usa muy poco (pág. 521)

right-to-work laws [leyes de libertad de sindicación] *n.* legislación que hace ilegal exigir que los trabajadores se asocien a los sindicatos (pág. 279)

risk [riesgo] *n.* posibilidad de sufrir pérdidas en una inversión (pág. 327)

S

safety net [red de protección] *n.* programas gubernamentales diseñados para proteger a las personas de las dificultades económicas (pág. 89)

sales tax [impuesto sobre las ventas] *n.* impuesto basado en el valor de los bienes o los servicios en el momento de la venta (pág. 412)

savings [ahorros] *n.* ingresos que no se utilizan para el consumo (pág. 318)

scarcity [carencia] *n.* situación en la que los recursos no son suficientes para satisfacer los deseos humanos (pág. 4)

seasonal unemployment [desempleo estacional] *n.* desempleo asociado al trabajo estacional (pág. 384)

secondary market [mercado secundario] *n.* mercado en el que los activos financieros se venden de nuevo (pág. 322)

service [servicios] *n.* trabajo que una persona realiza para otra a cambio de un pago (pág. 5)

shadow economy [economía sumergida] *véase* underground economy [economía subterránea]

share [acción] *n.* unidad del conjunto de acciones de una sociedad anónima (pág. 238); *véase* stock [acciones]

shock therapy [terapia de choque] *n.* programa económico en el que se pasa abruptamente de una economía autoritaria a una economía de libre mercado (pág. 563)

shortage [escasez] *n.* situación en la que la demanda es mayor que la oferta y la causa suele ser la fijación de precios excesivamente bajos (pág. 167)

shoulder surfing [navegar por el hombro] *n.* técnica utilizada por los ladrones de identidad para recoger información personal cuando se revela información privada en público (pág. 588)

socialism [socialismo] *n.* sistema económico en el que el gobierno posee algunos o todos los factores de producción (pág. 43)

Social Security [Seguridad Social] *n.* programa federal que proporciona ayuda a los ciudadanos mayores, a los niños huérfanos y a los incapacitados (pág. 423)

sole proprietorship [empresa unipersonal] *n.* empresa que pertenece a una sola persona y que es controlada por esa persona (pág. 226)

spamming [spamming] *n.* técnica utilizada por los ladrones de identidad para recoger información personal mediante correos electrónicos engañosos (pág. 588)

special economic zone (SEZ) [zona económica especial (ZEE)] *n.* región geográfica que tiene leyes económicas diferentes de las leyes económicas normales de un país, con el objetivo de aumentar las inversiones extranjeras (pág. 567)

specialization [especialización] *n.* situación en la que las personas o las empresas centran sus esfuerzos comerciales en los campos en que presentan una ventaja para una mayor productividad y mayores ganancias (págs. 50, 138, 510)

spending multiplier effect [efecto multiplicador de los gastos] *n.* situación en la que un pequeño cambio en los gastos acaba produciendo un cambio mucho más grande en el PIB (pág. 455)

stabilization programs [programas de estabilización] *n.* programas en los que los países en dificultades se ven obligados a realizar reformas, como reducir el déficit comercial exterior y el endeudamiento externo, eliminar los controles de precios, cerrar las empresas públicas ineficientes y bajar radicalmente el déficit presupuestario (pág. 559)

stagflation [estanflación] *n.* períodos durante los que suben los precios a la vez que se reduce la actividad económica (pág. 359)

standardized product [producto estandarizado] *n.* producto que los consumidores consideran idéntico en todas sus características esenciales a otros productos del mismo mercado (pág. 192)

standard of value [patrón de valor] *n.* forma de medir el valor económico en el proceso de cambio de divisas (pág. 289)

start-up costs [costos de puesta en marcha] *n.* gastos que una nueva empresa debe pagar para entrar en un mercado y empezar a vender a los consumidores (pág. 209)

state bank [banco estatal] *n.* banco autorizado por el gobierno de un estado (pág. 296)

statistics [estadísticas] *n.* datos numéricos (pág. 24)

stock [acciones] *n.* participaciones en la propiedad de una sociedad anónima (pág. 238)

stockbroker [agente de bolsa] *n.* agente que compra y vende valores para los clientes (pág. 332)

stock exchange [bolsa de valores] *n.* mercado secundario donde se venden y compran valores (pág. 330)

stock index [índice bursátil] *n.* instrumento utilizado para medir e informar sobre el cambio en los precios de un conjunto de acciones (pág. 334)

stored-value card [tarjeta de valor almacenado] *n.* tarjeta que representa dinero que el titular tiene en forma de depósito con la compañía emisora (pág. 308)

store of value [depósito de valor] *n.* algo que conserva su valor con el paso del tiempo (pág. 289)

strike [huelga] *n.* paralización del trabajo utilizada para ejercer presión en las negociaciones mientras se trata de convencer al empleador de que mejore los salarios, las condiciones laborales u otros asuntos relacionados con el trabajo (pág. 274)

structural unemployment [desempleo estructural] *n.* desempleo que existe cuando los puestos de trabajo disponibles no se corresponden con las aptitudes de las personas en condiciones de trabajar (pág. 384)

subsidy [subsidio] *n.* pago gubernamental que ayuda a cubrir el costo de una actividad económica que puede beneficiar al público en su conjunto (pág. 88)

substitutes [sustitutos] *n.* productos que se pueden usar en lugar de otros productos, para satisfacer los deseos de los consumidores (pág. 112)

substitution effect [efecto sustitución] *n.* patrón de comportamiento que se presenta cuando los consumidores, al reaccionar ante un cambio en el precio de un producto, compran un producto sustitutivo que ofrece un mejor valor relativo (pág. 107)

supply [oferta] *n.* disponibilidad y capacidad para producir y vender un producto (pág. 130)

supply curve [curva de la oferta] *n.* gráfica que muestra los datos de una tabla de oferta (pág. 134)

supply schedule [tabla de oferta] *n.* tabla que muestra la cantidad de un bien o de un servicio que un productor individual puede y está dispuesto a ofrecer para su venta a cada precio (pág. 132)

supply-side fiscal policy [política fiscal sobre la oferta] *n.* plan diseñado para ofrecer incentivos a los productores para que aumenten la oferta agregada (pág. 458)

surplus [excedente] *n.* situación en la que la oferta es mayor que la demanda y la causa suele ser la fijación de precios excesivamente altos (pág. 167)

T

tariff [arancel] *n.* cargo aplicado a los bienes transferidos a un país procedentes de otro país (pág. 521)

tax [impuesto] *n.* pago obligatorio a un gobierno (pág. 410)

taxable income [renta gravable] *n.* aquella parte de la renta sujeta a impuestos después de descontar todas las deducciones y exenciones (págs. 421, 604)

tax assessor [asesor fiscal] *n.* funcionario gubernamental que determina el valor de una propiedad sujeta a impuestos (pág. 437)

tax base [base imponible] *n.* forma de riqueza, como la renta, la propiedad, los bienes o los servicios, que está sujeta a impuestos (pág. 412)

tax incentive [incentivo fiscal] *n.* uso de impuestos para estimular o desalentar ciertos comportamientos económicos (pág. 417)

tax return [declaración de la renta] *n.* formulario utilizado para declarar la renta y los impuestos que deben pagarse al gobierno (pág. 421)

technological monopoly [monopolio tecnológico] *n.* monopolio que existe debido a que una empresa controla un método de fabricación, un invento o un tipo de tecnología (pág. 201)

technology [tecnología] *n.* aplicación de métodos e innovaciones científicos a la producción (pág. 149)

telecommuting [trabajo a distancia] *n.* práctica de realizar el trabajo de oficina en un lugar distinto a la propia oficina (pág. 270)

telework [teletrabajo] *véase* telecommuting [trabajo a distancia]

temp, temps, temping [trabajo temporal] *véase* contingent employment [empleo contingente]

thrift institution [entidad de ahorros] *n.* institución financiera que sirve a los ahorradores (pág. 478)

tight-money policy [política de dinero escaso] *véase* contractionary monetary policy [política monetaria restrictiva]

total cost [costo total] *n.* suma de los costos fijos y variables (pág. 140)

total revenue [ingreso total] *n.* ingreso que recibe una empresa al vender sus productos (págs. 122, 142)

total revenue test [prueba del ingreso total] *n.* método para medir la elasticidad comparando el ingreso total que obtendría una empresa al ofrecer su producto a diferentes precios (pág. 122)

trade barrier [barrera al comercio] *n.* toda ley aprobada para limitar el libre comercio entre los países (pág. 520)

trade deficit [déficit comercial] *n.* balanza de comercio desfavorable que se produce cuando un país importa más de lo que exporta (pág. 529)

trade-off [compensación] *n.* alternativa que se rechaza al tomar una decisión económica (pág. 14)

trade surplus [superávit comercial] *n.* balanza de comercio favorable que se produce cuando un país exporta más de lo que importa (pág. 529)

trade union [sindicato] *véase* labor union [sindicato laboral]

trade war [guerra comercial] *n.* serie de barreras al comercio entre los países (pág. 522)

trade-weighted value of the dollar [valor ponderado del dólar] *n.* medida del valor internacional del dólar que determina si el dólar es fuerte o débil al compararse con otra divisa (pág. 528)

traditional economy [economía tradicional] *n.* sistema económico en el que las personas toman decisiones económicas basándose en costumbres y creencias que se han pasado de una generación a la siguiente (pág. 38)

transfer payment [pago de transferencia] *n.* dinero distribuido a los contribuyentes sin que éstos proporcionen bienes o servicios a cambio (págs. 89, 432)

transitional economy [economía transicional] *n.* país que ha pasado (o está pasando) de una economía autoritaria a una economía de mercado (pág. 545)

Treasury bill (T bill) [letra del Tesoro] *n.* bono a corto plazo cuyo vencimiento es de menos de un año (pág. 464)

Treasury bond [bono del Tesoro a largo plazo] *n.* bono a largo plazo cuyo vencimiento es de 30 años (pág. 464)

Treasury note [pagaré del Tesoro] *n.* bono a medio plazo cuyo vencimiento es de entre dos y diez años (pág. 464)

trough [punto mínimo] *n.* fin de una contracción de la economía (pág. 359); *véase* business cycle [ciclo económico]

trust [grupo de empresas] *n.* grupo de compañías que se combinan para reducir la competencia en una industria (pág. 214)

trust fund [fondo fiduciario] *n.* fondo creado para un fin determinado y para un uso futuro (pág. 465)

U

underemployed [subempleados] *n.* personas que trabajan a tiempo parcial pero que quieren trabajar a tiempo completo, o personas que tienen un trabajo que requiere una capacidad inferior a la suya (pág. 383)

underground economy [economía subterránea] *n.* actividades de mercado que no se declaran por ser ilegales o porque los participantes quieren evitar pagar impuestos (pág. 354)

underutilization [infrautilización] *n.* condición en la que los recursos económicos se usan por debajo de su potencia total, dando lugar a menos bienes y servicios (pág. 20)

unemployment rate [tasa de desempleo] *n.* porcentaje de la fuerza laboral que no tiene empleo y que está buscando activamente un trabajo (pág. 382)

union [sindicato] *véase* labor union [sindicato laboral]

union shop [compañía de exclusividad sindical] *n.* empresa en la que los trabajadores están obligados a asociarse a un sindicato durante un período de tiempo establecido después de ser contratados (pág. 279)

unit elastic [elasticidad unitaria] *n.* situación en la que el cambio porcentual del precio y el de la cantidad demandada son iguales (pág. 118)

unlimited liability [responsabilidad ilimitada] *n.* situación en la que el propietario de una empresa es responsable de todas las pérdidas y deudas de la empresa (pág. 228)

unlimited life [vida ilimitada] *n.* situación en la que una sociedad anónima continúa existiendo aun después de un cambio de propietario (pág. 240)

user fee [cargo de usuario] *n.* impuesto cobrado por el uso de un bien o un servicio (pág. 425)

utility [utilidad] *n.* beneficio o satisfacción obtenido del consumo de un bien o un servicio (pág. 12)

V

variable costs [costos variables] *n.* costos comerciales que varían con el nivel de producción (pág. 140)

vertical merger [fusión vertical] *n.* combinación de dos o más empresas relacionadas con diferentes fases de la producción o de la comercialización de un producto o un servicio (pág. 243)

voluntary exchange [intercambio voluntario] *n.* intercambio en el que las partes participantes prevén que los beneficios serán más importantes que el costo (pág. 49)

voluntary export restraint (VER) [retricción voluntaria a la exportación (RVE)] *n.* autolimitación sobre las exportaciones a ciertos países para evitar cuotas o aranceles (pág. 521)

W

wage and price controls [controles de precios y salarios] *n.* limitaciones gubernamentales sobre el aumento de los precios y los salarios (pág. 501)

wage-price spiral [espiral de precios y salarios] *n.* ciclo que empieza con el aumento de los salarios, lo cual da lugar a costos de producción más altos, que a su vez produce precios más altos; esto provoca la demanda de salarios incluso más altos (pág. 400)

wage rate [escala de salarios] *n.* salario establecido para un determinado puesto de trabajo o tarea realizada (pág. 261)

wages [salarios] *n.* pagos que reciben los trabajadores a cambio de su trabajo (pág. 258)

wants [deseos] *n.* deseos que pueden satisfacerse mediante el consumo de un bien o un servicio (pág. 4)

welfare [asistencia social] *n.* programas económicos y sociales del gobierno que proporcionan ayuda a los necesitados (pág. 392)

withholding [retención] *n.* dinero descontado del pago de un trabajador antes de que reciba ese pago (pág. 421)

workfare [programa de empleo público] *n.* programa que obliga a los beneficiarios de la asistencia social a realizar algún tipo de trabajo a cambio de sus beneficios (pág. 393)

World Bank [Banco Mundial] *n.* institución financiera que proporciona préstamos, consejos relacionados con la política y ayuda técnica a países de ingresos bajos o medios, para reducir la pobreza (pág. 559)

World Trade Organization (WTO) [Organización Mundial del Comercio (OMC)] *n.* organización que negocia y gestiona acuerdos comerciales, resuelve conflictos comerciales, supervisa las políticas comerciales y apoya los países en vías de desarrollo (pág. 535)

Y

yield [rendimiento] *n.* tasa de rentabilidad anual sobre un bono (pág. 338)

Page numbers in **bold** indicate that the term is defined on that page. Page numbers in *italics* indicate an illustration. A letter after a number indicates a specific kind of illustration: *c* – chart; *i* – photograph; *m* – map. An *a* after an italicized page number indicates an Animated Economics feature.

law of, *131*, **131**

and production costs, 138–143, 148

supply curve, **134**–136, *134a*, *135*, 137, 147, *150*, R15

aggregate, *360*, *361a*, *403*

elastic/inelastic, 155, *155a*

labor, *259*

market demand curve and, 166, *166*, *337*

shifts in supply, *148a*

supply schedule, 132–133, *132a*, 133, 165, *165a*

supply-side fiscal policy, *458*, **458**–460

surplus, *167*, **167**–168, 176

trade, **529**

surveys, 63, 208

Sweden, 59–60, *90*

symbolism, 114

synthesizing data, 356, R23

T

tables, 25, R30

Taft-Hartley Act, 277, 279

Tajikistan, 569

taking notes

cause-and-effect chart, *498c*, *520c*, R20

cluster diagram, 4, 12, 38, 58, 70, 78, 84, 98, 116, 130, 154, 164, 192, 238, 258, 288, 330, 358, 382, 396, 410, 420, 446, 474, 526, 552, 562

comparison and contrast chart, *206c*, *232c*, *462c*

concepts chart, *24c*, *48c*, *106c*, *146c*, *174c*, *198c*, *226c*, *296c*, *324c*, *338c*, *434c*, *454c*, *480c*, *510c*, R13

hierarchy chart, *42c*, *138c*, *180c*, *214c*, *266c*, *304c*, *318c*, *352c*, *428c*, *490c*

summary chart, *18c*, *248c*, *274c*, *368c*, *388c*, *532c*, *544c*, R26, R27

summary paragraph, R29, R30

Tanzania, 546

tariff, 425, *515*, **521**, *522*, 522–523. *See also* international trade.

less developed countries and, 556

rates, *521*, 525

sugar prices, 538–539

tax, **410.** *See also* income tax.

assessor, **437**

base, **412**

bracket, 422

deduction, 421, *421*

equity, 411

estate, **425**

excise, **149**, **425**

exemption, 421

filing, 608–611

incentive, **417**

incidence, **415**, *415a*

indexing, 422

return, **421**

schedule, 427

taxable income, **421**, **608**

taxation, 410–438

ability-to-pay, 411

bases and structures, 412–414

benefits-received, 411

calculating, 427

corporate, **412**, *424*, *424*

double, 242, 424

economic impact of, *368*, 416–417

evaluating, 419

Federal, 420–426, *425*

fiscal policy and, 448, 450, 458–460

principles of, 410–411

regressive, **412**, *414*, *414*

social spending and, 90

state and local, 434–435, *435*, 437, *437*

U.S. households, *90*

Taylor, Paul, 124

technological monopoly, 201–202

technology, 149

computers, 178, 268–269

economic growth and, 371

productivity and, 373

Tel Aviv Stock Exchange (TASE), *336*

telecommuting, 270

telework, 270

temping, 270–271

Temporary Assistance for Needy Families (TANF), 393

1040 form, **605**–606, *606*

1099 form, 609

tertiary sector, 268

test-taking strategies

extended response, S14–S15

interpreting charts, S8–S9

interpreting graphs, S10–S13

multiple choice, S6–S7

Texaco, 244

Texas Instruments, 62

textile quotas, 520

Thailand, A15

Theory of Monopolistic Competition, 212

thrift institution, **478**

TicketMaster, 186–187

ticket prices, 180

tight-money policy, **493**

time deposit, 293

Toos, Andrew, 283, 345

total cost, 140

total revenue, 142–143

total revenue test, 122

Toyota, 154, 158

toys, 168

trade. *See also* international trade.

balance of, **529**–530

Acknowledgments

Text Acknowledgments

Chapter 1, page 32: Excerpts from "O'Hare International Airport (ORD/KORD), Chicago, IL, USA," from the Airport-Technology Web site. Reprinted by permission of SPG Media Limited.

Chapter 1, page 33: Excerpt from "Organization and Introduction," from the AReCO Web site. Reprinted by permission of The Alliance of Residents Concerning O'Hare, Inc. (AReCO).

Chapter 2, page 64: Excerpt from "The North Korean Famine," from *Peace Watch,* June 2002. Reprinted by permission of the United States Institute of Peace.

Chapter 2, page 65: Excerpt from "Masters of the Digital Age," by Rana Foroohar and B. J. Lee, *Newsweek,* October 18, 2004. Copyright © 2004 *Newsweek,* Inc. All rights reserved. Reprinted by permission.

Chapter 3, page 92: Excerpt from "The Industry: Message in a Bottle" by Matt Lee and Ted Lee, *The New York Times,* June 28, 2005. Copyright © 2005 by The New York Times Co. Reprinted with permission.

Chapter 3, page 93: Excerpt from "Growing Occupation: Being Your Own Boss" by Stacey Hirsh, *Baltimore Sun,* April 21, 2006. Copyright © 2006 The Baltimore Sun. Reprinted by permission.

Chapter 4, page 124: Excerpts from "Volkswagen Tries 12 Months of Free Car Insurance to Lure Buyers" by Jeff Green, December 31, 2004, Bloomberg Web site. Copyright © 2004 Bloomberg L.P. All rights reserved. Reprinted by permission of Bloomberg L.P.

Chapter 4, page 125: Excerpt from "2005 – The Year of the Hybrid," from the InvoiceDealers Web site. Reprinted by permission of Dealix Corporation, a Division of The Cobalt Group.

Chapter 5, page 144: Excerpt from "Why is the Supply of Cement Falling Short of Demand?" from the Portland Cement Association Web site. Reprinted by permission of the Portland Cement Association.

Chapter 5, 158: Excerpts from "Robots for Babies: Toyota at the Leading Edge" by Burritt Sabin, Japan Inc. Web site. Reprinted by permission of Japan Inc.

Chapter 5, page 159: Excerpt from "Cake Decorating" from the EPSON Robots Web site. Reprinted by permission of EPSON America Inc.

Chapter 6, page 187: Figure 1 from "The Economics of Real Superstars: The Market for Concerts in the Material World" by Alan B. Krueger, *Journal of Labor Economics,* 23(1), 2005. Reprinted by permission of The University of Chicago Press.

Chapter 7, page 220: Excerpts from "Anyone for Telly?," The Economist, September 10, 2005. The Economist Newspaper Ltd. All rights reserved. Reprinted with permission. Further reproduction prohibited. www.economist.com.

Chapter 7, page 221: Excerpt from "Gartner Says Mobile Phone Sales Will Exceed One Billion in 2009," from the Gartner Web site. Reprinted with permission.

Chapter 8, page 248: "World's Leading Franchises," from Franchise Facts. Copyright © International Franchise Association. Reprinted by permission of the International Franchise Association.

Chapter 8, page 252: Excerpt from "Steve Jobs and Steve Wozniak: The Personal Computer" from the Lemelson-MIT Program Web site. Courtesy of Inventor of the Week, Lemelson-MIT Program, http://web.mit.edu/invent.

Chapter 8, page 253: Excerpts from "Interview with Evelyn Richards" by Wendy Marinaccio, appearing on the "Making the Mac/Technology and Culture in Silicon Valley" Web page, Stanford University Library. Reprinted by permission of the Stanford University Library.

Chapter 8, page 253: "Highlights in Apple Company History" adapted from Apple timeline appearing in *Macworld,* February 2004. Copyright © 2004 Mac Publishing LLC. All rights reserved. Reprinted by permission.

Chapter 8, page 255: "Mergers in the United States" *MergerStat Review,* 2004. Copyright © 2004 Mergerstat Holdings, LLP. Reprinted by permission of FactSet Mergerstat LLC.

Chapter 9, page 282: Excerpt from "Subcontinental Drift" by Nandini Lakshman, *Business Week,* January 16, 2006. Copyright © 2006 by The McGraw-Hill Companies, Inc. Reprinted by special permission.

Chapter 9, page 283: Excerpt from "Foreign Firms Come Bearing Jobs" by Mike Meyers, *Star Tribune,* September 5, 2004. Copyright © 2004 Star Tribune. All rights reserved. Reprinted by permission of the Star Tribune, Minneapolis – St. Paul, Minnesota.

Chapter 10, page 312: Excerpts from "Congress Cuts Funding for Student Loans" by Anne Marie Chaker, *The Wall Street Journal,* December 22, 2005. Copyright © 2005 The Wall Street Journal. Reprinted by permission.

Chapter 10, page 313: Excerpts from "It's Payback Time" by Jonathan D. Glater, *The New York Times,* April 23, 2006. Copyright © 2006 by The New York Times Co. Reprinted with permission.

Chapter 11, page 334: "Dow Jones Industrial Average, 1929-2006," from Yahoo! Finance Web site. Copyright © 2006 Yahoo! Inc. YAHOO! and the YAHOO!

logo are trademarks if Yahoo! Inc. Reprinted by permission of Yahoo! Inc.

Chapter 11, page 342: "Apple Computer (AAPL-Q)," from *The Globe and Mail,* April 19, 2006. Reprinted by permission of the Globe and Mail

Chapter 11, page 344: "Kozmo.com," from the Wikipedia Web site. Reprinted by permission.

Chapter 11, page 345: Excerpt from "The Bubble Bowl" by David M. Ewalt, Forbes Web site, January 27, 2005. Copyright © 2005 Forbes.com Inc. Reprinted by permission.

Chapter 12, page 364: "U.S. Leading Economic Indicators (LEI) and Real GDP". The Conference Board, United States Bureau of Economic Analysis, National Bureau of Economic Research. Reprinted by permission of The Conference Board Inc.

Chapter 12, page 376: Excerpts from "Europe's Capitalism Curtain" by Steve Pearlstein, *The Washington Post,* July 23, 2004. Copyright © 2004, The Washington Post. Excerpted with permission.

Chapter 12, page 377: Excerpts from "Reaping the European Union Harvest," *The Economist,* January 8, 2005. The Economist Newspaper Ltd. All rights reserved. Reprinted with permission. Further reproduction prohibited. www.economist.com.

Chapter 13, page 404: Excerpt from "The Search for a New Economic Order" by Robert Tolles, *Ford Foundation,* New York, 1982, p. 24. Reprinted by permission of the Ford Foundation.

Chapter 13, page 405: Excerpts from "Open Editorial" by Bernice Davidson, *The New York Times,* September 29, 1972. Copyright © 1972 by The New York Times Co. Reprinted with permission.

Chapter 14, page 440: Excerpts from "iPod Tax Planned for Music Downloads?" from the CNET Web site, March 10, 2006. Copyright © 2006 CNET Networks, Inc. All rights reserved. Reprinted by permission of Reprint Management Services.

Chapter 14, page 441: Excerpt from "Internet Sales Tax," from *The New York Times,* July 5, 2005. Copyright © 2005 by The New York Times Co. Reprinted with permission.

Chapter 15, page 468: Excerpts from "Federal Budget Deficit Sparks Worries," *The Associated Press,* January 15, 2006. Copyright © 2006 The Associated Press. All rights reserved. Reprinted by permission of Reprint Management Services.

Chapter 15, page 469: Excerpt from "Snow Sets Sights on Deficits" by Edward Alden, Andrew Balls, and Holly Yeaser, *Financial Times,* November 4, 2005. Copyright © The Financial Times Ltd. 2005. Reprinted with permission.

Chapter 16, page 504: Excerpts from "Fed Expected to Boost Key Interest Rates," *The Associated Press,* May 10, 2006. Copyright © 2006 The Associated Press. All rights reserved. Reprinted by permission of Reprint Management Services.

Chapter 16, page 505: Excerpts from "Bernanke Talks Tough on Inflation" by Edmund L. Andrews, *The New York Times,* June 6, 2006. Copyright © 2006 by The New York Times Co. Reprinted with permission.

Chapter 17, page 521: "Tariffs are Falling," from the *Human Development Report,* 2005, United Nations Development Programme. Reprinted by permission of the United Nations Publications Department.

Chapter 17, page 538: Excerpt from "Sugar Daddies" by Jason Lee Steorts, *National Review,* July 18, 2005. Copyright © 2005 National Review. Reprinted by permission.

Chapter 17, page 539: Excerpts from "Sweetener Impact on US Economy," from the American Sugar Alliance Web site. Copyright © 2005 American Sugar Alliance. Reprinted by permission.

Chapter 18, page 570: Excerpt from "From T-shirts to T-bonds," *The Economist,* July 28, 2005. The Economist Newspaper Ltd. All rights reserved. Reprinted with permission. Further reproduction prohibited. www.economist.com.

Chapter 18, page: Excerpts from "China's Economic Miracle: The High Price of Progress," from CBC News, April 20, 2006, Canadian Broadcasting Corporation Web site. Copyright © CBC 2006. Reprinted by permission.

Skillbuilder Handbook

Page R15: Excerpts from "Crude Oil Prices Sink Below $66 a Barrel," *The Associated Press,* September 11, 2006. Copyright © 2006 The Associated Press. All rights reserved. Reprinted by permission of Reprint Management Services.

Page R21: Excerpt from "U.S. Trade Deficit Hit Record High in 2005"by Vikas Bajaj, *The New York Times,* February 10, 2006. Copyright © 2006 by The New York Times Co. Reprinted with permission.

Page R23: Excerpt from "Not Business as Usual" by Elizabeth Bauman, *Online NewsHour Extra,* January 30, 2002. Copyright © 2002 MacNeil-Lehrer Productions. Reprinted by permission.

Page R27: Excerpt from "1942: Beveridge Lays Welfare Foundations," from BBC Web site. Copyright © BBC. Reprinted by permission.

Frontmatter

cov *top* © Randy Faris/Corbis; *bottom left* © Peter Horree/Alamy Images; *top right* © Scott Olson/Getty Images; *center right* © Jochem D. Wijnands/Getty Images; *bottom right* © ShutterStock; **iii** *top* © Mark Lewis/Getty Images; *second from top* © Paul A. Souders/Corbis; *third from top* © Veer; *third from bottom* © Joeseph Sohm-Visions of America/Getty Images; *second from bottom* © Jack Dagley Photography/ShutterStock; *bottom* © Jose Luis Pelaez, Inc./Corbis; **iv** *Sally Meek* Photo courtesy of Isaac Portrait Photography, Dallas, Texas, isaacphotography.com; *Mark Schug* Photo courtesy of Diana Johnson, Northwestern University; *John Morton* Photo courtesy of Kathryn S. Morton; **4** © Getty Images.

Unit 1

2–3 © Charles Gupton/Corbis; **5** AP/Wide World Photos; **6** AP/Wide World Photos; **7** *left* © Peter Dean/Grant Heilman Photography; *right* © Grant Heilman/Grant Heilman Photography; **8** © Karen Kasmauski/Corbis; **11** © PictureQuest; **12** © Michelle Pedone/zefa/Corbis; **13** *right* © GDT/Getty Images; *center* © RNT Productions/Corbis; *left* © Getty Images; **14** © Nancy Ney/Getty Images; **16** *left* © Getty Images;center © Corbis; *right* © Peter Mason/Getty Images; **17** © Bryan Bedder/Getty Images; **18** © C Squared Studios/Getty Images; **21** *left* © Frank Rossoto Stocktrek/Getty Images; *right* © David Hancock/Alamy Images; **23** AP/Wide World Photos; **25** AP/Wide World Photos; **27** © Baerbel Schmidt/Getty Images; **29** © Matthew Mcvay/Corbis; **30** *left* The Granger Collection, New York; *right* The Granger Collection, New York; **31** © Bettmann/Corbis; **32** © Lawrence Manning/Corbis; **33** © CartoonStock; **36** © Keren Su/Corbis; **39** *left* © Frans Lanting/Corbis; *center* © Peter Turnley/Corbis; *right* © Burt Glinn/Magnum Photos; **40** © Frank Herholdt/Alamy Images; **41** © Robert Harding Picture Library Ltd/Alamy Images; **44** *bottom* © Dagli Orti/The Art Archive; center The Granger Collection, New York; **46** *left* © Thomas Hoepker/Magnum Photos; *right* © Wolfgang Kaehler/Corbis; **47** © Peter Turnley/Corbis; **48** © Rolf Bruderer/Corbis; **50** *left* © Getty Images ; *center* © Tim Boyle/Getty Images; *right* © Mario Tama/Getty Images; **52** © Juan Silva/Getty Images; **54** © Sue Cunningham Photographic/Alamy Images; **55** © image100/Getty Images; **57** © Stockbyte/Getty Images; **59** © David Woods/Corbis; **61** © Martin Guhl/CartoonStock; **62** © Rubberball/Jupiter Images; **63** © Fotosearch Stock Photography; **64** Lasse Norgaard/Red Cross/AP/Wide World Photos; **67** © Cathrine Wessel/Corbis; **68–69** © Cohen/Ostrow/Getty Images; **70** Photo courtesy of Monica Ramirez; **72** © Russell Gordon/Danita Delimont; **73** © Al Freni/Getty Images; **75** *center* © Jeff Greenberg/age fotostock america, inc.; *right* © Susan Van Etten/PhotoEdit; *left* © Getty Images; **76** *bottom* © Roger Ressmeyer/Corbis; *book image* © John Labbe/Getty Images; *book cover Free to Choose,* © 1980 by Milton Friedman and Rose Friedman, reproduced by permission of Harcourt, Inc. This material may not be reproduced in any form or by any means without prior written permission of the publisher.; **77** © Veer Wild Bill Melton/Getty Images; **78** © Creatas/Alamy Images; **83** © Time Life Pictures/Getty Images; **84** © Seth Joel/Getty Images; **85** © Joe Drivas/Getty Images; **86** *left* © Getty Images; center © Gideon Mendel/Corbis; right © David McNew/Getty Images; **87** © Ashley Cooper/Corbis; **88** © LADA/Photo Researchers, Inc.; **89** © David Young-Wolff/PhotoEdit; **91** © Gabe Palmer/Corbis; **92** © Ben Stechschulte/Redux; **95** © Niall McDiarmid/Alamy Images.

Unit 2

96-97 © Ryan McVay/Getty Images; **97** © Issei Kato/Reuters/Corbis; **98** © Jupiter Images; **99** © Getty Images; **102** © Scott Barbour/Getty Images; **104** *bottom* © Matthew Peyton/Getty Images; *center* Thomas Iannaccone/Fairchild Publications/AP/Wide World Photos; **107** © Getty Images; **108** © Getty Images; **110** *left* © Getty Images; *center* © Getty Images; *right* © Ron Kimball/Ron Kimball Stock; **112** *left* © Getty Images; *center* © Benjamin Rondel/Corbis; *right* © Martyn Goddard/Corbis; **114** © Kevin Kallaugher, www.kaltoons.com; **115** © Corbis; **116** © Vehbi Koca/Alamy Images; **117** *left* © Getty Images; *bottom inset* © Corbis; *bottom right* © Wayne Eastep/Getty Images; **119** *left* © Altrendo images/Getty Images; *center* © Getty Images; *right* Photograph by Tricia Bauman/Clik Photography; **123** © Mark E. Gibson; **124** © David Young-Wolff/Getty Images; **125** *top* © Brian Duffy/The Des Moines Register; *center* © Issei Kato/Reuters/Corbis; **128-129** © AFP/Getty Images; **129** © Lucas Schifres/Corbis; **130** © Mason Morfit/Getty Images; **131** © Jupiter Images; **132** © Chris Thomaidis/Getty Images; **136** © Martin Thiel/Getty Images; **137** © Spencer Grant/PhotoEdit; **138** © David A. Barnes/Alamy Images; **140** *clockwise from top left* © Michael Goldman/Getty Images; © Brownie Harris/Corbis; © Corbis; © Danish Khan/ShutterStock; © Todd S. Holder/ShutterStock; © Image Source/Getty Images; **142** © C Squared Studios/Getty Images (Royalty-Free); **145** © David McNew/Getty Images; **146** *left* © James L. Amos/Corbis; *right* © David Young-Wolff/PhotoEdit; **149** *left* © Albo/ShutterStock; right © Doug Priebe/ShutterStock; **152** *bottom* AP/Wide World Photos; center Stephen Chernin/AP/Wide World Photos; **153** © /Getty Images; **154** AP/Wide World Photos; **156** *left* © Getty Images; *center* © David Joel/Getty Images; *right* © Jupiter Images; **157** © Thinkstock; 158 © Lucas Schifres/Corbis; 159 © John Morris/CartoonStock; **162–163** © Peter M. Fisher/Corbis; **163** © Tim Mosenfelder/Getty Images; **164** © Eric Futran/FoodPix/Jupiter Images; **168** AP/Wide World Photos; **171** © Danny Lehman/Corbis; **173** © Dennis Wise/Getty Images; **174** © Tom Stewart/Corbis; **177** *center* © Yoshikazu Tsuno/AFP/Getty Images; *right* © Getty Images; *left* © Getty Images; **178 top** Harry Cabluck/AP/Wide World Photos; *center* © Bob Riha, Jr./Dell/Handout/Reuters/Corbis; *bottom* © Elipsa/Corbis; **179** © Sally and Richard Greenhill/Alamy Images; **180** © David Bergman/Corbis; **183** © Corbis; **184** © Forrest Anderson/Getty Images; **185** © Robert Barclay/Grant Heilman Photography; **186** © Tim Mosenfelder/Getty Images; **190–191** © Chuck Pefley/Alamy Images; **191** Kai-Uwe Knoth/AP/Wide World Photos; **193** © Veer; **195** © Sandra Ivany/Botanica/Jupiter Images; **197** © Brigitte Sporrer/zefa/Corbis; **198** © Dave G. Houser/Post-Houserstock/Corbis; **201** © Will & Deni McIntyre/Corbis; **202** *top left* © Getty Images; *top right* © BananaStock/Alamy Images; *top center* © Dynamic Graphics Group/i2i/Alamy Images; *bottom right* © istockphoto.com; **203** © Rob Leiter/MLB Photos via Getty Images; **204** © Harley Schwadron/CartoonStock; **205** © Royalty-Free/Corbis; **206** © Judy Griesedieck/Corbis; **207** © Matt Bowman/Foodpix/Jupiter Images; **208** © Justin Kase/Alamy Images; **209** © Chuck Savage/Corbis; **210** © Sue Cunningham Photographic/Alamy Images; **212** © Peter Lofts Photography; **213** © Royalty-Free/Corbis; **214** © Stock Montage/Getty Images; **215** Caleb Jones/AP/Wide World Photos; **218** © 2006 by R. J. Matson/Caglecartoons.com. All rights reserved.; **219** © Joseph Sohm/Visions of America/Corbis; **220** Kai-Uwe Knoth/AP/Wide World Photos; **221** © Richard Sly/CartoonStock; **223** © Hans-Peter Merten/Digital Vision/Getty Images.

Unit 3

224–225 © Comstock Images/Jupiter Images; **225** Paul Sakuma/AP/Wide World Photos; **226** © Getty Images; **227** © Stockbyte Platinum/Alamy Images; **228** © Brand X Pictures/Alamy Images; **230** Photo courtesy of Mary Kay Inc.; **231** © Viviane Moos/Corbis; **232** © Yuri Arcurs/ShutterStock; **233** © Arthur Tilley/Getty Images; **235** © Creasource/Corbis; **237** © Michael Keller/Corbis; **241** © Chris Wildt/CartoonStock; **244** © John Morris/CartoonStock; **246** © Lynn Goldsmith/Corbis; **247** © LWA-Dann Tardif/Corbis; **249** *top left* © Getty Images; *top right* © Thinkstock/Alamy Images; *top center* © Douglas Freer/ShutterStock; **250** *bottom* Courtesy of Salvation Army; *top* Courtesy of The American Lung Association; **251** Alan Diaz/AP/Wide World Photos; **252** Paul Sakuma/AP/Wide World Photos; **253** © Bernard Gotfryd/Getty Images; **255** © Dave G. Houser/Post-Houserstock/Corbis; **256–257** © Bruce Avres/Getty Images; **257** © Andrew Toos/CartoonStock; **258** © Ariel Skelley/Corbis; **262** © Roger Ressmeyer/Corbis; **264** *right* Joshua Lott/AP/Wide World Photos; *left* Human Capital: A Theoretical and Empirical Analysis with Special Reference to Education, by Gary S. Becker. © 1993. Reprinted with permission of The University of Chicago Press.; **265** © Brenda Prince/Photofusion Picture Library/Alamy Images; **266** © Getty Images; **269** *top* right © Robert Llewellyn/Corbis; top left © H. Armstrong Roberts/Corbis; **270** *bottom left* © Getty Images; *bottom center* © David Sacks/Getty Images; *bottom right* © Terry McCormick/Getty Images; **271** © Charles Thatcher/Getty Images; **273** © Alamy Images; **275** © Time Life Pictures/Getty Images; **276** *left* © Hulton Archive/Getty Images; *second from right* © Bettmann/Corbis; *right* The Granger Collection, New York; *second from left* The Granger Collection, New York; **277** *left* © Ted Streshinsky/Corbis; *right* © Roger Ressmeyer/Corbis; **280** © Jeff Kowalsky/AFP/Getty Images; **281** © H. P. Merten/zefa/Corbis; **282** © Jagadeesh/Reuters/Corbis; **283** © Andrew Toos/CartoonStock.

Unit 4

286–287 © George Diebold Photography/Getty Images; **287** © Ralph Hagen/CartoonStock; **288** © Comstock Images/Alamy Images; **290** © Lowell Georgia/Corbis; **291** © W. Perry Conway/CORBIS; **292** © Dennis Galante/Corbis; *all flags this page* © FOTW Flags of the World website at http://flagspot.net/flags; **295** © Klaus Hackenberg/zefa/Corbis; **296** Counting House (about 1375–1400). British Library, London. Photo © HIP/Art Resource, New York; **297** *center* © Archivo Iconografico, S.A./Corbis; *bottom right* The Granger Collection, New York; **298** *top left* © The Granger Collection, New York; *bottom right* The Granger Collection, New York; *top right* © The British Museum; *right* The Granger Collection, New York; **299** *left* © Getty Images; *top* © Bettmann/Corbis; *right* © Wally McNamee/Corbis; 300 © Marty Katz/Time Life Pictures/Getty Images; **303** © Don Smetzer/PhotoEdit; **307** *bottom left* © Bettmann/Corbis; *bottom right* © Getty Images; **308** © Brandtner & Staedeli/Getty Images; **309** *right* © Chuck Savage/Corbis; *bottom left* © Altrendo images/Getty Images; *center* © Chuck Savage/Corbis; **310** © Michael Keller/Corbis; **311** © Ryan McVay/Getty Images; **313** © Ralph Hagen/CartoonStock; **315** © Antonio M. Rosario/The Image Bank/Getty Images; **316–317** © Jean Miele/Corbis; **317** © Andrew Toos/CartoonStock; **318** © Graca Victoria/ShutterStock; **320** © Free Agents Limited/Corbis; **322** © Susan Van Etten/PhotoEdit; **323** © White Packert/Getty Images; **324** © Marc Romanelli/Getty Images; **325** *top left* © Getty Images; *top center* © Peter Adams/zefa/Corbis; *top right* © Chuck Savage/Corbis; **326** © Peter Kramer/Getty Images; **328** *top left* © Altrendo images/Getty Images; *top center* © Royalty-Free/Corbis; *top right* © Alan Schein/zefa/Corbis; **329** © Robert Mizerek/ShutterStock; **330** © Alan Schein/zefa/Corbis; **331** © Harley Schwadron/CartoonStock; **332** © Scott Barrow, Inc./SuperStock; **333** © Tonis Valing/ShutterStock; **335** © J. McGillen/CartoonStock; **336** © The Cover Story/Corbis; **337** © Ethan Miller/Getty Images; **339** *right* ©

Glowimages/Getty Images; *top* © Peter Bowater/Alamy Images; *center* © Zina Seletskaya/ShutterStock; 341 © Jim Sizemore/CartoonStock; 343 © Kai Hecker/ShutterStock; 344 © Erik Freeland/Corbis; 345 © Andrew Toos/CartoonStock; 347 © Royalty-Free/Corbis.

Unit 5

348–349 © Royalty-Free/Corbis; 349 © Wojtek Laski/East News via Getty Images; 350 © Jason Hawkes/Corbis; 354 © Ariel Skelley/Corbis; 357 © Royalty-Free/Corbis; 358 © Best of Latin America/Caglecartoons.com; 362 © Andersen Ross/Getty Images; 363 © Stan Honda/AFP/Getty Images; 365 *top* © Archive Holdings Inc./Getty Images; *bottom* The Granger Collection, New York; 371 © Ed Kashi/Corbis; 374 The Granger Collection, New York; 375 © Gary Braasch/Corbis; 376 © Wojtek Laski/East News via Getty Images; 377 © Peter Schrank; 380–381 © David Trood/Getty Images; 381 © Time & Life Pictures/Getty Images; 382 © Chris Hondros/Getty Images; 384 © Adam Crowley/Getty Images; 385 © AFP/Getty Images; 387 © Cleo Photography/PhotoEdit; 392 © Justin Sullivan/Getty Images; 393 © Photofusion Library/Alamy Images; 394 *top* Photo Courtesy of the Institute for Liberty and Democracy, Lima, Peru; *bottom* © Getty Images; 395 © Khaled El Fiqui/epa/Corbis; 396 © Dave Einsel/Getty Images; 400 © Stephanie Davis/ShutterStock; 401 *right* © Danny Bailey/istockphoto.com; *center* © James Leynse/Corbis; *left* © Getty Images; 402 © James Leynse/Corbis; 404 © Time & Life Pictures/Getty Images; 405 © Larry Katzman/CartoonStock; 407 © David Lees/Getty Images.

Unit 6

408–409 © Tom Bean/Getty Images; 411 Frank and Ernest reprinted with permission of Thaves; 416 © Ljupco Smokovski/ShutterStock; 419 Phil Coale/AP/Wide World Photos; 420 © Tim Boyle/Getty Images; 422 © Myrleen Ferguson Cate/PhotoEdit; 423 © Harley Schwadron/CartoonStock; 426 Photo courtesy of Sarah Brennan; 427 © Elizabeth Simpson/Getty Images; 428 © George Mattei/Photo Researchers, Inc.; 429 © Spencer Platt/Getty Images; 430 *left* © Getty Images; *center* © Jose Luis Pelaez, Inc./Corbis; *right* © Mark Wilson/Getty Images; 432 © Royalty-Free/Corbis; 433 Rachel Denny Clow/Corpus Christi Caller-Times/AP/Wide World Photos; 436 © Mike Lane/Caglecartoons.com; 438 © Dan Brandenburg/istockphoto.com; 439 © Michael Newman/PhotoEdit; 440 © G. Schuster/zefa/Corbis; 444–445 © I. Vanderharst/Getty Images; 445 © Harley Schwadron/www.CartoonStock.com; 447 © Joel Stettenheim/Corbis; 448 © John Humble/Getty Images; 452 © Larry Wright/Caglecartoons.com; 453 © Jeff Metzger/ShutterStock; 454 The Granger Collection, New York; 456 From *The General Theory of Employment, Interests, and Money,* by John Maynard Keynes (1997), book cover. (Amherst, NY: Prometheus Books). Book cover © 1997 by Prometheus Books. Reprinted with permission of the publisher.; *Time cover* © Time Life Pictures/Getty Images; 457 © Hulton-Deutsch Collection/Corbis; 460 *left* © Altrendo images/Getty Images; center Mel Evans/AP/Wide World Photos; *right* © Jim West/Alamy Images; 461 © Charles Luzier/Reuters/Corbis; 462 Harley Schwadron/www.CartoonStock.com; 467 © Peter Beck/Corbis; 468 © Stan Honda/AFP/Getty Images; 469 © Harley Schwadron/www.CartoonStock.com; 472–473 © Brooks Kraft/Corbis; 475 The Granger Collection, New York; 478 *bottom* © Kitt Cooper-Smith/Alamy Images; *top* © James Leynse/Corbis; 479 © Louie Psihoyos/Corbis; 480 © Janis Christie/Getty Images; 483 *top* U. S. Treasury/AP/Wide World Photos; *bottom* U. S. Treasury/AP/Wide World Photos; 486 David Zalubowski/AP/Wide World Photos; 489 © Jim Pathe/Star Ledger/Corbis; 492 Frank and Ernest reprinted with permission of Thaves.; 494 © Time & Life Pictures/Getty Images; 496 © James Leynse/Corbis; 497 © Don Mason/Corbis; 498 © Royalty-Free/Corbis; 501 *left* © Getty Images; *center* © Greg Henry/istockphoto.com; *right* © Sharon Meredith/istockphoto.com; 503 © Stocksearch/Alamy Images; 504 © J. Scott Applewhite/AP/Wide World Photos; 505 © Harley Schwadron/www.CartoonStock.com.

Unit 7

508–509 © Paul Chesley/Getty Images; 509 © Jack Kurtz/ZUMA/Corbis; 510 *left* © KCNA/epa/Corbis; *right* © Benelux Press/Getty Images; 511 *left* © Altrendo images/Getty Images; *center* © Tom Stewart/Corbis; *right* © Anita Patterson Peppers/ShutterStock; 512 The Granger Collection, New York; 513 *left* © Robert Garvey/Corbis; *right* © Royalty-Free/Corbis; 515 © Barry Mason/Alamy Images; 517 © Andrew Brookes/Corbis; 519 © Gordon Swanson/ShutterStock; 520 © Stephane Peray/Caglecartoons.com; 523 © Pierre Verdy/AFP/Getty Images; 524 © images-of-france/Alamy Images; 525 © Karl Weatherly/Getty Images; 526 *top* © Danita Delimont/Alamy Images; *center* © B.A.E. Inc./Alamy Images; *bottom* © Pacific Press Service/Alamy Images; 527 © You Sung-Ho/Reuters/Corbis; 528 *left* © Getty Images; *center* © Blue Line Pictures/Getty Images; *right* © Jerry Arcieri/Corbis; 531 © Alan Schein Photography/Corbis; 532 Mindaugas Kulbis/AP/Wide World Photos; 535 *right* Gautam Singh/AP/Wide World Photos; *second from right* © Ralph Orlowski/Getty Images; *second from left* © Chung Sung Jun/Getty Images; *left* Newscast/AP/Wide World Photos; 537 © PhotoLink/Getty Images; 538 © Jack Kurtz/ZUMA/Corbis; 541 *left* © Royalty-Free/Corbis; *right* © Steven Collins/ShutterStock; 542–543 © Mark Daffey/Getty Images; 543 © Best of Latin America/Caglecartoons.com; 545 *left* © Ed Kashi/Corbis; *right* © Justin

Guariglia/Corbis; 547 © Caroline Penn/Corbis; 549 © Bob Sacha/Corbis; 550 © Juda Ngwenya/Reuters/Corbis; 551 © Rafiqur Rahman/Reuters/Corbis; 552 © Royalty-Free/Corbis; 554 © Bill Fritsch/Age Fotostock America, Inc.; 555 *right* © SW Productions/Getty Images; *left* © Three Lions/Hulton Archive/Getty Images; 556 © Penny Tweedie/Alamy Images; 558 *bottom left* © Lisa Ryder/Alamy Images; *top left* © picturesbyrob/Alamy Images; *bottom right* © Jeff Morgan/Alamy Images; *top right* © Peter Kneffel/dpa/Corbis; 560 © Dieter Nagl/AFP/Getty Images; 561 © James Marshall/Corbis; 562 © Javier Larrea/Age Fotostock; 564 © Christo Komarnitski/Caglecartoons.com; 565 © Jon Hicks/Corbis; 566 *left* © Panorama Media (Beijing) Ltd./Alamy Images; *right* © Raymond Gehman/NGSImages.com; 569 © Directphoto.org/Alamy Images; 570 © Best of Latin America/Caglecartoons.com; 571 © Best of Latin America/Caglecartoons.com; 573 © Bob Krist/Corbis; 574 © George Shelley/Corbis; © Getty Images; 576 © Tara Urbach/ShutterStock; 577 © Digital Vision/Getty Images; 579 © Ariel Skelley/Corbis; 582 *top left* © Getty Images; *bottom right* © Mike Lane/Caglecartoons.com; 588 © BananaStock/Jupiter Images; 590 *top left* © Getty Images; *right* © Gabe Palmer/Corbis; 591 © Alexander Walter/Getty Images; 592 © David Young-Wolff/PhotoEdit; 594 © Mike Lane/Caglecartoons.com; 596 © Colorstock/Getty Images; 598 © John Morris/www.CartoonStock.com; 600 *top left* © Getty Images; *bottom right* Reprinted with permission of the Employment Development Department, State of California; 603 © Creatas Images/Jupiter Images; 605 © Mario Tama/Getty Images; 606 © Ken Reid/Getty Images; 608 © PM Images/Getty Images.

Backmatter

R26 © Stan Eales/CartoonStock.

All Maps

© GeoNova Group.

Trademark Acknowledgement

ADIDAS and the Adidas design are registered trademarks of Adidas AG Joint Stock Company

AMERICAN RED CROSS design is a trademark of American Red Cross Inc.

AMOCO design is a registered trademark of Amoco Oil Company

BET.COM design is a trademark of Black Entertainment Television, Inc.

COCA-COLA and the Coca-Cola design are registered trademarks of The Coca-Cola Company

DELL design is a registered trademark of Dell Inc.

FANTASTIC SAM'S is a registered trademark of Fantastic Sam's Franchise Corporation

HABITAT FOR HUMANITY design is a registered trademark of Habitat of Humanity International, Inc.

INTERNATIONAL MONETARY FUND design is a trademark of The International Monetary Fund

KOZMO.COM design is a registered trademark of Kozmo.com, Inc.

MASTERCARD design is a registered trademark of MasterCard International Incorporated

MICROSOFT is a registered trademark of Microsoft Corporation

NASDAQ is a registered trademark of NASDAQ Stock Exchange, Inc.

NEWSWEEK is a registered trademark of Newsweek, Inc.

NOKIA is a registered trademark of Nokia Corporation

NYSE is a registered trademark of New York Stock Exchange, Inc.

PIONEER is a registered trademark of Pioneer Kabushiki Kaisha DAB Pioneer Electronic Corporation

SALVATION ARMY design is a registered trademark of The Salvation Army

SAMSUNG is a regisered trademark of Samsung Electronics Co., Ltd.

The **SHELL** emblem is a trademark of Shell International Limited

SONY is a registered trademark of Sony Kabushiki Kaisha TA Sony Corporation (you can include this with the VAIO acknowledgement as not to repeat)

TIME design is a registered trademark of Time, Inc.

TYCO is a trademark of Mattel, Inc.

U.S. NEWS & WORLD REPORT design is a registered trademark of U.S. News & World Report, L.P.

VAIO design is a registered trademark of Sony Kabushiki Kaisha TA Sony Corporation

VISA design is a registered trademark of Visa International Service Association

VOLVO is a registered trademark of Volvo Trademark Holding AB Corporation

WWF design is a registered trademark of World Wide Fund for Nature

All other trademarks are property of their respective owners and are in no way affiliated with, connected to or sponsored by McDougal Littell, a division of Houghton Mifflin Company. Trademarks, trade names, logos and graphics are shown in this book strictly for illustrative purposes.